# Systems Behaviour

# The Open University Systems Behaviour Course Team

R. J. Beishon (Chairman)
J. H. Baily
J. Cannell
G. Einon
D. Elliott
E. Goldwyn (B.B.C.)
J. Groom (B.B.C.)
G. Harland
L. Jones
R. Jones (B.B.C.)
O. Lawrence
R. Morris
J. Naughton
D. Nelson (B.B.C.)
G. Peters
L. Suss
B. Whatley (B.B.C.)
P. Zorkoczy

# Systems Behaviour

*Edited by* **John Beishon and Geoff Peters**
*at The Open University*

*Published for*
The Open University Press
by Harper & Row, Publishers    London   New York   Evanston   San Francisco

Published by Harper & Row Ltd
28 Tavistock Street, London WC2E 7PN

Standard Book Number 06-318010-3 (cloth)
Standard Book Number 06-318011-1 (paper)

Printed in Great Britain by
Richard Clay (The Chaucer Press), Ltd
Bungay, Suffolk

# Preface

This book is a collection of papers and articles on systems. It arose out of the development of a course at the Open University on Systems Behaviour. In common with most Open University courses, the Systems Behaviour course adopts a multi-disciplinary and inter-disciplinary approach and it covers a range of topics not normally dealt with in a conventional university course. One of the problems in developing new courses is that suitable reference and back-up material is difficult to find and is usually spread across a wide variety of sources. This is particularly true of new areas such as Systems where there are few, if any, "standard" texts and most of the books available cover specific subject or technique areas. The Systems Behaviour course does not, for example, have any books set as "required reading", for the reason that no book dealing with more than a few parts of the course can be found. So one of our main reasons for producing a book of readings is that material on Systems is scattered far and wide in the literature, often in journal articles or reports which are relatively difficult to obtain.

Collections of readings suffer from a number of disadvantages: they are uneven in style and level, gaps in arguments and in the development of ideas occur, the coverage of a field is sometimes very patchy, and it is always possible to criticize the selection of material on one ground or another. Editors make valiant attempts to overcome these problems by providing linking passages and by careful editing where possible, but the results are not always satisfactory. However, one of the great advantages of readings from our point of view is that students can consult original sources and can compare and evaluate the different ideas and concepts presented. This is an essential part of the Systems Behaviour course.

It is worth pointing out, however, that the final choice of articles is not always what one would like. Material which would logically appear at a certain point is sometimes left out because it is readily available elsewhere, or because it would make the book unduly long, or more simply because permission to reprint it is not forthcoming. We have selected articles which seem to us to be of general interest as well as of direct relevance to the Systems Behaviour course, and we have inserted recommendations for other reading at appropriate places in the linking texts between sections.

A final point – the articles we have selected supply essential background reading for students taking the Systems Behaviour course, hence the title of this Reader. The articles therefore deal more with the systems approach than with the actual behaviour of systems.

*The Open University*                                    R. J. B.
                                                         G. P.

# Acknowledgements

The editors would like to thank Professor Peter Checkland of the University of Lancaster for valuable suggestions for articles for this reader, and Mrs. Judy Baily and Mr. Caryl Hunter-Brown of the Open University for collating and collecting the ancillary material. They would also like to thank David Hogg and Catherine Cahn at Harper & Row Ltd. for their patience and efficiency.

R. J. B.
G. P.

# The Open University Systems Behaviour Course

The basic idea of this course is to introduce students from many different backgrounds, scientists, technologists, social scientists, to the study and understanding of systems and system behaviour. It is a second level course and leads to a half-credit qualification. The course is presented in eight "modules" each containing about two weeks' worth of study involving a correspondence text, two television programmes, a radio programme, and various experimental and computer-based activities. The eight modules cover a number of different case studies each linked to the development of a theoretical idea and a technique for analysis or study.

The eight modules deal with:

Container handling
Air traffic control
Telephone systems
Work group systems in mines and motor manufacture
Local government corporation
Respiratory system
Economics of shipbuilding
Sheep farming

Techniques covered include:

Data collection and handling
Statistical methods
System representation
Modelling and simulation
Allocation of function and interface design
System dynamics

Students completing the course will have a detailed knowledge of eight different and important systems, will have acquired useful techniques for the analysis and prediction of systems behaviour, and will, hopefully, be able to make a start on tackling system designs (or redesigns) from a more systematic and systems orientated point of view.

# Contents

# Introduction
## Systems and Systems Behaviour

The concepts of systems have slowly emerged in the present century to assume a central importance in the thinking and approach of many scientists and technologists. The ideas are now having an increasing impact on the approach of social and political scientists and economists. In the slow development of knowledge about the physical and biological world the most significant advances generally come from painstaking, detailed study and analysis of ever smaller areas of knowledge and application. The natural philosophy of the earliest scientists gradually developed into the major natural sciences, physics, chemistry, and biology; these in turn have been increasingly subdivided into subjects such as nuclear physics, polymer chemistry, molecular biology, and so on. By the middle of the 20th century this subdivision process had chopped reality and the phenomena of the real world into hundreds of individual subjects and areas of professional expertise. Knowledge was compartmentalized and departmentalized into small and seemingly more manageable chunks.

The success of analytical techniques, and in particular structural analysis, tended to concentrate attention even more on static and structural properties, and some writers have seen this as a reflection of the desire of men to live in well-ordered, static social and political environments. Victorian man might fit into this picture but not the more modern variety. At least two groups found this approach limiting and unhelpful: the mechanical and later the electrical engineer who wanted to build and run mechanisms and devices which *worked*, and the psychologist or ethologist who was interested less in the anatomy of the human or animal system than in the *behaviour* of the complete organism. The full history of the emergence and effects of the systems-thinking "revolution" has yet to be written although some of the ground has been covered ably by one of the pioneers in the field, L. von Bertalanffy.*

The impetus towards systems thinking and the systems approach has come from a recognition (some would say a belated recognition) of the complex behaviour which can and does arise from both natural and man-made systems.

* See Article 2, p. 29.

The longer term implications of system behaviour only gradually become apparent. It is often only when these are seen to threaten human life or living styles that attention is directed to the system's activity, often in a dramatic way. Another stimulus to adopt a system approach arises from our attempts to predict and control the *behaviour* of systems instead of passively suffering from, or just reacting to, the often mysterious changes which occur in the surrounding physical, biological, social, economic, and political climate. Attempts to exercise control over systems, whether human or economic, have not been notably successful and, for example, there are real fears being expressed that control is no longer even possible over some of the ecosystems we have constructed or interfered with.

System problems appear intractable since we know so little about systems, about systems analysis, about control over system behaviour, or about system design. Even the first step of recognizing the system we are trying to deal with, of drawing its boundaries, presents formidable difficulties. Most scientific disciplines have a large body of facts and knowledge to draw on which have been accumulated over years of testing and experimenting. Theories can be tested against this body of knowledge and gaps identified. But with systems behaviour we have surprisingly little in the way of studies or documented experience. The structure of a system is often known but its behaviour is another matter. It is unfortunate that we often have to wait for a system failure to reveal its possible behaviours and there are many vested interests engaged in seeing that full records of what happened are not readily available! There are other difficulties, of course, system malfunctioning often occurs suddenly and catastrophically and people are not going to start making detailed observations when all is falling about their ears. This is one reason why black box flight recorders are now used on aircraft, so that a disaster can be analysed in detail after the event. The cost, a relatively small one, is that thousands of perfectly normal operations are recorded.

Systems thinking and the systems approach is now a growth area. Systems ideas appear in different guises in cybernetics, systems engineering, general system theory, operations research, systems analysis, computer systems, and many other fields. New jargon abounds: open and closed systems, purposive systems, adaptive systems; the ideas are new and exciting and innovators rush to apply them to different problem areas. There must be many a bewildered manager, administrator, or scientist gazing at the brand-new, shiny, systems approach and wondering quite what hit him. Yet it is becoming clear that a systems approach is essential if we are to have any hope of coping with the complexity of modern life with its multi-national organizations, space modules, international monetary policies, high-speed transport systems, and so on.

This book of readings contains 19 different articles or extracts, all concerned with systems. They have been chosen to illustrate something of the systems approach itself and the way it can be applied to different subjects or activities. The articles are grouped into a number of sections to give some organization to the book but it is a feature of system design that it is always difficult to bring the components of a system into a relationship which is useful and yet can serve a number of different purposes. In a sense this book is a multi-purpose system. People will read separate articles for one purpose, a combination of articles for another, and some will want to read progressively through the book. An order of presentation which might suit a social science student might be inappropriate for a biology student, so our order is only one arrangement designed to serve one, fairly general, purpose. One of the messages of the systems approach is that very simple systems can nevertheless show remarkable complexity of behaviours. Our 19 articles could be arranged in 19!* different ways, which is about $1 \cdot 2 \times 10^{17}$ ways. Enough for a different order for every person on Earth with a good few

* That is $19 \times 18 \times 17 \times 16 \ldots 3 \times 2 \times 1$ different ways.

left over.

Ideally the book should be produced in looseleaf form so that each reader could assemble, and reassemble, the articles into any desired order, and also reject or add material to suit individual need. The articles are grouped as follows:

*Section I*
Introductory material describing the system approach and defining systems concepts.

*Section II*
Two articles dealing with man–machine systems.

*Section III*
Five articles concerned with the impact and development of systems approaches to social systems and organizations.

*Section IV*
Three articles on biological and ecosystems.

*Section V*
The first two articles in this section deal with examples of systems operation, planning and implementation of change.
The final two articles are case studies showing something of the systems approach in action. One studies the New York water supply system, the other the City as a system.

We have provided linking passages where appropriate and references to other articles which could usefully be read at certain points or which complement the existing material. Since the articles cover such a wide range of scientific and organizational matters we have provided a glossary to assist people who are not familiar with all the different areas.

# Section I
# Introduction

The first five articles deal with introductory material about systems and systems concepts. Kast and Rosenzweig give a broad general introduction to a number of basic systems concepts, and then show how the systems approach can be applied to organizations. This article is followed by a more detailed, in depth review of General Systems Theory by one of the pioneers in this field, L. von Bertalanffy. His article gives some of the historical background to the emergence of systems ideas since the 1930s, and he also deals with some of the controversies and objections which have since arisen. This is an article written, as it were, from the insider's position and consequently will be difficult reading for anyone unfamiliar with the systems field. It is probably best to read it through, bypassing any difficult parts, and to come back to it again after reading other articles.

Next Peter Checkland presents a "systems map of the universe" which stems from the approach to systems engineering pioneered at Lancaster University by Jenkins and Checkland. This is valuable in showing how systems can be classified and how an enormously wide range of different phenomena can be looked at from a systems point of view. A full exposition of the systems approach, and how it can be used to solve problems, is contributed by Checkland's colleague, Gwilym Jenkins. This is a particularly valuable contribution because it really does try to set out clear guide lines for tackling typical problems in organizations and systems.

This first section ends with a shorter paper by Russell Ackoff, which presents for the management scientist a set of definitions of the variety of concepts used in the systems approach. Using this, we can at least be fairly sure what the different terms we use really mean.

## Associated reading

There are many general introductions to system concepts and most books with the term "systems" in the title include an opening section dealing with broadly similar ground.

A good straightforward coverage is given by C. W. Churchman in *The Systems Approach* (Dell Publishing Co.), 1968. Another useful general introduction is *Systems Engineering: a unifying approach in industry and society* (C. A. Watts, 1971), by Jenkins and Youle, which interprets systems engineering in the broader terms associated with the Lancaster University's System Engineering Department's approach. General concepts are dealt with in several books on cybernetics, e.g. Ross Ashby, *Introduction to Cybernetics* (Chapman and Hall, 1956); Stafford Beer, *Decision and Control* (Wiley, 1966); Van Court Hare Jr. in *Systems Analysis: a diagnostic approach* (Harcourt Brace Jovanovich, 1967) gives a more detailed introduction to the whole field of systems definition, analysis, and treatment, and we have included a chapter from his book later in these readings.

A full account of General Systems Theory is given in a book of that title by von Bertalanffy, *General system theory: essays on its foundation and development* (Braziller, 1969). Other articles in this area can be found in General Systems Year Books published by the Society for General Systems Research edited by L. von Bertalanffy and A. Rapoport, 1956–1972. Some relevant extracts from several of the above books together with other more specialized material can be found in *System Thinking*, edited by F. E. Emery (Penguin Books Ltd. 1969).

A simple introduction to systems concepts is also available in the Open University's first course unit of T100, *The Man-Made World*, entitled 'Systems' which is available from booksellers.

# 1 The modern view: a systems approach
*by F. E. Kast and J. E. Rosenzweig*

Organization theory and management practice have undergone substantial changes in recent years. Traditional theory has been modified and enriched by informational inputs from the management sciences and the behavioral sciences. These research and conceptual endeavors have, at times, led to divergent findings. During the past decade, however, an approach has emerged which can serve as a basis of convergence – the systems approach, which facilitates unification in many fields of knowledge. It has been used in the physical, biological, and social sciences as a broad frame of reference. It can also be used as a framework for the integration of a modern organization theory. General systems theory, its pervasiveness, its relationship to organization theory, and its potential usefulness are discussed in this chapter via the following topics:

General Systems Theory
Pervasiveness of Systems Theory
Systems Approach and Organization Theory
Organization: An Open System in Its Environment
Organization: A Structured Sociotechnical System
Other Properties of Organizational Systems
Managerial Systems
Systems Concepts for Organization and Management

## General Systems Theory

Over the past two decades the development of general systems theory has provided a basis for the integration of scientific knowledge across a broad spectrum.[1] *A system is an organized or complex whole: an assemblage or combination of things or parts forming a complex or unitary whole.* The term *system* covers a broad spectrum of our physical, biological, and social world. In the universe there are galaxial systems, geophysical systems, and molecular systems. In biology we speak of the organism as a system of mutually dependent parts, each of which includes many subsystems. The human body is a complex organism including, among others, a skeletal system, a circulatory system, and a nervous system. We come into daily contact with such phenomena as transportation systems, communication systems, and economic systems.

In considering the various types of systems in our universe, Kenneth Boulding provides a useful classification of systems which sets forth a hierarchy of levels as follows:

1. The first level is that of static structure. It might be called the level of *frameworks*; for example, the anatomy of the universe.
2. The next level is that of the simple dynamic system with predetermined, necessary motions. This might be called the level of *clockworks*.
3. The control mechanism or cybernetic system, which might be nicknamed the level of the *thermostat*. The system is self-regulating in maintaining equilibrium.
4. The fourth level is that of the "open system", or self-maintaining structure. This is the level at which life begins to differentiate from not-life: it might be called the level of the *cell*.
5. The next level might be called the genetic–societal level; it is typified by the *plant*, and it dominates the empirical world of the botanist.
6. The *animal* system level is characterized by increased mobility, teleological behavior, and self-awareness.
7. The next level is the *human* level, that is, of the individual human being considered as a system with self-awareness and the ability to utilize language and symbolism.
8. The *social system* or systems of human organization constitute the next level, with the consideration of the content and meaning of messages, the nature and dimensions of value systems, the transcription of images into historical record, the subtle symbolizations of art, music, and poetry, and the complex gamut of human emotion.
9. *Transcendental systems* complete the classification of levels.

These are the ultimates and absolutes and the inescapable unknowables, and they also exhibit systematic structure and relationship.[2]

The first three levels in this hierarchy can be classified as physical or mechanical systems and provide the basis of knowledge in the physical sciences such as physics and astronomy. The fourth, fifth, and sixth levels are concerned with biological systems and are the interest of biologists, botanists, and zoologists. The last three levels are involved with human and social systems and are the concern of the social sciences as well as the arts, humanities, and religion.

General systems theory provides a basis for understanding and integrating knowledge from a wide variety of highly specialized fields. In the past, traditional knowledge has been along well-defined subject-matter lines. Bertalanffy * suggests that the various fields of modern science have had a continual evolution toward a parallelism of ideas. This parallelism provides an opportunity to formulate and develop principles which hold for systems in general. "In modern science, dynamic interaction is the basic problem in all fields, and its general principles will have to be formulated in General System Theory."[3] General systems theory provides the broad macro view from which we may look at all types of systems. "So has arisen systems theory – the attempt to develop scientific principles to aid us in our struggles with dynamic systems with highly interacting parts."[4]

Bertalanffy made another major contribution in setting forth a distinction between closed systems and open systems. Physical and mechanical systems can be considered as closed in relationship to their environment. Thus, the first three levels in Boulding's hierarchy are closed systems. On the other hand, biological and social systems are not closed but are in constant interaction with their environment. This view of biological and social phenomena as open systems has profound importance for the social sciences and organization theory. Traditional theory assumed the organization to be a closed system, whereas the modern approach considers it an open system in interaction with its environment. While the development of general systems theory has provided an overall conceptual view for dealing with all types of phenomena – physical, biological, and social – there have been many additional threads in intellectual development which have contributed to the development of the systems approach.

## Pervasiveness of Systems Theory

In complex societies with rapid expansion of knowledge, the various scientific fields become highly differentiated and specialized. In many scientific fields, the concentration over the past several decades has been on analytical, fact-finding, and experimental approaches in highly specific areas. This

* [An article by Bertalanffy setting out the major ideas of General System Theory follows at p. 29. *Ed.*]

has been useful in helping to develop knowledge and to understand the details of specific but limited subjects. At some stage, however, there should be a period of synthesis, reconciliation, and integration, so that the analytical and fact-finding elements are unified into broader, multidimensional theories.[5] There is evidence that every field of human knowledge passes alternately through phases of analysis and fact finding to periods of synthesis and integration. Recently systems theory has provided this framework in many fields – physical, biological, and social. Even more important, it provides a basis for communication between scientists in the various disciplinary areas – a problem of immense importance with the high degree of specialization of knowledge.[6]

The application of systems thinking has been of particular relevance to the social sciences. There is a close relationship between general systems theory and the development of functionalism in the social sciences, as described by Martindale:

> The essential unity of the social sciences has been revealed in the flooding of the functionalistic point of view across the boundaries of the special disciplines. This point of view has had both theoretical and methodological dimensions. Theoretically, it consists in the analysis of social and cultural life from the standpoint of the primacy of wholes or systems. Epistemologically, it involves analysis of social events by methods thought peculiarly adapted to the integration of social events into systems.
>
> The functionalistic point of view has been manifest in all of the social sciences from psychology through sociology, political science, economics, and anthropology to geography, jurisprudence, and linguistics.[7]

Although there are several connotations of the word "functionalism", its basic emphasis is upon systems of relationships and the integration of parts and subsystems into a functional whole.[8] Functionalism attempts to look at social systems in terms of structures, processes, and functions and attempts to understand the relationship between these components. It emphasizes that each element of a culture or social institution has a function in the broader system.

Functionalism, under the influence of the earlier works of A. R. Radcliffe-Brown and Bronislaw Malinowski, has become the framework for modern anthropology.[9] They pioneered the view that social customs, patterns of behavior, and institutions do not exist independently but must be considered in relationship to the total culture. All aspects of social life form a related whole, and society can best be understood as an interconnected system. Thus each social action, such as a marriage ceremony or the punishment of a crime, has a function in the culture as a whole and contributes to the maintenance of the social structure.

In sociology, Talcott Parsons led in the adoption of functionalism and the general systems viewpoint.[10] Although Parsons acknowledges his debt to Pareto for the concept of systems in scientific theory, it is Parsons himself who has fully utilized the open-systems approach for the study of social structures.[11] He not only developed a broad social system framework but also related his ideas to the organization. Many of his concepts relating to the structure and processes of social systems will be used later in this book.

In the field of psychology, the systems approach has achieved prominence. The various types of behaviorism in psychological theory have given way to the holism of gestalt psychology and field theory. The very word *gestalt* is German for configuration or pattern.[12] "The Gestaltists early adopted the concept of system, which is more than the sum of its components, and which determines the activity of these components."[13] Kurt Lewin was among the first to apply to tenets of gestalt psychology to the field of individual personality. He found that purely psychological explanations of personality were inadequate and that sociocultural forces had to be taken into account. He viewed personality as a dynamic system, influenced by the individual's environment. Harry Stack Sullivan, in his *Interpersonal Theory of Psychiatry*, went even further in relating personality to the sociocultural system. He viewed the foundation of personality as an extension and elaboration of social relationships. A further extension of psychology to give greater consideration to broader interpersonal and social systems is seen in the rapidly expanding field of social psychology.[14]

Modern economics has increasingly used the systems approach. Equilibrium concepts are fundamental in economic thought, and the very basis of this type of analysis is consideration of subsystems of a total system. Economics is moving away from static equilibrium models appropriate to closed systems toward dynamic equilibrium considerations appropriate to open systems. Leontief and his followers in industrial input–output analysis utilize the systems approach. "Considered from the point of view of the input-output scheme any national economy can be described as a system of mutually interrelated industries or – if one prefers a more abstract term – interdependent economic activities. The interrelation actually consists in the more or less steady streams of goods and services which directly or indirectly link all the sectors of the economy to each other."[15]

The very foundation of the discipline of cybernetics is based upon a systems approach.[16] It is primarily concerned with communication and information flow in complex systems. Although cybernetics has been applied primarily to mechanistic engineering problems, its model of feedback, control, and regulation has a great deal of applicability for biological and social systems as well.

Another similar point of view permeating many of the social and physical sciences is the concept of holism which is closely related to functionalism and the systems approach. Holism is the view that all systems – physical, biological, and social – are composed of interrelated subsystems. The whole is not just the sum of the parts, but the system itself can be explained only as a totality. Holism is the opposite of elementarism, which views the total as the sum of its individual parts. The holistic view is basic to the systems approach. In traditional organization theory, as well as in many of the sciences, the subsystems have been studied separately, with the view to later putting the parts together into the whole. The systems approach emphasizes that this is not possible and that the starting point has to be with the total system.

The foregoing discussion has attempted to show how the systems approach and associate views have become the operating framework for many physical and social sciences. We agree with Chin, who says:

> Psychologists, sociologists, anthropologists, economists, and political scientists have been "discovering" and using the system model. In so doing, they find intimations of an exhilarating "unity" of science, because the system models used by biological and physical scientists seem to be exactly similar. Thus, the system model is regarded by some system theorists as universally applicable to physical and social events, and to human relationships in small and large units.[17]

It is important for the student of organization and management to recognize that the developing body of knowledge and applications of the systems approach to complex organizations is but a part of the broad trend in many of the physical and social sciences and that this field is part of a pervasive stream of thought. Furthermore, understanding that organization theory can be put in the context of general systems theory allows for a growing community of interest and understanding with widely diverse disciplines. We will now look more closely at the direct relationship between the systems approach and organization theory.

## Systems Approach and Organization Theory

Traditional organization theory used a highly structured, closed-system approach. Modern theory has moved toward the open-system approach. "The distinctive qualities of modern organization theory are its conceptual-analytical base, its reliance on empirical research data, and, above all, its synthesizing, integrating nature. These qualities are framed in a philosophy which accepts the premise that the only meaningful way to study organization is as a system."[18]

Chester Barnard was one of the first management writers to utilize the systems approach.[19] Herbert Simon and his associates viewed the organization as a complex system of decision-making processes. Simon has ranged widely in seeking new disciplinary knowledge to integrate into his organization theories. However, the one broad consistency in both his research and writings has been the utilization of the systems approach. "The term 'systems' is being used more and more to refer to methods of scientific analysis that are particularly adapted to the unraveling of complexity."[20] He not only emphasizes this approach for the behavioral view of organizations but also stresses its importance in management science.

The systems approach has been advocated by a number of other writers in management science. Churchman and his associates were among the earliest to emphasize this view. "The comprehensiveness of O. R.'s aim is an example of a 'systems' approach, since 'system' implies an interconnected complex of functionally related components. Thus a business organization is a social or man-machine system."[21] Although the systems approach has been adopted and utilized in management science, the models typically used are closed in the sense that they consider only certain variables and exclude from consideration those not subject to quantification.

The sociologist George Homans uses systems concepts as a basis for his empirical research on social groups. He developed a model of social systems which can serve as an appropriate basis for small groups and also for larger organizations.[22] In his view, an organization is comprised of an external environmental system and an internal system of relationships which are mutually interdependent. There are three elements in a social system. *Activities* are the tasks which people perform. *Interactions* occur between people in the performance of these tasks, and *sentiments* develop between people. These elements are mutually interdependent.

Philip Selznick utilizes structural functional analysis and the systems approach in his studies of organizations. The institutional leader is concerned with the adaptation of the organization to its external systems. The organization is a dynamic system, constantly changing and adapting to internal and external pressures, and is in a continual process of evolution. The organization is a formal system influenced by the internal social structure and subject to the pressure of an institutional environment. "Cooperative systems are constituted of individuals interacting as wholes in relation to a formal system of coordination. The concrete structure is therefore a resultant of the reciprocal influences of the formal and informal aspects of organization. Furthermore, this structure is itself a totality, an adaptive 'organism' reacting to influences upon it from an external environment."[23] Selznick used this systems frame of reference for empirical research on governmental agencies and other complex organizations.

The systems approach has not only been used by many students of organization theory in the United States but has also provided the model in other countries. The group of social scientists associated with Tavistock Institute of Human Relations in London is one of the strongest proponents of the open-systems approach. As a result of a number of research studies in the mining, textile, and manufacturing industries in England and other countries, this group developed the concept of the sociotechnical system.[24] They also stressed that the organization is an open system in interaction with its environment.

The systems approach has also been adopted by social psychologists as a basis for studying organizations. Using open-systems theory as a general conceptual scheme, Katz and Kahn present a comprehensive theory of organization.[14] They suggest that the psychological approach has generally ignored or has not dealt effectively with the facts of structure and social organization, and they use systems concepts to develop an integrated model.

There are numerous examples of the utilization of the systems approach at operational levels. For example, the trend toward automation involves implementation of these ideas. Automation suggests a self-contained system with inputs, outputs, and a mechanism of control. Automated production systems for processing of materials are becoming increasingly important in many industries. Another phase which has been automated is information flow. With the introduction of large-scale, electronic data processing equipment, information processing systems have been developed for many applications. Physical distribution systems have received increasing attention. The concepts of logistics, or material management, have been used to emphasize the flow of materials through distribution channels.

The systems approach has been utilized as a basis of organization for many of our advanced defense and space programs. Program management is geared to changing managerial requirements in research, development, procurement, and utilization. With the new, complex programs such as ballistic missiles and advanced space programs it became impossible to think of individual segments or parts of the program as separate entities, and it was necessary to move to a broader systems approach.[25] In many other types of governmental projects, which require the integration of many agencies and activities – transportation problems, pollution control, and urban renewal, for example – the systems approach is being used.

These examples of the increasing trend in adapting the systems approach to modern organization theory and management practice are by no means exhaustive; they merely illustrate current developments. However, they are sufficient to indicate that increasing attention is being given to the study of organizations as complex systems. This modern view treats the organization as a system of mutually dependent parts and variables, which is part of the whole system of society. Modern organization theory and general systems theory are closely related. Many systems concepts taken from the investigation of other types of physical, biological, and social systems are meaningful to the study of organizations.

## Organization: An Open System in Its Environment

Systems can be considered in two ways: (1) closed or (2) open and in interaction with their environments. This distinction is important in organization theory. Closed-system thinking stems primarily from the physical sciences and is applicable to mechanistic systems. Many of the earlier concepts in the social sciences and in organization theory were closed-system views because they considered the system under study as self-contained. Traditional management theories were primarily closed-system views concentrating only upon the internal operation of the organization and adopting highly rationalistic approaches taken from physical science models. The organization was considered as sufficiently independent so that its problems could be analyzed in terms of internal structure, tasks, and formal relationships – without reference to the external environment.

A characteristic of all closed systems is that they have an inherent tendency to move toward a static equilibrium and entropy. Entropy is a term which originated in thermodynamics and is applicable to all physical systems. It is the tendency for any closed system to move toward a chaotic or random state in which there is no further potential for energy transformation or work. "The disorder, disorganization, lack of patterning, or randomness of organization of a system is known as its *entropy*."[26] A closed system tends to increase in entropy over time, to move toward greater disorder and randomness.

Biological and social systems do not fall within this classification. The open-system view recognizes that the biological or social system is in a dynamic relationship with its environment and receives various inputs, transforms these inputs in some way, and exports outputs. The receipt of inputs in the form of material, energy, and information allows the open system to offset the process of entropy. These systems are open not only in relation to their environment but also in relation to themselves, or "internally" in that interactions between components affect the system as a whole. The open system adapts to its environment by changing the structure and processes of its internal components.[27]

The organization can be considered in terms of a general open-system model, as in Figure 1.1. The open system is in

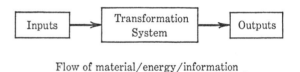

Flow of material/energy/information

**Figure 1.1** General model of organization as an open system.

continual interaction with its environment and achieves a "steady state" or dynamic equilibrium while still retaining the capacity for work or energy transformation. The survival of the system, in effect, would not be possible without continuous inflow, transformation, and outflow. In the biological or social system this is a continuous recycling process. The system must receive sufficient input of resources to maintain its operations and also to export the transformed resources to the environment in sufficient quantity to continue the cycle.

For example, the business organization receives inputs from the society in the form of people, materials, money, and information; it transforms these into outputs of products, services, and rewards to the organizational members sufficiently large to maintain their participation. For the business enterprise, money and the market provide a mechanism of the recycling of resources between the firm and its environment. The same kind of analysis can be made for all types of social organizations. Open-system views provide the basis for the development of a more comprehensive organization theory.

## Organization: A Structured Sociotechnical System

In addition to being considered as an open system in interaction with its environment, the organization can also be viewed as a structured sociotechnical system. This view of the organization is set forth by Trist and his associates at the Tavistock Institute. Technology is based upon the tasks to be performed and includes the equipment, tools, facilities, and operating techniques. The social subsystem is the relationship between the participants in the organization. The technological and social subsystems are in interaction with each other and are interdependent. "Trist's concept of the socio-technical system arose from the consideration that any production system requires both a technological organization – equipment and process layout – and a work organization – relating those who carry out the necessary tasks to each other. Technological demands limit the kind of work organization possible, but a work organization has social and psychological properties of its own that are independent of technology."[24]

Under this view an organization is not simply a technical or a social system. Rather, it is the structuring and integrating of human activities around various technologies. The technologies affect the types of inputs into the organization and the outputs from the system. However, the social system determines the effectiveness and efficiency of the utilization of the technology.

Technical subsystems are determined by the task requirements of the organization and vary widely. The technical subsystem for the manufacturing of automobiles differs significantly from that in an oil refinery or in an electronics or aerospace company. Similarly, the task requirements and technology in a hospital are substantially different from those in a university. The technological subsystem is shaped by the specialization of knowledge and skills required, the types of machinery and equipment involved, and the layout of facilities.

Technology frequently prescribes the type of human inputs required. For example, an aerospace company requires the employment of many scientists, engineers, and other highly trained people. Technology also is a prime factor in determining the structure and relationships between jobs.

In addition to the technical subsystem, every organization has within its boundaries a psycho-social subsystem, which consists of the interactions, expectations and aspirations,

sentiments, and values of the participants. However, it must be emphasized that these two subsystems, the technical and the social, cannot be looked at separately but must be considered in the context of the total organization. Any change in the technical subsystem will have repercussions on the social subsystem and conversely.

The organization *structure* can be considered as a third subsystem intermeshed between the technical and the social subsystems. The task requirements and technology have a fundamental influence upon the structure. Structure is concerned with the ways in which the tasks of the organization are divided into operating units and with the coordination of the units. In the formal sense, structure is set forth by the organization chart, by positions and job descriptions, and by rules and procedures. It also concerns the pattern of authority, communications, and work flow. In a sense, the organization structure provides for formalization of relationships between the technical and the psycho-social subsystems. However, it should be emphasized that this linkage is by no means complete and that many interactions and relationships occur between the technical and the psycho-social subsystems which bypass the formal structure.

One way of visualizing the organization as a structured sociotechnical system is shown in Figure 1.2. The goals and

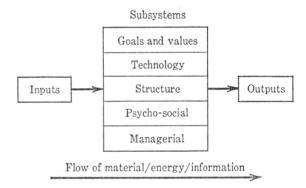

Figure 1.2 Organization as a sociotechnical system.

values, as well as the technical, structural, psycho-social, and managerial subsystems are shown as integral parts of the overall organization. This figure is an aid to understanding the evolution in organization theory. Traditional management theory emphasized the structural and managerial subsystems and was concerned with developing principles. The human relationists and behavioral scientists emphasized the psycho-social subsystem and focused their attention on motivation, group dynamics, and other related factors. The management science school emphasized the economic–technical subsystem and techniques for quantifying decision-making and control processes. Thus each approach to organization and management has emphasized particular primary subsystems, with little recognition of the importance of the others. The modern approach views the organization as a structured, sociotechnical system and considers *each* of the primary subsystems *and* their interactions.

## Other Properties of Organizational Systems

The systems approach emphasizes that an organization has a number of interacting subsystems and can only be considered in a holistic or synergistic framework. A number of other characteristics of organizational systems can be identified.

### Contrived systems

Social organizations are not natural like mechanical or biological systems; they are contrived. They have structure, but the structure of events rather than of physical components, and it cannot be separated from the processes of the system. The fact that social organizations are contrived by human beings suggests that they can be established for an infinite variety of objectives and do not follow the same life-cycle pattern of birth, maturity, and death as biological systems. Katz and Kahn say:

> Social structures are essentially contrived systems. They are made of men and are imperfect systems. They can come apart at the seams overnight, but they can also outlast by centuries the biological organisms which originally created them. The cement which holds them together is essentially psychological rather than biological. Social systems are anchored in the attitudes, perceptions, beliefs, motivations, habits, and expectations of human beings.[14]

Recognizing that the social organization is a contrived system cautions us against making an exact analogy between it and physical or biological systems.

### Boundaries

The view of the organization as an open sociotechnical system suggests that there are boundaries which separate it from the environment. The concept of boundaries helps us understand the distinction between open and closed systems. The closed system has rigid, impenetrable boundaries, whereas the open system has permeable boundaries between itself and a broader supersystem. "Boundaries are the demarcation lines or regions for the definition of appropriate system activity, for admission of members into the system, and for other imports into the system. The

boundary constitutes a barrier for many types of interaction between people on the inside and people on the outside, but it includes some facilitating device for the particular types of transactions necessary for organizational functioning."

The boundaries set the "domain" of the organization's activities. In a physical, mechanical, or biological system the boundaries can be identified. In a social organization, the boundaries are not easily definable and are determined primarily by the functions and activities of the organization. It is characterized by rather vaguely formed, highly permeable boundaries. Frequently, in the study of social organizations, where to draw the boundaries is a matter of convenience and strategy. Thus, in the study of a small work group, we may artificially establish the boundary to include only the activities of the immediate group and may consider interactions with other groups as outside these boundaries. Or, we might set our boundaries to include an entire department, division, company, industry, or total economic system. The boundaries of a social organization are often quite flexible and changeable over time, depending upon its activities and functions.

One of the key functions within any organization is that of boundary regulation between systems. A primary role of management is serving as a linking pin or boundary agent between the various subsystems to ensure integration and cooperation.[28] Furthermore, an important managerial function is that of serving as boundary agent between the organization and environmental systems.

The concept of *interface* is useful in understanding boundary relationships. An interface may be defined as the area of contact between one system and another. Thus, the business organization has many interfaces with other systems: suppliers of materials, the local community, prospective employees, unions, customers, and state, local, and federal governmental agencies. There are many transactional processes across systems boundaries at the interface involving the transfer of energy, materials, people, money, and information.

### Hierarchy of systems

In general, all systems – physical, biological, and social – can be considered in a hierarchical sense. A system is composed of subsystems of a lower order and is also part of a supersystem. Thus, there is a hierarchy of the components in the system. Large organizations are almost universally hierarchical in structure. People are organized into groups; groups are organized into departments; departments are organized into divisions; divisions are organized into companies; and companies are part of an industry and economy. Many general systems writers have concluded that this hierarchical relationship is paramount in all types of systems. "Hierarchical subdivision is not a characteristic that is peculiar to human organizations. It is common to virtually all complex systems of which we have knowledge. [There are] strong reasons for believing that almost any system of sufficient complexity would have to have the rooms-within-rooms structure that we observe in actual human organizations. The reasons for hierarchy go far beyond the need for unity of command or other considerations relating to authority."[29]

The hierarchical structure is not only related to levels but is based upon the need for more inclusive clustering or combination of subsystems into a broader system, in order to coordinate activities and processes. In complex organizations there is a hierarchy of processes as well as structure.

## Negative entropy

Closed physical systems are subject to the force of entropy which increases until eventually the entire system stops. The tendency toward maximum entropy is a movement to disorder, complete lack of resource transformation, and death. In a closed system, the change in entropy must always be positive. However, in the open biological or social system, entropy can be arrested and may even be transformed to negative entropy – a process of more complete organization and ability to transform resources. This is possible because in open systems and resources (material, energy, and information) utilized to arrest the entropy process are imported from the external environment. "Living systems, maintaining themselves in a steady state, can avoid the increase of entropy, and may even develop towards states of increased order and organization."[30] Obviously, for the biological system, this process of negative entropy is never perfect. The organism lives and grows for a period of time but is subject to deterioration and death. The contrived, or social, organization which can continue to import new human components and other resources in order to continue its functioning may be capable of indefinitely offsetting the entropy process. However, the only way in which the organization can offset entropy is by continually importing material, energy, and information in one form or another, transforming them, and redistributing resources to the environment.

## The steady state or dynamic equilibrium

The concept of *steady state* is closely related to that of negative entropy. A closed system must eventually attain an equilibrium state with maximum entropy – death or disorganization. An open system, however, may attain a state where the system remains in dynamic equilibrium through the continuous inflow of material, energy, and information. This is called a steady state. This relationship between negative entropy and the steady state for living organisms and social systems is suggested by Emery and Trist.

> In contradistinction to physical objects, any living entity survives by importing into itself certain types of material from its environment, transforming these in accordance with its own system characteristics, and exporting other types back into the environment. By this process the organism obtains the additional energy that renders it "negentropic"; it becomes capable of attaining stability in a time-independent steady state – a necessary condition of adaptability to environmental variance.[31]

The steady state for the open system, as contrasted to the closed system subject to entropy, occurs while the system can still maintain its functions and perform effectively. Under this concept, an organization is able to adapt to changes in its environment and to maintain a continual steady state. An analogy can be seen in a biological system. The human body is able to maintain a steady state of body temperature in spite of wide variations in the environmental temperature. Obviously, there are limits to the degree to which the biological organism or the social organization can maintain a steady state in response to environmental changes. Massive environmental changes may be so great that it is impossible for the system to adapt. The organism dies, or the social organization is disbanded.

The steady state has an additional meaning; within the organizational system, the various subsystems have achieved a balance of relationships and forces which allows the total system to perform effectively. In biological organisms, the term *homeostasis* is applied to the organism's steady state. For social organizations, it is not an absolute steady state but rather a dynamic or moving equilibrium, one of continual adjustment to environmental and internal forces. The social organization will attempt to accumulate a certain "slack" of resources which helps it to maintain its equilibrium and to mitigate some of the possible variations in the inflow and environmental requirements.

## Feedback mechanisms

The concept of feedback is important in understanding how a system maintains a dynamic equilibrium. Through the process of feedback, the system continually receives information from its environment which helps it adjust.

The concept of feedback has been used in looking at a number of biological phenomena. The maintenance of homeostasis, or the balance in a living organism, depends on a continual feedback of information to that organism from its environment. For example, the cooling of the blood from a drop in external temperatures stimulates certain centers in the brain which activate heat-producing mechanisms of the body, and the organism's temperature is monitored back to the center so that temperature is maintained at a steady level. Man uses principles of feedback in many of his physical activities. For example, in riding a bicycle, he receives feedback in regard to direction and balance which cause him to take corrective actions. Feedback can be both positive and negative, although for our purposes the most important consideration is that of negative feedback. Negative feedback is informational input which indicates that the system is deviating from a prescribed course and should readjust to a new steady state. Feedback is of vital importance in the complex organization which must continually receive informational inputs from its environment. Management is involved in interpreting and correcting for this information feedback. This is a vital part of the organizational control function.[32]

## Adaptive and maintenance mechanisms

Systems must have two mechanisms which are often in conflict. First, in order to maintain an equilibrium, they must have maintenance mechanisms which ensure that the various subsystems are in balance and that the total system is in accord with its environment. The forces for maintenance are conservative, and attempt to prevent the system from changing so rapidly that the various subsystems and total system become out of balance. Second, adaptive mechanisms are necessary in order to provide a *dynamic* equilibrium, one which is changing over time. Therefore, the system must have adaptive mechanisms which allow it to respond to changing internal and external requirements.

Some forces within the social organization are geared to the maintenance of the system, and other forces and subsystems are geared to adaptation. These counteracting forces will often create tensions, stresses, and conflicts which are natural and should not be considered as totally dysfunctional.[33] Katz and Kahn describe the importance of maintenance and adaptive mechanisms for social organizations.

If the system is to survive, *maintenance substructures*

must be elaborated to hold the walls of the social maze in place. Even these would not suffice to insure organizational survival, however. The organization exists in a changing and demanding environment, and it must adapt constantly to the changing environmental demands. *Adaptive structures* develop in organizations to generate appropriate responses to external conditions.[14]

## Growth through internal elaboration

In the closed system subject to the laws of physics, the system moves toward entropy and disorganization. In contrast, open systems appear to have the opposite tendency and move in the direction of greater differentiation and a higher level of organization. Bertalanffy points to the continual elaborations of biological organisms: "In organic development and evolution, a transition toward states of higher order and differentiation seems to occur. The tendency toward increasing complication has been indicated as a primary characteristic of the living, as opposed to inanimate, nature."[34]

This same process appears to hold true for most social systems. There is a tendency for them to elaborate their activities and to reach higher levels of differentiation and organization. An examination of certain attributes of complex organizations may help explain this tendency. Complex social organizations are made up of many subsystems, some of which have excess capacity or resources which create a continual pressure toward growth. Furthermore, social organizations will often try to encompass within their boundaries additional activities in order to limit uncertainties and to ensure their survival. The business organization may use vertical integration in order to ensure a continual source of raw materials. The pattern of conglomerate diversification and mergers by many corporations in the United States is another indication of this process. In many cases, these mergers result from product innovation and technological breakthroughs which provide opportunities for the organization to extend its boundaries into new areas. Or it may be attributed to an imbalance of managerial and technical skills which are seeking outlets for their activities and creativity. An indication of this elaboration has been the expansion of many of our large corporations into international activities, significantly increasing the boundaries of their operations.

There is also a tendency for complex organizations to achieve greater differentiation and specialization among internal subsystems. The increased number of specialized departments and activities in complex business organizations is readily apparent. The great proliferation of departments, courses, and subject matter in universities is another example of differentiation and elaboration.

## Equifinality of open systems

In physical systems there is a direct cause and effect relationship between the initial conditions and the final state. Biological and social systems operate differently. The concept of *equifinality* says that final results may be achieved with different initial conditions and in different ways. This view suggests that the social organization can accomplish its objectives with varying inputs and with varying internal activities. Thus, the social system is not restrained by the simple cause and effect relationship of closed systems.

The equifinality of social systems has major importance for the management of complex organizations. The closed-system cause and effect relationship adopted from the physical sciences would suggest that there is *one best way* to achieve a given objective. The concept of equifinality suggests that the manager can utilize a varying bundle of inputs into the organization, can transform these in a variety of ways, and can achieve satisfactory output. Extending this view further suggests that the management function is not necessarily one of seeking a rigid optimal solution but rather one of having available a variety of satisfactory solutions to his decision problems.

The foregoing are a few of the characteristics of open systems. To the student who is initially exposed to some of these concepts, they may seem complicated. Much of our educational experience emphasizes closed-system approaches – mathematics and the physical sciences, for example. The open-system view, with the properties set forth in the previous sections, is pertinent for organization theory.

## Managerial Systems

Having looked at the characteristics of organizations as open sociotechnical systems, we now turn to a more detailed consideration of managerial systems. Parsons provides a useful framework. He suggests that there are three managerial levels in the hierarchical structure of complex organizations: the technical or production level, the organizational (managerial) level, and the institutional or community level.[35]

The *technical* system is involved with the actual task performance in the organization. In the business firm, the technical functions involve the actual production and distribution of the products or services – the task performance activities of the organization. The technical system is not just involved with physical work but includes many types of technical activities utilizing knowledge. For example, research and development, production control, market research, operations research, and most accounting functions are part of the technical system. The teacher performs a technical task in the school, the doctor a technical task in the hospital, and scientists a technical task in the research laboratory. In complex organizations, many of the technical tasks are performed by professionals and highly trained experts, as well as by skilled and unskilled employees.

The second level, the *organizational*, coordinates and integrates the task performance of the technical system. A primary function of management at this level is to integrate the input of material, energy, and information to the technical level.

The *institutional* level is involved in relating the activities of the organization to its environmental system. The organization must continually receive supporting inputs from the society in order to carry on its transformation activities.

The managerial system spans the entire organization by directing the technology, organizing people and other resources, and relating the organization to its environment. However, there are basic differences in the orientation of the managerial system at these different levels. The technical level is concerned primarily with economic–technical rationality and tries to create certainty by "closing the technical core" to many variables. Thompson says, "Under norms of rationality, organizations seek to seal off their core technologies from environmental influences. Since complete closure is impossible, they seek to buffer environmental influences by surrounding their technical cores with input and output components."[36] The closed-system view is applicable to the "technical core" of the organization.

By contrast, at the institutional level the organization faces the greatest degree of uncertainty in terms of inputs from its environment over which it has little or no control. Therefore, management at this level should have an open-system view and concentrate on adaptive and/or innovative strategies. The organizational manager operates between the technical core and the institutional level and serves to mediate and coordinate the two. This level transforms the uncertainty of the environment into the economic-technical rationality necessary for input into the technical core. Figure 1.3 shows the organization as a composite system using these concepts. In describing this figure, Petit says:

The technical level has a boundary that does not seal it off entirely from the firm's environment but does have a high degree of closure. The organizational level has less closure and consequently is more susceptible to the intrusion of external elements. The institutional level has a highly permeable boundary and therefore is strongly affected by uncontrollable and unpredictable elements in the environment. Inputs enter the firm, are transposed into outputs in the technical subsystem, and then disposed of in the environment.[37]

relatively independently and that therefore it is not realistic to talk of a "line authority" extending from the top or institutional level, through the organization level, and down to the technical level. "I have emphasized the relative independence of the three level-types of organization, an independence that constitutes my main objection to the continuous line-authority picture of formal organization. This relative independence means that there is, at each

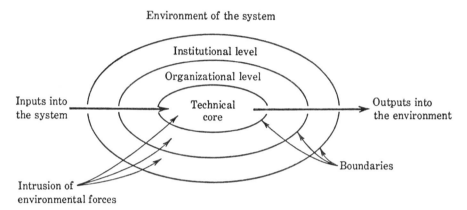

**Figure 1.3** The firm as a composite system (Thomas A. Petit, "A Behavioral Theory of Management", *Academy of Management Journal,* December, 1967, p. 346).

Thus the managerial system in the organization involves three levels – the technical core activities, intraorganizational interactions, and inter-institutional relationships. In many organizations these roles are separated theoretically. For example, in the university, the board of regents is thought of as fulfilling the institutional role, whereas the president, deans, and department heads are involved with organizational aspects. The professors, under this concept, perform the technical functions. In a hospital, the board of trustees performs the institutional role, the hospital administrator's staff is involved with organizational aspects, while the doctors, nurses, and other specialists perform the technical functions. Theoretically, in the business organization the board of directors relates the institution to its environment, upper and middle management deal with organizational aspects, and other employees perform the technical tasks. However, this distinction is not clear-cut in any of these organizations. For example, the president of a corporation usually has both institutional and organizational roles.

Parsons makes an interesting observation regarding these three levels. He stresses that they frequently are performed

linkage point, a range of possible *different* types of articulation."[38] He suggests that there is a break in the line authority between these three levels.

This view represents a major departure from the traditional scalar chain of command. There is a break between the organizational level and the technical level, particularly in the case of professional personnel. The manager cannot, because of his limited knowledge in a specific area, exert absolute authority over professional personnel. He must rely upon them to provide specialized technical expertise which he cannot develop himself. The manager can veto recommendations of the highly trained specialist; however, he cannot propose alternatives. Thus, it is necessary to develop means of articulation and adjustment at the boundaries between these various levels.

However, this does not mean that these different managerial levels can operate independently. Quite the contrary, they are interdependent. For example, the institutional level must perform effectively if the organization is to receive the necessary inputs for the technical level. Also, the technical level must produce outputs efficiently to ensure that the organization receives environmental support.

### Role of manager

The view of the organization as a sociotechnical system suggests a substantially different role for management than in traditional theory. In the traditional theory, the emphasis was upon economic–technical rationality. This closed-system view was appropriate for the technical level but not for the organizational and institutional levels. The human relations revolution did bring into focus the psycho-social subsystem but neglected the technical, structural, and environmental aspects. The management science approach adopted a closed-system view, focusing on the techniques of managerial decision making.

The view of an open sociotechnical system creates a more difficult role for the management system. It must deal with uncertainties and ambiguities and, above all, must be concerned with adapting the organization to new and changing requirements. Management is a process which spans and links the various subsystems of the organization. Thompson describes the management role as follows:

> The basic function of administration appears to be co-alignment, not merely of people (in coalition) but of institutionalized action – of technology and task environment into a viable domain, and of organizational design and structure appropriate to it. Administration, when it works well, keeps the organization at the nexus of the several necessary streams of action. Paradoxically, the administrative process must reduce uncertainty but at the same time search for flexibility.[36]

It is useful to consider the different types of managers necessary at the three levels in the managerial system. Petit suggests a basis for this classification in terms of the task performed, point of view, technique employed, time horizon, and decision-making strategy (see Figure 1.4).

The task at the technical level is primarily economic–technical and is concerned with efficiency of output with a given technology. Managers tend to adopt a closed-system view and utilize the methods of scientific management and management science. They have a task orientation with a short time perspective and utilize computational decision-making strategies.

The manager at the organizational level must integrate the technical level with the institutional level. He is more concerned with the psycho-social system of the organization. He serves as a mediator between levels. The decision-making strategy is to effect compromise between the demands of the other levels.

Institutional management must have a broad conceptual frame of reference. Top executives have a long-run perspective and prepare the organization to adapt to environmental changes. Because of the uncertainties in the environment, their decision-making strategy is primarily judgmental.

The systems view suggests that management faces situations which are dynamic, inherently uncertain, and frequently ambiguous. Management is not in full control of all the factors of production as suggested by traditional theory. It is strongly restrained by many environmental and internal forces. The technical system, the psycho-social system, and the environmental system all constrain the management system. Sayles outlines the role of management under the systems approach:

**Figure 1.4** The managerial system: technical, organizational, and institutional levels

| TYPE OF MANAGER | TASK | VIEWPOINT | TECHNIQUE | TIME HORIZON | DECISION-MAKING STRATEGY |
|---|---|---|---|---|---|
| Technical | Technical rationality | Engineering | Scientific management, operations research | Short run | Computational |
| Organizational | Coordination | Political | Mediation | Short run and long run | Compromise |
| Institutional | Deal with uncertainty, relate organization to environment | Conceptual and philosophical | Opportunistic surveillance, negotiate with environment | Long run | Judgmental |

SOURCE: Adapted from Thomas A. Petit, "A Behavioral Theory of Management", *Academy of Management Journal*, December, 1967, p. 349.

A systems concept emphasizes that managerial assignments do not have these neat, clearly defined boundaries; rather, the modern manager is placed in a network of mutually dependent relationships. . . . The one enduring objective is the effort to build and maintain a predictable, reciprocating system of relationships, the behavioral patterns of which stay within reasonable physical limits. But this is seeking a moving equilibrium, since the parameters of the system (the division of labor and the controls) are evolving and changing. Thus the manager endeavors to introduce regularity in a world that will never allow him to achieve the ideal . . . Only managers who can deal with uncertainty, with ambiguity, and with battles that are never won but only fought well can hope to succeed.[39]

One of the most pervasive functions of management at all levels is decision making. Figure 1.4 indicates that the decision-making strategy differs for various managerial levels. At the technical level, closed-system approaches are appropriate. However, at the organizational and institutional levels, open-system decision-making approaches are necessary.

## Summary

The systems approach provides an integrative framework for modern organization theory and management practice. General systems theory includes concepts for integrating knowledge in the physical, biological, and social sciences.

There is a close relationship between general systems theory and the development of functionalism in the social sciences. Functionalism emphasizes integration of parts and subsystems into a functional whole. It has been used as a primary frame of reference in anthropology and sociology. In the field of psychology, the systems concept has achieved prominence. Modern economics also uses this approach, particularly in dynamic equilibrium analysis and input-output studies. The discipline of cybernetics is founded on the systems approach, focusing on communication and information flow in complex systems. Although it has been applied primarily to mechanistic systems, its model of feedback, control, and regulation has applicability for social systems as well.

The systems approach is directly related to organization theory. Traditional theory used closed-system thinking. Modern theory has moved toward considering the organization as an open system interacting with its environment. In contrast to the closed or mechanical system, the open system is not subject to the process of entropy – it can maintain a dynamic equilibrium by importing material, energy, and information from its environment.

The organization can be viewed as a structured sociotechnical system with five primary components – goals and values, and technical, structural, psycho-social, and managerial subsystems.

There are several key characteristics of organizational systems. They are not natural, like physical or biological systems, but are *contrived*. There are *boundaries* which separate the organization from its environment. In general, a system is composed of subsystems of a lower order and is also part of a supersystem; there is a *hierarchy* of systems. In open biological or social systems, entropy can be arrested and may even be transformed to *negative entropy* – a process of more complete organization. The concept of *steady state* is closely related to that of negative entropy. The organization is able to adapt to changes in its environment and to maintain a continual dynamic equilibrium.

The concept of *feedback* is important in understanding how a system maintains a steady state. Through the process of feedback, it continually receives information from its environment which helps it to adjust. A system must have both *adaptive and maintenance mechanisms*. The forces for maintenance are conservative and attempt to prevent the system from changing so rapidly that the various subsystems become out of balance. In contrast, adaptive mechanisms are necessary in order to provide for change. Open systems display *growth through internal elaboration*. They tend to move in the direction of greater differentiation and to a higher level of organization. Finally, open systems have the characteristic of *equifinality* – objectives may be achieved with varying inputs and in different ways.

There are three levels in the managerial system of complex organizations; technical, organizational, and institutional. The *technical level* is involved with actual task performance. The *organizational level* integrates the technical and institutional levels. The *institutional level* relates the activities of the organization to its environment. The view of the organization as a sociotechnical system creates a different role for the manager. He must integrate and balance the various subsystems and their activities in the environmental setting.

## References

1 The name "general systems theory" and many of the basic concepts were set forth by the biologist Ludwig von Bertalanffy. For a general discussion of his views, see "The Theory of Open Systems in Physics and Biology", *Science*, Jan. 13, 1950, pp. 23–9; and

"General System Theory: A New Approach to Unity of Science", *Human Biology*, December 1951, pp. 302–61.

2 Boulding, Kenneth E. (1956) "General Systems Theory: The Skeleton of Science", *Management Science*, April, pp. 197–208.

3 von Bertalanffy, Ludwig (1952) *Problems of Life*, John Wiley & Sons, Inc., New York, p. 201. On page 176 he stresses this view: "If we survey the various fields of modern science, we notice a dramatic and amazing evolution. Similar conceptions and principles have arisen in quite different realms, although this parallelism of ideas is the result of independent developments, and the workers in the individual fields are hardly aware of the common trend. Thus, the principles of wholeness, of organization, and of the dynamic conception of reality become apparent in all fields of science."

4 Ashby, W. Ross (1964) in Mesarovic, Mihajlo D. (ed.), *Views on General Systems Theory*, John Wiley & Sons, Inc., New York, p. 166.

5 Eddington suggests that attention has been focused more and more on overall systems as frames of reference for analytical work in various areas. This synthesizing process "marked a reaction from the view that everything to which science need pay attention is discovered by microscopic dissection of objects. It provided an alternative stand-point in which the centre of interest is shifted from the entities reached by the customary analysis (atoms, electric potentials, etc.) to qualities possessed by the system as a whole, which cannot be split up and located – a little here and a little bit there." Eddington, Sir Arthur (1958) *The Nature of the Physical World*, The University of Michigan Press, Ann Arbor, Mich., pp. 103–4.

6 For an overview of the integrative possibilities of the systems approach, see Walter Buckley (ed.) (1968) *Modern Systems Research for the Behavioral Scientist*, Aldine Publishing Company, Chicago.

7 Martindale, Don (1965) *Functionalism in the Social Sciences*, Monograph 5, American Academy of Political and Social Science, February, pp. viii–ix.

8 Robert K. Merton discusses various connotations of the word *function* in *Social Theory and Social Structure*, rev. ed., The Free Press of Glencoe, New York, 1957, pp. 20–25.

9 Radcliffe-Brown, A. R. (1952) *Structure and Function in Primitive Society*, Cohen & West, London, and Bronislaw Malinowski (1960) *A Scientific Theory of Culture*, Oxford University Press, New York.

10 Talcott Parsons uses the systems approach in much of his writings. His *The Social System*, The Free Press of Glencoe, New York, 1951, presents a comprehensive treatise on his views.

11 For a view of Pareto's works, see Lawrence J. Henderson (1935) *Pareto's General Sociology*, Harvard University Press, Cambridge, Mass.

12 "A *gestalt* is an organized entity or whole in which the parts, though distinguishable, are interdependent; they have certain characteristics produced by their inclusion in the whole, and the whole has some characteristics belonging to none of the parts. The gestalt thus constitutes a 'unit segregated from its surroundings', behaving according to certain laws of energy distribution. It is found throughout human behaviour as well as in physiological and physical events and is thus a fundamental aspect of scientific data." Gould, Julius and Kolb, William L. (eds.) (1964) *A Dictionary of the Social Sciences*, The Free Press of Glencoe, New York, p. 287.

13 Whitaker, Ian (1965) "The Nature and Value of Functionalism in Sociology", in *Functionalism in the Social Sciences*, Monograph 5, American Academy of Political and Social Science, February, pp. 137–8.

14 Katz, Daniel and Kahn, Robert L. (1966) *The Social Psychology of Organizations*, John Wiley & Sons, Inc. New York, is an example of the movement of social psychology into broader systems of analysis.

15 Leontief, Wassily *et al.* (1953) *Studies in the Structure of the American Economy*, Oxford University Press, New York, p. 8.

16 Wiener, Norbert (1948) *Cybernetics*, John Wiley & Sons, Inc., New York.

17 Chin, Robert (1961) "The Utility of System Models and Developmental Models for Practitioners", in Warren G. Bennis, Kenneth D. Benne, and Robert Chin (eds.), *The Planning of Change*, Holt, Rinehart & Winston, Inc., New York, p. 202.

18 Scott, William G. (1967) *Organization Theory*, Richard D. Irwin, Inc., Homewood, Ill., pp. 122–3.

19 Barnard, Chester I. (1938) *The Functions of the Executive*, Harvard University Press, Cambridge, Mass.

20 Simon, Herbert A. (1964) "Approaching the Theory of Management", in Harold Koontz (ed.), *Toward a Unified Theory of Management*, McGraw-Hill Book Company, New York, pp. 82–3.

21 Churchman, C. West, Ackoff, Russell L. and Arnoff, E.

Leonard (1957) *Introduction to Operations Research*, John Wiley & Sons, Inc., New York, p. 7.

22 Homans, George C. (1950) *The Human Group*, Harcourt, Brace & World, Inc., New York.

23 Selznick, Philip (1948) "Foundations of the Theory of Organization", *American Sociological Review*, February, pp. 23–35.

24 Emery, F. E. and Trist, E. L. (1960) "Socio-technical Systems", in C. West Churchman and Michel Cerhulst (eds.), *Management Sciences: Models and Techniques*, Pergamon Press, New York, vol. 2, pp. 83–97; and Rice, A. K. (1963) *The Enterprise and Its Environment*, Tavistock Publications, London.

25 For a discussion of the evolution of this approach in military and space programs, see Kast, Fremont E. and Rosenzweig, James E. (1965) "Organization and Management of Space Programs", in Ordway, Frederick I. III (ed.), *Advances in Space Science and Technology*, Academic Press, Inc., New York, vol. 7, pp. 273–364.

26 Miller, James G. (1965) "Living Systems: Basic Concepts", *Behavioral Science*, July, p. 195.

27 Buckley, Walter, "Society as a Complex Adaptive System", in Buckley, *op. cit.*, pp. 490–1 (see Article 9).

28 This point is made by Rensis Likert in *New Patterns of Management*, McGraw-Hill Book Company, New York, 1961. In his interaction-influence system, he recommends the overlapping-group form of organization in which a "linking-pin function" is performed to integrate activities of the various subsystems in the organization.

29 Simon, Herbert A. (1960) *The New Science of Management Decision*, Harper & Row, Publishers, Incorporated, New York, pp. 40–2.

30 von Bertalanffy, Ludwig (1956) "General System Theory", in *General Systems*, Yearbook of the Society for the Advancement of General Systems Theory, vol. I, p. 4.

31 Emery, F. E. and Trist, E. L. (1965) "The Causal Texture of Organizational Environments", *Human Relations*, February, p. 2.1.

32 The concept of negative feedback is fundamental to the discipline of cybernetics. Mechanisms of feedback are basic to the purposeful behavior in man-made machines, as well as in living organisms and social systems. In discussing the cybernetic hypothesis, Wisdom says, "We may describe machines that embody negative feed-back mechanisms as proceeding by 'trial and error', or as 'error-compensating', or – best – as 'self-correcting'; and we may define 'a simple negative feed-back mechanism' as a mechanism by which part of the input-energy of a machine is utilized at intervals to impose a check on the output-energy. The basic hypothesis of cybernetics is that the chief mechanism of the central nervous system is one of negative feed-back." Wisdom, J. O. (1956) "The Hypothesis of Cybernetics", *General Systems*, Yearbook of the Society for the Advancement of General Systems Theory, vol. I, p. 112.

33 Robert Chin says, "The presence of tensions, stresses or strains, and conflict within the system often are reacted to by people in the system as if they were shameful and must be done away with. Tension reduction, relief of stress and strain, and conflict resolution become the working goals of practitioners but sometimes at the price of overlooking the possibility of increasing tensions and conflict in order to facilitate creativity, innovation, and social change." Chin, *op. cit.*, p. 204.

34 von Bertalanffy, Ludwig, (1950) "The Theory of Open Systems in Physics and Biology", *Science*, Jan. 13, p. 26.

35 Parsons, Talcott (1960) *Structure and Process in Modern Societies*, The Free Press of Glencoe, New York, pp. 60–96. Parsons calls the middle level in the managerial hierarchy "the managerial level". Actually management is involved in each of the three levels, and for our purpose it is more appropriate to call this "the organizational level".

36 Thompson, James D. (1967) *Organizations in Action*, McGraw-Hill Book Company, New York, p. 24.

37 Petit, Thomas A. (1967) "A Behavioral Theory of Management", *Academy of Management Journal*, December, p. 346.

38 Parsons, *Structure and Process in Modern Societies*, p. 95.

39 Sayles, Leonard (1964) *Managerial Behavior*, McGraw-Hill Book Company, New York, pp. 258–9.

# 2 General system theory – a critical review

## by Ludwig von Bertalanffy

*Since creative thought is the most important thing that makes people different from monkeys, it should be treated as a commodity more precious than gold and preserved with great care.* – A. D. Hall, A Methodology for Systems Engineering.

It is more than 15 years since the writer has first presented, to a larger public, the proposal of a General System Theory.* Since then, this conception has been widely discussed and was applied in numerous fields of science. When an early reviewer found himself "hushed into awed silence" by the idea of a General System Theory, now in spite of obvious limitations, different approaches and legitimate criticism, few would deny the legitimacy and fertility of the interdisciplinary systems approach.

Even more: The systems concept has not remained in the theoretical sphere, but became central in certain fields of applied science. When first proposed, it appeared to be a particularly abstract and daring, theoretical idea. Nowadays "systems engineering" "research", "analysis" and similar titles have become job denominations. Major industrial enterprises and government agencies have departments, committees or at least specialists to the purpose; and many universities offer curricula and courses for training.

Thus the present writer was vindicated when he was among the first to predict that the concept of "system" is to become a fulcrum in modern scientific thought. In the words of a practitioner of the science [R. L. Ackoff]:

In the last two decades we have witnessed the emergence of the "system" as a key concept in scientific research. Systems, of course, have been studied for centuries, but something new has been added. . . . The tendency to study systems as an entity rather than as a conglomeration of parts is consistent with the tendency in contemporary science no longer to isolate phenomena in narrowly confined contexts, but rather to open interactions for examination and to examine larger and larger slices of nature. Under the banner of *systems research* (and its many synonyms) we have also witnessed a convergence of many more specialized contemporary scientific developments. . . . These research pursuits and many others are being interwoven into a cooperative research effort involving an ever-widening spectrum of scientific and engineering disciplines. We

* This article first appeared in 1962.

are participating in what is probably the most comprehensive effort to attain a synthesis of scientific knowledge yet made.

This, however, does not preclude but rather implies that obstacles and difficulties are by no means overcome as is only to be expected in a major scientific reorientation. A reassessment of General Systems Theory, its foundations, achievements, criticisms and prospects therefore appears in place. The present study aims at this purpose.

According to the Preface to the VIth volume of *General Systems* by Meyer, the greatest number of enquiries made asks for "new statements describing the method and significance of the idea". Another central theme is "the organismic viewpoint". As one of the original proponents of the *Society for General Systems Research* and founders of the organismic viewpoint in biology, the author feels obliged to answer this challenge as well as readily admitted limitations of his knowledge and techniques permit.

## 1 The rise of interdisciplinary theories

The motives leading to the postulate of a general theory of systems can be summarized under a few headings.

1. Up to recent times the field of science as a nomothetic endeavor, i.e., trying to establish an explanatory and predictive system of laws, was practically identical with theoretical physics. Few attempts at a system of laws in non-physical fields gained general recognition; the biologist would first think of genetics. However, in recent times the biological, behavioral and social sciences have come into their own, and so the problem became urgent whether an expansion of conceptual schemes is possible to deal with fields and problems where application of physics is not sufficient or feasible.

2. In the biological, behavioral and sociological fields, there exist predominant problems which were neglected in classical science or rather which did not enter into its considerations. If we look at a living organism, we observe an amazing order, organization, maintenance in continuous change, regulation and apparent teleology. Similarly, in

human behavior goal-seeking and purposiveness cannot be overlooked, even if we accept a strictly behavioristic standpoint. However, concepts like organization, directiveness, teleology, etc., just do not appear in the classic system of science. As a matter of fact, in the so-called mechanistic world view based upon classical physics, they were considered as illusory or metaphysical. This means, to the biologist for example, that just the specific problems of living nature appeared to lie beyond the legitimate field of science.

3. This in turn was closely connected with the structure of classical science. The latter was essentially concerned with two-variable problems, linear causal trains, one cause and one effect, or with few variables at the most. The classical example is mechanics. It gives perfect solutions for the attraction between two celestial bodies, a sun and a planet, and hence permits one to exactly predict future constellations and even the existence of still undetected planets. However, already the three-body problem of mechanics is unsolvable in principle and can only be approached by approximations. A similar situation exists in the more modern field of atomic physics. Here also two-body problems such as that of one proton and electron are solvable, but trouble arises with the many-body problem. One-way causality, the relation between "cause" and "effect" or of a pair or few variables cover a wide field. Nevertheless, many problems particularly in biology and the behavioral and social sciences, essentially are multivariable problems for which new conceptual tools are needed. Warren Weaver, cofounder of information theory, had expressed this in an often-quoted statement. Classical science, he stated, was concerned either with linear causal trains, that is, two-variable problems; or else with unorganized complexity. The latter can be handled with statistical methods and ultimately stems from the second principle of thermodynamics. However, in modern physics and biology, problems of organized complexity, that is, interaction of a large but not infinite number of variables, are popping up everywhere and demand new conceptual tools.

4. What has been said are not metaphysical or philosophic contentions. We are not erecting a barrier between inorganic and living nature which obviously would be inappropriate in view of intermediates such as viruses, nucleoproteins and self-duplicating units in general which in some way bridge the gap. Nor do we protest that biology is in principle "irreducible to physics" which also would be out of place in view of the tremendous advances of physical and chemical explanation of life processes. Similarly, no barrier between biology and the behavioral

and social sciences is intended. This, however, does not obviate the fact that in the fields mentioned we do not have appropriate conceptual tools serving for explanation and prediction as we have in physics and its various fields of application.

5. It therefore appears that an expansion of science is required to deal with those aspects which are left out in physics and happen to concern just the specific characteristics of biological, behavioral, and social phenomena. This amounts to new conceptual models to be introduced. Every science is a model in the broad sense of the word, that is a conceptual structure intended to reflect certain aspects of reality. One such model is the system of physics – and it is an incredibly successful one. However, physics is but *one* model dealing with certain aspects of reality. It needs not to have monopoly, nor is it *the* reality as mechanistic methodology and metaphysics presupposed. It apparently does not cover all aspects and represents, as many specific problems in biology and behavioral science show, a limited aspect. Perhaps it is possible to introduce other models dealing with aspects outside of physics.

These considerations are of a rather abstract nature. So perhaps some personal interest may be introduced by telling how the present author was led into this sort of problem.

When, some 40 years ago, I started my life as a scientist, biology was involved in the mechanism–vitalism controversy. The mechanistic procedure essentially was to resolve the living organism into parts and partial processes: the organism was an aggregate of cells, the cell one of colloids and organic molecules, behavior a sum of unconditional and conditioned reflexes, and so forth. The problems of organization of these parts in the service of maintenance of the organism, of regulation after disturbances and the like were either by-passed or, according to the theory known as vitalism, explainable only by the action of soul-like factors, like hobgoblins as it were, hovering in the cell or the organism – which obviously was nothing less than a declaration of bankruptcy of science. In this situation, I was led to advocate the so-called organismic viewpoint. In one brief sentence, it means that organisms are organized things and, as biologists, we have to find out about it. I tried to implement this organismic program in various studies on metabolism, growth, and biophysics of the organism. One way in this respect was the so-called theory of open systems and steady states which essentially is an expansion of conventional physical chemistry, kinetics and thermodynamics. It appeared, however, that I could not stop on the way once taken and so I was led to a still further generalization which I called "General System Theory". The idea goes back for some considerable time – I presented it first in 1937 in Charles Morris' philosophy seminar at the University of Chicago. However, at this time theory was in bad reputation in biology, and I was afraid of what Gauss, the mathematician, called the "clamor of the Boeotians". So I left my drafts in the drawer, and it was only after the war that my first publications in this respect appeared.

Then, however, something interesting and surprising happened. It turned out that a change in intellectual climate had taken place, making model building and abstract generalizations fashionable. Even more: quite a number of scientists had followed similar lines of thought. So General Systems Theory, after all, was not isolated or a personal idiosyncrasy as I have believed, but rather was one within a group of parallel developments.

Naturally, the maxims enumerated above can be formulated in different ways and using somewhat different terms. In principle, however, they express the viewpoint of the more advanced thinkers of our time and the common ground of system theorists. The reader may, for example, compare the presentation given by Rapoport and Horvath which is an excellent and independent statement and therefore shows even better the general agreement.

There is quite a number of novel developments intended to meet the goals indicated above. We may enumerate them in a brief survey:

(1) Cybernetics, based upon the principle of feedback or circular causal trains providing mechanisms for goal-seeking and self-controlling behavior.

(2) Information theory, introducing the concept of information as a quantity measurable by an expression isomorphic to negative entropy in physics, and developing the principles of its transmission.

(3) Game theory, analyzing in a novel mathematical framework, rational competition between two or more antagonists for maximum gain and minimum loss.

(4) Decision theory, similarly analyzing rational choices, within human organizations, based upon examination of a given situation and its possible outcomes.

(5) Topology or relational mathematics, including non-metrical fields such as network and graph theory.

(6) Factor analysis, i.e., isolation by way of mathematical analysis, of factors in multivariable phenomena in psychology and other fields.

(7) General system theory in the narrower sense (G.S.T.), trying to derive from a general definition of "system" as complex of interacting components, concepts characteristic of organized wholes such as interaction, sum, mechanization, centralization, competition, finality, etc., and to apply them to concrete phenomena.

While systems theory in the broad sense has the character of a basic science, it has its correlate in applied science, sometimes subsumed under the general name of Systems Science. This development is closely connected with modern automation. Broadly speaking, the following fields can be distinguished:

Systems Engineering, i.e., scientific planning, design, evaluation, and construction of man–machine systems;

Operations research, i.e., scientific control of existing systems of men, machines, materials, money, etc.

Human Engineering, i.e., scientific adaptation of systems and especially machines in order to obtain maximum efficiency with minimum cost in money and other expenses.

A very simple example for the necessity of study of "man–machine systems" is air travel. Anybody crossing continents by jet with incredible speed and having to spend endless hours waiting, queuing, being herded in airports can easily realize that the physical techniques in air travel are at their best, while "organizational" techniques still are on a most primitive level.

Although there is considerable overlapping, different conceptual tools are predominant in the individual fields. In systems engineering, cybernetics and information theory, also general system theory are used. Operations research uses tools such as linear programming and game theory. Human engineering, concerned with the abilities, physiological limitations and variabilities of human beings, includes biomechanics, engineering psychology, human factors, etc., among its tools.

The present survey is not concerned with applied systems science; the reader is referred to Hall's book as an excellent textbook of systems engineering. However it is well to keep in mind that the systems approach as a novel concept in science has a close parallel in technology. The systems viewpoint in recent science stands in a similar relation to the so-called "mechanistic" viewpoint, as stands systems engineering to physical technology.

All these theories have certain features in common. *Firstly*, they agree in the emphasis that something should be done about the problems characteristic of the behavioral and biological sciences, but not dealt with in conventional physical theory. *Secondly*, these theories introduce concepts and models novel in comparison to physics: for example, a generalized system concept, the concept of information compared to energy in physics. *Thirdly*, these theories are particularly concerned with multivariable problems, as mentioned before. *Fourthly*, these models are inter-disciplinary and transcend the conventional fields of science. If, for example, you scan the *Yearbooks* of the *Society for General Systems Research*, you notice the breadth of application: Considerations similar or even identical in structure are applied to phenomena of different kinds and levels, from networks of chemical reactions in a cell to populations of animals, from electrical engineering to the social sciences. Similarly, the basic concepts of cybernetics stem from certain special fields in modern technology. However, starting with the simplest case of a thermostat which by way of feedback maintains a certain temperature and advancing to servomechanisms and automation in modern technology, it turns out that similar schemes are applicable to many biological phenomena of regulation or behavior. Even more, in many instances there is a formal correspondence or isomorphism of general principles or even of special laws. Similar mathematical formulations may apply to quite different phenomena. This entails that general theories of systems, among other things, are labor-saving devices: A set of principles may be transferred from one field to another, without the need to duplicate the effort as has often happened in science of the past. *Fifthly*, and perhaps most important: Concepts like wholeness, organization, teleology and directiveness appeared in mechanistic science to be unscientific or metaphysical. Today they are taken seriously and as amenable to scientific analysis. We have conceptual and in some cases even material models which can represent those basic characteristics of life and behavioral phenomena.

An important consideration is that the various approaches enumerated are not, and should not be considered to be monopolistic. One of the important aspects of the modern changes in scientific thought is that there is no unique and all-embracing "world system". All scientific constructs are models representing certain aspects or perspectives of reality. This even applies to theoretical physics: far from being a metaphysical presentation of ultimate reality (as the materialism of the past proclaimed and modern positivism still implies) it is but one of these models and, as recent developments show, neither exhaustive nor unique. The various "systems theories" also are models that mirror different aspects. They are not mutually exclusive and often combined in application. For example, certain phenomena may be amenable to scientific exploration by way of cybernetics, others by way of general system theory; or even in the same phenomenon, certain aspects may be describable in the one or the other way. Cybernetics combine the information and feedback models, models of

the nervous system net and information theory, etc. This, of course, does not preclude but rather implies the hope for further synthesis in which the various approaches of the present toward a theory of "wholeness" and "organization" may be integrated and unified. Actually, such further syntheses, e.g., between irreversible thermodynamics and information theory, are slowly developing.

The differences of these theories are in the particular model conceptions and mathematical methods applied. We therefore come to the question in what ways the program of systems research can be implemented.

## 2 Methods of general systems research

Ashby has admirably outlined two possible ways or general methods in systems study:

> Two main lines are readily distinguished. One, already well developed in the hands of von Bertalanffy and his co-workers, takes the world as we find it, examines the various systems that occur in it – zoological, physiological, and so on – and then draws up statements about the regularities that have been observed to hold. This method is essentially empirical. The second method is to start at the other end. Instead of studying first one system, then a second, then a third, and so on, it goes to the other extreme, considers the set of all conceivable systems and then reduces the set to a more reasonable size. This is the method I have recently followed.

It will easily be seen that all systems studies follow one or the other of these methods or a combination of both. Each of these approaches has its advantages as well as shortcomings.

1. The first method is empirico-intuitive; it has the advantage that it remains rather close to reality and can easily be illustrated and even verified by examples taken from the individual fields of science. On the other hand, the approach lacks mathematical elegance and deductive strength and, to the mathematically minded, will appear naïve and unsystematic.

Nevertheless, the merits of this empirico-intuitive procedure should not be minimized.

The present writer has stated a number of "system principles", partly in the context of biological theory and without explicit reference to G.S.T., partly in what emphatically was entitled an "Outline" of this theory. This was meant in the literal sense: It was intended to call attention to the desirability of such field, and the presentation was in the way of a sketch or blueprint, illustrating the approach by simple examples.

However, it turned out that this intuitive survey appears to be remarkably complete. The main principles offered such as wholeness, sum, centralization, differentiation, leading part, closed and open system, finality, equifinality, growth in time, relative growth, competition, have been used in manifold ways (e.g., general definition of system; types of growth; systems engineering; social work). Excepting minor variations in terminology intended for clarification or due to the subject matter, no principles of similar significance were added – even though this would be highly desirable. It is perhaps even more significant that this also applies to considerations which do not refer to the present writer's work and hence cannot be said to be unduly influenced by it. Perusal of studies such as those by Beer and Kremyanskiy on principles, Bradley and Calvin on the network of chemical reactions, Haire on growth or organizations, etc., will easily show that they are also using the "Bertalanffy principles".

2. The way of deductive systems theory was followed by Ashby. A more informal presentation which summarizes Ashby's reasoning lends itself particularly well to analysis.

Ashby asks about the "fundamental concept of machine" and answers the question by stating "that its internal state, and the state of its surroundings, defines uniquely the next state it will go to". If the variables are continuous, this definition corresponds to the description of a dynamic system by a set of ordinary differential equations with time as the independent variable. However, such representation by differential equations is too restricted for a theory to include biological systems and calculating machines where discontinuities are ubiquitous. Therefore the modern definition is the "machine with input": It is defined by a set $S$ of internal states, a set $I$ of input and a mapping $f$ of the product set $I \times S$ into $S$. "Organization", then, is defined by specifying the machine's states $S$ and its conditions $I$. If $S$ is a product set $S = \pi_i T_i$, with $i$ as the parts and $T$ is specified by the mapping $f$. A "self-organizing" system, according to Ashby, can have two meanings, namely: (1) The system starts with its parts separate, and these parts then change toward forming connections (example: cells of the embryo, first having little or no effect on one another, join by formation of dendrites and synapses to form the highly interdependent nervous system). This first meaning is "changing from unorganized to organized". (2) The second meaning is "changing from a bad organization to a good one" (examples: a child whose brain organization makes it fire-seeking at first, while a new brain organization makes him fire-avoiding; an automatic pilot and plane coupled first by deleterious positive feedback and then

improved). "There the organization is bad. The system would be 'self-organizing' if a change were automatically made" (changing positive into negative feedback). But "*no machine can be self-organizing in this sense*" (author's emphasis). For adaptation (e.g., of the homeostat or in a self-programming computer) means that we start with a set $S$ of states, and that $f$ changes into $g$, so that organization is a variable, e.g., a function of time $\alpha(t)$ which has first the value $f$ and later the value $g$. However, this change "cannot be ascribed to any cause in the set $S$; *so it must come from some outside agent, acting on the system* $S$ *as input*" (our emphasis). In other terms, to be "self-organizing" the machine $S$ must be coupled to another machine.

This concise statement permits observation of the limitations of this approach. We completely agree that description by differential equations is not only a clumsy but, in principle, inadequate way to deal with many problems of organization. The author was well aware of this emphasizing that a system of simultaneous differential equations is by no means the most general formulation and is chosen only for illustrative purposes.

However, in overcoming this limitation, Ashby introduced another one. His "modern definition" of system as a "machine with input" as reproduced above, supplants the general system model by another rather special one: the cybernetic model, i.e., a system open to information but closed with respect to entropy transfer. This becomes apparent when the definition is applied to "self-organizing systems". Characteristically, the most important kind of these has no place in Ashby's model, namely, systems organizing themselves by way of progressive differentiation, evolving from states of lower to states of higher complexity. This is, of course, the most obvious form of "self-organization", apparent in ontogenesis, probable in phylogenesis, and certainly also valid in many social organizations. We have here not a question of "good" (i.e., useful, adaptive) or "bad" organization which, as Ashby correctly emphasizes, is relative on circumstances; increase in differentiation and complexity – whether useful or not – is a criterion that is objective and at least on principle amenable to measurement (e.g., in terms of decreasing entropy, of information). Ashby's contention that "no machine can be self-organizing", more explicitly, that the "change cannot be ascribed to any cause in the set $S$" but "must come from some outside agent, an input" amounts to exclusion of self-differentiating systems. The reason that such systems are not permitted as "Ashby machines" is patent. Self-differentiating systems that evolve toward higher complexity (decreasing entropy) are, for thermodynamic reasons, possible only as open systems, i.e., systems importing matter containing free energy to an amount over-compensating the increase in entropy due to irreversible processes within the system ("import of negative entropy"). However, we cannot say that "this change comes from some outside agent, an input"; the differentiation within a developing embryo and organism is due to its internal laws of organization, and the input (e.g., oxygen supply which may vary quantitatively, or nutrition which can vary qualitatively within a broad spectrum) makes it only possible energetically.

than an inanimate communication channel. Both, however, are consequences of the organism's character as an open system.

Incidentally, it is for similar reasons that we cannot replace the concept of "system" by the generalized "machine" concept of Ashby. Even though the latter is more liberal compared to the classic one (machines defined as systems with fixed arrangement of parts and processes), the objections against a "machine theory" of life remain valid.

These remarks are not intended as adverse criticism of

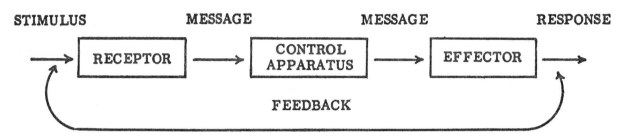

**Figure 2.1** Simple feedback model.

The above is further illustrated by additional examples given by Ashby. Suppose a digital computer is carrying through multiplications at random; then the machine will "evolve" toward showing even numbers (because products even × even as well as even × odd give numbers even), and eventually only zeros will be "surviving". In still another version Ashby quotes Shannon's Tenth Theorem, stating that if a correction channel has capacity $H$, equivocation of the amount $H$ can be removed, but no more. Both examples illustrate the working of closed systems: The "evolution" of the computer is one toward disappearance of differentiation and establishment of maximum homogeneity (analog to the Second Principle in closed systems); Shannon's Theorem similarly concerns closed systems where no negative entropy is fed in. Compared to the information content (organization) of a living system, the imported matter (nutrition, etc.) carries not information but "noise". Nevertheless, its negative entropy is used to maintain or even to increase the information content of the system. This is a state of affairs apparently not provided for in Shannon's Tenth Theorem, and understandably so as he is not treating information transfer in open systems with transformation of matter.

In both respects, the living organism (and other behavioral and social systems) is not an Ashby machine because it evolves toward increasing differentiation and inhomogeneity, and can correct "noise" to a higher degree

Ashby's or the deductive approach in general; they only emphasize that there is no royal road to General Systems Theory. As every other scientific field, it will have to develop by an interplay of empirical, intuitive and deductive procedures. If the intuitive approach leaves much to be desired in logical rigor and completeness, the deductive approach faces the difficulty of whether the fundamental terms are correctly chosen. This is not a particular fault of the theory or of the workers concerned but a rather common phenomenon in the history of science; one may, for example, remember the long debate as to what magnitude – force or energy – is to be considered as constant in physical transformations until the issue was decided in favor of $mv^2/2$.

In the present writer's mind, G.S.T. was conceived as a working hypothesis; being a practicing scientist, he sees the main function of theoretical models in the explanation, prediction, and control of hitherto unexplored phenomena. Others may, with equal right, emphasize the importance of axiomatic approach and quote to this effect examples like the theory of probability, non-Euclidean geometries, more recently information and game theory, which were first developed as deductive mathematical fields, and later applied in physics or other sciences. There should be no quarrel about this point. The danger, in both approaches, is to consider too early the theoretical model as being closed and definitive – a danger particularly important in a field like general systems which is still groping to find its correct foundations.

# 3 Homeostasis and open systems

Among the models mentioned, cybernetics in its application as homeostasis, and G.S.T. in its application to open systems lend themselves most readily for interpretation of many empirical phenomena. The relation of both theories is not always well understood, and hence a brief discussion is in place.

The simplest feedback scheme can be represented as follows (Fig. 2.1). Modern servomechanisms and automation, as well as many phenomena in the organism, are based upon feedback arrangements far more complicated than the simple scheme (Fig. 2.1) but the latter is the elementary prototype.

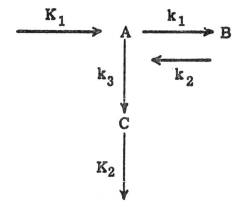

**Figure 2.2** Model of a simple open system. The component A is introduced into the system and transformed, in a reversible reaction, into B; it is catabolized in an irreversible reaction, into C which eventually is excreted. $K_1$, $K_2$ are constants of import and export, respectively; $k_1$, $k_2$, $k_3$ are reaction constants. The model approximately corresponds, for example, to protein turnover in an animal organism, A representing amino acids, B proteins, and C products of excretion.

In application to the living organism, the feedback scheme is represented by the concept of homeostasis.

Homeostasis, according to Cannon, is the ensemble of organic regulations which act to maintain the steady states of the organism and are effectuated by regulating mechanisms in such a way that they do not occur necessarily in the same, and often in opposite, direction to what a corresponding external change would cause according to physical laws. The simplest example is homeothermy. According to Van't Hoff's rule in physical chemistry, a decrease in temperature leads to slowing down of the rate of chemical reactions, as it does in ordinary physico-chemical systems

and also in poikilothermic animals. In warm-blooded animals, however, it leads to the opposite effect, namely, to an increase of metabolic rate, with the result that the temperature of the body is maintained constant at approximately 37°C. This is effectuated by a feedback mechanism. Cooling stimulates thermogenic centers in the brain thalamus which "turn on" heat-producing mechanisms in the body. A similar feedback pattern is found in a great variety of physiological regulations. Regulation of posture and the control of actions in animals and man toward a goal are similarly controled by feedback mechanisms.

In contradistinction to cybernetics concerned with feedback arrangements, G.S.T. is interested in dynamic interaction within multivariable systems. The case particularly important for the living organism is that of open systems. It amounts to saying that there is a system into which matter is introduced from outside. Within the system, the material undergoes reactions which partly may yield components of a higher complexity. This is what we call anabolism. On the other hand, the material is catabolized and the end products of catabolism eventually leave the system. A simple model of an open system is indicated in Figure 2.1.

A few main characteristics of open as compared to closed systems are in the fact that, appropriate system conditions presupposed, an open system will attain a steady state in which its composition remains constant, but in contrast to conventional equilibria, this constancy is maintained in a continuous exchange and flow of component material. The steady state of open systems is characterized by the principle of equifinality; that is, in contrast to equilibrium states in closed systems which are determined by initial conditions, the open system may attain a time-independent state independent of initial conditions and determined only by the system parameters. Furthermore, open systems show thermodynamic characteristics which are apparently paradoxical and contradictory to the second principle. According to the latter, the general course of physical events (in closed systems) is toward increasing entropy, leveling down of differences and states of maximum disorder. In open systems, however, with transfer of matter import of "negative entropy" is possible. Hence, such systems can maintain themselves at a high level, and even evolve toward an increase of order and complexity – as is indeed one of the most important characteristics of life processes.

The open-system model also has a wide application. According to its character, it is particularly applicable to phenomena showing non-structural, dynamic interaction of processes, such as those of metabolism, growth, metabolic aspects of excitation, etc.

Speaking more generally, living systems can be defined as hierarchically organized open systems, maintaining themselves, or developing toward a steady state. Disease is the life process regulating toward normalcy after disturbance, owing to the equifinality of biological systems and with the assistance of the physician. In this way, the *vis medicatrix naturae* of old is divested of its metaphysical paraphernalia; it is not a vitalistic agent but an expression of the dynamics of living systems, maintaining and reestablishing, so far as possible, the steady state.

In this way, the theory of open systems accounts for basic characteristics of the living organism which have baffled physicists, biologists, and philosophers, and appeared to be violations of the laws of physics, explainable only by vitalistic factors beyond the competence of science and scientific explanation.

Thus "feedback" and "open systems" are two models for biological and possibly behavioral phenomena. It should be made clear that the term "homeostasis" can be used in two ways. It is either taken in the original sense as proferred by Cannon and illustrated by examples like maintenance of body temperature and other physiological variables by feedback mechanisms – or else the term is often used as a synonym for organic regulation and adaptation in general. This is a question of semantics. However, it is a wise rule in the natural sciences to use terms in the sense originally attached to them by their authors. So I propose to use the word homeostasis in its narrower but well-defined sense, and this has important consequences, as it reveals certain limitations which are often forgotten.

As was already emphasized, regulations of the homeostasis or feedback type are abundant in the mature higher organism. However, it is clear from the scheme (Fig. 2.1) or any other flow diagram that feedback represents a machine-like arrangement, that is, an order of processes based upon fixed arrangements and representing linear, though circular, causal trains. The primary phenomena of organic regulation, e.g. the regulations in early embryonic development, in regeneration, etc., appear to be of a different nature. It seems that the primary regulations in the organism result from dynamic interaction within a unitary open system that reestablishes its steady state. Superimposed upon this by way of progressive mechanization are secondary regulatory mechanisms governed by fixed structures especially of the feedback type.

Although the homeostasis model transcends older mechanistic models by acknowledging directiveness in self-regulating circular processes, it still adheres to the machine theory of the organism. This also applies to a second aspect. An essential component of the mechanistic view is a utilitarian conception which is deeply connected with the economic outlook of the 19th and early 20th centuries. This is well known, for example, in the history of Darwinism: Struggle for existence and survival of the fittest are a biological version of the economic model of free competition. This utilitarian or economic viewpoint also prevails in the concept of homeostasis: The organism is essentially envisaged as an aggregate mechanism for maintenance of minimum costs. However, there seem to be plenty of non-utilitarian structures and functions in the living world.

The concept of homeostasis also retains a third aspect of the mechanistic view. The organism is essentially considered to be a reactive system. Outside stimuli are answered by proper responses in such a way as to maintain the system. The feedback model (Fig. 2.1) is essentially the classical stimulus-response scheme, only the feedback loop being added. However, an overwhelming amount of facts shows that primary organic behavior as, for example, the first movements of the fetus, are not reflex responses to external stimuli, but rather spontaneous mass activities of the whole embryo or larger areas. Reflex reactions answering external stimuli and following a structured path appear to be superimposed upon primitive automatisms, ontogenetically and phylogenetically, as secondary regulatory mechanisms. These considerations win particular importance in the theory of behavior as we shall see later on.

In this sense, it appears that in development and evolution dynamic interaction (open system) precedes mechanization (structured arrangements particularly of a feedback nature). In a similar way, G.S.T. can logically be considered the more general theory; it includes systems with feedback constraints as a special case, but this assertion would not be true vice versa. It need not be emphasized that this statement is a program for future systematization and integration of G.S.T. rather than a theory presently achieved.

## 4  Criticism of general system theory

A discussion of G.S.T. must take account of the objections raised, both to clarify misunderstanding and to utilize criticism for improvement.

A "devastating" criticism of "General Behavior Systems Theory" by Buck would hardly deserve discussion were it not for the fact that it appeared in the widely read *Minnesota Studies in the Philosophy of Science*, a leading publication of modern positivism. In passing, it should be noted that the lack of interest in, or even hostility of logical positivists against, G.S.T. is a rather remarkable phenomenon. One would expect that a group whose program is "Unified Science" should be concerned with a novel approach to this problem, however immature it may still be. The opposite is the case; no contribution or even pertinent criticism came forward from these quarters. The reason is not difficult to see. Abandoning the debatable but challenging position of Logical Positivism and replacing it by a rather tame "Empirical Realism", modern positivists have come back to what is generally agreed among modern scientists, avoiding commitments which trespass and would imply an adventure of thought. It needs to be said that modern positivism has been a singularly sterile movement. It is paradoxical that the declared "philosophers of science" have neither contributed any empirical research nor new idea to modern science – while professional or half-time philosophers who were justly censored for their "mysticism", "metaphysics", or "vitalism", indubitably did. Eddington and Jeans in physics, Driesch in biology, Spengler in history are but a few examples.

Buck's critique is not directed against the present author but against J. G. Miller and his Chicago group. Its essence is in the "So what?" argument: Supposing we find an analogy or formal identity in two "systems", it means nothing. Compare, for example, a chessboard and a mixed dinner party; a general statement expressing the alternation of black and white squares on the one hand, and of men and women on the other can be made. "If one is tempted to say 'All right, so they're structurally analogous, so what?' my answer is 'So, nothing.' " In the same vein, Buck pokes fun at some of Miller's more hazardous comparisons, such as the behavior of slime molds and Londoners during the *blitz*. He asks, "What are we to conclude from all this? That Londoners are a form of slime mold? That myxamoebae are a sort of city dweller?" Or "if no conclusion, why bother with the analogy at all?"

As proof of the emptiness of analogies Buck offers the example of a scientist, A, who finds a formula for the rate of formation of frost in a refrigerator; of another, B, formulating the rate of carbon deposit in an automobile motor; and a "general systems theorist," C, who notices that both formulas are the same. The similarity of mathematical expressions and models is, according to Buck, "sheer coincidence" – it does not prove that a refrigerator is an automobile or vice versa, but only that both are "systems" of some sort. This, however, is a meaningless statement; for

One is unable to think of anything, or of any combination of things, which could not be regarded as a system. And, of course, a concept that applies to everything is logically empty.

Regardless of the question whether Miller's is a particularly felicitous presentation, Buck has simply missed the issue of a general theory of systems. Its aim is not more or less hazy analogies; it is to establish principles applicable to entities not covered in conventional science. Buck's criticism is, in principle, the same as if one would criticize Newton's law because it draws a loose "analogy" between apples, planets, ebb and tide and many other entities; or if one would declare the theory of probability meaningless because it is concerned with the "analogy" of games of dice, mortality statistics, molecules in a gas, the distribution of hereditary characteristics, and a host of other phenomena.

The basic role of "analogy" – or rather of isomorphisms and models in science – has been lucidly discussed by Ashby. Hence a few remarks in answer to Buck will suffice.

The "So what?" question mistakes a method which is fundamental in science although – like every method – it can be misused. Even Buck's first example is not a meaningless pseudoproblem; in the "analogy" of chessboard and dinner party topology may find a common structural principle that is well worth stating. Generally speaking, the use of "analogy" (isomorphism, logical homology) – or, what amounts to nearly the same, the use of conceptual and material models – is not a half-poetical play but a potent tool in science. Where would physics be without the analogy or model of "wave", applicable to such dissimilar phenomena as water waves, sound waves, light and electromagnetic waves, "waves" (in a rather Pickwickian sense) in atomic physics? "Analogies" may pose fundamental problems, as for example, the analogy (logically not dissimilar from that of chessboard and dinner party) of Newton's and Coulomb's law which raises the question (one of the most basic for "Unified Science") of a general field theory unifying mechanics and electrodynamics. It is commonplace in cybernetics that systems which are different materially; e.g., a mechanical and an electrical system, may be formally identical; far from considering this as a meaningless So what? the researcher has to work out the common structure (flow diagram), and this may be of incomparable value for practical technology.

A similar lack of understanding is manifest in the criticism of the system concept. By the same token ("One is unable to think of anything" which would not show the properties in question) mechanics would have to be refused as "logically empty" because every material body shows mass, acceleration, energy, etc. In the following paragraphs of his paper, Buck has some glimpse of this truism, but he soon comes back to ridiculing Miller's use of "analogies".

Although Buck justly criticizes certain unfortunate formulations, his misunderstanding of the basic problems involved makes one wonder how his essay found its way into a treatise on "Philosophy of Science".

At an incomparably higher level stands the criticism by the Soviet authors, Lektorsky and Sadovsky. The writers give a sympathetic and fair presentation of Bertalanffy's G.S.T. sketching diligently its gradual evolution from "organismic biology" and the theory of open systems. In view of the above criticism by Buck, the following quotation is of interest:

> Bertalanffy emphasizes the idea that a general system theory is not an investigation of hazy and superficial analogies. . . . Analogies as such have little value, since differences can always be found among phenomena as well as similarities. Bertalanffy declares that the kind of isomorphism with which general system theory is concerned is a consequence of the fact that in some respects corresponding abstractions and conceptual models can be applied to different phenomena.

"We can only welcome [the] goal [of G.S.T.]," write Lektorsky and Sadovsky, "i.e., the attempt to give a general definition of the concept of 'organized system', to classify logically various types of systems and to work out mathematical models for describing them . . . Bertalanffy's theory of organization and of organized complexes is a special scientific discipline. At the same time it certainly fulfills a definite methodological function" (i.e., avoiding duplication of effort in various disciplines by a single formal apparatus). "Its mathematical apparatus can be utilized for analyzing a comparatively large class of systemed objects of interest to biologists, chemists, biochemists, biophysicists, psychologists and others."

The criticism of the Russian authors is directed against imperfections of G.S.T. which, unfortunately, cannot be denied: "Bertalanffy's definition is rather a description [not pretending to precision] of the class of events which we may call systems than a strictly logical definition." "The description contains no trace of logical elegance." "Elementary methods of analysis and synthesis are insufficient for the analysis of systems." Fairly enough the authors concede that "The flaws we have noted speak only for the fact that general system theory, like any scientific theory, should

develop further and in the process of development should strive for more adequate reflection of the objects of investigation."

The "main flaws of the theory", according to Lektorsky and Sadovsky, are in the lack of "methodology" (i.e., presumably of rules to establish and to apply system principles) and in considering G.S.T. "a philosophy of modern science". With respect to the first item, the present study is devoted to just this problem. The second point is a misunderstanding. G.S.T. in its present form is one – and still very imperfect – model among others. Were it completely developed, it would indeed incorporate the "organismic" world view of our time, with its emphasis on problems of wholeness, organization, directiveness, etc., in a similar way as when previous philosophies have presented a mathematical world view (philosophies *more geometrico*), a physicalistic one (the mechanistic philosophy based upon classical physics), etc., corresponding to scientific development. Even then, this "organismic" picture would not claim to be a "Nothing-but" philosophy: It would remain conscious that it only presents certain aspects of reality (richer and more comprehensive than previous ones, as corresponds to the advance of science), but never exhaustive, exclusive or final.

According to the authors, Marxist–Leninist philosophy "formulates a series of most important methodological principles of analysis of complex systems"; Soviet scientists "attempt to give a general definition of the notion of systems and to obtain a classification". Difficulties in international communication make it unfortunately impossible to the present writer to evaluate these claims.

Another criticism backed by the same *weltanschauung* is that of Kamaryt. The main arguments are:

1. Underestimation of the structural and morphologic aspects of organization of the theory of open systems (and implicitly in G.S.T.). The theory of open system does not "solve" the problem of life, its origin and evolution which is successfully attacked in modern biochemistry, submicroscopic morphology, physiological genetics, etc. The reply to this is that the functional and processual aspect has been emphasized in the theory, particularly in contradistinction to structural, homeostatic mechanisms. But neither the importance of the latter is denied, nor of course the specificity of the material basis of life. "Morphology and physiology are different and complementary ways of studying the same integrated object." If one wishes, this may be called a "dialectic unity of structure and function".

2. Neglect of "qualitative specificity" of biological open system and of the specific "chemodynamics" of the first.

The reply is: Thermodynamic considerations (of machines, chemical reactions, organisms, etc.) permit balance statements regarding the system as a whole, without entering into, or even knowing partial reactions, components, organization, etc., in detail. Hence part of the "theory of open systems" is concerned with such over-all balances of the system as a whole. If, however, the theory is applied to individual processes such as formation of proteins, behavior of tracers in the organism, ionic steady states, etc., the "specifity" of the respective components enters as a matter of course.

## 5 Advances of general system theory

The decisive question is that of the explanatory and predictive value of the "new theories" attacking the host of problems around wholeness, teleology, etc. Of course, the change in intellectual climate which allows us to see new problems which were overlooked previously, or to see problems in a new light, is in a way more important than any single and special application. The "Copernican Revolution" was more than the possibility somewhat better to calculate the movement of the planets; general relativity more than an explanation of a very small number of recalcitrant phenomena in physics; Darwinism more than a hypothetical answer to zoological problems; it was the changes in the general frame of reference that mattered. Nevertheless, the justification of such change ultimately is in specific achievements which would not have been obtained without the new theory.

There is no question that new horizons have been opened up but the relations to empirical facts often remain tenuous. Thus, information theory has been hailed as a "major breakthrough" but outside the original technological field contributions have remained relatively scarce. In psychology, they are so far limited to rather trivial applications such as role learning, etc. When, in biology, DNA is spoken of as "coded information" and of "breaking the code" when the structure of nucleic acids is elucidated, this is more a *façon de parler* than added insight into the control of protein synthesis. "Information theory, although useful for computer design and network analysis, has so far not found a significant place in biology." Game theory, too, is a novel mathematical development which was considered to be comparable in scope to Newtonian mechanics and the introduction of calculus; again, "the applications are meager and faltering" (the reader is urgently referred to Rapoport's discussions on information and game theory which admirably analyze the problems here mentioned). The same is seen in decision theory from which considerable gain in applied systems science was expected; but as regards the much-advertised military and business games, "there has been no controlled evaluation of their performance in training, personnel selection, and demonstration".

A danger in recent developments should not remain unmentioned. Science of the past (and partly still the present) was dominated by one-sided empiricism. Only collection of data and experiments were considered as being "scientific" in biology (and psychology); "theory" was equated with "speculation" or "philosophy", forgetting that a mere accumulation of data, although steadily piling up, does not make a "science". Lack of recognition and support for development of the necessary theoretical framework and unfavorable influence on experimental research itself (which largely became an at-random, hit-or-miss endeavor) was the consequence. This has, in certain fields, changed to the contrary in recent years. Enthusiasm for the new mathematical and logical tools available has led to feverish "model building" as a purpose in itself and often without regard to empirical fact. However, conceptual experimentation at random has no greater chances of success than at-random experimentation with biological, psychological, or clinical material. In the words of Ackoff, there is the fundamental misconception in game (and other) theory to mistake for a "problem" what actually is only a mathematical "exercise". One would do well to remember the old Kantian maxim that experience without theory is blind, but theory without experience a mere intellectual play.

The case is somewhat different with cybernetics. The model here applied is not new; although the enormous development in the field dates from the introduction of the name, Cybernetics, application of the feedback principle to physiological processes goes back to R. Wagner's work nearly 40 years ago. The feedback and homeostasis model has since been applied to innumerable biological phenomena and – somewhat less persuasively – in psychology and the social sciences. The reason for the latter fact is, in Rapoport's words that

> usually, there is a well-marked negative correlation between the scope and the soundness of the writings. . . . The sound work is confined either to engineering or to rather trivial applications; ambitious formulations remain vague.

This, of course, is an ever-present danger in all approaches to general systems theory: doubtless, there is a new compass of thought but it is difficult to steer between the scylla of the trivial and the charybdis of mistaking neologisms for explanation.

The following survey is limited to "classical" general system theory – "classical" not in the sense that it claims any priority or excellence, but that the models used remain in the framework of "classical" mathematics in contradistinction to the "new" mathematics in game, network, information theory, etc. This does not imply that the theory is merely application of conventional mathematics. On the contrary, the system concept poses problems which are partly far from being answered. In the past, system problems have led to important mathematical developments such as Volterra's theory of integro-differential equations, of systems with "memory" whose behavior depends not only on actual conditions but also on previous history. Presently important problems are waiting for further developments, e.g., a general theory of non-linear differential equations, of steady states and rhythmic phenomena, a generalized principle of least action, the thermodynamic definition of steady states, etc.

It is, of course, irrelevant whether or not research was explicitly labeled as "general system theory". No complete or exhaustive review is intended. The aim of this unpretentious survey will be fulfilled if it can serve as a sort of guide to research done in the field, and to areas that are promising for future work.

## Open systems

The theory of open systems is an important generalization of physical theory, kinetics and thermodynamics. It has led to new principles and insight, such as the principle of equifinality, the generalization of the second thermodynamic principle, the possible increase of order in open systems, the occurrence of periodic phenomena of overshoot and false start, etc. The possibility of measuring organization in terms of entropy ("chain entropy" of high molecular compounds showing a certain order of component molecules) deserves further attention.

The extensive work done cannot be reviewed here. . . . It should be briefly mentioned, however, that apart from theoretical developments, the field has two major applications, i.e., in industrial chemistry and in biophysics.

The applications of "open systems" in biochemistry, biophysics, physiology, etc., are too numerous to permit more than brief mentioning in the present study. The impact of the theory follows from the fact that the living organism, the cell as well as other biological entities essentially are steady states (or evolving toward such states). This implies the fundamental nature of the theory in the biological realm, and a basic reorientation in many of its specialties. Among others, the theory was developed and applied in such fields as e.g., the network of reactions in photosynthesis, calculation of turnover rates in isotope experiments, energy requirements for the maintenance of body proteins, transport processes, maintenance of ion concentrations in the blood, radiation biology, excitation and propagation of nerve impulses, and others. The organism is in a steady state not only with respect to its chemical components, but also to its cells; hence the numerous modern investigations on cell turnover and renewal have also to be included here. Beside the work already cited, results and impending problems in biophysics and related fields may be found in Netter (1959).

There are certainly relations between irreversible thermodynamics of open systems, cybernetics, and information theory, but they are still unexplored. First approaches to these problems are those by Foster, Rapoport and Trucco, and by Tribus. Another interesting approach to metabolizing systems was made by Rosen (1960) who instead of conventional reaction equations, applied "relational theory" using mapping by way of block diagrams.

Beyond the individual organism, systems principles are also used in population dynamics and ecologic theory. Dynamic ecology, i.e., the succession and climax of plant populations, is a much-cultivated field which, however, shows a tendency to slide into verbalism and terminological debate. The systems approach seems to offer a new viewpoint. Whittacker has described the sequence of plant communities toward a climax formation in terms of open systems and equifinality. According to this author, the fact that similar climax formations may develop from different initial vegetations is a striking example of equifinality, and one where the degree of independence of starting conditions and of the course development has taken appears even greater than in the individual organism. A quantitative analysis on the basis of open systems in terms of production of biomass, with climax as steady state attained, was given by Patten.

The open-system concept has also found application in the earth sciences, geomorphology and meteorology, drawing a detailed comparison of modern meteorological concepts and Bertalanffy's organismic concept in biology. It may be remembered that already Prigogine in his classic mentioned meteorology as one possible field of application of open systems.

## Growth-in-time

The simplest forms of growth which, for this reason, are particularly apt to show the isomorphism of law in different fields, are the exponential and logistic. Examples are, among many others, the increase of knowledge of number of animal species, publications on drosophila, of manufacturing companies. Boulding and Keiter have emphasized a general theory of growth.

The theory of animal growth after Bertalanffy (and others) – which, in virtue of using overall physiological parameters ("anabolism", "catabolism") may be subsumed under the heading of G.S.T. as well as under that of biophysics – has been surveyed in its various applications.

## Relative growth

A principle which is also of great simplicity and generality concerns the relative growth of components within a system. The simple relationship of allometric increase applies to many growth phenomena in biology (morphology, biochemistry, physiology, evolution).

A similar relationship obtains in social phenomena. Social differentiation and division of labor in primitive societies as well as the process of urbanization (i.e., growth of cities in comparison to rural population) follow the allometric equation. Application of the latter offers a quantitative measure of social organization and development, apt to replace the usual, intuitive judgments. The same principle apparently applies to the growth of staff compared to total number of employees in manufacturing companies.

## Competition and related phenomena

The work in population dynamics by Volterra, Lotka, Gauss and others belongs to the classics of G.S.T., having first shown that it is possible to develop conceptual models for phenomena such as the "struggle for existence" that can be submitted to empirical test. Population dynamics and related population genetics have since become important fields in biological research.

It is important to note that investigation of this kind belongs not only to basic but also to applied biology. This is true of fishery biology where theoretical models are used to establish optimum conditions for the exploitation of the sea (survey of the more important models: Watt). The most elaborate dynamic model is by Beverton and Holt developed for fish populations exploited in commercial fishery but certainly of wider application. This model takes into account recruitment (i.e., entering of individuals into the population), growth (assumed to follow the growth equations after Bertalanffy), capture (by exploitation), and natural mortality. The practical value of this model is illustrated by the fact that it has been adopted for routine purposes by the Food and Agriculture Organization of the United Nations, the British Ministry of Agriculture and Fisheries and other official agencies.

Richardson's studies on armaments races, notwithstanding their shortcomings, dramatically show the possible impact of the systems concept upon the most vital concerns of our time. If rational and scientific considerations matter at all, this is one way to refute such catch words as *Si vis pacem para bellum*.

The expressions used in population dynamics and the biological "struggle for existence", in econometrics, in the study of armament races (and others) all belong to the same family of equations. A systematic comparison and study of these parallelisms would be highly interesting and rewarding. One may, for example, suspect that the laws governing business cycles and those of population fluctuations according to Volterra stem from similar conditions of competition and interaction in the system.

In a non-mathematical way, Boulding has discussed what he calls the "Iron Laws" of social organizations: the Malthusian law, the law of optimum size of organizations, existence of cycles, the law of oligopoly, etc.

## Systems engineering

The theoretical interest of systems engineering and operations research is in the fact that entities whose components are most heterogeneous – men, machines, buildings, monetary and other values, inflow of raw material, outflow of products and many other items – can successfully be submitted to systems analysis.

As already mentioned, systems engineering employs the methodology of cybernetics, information theory, network analysis, flow and block diagrams, etc. Considerations of G.S.T. also enter. The first approaches are concerned with structured, machine-like aspects (yes-or-no decisions in the case of information theory); one would suspect that G.S.T. aspects will win increased importance with dynamic aspects, flexible organizations, etc.

## Personality theory

Although there is an enormous amount of theorizing on neural and psychological function in the cybernetic line based upon the brain–computer comparison, few attempts have been made to apply G.S.T. in the narrower sense to the theory of human behavior. For the present purposes, the latter may be nearly equated with personality theory.

We have to realize at the start that personality theory is at present a battlefield of contrasting and controversial theories. Hall and Lindzey have justly stated: "All theories of behavior are pretty poor theories and all of them leave much to be desired in the way of scientific proof" – this being said in a textbook of nearly 600 pages on "Theories of Personality".

We can therefore not well expect that G.S.T. can present solutions where personality theorists from Freud and Jung to a host of modern writers were unable to do so. The theory will have shown its value if it opens new perspectives and viewpoints capable of experimental and practical application. This appears to be the case. There is quite a group of psychologists who are committed to an organismic theory of personality, Goldstein and Maslow being well-known representatives. Biological considerations may therefore be expected to advance the matter.

There is, of course, the fundamental question whether, first, G.S.T. is not essentially a physicalistic simile, inapplicable to psychic phenomena; and secondly whether such model has explanatory value when the pertinent variables cannot be defined quantitatively as is in general the case with psychological phenomena.

1. The answer to the first question appears to be that the systems concept is abstract and general enough to permit application to entities of whatever denomination. The notions of "equilibrium", "homeostasis", "feedback", "stress", etc., are no less of technologic or physiological origin but more or less successfully applied to psychological phenomena. System theorists agree that the concept of "system" is not limited to material entities but can be applied to any "whole" consisting of interacting "components". . . . Systems engineering is an example where components are partly not physical and metric.

2. If quantitation is impossible, and even if the components of a system are ill-defined, it can at least be expected that certain principles will qualitatively apply to the whole *qua* system. At least "explanation on principle" (see below) may be possible.

Bearing in mind these limitations, one concept which may prove to be of a key nature is the organismic notion of the organism as a spontaneously active system. In the present author's words:

Even under constant external conditions and in the absence of external stimuli the organism is not a passive but a basically active system. This applies in particular to the function of the nervous system and to behavior. It appears that internal activity rather than reaction to stimuli is fundamental. This can be shown with respect both to evolution in lower animals and to development, for example, in the first movements of embryos and fetuses.

This agrees with what von Holst has called the "new conception" of the nervous system, based upon the fact that primitive locomotor activities are caused by central automatisms that do not need external stimuli. Therefore, such movements persist, for example, even after the connection of motoric to sensory nerves had been severed. Hence the reflex in the classic sense is not the basic unit of behavior but rather a regulatory mechanism superimposed upon primitive, automatic activities. A similar concept is basic in the theory on instinct. According to Lorenz, innate releasing mechanisms (I.R.M.) play a dominant role, which sometimes go off without an external stimulus (in-vacuo or running idle reactions): A bird which has no material to build a nest may perform the movements of nest building in the air. These considerations are in the framework of what Hebb called the "conceptual C.N.S. of 1930–1950". The more recent insight into activating systems of the brain emphasizes differently, and with a wealth of experimental evidence, the same basic concept of the autonomous activity of the C.N.S.

The significance of these concepts becomes apparent when we consider that they are in fundamental contrast to the conventional stimulus-response scheme which assumes that the organism is an essentially reactive system answering, like an automaton, to external stimuli. The dominance of the S–R scheme in contemporary psychology needs no emphasis, and is obviously connected with the *zeitgeist* of a highly mechanized society. This principle is basic in psychological theories which in all other respects are opposite, for example, in behavioristic psychology as well as in psychoanalysis. According to Freud it is the supreme tendency of the organism to get rid of tensions and drives and come to rest in a state of equilibrium governed by the "principle of stability" which Freud borrowed from the German philosopher, Fechner. Neurotic and psychotic behavior, then, is a more or less effective or abortive defense mechanism tending to restore some sort of equilibrium (according to D. Rappaport's analysis of the structure of psychoanalytic theory: "economic" and "adaptive points of view").

Charlotte Buhler, the well-known child psychologist, has aptly epitomized the theoretical situation:

In the fundamental psychoanalytic model, there is only one basic tendency, that is toward *need gratification* or *tension reduction*. . . . Present-day biologic theories emphasize the "spontaneity" of the organism's activity which is due to its built-in energy. The organism's autonomous functioning, its "drive to perform certain movements" is emphasized by Bertalanffy. . . . These concepts represent *a complete revision of the original homeostasis principle* which emphasized exclusively the tendency toward equilibrium. It is the original homeostasis principle with which psychoanalysis identified its theory of discharge of tensions as the only primary tendency. (Emphasis partly ours.)

In brief, we may define our viewpoint as "Beyond the Homeostasis Principle":

(1) The S–R scheme misses the realms of play, exploratory activities, creativity, self-realization, etc.;
(2) The economic scheme misses just specific, human achievements – the most of what loosely is termed "human culture";
(3) The equilibrium principle misses the fact that psychological and behavioral activities are more than relaxation of tensions; far from establishing an optimal state, the latter may entail psychosis-like disturbances, as e.g., in sensory-deprivation experiments.

It appears that the S–R and psychoanalytic model is a highly unrealistic picture of human nature and, in its consequences, a rather dangerous one. Just what we consider to be specific human achievements can hardly be brought under the utilitarian, homeostasis, and stimulus–response scheme. One may call mountain climbing, composing of sonatas or lyrical poems "psychological homeostasis" – as has been done – but at the risk that this physiologically well-defined concept loses all meaning. Furthermore, if the principle of homeostatic maintenance is taken as a golden rule of behavior, the so-called well-adjusted individual will be the ultimate goal, that is a well-oiled robot maintaining itself in optimal biological, psychological and social homeostasis. This is a *Brave New World* – not, for some at least, the ideal state of humanity. Furthermore, that precarious mental equilibrium must not be disturbed. Hence in what somewhat ironically is called progressive education, the anxiety not to overload the child, not to impose constraints and to minimize all directing influences – with the result of a previously unheard-of crop of illiterates and juvenile delinquents.

In contrast to conventional theory, it can safely be maintained that not only stresses and tensions but equally complete release from stimuli and the consequent mental void may be neurosogenic or even psychosogenic. Experimentally this is verified by the experiments with sensory deprivation when subjects, insulated from all incoming stimuli, after a few hours develop a so-called model psychosis with hallucinations, unbearable anxiety, etc. Clinically it amounts to the same when insulation leads to prisoners' psychosis and to exacerbation of mental disease by isolation of patients in the ward. In contrast, maximal stress need not necessarily produce mental disturbance. If conventional theory were correct, Europe during and after the war, with extreme physiological as well as psychological stresses, should have been a gigantic lunatic asylum. As a matter of fact, there was statistically no increase either in neurotic or psychotic disturbances, apart from easily explained acute disturbances such as combat neurosis.

We so arrive at the conception that a great deal of biological and human behavior is beyond the principles of utility, homeostasis and stimulus-response, and that it is just this which is characteristic of human and cultural activities. Such new look opens new perspectives not only in theory, but in practical implications with respect to mental hygiene, education, and society in general.

What has been said can also be couched in philosophical terms. If existentialists speak of the emptiness and meaninglessness of life, if they see in it a source not only of anxiety but of actual mental illness, it is essentially the same viewpoint: that behavior is not merely a matter of satisfaction of biological drives and of maintenance in psychological and social equilibrium but that something more is involved. If life becomes unbearably empty in an industrialized society, what can a person do but develop a neurosis? The principle which may loosely be called spontaneous activity of the psychophysical organism, is a more realistic formulation of what the existentialists want to say in their often obscure language. And if personality theorists like Maslow or Gardner Murphy speak of self-realization as human goal, it is again a somewhat pompous expression of the same.

## Theoretical history

We eventually come to those highest and ill-defined entities that are called human cultures and civilizations. It is the field often called "philosophy of history". We may perhaps better speak of "theoretical history", admittedly in its very first beginnings. This name expresses the goal to form a connecting link between "science" and the "humanities"; more in particular, between the "social sciences" and "history".

It is understood, of course, that the techniques in sociology and history are entirely different (polls, statistical analysis against archival studies, internal evidence of historic relics, etc.). However, the object of study is essentially the same. Sociology is essentially concerned with a temporal cross-section as human societies *are*; history with the "longitudinal" study how societies *become* and develop. The object and techniques of study certainly justify practical differentiation; it is less clear, however, that they justify fundamentally different philosophies.

The last statement already implies the question of constructs in history, as they were presented, in grand form, from Vico to Hegel, Marx, Spengler and Toynbee. Professional historians regard them at best as poetry, at worst as fantasies pressing, with paranoic obsession, the facts of history into a theoretical bed of Procrustes. It seems history can learn from the system theorists, not ultimate solutions but a sounder methodological outlook. Problems hitherto considered to be philosophical or metaphysical can well be defined in their scientific meaning, with some interesting outlook at recent developments (e.g., game theory) thrown into the bargain.

Empirical criticism is outside the scope of the present study. For example, Geyl and many others have analyzed obvious misrepresentations of historical events in Toynbee's work, and even the non-specialist reader can easily draw a list of fallacies especially in the later, Holy-Ghost inspired volumes of Toynbee's *magnum opus*. The problem, however, is larger than errors in fact or interpretation or even the question of the merits of Marx's, Spengler's or Toynbee's theories; it is whether, in principle, models and laws are admissible in history.

A widely held contention says that they are not. This is the concept of "nomothetic" method in science and "idiographic" method in history. While science to a greater or less extent can establish "laws" for natural events, history, concerned with human events of enormous complexity in causes and outcome and possibly determined by free decisions of individuals can only describe, more or less satisfactorily, what has happened in the past.

Here the methodologist has his first comment. In the attitude just outlined, academic history condemns constructs of history as "intuitive", "contrary to fact", "arbitrary", etc. And, no doubt, the criticism is pungent enough vis-à-vis Spengler or Toynbee. It is, however, somewhat less convincing if we look at the work of conventional historiography. For example, the Dutch historian, Peter Geyl, who made a strong argument against Toynbee from such methodological considerations, also wrote a brilliant book about Napoleon, amounting to the result that there are a dozen or so different interpretations – we may safely say, *models* – of Napoleon's character and career within academic history, all based upon "fact" (the Napoleonic period happens to be one of the best documented) and all

flatly contradicting each other. Roughly speaking, they range from Napoleon as the brutal tyrant and egotistic enemy of human freedom to Napoleon the wise planner of a unified Europe; and if one is a Napoleonic student (as the present writer happens to be in a small way), one can easily produce some original documents refuting misconceptions occurring even in generally accepted, standard histories. You cannot have it both ways. If even a figure like Napoleon, not very remote in time and with the best of historical documentation, can be interpreted contrarily, you cannot well blame the "philosophers of history" for their intuitive procedure, subjective bias, etc., when they deal with the enormous phenomenon of universal history. What you have in both cases is a conceptual model which always will represent certain aspects only, and for this reason will be one-sided or even lopsided. Hence the construction of conceptual models in history is not only permissible but, as a matter of fact, is at the basis of any historical interpretation as distinguished from mere enumeration of data, i.e., chronicle or annals.

If this is granted, the antithesis between idiographic and nomothetic procedure reduces to what psychologists are wont to call the "molecular" and "molar" approach. One can analyze events within a complex whole – individual chemical reactions in an organism, perceptions in the psyche, for example; or one can look for over-all laws covering the whole such as growth and development in the first or personality in the second instance. In terms of history, this means detailed study of individuals, treaties, works of art, singular causes and effects, etc., or else over-all phenomena with the hope of detecting grand laws. There are, of course, all transitions between the first and second considerations; the extremes may be illustrated by Carlyle and his hero worship at one pole and Tolstoy (a far greater "theoretical historian" than commonly admitted) at the other.

The question of a "theoretical history" therefore is essentially that of "molar" models in the field; and this is what the great constructs of history amount to when divested of their philosophical embroidery.

The evaluation of such models must follow the general rules for verification or falsification. First, there is the consideration of empirical bases. In this particular instance it amounts to the question whether or not a limited number of civilizations – some twenty at the best – provide a sufficient and representative sample to establish justified generalizations. This question and that of the value of proposed models will be answered by the general criterion; whether or not the model has explanatory and predictive value, i.e., throws new light upon known facts and correctly foretells facts of the past or future not previously known.

Although elementary, these considerations nevertheless are apt to remove much misunderstanding and philosophical fog which has clouded the issue.

1. As had been emphasized, the evaluation of models should be simply pragmatic in terms of their explanatory and predictive merits (or lack thereof); *a priori* considerations as to their desirability or moral consequences do not enter.

Here we encounter a somewhat unique situation. There is little objection against so-called "synchronic" laws, i.e., supposed regularities governing societies at a certain point in time; as a matter of fact, beside empirical study this is the aim of sociology. Also certain "diachronic" laws, i.e., regularities of development in time, are undisputed such as, e.g., Grimm's law stating rules for the changes of consonants in the evolution of Indo-Germanic languages. It is commonplace that there is a sort of "life-cycle" – stages of primitivity, maturity, baroque dissolution of form and eventual decay for which no particular external causes can be indicated – in individual fields of culture, such as Greek sculpture, Renaissance painting or German music. Indeed, this even has its counterpart in certain phenomena of biological evolution showing, as in ammonites or dinosaurs, a first explosive phase of formation of new types followed by a phase of speciation and eventually of decadence.

Violent criticism comes in when this model is applied to civilization as a whole. It is a legitimate question – Why often rather unrealistic models in the social sciences remain matters of academic discussion, while models of history encounter passionate resistance? Granting all factual criticism raised against Spengler or Toynbee, it seems rather obvious that emotional factors are involved. The highway of science is strewn with corpses of deceased theories which just decay or are preserved as mummies in the museum of history or science. In contrast, historical constructs and especially theories of historical cycles appear to touch a raw nerve, and so opposition is much more than usual criticism of a scientific theory.

2. This emotional involvement is connected with the question of "Historical Inevitability" and a supposed degradation of human "freedom". Before turning to it, discussion of mathematical and non-mathematical models is in place.

Advantages and shortcomings of mathematical models in the social sciences are well known. Every mathematical model is an oversimplification, and it remains questionable whether it strips actual events to the bones or cuts away vital parts of their anatomy. On the other hand, so far as it goes, it permits necessary deduction with often unexpected results which would not be obtained by ordinary "common sense".

In particular, Rashevsky has shown in several studies how mathematical models of historical processes can be constructed.

On the other hand, the value of purely qualitative models should not be underestimated. For example, the concept of "ecologic equilibrium" was developed long before Volterra and others introduced mathematical models; the theory of selection belongs to the stock-in-trade of biology, but the mathematical theory of the "struggle for existence" is comparatively recent, and far from being verified under wildlife conditions.

In complex phenomena, "explanation on principle" by qualitative models is preferable to no explanation at all. This is by no means limited to the social sciences and history; it applies alike to fields like meteorology or evolution.

3. "Historical inevitability" – subject of a well-known study by Sir Isaiah Berlin – dreaded as a consequence of "theoretical history", supposedly contradicting our direct experience of having free choices and eliminating all moral judgment and values – is a phantasmagoria based upon a world view which does not exist any more. As, in fact, Berlin emphasizes, it is founded upon the concept of the Laplacean spirit who is able completely to predict the future from the past by means of deterministic laws. This has no resemblance with the modern concept of "laws of nature". All "laws of nature" have a statistical character. They do not predict an inexorably determined future but probabilities which, depending on the nature of events and on the laws available, may approach certainty or else remain far below it. It is nonsensical to ask or fear more "inevitability" in historical theory than is found in sciences with relatively high sophistication like meteorology or economics.

Paradoxically, while the cause of free will rests with the testimony of intuition or rather immediate experience and can never be proved objectively ("Was it Napoleon's free will that led him to the Russian Campaign?"), determinism (in the statistical sense) can be proved, at least in small-scale models. Certainly business depends on personal "initiative", the individual "decision" and "responsibility" of the entrepreneur; the manager's choice whether or not to expand business by employing new appointees, is "free' in precisely the sense as Napoleon's choice whether or not to accept battle at Austerlitz. However, when the growth curve of industrial companies is analyzed, it is found that "arbitrary" deviations are followed by speedy return to the normal curve, as if invisible forces were active. Haire states that "the return to the pattern predicted by earlier growth suggests the operation of *inexorable forces* operating on the social organism" (our emphasis).

It is characteristic that one of Berlin's points is "the fallacy of historical determinism (appearing) from its utter inconsistency with the common sense and everyday life of looking at human affairs". This characteristic argument is of the same nature as the advice not to adopt the Copernican system because everybody can see that the sun moves from morning to evening.

4. Recent developments in mathematics even allow to submit "free will" – apparently the philosophical problem most recalcitrant against scientific analysis – to mathematical examination.

In the light of modern systems theory, the alternative between molar and molecular, nomothetic and idiographic approach can be given a precise meaning. For mass behavior, system laws would apply which, if they can be mathematized, would take the form of differential equations of the sort of those used by Richardson mentioned above. Free choice of the individual would be described by formulations of the nature of game and decision theory.

Axiomatically, game and decision theory are concerned with "rational" choice. This means a choice which "maximizes the individual's utility or satisfaction", that "the individual is free to choose among several possible courses of action and decides among them at the basis of their consequences", that he "selects, being informed of all conceivable consequences of his actions, what stands highest on his list", he "prefers more of a commodity to less, other things being equal", etc. Instead of economical gain, any higher value may be inserted without changing the mathematical formalism.

The above definition of "rational choice" includes everything that can be meant by "free will". If we do not wish to equate "free will" with complete arbitrariness, lack of any value judgment and therefore completely inconsequential actions (like the philosopher's favorite example: It is my free will whether or not to wiggle my left little finger) it is a fair definition of those actions with which the moralist, priest, or historian is concerned: free decision between alternatives based upon insight into the situation and its consequences and guided by values.

The difficulty to apply the theory even to simple, actual situations is of course enormous; so is the difficulty in establishing over-all laws. However, without explicit

formulation, both approaches can be evaluated in principle – leading to an unexpected paradox.

The "principle of rationality" fits – not the majority of human actions but rather the "unreasoning" behavior of animals. Animals and organisms in general do function in a "ratio-morphic" way, maximizing such values as maintenance, satisfaction, survival, etc.; they select, in general, what is biologically good for them, and prefer more of a commodity (e.g., food) to less.

Human behavior, on the other hand, falls far short of the principle of rationality. It is not even necessary to quote Freud to show how small is the compass of rational behavior in man. Women in a supermarket, in general, do not maximize utility but are susceptible to the tricks of the advertiser and packer; they do not make a rational choice surveying all possibilities and consequences; and do not even prefer more of the commodity packed in an inconspicuous way to less when packed in a big red box with attractive design. In our society, it is the job of an influential specialty – advertisers, motivation researchers, etc. – to *make* choices irrational which essentially is done by coupling biological factors – conditioned reflex, unconscious drives – with symbolic values.

And there is no refuge by saying that this irrationality of human behavior concerns only trivial actions of daily life; the same principle applies to "historical" decisions. That wise old mind, Oxenstierna, Sweden's Chancellor during the Thirty Years' War, has perfectly expressed this by saying: *Nescis, mi fili, quantilla ratione mundus regatur* – you don't know, my dear boy, with what little reason the world is governed. Reading newspapers or listening to the radio readily shows that this applies perhaps even more to the 20th than the 17th century.

Methodologically, this leads to a remarkable conclusion. If one of the two models is to be applied, and if the "actuality principle" basic in historical fields like geology and evolution is adopted (i.e., the hypothesis that no other principles of explanation should be used than can be observed as operative in the present) – then it is the statistical or mass model which is backed by empirical evidence. The business of the motivation and opinion researcher, statistical psychologist, etc., is based upon the premise that statistical laws obtain in human behavior; and that, for this reason a small but well-chosen sample allows for extrapolation to the total population under consideration. The generally good working of a Gallup poll and prediction verifies the premise – with some incidental failure like the well-known example of the Truman election thrown in, as is to be expected with statistical predictions. The opposite contention – that history is governed by "free will" in the philosophical sense (i.e., rational decision for the better, the higher moral value or even enlightened self-interest) is hardly supported by fact. That here and there the statistical law is broken by "rugged individualists" is in its character. Nor does the role played in history by "great men" contradict the systems concept in history; they can be conceived as acting like "leading parts", "triggers" or "catalyzers" in the historical process – a phenomenon well accounted for in the general theory of systems.

5. A further question is the "organismic analogy" unanimously condemned by historians. They combat untiringly the "metaphysical", "poetical", "mythical" and thoroughly unscientific nature of Spengler's assertion that civilizations are a sort of "organisms", being born, developing according to their internal laws and eventually dying. Toynbee takes great pains to emphasize that he did not fall into Spengler's trap – even though it is somewhat difficult to see that his civilizations, connected by the biological relations of "affiliation" and "apparentation", even (according to the latest version of his system) with a rather strict time span of development, are not conceived organismically.

Nobody should know better than the biologist that civilizations are no "organism". It is trivial to the extreme that a biological organism, a material entity and unity in space and time, is something different from a social group consisting of distinct individuals, and even more from a civilization consisting of generations of human beings, of material products, institutions, ideas, values, and what not. It implies a serious underestimate of Vico's, Spengler's (or any normal individual's) intelligence to suppose that they did not realize the obvious.

Nevertheless, it is interesting to note that, in contrast to the historians' scruples, sociologists do not abhor the "organismic analogy" but rather take it for granted. For example, in the words of Rappoport and Horvath:

There is some sense in considering a real organization as an organism, that is, there is reason to believe that this comparison need not be a sterile metaphorical analogy, such as was common in scholastic speculation about the body politic. Quasibiological functions are demonstrable in organizations. They maintain themselves; they sometimes reproduce or metastasize; they respond to stresses; they age, and they die. Organizations have discernible anatomies and those at least which transform material inputs (like industries) have physiologies.

Or Sir Geoffrey Vickers:

Institutions grow, repair themselves, reproduce themselves, decay, dissolve. In their external relations they show many characteristics of organic life. Some think that in their internal relations also human institutions are destined to become increasingly organic, that human cooperation will approach ever more closely to the integration of cells in a body. I find this prospect unconvincing (and) unpleasant. [N.B. so does the present author.]

And Haire:

The biological model for social organizations – and here, particularly for industrial organizations – means taking as a model the living organism and the processes and principles that regulate its growth and development. It means looking for lawful processes in organizational growth.

The fact that simple growth laws apply to social entities such as manufacturing companies, to urbanization, division of labor, etc., proves that in these respects the "organismic analogy" is correct. In spite of the historians' protests, the application of theoretical models, in particular, the model of dynamic, open and adaptive systems to the historical process certainly makes sense. This does not imply "biologism", i.e., reduction of social to biological concepts, but indicates system principles applying in both fields.

6. Taking all objections for granted – poor method, errors in fact, the enormous complexity of the historical process – we have nevertheless reluctantly to admit that the cyclic models of history pass the most important test of scientific theory. The predictions made by Spengler in the *Decline of the West*, by Toynbee when forecasting a time of trouble and contending states, by Ortega y Gasset in the *Uprise of the Masses* – we may as well add *Brave New World* and *1984* – have been verified to a disquieting extent and considerably better than many respectable models of the social scientists.

Does this imply "historic inevitability" and inexorable dissolution? Again, the simple answer was missed by moralizing and philosophizing historians. By extrapolation from the life cycles of previous civilizations nobody could have predicted the Industrial Revolution, the Population Explosion, the development of atomic energy, the emergence of underdeveloped nations, and the expansion of Western civilization over the whole globe. Does this refute the alleged model and "law" of history? No – it only says that this model – as every one in science – mirrors only certain aspects or facets of reality. Every model becomes dangerous only when it commits the "Nothing-but" fallacy which mars not only theoretical history, but the models of the mechanistic world picture, of psychoanalysis and many others as well.

We have hoped to show in this survey that General System Theory has contributed toward the expansion of scientific theory; has led to new insights and principles; and has opened up new problems that are "researchable", i.e., are amenable to further study, experimental or mathematical. The limitations of the theory and its applications in their present status are obvious; but the principles appear to be essentially sound as shown by their application in different fields.

# References

Ackoff, R. L. (1959) "Games, decisions, and organizations". *General Systems* IV, 145–50.

—— (1960) "Systems, organizations, and interdisciplinary research", *General Systems* V, 1–8.

Arrow, K. J. (1956) "Mathematical models in the social sciences", *General Systems* I, 29–47.

Ashby, W. R. (1958a) "General systems theory as a new discipline", *General Systems* III, 1–6.

—— (1958b) *An Introduction to Cybernetics*, 3rd impr., Wiley, New York.

—— (1962) "Principles of the self-organizing system", in H. von Foerster, G. W. Zopf, Jr. (eds.), *Principles of Self-organization*, Pergamon Press, New York, pp. 255–78.

Attneave, F. (1959) *Application of Information Theory to Psychology*, Holt, New York.

Beer, St. (1960) "Below the twilight arch. A mythology of systems", *General Systems* V, 9–20.

Bell, E. (1962) "Oogenesis", C. P. Raven (review), *Science* 135, 1056.

von Bertalanffy, L. (1947) "Vom Sinn und der Einheit der Wissenschaften", *Der Student*, Wien, 2, No. 7/8.

—— (1949) "Zu einer allgemeinen systemlehre", *Biologia Generalis* 19, 114–29.

—— (1950) "An outline of general system theory", *Brit. J. Philos. Sci.* 1, 134–65.

—— (1953) *Biophysik des fliessgleichgewichts*, (Transl. by W. Westphal), Vieweg, Braunschweig.

—— (1956) "General system theory", *General Systems* I, 1–10.

—— (1956) "A biologist looks at human nature", *Scientific Monthly* 82, 33–41.

—— (1952) *Problems of Life. An evaluation of Modern Biological and Scientific Thought*. Torchbook edition, Harper, New York, 1960a.

—— (1960b) "Principles and theory of growth", in W. W. Nowinski (ed.), *Fundamental Aspects of Normal and Malignant Growth*, Elsevier, Amsterdam, pp. 137–259.

—— (1933) *Modern Theories of Development. An Introduction to Theoretical Biology*. Torchbook edition, Harper, New York, 1962.

von Bertalanffy, L., Hempel, C. G., Bass, R. E., and Jonas, H. (1951) "General system theory: A new approach to unity of science", *Human Biol.* 23, 302–61.

Beverton, R. J. H. and Holt, S. J. (1957) "On the dynamics of exploited fish populations", *Fishery Investigation*, Ser. II, vol. XIX, H.M.S.O. London.

Boulding, K. E. (1953) *The Organizational Revolution*, Harper, New York.

—— (1956) "Toward a general theory of growth", *General Systems* I, 66–75.

Bradley, D. F. and Calvin, M. (1956) "Behavior: Imbalance in a network of chemical transformation", *General Systems* I, 56–65.

Bray, J. R. (1958) "Notes toward an ecology theory". *Ecology* 9, 770–6.

Bray, H. G. and White, K. (1957) *Kinetics and Thermodynamics in Biochemistry*, Academic Press, New York.

Buck, R. C. (1956) "On the logic of general behavior systems theory", in H. Feigel and M. Scriven (eds.), *Minnesota Studies in the Philosophy of Science*, vol. I, Univer. of Minnesota Press, Minneapolis, pp. 223–38.

Buhler, Ch. (1959) "Theoretical observations about life's basic tendencies", *Amer. J. Psychother.* 13, 501–81.

Chorley, R. J. "Geomorphology and general systems theory", in press.

Dost, R. H. (1953) *Der Blutspiegel. Kinetik der Konzentrationsabläufe in der Körperflussigkeit*. Thieme, Leipzig.

Egler, F. E. (1953) "Bertalanffian organismicism", *Ecology* 34, 443–6.

Feigl, H. (1956) "Some major issues and developments in the philosophy of science of logical empiricism", in H. Feigl and M. Scriven (eds.), *Minnesota Studies in the Philosophy of Science*, vol. I, Univer. of Minnesota Press, Minneapolis, pp. 3–37.

Foster, C., Rappoport, A., and Trucco, E. (1957) "Some unsolved problems in the theory of non-isolated systems", *General Systems* II, 9–29.

Gessner, F. (1952) "Wieviel Tiere bevölkern die Erde?", *Orion*, 33–5.

Geyl, P. (1957) *Napoleon for and Against*, Cape, London.

—— (1958) *Debates with Historians*, Meridian Books, New York.

Haire, M. (1959) "Biological models and empirical histories of the growth of organizations", in M. Haire (ed.),

*Modern Organization Theory*, Wiley, New York, pp. 272–306.

Hall, A. D. (1962) *A Methodology for Systems Engineering*, Nostrand, Princeton.

Hall, A. D. and Fagen, R. E. (1956) "Definition of system", *General Systems* I, 18–28.

Hall, C. S. and Lindzey, G. (1957) *Theories of Personality*, Wiley, New York.

Hayek, F. A. (1955) "Degrees of explanation", *Brit. J. Philos. Sci.* **6**, 209–25.

Hearn, G. (1958) *Theory Building in Social Work*, Univer. of Toronto Press, Toronto.

Hersh, A. H. (1942) "Drosophila and the course of research", *Ohio J. of Science* **42**, 198–200.

Holt, S. J. "The application of comparative population studies to fisheries biology – an exploration", in E. D. Le Cren and M. W. Holdgate (eds.), *The Exploitation of Natural Animal Populations*, Blackwell, Oxford.

Kamaryt, J. (1961) "Die Bedeutung der Theorie des offenen Systems in der gegenwaertigen Biologie", *Deutsche Z. fuer Philosophie* **9**, 2040–59.

Keiter, F. (1951–2) "Wachstum und Reifen im Jugendalter", *Koelner Z. fuer Soziologie* **4**, 165–74.

Kment, H. (1959) "The problem of biological regulation and its evolution in medical view", *General Systems* IV, 75–82.

Kremyanskiy, V. I. (1960) "Certain peculiarities of organisms as a 'system' from the point of view of physics, cybernetics, and biology", *General Systems* V, 221–30.

Lektorsky, V. A. and Sadovsky, V. N. (1960) "On principles of system research (related to L. Bertalanffy's general system theory)", *General Systems* V, 171–9.

McClelland, Ch. A. (1958) "Systems and history in international relations. Some perspectives for empirical research and theory", *General Systems* III, 221–47.

Meyer, R. L. (1961) Preface, *General Systems* VI, III–IV.

Miller, J. G. *et al.* (1953) Symposium. "Profits and problems of homeostatic models in the behavioral sciences", *Chicago Behavioral Sciences Publications No. 1.*

Naroll, R. S. and von Bertalanffy, L. (1956) "The principle of allometry in biology and the social sciences", *General Systems* I, 76–89.

Netter, H. (1959) *Theoretische Biochemie*, Springer, Berlin.

Oppenheimer, R. (1956) "Analogy in science", *Amer. Psychol.* **11**, 127–35.

Patten, B. C. (1959) "An introduction to the cybernetics of the ecosystem: The trophic-dynamic aspect", *Ecology* **40**, 221–31.

Prigogine, I. (1947) *Etude thermodynamique des phénomènes irréversibles*, Dunod, Paris.

Rapoport, A. (1956) "The promise and pitfalls of information theory", *Behav. Sci.* **1**, 303–15.

—— (1957) "Lewis F. Richardson's mathematical theory of war", *General Systems* II, 55–91.

—— (1959) "Critiques of game theory", *Behav. Sci.* **4**, 49–66.

—— (1960) *Fights, Games, and Debates*, Univer. of Mich. Press, Ann Arbor.

Rapoport, A. and Horvath, W. J. (1959) "Thoughts on organization theory and a review of two conferences", *General Systems* IV, 87–93.

Rappaport, D. (1960) "The structure of psycho-analytic theory", *Psychol. Issues* **2**, Monogr. 6, pp. 39–64.

Rashevsky, N. (1952) "The effect of environmental factors on the rates of cultural development", *Bull. Math. Biophysics* **14**, 193–201.

Rosen, R. (1960) "A relational theory of biological systems", *General Systems* V, 29–55.

Schulz, G. V. (1951) "Energetische und statistische Voraussetzungen fuer die Synthese der Makromolekuele im Organismus", *Z. Elektrochem. u. angew. phys. Chemie* **55**, 569–74.

Thompson, J. W. (1961) "The organismic conception in meteorology", *General Systems* VI, 45–9.

Toynbee, A. J. (1961) *A Study of History, Vol. XII. Reconsiderations*, Oxford Univer. Press, New York.

Tribus, M. (1961) "Information theory of the basis for thermostatics and thermodynamics", *General Systems* VI, 127–38.

Vickers, G. (1957) "Control, stability and choice", *General Systems* II, 1–8.

Watt, K. E. F. (1958) "The choice and solution of mathematical models for predicting and maximizing the yield of a fishery", *General Systems* III, 101–21.

Weaver, W. (1948) "Science and complexity", *American Scientist* **36**, 536–644.

Whittaker, R. H. (1953) "A consideration of climax theory: The climax as a population and pattern", *Ecol. Monographs* **23**, 41–78.

Weiss, P. (1962) "Experience and experiment in biology", *Science* **136**, 468–71.

Wiener, N. (1948) *Cybernetics*, Wiley, New York.

Zacharias, J. R. (1957) "Structure of physical science", *Science* **125**, 427–8.

Reprinted from von Bertalanffy, L. (1962) "General System Theory – A Critical Review", in *General Systems* VII, 1–20.

# 3 A systems map of the universe
## by P. B. Checkland

## Introduction

Professional engineers often use the words "systems engineering" to refer to the literal engineering of large systems involving many pieces of equipment united for some complex purpose. The concentration is on those aspects relevant to the assemblage as a whole, rather than on the design of individual pieces of equipment, and the considerations will include broader aspects of cost–benefit analysis and logistic support as well as purely technical aspects.

The definition of systems engineering implicit in this *Journal of Systems Engineering*, however, is a yet wider one, of which the relatively "hard" (technical) definition above is one example. (The design of computer systems by Computer Systems Engineers is another.) The wider definition embodies a "softer" definition of both "system" and "engineer". At its most fundamental this definition of "systems engineering" is that given by Kline and Lifson,[1] it is "the application of the systems approach". It is the use of systems concepts to *analyse* and hence *see a structure* in complex problem situations in order that improvements may be effected through systems design, implementation and subsequent appraisal.[2]

If we are to understand more deeply this wide-ranging kind of systems engineering, and to develop its methodologies, it is useful to examine its intellectual base, to differentiate this from the basis of other disciplines concerned with methodologies useful for problem solving, and to construct an intellectual platform capable of supporting the discipline as it develops. This paper attempts to make a start on that task.

## "The systems proposition"

We may reasonably postulate that any intellectual discipline rests ultimately upon some *proposition* which must be "true" if the discipline is valid. In the case of scientific disciplines this is clearly so: the propositions underlying the development of the sciences are of the form "it is reasonable to study together, phenomena characterized by . . .". Developing a discipline called "physics" assumes that it is reasonable to study together phenomena in which there are changes of energy, momentum, position but not of molecular form. Making "chemistry" a discipline in its own right assumes the fundamental similarity of phenomena in which free energy considerations lead to the spontaneous rearrangement of molecules or compounds into other molecular forms.

In the case of the more recent twentieth-century disciplines, which aim not so much to describe and understand the natural world as to solve the problems which arise in real-life situations, the basic propositions upon which they are based are less obvious, but no less real.

Examination of both the literature of Operational Research and the activity of its practitioners, for example, reveals an emphasis on the *scientific* nature of the activity and most especially on the value, in decision-taking situations, of the *quantitative model*. Thus a standard text[3] begins "No science was born on a specific day . . . Operations Research (O.R.) is no exception," and summarizes the O.R. methodology as:

1. Formulating the problem.
2. Constructing a mathematical model to represent the system under study.
3. Deriving a solution from the model . . .", etc.

A later text[4] defines O.R. as being "The application of the scientific method . . .", etc., and the Operational Research Society's official definition speaks of O.R. as "the application of the methods of science to complex problems. . . . The distinctive approach is to develop a scientific model. . . . The purpose is to help management determine its policy and actions scientifically." Clearly the basic proposition upon which O.R. is based is something like the following:

*The quantitative methods of science are an appropriate means of studying problems which arise in the operations of organizations.*

When we examine the applied social sciences and the activities of behavioural scientists in the context of problems in organizations, currently much in vogue, naturally we find a concentration on the human components. The concern is for the human being in an organization as a particular kind of animal, one possessing not only skills for the performance of tasks required by the organization but also emotional needs which must be satisfied within the various groups to which he belongs within the organization.[5] A distinguished social scientist has written:[6] "If an organization is advised to become a rational, a-historical system it will change its advisers," and no one who has worked on problems within organizations will deny the truth of that! Thus, the proposition upon which applied social science is based is that

*problems in organizations will require for their solution methods based upon knowledge of individual and group psychology.*

What of the proposition underlying the development of Systems Engineering defined as "the application of the systems approach"? "The systems proposition" can be stated in some such terms as the following:

*It is reasonable, and useful, to take the apparently chaotic universe to be a complex of interacting systems. If a system has definable objectives then we may hope to be able to engineer it in order that they are achieved. Even if this systems engineering is not possible, the systems view still provides the best framework for relevant debate concerning the problems which arise in the real world.*

The proposition may be amplified in a number of ways.

1. It is a general proposition, but only a general concept can hope to have general validity. Problems are multi-faceted; the aim of systems concepts is to sort out the chaos into a defined problem without distortion and over-simplification. The problem is stated in such a way that rational means can be used to tackle it. The method involves stating the problem *in systems terms*.

2. It does not imply that because the world is seen as a set of interacting systems the approach necessarily involves making a model of the relevant systems in the problem situation being studied. Life is too quixotic to be modelled. Rather it aims to define a context within which specific model making may be made relevant, and this from the stance that the concept of "a system" is more powerful than that of "a model".

3. The proposition does not say that the world *is* a set of interacting systems – we cannot say, ultimately, what the world *is* – only that we may structure unstructured prob-

lems within it on the assumption that the world may usefully be regarded as a complex of systems.

If this proposition is valid, then it ought to be possible to represent the world – or, indeed, the universe, on a "systems map", a diagrammatic representation of the systems which in their complex mixtures make up this picture of the real world as we know it. Such a "map" cannot of course be proved to be accurate: but it must be intuitively convincing.

A number of systems taxonomies have been proposed and Ackoff[7] has provided a useful round-up of systems concepts. Jones[8] sets out a classification useful from the ergonomist's point of view:

Manual, Mechanized, Automatic, Collaborative man–machine systems, Mechanical subsystems, Administrative, Voluntary, Environmental, Biological, Physical and Symbol systems.

But there are recognized types rather than types derived from some principle.

The most famous classification is that of Boulding[9] who makes an intuitively convincing attempt to build by examples a sequence of gradually increasing complexity, a hierarchic order of systems in which higher levels presuppose the existence of lower ones:

Static structures, Clockworks, Control Mechanisms, Open systems, Lower organisms, Animals, Man, Sociocultural systems, Transcendental systems.

The implication of such a hierarchy is that we must develop methodologies for dealing with each level of complexity. Many such methodologies exist, and Boulding sees his hierarchy as "a framework . . . on which to hang the flesh and blood of particular disciplines . . . in an orderly and coherent body of knowledge".

But if the systems proposition stated above is to be accepted as valid, and if systems concepts are to be useful in tackling real-world problems, we need more than a scale of system complexity on which any particular system may be placed; we need a picture of the universe in systems terms, one which will separate man-made and natural systems and delineate the area within which we may hope to "engineer" systems so that their performance may be improved.

## The systems map

The systems map presented here is developed from an idea of Blair and Whitston,[10] who chart some physical systems. The present map sees the universe as a mixture of system types, both physical and abstract, natural and man-made, and accords a special place to social and cultural systems which underlines the special difficulties facing methodologies aimed at problem-solving in the real world.

The basic definition of "system" upon which the map is based is that most commonly accepted, the dictionary definition:

> A system is a structured set of objects and/or attributes, together with the relationships between them.

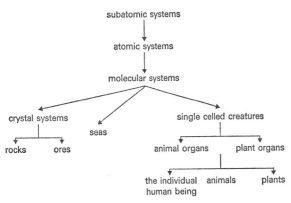

**Figure 3.1** The beginnings of a hierarchy of natural systems.

## Natural and transcendental systems

Natural systems are the physical systems which make up the universe, from the subatomic systems of atomic nuclei through life systems to galactic systems at the other extreme. They and all the other systems are set within a boundary beyond which are transcendental systems – systems, whether physical or abstract, which are beyond present knowledge. (The presence of a system within the boundary does not of course mean that it is, or even can be, fully understood: some degree of mystery is an element in all but some relatively simple man-made systems.) From subatomic systems we have a sequence which splits into inorganic and organic branches. One leads to the crucial "ore" systems and the other via cells and lower organisms to the even more crucial system "the individual human being".

## Human activity systems

The system "man" is crucial because of man's ability, as tool maker, myth maker and doer, to change his environment and his circumstances within it. Given man and his abilities, we have the huge area of "human activity systems", from the one-man-with-a-hammer at one extreme to the

international political systems which we shall have to forge if life is to remain tolerable for the human race on this finite planet.

Human activity systems must be designated in two different ways. Firstly there are the physical collections of components which are the "structured set" which make up the system; and secondly, because of the nature of the human component, there are the activity systems which are concerned with the management, in the broadest sense, of these systems. These are the abstract, but real systems concerned with processing information, making plans, carrying out operations, monitoring performance, taking control action, taking leisure, finding things out, and so on. The distinction between them and the physical systems within which they are relevant is that same distinction between *process* and *structure* which is so fundamental a concept in analysing any area of human endeavour.*

## Designed physical and designed abstract systems

"Ore" systems were stated to be crucial because of man's ability to obtain from them the metals upon which our civilization is based. Metals (and other materials) provide tools which man can design for some specific purpose within human activity systems – whether a hammer or a large scale automated equipment complex.

Also within this category of "designed physical systems" will be any automatic system not requiring human intervention, for example an information system mechanized so that a computer prints out reports automatically under the terms of programmed rules.

Man can design abstract as well as physical systems, and this leads to a special category of designed systems which will include philosophical systems built according to guiding principles as well as knowledge systems such as those of the various forms of mathematics. Also included here will be the knowledge systems of the sciences, in this case depending for their development upon the human activity system of scientific experimentation, an "enquiring system". Figure 3.2 illustrates the overall classification.

## Social and cultural systems

Within the terms of Figure 3.2 social systems are a special case.

---

* Some systems will have the same name for a "structure" and a "process" system. This is exampled on the map by "leisure systems" which will cover structure systems of the kind: football pitches, swimming baths, etc., as well as the process system: taking leisure.

Most human activity systems will exist as, or within, social systems, and there will be some human activity systems whose objectives are largely social, for example a drinking club, or the Boy Scout Movement. But it would be wrong to place social and cultural systems within the boundary of human activity systems. On the map they are deliberately placed *astride* the boundary between human activity systems and natural systems because of their equivocal nature. They are the context of virtually all human activity but at the same time they are also natural systems due to the fact that man is a gregarious animal who has a basic need for the supports provided by his fellow human beings in community life. It is not surprising that systems studies in social systems are exceptionally difficult and that in this area the systems approach is more likely to lead to illumination by systems analysis than to systems engineering to achieve objectives. And the systems analysis must somehow manage to embody human values, as has been argued in a previous paper.[11]

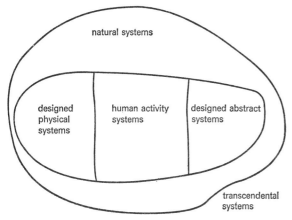

**Figure 3.2** Basic classes of systems.

## Discussion

The map (Figure 3.3) combines systems named according to the *nature of their components* (usually physical but sometimes intellectual) with, inside dotted boundaries, system types named according to the nature of their *activity*. The systems in the map are not mutually exclusive, and any system in the real world may well combine different systems. Thus "ecological systems" will contain "rocks"; and an industrial company in the real world is, among other things, a social system. A system may contain, for example, tools and machines, and a whole hierarchy of systems culminating in "manufacturing plants", as well as operational, planning, information, administrative and control systems.

Consider another example: carbon is an atomic system; it forms several molecular systems, one of which involves a tetrahedral arrangement of carbon atoms: the unique crystal system of a diamond; a diamond may be included in a cutting tool in a designed physical system; the tool itself may be one component in a man–machine human activity system and this system may itself by a subsystem of a manufacturing plant which has a production planning and control system; designing the latter may require use of an abstract "knowledge system".

The map divides into the basic areas of

natural systems
designed physical systems
designed abstract systems
human-activity systems.

It is important to recognize the different nature of these four kinds of system in order to be clear about the role of the systems engineer in relation to them.

A natural system simply *is* a natural system. It exists, implacably; it represents at least a temporary balance of forces which lead to a structure in static or slowly-moving equilibrium; and the sum total of changes in natural systems, if there is no human intervention, will be in the direction of increasing disorder, increasing entropy. Natural systems cannot in any meaningful way be said to have objectives, and to postulate objectives for natural systems is to lapse into theological speculation.

A designed physical system resembles a natural system but is man-made. A designed physical system exists because it is needed within a human activity system and does not exist in the natural world. The systems approach can be used in the design of a physical system of this kind but once the artefact exists it cannot be said in any meaningful way to have objectives: it simply serves a purpose. Thus climbers may use the systems approach to design an ice hammer, but once the hammer is constructed it simply exists, it is a component needed in the human activity system of climbing ice-covered cliffs, itself a sub-system of "leisure systems"; it is the system "climbing ice-covered cliffs" which has objectives, not the hammer. (Of course, in the higher reaches of debate about designed physical systems there is the speculation that it might be possible to construct a machine which is "intelligent" and can think for itself in the sense of acting in a way *not envisaged in its programmed instructions*. This has not been achieved but the dream is a powerful one and underlies the whole subject of cybernetics.)

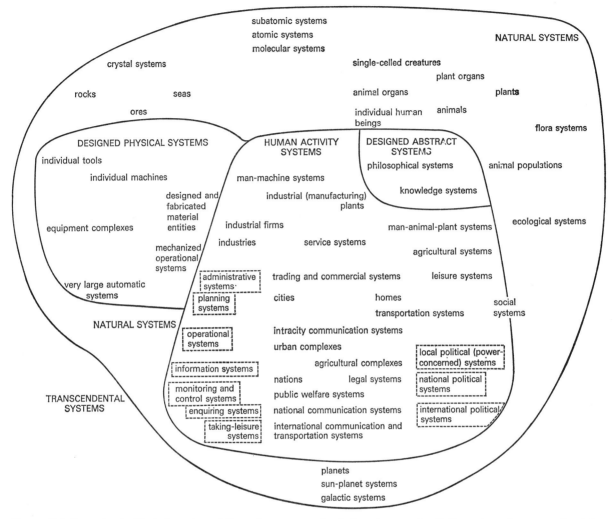

**Figure 3.3** Examples to illustrate a view of the universe as a complex of system types.

A designed abstract system is a system of thought, a philosophy, a structured set of ideas. Like a designed physical system, an abstract system will be constructed having in mind some objective related to its use – elucidation, maybe, or the enlargement of the sum total of knowledge.

The human activity systems comprise the area in which objectives can be originated. If they can be stated with some clarity then it is the area in which we can have some hope of being able to engineer systems so that objectives can be achieved. Systems Engineering is concerned with developing ways of doing this. A systems study will frequently involve the design and implementation of both physical systems and activity systems in a complex inter-relation. It may draw upon abstract systems of thought and also knowledge of natural systems. The map is not intended to be complete, but to include enough examples to illuminate the main areas. The special area for seeking to engineer systems is that of human activity systems but all the other areas are relevant:

We may *seek to engineer* human activity systems,
We may *use* designed physical and designed abstract systems,
We may *learn* from the behaviour of natural systems.

Within the main area for the application of systems engineering we note the special difficulties which arise in social systems. Although they are capable of having definable objectives they are at the same time natural and hence in a sense unchangeable.

And also within the area of human activity systems we note that there is a great variety of system type. We may discern a spectrum of systems of different types. At one extreme are the relatively "hard" systems involving industrial plants, characterized by easy-to-define objectives, clearly defined decision-taking procedures and quantitative measures of performance. At the other extreme are the "soft" systems in which objectives are hard to define, decision-taking is uncertain, measures of performance are at best qualitative and human behaviour is (thank goodness) irrational.

The challenge facing systems engineering defined as "the application of the systems approach" is to develop methodologies appropriate to this spectrum from "hard" to "soft" systems.

## Acknowledgement

The author is grateful to student and staff colleagues with whom he has profitably discussed the ideas in this paper.

## References

1 Kline, M. B. and Lifson, M. W. (1971) "Systems Engineering and its Applications to the Design of an Engineering Curriculum", *Journal of Systems Engineering*, **2**, 1.

2 Jenkins, G. M. (1969) "The Systems Approach", *Journal of Systems Engineering*, **1**, 1. (See Article 4.)

3 Churchman, C. W., Ackoff, R. L. and Arnoff, E. L., *Introduction to Operations Research*, John Wiley & Sons.

4 Ackoff, R. L. and Sasieni, M. W. (1968) *Fundamentals of Operations Research*, John Wiley & Sons.

5 See, for example, the papers in three Penguin anthologies:
   Vroom, V. H. and Deci, E. L. (eds.) (1970) *Management and Motivation*.
   Pugh, D. S. (ed.) (1971) *Organisation Theory*.
   Burns, T. (ed.) (1969) *Industrial Man*.

6 Emery, F. E. (1970) "Organisational Behaviour: an Introduction", in *Approaches to the Study of Organisational Behaviour*, Heald, G. (ed.), Tavistock.

7 Ackoff, R. L. (1971) "Towards a System of Systems Concepts", *Management Science*, **17**, 11. (See Article 7.)

8 Jones, J. C., "The Designing of Man–Machine Systems", in *The Human Operator in Complex Systems*, Singleton, W. Y. *et al.* (ed.), Taylor and Francis.

9 Boulding, K. E. (1956) "General Systems Theory – the Skeleton of Science", *Management Science*, **2**, 3.

10 Blair, R. N. and Whitston, C. W. (1971) *Elements of Industrial Systems Engineering*, Prentice Hall.

11 Checkland, P. B. (1970) "Systems and Science, Industry and Innovation", *Journal of Systems Engineering*, **1**, 2.

(Reprinted from Checkland, P. B. (1971) "A Systems Map of the Universe", *Journal of Systems Engineering*, **2**, 2, Winter 1971.)

# 4 The systems approach
## by Gwilym M. Jenkins

**Summary**

The objective of this paper is to discuss the philosophy underlying a systems approach to the solution of problems. The most important conclusion may be summarized as follows:

1. A *piecemeal approach* to problems within firms and in local and national government is *no longer good enough* if firms and nations are to compete, and indeed to collaborate, efficiently.

2. This is so because technology, firms, organizations and affairs in general are becoming *increasingly complex* and because policy decisions *increasingly require the expenditure of large sums of money* – so that the consequences of *bad decision making* are becoming *increasingly costly*.

3. A *systems approach* to problems demands that a *piecemeal approach* is replaced by an *overall approach*. Systems Engineering is the science of designing complex systems, by the efficient use of resources in the form of *Men, Money, Machines* and *Materials*, so that the individual sub-systems making up the overall system can be designed, fitted together, checked and operated so as to achieve the *overall objective* in the most efficient way.

4. The rapid development of Systems Engineering during the last few years has been stimulated not only by the increasing complexity of businesses but also by the increasing potential of large analogue, digital and hybrid computers which enable an overall *model* of the system to be *optimized*.

5. One of the greatest benefits of Systems Engineering is that it exerts a *unifying influence* on management by tying together the many specialist techniques needed to solve complex problems.

6. The systems engineer is seen as the *generalist* who always takes an overall view and who always takes particular care to ensure that the system objectives are correct, are communicated to all concerned, and are achieved with maximum efficiency.

7. One of the most important consequences of the systems approach is that it highlights the fact that *fundamental changes* are needed in the way that both individuals and organizations go about their work. In particular, it demands that problem solving needs to be carried out on a more *interdisciplinary* basis and that many firms and organizations need to be organized in a more *integrated* way than at present.

8. Thus, Systems Engineering is seen as a *key factor* in improving *management practice*, and hence, in making big improvements to the efficiency of firms and organizations.

9. Finally, the paper draws attention to the *urgent need* at this point in time to inject *systems thinking* at all levels into industry, commerce, and into local and national government.

The paper is in three parts. Part A is concerned with answering the questions "What is Systems Engineering?" and "What is a Systems Engineer?" Part B answers the question "How does a Systems Engineer go about solving any problem?" *

## A. The nature and objectives of Systems Engineering
### A.1. Systems and their properties

The expression "All Systems Go" is now an established part of popular jargon. It means that the overall system, consisting of millions of electronic components, making up a space rocket and hundreds of men, making up the management and technical teams, has been designed in such a way that each component and human being is ready to play its *designed role* efficiently in making the rocket achieve its predetermined objective. Such an impressive feat of engineering and project management calls for sophisticated systems engineering skills. Before discussing these skills in

---

* [The original article contained a further part discussing the question, "How can systems thinking help to improve efficiency within firms and other organizations?" *Ed.*]

greater detail, it is useful by way of introduction to say what is meant by a system.

The notion that it is useful to regard such diverse entities as a domestic water heater, an industrial plant, a company, a space rocket, a hospital, a port and the entire regional government set-up of a country as *systems*, must surely go down as a very important contribution to twentieth-century thought. That the word is not new is seen from its Greek origin "systema", which derives from "syn" meaning "together" and "histemi", which means "to set". A typical dictionary definition of a system would read "A *plan* or scheme according to which things are *connected* into a *whole*", as in a system of philosophy or in the solar system. Thus, the key words, *plan, connected* and *whole*, which will recur throughout this paper, are present even in popular definitions of the word system.

Although a system has a well-established popular meaning, from the point of view of systems engineering a more precise and extended definition is needed [1]. In the following discussion, six important properties of systems are listed and illustrated by considering a relatively simple system in the form of a chemical plant.

## Systems as complex groupings of human beings and machines

A chemical plant usually consists of a very large number of different items of equipment, together with stocks of raw materials, intermediate products and finished products and also services in the form of water, steam and electricity. To operate the plant, a plant manager is required, and he will need to be assisted by several foremen and process workers, usually working three eight-hour shifts per day. For efficient running of the plant, these "line personnel" must be backed up by a host of technical and commercial "service personnel", for example maintenance engineers, research chemists accountants and salesmen. Thus, the first property of a system is that it is *a complex grouping of human beings and machines*.

## Sub-systems and flow-block diagrams

An important characteristic of systems is that they may be broken down into *sub-systems*. The way in which this breaking down is done in any particular situation will depend on the nature of the system being studied and therefore on the extent to which detail is important. To decide on the amount of sub-system detail needed may require an analysis in depth of the system and its interactions.

A convenient and readily understood way of displaying how systems may be broken down into sub-systems is provided by a *flow-block diagram*, as indicated in Figure 4.1. This shows a simplified flow-block diagram of a chemical plant for making acrolein ($C_3H_4O$) by the catalytic oxidation of propylene ($C_3H_6$) * [2]. The diagram displays the individual sub-systems or process units, making up the whole plant, as *blocks* and the links or *flows* between them, as arrows. In the present example, the flows refer to materials and energy. More generally, the flows between individual sub-systems may refer to Money, Materials, Energy, Information or Decisions.

Flow-block diagrams provide an invaluable tool for helping to clarify one's thinking about a particular system. It is remarkable how much light can be shed on a complex problem by the mere act of constructing a flow-block diagram.

## Sub-systems interact with each other

The overall efficiency of the acrolein plant depends on the correct functioning of all the sub-systems shown in Figure 4.1. This is because the plant units have *interacting tasks* to perform. In addition, some material is *recycled* from one part of the plant to an earlier stage and this in turn produces further interactions. An example of a simple interaction is provided by the fact that the more concentrated the acrolein leaving the absorption column, the less is the demand on the distillation column; thus the design of the absorption and distillation columns may be balanced against each other. Similarly, a small reactor will be cheaper but may give a lower conversion to acrolein and hence may demand more recycling of unconverted raw materials and also bigger absorption and distillation columns. At the same time the catalyst is expensive and has a limited life; it can be shown that this has an effect on the most economic size of the reactor tubes. Because of these interactions, and many more besides, it is impossible to arrive at the best design of the plant, or even at the best design for an individual piece of equipment, by considering each item separately. This brings us to the third general property of systems, namely that *the individual sub-systems interact with each other*. The performance of a given sub-

* In the process propylene and air are mixed with recycle gas and passed into a tubular reactor where they react over a catalyst to produce acrolein plus other gases. The outlet gases are cooled and then passed on to an absorption column where some gases are absorbed in water, the undissolved gases from the top of the column being recycled to the reactor. The liquid from the bottom stream of the absorber is passed into the distillation column where the acrolein is distilled and removed at the top of the column and the liquid (mostly water) from the bottom of the column is then returned to the absorption column for further use.

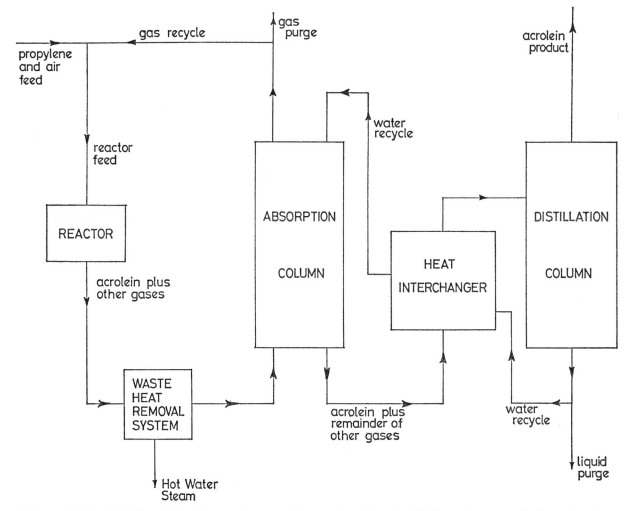

**Figure 4.1** Simplified flow-block diagram of an acrolein plant as an example of a simple system with interacting sub-systems.

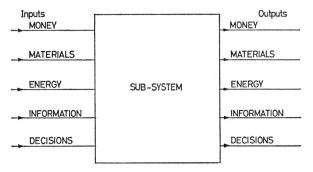

**Figure 4.2** A sub-system as some process which transforms input flows of money, materials, energy, information and decisions into corresponding output flows.

system interacts with the performance of other sub-systems and hence it cannot be designed in isolation from these other sub-systems.

In general, a sub-system may be regarded as some process which *transforms* certain *input* flows of money, materials, energy, information or decisions into corresponding *outputs*, as shown in Figure 4.2.

It is a fact that the outputs from one sub-system provide the inputs for other sub-systems which is responsible for the interactions between the various sub-systems. Understanding the detailed nature of these interactions is one of the primary concerns of the Systems Engineer.

## Systems form part of hierarchies of systems

The process of breaking down a system into sub-systems can be taken further as we look at the system in greater detail. Thus, at a later stage in the design of a chemical process, it will be necessary to specify individual plant units in much greater detail and to include their instrumentation and control equipment. The breaking down process could be continued even further until one was concerned with minute detail such as the frequency with which pumps should be serviced or even the ordering of the grease for the maintenance mechanic's grease gun!

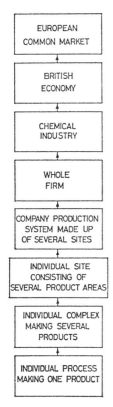

**Figure 4.3** Hierarchy of systems associated with the wider system of which an individual plant forms part.

In turn, as indicated in Figure 4.3, the plant being studied may be part of a complex of plants making several products from common feedstocks and using common and interlocking utility supplies. Again, the complex may be one of several plants and complexes on a single large industrial site. In turn, the production facilities of the entire company may consist of several manufacturing sites *to which* raw materials have to be transported, *at which* production has to be planned on a company-wide basis and *from which* finished products have to be delivered to marketing areas. If the whole firm is to operate efficiently, it must *coordinate* and *integrate* the functions of planning and investment,

research, design and development, production and equally importantly, selling and marketing. This can be done efficiently only if proper account is taken of other firms, especially those in the chemical industry. In turn the chemical industry, along with other industries, forms part of an even wider system, the British Economy of this country, possibly itself to form part of an even wider system, the European Common Market.

Thus, the fourth property of systems is that *they form part of a hierarchy of systems.* There will usually be strong interactions between the various systems which occur at the same level of a hierarchy and between systems at different levels in the hierarchy. However, the systems "at the top" are the most important because they exert considerable influence on the systems lower down in the hierarchy.

## Systems have conflicting objectives

The fifth property of a *system is that it should have an objective.* Getting the objectives right is not an easy matter but it is the key to successful systems design. For example, in the case of designing a plant, is the objective "to minimize capital costs" or "to minimize operating costs" or "to achieve the highest possible safety standards" or "to maximize reliability" or "to maximize the ease of maintenance" or what? In fact, for a given system, it is not difficult to write down a long list of possible objectives. However, these objectives will usually tend to be in conflict with each other. For example, lower capital costs result in higher operating costs, higher safety and reliability standards increase both capital and operating costs but may increase throughput and profit, and so on.

In general, *all systems have conflicting objectives*, so that some form of compromise is essential. Therefore, a balance or *trade-off* must be sought between the conflicting objectives if the best overall result is to be obtained. Thus, in the present example, a compromise between the conflicting requirements of low capital costs, low operating costs, high safety standards, high reliability and ease of maintenance must be obtained by calculating their contribution to some overall objective, such as the financial rate of return on the plant over its expected future lifetime. Reaching the best compromise between conflicting objectives poses many important questions which usually require detailed investigation at the beginning of a systems study.

## Systems must be designed to be able to achieve their objectives

The sixth, and most important, property of a system is that it must be *designed* in such a way that it is capable of achieving its overall objective. Achieving the overall objective may be a difficult and complicated question and may involve analysis, planning and designing over a long time period. This is what Systems Engineering is all about. Before going on to discuss its role in greater detail, a summary is given of the main properties of systems.

## Summary of properties of systems

1. A system is a *complex grouping* of human beings and machines.

2. Systems may be broken down into *sub-systems*, the amount of sub-system detail depending on the problem being studied. *Flow-block diagrams* provide a readily understood way of describing these sub-systems.

3. The *outputs* from a given sub-system provide the *inputs* for other sub-systems. Thus the performance of a given sub-system *interacts* with the performance of other sub-systems and hence can not be studied in isolation.

4. The system being studied will usually form part of a *hierarchy* of such systems. The systems at the top are very important and exert considerable influence on the systems lower down.

5. To function at all, a system must have an *objective*, but this is influenced by the wider system of which it forms part. Usually, systems have multiple objectives which are in conflict with one another, so that an *overall objective* is required which effects a compromise between these conflicting objectives.

6. To function at maximum efficiency, a system must be *designed* in such a way that it is capable of achieving its overall objective in the best way possible.

## A.2. The four M's and Systems Engineering

A system has been defined as any complex grouping of human beings and machines with a definite objective, such as an entire industrial plant, a whole firm or a rocket system, which is made up of a very large number of electronic components, each affecting the overall performance of the rocket. *Systems Engineering is the science of designing complex systems in their totality* to ensure that the component sub-systems making up the system are designed, fitted together, checked and operated in the most efficient way [1], [3]. It is not a new discipline, since its history is deeply rooted in good industrial design practice. However, it brings a new emphasis on *overall performance*, as opposed to the performance of individual parts of the system.

An important central feature of Systems Engineering is the building of *quantitative models* so that some overall measure of the performance of the system can be *optimized*. One of the advantages of the systems approach is that it is possible to look at entirely different problems coming from different areas of technology and business in a way that emphasizes their common features when regarded as systems.

The word "engineer" in Systems Engineering is used in the everyday sense of "designing, constructing and operating works of public utility", a definition which includes a much wider range of people than would be recognized as engineers by the professional engineering institutions! Hence, Systems Engineering is the activity of planning, designing, constructing, checking and operating complex systems. This definition has much in common with the original Greek meaning of the word system, namely "to set together". Many sub-systems need to be integrated together for the whole system to work effectively. Thus, systems engineering is the science of setting, or knitting together, or engineering, systems so that jointly they perform more efficiently in pursuit of a common objective.

It is now possible to state more precisely what is meant by the expression "All systems go", mentioned in the introduction. "All systems go" means that in the launch controller's view, each piece of electronic equipment is working properly and is making its designed contribution to the overall performance of the rocket. To reach a state where the launch controller is able to say with confidence that "All systems go", the rocket designers must have previously defined the total system and its objective. Its objective may be to launch a capsule into a predetermined path to reach the Moon. The total system consisting of rocket, launching pad and technical crew must then be designed to achieve this objective. The designers will need to analyse the requirements of the total system and then break them down into smaller systems capable of finer definition until every component and human being *has its planned place and role* in a suitably defined subsidiary system. Nothing less is acceptable from a systems engineering point of view.

## The four M's

Perhaps a simpler way of saying all this is that Systems Engineering is concerned with the *optimal use of resources* of all kinds. The major resources are the four M's, namely Men, Money, Machines and Materials or, as once translated by an earthy Yorkshire executive, Blokes, Brass, Gadgets and Muck! It has been objected by some that Systems Engineering will result in the regimentation of people to such an extent that they may become technological robots. On the contrary – a systems approach to many problems in British industry during the last twenty-five years would have shown that too much emphasis was being placed on Money, Machines and Materials and not enough on Blokes. Greater emphasis on people would have achieved the dual result of making firms much better places in which to work and also of increasing efficiency, profits and benefits all round.

## Reasons for the rapid development of Systems Engineering

Systems Engineering is becoming increasingly important because of the increasing *complexity* of business and of modern affairs in general. If all that were concerned was running a small family business, or the local parish council, there would be no particular need for Systems Engineering. However, many problems nowadays are far more complicated. Governments are forced to consider future national energy requirements and to balance up supply and demand of oil, coal, natural gas, hydro-electric power and atomic power. City administrations have to control vast financial resources in the areas of health, sanitation, education and transport. Large oil companies operate huge refineries where plant units are strung together in series and in parallel so that the performance of any one affects the efficiency of the whole. Many separate systems need to come together if a satisfactory solution is to be obtained for such complex problems. Thus, the science of knitting together separate systems is rapidly becoming an important branch of science – the science of Systems Engineering.

Alongside the increasing complexity of affairs, the ability to perform the sometimes very complicated calculations needed for systems engineering studies has been made possible by rapid developments in the development of large digital, analogue and hybrid computers. Such computers have now become indispensable weapons in the system engineer's armoury since they enable him to explore in considerable detail the economics of different ways of operating a system and to select those ways that are most efficient, resulting in optimization of the system.

## Interdisciplinary approach

In addition to providing a method by which complex problems, activities and organizations can be analysed, Systems Engineering also provides a framework within which to tie together many separate and possibly divergent disciplines, which otherwise might fail to make an effective contribution to the overall optimization of the problem. Thus Systems Engineering is a team activity and brings together specialists with such diverse backgrounds as natural science, engineering, mathematics, statistics, economics, accountancy and behavioural science. By contrast, the Systems Engineer himself is a generalist, a man trained to think in terms of an overall approach to problem solving, of getting the objectives right and seeing that they are achieved efficiently. As such, it is essential that he is able to liaise and *communicate* effectively with the various specialists whose advice is essential and to stimulate their creativity within this interdisciplinary approach. In fact, the role of the Systems Engineer is very much like that of the general practitioner whose main concern is with the general health of his patient but who, from time to time, will call in specialists for guidance. The systems team will contain specialists and Systems Engineers but the main job of the Systems Engineer is to sort out what is happening, and why, and how it can be done better. Then, together with the specialists, he ensures that the agreed objectives are realized as efficiently as possible in minimum time and at minimum cost and that a good case is presented to the decision makers who will eventually have to sanction the implementation of the designed system.

## Disasters that could have been avoided with Systems Engineering

That there is urgent need to apply a systems approach throughout industry is highlighted by the following examples of the consequences of a piecemeal approach which the writer has seen during the last few years:

1. A plant translated too quickly from laboratory stage to full-scale plant, without a proper systems study, failed to operate at all on the large scale and had to be re-designed at considerable expense.
2. A plant, which had been engineered excellently, was built but was written off immediately and did not manufacture a single ton of product. This was because the firm's assessment of the market had been at fault and was outstripped by the assessment of a rival company.
3. A large integrated plant complex lost a great deal of money during the first two years of its life because plant reliability and raw material availability had not been assessed properly.
4. A fibre manufacturer responded quickly to an increase in demand by installing additional spinning capacity without ensuring that its raw material supply was adequate and so lost money by tying up valuable capital resources.

Mistakes of this kind, which are so obvious in hindsight, are caused by a piecemeal approach to problems. It is such disasters that the disciplined approach of Systems Engineering is designed to prevent and can prevent.

## Success stories that went with good Systems Engineering

By contrast, the following represent some successful applications of systems engineering which the author has seen at close quarters during the past few years:

1. A plant designed using a systems engineering approach was estimated to be at least 10% cheaper than a plant designed by conventional methods [2].

2. A systems study leading to the installation of an on-line computer on a paper making machine led to an increase in profitability of 9% and the cost of the computer was recovered within two years [4].

3. Short term production planning of an olefines complex resulted in savings of the order of £200,000 per annum [5, 6].

4. A systems study of a petrochemical plant resulted in improvements to the process and in savings of approximately £80,000 per annum at a total cost of £6,000, including the cost of systems effort [7].

Such examples could be multiplied several times over and testify to the efficiency of the extra discipline instilled by a systems approach. Detailed stages in the development of a systems engineering project will be described later. Figure 4.4 and the following discussion summarize the main sequence of events in a typical systems study.

## Summary of stages in a systems approach to problems

1. *Systems analysis.* Systems Engineering starts with a common-sense analysis of what is going on, and why, and whether it might be done better. Then the system and its objectives have to be defined and data gathered about its likely performance.

2. *Systems design* (*or systems synthesis*). First, the future environment of the system has to be *forecast*. Then a quantitative *model* has to be built and used to *simulate* or explore a number of different ways of operating the system, finally choosing the system or systems which are in some sense "best", thus optimizing the system.

3. *Implementation.* The results of the system study must be presented and approval sought for their implementation. The optimized system will then have to be built, that is suitable hardware and/or software constructed. The project will require careful planning at this stage to ensure that the full benefits of the system approach are realized.

After construction, the system will need to be checked for performance, reliability, etc.

4. *Operation.* A point will be reached when the system will need to be handed over to those who have to operate the system on a routine basis. This is where great care is needed to avoid misunderstanding and inefficiency and probably represents *the area which is least well done in any project*. Finally the effectiveness of the operational system will need to be assessed, and if unsatisfactory, the system "tuned", or reoptimized, to operate in an environment which may turn out to be different from that for which it was designed.

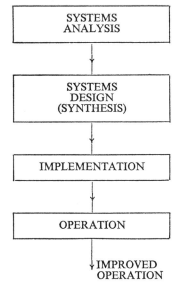

**Figure 4.4** Broad stages in the development of a systems engineering project.

## Benefits which follow from using a Systems Engineering approach

Several benefits follow from applying a systems approach. The following are the most important:

1. The majority of systems in industry and government have not been designed at all – like Topsy, they have just happened! New systems get added on to old systems and the result becomes a mess. An example of this is provided by the piecemeal development of an industrial site where plant after plant is added without a full examination of the consequences in terms of overall efficiency. Even if there were well defined objectives originally, these change gradually in time without any consequent change in the

system. Hence, the most important benefit of taking an overall systems approach is *that it affords an opportunity to stand back, take a good look at the system and to start formulating new objectives.*

2. Getting the objectives right is the most important part of any study. If the objectives are wrong, most of the subsequent effort is going to be wasted. In this context, it is easy to delude oneself into thinking that a well-defined mathematical objective is relevant. It may be that the real objective is more difficult to define and more vague. Nevertheless, it must be brought out into the open, no matter how subjective certain features of it turn out to be. Hence the second benefit of Systems Engineering is that by its disciplined method of attack on problems, it focuses attention on the important issues – *the correct objective will tend to be brought to the foreground as opposed to an irrelevant objective which might be kept in the background.* Once the objective has been formulated and agreed, it should be explained carefully to all those involved with the system, *down* to the men who will have to operate the system and *up* to the senior managers whose support is necessary both for implementation and efficient operation. Because of his overall approach, the systems engineer is the best person to define *what* should be optimized and hence is the best man to carry out the optimization.

3. There is still a great tendency in industry and in government to base decisions on *guesswork*. For example, the use of guesswork in the design of industrial plants has often led in the past to large safety factors being used in the design, resulting in excessive capital and operating costs. The third important benefit of Systems Engineering is that it *replaces guesswork by model building and optimization.* Careful consideration is then given to the consequences of alternative ways of designing the system. However, it should be emphasized that model building and optimization, if they are to be effective, must supplement and enhance intuition, judgement and inventiveness and not replace them!

4. The fourth important benefit is that by taking an overall view, *problems will be tackled in their correct order of importance.* Time will not be wasted in exploring avenues which, although interesting in themselves are not important to the realization of the overall objective. For example, there is little point in worrying about what is happening on the 17th plate of a distillation column in a chemical plant if the 17th plate has no effect on the overall economic performance of the plant. By contrast, the objectives of Systems Engineering are to pin-point those

areas which are cost sensitive and to see that these are studied carefully.

5. Related to the fourth benefit is the fact that if simple devices and techniques result in big improvements, *these will be applied as soon as possible,* leaving the last 5% or 10%, say, of the improvements to the development of more sophisticated techniques later on, provided, of course, that the effort involved in getting this last 10% of improvement is worthwhile and could not more usefully be spent elsewhere. In other words, a good systems engineer should be applying Systems Engineering to find out where he should be doing Systems Engineering!

## A.3. The origins and scope of Systems Engineering

It is claimed by Schlager in [8] that the term "Systems Engineering" was probably first used in the Bell Telephone Laboratories in the early 1940s. The widespread development of Systems Engineering since that time is demonstrated by references [9] to [29], which represent a few of the many books and articles written on the subject during the last 15 years. Systems Engineering was born and has been developed in two quite distinct areas – in military and space technology systems during and since World War II and also in industrial problems, particularly in the oil, chemical and power generation industries.

Systems Engineering in military and space applications has been dominated by the U.S.A. and has fitted in very well with the practice whereby government agencies specify the overall system requirements and then sub-contract major sub-systems to individual firms. By contrast, in the non-military area, British development, although as yet in its infancy, compares very favourably with that in other countries. This is especially true in relation to the application of systems thinking to the activities of a whole firm.

### Engineering and Systems Engineering

Differences of opinion seem to exist as to the scope and nature of Systems Engineering. There are many engineers who would argue that good engineering and Systems Engineering are synonymous. For example, Affel in [22] writes "I still find it hard to convince myself that there is a difference between systems engineering and just good engineering". In a similar vein, J. M. English [29] says "Since engineers have always been concerned with developing systems, they always have been doing systems engineering or (synonymously) engineering design. . . . Design is the function which characterises the engineer." The author would agree that "Design" is the central activity in engineering (and unfortunately an activity which is sadly neglected in many university engineering departments) and, therefore, that good engineering and good systems engineering go hand-in-hand. However, in the author's opinion, such a narrow view of Systems Engineering seems to miss two very important points.

The first is that even in situations where an engineer is usually involved, for example in the design of a chemical plant, there is a systems problem to be solved before conventional engineering can begin. Thus the design of a plant must be seen as part of the Investment Planning System of the Company. The systems problem is concerned with answering such questions as "Why should we make this product anyway as compared with other products?" If the answer to this is in the affirmative, "What is the best way to manufacture it as cheaply as possible on a large scale?" "Does the venture still look economically viable, bearing in mind the activities of competitors?" "How big should the plant be and where should it be located?", and so on. Finally, a systems problem has to be solved first to determine the interactions which the various plant units must meet in order that they can play their designed role in optimizing an overall economic criterion. It follows that when the systems job is finished, there is still a major engineering job to be done to convert the system specifications for each individual unit into detailed engineering design and hardware. However, this detailed engineering design can turn out to be pointless and wasteful in resources unless the systems job has been properly executed.

The second and more important reason that there is a difference between engineering and Systems Engineering is that the same systems thinking which can be applied to the design of hardware systems, such as space rockets, plants or ships, can also be applied, for example, to parts of firms, or whole firms, or to local government. Conventionally a firm is not regarded as a system analogous to a space rocket. But the systems engineer claims that, by definition, a firm is a system of at least similar complexity and, moreover, that to look at a firm in this way provides an opportunity for improving its efficiency markedly. Thus the systems approach to design can be applied to these much wider Commercial, Management and "software" systems just as well as to the "hardware" systems with which the engineer is more familiar.

## Operations (Operational) Research and Systems Engineering

Whereas Systems Engineering has its origins in the design of Engineering Systems, Operations Research is said to have been born in the Battle of Britain which led to the, by now, legendary studies into the optimal size of convoys. Operations Research is defined by the British Operational Research Society as "The application of the methods of science to complex problems arising in the direction and management of large systems of men, machines, materials and money in industry, business, government, and defence. The distinctive approach is to develop a scientific model of the system, incorporating measurements of factors such as chance and risk, with which to predict and compare the outcomes of alternative decisions, strategies or controls. The purpose is to help management determine its policy and actions scientifically." Hence, it is clear that Operations Research and Systems Engineering have much in common. In fact, during an article in a book entitled "Operations Research and Systems Engineering", Roy [13] states that "in a certain sense, operations research and systems engineering *are* the same". However, in the same breath he goes on to say that "The operations research team is more likely to be concerned with operations *in being* rather than with operations *in prospect*" and "systems engineers are more likely to be engaged in the design of systems yet to be, rather than in the operation of systems in being". This supposed difference has also been suggested by several other people, including Hall [19]. However, it is a false and artificial distinction since Systems Engineering is just as much concerned with redesigning existing systems as in designing new ones. In fact, designing a new system is usually the most satisfactory of situations since a fresh start can be made. However, the majority of systems have just evolved in a haphazard way without any clear objectives, or if there were clear objectives originally, these have now changed without any consequent change in the system. In such a situation, the application of systems engineering is as valuable, or even more valuable, as when a fresh start can be made.

To a certain extent it is true that, in its early days, Systems Engineering was more concerned with the design of what may be called Technical Systems, such as military and space systems, new plants, the improvement of existing plants and systems engineering studies leading to the installation of on-line computers on plants. (These are areas which involve the development of new technology and as such lie outside the field of practice of operational research workers.) However, in recent years, this activity has been extended considerably and the systems approach is now being applied, for example, to such wide ranging problems as the design of integrated production–distribution planning and control systems, corporate planning systems, transportation systems and to improving the efficiency of departments in a city administration.

The writer cannot speak for Operational Research but can only repeat that Systems Engineering is concerned with placing a big emphasis on the design of the total system and not individual sub-systems. It is difficult to escape the conclusion that if Operational Research is really concerned with the overall design of complex human-machine systems, the subject has a rather unfortunate title and that many of its exponents are nevertheless content to tinker with the sub-systems.

## Systems Analysis and Systems Engineering

The word Systems Analysis has been used, for example by the RAND Corporation [30] and the Systems Development Corporation [31] to describe the application of the systems approach to the wider "non-hardware" systems mentioned earlier. It is unfortunate perhaps that, in their attempts to emphasize that Systems Analysis is concerned with the design of much wider systems than "engineering" or "hardware" systems, the users of this word have only told part of the story. This is because systems synthesis is an equally important step as systems analysis in the design of systems. However, the word "engineering" covers the processes of analysis and synthesis and it is for this reason that the Department of Systems Engineering at the University of Lancaster has been so named. The word "engineer" has been used in the general sense of the man who designs or engineers systems whether they be composed of hardware or software or just people.

Clearly, semantic discussions resolve nothing. However, since Operational Research, Systems Analysis and Systems Engineering have a great deal in common, then the systems approach would suggest that there is need for better communication between them.

## B. Stages in the application of Systems Engineering

This section gives some general guide lines as to how a systems engineer would tackle any problem. The various stages to be described represent a breakdown and amplification of the four steps

1. Systems Analysis,
2. Systems Design,
3. Implementation,
4. Operation,

mentioned earlier and are summarized in the flow diagram of Figure 4.5. It is *not* suggested that all systems projects will proceed along the following lines. Rather, the stages are intended as rough guide lines to aid clear thinking and to emphasize above all that *Systems Engineering is an orderly and well-disciplined way of getting things done*.

### 1. SYSTEMS ANALYSIS

1.1. Formulation of the problem
1.2. Organization of the project
1.3. Definition of the system
1.4. Definition of the wider system
1.5. Objectives of the wider system
1.6. Objectives of the system
1.7. Definition of overall economic criterion
1.8. Information and data collection

↓

### 2. SYSTEMS DESIGN

2.1. Forecasting
2.2. Model building and simulation
2.3. Optimization
2.4. Control
2.5. Reliability

↓

### 3. IMPLEMENTATION

3.1. Documentation and Sanction Approval
3.2. Construction

↓

### 4. OPERATION

4.1. Initial operation
4.2. Retrospective appraisal
4.3. Improved operation

**Figure 4.5** Detailed stages in a Systems Approach to problems.

### B.1. Systems Analysis

The first step in Systems Engineering is Systems Analysis. This involves the following stages:

1.1. Recognition and formulation of the problem.
1.2. Organization of the systems project.
1.3. Definition of the system.
1.4. Definition of the wider system of which the system being studied forms part.
1.5. Definition of the objectives of the wider system.
1.6. Definition of the objectives of the system being studied.
1.7. Definition of the overall economic criterion.
1.8. Information and data collection.

## 1.1. *Recognition and formulation of the problem*

Firms and organizations do not exist to provide employment for systems engineers! Rather, they have problems which arise in the day-to-day running of their organizations, the solution of which would lead to improved efficiency and profitability. The job of the systems engineer is to provide effective solutions to those problems.

A problem arises because some manager needs *help* – he may have noticed that something is going wrong or he may need help to make a planning decision or to implement a planning decision made higher up. He may then decide to consult the systems engineer as an individual accustomed to taking an overall point of view towards solving problems. In these circumstances the systems engineer should interrogate the manager very thoroughly and also all other persons within the organization who are likely to be able to help. In particular he should ask

(1) How did the problem arise?

(2) Who are the people who believe it to be a problem?

(3) If it involves implementing a planning decision made higher up, what is the chain of argument leading to the making of the decision?

(4) Why is the solution important? How much money might it save?

(5) Is it the right problem anyway? Might it not be just a manifestation of a much deeper problem? Would greater benefits accrue if that problem were solved rather than the one posed by the manager?

(6) Inevitably, the resources available to the firm are limited. On the evidence available at this stage, does it seem that there would be a reasonable return on systems effort if applied to the project or would this effort be better employed in tackling a different problem?

As a result of this dialogue, a clearer picture should now begin to emerge about the scope of the problem and the likely benefits which would result from its solution.

## 1.2. *Organization of the project*

1. *Composition of the systems team.* Once the scope of the problem has been defined, the way in which it is to be tackled should be mapped out. Systems Engineering is a team activity not an individual activity and an *ad hoc* systems team should now be set up. Ideally this should be able to draw some of its members from a small central systems department within the company. In addition, it will be necessary to supplement these systems men by people, drawn from various departments within the company, whose specialist knowledge can be brought to bear upon the problem.

Many companies do not have a central systems organization nor a great deal of systems experience. This does not mean that a systems team cannot be formed. The best resources available within the organization for tackling the problem should be brought together and, with efficient leadership, they can develop into a systems team very quickly.

A typical systems team would contain some or all of the following:

(*a*) *Team leader* – ideally an experienced systems engineer, or alternatively, someone with a keen intellect and a great deal of knowledge of the problem which is to be tackled.

(*b*) *User* – a representative of the team which will operate the engineered system. For example, if the problem is to design and build a chemical plant, production department should be represented, preferably by the plant manager designate.

(*c*) *Model builders* – to take part in the model building itself and also to liaise with and stimulate those specialist functional departments (such as research, process development and sales departments) which will be able to provide information for the sub-systems models.

(*d*) *Designers* – if the system involves the building of hardware, representatives of the engineering team who will be responsible for the design of this hardware to meet the system specification. Similarly, if the system involves software, representatives of the team which will design this software, for example computer programmers, data processing and computer experts.

(*e*) *Computer Programmers/Mathematicians* – to programme the systems models and to help with the optimization of the design.

(*f*) *An economist or accountant* – to provide information on the general economic environment of the problem which will help in defining the overall economic criterion, and to assist in obtaining cost information for the model.

(*g*) *Systems engineers* – these may contribute to a greater or lesser extent in the model building, programming, optimization, economic evaluation, etc. In some situations, they may have to do most of this work themselves. Above all, however, they should be taking an overall view of the development of the project.

2. *Terms of reference.* The systems team should take steps to ensure that they are given the widest possible terms of reference and are given access to any information or

person. In other words, they should be given the maximum opportunity to stand back and take a fresh look at the problem.

3. *Scheduling the project*. The systems engineering team should apply the systems approach to the conduct of its own activities to ensure that the work is carried out logically and systematically and that the implementation of the systems study can take place by an allotted time. Thus a decision network should be constructed (for example a critical path schedule), targets set and duties allocated. In this way, maximum effort can be concentrated in areas which are most important. The systems team will then ensure, by its critical approach to its own method of working, that problems are tackled in their correct order of importance.

## 1.3. *Definition of the system*

The next task of the systems engineering team is to define in precise terms the system which is to be studied. This is a process of *analysis* in which the system has to be broken down into its important sub-systems and the interactions between these sub-systems indicated by drawing a *flow-block diagram*. The subsequent task of the systems engineer is one of *synthesis*, that is to design or engineer the individual sub-systems so that they work together towards achieving an overall objective. As indicated in Section A.1, the flows typically appearing in a flow-block diagram represent money, energy, materials, information and decisions. In constructing a flow diagram, it is sometimes helpful to use a different flow convention for these different types of flow, or alternatively, the flows should be clearly labelled.

The extent to which the system needs to be broken down into sub-systems may not be known initially. For example, certain processing units in a chemical plant may usefully be lumped together and considered as one unit for the purpose of building a model to establish the overall system requirements. To avoid making the system description too complex, it is usually better to work with a simple representation of the system first and then elaborate later if necessary. If the system already exists, as for example in a process improvement study of an existing plant, the simplicity of the system diagram, and its description, is justified if the resulting model is able to describe those areas which are sensitive to cost. Even when nothing very much is known about the system, as in the initial stages of the design of a new plant, there is a great deal to be said for making the system description simple to start with and then examining the consequences of gradual elaboration later.

A related question to the simplicity of the system description is that the systems design process must be sufficiently *flexible*, so that this description can be changed as further knowledge and experience is accumulated during the course of the project. This is especially important in the design of a new system when there may be very inadequate knowledge at the start of a project. As the project proceeds, the system description will become clearer as the process of *innovation* develops. Indeed, there may have to be several iterations of the design process before a satisfactory solution can be found.

## 1.4. *Definition of the wider system which contains the system being studied*

To define the objectives of the system, it is necessary to display very clearly the role which the system plays in the wider system of which it forms part. A separate flow-block diagram should be constructed to display this role very clearly. By contrast to the flow-block diagram of the system itself, the flow-block diagram of the system as part of a wider system should include as much detail as is available. Invariably, it happens that the relationship of the system to the wider system is hazy and unclear to most people at the beginning. Hence a great deal of clear thinking will be necessary to fill in sufficient detail on this flow-block diagram so that proper account is taken of the interactions between the system and the wider system when formulating objectives. The flow diagram of the wider system provides an excellent tool for clarifying this thinking.

## 1.5. *Definition of the objectives of the wider system*

The block diagrams of the system and of the wider system provide invaluable tools for analysing and then formulating objectives. Because systems form part of a hierarchy of systems, it is impossible to dissociate the objectives of the system being studied from those of the wider system of which it forms part. In fact, it is the objectives of the wider system which are the crucial ones since they determine the *environment* within which the system has to function. If this environment changes, then so will the objectives of the system change. To take a very simple example, the objectives of a single chemical plant must fit into the overall production plan of the company. At different times the company plan may stipulate one of several objectives.

For example,

(1) the plant must make a fixed tonnage of the right quality product at minimum cost per ton. This is commonly referred to as a *production limited* situation, or

(2) the plant must make as much product as possible while satisfying the same or possibly less stringent quality constraints than in (1), or

(3) the plant must make a fixed tonnage at minimum cost per ton but using a cheaper, less pure, raw material, and so on.

Therefore, in a process improvement exercise, there may not be one unique objective but rather a *catalogue* of possible objectives, each resulting in a different way of operating the plant. Thus the relevant objective at any given instant must be dictated by the needs of the wider system. Definition of the objectives of the wider system brings several advantages:

(1) It focuses attention on the fact that systems must be designed so that:

> (*a*) junior systems in a hierarchy should play their designed role in achieving the objectives of more senior systems in the hierarchy,
>
> (*b*) senior systems in the hierarchy should make a clear, unambiguous statement of what the junior systems are expected to contribute.

Without such clearly defined responsibilities a system may operate very inefficiently, or if the objectives are very vague, anarchy may result.

(2) We have seen that the objectives of systems at the same level in the hierarchy are usually in conflict – such systems are usefully described as *interlocking* or *competitive* systems. Thus, defining the objectives of the wider system is essential so that the objectives of the competitive systems can be formulated in such a way that they contribute effectively to the objectives of the wider system instead of pulling in different directions. For example, two plant managers can very easily operate their own plants in such a way that they optimize their performance individually but at the expense of not meeting the company's objectives efficiently. Such conflicts are of frequent occurrence in industry and in other walks of life and stem from a failure to define objectives clearly.

(3) Facing up to the objectives of the senior systems in the hierarchy will counteract the tendency to omit these systems altogether. There will always be a tendency to omit the systems at the top because they seem too vague, or more importantly, *too difficult* to formulate. In fact, the systems at the top should not be omitted until the consequence of doing so on the system being studied have been carefully ascertained and shown to be of no consequence. For example, it might be sensible to omit the influence of the British Economy in deciding how to operate a plant but to omit the influence of raw material availability within the company might be very short sighted.

(4) By defining the objectives of the senior systems in the hierarchy, the system under study can be designed so that it is capable of *adapting itself to change* quickly. For example, by knowing that the production system of a company may make changing demands on an individual plant, the operation of that plant can be planned so that it is able to react quickly to the changes when they occur. This can be achieved, for example, by tabulating the best operating conditions for different values of the throughput.

(5) The performance of junior systems in the hierarchy may improve, especially the performance of the people involved. By communicating the objectives of the higher systems to those involved in the junior systems, their sense of involvement is increased, with a consequent increase in efficiency. Sometimes immediate and worthwhile benefits can result by communicating objectives of the senior systems since it can pin-point areas where conflicts are leading to a deterioration in efficiency.

## 1.6. *Definition of the objectives of the system*

The end product of any definition of objectives is the formulation of the criterion, usually an economic one, which measures the efficiency with which the system is achieving its objective. The formulation of the economic criterion may require a careful study in its own right. However, in the early stages it is better to define the objectives in broad terms.

There will usually be conflicting objectives and at the start of a systems study it is essential to make a *comprehensive list* of all possible objectives in *their anticipated order of importance*. One, or possibly a few, objectives might then be singled out as being the most important ones. What weight to give these conflicting objectives in the formulation of the overall economic criterion will have to be considered later.

At this important stage of any systems study, much questioning will have to be done and many different points of view listened to. In the end the systems engineer must make up his own mind about the correct objectives, then get agreement with all concerned and finally communicate his findings to everybody so that their future cooperation can be relied upon.

Important points to be borne in mind at this stage are:

(1) The systems engineer may meet resistance when he tries to define objectives. People who have got along quite well in the past with vague objectives may object to the influx of new ideas. However, the systems engineer must persist because no system can be designed properly unless it is clearly known what it is trying to achieve.

(2) He may be frustrated because the objectives are not clear. If after persistent attempts, objectives are still not satisfactorily defined, this must be faced up to. This means that the resulting system will have to be acknowledged to be imperfect and improved later if more precise information becomes available. His motto should be "It ain't much but it's all I've got" rather than "I'm sorry mate but I don't know enough to start!"

(3) Where possible, objectives should be *simple and direct*. If simple quantitative objectives are not possible, they should be replaced by simple subjective objectives. Failure to quantify objectives should be recorded and brought to the attention of people so that attempts can be made at some future stage to improve precision. In other words, the systems engineer can make a big contribution by being objective about subjective matters!

## 1.7. *Definition of the overall economic criterion*

Once the objectives have been agreed, the next step is to define, in as precise terms as possible, a criterion which measures the efficiency with which the system can achieve its objective. Usually, but not invariably, this criterion will be an economic one, for example a company may measure performance by its rate of return on capital, or the performance of a chemical plant may be measured by the cost per ton of manufacturing the main product. The more precise the objectives, the easier it is to set up quantitative criteria. Conversely, if the overall objectives are not precise, then there will have to be some subjective criterion of performance.

An overall economic criterion should be:

(1) *Related to objectives* – care should be taken to avoid a precise mathematical criterion which does not embrace all the objectives.
(2) *Simple and direct* – if possible, both objectives and performance criterion should be expressed as concisely and simply as possible.
(3) *Clearly agreed and accepted, even if qualitative* – in practice confusion often arises because of the application of contradictory criteria. For example, one manager may decide that a certain course of action is desirable because

it is based on a certain criterion, whereas another manager in the same company may reach the opposite decision because his criterion is different. It is very important that criteria of performance be agreed by everyone, notified to everyone and applied by everyone in the same way – otherwise confusion results and efficiency is impaired.

*Resolution of conflicting objectives.* To formulate an economic criterion, it is necessary to decide on the compromises which have to be achieved between the conflicting objectives of a system. There are two basic ways in practice in which conflicting objectives can be met.

(1) By *weighting* alternative objectives in the overall criterion.
(2) By imposing *constraints* (sometimes objective, sometimes subjective) on certain variables which enter into the economic criterion.

These two methods are now discussed briefly.

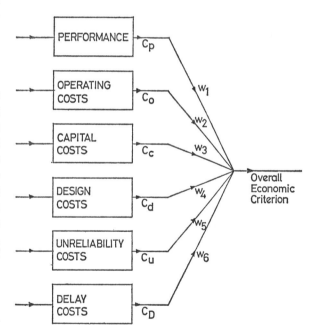

**Figure 4.6** Conflicting objectives in the design of a system.

1. *Weighting of objectives.* Figure 4.6 summarizes typical conflicting objectives which have to be met by any system. This shows that the overall economic criterion has to be obtained by attaching weights $w_1, w_2, \ldots, w_6$ to:

1. The performance of the system.
2. Operating and production costs.

3. Capital costs.
4. Design costs.
5. Unreliability costs.
6. "Delay to build" costs.

Very often these weights will not be known exactly and it may be necessary to make *value judgements* of what the real weights are. This does not detract from the exercise but on the contrary forces designers to think more clearly about the subjective judgements that they have to make. For example, in the case of a plant design study, the influence of these costs on total cash flow as the project develops is illustrated in Figure 4.7. Thus the time and money spent on each of the four stages – research, development, construction and start-up – can have a considerable effect on the profitability of the project.

Most plant design studies nowadays try to balance capital against operating costs. Unfortunately, insufficient attention seems to be paid to unreliability and "delay to build" costs. Bad judgement of these costs can result in poor performance during the early years of a plant and convert what would otherwise have been a highly profitable project into one whose profitability is unacceptably low.

Figure 4.6 gives the impression that the weighting of objectives is *static*. However, in most systems design, the weighting must be *dynamic* so that the contribution of the various costs to project profitability can be discounted over the life time of the project. Discussion of the various forms of discounted cash flow criteria now being used to weight conflicting objectives lies outside the scope of the present paper. However, all criteria are based on the fact that a predicted net cash flow of £$a_i$ for the project in year $i$ is worth £$a_i/(1 + r)^i$ *now*, where $r$ is the interest rate one could reasonably expect to earn by investing one's money in other projects inside the company, or possibly outside. For example, the *net present worth* (N.P.W.) of a project is defined by

$$\text{N.P.W.} = \sum_{i=1}^{n} a_i/(1+r)^i,$$

where $n$ is the expected life time of the project. Again, from the point of view of systems design, such criteria should not be used in a mechanical fashion. In practice, it is necessary to look at the individual predicted cash flows and their *uncertainty* in greater detail because two projects with widely different cash flows can give rise to the same net present worth. Therefore, it is usually necessary to compare the *risks* associated with two projects before a decision in favour of one or the other can be made.

2. *Constraints*. It is not always possible to achieve a compromise between conflicting objectives by weighting alone. In addition, the conflicts may have to be resolved by imposing certain constraints on the design of the system. These constraints are usually of two kinds:

(*a*) physical constraints,
(*b*) constraints which are a recognition of the fact that *it is sometimes difficult to quantify*.

Once again, this is illustrated by considering the design of a chemical process. Under (*a*) come constraints on quality and physical properties imposed by customers and by equipment performance, etc. Under (*b*) come, for example, factors associated with the safe running of the process at conditions as near as possible to the inflammable or explosive limits or other process constraints. If an explosion happens, there may be a loss of human life and the plant may be shut down for long periods.

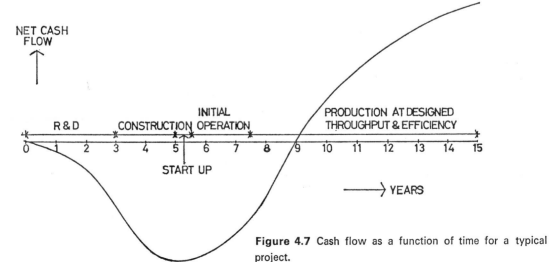

**Figure 4.7** Cash flow as a function of time for a typical project.

To allow for such factors in a quantitative way would be too difficult or too complex. As mentioned earlier, much is to be gained by making the overall economic criterion simple. In other words, one should try to build in those main economic features which are well understood and then impose certain constraints on the freedom of choice of certain variables in the design to allow for factors which are much more difficult to quantify, such as the loss in customers due to bad quality and to shutdowns due to explosions, the loss of lives, etc.

This illustrates the general point made about objectives earlier, namely that a detailed analysis of the economics of a situation may reveal areas which are difficult to quantify. As with objectives, it is better to bring to the foreground these subjective elements rather than bury one's head in the sand and to pretend that one is making progress by using a criterion which is easy to quantify but *irrelevant* to the real-life situation. The fact that subjective elements are present does not mean that nothing can be done. On the contrary, it means that subjective economic judgements have to be made and these are usually best expressed in the form of constraints imposed on the design. Indeed, once this is done, the possibility arises of varying the constraints to see what effect they have on the economic performance of the system.

## 1.8. *Information and data collection*

The final, and probably most extensive, stage in Systems Analysis is the gathering of data and information which will form the basis of any future modelling of the system. If the system is not in existence, then the fact finding will have to be based on new research and development and on other similar systems if they exist. Data will be required not only to provide information about the operation of the system but also to make *forecasts* of the *environment* in which the system will have to operate in future.

Efficient information and data collection requires

(i) *Clear thinking* about the problem so that relevant sources of information can be tapped.
(ii) *Ability to communicate* in speech and in writing so that people are stimulated into parting with information and into volunteering new information.
(iii) *A grasp of statistical techniques* so that the significance of the data can be appreciated and used in subsequent model building and decision making.

## B.2. Systems Design (or Synthesis)

The systems analysis stage should have opened up the problem, enabled objectives to be defined and initiated fact finding. Based on these foundations, the Systems Design stage can then be tackled with confidence. It is convenient to discuss the design stage under the five headings

2.1. Forecasting,
2.2. Model Building and Simulation,
2.3. Optimization,
2.4. Control,
2.5. Reliability.

## 2.1. *Forecasting*

Forecasting is the first important step in the design of any system. For example, in the design of a production control or production planning system, forecasts of demand may be needed for each fortnight or month for up to a year ahead (short term forecasting). Similarly, to design a plant, forecasts of demand will be needed for a period of several years ahead (medium term forecasting) and to design a Corporate Plan for a company, forecasts of the firm's activities and environment will be needed for up to 15 or even 20 years ahead (long term forecasting, technological forecasting).

Accurate forecasts are essential for the efficient design of any system. By contrast, if the forecasts are inaccurate, they can not be compensated for by sophisticated model building and optimization at a later stage. Indeed such sophistication at a later stage may then turn out to be a complete waste of time.

Forecasts of future values are not of much use on their own. In addition, it is essential to obtain estimates of their *accuracy*, so that this can be allowed for in assessing the *risk* associated with the design of the system.

## 2.2. *Model building and simulation*

To compute the costs associated with different ways of running a system, it is necessary to predict the performance of the system over a wide range of operational conditions. To do this, a *model* of the system needs to be built. By a model is meant a *quantitative* description of the behaviour of the system which can be used to predict performance over a relevant range of operating conditions and real life environments. In its crudest form, a model could consist of a set of tables or graphs; at a more sophisticated level it might be written in mathematical form, namely as a set of algebraic or differential equations.

Model building is not a straightforward, but rather, a highly creative activity. It is of necessity an *iterative* or *adaptive* process in which one moves from a state of little knowledge to one of greater knowledge – in other words, it is a process of hauling oneself up by one's bootstraps. To design a system, many different types of model may need to be developed. Experience and good judgement are needed to decide which type of model should be used for any particular situation, so that the system can then be designed as efficiently as possible with the minimum expenditure of time and money.

Quantitative models useful in Systems Engineering may be classified into four types:

(i) *Descriptive* models, which provide a qualitative description and insight, as compared with *predictive* models, which should be able to give predictions of the economic performance of a system to a required degree of accuracy.

(ii) *Mechanistic* models, which are based on a mechanism by the way that the system behaves, as compared with *empirical* or *statistical* models, obtained by fitting data obtained from the system.

(iii) *Steady state* models, which are based on average performance, as compared with *dynamic* models which allow for the way that performance fluctuates with time.

(iv) *Local* models, which describe the behaviour of sub-systems, as compared with *global* models which tie together the sub-system models into a model for the overall system.

Model building is the cornerstone of any scientific activity and, as such, plays a very important role in systems engineering – as mentioned in Section 1.2, a model replaces guesses by facts. However, there are important differences between the approach required for model building in systems engineering compared with that required for other scientific subjects. For example, in physics and chemistry, model building is almost an end in itself since the objective is to subsume as many facts as possible under the umbrella of a single model. In Systems Engineering, on the other hand, the end objective is to *optimize* the performance of a system and hence model building must be subservient to this objective. Thus a Systems Engineering team must:

(1) Ensure that model building is carried out *with a sense of purpose*, that is to enable a system to be designed as cheaply and efficiently as possible.

(2) *Tie together* the various specializations that may be needed for building models of the sub-systems. In particular, the systems team will always be emphasizing to the specialist model builders that the important thing is to model those areas to which the overall economic criterion is sensitive.

(3) *Ensure that work is concentrated where it is most needed.* Because it takes an overall view, the systems team will be in a much better position to pin-point those areas which are cost sensitive and, if necessary, to ask for more work to be done in those areas. Conversely, it will be in a better position to stop activity in those areas which are not cost sensitive. For example, in a plant design project an over-enthusiastic chemist may believe that it is necessary to predict a certain physical property to say within 1%, whereas from a systems viewpoint it may only be necessary to predict it to within 5% or even 10%. *As a general rule, models should be kept as simple as possible.*

(4) *Decide when the model is adequate* for the purposes for which it is needed, namely to predict overall system performance to a sufficient degree of accuracy. Model building is a fascinating activity and people, if left to their own initiative, tend to be carried away, tend to become emotionally involved and tend to waste time and money by over-elaborating the model. By contrast, the systems approach requires discipline to ensure that when the model is adequate, model building is terminated and the optimization stage begun as soon as possible.

(5) If the model is to be used for planning, see that an *effective dialogue* is conducted between the systems team and the managers who will use the model. Experience suggests that in such areas as production, investment and corporate planning, that this *dialogue must start whilst the model is being built* and not when the model is handed over. This is because models must be thoroughly understood by management if they are to be used effectively and moreover, because it is management that makes the decisions, their involvement at an early stage can often lead to suggestions resulting in substantial improvements and simplifications in the models themselves.

*Simulation.* Once a model of the overall system has been built, the model has to be converted from a *passive* device (a set of graphs or equations) into an *active* device which can then be used to *simulate* the behaviour of the system when subjected to:

(a) realistic inputs typical of those which the operational system will have to meet in practice,

(b) realistic disturbances, which will cause the behaviour of the system to fluctuate from its average or steady state performance.

Hence a simulation is a *working* or *operational* model of the system which should be able to reproduce the actual behaviour of the real system to an accepted degree of accuracy. If the simulation is accurate, data generated from the simulation should agree closely with data from the operational system. In other words, from the point of view of systems design, we can treat the simulation *as if it were* the actual system and make changes to the parameters in the simulation to see how to optimize the system.

The inputs or disturbances, in the simulation may be:

(i) deterministic, or
(ii) statistical,

and correspondingly, the simulation is said to be *deterministic* or *statistical*. An example of a deterministic simulation is provided by a model of a chemical plant which is set up in such a way that it can be fed with average values of process inputs and used to calculate the corresponding values of the average outputs. An example of a statistical simulation is provided by a model which describes the random times of arrival of tankers at a port with a view to optimizing the berthing facilities.

In a statistical simulation, it may be possible to collect enough data relating to the statistically fluctuating variables directly from an operating system. However, it often happens that insufficient data is available to simulate the behaviour of the system over a sufficiently long period for the results to have meaning. In these cases, a statistical analysis will be needed to analyse the data so that a statistical (probability) model can be set up to describe the data. Armed with a statistical model, unlimited amounts of hypothetical data can then be generated so that the system can be simulated over a sufficiently long period of time.

In recent years, powerful computer simulation languages have been developed to speed up the simulation stage of a systems design. As with modelling, the systems engineer will emphasize that a simulation should be made as simple as possible so that optimization can go ahead with minimum delay.

## 2.3. *Optimization*

The next step after simulation is to optimize the system. Armed with a model which can predict performance, it is then possible to compute the value of the economic criterion corresponding to different modes of operating the system. For example, when designing an industrial plant, it enables the rate of return on capital to be calculated for different sizes of equipment and operating conditions, and so on. Choosing the system which results in the most favourable value of the economic criterion is what is meant by optimization. It is at this point that the importance of defining the overall objectives should become apparent. If the system

and its objectives are too narrow, then the most profitable mode of operation for this narrow system will almost certainly be in conflict with the most profitable conditions for the wider system which has been overlooked. This is usually referred to as *sub-optimization*.\* One of the most important jobs of the systems engineer is to ensure that sub-optimization does not take place. He will constantly need to emphasize that the optimization of each sub-system independently will not in general lead to a system optimum. More strongly, he will have to emphasize that improvement to a particular sub-system *may actually worsen* the overall system.

During the last fifteen years, the need to optimize systems has stimulated the development of a number of mathematical techniques called *optimization techniques*.†

Although these mathematical techniques are very important, from a systems engineering point of view, optimization involves a great deal more than a mathematical problem. Assuming that the problem is one of maximization, optimization is equivalent to climbing a multi-dimensional hill. Very often one is debarred from climbing to the top because of the constraints on the design variables. However, in systems engineering work, one is not only interested in getting to the highest point possible on the hill and then planting the Union Jack at the summit! In the design of a system, three other much more important considerations have to be investigated, namely:

(1) The sensitivity of the economic criterion to changes in the parameters near the "optimum".

---

\* It is stated [25] that the word "sub-optimize" was first used by C. J. Hitch [32]. In his analysis of the wartime problem where it was shown that convoys should be made as large as possible, he points out that although the final answer reached was approximately correct, it was arrived at for the wrong reasons. He argues that the reasons were wrong because too much emphasis was placed on a sub-system, namely a skirmish between a convoy and a submarine pack, rather than on the wider system, that is winning the Battle of the Atlantic or more importantly still, optimizing an even wider system, namely winning the war.

† From a mathematical point of view, the problem of optimization is one of maximizing or minimizing an overall economic criterion

$$f(x_1, x_2, \ldots, x_n)$$

which depends on various design parameters $x_1, x_2, \ldots, x_n$, (e.g. operating conditions, sizes of equipment, when designing a plant) and is subject to certain inequality constraints

$$g_i(x, x_{21}, \ldots, x_n) \leqslant c, i = 1, 2, \ldots, l$$

and certain equality constraints

$$h_j(x_1, x_2, \ldots, x_n) = d_j, j = 1, 2, \ldots, m.$$

(2) The sensitivity of the economic criterion to various assumptions made in the design.

(3) The effect of uncertainty in the forecasts of the environment in which the system will have to operate.

(1) In many optimization studies, there are usually more design variables to choose from than one usually can, or wants to, work with. As a first approach, one can choose those variables which appear to be the most important on intuitive grounds and optimize with respect to these. It is useful then to plot the economic criterion as a function of each variable, holding the others fixed at their best values – in this way one can identify the variables to which the value of the economic criteria is sensitive. Those variables to which it is insensitive can be left out and further optimization runs made with these insensitive variables replaced by new variables.

When all the sensitive variables have been discovered, the end point of any optimization study should be:

(a) to quote the best values of all variables.

(b) to give plots of the economic criterion with respect to each variable, holding all other variables at their best values.

(c) if possible, to give contour plots for certain pairs of variables, holding all other variables at their best values. This type of exercise can be very useful in discovering how one can "trade-off" one parameter against another in achieving a given cost or performance.

When (a), (b) and (c) are completed, it should be possible to obtain a clear picture of how the system is sensitive to cost.

Thus, if the overall economic criterion is smooth with respect to changes in the design parameters, then this information tells us that a wide range of systems is acceptable, each with a value of the economic criterion that is roughly the same as that of the "best" system.

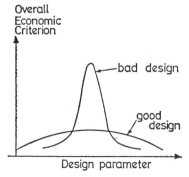

**Figure 4.8** Sensitivity of a design to the design parameters.

This constitutes a good design, as indicated in Figure 4.8. On the other hand, if the economic criterion is steep and pointed, small changes in the design of the system will produce very marked changes in its profitability. Such sensitivity to small changes in the design parameters is undesirable and leads to a bad design since one cannot be absolutely certain that the assumptions, on which the design was based, are valid. If the assumptions are wrong, there might be a high probability that the realized economic performance will occur in the foothills of the surface rather than near the top.

(2) This brings us to a very important part of the optimization stage, namely that it is essential that changes should be made in the assumptions on which the design is based and an examination made of the effects which these changes have on the system. If the changes produce markedly different systems, then one will have to think again. On the other hand, if they produce systems having the same general features, then one can feel more assured about recommending the design. The system can then be said to be *robust* with respect to the underlying assumptions.

(3) Not only must sensitivity to assumptions about performance of sub-systems be investigated but also sensitivity to the uncertainty in the forecasts of the environment within which the system will have to operate. For example, in designing a plant, if the sales forecasts are very uncertain, it has to be faced up to that the most pessimistic forecasts might be the ones that actually occur, and hence that low profitability may result. However, one should clearly not design in the expectation that the most pessimistic forecasts will be realized. A *risk analysis* is then very important in helping to assess the most reasonable approach to the design problem. For example, this form of analysis can be especially helpful if a multi-product complex is being designed when the sales forecasts for each product are subject to different degrees of uncertainty. The size of these uncertainties can have an appreciable effect on the way in which the complex is designed.

*To summarize*, at the optimization stage the systems engineer should pay particular attention to the following:

(1) He should be aware of the dangers of sub-optimization and indeed of *leaving out altogether* certain important variables.

(2) After locating the optimum design conditions, he should examine very carefully the economic criterion surface to see which parameters are cost sensitive.

(3) He should guard against "very sharp optima" since a system which is very cost sensitive may be highly dependent on the assumption made in the design.

(4) He should make a *sensitivity analysis* to see whether changes in the assumptions lead to systems with the same general features. If not, he should think again.

(5) Finally, he should be very conscious of the fact that, when optimization is complete, a *very costly decision* may have to be made to allow the optimized design to be built. Therefore, at the optimization stage, he should be guided by certain techniques for making decisions in the presence of uncertainty, such as risk analysis.

## 2.4. *Control*

When a system has been optimized, a control system must be set up so that the most profitable design conditions can be realized when the system is operated in a real life environment. Control is necessary because unpredictable *disturbances* enter a system which cause its *actual* performance to deviate from its *predicted* performance. For example, local control devices will need to be installed on a chemical plant to regulate automatically the flow of materials, the levels of liquids in tanks and the temperatures and pressures required to achieve the most profitable operating conditions. Similarly, a management control system is needed to control a company production plan. This means that when a company production plan has been formulated, it must be backed up by an accounting system which feeds information to senior managers indicating whether the plan is being "kept on target". Management can then be helped to take corrective action to compensate for deviations from the plan. As argued elsewhere [4]:

(1) Control should be thought of as an integral part of the design of the system and not an afterthought, as often happens for example in the design of an industrial plant.

(2) A systems approach takes away the undue attention that is sometimes given to the mechanics of the control of local loops and focuses attention on the wider questions of where should control be exercised, how sophisticated should it be, what equipment is needed, whether an on-line computer is justifiable, and so on.

(3) A systems approach focuses attention on the economic benefits, both tangible and intangible, which result from control and demands that the cost should be justified as part of the design of the overall system.

(4) Most important of all, the advantages of local control within a firm can only be realized effectively when it plays its planned role within a hierarchy of technical and financial control systems within the company.

## 2.5. *Reliability*

The importance of system reliability has already been mentioned in the section dealing with the definition of the economic criterion (stage 1.7). A good control system will go part of the way towards ensuring good reliability. For example, if there are process constraints which must not be isolated in the operation of a plant, the control system will have to be both efficient and reliable to keep clear of these constraints. However, systems reliability involves looking at aspects other than control by considering the overall effect of *uncertainty* on the design of the system. Uncertainty in forecasting environmental factors has already been discussed in Section 2.1. Other sources of unreliability are, for example, breakdown of equipment, non-availability of resources in the form of raw materials and men to perform operating and maintenance tasks. To cope with such unpredictable events requires redundant or stand-by equipment, extra storage and capacity, extra manpower and so on. This inevitably leads to higher capital and operating costs so that reliability questions must be considered as an integral part of the overall optimization of the design. The singling out of systems reliability as a separate stage in this paper is a reflection of the fact that reliability questions are all too often regarded as an *after thought*, invariably resulting in disastrous effects on performance and profitability. It is hoped to prepare a paper for a later issue of this journal to illustrate how neglect of reliability problems had serious consequences on the profitability of a large petrochemical complex.

Another reason for separating out reliability from optimization is that extensive simulation and modelling may be needed after the optimization stage to check that system unreliability has been reduced to an acceptable level.

## B.3. Implementation

No systems study, however well carried out, is of much use unless it leads to positive action and is properly implemented. The important steps in this stage are:

3.1. Documentation and sanction approval.
3.2. Construction.

## 3.1. *Documentation and sanction approval*

The end product of a systems engineering study is a report (or reports) which should highlight proposals for ACTION.

Failure of *communication* at this very important stage can sometimes ruin what is otherwise a perfectly good systems study. To avoid this happening,

(1) *before issue*, the form and content of the final reports should be discussed and agreed with those senior managers whose backing will be needed to implement the results of the study, and not planted on their desks as a "fait accompli" before any discussion has taken place.

(2) the report should be simple, direct and logical. A three tier report is recommended for work of this kind.

(i) (*a*) A brief statement of the problem,
(*b*) a summary of the main conclusions and benefits of the study,
(*c*) a summary of the recommendations, including an overall figure for the savings and the cost of implementing them.

Many senior managers will only have time to read this part of the report so that it should make the maximum impact in the smallest amount of space.

(ii) A middle section where the main substance of the recommendations and benefits are argued so that any intelligent manager can understand them.
(iii) A final, more detailed, section containing the technical details of the study.

(3) a separate document will usually be needed within the organization to highlight the recommendations and to draw up a time-table or critical path schedule for their implementation. Such a sanctioning document may need to go to higher management to obtain approval for the project to proceed.

This is the most critical stage of any systems study since a *decision* has now to be reached as to whether to go ahead and build the system. Clearly, this decision should be made in an objective way and no attempt should be made to "dress up" the sanction proposal. On the other hand, the systems engineer should avoid the all-too-common mistake of putting forward bad arguments for a good case. In this way, not only does he not do justice to himself and his team but will have turned out to be a bad systems engineer.

## 3.2. *Construction*

Some projects may require the building of special hardware and software before implementation is possible. For example, if a plant is to be built, site works must be con-structed and equipment ordered, delivered and installed on site. Similarly, if an on-line computer is to be installed on a plant, hardware in the form of instrumentation, control equipment and the computer itself must be ordered, delivered and installed. In addition, software in the form of computer programmes must be designed to implement the control and optimization algorithms.

The majority of the systems team may have moved on to other work by this stage. However, it is important to realize that the construction stage is still a part of the overall systems design. Thus, bad planning at the construction stage can have a big effect on the profitability of a project by holding up its start-up date. A systems approach at this stage would ensure that

(i) the systems team has specified the system in a clear and unambiguous way down to the minutest detail of all subsidiary sub-systems.
(ii) by the continued involvement of the systems team, the builders of the system are kept constantly in touch with the philosophy underlying the design and the way that it is to be implemented when in operation,
(iii) the project is well planned, duties allocated and targets met on time. Critical path scheduling emerges as the important technique in this area. One of the big advantages of C.P.S. is that it forces planners to concentrate attention on those areas which are critical for completion of the project.

## B.4. Operation

After the system has been designed, built and installed in its working environment, then follow the steps:

4.1. *Initial Operation* of the system.
4.2. *Retrospective Appraisal* of the system in the light of operational experience, and if necessary,
4.3. *Improved Operation* of the system.

## 4.1. *Initial operation*

Effective liaison between the systems team and the users of the system is essential if the full benefits of the systems study are to be realized. In the writer's experience, this is the part of the exercise which is least well done in practice. The process of handing over is helped if:

(1) adequate documentation and training have been provided in advance,
(2) one of the users of the operational system has been involved as a member of the systems team, so that he is fully conversant with the design philosophy,

(3) adequate communication is maintained between the systems team and the users so that any defects and misunderstandings can be cleared up without delay.

Difficulties can usually be expected at the *start-up* of the system. However, good systems thinking will ensure that these upsets are minimized and that the operation works smoothly according to plan.

## 4.2. *Retrospective appraisal of the project*

After the new system has been operating for a sufficiently long period, the systems team should collaborate with the users of the system in making a retrospective appraisal of system performance. If the system is shown to be working according to plan, or better, everyone will be happy and the original systems thinking will have been vindicated. On the other hand, if system performance is not up to expectation, a postmortem will be needed. Nothing but harm, both to himself and to the systems approach, will be achieved if the systems engineer regards his job as finished when the original systems study has been completed. He must be prepared to accept full responsibility for the successful operation of the system and to identify himself with its success or failure. The retrospective appraisal may show that

(1) the original system study has overlooked certain factors, or
(2) the system has had to operate in an environment which is different from that for which it was designed. For example, a chemical plant may have had to switch to feedstocks of different quality, or the plant may have to operate at throughput in excess of design, and so on.

In either of the situations (1) or (2), a certain amount of reoptimization will be inevitable, however painful this may turn out to be. In the retrospective appraisal, a splendid opportunity arises of checking the economic assessment that was made at the design stage and hence to check the systems thinking. For example, in a computer control scheme, a list should be made of all the benefits, both tangible and intangible, which have been achieved. This is usually a very worthwhile exercise despite the fact that some of the benefits may be difficult to assess.

## 4.3. *Improved operation*

Improved operation of the system may be needed

(i) if the retrospective appraisal of the system shows that actual performance is falling short of plan, or

(ii) in certain cases, because certain parameters can only be optimized when operational experience has been obtained.

The system must then be "tuned" to its environment, leading to improved operation. If the retrospective appraisal shows that reoptimization is necessary, the systems engineering work at the design stage may have to be re-examined and modified. If the original systems study was conducted in an orderly way and well documented, this should not prove difficult. However, if this was not well done and people have left the company in the meantime, chaos may result – Joe Bloggs will have disappeared into thin air taking away in his head all the details of the system!

Finally, if redesign or retuning of the system is necessary, a decision will have to be made as to whether the improved system performance is acceptable.

## Summary of stages in the application of Systems Engineering

The various stages in a Systems Approach are summarized below in the form of certain key questions which need to be answered.

### 1. *Systems Analysis*

1.1. *Formulation of the problem.* What is the problem? How did it arise? Who believes it to be important? Why is it important? Is it the right problem anyway? Will it save money? Is there the prospect of a reasonable rate of return on systems effort to justify tackling it as compared with some other problem?

1.2. *Organization of project.* What is the best composition for the systems team? Are its terms of reference sufficiently wide? When is the project to be completed? Has a preliminary project schedule been constructed? Have duties been allocated so that a more detailed critical path schedule can be set up?

1.3. *Definition of the system.* What is the precise nature of the system being studied? How is it best broken down into convenient sub-systems? What are the interactions between these sub-systems? Has a flow-block diagram been constructed?

1.4. *Definition of the wider system.* What is the environment (commercial, social, political) in which the system will have to operate? How does the system fit into the flow-block diagram of the wider system?

1.5. *Definition of the objectives of the wider system.* Have *competitive* and *senior* systems been properly taken into account? How do they influence the objectives of the system being studied? Is there a danger of sub-optimization?

1.6. *Definition of the objectives of the system.* Has a list of objectives in order of importance been drawn up? Have the constraints been listed? Are the objectives simple and direct? Are there some subjective features which are difficult to quantify? Have the objectives been agreed? Have they been communicated to all concerned with the design of the system?

1.7. *Precise definition of economic criterion.* Have conflicting objectives been properly weighted? Are the constraints reasonable? Are both criterion and constraints simple and direct? Have they been clearly agreed and accepted, even if qualitative?

1.8. *Information and data collection.* Have all important persons and sources of data been interrogated? Has all relevant data been assembled and presented in the best way?

## 2. *Systems Design*

2.1. *Forecasting.* Has all relevant data been used to forecast system environments? How accurate are these forecasts?

2.2. *Model building and simulation.* What type of model is best suited to the purposes at hand? Is the model building concentrated where it is most needed? Does the simulation performance agree sufficiently well with actual or conjectured performance for optimization to proceed?

2.3. *Optimization.* What optimization technique should be used? Have the performance sensitive variables been isolated? Have plots of the economic criterion with respect to the main variables been prepared? Has the sensitivity of the design to assumptions been checked? Would a risk analysis help?

2.4. *Control.* How can the optimized conditions be realized most economically as part of the overall design by installing a control system? Where should control be exercised and what instrumentation is needed? What type of control is required? How sophisticated should it be?

2.5. *Reliability.* Has the effect of uncertainty on system reliability been properly taken into account? Has the unreliability been reduced to an acceptable level?

## 3. *Implementation*

3.1. *Documentation and sanction approval.* Have the conclusions been agreed? Is the report well written so as to make the maximum impact? Has a time-table been prepared for implementation? Have the users of the system been fully involved and briefed?

3.2. *Construction.* Is the hardware and/or software fully integrated into the system specification? Have the users of the system been kept in touch with the philosophy underlying the design? Has a critical path schedule been drawn up for building and installation?

## 4. *Operation*

4.1. *Initial operation.* Have adequate plans been made for start up? Is there effective liaison with the users so that the system can be handed over? Have all the operational snags been ironed out?

4.2. *Retrospective appraisal.* Is the actual performance as predicted at the design stage? If not, why not? Has the retrospective appraisal been adequately documented?

4.3. *Improved operation.* Does the system need reoptimizing either by retraining or redesign? How is this best achieved? Finally, is the resulting improved operation now adequate?

## Role of the Systems Engineer

A great deal of the work described above will involve people other than systems engineers. In this interdisciplinary approach, it is useful to highlight the *key roles* played by the systems engineer.

(1) He tries to distinguish the wood from the trees – what's it all about?

(2) He stimulates discussion about objectives – obtains agreement about objectives.

(3) He communicates the finally agreed objectives to all concerned so that their co-operation can be relied upon.

(4) He always takes an overall view of the project and sees that techniques are used sensibly.

(5) By his overall approach, he ties together the various specializations needed for model building.

(6) He decides carefully when an activity stops.

(7) He asks for more work to be done in areas which are sensitive to cost.

(8) He challenges the assumptions on which the optimization is based.

(9) He sees that the project is planned to a schedule, that priorities are decided, tasks allocated, and above all that the project is finished on time.

(10) He takes great pains to explain carefully what the systems project has achieved, and presents a well-argued and well-documented case for implementation.

(11) He ensures that the users of the operational system are properly briefed and well trained.

(12) He makes a thorough retrospective analysis of system performance.

# References

[1] Jenkins, G. M. (1967) "Systems and their Optimisation", Inaugural lecture, University of Lancaster publication.

[2] Andrew, S. M. (1969) "Computer Modelling and Optimisation in the Design of a Complete Chemical Process", *Trans. Inst. Chem. Eng.* **47** (4), T79–T84.

[3] Jenkins, G. M. and Youle, P. V. (1968) "A Systems Approach to Management", *Opl. Res. Quart.* **19**, 5.

[4] Jenkins, G. M. (1968) "Control as Part of a Wider Systems Philosophy", *Meas. and Contr.* **1**, 105.

[5] Stephenson, G. G. (1965) "Production Optimisation at I.C.I.'s Complex at Wilton", *Chem. Proc.* **11**, 48.

[6] Taylor, A. W. and Youle, P. V. (1969) "The Optimisation of a Large Petrochemical Complex", *Jour. Syst. Eng.* **1**, 55.

[7] Jenkins, G. M. (1969) "A Systems Study of a Petrochemical Plant", *Jour. Syst. Eng.* **1**, 99.

[8] Schlager, K. J. (1956) "Systems Engineering – Key to Modern Development", *IRE Trans., Prof. Group Eng. Man.* **3**, 64.

[9] Schlager, K. J. (1957) "Organisation for Effective Systems Engineering", *Problems and Practices in Engineering Management*, Amer. Man. Assoc. Special Report **24**, 115.

[10] Goode, H. H. and Machol, R. E. (1959) *Systems Engineering*, McGraw-Hill, New York.

[11] Engstrom, E. W. (1957) "Systems Engineering – A Growing Concept", *Elec. Eng.* **76**, 113.

[12] Morton, J. A. (1959) "Integration of Systems Engineering with Component Development", *Elec. Man.* **64**, 85.

[13] Flagle, C. D., Huggins, W. H. and Roy, R. H. (eds.) (1960) *Operations Research and Systems Engineering*, Johns Hopkins Press, Baltimore.

[14] Williams, T. J. (1961) *Systems Engineering in the Process Industries*, McGraw-Hill, New York.

[15] Williams, T. J. (1962) "Systems Engineering a Large Chemical Plant Complex", *Elec. Eng.*, **82**, 590, August.

[16] Levine, S. and Buegler, R. J. (1962) "Large-Scale Systems Engineering for Airline Reservations", *Elec. Eng.*, **82**, 604, August.

[17] Chadwick, W. L. (1962) "Systems Engineering for Automation of a Large Power Station", *Elec. Eng.*, **82**, 598, August.

[18] Dommasch, D. O. and Landeman, C. W. (1962) *Principles Underlying Systems Engineering*, Pitman Publish. Corp., New York.

[19] Hall, A. D. (1962) *A Methodology for Systems Engineering*, Van Nostrand, Princeton, N.J.

[20] Feigenbaum, D. S. (1963) "Systems Engineering – A Major New Technology", *Ind. Qual. Con.* **20**, 9.

[21] Johnson, R. A., Kast, F. E. and Rosenzweig, J. E. (1963) *The Theory and Management of Systems*, McGraw-Hill, New York.

[22] Affel, H. A. (1964) "Systems Engineering", *Intern. Sci. Technol.* **35**, 18.

[23] Rosenstein, A. B. (1964) "Systems Engineering and Modern Engineering Design", *Amer. Ceram. Soc. Symposium Proc.* (Chicago, Ill., April 19), Miscellaneous Publication 267, Nat. Bur. Stand., Washington, D.C.

[24] Chestnut, H. (1965) *Systems Engineering Tools*, John Wiley, New York.

[25] Machol, R. E. (1965) *Systems Engineering Handbook*, McGraw-Hill, New York.

[26] Savas, E. S. (1965) *Computer Control of Industrial Processes*, McGraw-Hill.

[27] Chestnut, H. (1967) *Systems Engineering Methods*, John Wiley, New York.

[28] Jeffreys, T. O. (1967) "Nuclear Power and the Systems Engineer", Inaugural Lecture, University of Swansea Publication.

[29] Kline, M. B. and Lifson, M. W. (1968) "Systems Engineering", Chapter 2 of *Cost Effectiveness*, J. M. English (ed.), John Wiley, New York.

[30] Kahn, H. and Mann, I. (1957) *Techniques of Systems Analysis*, R. M. – 1829 – 1, The Rand Corporation.

[31] Adelson, M. (1966) "The System Approach – a Perspective", *Systems Development Corporation Magazine*, **9** (10), 1.

[32] Hitch, C. (1953) "Sub-optimisation in Operations Problems", *Jour. Op. Res. Soc. Am.* **1**, 87.

[33] Anthony, R. N. (1965) *Planning and Control Systems: A Framework for Analysis*, Harvard Grad. School of Bus. Admin., Boston, Mass.

[34] Schoderbek P. (ed.) (1967) *Management Systems*, John Wiley, New York.

# Appendix
## Techniques useful in Systems Engineering

The following table lists, alongside the various stages in the development of a system project, the techniques which are most relevant at each stage. The final column in the table gives a selected list of references which describe these techniques – note that the numbering refers to a selected

**1. *Systems Analysis***

| | | |
|---|---|---|
| 1.1. Formulation of the problem | Critical Examination | 1, 2 |
| 1.2. Organization of the project | Critical path scheduling | 3, 4, 5 |
| 1.3. Definition of the system | | |
| 1.4. Definition of the wider system | | |
| 1.5. Objectives of the wider system | Corporate Planning | 6, 7, 8 |
| 1.6. Objectives of the system | Management by Objectives | 9 |
| 1.7. Definition of overall economic criterion | Financial Practice and Economic Modelling | 10 |
| | Discounted cash flow techniques | 11, 12 |
| 1.8. Information and data collection | Statistical techniques | 13 |

**2. *Systems Design***

| | | |
|---|---|---|
| 2.1. Forecasting | Short and medium term forecasting | 14 |
| | Technological forecasting | 15, 16 |
| 2.2. Model Building | Empirical – steady state models | 17, 18, 19 |
| | Empirical – dynamic models | 14 |
| | Mechanistic – steady state models | 20, 21 |
| | Mechanistic – dynamic models | 22 |
| | Probabilistic models | 23 |
| | Economic Modelling | 10 |
| | Numerical Mathematics | 24 |
| Simulation | Statistical (Monte Carlo) Simulation | 25, 26, 27, 28 |
| | Deterministic Simulation | 29 |
| | Analogue Computer Simulation | 30 |
| 2.3. Optimization | Linear Programming | 31, 32 |
| | Hill climbing | 33, 34 |
| | Variational methods (Dynamic programming) | 35, 36 |
| | Risk Analysis | 37 |
| | Decision Theory | 38 |
| 2.4. Control | Technical Control | 39 |
| | Computer Control | 40 |
| | Statistical Control | 14 |
| | Production Control | 41, 42 |
| | Management Control | 43, 44 |
| 2.5. Reliability | Reliability Techniques | 45 |

**3. *Implementation***

| | | |
|---|---|---|
| 3.1. Documentation and Sanction Approval | Report Writing | 46 |
| 3.2. Construction | Critical path scheduling | 3, 4, 5 |

**4. *Operation***

| | | |
|---|---|---|
| 4.1. Initial operation | Systems Analysis | |
| 4.2. Retrospective appraisal | Techniques | |
| 4.3. Improved operation | Systems Design Techniques | |

bibliography of techniques given at the end of this appendix and is quite distinct from the reference numbering used in the main body of the paper. Most of the references are to books, but in some cases, recent papers are included.

Finally, there is a brief reference to the literature on Operational Research, including a very valuable survey by P. G. Moore.

## Selected Bibliography of Techniques

1 Currie, R. M. (1963) Chapter 7 of *Work Study*, Pitman, London (2nd ed.).

2 Whitmore, D. A. (1968) Chapter 5 of *Work Study and Related Management Sciences*, Heinemann, London.

3 Lambourne, S. (1967) *Network Analysis in Project Management*, Industrial and Commercial Techniques, Ltd. Handbook.

4 Battersby, A. (1964) *Network Analysis for Planning and Scheduling*, Macmillan, London.

5 Archibald, R. D. and Villoria, R. L. (1967) *Network based Management Systems (PERT/CPM)*, John Wiley, New York.

6 Argenti, J. (1968) *Corporate Planning*, George Allen and Unwin, London.

7 Jackson, A. S., Stephenson, G. G. and Townsend, E. C. (1968) "Financial Planning with a Corporate Financial Mode", *The Accountant*, Jan. 27th–Feb. 17th.

8 Spencer, R. S. (1966) "Modelling strategies for corporate growth. Paper presented at the Society for General Systems Research session at the conference of the American Association for the Advancement of Science, Washington, D.C., Dec. 27th.

9 Odiorne, G. S. (1965) *Management by Objectives*, Pitman, London.

10 Baumol, W. J. (1965) *Economic Theory and Operations Analysis*, Prentice-Hall, Englewood Cliffs, N.J. (2nd ed.).

11 Merrett, A. J. and Sykes, A. (1963) *The Finance and Analysis of Capital Projects*, Longmans, London.

12 English, J. M. (ed.) (1968) *Cost-Effectiveness, The Economic Evaluation of Engineered Systems*, John Wiley, New York.

13 Lowe, C. W. (1968) *Industrial Statistics, Vol. 1*, Business Books, London.

14 Box, G. E. P. and Jenkins, G. M. (in the press) *Time Series Analysis, Forecasting and Control*, Holden-Day, San Francisco.

15 Jantsch, E. (1967) *Technological Forecasting in Perspective*, O.E.C.D. Publication, Paris.

16 Quinn, J. B. (1967) "Technological Forecasting", *Harvard Bus. Rev.* **45**, 89.

17 Draper, N. R. and Smith H. (1966) *Applied Regression Analysis*, John Wiley, New York.

18 Davis, O. L. (ed.) (1963) *The Design and Analysis of Industrial Experiments*, Oliver and Boyd, Edinburgh (2nd ed.).

19 Box, G. E. P. and Draper, N. R. (1969) *Evolutionary Operation*, John Wiley.

20 Himmelblan D. M. and Bischoff, K. B. (1968) *Process Analysis and Simulation*, John Wiley, New York.

21 Hunter, W. G., Kittrell, J. R. and Mezaki, R. (1967) "Experimental Strategies for Mechanistic Model Building", *Trans. Inst. Chem. Eng.* **45**, 146.

22 Campbell, D. P. (1958) *Process Dynamics*, John Wiley, New York.

23 Feller, W. (1966) *Probability Theory and its Applications*, John Wiley, New York, Vol. 1, 1950, Vol. 2.

24 Conte, S. D. (1965) *Elementary Numerical Analysis*, McGraw-Hill, New York.

25 Tocher, K. D. (1964) *The Art of Simulation*, English Universities Press, London.

26 Naylor, T. H. *et al.* (1966) *Computer Simulation Techniques*, John Wiley, New York.

27 *Bibliography on Simulation*, I.B.M. publication (Form 320-0924-0), White Plains, New York.

28 Lee, A. M. (1966) *Applied Queuing Theory*, Macmillan, London.

29 Sargent, R. W. H. (1968) "Developments in Computer Aided Process Design", *Chem. Eng. Prog.* **64** (4), 39.

30 Rogers, A. E. and Connolly, T. W. (1960) *Analogue Computers in Engineering Design*, McGraw-Hill, New York.

31 Beale, E. M. L. (1968) *Mathematical Programming in Practice*, Pitman, London.

32 Gass, S. I. (1958) *Linear Programming*, McGraw-Hill, New York.

33 Box, M. J., Davies, D., Swann, W. H. (1969) *Non-Linear Optimisation Techniques*, I.C.I. Monographs in Mathematics and Statistics, No. 5, Oliver and Boyd, Edinburgh.

34 Wilde, D. and Beightler, C. (1966) *Foundations of Optimisation*, Prentice-Hall.

35 Jacobs, O. L. R. (1967) *An Introduction to Dynamic Programming*, Chapman and Hall, London.

36 Rosenbrock, H. H. and Storey, C. (1966) *Computational Techniques for Chemical Engineers*, Pergamon, London.

37 Adelson, R. M. (1965) "Criteria for Capital Investment: An Approach Through Decision Theory", *Opl. Res. Quart.*, **16**, 19 .

38 Morris, W. T. (1964) *The Analysis of Management Decisions*, Irwin, Homewood, Ill.

39 Kuo, B. C. (1962) *Automatic Control Systems*, Prentice-Hall, Englewood Cliffs.

40 Savas, E. S. (1965) *Computer Control of Industrial Processes*, McGraw-Hill, New York.

41 Magee, J. F. (1967) *Production Planning and Inventory Control*, McGraw-Hill, New York, 1958 2nd ed. J. F. Magee and D. Boodman, McGraw-Hill, New York.

42 Forrester, J. W. (1961) *Industrial Dynamics*, M.I.T. Press, Cambridge, Mass. (and see Article 12).

43 Boyce, R. O. (1967) *Integrated Managerial Control*, Longmans, London.

44 Anthony, R. N. (1965) *Planning and Control Systems: A Framework for Analysis*, Harvard Grad. School of Bus. Admin., Boston, Mass.

45 Sandler, G. H. (1963) *Systems Reliability Engineering*, Prentice-Hall, Englewood Cliffs, N.J.

46 Cooper, B. M. (1969) *Writing Technical Reports*, Penguin Books Ltd., Harmondsworth.

## Bibliography of Operations Research

1 *Philosophy*
   (*a*) Rivett, B. H. P. and Ackoff, R. L. (1963) *The Manager's Guide to Operational Research*, John Wiley, New York.
   (*b*) Rivett, B. H. P. (1968) *Concepts of Operational Research*, C. A. Watts, London.

2 *Techniques*
   Sasieni, M. Yaspan, A. and Friedman, L. (1959) *Operational Research – Methods and Problems*, John Wiley, New York.

3 *Survey*
   Moore, P. G. (1966) "A Survey of Operational Research", *Jour. Roy. Stat. Soc. A*, **129**, 399.

Reprinted from Jenkins, G. M. (1969) "The Systems Approach", *Journal of Systems Engineering*, **1**, 1.

# 5 Towards a system of systems concepts
## *by Russell L. Ackoff* [1]

*The concepts and terms commonly used to talk about systems have not themselves been organized into a system. An attempt to do so is made here. System and the most important types of system are defined so that differences and similarities are made explicit. Particular attention is given to that type of system of most interest to management scientists: organizations. The relationship between a system and its parts is considered and a proposition is put forward that all systems are either variety-increasing or variety-decreasing relative to the behavior of its parts.*

## Introduction

The concept *system* has come to play a critical role in contemporary science.[1,2,3] (Churchman, Emery.) This preoccupation of scientists in general is reflected among Management Scientists in particular for whom the *systems approach* to problems is fundamental and for whom *organizations*, a special type of system, are the principal subject of study.

The systems approach to problems focuses on systems taken as a whole, not on their parts taken separately. Such an approach is concerned with total-system performance even when a change in only one or a few of its parts is contemplated because there are some properties of systems that can only be treated adequately from a holistic point of view. These properties derive from the *relationships* between parts of systems: how the parts interact and fit together. In an imperfectly organized system even if every part performs as well as possible relative to its own objectives, the total system will often not perform as well as possible relative to its objectives.

Despite the importance of systems concepts and the attention that they have received and are receiving, we do not yet have a unified or integrated set (i.e., a system) of such concepts. Different terms are used to refer to the same thing and the same term is used to refer to different things. This state is aggravated by the fact that the literature of systems research is widely dispersed and is therefore difficult to track. Researchers in a wide variety of disciplines and interdisciplines are contributing to the conceptual development of the systems sciences but these contributions are not as interactive and additive as they might be. Fred Emery[3] has warned against too hasty an effort to remedy this situation:

It is almost as if the pioneers [of systems thinking], while respectfully noting each other's existence, have felt it incumbent upon themselves to work out their intuitions in their own language, for fear of what might be lost in trying to work through the language of another. Whatever the reason, the results seem to justify the stand-offishness. In a short space of time there has been a considerable accumulation of insights into system dynamics that are readily translatable into different languages and with, as yet, little sign of divisive schools of thought that for instance marred psychology during the 1920s and 1930s. Perhaps this might happen if some influential group of scholars prematurely decide that the time has come for a common conceptual framework (p. 12).

Although I sympathize with Emery's fear, a fear that is rooted in a research perspective, as a teacher I feel a great need to provide my students with a conceptual framework that will assist them in absorbing and synthesizing this large accumulation of insights to which Emery refers. My intent is not to preclude further conceptual exploration, but rather to encourage it and make it more interactive and additive. Despite Emery's warning I feel benefits will accrue to systems research from an evolutionary convergence of concepts into a generally accepted framework. At any rate, little harm is likely to come from my effort to provide the beginnings of such a framework since I can hardly claim to be, or to speak for, "an influential group of scholars".

The framework that follows does not include all concepts relevant to the systems sciences. I have made an effort, however, to include enough of the key concepts so that building on this framework will not be as difficult as construction of the framework itself has been.

One final word of introduction. I have not tried to identify the origin or trace the history of each conceptual idea that is presented in what follows. Hence few credits are provided. I can only compensate for this lack of bibliographic bird-dogging by claiming no credit for any of the elements in what follows, only for the resulting system into which they have been organized. I must, of course, accept responsibility for deficiencies in either the parts or the whole.

# Systems

1. A *system* is a set of interrelated elements. Thus a system is an entity which is composed of at least two elements and a relation that holds between each of its elements and at least one other element in the set. Each of a system's elements is connected to every other element, directly or indirectly. Furthermore, no subset of elements is unrelated to any other subset.

2. An *abstract system* is one all of whose elements are concepts. Languages, philosophic systems, and number systems are examples. *Numbers* are concepts but the symbols that represent them, *numerals*, are physical things. Numerals, however, are not the elements of a number system. The use of different numerals to represent the same numbers does not change the nature of the system.

In an abstract system the elements are created by defining and the relationships between them are created by assumptions (e.g., axioms and postulates). Such systems, therefore, are the subject of the so-called "formal sciences".

3. A *concrete system* is one at least two of whose elements are objects. It is only with such systems that we are concerned here. Unless otherwise noted, "system" will always be used to mean "concrete system".

In concrete systems establishment of the existence and properties of elements and the nature of the relationships between them requires research with an empirical component in it. Such systems, therefore, are the subject of study of the so-called "non-formal sciences".

4. The *state of a system* at a moment of time is the set of relevant properties which that system has at that time. Any system has an unlimited number of properties. Only some of these are relevant to any particular research. Hence those which are relevant may change with changes in the purpose of the research. The values of the relevant properties constitute the state of the system. In some cases we may be interested in only two possible states (e.g., off and on, or awake and asleep). In other cases we may be interested in a large or unlimited number of possible states (e.g., a system's velocity or weight).

5. The *environment of a system* is a set of elements and their relevant properties, which elements are not part of the system but a change in any of which can produce* a change in the state of the system. Thus a system's environment con-

---

*One thing ($x$) can be said to produce another ($y$) in a specified environment and time interval if $x$ is a necessary but not a sufficient condition for $y$ in that environment and time period. Thus a producer is a "probabilistic cause" of its product. Every producer, since it is not sufficient for its product, has a coproducer of that product (e.g., the producer's environment).

sists of all variables which can affect its state. External elements which affect irrelevant properties of a system are not part of its environment.

6. The *state of a system's environment* at a moment of time is the set of its relevant properties at that time. The state of an element or subset of elements of a system or its environment may be similarly defined.

Although concrete systems and their environments are *objective* things, they are also *subjective* insofar as the particular configuration of elements that form both is dictated by the interests of the researcher. Different observers of the same phenomena may conceptualize them into different systems and environments. For example, an architect may consider a house together with its electrical, heating, and water systems as one large system. But a mechanical engineer may consider the heating system as a system and the house as its environment. To a social psychologist a house may be an environment of a family, the system with which he is concerned. To him the relationship between the heating and electrical systems may be irrelevant, but to the architect it may be very relevant.

The elements that form the environment of a system and the environment itself may be conceptualized as systems when they become the focus of attention. Every system can be conceptualized as part of another and larger system.

Even an abstract system can have an environment. For example, the metalanguage in which we describe a formal system is the environment of that formal system. Therefore logic is the environment of mathematics.

7. A *closed system* is one that has no environment. An *open system* is one that does. Thus a closed system is one which is conceptualized so that it has no interaction with any element not contained within it; it is completely self-contained. Because systems researchers have found such conceptualizations of relatively restricted use, their attention has increasingly focused on more complex and "realistic" open systems. "Openness" and "closedness" are simultaneously properties of systems and our conceptualizations of them.

Systems may or may not change over time.

8. A system (or environmental) *event* is a change in one or more structural properties of the system (or its environment) over a period of time of specified duration; that is, a change in the structural state of the system (or environment). For example, an event occurs to a house's lighting system when a fuse blows, and to its environment when night falls.

9. A *static (one-state) system* is one to which no events occur. A table, for example, can be conceptualized as a

static concrete system consisting of four legs, top, screws, glue, and so on. Relative to most research purposes it displays no change of structural properties, no change of state. A compass may also be conceptualized as a static system because it virtually always points to the Magnetic North Pole.

10. A *dynamic (multi-state) system* is one to which events occur, whose state changes over time. An automobile which can move forward or backward and at different speeds is such a system, or a motor which can be either off or on. Such systems can be conceptualized as either open or closed; closed if its elements react or respond only to each other.

11. A *homeostatic system* is a static system whose elements and environment are dynamic. Thus a homeostatic system is one that retains its state in a changing environment by internal adjustments. A house that maintains a constant temperature during changing external temperatures is homeostatic. The behavior of its heating subsystem makes this possible.

Note that the same object may be conceptualized as either a static or dynamic system. For most of us a building would be thought of as static, but it might be taken as dynamic by a civil engineer who is interested in structural deformation.

## System Changes

12. A *reaction* of a system is a system event for which another event that occurs to the same system or its environment is sufficient. Thus a reaction is a system event that is deterministically caused by another event. For example, if an operator's moving a motor's switch is sufficient to turn that motor off or on, then the change of state of the motor is a reaction to the movement of its switch. In this case, the turning of the switch may be necessary as well as sufficient for the state of the motor. But an event that is sufficient to bring about a change in a system's state may not be necessary for it. For example, sleep may be brought about by drugs administered to a person or it may be self-induced. Thus sleep may be determined by drugs but need not be.

13. A *response* of a system is a system even for which another event that occurs to the same system or to its environment is necessary but not sufficient; that is, a system event produced by another system or environmental event (the *stimulus*). Thus a response is an event of which the system itself is a coproducer. A system does not have to respond to a stimulus, but it does have to react to its cause. Therefore, a person's turning on a light when it gets dark is

a response to darkness, but the light's going on when the switch is turned is a reaction.

14. An *act* of a system is a system event for the occurrence of which no change in the system's environment is either necessary or sufficient. Acts, therefore, are self-determined events, autonomous changes. Internal changes – in the states of the system's elements – are both necessary and sufficient to bring about action. Much of the behavior of human beings is of this type, but such behavior is not restricted to humans. A computer, for example, may have its state changed or change the state of its environment because of its own program.

Systems all of whose changes are reactive, responsive, or autonomous (active) can be called reactive, responsive, or autonomous (active), respectively. Most systems, however, display some combination of these types of change.

The classification of systems into reactive, responsive, and autonomous is based on consideration of what brings about changes in them. Now let us consider systems with respect to what kind of changes in themselves and their environments their reactions, responses, and actions bring about.

15. A system's *behavior* is a system event(s) which is either necessary or sufficient for another event in that system or its environment. Thus behavior is a system change which initiates other events. Note that reactions, responses, and actions may themselves constitute behavior. Reactions, responses, and actions are system events *whose antecedents are of interest*. Behavior consists of system events *whose consequences are of interest*. We may, of course, be interested in both the antecedents and consequences of system events.

## Behavioral Classification of Systems

Understanding the nature of the classification that follows may be aided by Table 1 in which the basis for the classification is revealed.

16. A *state-maintaining system* is one that (1) can react in only one way to any one external or internal event but (2) it reacts differently to different external or internal events, and (3) these different reactions produce the same external or internal state (outcome). Such a system only reacts to changes; it cannot respond because what it does is completely determined by the causing event. Nevertheless it can be said to have the *function* of maintaining the state it produces because it can produce this state in different ways under different conditions.

Thus a heating system whose internal controller turns it

**Table 1** Behavioral Classification of systems

| TYPE OF SYSTEM | BEHAVIOR OF SYSTEM | OUTCOME OF BEHAVIOR |
|---|---|---|
| State-Maintaining | Variable but determined (reactive) | Fixed |
| Goal-Seeking | Variable and chosen (responsive) | Fixed |
| Multi-Goal-Seeking and Purposive | Variable and chosen | Variable but determined |
| Purposeful | Variable and chosen | Variable and chosen |

on when the room temperature is below a desired level, and turns it off when the temperature is above this level, is state-maintaining. The state it maintains is a room temperature that falls within a small range around its setting. Note that the temperature of the room which affects the system's behavior can be conceptualized as either part of the system or part of its environment. Hence a state-maintaining system may react to either internal or external changes.

In general, most systems with "stats" (e.g. thermostats and humidistats) are state-maintaining. Any system with a regulated output (e.g., the voltage of the output of a generator) is also state-maintaining.

A compass is also state-maintaining because in many different environments it points to the Magnetic North Pole.

A state-maintaining system must be able to *discriminate* between different internal or external states to changes in which it reacts. Furthermore, as we shall see below, such systems are necessarily *adaptive*, but unlike goal-seeking systems they are not capable of learning because they cannot choose their behaviour. They cannot improve with experience.

17. A *goal-seeking system* is one that can respond differently to one or more different external or internal events in one or more different external or internal states and that can respond differently to a particular event in an unchanging environment until it produces a particular state (outcome). Production of this state is its goal. Thus such a system has a *choice* of behavior. A goal-seeking system's behavior is responsive, but not reactive. A state which is sufficient and thus deterministically causes a reaction cannot cause different reactions in the same environment.

Under constant conditions a goal-seeking system may be able to accomplish the same thing in different ways and it may be able to do so under different conditions. If it has *memory*, it can increase its efficiency over time in producing the outcome that is its goal.

For example, an electronic maze-solving rat is a goal-seeking system which, when it runs into a wall of a maze, turns right and if stopped again, goes in the opposite direction, and if stopped again, returns in the direction from which it came. In this way it can eventually solve any solvable maze. If, in addition, it has memory, it can take a "solution path" on subsequent trials in a familiar maze.

Systems with automatic "pilots" are goal-seeking. These and other goal-seeking systems may, of course, fail to attain their goals in some situations.

The sequence of behaviour which a goal-seeking system carries out in quest of its goal is an example of a process.

18. A *process* is a sequence of behavior that constitutes a system and has a goal-producing function. In some well-definable sense each unit of behavior in the process brings the actor closer to the goal which it seeks. The sequence of behavior that is performed by the electronic rat constitutes a maze-solving process. After each move the rat is closer (i.e., has reduced the number of moves required) to solve the maze. The metabolic process in living things is a similar type of sequence the goal of which is acquisition of energy or, more generally, survival. Production processes are a similar type of sequence whose goal is a particular type of product.

Process behavior displayed by a system may be either reactive, responsive, or active.

19. A *multi-goal-seeking* system is one that is goal-seeking in each of two or more different (initial) external or internal states, and which seeks different goals in at least two different states, the goal being determined by the initial state.

20. A *purposive system* is a multi-goal-seeking system the different goals of which have a common property. Production of that common property is the system's purpose. These types of system can pursue different goals but they do not select the goal to be pursued. The goal is determined by the initiating event. But such a system does choose the means by which to pursue its goals.

A computer which is programmed to play more than one game (e.g., tic-tac-toe and checkers) is multi-goal-seeking. What game it plays is not a matter of its choice, however; it is usually determined by an instruction from an external source. Such a system is also purposive because 'game winning' is a common property of the different goals it seeks.

21. A *purposeful system* is one which can produce the same outcome in different ways in the same (internal or external) state and can produce different outcomes in the same and different states. Thus a purposeful system is one which can change its goals under constant conditions; it selects ends as well as means and thus displays *will*. Human beings are the most familiar examples of such systems.

Ideal-seeking systems form an important subclass of purposeful systems. Before making their nature explicit we must consider the differences between goals, objectives, and ideals and some concepts related to them. The differences to be considered have relevance only to purposeful systems because only they can choose ends.

A system which can choose between different outcomes can place different values on different outcomes.

22. The *relative value of an outcome* that is a member of an exclusive and exhaustive set of outcomes, to a purposeful system, is the probability that the system will produce that outcome when each of the set of outcomes can be obtained with certainty. The relative value of an outcome can range from 0 to 1.0. That outcome with the highest relative value in a set can be said to be *preferred*.

23. The *goal* of a purposeful system in a particular situation is a preferred outcome that can be obtained within a specified time period.

24. The *objective* of a purposeful system in a particular situation is a preferred outcome that cannot be obtained within a specified period but which can be obtained over a longer time period. Consider a set of possible outcomes ordered along one or more scales (e.g., increasing speeds of travel). Then each outcome is closer to the final one than those which precede it. Each of these outcomes can be a goal in some time period after the "preceding" goal has been obtained, leading eventually to attainment of the last outcome, the objective. For example, a high-school freshman's goal in his first year is to be promoted to his second (sophomore) year. Passing his second year is a subsequent goal. And so on to graduation, which is his objective.

Pursuit of an objective requires an ability to change goals once a goal has been obtained. This is why such pursuit is possible only for a purposeful system.

25. An *ideal* is an objective which cannot be obtained in any time period but which can be approached without limit. Just as goals can be ordered with respect to objectives, objectives can be ordered with respect to ideals. But an ideal is an outcome which is unobtainable in practice, if not in principle. For example, an ideal of science is errorless observations. The amount of observer error can be reduced

without limit but can never be reduced to zero. Omniscience is another such ideal.

26. An *ideal-seeking system* is a purposeful system which, on attainment of any of its goals or objectives, then seeks another goal and objective which more closely approximates its ideal. An ideal-seeking system is thus one which has a concept of "perfection" or the "ultimately desirable" and pursues it systematically; that is, in interrelated steps.

From the point of view of their output, six types of system have been identified: state-maintaining, goal-seeking, multi-goal-seeking, purposive, purposeful, and ideal-seeking. The elements of systems can be similarly classified. The relationship between (1) the behavior and type of a system and (2) the behavior and type of its elements is not apparent. We consider it next.

## Relationships between systems and their elements

Some systems can display a greater variety and higher level of behavior than can any of their elements. These can be called *variety increasing*. For example, consider two state-maintaining elements, $A$ and $B$. Say $A$ reacts to a decrease in room temperature by closing any open windows. If a short time after $A$ has reacted the room temperature is still below a specified level, $B$ reacts to this by turning on the furnace. Then the system consisting of $A$ and $B$ is goal-seeking.

Clearly, by combining two or more goal-seeking elements we can construct a multi-goal-seeking (and hence a purposive) system. It is less apparent that such elements can also be combined to form a purposeful system. Suppose one element $A$ can pursue goal $G_1$ in environment $E_1$ and goal $G_2$ in another environment $E_2$; and the other element $B$ can pursue $G_2$ in $E_1$ and $G_1$ in $E_2$. Then the system would be capable of pursuing $G_1$ and $G_2$ in both $E_1$ and $E_2$ if it could select between the elements in these environments. Suppose we add a third (controlling) element which responds to $E_1$ by "turning on" either $A$ or $B$, but not both. Suppose further that it turns on $A$ with probability $P_A$ where $0 < P_A < 1.0$ and turns on $B$ with probability $P_B$ where $0 < P_B < 1.0$. (The controller could be a computer that employs random numbers for this purpose.) The resulting system could choose both ends and means in two environments and hence would be purposeful.

A system can also show less variety of behavior and operate at a lower level than at least some of its elements. Such a system is *variety reducing*. For example, consider a simple system with two elements one of which turns lights on in a room whenever the illumination in that room drops below a certain level. The other element turns the lights off whenever the illumination exceeds a level that is lower than that provided by the lights in the room. Then the lights will go off and on continuously. The system would not be state-maintaining even though its elements are.

A more familiar example of a variety-reducing system can be found in those groups of purposeful people (e.g., committees) which are incapable of reaching agreement and hence of taking any collective action.

*A system must be either variety-increasing or variety-decreasing.* A set of elements which collectively neither increase nor decrease variety would have to consist of identical elements either only one of which can act at a time or in which similar action by multiple units is equivalent to action by only one. In the latter case the behavior is non-additive and the behavior is redundant. The relationships between the elements would therefore be irrelevant. For example, a set of similar automobiles owned by one person do not constitute a system because he can drive only one at a time and which he drives makes no difference. On the other hand a radio with two speakers can provide stereo sound; the speakers each do a different thing and together they do something that neither can do alone.

## Adaptation and Learning

In order to deal with the concepts "adaptation" and "learning" it is necessary first to consider the concepts "function" and "efficiency".

27. The *function*(s) of a system is production of the outcomes that define its goal(s) and objective(s). Put another way, suppose a system can display at least two structurally different types of behavior in the same or different environments and that these types of behavior produce the same kind of outcome. Then the system can be said to have the function of producing that outcome. To function, therefore, is to be able to produce the same outcome in different ways.

Let $C_i$ $(1 \leq i \leq m)$ represent the different actions available to a system in a specific environment. Let $P_i$ represent the probabilities that the system will select these courses of action in that environment. If the courses of action are exclusive and exhaustive, then $\sum_{i=1}^{m} P_i = 1.0$. Let $E_{ij}$ represent the probability that course of action $C_i$ will produce a particular outcome $O_j$ in that environment. Then:

28. The *efficiency* of the system with respect to an outcome $O_j$ which it has the function of producing is $\sum_{i=1}^{m} P_i E_{ij}$.

Now we can turn to "adaptation".

29. A system is *adaptive* if, when there is a change in its environmental and/or internal state which reduces its effi-

ciency in pursuing one or more of its goals which define its function(s), it reacts or responds by changing its own state and/or that of its environment so as to increase its efficiency with respect to that goal or goals. Thus adaptiveness is the ability of a system to modify itself or its environment when either has changed to the system's disadvantage so as to regain at least some of its lost efficiency.

The definition of "adaptive" implies four types of adaptation:

29.1. *Other-other adaptation:* A system's reacting or responding to an external change by modifying the environment (e.g., when a person turns on an air conditioner in a room that has become too warm for him to continue to work in).

29.2. *Other-self adaptation:* A system's reacting or responding to an external change by modifying itself (.e.g., when the person moves to another and cooler room).

29.3. *Self-other adaptation:* A system's reacting or responding to an internal change by modifying the environment (e.g., when a person who has chills due to a cold turns up the heat).

29.4. *Self-self adaptation:* a system's reacting or responding to an internal change by modifying itself (e.g., when that person takes medication to suppress the chills). Other-self adaptation is most commonly considered because it was this type with which Darwin was concerned in his studies of biological species as systems.

It should now be apparent why state-maintaining and higher systems are necessarily adaptive. Now let us consider why nothing lower than a goal-seeking system is capable of learning.

30. To *learn* is to increase one's efficiency in the pursuit of a goal under unchanging conditions. Thus if a person increases his ability to hit a target (his goal) with repeated shooting at it, he learns how to shoot better. Note that to do so requires an ability to modify one's behavior (i.e., to display choice) and memory.

Since learning can take place only when a system has a choice among alternative courses of action, only systems that are goal-seeking or higher can learn.

If a system is repeatedly subjected to the same environmental or internal change and increases its ability to maintain its efficiency under this type of change, then it *learns how to adapt.* Thus adaptation itself can be learned.

## Organizations

Management Scientists are most concerned with that type of system called "organizations". Cyberneticians, on the other hand, are more concerned with that type of system called "organisms", but they frequently treat organizations as though they were organisms. Although these two types of system have much in common, there is an important difference between them. This difference can be identified once "organization" has been defined. I will work up to its definition by considering separately each of what I consider to be its four essential characteristics.

(1) An organization is a purposeful system that contains at least two purposeful elements which have a common purpose.

We sometimes characterize a purely mechanical system as being well organized, but we would not refer to it as an "organization". This results from the fact that we use "organize" to mean, "to make a system of", or, as one dictionary puts it, "to get into proper working order", and "to arrange or dispose systematically". Wires, poles, transformers, switchboards, and telephones may constitute a communication system, but they do not constitute an organization. The employees of a telephone company make up the organization that operates the telephone system. Organization of a system is an activity that can be carried out only by purposeful entities; to be an organization a system must contain such entities.

An aggregation of purposeful entities does not constitute an organization unless they have at least one common purpose: that is, unless there is some one or more things that they all want. An organization is always organized around this common purpose. It is the relationships between what the purposeful elements do and the pursuit of their common purpose that give unity and identity to their organization.

Without a common purpose the elements would not work together unless compelled to do so. A group of unwilling prisoners or slaves can be organized and forced to do something that they do not want to do, but if so they do not constitute an organization even though they may form a system. An organization consists of elements that have and can exercise their own wills.

(2) An organization has a functional division of labor in pursuit of the common purpose(s) of its elements that define it.

Each of two or more subsets of elements, each containing one or more purposeful elements, is responsible for choosing from among different courses of action. A choice from each subset is necessary for obtaining the common purpose. For example, if an automobile carrying two people stalls on a highway and one gets out and pushes while the other sits in the driver's seat trying to start it when it is in motion, then there is a functional division of labor and they consti-

tute an organization. The car cannot be started (their common purpose) unless both functions are performed.

The classes of courses of action and (hence) the subsets of elements may be differentiated by a variety of types of characteristics; for example:

(a) by *function* (e.g., production, marketing, research, finance, and personnel, in the industrial context),
(b) by *space* (e.g., geography, as territories of sale offices),
(c) by *time* (e.g., waves of an invading force).

The classes of action may, of course, also be defined by combinations of these and other characteristics.

It should be noted that individuals or groups in an organization that *make* choices need not *take* them: that is, carry them out. The actions may be carried out by other persons, groups, or even machines that are controlled by the decision makers.

(3) The functionally distinct subsets (parts of the system) can respond to each other's behavior through observation or communication.*

In some laboratory experiments subjects are given interrelated tasks to perform but they are not permitted to observe or communicate with each other even though they are rewarded on the basis of an outcome determined by their collective choices. In such cases the subjects are *unorganized*. If they were allowed to observe each other or to communicate with each other they could become an organization. The choices made by elements or subsets of an organization must be capable of influencing each other, otherwise they would not even constitute a system.

(4) At least one subset of the system has a system-control function.

This subset (or subsystem) compares achieved outcomes with desired outcomes and makes adjustments in the behavior of the system which are directed toward reducing the observed deficiencies. It also determines what the desired outcomes are. The control function is normally exercised by an executive body which operates on a feed-back principle. "Control" requires elucidation.

31. An element or a system *controls* another element or system (or itself) if its behavior is either necessary or sufficient for subsequent behavior of the other element or system (or itself), and the subsequent behavior is necessary or sufficient for the attainment of one or more of its goals.

* In another place, Ackoff [1], I have given operational definitions of "observation" and "communication" that fit this conceptual system. Reproduction of these treatments would require more space than is available here.

Summarizing, then, an "organization" can be defined as follows:

32. An *organization* is a purposeful system that contains at least two purposeful elements which have a common purpose relative to which the system has a functional division of labor; its functionally distinct subsets can respond to each other's behavior through observation or communication; and at least one subset has a system-control function.

Now the critical difference between organisms and organizations can be made explicit. Whereas both are purposeful systems, organisms do not contain purposeful elements. The elements of an organism may be state-maintaining, goal-seeking, multi-goal-seeking, or purposive; but not purposeful. Thus an organism must be variety increasing. An organization, on the other hand, may be either variety increasing or decreasing (e.g., the ineffective committee). In an organism only the whole can display will; none of the parts can.

Because an organism is a system that has a functional division of labor it is also said to be "organized". Its functionally distinct parts are called "organs". Their functioning is necessary but not sufficient for accomplishment of the organism's purpose(s).

## Conclusion

Defining concepts is frequently treated by scientists as an annoying necessity to be completed as quickly and thoughtlessly as possible. A consequence of this disinclination to define is often research carried out like surgery performed with dull instruments. The surgeon has to work harder, the patient has to suffer more, and the chances for success are decreased.

Like surgical instruments, definitions become dull with use and require frequent sharpening and, eventually, replacement. Those I have offered here are not exceptions.

Research can seldom be played with a single concept; a matched set is usually required. Matching different researches requires matching the sets of concepts used in them. A scientific field can arise only on the base of a system of concepts. Systems science is not an exception. Systems thinking, if anything, should be carried out systematically.

## References

1 Ackoff, R. L. (1967) *Choice, Communication, and Conflict*, a report to the National Science Foundation under Grant GN-389, Management Science Center, University of Pennsylvania, Philadelphia.
2 Churchman, C. W. (1968) *The Systems Approach*, Delacorte Press, New York.
3 Emery, F. E. (1969) *Systems Thinking*, Penguin Books Ltd., Harmondsworth, Middlesex, England.

Reprinted from Ackoff, R. L. (1971) "Towards a system of systems concepts", *Management Science*, **17**, 11.

# Section II
## Introduction

The demands made upon men by society and technology are constantly increasing. Machines operate faster, organizations become large and more complex, simple manual control is no longer adequate to cope with industrial and military equipment. Since the Second World War there has been a steady growth in the study of the interactions and combinations of man and machine. Engineers and psychologists together with physiologists, anthropologists, and others have come to work together as human factors engineers, or engineering psychologists to tackle the problems which arise. For some time attention was directed to the smaller-scale problems, the design of easy-to-grip knobs and easy-to-read dials for example, but latterly it has been realized that there is a larger, systems aspect to the design of even the small parts of a system.

Kenyon De Greene's article sets out the development of systems thinking in psychology, particularly in relation to the problems of engineering psychology. Many of the terms and ideas presented in earlier articles are repeated but with different examples. We have left these in to provide alternative explanations which we feel will assist in making some of the more difficult concepts clearer. The second article by George Bekey deals more specifically with problems of control by human operators and the design of displays and controls in relation to the whole system.

## Associated reading

Several general books on Human Factors Engineering, or Ergonomics as it is sometimes called in Britain, are available which deal with the much wider field.

The more systems oriented approach which is slowly spreading is well expressed by Singleton "Psychological aspects of man—machine systems". In: Warr, P. B. (ed.) *Psychology at Work*; Penguin, 1971, pp. 97–120.

# 6 Systems and psychology
## by Kenyon B. De Greene

## Introduction

It's a typical day. The car starts OK, but you think with a flash of irritation that it really shouldn't have been necessary to remove the engine just to replace the starter motor. At the stop signal, it seems the flow of cross traffic will never end. You've got to present a briefing to military higher management at the other end of the country this afternoon and you're not satisfied. The pieces just don't seem to fit together. Perhaps that combination of tranquilizers and sleeping pills had left you unduly grouchy, but your wife shouldn't have bugged you about spending so much time on your job and neglecting the kids and all. An hour to catch your plane and cars piled up on the freeway as far as the eye can see. Start, move a few feet, and stop, start. . . . You reflect on the events in this morning's paper. Big jet pancakes down in the ocean eight miles short of the runway, killing 147. More student and minority group riots. Danger of imminent starvation in Africa and Asia. Strikes curtail services in still another city. You're still worried about your briefing. If you only had a better gauge that the men (how many *are* really necessary) could really do the job in that environment. You glance over your left shoulder. Traffic going the other way isn't much better. Car piled with skis and boats and people headed for the mountains and desert, even though it's a weekday. Airport's a couple of miles ahead now, but you can't see the tower through the smog. Surely there ought to be a way of getting an overall grasp of things, things that should fit nicely together but always seem to be operating at cross purposes. People pretty well manage to foul things up. People. Human nature again. If only the headshrinkers. . . . You'll have to walk about half a mile to your plane from the parking place you were just able to ace away from that other guy. But no sweat, there's still time for a quick cup of coffee, and you'll get points from your brisk walk in that new exercise system. System! You remember a book you leafed through at the company book stall on the quad. There was sort of a catchy quotation: "When we try to pick out anything by itself, we find it hitched to everything else in the universe." McGraw-Hill as you recall. Right!

*Systems Psychology*. Have to look into it when you get a chance and see what it's about. . . .

This book* is about people and how they relate to complex technology and its consequences – how they relate to machines, buildings, communications, roads, and one another. Because human behavior varies from one situation to another, it is also about how people relate to environments. You may already be familiar with the *Three-M –* man–machine–medium – concept of interaction and its more recent extension to include a fourth and fifth *M*, mission and management. In this book, we determine whether apparently diverse and unrelated problems can be investigated in a *general yet systematic* manner, a manner that at once provides a basis for both definition and solution of these problems. Of basic concern is the *effectiveness* of people and the missions to which they contribute. We look at the way people behave and the effects of various conditions on their behavior.

At the same time, we examine the capabilities and limitations of machines. We thus are concerned with the man–machine *interface* – how man and machine can complement one another most effectively in accomplishing some end. Optimum design of the man–machine package alone does not guarantee the effectiveness we desire, however, and our success in man–machine design, even optimized to meet the constraints of a physicochemical environment, may introduce problems that seem less easy to handle. Our concept of effectiveness must be extended to include the variables of individual need, reward, expectation, and attitude. Not all problem situations structured through engineering will involve the same *psychological factors*. Sometimes it is necessary to single out specific factors – for example, alertness, vigilance, or decision making – for special study and consideration. However, under operating conditions of, say, piloting an aircraft, vigilance and decision making are functions of the pilot's needs at a given moment.

* [i.e., *Systems Psychology*, Ed.]

Clearly, *interrelatedness* and *interaction* among things are important themes in systems science. As we attempt to lend order and meaning to complicated situations, we apply the framework concepts and methods of *systems*, represented along the two dimensions of *time* and *depth*, which characterize, respectively, the sequence of activities by which a system accomplishes a given *purpose*, and the amount of knowledge available and applicable at given times. It is necessary first to postulate a hierarchy of subwholes,* leading eventually to the level of the individual human being, who can conveniently be viewed as a "*blackbox* component" that, by some poorly understood *transfer function*, converts *inputs* into *outputs*. Unraveling the mechanisms involved in the human transfer function is a primary ongoing responsibility of psychology and physiology. You will notice the engineering language used here: Blackbox component can be translated into the more psychological *stimulus–organism–response (S–O–R) paradigm*, or model.

It is sometimes convenient to single out constructs such as perception, motivation, learning, thinking, and intelligence. But these constructs are interrelated and are, in turn, reflections of other, perhaps more basic processes and of the environment at any instant. This difficulty has long been evident in the field of accident investigation. Suppose a pilot has had a quarrel with his wife and later, on a routine flight, in good weather, collides with another aircraft. Is the "cause" of this accident perception, attention, emotion, poor judgment, or what? Let's say we attribute it to degraded attention. We must then ask: Was attention degraded because of poor equipment design, conflicting task demands, boredom, or preoccupation with marital difficulties? The point we must never forget is this: While it is necessary to identify an abstraction such as "vigilance" for study in the laboratory, the vigilance of one situation may have little predictive value for the vigilance in another situation.

This book† attempts to integrate several established practices in psychology and in engineering. Part I covers the sequence of processes of analysis, synthesis, and evaluation applicable to the engineering of all systems. Because we are concerned primarily with human behavior, matters of particular interest to psychology applied within the context of systems engineering are covered in greater detail; specific-

* This process introduces epistemological difficulties, discussed later, that are associated with terminology and the meaningfulness of constituents and abstractions. (Note the use of *constituents* rather than *units*, *components*, or *elements*.)

† [i.e., *Systems Psychology*, Ed.]

ally, this is the field of *human factors*‡ or engineering psychology.

As viewed by the U.S. Air Force, the management of human factors within systems engineering involves development of partially sequential, partially parallel, but interrelated specialties. These *personnel subsystem elements* (see the preceding footnote and the last section of this chapter) are considered in Parts I and IV of this book. The concept of man as a constituent of man–machine systems is expressed n Part II, where we examine input, throughput, and output in terms of *information*, *decision*, and *control theory*, respectively. In Parts II, III, and V, we discuss perception, attention, cognitive processes, perceptual-motor behavior, individual differences, and motivation, usually in the context of a particular system operational requirement. The modifying effects of physicochemical and psychosocial environmental factors on behavior are discussed in Part V.

Specific system problem areas of salient concern to the psychologist, and not treated widely elsewhere, are considered in detail in Parts III and VI. Throughout the book, attempts are made to integrate psychology with other disciplines, to determine a common language for the intercommunication of ideas, and to develop a body of systems psychological methods applicable to the study of any system problem. Particular emphasis is placed on the recognition, definition, measurement, and, where possible, quantification of basic psychological factors; the identification of human capabilities and limitations; the relating of psychological factors to systems factors; the prediction of effective and ineffective human behavior; and the highlighting of situations in which failure to follow these procedures leads to degraded human and system performance, human frustration or misery, danger, waste of resources, and other unsatisfactory results. Applications include those in which psychologists have had extensive experience and those in which we urge far greater participation.

‡ For the benefit of our human factors readers who are not psychologists, we acknowledge the important contributions of physiologists, physicians, anthropologists, sociologists, engineers, and mathematicians to the field. Choice of either term – *human factors* or *engineering psychology* – is a matter of personal preference, in part reflecting the professional organization addressed (Human Factors Society or Society of Engineering Psychologists, a division of the American Psychological Association).

Here, human factors is considered a broader term, which includes training, manpower determinations, analysis, evaluation, equipment design, and so forth. On the other hand, engineering psychology can be equated most readily to human engineering – equipment, facilities, and environments designed for compatibility with human capabilities and limitations.

In the remainder of this chapter, we examine, in some detail, different ways of looking conceptually at systems, at psychology, and at psychology within the systems context. A number of dramatic examples are provided of failure to see things as systems, particularly with regard to psychological factors in systems. The chapter concludes with an examination of the practical aspects of systems engineering and management.

## Systems science and psychology

Every educated person recognizes that a "system" imposes an order or consistency on similar interrelated constituents (for example, solar system, nervous system, tax-evasion system); yet there is no integrated body of system knowledge acceptable to the educated public as a whole. We will use the term *systems science* here in the most inclusive sense to include conceptual, theoretical, and applied developments.* There usually is no close relationship between the theoretical, as represented most typically in the *Yearbook of the Society for General Systems Research*, and the applied, as represented by the burgeoning advances in systems engineering and the derived systems management. In fact, it is often stated that applications lack valid theoretical underpinnings. This is perhaps as it should be for a field in the stage of initial rapid growth, but we should caution against theorizing apart from insightful interpretation of our experiences building systems, and conversely, continuing to implement outside of a conceptual *system for systems*. (Following popular practice, we use the term *systems*, instead of *system*, as a noun modifier.)

In this section, we examine various conceptual ways of approaching the study of systems and then attempt to integrate psychology and systems. Systems engineering and management methodology are discussed later in this chapter.

### What is a system?

A look into a dictionary reveals that definition of the word *system* entails consideration of a set or arrangement, of relationship or connection, and of unity or wholeness. Further, the term has had longstanding use both as general methodology for achieving order and as a specific modifier in sciences such as astronomy, mathematics, chemistry, geology, and biology. In the most general sense, then,

*system* can be thought of as synonymous with *order*; the opposite of chaos.

Experience has led to modification of this simple definition, in most cases in terms of *level* or *hierarchy*, *purpose*, and *environment*. Hall and Fagen (1956) provide the following definition:

> A system is a set of objects together with relationships between their attributes.

As Hall and Fagen see it, *objects* are simply the parts, or components of a system – for example, stars, atoms, neurons, switches, and mathematical laws. *Attributes* are the properties of objects – for example, the temperature of a star. *Relationships* tie the system components together, and which relationships are meaningful at a given time is a matter of discretion by the investigator. It is important to determine interconnections and dependencies, as well as the static or dynamic nature of the relationship.

The *environment* of a system has been defined by Hall and Fagen as follows:

> For a given system, the environment is the set of all objects a change in whose attributes affects the system and also those objects whose attributes are changed by the behavior of the system.

Subdivision of a universe into system and environment is obviously often quite arbitrary. Yet to specify completely an environment, one must know all the factors affecting or affected by the system. This is easier in the physical sciences than in the life, behavioral, and social sciences. Differentiation between system and environment is an immensely complex problem in the last two.

Any system can be further subdivided hierarchically into subsystems, which can in turn by subdivided into sub-subsystems, components, units, parts, and so forth (Figure 6.1 and Table 6.2).†

Objects that are parts of one system or subsystem can be considered parts of the environment of another system or subsystem. Also, systems may unite as subsystems of a still larger system, and under some conditions subsystems can be considered systems. Often the behavior of subsystems is not completely analogous to that of the system itself.

Systems may be studied at macroscopic or microscopic levels, depending on one's training, specialization, and philosophy. Analytic, "atomistic", "elementaristic", or "molecular" approaches versus "holistic" or "molar" approaches are discussed later.

---

* For example, a definition of systems science given by the Institute of Electrical and Electronic Engineers professional group in Systems Science and Cybernetics (see Rowe, 1965) is: *The scientific theory and methodology that is common to all large collections of interacting functional units that together achieve a defined purpose.*

† We discuss problems of terminology involving these subdivisions later in this section.

Many workers do not consider as systems those natural organizations or structures that lack *purpose*, where purpose is construed to be the discharge of some function. For example, minerals can be classified into one of six systems (halite into the cubic system and calcite into the hexagonal system); however, some authors (Gérardin, 1968) argue that crystals cannot be said to form a system, because they perform no function, are end-products in themselves, and do not change except by application of external force. For man-made systems, purpose or mission is an important, integral feature. A general definition of such a system might be: an assemblage of constituents (people and/or hardware and/or software) that interact to fulfill a common purpose transcending the individual purposes of the constituents.

## Systems properties and types

A survey of the systems literature reveals a plethora of definitions, but there is almost universal acceptance of the following:

1. Basic system constituents (components, elements, parts, objects) may or may not be similar and possess peculiar characteristics (attributes, behaviors).
2. What constitutes a *basic* constituent is an arbitrary decision within a hierarchical arrangement and a function of one's specialization and the exigencies of the moment.
3. Upon incorporation into the system, constituents are modified through *interactions* with other constituents.
4. The system's characteristics are usually quantitatively greater than, and qualitatively different from, the inferred sum of the characteristics of the constituents.
5. The system exists within an environment, defined as a function of the hierarchical level chosen, that modifies the behavior of the system and may be modified by it: The *boundary* between system and environment should be clearly recognizable.
6. Some systems have a recognized purpose.

Systems are often considered to possess other, often interrelated properties (see, for example, von Bertalanffy, 1956; Hall and Fagen, 1956). The properties outlined below represent a good approximation of *first-order* properties from which it is possible to make second-order derivations, third-order derivations, and so on. For example, out of the disruption of equilibrium, we can observe what might be called *drive* or goal-direction, which in turn can lead to *competition*. Recognition of secondary and tertiary properties is particularly important in biological and social sciences.

From certain dominant properties, we can designate *types* of systems – for example, feedback control systems,* adaptive control systems, self-organizing systems, or information systems.

*Equilibrium.* Equilibrium may be static but is usually dynamic and occurs in concepts of chemistry, geology, biology, and other sciences. A familiar example is *homeostasis.*†

*Change over time.* Changes that occur over time (especially *growth* and *decay*) are important in almost all sciences.

*Dominance or centralization.* On subsystem may play a dominant role in the behavior of the system. With caution, we can offer the nervous and endocrine systems in vertebrates as examples.

*Independence.* The hierarchical nature of systems has been noted, as well as the arbitrary nature of system designation. However, there is some virtue in excluding from consideration as systems those entities that cannot exist independently. Thus, the nervous system cannot operate outside the body; the propulsion system of a spacecraft has no ongoing function outside that spacecraft.

*Feedback.* The system output is sampled, measured, and fed back to the input with subsequent modification, if necessary, of the output. Feedback is especially important to the control mechanisms of organisms and machines, and it provides one of the major bases for cybernetics, discussed later in this section. Feedback systems are typically called *closed-loop* systems. Systems without feedback are called *open-loop* systems. These terms should not be confused with *open* and *closed systems*, respectively (see below).

The type and amount of feedback is important to system stability and equilibrium. The terms *positive and negative feedback* are commonly used. Familiar machine examples of feedback are servomechanisms such as antiaircraft fire-control mechanisms, ship-steering mechanisms, and target-seeking guided missiles. In mammalian psychophysiology, increased secretions of adrenal cortical, thyroid, and gonadal hormones inhibit the secretion of the relevant anterior pituitary hormones in a negative-feedback loop; the release of epinephrine by the adrenal medulla in stress helps enhance the action of the sympathetic nervous system by a positive-feedback mechanism. Integration of control mechanisms in animal and machine is, of course, the main role of *cybernetics* discussed later.

* [See Article 7. *Ed.*]        † [See Article 13. *Ed.*]

*Entropy and information.* In the strictest sense, entropy indicates the theoretical amount of energy (as in steam) in a thermodynamic system that cannot be transformed into mechanical work. It is a function of the probabilities of the states of gas particles. In a closed system, entropy must increase to a maximum with eventual cessation of the physical process and equilibrium. The concept of entropy has also been applied to information systems, where one can speak of "source entropy", "channel entropy", and the like. Entropy can be considered a measure of probability in that the most probable distribution is one of randomness or disorder. It is thus the opposite of information, which can be used as a measure of order in a system.

*Open and closed systems.* Open systems exchange information, energy, or materials with their environments. Biological systems are the best examples of open systems. One of the most important jobs of the biologist and psychologist is understanding the transfer function whereby inputs (information, energy, or materials) are converted into outputs. Many "test-tube" physical–chemical reactions occur in closed systems (see entropy above), which are considered isolated from their environments.

*Differentiation.* Related to growth and especially characteristic of biological systems, differentiation refers to the formation, over time, of new constituents from old. *Reproduction* is closely related to differentiation.

*Adaptation.* Adaptation refers to the ability to modify a system in accord with environmental demands to assure continued function. Individual learning and biological evolution are examples. There is tremendous interest in developing artificial systems possessing qualities of biological systems. Such systems are referred to as *self-regulating*, *self-adapting*, or *self-organizing*. The self-organizing system is described by Yovits *et al.* (1962) as one "which changes its basic structure as a function of its experience and environment".

*Predetermined control.* Predetermined control of a sequence of structural or functional changes is a consequence of information coding. It is characteristic of living systems in which control over reproduction, growth, differentiation, and behavior reflects information coded in all genes, in organizer tissues in embryological development, and in nervous tissue. Predetermined control is an important feature also of computerized systems. In some man–machine systems, termed *procedural* systems, it is possible to specify beforehand the sequence of operator tasks. The alternative is a *contingency* system.

*Naturalness or artificiality.* This might appear to be a simple dichotomy, but the distinction fades with man's ability to synthesize proteins and to design systems on the basis of natural bionic analogs.

*Compatibility with the environment.* The biological world provides myriad examples of organisms marvelously adapted to an environment or, conversely, extinct because the changing environment has passed them by. In a related sense, artificial systems may not function if the environment for which they were designed changes (*cf.* general-purpose and special-purpose computers). Similarly, we may find that one system does not interface well with another when we attempt to build a new system on an old base (the "grow like Topsy" approach) or to effect retrofits. The job of system integration indeed may be formidable in such cases.

*Randomness.* If constituents are assembled at random, the situation is chaos and a system cannot be said to exist. Yet all physical, biological, and social systems have random properties or functions. Vacuum-tube noise is considered due to random emission of electrons from the cathode. Many people believe that, at first, connections among neurons in the retina and brain may be purely random. There is evidence that random errors and accidents occur in complex systems.

## Ways of looking at systems

Systems are observed, studied, and evaluated primarily to: (1) improve the system or its successor; (2) determine general theories or methods for new system development; and (3) advance science. Study of man-made, natural, and semi-natural systems more or less fulfills all three objectives, depending on the purposive or adventitious human contribution to the original "design".

A growing body of systems science methods is beginning to reconcile the conflicting definitions of what a system is and differences among systems. These methods include: (1) generalization across systems; (2) analysis and synthesis; and (3) modeling and simulation. These general approaches must be modified in terms of system level and definition of environment and the degree of practical relationship to the "real world".

*Generalization across systems.* Examination of the examples given in the earlier discussion of system properties reveals that different systems may have much in common. In several cases, workers in different specialties have arrived independently at similar concepts. The term *isomorphism* (*an* isomorphy) refers to structural similarities among systems in different fields. The concept of isomorphism suggests that the various fields of science can be united at basic levels through underlying principles. An analog based on only two variables – input and output – has the lowest degree of isomorphism, and the underlying function may be vastly dissimilar. Such an oversimplified model is most useful as a representation of a subsystem, which is then linked to other simplified subsystems. *The lack of precision and detail should not transcend the subsystems.* Isomorphism can also refer to structural–functional relationships between a living prototype and a model. Practical attempts to determine isomorphic properties of different systems are particularly spectacular in bionics.

*Analysis and synthesis.* Complexity in all systems can be approached by breaking the whole into simpler constituents – that is, by analysis. Often, however, there is reason to suspect the significance of the abstracted constituents when we attempt to synthesize them as a means of explaining and predicting the whole. This has long been a major problem within psychology, a most recent example of which is provided by efforts to predict human error.

*Modeling and simulation.* Models and simulations are analogies ranging from physical operating devices with definite shapes to block diagrams, figures, and computer programs (*abstract* or *mathematical models*). They aid in explaining natural phenomena. Whether present mathematics can be applied is a function of the extent to which a given system can be analyzed. Realistic models can be constructed fairly easily for physical systems but not for complete biological and social systems, in which real system relationships are obscure, the actual number of variables may not be known, and quantification poses a formidable problem. Modeling and simulation have an advantage for these systems, however, in that they allow detachment of the observer from the system he is studying and therefore reduce personal bias.

*Selection of level and environment.* All systems possess hierarchical structure: A system at one level may be considered a subsystem at another. Similarly, how much of the environment is included in the system helps determine the system properties. Knowledge gleaned at one level may have limited applicability to another level.

*Relationship to the "real world".* Even if a particular level and environment are chosen for study, only some of the properties of systems may find application in the study of real-world engineering problems. The systems engineer and manager are particularly concerned with interactions, pro-

cessing, feedback, environmental compatibility, evolution and change, and purpose (mission); the systems theorist is more concerned with such factors as entropy and differentiation. Accordingly, we can recognize a "systems approach" that may be partially qualitative, even intuitive, and lack the theoretical basis of systems science.

## Examples of systems

Over the years, systems have been classified in a number of ways on the basis of properties such as those discussed earlier. It is interesting to combine the properties in different ways or to describe definite entities in terms of relevant properties. A more formidable problem arises, however, when we try to achieve unanimity of agreement as to what *is* and *is not* a system. Most people will agree that a man is a system and that a submarine is a system, and that each can be characterized in terms of certain properties; most also will agree that a single perceptual-motor action is not a system and that an electron is not a system. On the other hand, many will disagree as to whether a crystal or a city is a system, primarily because of differing conceptions of *purpose, normal independence,* and *clearly recognizable boundary.* Ultimate resolution of these disparities *is* a responsibility of systems science, but for purposes of this discussion, we will consider some nonequivocal examples of systems arranged in order of complexity.

Wilson (1965) illustrates a simple mechanical system that shows rudimentary features of negative and positive feedback and exemplifies that the whole is greater than sum of the parts. This system has only five constituents: a pipe, a valve, a supportive arm, a spring, and a container. Its mission is to fill the container to a certain level and shut off the valve automatically. When the constituents are *properly connected* – that is, the fulcrum is placed near the container – the increasing weight of the liquid results in greater tension on the spring, which closes the valve. The system mission is faithfully discharged. Conversely, an improper connection of the constituents – moving the fulcrum to the middle of the pipe – precludes start of the mission. If the system is started in the middle of its operating cycle, the valve opens progressively wider as the container fills. The miller's grain-feeder (Gérardin, 1968), known by at least the eighteenth century, illustrates an early practical design of a similar mechanical system with aspects of automatic control.

A telephone network illustrates an intermediate level of complexity. It can be viewed at the level of a local exchange, a nationwide network, or a worldwide network connected by radio, undersea cable, and communications satellites.

Each succeeding level can be viewed as a system or a subsystem of a larger system. At different levels, specialty subsystems, such as central switching and direct dialing, can be recognized. Despite its immense number of constituents, a telephone network is not the most complicated of systems. Its several basic functions are relatively simple, straightforward, and generalizable from one level to the next, and thus are amenable to considerable automation.

*Nearly* the most complicated systems are the large-scale, computerized information-acquisition, -processing, and -display, control and command-and-control systems. In the broadest sense, these systems acquire radar, sonar, microwave, ionizing radiation, system status, biomedical, voice, and other data from a variety of terrestrial and solar system environments. Conversions of information, digital to analog, parallel to serial, and vice versa, and data compressions are almost always necessary. Almost every aspect of computer and display technology is relevant. Large numbers of personnel are required, sometimes in a great variety of types and skills. The many environmental stresses are both acute and chronic. Vehicles are controlled directly or indirectly and are themselves complex systems that may or may not cooperate with the system. This large systems category includes the various Air Force "L" systems, the manned spaceflight systems, and the naval control systems. The Semi-Automatic Ground Environment (SAGE) air defense system, the Air Force Satellite Control Facility, and the Apollo manned spacecraft system are considered in some detail throughout this book, because they exemplify system problem areas particularly well and because several of the authors have had experience with them.

The mission of SAGE is to detect, track, identify, intercept, and destroy enemy bomber aircraft. It has no antiballistic missile destruction capability. Major inputs are the dynamic position and speed data from radar and flight plans. Large, duplexed, digital computers compute aircraft tracks, determine identifications, calculate intercept points, etc. Various data are displayed on computer-related cathode-ray tubes. Enemy bombers are intercepted by manned aircraft or by Nike or Bomarc missiles. At one time, four-storied, duplexed SAGE Direction Center blockhouses were distributed over most of the contiguous United States and Canada. Now being phased out, SAGE is of particular interest because: (1) it can be viewed as the "granddaddy" of the electronic command and control systems, a laboratory of what was done correctly and incorrectly; (2) it exemplifies the long lead times between system conceptualization and system implementation; (3) in a related sense, it dramatizes the possibility that by the

time a system is operational, its mission may be quite incidental – SAGE went into operation just as the enemy threat changed from "air-breathing" bomber to ballistic missile, a still unsolved problem; (4) almost no attention was paid at high engineering and management levels to human factors and other psychological problems; and (5) it contributed a great deal to the design of computerized systems – for example, the presently important concepts of man–computer interaction, time-sharing, and display buffer design owe much to SAGE.

The Air Force Satellite Control Facility (SCF) has evolved considerably since its inception. The general aspects of the system and its mission can be gleaned from an article by White (1963), although the system has changed in detail since White's publication appeared. The mission of the SCF is to track, receive, and process telemetry data, test and check out, and control satellites. The SCF does not launch satellites, although it monitors prelaunch checkout and launch, which is a responsibility of other agencies at Cape Kennedy and at Vandenberg Air Force Base in California. Once launched, the satellite is tracked by, and telemetry data are received from, a worldwide network of tracking stations. Raw data received by these tracking stations are processed, compressed if necessary, converted, and transmitted mostly via digital data link to the Satellite Test Center in Sunnyvale, near San Francisco, California. After analysis of the tracking and telemetry data, especially the latter, voice commands are sent to the tracking station, which transmits them in nonvoice form to the satellite, correcting its attitude and so on. This is an oversimplification, and data are not always easily transmitted or easily analyzed. For our purposes, the major lessons learned from the SCF are: (1) it is an outstanding example of system development wherein operation requirements came too fast, too heavily, and from too many separate users, without central planning – what had started out as a fairly simple research and development (R&D) effort for testing the Discoverer unmanned satellite within several years became a superimposed mass of satellite-support equipment, methods, and personnel; (2) it provides an example of managerial debate as to whether a system is "operational" or "R&D", raising questions as to the applicable type of management control; (3) it has long demonstrated a challenging number of human factors problems connected with the allocation of functions between man and computer, automation of other functions, information availability, diagnosis and troubleshooting, problem solving, display and control design, personnel numbers and training, and formulation of operational procedures.

The mission of Apollo 11 was to bring three American men into a lunar orbit, land two of them on the moon, bring all three together again, and return them to Earth. Apollo involves a marvelous integration of test and checkout, launch, tracking and telemetry, data processing and display, control and recovery capabilities. It is perhaps *par excellence* the example of successful planning and the management of thousands of contractors and tens of thousands of specialist workers to bring about the successful implementation of a mission. For our purposes, it is of particular interest because: (1) it demonstrates that sophisticated management of complex processes can lead to the solution of quite formidable *technical* problems; (2) it can serve as a type example for application to the sociotechnical area; (3) in all systems, unforeseen interactions can result in costly waste and in tragedy; and (4) it exemplifies the concept of system hierarchy. The "system" can be considered the complete spacecraft-launch vehicle assemblage plus the worldwide network of tracking stations, the launch and recovery facilities, the Integrated Mission Control Center (IMCC) in Houston, Texas, and the simulation and training facilities; or we could consider the "system" as comprising only the spacecraft itself, consisting of an Escape Module (Launch Escape System jettisoned shortly after earth launch), Service Module, Command Module, and Lunar Module.* During descent to and ascent from the moon, the system could consist of either the Lunar Module (containing two astronauts) or Command Module (containing one astronaut). During the return cislunar voyage, and reentry and earth recovery, the system is the combined Service-Command Modules and the Command Module, respectively. Of course, the unmanned spacecraft or an individual astronaut can also be considered the system.

Systems such as those discussed above are *nearly* the most complicated with which we must deal. What then is more complex? The entire universe? Probably not, if complexity may be defined in terms of the overall problems with which we must live – and survive. The universe is complex and inspiring, but *in toto* has little effect upon our everyday lives. The most complicated system, or system environment, can be delineated as comprising the earth, Earth's moon, the sun and the five nearest planets to the sun. How is this a system? Consider our earlier properties and the concept of boundary. Boundary need not be a

* At earth launch, the Lunar Module is physically separated from the Command and Service Modules by the S-IVB (third) stage of the three-stage Saturn V launch vehicle. A reconfiguration of the modules is required shortly after injection into the cislunar path.

physical wall or even the effective force of the sun's gravitation. It can also be managerial, organizational, economic, psychological, conceptual. There is no question that space exploration, undersea exploration, poverty, automation and technological change, education, population growth, human happiness, democracy, and communism are today inextricably intertwined. This monstrous system, absolutely the most important for you and for us during our lifetimes and probably for a long time thereafter, can be characterized, however crudely, in terms of boundary; inputs, throughputs, and outputs; equilibrium; feedback loops; growth, differentiation, and decay; dynamic interactions; control and other properties. In this most macroscopic of macrosystems, the North American air defense network (NORAD) of which SAGE can be viewed a subsystem, the SCF, and Apollo, as well as individual cities and nations, can be recognized only as important subsystems (Figure 6.1). The interactions are quite evident. Important contributory factors of this system are discussed in the last three chapters of this book. We believe that one of the most useful discoveries of the twentieth century will be the application of systems know-how to the solution of problems in *sociotechnical* systems.

The partially human-designed, semispontaneous, and fortuitous systems and organizations of mankind possess many of the systems properties defined earlier. Yet there are important differences: man-made equipment-oriented systems reflect the purposes of a few users and are designed largely to function *in spite of* environments. Seminatural systems reflect the vagaries of numerous economic, social, and political needs, and geographic and climatic environments. Organizations, as in business and industry, are examples of systems in which man–man interactions predominate over man–machine interactions.

System interactions occur in these less, as well as in the more, structured systems. The interactions and their results may be apparently *unpredictable, uncontrollable,* and as in our present technological society, *unmanageable.* Psychology has the chance of its lifetime to demonstrate its worth in dealing with these late twentieth-century problem areas, especially in relation to growth and decline, need and goal direction, stability, and internally and externally generated stress and change.

## The search for universals

Three separate approaches to the identification of underlying principles of structure and behavior have developed in response to observations of isomorphies among systems and the development of similar concepts in different fields on the one hand, and the increasing specialization of knowledge on the other. To varying extents, general systems theory, cybernetics, and bionics seek universals that can relate the specifics of different sciences and technologies.

*General systems theory.* By the 1950s, it was evident that scientific specialization was leading to increasing difficulties of communication across disciplines. A number of philosophies, methods, and approaches, based on attempts to understand organization and the behavior of wholes, integrative mechanisms, dynamic interaction, and environmental effects, had evolved over the last 100 years in several sciences. However, this evolution took place in one discipline independently of developments in other disciplines. Examples include the field concept of physics, homeostasis and synergy in biology, servo theory in engineering, and Gestalt psychology.

Pressures to integrate similarities and relationships among the sciences, to enhance communication across disciplines, and to derive a theoretical basis for *general* scientific education had several philosophical roots, of which we will mention three (see von Bertalanffy, 1956; Boulding, 1964).*

1. Science in the late nineteenth and early twentieth centuries was largely analytic, with the whole being reduced to even smaller units, the study of which would allegedly result in understanding the whole. Eventually, many theorists hoped to achieve unity within science by reduction to the particles and mechanisms of physics. Thus, molecules were broken down into atoms; atoms into electrons, protons, and other particles; organisms into cells; behavior into reflexes; perception into sensations; the mind into ideas; and so forth. Simple additive and static cause–effect explanations were offered in describing the properties of the whole. Concepts of organization and of interaction were ignored. Countering this *reductionistic* approach was the increasing awareness of the importance of interaction and of dynamics that emerged in several fields of science during the first third of the twentieth century. Such terms as *field theory*, *Gestalt*, *holistic*, *organismic*, *adaptiveness*, and *goal-direction* reflect this newer tenor. The independent development of these concepts in different sciences can be considered a forerunner of the development of a general systems theory.

2. The second stimulus toward development of a general systems theory – and limitation of specific-system ap-

proaches – came from the so-called Heisenberg Principle of Indeterminacy. Thus, information cannot be applied to or withdrawn from a system without changing it, and the very process of observation or study distorts the system itself and hence the meaning of results. A wide variety of experiences, especially in the biological, behavioral, and social sciences, substantiates this objection. For example, in experimental psychology the experimenter's behavior itself or the design of his equipment may offer subtle cues to the human subjects; in opinion polling, respondents tend to give answers they believe will seem "right" to the pollster.

3. Many systems are probabilistic or stochastic rather than deterministic. A single observation can tell us little or nothing about the probability of occurrence of the event observed. Again this holds especially true in the biological, behavioral, and social sciences.

In 1956, a group of scientists established the Society for General Systems Research (originally called the Society for the Advancement of General Systems Theory). The Society issues a yearbook of articles on systems approaches from virtually all the sciences. Young (1964) has surveyed general systems theory after nearly a decade of its existence, summarizing the attempts of workers to apply general systems theory to their specific fields. *Emphasis on specific applications to enhance the general theory was found to be far greater than the applications of general systems theory to specific disciplines.* Work could be broken down into four categories:

1. *Systematic and descriptive factors.* This category dealt with classifications of types of systems, their data and internal organization, and system environments. Particular attention was given to openness and closedness, organismic or nonorganismic properties, centralization, independence, differentiation, interaction, and boundaries.

2. *Regulation and maintenance.* This category dealt with control and stabilization. Concepts of equilibrium, feed-back and communication, and control were important.

3. *Dynamics and change.* This category dealt with nondisruptive internal and external environmental changes. Of particular importance were adaptation, learning, growth, and goal-seeking.

4. *Decline and breakdown.* This category dealt with disruption and dissolution, and emphasized stress, overload, entropy, and decay.

* The term "general systems theory" was coined by von Bertalanffy.

Young states that the typical literature is strong on regulation and maintenance and weak on decline and breakdown. Social scientists are showing an increased, sometimes overriding, interest in the general systems field, perhaps because of training and interests at the given time. The usefulness of the literature is diminished by the tendency of some authors to cite general concepts without indicating how these concepts helped specific applications.

Material on general systems can be found in the *Yearbook of the Society for General Systems Research* and in the Institute of Electrical and Electronic Engineers *Transactions on Systems Science and Cybernetics*. Boulding (1956) is a good general reference.

*Cybernetics*. Since World War II, there have been several concerted, often highly mathematical attempts to determine universals applicable to the explanation of the behavior of both organisms and machines. Work has been directed to increasing understanding of organisms (and societies) and making machines more adaptive, more flexible, and more in tune with given environments. In this book, we will consider two main developments: *cybernetics* and *bionics*.* Cybernetics can be thought of as an attempt to understand organisms through making analogies to machines, and bionics as an attempt to develop better machines through understanding of biological design principles. Cybernetics traditionally has emphasized understanding of a given process *per se*, while bionics seeks understanding of a given process as a means of generalizing to another situation. Both cybernetics and bionics involve theory, model building, experimentation, and application; they have been compared with the two sides of a coin.

A few individuals have participated in developments in both cybernetics and bionics; similarly, there have been tangential developments, closely akin to these, but given other names such as *self-organizing systems* (Yovits *et al.*, 1962), *adaptive systems, learning machines, automata*, and *artificial intelligence*, which have yet to be interrelated. These approaches appear to rely more heavily on "armchair", rational, and intuitive methods, while cybernetics and bionics emphasize empirical and experimental methods.

As we attempt to deal with the increasing complexity of our world, those most complex of things, living organisms, can provide clues to better design for small and compact power supplies, for reliability, for greater adaptability, for

more effective organization, and so forth. Of particular interest to both cybernetics and bionics are the following:

1. The reception ("sensation") and recognition ("perception") of information.
2. Integrative processes.
3. Storage and retrieval of information.
4. Self-regulatory ("homeostatic") processes.
5. Adaptive ("learning") processes.
6. Control processes.

The world first became widely aware of cybernetics in 1948 when Norbert Wiener published the first edition of *Cybernetics or Control and Communication in the Animal and the Machine* (the second edition appeared in 1961). However, Wiener had formulated his ideas earlier in World War II, when he was faced with problems of automatic aiming of antiaircraft guns. It was necessary to shoot the projectile not at the aircraft itself, but along a trajectory such that the two would intersect in space sometime in the future. Accordingly, it was necessary to predict the future position of the aircraft. Wiener was able to formulate equations describing a closed-loop system (the input to a computer was part of the output signal). Thus, the computer, utilizing a feedback loop, could calculate the time of the trajectory of a projectile and predict the point at which the gun should aim. Working with Arturo Rosenblueth, a biologist, and with other prominent engineers, mathematicians, biologists, and psychologists, Wiener formulated principles common to machines, animals, and societies. The term *cybernetics* itself comes from the Greek word for *steersman*, a tribute to the fact that a ship's steering engines provide one of the earliest types of feedback mechanism. Wiener's book was eclectic and contained discussions of normal and abnormal physiological, psychological, and sociotechnical processes, as well as of information, communications and feedback *per se*.

Wiener viewed cybernetics as encompassing the entire field of control and communication theory, whether in the animal or the machine. The study of *automata*, machine or animal, was regarded as a branch of communication engineering, and was concerned with the concepts of information amount, coding and message, with noise, and so on. Automata are related to the outside world through sensors/receptors and control mechanisms/effectors, which are interconnected by central integrating mechanisms.

Wiener recognized that the value of cybernetics would be shaped by the limitations of the data we can obtain. Yet he felt there were two areas in particular offering practical results: the development of prostheses and the development

---

* In some parts of Europe, bionics is considered to be synonymous with applied cybernetics.

of automatic computing machines. Subsequent developments have borne out Wiener's expectations, particularly in the second area.

The importance of cybernetics to the psychologist or physiologist interested in neuro-endocrine integrative action, self-organizing behavior, homeostasis, perception, learning, and so forth should be quite evident. In another area, Wiener was remarkably prophetic: he expressed concern over our abilities to construct machines of almost any degree of sophistication of performance, believing that we are confronted with "... *another social potentiality of unheard-of-importance for good and for evil* ..." (emphasis added). Just as the industrial revolution *devalued* the human arm through competition with machinery, so the present technological revolution is bound to devalue the human brain, at least in its more routine processes. Wiener believed, as we emphasize later, that the alternative is a society based on human values other than buying and selling – *a society that would require a great deal of planning and struggle*. He hoped that a better understanding of man and society, as "fall-out" of cybernetics efforts, would outweigh the concentration of power (in the hands of the most unscrupulous) incidental to the applications of cybernetics, but he concluded in 1947, "... that it is a very slight hope".

Cybernetics is an integrated body of concepts applicable to orderly study within physical, biological, and social sciences, and in the "crossroads" interdisciplinary sciences between. In each case, problems can be represented in terms of information content and flow and in terms of feedback and control. Yet, like some other concepts, cybernetics has proved no universal panacea. Its initial reception was lurid with the connotation, "The robots are here." Extensions were interesting and led to coining of new terms – *cyborg* for an organism with a machine built into it with consequent modification of function, *cybernation* for automation involving especially information and control systems – but cybernetics generally did not live up to expectations. The term itself remained an obscure one in the United States, although it became popular in Germany and in the Soviet Union, where theoretical cybernetics is considered to include information theory, automata theory, programming theory, and the theory of games. More recently, interest in cybernetics has renewed in the United States, as reflected in the establishment of the Professional Group in Systems Science and Cybernetics (1965) within the Institute of Electrical and Electronics Engineers and the American Society for Cybernetics (1968).

Cybernetics applications include adaptive teaching machines and pattern perception devices; the best examples are provided by automata and by prostheses. *Locomotion automata*, which may be bi- or quadrupedal, are of potential value for use in difficult terrain, such as mountains, polar regions, swamps, and the lunar surface. In a simple quadruped automaton, each leg has only two output states: on the ground pushing backward and in the air pushing forward. The sequence of motions for each leg and the gait are controlled by a binary-sequence generator using a different program for each gait and based on *finite-state* logic (the machine can have only a finite number of states) (Kalisch, 1968; Swanson, 1968). Other applications deal with powered prostheses. The most sophisticated concepts involve sensing and amplifying bioelectric potentials from muscles, or even better, nerves in the stump of the severed limb itself. Devices based on utilization of muscle potentials and including an electric motor enable the patient to perform fairly precise activities such as writing and to lift weights of about 10 pounds. Other cybernetic machines under study include those that amplify a normal operator's strength, enabling him to lift 1,500 pounds, or increase his locomotion speed to 35 mph over rough or dangerous terrain.

An automaton possessed of adaptive ("homeostatic") behavior was Ashby's (1960) *homeostat*, an electromechanical device, which always returned to equilibrium by means of switches, regardless of input. Another was Shannon's mechanical mouse, which was programmed to "learn" a checkerboard maze after one trial by "remembering" the direction in which it had left a given square for the last time (Lindgren, 1968). A Russian automaton, based on a hierarchy of heuristic computer programes, purportedly also possesses feeling and consciousness (Lindgren, 1968).

*Bionics.* Bionics is another of the important interdisciplinary areas that emerged toward the late 1950s and early 1960s. The term was coined by U.S. Air Force Major J. E. Steele in 1958, but first received widespread recognition at the first bionics symposium in 1960 (*Bionics Symposium: Living Prototypes – the Key to New Technology*, 1960). Since 1960, other bionics congresses have been held (e.g., *Bionics Symposium: Information Processing by Living Organisms and Machines*, 1964). The word "bionics" suggests a coalescence of biology and electronics, but bionics protagonists emphasize the integration of *analysis* (from biology) and *synthesis* (from engineering design). This is reflected in an official insignia: the scalpel representing analysis, an integral sign representing synthesis. Over the years biologists, psychologists, engineers, and mathematicians have participated in bionics efforts.

Bionics can be defined as the study of living systems to identify concepts applicable to the design of artificial systems; alternatively, it can be defined as the study of systems whose functions have been derived from the study of living systems.

The philosophical and rational basis for bionics rests on the time-based, dynamic organism–environment interactions that have characterized all living systems since the first appearance of life on earth some two to three billion years ago. The environment stresses the organism, which either adapts to fit a particular ecological niche at a given time or perishes. Hence, living systems can be thought of as being good, sometimes even the best, approximations of adjustments to the demands of given environments at a given time.

The next question concerns the appropriate degree of isomorphism between the natural and artificial system. Attempts to pattern design too rigidly after the living prototype often lead to dead ends, as shown by early (sometimes fatal) attempts to fly by avian methods. Modeling is widely used in bionics and provides a bridge between different specialists. Model building, however, always presents the possibility of too great abstraction and mathematical precision at the cost of minimum relation to the real world. Also, there has long been a tendency both in biology and in psychology, and now perhaps also in bionics, to concentrate on knowledge that may be incomplete, distorted out of context, incidental, or artifactual. Examples are the undue emphasis on the electrical activity of the nervous system and on reflex activity, and attempts to equate nervous system and computer functioning. Nevertheless, a rigid insistence on complete understanding of a biological process may retard useful serendipitous discovery. It seems desirable, therefore, to qualify the definition of bionics to include processes that directly and wholly explain a natural phenomenon, those that seem to explain *some* aspects of a natural phenomenon, those recognized as incidental, and those that clearly are only analogies.

Bionics thus can be seen to be the study of living organisms with the intention of deriving technological knowledge. As the flight of aircraft and of spacecraft demonstrate, the capabilities of the artificial systems – *along some dimensions* – may greatly exceed those of the original prototypes. Actual or potential system design applications based on *living prototypes* are summarized in Table 6.1.

Often the living prototype indicates only that a process *is* possible, but information as to how the process works is scant. Thus, in many bionics studies, limited biological or psychological knowledge is extended by simulation and modeling and by intuition on the part of the bionicist.

The question has been raised as to the usefulness of the bionics approach. That there are probably more workers in the area of artificial neurons or *neuromimes*\* than in any other derives from the hope that greater understanding of the nervous system will aid in the construction of smaller, more flexible computers. On the other hand, neural modeling should provide better understanding of the nervous system *per se*. What we know about the neuron has enabled us to build electronic analogs that simulate neuron behavior. Many different kinds of neuromimes have been built, depending on the interests of the designers. Some emphasize central processes such as memory; others emphasize peripheral processes such as excitation-inhibition, threshold, summation, and refractoriness. Van Bergéijk and Harman (1960) have attempted to produce as precise an analog of the peripheral nervous system as possible, and report that this approach has helped elucidate both anatomical and physiological features.

Reichardt (1961) and his interdisciplinary coworkers at the Max Planck Institut für Biologie, Tübingen, Germany, have studied visual processes in the beetle *Chlorophanus*. This beetle responds optokinetically (in terms of head or eye movements) to relative movements of light in its optical environment. The most elementary succession of light changes found capable of eliciting an optomotor response consisted of two stimuli in adjacent ommatidia (facets) of the compound eye. A stimulus received by one ommatidium can interact only with that received by the adjacent ommatidium or those adjacent to the latter. Transformation and interaction within the central nervous system were found to agree with known principles. The results were expressed in the language of control systems, suggesting that the beetle could derive velocity information from a moving, randomly shaded background. This finding led to the design of a ground-speed indicator for aircraft based on the function of two of the hundreds of facets comprising the compound eye (see Savely's article in Steele, 1960).

A very readable book that discusses most of the developments in bionics has been written by Gérardin (1968). Specific original papers of representative interest are those of Rosenblatt (1958), Lettvin *et al.* (1959), Newell and Simon (1961), and Simon (1961).

---

\* There is a need for nomenclature to differentiate between the natural and analog entity. Following van Bergéijk (1960), we can consider the suffix *mime* to indicate the most general type of artificial cell or organ. Accordingly, a neuristor would be one type of neuromime.

**Table 6.1** Bionic developments (Prepared partially from text in Gérardin, 1968)

| PROTOTYPE | APPLICATION |
| --- | --- |
| Olfactory receptors of moths and butterflies; infrared receptors of pit vipers | Lightweight sensors |
| Compound eye of beetle *Chlorophanus* | Aircraft ground-speed indicator |
| Compound eye of king crab *Limulus*; retina of frog | Automatic recognition of pattern, movement |
| Eel and ray electrical-field generation, detection | Submarine detection |
| Bat and cetacean echo-location behavior and related physiology; bat–moth interactions | Radar and sonar with better antijamming and antievasive capabilities |
| Bat ear structure and echo location | Location aid to the blind |
| Neuronal (generally peripheral) electrophysiology | Artificial neuron or neuristor to propagate a "signal" without attenuating it* |
| Retina and brain of higher vertebrates | Pattern-perception and learning machines (perceptrons) |
| Animal short-term memory (apparently electro-chemical or synaptic) and long-term memory (apparently chemical and inter- and intracellular involving both neurons and neuroglia) | Computer memory |
| Human problem solving | Adaptive (heuristic) problem-solving computer programs |
| Dolphin swimming behavior and double (turbulence-reducing) skin | Streamlined torpedo |
| Migratory, orientation, homing behavior; related physiology of birds, turtles, fish, insects | Navigation devices |
| Bioluminescence | Cold (100% efficient) light |

* Neuristors are capable of performing complex calculations, leading to attempts to build computers using them as basic constituents.

## Systems psychology: a new field

Conceptually, systems theory and psychology have long had much in common. Concepts that have arisen independently include those of field and environment, dynamics, interaction, and evolution and change. Most significantly, both organisms and systems consist of wholes that transcend the sum of the dynamically interacting parts. In turn, each part affects the properties of the whole. The organism can be thought of in terms of a hierarchy expressed from most general and tenuous to most elementary and precise: the social grouping of organisms and the man–machine system; the total intact organism; the organ system such as the nervous system; the tissue such as nervous tissue; the individual cell such as the neuron; the cell nucleus; the complex molecule or colloid such as deoxyribonucleoprotein; the simpler molecules such as the nucleotides, nucleosides, purines, and pyrimidines; and finally the atom and subatomic particle. At the upper end of this hierarchy, psychology interrelates with sociology, cultural anthropology, economics, and political science; at the lower end with physiology, biochemistry, and biophysics. Systems concepts and methods are applicable at all levels, and psychological problems at each level can be couched in systems terms. Examples at each end of the continuum are provided by simulation studies of the industrial organiza-

tion and by relating memory to nucleic acid and protein metabolism within the neuron cell body and associated neuroglia.

In a similar vein, systems are arranged as *macrosystems* such as the Apollo systems as defined earlier; as *systems* such as the Apollo spacecraft; and as *subsystems*, *sub-subsystems*, or *modules*, *components* (individual subassemblies), *units*, and *parts*. Psychological factors or psychology-related problems can be defined at each level, for example, by the use of computers in military decision making involving national defense, at one extreme, and by training required for the assembly of printed-circuit boards at the other. A major problem derives from the lack of consistency in use of systems terminology. Such terms as *unit*, *part*, *component*, and *element* are used interchangeably. We have used the neutral term *constituent*, as appropriate, to indicate the most general case. The same semantic difficulties apply to such terms as *job*, *task*, *element*, and others in the behavioral hierarchy. In some chapters, the term *element* is used in a general sense, although there are objections to doing so. The nomenclature and definitions given in Table 6.2, and used throughout this book, are based generally on usage in the aerospace industry and specifically on practice at Northrop Corporation on the Skybolt air-to-ground missile project.

**Table 6.2** Definitions of basic terms in systems hierarchy

GENERAL

*Mission.* A statement of *what* the system is to do to solve a given problem and *when* and *where* – an expression of purposes and objectives. It can be arbitrarily segmented in terms of identifiable beginning and end points. Mission determination involves many subjective or judgmental factors.

*Requirement.* A statement of an obligation the system must fulfill to effect the mission. Requirements are expressed first in qualitative terms and progressively in quantitative performance terms relative to some criterion(ia). They further delineate the system mission.

*Function.* A general means or action by which the system fulfills its requirements. Functions are usually expressed in verb form (monitor, control) or participial form (monitoring, controlling). They are the first expression of the *hows* of the system. They are expressed progressively more precisely. Ideally, functions are conceived apart from implementation by men and/or by machines; in practice, they are usually expressed along with machine design implications.

| EQUIPMENT | BEHAVIORAL |
|---|---|
| *Subsystem.* At its *most basic level*, a single module, or combination of modules, plus independent components that contribute to modular functions, all interconnected and interrelated within a system and performing a specific function. Examples: guidance and control subsystem, propulsion subsystem. | *Job operation.* A combination of duties and tasks necessary to accomplish a system function. A job operation may involve one or more positions or career specialties or fields. |
| *Module (sub-subsystem).* A combination of components contained in one package or so arranged that together they are common to one mounting, which provides a complete function(s) to the subsystem and/or systems in which they operate. Examples: guidance and control computer, astrotacker. | *Position.* A grouping of duties and responsibilities constituting the principal work assignment of *one* person. The position may be that of operator, maintainer, controller, etc. Positions related in terms of ability, education, training, and experience can be grouped as career specialties and fields. Synonym: *job.* |
| *Component.* A combination of units or parts independent of, or an independent entity within, a complete operating module or subsystem, providing a self-contained capability necessary for proper module, subsystem, and/or system operation. Can be replaced as a whole. Examples: DC power supply, digital display readout. | *Duty.* A set of operationally related tasks within a given position. These may involve operating, maintaining, training, and supervising, etc. |
| *Unit.* A combination of parts constituting a definable entity of a component, possessing a functional potential essential to the proper operation of that component. Example: chip. | *Task.* A composite of related (discriminatory–decision–motor) activities performed by an individual, and directed toward accomplishing a specific amount of work within a specific work context. Involves, for example, a group of associated operations or inspections. |
| *Part.* The smallest *practical* equipment subdivision of a system; an individual piece having an inherent functional capability, but unable to function without the interaction of other parts or forces; ordinarily not subject to further disassembly without destruction. Examples: transistor, diode, resistor, capacitor. | *Subtask.* Actions fulfilling a limited purpose within a task – for example, making a series of related machine adjustments. |
| | *Task element.* A basic S–O–R constituent of behavior comprising the smallest *logically* definable set of perceptions, decisions, and responses required to complete a task or sub-task. Involves, for example, identifying a specific signal on a specific display, deciding on a single action, actuating a specific control, and noting the feedback signal of response adequacy. Synonym: *behavior* or *job behavior.* |

SOURCE: Modified from text in Headquarters Air Force Systems Command, *Personnel Subsystems*, (1969) and from practices at Northrop Corporation.

Figure 6.1 summarizes the above aspects of systems hierarchy. Macro-macrosystems can be subdivided into many other ways – for example, in terms of communications; transportation, or use of resources. An immensely complicated figure would be required to indicate *organizational* hierarchy and all subdivisions at the lower hierarchical levels. Identification and analysis of all segments of the mission profile and the constituent functions, tasks, and the like require detailed documentation, and constitute one of the main businesses of *human factors. Systems* science is concerned with determination of interrelationships among the various concepts, levels, and terms. This does not imply, however, simple linear, additive, multiplicative, or deterministic relationships, either laterally or hierarchically. For example, at the moment we can clearly relate system job performance neither to the biochemistry of the brain nor to task-element performance. Hopefully someday we will be able to do much of both.

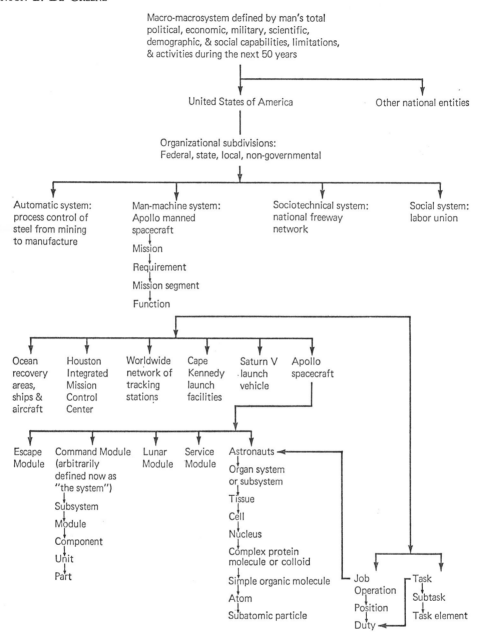

**Figure 6.1** Examples of systems subdivision and organismic, equipment, and behavioral hierarchy (see Table 6.2 for definitions of basic terms).

Systems and organisms can also be studied and described in terms of *feedback control*. Independently of physical scientists, biologists and psychologists came up with the concepts of *milieu internale* and homeostasis, and extensions thereof, which describe the maintenance of constancy of physiological, behavioral, and social parameters, internal to the organism or group, despite wide variations in stimuli. However, the organism is immensely complex when compared to the machine: Control loops in the organism are superimposed upon one another, and its internal nonlinear feedback mechanisms may be dissimilar to those in the machine.

Conceptualization of organisms and systems in hierarchical terms like those indicated earlier has been associated with the development of philosophies concerned with methods of approach. Can the complex whole best be understood at that level, or by studying the individual constituents? Is analysis that defines the behavior of these constituents isolated from the system a more meaningful approach than synthesis, the attempt to deduce behavior of the system from knowledge of the constituent functions? Terms such as *holism, Gestalt, molar, molecular, atomism, elementarism, associationism, reductionism, stimulus-response unit, mechanism,* and *vitalism,* long used by psychologists or biologists, attest to the continuing lack of agreement.

Finally, systems techniques have the heuristic or epistemological benefit of providing rigor in the definition of psychological terms such as *intelligence, learning, thinking,* and *feeling.* This is especially evident when we try to answer such questions as: Do machines think? What is artificial intelligence? How does problem solving relate to decision making? In our attempts to provide answers to these questions, assist colleagues in other fields to understand how psychology can contribute to solving their problems, and evaluate the statements they so frequently vouchsafe, we are forced to consider even more far-reaching questions. For example: What *is* psychology? How good are its basic methods? Are the right problems being recognized, defined, and attacked? Does psychology have a body of theory and an approach amenable to the study of *real-world* problems? How good and how useful is psychological research? How can we better apply psychological research to the crushing problems of technology and society? Is psychology poorly understood by the layman and by other scientists and engineers so that its findings, while valid and generalizable, are poorly applied? Throughout this book, we attempt to provide answers to each of these questions, mostly within the context of specific subject areas.

*The nature of psychology and psychological theory.* A science must be defined in terms of the events of a given time in history; the efforts of its practitioners, the problems they recognize and identify, the tools they use, and interfaces with other sciences. It is not always clear just *what* psychology is. Certainly, the customary definitions do not provide a realistic framework for a science that encompasses a greater vertical range than any other, including at one extreme human behavior in groups and organizations, and at the other the biophysics and biochemistry of learning. More and more, psychologists find themselves associated with specialists in other fields – clinicians with psychiatrists, educational psychologists with teachers, engineering psychologists with engineers – cut off from their fellows who share the science of mind, of man, of behavior, and of experience.

We can expect a shifting of boundaries within science, the emergence of interdisciplinary "cross-roads sciences", which eventually achieve an intrinsic sufficiency of their own, and the absorption of subsciences that have not proved their worth. This may sound like an unduly pragmatic view, and there is indeed danger in compromising development of basic knowledge in the name of immediate returns on research grants. There is just as great a danger in retreating into the contented isolation of our laboratories while the world collapses without, secure in our grasp of an idea, or method, or shibboleth of questionable relevance.

The history of science provides us with many examples of intellectual *culs de sac.* There is always the risk of misunderstanding the problem, selecting the wrong level or the fortuitous artifactual, rather than the lasting and real, or of simply grasping the most convenient. It is always tempting to build elaborate theories on limited or premature data, only to become caught up in the excitement and momentum of the times and pushing applications that may be invalid at best and downright harmful at worst. Jones and Gray (1963) cite the selection of neuron pulse interval or pulse frequency, while ignoring pulse amplitude or width, as an example of grasping a phenomenon that is easier to deal with conceptually or mathematically in model building: the problem and unit of measure has been selected to fit available mathematics, rather than new mathematics developed to fit the problem. The traditional attempts of psychology to explain learning and memory in terms of simple conditioned reflexes or in terms of electrophysiological events (ignoring the chemical) probably represent premature theorizing based on limited fact. Goslin (1968) has reviewed the field of standardized ability tests and testing, and has pointed out the many questions of validity and predictability and the real danger of individual and social harm.

A considerably body of psychological theory and data has been based on experimentation with the albino variety of the brown rat, *Rattus norvegicus.* What if all this research is at best incidental and at worst artifactual and decidedly wrong? Some insight into this serious problem is offered by Lockard (1968), who presents considerable evidence that the albino rat is an *atypical* organism – a poor one, indeed, on which to base generalizations of behavior – that its very evolution is adventitious and artificial, and that results based thereon are bound to be distorted. Here is an excellent example of our misguided hope in finding a standard unit (as in physical science); there are biologically many types of white rats.

When the engineering psychologist turns to the experimental psychologist and asks for basic data on human performance, he is likely to find that there are no data or that the data are inapplicable to real-world problems of analysis, design, and operation. Again and again, workers have complained about the lack of application, even relevancy, of the results of psychological experimentation to pressing engineering and social requirements (Chapanis, 1967; Alluisi, 1967, and Meister, 1964; and Boulding, 1967, and Mackie and Christensen, 1967). At the same time engineers, computer programmers, chemists, mathematicians, and others are assuming, and – to an extent more than psychologists – mastering problems long considered within the domain of psychology. At present, problem solving, especially man–computer problem solving, is quite *in*. But where is the basic groundwork in psychology developed over the years as an aid to the psychologists and others now specializing in the field? Why were so many of us psychologists running rats through mazes over several decades and so few studying human thinking and problem solving? Simultaneously, in the streets throughout the world, social and sociotechnical problems cry out for solution – and the cry is becoming louder – in terms of skill definitions *vis-à-vis* automation and technological change, in terms of training, education, attitudes, emotions, mental disease, and so forth. Psychology's record of accomplishment in helping to ameliorate the world's woes, perhaps also in advancing basic science, has not been great, especially considering the number of psychologists. Demonstrable results often come from outside psychology. The major advance in the treatment of the mentally ill in the last decade or so has stemmed from developments in pharmacology, not from developments in clinical psychological analysis and therapy. Separate abstractions such as personality, mental illness, intelligence, learning, and memory may see unity through extension of Pauling's (1968) concept of *orthomolecular psychiatry* to include gene action and specified biophysical and biochemical processes involving membrane permeability, metabolism, waste product accumulation, and the like.

Psychology, as we have now seen, s a remarkably diverse science that often seems at odds with itself and with its neighbor sciences. Internecine battle has long raged within psychology: clinician against experimentalist, "brass-instrument" man against "field theorist", "rat man" against "head shrinker", pure scientist against applied worker. Many psychologists believe that this conflict has been for the better and will lead to a truly stable eclectic science. Actually, this is far from true, and at no time more evident than when we try to answer the question, just what *are* the psychological factors in systems? At first the answer seems deceptively simple. We could say, why they're perception, learning, memory, motivation, emotion, psychomotor behavior, and so on. Closer inspection, however, reveals that these entities themselves are interrelated, varied within themselves, and time- and context-dependent. There seem to be at least two types of memory, for example, short term and long term, differing at the cellular level. There are undoubtedly several levels of perception, learning, and emotion, which might be called "peripheral", "subcortical", and "cortical".

Further, in operational situations we find it necessary to deal with factors like judgment and intuition that have long been pariahs to objective psychology. Even when we reduce the psychological factors to basics like visual acuity, vigilance, and reaction time, we find that these are dependent on the temporal and environmental context. Clearly what is needed is a *general* and *flexible* approach, adaptable to different problems, levels, times and environments. Systems theory seems to provide this approach. Throughout psychology, it is meaningful to conceptualize a person – or a human group, or a brain, or a mitochondrion – as a constituent processing energy, materials, and information; interacting within a given environment, at a given time, and at a given state of equilibrium and internal consistency. Systems theory should provide a common framework for posing, studying, and solving systems problems that seem to involve as apparently disparate factors as pattern perception, alertness, decision making, language, fatigue and stress, individual skill and performance differences, morale, and interpersonal relations.

It is probably premature to try to develop a comprehensive theory encompassing the *continuum*: automatic – man–machine – sociotechnical – social systems. An intermediate step is to use various models: information processing, feedback control, probabilistic, input–throughput–output, and man–machine–environmental. Further, it is probably fair to state that *there is no comprehensive theory tying together what we know about human behavior in systems*. In view of the many problems discussed later in this book, any systems psychological theory clearly must account for factors long faced by psychological theory in general. What are these factors? One approach is suggested by Coan's (1968) recent study of basic trends in psychological theory over time and at any given time. Coan determined 34 variables (divided into emphasis on content, methodology, basic assumption or mode of conceptualization) related to 54 theorists by the ratings of a couple of hundred experts in the history and theory of psychology. The theories included those of personality, abnormal behavior, learning, brain mechanisms, homeostasis, peripheral nervous activity, mental abilities, individual differences, sensation, integrative activity of the nervous system, and so forth.* For each psychological theorist, the experts' ratings were averaged and a 54 × 34 matrix obtained. Factor analysis and multiple-regression analysis revealed six factors and a placement of each theorist along a continuum represented by that factor. The factors are summarized as follows:

1. Subjectivistic versus objectivistic.
2. Holistic versus elementaristic; these two factors emerged as the factors of greatest variance, but other factors were also necessary.
3. Transpersonal versus personal, or experimental versus clinical.
4. Quantitative versus qualitative.
5. Dynamic versus static.
6. Endogenist ("biological") versus exogenist ("social" or, we might add, "environmental").

The six factors were intercorrelated and further analysis revealed two more general factors:

1. Synthetic (subjectivistic, holistic, and qualitative) versus analytic (objectivistic, elementaristic, and quantitative).
2. Functional (dynamic, personal, and internal and biological) versus structural (static and transpersonal).

In turn, the two second-order factors had a correlation of 0·55, leading to isolation of a final general factor: fluid (relaxed) orientation versus restrictive (controlling, compartmentalized) orientation. These theoretical orientations were seen to be a function of the personality of the scientist, a point systems researchers could do well to bear in mind. Does the need for systematization or mathematical rigor in fact reflect inner insecurities? Coan's work is summarized in Figure 6.2.

From the trends revealed in his work, Coan observes that neither at the factor level nor at the variable level is there a basis for confidently extrapolating to future developments. The clearest trend was toward greater objectivism. The

* Unfortunately, Coan emphasized classical theorists to the detriment of pragmatic theorists such as organization theorists.

participation of psychologists in system theory and system development over the past two and one-half decades suggests an approach (remember there is not yet a theory) that can be characterized as objectivistic, elementaristic, transpersonal, quantitative, dynamic, and exogenist. This approach *could* serve as a launching point for a comprehensive theory of human behavior in both man–machine and sociotechnical systems (which should be viewed not as dichotomous but rather as operating along a continuum). This theory must incorporate the input–throughput–output paradigm, and it must be expressible in terms of the modification or processing of inputs, probably in terms of information processing. Most important, it must express interactions at different levels and the same level, and predict the effects of interactions on the disruption and maintenance of equilibrium. Other systems properties could be factored in to a lesser extent. From here there could be an infinite quest for universals, perhaps the "elements" or "tasks" or "behaviors". One factor of particular importance is *expectation*: when the system situation, operation, or environment does not accord with an individual's expectation, degraded behavior occurs: the pilot loses control of his aircraft, the maintenance man's morale decreases, the minority group member or college student riots.

*The definition, value, and directions of systems psychology.* What we've said so far suggests the time has arrived to say, "Whoa, let's take stock of ourselves!" We must define systems psychology within its context of the other sciences, and carefully evaluate its future directions. Formally we define systems psychology as *the science and technology of understanding, describing and predicting; and generalizing the total effective performance and need-gratification behavior of intact organisms (usually human beings) under conditions of interaction with other intact organisms or machines within given environments.*

From preceding discussions, we may define *systems psychology* more generally as a new interdisciplinary specialty characterized by a *level*, a *breadth*, and a *method of approach*. At its most basic, the *level* is that of the individual intact organism (almost invariably, but not exclusively, a human being) interacting with at least one other entity, either man or machine, at about the same hierarchical level of complexity. Usually, at least ten of these basic constituents are involved. *Breadth* refers to similar consideration of man–man interactions within an environment, and man–machine interactions within an environment, and combinations thereof. The *method of approach* is that of systems

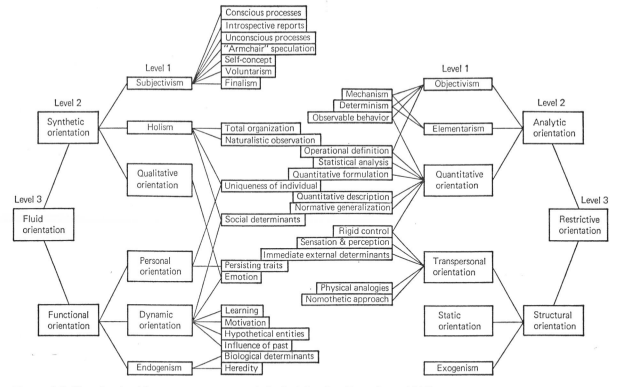

**Figure 6.2** Three levels of factors common to psychological theories (From Coan, 1968).

theory *and* practice as discussed in detail throughout this chapter. It is general enough to permit qualitative, quantitative, or mixed techniques as appropriate.

Clearly, systems psychology cannot stand alone, and recognition of its relationships to other fields is important. If the same methods are applied at the level of the brain, the scientist is a physiological psychologist or physiologist. If the focus is on applying knowledge as to *specific* human capabilities and limitations, especially performance capabilities and limitations, to equipment design, the worker is an engineering psychologist; finding the requisite information is the work of an experimental psychologist. The man interested in the interaction of people in groups is a social psychologist.

We already have *specialists* capable of dealing with all sorts of system-related problems. Why establish still another science? One reason is that it is often difficult to relate problems to disciplines. Is self-regulated decrease in viable births, consequent to over-crowding, apparently involving sensory–neural–endocrine mechanisms and observed in mammals from rats to elephants, the province of physiological psychology or social psychology? Is the study of attitudes toward machines a concern of engineering psycho-

logy, industrial psychology, or social psychology? The choice of problems within our discipline is largely a function of how we define our jobs. A second reason is that, in practice, scientific generalists are few and far between. Industrial psychology, nominally broad, has proved to be rather static and has generated few, if any, exciting ideas. Human factors has made much progress in integrating human engineering, training, and man-power determination, but so far has largely ignored motivation, attitudes, and social factors in systems.

Systems psychology has roots in physiological, experimental, general, individual, and social psychology, as well as in physiology, the other social sciences, engineering, the computer and information sciences, and mathematics. It is both an applied and a theoretical/conceptual field, but at the present time, emphasis is on applications. Although systems psychology possesses methods appropriate to its level (for example, computer modeling and simulation), it is reciprocally dependent on other sciences and technologies: *One of the most healthful relationships entails recognizing and defining complex real-world problems in terms amenable to solution by the contributory sciences and referring these problems to the relevant specialty science.*

It is not sufficient to establish systems psychology as a well-defined and worthwhile science: We must insist on a careful evaluation of where we are going. Your response might now be, "Eureka! The millenium has arrived." A look to the past in psychology suggests caution, however. Uncertain of its own identity, psychology has all too often tried to emulate the rigor of the physical sciences. We have already mentioned the "standard rat". In the early days of experimental psychology, the human subject was known as the "reagent". The present author, whose initial university education was in chemistry and biology, is still uncomfortable with applications to psychology of such terms as *genotype* and *phenotype*, *molar* and *molecular*. Currently, many of the *in*-concepts and terms derive from information and control theory, but terms like *bit* and *coding* and *channel* should not be used to camouflage a poorly defined problem. Psychology must stand on its own two feet.

We must encourage the development of theory of man-related systems, but not at the expense of basic data collection. As psychologists, we should not be ashamed of perhaps emphasizing fieldwork over experiment. Meteorology, astronomy, geology, zoology, botany, anthropology, and sociology too must rely largely on field observations and measurements. Attempts to predict novae, earthquakes, or volcanic eruptions largely on the basis of laboratory abstractions would seem doomed to failure. Complex sociotechnical systems in particular require that basic field data be collected before subaspects of the systems problem can be relegated to the laboratory for detailed study.

Finally, we must urge the expansion of interdisciplinary, systems-related education in a changing psychology. One example is Fein's (1961) discussion of education in the computer-based sciences in 1975; the present book is another.

Systems science is general, widely applicable; we believe that, when judiciously used, it will reshape psychology and psychology's effect upon the world. And you, the reader, should you care to launch yourself into a career as a systems psychologist, will find your world very exciting indeed – and pleasantly remunerative, if you plan carefully, discipline yourself, and don't mind some risk and uncertainty.

## How systems come into being

In the last section, we examined the theoretical basis of systems and psychology, an area that we will help advance. At the same time, however, there is a multitude of immediate systems to implement, of "brush fires to put out". The remainder of this chapter and much of the rest of this book is devoted to the practical demands of systems analysis, engineering, evaluation, and management. The most relevant theoretical, experimental, and empirical findings that provide substance to human factors will be discussed in appropriate sequence. A first step in learning to work with systems involves understanding how they originate and develop. In this section, we offer four examples of levels of rigor, taken from the natural and artificial worlds.

The origin, development, and evolution of systems can be conceptualized in terms of spontaneity, type, and degree of control; prior planning and integration; and exigencies of the time. Thus, the development of biological systems is mainly a function of control coded in the genes by the sequence of the nitrogenous bases adenine, cytosine, thymine, and guanine within the deoxyribonucleic acid molecule; by organizers within certain tissues during embryonic development (as appropriate); and by environmental constraints introduced, especially by the presence of chemical and ionizing radiation agents. Such systems are effectively preprogrammed and integrated.

Next come systems based on the most thorough possible long-range analyses of mission, operational, and performance requirements (Ferguson, 1965), involving much prior planning and freedom from ephemeral exigencies. This category includes most modern engineering systems such as the Apollo manned spacecraft system.

In the past, however, and to some extent still, systems have "grown like Topsy". Long-range planning has been absent, often because of military pressures to "get the system operational on schedule". In other cases, subsystems have been superimposed on subsystems, as, for example, in the SCF, outlined earlier, which included specialized – that is, "program-peculiar" – test support facilities (antennas, computers, communications, recorders, conversion equipment, telemetry ground stations, and so on). This specialization reduced the effectiveness of the network of control, tracking, and communications facilities by increasing station "turnaround time", and by necessitating replicate and redundant equipment, additional specialized personnel, and computer programs, and so on. Subsequently, attempts have been made to simplify and integrate the network toward development of a real system. But many interesting human factors problems still remain unsolved in the areas of display, control, man–machine task allocation, and personnel numbers. Unpublished studies by the present author, for example, suggest that personnel reallocations could result in cost savings sufficient to pay for a new computer-generated cathode-ray-tube display system.

Most civil or social systems are just reaching this state. Hence, we can expect obsolescent or obsolete transportation or urban networks superimposed on one another before a true system is evolved. Similarly, buildings in cities tend to be designed apart from their function in the total urban ecology.

## Human roles in systems: the degree of mannedness

Human capabilities in the *operation* of such equipment as aircraft and radar were recognized as long ago as World War II. This recognition gave rise to fields variously called aviation psychology, applied experimental psychology, engineering psychology, human engineering, and ergonomics. Even after the importance of human capabilities and limitations in the operation of equipment had been recognized, albeit at the subsystem or "knob and dial" level, equipment continued to be poorly designed for *maintainability*. Still later, it was recognized that *controllability* is an attribute that can be differentiated from operability by virtue of complexity and the dynamic behavior of at least some equipment or vehicles.

At the present time there is considerable interest in man's role as *decision maker* and *manager*. A related role, particularly in complex military and space systems, is that of *analyst*. For example, analysts help evaluate the military threat, and are indispensable to the evaluation and interpretation of satellite tracking, trajectory, and telemetry (both hardware and biomedical) data. The role of analysis in system development is self-evident.

Other roles of men in systems include those of *planner*, *designer*, *producer*, and *evaluator*. These roles can be conceptualized and studied in terms of the amount of human involvement, and real-time or non-real-time nature of human participation, and the types of psychological factors involved. Systems are sometimes dichotomized as manned, e.g., projects Mercury, Gemini, and Apollo; or unmanned, e.g., projects Ranger, Surveyor, and Mariner (all these involve space missions). However, it is more meaningful to speak of *degrees of mannedness*. By definition, all man-made systems involve the participation of human beings.

Human roles also vary with time. Most attention has been paid to the more dramatic real-time operations and control activities. There *is* justifiable concern with human capabilities and limitations involved in, say, piloting an aircraft or spacecraft and in ground-based air traffic control. Yet system success or failure may depend as much on planning, inspection, quality control, computer program design, maintenance, and similar factors.

Finally, behavioral and life scientists have long emphasized clearly identifiable perceptual-motor skills and related physiological (e.g., reaction to high g forces) and anthropometric (reach and dimension) parameters. Poorly understood concepts such as "judgment" were implied. Today, decision making, short- and long-term memory, problem solving, and creativity are receiving much attention. Motivational and emotional factors are still largely ignored in systems contexts, although they are of considerable importance to the field of psychology as a whole. The problem of interfacing these psychological factors with equipment and environmental parameters and with anticipation, analysis, planning, management, and real-time operations is a major one in systems psychology – and in this book.

## What happens when the systems approach is not followed?

In conceptualizing and experimenting in the laboratory, if we make a mistake, leave out a variable, or neglect an interaction, we end up with an imprecise theory or limited or misleading results. The same type of mistake in the design or operation of a system can kill hundreds or potentially millions of people, can cost millions or billions of dollars, or can degrade the dignity of our lives.

For example, as this manuscript goes to press, there is considerable congressional, military, industrial, and public concern with military systems that have "gone wrong" in one way or another. In some cases, system hardware was never constructed. In other cases the systems were cancelled, prototype equipment and all, before they became operational. It is estimated that the cost of 68 such "historic" weapons systems over the past 15 years was about $10 billion.* Examples are the B-70 manned supersonic bomber, Skybolt B-52-launched air-to-ground missile, and a nuclear-powered aircraft. In addition to these historic examples, we must consider the contemporary F-111A and B fighter-bomber aircraft, C5A heavy transport aircraft, Cheyenne jet combat helicopter, and Air Force Manned Orbital Laboratory (MOL) spacecraft. We discuss some of these systems in more detail later. The point we emphasize is that we can learn much from our mistakes. We all make mistakes – whether government planner, military planner, industrial system developer, or urban planner. A critical look at what we have done, where we stand, and where we are going is in no way to be interpreted as "finger pointing".

The systems method provides a means for the orderly, integrated, and timely development of systems. Where

* For a list of these "systems that failed", see the *Congressional Record*, vol. 115, no. 59, April 15, 1969.

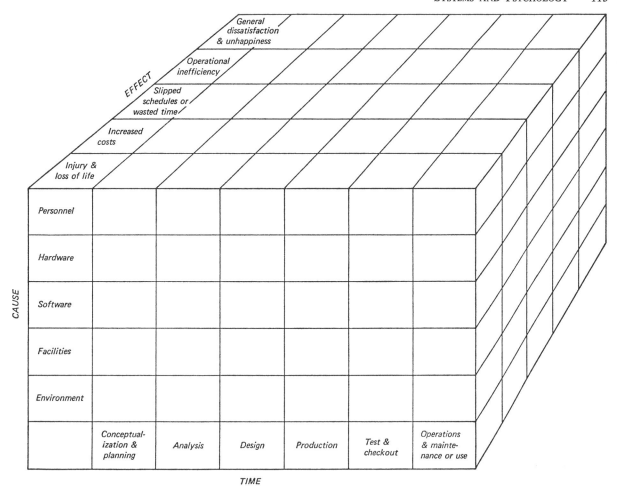

**Figure 6.3** First-level cause-effect-time matrix for indicating system degradation. *Note:* Progressively more refined matrices may be constructed. Use extreme caution in establishing cause-effect relationships.

people are involved, careful consideration must be given to human capabilities and limitations. *When these guidelines are not followed, penalties must be paid in terms of increased costs, decreased performance, slipped schedules, accidents, and loss of life.*

A number of examples of failure to follow systems guidelines are outlined in this section. Whereas the *individual events* within each example are probably stochastic, the gross picture in each case has been qualitatively replicated and the cases are of *unequivocal* pedagogic value. Thus, there *have* been several Boeing 727 landing crashes under similar conditions, several midair aircraft collisions under similar conditions, several misinstallations of constituents in missile systems under similar conditions, and so on. All the examples demonstrate some aspect of "human error" (whatever the scientific limitations of that term).

The study of human errors and accidents – classification, prediction, investigation, and prevention – is, of course, an organized specialty in human factors. Accidents themselves provide a valuable source of data to systems psychological understanding of human capabilities and limitations and to design. Throughout this book, however, the theme recurs of human error and how to prevent it. The hardware- and software-related* examples that follow stress dollar losses, loss of lives, decreased operation efficiency, and near

* In this chapter, *hardware* means equipment, including communications equipment; *software* means computer programs and documentation; *facilities* means buildings, roads, airstrips, docks, etc. These three, plus *personnel*, are the four major constituent subdivisions of the systems with which we will deal most of the time. Interfaces are important both between and within major constituents.

national chaos. System degradations can be roughly classified using the matrix illustrated in Figure 6.3. As more information becomes available, progressively finer matrices can be employed. Remember that *every event occurs within a context; therefore, simple cause–effect relationships are usually impossible to establish.* Even a concatenation or field of interacting events may be much harder to establish than the causal events in the cases we now discuss.

## Effect of failure to plan for multiple contingencies

*The great Northeast power failure: national chaos narrowly avoided.* The great Northeast power failure, the largest in American history (see Friedlander, 1966), provides a dramatic example of failures in systems thinking, planning, and management. On November 9, 1965, because of an unexpected flow of power, a circuit breaker tripped at a hydroelectric plant on the Niagara River in Ontario, triggering a power blackout that lasted many hours and involved 30 million people in the Northeast United States and parts of Canada.

Interconnected power systems comprise previously isolated local power company utilities tied together. But *system integration is often poorly advanced.* Each constituent utility company has different output capacities, dynamic inertia, speed-regulating methods, and loading systems. The interconnected systems are designed to meet a *single* large-scale contingency, but not a *combination* of simultaneous disturbances. Thus, when the circuit breaker in Ontario tripped, power shifted to other lines, which, because their own load-carrying capacities were now overloaded, tripped out in *cascade.* Significantly, the backup relay that triggered the disturbance had been set in 1963 at a capacity below that of the line, and perhaps unrelated to subsequent actual power flows. Thus, at about 5.16 P.M. on November 9, 1965, the power flow apparently reached the level at which the relay was set. The relay functioned properly, and its circuit breaker tripped out the line. *Operating personnel were not aware of the relay setting.*

Normally, in power systems, design provides for protection against loss of power generation, not against loss of a very large block of load. In this case, the outage of five transmission lines separated the Canadian power generation from its normal load, leading to a power reversal and superimposing additional power onto New York lines, exceeding the capacity of the New York system and leading to its breakup.

Thus, a simple power-limit pullout led to a chain reaction of power failures. This involved direction reversals of load, cascade tripping off of other units, loss of synchronization among utility units, automatic shutdown of generators to prevent damage, severing of lines to other power pools, and fragmentation of the Northeast power pool into four constituents, some of which possessed an excess of load and some an excess of generation. All this took only four seconds. Further sequential breakdowns of similar nature then occurred, with an end result of a widespread power blackout within about 12 minutes.

The results of the power failure included both damages to the generators themselves and interesting side effects relative to communications, transportation, and mass human behavior. These latter events dramatize that no system, whether power, transportation, communication, air defense, police, or what, exists out of context of parallel, subordinate, and supraordinate systems. In this case, television, some radio, teletype, and news printing were lost; railway and traffic lights ceased functioning; electrically driven gasoline pumps at service stations would not operate; 600,000 people were trapped for hours in subways, and thousands more in elevators; and operations were not possible at most airports. Fortunately, the telephone company, some hospitals, and other agencies possessed auxiliary power sources. Had the power failure taken place on a moonless, blizzardy night, a major catastrophe could have occurred. Implications for sabotage or attack on the nation are self-evident, as for mass panic behavior of the "War of Worlds" sort.

Further, restoration of power after the failure took many hours: Each utility company checked its own relays, circuit breakers, and switches; these companies' frequencies were synchronized with other parts of the system; city underground grid circuits were checked; the power generation sources, themselves to a greater (thermal) or lesser (hydro) extent dependent on electricity, were restored. At the time, the nature and location of the failure were unknown. This dramatizes again the need for sensing mechanisms, display of system status, and personnel trained in recognition of symptoms and contingency procedures.

Major lessons learned were recognition of the need for close human override of automatic equipment; planning for contingencies and improbable events; sensing, display, and monitoring of dynamic system status; better personnel training; and some backup, redundant, or emergency equipment. Further, the system failure dramatically demonstrated the integrated power system interface with other systems, and the resulting, even larger metropolitan or regional system. In avoiding a recurrence, guidance could perhaps be taken from such aerospace systems as SAGE (where track and other data must be maintained by Direction Centers adjacent to an "outage") or the SCF (where contact can be lost between the main control center and an outlying tracking station). An overall supervisory control system is also indicated.

Other power failures have occurred since the great November 9, 1965, power blackout.

## Effects of improper analysis of operator requirements

*SAGE: blue light and blinking displays.* The SAGE air defense system is a salient example of increased computer programming and environmental costs, and reduced efficiency, resulting from the failure to analyze, in depth, operator and controller task information requirements. Too much information – and clutter – was displayed at each console. This increased the load on the display-generating computer program, which then was unable to refresh the (flickering) display on each cathode-ray tube rapidly enough to maintain a character brightness level legible under the conditions of tube and phosphor development of the time. To avoid this problem, the familiar broad-band blue lighting system was used, involving blue filters over ordinary fluorescent light sources and orange filters over the cathode-ray tube faces. The displays could be read and certain other tasks performed under the same level of blue illumination. However, the lighting system imparted an eerie atmosphere to SAGE Direction and Combat Centers, and personnel often complained of headaches after exposure to the blue light. To our knowledge, no studies were made of the behavioral or physiological consequences of exposure to this atypical environment. The system interactions among personnel information requirements, computer programming design, hardware availability, display design, and environmental design are evident. For a consideration of other problems in SAGE and similar systems, see Israel (1965).

*Apollo Command Module: fire kills three astronauts.* The launch pad fire in the Apollo Command Module in January 1967 exemplifies dramatically a failure of systems engineering and management. The interacting factors included the 100 percent oxygen breathing atmosphere (selected for all U.S. manned space programs), increased combustibility of normally noncombustible materials in a pure-oxygen atmosphere, failure to apply available knowledge of such fire danger, nonfireproof space suit worn by the astronauts, the length of time required to open the escape hatch, and the electric arcing permitted by the circuitry design. Three

men died – yet prevention of this accident required no new advances in science or engineering. In systems work, little "knowns" seem often to add up to big "unknowns". The aftereffects of this accident included widespread managerial changes within both the National Aeronautics and Space Administration (NASA) and the contracting organizations, and a year's delay in implementation of the United States manned space program.

## Effects of improper methods in design, production, and test and checkout

*Nimbus B/Thorad/Agena: incorrect gyro installation leads to spacecraft destruction.* On May 18, 1968, a Nimbus B/Thorad/Agena space vehicle was launched at the Western Test Range, Vandenberg Air Force Base, California. The space vehicle consisted of a Thorad (long-tank Thor) primary launch vehicle, a second-stage Agena orbital vehicle, and a Nimbus B spacecraft. The Nimbus was the largest, most heavily instrumented NASA meteorological (weather-mapping) satellite. Within two minutes after launch, during the Thorad-powered portion of the flight, direct visual, tracking, and telemetry data indicated that the vehicle was exhibiting increasing oscillations in yaw and deviating considerably to the left of the prescribed trajectory, finally crossing the range safety boundary. The range safety officer than destroyed the vehicle.

The accident investigation board* found that the malfunction of the Thorad launch vehicle was caused by a misinstallation of the yaw-rate gyro, which provided negative pitch-rate data to the autopilot yaw-control channel, rather than the correct yaw-rate feedback signals. Such a misinstallation required rotation of the gyro (looking forward) 90 degrees clockwise about its long axis. *It was a clear case of human error* associated with: (1) "incorrect installation of the gyro in a correctly fabricated and installed gyro-mounting bracket", or (2) "installation of the gyro in an improperly made gyro bracket", according to the accident investigation report. Specific deficiencies are outlined below.

*Manufacturing.* Dowel pin holes were drilled in a fixture permitting their mislocation, which resulted in a "proper appearing", but actually incorrect, installation.
*Installation.* The installation drawings did not show the dowel pin holes in place, and the projections used did not accord with the natural view of the worker. In addition,

* This discussion is based partially on the board's report; see also *Aviation Week*, May 27 and August 19, 1968.

it was possible to depress the guide pin inadvertently, thus losing an orientation to correct installation.

Installation of the long-tank Thor gyro in the vertical position was awkward because of the physical location of the mounting bracket. The installer had to reach 2 to 3 feet above his head to mount the gyro (a one-man operation) because the permanent step ladder was too low. A variety of rate gyro brackets, intended for use on different models of the Thor booster, could be interchanged, installed on the wrong vehicle, or misinstalled. *Test and Inspection Procedures.* Procedural inadequacies made it impossible to accurately determine correctness of installation. For example:

- It was possible to obtain valid-appearing data even from an improperly installed gyro, because it was nearly impossible physically for the operator to move the gyro precisely into its intended plane.
- Check lists of *critical items* to inspect when verifying an installation were not provided.
- Even when members of the accident investigation board were present (such observation was known to the personnel concerned), numerous attempts were made to misconnect electrical connectors, sensitive equipment was nearly damaged, etc.
- The acceptance testing procedures and specifications of the primary contractor permitted acceptance of an incorrectly installed gyro.
- Procedures for conducting gyro tests (not related to differences in test equipment) differed among launch sites, at the factory, and even on the same launch complex during different phases of prelaunch testing.
- During testing, operators did not wear their headsets, leading to miscommunication of information.

This case exemplifies the omission of long understood human factors principles associated with design, manufacture, testing, procedures, and supervision. We also can note again the importance of taking a systems overview that recognizes the reinforcing of interacting effects of a sequence of events. *The cost: estimated at $62 million!*

*Apollo/Saturn: improper labeling leads to engine shutdown.* An improper installation of signal wires led to premature shutdown of two of the five second-stage engines on the Apollo 6/Saturn 502 space vehicle launched April 4, 1968 (*Aviation Week*, April 15, 1968). This was the second unmanned flight of the Saturn 5, and the error might well have contributed to the requirement for an additional unmanned

flight prior to the first manned flight and precluded hoped-for cost and time savings. NASA had hoped that a third unmanned flight, already programmed, could be cancelled. Postflight analysis revealed that a workman had followed the installation instructions properly, but that the wires had been mislabeled. The cost of another unmanned flight, if necessary to man-rate the launch vehicle, would be approximately $200 million. From the system standpoint, such an error could result from poor human engineering design for maintainability (including technical manuals), inadequate training or personnel selection, lack of motivation, inferior management, or some combination of these factors.

*Mariner/Atlas/Agena Venus flyby: computer program error leads to vehicle destruction.* In mid-1962, a Mariner/Atlas/Agena combination was launched from Cape Canaveral, Florida. The mission involved flight of the Mariner to the vicinity of the planet Venus. During operation of the second or sustainer stage of the Atlas, it was determined that the vehicle was off course and had to be destroyed. Subsequent investigation revealed a transcription error in coding the computer program, which resulted in the omission of *a hyphen* from the guidance equations before the equations were fed into the missile-guidance computer. The cost: over $35 million! This case exemplifies the importance of designing computer programs that do not assign rigidly prescribed meanings to easily overlooked or forgotten things like commas, spaces, and hyphens, and that ensure the identification of errors as they occur. It also illustrates that, although the actual perpetrator of an error or accident is usually an operator, factory worker, maintenance man, clerk, and so on, the error or accident situation may have received its essential structure long before, during problem formulation, analysis, or design.

## *Effects of failure to predict man–machine–environmental interactions in operations*

*DC-7B takeoff crash: evasive maneuver in response to optical illusion.* That degraded perception can lead to fatal aircraft accidents is illustrated by the following two cases attributed to optical illusions. In the first case (*Aviation Week*, January 2, 1967),* an Eastern Airlines DC-7B climbing on departure from John F. Kennedy International Airport (New York City) on February 8, 1965, crashed in the Atlantic Ocean off Long Island about 6.26 P.M. (and hence in

* From time to time, the weekly *Aviation Week and Space Technology* presents detailed reports on the results of aircraft accident investigations. It is recommended that you keep a file of these if you wish to begin specializing in this field.

darkness), killing all 84 persons aboard. The Civil Aeronautics Board (CAB) determined the probable cause to be evasive action taken by the DC-7B to avoid an *apparent* collision with a Pan American Boeing 707 descending to land. This maneuver placed the DC-7B aircraft in an attitude from which recovery in time was not possible.

Detailed analysis indicated that one or more illusions, associated with a paucity of stimuli, misleading cues, or a conflict among sensory cues – separately amenable to laboratory study but difficult to isolate operationally – may have been involved. Other perceptual factors such as vertigo led to disorientation. Following recognition of disorientation, as much as 36 seconds would have been required to reestablish orientation using instruments. Under conditions of this particular flight, this period was too long.

The abrupt avoidance maneuver had originally been precipitated by the belated ability of the pilot of the DC-7B to detect the jet aircraft visually. The initial evasive maneuver of the DC-7B was paralleled by an evasive maneuver by the 707, which appeared to negate the former. A second evasive maneuver, a rapid pull up and roll to the right, led to spatial disorientation of the crew of the DC-7B. This vertical bank could be corrected only within a time period less than that required for instruments. Postaccident flight tests indicated five out of six pilots experienced similar illusions of collision under equivalent flight conditions.

Ground radar separation of the two aircraft had disappeared at the time of the initial turn of the DC-7B toward the 707, although in reality the aircraft were separated by 1,000 feet vertical elevation. The CAB recommends that pilots avoid vectoring aircraft on directly converging courses because of problems associated with spatial disorientation. Also, the Federal Aviation Administration (FAA) promulgated a procedure requiring that 2,000- rather than 1,000-foot vertical separation be maintained between inbound and outbound flights in areas where illusions have occurred. Development of automatic collision-sensing and display systems also show promise in preventing future accidents of this kind.

The above case exemplifies the interactions among visual angle and visual field, themselves a function of cockpit design, window size, and placement; depth and movement perception based on size, change, and rate-of-change cues; decision making; mission profile and maneuvers; lack of a horizon and night-time flying conditions; contingency phenomena and operational procedures in both aircraft and at ground control; psychophysiological cues and responses to visual, labyrinthine, and probably kinesthetic stimuli; reaction times and other aspects of task time stress; and

cockpit display design. There is no alternative to our development of a total systems understanding.

*Boeing 707-Lockheed 1049C midair collision: cloud forms distort perception.* The midair collision of a Trans World Airlines (TWA) Boeing 707 and an Eastern Airlines Lockheed 1049C (*Aviation Week*, January 9, 1967) is another example of failure to consider all the variables in a dynamically operating system. This accident occurred on December 4, 1965, while the TWA and Eastern aircraft were enroute to John F. Kennedy International Airport and to Newark (New Jersey) Airport, respectively. The Boeing 707 was approaching the New York area, under an Instrument Flight Rules (IFR) flight plan at an assigned altitude of 11,000 feet. The Lockheed aircraft was approaching the area under an IFR flight plan at an assigned altitude of 10,000 feet. In close sequence, the crews of both aircraft perceived an apparent collision course and took evasive maneuvers, the Lockheed aircraft being pulled up and the Boeing then being rolled first to the right and then to the left. The aircraft then collided at approximately 11,000 feet. Both aircraft suffered structural damage; the Lockheed aircraft, forced to land in an open field, was destroyed by impact and fire. Four persons on the Lockheed aircraft suffered fatal injuries and 49, nonfatal injuries. There were no injuries aboard the Boeing 707. The CAB attributed the collision to misjudgment of altitude separation by the crew of the Lockheed aircraft because of an optical illusion created by the up-slope effect of cloud tops, followed by the previously described evasive measures. At the time of the collision, the area was overcast with cloud tops at just above 10,000 feet. Cloud tops tended to be higher to the north than to the south, resulting in an illusion of upward slope toward the north.

The above example dramatizes better than any laboratory abstraction the figure/ground relationships in perception. In this case, illusion appears to have been a function of the distances between the aircraft, their angular velocities, and the observed rate of change of the range-rate of each aircraft, all superimposed on the false horizon cues provided by the sloping clouds.

*Boeing 727 landing crash: display design and inclement weather.* A landing crash and burn of an American Airlines Boeing 727 aircraft occurred during darkness and inclement weather at Greater Cincinnati Airport. Fifty-eight of the 62 persons on board were fatally injured (*Aviation Week*, October 24, 1966). The CAB determined that the probable cause of the accident lay in the crew's failure to monitor properly the altimeters during a visual landing approach into environmental conditions leading to reduced visibility. However, careful scrutiny provides detail of a subtler nature involving psychological factors of attention, perception, motivation, and judgment interacting with task structure and load and with display design:

- Late departure from La Guardia (New York) Airport, together with increasing thunderstorm activity around Cincinnati, apparently prompted the crew to expedite their landing. A landing delay or instrument approach would have been a more prudent judgment. Much more psychological research should be performed on motivation, decision making, problem solving, and judgment under conditions of time- and load-stress and fatigue.
- Just before the crash, both pilots were preoccupied with maintaining visual reference to the runway, so that they neglected the altimeters.
- It is well known to human factors scientists that poor altimeter design has been associated with numerous aircraft accidents over the years. In this case, the three altimeters were Kollsman drum-pointer types; thousands of feet were indicated on a rotating drum visible through a slot, and hundreds of feet were indicated by a radial pointer. The range of the altimeters was from minus 1,500 feet to plus 50,000 feet. Crosshatching was printed on the drum adjacent to the critical values between plus 1,000 and minus 1,500 feet. Human factors and other developments leading to the incorporation of audible and additional visual alarms at low altitudes should prove valuable.
- System design should reflect contingency, low-probability, stress factor, and interaction events, particularly for critical segments of a mission profile, such as aircraft takeoff, approach, and landing. These factors should receive particular attention in information display design.

## The systems approach as a problem-solving and decision-making methodology

Systems methods applied to practical engineering problems are now intrinsic facets of our technology. These are largely pragmatic, even intuitive, and have grown through trial and error in the face of complex, previously unmanageable problems. Thus, in many ways, the systems approach is one of conceptual problem solving, an attitude or ability to perceive wholes, different levels, and interrelationships, rather than a formal regimen! It cannot be said that practice usually follows the general systems theory discussed

earlier in this chapter; on the contrary, theory often has been derived from observation of, and experience with, real-life problem areas and cases. The large-scale systems methods employed so far can thus be said to be more rational, empirical, and observational than experimental. Nevertheless, an appreciable engineering and management methodology has emerged, which has been associated with rather spectacular improvements in costs, efficiency, safety, and timeliness, and which is currently being applied to broader and broader vistas. For purposes of discussion, this methodology can be considered to have four iterative, usually overlapping and reinforcing segments: *analysis*, *engineering*, *management*, and *evaluation*. Collectively, these contribute to the *system-development process*, usually more realistically considered the *system-development cycle*.

### Systems analysis

Systems analysis may have a future orientation in which the realism of requirements is degraded by increasing uncertainties (see, for example, Quade, 1966). Ferguson (1965) cautions against expecting formalized, unchanging requirements. Further, in dealing with social systems, most of the input derives from the poorly understood, poorly quantifiable, and the uncertain.

Two examples of the uses and limitations of systems analysis are provided by the B-70 high-altitude supersonic bomber and the F-111 (TFX) fighter-bomber, both reflecting decisions from high levels within the United States government.

In each case, lively political controversy was generated, involving the Department of Defense, the Congress, the Air Force, and other agencies; the Department of Defense's insistence on rigor in the analysis of weapons systems requirements prevailed over more partisan political pressures. The B-70 eventually cost about $1·5 billion; two experimental aircraft were built, one of which eventually crashed, with loss of the pilot's life, during a public relations filming (see Carter, 1968). As originally planned, the program was to lead to a $20 billion fleet of these aircraft. The program was, in Carter's words, "a classic example of failure to analyze rigorously the mission to be performed and the state of the technology the mission requires". One of the most severe limitations of the program was its dependence on the development of an extremely high-resolution radar, associated processing and display equipment, and (perhaps an impossible) *human interpretation capability*. The Department of Defense questioned that this equipment could be available by 1967, as planned, or, indeed, even by 1970. Further, even if the aircraft (later renamed the RS-70) could be developed, *cost/effectiveness* studies indicated that cheaper, less vulnerable, and more effective weapons systems were available. The RS-70 made a poor showing when compared to the Polaris missile-carrying submarine and even to the antiquated B-52. In retrospect, it appears that application of rigorous systems analysis saved the taxpayers some $8·5 billion.

The case of the F-111 aircraft is still unclear. Development of this aircraft was also clouded by political factors, in this case involving industrial contractors as well. Further consideration of these factors is beyond the scope of this book. Suffice it to say that the Department of Defense attempted to reduce the cost of developing separate weapons systems for the Air Force and Navy by developing two versions, the Air Force F-111A and Navy F-111B, of the same basic aircraft. Unfortunately, the program has been plagued with difficulties. Both versions have cost considerably more than originally programmed. The Navy version has been cancelled; among other reasons, the Navy maintains the aircraft is too heavy and cumbersome to operate off a carrier. Several F-111A aircraft have crashed, both in the United States and, under combat conditions, in Southeast Asia.

## Systems engineering

Systems engineering connotes design of equipment, communications, computer programs, documentation, job or task assignments for personnel, or usually, some combination of all these factors. Where systems analysis leaves off and systems engineering begins is an arbitrary judgment: Systems analysis can be considered an integral part of systems engineering; alternatively, following Gilmore *et al.* (1967), for example, we might consider the dividing line to be the selection of performance requirements by the customer, user, or design team. Systems engineering, of course, usually has a hardware-design implication, as opposed to a pencil/paper or computer model and simulation implication. Systems engineering design starts when a system is fairly well defined. Traditionally, intuitions, judgments, economics, politics, and expediency have played as great a role in the selection of a design as has analysis, whether poor, good, or nonexistent.

*The essence of systems engineering lies within recognizing and understanding constituent specialties – for example, structures, electronics, power and fuel, and crew – and allowing these to function only within the context of integrating these efforts into a whole.* The systems engineer must be able to stimulate, direct, and utilize much work that is not

"systems engineering", but only specialty or constituent engineering.

Systems engineering developments have taken place within industry; methodology has been generalized from case histories and is based more on inference derived from direct observation than on experimentation or model building. According to Hall (1966), the universities have been rather uncritical in accepting even extreme claims from industry; there is a need for the active development of better curricula, more scholarly analysis and less promotionalism in the present literature, and the formulation and testing of models against actual situations.

## Systems management

We have seen that there are systems of all levels of complexity. The systems of primary concern in this book – weapons, aerospace, sociotechnical – are of *immense* complexity. The United States civilian space program, for example, has involved 20,000 contractors; some 300,000 engineers, technicians, and production workers; and expenditures of $35 billion over a decade, of which $24 billion alone has been spent on the manned space effort. This complexity of techniques, disciplines, specialists, contractors, concepts, resources, and building blocks must be brought together in an orderly manner. Engineering systems management or, more simply, systems management techniques have provided an impressive start in the right direction: that of *total system design and management.*

Systems management encompasses techniques developed since the early 1950s, primarily by the Air Force in connection with advanced aircraft, missile, and space systems. NASA's unmanned and manned space programs and the Navy's nuclear submarine projects have also contributed substantive ideas.* Systems management is a time-phased, monitorial, evaluative, and integrative activity involving the recognition of technical (for example, analytic) criteria; the assignment of organizational and contractual responsibilities; the definition of milestones; and the assignment of required documentation, hierarchies of contributing organizations, and feedback responses to initial documentation. In parallel with, and utilizing, systems analysis and engineering, it proceeds from the general to the specific, from the hypothetical to the real, and from the conceptual through research and development and production to the operational. The systems concepts of interface, evolution, and integration are of paramount importance.

* The Program Evaluation and Review Technique (PERT), a form of *network analysis* developed for the Navy, deserves special mention.

Before examining the main ideas of systems management in more detail, we will first review the situation before the early and mid-1960s. Neither the user nor the contractor was certain how the system would turn out until it appeared in the field. Often hardware was delivered, but no crews; if there were crews, they were untrained. Often, the operations and maintenance philosophy had not been thought out. Typically, the system was not available on schedule, was difficult to use, and required costly and time-consuming retrofit changes. To determine and correct deficiencies in the management of systems engineering, Air Force Systems Command (AFSC) of the U.S. Air Force conducted a series of management surveys (see, for example, AFSCP 375-2, 1963). Significant lessons were gained from 24 major contractors. Twenty-six major findings were cited. Those of particular relevance to this book include:

- Underestimation of costs.
- Limited standards of manpower utilization (the largest single element of costs) and the related, inefficient utilization of engineering manpower.
- Costly proliferation and duplication of reports.
- Insufficient systems analysis, systems design, and detailed design integration, leading to a cascading effect on production, logistics, and the like, and requiring costly design changes to correct early over-sights.
- Inadequate consideration of reliability in detailed design.
- Unrealistic engineering development and test schedules, leading to slipped schedules and increased costs.
- Late delivery of end items.
- Technical data late, costly, and inaccurate; related technical manuals not validated, late, and of poor quality.

As you might expect from the points emphasized so far, these deficiencies were seldom isolated problems but were *interrelated*, symptomatic of common management problems. As a result of these and other findings, the U.S. Air Force has developed a comprehensive body of systems management techniques, which have been extended to other branches of the Department of Defense. Much of applied systems management has also been derived from the cost/effectiveness systems analysis studies of the RAND school, which has received enthusiastic support in the Department of Defense. A descendant of the concept, the Planning–Programming–Budgeting System (PPBS), which attempts to provide a bridge between the already extant military planning and budgeting, is becoming rather widely accepted in state governments as well.

Systems management can be defined as *the process of planning, organizing, coordinating, controlling, and directing the combined efforts of contractors and other relevant organizations to accomplish system program objectives. It involves an integration, in a time-phased manner, of organizations, responsibilities, knowledge, and data and documentation.* The details of the Air Force program are given in the AFR 375-1 through 375-5 series and the AFSCM 375-1 through 375-5 series. Systems management concepts as applied to personnel subsystem (human factors) management are presented in the *Handbook of Instructions for Aerospace Personnel Subsystem Design* (HIAPSD), AFSCM 80-3.* Most important of the 375 series for our purposes is AFSCM 375-5, *Systems Engineering Management Procedures* (1964). A review of this document and its uses, available to the general reader, is provided by Gelbwaks (1967).

The management of the systems engineering process entails as early and accurate an identification as possible of *total system* requirements, control over the evolution of requirements and designs, integration of technical specialty efforts including human factors, and development of basic data and documentation. In the broadest sense, systems management is applied over the life cycle of the system, including conceptualization, design, development, test and evaluation, operations and maintenance, and senescence and replacement. In actuality, one could make a distinction between *systems development management* and *systems operational management*: The basic Air Force regulation AFR 375-1 states, for example, "systems management does not apply to *actual use* of a system during the operational phase". Thus, the degree and type of management control, the nature of the scientific or technical and engineering processes, and the organizations involved differ among say a conceptual system, an operational system, and a system about to be phased out. In the past, so-called "R&D systems" have been largely free of management control.

The heart of the management of complex systems lies in the identification and control over specific events in the life history of the system. The life cycle of *Air Force Systems* is divided into four formal phases which in turn may be further divided into subphases. The four phases and their salient events can be summarized as follows:

1. *Conceptual phase:* determination of a system concept that will satisfy the stated (mission) requirements and is

---

* The names and codes for military organizations frequently change, as does the nomenclature for documentation. HIAPSD has been revised and updated, and the design (but not the management) portions have been reissued as AFSC DH 1-3 (1969).

indicated by analysis as suitable, feasible, and acceptable in terms of *performance*, *cost*, and *schedule*; and specification of functions, system interfaces, and gross performance and design requirements.

2. *Definition phase:* definition in greater detail of the basic concept, personnel, computer programs, equipment, facilities, costs, and schedules leading to acquisition phase contractor selection.

3. *Acquisition phase:* design, production, and test (Categories I and II) of the system; the acquisition phase may overlap with the operational phase.

4. *Operational phase:* system test (Category III) and evaluation to determine accomplishment of the mission objectives; and actual operation of the system.

Within and, particularly, among the phases, specific documents are prepared and released by given organizations; these documents call for responses on the part of other organizations and are reflected in feedback modifications of the original documentation.

Such system development depends at each phase on the *previous* development of *basic building blocks*. A series of R&D categories has been established by the Department of Defense in the sequence: basic research, exploratory development, advanced development, and so on, eventually leading to the operational system. Psychologists have the opportunity to participate in basic research and all phases of the system life cycle. They have made contributions in universities, industry, and military and associated non-military organizations.*

There is a burgeoning specialty area dealing with management and the manager, and psychologists have the opportunity to make major contributions both within the field of management, viewed as a system, and with regard to the interpersonal capabilities and limitations of the individual manager. The term *behavioral science* sometimes is used in a very specialized sense to describe the study of human behavior in organizations; in practice, it is more circumscribed with a small-group-dynamics emphasis. Fields of concentration include such areas as leadership, sensitivity

---

* Systems analysis, engineering, and management skills, as opposed to specialty training, are not common. For this reason, the Air Force has used intermediary "think tank" organizations such as the RAND, Aerospace, and Mitre corporations, which perform advanced research, study, and planning, or act as intermediaries between the military user and the design, and frequently operations and maintenance, industrial contractor. Such organizations frequently have General Systems Engineering and Technical Direction (GSE/TD) responsibilities.

training in which the manager hopes to develop a better awareness of himself and his effect on other people, and organizational change.

*Management information and control systems* are bona fide systems that present all the challenges of complex systems and provide the psychologist with all the opportunities to apply the techniques and information to which this book is devoted. Later, we discuss motivation, morale, job satisfaction, supervision, and group relations – all topics of particular interest to management psychology. For additional general reading on systems management see Johnson *et al.* (1967); on management psychology, see Leavitt (1964) and Leavitt and Pondy (1964); and on management systems, see Schoderbek (1967).

Experience with systems management programs has shown that effective documentation (including use of computer methods) is an absolute necessity for systems development. However, there is evidence of too strict adherence to *procedure*. Numerous industrial contractors have complained about stifled creativity and enforced conformity especially during the early conceptual phase, tight control over their design activities, and the time spent filling out and maintaining accountability forms that (the contractors maintain) could better be spent on design itself. Similarly, there is some evidence of misapplication of tight control to smaller, one-of-a-type or conceptual systems.

Also, it must be remembered that systems management approaches and techniques are evolving. We have a good thing, but it's not foolproof. Consider the C5A heavy-transport aircraft, developed under sophisticated systems management concept, which nevertheless has been estimated to cost twice as much per aircraft as originally budgeted. We must constantly refine our methods, adapt our techniques to fit experiences, and work toward the advancement of systems theory.

## Systems evaluation

Systems evaluation begins with the first consideration of pencil–paper alternatives and continues through the use of nonwired, wired but static, and dynamic *mockups* and *simulators*, related in various degrees of fidelity to expected environmental conditions. Sophisticated simulations play a large role in such systems evaluations. As the operational date draws nearer, more and more realistic evaluations become possible. Thus, in the Air Force systems management terminology, *Category I testing* typically involves in-plant (within the factory) subsystem testing and evaluation utilizing design engineer personnel; *Category II testing* is system testing in the field, usually with mixed design and user personnel; and *Category III testing* is system testing in the field under near-operational conditions. "Testing" cannot be separated from "evaluation" in these contexts. Personnel subsystem testing and evaluation is a specialized aspect of particular importance to this book.

The value of systems testing and evaluation – and of systems analysis – rests on successful *definition of criteria*, which presents a major, largely unresolved problem, especially in social systems.

## Applied systems psychology: engineering psychology and human factors

In the practical, applied sense, systems psychology has meant engineering psychology and human factors. Engineering psychology, originally largely an outgrowth of experimental psychology,* is concerned mainly with the design of equipment, facilities, and environments to match the capabilities and limitations of people; and to a lesser extent with the selection and training of personnel. Engineering psychology originated in World War II (see Christensen, 1964; Grether, 1968), when it became clear that operational deficiencies in bombing, artillery targeting, submarine sonar detection, and aircraft were associated with poor equipment design and personnel selection and training.† Psychologists were asked to examine these problems, and when the war ended, several research laboratories and independent consulting companies were established. Interdisciplinary work with engineers began with the study of aircraft cockpits, radar and sonar displays, panel layouts, individual displays and controls, fire-control systems, and so on. Human factors groups were founded, grew, and proliferated in numerous military and industrial organizations. Many significant books were published and well received; some were revised and published in later editions (see especially Chapanis *et al.*, 1949; Morgan *et al.*, 1963‡ Gagné, 1963; Woodson and Conover, 1964; and Meister and Rabideau, 1965). The military released *design-criterion* documentation – guidance and specifications – which generally is evolving toward applicability across all departments of the Department of Defense.

* The term *applied experimental psychology* was an early synonym.

† Even before World War II, designers were concerned with simplifying the aircraft pilots' job. Information from such instruments as the artificial horizon, rate-of-turn indicator, altimeter, and directional gyro was integrated at a single point of observation and displayed on a cathode-ray tube (Anonymous, 1938).

‡ This so-called "Joint Services (Army-Navy-Air Force) Guide" is scheduled for release in an updated version.

Considerable progress in engineering psychology has been made, but the route has not always been clear, the road often rough, and much remains to be done by imaginative, aggressive people interested in specializing in the field. For example, there is considerable confusion in terminology. Engineering psychology and human factors are *not* synonymous: Some 40 percent of people who consider themselves to be human factors experts are *not* psychologists. Further, in practice it is easy to confuse engineering psychology with human engineering, which as we shall see is a single aspect of human factors. Also, in practice, human engineering has been much more subsystem-, even modular-oriented (we should say subsystem- or modular-limited) than should be the case. Then there is a whole group of people who variously call themselves training experts and training directors, who have their own society, the *American Society of Training Directors*, and who may have little association with human factors people. The same is true of the aerospace medicine specialists and the *Aerospace Medical Association*. Finally, we must consider our colleagues in Europe whose specialty, ergonomics, entails both the work of human engineers in the United States and things like work measurement (see, for example, Murrell, 1965). For these reasons, we will use the terms *human factors scientist* and *human factors psychologist* to indicate the expert, psychologist and otherwise, who is concerned with all the interacting elements of the personnel subsystem discussed in the next section. However, he is usually also a specialist in one area – for example, engineering psychology or anthropometry. With regard to psychology in the development of a *given* system, engineering psychology, training psychology, and personnel psychology might be thought of as specialties of human factors psychology. When the human factors psychologist begins to generalize across systems at all levels and to work toward development of basic theories and methods of application, he becomes a *systems psychologist*.

Even more crucial than semantic problems has been that of securing the rightful place of systems psychology among the other sciences and establishing the practical value of its findings. The early work cited above made good sense to most observers, including military managers, and after 1957, contractual requirements, particularly within the Air Force "family", forced the inclusion of human factors considerations – and the hiring of human factors specialists! Release of design-criterion documentation aided this effort immensely. Yet the human factors man, as a human engineer, usually found himself doing what became known as "knob-and-dial" work, minutiae such as indicating the color coding of controls. Design was already frozen when he came into the picture, and isolated from the planning phase, he was powerless to alter situations that, according to his expertise, clearly violated sound principles relating to human capabilities and limitations. At the same time, in other parts of the organization, other human factors specialists were working, usually with great replication of effort, on training requirements, plans, and programs; manpower determinations; and test and evaluation. Appreciation of human factors contributions was often quite perfunctory. Many corporations, both profit and not-for-profit, employed thousands of engineers, but at most a few human factors workers.

*Clearly, there was a need both to integrate human factors efforts and to bring this integrated activity at least a couple of years "upstream" into the problem-definition, conceptualization, and planning stages of the system. Coupled with this management shift was the preeminent need to convince high-level decision makers in industrial organizations, the military, and government what human factors and psychology can do.*

The establishment of the personnel subsystem concept and program was a step of fundamental importance in meeting the first two needs. Meeting the last need is a matter of (1) diversification of effort; (2) taking a good look at ourselves and where we are going; (3) developing a basic body of theory and methodology, including, but not limited to, quantified methodology; and (4) education, training, and selling ourselves. Human factors scientists now participate at the several stages in the development of many different kinds of systems: weapons and nonweapons; aerospace, ground-based, and undersea; governmental and commercial. They study problems as varied as those involving communication with computers, automobile safety, telephone-user preferences, and aerospace pilot models. For a review of human factors activities up to the mid 1960s, see Lindgren (1966a, 1966b).

## The personnel subsystem: a framework for systems management

The importance of the total systems approach, involving development of the appropriate subsystems in *parallel*, is now widely recognized. Thus, a human or crew or personnel subsystem can be recognized and defined, and planned and designed in relation to the structure, power, electronic, environmental control, and other subsystems. Gone are the days, hopefully forever, when aircraft are delivered with no (trained) crews; or costly retrofits are required to make the aircraft or ground system operable or safe.

Systems interactions *within* human factors must also be

recognized. The relationships among oxygen partial pressure breathing requirements of Apollo astronauts, the flammability of materials and consequent degradation of safety, the design of the space suit, and the design of the escape hatch have been mentioned. Similarly, there is a clearly recognizable tradeoff among human engineering, training, and personnel selection. The better human engineered a system, the easier and less specialized the training and the more typical the crew member chosen. For example, flexibility in personnel assignment is reduced by a lack of standardization in type and layout of equipment performing similar or identical functions in satellite tracking stations. And placement of some controls in the navigator's position of certain models of the B-52 manned bomber appear to require the arm reach of an orangutan, an Air Force (personnel) Specialty Code hard to fill!

To manage the integrated development of human factors both internally and in relation to other efforts such as reliability engineering, civil engineering, and equipment design, and in the overall context of systems management, the Air Force (about 1960) defined the personnel subsystem (PS) program. PS is a time-phased program involving management, analysis, design, selection, training, and test and evaluation.* It emphasizes man's capabilities and limitations, and their effects on system performance, from the earliest phases of consideration of a (possible) system, through the conceptual, definition, acquisition, and operational phases. Even an obsolescent or senescent system can provide general concepts and specific performance data for incorporation into a new-generation system.

The personnel subsystem concept involves definition of a number of so-called *elements*, which can be interpreted roughly as subfields within human factors and aggregates of the subfields. The number of these elements changes with experience. The 14 defined in Table 6.3 are now in the process of being integrated into a more manageable number; this involves some change in nomenclature. For example, many of the PS elements deal with training and could be grouped together for purposes of generalization. However, it should be noted that the listing in Table 6.3 is to some extent sequential. Thus, for the most part, analysis precedes design and the determination of types and numbers of personnel or training requirements and plans. The personnel equipment data can be thought of as prerequisite to human engineering, QQPRI, and so forth. Similarly, training concepts are basic to the preparation of training

---

* The term *effectiveness engineering* has been utilized to describe an integrated approach to human factors, maintainability, reliability, safety, cost analysis, and value engineering.

**Table 6.3** Personnel subsystem elements (Prepared from text in Headquarters Air Force Systems Command, 1967)

1. *Personnel equipment data (PED)*. Centrally controlled, multilevel, multisource, analytic data on personnel interactions with equipment, environments, etc.
2. *Human engineering*. Application of knowledge of man's capabilities and limitations relative to equipment, facilities, environments, jobs, procedures, computer programs, and performance aids, to achieve optimum safety, comfort, and effectiveness compatible with system requirements
3. *Life support*. Application of physiological, anthropometric, and psychological principles to ensure man's integrity, health, safety, and comfort
4. *Qualitative and quantitative personnel requirements information (QQPRI)*. Determination of the kinds and numbers of persons required in the system for operating, maintaining, controlling, etc.
5. *Trained personnel requirements*. List of personnel requiring system-specific training to support the system through the acquisition phase
6. *Training concepts*. Early planing based on estimates of Air Training Command and of the User Command
7. *Manpower authorizations*. Early allocations required for advanced planning
8. *System manning and trained personnel requirements*. Specialized planning produced for higher headquarters when special manpower problems are anticipated
9. *Training equipment planning information*. Recommendations on the types and quantities of training equipment required
10. *Training equipment development*. Procedures for developing and producing training equipment
11. *Training facilities*. Real estate and buildings used exclusively for training
12. *Technical publications*. Development of manuals to support operations, maintenance, and training
13. *Training plans*. Methods and schedules to effect training
14. *Personnel subsystem test and evaluation (PST&E)*. Coordinated subsystem and system testing under preoperational conditions

plans. Note, however, that system development is usually *iterative*: Test and evaluation data may modify the original requirements and initial design.

## Summary and conclusions

This chapter has set the theme of the book.* The artificial systems with which we are primarily concerned lie along a continuum of different types, degrees, and relative directness of human participation. For convenience, we can designate four types of systems: *automatic, man–machine, sociotechnical*, and *social*. Man does participate as manager, planner, analyst, designer, production worker, operator, controller, maintainer, supervisor, evaluator, and user. In any given position, error, accident, or inefficiency may occur. A consideration of man's capabilities and limitations thus is critical to successful system operation.

It is tempting to seek guidance in the traditional fields of psychology: perception, intelligence, learning, motivation, and so on. To an extent we have done so, as reflected in some of the chapter titles, but this is an insufficient model. It can be embellished by viewing man as a system constituent, which at a given time and in a given environmental context acts on, changes, or processes something – at the level of psychology, usually information, but also energy or materials.

* [*Systems Psychology*, Ed.]

As a system constituent, man modifies and is modified by his fellow constituents – the machines, other men, and facilities; by the communicative connections among these constituents; and by the general ambiance. When the outside forces – physical, chemical, biological, and social – exceed a tolerance level set at the moment within the man, or these forces interact with internal psychological forces to reduce that tolerance, we can say that *stress* has occurred. Associated with stress can be severely degraded performance, both on specific tasks and in terms of general efficiency. In all cases, inputs to the system constituent are converted somehow into outputs. The search for the appropriate transfer functions is one of our ongoing responsibilities; therefore, the S–O–R paradigm can be added to the model for the book and is accordingly reflected in the chapter organization.

It is probably futile for psychology to proceed by itself apart from integration within the mainstream of science and technology. The body of a science can be an ephemeral thing. This does not mean aping the terminology of physics, chemistry, biology – or of information theory! Sciences can mutually reinforce themselves, each science both giving specifics and receiving generalities. General systems theory, cybernetics, and bionics are attempts toward this mutual support. Progress in psychology should follow from using the generally applicable systems concepts and methods. Otherwise, there is a formidable communications barrier in trying to translate psychological terms into, for example, engineering terms; there is a real danger in being left by the wayside. We have defined a new field, *systems psychology*, because there is no appropriate term within psychology, and because specialties like engineering psychology, industrial psychology, and human factors have been limited in practice. Systems psychology is necessary because of the shifting boundaries of knowledge; because all new science and technology *must* be interdisciplinary; and because of the hierarchical nature, complexity, and generalizability of our effort. Systems psychology, a branch of systems science, then, provides the theoretical framework of our effort.

Burgeoning almost completely apart from the somewhat erratic developments of systems theory, the pragmatic advances of systems analysis, systems engineering, and systems management have shaken our society to its roots. Psychology itself has found expression in human factors. Since World War II, great progress has been made, but major battles remain to be won. A major advance has been the development of the personnel subsystem concept and program within systems engineering and management. This concept also is reflected in the chapter structure of this book.

A major problem still derives from the self-identity of psychology and of human factors; their direction, orientation, and extension; and general education in their practical usefulness. When a systems approach incorporating psychological factors is *not* followed in design and management, literally *terrible* things can result at worst, frustrating and costly things at best. We can be of greatest service to our organization, our society, our nation, and our world by developing our theory, coalescing our methods, assuming a large-scale perspective of problems, and *aggressively* attacking these problems. It's an exciting world, offering adventure at each step. You, our young champion, are a far cry from the poor, jaded chap who entered this chapter.

## References and bibliography

Anonymous (1938) "Simplifying the Pilot's Task", *Scientific American*, December, 159(6), 308.

Anonymous (1968a) "Use of Existing Spares Urged for Early Nimbus Replacement", *Aviation Week and Space Technology*, May 27, 88(22), 31.

Anonymous (1968b) "Nimbus Abort Laid to Gyro Misalignment", *Aviation Week and Space Technology*, Aug. 19, 89(8), 17.

Ashby, W. R. (1960) *Design for a Brain*, New York: Wiley.

Boulding, K. E. (1956) "General Systems Theory: The Skeleton of Science", *Management Science*, April 2, 197–208.

Boulding, K. E. (1964) "General Systems as a Point of View", in Mesarovic, M. D. (ed.), *Views on General Systems Theory*, Proceedings of Second Systems Symposium at Case Institute of Technology, New York: Wiley.

Butsch, L. M. and H. L. Oestreicher (Cochairmen) (1964) *1963 Bionics Symposium: Information Processing by Living Organisms and Machines*, Wright-Patterson AFB, Ohio: Aeronautical Systems Division, Technical Report ASD-TDR-63-946, March.

Carter, L. J. (1968) "The McNamara Legacy: A Revealing Case History – Death of the B-70", *Science*, Feb. 23, 159(3817), 859–63.

Christensen, J. M. (1964) *The Emerging Role of Engineering Psychology*, Wright-Patterson AFB, Ohio: Aerospace Medical Research Laboratories, Technical Report AMRL TR-64-88, September.

Chapanis, A., *et al.* (1949) *Applied Experimental Psychology: Human Factors in Engineering Design*, New York: Wiley.

Coan, R. W. (1968) "Dimensions of Psychological Theory", *American Psychologist*, 23(10), 715–22.

Fein, L. (1961) "The Computer-Related Sciences (Synnoetics) at a University in the Year 1975", *American Scientist*, June, 49(2), 149–68.

Ferguson, J. (1965) "Military Electronic Systems for Command and Control", *IEEE Transactions on Military Electronics*, April, MIL-9(2), 80–7.

Friedlander, G. D. (1966) "The Northeast Power Failure – A Blanket of Darkness", *IEEE Spectrum*, 3(2), 54–73.

Gagné, R. M. (ed.) (1963) *Psychological Principles in System Development*, New York: Holt, Rinehart and Winston.

Gelbwaks, N. L. (1967) "AFSCM 375-5 As a Methodology for System Engineering", *IEEE Transactions on Systems Science and Cybernetics*, June, SSC-3(1), 6–10.

Gérardin, L. (1968) *Bionics*, New York: McGraw-Hill.

Gilmore, J. S., *et al.* (1967) *Defense Systems Resources in the Civil Sector: An Evolving Approach, an Uncertain Market*, Washington, D.C.: U.S. Arms Control and Disarmament Agency, Paper E-103, July.

Goslin, D. A. (1968) "Standardized Ability Tests and Testing", *Science*, Feb. 23, 159(3817), 851–5.

Grether, W. F. (1968) "Engineering Psychology in the United States", *American Psychologist*, 23(10), 743–51.

Hall, A. D. and R. E. Fagen (1956) "Definition of System", in Bertalanffy, L. von and Rapoport, A. (eds.), *General Systems Yearbook of the Society for the Advancement of General Systems Theory*, I, 18–28.

Hall, A. D. (1966) "The Present Status and Trends in Systems Engineering", *IEEE Transactions on Systems Science and Cybernetics*, August, SSC-2(1), 1–2.

Headquarters Air Force Systems Command (1967) *Handbook of Instructions for Aerospace Personnel Subsystems Design*, Andrews AFB, Washington, D.C.: AFSCM 80–3.

Headquarters Air Force Systems Command (1969) *Personnel Subsystems*, Andrews AFB, Washington, D.C.: AFSC DH 1–3.

Israel, D. R. (1965) *System Design and Engineering for Real-Time Military Data Processing Systems*, Bedford, Mass.: Electronic Systems Division, Technical Report ESD-TDR 64-168, January (AD 610 392*).

Johnson, R. A., *et al.* (1967) *The Theory and Management of Systems*, New York: McGraw-Hill.

Jones, R. W. and J. S. Gray (1963) "System Theory and Physiological Processes", *Science*, May 3, 140(3566), 461–6.

Kalisch, R. B. (1968) "The Locomotion Quadruped", *OAR Research Review*, VII(8), 4–5.

Leavitt, H. J. (1964) *Managerial Psychology* (2nd ed.), Chicago: The University of Chicago Press.

Leavitt, H. J. and L. R. Pondy (eds.) (1964) *Readings in Managerial Psychology*, Chicago: The University of Chicago Press.

Lettvin, J. Y., *et al.* (1959) "What the Frog's Eye Tells the Frog's Brain", *Proceedings of the IRE*, 47(11), 1940–51.

Lindgren, N. (1966a) "Human Factors in Engineering: Part I – Man in the Man-Made Environment", *IEEE Spectrum*, 3(3), 132–9.

Lindgren, N. (1966b) "Human Factors in Engineering: Part II – Advanced Man–Machine Systems and Concepts", *IEEE Spectrum*, 3(4), 62–72.

Lindgren, N. (1968) "Purposive Systems: The Edge of Knowledge", *IEEE Spectrum*, 5(4), 89–100.

Lockard, R. B. (1968) "The Albino Rat: A Defensible Choice of a Bad Habit?", *American Psychologist*, 23(10), 734–42.

Meister, D. and G. F. Rabideau (1965) *Human Factors Evaluation in System Development*, New York: Wiley.

Morgan, C. T., *et al.* (eds.) (1963) *Human Engineering Guide to Equipment Design*, New York: McGraw-Hill.

Murphy, C. S. (Chairman) (1966) "Crew Monitoring Cited in 727 Crash (Civil Aeronautics Board Accident Investigation Report)", *Aviation Week and Space Technology*, Oct. 24, 95–122.

* Defense Documentation Center (DDC) Acquisition Number.

Murphy, C. S. (Chairman) (1967a) "Collision-Course Illusion Cited in Accident (CAB Accident Investigation Report)", *Aviation Week and Space Technology*, Jan. 2, 86(1), 84–98.

Murphy, C. S. (Chairman) (1967b) "Optical Illusion Cited as Cause of Collision (CAB Accident Investigation Report)", *Aviation Week and Space Technology*, Jan. 9, 86(2), 81–97.

Murrell, K. F. H. (1965) *Human Performance in Industry*, New York: Reinhold.

Newell, A. and H. A. Simon (1961) *Computer Simulation of Human Thinking*, Santa Monica, Calif.: The RAND Corporation Paper, P-2276, April 20.

Normyle, W. J. (1968) "Nimbus B to Test New Weather Sensors", *Aviation Week and Space Technology*, May 6, 88(19), 71–9.

Pauling, L. (1968) "Orthomolecular Psychiatry", *Science*, April 19, 160(3825), 265–71.

Quade, E. S. (1966) *Some Problems Associated with Systems Analysis*, Santa Monica, Calif.: The RAND Corporation Paper, P-3391, June (AD 634 375).

Reichardt, W. (1961) "Autocorrelation, a Principle for the Evaluation of Sensory Information by the Central Nervous System", in Rosenblith, W. A. (ed.), *Sensory Communication*, 303–17, M.I.T. Press and Wiley.

Rosenblatt, F. (1958) "The Perceptron: A Probabilistic Model for Information Storage and Organization in the Brain", *Psychological Review*, November, 65(6), 386–408.

Rowe, W. D. (1965) "Why Systems Science and Cybernetics?", *IEEE Transactions on Systems Science and Cybernetics*, November, SSC-1(1), 2–3.

Schoderbek, P. P. (ed.) (1967) *Management Systems: A Book of Readings*, New York: Wiley.

Simon, H. A. (1961) *Modeling Human Mental Processes*, Santa Monica, Calif.: The RAND Corporation Paper, P-2221, February.

Steele, J. E. (Chairman) (1960) *Bionics Symposium: Living Prototypes – The Key to New Technology.* Wright-Patterson AFB, Ohio: Wright Air Development Division, Technical Report 60-600, December.

Swanson, R. W. (1968) "Automata in Motion", *OAR Research Review*, VII(10), 12–13.

Thomas, B. K., Jr (1968) "Apollo 6 Wiring Flaw Found as Next Mission Is Studied", *Aviation Week and Space Technology*, April 15, 88(16), 28–9.

van Bergéijk, W. A. (1960) "Nomenclature of Devices Which Simulate Biological Functions", *Science*, Oct. 28, 132(3435), 1248–9.

van Bergéijk, W. A. and L. D. Harman (1960) "What Good Are Artificial Neurons?", *Bionics Symposium: Living Prototypes – The Key to New Technology*, Wright-Patterson AFB, Ohio: Wright Air Development Division, Technical Report 60-600, December, 395–406.

von Bertalanffy, L. (1956) "General Systems Theory", *General Systems Yearbook of the Society for the Advancement of General Systems Theory*, I, 1–10.

White, V. (1963) "A Multiple Satellite Real-Time Control Network", *IEEE Transactions on Military Electronics*, October, MIL-7(4), 285–95.

Wiener, N. (1948) *Cybernetics, or Control and Communication in the Animal and the Machine*, New York: Wiley.

Wilson, W. E. (1965) *Concepts of Engineering System Design*, New York: McGraw-Hill.

Woodson, W. E. and D. W. Conover (1964) *Human Engineering Guide for Equipment Designers* (2nd ed.), Berkeley, Calif.: University of California Press.

Young, O. R. (1964) "A Survey of General Systems Theory", in von Bertalanffy, L. and Rapoport, A. (eds.), *General Systems Yearbook of the Society for General Systems Research*, IX, 61–80.

Yovits, M. C., *et al.* (eds.) (1962) *Self-Organizing Systems 1962*, Washington, D.C.: Spartan Books.

# 7 The human operator in control systems
## *by George A. Bekey*

## Introduction

The ultimate responsibility of the human element in a man–machine system is to take *action* that influences the system. The automobile driver receives inputs from the road ahead, from his instruments, from the sound of the engine, from the acceleration forces on his body, and so forth. He processes all this information to arrive at decisions regarding appropriate actions. Finally, he must act – by braking, turning the steering wheel, accelerating, or perhaps by some combination of these actions. This action is the man's *control input* to the machine. Thus, control may be viewed as *the end product of a chain of processes, which begin with information processing and continue through decisions.\**

The *relation* between information theory, decision theory, and control theory may also be viewed from a mathematical point of view. Thus, a decision to act may be viewed from the standpoint of ultimate *utility* to the human controller. The relevant mathematical disciplines here are *value theory* or *utility theory*. On the other hand, a decision may be viewed from the standpoint of *maximizing* the information transfer through a system. The relevant dimension of decision theory here would be the *probability theory*. Finally, the decision to act, in the presence of uncertainty, may be constrained by system stability considerations, in which case the relevant discipline is *control theory*. In many practical situations (for example, the pilot's control of an aircraft following failure of a stability augmentation system) the maximization of information transfer or the evaluation of a rational basis for decisions may both have to be subordinated to a need to maintain stability or face complete disaster. Nevertheless, it should be clear that even in such extreme situations, the pilot receives and processes information, makes decisions and exerts control.

In the past, information theory, decision theory, and control theory have developed as *separate* disciplines. Only now is control theory beginning to use the available tools in the other disciplines. Thus, interest is beginning to focus on the adaptive and decision-making behavior of human controllers in complex systems. Although each discipline is treated separately in this book, as the reader reviews the classical problems of manual control at the beginning of this chapter, he should bear in mind the applicability of the concepts as discussed in earlier chapters. *It is quite possible that the most significant developments in the study of man–machine systems in the next decade will include those based on a synthesis of information theory, decision theory, and control theory.*

This chapter surveys the role of man as an element or constituent in a *control system*. Such systems include the steering of an automobile, manual attitude control of a spacecraft, the control of piloted aircraft, manual process control, air traffic control, and, in certain cases, man–computer systems. In all these systems, the human element provides certain inputs to a group of machines, devices, or other fixed elements (sometimes known collectively as "the plant"), and he receives feedback information regarding the state of the system. In general, *a control system involves the manipulation of certain variables to achieve desired or reference values.* Such a reference value may be *fixed*, as for instance the "set point" in the control of a furnace or chemical reactor, or it may be *variable*, as in the pursuit of an evasive target by means of an adjustable set of crosshairs. In general, the fundamental man–machine control system can be viewed as in the block diagram of Figure 7.1, where inputs to the plant are provided by means of a set of *controls* and feedback is obtained by means of *displays*. The man's receptors provide sensory inputs to the central nervous system from which a response $R$ originates. Thus, *from a systems point of view, man can be viewed as an information-processing device. He converts sensory inputs into appropriately coded muscular outputs.* A complete analysis of man as an element in the system of Figure 7.1 requires an understanding of the characteristic of the receptors and effectors, the nature of the information processing in the central nervous system, the psycho-physical relationships existing between displays and receptors on the

---

\* The application of information theory to the study of man's data processing is discussed in Chapters 6 and 7, and decision theory is covered in Chapter 8, of De Greene's book. *Ed.*

one hand and effectors and controls on the other, and the nature of the plant or controlled process. These will be reviewed briefly in the following pages.

Much basic study has gone into understanding the interaction between man and machine. Nevertheless, it is probably fair to say that, *except in certain simple cases, it is not possible at the present time to obtain a clear quantitative measure of the usefulness of man as a system constituent, in contrast to an automatic control device.* Man excels in environmental adaptability, versatility, and ability to dis-

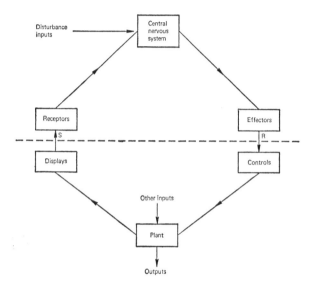

**Figure 7.1** Structure of man–machine control system.

cern signals in the presence of noise; his presence makes a control system adaptive and self-optimizing, within certain limits. However, the relative importance of these factors is hard to assess. The optimum selection of a control strategy for a proposed system involves a wide range of disciplines, including psychology, physiology, control systems theory, mechanics, and simulation techniques.

In this chapter, we first introduce some of man's input–output characteristics that are important to the design of man–machine systems. The psychological and engineering approaches to the description of man as a control element are then discussed. Display and control factors are reviewed briefly, with some examples of actual and proposed systems. The engineering approach to control systems is then indicated, and some mathematical models of the human operator's function are presented. Finally, simulation of manned systems is examined briefly in terms of stimuli, experimental design, and evaluation criteria.

## Characteristics of human input and output channels

The design of a man–machine system, such as a manually controlled spacecraft, requires an understanding of man's characteristics. The effects of these characteristics, notably of the input channels (the senses) and the output channels (largely limb movements and speech) must be analyzed. Details on human characteristics may be found in Sinaiko (1961), Fogel (1963), Pew (1965), Kelley (1968), Lyman and Fogel (1961), and Gagné (1962). To aid in the allocation of sensing and operating functions in man–machine systems, it is convenient to refer to the apparent functional advantages and disadvantages of man and machine in typical system situations.* Nontechnical factors (e.g., government policies), a well as man or machine capabilities, must almost always be considered. A careful comparison of man and machine capabilities and limitations is presented in Table 7.1.

The major input channels useful in system operation are vision and audition, but other senses such as the kinesthetic sense and the perception of acceleration forces are extremely important in many cases. The major output channels are those requiring muscular movement by activation of hand controls, levers, pedals, and similar devices. The human voice is another important output channel.

### Input channels

*Vision.* The major dimensions of *vision* are brightness discrimination, color discrimination, and spatial and time discrimination. Approximately 570 *relative* brightness and three to five *absolute* brightness levels can be distinguished. Spatial discrimination, usually considered excellent, involves visual acuity, depth, form, and movement sensitivity. Typically, the accuracy of spatial discrimination depends on exposure time, as do threshold levels. Temporal discrimination involves 0·04 to 0·4 second at the retina.

These features are important to man–machine systems design because:

- Displays can be coded by color and shape.
- Brightness sensitivity is used in display design.
- Vision is *the* major input sense in man–machine systems.

*Audition.* The major dimensions of *audition* are pitch, loudness, and duration. Aural spatial discrimination is poor compared with that of vision while time discrimination between sounds is one of audition's best features.

* [Limitations of this approach were discussed in Chapter 2 of De Greene's book. *Ed.*]

**Table 7.1** Functional advantages and disadvantages of men and machines (Modified from Lyman and Fogel, 1961)

| FUNCTIONAL AREA | MAN | MACHINE |
|---|---|---|
| Data sensing | Can monitor low probability events not feasible for automatic systems because of number of events possible | Limited program complexity and alternatives; unexpected events cannot be handled adequately |
| | Absolute thresholds of sensitivity are very low under favorable conditions | Generally not as low as human thresholds |
| | Can detect masked signals effectively in overlapping noise spectra | Poor signal detection when noise spectra overlap |
| | Able to acquire and report information incidental to primary activity | Discovery and selection of incidental intelligence not feasible in present designs |
| | Not subject to jamming by ordinary methods | Subject to disruption by interference and noise |
| Data processing | Able to recognize and use information, redundancy (pattern) of real world to simplify complex situations | Little or no perceptual constancy or ability to recognize similarity of pattern in spatial or temporal domain |
| | Reasonable reliability in which the same purpose can be accomplished by different approach (corollary of reprogramming ability) | High reliability may increase cost and complexity; particularly reliable for routine repetitive functioning |
| | Can make inductive decisions in new situations; can generalize from few data | Virtually no capacity for creative or inductive functions |
| | Computation weak and relatively inaccurate; optimal game theory strategy cannot be routinely expected | Can be programmed to use optimum strategy for high-probability situations |
| | Channel capacity limited to relatively small information throughput rates | Channel capacity can be enlarged as necessary for task |
| | Can handle variety of transient and some permanent overloads without disruption | Transient and permanent overloads may lead to disruption of system |
| | Short term memory relatively poor | Short term memory and access times excellent |
| Data | Can tolerate only relatively low imposed forces and generate relatively low forces for short periods | Can withstand very large forces and generate them for prolonged periods |
| | Generally poor at tracking though satisfactory where frequent reprogramming required; can change to meet situation. Is best at position tracking where changes are under 3 radians per second | Good tracking characteristics over limited requirements |
| | Performance may deteriorate with time; because of boredom, fatigue, or distraction; usually recovers with rest | Behavior decrement relatively small with time; wear maintenance and product quality control necessary |
| | Relatively high response latency | Arbitrarily low response latencies possible |
| Economic properties | Relatively inexpensive for available complexity and in good supply; must be trained | Complexity and supply limited by cost and time; performance built in |
| | Light in weight, small in size for function achieved; power requirement less than 100 watts | Equivalent complexity and function would require radically heavier elements, enormous power and cooling resources |
| | Maintenance may require life support system | Maintenance problem increases disproportionately with complexity |
| | Nonexpendable; interested in personal survival; emotional | Expendable; non-personal; will perform without distraction |

*Kinesthesis.* An important sensory function in man–machine systems is that provided by the specialized receptors, known as *kinesthetic proprioceptors*, in muscles and joints; these provide feedback information on limb movement, its duration, and, to some extent, the applied force. Joint movements of 0·2 to 0·7 degree can be detected at a minimum rate of 10 degrees per minute.

*Other senses.* Smell and temperature senses are used mainly as alarm detectors, rather than for fine control. The sense of touch is incorporated in control systems mainly by the shape coding of knobs and other control devices. Note, however, that questions of tactile feedback also are important in connection with remote planetary exploration. In fact, it may be desirable to transmit back to earth signals that can be interpreted by earthbound observers as tactile stimuli regarding the nature of the surface of rocks or other planetary objects.

Angular and linear acceleration senses are of considerable importance in the design of aerospace vehicles. They are responsible in part for "seat of the pants" impressions regarding the movement of a vehicle. They also impose design limits on the acceleration rates of such vehicles to avoid vertigo and consequent disorientation and loss of control.

The ability of human controllers to be aware of the passage of time, and to detect the probability distribution of random events can also be considered as senses. Quantitative data regarding these "senses" are lacking, except under carefully controlled circumstances. It is also significant to note that the human being completely lacks sensors for ionizing and ultraviolet radiation. The detection of x-rays, certain radioactive particles, lethal but odorless gases, and so forth requires the use of specialized detection devices.

*Problems with sensory inputs.* In many cases there is "cross talk" between different dimensions of the same sense (such as brightness and color in vision) and between different sensory modalities. For example, the effect of strong auditory stimuli on pain thresholds is well known. From a systems viewpoint, such interaction makes it difficult to isolate particular stimulus–response relationships for mathematical analysis. This is particularly so in a complex system in which the human operator receives stimuli simultaneously through a number of sensory modalities, e.g., in a space vehicle where strong visual stimuli occur simultaneously with auditory alarms and violent pitching and rolling movements of the vehicle.

*All the sensors are nonlinear.* Nonlinearities are of particular importance:

1. The *threshold* phenomena present in all sensory modalities depend on a number of other variables such as vigilance and interaction from other senses.
2. There is a maximum signal that any particular sense is capable of receiving. Stimulation beyond this *saturation* level will produce organic damage or simply no additional change in the receptor output.
3. *Psychophysical* nonlinearities exist between a given stimulus and sensation. Even assuming that over the range between threshold and saturation stimuli a given sensor behaves as a linear transducer, this stimulus and the resulting subjective sensation are *not* linearly related. In some cases, the stimulus level $P$ can be related to the sensation level $S$ by means of approximate laws such as the Weber–Fechner law, $S = k_1 \log P$; or the Stevens power law, $S = k_2 P^n$, where $k_1$, $k_2$, and $n$ are constants that depend on the sensory modality involved and the type of continuum being observed (Stevens, 1951).

## Output channels

*Muscular output.* In most control systems, the human controller's input to the machine is obtained from the contraction of skeletal muscles. In manual control systems, the operator is dealing with such devices as toggle switches, buttons, knobs, levers, joysticks, cranks, and steering wheels. Footpedals are used as control devices in both aircraft and automobile applications. In extreme cases, other muscles have been used for control purposes. For example, tongue movement has been used as a control output by quadriplegics at the Rancho Los Amigos Hospital (Waring *et al.*, 1967). Ear movement has been used as a control output for the movement of artificial arms in experiments at the Case Institute of Technology (Bontrager, 1965). The accuracy of muscular movement depends on a number of factors, such as the muscles involved, the limb position and support, the amplitude and direction of motion, and the force required. Small movements tend to merge into involuntary tremors. Large movements tend to undershoot while small movements tend to overshoot the desired position. In general, muscular movement is of low accuracy unless monitored by appropriate feedback (usually visual) in both force and position.

*Voice.* The human voice is a control output of increasing importance. An aircraft "talked into a landing" by the control tower is evidently being controlled by a speech channel. Of growing significance is the availability of equipment that converts voice into a digital code, which is used directly as an input to a number of control devices. Voice control devices can be expected to assume a considerably larger share of man–machine system interaction in the next decade.

*Other human outputs.* Among other outputs available from a human operator are various electrophysical signals such as the electrocardiogram (ECG), the electroencephalogram (EEG), and the electromyogram (EMG); the galvanic skin response (GSR), eye movements, skin temperature, breathing rate, and blood pressure. Of these, only a few have been used for control purposes. EMG signals, which give an indication of muscle activity, can be detected and amplified and used as input to control devices. Eye movements can be detected by means of eye-movement cameras or simple biopotential electrodes mounted on the temples and forehead. Such electrodes can provide a useful signal, proportional to the position of the eyes, as an input to a control device.

*Problems of output channels.* From a systems point of view, two major problems of the output channels become readily apparent: *output rate limitations* and performance deterioration due to *fatigue*. The maximum rate of tapping with the fingers can be shown to be about 8 to 10 taps per second. Similarly, the maximum rate of repeating memorized syllables is about 8 per second. However, as accuracy requirements are imposed on movements, even these relatively low rates cannot be maintained. In fact, within certain limits, operators can trade speed for accuracy in a nearly linear relationship, thus implying a fixed information-processing capacity. It is also important to note that accurate movements, especially movements requiring considerable amounts of force, cannot be maintained for long periods because of muscular fatigue.

## The man–machine control loop: psychological and engineering approaches

The physiological and psychophysiological aspects of human input and output channels were introduced above. In a system design, however, the *overall* input–output transfer characteristics of the human element are of importance. *In many cases it is very difficult to isolate the specific physiological source for the human controller's behavior.*

### The basic control system

The block diagram of Figure 7.2 may be considered a representation of a "tracking task", in which the human operator observes on a visual display the difference between a desired input quantity $i(t)$ and the feedback or system response $r(t)$, and adjusts a manipulator, joystick, handwheel, or similar output device in such a manner that the system response agrees with the input as closely as possible. *Tracking research*, involving an investigation of human behavior in systems of the type represented in Figure 7.2, has been performed by both psychologists and engineers for a number of years. It was initiated in connection with problems of tank-turret control and antiaircraft fire control during World War II. More recently, it has been applied to

problems of aircraft control, spacecraft control, submarine control, and automobile control (Fogel, 1963; Kelley, 1968; Cooper, 1957; Brissenden *et al.*, 1961). Two overlapping classes of questions may be asked in connection with the block diagram of Figure 7.2. The first category, referred to loosely as the "psychological approach", is concerned with such factors as task difficulty, task loading, human operator vigilance, display–control compatibility, human operator training, learning effects, motivation, and stress. The second group of questions, which characterize the "engineering approach", includes such items as the effect of display gain on the stability of the feedback system, choice of forcing function frequency, the nature of the probability distribution of error, the relation between human operator performance and the performance of an appropriately defined "optimum controller", and the stability of the system with the human operator present. Both classes of questions are concerned with system performance; experience has shown that the degree of training of the human operator, for example, has a significant effect on loop stability margins.

Although the "psychological" and "engineering" approaches in the study of manual control systems are difficult to separate, there are differences of emphasis and motivation. Some psychologists (e.g., Adams and Webber, 1963) have found the engineering approach inadequate and overly confining for describing the details of human information processing. In many cases, psychologists have been concerned with variables such as training, motivation, and stress, while engineers have been concerned with variables such as spring loading and forcing function frequency. However, a more fundamental difference has arisen as a result of the variety of performance measures used in evaluating the quality or state of the complete tracking system. Engineers, as a result of their greater mathematical training, tend to specify the process in such a way as to permit the *deduction* of an appropriate measure. For example, much control system design is concerned with the use of mean-square performance criteria, since it is known that such criteria, when used as a basis of optimum design, lead to linear controllers. Tracking research in the psychological literature, on the other hand, has often been based on a convenient performance measure without a careful analysis of the limitations that may arise from its use. For example, "time-on-target" has been used as a performance measure for some time even though difficulties if interpretation of results have occasionally been demonstrated. An additional problem has arisen in connection with measures of task difficulty, which has been shown to be related in a complex and anomalous way to so many other system variables that it indicates little about the physical requirements of the task.

## Types of tracking systems

Two basic types of tracking systems can be distinguished on the basis of the kind of display information presented to the operator:

1. *Pursuit tracking* refers to a situation where the target motion and response motion are separately displayed. The operator attempts to make his response output correspond to the target position, whether it be positioning an instrument needle to follow another one, or making a spot on a cathode-ray screen follow another.

2. *Compensatory tracking* refers to a situation where the display presents the error or difference between the target position and the controlled system response. Thus, in terms of Figure 7.2, the compensatory display presents only the difference between the input or forcing function $i(t)$ and the system output $r(t)$.

The two configurations are presented in more detail in Figure 7.3 (see also Licklider, 1960; McRuer and Krendel, 1957; Tustin, 1947).

## Displays

Display design is an important part of manual control. As noted earlier, visual inputs are the most commonly used input channels. Most of the information used by automobile

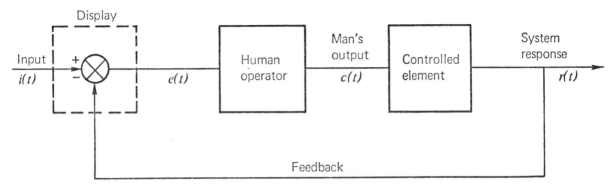

**Figure 7.2** Block diagram of manual control systems.

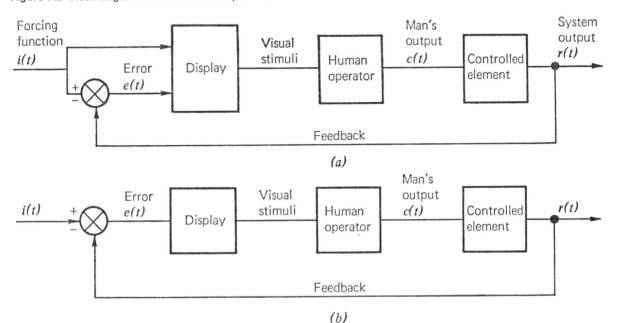

**Figure 7.3** (*a*) Pursuit tracking and (*b*) compensatory tracking.

drivers or astronauts for control purposes comes by way of the visual channel, either by direct observation of the "outside world" or by reference to displays. Improved display design can substantially improve operator performance, ease the workload, and reduce skill requirements. A detailed discussion of the problems of display system design are beyond the scope of this chapter; the interested reader is urged to consult Poole (1966) and Luxenberg and Kuehn (1968). However, some aspects of display design are enumerated briefly here.

*Separated versus integrated displays.* The most common display concepts are based on the use of a separate indicator for each variable to be displayed, along with auditory alarms and warning lights for special purposes. The clear advantage of this approach is that, in general, failure of a given instrument will not be catastrophic. On the other hand, in recent years, multipointer and integrated instruments such as "three-axis eight-ball" attitude indicators have been used. With these instruments it is possible to display three, six, or more variables with a single instrument. While this approach minimizes display panel clutter, failure of such an instrument may indeed be catastrophic to the system.

*Literal versus symbolic displays.* A literal display, such as a photograph, has a one-to-one correspondence with the features of the actual situation. A symbolic display, such as a map, contains symbols that represent the actual objects but may have no necessary correspondence with them.

*Analog versus digital displays.* Analog displays represent magnitudes by distances along a scale (whether it be circular or linear), while digital displays use numerical readouts.

*Display–control compatibility.* This term refers to the relationship between movement of the display needle or indicator and movement of the control. Thus, to minimize both training time and errors, it is desirable to have a clockwise display-needle movement correspond to a clockwise control displacement. This area continues to be an important research problem, particularly in connection with spacecraft displays.

*Inside-out versus outside-in displays.* This is a special case of control–display compatibility, which is particularly important in aircraft, spacecraft, and submarines. The artificial horizon display shows the motion of the horizon in the cockpit as it would be seen looking out of the window. If the display horizon bar moves relative to a fixed aircraft symbol, it is an "inside-out" display. If an aircraft symbol

moves relative to a fixed horizon, it is an "outside-in" display.

*Types of displays.* In addition to the commonly used dials and tapes, electroluminescent displays recently have been used, cathode-ray tubes are common in many modern display systems, three-dimensional displays are coming into use to provide the proper stimulus to spatial variables, and contact analogs have been in use since 1956. Predictor displays represent another important class. The *contact analog* display (Figure 7.4) is a computed pictorial display, which is an analog of the real-world and real-time situation presented in perspective to the observer. The pattern usually includes an artificial horizon, perspective information, and a textured ground plane. A flight-path generator produces a commanded path for the pilot. *Predictor* displays indicate not only the present condition of the vehicle, but also the expected condition of the vehicle at some time in the future if present velocities and accelerations were maintained without change. Such a prediction is based on the use of a mathematical model and a *faster-than-real-time* computation. Predictor displays are discussed further in a subsequent section.

## Controls

The proper design of control devices is equally important to the design of displays in manual control systems. Controls may be hand- or foot-operated. For example, in many aircraft, pedals are used for rudder control, while levers are manually operated for elevator control. Typical control devices include:

- *Joysticks:* for attitude control in aircraft.
- *Fingertip controls:* for attitude control under conditions of high acceleration, such as in spacecraft.
- *Wheels:* for steering on ships, automobiles, etc.
- *Thumbwheels:* for a number of purposes on aircraft, spacecraft, and in other vehicles.

An interesting design for a spacecraft control (Besco *et al.*, 1964) uses a three-dimensional model of the spacecraft that can be rotated to the desired orientation. Appropriate sensors then pick up the model orientation and generate the necessary signals to reorient the vehicle.

Even from our brief discussion, it is evident that modern display and control systems are strongly *computer dependent.* The generation of a contact analog display or a situation display for the spatial orientation of an Apollo spacecraft requires a computer to provide the necessary information from the appropriate data sensors. Similarly, computers are necessary in the control systems of a modern passenger aircraft or a space vehicle, where the forces available to the human operator require augmentation by means of appropriate power assist devices, and where the integrated action of a number of controllers is required to maintain appropriate flight profile and stability. It is probably fair to state that advanced control systems involving human operators will continue to augment human capabilities by the use of computers to generate synthetic displays on which the operator can act and to process the relatively low levels of force under his limited degrees of freedom to obtain the desired vehicle performance.

## The engineering approach to manual control systems

The engineering approach to the study of manual control systems considers the human being as a control system element that can be represented mathematically (at least approximately) to predict the system performance. In this section, we shall review briefly the characteristics of a human controller as a system element, examine once again the question of control and display design, and sketch briefly some mathematical models of the human controller's performance.

### The human operator as a control system element

The behavior of a human operator in a control system, when viewed as a system element, has several major characteristics, some of which form the basis for the engineering models of human performance. These characteristics, which were identified through the efforts of both psychological and engineering investigators (Licklider, 1960; Tustin, 1947; McRuer and Krendel, 1957; Bates, 1947), include:

*Reaction time.* There is a pure time delay or transport lag, since muscular response to a sensory input cannot take place instantaneously. A portion of this delay is due to transmission time along both sensory and motor peripheral nerve fibers, a portion is due to data processing in the receptor, and a portion is due to the information-processing activity of the cerebral cortex. Reaction time can be clearly observed in the response to step function inputs, but cannot be measured directly in closed-loop tracking situations, where it is impossible to distinguish individual stimuli and responses.

*Low-pass behavior.* Visual examination (and Fourier analysis) of tracking records reveals that the tracker tends to

attenuate high frequencies, the amount of attenuation increasing as the frequency increases.

*Situational demand.* The operator is able to adjust his input–output characteristics in order to perform his control function with a wide range of controlled element dynamics.

*Time dependence.* The operator's characteristics depend on time in two ways: First, his performance changes with time as he learns, and second, he is capable of sensing changes in environmental parameters and controlled system parameters and adjusting his characteristics accordingly.

*Prediction.* The ability of the human operator to predict the course of a target based on past performance is well known (Gottsdanker, 1952). This ability to extrapolate is important in tacking: Tracking behavior is different with "predictable inputs" (such as sine waves or constant-frequency square waves) than it is with random or random-appearing inputs. Tracking with a predictable input has been called "precognitive" tracking (McRuer and Krendel, 1957).

*Nonlinearity.* For certain tracking tasks the operator's behavior appears to be approximately linear, while for other tasks his behavior is nonlinear.

*Determinacy.* A human operator is a nondeterministic system, since his performance is different in successive trials of the same experiment. However, his variability is slight in situations where training time is adequate and the task is not difficult. Consequently, a deterministic model may be used to describe his performance in a statistical sense.

*Intermittency.* A considerable body of evidence indicates that the human operator behaves as a discrete or sampling system in certain tracking operations (Bekey, 1962).

### Types of manual control systems

*To represent mathematically a manual control system, it is necessary to describe quantitatively the plant or controlled element, control device, the display system, and the human operator himself.* The dynamics of the controlled element in Figure 7.2 represent a combination of the dynamics of control and mechanism. If we neglect mechanism dynamics for the moment, we can distinguish the following basic types of manual control systems.

*Position–position control.* Displacement of the control handle produces a corresponding displacement of the output. If the linkage between handle and output member is

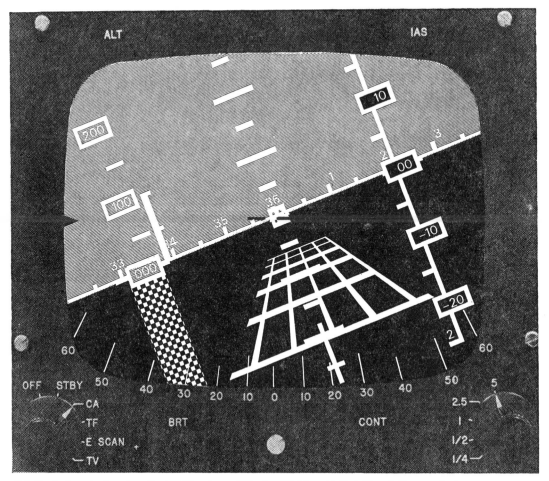

**Figure 7.4** Typical contact analog display (Courtesy of Norden Division, United Aircraft Corporation).

rigid (a gear train, for example) the positional control may be instantaneous. If a power servo is introduced into the system, there may be an appreciable lag between handle displacement and output displacement.

*Position–velocity control.* Displacement of the handle produces a corresponding output velocity of the controlled element – for example, a rheostat controlling the speed of an electric motor. This can be expressed mathematically as

$$\frac{dr}{dt} = kc \qquad (1)$$

where $c$ and $r$ are the control and output motions, respectively, as indicated in Figure 7.7$b$, and $k$ is a constant. It should be noted that the motion of the output is now given by integration of input displacement, i.e.,

$$r(t) = k \int c(t) \, dt \qquad (2)$$

*Position–acceleration control.* Displacement of the control handle produces a corresponding output acceleration, or

$$\frac{d^2 r}{dt^2} = kc(t) \qquad (3)$$

*Rate-aided control.* Control-handle displacement can give the output not only a proportional displacement but an increment of velocity as well. In this case we can write,

$$r(t) = k_1 c(t) + k_2 \int c(t) \, dt \qquad (4)$$

The basic control configurations are illustrated in the block diagrams of Figure 7·5, where $H$ represents the human operator, and $s$ is the "Laplace operator". Thus, for example, if a displacement of a knob results in the proportional increase in the speed of a motor, this is evidently a rate-control device. On the other hand, if an angular displacement of a joystick produces a proportional angular change in an elevator surface of an aircraft, this would be referred to as a position–position control.

## Dynamics of control devices

The control devices themselves may include nonnegligible inertia or damping, and may or may not be spring restrained. For example, a hand control often is so constructed that in a "hands off" situation, springs return it to a center null position. If one considers man's primary output as force, applied to a control device with non-negligible dynamics, the displacement resulting from a force input will be described by the equation

$$I\frac{d^2x}{dt^2} + B\frac{dx}{dt} + Kx = f(t) \tag{5}$$

where $I$ is the control inertia, $B$ is the control damping coefficient, $K$ is the control spring constant, $x$ is the resulting displacement, and $f(t)$ is the force input. The selection of a control device can be viewed as a selection of the magnitude of the terms $I$, $B$, and $K$ in the above equation. As we shall see below, the selection of control devices has an important

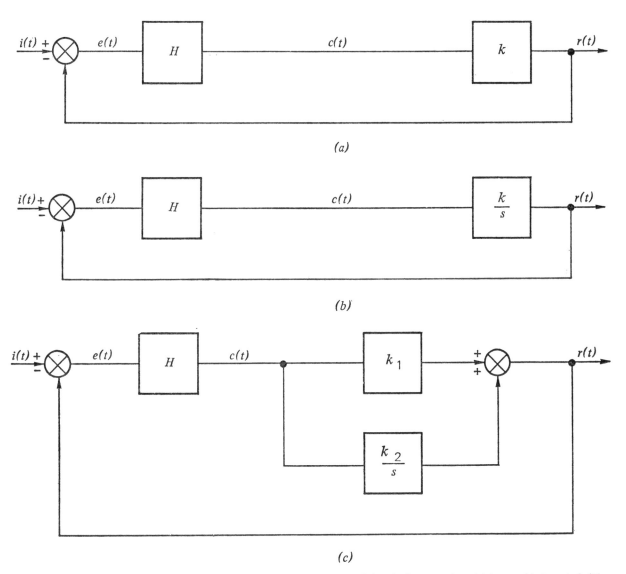

Figure 7.5 Simple manual control system showing (a) position control, (b) velocity control, and (c) rate-aided control. (The Laplace Operator $1/s$ represents integration with respect to time.)

bearing on system stability and thus on the kind of compensation that must be introduced for stable operation, either by the designer or by the control strategy of the operator himself.

The control dynamics indicated by Eq. (5) are based on the assumption that the control is linear. In many control system applications this is not true. For example, on–off switches, bang–bang controls, and similar devices produce no ouput until the control displacement exceeds some specified amount. In other controls, the output may be proportional to an input force over a given range, after which limits are encountered. These are nonlinear effects that further complicate the analysis of both stability and human performance in manual control systems.

## Performance criteria

If one examines the compensatory tracking scheme of the type illustrated in Figure 7.2, it is evident that a measure of the operator's tracking ability must be based in some way on the loop error, indicated by $e(t)$ in the figure. Common measures used in the past are outlined below (Obermayer and Muckler, 1963).

*Time on target.* This is simply a measure of the fraction of time during which the tracking error remains within a specified distance of the desired zero error or center of the screen. It can be obtained by scoring the tracker's performance on the basis of the percentage of time during which a dot on the oscilloscope screen remains within a small circle of specified radius.

*Mean value of error.* This measure is defined as

$$\bar{e} = \frac{1}{T}\int_0^T e(t)\, dt \qquad (6)$$

where $T$ is the time interval over which the averaging is performed. It is evident that the mean value of the error can be zero, while the tracker's performance may in fact involve instantaneously large excursions away from zero. However, this criterion is useful in revealing the possible presence of a bias, positive or negative, in the error signal.

*Mean square error.* This measure is defined by

$$\overline{e^2} = \frac{1}{T}\int_0^T e^2(t)\, dt \qquad (7)$$

It can be seen that this error criterion penalizes large errors much more severely than small errors, because of the squaring operation.

A question of some interest in the study of manual control systems has been to determine whether these or any similar criteria can be used to judge the *quality* of a man–machine system. There is some evidence to indicate that manual control systems that are *judged* by the operator as *vastly different* in quality nevertheless yield *similar* values of mean square error. Scales such as the Cooper Rating Scale (Cooper, 1957) that are used as a subjective measure of a pilot's evaluation of an aircraft control system show very little correspondence with the mean square error. It may be hypothesized that pilots control their craft in such a way as to minimize the mean square tracking errors, but that depending on the aircraft design this minimization may require considerably different degrees of effort and concentration on the part of the pilot. A quantitative approach to this difference among systems is provided by the use of mathematical models of pilot performance, discussed in a later section.

## Stability criteria

From a control system point of view, a system is defined as *stable* if an error due to temporary disturbance does not continue to grow indefinitely. A system is described as *asymptotically stable* if the errors resulting from a disturbance progressively decrease to zero. If a system is *unstable*, any input disturbance will either cause the output to grow without limit or will cause it to oscillate with progressively larger amplitudes. In a completely linear system, the stability criteria can be formulated mathematically quite simply. The presence of the human operator, however, renders the problem considerably more complex. Man has a sensory threshold. This dead zone may result in a small amplitude oscillation, with the error oscillating within the threshold region, which is known as a *limit cycle*. If a threshold is a small proportion of the total excursion allowed, the system can still be stable insofar as large input signals are concerned. In addition, man's reaction time introduces a finite time delay into a system. It is easy to show that any stable system with greater than unity loop gain can be made unstable by the insertion of sufficient time delay into the loop. An example of this situation is a problem of "pilot-induced oscillations" in which the pilot's corrective maneuvers are always too late to check the increasing amplitude of oscillation of his aircraft, and his attempt to control it results only in larger and larger oscillation. In some cases, the solution to pilot-induced oscillation is simply for the pilot to abandon all attempt to control, relying on the damping effect of the atmosphere and the structural design of the vehicle to reduce the oscillations. In other words, *a human controller by his very presence introduces destabilizing effects into a control system that require compensation to ensure stability*. Hence, the human operator is required to adjust his performance strategy (or, in mathematical terms, his gain and other parameters) to produce optimum response consistent with stability.

## Compensation

Consider a tracking task in which the operator is required to follow a constant velocity input (a ramp signal) with zero error. It can be shown that the design of such a system requires at least two integrations in the forward loop (Murphy, 1962). Let us now assume that the controlled system or mechanism has negligible dynamics and can be represented simply by a proportional factor, and that the man is provided with a damped joystick that introduces a single integration into the system. This situation is depicted in Figure 7.6*a*. The requirements on the man's tracking strategy can now be stated from a servo point of view as follows:

1. The man must introduce at least one integration to enable him to maintain zero error as desired.
2. A system with two integrations and time delay (reaction time) can be shown to be unstable.
3. The man therefore also must introduce some anticipation, in the form of a derivative term that introduces "lead" into the control system. Hence, the human controller is required to introduce an integral and a derivative term to maintain the desired system performance (as shown in Figure 7.6*b*), in addition to whatever subjective additional criteria he may use.

Evidently, a human controller does not *literally* perform the operations of differentiation and integration in a mathematical sense. Nevertheless, his tracking strategy, learned by experience and practice, results in control signals that can be closely approximated by devices having the required compensation characteristics. It is intuitively clear that the more complex the mathematical operations required of the operator are, the more "difficult" the task will be, and the longer it will take to acquire the necessary skills. In a classical paper Birmingham and Taylor (1954) suggested that an ideal criterion for the design of man–machine systems is to ensure that the human operator's role reduces to that of a simple amplifier, i.e., that he is required to perform no integrations and no differentiations. (It may of course be argued that in this case, from a systems point of view, it may be more economical to replace the human operator by a simple amplifier, as in fact has been done in many systems.)

Relieving the operator of the necessity of differentiating or integrating is generally known as *aiding*. The removal of differentiations from the task is called *quickening*. Figure 7.6*c* shows a derivative term inserted into the feedback loop of a system; now the operator no longer sees the *actual* system error, but rather an error signal that includes some element proportional to the rate of change of the control variable. In some cases such derivative terms can be added directly to the display devices, which are then known as *rate-aided* displays.

An aided display is *anticipatory* in the sense that it informs the operator of the results of his own actions. This anticipation is not true *prediction*, however, since it does not account for the dynamics of the controlled element (airplane or submarine, for example). The inclusion of error derivatives in the display simply indicates to the operator the trends resulting from his actions and thus prevents excessive overshoots. Actual prediction can be obtained if the display is produced by a computer that uses a mathematical model of the system to compute its behavior. The display may then show, for example, the predicted error at some time in the future, as calculated by the computer. Clearly, the accuracy of prediction depends on the adequacy of the equations representing system behavior. Predictive displays are considerably more complex than aided displays, but they further simplify man's task and tend to null the reaction time. A predictive control system is shown in Figure 7.7. Predictive displays have been extensively studied by Kelley (1962, 1968), who has used them with considerable success in a variety of applications. Typical three-trace predictive displays during a submarine dive are shown in Figure 7.8.

## The operator's function in a manual control system

We have reviewed some of the characteristics of manual tracking systems, and the relation of the human operator to the dynamics of control and mechanism. It was shown that performance and stability were *systems* attributes that depend on both man and machine, as well as on the communication links between them – namely, display and control. If the operator is required to provide a complex computing function, he can do so only at the expense of increased reaction time, i.e., reduced system bandwidth. Methods of alleviating the man's computational function were discussed.

You might ask why the operator should be included in

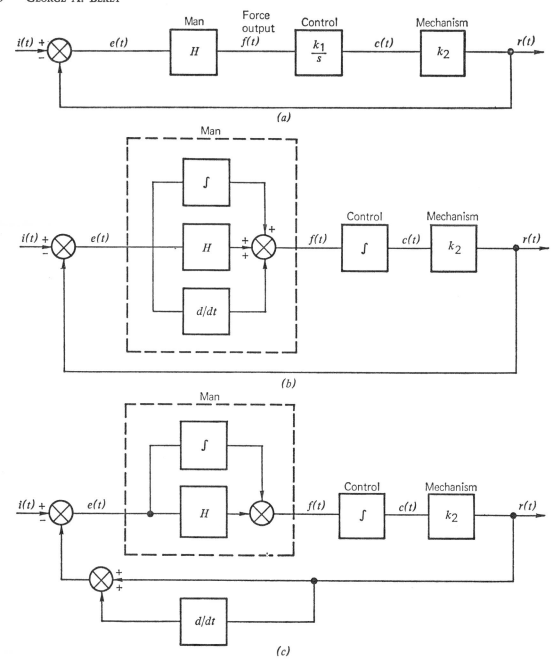

**Figure 7.6** Human operator compensation: (*a*) basic system, (*b*) compensation requirement, and (*c*) system with rate aiding in feedback loop.

the loop at all when all the complex functions are taken away from him. There are several answers to this question. In the first place, even with all differentiating and integrating operations removed, the human being still does not act as a "simple amplifier" (Birmingham, 1958; Birmingham and Taylor, 1954; McRuer *et al.*, 1965). He is still required to translate sensory inputs to motor outputs, e.g., meter deflections or spot displacements to crank motion. Clearly, this function is at least that of a transducer, rather than an amplifier. If the task calls for simple amplification, an electronic amplifier may serve this function more efficiently than a man could.

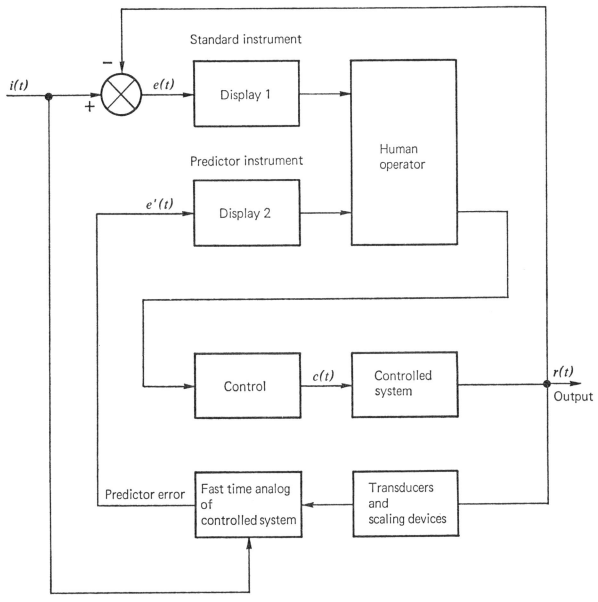

**Figure 7.7** Predictive control system block diagram.

Second, although not evident from the simple block diagrams, man's function in the loop is more complex and demanding than that of an information translator. Man is capable of detecting quite efficiently a signal masked by noise, even with very low signal-to-noise ratios. Furthermore, man is adaptive, and his ability to function can be adjusted to the task requirement. He can monitor low-probability events and quickly adjust his gain and compensation to meet the situation. This does not imply that an autopilot could not be designed to perform all these functions. It merely says that the versatility and adaptability of man make him a desirable element of many control situations, not merely to amplify, but to translate, interpret, compute, modify, plan, predict, guess, or perhaps to react, with his usual cussedness, in an unpredictable manner.

## Mathematical models of the human operator

We have reviewed some psychophysiological characteristics of the human operator in a tracking situation, and

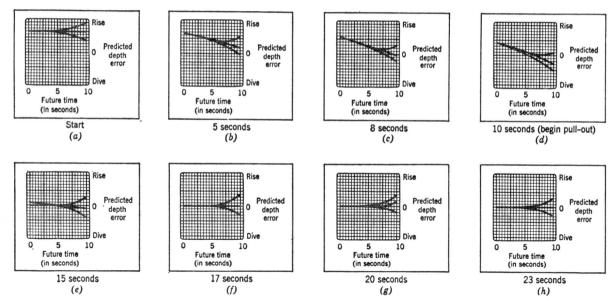

**Figure 7.8** Typical traces from a predictive display. The inner trace represents the predictions if the submarine diving planes are returned to center, the outer two traces represent the predictions if they are moved to either extreme. (From Kelley, 1968.)

briefly analyzed several tracking situations from the point of view of performance and stability. It is clear that *the human element is the limiting factor in the tracking loop. Adequate compensation cannot be designed unless the operator's behavior can be expressed in mathematical terms, thus making the entire loop amenable to analysis.*

Several types of models have been proposed. A *linear model* with constant parameters is the easiest to formulate and use. Unfortunately, such models cannot account for the nonlinear and adaptive behavior of man. *Quasilinear* describing-function models with various types of remnants are rather complex to evaluate but give good agreement with experimental data. Nonlinear and adaptive models can be formulated but require computer *simulation*, since general techniques for the analysis and synthesis of nonlinear systems are not available. A *stochastic model* (Fogel, 1957) has been proposed that promises to give excellent results in terms of probabilities of certain events; however, it cannot give transient-response information directly in the time domain. *Sampled-data models* have been suggested that give some promise of representing correctly the intermittency and "refractory period" of the human operator (Bekey, 1962).

In recent years the quasilinear describing-function models have been further developed to include some representation of the neuromuscular portion of operator physiology (McRuer *et al.*, 1968). There also has been considerable emphasis on obtaining mathematical models of human operators in multiloop and -instrument situations (Todosiev *et al.*, 1966), as well as on attempts to describe the adaptive and learning characteristics of human controllers.

### A quasilinear describing-function model

This technique of representing human operator dynamics was pioneered by McRuer and Krendel (1957) and is widely accepted as a representation of human performance in many aerospace systems. Basically, this is an engineering-oriented approach to modeling in which the operator characteristics are represented by the sum of two terms, as illustrated in Figure 7.9. The first term is a linear differential equation that is the best possible linear approximation to the operator's response (in the sense of minimizing the mean square error of approximation). However, in this describing function, the coefficients are constant, while human operator characteristics change with changes in the environment as well as with variable processes within the operator himself. Hence, the describing function does not represent the totality of the human operator's output. The second term, known as the *remnant*, includes all those response elements that are not linearly correlated with the input to the control system. These elements are assumed to be due primarily to time-varying elements in the operator's characteristics and, to a lesser extent, to the human operator's nonlinearities. The describing functions com-

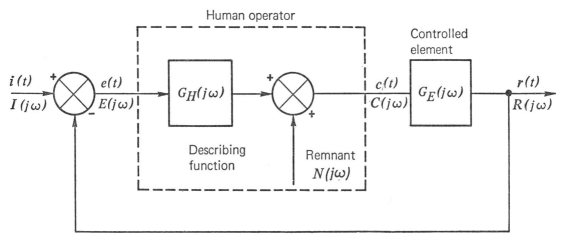

**Figure 7.9** Quasilinear model of human operator.

monly are measured by *spectral analysis* techniques (McRuer and Krendel, 1957) under conditions where the operator tracks a random-appearing sum of nonharmonic sinusoids. An alternative method of determining the describing function, linear regression or "measurement by mimicking", was pioneered by Elkind and Green (1961). In general, in the frequency domain, the describing function takes the form:

$$G_H(j\omega) = \frac{K(1 + T_L j\omega)(\exp - \tau j\omega)}{(1 + T_I j\omega)(1 + T_N j\omega)} \quad (8)$$

where $\tau$ is the reaction time, $T_N$ is an approximation to the neuromuscular system time constant, and $T_I$ and $T_L$ represent the compensation introduced by the operator to the system to maintain stability and satisfactory response; $K$ is a gain factor, and $\omega$ is the frequency variable.

This model is known as "quasilinear" because the values of the coefficients in Eq. (8) depend on the controlled-element dynamics and on the nature of the forcing function. It has been shown that the human operator adjusts his open-loop gain $K$ to correspond to the gain of the controlled element so that the closed-loop gain will be unity in the frequency range being tracked. The gain adjustment appears to be a function of individual training and motivation in each particular situation. The equalization terms $T_I$ and $T_L$ have been shown to vary in an adaptive manner depending on the controlled elements. The adjustment rules used by the human operator have been summarized by McRuer and Graham (1964) and may be stated as follows: (1) the human operator adapts so that the gain and equalization characteristics are appropriate

for stable control, and (2) the human operator adapts so that the form of equalization characteristics is appropriate for good low frequency closed-loop system response to the forcing function, in the sense of control system performance.

It has been shown that the parameter values of the human describing function vary with learning and become stabilized only after many hours of learning trials. For highly experienced aircraft pilots, the parameters have less variability and the lead-time constants are larger. Detailed discussions of quasilinear describing functions may be found in McRuer *et al.* (1965).

## A model of the adaptive behavior of the human operator

The adaptive behavior of human controllers has been the subject of considerable research. In fact, it is this adaptability that makes the human controller a desirable element in space vehicles and other advanced systems. For example, it is known that a human pilot of a high-performance jet aircraft is capable of modifying his control strategy within 2 to 5 seconds following the failure of the stability augmentation system. A recent study that attempts to model the adaptation strategy (Phatak and Bekey, 1969) is exemplified in the flowchart of Figure 7.10, which depicts a sequence of decisions made by the human controller on the basis of his observations of the tracking error, and the rate of change of the tracking error. On the basis of these observations, he makes choices between various pre-stored control strategies, always testing the response against learned stability and performance criteria until adequate performance is achieved. Elkind and Miller (1967) have pursued the ques-

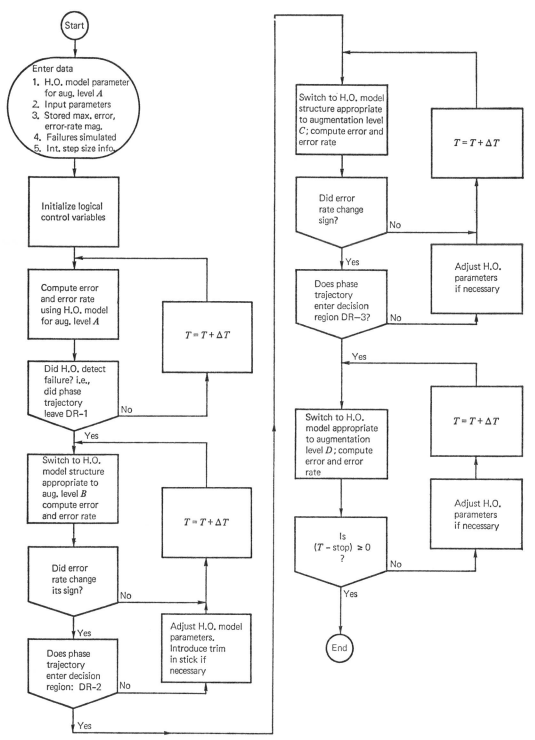

**Figure 7.10** Flowchart of adaptation strategy of human pilot following failure of stability augmentation system. The pre-failure system is described as augmentation level (aug. level) A. The pilot (H.O.) chooses among possible post-failure structures B, C, and D. The digital computer integration step size (int. step) in the simulation of this process is given by $\Delta T$. Decision regions are given by DR. (From Phatak and Bekey 1969.)

tions of adaptation and learning in considerable detail, using learning theory and Bayes' theorem statistics.

## Simulation of man–machine systems*

One of the most important applications of the simulation method is in the study of systems in which a human being participates, either as an element of the system such as the pilot of a vehicle or as a passenger whose tolerance to environmental characteristics is limited. Simulation techniques are so common in the design of piloted vehicles that in some quarters the term *simulator* is reserved for this type of activity.

### *Characteristics of manned simulation*

In addition to all the characteristics of unmanned simulation, simulation involving man includes the following particular characteristics of human performance:

1. Human performance is inherently time varying. There is variation in successive trials of the same task by the same operator, and there is a variation in the responses of several operators trying the same task.

2. Human response includes elements that apparently are not determined by the input and can only be accounted for by statistical descriptions. Consequently, the description of systems involving human operators must make use of statistical methods, and the resulting descriptions will be in some sense statistical averages defined over particular populations.

3. The inherent variability of human performance implies that many repetitions of each particular experiment must be tried.

4. Simulation studies involving human operators must be run in real time, whereas studies involving nonhuman elements may be run in an accelerated time scale in many cases.

5. The simulation method and the experimental situation must be selected in such a way as to avoid any possible injury to the operators involved.

Simulation of manned systems takes on two primary forms: *environmental simulation* and *man-in-the-loop simulation*. Environmental simulation involves creation of an environment that reproduces one or more unusual system situations in which human beings may have to operate.

* A portion of this section is based on a chapter entitled "Simulation", by Bekey, G. A. and Gerlough, D. L. in Machol, R. E. (ed.), *System Engineering Handbook*, McGraw-Hill (1965).

Man-in-the-loop simulation involves an interaction between man and equipment.

*Environmental simulation.* Environmental simulators are needed because human beings are often subjected to environments drastically different from those of ordinary life. For example, man may be exposed to situations where high temperatures and high levels of pressure are involved, such as in certain types of mining or underground operations. Man may be asked to undergo long periods of weightlessness such as those occurring in interplanetary flight, or he may be asked to operate in atmospheres different from that of his normal habitat.

To test the adequacy of the proposed design techniques and to ensure human survival, it is absolutely necessary to simulate the characteristics of the particular environment before a vehicle is constructed. Generally, a characteristic problem in the design of such simulators is the selection of the particular quantities or variables to be investigated. For example, it may be decided to construct a simulated space cabin for an interplanetary voyage in which human passengers may be subjected to temperatures, radiation levels, and illumination levels similar to those encountered in the actual flight; it may be decided, however, that no attempt will be made to simulate the gravitational environment of free space. Other simulations may be designed for examining the ability of operators to perform certain tasks under conditions of reduced gravity; certain kinds of supporting harness structures have been used for this purpose. Note that decisions on what is to be simulated and what is to be omitted, what is important, and what is negligible must be made in connection with every simulation.

Environmental simulation has the following major characteristics:

1. *Temperature simulation.* Variable climate chambers and hangars have been constructed, some with temperatures ranging from $-300°$ to $+1,000°$F. Such a chamber may range in size from a cell barely adequate to accommodate one man to a chamber sufficient to accommodate an entire airplane or space vehicle.

2. *Acceleration.* The effect of acceleration and deceleration on human operators and passengers is usually measured using centrifuges and rocket sleds capable of imparting wide ranges of acceleration and deceleration. For example, the human centrifuge at Johnsville, Pennsylvania, has a cabin located at the end of a 50-foot arm. The centrifugal acceleration to which the operator

is exposed may reach 40 and 50g. Rocket sleds, such as one located at Holloman Air Force Base, provide acceleration as high as 50 or 60g.

3. *Unusual atmospheric conditions.* Altitude chambers and environmental chambers have been constructed with a capability of generating ice and snow with atmospheric conditions ranging from sea level to 100,000 feet in altitude. Simulated desert sand and dust storms can be generated in certain simulators. Humidity ranges from 0 to 100 percent, salt spray, tropical rain storms, and similar unusual conditions have been produced in the laboratory.

4. *Vibration.* Simulators have been constructed that provide vibration and shock excitation ranging from 5 to 2,000 cycles, as well as random vibration sources with various spectral characteristics. Shock in the range of 0 to 100g and of various durations has also been simulated.

5. *Zero gravity.* Conditions of null or zero gravity have been simulated in airplane cabins while the airplane flies a particular type of trajectory known as a parabolic flight, during which gravitational and centrifugal accelerations exactly cancel, resulting in periods of weightlessness as long as 15 to 35 seconds. Zero g has also been simulated by spinning a man submerged in a fluid.

6. *Lack of atmosphere.* The lack of atmospheric friction and resistance in space for the performance of particular tasks has been simulated by means of minimum friction air-bearing tables.

7. *Complete cabin simulations.* A number of tests have been performed in simulated space cabins that include complete closed-cycle ecological systems. Human volunteers have stayed under simulated space cabin conditions for a number of days. In many cases, such simulated cabins have included temperature, atmospheric composition, and other aspects of the environment in simulated form.

Other environmental simulators have been constructed for the testing of equipment that does not involve human operators. Such simulators include methods for determining the effect of extreme levels of solar radiation, nuclear explosion effects, and so forth.

Since no simulator takes into account each and every effect encountered by a human operator or a human passenger in a particular situation, the addition or superposition of effects observed in various portions of the simulation must be handled with great care. In many cases a simple linear superposition of effects may not be valid.

Performance decrement resulting from exposure to untoward environmental conditions is discussed in detail in Chapter 14;* see also Webb (1964).

*Flight trainers and piloted simulators.* Where a human pilot performs control or guidance functions in the operation of a system, some form of simulation is essential during the design phase. The simulation may be entirely an analog simulation, since in a control task the operator's input and output are generally continuous, or it may be a partially or entirely digital simulation, which may require some form of analog-to-digital and digital-to-analog conversion. In the design of flight-control systems, the simulation generally becomes some form of physical simulation in which there is an interrelationship between a human pilot, an actual or simulated portion of a vehicle control system (including manual controls, displays, dials, knobs, and so forth), and a general-purpose computer (analog or digital) that provides inputs, to the cockpit and operator, representing the variation of environmental characteristics during a particular flight mission. Where the pilot responds to simple dial movements, a general- or special-purpose computer may be adequate to provide the input signals. Where a more realistic simulation of the external environment is required, more elaborate equipment is also necessary.

Attempts to overcome various of the limitations of the fixed-base laboratory simulator of the type discussed above have resulted in a variety of more complex and generally considerably more costly simulators, some of which are outlined below.

1. *The moving-base simulator.* The simulated or actual cockpit is mounted on gimbals, suspended on chains, mounted in a sled, or supported in other similar fashion and subjected to movement similar to that of actual mission conditions. All moving-base simulations involve limitations of dynamic range and consequently may provide faithful movement over only certain particular ranges of angular or linear displacement. Furthermore, motion cues may be misleading since a pilot in a simulated space mission will be subjected to the motion in space without the gravitational environment of space. Effects on both physiology and performance may be different from those in space.

2. *The variable-stability airplane.* In an attempt to provide a more realistic simulation of flight-control systems of vehicles under investigation, certain airplanes, heli-

* [Of the original text. *Ed.*]

copters, and other vehicles with adjustable handling characteristics have been developed. These vehicles include an airborne computer, analog or digital, which alters their handling characteristics to simulate the performance of the system under design. Many such variable-stability aircraft have been built and have proven an invaluable research and design tool in the aerospace industry. In fact, the simulation of certain phases of reentry from space has been accomplished using the variable-stability aircraft as a simulator.

3. *Increasing sophistication in physical simulation.* It is possible to include in the simulation a whole range of equipment from a simple simulator cockpit to a complete mockup of the actual vehicle. In airplane simulators, for example, it is common to include not only the cockpit itself, but also the servos, actuators, tail assemblies, hydraulic mechanisms, and similar devices as portions of the simulation to ensure that the performance of the pilot will not be distorted by a possibly inaccurate mathematical description included on a computer.

It is clear that simulation in one form or another is essential for the development of manned vehicles: It is important that man be subjected to simulated conditions before he is exposed to actual and possibly hazardous operating conditions. Thus manned simulation is both a *research tool* and a *design tool*. As a research tool, it enables us to determine conditions that will govern the design of future systems by providing envelopes of satisfactory performance. As an invaluable design tool, it proves the absolutely necessary verification by human subjects of a proposed system configuration. Note, however, that *simulation cannot and should not be a substitute for design.*

*Computers used with manned simulators.* Some form of computer is required to generate the input signals to the cockpit and process the pilot's output signals in accordance with a predetermined mission such as a particular flight trajectory, a landing on a carrier deck, or a reentry from space. Historically, *analog* computers have been used for flight-control simulators because of: (1) bandwidth requirements, since the mission characteristics as well as the input and output signals contained frequencies sufficiently high as to preclude real-time digital computation; and (2) accuracy compatibility, since in many cases the physical characteristics of the airframe and the atmosphere were known only to levels of accuracy compatible with those of analog elements. Recently, the picture has changed in two respects: first, the increasing speed of digital computers has made possible the real-time digital simulation of certain

portions of aerospace missions; and second, airborne digital computers are being used to an increasing degree to handle the complex levels of data processing and computation characteristic of modern high-performance aerospace vehicles. Consequently, it is expected that an increasing use of *digital* computers in flight simulators will be seen in the future – in many cases, in the form of hybrid analog–digital equipment.

## Bibliography

Adams, J. A. and Webber, C. E. (1963) "A Monte Carlo Method of Tracking Behavior", *Human Factors*, February, 5(1), 81–102.

Bates, J. A. V. (1947) "Some Characteristics of a Human Operator", *IEE Journal* (London), 94(IIA), 298–304.

Bekey, G. A. (1962) "The Human Operator as a Sampled-Data System", *IRE Transactions on Human Factors in Electronics*, September, HFE-3, 43–51.

Besco, R. O., *et al.* (1964) *Manual Attitude Control Systems: Parametric and Comparative Studies of Operating Modes of Control*, Washington, D.C.: National Aeronautics and Space Administration, Contractor Report 56, June.

Birmingham, H. P. and Taylor, F. V. (1954) "A Design Philosophy for Man–Machine Control Systems", *Proceedings of the IRE*, 42(12), 1748–58.

Birmingham, H. P. (1958) "The Optimization of Man–Machine Control Systems", *1958 IRE Wescon Convention Record*, 272–6, New York: Institute of Radio Engineers.

Bontrager, E. (1965) *The Application of Muscle Education Techniques in the Investigation of Electromyographic Control*, Cleveland, Ohio: Case Institute, Technical Report 2DC-4-65-13.

Brissenden, R. F., *et al.* (1961) *Analog Simulation of a Pilot-Controlled Rendezvous*, Washington, D.C.: National Aeronautics and Space Administration, Technical Note D-747, April.

Cooper, G. E. (1957) "Understanding and Interpreting Pilot Opinion", *Aeronautical Engineering Review*, 16(3), 47–51, 56.

Elkind, J. I. and Green, D. M. (1961) *Measurement of Time Varying and Non-Linear Dynamic Characteristics of Human Pilots*, Wright-Patterson AFB, Ohio: Aeronautical Systems Division, Technical Report 61-225, December.

Elkind, J. I. and Miller, D. C. (1967) *Adaptive Characteristics of the Human Controller of Time-Varying Systems*, Edwards AFB, Calif.: Air Force Flight Dynamics Laboratory, Technical Report 66-60, December.

Fogel, L. J. (1957) "The Human Computer in Flight Control", *IRE Transactions on Electronic Computers*, September, EC-6, 195–201.

Fogel, L. J. (1963) *Biotechnology*, Englewood Cliffs, N.J.: Prentice-Hall.

Gagné, R. M. (1962) *Psychological Principles in System Design*, New York: Holt, Rinehart and Winston.

Gottsdanker, R. M. (1952) "The Accuracy of Prediction Motion", *Quarterly Journal of Experimental Psychology*, 43, 26–36.

Kelley, C. R. (1962) "Predictor Instruments Look into the Future", *Control Engineering*, 9(3), 86–90.

Kelley, C. R. (1968) *Manual and Automatic Control*, New York: Wiley.

Licklider, J. C. R. (1960) "Quasilinear Operator Models in the Study of Manual Tracking", in Luce, R. D. (ed.), *Developments in Mathematical Psychology*. Glencoe, Ill.: The Free Press.

Luxenberg, H. R. and Kuehn, R. L. (eds.) (1968) *Display Systems Engineering*, New York: McGraw-Hill.

Lyman, J. and Fogel, L. J. (1961) "The Human Component", in Grabbe, E. M. *et al.* (eds.), *Handbook of Automation, Computation and Control*, chap. 2, vol. 3. New York: Wiley.

McRuer, D. T. and Krendel, E. S. (1957) *Dynamic Response of Human Operators*, Wright-Patterson AFB, Ohio: Wright Air Development Division, Technical Report 56-524, October.

McRuer, D. T. and Graham, D. (1964) *Pilot–Vehicle Control System Analysis, Guidance and Control II, Progress in Astronautics and Aeronautics*, 13, 603–21, New York: Academic Press.

McRuer, D. T., *et al.* (1965) *Human Pilot Dynamics in Compensatory Systems*, Edwards AFB, Calif.: Air Force Flight Dynamics Laboratory, Technical Report 65-15, July.

McRuer, D. T., *et al.* (1968) *New Approaches to Human-Pilot/Vehicle Dynamic Analysis*, Edwards AFB, Calif.: Air Force Flight Dynamics Laboratory, Technical Report 67-150, February.

Murphy, G. J. (1962) *Basic Automatic Control Theory*, Princeton, N.J.: D. Van Nostrand.

Obermayer, R. W. and Muckler, F. A. (1963) "Performance Measures in Flight Studies", *Proceedings of the AIAA Simulation for Aerospace Flight Conference*, New York: American Institute of Aeronautics and Astronautics, August, 58–65.

Pew, R. (1965) "Human Information Processing Concepts for System Engineers", in Machol, R. E. (ed.), *System Engineering Handbook*. New York: McGraw-Hill.

Phatak, A. V. and Bekey, G. A. (1969) "Model of the Adaptive Behavior of the Human Operator in Response to a Sudden Change in the Control Situation", *IEEE Transactions on Man–Machine Systems*, September, MMS-10(3), 72–80.

Poole, H. H. (1966) *Fundamentals of Display Systems*, Washington, D.C.: Spartan Books.

Sinaiko, H. W. (1961) *Selected Papers on Human Factors in the Design and Use of Control Systems*, New York: Dover Publications.

Stevens, S. S. (ed.) (1951) *Handbook of Experimental Psychology*, New York: Wiley.

Todosiev, E. P., *et al.* (1966) *Human Tracking Performance in Uncoupled and Coupled Two-Axis Systems*, Washington, D.C.: National Aeronautics and Space Administration, Contract Report 532, August.

Tustin, A. (1947) "The Nature of the Operator's Response in Manual Control and Its Implications for Controller Design", *IEE Journal* (London), 94(IIA), 190–202.

Waring, W., *et al.* (1967) "Myoelectric Control for Quadriplegic Orthotics", *Prosthetics*, December, 21, 255–8.

Webb, P. (ed.) (1964) *Bioastronautics Data Book*, Washington, D.C.: National Aeronautics and Space Administration, Special Publication 3006.

# Section III
# Introduction

Systems ideas have had a considerable impact on sociological thinking. The concept of the organization as a system, of even nations and societies as systems, has been developed and used to try to explain their behaviour and the changes which occur in their structures. Buckley presents the system approach to the idea of society as an adaptive system and he uses the ideas of control and feedback to account for this adaptability. Easton uses a similar approach to model the political aspects of social systems and this short extract only gives the briefest flavour of his approach, which is developed in two books. The short extract from a booklet by Hoos rightly draws attention to the question of value-judgements in systems treatments and makes some pertinent criticisms of the systems analysis technique.

Modelling of social and political systems may seem ambitious in itself but the next two articles go further still. Milsum, a noted control engineer, takes up the challenge of modelling virtually the total system around us, the geosphere, the biosphere, sociosphere, and the technosphere. He comes down in favour of experimenting on a small scale to predict the effects of changes on these systems. But Forrester, in the last article in this section, goes still further and presents a modelling method called system dynamics which, it is claimed, can project the outcomes of our whole world. Forrester's work has generated much controversy, but many of the objections to his work stem from disagreements about the validity of his starting data and assumptions rather than from the method.

## Associated reading

Buckley's book *Sociology and Modern Systems Theory* (Prentice-Hall, 1967) presents his general ideas in more detail. An important work in this area is Katz and Kahn, *The Social Psychology of Organisations*, Wiley, 1966. Easton's two books are *A Framework for Political Analysis* and *A Systems Analysis of Political Life*, published by Prentice-Hall and Wiley respectively, in 1965.

Forrester's work and that of his colleagues is presented in several books. The original work on the method appears in *Industrial Dynamics* and *Urban Dynamics*, both by Forrester (M.I.T. Press). Later work is in *World Dynamics*, by Forrester, and *Limits to Growth*, by Meadows, D. H. *et al.*, Earth Island, 1972.

# 8 The technique and the technicians
## by I. R. Hoos

## Fitting social systems to systems analysis

The use of systems analysis in the realm of public affairs implies certain assumptions about the nature of social problems and certain presumptions about the state-of-the-art of systems techniques. Basic to this manifestation of technology transfer, whether local, national, or international, is the assumption that large-scale, complex social systems can be managed in much the same way and by the same mind of experts as large-scale, complex aerospace projects, military missions, and business endeavours. This implies that social systems can be reduced to measurable, controllable units all of whose relationships are fully recognized, appreciated, and amenable to manipulation. Implicit, too, is the notion that through systems analysis, new insights will be achieved and new solutions will emerge. Justification for this line of thought appears to be vested in the persuasion that experts from *outside* the discipline or the public agency will bring to the problem a fresh approach, unfettered by doctrinaire restraints.

In practice, none of these assumptions has found substantiation. Review of completed systems analyses indicates that, far from submitting gracefully to quantitative treatment, social systems are by their very nature so laden with intangible, human variables that concentration on their measurable aspects distorts the problem and confuses the issues. One might venture the proposition that instead of assuming that social systems should be approached as though readily subject to technical treatment, those which appear technical might more appropriately be treated as social in their essence. Concerns which are largely technological, when they impinge on our social, economic, and political environments, require a social orientation. Thus, transportation is not mere movement of people and goods nor miles of highways and location of airports. Rather, what is at stake here are the values of the society – how many acres of recreation land it is willing to forfeit to rights-of-way, whether it is willing to accept some mode of travel other than the one-man, one-car, whose priorities should be taken into account in assessing benefits of transport facilities?

A transportation system designed to enhance the life style of a society would have to be based on some utopian conception of the good life and would incorporate many of the analyst's own value-judgements. Reflected in such a system, there would have to be assumptions about people's preferences for location of home, forms of travel, means of recreation, use of leisure time. Also, account would have to be taken of their tolerance of land and air traffic noise, sonic booms, and the like; their concern for highway and air safety; their interest in curbing pollution. Even in so technical a matter as planning a transportation network the social costs and benefits are crucial, and these are outside the purlieu of quantification and beyond the proper limits of manipulation.

In pollution the problem is not simply one of disposal of unwanted products. A total waste management system is a complex network of technical inter-relationships and critical aesthetic, geographical, economic, political, jurisdictional, and administrative considerations. Here criteria, standards, and regulations of environmental quality are crucial. With the skies not spacious enough for all the debris and the seas not deep enough to swallow the fissionable wastes of this nuclear age, it is readily apparent that the design of the system has to take into account a broad range of value-laden uncertainties running the gamut from people's choice of fuels to their way of dealing with international tensions. Scarcity of resources imposes choices between alternatives that must be decided in large part subjectively; the pretence that they can be made scientifically, objectively, with the air of pre-determined quantified precision, is transparent.

## Information systems – a credibility trap

The aggregation and organization of data, superficially innocuous operations vital to the systems approach, are similarly fraught with deep social significance. Because business and government managers have allowed themselves to believe that computer technology will provide information systems that will expedite and improve policy-planning and decision-making, systems experts respond by replacing the overflowing files with busy-working computers. On the assumption that all information is relevant unless proved otherwise, and that economies of quantity superseded all other considerations, the engineers in all of the cases I have observed record every possible item and justify this procedure by the spectacular lowering of unit cost. In the California Welfare Study,[1] for example, the proposed system was designed to yield not only the routine facts about age, marital status, and the like but would also respond to special inquiries. It could tabulate the number of welfare cases in which the unemployed father was a migrant labourer, with a bad cardiac condition, with two years of schooling and little English. And, like the sorcerer's apprentice, it could keep on pouring out information – that the area in which the family lived had $x$ number of substandard dwellings, $y$ number of jobless bricklayers, and was $z$ miles from the nearest police station. This cornucopia failed, however, to supply government planners with the indicators they had sought in identifying populations-at-risk and intervention strategies for anticipating dependency on public welfare. Guided by the principle of the more information the better, analysts currently engaged in a California Criminal Justice Information Study (under a $350,000, largely federally-funded contract with Lockheed Missiles & Space Company) have made the discovery that their proposed information network calls for the same items of intelligence about potential jurors as criminals!

## Danger to democracy?

The reification and deification of data which dominate the systems approach could well be one of its most serious hazards to a democratic society. The planned California systems are only a small link in a national chain capable of providing an instant check on any American with complete details of his birth, colour, religious and political affiliations, club memberships, school performance, military record, criminal career, credit rating, and medical history. Even if a person's past contained nothing so damaging as a youthful brush with the law or a mental illness once suffered and now overcome, he could be tabbed by the system as a potential member of some designated "risk" population, such, for example, as criminal, welfare, or even politically subversive, and thus be subject to unwelcome attention if not discrimination and persecution. Information about people has become a high-priced and valuable commodity, bought and sold, used and misused more all the time.

The testimony of experts in the Congressional Hearings on "The Computer and Invasion of Privacy"[2] presented substantial evidence demonstrating how naïve and fatuous it is to rely on technological locks. One computer expert from the RAND Corporation[3] cautioned against accepting statements that ring seductively of safety when, in fact, a computer can generate its own cryptographic key.

One sociologist has said:

"The potential for evil, for official and unofficial blackmail, for the harassment of political minorities is virtually unlimited. One must realise that whatever safeguards may be proposed in the initial justification could later be removed by a powerful president or a stampeded Congress. Also, the safeguards probably would be circumvented on or off the record by our undercover agencies."[4]

Professor Alan Westin of Columbia University, in a definitive work entitled *Privacy and Freedom*,[5] made the cogent observation that while tyranny is not the necessary outcome of the new uses of information technology,

"tyranny can be tighter and more inclusive for more people, and more efficient and more inescapable with the contribution of computers and data processors".

Recognizing the threat of cradle-to-grave surveillance, Professor Thomas A. Cowan of Rutgers University Law School commented:

". . . it is a prime policy matter to determine what data shall be preserved, and among those that are preserved, which it is politic in any instance to suffer to be recalled. Data-retrieval experts make the blithe assumption that data are *ipso facto*, good".[6]

His recommendation for "creative unlearning" or purposeful forgetting comes from his experience in the practice and philosophy of law and is all the more *a propos* in view of the potential dangers to individual privacy inherent in the capability for the electronic matching and co-ordination of large masses of information. Some experts have observed that, until now, privacy has been protected by the inefficiency of the government to manipulate the huge amounts of data it already has. The establishment of a Federal Data Centre, justified by its contribution to government efficiency but insensitive to individual, private interests, and feared as a form of Frankenstein monster,[7] was halted by a special decision of Congress. Yet electronic accumulation of data continues at every level of government and in every agency. The linkages are a simple technicality. Complete and detailed dossiers are no longer an Orwellian fantasy nor a post-1984 nightmare.

During the testimony before a Committee on the Judiciary, four witnesses quoted the famous and prophetic statement of Justice Brandeis in a Supreme Court case in 1927.*

"The makers of the Constitution . . . recognized the significance of man's spiritual nature, of his feelings and of his intellect. . . . They sought to protect Americans in their beliefs, their thoughts, their emotions, and their sensations. They conferred as against the Government, the right to be let alone – the most comprehensive of rights and the most valued by civilized men. To protect that right, every unjustifiable intrusion by the Government upon privacy of the individual, whatever the means employed, must be deemed a Violation of the Fourth Amendment."

## Lack of theoretical framework

The implications of advancing information technology in social planning, where responsibility for determining what information shall be gathered and how it shall be used is a vital element, are extremely grave because of the trained incapacity of the systems analyst. Lacking the theoretical framework on which to draw, he has a different conception of data from that of the professional in the given field; he selects what he considers appropriate as "input", to be programmed and manipulated for the efficient functioning of a system. The analysts doing the Crime Study, for example, accepted as their data base the current statistics on convicted offenders and built all their assumptions and conclusions on these figures. Reliance on the precise quantification of these imprecise and unreliable data led them to an emphasis on crime-susceptible *individuals*, and away from crime-making *conditions*. Since the statistics used related only to persons apprehended by law enforcement officers, they revealed only the hapless and the helpless caught by such systems as Police Information Networks. High-lighted were individual characteristics of the offenders e.g. age, sex, colour, education, employment status, but ignored were the meaningful causal relations between social

---

* Olmstead v. U.S., 277 U.S. 438, 478 (1927). In this landmark case, a 5–4 majority of the Supreme Court held that a federal agent's use of wire-tapping on the telephones of Olmstead, a large-scale bootlegger on the Pacific Coast during Prohibition, was not a search and seizure covered by the Fourth Amendment. Professor Alan Westin, in *Privacy and Freedom* (*op. cit., p. 398*), cites this case as persuasive evidence of the need for a new Supreme Court ruling, because the *Olmstead* decision is no longer relevant in its technological assumptions or its legal foundations.

conditions and attitudes towards the law. Neglected also were the effects of the court system and the penal institutions on the criminal career. Moreover, no consideration was given to the changing conceptions of law with respect to such matters as use of marijuana or homosexuality between consenting adults. These have constituted punishable offences, but basic re-assessment is now under way. The objective of a "system of criminal justice" has not been articulated satisfactorily, and, despite the appearance of precision, we can only surmise that the purpose of the "technological improvement" was to catch more criminals. Hence, such "attacks on crime" as the recently established "Police Control Center" in New York.[8] Here, closed-circuit and helicopter-borne television cameras reporting to a computer-assisted telephone data system will undoubtedly increase the number of arrests. This "success" will bring more persons *into* the system, perhaps even incarcerate them, but whether society's interests *vis-à-vis* criminal justice will be served is quite another matter. This approach inevitably encouraged a neo-Lombroso taxonomy[9] of offender characteristics. If applied, the conclusions of the study would have resulted in a "system of criminal justice" which would have embodied a disastrous attack on the human liberty of the least protected sectors of the population.

The handling of a system's information system cannot be divorced from its theoretical and operational framework, its objectives and its *raison d'être*. Data collected, collated, and manipulated without sensitivity to their meaning, their relationships, and their appropriateness are not only dangerous for us as individuals but also a menace to society, for they can *impede* the efforts of social planners to understand social problems in their true and dynamic dimensions. The appropriate model, the significant frame of reference, sensitivity to the meaning of the subject-matter – these are essential to systematic analysis, and they are totally lacking in the technological approach to information.

There is a real possibility that through the misinterpretation, inappropriate weighting, or distortion by Procrustean treatment to force complex problems into analytically tractable shape, important questions will be ignored and unfortunate conclusions reached. The dangers to society are compounded when political expediency, inertia, or inexperience with quantitative techniques discourage critical evaluation of a system which satisfies only "technical" requirements.

Sir Isaiah Berlin,[10] in his admirable critique of 18th-century mechanists, lists certain prerequisites for adequate model construction:

"the sense of what is characteristic and representative, of what is a true sample suitable for being generalized, and, above all, of how the generalizations fit in with each other – that is, the exercise of judgement, a qualitative, quasi-intuitive form of thinking dependent on wide experience, memory, imagination, on the sense of 'reality', of what goes with what, which may need control by, but is not at all identical with, the capacity for logical reasoning and the construction of laws and scientific models – the capacity for perceiving the relations of the particular case to law, instance to general rule, theorems to axioms, not of parts to wholes or fragments to completed patterns".

The zeal of hardware and software merchants to sell their wares has made information a valuable commodity, to be bought and sold. This intertwining of technology and Madison Avenue could eventually remove information-handling, the heart of most government operations, from the very professionals who understand best the purposes and uses of the data.

Lack of appropriate professional orientation is equally apparent in proposed total systems designs when ignorance is mistaken for objectivity and analysts do not know when they are retreading worn ruts or rehashing tired hypotheses. This has occurred often and was recently brought to public attention. In their report to the Office of Civil Defense on "Management Requirements for Crisis Civil Defense Programs", the Hudson Institute was quoted as saying "The goal of this report is to show the importance of peacetime preparations for the management of crisis programmes".[11] This official evaluation by a technical monitor was that the report was superficial and provided no new information to the professionals in the field; moreover, he commented, the goal as set forth by Hudson had long been achieved.

Absence of guiding principles caused analysts in the California Welfare Study[11] to base their conclusions on a severely limited and not too closely related sample. On the basis of about 110 cases, they projected a possible target population of some 400,000 families and then declared that the evolving patterns that they discerned were "logical and consistent". Their prediction techniques, based on their own econometric model, reflected more their own bias about welfare recipients than a knowledge of the field. Concentration of economic factors, to the exclusion of social and behavioural influences, provided a set of formulae which suggested a chance coincidence between the actual and the predicted in the short run but in the long run generated discrepancies that demanded the introduction of other variables as explanation. The prediction results were found to be substantially less accurate than those reached by the professional research staff as part of their routine duties and without the "powerful tools of technology".

Far from seeking the guidance of professionals in the particular field, technical experts seem to have developed techniques for systematic avoidance of such involvement. "Progress reports" provide little information on which to evaluate progress and are almost invariably submitted so late that it is practically impossible to effect changes. For example, in the Office of Civil Defense's dealings with the Hudson Institute, the first report on contract 64–116 was submitted about seven months after the contractor had begun and when two-thirds of the research work had been completed. Under the second contract, the first report appeared five months after the inception of the project and with three-quarters of the estimated work done. In the California Welfare Study, "progress reports" which were supposed to ensure the active participation of the State Social Welfare Board and other members of a resource committee appeared on the very day of the scheduled meeting and sometimes right at the conference table. Resentment of criticism from the professionals in the field typifies the attitude of many technical systems experts. It may take the mild form of intolerance; it may, however, carry a contemptuous message which says, "You failed to solve this mess by *your* methods so stand aside while I straighten it out with mine."

# References

1 Space-General Corporation, *Systems Management Analysis of the California Welfare System* (SGC 1048 R-G), El Monte, California, 15 March, 1967.

2 Hearings of the Subcommittee of the Committee on Government Operations, US House of Representatives, 89th Congress, Second Session, 26, 27, 28 July, 1966.

3 Baran, Mr Paul, "Testimony at Hearings on 'The Computer and Invasion of Privacy' ", *ibid.*, pp. 119 ff.

4 Buckner, Professor H. Taylor (1967) "Letter to the Editor", *The American Sociologist*, February, p. 25.

5 Westin, Alan F. (Professor of Law, Columbia University, and Director of the Center for Research and Education in American Civil Liberties) (1967) *Privacy and Freedom*, Atheneum, New York.

6 Cowan, Thomas A. (1963) "Decision Theory in Law, Science, and Technology", *Science*, 7 June, p. 1070.

7 Senator Edward V. Long, at Hearings on Computer Privacy, Sub-committee on Administrative Practice and Procedure of the Committee on the Judiciary, US Senate, 90th Congress, First Session, 14 and 15 March, 1967, p. 1.

8 Burnham, David (1969) "City Opens 'World's Most Sophisticated Police Control Center' ", *New York Times*, 14 October.

9 Professor Cesare Lombroso, University of Turin, maintained in *Criminal Man* (1896) and other writings that all crime can be explained by anthropological factors, that motivations for criminal behavior are biological. Thus, some people are born criminal types.

10 "History and Theory: The Concept of Scientific History", *History and Theory* Vol. 1, No. 1 (1960), p. 17.

11 Staats, Elmer B. (1968) *Report to the Congress*, Comptroller General of the United States, *Observations on the Administration by the Office of Civil Defense of Research Study Contracts Awarded to Hudson Institute Inc.*, Report B-133209, 25 March, pp. 32, 33.

Reprinted from *Systems Analysis in Social Policy*, Ida R. Hoos, Institute of Economic Affairs, Westminster, London, S.W.1, 1969.

# 9 Society as a complex adaptive system
## *by Walter Buckley*

We have argued at some length in another place[1] that the mechanical equilibrium model and the organismic homeo-stasis models of society that have underlain most modern sociological theory have outlived their usefulness. A more viable model, one much more faithful to the *kind* of system that society is more and more recognized to be, is in process of developing out of, or is in keeping with, the modern systems perspective (which we use loosely here to refer to general systems research, cybernetics, information and communication theory, and related fields). Society, or the sociocultural system, is not, then, principally an equilibrium system or a homeostatic system, but what we shall simply refer to as a complex adaptive system.

To summarize the argument in overly simplified form: Equilibrial systems are relatively *closed* and *entropic*. In going to equilibrium they typically *lose structure* and have a *minimum of free energy*; they are affected only by external "disturbances" and have *no internal or endogenous sources of change*; their component elements are *relatively simple* and *linked directly via energy exchange* (rather than information interchange); and since they are relatively closed they have no feedback or other systematic self-regulating or adaptive capabilities. The homeostatic system (for example, the organism, apart from higher cortical functioning) is open and negentropic, maintaining a moderate energy level within controlled limits. But for our purposes here, the system's main characteristic is its functioning to *maintain the given structure of the system* within pre-established limits. It involves feedback loops with its environment, and possibly information as well as pure energy interchanges, but these are geared principally to *self-regulation* (structure maintenance) rather than adaptation (*change* of system structure). The complex adaptive systems (species, psychological and sociocultural systems) are also open and negentropic. But they are *open "internally" as well as externally* in that the interchanges among their components may result in *significant changes in the nature of the components themselves* with important consequences for the system as a whole. And the energy level that may be mobilized by the system is subject to relatively wide fluctuation.

Internal as well as external interchanges are mediated characteristically by *information flows* (via chemical, cortical, or cultural encoding and decoding), although pure energy interchange occurs also. True feedback control loops make possible not only self-regulation, but self-direction or at least adaptation to a changing environment, such that the system may *change or elaborate its structure* as a condition of survival or viability.

We argue, then, that the sociocultural system is fundamentally of the latter type, and requires for analysis a theoretical model or perspective built on the kinds of characteristics mentioned. In what follows we draw on many of the concepts and principles presented throughout this source-book to sketch out aspects of a complex adaptive system model or analytical framework for the socio-cultural system. It is further argued that a number of recent sociological and social psychological theories and theoretical orientations articulate well with this modern systems perspective, and we outline some of these to suggest in addition that modern systems research is not as remote from the social scientists' interests and endeavors as many appear to believe.

## Complex adaptive systems: a paradigm

A feature of current general systems research is the gradual development of a general paradigm of the basic mechanisms underlying the evolution of complex adaptive systems. The terminology of this paradigm derives particularly from information theory and cybernetics. We shall review these concepts briefly. The *environment*, however else it may be characterized, can be seen at bottom as a set or ensemble of more or less distinguishable elements, states, or events, whether the discriminations are made in terms of spatial or temporal relations, or properties. Such distinguishable differences in an ensemble may be most generally referred to as *"variety"*. The relatively stable "causal", spatial and/or temporal relations between these distinguishable elements or events may be generally referred to as *"constraint"*. If the elements are so "loosely" related that there is equal probability of any element or state being associated with any other, we speak of "chaos" or complete randomness, and hence, lack of "constraint". But our more typical natural environment is characterized by a relatively high degree of constraint, without which the development and elaboration of adaptive systems (as well as "science") would not have been possible. When the internal organization of an adaptive system acquires features that permit it to discriminate, act upon, and respond to aspects of the environmental variety and its constraints, we might generally say that the system has "*mapped*" parts of the environmental variety and constraints into its organization as structure and/or "information". Thus, a subset of the ensemble of constrained variety in the environment is coded and transmitted in some way via various channels to result in a change in the structure of the receiving system which is isomorphic in certain respects to the original variety. The system thus becomes selectively matched to its environment both physiologically and psychologically. It should be added that two or more adaptive systems, as well as an adaptive system and its natural environment, may be said to be selectively interrelated by a mapping process in the same terms. This becomes especially important for the evolution of social systems.

In these terms, then, the paradigm underlying the evolution of more and more complex adaptive systems begins with the fact of a potentially changing environment characterized by variety with constraints, and an existing adaptive system or organization whose persistence and elaboration to higher levels depends upon a successful mapping of some of the environmental variety and constraints into its own organization on at least a semi-permanent basis. This means that our adaptive system – whether on the biological, psychological, or sociocultural level – must manifest (1) some degree of "*plasticity*" and "*irritability*" vis-à-vis its environment such that it carries on a constant interchange with environmental events, acting on and reacting to it; (2) some source or mechanism for *variety*, to act as a potential pool of adaptive variability to meet the problem of mapping new or more detailed variety and constraints in a changeable environment; (3) a set of *selective* criteria or mechanisms against which the "variety pool" may be sifted into those variations in the organization or system that more closely map the environment and those that do not; and (4) an arrangement for *preserving and/or propagating* these "successful" mappings.[2]

It should be noted, as suggested above, that this is a *relational* perspective, and the question of "substance" is quite secondary here. (We might also note that it is this kind of thinking that gives such great significance to the rapidly developing relational logic that is becoming more and more important as a technical tool of analysis.) Also, as suggested, this formulation corresponds closely with the current conception of "information" viewed as the process of selection – from an ensemble of variety – of a subset which, to have "meaning", must match another subset taken from a similar ensemble.[3] Communication is the process by which this constrained variety is transmitted in one form or another between such ensembles, and involves coding and decoding such that the original variety and its constraints remains relatively invariant at the receiving end. If the source of the "communication" is the causally constrained variety of the natural environment, and the destination is the biological adaptive system, we refer to the Darwinian process of natural selection whereby the information encoded in the chromosomal material (for example the DNA) reflects or is a mapping of the environmental variety, and makes possible a continuous and more or less successful adaptation of the former system to the latter. If the adaptive system in question is a (relatively high-level) psychological or cortical system, we refer to "learning", whereby the significant environmental variety is transmitted via sensory and perceptual channels and decodings to the cortical centers where, by selective criteria (for example, "reward" and "punishment") related to physiological and/or other "needs" or "drives", relevant parts of it are encoded and preserved as "experience" for varying periods of time and may promote adaptation. Or, on the level of the symbol-based sociocultural adaptive system, where the more or less patterned actions of persons and groups are as crucial a part of the environment of other persons and groups as the non-social environment, the gestural variety and its more or less normatively defined constraints is encoded, transmitted, and decoded at the receiving end by way of the various familiar channels with varying degrees of fidelity. Over time, and again by a selective process – now much more complex, tentative, and less easily specified – there is a selective elaboration and more or less temporary preservation of some of this complex social as well as non-social constrained variety in the form of "culture", "social organization", and "personality structure".

On the basis of such a continuum of evolving, elaborating levels of adaptive system (and we have only pointed to three points along this continuum), we could add to and refine our typology of systems. Thus, we note that as adaptive systems develop from the lower biological levels through the higher psychological and sociocultural levels we can distinguish: (1) the *varying time span* required for exemplars of the adaptive system to map or encode within themselves changes in the variety and constraints of the environment; phylogenetic time scales for organic systems and for tropistic or instinctual neural systems; ontogenetic time scales for higher psychological or cortical systems; and, in the sociocultural case, the time span may be very short – days – or very long, but complicated by the fact that the relevant environment includes both intra- and inter-societal variety and constraints as well as natural environment variety (the latter becoming progressively less determinant); (2) the greatly *varying degrees of fidelity of mapping* of the environment into the adaptive system, from the lower unicellular organisms with a very simple repertoire of actions on and reactions to the environment, through the complex of instinctual and learned repertoire, to the ever-proliferating more refined and veridical accumulations of a sociocultural system; (3) the progressively greater separation and independence of the more refined "stored information" from purely biological processes as genetic information is gradually augmented by cortically imprinted information, and finally by entirely extrasomatic cultural depositories. The implications of these shifts, and others that could be included, are obviously far-reaching.

One point that will require more discussion may be briefly mentioned here. This is the *relative* discontinuity we note in the transition from the non-human adaptive system to the sociocultural system. (The insect society and the rudimentary higher animal society make for much less than a complete discontinuity.) As we progress from lower to higher biological adaptive systems we note, as a general rule, the gradually increasing role of other biological units of the same as well as different species making up part of the significant environment. The variety and constraints represented by the behavior of these units must be mapped along with that of the physical environment. With the transition represented by the higher primate social organization through to full-blown human, symbolically mediated, sociocultural adaptive systems, the mapping of the variety and constraints characterizing the subtle behaviors, gestures and intentions of the individuals and groups making up the effective social organization become increasingly central, and eventually equal if not overshadow the requirements for mapping the physical environment.[4]

It was these newly demanding requirements of coordination, anticipation, expectation and the like within a more and more complex *social* environment of interacting and interdependent others – where genetic mappings were absent or inadequate – that prompted the fairly rapid elaboration of relatively new system features. These included, of course: the ever-greater conventionalizing of gestures into true symbols; the resulting development of a "self", self-awareness, or self-consciousness out of the symbolically mediated, continuous mirroring and mapping of each unit's behaviors and gesturings in those of ever-present others (a process well described by Dewey, Mead, Cooley, and others); and the resulting ability to deal in the present with future as well as past mappings and hence to manifest goal-seeking, evaluating, self-other relating, norm-referring behavior. In cybernetic terminology, this higher level sociocultural system became possible through the development of higher order feedbacks such that the component individual subsystems became able to map, store, and selectively act toward, not only the external variety and constraints of the social and non-social environment, but also their own internal states. To speak of self-consciousness, internalization, expectations, choice, certainty and uncertainty, and the like, is to elaborate this basic point. This transition, then, gave rise to the newest adaptive system level we refer to as socio-cultural. As we argued earlier, this higher level adaptive organization thus manifests features that warrant its scientific study in terms as distinct from a purely biological system as the analytical terms of the latter are from physical systems.

## The sociocultural adaptive system

From the perspective sketched above, the following principles underlying the sociocultural adaptive system can be derived:

1. The principle of the "irritability of protoplasm" carries through to all the higher level adaptive systems. "Tension" in the broad sense – in which stress and strain are manifestations under conditions of felt blockage – is ever-present in one form or another throughout the socio-cultural system – how as diffuse, socially unstructured strivings, frustrations, enthusiasms, aggressions, neurotic or psychotic or normative deviation; sometimes as clustered and minimally structured crowd or quasi-group processes, normatively supportive as well as destructive; and now as socioculturally structured creativity and production, conflict and competition, or upheaval and destruction. As Thelen and colleagues put it:

> 1. Man is always trying to live beyond his means. Life is a sequence of reactions to stress: Man is continually meeting situations with which he cannot quite cope.
> 2. In stress situations, energy is mobilized and a state of tension is produced.

3. The state of tensions tends to be disturbing, and Man seeks to reduce the tension.

4. He has direct impulses to take action. . . . [5]

2. Only closed systems running down to their most probable states, that is, losing organization and available energy, can be profitably treated in equilibrium terms. Outside this context the concept of equilibrium would seem quite inappropriate and only deceptively helpful. On the other side, only open, tensionful, adaptive systems can elaborate and proliferate organization. Cannon coined the term "homeostasis" for biological systems to avoid the connotations of equilibrium, and to bring out the dynamic, processual, potential-maintaining properties of *basically unstable* physiological systems.[6] In dealing with the socio-cultural system, however, we need yet a new concept to express not only the *structure-maintaining* feature, but also the *structure-elaborating and changing* feature of the inherently unstable system. The notion of "steady state", now often used, approaches the meaning we seek if it is understood that the "state" that tends to remain "steady" is *not to be identified with the particular structure* of the system. That is, as we shall argue in a moment, in order to maintain a steady state the system may change its particular structure. For this reason, the term "morphogenesis" is more descriptive.[7] C. A. Mace recognizes this distinction in arguing for an extension of the concept of homeostasis:

> The first extension would cover the case in which what is maintained or restored is not so much an internal state of the organism as some relation of the organism to its environment. This would take care of the facts of adaptation and adjustment, including adjustment to the social environment . . . the second extension would cover the case in which the goal and/or norm is some state or relation which has never previously been experienced. There is clearly no reason to suppose that every process of the homeostatic type consists in the maintenance or restoration of a norm.[8]

3. We define a system in general as a complex of elements or components directly or indirectly related in a causal network, such that at least some of the components are related to some others in a more or less stable way *at any one time*. The interrelations may be mutual or unidirectional, linear, non-linear or intermittent, and varying in degrees of causal efficacy or priority. The particular kinds of more or less stable interrelationships of components that become established at any time constitute the particular *structure* of the system at that time.

Thus, the complex, adaptive system as a continuing entity is not to be confused with the structure which that system may manifest at any time. Making this distinction allows us to state a fundamental principle of open, adaptive systems: *Persistence or continuity of an adaptive system may require, as a necessary condition, change in its structure*, the degree of change being a complex function of the internal state of the system, the state of its relevant environment, and the nature of the interchange between the two. Thus, animal species develop and persist or are continuously transformed (or become extinct) in terms of a change (or failure of change) of structure – sometimes extremely slow, sometimes very rapid. The higher individual organism capable of learning by experience maintains itself as a viable system vis-à-vis its environment by a change of structure – in this case the neural structure of the cortex. It is through this principle that we can say that the "higher" organism represents a "higher" level of adaptive system capable, ontogenetically, of *mapping the environment more rapidly and extensively* and with *greater refinement and fidelity*, as compared to the tropistic or instinct-based adaptive system which can change its structure only phylogenetically. The highest level adaptive system – the sociocultural – is capable of an even more rapid and refined mapping of the environment (including the social and non-social environment, as well as at least some aspects of its own internal state) since sociocultural structures are partially independent of both ontogenetic and phylogenetic structures, and the mappings of many individuals are selectively pooled and stored extrasomatically and made available to the system units as they enter and develop within the system.

Such a perspective suggests that, instead of saying, as some do, that a prime requisite for persistence of a social system is "pattern maintenance", we can say, after Sommerhof and Ashby,[9] that persistence of an adaptive system requires as a necessary condition the maintenance of the system's "essential variables" within certain limits. Such essential variables and their limits may perhaps be specified in terms of what some have referred to as the "functional prerequisites" of any social system (for example, a minimal level organismal sustenance, of reproduction, of patterned interactive relations, etc.). But the maintenance of the system's essential variables, we are emphasizing, may hinge on (as history and ethnography clearly show) *pattern reorganization or change*. It is true, but hardly helpful, to say that *some* minimal patterning or stability of relations, or integration of components, is necessary – by the very definition of "system" or adaptive organization. Nor can we be be satisfied, with the statement that persistence, continuity, or social "order" is promoted by the "institutionalization" of interactive relations via norms and values, simply because we can say with equal validity that discontinuity or social "disorder" is *also* promoted by certain kinds of "institutionalization".

To avoid the many difficulties of a one-sided perspective it would seem essential to keep before us as a basic principle that the persistence and/or development of the complex sociocultural system depends upon structuring, destructuring, and restructuring – processes occurring at widely varying rates and degrees as a function of the external social and non-social environment. Jules Henry, among others, has made this point:

> ... the lack of specificity of man's genetic mechanisms has placed him in the situation of constantly having to revise his social structures because of their frequent failure to guide inter-personal relations without tensions felt as burdensome even in the society in which they originate ... thus man has been presented with a unique evolutionary task: because his mechanisms for determining inter-personal relations lack specificity, he must attempt to maximize social adaptation through constant conscious and unconscious revision and experimentation, searching constantly for social structures, patterns of inter-personal relations, that will be more adaptive, as he feels them. Man's evolutionary path is thus set for him by his constant tendency to alter his modes of social adaptation.[10]

More generally, we recall that Karl W. Deutsch has seen restructuring as a basic feature distinguishing society from an organism or machine. Speaking of "the critical property which makes a given learning net into a *society*", he says:

> A learning net functions as a society, in this view, *to the extent* that its constituent physical parts are capable of regrouping themselves into new patterns of activity in response to changes in the net's surroundings, or in response to the internally accumulating results of their own or the net's past.
>
> The twin tests by machine we can tell a society from an organism or a machine, on this showing, would be the freedom of its parts to regroup themselves; and the nature of the regroupings which must imply new coherent patterns of activity – in contrast to the mere wearing out of a machine or the aging of an organism, which are marked by relatively few degrees of freedom and by the gradual disappearance of coherent patterns of activity. ...

This in turn may rest on specific properties of their members: *their capacity for readjustment to new configurations, with renewed complementarity and sustained or renewed communication.*[11]

4. The cybernetic perspective of control or self-regulation of adaptive systems emphasizes the crucial role of "deviation", seen in both negative and positive aspects. On the negative side, certain kinds of deviations of aspects of the system from its given structural state may be seen as "mismatch" or "negative feedback" signals *interpreted by certain organizing centers* as a failure of the system's operating processes or structures relative to a goal state sought, permitting – under certain conditions of adaptive structuring – a change of those operating processes or structures toward goal-optimization. (Thus, one facet of the "political" process of sociocultural systems may be interpreted in this light, with the more "democratic" type of social organization providing the more extended and accurate assessment of the mismatch between goal-attainment on the one hand, and current policy and existing social structuring on the other.)

On the positive side, the cybernetic perspective brings out the absolute necessity of deviation – or, more generally, "variety" – in providing a pool of potential new transformations of process or structure that the adaptive systems might adopt in responding to goal-mismatch. On the lower, biological levels we recognize here the principle of genetic variety and the role of gene pools in the process of adaptive response to organismic mismatch with a changed environment. (And in regard to the other major facet of the "political" process, the more democratic type of social organization makes available a broader range of variety, or "deviation", from which to select new orientations.) Ashby, in developing his very general theory of the adaptive or self-regulating system, suggests the "law of requisite variety", which states that the variety within a system must be at least as great as the environmental variety against which it is attempting to regulate itself. Put more succinctly, only variety can regulate variety. Although such a general principle is a long way from informing more concrete analysis of particular cases, it should help provide a needed corrective to balance (not replace) the current emphasis in social science on conformity, the "control" (as against the cultivation) of "deviants", and "re-equilibration" of a given structure.

Thus, the concept of requisite deviation needs to be proferred as a high-level principle that can lead us to theorize: A requisite of sociocultural systems is the development and maintenance of a significant level of non-pathological deviance manifest as a pool of alternate ideas and behaviors with respect to the traditional, institutionalized ideologies and role behaviors. Rigidification of any given institutional structure must eventually lead to disruption or dissolution of the society by way of internal upheaval or ineffectiveness against external challenge. The student of society must thus pose the question – What "mechanisms" of non-pathological deviance production and maintenance can be found in any society, and what "mechanisms" of conformity operate to counteract these and possibly lessen the viability of the system?

Attempts to analyze a society from such a perspective make possible a more balanced analysis of such processes as socialization, education, mass communication, and economic and political conflict and debate. We are then encouraged to build squarely into our theory and research designs the full sociological significance of such informally well-recognized conceptions as socialization for "self-reliance" and relative "autonomy", education for "creativity", ideational flexibility and the "open mind", communications presenting the "full spectrum" of viewpoints, etc., instead of smuggling them in unsystematically as if they were only residual considerations or ill-concealed value judgments.

5. Given the necessary presence of variety or deviance in an adaptive system, the general systems model then poses the problem of the *selection* and more or less permanent *preservation* or systemic structuring of some of this variety. On the biological level, we have the process of "natural selection" of some of the genetic variety existing within the interfertile species and sub-species gene pool, and the preservation for various lengths of time of this variety through the reproductive process. On the level of higher order psychological adaptive systems, we have trial-and-error selection, by way of the so-called "law of effect", from the variety of environmental events and the potential behavioral repertoire to form learned and remembered experience and motor skills more or less permanently preserved by way of cortical structuring.[12] As symbolic mapping or decoding and encoding of the environment and one's self becomes possible,[13] the selection criteria lean less heavily on direct and simple physiological reward and more heavily on "meanings" or "significance" as manifested in existing self-group structural relations. In the process, selection from the full range of available variety becomes more and more refined and often more restricted, and emerges as one or another kind of "personality" system or "group character" structure. On the sociocultural level,

social selection and relative stabilization or institutionalization of normatively interpreted role relations and value patterns occurs through the variety of processes usually studied under the headings of conflict, competition, accommodation, and such; power, authority and compliance; and "collective behavior", from mob behavior through opinion formation processes and social movements to organized war. More strictly "rational" processes are of course involved, but often seem to play a relatively minor role as far as larger total outcomes are concerned.

It is clearly in the area of "social selection" that we meet the knottiest problems. For the sociocultural system, as for the biological adaptive system, analysis must focus on both the potentialities of the system's structure at a given time, and the environmental changes that might occur and put particular demands on whatever structure has evolved. In both areas the complexities are compounded for the sociocultural system. In developing a typology of systems and their internal linkages we have noted that, as we proceed from the mechanical or physical through the biological, psychic and sociocultural, the system becomes "looser", the interrelations among parts more tenuous, less rigid, and especially less directly tied to physical events as energy relations and transformations are overshadowed by symbolic relations and information transfers. Feedback loops between operating sociocultural structures and the surrounding reality are often long and tortuous, so much so that knowledge of results or goal-mismatch, when forthcoming at all, may easily be interpreted in non-veridical ways (as the history of magic, superstition, and ideologies from primitive to present amply indicate). The higher adaptive systems have not been attained without paying their price, as the widespread existence of illusion and delusions on the personality and cultural levels attest. On the biological level, the component parts have relatively few degrees of freedom, and changes in the environment are relatively directly and inexorably reacted to by selective structural changes in the species.

Sociocultural systems are capable of persisting within a wide range of degrees of freedom of the components, and are often able to "muddle through" environmental changes that are not too demanding. But of course this is part of the genius of this level of adaptive system: it is capable of temporary shifts in structure to meet exigencies. The matter is greatly complicated for the social scientist, however, by this system's outstanding ability to act on and partially control the environment of which a major determining part is made up of other equally loose-knit, more or less flexible, illusion-ridden, sociocultural adaptive systems. Thus, although the minimal integration required for a viable system does set limits on the kinds of structures that can persist, these limits seem relatively broad compared to a biological system.[14] And given the relatively greater degrees of freedom of internal structuring (structural alternatives, as some call them) and the *potentially* great speed with which restructuring may occur under certain conditions, it becomes difficult to predict the reactions of such a system to environmental changes or internal elaboration. Considering the full complexities of the problem we must wonder at the facility with which the functionalist sociologist has pronounced upon the ultimate functions of social structures, especially when – as seems so often the case – very little consideration is given either to the often feedback-starved social selective processes that have led to the given structures, or to the environmental conditions under which they may be presumed to be functional.

Although the problem is difficult, something can be said about more ultimate adaptive criteria against which sociocultural structures can be assessed. Consideration of the grand trends of evolution provides clues to very general criteria. These trends point in the direction of: (1) greater and greater flexibility of structure, as error-controlled mechanisms (cybernetic processes of control) replace more rigid, traditionalistic means of meeting problems and seeking goals; (2) ever more refined, accurate, and systematic mapping, decoding and encoding of the external environment and the system's own internal milieu (via science), along with greater independence from the physical environment; (3) and thereby a greater elaboration of self-regulating substructures in order – not merely to restore a given equilibrium or homeostatic level – but to purposefully restructure the system without tearing up the lawn in the process.[15]

With these and perhaps other general criteria, we might then drop to lower levels of generality by asking what restrictions these place on a sociocultural adaptive system if it is to remain optimally viable in these terms. It is possible that this might provide a value-free basis for discussing the important roles, for example, of a vigorous and independent science in all fields; the broad and deep dissemination of its codified findings; the absence of significant or long-lasting subcultural cleavages, power centers and vested interests, whether on a class or ethnic basis, to break or hinder the flow of information or feedback concerning the internal states of the system; and the promotion of a large "variety pool" by maintaining a certain number of degrees of freedom in the relations of the component parts – for example, providing a number of real choices of behaviors and goals. Thus we can at least entertain the feasibility of developing an objective rationale for the sociocultural "democracy" we shy from discussing in value terms.

6. Further discussion of the intricacies of the problem of *sociocultural selection processes* leading to more or less stable system *structures* may best be incorporated into the frame of discussion of the problem of "*structure versus process*". This is another of those perennial issues of the social (and other) sciences, which the modern systems perspective may illuminate.

Our argument may be outlined as follows:

– Much of modern sociology has analyzed society in terms of largely structural concepts: institutions, culture, norms, roles, groups, etc. These are often reified, and make for a rather static, overly deterministic, and elliptical view of societal workings.

– But for the sociocultural system, "structure" is only a relative stability of underlying, ongoing micro-processes. Only when we focus on these can we begin to get at the selection process whereby certain interactive relationships become relatively and temporarily stabilized into social and cultural structures.

– The unit of dynamic analysis thus becomes the systemic *matrix* of interacting, goal-seeking, deciding individuals and subgroups – whether this matrix is part of a formal organization or only a loose collectivity. Seen in this light, society becomes a continuous morphogenic process, through which we may come to understand in a unified conceptual manner the development of structures, their maintenance, and their change. And it is important to recognize that out of this matrix is generated, not only *social* structure, but also *personality* structure, and *meaning* structure. All, of course, are intimately interrelated in the morphogenic process, and are only analytically separable.

## Structure, process, and decision theory

Though the problem calls for a lengthy methodological discussion, we shall here simply recall the viewpoint that sees the sociocultural system in comparative perspective against lower-level mechanical, organic and other types of systems. As we proceed upward along such a typology we noted that the ties linking components become less and less rigid and concrete, less direct, simple and stable within themselves. Translation of energy along unchanging and physically continuous links gives way in importance to transmission of information via internally varying, discontinuous components with many more degrees of freedom. Thus for mechanical systems, and parts of organic systems, the "structure" has a representation that is concrete and directly observable – such that when the system ceases to operate much of the structure remains directly observable for a time. For the sociocultural system, "structure" becomes a theoretical construct whose referent is only indirectly observable (or only inferable) by way of series of events along a time dimension; when the system ceases to operate, the links maintaining the sociocultural structure are no longer observable.[16] "Process", then, points to the actions and interactions of the components of an ongoing system, in which varying degrees of structuring arise, persist, dissolve, or change. (Thus "process" should not be made synonymous simply with "change", as it tended to be for many earlier sociologists.)

More than a half century ago, Albion W. Small argued that, "The central line in the path of methodological progress in sociology is marked by the gradual shifting of effort from analogical representation of social structures to real analysis of social processes."[17] This was an important viewpoint for many social thinkers earlier in this century, possibly as part of the trend in physical science and philosophy toward a process view of reality developing from the work of such people as Whitehead, Einstein, Dewey, and Bentley. Such views have apparently had little impact on those of recent decades who had developed the more dominant structure-oriented models of current sociology, but it seems clear that – with or without the aid of the essentially process-conscious general systems approach – a more even balance of process with structure in the analysis of sociocultural systems is gradually regaining lost ground.

C. H. Cooley, in his *Social Process*, focused on the "tentative process", involving inherent energy and growth as the dynamic agents, with ongoing "selective development" set in motion by the interaction of "active tendencies" and surrounding "conditions". He argued that for the social process, "that grows which works" is a better phrase than "natural selection" or "survival of the fittest", since "it is not so likely to let us rest in mechanical or biological conceptions".[18] R. E. Park, with his recognition of the central importance of communication, kept the notion of process in the foreground whether developing the forms of interaction or the foundations of social ecology. We should also recall the leaders of the so-called "formal" school: Whereas Simmel focused on "forms of interaction", the emphasis was always on the "interaction" as

process rather than simply on the "forms"; and though the Wiese–Becker systematics developed in great detail a classification of action *patterns*, it gave equal attention to *action* patterns. For W. I. Thomas, all social becoming is viewed as a product of continual interaction of individual consciousness and objective social reality. (F. Znaniecki more recently reinforced this point of view.[19]) And at least one unbroken thread in this vein continuing from the early part of the century is the Dewey–Mead perspective referred to as social interactionism (which, we have noted, has established a strong base especially congenial to the modern cybernetic approach).[20] A reviewer of a recent collection of social interactionist essays was "reminded throughout of the continuous character of socialization, of the complexity and fluidity of interaction when it is viewed as a process rather than as the mere enactment of social forms . . .".[21]

We can take only brief note of a few of the more recent arguments for the process viewpoint. The anthropologists, for example, have become acutely concerned in the last few years with this issue. G. P. Murdock seems to be echoing Small when he says, 'All in all, the static view of social structure which seeks explanations exclusively within the existing framework of a social system on the highly dubious assumption of cultural stability and nearly perfect functional integration seems clearly to be giving way, in this country at least, to a dynamic orientation which focuses attention on the processes by which such systems come into being and succeed one another over time."[22] At about the same time, Raymond Firth was stating: "The air of enchantment which for the last two decades has surrounded the 'structuralist' point of view has now begun to be dispelled. Now that this is so, the basic value of the concept of social structure as an heuristic tool rather than a substantial social entity has come to be more clearly recognized."[23]

Soon after appeared the late S. F. Nadel's penetrating work, *The Theory of Social Structure*, which was preceded by his article on "Social Control and Self Regulation". This perspective is used effectively in *The Theory of Social Structure* as a basis for a critique of the current rather one-sided equilibrium model emphasizing the "complementarity of expectations" to the relative neglect of the several other crucial types of associative *and* dissociative social interrelationships considered equally important in earlier sociology.

Parsons' model has to do with "the conditions of relatively stable interaction in social systems", implying defined value "standards" and "institutionalized role expectations": any willful disagreement with them simply falls outside the stipulated stability and the model based on it.

I would argue that this is not necessarily so and that our model must allow for such disagreements. Even "relatively stable" social systems do not exclude them, or include them only in the form of purely fortuitous contingencies. Far from being fortuitous or idiosyncratic, the rejection of the sanctioning potentialities of other roles may itself be anchored in the existing institutions, reflecting the presence of diverse but equally legitimate "value patterns", ideologies or schools of thought, that is, that plurality of norms we spoke of before.[24]

Nadel's book as a whole explores the thesis that structural analysis is not, and should not be treated as, static analysis: "Social structure as Fortes once put it, must be 'visualized' as 'a sum of processes in time'. As I would phrase it, social structure is implicitly an event-structure. . . . "[25] And in concluding he reiterates his argument that

> . . . it seems impossible to speak of social structure in the singular. Analysis in terms of structure is incapable of presenting whole societies; nor, which means the same, can any society be said to exhibit an embracing, coherent structure as we understand the term. There are always cleavages, dissociations, enclaves, so that any description alleged to present a single structure will in fact present only a fragmentary or one-sided picture.[26]

As a final example in anthropology, we should mention the cogent argument of Evon Z. Vogt that the two concepts of structure and process must be integrated into a general theoretical model. As with Nadel, structure is seen as falsely conceived as static, with change pathological. Rather, Vogt feels, must we pose the primacy of change, considering structure the way in which moving reality is translated, for the observer, into an instantaneous and artificial observation: social and cultural structures are only the intersections in time and space of process in course of change and development.[27]

Among sociologists, a perennial critic of the overly-structural conception of the group is Herbert Blumer. Blumer has argued that it is from the process of ongoing interaction itself that group life gets its main features, which cannot be adequately analyzed in terms of fixed attitudes, "culture", or social structure – nor can it be conceptualized in terms of mechanical structure, the functioning of an organism, or a system seeking equilibrium, ". . . in view of the formative and explorative character of interaction as the participants *judge* each other and *guide* their own acts by that judgment."

> The human being is not swept along as a neutral and indifferent unit by the operation of a system. As an organism capable of self-interaction he forges his actions out of a process of definition involving *choice*, *appraisal*, and *decision*. . . . Cultural norms, status positions and role relationships are only *frameworks* inside of which that process [of formative transaction] goes on.[28]

Highly structured human association is relatively infrequent and cannot be taken as a prototype of a human group life. In sum, institutionalized patterns constitute only one conceptual aspect of society, and they point to only a part of the ongoing process (and, we might add, they must be seen to include deviant and disfunctional patterns: for conceptual clarity and empirical relevance, "institutionalization" cannot be taken to imply only "legitimacy", "consent", and ultimately adaptive values).

Finally, it should be noted that Gordon Allport, viewing personality as an open-system, stresses a very similar point concerning the organization of personality:

> . . . the best hope for discovering coherence would seem to lie in approaching personality as a total functioning structure, i.e., as a *system*. To be sure, it is an incomplete system, manifesting varying degrees of order and disorder. It has structure but also unstructure, function but also malfunction. As Murphy says, "all normal people have many loose ends". And yet personality is well enough knit to qualify as a system – which is defined merely as *a complex of elements in mutual interaction*.[29]

In the light of such views, we need only recall the many critiques pointing to the incapacity or awkwardness of the conventional type of framework before the facts of process, "becoming", and the great range of "collective behavior".[30]

Statements such as Blumer's, a continuation of the perspective of many neglected earlier sociologists and social psychologists, would seem to constitute a perspective that is now pursued by many under new rubrics such as "decision theory". For earlier antecedents it should be enough to mention W. I. Thomas's "definition of the situation", Znaniecki's "humanistic coefficient", Weber's "verstehen", Becker's "interpretation", and MacIver's "dynamic assessment".[31] Much of the current structural, consensus theory represents a break from this focus. As Philip Selznick has argued,

A true theory of social action would say something about goal-oriented or problem-solving behavior, isolating some of its distinctive attributes, stating the likely outcomes of determinate transformations. . . . In Parsons' writing there is no true embrace of the idea that structure is being continuously opened up and reconstructed by the problem-solving behavior of individuals responding to concrete situations. This is a point of view we associate with John Dewey and G. H. Mead, for whom, indeed, it had significant intellectual consequences. For them and for their intellectual heirs, social structure is something to be taken account of in action; cognition is not merely an empty category but a natural process involving dynamic assessments of the self and the other.[32]

It can be argued, then, that a refocusing is occurring via "decision theory", whether elaborated in terms of "role-strain" theory; theories of cognitive dissonance, congruence, balance, or concept formation; exchange, bargaining, or conflict theories, or the mathematical theory of games. The basic problem is the same: How do interacting personalities and groups define, assess, interpret, "verstehen", and act on the situation? Or, from the broader perspective of our earlier discussion, how do the processes of "social selection" operate in the "struggle" for socio-cultural structure? Instead of asking how structure affects, determines, channels actions and interactions, we ask how structure is created, maintained, and recreated.

Thus we move down from structure to social interrelations and from social relations to social actions and interaction processes – to a matrix of "dynamic assessments" and intercommunication of meanings, to evaluating emoting, deciding and choosing. To avoid anthropomorphism and gain the advantages of a broader and more rigorously specified conceptual system, we arrive at the language of modern systems theory.

Basic ingredients of the decision-making focus include, then: (1) a *process* approach; (2) a conception of *tension* as inherent in the process; and (3) a renewed concern with the role and workings of man's enlarged cortex seen as a complex adaptive subsystem operating within an *interaction matrix* characterized by *uncertainty, conflict,* and other dissociative (as well as associative) processes *underlying the structuring and restructuring of the larger psycho-social system.*

## Process focus

The process focus points to information-processing individuals and groups linked by different types of communication nets to form varying types of interaction matrices that may be characterized by "competition", "cooperation", "conflict", and the like. Newer analytical tools being explored to handle such processes include treatment of the interaction matrix over time as a succession of states described in terms of transition probabilities, Markoff chains, or stochastic processes in general. The Dewey–Mead "transactions" are now discussed in terms of information and codings and decodings, with the essential "reflexivity" of behavior now treated in terms of negative and positive feedback loops linking via the communication process the intrapersonal, interpersonal and intergroup subsystems and making possible varying degrees of matching and mismatching of Mead's "self and others", the elaboration of Boulding's "Image",[33] and the execution of Miller's "Plans". And herein we find the great significance for sociology of many of the conceptual tools (though not, at least as yet, the mathematics) of information and communication theory, cybernetics, or general systems research, along with the rapidly developing techniques of *relational* mathematics such as the several branches of set theory – topology, group theory, graphy theory, symbolic logic, etc.

## Conception of tension

Tension is seen as an inherent and essential feature of complex adaptive systems; it provides the "go" of the system, the "force" behind the elaboration and maintenance of structure. There is no "law of social inertia" operating here, nor can we count on "automatic" re-equilibrating forces counteracting system "disturbances" or "deviance", for, whereas we do find deviance-reducing negative feedback loops in operation we *also* find deviance-maintaining and deviance-amplifying *positive* feedback processes often referred to as the vicious circle or spiral, or "escalation".[34] It is not at all certain whether the resultant will maintain, change, or destroy the given system or its particular structure. The concepts of "stress" or "strain" we take to refer only to the greater mobilization of normal tension under conditions of more than usual blockage. And instead of a system's seeking to manage *tension*, it would seem more apt to speak of a system's seeking to manage *situations* interpreted as responsible for the production of greater than normal tension.

The "role strain" theory of William J. Goode is an illustrative attack on assumptions of the widely current structural approach, using a process and tension emphasis and contributing to the decision-theory approach. Goode analyzes social structure or institutions into role relations, and role relations into role transactions. "Role relations are seen as a sequence of 'role bargains' and as a continuing process of selection among alternative role behaviors, in which each individual seeks to reduce his role strain." [35] Contrary to the current stability view, which sees social system continuity as based primarily on normative consensus and normative integration, Goode thus sees "dissensus, nonconformity, and conflicts among norms and roles as the usual state of affairs. . . . The individual cannot satisfy fully all demands, and must move through a continuous sequence of role decision and bargains . . . in which he seeks to reduce his role strain, his felt difficulty in carrying out his obligations." [36] Goode also recognizes that there is no "law of social inertia" automatically maintaining a given structure.

> Like any structure or organized pattern, the role pattern is held in place by both internal and external forces – in this case, the role pressures from other individuals. Therefore, not only is role strain a normal experience for the individual, but since the individual processes of reducing role strain determine the total allocation of role performances to the social institutions, the total balances and imbalances of role strains create whatever stability the social structure possesses. [37]

It should be noted, however, that Goode accepts unnecessarily a vestige of the equilibrium or stability model when he states, "The total role structure functions so as to reduce role strain." [38] He is thus led to reiterate a proposition that – when matched against our knowledge of the empirical world – is patently false. Or, more precisely, not false, but a half-truth: it recognizes deviance-reducing negative feedback processes, but not deviance-amplifying positive feedback processes. Such a proposition appears reasonable only if we "hold everything else constant", that is, take it as a closed system. However, the proposition is unnecessary to his argument and, in fact, clashes with the rest of his formulation: ". . . though the sum of role performances ordinarily maintains a society it may also change the society or fail to keep it going. There is no necessary harmony among all role performances. . . . But whether the resulting societal pattern is 'harmonious' or integrated or whether it is even effective in maintaining that society, are separate empirical questions." [39]

## Study of cognitive processes

A more concerted study of cognitive processes, especially under conditions of *uncertainty* and *conflict*, goes hand in hand, of course, with a focus on decision-making and role transactions. Despite the evolutionary implications of man's enlarged cortex, much social (and psychological) theory seems predicted on the assumption that men are decorticated. Cognitive processes, as they are coming to be viewed today, are not to be simply equated with the traditional, ill-defined, concept of the "rational". That the data-processing system – whether socio-psychological or electro-mechanical – is seen as inherently "rational" tells us little about its outputs in concrete cases. Depending on the adequacy and accuracy of the effectively available information, the total internal organization or "Image", the character of the "Plans" or program, and the nature of the significant environment, the output of either "machine" may be sense or nonsense, symbolic logic or psychologic, goal-attainment or oscillation.

Beyond giving us a deeper perspective on the concept of the "rational", current theories of cognitive processes give promise of transcending the hoary trichotomy of the cognitive, the conative, and the moral as analytical tools. Whether this amounts to a rejection of the distinction, or simply an insistence that what was analytically rent asunder must now be reunified, the ferment appears significant. We refer here, not only to the many neurological and schematic studies of the brain, or the processes by which it solves problems and attains concepts, but especially to the several theories of cognitive "dissonance" or "congruence" or "balance" represented in the works of Heider, Cartwright and Harary, Osgood and Tannenbaum, Festinger, and others, as well as the symbol-processing and interpersonal communication perspectives represented by the "psycholinguistics" of Osgood, the "communicative acts" of Newcomb, and the "two factor" theory of Mowrer.

The intricate meeting of the cognitive, the affective and evaluative (or attitudinal), and the semantic or symbolic in such theories is well illustrated in Osgood's treatment of "cognitive dynamics". Equating "cognitive elements" with the *meanings* of signs, Osgood proposes that "congruity exists when the evaluative meanings of interacting signs are equally polarized or intense – either in the same or opposite evaluative directions . . .". [40] In contrast to the theories of Heider and Festinger, this theory *"assigns affective or attitudinal values to the cognitive elements themselves, and not to their relations . . .".* [41] And in discussing the "process of inference through psycho-logic", Osgood says:

> Much of what is communicated attitudinally by messages and by behavior is based on such inferences; . . . The syntax of language and of behavior provides a structural framework within which meaningful contents

are put; the structure indicates what is related to what, and how, but only when the meaningful values are added does the combination of structure and content determine psycho-logical congruence or incongruence.[42]

Despite the incorporation of aspects of these several elements into their theories, however, the psychologically oriented theorist usually leaves the sociologist something to be desired, namely, something that transcends "the individual" and "his" attempts to minimize inconsistency or dissonance and maintain stability, and which views the group situation as inadequately characterized in terms of "myriad decisions in individual nervous systems". Thus Osgood hypothesizes that

laws governing the thinking and behaving of individuals also govern the "thinking" and "behaving" of groups . . . with nothing but communication to bind us together, it is clear that "decisions" and "behaviors" of nations must come down to myriad decisions in individual nervous systems and myriad behaviors of individual human organisms.[43]

We are reminded here of Robert R. Sears' complaint that "psychologists think monadically. That is, they choose the behavior of one person as their scientific subject matter. For them, the universe is composed of individuals . . . the universal laws sought by the psychologist almost always relate to a single body."[44] Arguing for the desirability of combining individual and social behavior into a common framework, Sears noted that, "Whether the group's behavior is dealt with as antecedent and the individual's as consequent, or vice versa, the two kinds of event are so commonly mixed in causal relationships that it is impractical to conceptualize them separately."[45]

Fortunately, however, there are recent statements that rally to the side of the sociological interactionist theorists, whose perspective continues to be ignored or little understood by so many personality theorists who are nevertheless gradually rediscovering and duplicating its basic principles. A good beginning to a truly interpersonal approach to personality theory and the problem of stability and change in behavior is the statement of Paul F. Secord and Carl W. Backman, which remarkably parallels Goode's theory of stability and change in social systems discussed earlier. Pointing to the assumptions of several personality theorists that when stability of behavior occurs it is solely a function of stability in personality structure, and that this latter structure has, inherently, a strong resistance to change except when special change-inducing

forces occur, Secord and Backman see as consequences the same kinds of theoretical inadequacies we found for the stability view of social systems:

The first is that continuity in individual behavior is not a problem to be solved; it is simply a natural outcome of the formation of stable structure. The second is that either behavioral change is not given systematic attention, or change is explained independently of stability. Whereas behavioral stability is explained by constancy of structure, change tends to be explained by environmental forces and fortuitous circumstances.[46]

Their own theoretical view abandons these assumptions and "places the locus of stability and change in the interaction process rather than in intrapersonal structures." Recognizing the traditional two classes of behavioral determinants, the cultural-normative and the intrapersonal, their conceptualization

attempts to identify a third class of determinants, which have their locus neither in the individual nor the culture, but in the interaction process itself. In a general sense this third class may be characterized as the tendencies of the individual and the persons with whom he interacts to shape the interaction process according to certain requirements, i.e., they strive to produce certain patterned relations. As will be seen, the principles governing this activity are truly interpersonal; they require as much attention to the behavior of the other as they do to the behavior of the individual, and it cannot be said that one or the other is the sole locus of cause.[47]

They go on to analyze the "interpersonal matrix" into three components: an aspect of the self-concept of a person, his interpretation of those elements of his behavior related to that aspect, and his perception of related aspects of the other with whom he is interacting. "An interpersonal matrix is a recurring functional relation between these three components."

In these terms, Secord and Backman attempt to specify the conditions and forces leading to or threatening congruency or incongruency, and hence stability or change, in the matrix. Thus, four types of incongruency, and two general classes of resolution of incongruency, are discussed. One of these latter classes

results in restoration of the original matrix, leaving self and behavior unchanged (although cognitive distortions may occur), and the other leads to a new matrix in which self or behavior are changed.[48]

In sum, contrary to previous approaches, theirs emphasizes

that "the individual strives to maintain interpersonal relations characterized by congruent matrices, rather than to maintain a self, habits, or traits".

> Maintenance of intrapersonal structure occurs only when such maintenance is consistent with an ongoing interaction process which is in a state of congruency. That most individuals do maintain intrapersonal structure is a function of the fact that the behavior of others toward the individuals in question is normally overwhelmingly consistent with such maintenance.[49]

And this conception also, as most approaches do not (or do inadequately), predict or accounts for the fact that, should the interpersonal environment cease to be stable and familiar, undergoing great change such that others behave uniformly toward the individual in new ways, the individual "would rapidly modify his own behavior and internal structure to produce a new set of congruent matrices. As a result, he would be a radically changed person."[50]

As we have said, the Secord and Backman theory and Goode's role-strain theory may be seen as closely complementary views. The former argues that *personality* structure is generated in, and continues to have its seat in, the social interactive matrix; the latter argues that *social* structure is generated in, and continues to have its seat in, the social interactive matrix. Since it is the latter that we are focusing on here, we shall conclude with additional examples of current theory and research that explore further the mechanisms underlying the genesis or elaboration of social structure out of the dynamics, especially the role dynamics, of the symbolic interaction process.

## Further examples

Ralph Turner has addressed himself to the elaboration of this perspective in that conceptual area fundamental to the analysis of institutions – roles and role-taking.[51] The many valid criticisms of the more static and overdetermining conception of roles is due, he believes, to the dominance of the Linton view of role and the use of an over-simplified model of role functioning. Viewing role-playing and role-taking, however, as a process (as implied in Meadian theory), Turner shows that there is more to it than just "an extension of normative or cultural deterministic theory" and that a process view of role adds novel elements to the notion of social interaction.

The morphogenic nature of role behavior is emphasized at the start in the concept of "*role-making*". Instead of postulating the initial existence of distinct, identifiable roles, Turner posits "a tendency to create and modify conceptions of self- and other-roles" as the interactive orienting process. Since actors behave *as if* there were roles, although the latter actually exist only in varying degrees of definitiveness and consistency, the actors attempt to define them and make them explicit – thereby in effect creating and modifying them as they proceed. The key to role-taking, then, is the morphogenic propensity "to shape the phenomenal world into roles"; formal organizational regulation restricting this process is not to be taken as the prototype, but rather as a "distorted instance" of the wider class of role-taking phenomena. To the extent that the bureaucratic setting blocks the role-making process, organization is maximal, "variety" or alternatives of action minimal, actors are cogs in a rigid machine, and the morphogenic process underlying the viability of complex adaptive systems is frustrated.

Role interaction is a tentative process of reciprocal responding of self and other, challenging or reinforcing one's conception of the role of the other, and consequently stabilizing or modifying one's own role as a product of this essentially feedback-testing transaction. The conventional view of role emphasizing a prescribed complementarity of expectations thus gives way to a view of role-taking as a process of "devising a performance on the basis of an imputed other-role", with an important part being played by cognitive processes of inference testing. In a manner consistent with models of the basic interaction process suggested by Goode and by Secord and Backman, Turner views as a central feature of role-taking "the process of discovering and creating 'consistent' wholes out of behavior", of "devising a pattern" that will both cope effectively with various types of relevant others and meet some recognizable criteria of consistency. Such a conception generates empirically testable hypotheses of relevance of our concern here with institutional morphogenesis, such as: "Whenever the social structure is such that many individuals characteristically act from the perspective of two given roles simultaneously, there tends to emerge a single role which encompasses the action."[52]

Turning directly to the implications for formal, institutional role-playing, Turner argues that the formal role is primarily a "skeleton" of rules which evoke and set into motion the fuller roles built-up and more or less consensually validated in the above ways. Role behavior becomes relatively fixed only while it provides a perceived consistency and stable framework for interaction, but it undergoes cumulative revision in the role-taking process of accommodation and compromise with the simple conformity demanded by formal prescriptions.

The purposes and sentiments of actors constitute a unifying element in role genesis and maintenance, and hence role-taking must be seen to involve a great deal of selective perception of other-behavior and relative emphasis in the elaboration of the role pattern. This selection process operates on the great variety of elements in the situation of relevant objects and other-behaviors which could become recognized components in a consistent role pattern. Not all combinations of behavior and object relations can be classed into a single role; there must be criteria by which actors come to "verify" or "validate" the construction of a number of elements into a consistent role. This verification stems from two sources: "internal validation" of the interaction itself, and "external validation" deriving from "the generalized other" of Mead. The former hinges on successful prediction or anticipation of relevant other-behavior in the total role-set, and hence on the existence of role patterns whereby coherent selection of behaviors judged to constitute a consistent role can be made. But the notion of fixed role prescriptions is not thereby implied, since, first, roles – like norms – often or usually provide a *range of alternative* ways of dealing with any other-role, or, as is most common, the small segment of it activated at any one time, and secondly, the coherence and predictability of a role must be assessed and seen as "validated", not in terms of any one other-role, but in terms of the Gestalt of all the accommodative and adjusted requirements set by the number of other-roles in the actor's role-set and generated in the ongoing role-making process.

An example is provided by the study by Gross *et al.* of the school superintendent role. It is found that incumbency in this role (1) actually involved a great deal of choice behavior in selecting among the alternative interpretations and behaviors deemed possible and appropriate, and that (2) consistency and coherence of an incumbent's behavior could be seen only in terms of the total role as an accommodation with correlative other-roles of school board member, teacher, and parent, with which the superintendent was required to interact simultaneously. As Gross puts it, a "system model" as against a "position-centric" model involves an important addition by including the interrelations among the counter positions. "A position can be completely described only by describing the total system of positions and relationships of which it is a part. In other words, in a system of interdependent parts, a change in any relationship will have an effect on all other relationships, and the positions can be described only by the relationships."[53]

Thus Turner sees the internal criterion of role validation as insuring a constant modification, creation, or rejection of the content of specific roles occurring in the interplay between the always somewhat vague and incomplete ideal role conceptions and the experience of their concrete implications by the interpreting, purposive, selectively evaluating and testing self and others.

The basis of "external validation" of a role is the judgment of the behavior to constitute a role by others felt to have a claim to correctness of legitimacy. Criteria here include: discovery of a name in common use for the role, support of major norms or values, anchorage in the membership of recognized groups, occupancy of formalized positions, and experience of key individuals as role models acting out customary attitudes, goals and specific actions.

Under the "normal loose operation of society" these various internal and external criteria of validation are at best only partially conveyant and consistent in identifying the same units and content as roles. The resulting inevitable discrepancies between formal, institutional rules and roles, and the goals, sentiments and selective interpretations arising from the experience of actually trying to play them out, make role conceptions "creative compromises", and insure "that the framework of roles will operate as a hazily conceived ideal framework for behavior rather than as an unequivocal set of formulas".[54]

In sum, "institutions" may provide a normative framework prescribing roles to be played and thus assuring the required division of labor and minimizing the costs of general exploratory role-setting behavior, but the actual role transactions that occur generate a more or less coherent and stable working compromise between ideal set prescriptions and a flexible role-making process, between the structured demands of others and the requirements of one's own purposes and sentiments. This conception of role relations as "fully interactive", rather than merely conforming, contributes to the recent trends "to subordinate normative to functional processes in accounting for societal integration"[55] by emphasizing the complex adaptive interdependence of actors and actions in what we see as an essentially morphogenic process – as against a merely equilibrial or homeostatic process.

## Organization as a negotiated order

Next we shall look at a recently reported empirical study of a formal organization that concretely illustrates many facets of the above conceptualization of Turner and contributes further to our thesis. In their study of the hospital and its interactive order, Anselm Strauss and colleagues develop a model of organizational process that bears directly on the basic sociological problem of "how a measure of order is maintained in the face of inevitable changes (derivable from sources both external and internal to the organization)".[56] Rejecting an overly structural view, it is assumed that social order is not simply normatively specified and automatically maintained but is something that must be "worked at", continually reconstituted. Shared agreements, underlying orderliness, are not binding and shared indefinitely but involve a temporal dimension implying eventual review, and consequent renewal or rejection. On the basis of such considerations, Strauss and colleagues develop their conception of organizational order as a "negotiated order".

The hospital, like any organization, can be visualized as a hierarchy of status and power, of rules, roles and organizational goals. But it is also a locale for an ongoing complex of transactions among differentiated types of actors: professionals such as psychiatrists, residents, nurses and nursing students, psychologists, occupational therapists and social workers; and non-professionals such as various levels of staff, the patients themselves, and their families. The individuals involved are at various stages in their careers, have their own particular goals, sentiments, reference groups, and ideologies, command various degrees of prestige, esteem and power, and invest the hospital situation with differential significance.

The rules supposed to govern the actions of the professionals were found to be far from extensive, clearly stated, or binding; hardly anyone knew all the extant rules or the applicable situations and sanctions. Some rules previously administered would fall into disuse, receive administrative reiteration, or be created anew in a crisis situation. As in any organization, rules were selectively evoked, broken, and/or ignored to suit the defined needs of personnel. Upper administrative levels especially avoided periodic attempts to have the rules codified and formalized, for fear of restricting the innovation and improvisation believed necessary to the care of patients. Also, the multiplicity of professional ideologies, theories and purposes would never tolerate such rigidification.

In sum, the area of action covered by clearly defined rules was very small, constituting a few general "house rules" based on long-standing shared understandings. The basis of organizational order was the generalized mandate, the single ambiguous goal, of returning patients to the outside world in better condition. Beyond this, the rules ordering actions to this end were the subject of continual negotiations – being argued, stretched, ignored, or lowered as the occasion seemed to demand. As elsewhere, rules failed to act as universal prescriptions, but required judgment as to their applicability to the specific case.

The ambiguities and disagreements necessitating negotiation are seen by the researchers to be patterned. The various grounds leading to negotiation include: disagreement and tension over the proper ward placement of a patient to maximize his chances of improvement; the mode of treatment selected by the physician, which is closely related to his own psychiatric ideology and training; the multiplicity of purposes and temporal ends of each of the professional groups as they maneuver to elicit the required cooperation of their fellow workers; the element of medical uncertainty involved in treating the patient as a unique, "individual case", and the consequent large area of contingency lying of necessity beyond specific role prescription; and, finally, the inevitable changes forced upon the hospital and its staff by external forces and the unforeseen consequences of internal policies and the round of negotiations themselves. What is concretely observed, then, in researching the organizational order of the hospital, is negotiation between the neurologically trained and the psychotherapeutically oriented physician, between the nurses and the administrative staff, between the nonprofessional floor staff and the physician, between the patient and each of the others.

The negotiation process itself was found to have patterned and temporal features. Thus, different physicians institute their own particular programs of treatment and patient care and in the process develop fairly stable understandings with certain nurses or other institutional gatekeepers such as to effectuate an efficient order of behaviors with a minimum of communication and special instructions. Such arrangements are not called for by any organizational role prescriptions; nevertheless, they represent a concrete part of the actual organization generated in the morphogenic process of negotiation (or role-making and -taking, in Turner's terms). Thus, agreements do not occur by chance but are patterned in terms of "who contracts with whom, about what, as well as when . . .".[57] There is an important temporal aspect, also, such as the specification of a termination period often written into an agreement – as when a physician bargains with a head nurse to leave his patient in the specific ward for "two more days" to see if things will work themselves out satisfactorily.

In a final section of their paper, Strauss and his colleagues bring out the full implications of their negotiation model in dealing with genuine organizational change. The model presents a picture of the hospital – and perhaps most other institutionalized spheres of social life – as a transactional milieu where numerous agreements are "continually being established, renewed, reviewed, revoked, revised". But this raises the question of the relation between this process and the more stable structure of norms, statuses, and the like. The authors see a close systemic relation between the two. The daily negotiations periodically call for a reappraisal and reconstitution of the organizational order into a "new order, not the reestablishment of an old, as reinstituting of a previous equilibrium". And, we would add, it contributes nothing to refer to this as a "moving equilibrium" in the scientifically established sense of the term. The daily negotiative process not only allows the day-by-day work to get done, but feeds back upon the more formalized, stable structure of rules and policies by way of "a periodic appraisal process" to modify it – sometimes slowly and crescively, sometimes rapidly and convulsively. And, as a reading of history suggests, virtually every formal structure extant can be traced, at least in principle, from its beginnings to its present apparently timeless state through just such a morphogenic process – a process characteristic of what we have called the complex adaptive system.

## The school superintendent and his role

We turn to the study by Gross and his associates of the role system of the school superintendent and his counter-role partners, the school board member, the teacher, and the parent. A major burden of this empirical study is to demonstrate the research sterility of the Lintonian conception of role, and structural theories built on it, due principally to the postulate of consensus on role definition. The study showed a majority of significant differences in the definitions of their own roles by a sample of incumbents of the same social position and by incumbents of different but interrelated counter positions. This fact led Gross and his associates to the demonstration of a number of important theoretical consequences derived from rejection of the postulate of role consensus. It is often assumed, for example, that the socialization process by which roles are "acquired" provides for a set of clearly defined and agreed-upon expectations associated with any particular position. But the empirically discovered fact of differential *degrees of consensus* seriously challenged this assumption. From our systems model viewpoint, recognition of degrees of consensus is tantamount to the recognition of a continuous source of "variety" in the role system, as defined earlier, which leads us to seek the various *selective*, choice processes occurring in the role transactions. At least for the occupational positions studied, it was found that the assumption of socialization on the basis of prior consensus on role

definitions was untenable, and deserved "to be challenged in most formulations of role acquisition, including even those concerned with the socialization of the child".[58]

Secondly, the research showed that, instead of assuming role consensus and explaining variations of behavior of incumbents of the same position in terms of personality variables, one would better explain them in terms of the varying role expectations and definitions – which may be unrelated to psychological differences.

The implications are also great for a theory of social control. Instead of a model assuming that the application or threat of negative sanctions leads to conformity to agreed-upon norms, the research pointed to the numerous situations in which, due to variant or ambiguous role definitions, the same behavior resulted in negative sanctions by some role partners and positive sanctions by others, or failure to apply sanctions because of perceived ambiguity – or nonconformity to perceived expectations of another despite negative sanctions because other expectations were defined as more legitimate.

Another Lintonian postulate challenged by this research is that though an actor may occupy many positions, even simultaneously, he activates each role singly with the others remaining "latent". It is found, however, that individuals often perceive and act toward role partners as if simultaneous multiple roles were being activated. For example, one may hold different expectations regarding a teacher who is male, young and unmarried as against one who is female, older and married. In other words, standards and expectations are applied to the whole person as a result, in part, of the complex of positions the person is perceived as occupying at that time. A related consideration involves the time dimension over which two or more individuals interact; other positions they occupy enter progressively into their perception of each other and consequently modify evaluations and expectations. Thus the authors generalize their point to a broader theory of social interaction by suggesting that evaluative standards shift over time from those applied as appropriate to the incumbent of a particular position to those applied to a total person with particular personality features and capacities as the incumbent of multiple positions.

Finally, their rejection of the consensus model led these researchers to find a process of role-strain or role-conflict generation and resolution similar in principle to that conceptualized by others discussed above. Having defined the role set they were studying as a true *complex system* of interrelated components, and having then uncovered and analyzed the *variety* continuously introduced into the system by way of variant, ambiguous or changing role definitions, they then focused on the *selection process* whereby this variety was sifted and sorted in the give and take of role transactions. Thus, given the situation in which a role incumbent was faced with incompatible expectations on the part of two of his counter-role partners, a theory was constructed to answer the question of how the actor may choose from among four alternatives in resolving the role conflict. From our present perspective, the theoretical scheme suggested constitutes another important contribution to the forging of a conceptual link between the dynamics of the role transaction and the more stable surrounding social structure – a link that is too often skipped over by the consensus theorist's identification of social structure and consensual role playing.

This linkage is made in terms of the concepts of perceived *legitimacy* of the conflicting expectations, an assessment of the *sanctions* that might be applied, and predispositions to give primacy to a *moral* orientation, an *expedient* orientation, or a balance of the two. We face once again the reciprocal question of how role transactions are conditioned by the surrounding social structure and how that structure is generated and regenerated as a product of the complex of role transactions.

The four alternatives that Gross and colleagues see open to an actor to choose in attempting to resolve a role conflict between incompatible expectations A and B are: (1) conformity to expectation A; (2) conformity to expectation B; (3) compromise in an attempt to conform in part to both expectations; or (4) attempt to avoid conforming to either expectation. The first criterion that the theory postulates to underlie the particular alternative chosen is the actors' definition of the legitimacy of the expectations. Thus the prediction of behavior on this criterion is that, when only one expectation is perceived as legitimate the actor will conform to that one; when both are defined as legitimate he will compromise; and when neither is seen as legitimate he will engage in avoidance behavior. The second criterion is the actor's perception of the sanctions that would be applied for nonconformity, which would create pressures to conform if strong negative sanctions are foreseen otherwise. This predicts for three of the four combinations of two sets of expectations, but not for the case of both expectations being perceived as leading to weak or no negative sanctions.

It is assumed that for any role conflict situation an actor would perceive both of these dimensions and make his decision accordingly. Predictions on the basis of the theory so far provide for determinate resolutions of conflict in

seven of the sixteen combinations of the four types of legitimacy and the four types of sanctions situations, but the other nine are left indeterminate with only the two criteria. This is because the criteria predispose in different directions, and at least a third criterion is needed to determine the outcome. The authors thus appeal to the actor's predisposition to give primacy to either the legitimacy or to the sanctions dimension, or to balance the two, thus leading to the postulation of three types of predisposing orientations to expectations as listed above – the *moral*, the *expedient*, and the balanced *moral-expedient*. All the combinations of situations now become predictive.

The accuracy of the predictions was tested empirically with the data from the superintendent-role study for four "incompatible expectation situations", and the evidence supported the theory, though with some incorrect predictions.

The implications of this conceptualization and empirical analysis are far-reaching, as already suggested, for general sociological theory. The study is concerned with what must be considered "institutional" organization and process, and supports a model of that structure and process that is quite different from the more traditional models. As the authors point out, one strong advantage of the theory is its conceptualization of institutional role behavior in terms of "expectations", whether legitimate or illegitimate, rather than in terms of "obligations" (legitimate expectations) as is assumed in consensus theory. The theory thus allows for the possibility that illegitimate expectations constitute a significant part of institutional role behavior, and underlie much of the conflict occurring – as we feel intuitively to be the case – within the institutional process. It follows, further, that deviance – nonconformity to expectations – is a more intimate and normal element in institutional behavior than conformity theory would permit. And it also permits theoretical recognition of the possibility that, as Etzioni has suggested,[59] a great deal of organizational behavior is based, not on internalized norms and values, but on an expedient calculation of self-interests and of possible rewards and punishments. This, in turn, leaves open the theoretical possibility that non-legitimized power, as well as legitimized authority, may often be a controlling factor in institutional behavior.

## Role conflict and change among the Kanuri

The final empirical study we shall sketch is explicitly based on an understanding of the modern systems approach, focusing as it does on a theory of "self-generating internal change". Ronald Cohen, an anthropologist, reports a theoretically well-organized analysis of his field study of role conflict and change among the Kanuri of Nigeria.[60] The study focuses on "goal ambiguity" and "conflicting standards" within a facet of the joint native–colonial political administrative hierarchy, particularly on the pivotal position of native "district head" which had come to combine the quite diverse cultural orientations of the colonial British and the Kanuri. This diversity between, as well as within, the two cultures made for inconsistencies, ambiguity, and conflict in political goals and in role standards and performances, which were continuously exacerbated by the variety of pressures put on district heads by the central native administration, the colonial administration, and the colonial technical departments.

The consequences of this situation for the political system are analyzed in terms of A. G. Frank's theory of organizational process and change.[61] Given the conditions of ambiguity and conflict of standards and goals, it is postulated that a process of *selective performance* and *selective enforcement* of standards will occur, with subordinates being forced to decide on which expectations to meet, and superiors required to selectively evaluate performances and hence selectively enforce some standards over others. This postulate leads to a number of predictions that Cohen proceeded to test. In essence, a continuous process is set up that appears, though in more exaggerated form, much like the "role strain", "role-making", "negotiated order" situations we met earlier. Role players fail to meet, or feign meeting some standards, and differentially select those they will meet. As a result, the role system is postulated to exhibit a strain toward substantive rationality (in Weber's sense), shifting standards for members, widespread role innovation or "deviance", ready adaptation to environmental changes, and an active and widespread circulation of information about standards and goals by "intermediary dealers in information" and by members seeking to reduce the ambiguity and conflict concerning these standards and goals.

The process is thus a circular, feedback loop whereby superiors continuously modify their standards or expectations as definitions of political objectives change, and subordinates adapt their decisions and performances to these changing expectations and surrounding circumstances, which in turn changes the states of the situation toward which superiors are acting. The role system, then, is seen as continuously receptive and responsive to external and internal pressures which demand some kind of workable "mapping" of the abundantly available situational "variety", which in turn makes possible – though does not guarantee – the evolution of more or less adaptive, institutionalized internal system procedures.

Applying this theory to the Kanuri, Cohen found the predictions to be borne out to a substantial degree. We leave the detailed description of these phenomena to the original study, which drew the general practical conclusion that – in spite of its apparent conservative, anti-progressive traditionalism – the Kanuri political role system showed greater compliance to the varied pressures of superiors and situational exigencies than to the tenets of tradition and thereby proved to be a self-generating system containing mechanisms for its own transformation. The implications of this for policy relating to "developing countries" are of obvious importance.

On the theoretical side, Cohen clearly recognizes the implications of his mode of analysis for a genetic model of sociocultural evolution.

This model depends basically on two conditions. First, the evolving phenomenon must be shown to be *variable* in terms of its constituent units, and second, there must be analytically distinct *selective factors* which operate on the variation within the phenomenon to produce a constantly adapting and thus an evolving history of development. Although there are more or less stable orientations of tradition present in Bornu, conflicts in the political organization produce a variability of response by the actors upon which selective pressures exerted by superiors in the political hierarchy may operate to bring about innovations and changes that are incremental in their nature, i.e., evolutionary rather than revolutionary.[62]

We opened our discussion of the decision-making, process approach to complex adaptive systems with a turn-of-the-century prognosis of Albion Small. We might remind ourselves further of important ties with the past by closing with the early fundamental insight of Edward Sapir:

While we often speak of society as though it were a static structure defined by tradition, it is, in the more intimate sense, nothing of the kind, but a highly intricate network of partial or complete understandings between the members of organizational units of every degree of size and complexity. . . . It is only apparently a static sum of social institutions; actually it is being reanimated or creatively reaffirmed from day to day by particular acts of a communicative nature which obtain among individuals participating in it.[63]

# Conclusion

We have suggested that much current thinking represents the coming to fruition of earlier conceptions of which Sapir's and Small's statements are harbingers. Although a science should not hesitate to forget its founders, it would do well to remain aware of their basic thought.

We have argued that a promising general framework for organizing these valuable insights of the past and present may be derived from the recent general systems perspective, embracing a holistic conception of complex adaptive systems viewed centrally in terms of information and communication process and the significance of the way these are structured for self-regulation and self-direction. We have clearly arrived at a point in the development of the "behavioral" sciences at which synthesis or conceptual unification of subdisciplines concerned with social life is challenging simple analysis or categorization. Not only is there growing demand that the "cognitive", "affective" and "evaluative" be conceptually integrated, but that the free-handed parceling out of aspects of the sociocultural adaptive system among the various disciplines (e.g., "culture" to anthropology, the "social system" to sociology, and "personality" to psychology) be reneged, or at least ignored. The potential of the newer system theory is especially strong in this regard.[64] By way of conclusion we recapitulate the main arguments.

1. The advance of science has driven it away from concern with "substance" and toward a focus on *relations* between components of whatever kind. Hence the concern with complex organization or systems, generally defined in terms of the transactions, often mutual and usually intricate, among a number of components such that some kind of more or less stable structure – often tenuous and only statistically delineated – arises (that is, *some* of the relations between components show *some* degree of stability or repetitiveness *some* of the time). Extremely fruitful advances have been taking place, especially since the rapid scientific progress made during World War II, in specifying basic features common to substantively different kinds of complex adaptive systems, as well as delineating their differences. In contrast to some of the general systems theorists themselves as well as their critics, we have argued that this is not simply analogizing but generalizing or abstracting as well (although the former is important, and scientifically legitimate also, when performed with due caution). To say that physiological, psychological, and sociocultural processes of control all involve the basic cybernetic principles of information flow along feedback loops is no more a mere analogy than to say that the trajectories of a falling apple, an artificial satellite, or a planet all involve the basic principle of gravitational attraction.

2. Complex adaptive systems are open systems in intimate interchange with an environment characterized by a great deal of shifting variety ("booming, buzzing confusion") and its constraints (its structure of causal interrelations). The concept of equilibrium developed for closed physical systems is quite inappropriate and usually inapplicable to such a dynamic situation. Rather, a characteristic resultant is the elaboration of organization in the direction of the less probable and the less inherently stable.

Features common to substantively different complex adaptive systems can be conceptualized in terms of the perspective of information and control theory. "Information" in its most general sense is seen, not as a thing that can be transported, but as a selective interrelation or mapping between two or more subsets of constrained variety selected from larger ensembles. Information is thus transmitted or communicated as invariant constraint or structure in some kind of variety, such that subsystems with the appropriate matched internal ensembles, reacting to and acting upon the information, do so in a situation of decreased uncertainty and potentially more effective adaptation to the variety that is mapped. Unless mapping (encoding, decoding, correlating, understanding, etc.) occurs between two or more ensembles we do not have "information", only raw variety or noise.

In these terms, adaptive systems, by a continuous selective feedback interchange with the variety of the environment, come to make and preserve mappings on various substantive bases, which may be transmitted generationally or contemporaneously to other similar units. By means of such mappings (for example, via genes, instincts, learned events, culture patterns) the adaptive system may, if the mappings are adequate, continue to remain viable before a shifting environment. The transmission and accumulation of such information among contemporaneous adaptive systems (individuals) becomes more and more important at higher levels until it becomes the prime basis of linkage of components for the highest level sociocultural system.

Some of the more important differences between complex adaptive systems include the substantive nature of the components, the types of linkage of the components, the kinds and levels of feedback between system and environment, the degree of internal feedback of a system's own state (for example, "self-awareness"), the methods of transmission of information between subsystems and along generations, the degree of refinement and fidelity of mapping and information transfer, the degree and rapidity with which the system can restructure itself or the environmental variety, etc.

3. Such a perspective provides a general framework which meets the major criticisms leveled against much of current sociological theory: lack of time and process perspective, overemphasis on stability and maintenance of given structure, and on consensus and cooperative relations, to the relative neglect – or unsystematic treatment – of deviance, conflict and other dissociative relations underlying system destructuring and restructuring.

4. Thus, the concept of the system itself cannot be identified with the more or less stable structure it may take on at any particular time. As a fundamental principle, it can be stated that a condition for maintenance of a viable adaptive system may be a change in its particular structure. Both stability and change are a function of the same set of variables, which must include both the internal state of the system and the state of its significant environment, along with the nature of the interchange between the two.

5. A time perspective is inherent in this kind of analysis – not merely historical but evolutionary. (It can probably be said that the time was ripe by 1959 for a Darwinian centennial ramifying well beyond the purely biological.) This perspective calls for a balance and integration of structural and processual analysis. As others have pointed out, the Linnean system of classification of structures became alive only after Darwin and others discovered the processes of variation, selection and recombination that gave them theoretical significance, though these discoveries leaned heavily in turn on the classification of systematically varying structures.

And among the important processes for the sociocultural system are not only cooperation and conformity to norms, but conflict, competition and deviation which may help create (or destroy) the essential variety pool, and which constitute part of the process of selection from it, such that a more or less viable system structure may be created and maintained (or destroyed).

6. In sociological terms, the "complementarity of expectations" model is an ideal type constituting only one pole of a continuum of equally basic associative and dissociative processes characterizing real societies – although the particular "mix" and intensities of the various types may differ widely with different structural arrangements. Further, the systemic analysis of a sociocultural system is not exhausted by analysis of its institutionalized patterns. By focusing on process, we are more prepared to

include all facets of system operation – from the minimally structured end of the collective behavior continuum through the various degrees and kinds of structuring to the institutional pole. The particular characteristics of the process, especially the degrees and kinds of mappings and mismatchings of the interacting units, tell us whether we are in fact dealing with certain degrees of structuring and the dynamics underlying this structuring: de facto patterning may be anchored in coercive, normative, or utilitarian compliance, making for very different kinds of system.

7. "Institutionalized" patterns are not to be construed as thereby "legitimized" or as embracing only "conformity" patterns – at least for the sake of conceptual clarity and empirical adequacy. Processes of all degrees and kinds of structuring may be seen in terms of deviant as well as conformity patterns – relative to the point of reference selected by the observer. One may select certain institutional patterns and values (to be clearly specified) as an arbitrary reference point to match against *other* institutional patterns and values, along with less structured behaviors. The concept of *the* institutionalized common value system smuggles in an empirically dubious, or unverified, proposition – at least for complex modern societies.

8. The complex adaptive system's organization *is* the "control", the characteristics of which will change as the organization changes. The problem is complicated by the fact that we are dealing directly with two levels of adaptive system and thus two levels of structure, the higher level (sociocultural) structure being largely a shifting statistical or probability structure (or ensemble of constraints) expressing over time the transactional processes occurring among the lower level (personality) structures. We do not have a sociocultural system *and* personality systems, but only a sociocultural system *of* constrained interactions among personality systems.

We can only speak elliptically of "ideas" or "information" or "meanings" in the head of a particular individual: all we have is an ensemble of constrained variety embodied in a neurological net. "Meaning" or "information" is generated only in the process of interaction with other ensembles of similarly mapped or constrained variety (whether embodied in other neurological nets or as the ensemble of causally constrained variety of the physical environment), whereby ensemble is mapped or matched against ensemble via communication links, and action is carried out, the patterning of which is a resultant of the degree of successful mapping that occurred. (Of course, "meaning" on the symbolic level can be regenerated over a long period by the isolated individual through an internal interchange or "conversation" of the person with his "self", made possible by previous socially induced mappings of one's own internal state that we call "self-awareness". But in some respects, part of the world literally loses its meaning for such a person.)

If the ensembles of variety of two interacting units, or one unit and its physical environment, have no or little isomorphic structuring, little or no meaning can be generated to channel ongoing mutual activity; or in more common terms, there is no "common ground", no "meeting of minds" and thus no meaning or information exchange – only raw variety, uncertainty, lack of "order" or organization.

Unless "social control" is taken as simply the more or less intentional techniques for maintaining a given institutional structure by groupings with vested interests, it must refer to the above transactional processes as they operate – now to develop new sociocultural structures, now to reinforce existing ones, now to destructure or restructure older ones. Thus, we cannot hope to develop our understanding much further by speaking of one "structure" determining, "affecting", or acting upon another "structure". We shall have to get down to the difficult but essential task of (a) specifying much more adequately the distribution of essential features of the component subsystems' internal mappings, including both self-mappings and their mappings of their effective environment, (b) specifying more extensively the structure of the transactions among these units at a given time, the degree and stability of the given structuring seen as varying with the degree and depth of common meanings that are generated in the transaction process, and (c) assessing, with the help of techniques now developing, the ongoing process of transitions from a given state of the system to the next in terms of the deviation-reducing and deviation-generating feedback loops relating the tensionful, goal-seeking, decision-making subunits via the communication nets partly specified by (b). Some behavior patterns will be found to be anchored in a close matching of component psychic structures (for example, legitimized authority or normative compliance); others, in threats of goal-blockage, where there is minimal matching (for example, power or coercive compliance); still others, anchored in a partial matching, primarily in terms of environmental mappings of autonomous subunits and minimally in terms of collective mappings (for example, opportunism or utilitarian compliance). As the distribution of mappings shifts in the system (which normally occurs for a number of reasons), so will the transaction processes and communication nets, and thus will the sociocultural struc-

ture tend to shift as gradients of misunderstanding, goal-blockage, and tensions develop.

9. Finally, we have tried to show how this perspective bears on, and may help to integrate conceptually, the currently developing area of "decision theory" which recognizes individual components as creative nodes in an interactive matrix. In the complex process of transactions occurring within a matrix of information flows, the resulting cognitive mappings and mismappings undergo various stresses and strains as component units assess and reassess with varying degrees of fidelity and refinement their internal states and the shifting and partially uncertain, and often goal-blocking environment. Out of this process, as more or less temporary adjustments, arises the more certain, more expected, more codified sequences of events that we call sociocultural structure. In the words of Norbert Wiener, "By its ability to make decisions" the system "can produce around it a local zone of organization in a world whose general tendency is to run down".[65] Whether that structure proves viable or adaptive for the total system is the kind of question that cannot be reliably answered in the present state of our discipline. It most certainly demands the kind of predictive power that comes with the later rather than the earlier stages of development of a science. And later stages can arrive only at some sacrifice of ideas of earlier stages.

# References

1 *Sociology and Modern Systems Theory* (Englewood Cliffs, N.J.: Prentice-Hall, 1967).

2 See Campbell, Donald T. (1959) "Methodological Suggestions from a Comparative Psychology of Knowledge Processes", *Inquiry*, **2**, 152–67.

3 See, for example, Rapoport and MacKay, Chapters 16 and 24 of *Modern Systems Research for the Behavioral Scientist*.

4 For an excellent recent overview of this transition, see Hallowell, A. Irving, "Personality, Culture, and Society in Behavioral Evolution", in Koch, Sigmund (ed.), *Psychology: A Study of a Science*, Volume 6: Investigations of Man as Socius (New York: McGraw-Hill, 1963), 429–509.

5 Thelen, Herbert A. (1956) "Emotionality and Work in Groups", in Leonard D. White (ed.), *The State of the Social Sciences* (Chicago: University of Chicago Press), pp. 184–6.

6 See Cannon, Article 13, p. 219.

7 Or perhaps we might take Cadwallader's suggestion and use Ashby's term "ultrastability". I dislike, how-

ever, the connotative overemphasis on "stability", which is sure to be misunderstood by many.

I prefer the term "morphogenesis" as best expressing the characteristic feature of the adaptive system. Thus, we might say that physical systems are typically equilibrial, physiological systems are typically homeostatic, and psychological, sociocultural, or ecological systems are typically morphogenic. From this view, our paradigm of the mechanisms underlying the complex system becomes a basic paradigm of the morphogenic process, perhaps embracing as special cases even the structuring process below the complex adaptive system level.

8 Mace, C. A. (1953) "Homeostasis, Needs and Values", *British Journal of Psychology*, **44**, 204–5. Gordon Allport reinforces this view for personality (but note his terminology): "Some theories correctly emphasize the tendency of human personality to go beyond steady states and to elaborate their internal order, even at the cost of disequilibrium. Theories of changing energies . . . and of functional autonomy . . . do so. These conceptions allow for a continual increase of men's purposes in life and for their morphogenic effect upon the system as a whole. Although homeostasis is a useful conception for short-run 'target orientation', it is totally inadequate to account for the integrating tonus involved in 'goal orientation'. . . . Although these formulations differ among themselves, they all find the 'go' of personality in some dynamic thrust that exceeds the pale function of homeostatic balance. They recognize increasing order over time, and view change within personality as a recentering, but not as abatement, of tension." – Allport, Gordon W. (1961) *Pattern and Growth in Personality* (New York: Holt, Rinehart & Winston), p. 569.

9 See Chapters 34 and 35 of *Modern Systems Research for the Behavioral Scientist*.

10 Henry, Jules (1959) "Culture, Personality, and Evolution", *American Anthropologist*, **61**, 221–2.

11 Deutsch, Karl W. (1948–9) "Some Notes on Research on The Role of Models in Natural and Social Science", *Synthese*, pp. 532–3.

12 See Campbell, *op. cit.*

13 See Osgood, Charles E., "Psycholinguistics", in Koch, S. (ed.), *Psychology*, *loc. cit.*, pp. 244–316; Mowrer, O. Hobart (1960) *Learning Theory and the Symbolic Processes* (New York: John Wiley), esp. Chapter 7: "Learning Theory, Cybernetics, and the Concept of Consciousness." For less behavioristic and more genetic and emergent views, see, for example, Mead, George H. (1934) *Mind, Self and Society* (Chicago: University of Chicago Press), and more recently, Werner, Heinz and Kaplan, Bernard (1963) *Symbol Formation* (New York: John Wiley).

14 See, for example, Sahlins, Marshall D. (1964) "Culture and Environment: The Study of Cultural Ecology", in Sol Tax (ed.), *Horizons of Anthropology* (Chicago: Aldine), pp. 132–47.

15 See the selections from Nett (Chapter 48), Deutsch (Chapter 46), Hardin (Chapter 55), and Vickers (Chapter 56) in *Modern Systems Research for the Behavioral Scientist*.

16 However, we should not deemphasize the important structuring role of concrete artifacts, for example, the structure of physical communication nets, road nets, cities, interior layouts of buildings, etc., as limiting and channeling factors for sociocultural action and interaction.

17 Small, Albion W. (1905) *General Sociology* (Chicago: University of Chicago Press), p. ix.

18 Cooley, Charles H. (1918) *Social Process* (New York: Scribner's).

19 Znaniecki, Florian (1952) *Cultural Sciences* (Urbana: University of Illinois Press).

20 Consider the explicit "feedback" and "self-regulation" conceptions in the following statements of G. H. Mead in *Mind, Self and Society*: ". . . the central nervous system has an almost infinite number of elements in it, and they can be organized not only in spatial connection with each other, but also from a temporal standpoint. In virtue of this last fact, our conduct is made up of a series of steps which follow each other, and the later steps may be already started and influence the earlier ones. The thing we are going to do is playing back on what we are doing now" (p. 71). "As we advance from one set of responses to another we find ourselves picking out the environment which answers to this next set of responses. To finish one response is to put ourselves in a position where we see other things. . . . Our world is definitely mapped out for us by the responses which are going to take place. . . . The structure of the environment is a mapping out of organic responses to nature; any environment, whether social or individual, is a mapping out of the logical structure of the act to which it answers, an act seeking overt expression" (pp. 128–9, and footnote 32, p. 129). "It

is through taking this role of the other that [the person] is able to come back on himself and so direct his own process of communication. This taking the role of the other, an expression I have so often used, is not simply of passing importance. It is not something that just happens as an incidental result of the gesture, but it is of importance in the development of cooperative activity. The immediate effect of such role-taking lies in the control which the individual is able to exercise over his own response. . . . From the standpoint of social evolution, it is this bringing of any given social act, or of the total social process in which that act is a constituent, directly and as an organized whole into the experience of each of the individual organisms implicated in that act, with reference to which he may consequently regulate and govern his individual conduct, that constitutes the peculiar value and significance of self-consciousness in those individual organisms" (p. 254, including part of footnote 7).

See also the extended discussion based on Mead's essentially cybernetic perspective in Shibutani, Chapter 39.

21 Seeman, Melvin, review of Rose, Arnold (ed.) *Human Behavior and Social Processes*, in *American Sociological Review*, **27** (August 1962), 557.

22 Murdock, George P. (1955) "Changing Emphasis in Social Structure", *Southwestern Journal of Anthropology*, **11**, 366.

23 Firth, Raymond (1955) "Some Principles of Social Organization", *Journal of the Royal Anthropological Institute*, **85**, 1.

24 Nadel, S. F. (1957) *The Theory of Social Structure* (New York: The Free Press of Glencoe), pp. 54–5.

25 *Ibid.*, p. 128.

26 *Ibid.*, p. 153.

27 Vogt, Evon Z. (1960) "On the Concept of Structure and Process in Cultural Anthropology", *American Anthropologist*, **62**, 18–33.

28 Blumer, Herbert (1953) "Psychological Import of the Human Group", in Sherif, Muzafer and Wilson, M. O. (eds.) *Group Relations at the Crossroads* (New York: Harper), pp. 199–201. Emphasis added.

29 Allport, Gordon W. (1961) *Pattern and Growth in Personality* (New York: Holt, Rinehart, & Winston), p. 567.

30 For example, see Gouldner, Alvin W. (1956) "Some Observations on Systematic Theory, 1945–55", in Zetterberg, Hans L. (ed.) *Sociology in the United States of America* (Paris: UNESCO), pp. 39–40. See also Moore, Jr., Barrington (1955) "Sociological Theory and Contemporary Politics", *American Journal of Sociology*, **61** (September), 111–15.

31 Recall, for example, the excellent treatment of "decision theory" in MacIver, Robert M. (1942) *Social Causation* (New York: Ginn & Co.), esp. pp. 291 ff.

32 Selznick, Philip, (1961) "Review Article: The Social Theories of Talcott Parsons", *American Sociological Review*, **26** (December), 934.

33 Boulding, Kenneth E. (1956) *The Image* (Ann Arbor: University of Michigan Press).

34 Recall Maruyama's discussion in Chapter 36 of *Modern Systems Research for the Behavioral Scientist*.

35 Goode, William J. (1960) "A Theory of Role Strain", *American Sociological Review*, **25** (August), 483.

36 *Ibid.*, 495.

37 *Ibid.*

38 *Ibid.*, 487.

39 *Ibid.*, 494.

40 Osgood, Charles E. (1960) "Cognitive Dynamics in the Conduct of Human Affairs", *Public Opinion Quarterly*, **24**, 347.

41 *Ibid.*, 347–8.

42 *Ibid.*, 351.

43 *Ibid.*, 363.

44 Sears, Robert R. (1951) "A Theoretical Framework for Personality and Social Behavior", *American Psychologist*, **6**, 478–9.

45 *Ibid.*, 478.

46 Secord, Paul F. and Backman, Carl W. (1961) "Personality Theory and the Problem of Stability and Change in Individual Behavior: An Interpersonal Approach", *Psychological Review*, **68**, 22.

47 *Ibid.*

48 *Ibid.*, 26.

49 *Ibid.*, 28.

50 *Ibid.*

51 Turner, Ralph H. (1962) "Role-Taking: Process Versus Conformity", in Rose, Arnold M. (ed.) *Human Behavior and Social Processes* (Boston: Houghton Mifflin Co.), Chapter 2.

52 *Ibid.*, 26.

53 Gross, Neal, *et al.* (1958) *Explorations in Role Analysis* (New York: John Wiley), p. 53.

54 Turner, *loc. cit.*, p. 32.

55 *Ibid.*, p. 38.

56 Strauss, Anselm *et al.* (1963) "The Hospital and Its Negotiated Order", in Freidson, Eliot (ed.) *The*

*Hospital in Modern Society* (New York: The Free Press of Glencoe), p. 148.

57 *Ibid.*, p. 162.

58 Gross, Neal *et al.*, *op. cit.*, p. 321. Also see Kahn, Robert L. *et al.* (1964) *Organizational Stress: Studies in Role Conflict and Ambiguity* (New York: John Wiley).

59 Etzioni, Amitai (1961) *A Comparative Analysis of Complex Organizations* (New York: The Free Press of Glencoe).

60 Cohen, Ronald (1964) "Conflict and Change in a Northern Nigerian Emirate", in Zollschan, George K. and Hirsch, Walter (eds.) *Explorations in Social Change* (Boston: Houghton Mifflin Co.), Chapter 19.

61 Frank, A. G. (1959) "Goal Ambiguity and Conflicting Standards: An Approach to the Study of Organization", *Human Organization*, **17**, 8–13.

62 *Op. cit.*, 519. Emphasis supplied.

63 Sapir, Edward (1931) "Social Communication", *Encyclopedia of the Social Sciences* (New York: Macmillan), Vol. 4, p. 78.

64 This still remains primarily a potential, however; perusal of the general systems literature shows treatment of the sociocultural level systems to be sparse compared to that of biological, psychological and other systems. Part of the reason for this is the failure of sociologists to participate and to make what could be significant contributions to a field rapidly leaving us behind.

65 Wiener, Norbert (1954) *The Human Use of Human Beings* (Garden City, N.Y.: Doubleday Anchor, 2nd ed., rev.), p. 34.

Reprinted from *Modern Systems Research for the Behavioral Scientist: A Sourcebook* edited by Walter Buckley (1968). Published by permission of Aldine Publishing Company, Chicago.

# 10  A systems analysis of political life
*by David Easton*

In *A Framework for Political Analysis*[1] I spelled out in considerable detail the assumptions and commitments that would be required in any attempt to utilize the concept "system" in a rigorous fashion. It would lead to the adoption of what I there described as a systems analysis of political life. Although it would certainly be redundant to retrace the same ground here, it is nonetheless necessary to review the kinds of basic conceptions and orientations imposed by this mode of analysis. In doing so, I shall be able to lay out the pattern of analysis that will inform and guide the present work.

## Political life as an open and adaptive system

. . . The question that gives coherence and purpose to a rigorous analysis of political life as a system of behavior is as follows. How do any and all political systems manage to persist in a world of both stability and change? Ultimately the search for an answer will reveal what I have called the life processes of political systems – those fundamental functions without which no system could endure – together with the typical modes of response through which systems manage to sustain them. The analysis of these processes, and of the nature and conditions of the responses, I posit as a central problem of political theory.

Although I shall end by arguing that it is useful to interpret political life as a complex set of processes through which certain kinds of inputs are converted into the type of outputs we may call authoritative policies, decisions and implementing actions, at the outset it is useful to take a somewhat simpler approach. We may begin by viewing political life as a system of behavior imbedded in an environment to the influences of which the political system itself is exposed and in turn reacts. Several vital considerations are implicit in this interpretation and it is essential that we become aware of them.

First, such a point of departure for theoretical analysis assumes without further inquiry that political interactions in a society constitute a *system* of behavior. This proposition is, however, deceptive in its simplicity. The truth is that if the idea "system" is employed with the rigor it permits and with the implications currently inherent in it, it provides a starting point that is already heavily freighted with consequences for a whole pattern of analysis.

Second, to the degree that we are successful in analytically isolating political life as a system, it is clear that it cannot usefully be interpreted as existing in a void. It must be seen as surrounded by physical, biological, social and psychological *environments*. Here again, the empirical transparency of the statement ought not to be allowed to distract us from its crucial theoretical significance. If we were to neglect what seems so obvious once it is asserted, it would be impossible to lay the groundwork for an analysis of how political systems manage to persist in a world of stability or change.

This brings us to a third point. What makes the identification of the environments useful and necessary is the further presupposition that political life forms an *open* system. By its very nature as a social system that has been analytically separated from other social systems, it must be interpreted as lying exposed to influences deriving from the other systems in which empirically it is imbedded. From them there flows a constant stream of events and influences that shape the conditions under which the members of the system must act.

Finally, the fact that some systems do survive, whatever the buffetings from the environments, awakens us to the fact that they must have the capacity to *respond* to disturbances and thereby to adapt to the conditions under which they find themselves. Once we are willing to assume that political systems may be adaptive and need not just react in a passive or sponge-like way to their environmental influences, we shall be able to break a new path through the complexities of theoretical analysis.

As I have elsewhere demonstrated, in its internal organization, a critical property that a political system shares with all other social systems in this extraordinarily variable capacity to respond to the conditions under which it functions. Indeed, we shall find that political systems accumulate large repertoires of mechanisms through which they may seek to cope with their environments. Through these they may regulate their own behavior, transform their internal structure, and even go so far as to remodel their fundamental goals. Few systems, other than social systems, have this potentiality. In practice, students of political life could not help but take this into account; no analysis could even begin to appeal to common sense if it did not do so. Nevertheless it is seldom built into a theoretical structure as a central component; certainly its implications for the internal behavior of political systems have never been set forth and explored.

## Equilibrium analysis and its shortcomings

It is a major shortcoming of the one form of inquiry latent but prevalent in political research – equilibrium analysis – that it neglects such variable capacities for systems to cope with influences from their environment. The equilibrium approach is seldom explicitly elaborated, yet it infuses a good part of political research, especially group politics and international relations. Of necessity an analysis that conceives of a political system as seeking to maintain a state of equilibrium must assume the presence of environmental influences. It is these that displace the power relationships in a political system – such as a balance of power – from their presumed stable state. It is then customary, if only implicitly so, to analyze the system in terms of a tendency to return to a presumed pre-existing point of stability. If the system should fail to do so, it would be interpreted as moving on to a new state of equilibrium and this would need to be identified and described. A careful scrutiny of the language used reveals that equilibrium and stability are usually assumed to mean the same thing.

Numerous conceptual and empirical difficulties stand in the way of an effective use of the equilibrium idea for the analysis of political life. But among these there are two that are particularly relevant for my present purposes.

In the first place, the equilibrium approach leaves the impression that the members of a system are seized with only one basic goal as they seek to cope with change or disturbance, namely, to re-establish the old point of equilibrium or, at most, to move on to some new one. This is usually phrased, at least implicitly, as the search for stability as though this were sought above all else. In the second place, little if any attention is explicitly given to formulating the problems relating to the path that the system takes insofar as it does seek to return to this presumed point of equilibrium or to attain a fresh one. It is as though the pathways taken to manage the displacements were an incidental rather than a central theoretical consideration.

But it would be impossible to understand the processes underlying the capacity of some kind of political life to sustain itself in a society if either the objectives or the form of the responses are taken for granted. A system may well seek goals other than those of reaching one or another point of equilibrium. Even though this state were to be used only as a theoretical norm that is never achieved, it would offer a less useful theoretical approximation of reality than one that takes into account other possibilities. We would find it more helpful to devise a conceptual approach that recognized that at times members in a system may wish to take positive actions to destroy a previous equilibrium or even to achieve some new point of continuing disequilibrium. This is typically the case where the authorities may seek to keep themselves in power by fostering internal turmoil or external dangers.

Furthermore, with respect to these variable goals, it is a primary characteristic of all systems that they are able to adopt a wide range of actions of a positive, constructive and innovative sort for warding off or absorbing any forces of displacement. A system need not just react to a disturbance by oscillating in the neighborhood of a prior point of equilibrium or by shifting to a new one. It may cope with the disturbance by seeking to change the environment so that the exchanges between the environment and itself are no longer stressful; it may seek to insulate itself against any further influences from the environment; or the members of the system may even transform their own relationships fundamentally and modify their own goals and practices so as to improve their chances of handling the inputs from the environment. In these and other ways a system has the capacity for creative and constructive regulation of disturbances as we shall later see in detail.

It is clear that the adoption of equilibrium analysis, however latent it may be, obscures the presence of system goals that cannot be described as a state of equilibrium. It also virtually conceals the existence of varying pathways for attaining these alternative ends. For any social system, including the political, adaptation represents more than simple adjustments to the events in its life. It is made up of efforts, limited only by the variety of human skills, resources, and ingenuity, to control, modify or fundamentally change either the environment or the system itself, or both together. In the outcome the system may succeed in fending off or incorporating successfully any influences stressful for it.

## Minimal concepts for a systems analysis

A systems analysis promises a more expansive, more inclusive, and more flexible theoretical structure than is available even in a thoroughly self-conscious and well-developed equilibrium approach. To do so successfully, however, it must establish its own theoretical imperatives. Although these were explored in detail in *A Framework for Political Analysis*, we may re-examine them briefly here, assuming, however, that where the present brevity leaves unavoidable ambiguities, the reader may wish to become more familiar with the underlying structure of ideas by consulting this earlier volume. In it, at the outset, a system was defined as any set of variables regardless of the degree of interrelationship among them. The reason for preferring this definition is that it frees us from the need to argue about whether a political system is or is not really a system. The only question of importance about a set selected as a system to be analyzed is whether this set constitutes an interesting one. Does it help us to understand and explain some aspect of human behavior of concern to us?

To be of maximum utility, I have argued, a *political* system can be designated as those interactions through which values are authoritatively allocated for a society; this is what distinguishes a political system from other systems that may be interpreted as lying in its environment. This environment itself may be divided into two parts, the intra-societal and the extra-societal. The first consists of those systems in the same society as the political system but excluded from the latter by our definition of the nature of political interactions. Intra-societal systems would include such sets of behavior, attitudes and ideas as we might call the economy, culture, social structure or personalities; they are functional segments of the society with respect to which

the political system at the focus of attention is itself a component. In a given society the systems other than the political system constitute a source of many influences that create and shape the conditions under which the political system itself must operate. In a world of newly emerging political systems we do not need to pause to illustrate the impact that a changing economy, culture, or social structure may have upon political life.

The second part of the environment, the extra-societal, includes all those systems that lie outside the given society itself. They are functional components of an international society or what we might describe as the supra-society, a supra-system of which any single society is part. The international political systems, the international economy, or the international cultural system would fall into the category of extra-societal systems.

Together, these two classes of systems, the intra- and extra-societal, that are conceived to lie outside of a political system may be designated as its total environment. From these sources arise influences that are of consequence for possible stress on the political system. The total environment is presented in Table 10.1 as reproduced from *A Framework for Political Analysis*, and the reader should turn to that volume for a full discussion of the various components of the environment as indicated on this table.

*Disturbances* is a concept that may be used to identify those influences from the total environment of a system that act upon it so that it is different after the stimulus from what it was before. Not all disturbances need strain the

**Table 10.1** Components of the Total Environment of a Political System

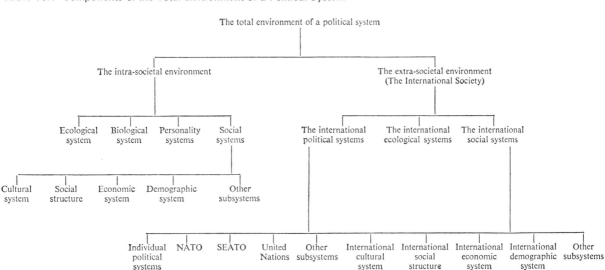

system. Some may be favorable with respect to the persistence of the system; others may be entirely neutral with respect to possible stress. But many can be expected to lead in the direction of stress.

When may we say that *stress* occurs? This involves us in a rather complex idea, one that has been treated at length. But since it does stand as a major pillar underpinning the analysis to be elaborated in the succeeding chapters, I must at least broadly sketch out its implications. It embodies several subsidiary notions. All political systems as such are distinguished by the fact that if we are to be able to describe them as persisting, we must attribute to them the successful fulfillment of two functions. They must be able to allocate values for a society; they must also manage to induce most members to accept these allocations as binding, at least most of the time. These are the two properties that help us to distinguish most succinctly political systems from other kinds of social systems.

By virtue of this very fact these two distinctive features – the allocations of values for a society and the relative frequency of compliance with them – are the *essential variables* of political life. But for their presence, we would not be able to say that a society has any political life. And we may here take it for granted that no society could exist without some kind of political system; elsewhere I have sought to demonstrate this in detail.

One of the important reasons for identifying these essential variables is that they give us a way of establishing when and how the disturbances acting upon a system threaten to stress it. Stress will be said to occur when there is a danger that the essential variables will be pushed beyond what we may designate as their *critical range*. What this means is that something may be happening in the environment – the system suffers total defeat at the hands of an enemy, or widespread disorganization in and disaffection from the system is aroused by a severe economic crisis. Let us say that as a result, the authorities are consistently unable to make decisions or if they strive to do so, the decisions are no longer regularly accepted as binding. Under these conditions, authoritative allocations of values are no longer possible and the society would collapse for want of a system of behavior to fulfill one of its vital functions.

Here we could not help but accept the interpretation that the political system had come under stress, so severe that any and every possibility for the persistence of a system for that society had disappeared. But frequently the disruption of a political system is not that complete; the stress is present even though the system continues to persist in some form. Severe as a crisis may be, it still may be possible for the authorities to be able to make some kinds of decisions and to get them accepted with at least minimal frequency so that some of the problems typically subjected to political settlements can be handled.

That is to say, it is not always a matter as to whether the essential variables are operating or have ceased to do so. It is possible that they may only be displaced to some extent as when the authorities are partially incapacitated for making decisions or from getting them accepted with complete regularity. Under these circumstances the essential variables will remain within some normal range of operation; they may be stressed but not in a sufficient degree to displace them beyond a determinable critical point. As long as the system does keep its essential variables operating within what I shall call their critical range, some kind of system can be said to persist.

As we have seen, one of the characteristic properties of every system is the fact that it has the capacity to cope with stress on its essential variables. Not that a system need take such action; it may collapse precisely because it has failed to take measures appropriate for handling the impending stress. But it is the existence of a capacity to respond to stress that is of paramount importance. The kind of response actually undertaken, if any, will help us to evaluate the probabilities of the system's being able to ward off the stress. In thus raising the question of the nature of the response to stress, it will become apparent, in due course, that the special objective and merit of a systems analysis of political life is that it permits us to interpret the behavior of the members in a system in the light of the consequences it has for alleviating or aggravating stress upon the essential variables.

## The linkage variables between systems

But a fundamental problem remains. We could not begin the task of applying this kind of conceptualization if we did not first pose the following question. How do the potentially stressful conditions from the environment communicate themselves to a political system? After all, common sense alone tells us that there is an enormous variety of environmental influences at work on a system. Do we have to treat each change in the environment as a separate and unique disturbance, the specific effects of which for the political system have to be independently worked out?

If this were indeed the case, as I have shown in detail before, the problems of systematic analysis would be virtually insurmountable. But if we can devise a way for generalizing our method for handling the impact of the environment on the system, there would be some hope of reducing the enormous variety of influences into a relatively few, and therefore into a relatively manageable number of indicators. This is precisely what I have sought to effect through the use of the concepts "inputs" and "outputs".

How are we to describe these inputs and outputs? Because of the analytic distinction that I have been making between a political system and its parametric or environmental systems, it is useful to interpret the influences associated with the behavior of persons in the environment or from other conditions there as *exchanges* or *transactions* that cross the *boundaries* of the political system. Exchanges can be used when we wish to refer to the mutuality of the relationships, to the fact that the political system and those systems in the environmental have reciprocal effects on each other. Transactions may be employed when we wish to emphasize the movement of an effect in one direction, from an environmental system to the political system, or the reverse, without being concerned at the time about the reactive behavior of the other system.

To this point, there is little to dispute. Unless systems were coupled together in some way, all analytically identifiable aspects of behavior in society would stand independent of each other, a patently unlikely condition. What carries recognition of this coupling beyond a mere truism, however, is the proposal of a way to trace out the complex exchanges so that we can readily reduce their immense variety to theoretically and empirically manageable proportions.

To accomplish this, I have proposed that we condense the major and significant environmental influences into a few indicators. Through the examination of these we should be able to appraise and follow through the potential impact of environmental events on the system. With this objective in mind, I have designated the effects that are transmitted across the boundary of a system toward some other system as the *outputs* of the first system and hence, symmetrically, as the *inputs* of the second system, the one they influence. A transaction or an exchange between systems will therefore be viewed as a linkage between them in the form of an input–output relationship.

## Demands and supports as input indicators

The value of inputs as a concept is that through their use we shall find it possible to capture the effect of the vast variety of events and conditions in the environment as they pertain to the persistence of a political system. Without the inputs it would be difficult to delineate the precise operational way in which the behavior in the various sectors of society affects what happens in the political sphere. In-

puts will serve as *summary variables* that concentrate and mirror everything in the environment that is relevant to political stress. Thereby this concept serves as a powerful tool.

The extent to which inputs can be used as summary variables will depend, however, upon how we define them. We might conceive of them in their broadest sense. In that case, we would interpret them as including any event external to the system that alters, modifies or affects the system in any and every possible way. But if we seriously considered using the concept in so broad a fashion, we would never be able to exhaust the list of inputs acting upon a system. Virtually every parametric event and condition would have some significance for the operations of a political system at the focus of attention; a concept so inclusive that it does not help us to organize and simplify reality would defeat its own purposes. We would be no better off than we are without it.

But as I have already intimated, we can greatly simplify the task of analyzing the impact of the environment if we restrict our attention to certain kinds of inputs that can be used as indicators to sum up the most important effects, in terms of their contributions to stress, that cross the boundary from the parametric to the political systems. In this way we would free ourselves from the need to deal with and trace out separately the consequences of every different type of environmental event.

As the theoretical tool for this purpose, it is helpful to view the major environmental influences as coming to a focus in two major inputs: demands and support. Through them a wide range of activities in the environment may be channeled, mirrored, and summarized and brought to bear upon political life, as I shall show in detail in the succeeding chapters. In this sense they are key indicators of the way in which environmental influences and conditions modify and shape the operations of the political system. If we wish, we may say that it is through fluctuations in the inputs of demands and support that we shall find the effects of the environmental systems transmitted to the political system.

## Outputs and feedbacks

In a comparable way, the idea of outputs help us to organize the consequences flowing from the behavior of the members of the system rather than from actions in the environment. Our primary concern is, to be sure, with the functioning of the political system. In and of themselves, at least for understanding political phenomena, we would have no need to be concerned with the consequences that political actions have for the environmental system. This is a problem that can or should be handled better by theories seeking to explore the operations of the economy, culture, or any of the other parametric systems.

But the fact is that the activities of the members of the system may well have some importance with respect to their own subsequent actions or conditions. To the extent that this is so, we cannot entirely neglect those actions that do flow out of a system into the environment. As in the case of inputs, however, there is an immense amount of activities that take place within a political system. How are we to sort out the portion that has relevance for an understanding of the way in which systems manage to persist?

Later we shall see that a useful way of simplifying and organizing our perceptions of the behavior of the members of the system, as reflected in their demands and support, is in terms of the consequences of these inputs for what I shall call the political outputs. These are the decisions and actions of the authorities. Not that the complex political processes internal to a system, and that have been the subject of inquiry for so many decades in political science, will be considered in any way irrelevant. Who controls whom in the various decision-making processes will continue to be a vital concern since the pattern of power relationships helps to determine the nature of the outputs. But the formulation of a conceptual structure for this aspect of a political system would draw us into a different level of analysis. Here I am only seeking economical ways of summarizing the outcomes of these internal political processes – not of investigating them – and I am suggesting that they can be usefully conceptualized as the outputs of the authorities. Through them we shall be able to trace out the consequences of behavior within a political system for its environment.

There would be little point in taking the trouble to conceptualize the results of the internal behavior of the members in a system in this way unless we could so something with it. As we shall see, the significance of outputs is not only that they help to influence events in the broader society of which the system is a part; in doing so, they help to determine each succeeding round of inputs that finds its way into the political system. As we shall phrase it later, there is a *feedback loop* the identification of which will help us to explain the processes through which the authorities may cope with stress. This loop has a number of parts. It consists of the production of outputs by the authorities, a response on the part of the members of the society with respect to them, the communication of information about this response to the authorities, and finally, possible succeeding actions on the part of the authorities. Thereby a new round of outputs, response information feedback, and

reaction on the part of the authorities is set in motion and is part of a continuous never-ending flow. What happens in this feedback loop will turn out to have the deepest significance for the capacity of a system to cope with stress.

## A flow model of the political system

It is clear from what has been said that this mode of analysis enables and indeed compels us to analyze a political system in dynamic terms. Not only do we see that it gets something done through its outputs but we are also sensitized to the fact that what it does may influence each successive stage of behavior. We appreciate the urgent need to interpret political processes as a continuous and interlinked flow of behavior.

If we apply this conceptualization in the construction of a rudimentary model of the relationships between a political system and its environment, we would have a figure of the kind illustrated in Figure 10.1. . . . In effect it conveys the idea that the political system looks like a vast and perpetual conversion process. It takes in demands and support as they are shaped in the environment and produces something out of them called outputs. But it does not let our interest in the outputs terminate at this point. We are alerted to the fact that the outputs influence the supportive sentiments that the members express toward the system and the kinds of demands they put in. In this way the outputs return to haunt the system, as it were. As depicted on the diagram, all this is still at a very crude level of formulation. It will be our task to refine these relationships as we proceed in our analysis.

But let us examine the model a little more closely since in effect this volume will do little more than to flesh out the skeleton presented there. In interpreting the diagram, we begin with the fact that it shows a political system surrounded by the two classes of environments that together form its total environment. The communications of the many events that occur here are represented by the solid lines connecting the environments with the political system. The arrowheads on the lines show the direction of flow into the system. But rather than attempting to discuss each disturbance in the environment uniquely or even in selected groups or classes of types, I use as an indicator of the impact that they have on the system, the way in which they shape two special kinds of inputs into the system, demands and support. This is why the effects from the environment are shown to flow into the box labelled "inputs". We must remember, however, that even though the desire for simplicity in presentation does not permit us to show it on

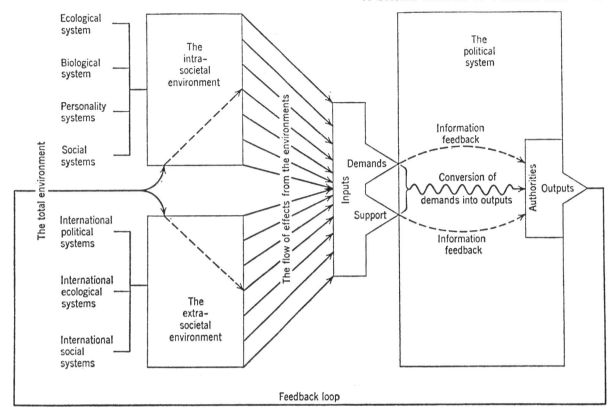

**Figure 10.1** A Dynamic Response Model of a Political System.

the diagram, events occurring within a system may also have some share in influencing the nature of the inputs.

As is apparent, the inputs provide what we may call the raw materials on which the system acts so to produce something we are calling outputs. The way in which this is done will be described as a massive conversion process cavalierly represented on the diagram by the serpentine line within the political system. The conversion processes move toward the authorities since it is toward them that the demands are initially directed. As we shall see, demands spark the basic activities of a political system. By virtue of their status in all systems, authorities have special responsibilities for converting demands into outputs.

If we were to be content with what is basically a static picture of a political system, we might be inclined to stop at this point. Indeed much political research in effect does just this. It is concerned with exploring all those intricate subsidiary processes through which decisions are made and put into effect. This constitutes the vast corpus of political research today. Therefore, insofar as we were concerned with how influence is used in formulating and putting into effect various kinds of policies or decisions, the model to

this point would be an adequate if minimal first approximation.

But the critical question that confronts political theory is not just the development of a conceptual apparatus for understanding the factors that contribute to the kinds of decisions a system makes, that is, for formulating a theory of political allocations. As I have indicated, theory needs to know how it comes about that any kind of system can persist long enough to continue to make such decisions. We need a theory of systems persistence as well. How does a system manage to deal with the stress to which it may be subjected at any time? It is for this reason that we cannot accept outputs as the terminal point either of the political processes or of our interest in them. Thus it is important to note on the diagram, that the outputs of the conversion process have the characteristic of feeding back upon the system and shaping its subsequent behavior. Much later I shall seek to demonstrate that it is this feature together with the capacity of a system to take constructive actions that makes it possible for a system to seek to adapt or to cope with possible stress.

In the figure, this feedback is depicted by the line that

shows the effects of the outputs moving directly back to the environments. As the broken lines within the environmental boxes indicate, the effects may reshape the environment in some way; that is to say, they influence conditions and behavior there. In this way the outputs are able to modify the influences that continue to operate on the inputs and thereby the next round of inputs themselves.

But if the authorities are to be able to take the past effect of outputs into account for their own future behavior, they must in some way be apprised of what has taken place along the feedback loop. The broken lines in the box labeled "The political system" suggest that, through the return flow of demands and support, the authorities obtain information about these possible consequences of their previous behavior. This puts the authorities in a position to take advantage of the information that has been fed back and to correct or adjust their behavior for the achievement of their goals.

It is the fact that there can be such a continuous flow of effects and information between system and environment, we shall see, that ultimately accounts for the capacity of a political system to persist in a world even of violently fluctuating changes. Without feedback and the capacity to respond to it, no system could survive for long, except by accident.

In this brief overview, I have summarized the essential features of the analytic structure. . . . If we condensed the figure still further, we would have the diagram shown on Figure 10.2. It reduces to its bare essentials the fundamental processes at work in all systems and starkly reveals the source of a system's capacity to persist. It may well stand temporarily as the simplest image, to carry in our minds, of the processes we are about to discuss in detail.

To summarize the conceptualization being reviewed here, our analysis will rest on the idea of a system imbedded in an environment and subject to possible influences from it that threaten to drive the essential variables of the system beyond their critical range. To persist, the system must be capable of responding with measures that are successful in alleviating the stress so created. To respond, the authorities

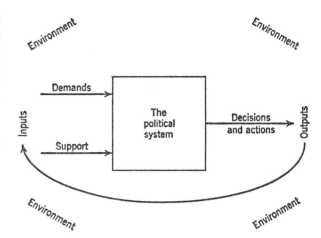

**Figure 10.2** A simplified model of a political system.

at least must be in a position to obtain information about what is happening so that they may react insofar as they desire or are compelled to do so.

In *A Framework for Political Analysis* each of these concepts and interrelationships was attended to in varying degrees of detail . . . It will be my task to begin to apply them in an effort to construct a much more elaborate structure for the analysis of political systems.

In doing so, we shall find ourselves confronted with a series of major questions. What precisely are the nature of the influences acting upon a political system? How are they communicated to a system? In what ways, if any, have systems typically sought to cope with such stress? What kinds of processes will have to exist in any system if it is to acquire and exploit the potential for acting so as to ameliorate these conditions of stress? . . .

## Reference

1 Easton, D. (1961) *A Framework for Political Analysis*, Prentice-Hall, Englewood Cliffs, N.J.

# 11 Technosphere, biosphere, and sociosphere: an approach to their systems modeling and optimization*

*by J. H. Milsum*

## Introduction

In the last century, technology and the science underlying it have been primary agents forcing the vast changes that have occurred in the geosphere and sociosphere which we inhabit. The pace of this change has, in addition, accelerated fantastically in more recent years. Consider, for example, that in the lifetime of almost all here present, the following list represents only the most dramatic examples which have been invented, developed, and have reached mass-production with great social effects upon our lives: gas turbine (jet) engines (providing nearly instantaneous transport of people anywhere around the world at a cost that many can afford); rockets and nuclear energy (providing for space travel and potential "over-kill" capability against the whole human population, as well as other less dramatic, but probably more useful activities); radar, television, and solid-state electronics (providing instantaneous and reasonably economic world-wide communication); electronic computers (providing essentially instantaneous computational ability of such great power that we are only beginning to understand its vastly-pervading influence upon our lives).

While there has not been complete agreement in our society that these changes all represent improvement, nevertheless no groups of significant size ever seriously try to operate their societies without utilizing available technological advances. Thus it may be said that the technologist has had society's tacit support, even if he has not formally represented the ideal prototype for its citizens to aspire to. Unfortunately, it has been largely true that during this early technological period when the advantages of technological advances have generally been so obvious to society, in contrast to the disadvantages which tend to become obvious somewhat later and to cost money to avoid, then the technologist does not seem to have felt it his prime duty to anticipate and point out to society the concomitant disadvantages in comparison to the expected advantages. Nor indeed would it seem justified to consider him particularly culpable here, since society has not really encouraged consideration of the aesthetic and ethical aspects which might arise from technological advance if it were to involve larger cost. Consequently, a naïve technologist would seem superficially justified in being puzzled when he finds himself apt to be as much blamed as praised for new technological developments. Clearly this tendency for blame to be attached comes when societies are beginning to realize that things are not going quite according to plan, and yet are not really clear why. Certainly few would now agree with the philosopher, Dr. Pangloss of *Candide*, that "All is necessarily for the best in the best of all possible worlds". In fact, in spite of the invention, development, and widespread production of vast numbers of useful consumer goods and services, which have turned most Western societies into very affluent ones, it is clear that we perceive ourselves to have some very urgent and perplexing problems.

As regards tackling these problems, it now seems clear that the technologist must increasingly take a systems view which is broad enough to include the problems of social values, and that he must be prepared to take more of a lead in pointing out to his less technically-literate confreres in society how some of the different aspects, such as beautification and prevention of pollution, will trade off in the overall optimization of the system under consideration. Then, while it will remain true that simple answers cannot be expected to the complex problems which we are now producing for ourselves as a result of the vast interlocking of our systems, nevertheless society will be encouraged into the dialogue in helping establish how human values should be entered into the complicated systems equations.

Despite such optimization attempts, it will almost undoubtedly remain true that the affluence available through maximum use of technology will bring at the same time many new problems and will also place constraints upon us. Inasmuch as certain of such constraints may be con-

* Presidential address presented at the Annual Meeting of the Society for General Systems Research, New York, December 1967.

sidered unacceptable by societies at any given time, then it is probable that not every technological advance will be automatically accepted. On the other hand, societies are always adapting, if only slowly, and therefore it will seldom be possible to predict with certainty whether any given innovation will remain unacceptable. It is both refreshing and sobering to realize that in the late twenties Freud was very concerned about these same problems (*Civilization and Its Discontents*, Norton, 1929).

In this talk, I hope to make a few useful suggestions towards how we may bring a systems approach to bear on analyzing our problems in the broad areas of geosphere, biosphere, technosphere, and sociosphere, and hopefully towards optimizing them. It should be mentioned that these of course represent only my own opinions, arising from my own background of control engineering, systems research, and biomedical engineering.

## Geosphere

Under this heading, we mention some of those vast natural processes in and upon the earth which do not either inherently or necessarily involve living processes. These physical systems involve such complicated interlocking dynamics that they are only now beginning to be understood, in the sense of adequate mathematical models being available.

Perhaps the most obvious dynamic phenomena in the geosphere are those cycles due to the varying exposure of the earth to the sun; namely the annual and daily cycles, and of course, although less noticeably, the lunar cycle. Thus genuine and fairly strict cycles exist in such atmospheric conditions as temperature and precipitation, which have in turn widespread influence upon our biosphere, technosphere, and sociosphere. Other major phenomena depend to a greater or lesser extent upon these cyclic-forcing inputs, in particular the circulation of water in the oceans, the circulation of air in the atmosphere, and the rainwater cycle itself. In turn, the latter is coupled to some extent with an electrical cycle which produces the familiar electrical discharges of lightning, among other things. Actually the word *circulation* may be much better than *cycle* to define these phenomena. The point here is that while a cycle may be traced, namely rain – surface and subsurface water flow – pooling in the seas (both ocean and landlocked) – evaporation – cloud formation – rainfall, the cycling is of given molecules between different phases; and that, from an information flow viewpoint, it is merely a relatively constant circulating flux rather than a true cycle. On the other hand, the circulation shows seasonal cyclicity

at any one point on earth, of course; and furthermore, the large spatial coverage of many rain-water systems means that spatio-temporal effects couple-up inextricably.

In these cyclic or circulatory phenomena, some of the effects are unidirectional only, in the sense that what goes in one "direction" is not necessarily returned in the other. A specific important example arising in the rainfall circulation of water is that of erosion of the earth, and specifically of minerals into the sea. As one consequence, the sea cannot itself constitute a constant long-term environment for living species, which has evolutionary implications in the biosphere. It should be noted that the fact that some land also gets thrown back from the sea does not effectively cancel the erosion effect in this biological sense.

At another level of conceptualization, it could be commented that this washing of the land into the oceans is of course in accord with the second law of thermodynamics, namely that closed systems tend towards a state of uniform low order. In fact, the earth is not a closed system; but the geosphere cannot open itself to trap energy from the sun, not at least permanently nor to the same extent as the biosphere can. A further comment is that, in searching for the appropriate physical laws which govern the physical phenomena such as those described, the use of "minimal" principles has often proved important. Minimal principles usually concern conservation of certain properties, that of energy being most generally applicable and valuable, as in the Hamiltonian function.

## Biosphere

Since all living organisms essentially exist close to the earth's surface, it is not surprising that many of the relevant major phenomena of the biosphere are closely coupled with those in the geosphere, such as already mentioned. Furthermore, some of the couplings in these combined systems is completely inextricable; for example, in circulatory cycles of such gases as oxygen and carbon dioxide, and indeed of many other materials, both solid and liquid. Again, there are also slow drifts in the sense that, while during the early stages of life on earth the earth may have been considered to provide a largely constant pool of basic materials, this is not necessarily true today when the biomass has become significantly large. Thus, as is obvious to us, the net result of these interactions is that the geosphere itself has been considerably modified from the relevant conditions which would otherwise exist were there no life on earth. In a parallel example to that of the increase of mineral concentrations in the sea of the geosphere, the carbon dioxide content of the atmosphere has increased as a result of life in general, and man's social system in particular. In turn, this is producing significant effects, both as to climate and net electromagnetic radiation conditions at the earth's surface.

The specific major new ability that living things have added over those exhibited in the non-living world is the ability of living organisms to trap high-energy electromagnetic radiations from the sun, on a relatively permanent basis in that the energy is transformed through photosynthesis into other forms useful in life, such as the so-called organic materials, cells, and high order organisms, and thus ultimately, our own societies.

Since apparently it has not proved practical to evolve organisms that live for an indefinitely extended period of time, then an essential feature of maintaining life has been the ability of these organisms to procreate. This ability provides the advantage that evolution can then operate through the competitive process of selection to allow refinement and improvement of the life forms. This expresses what is usually called the adaptive ability in systems theory, which is implemented in the form of some hill-climbing scheme. From a slightly different viewpoint, this ability of evolution to reject the worst results and retain the "best" may be considered a process which is of the positive-feedback, unstable type. Clearly this mechanism can potentially build up regimes of ever-increasing high order, rather than suffering the usual fate, as prescribed by the second law of thermodynamics, of degradation to uniform low order. The manifestly high-order regimes, which living forms have generated and continue to extend, therefore arises solely from the fact that living systems are able to "open" themselves to the high-energy source of the sun.

Inasmuch as the feeding patterns of living organisms represent a fantastically complicated predator–prey situation, a "balance of nature" is usually stated to express the phenomenon that there seems to be some sort of stability principle at work with regard to the populations to be found, both within species and their ecologies. Furthermore, and perhaps rather to the surprise of many, evidence is accumulating that a self-regulation of populations within species and groups exists, in order apparently to match the available food supplies with the size of the group concerned. Apparently this applies not only in the immediate sense of food supply available in a given short time period, but rather in the sense of the minimum amount available when statistical fluctuations are included over a much longer period. Social measures appear at least in part to be responsible for implementing this self-regulation in many different species, notably birds for example (see Wynn-

Edwards (1962) *Animal Dispersion in Relation to Social Behaviour*, Hafner.

## Technosphere

Historically, it is hardly justifiable to consider that technology started only in the last one, or at most two, centuries. However, such is the nature of exponential growth processes that, for all practical purposes, it suffices to consider that the industrial age started with a small initial condition in the 18th century. Specifically, the so-called first industrial revolution of the 18th–19th century essentially relieved man of the requirement to obtain all his nicely controlled mechanical power through the use of either his own or animal muscles by providing, instead and in succession, steam power, electric power, hydrocarbon fuel power, and finally, nuclear power. This revolution has of course had tremendous social implications, which have been widely discussed, but nevertheless they probably provide only a small component cause in producing the difficult complex problems we face today. The major component arises from the more recent second industrial revolution, which in turn has relieved man of the need to perform all his own data processing by providing, instead, the tremendous capacity of modern electronic (and other) computing machines. This particular revolution has been extremely rapid, for within the course of about twenty-five years from the computer's inception, we now find ourselves affected in a wide spectrum of important ways by this new slave, both helpfully, disturbingly, and frustratingly. Part of the trouble lies in the fact that this slave does accurately and fast so many of the tasks society has found necessary, but which humans themselves have found tedious and therefore do not in fact perform well. Nevertheless, while their work may have generally been decried by these workers, at the same time it has constituted much of the basis for their self-respect. Hence it becomes necessary to define much more carefully what might be considered to constitute the essential characteristics of man, as opposed to a computing machine; in particular, what is necessary to man for him to feel enjoyment in life and to experience emotional and purposeful activity. It is generally presumed that these latter areas are not ones in which a computer excels, and yet, when one tries to define exactly where man does differ in a "superior" way from the computer, the matter becomes very perplexing.

Consequent upon these industrial revolutions, our technosphere now seems capable of providing, at least in principle, large integrated industrial processes which are both automated and computer controlled; as one example, we could cite the possibility of integrating the steel industry through from the mining of metal ores to the inventory control of finished products such as automobiles, almost without human intervention. In other words, given certain sensible and yet fairly unrestrictive constraints on any of man's material needs, he can now aspire to a society in which it is not necessary for the national production of material and information products to be tied essentially to the amount of man power available and its productivity. Theoretically, this should leave him free to develop the higher human qualities with which he believes himself specially endowed. The unfortunate fact that this does not seem to be working out, at present, probably and hopefully relates to the problems of the sociosphere, which at least we may be able to tackle if we can first define them.

## Sociosphere

It has been noted that many of today's problems arise partly because the technological advances which have so greatly affected our social environment have occurred much faster than the normal rate at which adaptive changes in social behavior can accommodate to them. Stated slightly differently, the present time constants of technological change are probably at least one order of magnitude larger than that of social change. Some of these problems arise specifically because the result of technological change has been to call into question for needed re-evaluation certain relevant concepts and beliefs that were long thought either to have been handed down to the world by divine inspiration or else to have been adequately proven by long human experience. Indeed, for much of human history, the changes were of a sufficiently slow nature that they could be adapted to without doing great violence to traditional beliefs; that is, their evolution was possible rather than revolution. Today, however, we have seen reflected into society as a result of technological advancement such dramatic changes that it is clear to almost all that certain absurd situations are arising. Some outstanding examples in my view would seem to be:

1. The subject of *human population*, and the need for its rational control by the societies involved. Certainly there existed adequate justification throughout much of human history for attributing sacrosanct status to new human life, inasmuch as all population possible was desirable to offset the high wastage rate due to warfare and disease. Having now tampered very effectively with the death rate side of human population, sufficiently that a runaway condition is in progress, it would seem to represent elementary good husbandry for us to consider some overall objectives for the size of human populations, so as to be able to work towards achieving such conditions before panic measures prove necessary. Relevant criteria in such considerations obviously must relate to matters such as family health, wealth, and security; adequacy of national food supply; natural resources, etc., and finally a satisfactory population density to avoid unsatisfactory, if as yet unknown, psychological pressures.

2. The matter of *work–leisure relations* in an affluent and automated society. A specific basic problem here concerns how we may accomplish change in the deeply-ingrained protestant ethic which makes it difficult for people to feel themselves fulfilled, and thus to maintain their necessary self-pride, if they cannot be working members of the community, no matter how unrewarding the work might seem to be at first glance. It should be noted that this difficulty seems largely independent of whether they are provided adequate sustenance by their society even when they do not work, in fact possibly even *because* they do not work. Again, therefore, the inheritance of a non-technological age, that unremitting toil is good and necessary, has now rapidly become inappropriate, but too rapidly for society to adopt happily to this condition.

3. The problem of *aggression and interpersonal fear* which lead especially to the problems of warfare and ethnic strife within a particular state.

4. The problem of unacceptably *large and probably increasing differences* between the affluence of the developed societies on the one hand, and the developing societies on the other. It should be noted that this is one of the inevitable effects when subsystems having positive feedback pathways are placed in competition with each other. The process is in fact an example of the general competitive exclusion aspect of evolution, and can lead to the same ruthless solutions unless we impose, as civilized societies, some higher performance criteria upon the overall system.

5. The problem of *participation* by the members of society in their society, in such a meaningful way that they are able to feel part of it and therefore to fulfill themselves. This problem is related to the work–leisure problem mentioned in 2 above. The word alienation has been used to describe the general absence of participation that people feel in large remotely-run and apparently inflexible societies.

Let us ask what may in some reasonable sense be considered the purpose of the people within their societies, and then even of their societies themselves. It seems clear that there are many needs which can already be described for individuals: to be closely involved in a "family", and in contributing to the generation and training of the new generation; to be valued by his neighbors for contributions he can make to his immediate community; to be able to call upon his community in times of need; to be able to develop himself in various intellectual, cultural, and other social ways; and finally, in a less well-defined way, to be able to contribute towards the development of his society at large towards some sort of inspiring long-term goal. It is important to notice in this latter regard that people do not need to be in a state of great affluence as a prerequisite to feeling that they are fulfilling themselves satisfactorily in a society, but rather that they are moving towards a better state by their effort. This fact seems again an illustration of the general biological phenomenon that the rate of change seems to be more important than the absolute value itself. A further point is that it is also necessary to have a basis for comparing performance with another outside standard in order to produce an "error signal" for deciding which action should be taken.

A pertinent question follows from these comments in that it is being implicitly suggested that societies can meaningfully be planned with some overall optimization in view. Unfortunately, of course, it is very hard to find successful evidence for this in history, especially since we are necessarily restricted to a history on which many stages of editing have been performed. Furthermore, since societies contain so much positive feedback, there is always the danger that prophecies may become self-fulfilling. Such conditions could considerably obscure the data obtained from historical studies. This emphasizes from another viewpoint that it is not for trivial reasons that the sociosphere is an area of the "soft sciences". However, while the problems are admittedly extremely complex, this fact alone would seem to emphasize how urgent it is that we as societies bring many of our best scientists to work upon the problems.

## On the problems

Many of society's problems arise because change is necessary from some established conditions. The codification and implementation of these conditions has generally supported the development of a cadre of professionals, which then inherently tends to resist any changes suggested by its "lay electorate", even though the professionals themselves may generate amendments and even major changes in pursuing their maintenance task. In either case, it follows that changes, such as in amendments of laws, necessarily occur in discrete jumps and at discrete intervals of time,

since each change must be brought about by "the pressure to reform" having reached a threshold level after which the resistance may crumble. It may be useful to think of this process as a form of relaxation oscillation, analogous, for example, to the stick-slip friction by which a bow produces a note on the violin string. Furthermore, it should be noted that the decaying of resistance, as the actual change process gathers momentum, is equivalent to positive feedback in the local circuit.

The tendency of the establishment to resist change is not in itself necessarily unhealthy since this procedure represents a reasonable way in which to filter out the high-frequency "noise" for which no change in the rules is really required. On the other hand, society's non-trivial problem in this respect is that of judging how to match the desirable time constant of the filter to the time constant of "DC" or permanent change in the process, so that substantial changes in the "signal" can be adjusted for as rapidly as desirable, while the high-frequency noise is filtered out. Note that use of the word desirable in this sense rather begs the question since, in order to predict this effectively, an observer of godly powers is required.

When changes are made they may fall into either of two general types. In the first type, change is of the amendment or evolutionary type in the sense that the general principles of operation remain the same, but the particular parameter values are changed. The second is of a more revolutionary type in that the whole structure is changed, and obviously therefore this will only occur at a greater threshold of change in the system variables. One classic example of the second type arises when a small one-man business prospers so well that in a relatively short time period it becomes restructured to include professional managers, accountants, salesmen, etc. A frequent by-product of such a change is that the original owner, while still being proud of his success superficially, finds himself increasingly frustrated in that the business is now no longer a simple direct extension of himself, with everything proceeding under his own control. This points to the fact that, during different phases of the life cycle of sociological organisms, staffs of different strengths and weaknesses are required for the different regimes of operation.

Most of man's sociological and industrial enterprises involving many staff have grown more or less successfully to their present stage in a groping manner. Indeed, when the enterprise has been almost entirely focused to achieve the objective of some particular individual, then this type of growth has usually been the most efficient. On the other hand, once its growth reaches the stage where it is essentially a "corporate" business, then it is common experience that the overt objectives of the enterprise can become distinctly modified by these strong but publicly unexpressed motivations of the staff, especially the managers. Thus it has been the well-documented experience of the systems analyst that, when he attempts analysis of such enterprises, this very attempt immediately requires that many questions as to corporate purpose and information-flow details be asked, and that this process itself seems surprisingly revolutionary. The typical consequence is that significant improvements can easily be made in the operation, largely as a result of certain critical questions having been asked for the first time because of the point of view taken by the systems analyst. Stated slightly differently, the first cream of the optimization process can often be gained without resorting to any major refinements. The second stage as a result of the systems study is usually to introduce complicated data processing and hence control schemes for the organization. As the operation becomes closer to optimal, the cost of the analyst and of the computing time necessary for the optimization studies becomes very significant, until finally the diminishing-returns stage is reached in which the cost of the analytical effort exceeds the economy gained as a result.

On the other hand, it should also be noted that the advantages of analytical optimization studies may be realized only after a considerable time delay so that in such cases an immediate economic loss is quite acceptable in view of the profit to be gained later by the experience acquired.

In performing any optimization study, one focal point of the analysis concerns establishing an appropriate performance criterion, also often called cost function or profit function. When the analyst is searching for background knowledge to establish this criterion, he often finds that he must ask questions for which answers are not readily available, while many of the correct answers which are available are unfortunately not answers to useful questions! In defining the performance criterion, one of the most difficult tasks relates to establishing quantitative values for the social aspects, an extreme example being the value of a person's life. In fact, some react with horror to the idea that such an evaluation can even be considered. Such reactions are clearly not rational, since in fact we place great reliance upon insurance schemes, which necessarily quantify such matters; but they do point out the deep-seated nature of reactions that must be considered in any realistic analysis.

The fact that we have accepted a position of such dependence upon our technological processes, in contrast to the condition of being subject only to natural accidents, means that we have to accept the responsibility for setting safety standards, etc., which in turn determine, at least statistically, the risk rate of accidental mortality. To emphasize the case by taking the absurd extreme, almost all new technological innovations would be too expensive for us to utilize if we insisted as a society that under no circumstances could these machines conceivably take or damage human life. As a concrete example, we all recognize that accidents can happen to airplanes, with heavy loss of life, but we go on flying; and furthermore it is doubtful whether we as a society would legislate for significantly lower risk rate, in view of the rapidly increasing cost which would probably be involved. In summary, there is some incompatibility between what might be called the public and private attitudes of society, or the conscious and unconscious attitudes, and all this is borne in mind by the managers of the various important undertakings of our society, for otherwise the society certainly could not function as relatively smoothly as it does.

This consideration suggests another problem concerning inquiries into social beliefs and behaviour, namely that there are strong feedback effects especially on the positive type. To amplify this point, recall that in the physical sciences it is usually possible to design instrumentation with sufficiently high input impedance that no significant power drain is placed upon the system being observed and therefore no significant changes caused upon it. Unfortunately, the position is much worse in the social field, in that it is almost impossible to ask any question of a human being without in some way either "loading the question" or the responder feeling that the question is loaded because of his own subjective reaction. In any case, he may not answer in an entirely frank way, and may even be quite dishonest. Of course, in view of the simultaneously-held, incompatible beliefs that any responder holds, it is probably begging the question to attach any value judgment to the word "dishonest" in this context.

## On the phenomena

In this section are considered a number of the most important phenomena concerned in complex systems such as we have been discussing, as follows: growth and positive feedback; oscillations; unidirectionality; psychological and man–machine interactions; minimal principles; and extreme value statistics.

### Growth and positive feedback

The expression "positive feedback" conveys some common meaning to most people in a qualitative way, but care must be taken before it is used in a quantative way, especially if any value judgments are to be involved in the matter. For example, the term "vicious circles" is commonly used to connote that a chain of vicious effects circulates in an increasing way. On the other hand, positive feedback is fundamental to all growth processes, whether in living or non-living systems. In this growth, positive feedback is responsible for the rapid growth in the initial stages, although the subsequent decay of growth rate to zero so that some steady state value is reached is due to other feedbacks. Actually, it is very hard to see how social life, as we know it, could be continued without this initiating effect. A few examples are now mentioned from the several domains considered earlier:

*Fire*, an essential tool in our life, must necessarily start as a small initial condition and then grow rapidly until the equilibrium conditions are approached when a leveling out of growth occurs. Although perhaps trite, it seems worth pointing out that when fire gets out of hand, as in forest and house fire, etc., then the exponential growth stage has merely been able to continue somewhat further than is considered desirable from the viewpoint of our own particular social system. The basic process, however, is the same as that which we consider desirable when we contain the fire within our household grates, oil furnaces, or internal combustion engines to pleasant and/or useful levels.

## Growth of organisms, journals, and capital

The very prototype of growth is that in which cells successively divide after relatively constant periods given adequate nutrition, and thus produce the classic exponential growth. To continue the classic picture, however, the usual later growth pattern is modeled reasonably well by the so-called logistic curve or S-curve, in that the decay of growth rate essentially follows a mirror image pattern to the initial increase of growth rate until a steady-state population is reached, typically under a constant nutrition condition (see for example *Positive Feedback*, J. H. Milsum, ed., Pergamon Press, 1968). At present, knowledge, journals, and information are in the stage of exponential explosion. De Solla Price points out that while specific subsets of such knowledge systems, for example, of universities, show more or less the classic S-curve of growth over defined periods, they often set off on a renewed growth curve after some dramatically new condition has appeared (*Science Since Babylon*, Yale University Press, 1961). As regards money, this obviously continues in principle to produce exponential growth if invested with compound interest at constant rate.

## Bandwagons, fashions, and vicious cycles

All these terms are used to describe phenomena exhibiting positive feedback in the social domain, the following constituting a few random examples: growth of discussion about a new and important subject, once somebody has first raised the matter; the arousal of passion in mobs; the spread of fashion in such matters as clothing, usage of words, and beliefs.

Another important aspect of growth in complicated systems is that while positive feedback may stimulate the growth of a particular subsystem, there must often be present inhibition for other similar but less successful subsystems in the surrounding domain. For example, there develops a competition between the individual tiny trees in the initial stages of growth of a number of seedlings in the forest so that once some particular examples prevail strongly enough, for example by an appropriate advantage in height, etc., then they can continue to grow preferentially with regard to the others, which latter are effectively inhibited and die off. In turn, of course, further stages of competition arise as these saplings grow larger, until the end result is the few "mighty oaks" for each acre of mature forest. Similar growth examples exist for animal species; for example, in a colony of flour beetles in a jar of flour, the female beetles lay eggs almost continually in the tunnels, but there is an extremely high probability that these eggs will be subsequently eaten by other perambulating mature beetles. Thus, while chance may set the initial conditions by which certain eggs are overlooked, once these newly-hatched beetles have survived to a certain size their probability of survival becomes successively larger. At higher levels of social organization, such as in bee colonies and in political parties, the same initial stage of selecting the queen bee or leader occurs, usually followed by a rallying around or "climbing onto the bandwagon", then elimination of competitors, then a period of comparative stability and unchallenged leadership, until eventually sufficient decay in the leader's performance occurs that the competition starts up again. It is also interesting to note that in certain neuronal data processing, such as in the retina, there is a strong tendency to emphasize contrast and/or movement of perceived objects, which is analogous to the aspect already described of enhancing some central feature and inhibiting the surround.

A common feature, worth noting in this matter of accepting a leader and then inhibiting competition, is that the first important feature in the emergence is to provide a sufficiently superior initial condition for one object to excel over its competition. Once this superiority has been accepted by the surrounding competition, then the survivor essentially loses most of its competition for a period, and usually therefore survives even for some significant period after its performance has fallen below that threshold of superiority which was originally necessary. In our common jargon we say that habits, laws, beliefs, and systems tend to be carried along by their own momentum even after people start to become dissatisfied with them. When we view the matter, however, in terms of the "capital" invested in the system, whether emotional or financial, then such tolerance is not unreasonable. In any case, the result is typically that of the stick-slip friction model already discussed.

An interesting and relevant socio-technological example concerns the circumstances by which the gauge separating the two tracks of railroads became standardized. It provides a classic example of those growth situations in which the apparently unimportant detail decisions at the early stages in fact become inevitably frozen into the design of huge systems. Thus today's railroads apparently developed from their embryonic form of horse-drawn coal carts. In the 19th century these were first carried over wooden planks, and then on iron plateways, and then on crude rails after the invention of the flanged wheel. The essentials of the modern system then started in England at the beginning of the 19th century, and, as the typical explosion of railroad building occurred, there did not seem any compelling reason at any stage to change from the first gauge which had "just happened", namely 4 ft. 8 1/2 in. No compelling reason, that is, for the original inventor Stephenson and subsequently his son, who were responsible for building most of England's railroad trackage. However, there was competition, symbolized by the engineer, Brunel, who realized that this gauge was not technically optimum, and therefore decided to build the Great Western Railway on a gauge of 9 ft. Considerable rivalry grew up over this matter, and technical passions were raised; but ultimately it was resolved on the matter of total capital investment, rather than on technical merit alone. Thus, when it was resolved to standardize in England after many years, there was about 80% of the narrower gauge compared to the remainder of the wider gauge, so the result may have been considered inevitable.

A further pertinent aspect may be pointed out concerning this case history. England, as the originator of railroads, had been more or less strongly involved in developing railroads all over the world. Thus the decision concerning the gauge standardization affected all, but was made only by a few.

## Oscillations

Oscillations occur in many systems, and in social systems especially in those where mutual interaction exists. Now, many ecologists consider that an ecology cannot be considered to have reached optimal conditions while considerable oscillation of more or less random patterns continues in the subpopulations of the system. Evidently as ecologies become more mature, then the magnitude of oscillatory behaviour decreases. This comment is probably pertinent for many of our own human social systems also. For example, as Boulding comments, we are no longer interested in merely understanding why our economic systems oscillate, because such oscillations produce profound human misery, but rather we wish to control these oscillations to a satisfactorily low level.

In contrast, it should be noted that, within animals, the perceptual mechanisms seem particularly designed for detection of changes, as characterized rather dramatically by the fact that in the absence of change in the stimuli most of the relevant receptors generally cease to be stimulated. Furthermore, it has been shown that if a large sensory loss is maintained for a considerable period of time, then the human psyche finds it very difficult to operate at all in a stable normal way.

The evidence is increasing that the normal condition of state variables within organisms such as man, animals, and even plants, is often one of continual cycling. This may be anywhere in the range from subcellular systems up to the level of the organism itself. In any one case, the oscillation is in relatively narrow spectral bands, typical examples being the approximately one-second heart cycle; a ten-second "engine" cycle at the capillary level of blood, as noted by Iberall; circadian cycles of temperature, metabolic activity, etc., of order one day; the three- to five-day water cycle; the monthly ovarian cycle; and finally, the various generational cycles of different species.

Most of the technological systems which have been designed to incorporate adaptive and optimizing aspects inherently require a more-or-less continuous cycling action. This is necessary both in theory and practice, because the performance criterion may be time varying, and the fact that the system had once adapted so as to reach maximum performance "on top of the hill" is not satisfactory in general, since the hill may subsequently have moved. A hill-climbing scheme is therefore necessary in which the relevant derivative must be measured so that direction and rate information can be provided for climbing again towards the optimal performance condition. It is therefore at least conceptually possible that much of the cycling found in living systems relates to the possibility of them continually optimizing themselves. However, there are other equally plausible explanations, for example, that the oscillation is difficult to filter out and in itself is not harmful, or that the oscillation may help implement the necessary sharing of materials which are competed for in such economies as those of cells.

## Unidirectionality

Asymmetry is a particular form of non-linearity which arises widely in the operation of systems, but perhaps especially those of the biological and social type. It is noteworthy that the relative infrequency of non-linearity in technological systems merely reflects the purpose of the designers, is that there is at least a fairly coherent linear system theory, which unfortunately is not true for the non-linear domain. However, with the advent of more powerful theories, and of the computer, the engineer is increasingly beginning to design his systems to be non-linear, which often has advantages as far as optimization is concerned.

A major reason for asymmetry in many living systems is that negative quantities cannot exist for many variables. Examples are the concentrations of active chemicals such as hormones in the endocrine system; that the force which a muscle can exert is restricted to pulling, rather than pushing; that the firing frequency of neurons can only be at a positive rate, since negative frequencies are meaningless; that such behavioral variables as hostility can have only one polarity, unless an anti-hostility effect is definable; and that the strength of an army is only significant for positive quantities. In the detailed design of biological systems, this fundamental unidirectional nature of certain of the components is overcome by providing another parallel channel which utilizes the same operating principle, but is connected in the reverse sense so as to provide effectively a variable for the negative polarity requirement of the variable. Particularly obvious examples are agonist–antagonist pairs of muscles, and the stimulatory–inhibitory connections of neurons. Note that in obtaining efficient operation, reciprocal-type information networks must be provided so that the two energetically-expensive variables cannot fight each other for no net effect in the system. However, as often is the case in biological systems, more subtle uses can also be made of the system in which in fact such apparently useless action is implemented; for example, a pair of muscles will be provided with "tone" in order to maintain a certain desired stiffness in the system, and furthermore, when the muscles are required to shiver in order to produce heat for the thermoregulation system, then it is clearly necessary for both muscles to shiver at the same time.

The above comments have essentially concerned static unidirectionality, but some very interesting and advantageous system characteristics arise from dynamic unidirectionality of the type specially pursued by Clynes ("Rein Control, or Unidirectional Rate Sensitivity, A Fundamental Dynamic and Organizing Function in Biology", to be published in *Annals of the N.Y. Acad. of Sci.*, 1968). The general effect is that dynamic asymmetry tends to emphasize changes of condition, a process noted earlier as being ubiquitous in living systems. Further, it emerges that such dynamic unidirectionality provides especially good response characteristics at the high-frequency end of the spectrum, but unfortunately this cannot be pursued further here.

There is another steady-state effect of static unidirectionality that is worth mentioning, which is that, in systems exhibiting oscillation or statistical variation, the rectifying effect of unidirectionality can result in an irrevocable loss of system capacity. The prototype for this is perhaps the service capacity of a facility given a waiting line. In particular, when the vehicles arrive with some statistical variation or if the service time is similarly distributed, there is an irrevocable loss of service capacity as compared to the situation when both arrivals and servicings are regular. The classic result is that as the mean arrival time reduces until it approaches the mean service time, then the length of the waiting line extends theoretically to infinity. The physical basis for this result is that there is a basic asymmetry operating, in that whenever chance decrees that no vehicles are waiting for service, then this otherwise available service time is lost forever. This condition applies equally for a neuron which must cut off information flow at zero frequency. Of course, effective bidirectionality can be introduced by incorporating a high spontaneous level of neural firing for which the information transfer is zero, but such a technique is metabolically expensive.

Other similar examples arise wherever material is pooled in some capacitor but tends to escape when the pressure rises above a certain amount; for example, if a bathtub has an overflow system, then the result of a statistical variation in the height of water due to waves will be that the mean height will be less than this threshold value at which overflow can first occur.

## Psychological and man–machine interactions

In man–machine systems, and indeed in any systems where the psychological characteristics of man contribute significantly, any satisfactory analysis depends upon obtaining good experimental data regarding the psychological aspects. This point is well illustrated by the study of how the flow of vehicles through a single-lane facility can be maximized. In the case of one of the New York tunnels, a well-defined curve was obtained relating the number of cars passing through the tunnel per hour to the steady-speed at which the cars were constrained to travel. To the untrained intuition, it may seem rather surprising that the maximum throughput rate occurred when the controlled speed was close to 20 mph, and that the hill characterizing the throughput was fairly steep sided. The explanation, why the throughput falls above the optimal speed, relates to the psychological considerations that, with very good reason, the driver is not prepared to remain as closely behind the car in front as he would at a lower speed. One base measure for his spacing would be if it increased as the square of the speed, therefore being proportional to kinetic energy, so that the driver would be assured of being able to brake to a full stop without an accident even if the car in front came to an instantaneous halt, such as could occur if he sustained a head-on collision. In practice, drivers can generally see conditions somewhat ahead of the car in front and, given certain other social pressures, the experienced driver then generally chooses some spacing relation intermediate between the quadratic type and a linear spacing with velocity, which in turn gives rise to the optimal condition already stated.

It should perhaps be pointed out that this particular optimal condition was not recognized as such until the appropriate experimental work had been done; indeed, most of the tunnels mentioned are frequently marked "maintain 40 mph". Furthermore, while the systems analyst can obtain such answers concerning optimality, it is most unlikely that any set of subsystems such as drivers themselves would ever arrive at this solution if left to their own resources. Indeed, as members of the social system, we have all experienced frustrating situations especially in traffic jams, of seeing the overall system degenerate to an obviously non-optimal condition in consequence of people operating individually and apparently in their own best interests; the resultant breakdown of the complete system, however, shows that this is not so; but on the other hand that the subsystems are equally powerless to do anything about it.

While man must necessarily set his own performance criteria, he may not necessarily be able to or even wish to reveal their nature to an experimenter. For example, if a person is asked to move a heavy weight with his arm as rapidly as possible across a smooth surface between two fixed points, then observation of the dynamic performance will reveal quite a lot about the subject's strategy. In fact, this does turn out to be generally similar to the "bang–bang" control which does produce the action in minimum time. However, the subject still has under his control the arbitrary choice of what strength of muscle force he shall utilize, and this never seems to be the very maximum that could be obtained. Furthermore, carefully detailed observation may reveal that the man does not in fact accept the verbally stated criterion as appropriate to him, in the light of his actual performance.

## Minimal principles and optimality

A number of minimal principles, that is, equivalently optimality principles, are recognized in physics. A generalized verbal formulation of such principles may be given roughly as follows: The particular solution "selected" by a process in a physical system will be that one out of the possible family of solutions, all consistent with given constraints, which minimizes a certain "cost". Thus a ray of light moves through media of arbitrary refractive indices in least time (Fermat's Principle), while a mechanical system which conserves total energy moves along that path which minimizes the quantity defined as "action" (Maupertuis' Principle of Least Action). When slightly generalized to minimize "virtual displacement" rather than action, Maupertuis' principle becomes consistent with that most general minimal principle of physics called Hamilton's Principle. The major drawback to universal application is that only conservative systems can be so treated. Other minimal principles concern lines of minimum length joining points on a given surface, and generalizations of this. There are implications for the latter principle in biology, for example, concerning the deduction that thin films enclosing material should assume configurations which minimize surface area.

Minimal principles have been of considerable philosophical importance in physics, but have not become necessary working tools for normal problems, such as those of the atmospheric and oceanic circulation mentioned earlier. In part this is because the mechanical, hydrodynamic, electrical and other laws which are derivable from the above principle are already well known (and indeed were discovered first usually), but also importantly because the ubiquity of dissipative phenomena render them ineligible.

With the recent development of a comprehensive control theory (see, for example, Bellman, *Adaptive Control Pro-*

*cesses: a Guided Tour*, Princeton University Press, 1961) the Hamiltonian and its derivative Euler–Lagrange equations have become of renewed importance. In this case the Hamiltonian represents a function of the performance criterion, being in detail comprised not only of the cost function itself but also of the constraints on the system behaviour. This has significant implications for equally direct optimization in the general types of systems we have been considering, if and when it becomes possible to define quantitatively both the performance criteria and the constraints.

The situation in biology is somewhat different and more promising than in physics, as Rosen points out in his recent book (R. Rosen, *Optimality Principles in Biology*, Butterworths, 1967) "... it is possible to give at the outset a coherent, if qualitative, argument which will to some extent justify a search for such principles in biology, and help in their formulation. This argument is based on the phenomenon of natural selection, and the pressure which selection exerts on nearly every aspect of the structure, function, and performance of biological individuals. ... It is now possible to make the fundamental hypothesis that biological structures, which are optimal in the context of natural selection, are also optimal in the sense that they minimize some cost functional derived from the engineering characteristics of the situation. This most natural assumption has been called the Principle of Optimal Design (N. Rashevsky, *Mathematical Biophysics*, 3rd edition, Dover, New York, 1960; see also D'Arcy Thompson, *On Growth and Form*, Macmillan, New York, 1945). ... Usually, however, the appropriate cost functional is not immediately obvious; therein lies the art and difficulty of the entire subject." We might add furthermore that it is not indeed likely that most cost functionals will prove simple enough to allow this direct analytical attack even when they can be plausibly defined. It is of interest that Rosen then considers the vascular system and, by assuming a reasonable cost functional related to the metabolic cost of maintaining the system plus the hydrodynamic power loss in the system, is able to show that the results of an optimality analysis are consistent with those obtained for dogs as regards blood vessel size and the geometry of branching.

The last example illustrates a "design optimization" in the sense that this is achieved at the genetic and growth level, presumably just once for any organism. On the other hand, there is evidence for on-going "operating optimization" in the sense that many organ system functions such as respiration, locomotion, posture, and swimming in fishes seem to be optimized on an energy related criterion (J. H.

Milsum, *Biological Control Systems Analysis*, McGraw-Hill, 1966; also J. H. Milsum in *Advances in Bio-Medical Engineering and Medical Physics*, edited by S. N. Levine, Wiley-Interscience, 1967).

There is some first rather qualitative evidence that optimality principles apply also in social systems, where the interacting variables are probably more related to information flow than to energy flow (for example, G. K. Zipf, *Human Behaviour and Principle of Least Effort*, Harvard Univ. Press, 1949).

## Extreme value statistics

Since nature's various populations and evolutionary experiments involve very large numbers, some of the small samples constituting our experimental research will inevitably differ from the mean by extremely large numbers of standard deviations, that is, falling into the area of extreme value statistics. For example, if the probability of an event such as a particular genetic combination is less than, say, ten to the minus nine, nevertheless such events may occur with reasonable regularity in some of nature's populations. In particular cases sufficient numbers of these extremely improbable events have happened, so that some form of evolution has even operated upon them. The simple animal hydra provides an example here in its evolution of unlikely methods of escaping either in space or time from unfavorable conditions such as by ballooning, etc. (see Slobodkin in *Positive Feedback*, J. H. Milsum, editor, Pergamon Press, 1968).

A trade-off situation is certainly involved in systems involving extreme value statistics, and some rather elementary examples will be considered; but in general it is certainly extremely difficult to attach quantitative values to the relevant variables. In these situations at least one new component is added to the performance criterion, representing the expected value or cost of the unlikely events. An *expected value* or *cost* equals the probability of the event multiplied by the value or cost of the event, should it happen. Numerically this value can be significant, and even comparable to other cost components of the performance criterion, even if the probability of the event is very small, provided that the cost attached to the event is large. Consider a simplified example of deciding what strength should be designed into buildings to combat the possibility of collapse due to earthquakes. If it is assumed that earthquakes are distributed in some reasonable and known statistical manner, then a probability value can be assigned concerning the occurrence of earthquakes of a given strength or larger during an appropriate period of time.

Clearly the construction cost will increase as the design strength against earthquakes is increased, and for an optimal design this must be traded off against the expected cost due to the finite possibility of building collapse. Thus, as design strength is increased, construction cost increases whereas the expected cost decreases because of the decreasing probability that a sufficiently strong earthquake will occur to cause building collapse. On the other hand, if construction strength is decreased, the latter cost is decreased whereas the expected cost of earthquake collapse is increased. It may be expected that an economic optimum point exists when mathematically the derivatives of the two costs, plotted as functions of construction strength, are equal in magnitude although opposite in sign.

Such an analysis forces us to confront the difficult issue of whether or not we are prepared to accept a possibility of building collapse "in cold blood". Clearly though, there is nothing wrong with the thinking of carrying out the analysis as long as we in society are prepared to say whether we are satisfied with the results, following upon incorporating into the performance criterion all values that concern us. Specifically, the difficult problem revolves about the cost of people's lives potentially lost in a collapse. This is certainly not an easy matter to resolve, but on the other hand, our society's nominal claim that we must not allow any risk of accidental death at all is clearly not carried out either individually or en masse in our normal affairs. As we increasingly generate new systems where such considerations will be forced upon us, as in universal systems of medical care, rational, but ethical guidelines will have to be developed. For example, in medical systems there is not only the problem of optimizing the system with regard both to the cost of medical care and the expected value of extended survival of life or mitigation of pain, but also whether or not the positive feedback dynamics of social pressures may allow any rational thinking about the value of prolonging life of individuals, and so on. Here the considerations move rapidly and increasingly confusingly into the technological, legal, ethical, moral, and religious domains.

## On tampering and optimizing; some conclusions

It is a basic concept that systems comprise collections of subsystems, and that the problem in optimizing a social system is especially difficult in that it is as yet almost impossible to define quantitatively a relevant performance criterion. The difficulty resides especially in the fact that hard facts regarding costs of concrete, etc., have to be compared with "soft facts" concerning such social aspects as aesthetics and fulfillment. Furthermore, a satisfactory overall criterion must consist of a weighted collection of criteria which comprise the preferences of all the subsystems, namely ourselves who constitute the electorate for the overall systems planners and controllers, and therefore hopefully the ultimate controllers of the latter. It should be noted that the criteria we then choose will certainly be different from the ones we would otherwise be forced to choose if we were in a "dog-eat-dog" condition where each would have to optimize his own subsystem without regard to his neighbors. As Freud points out, in the work quoted, this is why societies have successively adopted the otherwise undesirable constraints of a civilized system. However, resulting from the energy and information revolutions, such constraints can become increasingly irksome while at the same time we enjoy the advantages, and therefore we must arrange that our legal and social structures, and our systems planning, are adequately flexible and fairly rapidly adaptable. In particular, they must try to anticipate the impact of technological change upon the social scene. This requires a vastly greater acceptance by the technologist and scientist of responsibility for reporting to society their intelligent predictions regarding social effects of technological change, and a vastly greater acceptance by the social scientists and humanists of their need to understand something not only of the general systems approach, but also of technological principles. Morison, in his book *Men, Machines, and Modern Times* (MIT Press, 1966) suggests that it is important for society to get into a mood of continuous, small-scale but ubiquitous experimentation, to be carried on by all intelligent members of society. This would encourage a sense of participation by individuals, would enable multiple-parallel experiments to be carried out on a small scale to predict effects of change rather in the same way that evolution operates, and would be a wonderfully fruitful way of realizing the dream of "intelligence amplification".

If such an experimental mood could be widely cultivated in society, then an atmosphere could be created for multidisciplinary systems analysis on a large number of large-scale technological projects with important social implications. For example, recent suggestions of this type include damming the Bering Straits, and widespread modifications of the North American fresh-water systems. A number of other vast projects are interestingly presented in *Engineer's Dreams* by Willy Ley (Viking, 1954).

Along with these new projects, society will also naturally tackle the pressing socio-technological problems such as that of air and water pollution due to pollutants of all types such as chemicals, noise, visual objects, and so on. A further aspect merging more towards the pure biological domain will be that of improving our attempts to control or eradicate what we conceive of as hostile species of animals, insects, etc., by use of the evolutionary process (by attracting and then sterilizing males, for example) rather than making it work continually against us, as in current pesticides. Furthermore, because of the huge and delicate balances of nature of the ecologies with which we tamper, we shall be forced to study the whole problem in a systems light. Finally, what can we say of man himself? We largely believe that we have provided the technological capability for fulfilling ourselves, but we have yet to define what this consists of, and how we must plan our society so as to be able to achieve it.

Reprinted from Milsum, J. H. (1968) "Technosphere, Biosphere and Sociosphere", *General Systems*, **13**.

# 12 Understanding the counterintuitive behaviour of social systems*

## by Jay W. Forrester

*System dynamics has demonstrated how companies and how urban systems behave in ways that run against most of what man would do to correct their ills. Now the same obtuse behaviour can be assigned to the largest social issues which confront the world. Although this article is written with the United States in mind, the analytical techniques described and the conclusions derived from them can be applied to all industrialized countries.*

This paper addresses several issues of broad concern in the United States: population trends; the quality of urban life; national policy for urban growth; and the unexpected, ineffective, or detrimental results often generated by government programmes in these areas.

The nation exhibits a growing sense of futility as it repeatedly attacks deficiencies in our social system while the symptoms continue to worsen. Legislation is debated and passed with great promise and hope. But many programmes prove to be ineffective. Results often seem unrelated to those expected when the programmes were planned. At times programmes cause exactly the reverse of desired results.

It is now possible to explain how such contrary results can happen. There are fundamental reasons why people misjudge the behaviour of social systems. There are orderly processes at work in the creation of human judgment and intuition that frequently lead people to wrong decisions when faced with complex and highly interacting systems. Until we come to a much better understanding of social systems, we should expect that attempts to develop corrective programmes will continue to disappoint us.

The purpose of this paper is to leave with its readers a sense of caution about continuing to depend on the same past approaches that have led to our present feeling of frustration and to suggest an approach which can eventually lead to a better understanding of our social systems and thereby to more effective policies for guiding the future.

## A new approach to social systems

It is my basic theme that the human mind is not adapted to interpreting how social systems behave. Our social systems belong to the class called multiloop nonlinear

* This paper is based on testimony for the Subcommittee on Urban Growth of the Committee on Banking and Currency, US House of Representatives, on October 7, 1970.

feedback systems. In the long history of evolution it has not been necessary for man to understand these systems until very recent historical times. Evolutionary processes have not given us the mental skill needed to properly interpret the dynamic behaviour of the systems of which we have now become a part.

In addition, the social sciences have fallen into some mistaken "scientific" practices which compound man's natural shortcomings. Computers are often being used for what the computer does poorly and the human mind does well. At the same time the human mind is being used for what the human mind does poorly and the computer does well. Even worse, impossible tasks are attempted while achievable and important goals are ignored.

Until recently there has been no way to estimate the behaviour of social systems except by contemplation, discussion, argument, and guesswork. To point a way out of our present dilemma about social systems, I will sketch an approach that combines the strength of the human mind and the strength of today's computers. The approach is an outgrowth of developments over the last 40 years, in which much of the research has been at the Massachusetts Institute of Technology. The concepts of feedback system behaviour apply sweepingly from physical systems through social systems. The ideas were first developed and applied to engineering systems. They have now reached practical usefulness in major aspects of our social systems.

I am speaking of what has come to be called industrial dynamics. The name is a misnomer because the methods apply to complex systems regardless of the field in which they are located. A more appropriate name would be *system dynamics*. In our own work, applications have been made to corporate policy, to the dynamics of diabetes as a medical system, to the growth and stagnation of an urban area, and most recently to world dynamics representing the interactions of population, pollution, industrialization, natural resources, and food. System dynamics as an extension of the earlier design of physical systems, has been under development at MIT since 1956. The approach is easy to understand but difficult to practice. Few people have a high level of skill; but preliminary work is developing all over the world. Some European countries and especially Japan have begun centres of education and research.

## Computer models of social systems

People would never attempt to send a space ship to the moon without first testing the equipment by constructing prototype models and by computer simulation of the anticipated space trajectories. No company would put a new kind of household appliance or electronic computer into production without first making laboratory tests. Such models and laboratory tests do not guarantee against failure, but they do identify many weaknesses which can then be corrected before they cause full-scale disasters.

Our social systems are far more complex and harder to understand than our technological systems. Why, then, do we not use the same approach of making models of social systems and conducting laboratory experiments on those models before we try new laws and government programmes in real life? The answer is often stated that our knowledge of social systems is insufficient for constructing useful models. But what justification can there be for the apparent assumption that we do not know enough to construct models but believe we do know enough to directly design new social systems by passing laws and starting new social programmes? I am suggesting that we now do know enough to make useful models of social systems. Conversely, we do not know enough to design the most effective social systems directly without first going through a model-building experimental phase. But I am confident, and substantial supporting evidence is beginning to accumulate, that the proper use of models of social systems can lead to far better systems, laws, and programmes.

It is now possible to construct in the laboratory realistic models of social systems. Such models are simplifications of the actual social system but can be far more comprehensive than the mental models that we otherwise use as the basis for debating governmental action.

Before going further, I should emphasize that there is nothing new in the use of models to represent social systems. Each of us uses models constantly. Every person in his private life and in his business life instinctively uses models for decision making. The mental image of the world around you which you carry in your head is a model. One

does not have a city or a government or a country in his head. He has only selected concepts and relationships which he uses to represent the real system. A mental image is a model. All of our decisions are taken on the basis of models. All of our laws are based on the basis of models. All executive actions are taken on the basis of models. The question is not to use or ignore models. The question is only a choice among alternative models.

The mental model is fuzzy. It is incomplete. It is imprecisely stated. Furthermore, within one individual, a mental model changes with time and even during the flow of a single conversation. The human mind assembles a few relationships to fit the context of a discussion. As the subject shifts so does the model. When only a single topic is being discussed, each participant in a conversation employs a different mental model to interpret the subject. Fundamental assumptions differ but are never brought into the open. Goals are different and are left unstated. It is little wonder that compromise takes so long. And it is not surprising that consensus leads to laws and programmes that fail in their objectives or produce new difficulties greater than those that have been relieved.

For these reasons we stress the importance of being explicit about assumptions and interrelating them in a computer model. Any concept or assumption that can be clearly described in words can be incorporated in a computer model. When done, the ideas become clear. Assumptions are exposed so they may be discussed and debated.

But the most important difference between the properly conceived computer model and the mental model is in the ability to determine the dynamic consequences when the assumptions within the model interact with one another. The human mind is not adapted to sensing correctly the consequences of a mental model. The mental model may be correct in structure and assumptions but, even so, the human mind – either individually or as a group consensus – is most apt to draw the wrong conclusions. There is no doubt about the digital computer routinely and accurately tracing through the sequences of actions that result from following the statements of behaviour for individual points in the model system. This inability of the human mind to use its own mental models is clearly shown when a computer model is constructed to reproduce the assumptions held by a single person. In other words, the model is refined until it is fully agreeable in all its assumptions to the perceptions and ideas of a particular person. Then, it usually happens that the system that has been described does not act the way the person anticipated. Usually there is an internal contradiction in mental models between the assumed structure and the assumed future consequences. Ordinarily the assumptions about structure and internal motivations are more nearly correct than are the assumptions about the implied behaviour.

The kind of computer models that I am discussing are strikingly similar to mental models. They are derived from the same sources. They may be discussed in the same terms. But computer models differ from mental models in important ways. The computer models are stated explicitly. The "mathematical" notation that is used for describing the model is unambiguous. It is a language that is clearer, simpler, and more precise than such spoken languages as English or French. Its advantage is in the clarity of meaning and the simplicity of the language syntax. The language of a computer model can be understood by almost anyone, regardless of educational background. Furthermore, any concept and relationship that can be clearly stated in ordinary language can be translated into computer model language.

There are many approaches to computer models. Some are naïve. Some are conceptually and structually inconsistent with the nature of actual systems. Some are based on methodologies for obtaining input data that commit the models to omitting major concepts and relationships in the psychological and human reaction areas that we all know to be crucial. With so much activity in computer models and with the same terminology having different meanings in the different approaches, the situation must be confusing to the casual observer. The key to success is not in having a computer; the important thing is how the computer is used. With respect to models, the key is not to computerize a model, but to have a model structure and relationships which properly represent the system that is being considered.

I am speaking here of a kind of computer model that is very different from the models that are now most common in the social sciences. Such a computer model is not derived statistically from time-series data. Instead, the kind of computer model I am discussing is a statement of system structure. It contains the assumptions being made about the system. The model is only as good as the expertise which lies behind its formulation. Great and correct theories in physics or in economics are few and far between. A great computer model is distinguished from a poor one by the degree to which it captures more of the essence of the social system that it presumes to represent. Many mathematical models are limited because they are formulated by techniques and according to a conceptual structure that will not accept the multiple-feedback-loop and nonlinear nature of real systems. Other models are defective because of lack of knowledge or deficiencies of perception on the part of the persons who have formulated them.

But a recently developed kind of computer modelling is now beginning to show the characteristics of behaviour of actual systems. These models explain why we are having the present difficulties with our actual social systems and furthermore explain why so many efforts to improve social systems have failed. In spite of their shortcomings, models can now be constructed that are far superior to the intuitive models in our heads on which we are now basing national social programmes.

This approach to the dynamics of social systems differs in two important ways from common practice in social sciences and government. There seems to be a common attitude that the major difficulty is shortage of information and data. Once data is collected, people then feel confident in interpreting the implications. I differ on both of these attitudes. The problem is not shortage of data but rather our inability to perceive the consequences of the information we already possess. The system dynamics approach starts with the concepts and information on which people are already acting. Generally these are sufficient. The available perceptions are then assembled in a computer model which can show the consequences of the well known and properly perceived parts of the system. Generally, the consequences are unexpected.

## Counterintuitive nature of social systems

Our first insights into complex social systems came from our corporate work. Time after time we have gone into a corporation which is having severe and well-known difficulties. The difficulties can be major and obvious such as a falling market share, low profitability, or instability of employment. Such difficulties are known throughout the company and by anyone outside who reads the management press. One can enter such a company and discuss with people in key decision points what they are doing to solve the problem. Generally speaking we find that people perceive correctly their immediate environment. They know what they are trying to accomplish. They know the crises which will force certain actions. They are sensitive to the power structure of the organization, to traditions, and to their own personal goals and welfare. In general, when circumstances are conducive to frank disclosure, people can state what they are doing and can give rational reasons for their actions. In a troubled company, people are usually trying in good conscience and to the best of their abilities to solve the major difficulties. Policies are being followed at the various points in the organization on the presumption that they will alleviate the difficulties. One can combine these policies into a computer model to show the consequences of how the policies interact with one another. In many instances it then emerges that the known policies describe a system which actually causes the troubles. In other words, the known and intended practices of the organization are fully sufficient to create the difficulty, regardless of what happens outside the company or in the marketplace. In fact, a downward spiral develops in which the presumed solution makes the difficulty worse and thereby causes redoubling of the presumed solution.

The same downward spiral frequently develops in government. Judgment and debate lead to a programme that appears to be sound. Commitment increases to the apparent solution. If the presumed solution actually makes matters worse, the process by which this happens is not evident. So, when the troubles increase, the efforts are intensified that are actually worsening the problem.

## Dynamics of urban systems

Our first major excursion outside of corporate policy began in February 1968, when John F. Collins, former mayor of Boston, became Professor of Urban Affairs at MIT. He and I discussed my work in industrial dynamics and his experience with urban difficulties. A close collaboration led to applying to the dynamics of the city the same methods that had been created for understanding the social and policy structure of the corporation. A model structure was developed to represent the fundamental urban processes. The proposed structure shows how industry, housing, and people interact with each other as a city grows and decays. The results are described in my book *Urban Dynamics*, and some were summarized in *Technology Review* (*April, 1969, pp. 21–31*).

I had not previously been involved with urban behaviour or urban policies. But the emerging story was strikingly similar to what we had seen in the corporation. Actions taken to alleviate the difficulties of a city can actually make matters worse. We examined four common programmes for improving the depressed nature of the central city. One is the creation of jobs as by bussing the unemployed to the suburbs or through governmental jobs as employer of last resort. Second was a training programme to increase the skills of the lowest-income group. Third was financial aid to the depressed city as by federal subsidy. Fourth was the construction of low-cost housing. All of these are shown to lie between neutral and detrimental almost irrespective of the criteria used for judgment. They range from ineffective to harmful judged either by their effect on the economic health of the city or by their long-range effect on the low-income population of the city.

The results both confirm and explain much of what has been happening over the last several decades in our cities.

In fact, it emerges that the fundamental cause of depressed areas in the cities comes from *excess* housing in the low-income category rather than the commonly presumed housing shortage. The legal and tax structures have combined to give incentives for keeping old buildings in place. As industrial buildings age, the employment opportunities decline. As residential buildings age, they are used by lower-income groups who are forced to use them at a higher population density. Therefore, jobs decline and population rises while buildings age. Housing, at the higher population densities, accommodates more low-income urban population than can find jobs. A social trap is created where excess low-cost housing beckons low-income people inward because of the available housing. They continue coming to the city until their numbers so far exceed the available income opportunities that the standard of living declines far enough to stop further inflow. Income to the area is then too low to maintain all of the housing. Excess housing falls into disrepair and is abandoned. One can simultaneously have extreme crowding in those buildings that are occupied, while other buildings become excess and are abandoned because the economy of the area cannot support all of the residential structures. But the excess residential buildings threaten the area in two ways – they occupy the land so that it cannot be used for job-creating buildings, and they stand ready to accept a rise in population if the area should start to improve economically.

Any change which would otherwise raise the standard of living only takes off the economic pressure momentarily and causes the population to rise enough that the standard of living again falls to the barely tolerable level. A self-regulating system is thereby at work which drives the condition of the depressed area down far enough to stop the increase in people.

At any time, a near-equilibrium exists affecting population mobility between the different areas of the country. To the extent that there is disequilibrium, it means that some area is slightly more attractive than others and population begins to move in the direction of the more attractive area. This movement continues until the rising population drives the more attractive area down in attractiveness until the area is again in equilibrium with its surroundings. Other things being equal, an increase in population of a city crowds housing, overloads job opportunities, causes congestion, increases pollution, encourages crime, and reduces almost every component of the quality of life.

This powerful dynamic force to re-establish an equilibrum in total attractiveness means that any social programme must take into account the eventual shifts that will occur in the many components of *attractiveness*. As used here, attractiveness is the composite effect of all factors that cause population movement towards or away from an area. Most areas in a country have nearly equal attractiveness most of the time, with only sufficient disequilibrium in attractiveness to account for the shifts in population. But areas can have the same composite attractiveness with different mixes in the components of attractiveness. In one area component A could be high and B low, while the reverse could be true in another area that nevertheless had the same total composite attractiveness. If a programme makes some aspect of an area more attractive than its neighbour's, and thereby makes total attractiveness higher momentarily, population of that area rises until other components of attractiveness are driven down far enough to again establish an equilibrium. This means that efforts to improve the condition of our cities will result primarily in increasing the population of the cities and causing the population of the country to concentrate in the cities. The overall condition of urban life, for any particular economic class of population, cannot be appreciably better or worse than that of the remainder of the country to and from which people may come. Programmes aimed at improving the city can succeed only if they result in eventually raising the average quality of life for the country as a whole.

## On raising the quality of life

But there is substantial doubt that our urban programmes have been contributing to the national quality of life. By concentrating total population, and especially low-income population, in urban locations, undermining the strength and cohesiveness of the community, and making government and bureaucracy so big that the individual feels powerless to influence the system within which he is increasingly constrained, the quality of life is being reduced. In fact, if they have any effect, our efforts to improve our urban areas will in the long run tend to delay the concern about rising total population and thereby contribute directly to the eventual overcrowding of the country and the world.

Any proposed programme must deal with both the quality of life and the factors affecting population. "Raising the quality of life" means releasing stress and pressures, reducing crowding, reducing pollution, alleviating hunger, and treating ill health. But these pressures are exactly the sources of concern and action aimed at controlling total population to keep it within the bounds of the fixed world within which we live. If the pressures are relaxed, so is the concern about how we impinge on the environment. Population will then rise further until the pressures reappear with an intensity that can no longer be relieved. To try to raise quality of life without intentionally creating compensating pressures to prevent a rise in population density will be self-defeating.

Consider the meaning of these interacting attractiveness components as they affect a depressed ghetto area of a city. First we must be clear on the way population density is, in fact, now being controlled. There is some set of forces determining that the density is not far higher or lower than it is. But there are many possible combinations of forces that an urban area can exert. The particular combination will determine the population mix of the area and the economic health of the city. I suggest that the depressed areas of most American cities are created by a combination of forces in which there is a job shortage and a housing excess. The availability of housing draws the lowest-income group until they so far exceed the opportunities of the area that the low standard of living, the frustration, and the crime rate counter-balance the housing availability. Until the pool of excess housing is reduced, little can be done to improve the economic condition of the city. A low-cost housing programme alone moves exactly in the wrong direction. It draws more low-income people. It makes the area differentially more attractive to the poor who need jobs and less attractive to those who create jobs. In the new population equilibrium that develops, some characteristic of the social system must compensate for the additional attractiveness created by the low-cost housing. The counterbalance is a further decline of the economic condition for the area. But as the area becomes more destitute, pressures rise for more low-cost housing. The consequence is a downward spiral that draws in the low-income population, depresses their condition, prevents escape, and reduces hope. All of this is done with the best of intentions.

My paper, "Systems Analysis as a Tool for Urban Planning" from a symposium in October 1969, at the National Academy of Engineering, suggests a reversal of present practice in order to simultaneously reduce the aging housing in our cities and allocate land to income-earning opportunities. The land shifted to industry permits the "balance of trade" of the area to be corrected by allowing labour to create and export a product to generate an income stream with which to buy the necessities of modern life from the outside. But the concurrent reduction of excess housing is absolutely essential. It supplies the land for new jobs. Equally important, the resulting housing shortage creates the population-stabilizing pressure that allows economic revival to proceed without being inundated by rising population. This can all be done without driving the present low-income residents out of the area. It can create *upward economic mobility* to convert the low-income population to a self-supporting basis.

The first reaction of many people to these ideas is to believe that they will never be accepted by elected officials or by residents of depressed urban areas. But some of our strongest support and encouragement is coming from those very groups who are closest to the problems, who see the symptoms first-hand, who have lived through the failures of the past, and who must live with the present conditions until enduring solutions are found.

Over the last several decades the country has slipped into a set of attitudes about our cities that are leading to actions that have become an integral part of the system that is generating greater troubles. If we were malicious and wanted to create urban slums, trap low-income people in ghetto areas, and increase the number of people on welfare, we could do little better than follow the present policies. The trend towards stressing income and sales taxes and away from the real estate tax encourages old buildings to remain in place and block self-renewal. The concessions in the income tax laws to encourage low-income housing will in the long run actually increase the total low-income population of the country. The highway expenditures and the government loans for suburban housing have made it easier for higher-income groups to abandon urban areas than to revive them. The pressures to expand the areas incorporated by urban government, in an effort to expand the revenue base, have been more than offset by lowered administrative efficiency, more citizen frustration, and the accelerated decline that is triggered in the annexed areas. The belief that more money will solve urban problems has taken attention away from correcting the underlying causes and has instead allowed the problems to grow to the limit of the available money, whatever that amount might be.

## Characteristics of social systems

I turn now to some characteristics of social systems that mislead people. These have been identified in our work with corporate and urban systems and in more recent work that I will describe concerning the worldwide pressures that are now enveloping our planet.

First, social systems are inherently insensitive to most policy changes that people select in an effort to alter the behaviour of the system. In fact, a social system tends to draw our attention to the very points at which an attempt to intervene will fail. Our experience, which has been developed from contact with simple systems, leads us to look close to the symptoms of trouble for a cause. When we look, we discover that the social system presents us with an apparent cause that is plausible according to what we have learned from simple systems. But this apparent cause is usually a coincident occurrence that, like the trouble symptom itself, is being produced by the feedback-loop dynamics of a larger system. For example, as already discussed, we see human suffering in the cities; we observe that it is accompanied (some think caused) by inadequate housing. We increase the housing and the population rises to compensate for the effort. More people are drawn into and trapped in the depressed social system. As another example, the symptoms of excess population are beginning to overshadow the country. These symptoms appear as urban crowding and social pressure. Rather than face the population problem squarely we try to relieve the immediate pressure by planning industry in rural areas and by discussing new towns. If additional urban area is provided it will temporarily reduce the pressures and defer the need to face the underlying population question. The consequence, as it will be seen 25 years hence, will have been to contribute to increasing the population so much that even today's quality of life will be impossible.

A second characteristic of social systems is that all of them seem to have a few sensitive influence points through which the behaviour of the system can be changed. These influence points are not in the locations where most people expect. Furthermore, if one identifies in a model of a social system a sensitive point where influence can be exerted, the chances are still that a person guided by intuition and judgment will alter the system in the wrong direction. For example in the urban system, housing is a sensitive control point but, if one wishes to revive the economy of a city and make it a better place for low-income as well as other people, it appears that the amount of low-income housing must be reduced rather than increased. Another example is the world-wide problem of rising population and the disparity between the standards of living in the developed and the underdeveloped countries, an issue arising in the world system to be discussed in the following paragraphs. But it is beginning to appear that a sensitive control point is the rate of generation of capital investment.

And how should one change the rate of capital accumulation? The common answer has been to increase industrialization, but recent examination suggests that hope lies only in reducing the rate of industrialization. This may actually help raise quality of life and contribute to stabilizing population.

As a third characteristic of social systems, there is usually a fundamental conflict between the short-term and long-term consequences of a policy change. A policy which produces improvement in the short run, within five to ten years, is usually one which degrades the system in the long run, beyond 10 years. Likewise, those policies and programmes which produce long-run improvement may initially depress the behaviour of the system. This is especially treacherous. The short run is more visible and more compelling. It speaks loudly for immediate attention. But a series of actions all aimed at short-run improvement can eventually burden a system with long-run depressants so severe that even heroic short-run measures no longer suffice. Many of the problems which we face today are the eventual result of short-run measures taken as long as two or three decades ago.

## A global perspective

I have mentioned social organizations at the corporate level and then touched on work which has been done on the dynamics of the city. Now we are beginning to examine issues of even broader scope.

In July 1970 we held a two-week international conference on world dynamics. It was a meeting organized for the Club of Rome, a private group of about 50 individuals drawn from many countries who have joined together to attempt a better understanding of social systems at the world level. Their interest lies in the same problems of population, resources, industrialization, pollution, and world-wide disparities of standard of living on which many groups now focus. But the Club of Rome is devoted to taking actions that will lead to a better understanding of world trends and to influencing world leaders and governments. The July meeting at MIT included the general theory and behaviour of complex systems and talks on the behaviour of specific social systems ranging from corporations through commodity markets to biological systems, drug addiction in the community, and growth and decline of a city. Especially prepared for this conference was a dynamic model of the interactions between world population, industrialization, depletion of natural resources, agriculture, and pollution. A detailed discussion on this world system will soon appear in my book *World Dynamics*, and its further development is the purpose of the "Project on the Predicament of Mankind" being sponsored by the Club of Rome at MIT for a year under the guidance of Professor Dennis Meadows. The plan is to develop a research group of men from many countries who will eventually base their continuing efforts in a neutral country such as Switzerland. The immediate project will re-examine, verify, alter, and extend the preliminary dynamic study of the world system and will relate it to the present world-wide concern about trends in civilization.

The simple model of world interactions as thus far developed shows several different alternative futures depending on whether population growth is eventually suppressed by shortage of natural resources, by pollution, by crowding and consequent social strife, or by insufficient food. Malthus dealt only with the latter, but it is possible for civilization to encounter other controlling pressures before a food shortage occurs.

It is certain that resource shortage, pollution, crowding, food failure, or some other equally powerful force will limit population and industrialization if persuasion and psychological factors do not. Exponential growth cannot continue forever. Our greatest immediate challenge is how we guide the transition from growth to equilibrium. There are many possible mechanisms of growth suppression. That some one or combination will occur is inevitable. Unless we come to understand and to choose, the social system by its internal processes will choose for us. The natural mechanisms for terminating exponential growth appear to be the least desirable. Unless we understand and begin to act soon, we may be overwhelmed by a social and economic system we have created but can't control.

The diagram* shows the structure that has been assumed. It interrelates the mutual effects of population, capital investment, natural resources, pollution, and the fraction of capital devoted to agriculture. These five system "levels" are shown in the rectangles. Each level is caused to change by the rates of flow in and out, such as the birth rate and death rate that increase and decrease population. As shown by the dotted lines, the five system levels, through intermediate concepts shown at the circles, control the rates of flow. As an example, the death rate at Symbol 10 depends on population P and the "normal" lifetime as stated by death rate normal DRN. But death

* All figures are taken from *World Dynamics* by Jay W. Forrester, Wright–Allen Press, 238 Main Street, Cambridge, Mass. 02142.

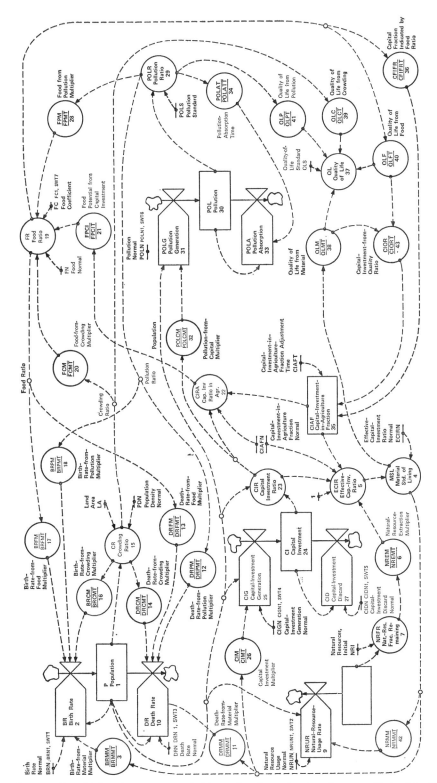

**Figure 12.1** Flow diagram of world. Levels are represented by rectangles; rates by valves; auxiliaries (significant components of rates) by circles; dotted lines indicate directions, shown by arrows.

rate depends also on conditions in other parts of the system. From Circle 12 comes the influence of pollution that here assumes death rate to double if pollution becomes 20 times as severe as in 1970; and, progressively, that death rate would increase by a factor of 10 if pollution became 60 times as much as now. Likewise from Circle 13 the effect of food per capita is to increase death rate as food becomes less available. The detailed definition of the model states how each rate of flow is assumed to depend on the levels of population, natural resources, capital investment, capital devoted to food, and pollution.

Individually the assumptions in the model are plausible, create little disagreement, and reflect common discussions and assertions about the individual responses within the world system. But each is explicit and can be subjected to scrutiny. From one viewpoint, the system of Figure 12.1 is very simplified. It focuses on a few major factors and omits most of the substructure of world social and economic activity. But from another viewpoint, Figure 12.1 is comprehensive and complex. The system is far more complete and the theory described by the accompanying computer model is much more explicit than the mental models

that are now being used as a basis for world and governmental planning. It incorporates dozens of nonlinear relationships. The world system shown here exhibits provocative and even frightening possibilities.

## Transition from growth to equilibrium

With the model specified, a computer can be used to show how the system, as described for each of its parts, would behave. Given a set of beginning conditions, the computer can calculate and plot the results that unfold through time.

The world today seems to be entering a condition in which pressures are rising simultaneously from every one of the influences that can suppress growth – depleted resources, pollution, crowding, and insufficient food. It is still unclear which will dominate if mankind continues along the present path. Figure 12.2 shows the mode of behaviour of this world system given the assumption that population reaches a peak and then declines because industrialization is suppressed by falling natural resources. The model system starts with estimates of conditions in 1900. Adjustments have been made so that the generated paths pass through the conditions of 1970.

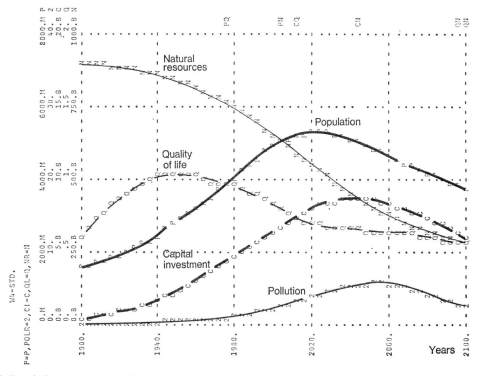

**Figure 12.2** Population reaches a peak and then declines because industrialization is suppressed by falling natural resources.

In Figure 12.2 the quality of life peaks in the 1950's and by 2020 has fallen far enough to halt further rise in population. Declining resources and the consequent fall in capital investment then exert further pressure to gradually reduce world population.

But we may not be fortunate enough to run gradually out of natural resources. Science and technology may very well find ways to use the more plentiful metals and atomic energy so that resource depletion does not intervene. If so, the way then remains open for some other pressure to arise within the system. Figure 12.3 shows what happens within this system if the resource shortage is foreseen and avoided. Here the only change from Figure 12.2 is the usage rate of natural resources after the year 1970. In Figure 12.3 resources are used after 1970 at a rate 75 per cent less than assumed in Figure 12.2. In other words, the standard of living is sustained with a lower drain on the expendable and irreplaceable resources. But the picture is even less attractive! By not running out of resources, population and capital investment are allowed to rise until a pollution crisis is created. Pollution then acts directly to reduce birth rate, increase death rate, and to depress food production.

Population which, according to this simple model, peaks at the year 2030 has fallen to one-sixth of the peak population within an interval of 20 years – a world-wide catastrophe of a magnitude never before experienced. Should it occur, one can speculate on which sectors of the world population will suffer most. It is quite possible that the more industrialized countries (which are the ones which have caused such a disaster) would be the least able to survive such a disruption to environment and food supply. They might be the ones to take the brunt of the collapse.

Figure 12.3 shows how a technological success (reducing our dependence in natural resources) can merely save us from one fate only to fall victim to something worse (a pollution catastrophe). There is now developing throughout the world a strong undercurrent of doubt about technology as the saviour of mankind. There is a basis for such doubt. Of course, the source of trouble is not technology as such but is instead the management of the entire technological–human–political–economic–natural complex.

Figure 12.3 is a dramatic example of the general process

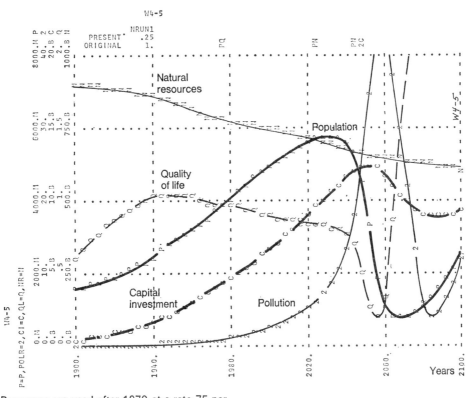

**Figure 12.3** Resources are used after 1970 at a rate 75 per cent less than assumed in Fig. 12.2.

discussed earlier wherein a programme aimed at one trouble symptom results in creating a new set of troubles in some other part of the system. Here the success in alleviating a natural resource shortage throws the system over into the mode of stopping population caused by industrialization which has been freed from natural resource restraint. This process of a solution creating a new problem has defeated many of our past governmental programmes and will continue to do so unless we devote more effort to understanding the dynamic behaviour of our social systems.

## Alternatives to decline or catastrophe

Suppose in the basic world system of Figures 12.1 and 12.2 we ask how to sustain the quality of life which is beginning to decline after 1950. One way to attempt this, and it is the way the world is now choosing, might be to increase the rate of industrialization by raising the rate of capital investment. Models of the kind we are here using make such hypothetical questions answerable

in a few minutes and at negligible cost. Figure 12.4 shows what happens if the "normal" rate of capital accumulation is increased by 20 per cent in 1970. The pollution crisis reappears. This time the cause is not the more efficient use of natural resources but the upsurge of industrialization which overtaxes the environment before resource depletion has a chance to depress industrialization. Again, an "obvious" desirable change in policy has caused troubles worse than the ones that were originally being corrected.

This is important, not only for its own message but because it demonstrates how an apparently desirable change in a social system can have unexpected and even disastrous results.

Figure 12.4 should make us cautious about rushing into programmes on the basis of short-term humanitarian impulses. The eventual result can be anti-humanitarian. Emotionally inspired efforts often fall into one of three traps set for us by the nature of social systems: The programmes are apt to address symptoms rather than

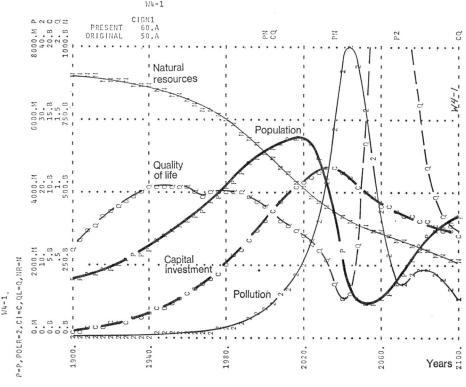

**Figure 12.4** In 1970, the rate of capital accumulation is increased by 20 per cent in an effort to reverse the beginning decline in quality of life. The pollution crisis occurs before natural resources are depleted.

causes and attempt to operate through points in the system that have little leverage for change; the characteristic of systems whereby a policy change has the opposite effect in the short run from the effect in the long run can eventually cause deepening difficulties after a sequence of short-term actions; and the effect of a programme can be along an entirely different direction than was originally expected, so that suppressing one symptom only causes trouble to burst forth at another point.

Figure 12.5 retains the 20 per cent additional capital investment rate after 1970 from Figure 12.4 but in addition explores birth reduction as a way of avoiding crisis. Here the "normal" birth rate has been cut in half in 1970. (Changes in normal rates refer to coefficients which have the specified effect if all other things remain the same. But other things in the system change and also exert their effect on the actual system rates.) The result shows interesting behaviour. Quality of life surges upward for 30 years for the reasons that are customarily asserted. Food-per-capita grows, material standard of living rises, and crowding does not become as great. But the more affluent world population continues to use natural resources and to accumulate capital plant at about the same rate as in Figure 12.4. Load on the environment is more closely related to industrialization than to population and the pollution crisis occurs at about the same point in time as in Figure 12.4.

Figure 12.5 shows that the 50 per cent reduction in "normal" birth rate in 1970 was sufficient to start a decline in total population. But the rising quality of life and the reduction of pressures act to start the population curve upward again. This is especially evident in other computer runs where the reduction in "normal" birth rate is not so drastic. Serious questions are raised by this investigation about the effectiveness of birth control as a means of controlling population. The secondary consequence of starting

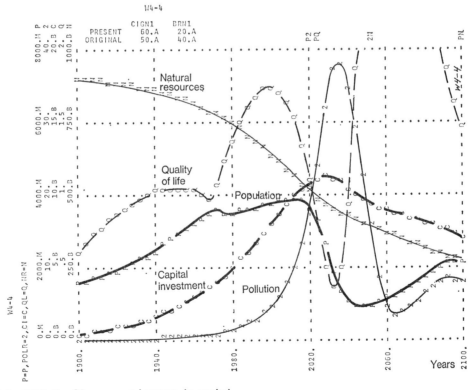

**Figure 12.5** In 1970 the 20 per cent increase in capital accumulation from Fig. 12.4 is retained, and "normal" birth rate is reduced 50 per cent. Capital investment continues to grow until the pollution crisis develops. After an initial decline, population is again pushed up by a rapid rise in quality of life that precedes the collapse.

a birth control programme will be to increase the influences that raise birth rate and reduce the apparent pressures that require population control. A birth control programme which would be effective, all other things being equal, may largely fail because other things will not remain equal. Its very incipient success can set in motion forces to defeat the programme.

Figure 12.6 combines the reduced resource usage rate and the increased capital investment rate of Figures 12.3 and 12.4. The result is to make the population collapse occur slightly sooner and more severely. Based on the modified system of Figure 12.6, Figure 12.7 then examines the result if technology finds ways to reduce the pollution generated by a given degree of industrialization. Here in Figure 12.7, the pollution rate, other things being the same, is reduced by 50 per cent from that in Figure 12.6. The result is to postpone the day of reckoning by 20 years and to allow the world population to grow 25 per cent greater before the population collapse occurs. The "solution" of reduced pollution has, in effect, caused more people to suffer the eventual consequences. Again we see the dangers

of partial solutions. Actions at one point in a system that attempt to relieve one kind of distress produce an unexpected result in some other part of the system. If the interactions are not sufficiently understood, the consequences can be as bad or worse than those that led to the initial action.

There are no utopias in our social systems. There appear to be no sustainable modes of behaviour that are free of pressures and stresses. But there are many possible modes and some are more desirable than others. Usually, the more attractive kinds of behaviour in our social systems seem to be possible only if we have a good understanding of the system dynamics and are willing to endure the self-discipline and pressures that must accompany the desirable mode. The world system of Figure 12.1 can exhibit modes that are more hopeful than the crises of Figures 12.2 through 12.7. But to develop the more promising modes will require restraint and dedication to a long-range future that man may not be capable of sustaining.

Figure 12.8 shows the world system if several policy changes are adopted together in the year 1970. Population

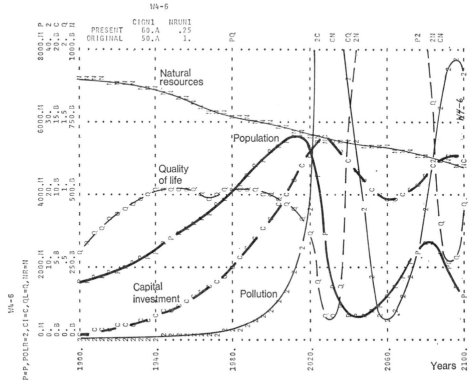

**Figure 12.6** The 20 per cent increase of capital investment from Fig. 12.4 and the 75 per cent reduction of natural resource usage from Fig. 12.3 are combined.

is stabilized. Quality of life rises about 50 per cent. Pollution remains at about the 1970 level. Would such a world be accepted? It implies an end to population and economic growth.

In Figure 12.8 the normal rate of capital accumulation is *reduced* 40 per cent from its previous value. The "normal" birth rate is reduced 50 per cent from its earlier value. The "normal" pollution generation is reduced 50 per cent from the value before 1970. The "normal" rate of food production is *reduced* 20 per cent from its previous value. (These changes in "normal" values are the changes for a specific set of system conditions. Actual system rates continue to be affected by the varying conditions of the system.) But reduction in investment rate and reduction in agricultural emphasis are counterintuitive and not likely to be discovered or accepted without extensive system studies and years of argument – perhaps more years than are available. The changes in pollution generation

and natural resource usage may be easier to understand and to achieve. The severe reduction in worldwide birth rate is the most doubtful. Even if technical and biological methods existed, the improved condition of the world might remove the incentive for sustaining the birth reduction emphasis and discipline.

## Future policy issues

The dynamics of world behaviour bear directly on the future of the United States. American urbanization and industrialization are a major part of the world scene. The United States is setting a pattern that other parts of the world are trying to follow. That pattern is not sustainable. Our foreign policy and our overseas commerical activity seem to be running contrary to overwhelming forces that are developing in the world system. The following issues are raised by the preliminary investigations to date. They must, of course, be examined more deeply and confirmed

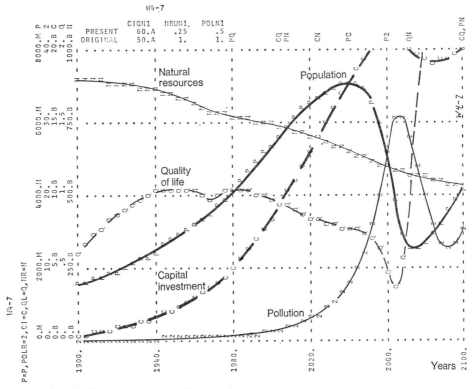

**Figure 12.7** Increased capital investment rate and reduced natural resource usage from Fig. 12.6 are retained. In addition in 1970 the "normal" rate of pollution generation is reduced 50 per cent. The effect of pollution control is to allow population to grow 25 per cent further and to delay the pollution crisis by 20 years.

by more thorough research into the assumptions about structure and detail of the world system.

Industrialization may be a more fundamentally disturbing force in world ecology than is population. In fact, the population explosion is perhaps best viewed as a result of technology and industrialization. I include medicine and public health as a part of industrialization.

Within the next century, man may be facing choices from a four-pronged dilemma – suppression of modern industrial society by a natural resource shortage, collapse of world population from changes wrought by pollution, population control by war, disease, and social stresses caused by physical and psychological crowding.

We may now be living in a "golden age" where, in spite of the world-wide feeling of malaise, the quality of life is, on the average, higher than ever before in history and higher than the future offers.

Efforts for direct population control may be inherently self-defeating. If population control begins to result as

hoped in higher per capita food supply and material standard of living, these very improvements can generate forces to trigger a resurgence of population growth.

The high standard of living of modern industrial societies seems to result from a production of food and material goods that has been able to outrun the rising population. But, as agriculture reaches a space limit, as industrialization reaches a natural-resource limit, and as both reach a pollution limit, population tends to catch up. Population then grows until the "quality of life" falls far enough to generate sufficiently large pressures to stabilize population.

There may be no realistic hope for the present underdeveloped countries reaching the standard of living demonstrated by the present industrialized nations. The pollution and natural resource load placed on the world environmental system by each person in an advanced country is probably 10 to 20 times greater than the load now generated by a person in an underdeveloped country. With four

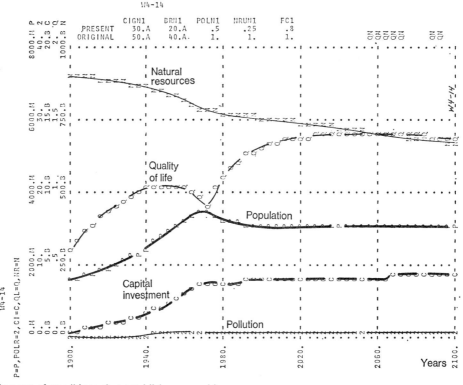

**Figure 12.8** One set of conditions that establishes a world equilibrium. In 1970 capital investment rate is reduced 40 per cent, birth rate is reduced 50 per cent, pollution generation is reduced 50 per cent, natural resource usage rate is reduced 75 per cent, and food production is reduced 20 per cent.

times as much population in underdeveloped countries as in the present developed countries, their rising to the economic level of the United States could mean an increase of 10 times in the natural resource and pollution load on the world environment. Noting the destruction already occurring on land, in the air, and especially in the oceans, no capability appears to exist for handling such a rise in standard of living for the present total population of the world.

A society with a high level of industrialization may be nonsustainable. It may be self-extinguishing if it exhausts the natural resources on which it depends. Or, if unending substitution for declining natural resources is possible, the international strife over "pollution and environmental rights" may pull the average world-wide standard of living back to the level of a century ago.

From the long view of a hundred years hence, the present efforts of underdeveloped countries to industrialize along Western patterns may be unwise. They may now be closer to the ultimate equilibrium with the environment than are the industrialized nations. The present underdeveloped countries may be in a better condition for surviving the forthcoming world-wide environmental and economic pressures than are the advanced countries. When one of the several forces materializes that is strong enough to cause a collapse in world population, the advanced countries may suffer far more than their share of the decline.

## A new frontier

It is now possible to take hypotheses about the separate parts of a social system, to combine them in a computer model, and to learn the consequences. The hypotheses may at first be no more correct than the ones we are using in our intuitive thinking. But the process of computer modelling and model testing requires these hypotheses to be stated more explicitly. The model comes out of the hazy realm of the mental model into an unambiguous model or statement to which all have access. Assumptions can then be checked against all available information and can be rapidly improved. The great uncertainty with mental models is the inability to anticipate the consequences of interactions between the parts of a system. This uncertainty is totally eliminated in computer models. Given a stated set of assumptions, the computer traces the resulting consequences without doubt or error. This is a powerful procedure for clarifying issues. It is not easy. Results will not be immediate.

We are on the threshold of a great new era in human pioneering. In the past there have been periods characterized by geographical exploration. Other periods have dealt with the formation of national governments. At other times the focus was on the creation of great literature. Most recently we have been through the pioneering frontier of science and technology. But science and technology are now a routine part of our life. Science is no longer a frontier. The process of scientific discovery is orderly and organized.

I suggest that the next frontier for human endeavour is to pioneer a better understanding of the nature of our social systems. The means are visible. The task will be no easier than the development of science and technology. For the next 30 years we can expect rapid advance in understanding the complex dynamics of our social systems. To do so will require research, the development of teaching methods and materials, and the creation of appropriate educational programmes. The research results of today will in one or two decades find their way into the secondary schools just as concepts of basic physics moved from research to general education over the past three decades.

What we do today fundamentally affects our future two or three decades hence. If we follow intuition, the trends of the past will continue into deepening difficulty. If we set up research and educational programmes, which are now possible but which have not yet been developed, we can expect a far sounder basis for action.

## The nation's real alternatives

The record to date implies that our people accept the future growth of United States population as preordained, beyond the purview and influence of legislative control, and as a ground rule which determines the nation's task as finding cities in which the future population can live. But I have been describing the circular processes of our social systems in which there is no unidirectional cause and effect but instead a ring of actions and consequences that close back on themselves. One could say, incompletely, that the population will grow and that cities, space, and food must be provided. But one can likewise say, also incompletely, that the provision of cities, space, and food will cause the population to grow. Population generates pressure for urban growth, but urban pressures help to limit population.

Population grows until stresses rise far enough, which is to say that the quality of life falls far enough, to stop further increase. Everything we do to reduce those pressures causes the population to rise farther and faster and hastens the day when expediencies will no longer suffice. The United States is in the position of a wild animal running from its pursuers. We still have some space, natural resources, and agricultural land left. We can avoid the question of rising population as long as we can flee this bountiful reservoir that nature provided. But it is obvious that the reservoirs are limited. The wild animal usually flees until he is cornered, until he has no more space. Then he turns to fight, but he no longer has room to manoeuvre. He is less able to forestall disaster than if he had fought in the open while there was still room to yield and to dodge. The United States is running away from its long-term threats by trying to relieve social pressures as they arise. But if we persist in treating only the symptoms and not the causes, the result will be to increase the magnitude of the ultimate threat and reduce our capability to respond when we no longer have space to flee.

What does this mean? Instead of automatically accepting the need for new towns and the desirability of locating industry in rural areas, we should consider confining our cities. If it were possible to prohibit the encroachment by housing and industry onto even a single additional acre of farm and forest, the resulting social pressures would hasten the day when we stabilize population. Some European countries are closer to realizing the necessity of curtailing urban growth than are we. As I understand it, farm land surrounding Copenhagen cannot be used for either residence or industry until the severest of pressures forces the government to rezone small additional parcels. When land is rezoned, the corresponding rise in land price is heavily taxed to remove the incentive for land speculation. The waiting time for an empty apartment in Copenhagen may be years. Such pressures certainly cause the Danes to face the population problem more squarely than do we.

Our greatest challenge now is how to handle the transition from growth into equilibrium. Our society has behind it a thousand years of tradition that has encouraged and rewarded growth. The folklore and the success stories praise growth and expansion. But that is not the path of the future. Many of the present stresses in our society are from the pressures that always accompany the conversion from growth into equilibrium.

In our studies of social systems, we have made a number of investigations of life cycles that start with growth and merge into equilibrium. There are always severe stresses in the transition. Pressures must rise far enough to suppress the forces that produced growth. Not only do we face the pressure that will stop the population growth; we also encounter pressures that will stop the rise of industrialization and standard of living. The social stresses will rise.

The economic forces will be ones for which we have no precedent. The psychological forces will be beyond those for which we are prepared. Our studies of urban systems demonstrated how the pressures from shortage of land and rising unemployment accompany the usual transition from urban growth to equilibrium. But the pressures we have seen in our cities are minor compared to those which the nation is approaching. The population pressures and the economic forces in a city that was reaching equilibrium have in the past been able to escape to new land areas.

But that escape is becoming less possible. Until now we have had, in effect, an inexhaustible supply of farm land and food-growing potential. But now we are reaching the critical point where, all at the same time, population is over-running productive land, agricultural land is almost fully employed for the first time, the rise in population is putting more demand on the food supplies, and urbanization is pushing agriculture out of the fertile areas into the marginal lands. For the first time demand is rising into a condition where supply will begin to fall while need increases. The crossover from plenty to shortage can occur abruptly.

The fiscal and monetary system of the country is a complex social–economic–financial system of the kind we have been discussing. It is clear the country is not agreed on behaviour of the interactions between government policy, growth, unemployment, and inflation. An article by a writer for *Finance* magazine in July 1970, suggests that the approach I have been discussing be applied in fiscal and monetary policy and their relationships to the economy. I estimate that such a task would be only a few times more difficult than was the investigation of urban growth and stagnation. The need to accomplish it becomes more urgent as the economy begins to move for the first time from a history of growth into the turbulent pressures that will accompany the transition from growth to one of the many possible kinds of equilibrium. We need to choose the kind of equilibrium before we arrive.

In a hierarchy of systems, there is usually a conflict between the goals of a subsystem and the welfare of the broader system. We see this in the urban system. The goal of the city is to expand and to raise its quality of life. But this increases population, industrialization, pollution, and demands on food supply. The broader social system of the country and the world requires that the goals of the urban areas be curtailed and that the pressures of such curtailment become high enough to keep the urban areas and population within the bounds that are satisfactory to the larger system of which the city is a part. If this nation chooses to continue to work for some of the traditional urban goals, and if it succeeds, as it may well do, the result will be to deepen the distress of the country as a whole and eventually to deepen the crisis in the cities themselves. We may be at the point where higher pressures in the present are necessary if insurmountable pressures are to be avoided in the future.

I have tried to give you a glimpse of the nature of multi-loop feedback systems, a class to which our social systems belong. I have attempted to indicate how these systems mislead us because our intuition and judgment have been formed to expect behaviour different from that actually possessed by such systems. I believe that we are still pursuing national programmes that will be at least as frustrating and futile as many of the past. But there is hope. We can now begin to understand the dynamic behaviour of our social systems. Progress will be slow. There are many cross-currents in the social sciences which will cause confusion and delay. The approach that I have been describing is very different from the emphasis on data gathering and statistical analysis that occupies much of the time of social research.

But there have been breakthroughs in several areas. If we proceed expeditiously but thoughtfully, there is a basis for optimism.

## Suggested readings

Forrester, Jay W. (1961) *Industrial Dynamics*, The MIT Press, Cambridge, Mass.

Forrester, Jay W. (1968) *Principles of Systems*, Wright-Allen Press, Cambridge, Mass.

Forrester, Jay W. (1969) *World Dynamics*, The MIT Press, Cambridge, Mass.

Forrester, Jay W. (1971) *World Dynamics*, Wright-Allen Press, Cambridge, Mass.

Meadows, Dennis L. (1970) *Dynamics of Commodity Production Cycles*, Wright-Allen Press, Cambridge, Mass.

# *Section IV*
# Introduction

Although it is true that we are creating complex systems with technology and in our organizations, we are nowhere near approaching the complexity and behavioural richness of living systems. The highly evolved higher animals, and in particular their nervous systems, are systems of a complexity well beyond anything we can at present construct. Two different systems can be identified: the internal physiological and biochemical control systems, and the system of inter-relations of animals and plants with their ecological environment.

By now, a reader will be familiar with the ideas stemming from von Bertalanffy about the special nature of open biological systems. One of the most important concepts here is that of "stability" in organisms, and we have reproduced a small portion of a classic work by Cannon on homeostasis. The two following articles each deal with one aspect of the two different systems mentioned above. The first, by Priban, discusses modelling the respiratory system, and we have chosen this because it deals with a typical physiological function which is the subject of one module in the Open University course. The second article by Dale suggests how the ideas of Systems analysis can be applied to ecology.

## Associated reading

Biological control systems have become of great interest to engineers in recent years, partly because engineering analysis can be hoped to reveal more of the functioning of important physiological systems and partly because engineers learn much from these extremely "well-engineered" systems. There are a number of fairly detailed books on control theory and systems ideas applied to biological systems. Milsum's book *Biological control systems analysis* (McGraw-Hill, 1966) is a comprehensive treatment, *The application of control theory to physiological systems* (W. B. Saunders, 1966) by H. T. Milhorn is another. Work on the respiratory system is covered by J. H. Comroe in the *Physiology of respiration* (Year Book Pub., 1965) and in his article "The Lung" in *Scientific American* (February 1966).

# 13 Self-regulation of the body

## *by Walter B. Cannon*

### I

Our bodies are made of extraordinarily unstable material. Pulses of energy, so minute that very delicate methods are required to measure them, course along our nerves. On reaching muscles they find there a substance so delicately sensitive to slight disturbance that, like an explosive touched off by a fuse, it may discharge in a powerful movement. Our sense organs are responsive to almost incredibly minute stimulations. Only recently have men been able to make apparatus which could even approach the sensitiveness of our organs of hearing. The sensory surface in the nose is affected by vanillin, 1 part by weight in 10,000,000 parts of air, and by mercaptan $1/23,000,000$ of a milligram in a liter (approximately a quart) of air. And as for sight, there is evidence that the eye is sensitive to $5/1,000,000,000,000$ erg, an amount of energy, according to Bayliss, which is $1/3,000$ that required to affect the most rapid photograph plate.

The instability of bodily structure is shown also by its quick change when conditions are altered. For example, we are all aware of the sudden stoppage of action in parts of the brain, accompanied by fainting and loss of consciousness, that occurs when there is a momentary check in the blood flow through its vessels. We know that if the blood supply to the brain wholly ceases for so short a time as seven or eight minutes certain cells which are necessary for intelligent action are so seriously damaged that they do not recover. Indeed, the high degree of instability of the matter of which we are composed explains why drowning, gas poisoning, or electric shock promptly brings on death. Examination of the body after such an accident may reveal no perceptible injury that would adequately explain the total disappearance of all the usual activities. Pathetic hope may rise that this apparently normal and natural form could be stirred to life again. But there are subtle changes in the readily mutable stuff of the human organism which prevent, in these conditions, any return of vital processes.

When we consider the extreme instability of our bodily structure, its readiness of disturbance by the slightest application of external forces and the rapid onset of its decomposition as soon as favoring circumstances are withdrawn, its persistence through many decades seems almost miraculous. The wonder increases when we realize that the system is open, engaging in free exchange with the outer world, and that the structure itself is not permanent but is being continuously broken down by the wear and tear of action, and as continuously built up again by processes of repair.

### II

The ability of living beings to maintain their own constancy has long impressed biologists. The idea that disease is cured by natural powers, by a *vis medicatrix naturae*, an idea which was held by Hippocrates (460–377 B.C.), implies the existence of agencies which are ready to operate correctively when the normal state of the organism is upset. More precise references to self-regulatory arrangements are found in the writings of modern physiologists. Thus the German physiologist, Pflüger, recognized the natural adjustments which lead toward the maintenance of a steady state of organisms when (1877) he laid down the dictum, "The cause of every need of a living being is also the cause of the satisfaction of the need." Similarly, the Belgian physiologist, Léon Fredericq, in 1885, declared, "The living being is an agency of such sort that each disturbing influence induces by itself the calling forth of compensatory activity to neutralize or repair the disturbance. The higher in the scale of living beings, the more numerous, the more perfect and the more complicated do these regulatory agencies become. They tend to free the organism completely from the unfavorable influences and changes occurring in the environment." Again, in 1900, the French physiologist, Charles Richet, emphasized the remarkable fact. "The living being is stable," he wrote. "It must be so in order not to be destroyed, dissolved or disintegrated by the colossal forces, often adverse, which surround it. By an apparent contradiction it maintains its stability only if it is excitable and capable of modifying itself according to external stimuli and adjusting its response to the stimulation. In a sense it is stable because it is modifiable – the slight instability is the necessary condition for the true stability of the organism."

Here, then, is a striking phenomenon. Organisms, composed of material which is characterized by the utmost inconstancy and unsteadiness, have somehow learned the methods of maintaining constancy and keeping steady in the presence of conditions which might reasonably be expected to prove profoundly disturbing. For a short time men may be exposed to dry heat at 115 to 128 degrees Centigrade (239 to 261 degrees Fahrenheit) without an increase of their body temperature above normal. On the other hand arctic mammals, when exposed to cold as low as 35 degrees Centigrade below freezing (31 degrees below zero Fahrenheit) do not manifest any noteworthy fall of body temperature. Furthermore, in regions where the air is extremely dry the inhabitants have little difficulty in retaining their body fluids. And in these days of high ventures in mountain climbing and in airplanes human beings may be surrounded by a greatly reduced pressure of oxygen in the air without showing serious effects of oxygen want.

Resistance to changes which might be induced by external circumstances is not the only evidence of adaptive stabilizing arrangements. There is also resistance to disturbances from within. For example, the heat produced in maximal muscular effort, continued for twenty minutes, would be so great that, if it were not promptly dissipated, it would cause some of the albuminous substances of the body to become stiff, like a hard-boiled egg. Again, continuous and extreme muscular exertion is accompanied by the production of so much lactic acid (the acid of sour milk) in the working muscles that within a short period it would neutralize all the alkali contained in the blood, if other agencies did not appear and prevent that disaster. In short, well-equipped organisms – for instance, mammalian forms – may be confronted by dangerous conditions in the outer world and by equally dangerous possibilities within the body, and yet they continue to live and carry on their functions with relatively little disturbance.

## III

The statement was made above that somehow the unstable stuff of which we are composed had learned the trick of maintaining stability. As we shall see, the use of the word "learned" is not unwarranted. The perfection of the process of holding a stable state in spite of extensive shifts of outer circumstance is not a special gift bestowed upon the highest organisms but is the consequence of a gradual evolution. In the eons of time during which animals have developed on the earth probably many ways of protecting against the forces of the environment have been tried. Organisms have had large and varied experience in testing different devices for preserving stability in the face of agencies which are

potent to upset and destroy it. As the construction of these organisms has become more and more complex and more and more sensitively poised, the need for more efficient stabilizing arrangements has become more imperative. Lower animals, which have not yet achieved the degree of control of stabilization seen in the more highly evolved forms, are limited in their activities and handicapped in the struggle for existence. Thus the frog, as a representative amphibian, has not acquired the means of preventing free evaporation of water from his body, nor has he an effective regulation of his temperature. In consequence he soon dries up if he leaves his home pool, and when cold weather comes he must sink to its muddy bottom and spend the winter in sluggish numbness. The reptiles, slightly more highly evolved, have developed protection against rapid loss of water and are therefore not confined in their movements to the neighborhood of pools and streams; indeed, they may be found as inhabitants of arid deserts. But they, like the amphibians, are "cold-blooded" animals, that is, they have approximately the temperature of their surroundings, and therefore during the winter months they must surrender their active existence. Only among the higher vertebrates, the birds and mammals, has there been acquired that freedom from the limitations imposed by cold that permits activity even though the rigors of winter may be severe.

The constant conditions which are maintained in the body might be termed *equilibria*. That word, however, has come to have fairly exact meaning as applied to relatively simple physico-chemical states, in closed systems, where known forces are balanced. The coordinated physiological processes which maintain most of the steady states in the organism are so complex and so peculiar to living beings – involving, as they may, the brain and nerves, the heart, lungs, kidneys and spleen, all working cooperatively – that I have suggested a special designation for these states, *homeostasis*. The word does not imply something set and immobile, a stagnation. It means a condition – a condition which may vary, but which is relatively constant.

It seems not impossible that the means employed by the more highly evolved animals for preserving uniform and stable their internal economy (i.e., for preserving homeostasis) may present some general principles for the establishment, regulation and control of steady states, that would be suggestive for other kinds of organization – even social and industrial – which suffer from distressing perturbations. Perhaps a comparative study would show that every complex organization must have more or less effective self-righting adjustments in order to prevent a check on its functions or a rapid disintegration of its parts when it is subjected to stress. And it may be that an examination of the self-righting methods employed in the more complex living beings may offer hints for improving and perfecting the methods which still operate inefficiently and unsatisfactorily. At present these suggestions are necessarily vague and indefinite. They are offered here in order that the reader, as he continues into the concrete and detailed account of the modes of assuring steady states in our bodies, may be aware of the possibly useful nature of the examples which they offer. . . .

Reprinted from Cannon, W. B. (1939) *The Wisdom of the Body*, W. W. Norton & Co. Inc.

# 14 Models in medicine

## by Ian Priban

Although medical diagnosis has been analysed frequently in the hope of improving the treatment of disease, doctors still often find themselves obliged to treat symptoms rather than causes of illnesses. Consider, for example, the task facing a physician who is trying to identify the cause of clinical symptoms which could result from a malfunction in one of any number of different physiological mechanisms. He may be able to make key diagnostic tests but the process of detection is generally slow, routine and possibly tedious. What the physician needs is some fault finding strategies akin to those used by the computer engineer which will enable him to test the "biological circuitry" quickly and conveniently. And this is where mathematical models representing physiological functions can help. Equipped with the relevant model, the physician could systematically examine the suspect mechanisms and select the most effective treatment for the patient.

A mathematical model of any system can be constructed only after the relevant variables and their inter-relationships have been determined. This fundamental information can then be incorporated into a model which simulates the real system – anatomical structures and all. Unfortunately building such models inevitably involves some kind of compromise; any living system has so many variables that, even with modern powerful computers, only a small part of it can be dealt with at any one time. Nevertheless, I feel that some models are becoming sufficiently sophisticated and analogous to the natural activities which they represent to help in tracking down the cause of observed symptoms and even, in some cases, to forecast failures in health.

On the other hand, many details of the physiology of even such intensely studied tissues as muscle still have to be worked out in the context of the whole body. To be successful medical models cannot be restricted to the isolated systems so familiar in traditional physiological studies; the data used to construct the model must reflect the influence of other relevant systems in the body.

In order to indicate the kind of problem inherent in providing medically valuable models, I will confine my discussion to just one topic: the control of respiration. In this way I hope to impress upon the reader the innumerable controlled reactions and restraints which together maintain a stable internal environment within the body in spite of sudden fluctuations in both internal and external conditions. I also hope to emphasize that it is not beyond scientific ingenuity to provide a model which will help to relieve the physician of routine tasks and enable his effort to be diverted to areas more rewarding both for him and for his patient.

Most mathematical descriptions of living systems are expressed in the language of the control systems engineer, since this is more amenable to quantitative manipulation than that of the biologist. The late Norbert Wiener pointed out some 20 years ago the similarities between automatically controlled systems and living ones. In fact, control engineers have investigated and modelled certain aspects of human activity for some time – particularly during and since World War 2. Now biologists also are beginning to appreciate what Wiener was saying and as a result they are starting to draw more freely on the experience, methods and theories of the control engineer in their analysis of living systems.

One of the most important concepts in control theory is that of feedback, which is familiar to most people through the control of heating systems by a thermostat. The thermostat compares the ambient temperature with a preset value and an error signal based on the difference is fed back to the heater. The objective of this feedback is to keep the temperature steady at a predetermined level even in the face of large changes in the surroundings. When applied to biological mechanisms, such as the control of body temperature and the level of blood glucose, this concept greatly enhanced the physiologist's understanding; but, paradoxically, by enabling him to look at the control of living systems in more detail, it soon exposed a major problem. How could he explain the close simultaneous control of many variables even when some of the parameters of the system were being subjected to large changes?

Use of the theory of self-adaptive, multilevel control

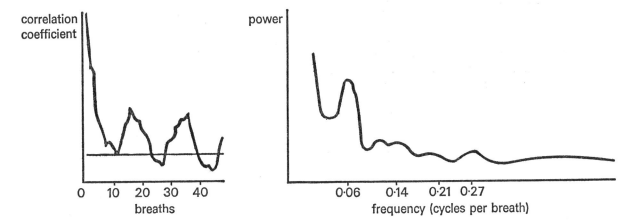

**Figure 14.1** Statistical techniques reveal the relationships between different breaths in the respiratory pattern. The graph (left) reveals a direct relationship between the amplitude of any breath and those removed in time by 16 breaths or multiples of this. The prominences seen in the power density spectrum (right) based on two closely related variables, the amplitude and duration of breaths, indicate that four control loops each with a different time delay are concerned with the mutual adjustment of these two variables

systems and of predictive control can go a long way to finding a solution. A classical example of adaptive control – also called self-optimizing control – is the minimizing of the fuel consumption of aircraft piston engines by controlling ignition timing and the composition of the fuel/air mixture. In this adaptive system the "performance index" in kilometres per litre is measured continually, compared with the ideal index, and the error signal used to adjust the mixture and timing to achieve the optimum value. The important feature with adaptive control is that the operating state is determined by the existing physical or physical–chemical characteristics of the process, which may be changing, rather than by the properties of the controller. The best possible performance is achieved by continually evaluating the operation of the system with a test signal which is used to measure the deviation from the optimum. The result of the evaluation is a control signal which adjusts the inputs to the process to attain the optimum performance.

To represent living systems in terms of adaptive control requires that these systems have some unique optimum value and a physiological equivalent of the test signal. Considerable evidence exists for the former in many biological processes. In fact, many so-called "normal" values are the optimum ones in terms of the energy expenditure for the particular processes concerned. The evidence for the existence of test signals, however, is accumulating only slowly; this is due mainly to their being extremely small and difficult to measure.

To build up a model it is necessary also to know how to dissect living systems in a mathematical sense. The respiratory system is suited to such treatment because it is relatively accessible for investigation and making measurements causes little interference to subjects. One of the aims of the work in our laboratory is to show how parts of the respiratory system interact and are co-ordinated. Many of the mechanisms are being investigated individually in detail in laboratories through the world and provide much of the information needed for an operational model.

Breathing is rhythmical but each breath is different from the previous one and the next. The pattern varies continuously even when a person is in a steady state – as, for example, during sleep. Applying "random process" analysis to the breathing pattern, breaking this down into definite amplitude and time or frequency components, yields information about the system generating the pattern which can then be related to anatomical structures.

To do this the true signals must be separated from the random variations which have no explicit mathematical relationship and therefore, on average, cancel one another out. The results of the analysis indicate whether mathematical relationships exist between an event at one time and an event or events at other times. For instance, a recording of a sequence of several hundred to a thousand breaths can be fed into a computer to obtain a series of values of amplitude – the tidal volume. If each value is simply multiplied by itself the average of the products gives a single value. If the original sequence is copied and the copy is moved along by one breath, by multiplying the two, now out of phase, series and again averaging the products another single value is given. This process is then repeated many times to give a series of average values. The illustration Fig. 14.1, shows the final result. There is a direct relationship between any breath and those removed in time by 16 breaths and multiples of this. More simply, this means that the tidal volume of a particular breath is determined partly by what happened 16 breaths earlier.

The "power density spectrum" is a related method for extracting signals and highlighting relationships – in this case in terms of frequency components. The relationship illustrated is between the amplitude of a breath and its duration – two closely related variables. These results were selected from a large number of records. Usually a sequence of breaths shows fewer prominences at any one time, but these features are found when results from different sequences are combined. They indicate that breathing is controlled by signals fed back through at least four control loops with different time delays.

Before relating these results to anatomical structures it is necessary to decide exactly what process is being controlled. In normal man the mean values of the respiratory variables in the arterial blood – the $pH$ and the partial pressures of carbon dioxide and oxygen – are nearly constant. It seems that the rate of exchange of both oxygen and carbon dioxide between the environment and the body is controlled, and that the controls ensure that respiration keeps pace exactly with metabolism. The important constituent in this exchange process is blood. Its chemical state depends upon the relative exchange flow rates of carbon dioxide and oxygen from the blood; carbon dioxide moves into the blood and oxygen out as it passes the body tissues and *vice versa* as the blood passes through the lungs.

The respiratory function of blood depends largely on the red pigment, haemoglobin. Its most important property, pointed to by Professor F. J. W. Roughton in Cambridge, is that it can carry the maximum number of molecules of carbon dioxide in exchange for molecules of oxygen and *vice versa* at the partial pressure and $pH$ values normally found in arterial blood. These are the values at which the blood accomplishes its respiratory function with the minimum expenditure of energy with respect to the circulation, the ventilation of the lungs and with respect to its own metabolism. Since the purpose of feedback systems is to maintain the stability of a process in face of major disturbances, the gas exchange is obviously being controlled by keeping the blood as nearly as possible in its optimal state. Why have more than one feedback loop to control this

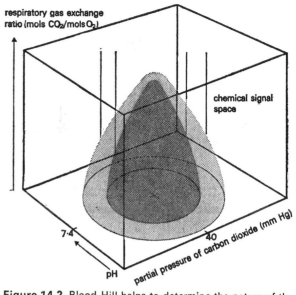

**Figure 14.2** Blood Hill helps to determine the nature of the chemical signal which is passed on to the sensors responsible for continually monitoring the blood. The chemical signal is determined by the slope and shape of the hill. Obviously at its peak all the factors combine to give the optimum conditions but as the slope is descended changes in one variable necessitate substantial changes in the others to maintain the respiratory function of the blood. The inner hill shows the effect of reducing the partial pressure of oxygen from about 90 millimetres of mercury to about 50. Clearly such a reduction leads to a considerable increase in the chemical signal and hence a greater change in the pattern of respiration.

process? A simple answer is that the faster a control cycle is, the more rapid the response to small disturbances and the more efficient is the use of available energy. Such a rapid response is important in any condition involving more than resting muscular effort. In rest and sleep the slower loops alone can maintain an adequate respiratory gas exchange. Many of the structures which are part of the fastest control loop are also part of the slower loops – such as the circulatory system. The main differences between the loops are their transport times, which depend on the structures that modify and delay the signals before they arrive at the parts of the brain controlling breathing.

The fastest control loop is a most interesting one. To keep the functional state of blood at the optimum values three processes have to be controlled simultaneously, so that three sub-loops are involved. One of these almost exactly matches the level of pulmonary ventilation to the body's oxygen and carbon dioxide exchange requirements;

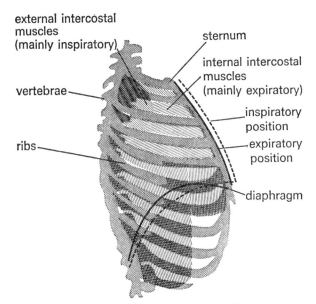

external intercostal
muscles
(mainly inspiratory)

sternum

internal intercostal
muscles
(mainly expiratory)

vertebrae

inspiratory
position

ribs

expiratory
position

diaphragm

**Figure 14.3** Control of the chest muscles which determine the change in volume of the chest and hence the potential gaseous exchange is fundamental to any respiratory system. In fact these respiratory muscles are subject to the finest control which is continually updated by feedback from receptors within the muscles. This feedback also provides additional information for the control of the overall pattern of respiration.

the second ensures that the respiratory muscles accomplish this ventilation with a minimum of energy expenditure, and the third makes sure that the energy used in ventilating the dead space – the conducting part of the lung airways – is kept at a minimum.

A signal which plays a part in evaluating the effectiveness of the gas exchange is caused by the rhythmical nature of breathing. The two way gas exchange associated with each breath causes the state of the blood to fluctuate about a mean value. Recently, W. S. Yamamoto at the University of Pennsylvania suggested that this fluctuation might be a signal controlling breathing. This is highly likely because, when blood is in the optimal state, the gas exchange can be accomplished with the smallest fluctuations or variations of state. By adjusting the level of ventilation in the direction that will minimize the magnitude of these variations, which would appear to be the error signals, the controller ensures that the level of ventilatory gas exchange will tend to keep pace exactly with that required by metabolism. The objective of this control system is very similar to that of a control engineer regulating an electrical power supply network so that generators are brought into action to meet the demands of the consumer.

In order that the ventilatory gas exchange can occur efficiently the activity of numerous respiratory muscle units has to be finely controlled and co-ordinated. In exercise these may have to pump air in and out of the lungs at more than ten times the resting rate. In addition, many of these muscles also have other important functions associated, for example, with posture, movement and speech.

One of the oldest observations about the efficiency of the energy cost of breathing was made by F. Rohrer in 1925. He showed that the natural frequency of breathing is that at which the average power requirement for ventilation is at a minimum. For breaths of shorter duration and small tidal volumes, on the one hand, high input power is required to produce the relatively large changes in velocity of muscle shortening; on the other hand, for larger tidal volumes more sustained muscle action is required and the power needed to distend the chest wall rises steeply as the tidal volume increases.

An examination of the structure and physical properties of the chest respiratory apparatus, which is made up of many different muscles and bones as shown above, provides the important clue to how the control objective – the minimization of the muscular energy cost – can be accomplished. Professor A. V. Hill and his colleagues at University College, London, have established that the efficiency of energy conversion by a muscle depends on its average length and its load or rate of shortening. At any time, therefore, depending on an individual's posture and movement, some muscle units must be able to bring about ventilation of the lungs more efficiently than others. The objective of the control must be to select these units. And to visualize how this is accomplished I have represented the structural arrangement of the muscles by a two dimensional grid, each sector of which contains muscle units with particular performance characteristics (see illustrations). The obvious goal of the controller is to match the "contours" of the muscle activity with contours of the highest value of the performance index (defined as the maximum number of units of ventilation obtained per unit energy expenditure in the muscles).

The following explanation of the mechanisms of control is new and partly hypothetical. It is also part of the operational model which itself provides the basis for new experiments aimed at validating or rejecting the model. The control is seen as being accompanied by a sequence of control actions involving a hierarchial system with three levels. The organization of the respiratory system may be compared with that of a large industrial organization – a

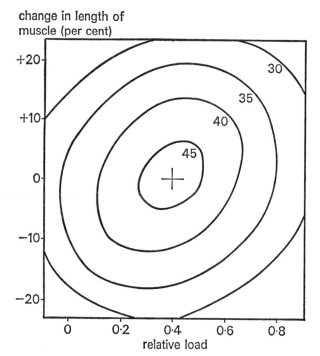

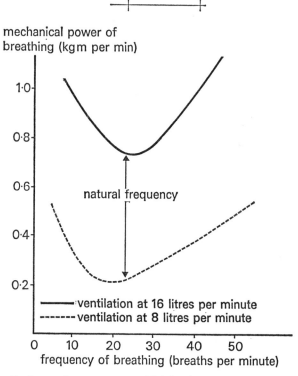

**Figure 14.4** Performance contours (above) express the working efficiency of the respiratory muscles – the contour values give the percentage efficiency. The objective of the control system is to call into action those muscles which will bring about the required ventilation of the lungs with the least expenditure of muscular effort. Since the chest muscles are also concerned with posture and other functions, different levels of ventilation and different postures generally involve different contours. The fundamental goal of the body's control system is to keep the balance of energy used by it to the lowest possible level.

The natural frequency (right) of breathing is found to require the least mechanical power. For the same ventilation of the lungs any increase or decrease in the rate of breathing increases the power required for respiration and therefore the amount of work. For example, short rapid breaths demand extra power for the rapid rate of change in the muscle length whereas in slower, deeper breaths the power needed to distend the chest wall rises steeply.

kind of microeconomy. Here information is evaluated, decisions are made in the planning and predicting process and the management takes steps to ensure that the factory, the suppliers and the sales department all fulfil their jobs as predicted.

In the respiratory system a high level overall controller in the brain predicts the total amount of energy to be expended in a breath and the time over which it is to be dissipated in order to keep ventilation in step with metabolism. The prediction is conditioned by the responses of the system during previous breaths and, because living systems are evolutionary systems, also by its own past history as well as that of its ancestors. An intermediate level controller in the brain, also containing memory of past activity, takes the orders from the higher level and produces a more detailed temporal distribution of the pattern of activity. Finally, a lower level controller in the spinal cord takes the orders from the intermediate level and acts by selecting in detail the appropriate respiratory muscle units. Such selection can be accomplished only by a continual evaluation of muscle performance relative to the input signal as determined by the receptors or "spindles" in the muscles. The output from these muscle spindles also feeds back to the highest level of control. If the muscles shorten and effect ventilation as predicted, no correction is required of the higher control activity. But if the load on the muscles has changed the predicted activity will differ from the actual activity. This difference, the error signal, is fed back to the brain via the relay stations and enables a new prediction to be made.

How can experimental evidence be obtained to reject or confirm and make a more quantitative assessment of the model? The whole process of formulating a model exposes many gaps in existing knowledge, some of which are filled by current experimental work on animals, while others can be better filled by devising new experiments. One new experiment developed by my colleague, Dr Bill Fincham, employs an interrogation technique. His objective was to obtain information about the neural policy and decision processes concerned with predicting the optimal breath. In the experiment a subject was connected to recording instruments. He breathed in the usual way; then, in response to a visual or aural signal lasting about one second, he would hold his breath until the signal stopped. By analysing the "hold" response and the subsequent breathing pattern Fincham concluded that the neural respiratory activity of the brain is modified after the "hold" signal in such a way as to compensate for the lost respiratory time. To represent these features the model has to include a storage device – the equivalent of memory – and sampled data elements which prevent the breath design from being radically modified. This means that while the brain and spinal cord are controlling the activity of muscles in one breath, the brain is also computing the best design for the next breath, using both the information stored from previous breaths and that being fed back from the periphery associated with the present one. Breathing is therefore a discontinuous process – a sequence of phasic events.

The efficiency of ventilation also depends on the control of the airway dimensions. It is well established that the airway diameter is actively controlled by means of so-called "smooth" muscles in its walls. If the nerves which normally convey the information to and from the airways are blocked using a local anaesthetic, or are cut, a pattern of breathing is produced which shows that the energy consumption for flushing the airway is increased for the same average level of ventilation in the minute sac-like air spaces – the alveoli – in the lungs.

The overall efficiency of the respiratory system as a whole is undoubtedly due to the well co-ordinated control of the different individual mechanisms. For example, the airway dimensions determine the resistance to air flow and the rate of filling of the alveolar space in which the gas exchanges occur, and both of these are governed also by the rate of shortening of the respiratory muscles. The overall mechanism can be visualized by drawing a grid of any respiratory sub-system and representing on this the operational characteristics in the form of a performance index of the parts of the system, as was done previously for the respiratory muscles. Evidence from different laboratories is now accumulating, which shows that the performances of many living systems, when presented in this form, have the shape of a hill – they have unique optima. The overall objective of the main controller is to regulate the different processes in such a way that the hills representing different sub-systems coincide. In other words, the performance of each sub-system is regulated so that the system as a whole will attain the optimum level of performance.

Consider a control sequence when the operating point of blood has moved away from the optimum. This move may result from a change in ventilation, metabolism or efficiency of the airway control mechanism. The chemo-sensor, by comparing the chemical state of the blood in the last few breaths with that in earlier breaths, obtains a measure of both the direction and the distance of the operating point from the optimum value. This comparison enables the decision to be made whether or not to change the level of ventilation and hence the energy used in respiration. To resolve ventilation into tidal volume and breath duration, the main controller uses the previous prediction stored in the form of memory, the pattern of activity controlling the present breath and the error signals fed back from the muscular and airway sub-systems. These error signals contain the information about the mismatch in performance with respect to the best predicted input to the process in the sub-system. The information content of these signals is reduced at the low and intermediate level controllers, so that only the information concerning the accuracy of the prediction or change in state in the periphery is fed back to the main controller. Part of the information is stored in the lower levels and is then used in the next breath to increase the detail of the neural signal controlling the muscle activity.

I have not used the term "reflex" because this is usually associated with non-anticipatory systems. Instead predictive control has been introduced which is more suited for explaining simply and accurately the behaviour of the neural mechanisms and of naturally operating systems such as those which are part of the respiratory control system.

The fastest control cycle occupies, on average, 3·8 breaths. Most of this time is taken up by the signal, the state of blood being transported in the circulation from the lungs to the chemo-sensitive region in the brain. The transmission and evaluation of the signals in the nervous system is fast and takes relatively little time. The fastest control loop involves three simultaneous sub-processes, resulting in the high efficiency needed by an active working organism.

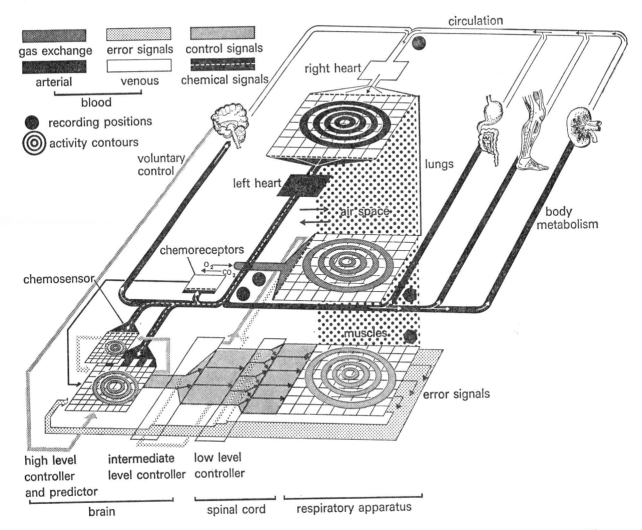

**Figure 14.5** Control of respiration, mapped out schematically here, is carried out at three levels with an over-riding "executive" level in the brain itself. The entire system is geared to maintaining the most efficient exchange of respiratory gases and the different levels of control are required both for sensitivity of control and to avoid any violent fluctuations which might occur locally in the system. The different levels also show a gradation in control with the fine control residing in the lowest level which sends signals to the respiratory muscles. Since respiration is a dynamic process, conventional graphic methods cannnot really explain the relationships between the various subsystems such as the pulmonary circulation and the respiratory muscles but data can be recorded and processed to give maps showing "activity contours". Briefly, the diagram shows how the performance of the lungs is assessed by comparing the chemical state of the blood in the arteries with the predicted performance of the respiratory system. The difference between predicted and actual performance gives rise to an error signal which is used by the predictor in controlling the next breath. This coarse control receives additional information from an error signal arising in the respiratory muscles which ultimately determines the potential gaseous exchange within the lungs. As this error signal feeds back it adjusts the control at successive levels continuously modifying the respiratory pattern.

During inactivity or sleep high efficiency is no longer necessary and then the slower loops can adequately control the respiratory gas exchange – but it is still necessary to protect the organism from large disturbances. Important structures concerned with this are the so-called chemo-receptors which are stimulated by more abrupt and large changes in the chemical state of the blood. The still slower cycles probably result from the direct effect of the chemical state of the blood on that of the brain.

Obviously the value of a model lies in how accurately it can be used to predict naturally occurring events. In turn this depends on how realistically the model represents the conditions found in real life. Life is governed by innumerable variables, but to make modelling manageable their number and level of accuracy must be restricted. We have done this by defining the area of interest in terms of the structural elements, their properties and by the generally observable behaviour, and then arranging these features systematically using block diagrams. A block represents a process (for instance, the illustration of the blood characteristic) and the lines connecting these variables correspond to flow of material, energy or information. Thus the whole system is mapped out using, in our case, nearly 50 blocks, the characteristic of some being represented by the appropriate graph or equation, while the empty blocks call for experiments to be done. So far only different aspects of the system are being simulated, using analogue or digital computers depending on which is appropriate to the problem.

The body is complex and because of the innumerable adaptive feedback systems it is difficult to separate cause from effect. But the very fact that the systematic nature of its dynamic organization has been recognized and is being examined quantitatively means that in the foreseeable future we will be using mathematical terms to define an individual's health. Already some patients have been found who apparently lack the fastest and most efficient control loop. Moreover, prominences associated with the control loops can usually be found more easily in the spectra of certain types of patient than in those of normal subjects. The implications are that in these patients the impaired structures tend to exert a more marked effect on breathing. In normal subjects the functioning of the component structures is well matched and controlled so that no one structure or mechanism significantly influences breathing on its own. These tests are therefore of use in assessing the health of individuals.

A particular application of models is in the field of intensive care. With a model it becomes possible to assess automatically certain aspects of a patient's health or even to predict that a patient is moving towards a critical state. For example, some patients suffer from a severe asthmatic condition in which the attacks can be fatal and may occur with little or no warning at any time. Provided we have both adequate means for measuring the patient's respiration and the relevant computer model, we can predict the likelihood of occurrence of an attack. This will permit the medical staff to take precautions at the most appropriate time leaving them free at other times. With the use of a computer and the appropriate model it should be possible to evaluate automatically the state of any one patient in a group. This use of computers will help the medical staff to solve the priority problem by permitting them to give their attention to the patients requiring it most.

Only a few patients are at present benefiting from this type of work because the necessary instruments and computers, along with know-how on their use, are not yet available even in large modern hospitals and medical institutions. So far, the rapid advances in control technology have not been exploited in the study of living systems except in the few institutes specializing in these aspects of technology such as Imperial College of Science and Technology and the Autonomics Division of the National Physical Laboratory in the United Kingdom, MIT and Caltech in the United States and the Institute of Automatics and Telemechanics in Moscow. For biological systems research to be successful the close association between physicians, engineers, scientists, mathematicians and programmers is essential. In my own case this involves association with physicians in a number of London hospitals, both for obtaining new experimental data and in ensuring that the results of the work can be of benefit to patients, and also with my colleagues at the laboratory.

As more centres of automation spring up and more biologists and physicians begin to use the language of the control systems engineer, so the effects and benefits of this type of work must spread more widely. The extent and speed with which this occurs, especially in the clinical application, depends particularly on how readily the medical profession becomes more technologically orientated.

## Bibliography

Meethan, A. R. and Hudson, R. A. (eds.) (1968) *Encyclopaedia of Linguistics, Information and Control*, Pergamon Press, Oxford.

Comroe, J. H. (1965) *Physiology of Respiration*, Year Book Med. Pub. Inc.

Milhorn, H. T. (1966) *The Application of Control Theory to Physiological Systems*, W. B. Sanders, London.

Hammond, P. H. (1967) "Living Control Systems", in *Electronics and Power I.E.E.*, **13**, pp. 338–42.

Priban, I. P. and Fincham, W. F. (1965) "Self-adaptive Control and the Respiratory System", in *Nature*, **208**, pp. 339–43.

Yamamoto, W. S. and Raub, W. F. (1967) "Models of the Regulation of External Respiration in Mammals", in *Computers and Biomedical Research*, **1**, pp. 65–104.

Reprinted from Priban, I. (1968) "Models in medicine", *Science Journal*, June, 1968.

# 15 Systems analysis and ecology

## *by M. B. Dale*

*Systems analysis is defined as the use of scientific method with conscious regard for the complexity of the object of study. It has strong relationships with problem solving, in that the same four phases – lexical, parsing, modelling, and analysis – are identifiable in both. Examination of each of these phases reveals some of the problems involved in the use of systems methods in ecology. A model of the precipitation–evaporation system is presented as an example Problems in experimenting with models of systems and with control, optimization, and comparison of such models are considered.*

## Introduction

Systems analysis has been presented as a desirable framework on which the investigation and comparison of ecosystems can be hung. This approach has been especially emphasized by the productivity subgroups of the International Biological Program (IBP). Claims of the importance of systems analysis are not restricted to ecology, for in other fields the results of employing these methods have been claimed to give additional insight and clarity (see e.g. Halmos and Vaughan 1950, Bush and Mosteller 1955, Glanzer and Glaser 1959, Orcutt 1960, Harary and Lipstein 1962, Keeney, Koenig and Zemach 1967). Examples of explicit use of systems methods in ecology are few (Olson 1963, Patten 1965, Holling 1966, Watt 1968), and it is by no means clear from these examples what systems analysis is, what it does, what restrictions it imposes, nor how the variety of ecology (or more precisely ecological methodology) can be attached to this framework. This paper attempts to clarify some of the questions an ecologist must answer and the problems he must resolve before using systems methods, and to introduce some of these methods in the context of a general systems approach. It does not provide the mathematical, statistical, and other details of the use of the methods, although it is hoped that sufficient references are included to enable the interested ecologist to obtain this information. Necessary definitions are provided and the general nature of systems considered. The relationship between systems analysis and problem solving is established, and the ecosystem is examined in the framework of the problem-solving processes. An example of a systems model is presented and the problems of investigating and manipulating systems and of organizing ecosystem descriptions are considered.

## Systems analysis, systems, and ecosystems

### *Systems analysis*

Systems analysis has rarely been defined when introduced into ecological studies. Watt (1968) suggests that it is the determination of those variables which are important in a system, and further adds that systems simulation, systems optimization, and systems measurement are other facets of the systems approach. Others, such as Priban (1968),[*] view model building as the essence of the systems approach. Morton (1964) has suggested that systems analysis is no more nor less than scientific method itself, and that the distinguishing feature of the systems approach is the conscious application of scientific method to complex organizations in order that no important factor be overlooked, a view expressed by Pascal as "error comes from exclusion". These viewpoints are not necessarily mutually exclusive. Systems analysis is the application of scientific method to complex problems, and this application is further distinguished by the use of advanced mathematical and statistical techniques and by the use of computers. The computers are used as "number-crunching" calculating machines and as convenient tools for modelling systems too complex for analytic solutions to be presently possible. This modelling function is of great importance in studies of complex natural systems, for, provided the model can be treated as representing the real system for the purposes of the investigation, experiments can be performed on the model with a consequent gain in control and rapidity of response. A good model will obviously contain the important variables, so Watt's comments are pertinent. Equally, if natural systems are complex than the modelling phase of the systems analysis will be emphasized and Priban's emphasis accepted. Morton's more general view, since it includes both the others, seems the most acceptable since it does not presuppose some a priori emphasis on certain parts of the analysis.

### *Systems*

A system is a collection of interacting entities, or alternatively it is a collection of parts, together with statements

[*] [Ed.] Article 14 in this collection of readings.

on the relationships, of some kind, between these parts. The interpretation to be given to the entities is the choice of the investigator, but the entities need not, and in general are not, in one-to-one correspondence with "real" things. They can represent classes of things, or classes of processes if this seems necessary. The state of the system at some point in space and time is described by the values of properties of the entities, and all properties used to so describe the system are termed endogenous. Variables which affect the interrelationships between entities, but which are not included in the state description, are called exogenous and form the environment in which the system acts. If endogenous properties are interchanged with other systems outside the defined one, then the system is said to be "open" for these properties. If there is no import or export, the system is closed. Representations of systems can take a variety of forms. Perhaps the commonest is as a network (Ford and Fulkerson 1962, Harary, Norman, and Cartwright 1965) or as a matrix derived from such a network. An alternative mathematical representation is given by Rosen (1958), and an ecological example is the structural description diagrams of Dansereau, Buell, and Dagon (1966). Such general descriptions permit discussions about systems, but a computer program modelling a system is equally a representation of that particular system.

Any system is composed of subsystems defined for subsets of the entities. Each of these subsystems can be treated as a system in its own right, so that the definition of a system is recursive.* An open system, that is, one open for at least one property, can be considered as a subsystem of some "higher" order system (Cooper 1969), and since each subsystem can be decomposed into sub-subsystems, a hierarchy of systems is produced. A familiar example of such a hierarchy is . . . –organism–organ–tissue–cell–organelle– . . . Obviously some means is required to prevent infinite regress, and in practical work this termination depends on the fidelity of the model of the system to the "real" system. This fidelity requirement will be discussed later.

Finally, it is necessary to define an ecosystem. An ecosystem is a system open for at least one property, in which at least one of the entities is classed as living. This definition

* A simple example of recursive definition is the factorial of an integer number written $n!$. This can be calculated as follows:

$$n! = n \times (n-1) \times (n-2) \times (n-3)$$
$$\times \ldots \times 3 \times 2 \times 1$$

Equally the value can be calculated from the following rule.

$$n! = if \, n = 1 \, then \, 1 \, else \, n \times (n-1)!$$

is very broad, but restrictions imposed by ecologists to limit this definition for particular studies have not received much consideration. It must be remembered that an ecosystem is a special case of the general system and will possess all properties of the general system. Thus there is no restriction on the number of properties which may be used to describe the system, although many ecologists have so restricted themselves, with the consequent introduction of difficulties with an excessively large number of exogenous variables. There is certainly no restriction to studies of productivity or energy transfer, although many applications of systems analysis in ecology have been on these problems. Population models are systems models and so is the physiognomic description of vegetation. However, since the preponderance of systems studies in ecology have been studies of productivity, it will be convenient to phrase examples in these terms.

## Systems and problem solving

The recursive hierarchical nature of systems is closely paralleled in some theories of human problem solving (e.g., Simon and Newall 1962, Feigenbaum and Feldman 1963). Here an attempt is made to decompose insoluble problems into sub-problems. Any subproblems remaining insoluble are further decomposed, until hopefully all subproblems and their derivatives are soluble, when an attempt is made to reintegrate the solutions into a single solution of the original problem. The parallel between problem solving and systems can be drawn more closely, however. Ross (1967) distinguishes four phases in problem solving: (i) lexical, (ii) parsing, (iii) modelling, and (iv) analysis (see also Morton 1964). In systems analysis these same four phases can also be identified: (i) delimination of the entities or parts; (ii) the choice of relationships between entities which are of interest; (iii) the specification of the mechanism by which these interrelationships take place; and (iv) validation of the model of the system so produced and investigation of its properties.

Ross points out that the rules under which these phases are carried out must be agreed upon a priori, which is not a simple task. An obvious example of changing rules is given by the diversity of human language, which has an additional complication due to the possible existence of several scripts for one spoken language. Some of the phytosociological arguments on vegetation description appear to be arguments regarding rules of procedure, although the situation is complicated here because it is not clear that each system is intended to contain the same information. Ecologists must therefore agree on the rules to be used, otherwise comparison of systems will not be possible. Much of the difficulty lies in the choice of entities, and this will be discussed later.

The four phases of problem solving and systems analysis are used in the following sections as a framework in which to discuss problems in systems analysis.

## The lexical phase

One of the most neglected problems in systems studies is the choice of the entities or parts which compose the system. It is commonly assumed that these are self-evident; yet the arguments which have taken place in areas such as the classification of organisms or vegetation concerning sampling, description, and measures of similarity suggest that this is not true. In taxonomy a hierarchy similar to the systems hierarchy is apparent – family, genus, species, etc., and taxonomists have agreed that while studies at any level are possible, the species level is in some way more important. It is by no means clear that the species level is a consistent level: the occurrence of "difficult" genera such as *Hieracium*, *Rubus*, or *Quercus*, and the varied degree of subtlety in characters used to describe and distinguish species in different families such as the Umbelliferae and the Magnoliaceae, attests some inconsistency. Yet the taxonomist has a distinct advantage over the ecologist in that there exists a generating system (Williams 1967), the genetic system, which constrains the possible variation, so that the lexical phase in taxonomy rests on the interpretation of genetic event patterns; that much of the genetic information available is not at the species level but within it is a practical problem though an unfortunate one. The ecologist has no such system presently available, and in the opinion of some ecologists there is no such system.

The choice of entities for the ecosystem is in part determined by the parsing phase, that is, by the nature of the relationships with which the system is concerned. The commonest choices have been between taxonomic, structural, and functional entities. Taxonomic is a convenient adjective to describe entities based on individual organisms, populations, and the commoner taxonomic categories of species, genera, and so on. Structural entities are based on life-form criteria, trees, shrubs, herbs, and bryoids providing a simple botanical example. Life-form criteria are in general more responsive to local environmental fluctuations than taxonomic criteria, since these latter employ characters selected to be invariant within taxa, wherever possible. Functional entities have perhaps received more attention in animal ecology, e.g., herbivore,

carnivore, omnivore, although a variety of similar units exists in plant ecology, though less precisely defined, e.g., xerophyte, halophyte, and saprophyte. The definition of entities is not of course concerned with the ease of identification of these parts, although it may well be essential to provide common means of identifying the entities if different systems are to be compared. Of more consequence is the possibility of conversion from one set of entities to another. If one description employs structural categories and another taxonomic categories, how can the two be compared? *Liriodendron tulipifera* is a taxon which could certainly fall into the categories of shrub or tree, and on some definitions the seedlings would be classed as herbs. Even restriction to species as entities fails to resolve the problem, for this ignores all ecotypic and ontogenetic variation and the inconsistencies in the species level noted above.

It may be true that some ecosystems can only be compared at gross levels such as autotroph and heterotroph, for example marine and terrestrial systems. Yet because the United Kingdom has some 1,700 species of vascular plants, 900 bryoids, and various numbers of lichens and fungi, whereas Oak Ridge, Tennessee, has some 2,000 species of vascular plants alone, does not imply that comparisons of the two areas are only possible at some very gross level, even though the species complements are widely different. To demand that comparisons be possible with both very similar and very different ecosystems places severe restrictions on the possible choices of entities which can be employed to describe the systems. It may also be possible to describe systems in terms of a few simple ratios, such as the efficiencies which have been proposed, but this could equally reflect the well-known half-truth that biologists, when given two numbers, divide one by the other.

Functional entities do not resolve the problems of choice any more than structural or taxonomic entities. Omnivores, for example, are both herbivorous and carnivorous, while insectivorous plants are both autotrophic and heterotrophic. Nonliving materials within the ecosystem are less well served with possibilities, while still having problems of ontogeny and chemical equilibrium, such as that between the various forms of nitrogen in the soil. Perhaps a distinction between solid, liquid, and gaseous phases is possible, but is this all?

Since the first phase of a systems analysis is the choice of entities, it is very necessary that an ecologist give considered thought to these problems. In a study of a single system, the problems may well be less acute than when comparison of systems is necessary. But the choice of entities is the ecologists' task and must not be given to the systems analysts by default.

## The parsing phase

The second phase is concerned with the definition of the relationships between the selected entities. These relationships can be of any kind and need not be restricted to materials. If has been common practice in ecology to assume that the relationships are those relating to material which the system can reorder or reallocate among its parts. The relationships can, however, be spatial or temporal and need not concern materials at all. Such relationships are important in physiognomic description of vegetation. In view of the present great interest in productivity, however, attention will be concentrated on ecosystems models produced by such studies, and the properties relevant to them. These properties include energy, biomass, carbon, mineral nutrients, populations, individuals, water, and possibly information (in the form of genetic material). It does not include diversity in the sense in which this has been commonly used in ecology (Margalef 1947), which is a measure of the distribution of some property or properties over the entities, or some subset of them, in a single state description. Changes in diversity can provide useful indices of changes in this distribution caused by exogenous variables.

There is no restriction in the definition of the ecosystem given earlier on the use of several properties to describe the state of the system. The description can be multivariate. The importance of interaction between properties in such a multivariate system can be seen in work on mineral nutrient interactions and their effects on yield (Figure 15.1). Such interactions are not of course limited to these particular variables. The difficulties of modelling and experimenting with multivariate systems do impose practical constraints on the investigator (Jacoby and Harrison 1962). The problem can be reduced to a univariate one by treating other properties as exogenous, although this increases the experimentation required. In comparing two systems which have been made univariate, it is essential to ensure that differences between systems do not become confounded with differences in treatment of the relocated exogenous variables.

In the context of the International Biological Program the property most favored has been energy fixed as carbon, usually as total biomass. This implies a preference against edible, palatable, or otherwise desirable biomass such as protein, which preference may not always be desirable. Thus wool growth in sheep may well be related to amounts of sulfur-containing protein rather than total biomass

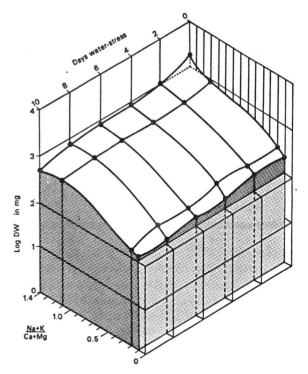

**Figure 15.1** Dry weight response of *Atriplex inflata* after 8 weeks in relation to days of withholding water and the ratio (Na + K)/(Ca + Mg).

consumed. This is not to deny the importance of energy transfer as measured by total biomass, but merely to indicate that it alone will be but a partial representation of the "real" system and may not always be the most desirable. Other choices have been made including mineral nutrients, water, radioactive contaminants, and, with growing emphasis in the United States, pollutants in general. In all these cases, however, the possibility that a multivariate system might be more useful than the univariate one must be accepted and consideration given to the requirements of such a system model.

## Modelling

*Fidelity.* Having fixed the entities and the properties, the next phase is the specification of the mechanisms by which changes in the system, that is in the distribution of the properties across the entities, take place. In choosing these processes, an attempt is made to make the model of the system "mimic" the real system, either to increase understanding of the system or to attain control of the system over some range of states. This difference in possible objective is characterized by differing degrees of fidelity.

High fidelity implies that the model resembles the real system for a wide range of states and changes in state and as a corollary, that this similitude is obtained by designing the model to follow presumed or known processes of the real system. The range of property values, for a given range of values of exogenous variables and for some entities, are called the outputs of the system, these being the particular values of interest. Knowledge of the sensitivity of the system to changes in some processes would be used to gain greater understanding of the mechanism of action of the system, and hence higher fidelity.

However, high fidelity is not always required. Provided that the model mimics the real system over some restricted range, that is, that the model outputs and the real system outputs are highly correlated, then the processes used in the model need not reflect the real system at all. As an example, in the description of spatial distributions of plants, several mathematical expressions may fit the data equally well, for example, Thomas' double poisson and the negative binomial distribution (Archibald 1948, Greig-Smith 1964). The mathematical expressions may well imply different models of the underlying real system, which may in fact agree with neither model, yet the results may be adequate. The simplest and most common ecosystem model is

### Input–Ecosystem–Output

where the system itself is treated as a closed "black" box. This has been widely used in ecology (Van Dyne, Wright, and Dollar 1968), since it is the basis of univariate multiple regression. The attainment of high fidelity is expensive in time and in the effort required to obtain the precise and accurate data on which to build and validate the model. An analogy with sound reproduction is reasonably drawn. Telephone voice communication neither requires nor uses equipment necessary for the high-quality reproduction of music.* The complexity of model required to attain high fidelity must be matched by the quality of the data. To continue the sound-reproduction analogy, a scratched recording is still scratched on the best equipment. The collection of adequate and relevant data in studies of ecosystems will often be difficult if not impossible. For example, in studies of the interaction of radiant energy and a plant canopy, account must be taken of the spatial distribution of the stems and leaves. The collection of precise and detailed information on this feature is extremely difficult.

* In statistics the problem of fidelity appears in the use of one distribution to provide an approximation to another. One example is the use of the normal distribution to approximate others such as the binomial, poisson, or Mann-Whitney U (see Siegel 1956).

The processes to be defined must obviously depend on the choice of properties and entities. Changes in state of plant entities, for example, will require processes defining fixation of energy, carbon, nitrogen, and water, and other processes defining the reallocation of these properties among the entities. Some of the processes operate in sequence, the results of one forming an input to the next. They may also of course operate in parallel, that is, over the same time interval. This parallelism can be troublesome in some methods of investigating systems, such as simulation on digital computers which are essentially serial in operation. Special processing techniques (including special languages such as the SIMULA extension to ALGOL (Dahl and Nygaard 1966)) may be required.

The processes only change endogenous variables although they may employ both previous values of endogenous variables and exogenous variables in the calculation. It must also be realized that high fidelity in the definition of the processes does not guarantee high correlation between model and real outputs. The choice of exogenous variables also constrains the fidelity of the model. For example, consider two models of photosynthesis, one using mean day length to predict amount of carbon dioxide fixed, the other being more sophisticated and employing temperature, carbon dioxide, humidity, and radiation fluxes, together with data on spatial distribution of leaves to estimate the same value. The second might be expected to be of higher fidelity, yet by introducing appropriate stochastic variation into the first model it might be possible to make it of higher fidelity. This prediction requires less data, but the selection of the appropriate stochastic inputs would be troublesome. This emphasizes the importance of considering data-collection techniques when choosing the form of the processes (Watanabe and Abraham 1960). More than this, however, it reinforces the comment made earlier that the definition of the system in the ecologists' problem and is the result of interaction between available, or potentially available, information and the purposes for which the model is required. The modelling process may suggest areas where data-collection techniques might be improved so that a more faithful model becomes possible. One indication can be gleaned from economic models. The choice of interesting and practical models appears to be those models with 30–300 variables, with the experienced worker reducing the number (Forrester, *personal communication*).

*Practical considerations.* – Watt (1968) has presented a variety of approaches to the problem of defining processes; these by no means exhaust the possibilities. A very simple model of an ecosystem can be constructed consisting of four

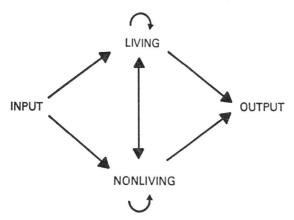

**Figure 15.2** The primitive model.

| | INPUT | LIVING | NONLIVING | OUTPUT |
|---|---|---|---|---|
| INPUT | 0 | $a_{IL}$ | $a_{IP}$ | 0 |
| LIVING | 0 | $a_{LL}$ | $a_{LP}$ | $a_{LO}$ |
| NONLIVING | 0 | $a_{PL}$ | $a_{PP}$ | $a_{PO}$ |
| OUTPUT | 0 | 0 | 0 | 0 |

**Figure 15.3** Transition matrix for the primitive model.

entities each of which represents a class and the properties and processes remain unspecified (Figure 15.2). The same system can be presented in the form of a transition matrix, where each $a_{jk}$ represents the probability of transfer of a property between the $j$th and $k$th entity (Figure 15.3). Similar matrices could be constructed for all properties, so that the entries can be interpreted as arrays of coefficients. To each of these there must be attached a corresponding process giving the next value of the $a_{jk}$ in terms of the present and previous values of the whole matrix and any additional exogenous variables. The nature of these functions is, of course, of great interest to ecologists. The model does not include some features of human information transfer where questions of the value, reliability, and credibility of information are involved. It would include demographic or population models which form the bulk of ecological work on systems (see Kerner 1957, 1959, Whittle 1962, Bellman, Kagiwada, and Kalaba 1966, Garfinkel 1967a, b, Watt 1968, and others). Demographic models conveniently illustrate the duality between continuous and discrete models of systems. Many population models employ systems of differential equations which provide a continuous model of the system, including fractional values for the population total. But the population in most cases is discrete, being an integer number of individuals. Of the references given above only Whittle employs a discrete model (a discrete branching Markov process), probably because of the extra effort involved in the mathematics if restriction to integer solutions is imposed.

While demographic models can certainly be included in the ecosystem concept, it is also common to restrict the definition of ecosystem to models of the movement of materials or energy (e.g., Golley 1960, Olson 1963, Witherspoon, Auerbach, and Olson 1964, Patten 1965). If this restriction is accepted, then a slightly more complex model, as shown in Figure 15.4, hopefully would improve in fidelity over the primitive model of Figure 15.2. Autotroph in this model includes both energy and chemical fixation. Minor variants of this model in Figure 15.5 show its generality.

While the network representations of Figures 15.2, 15.4 and 15.5 are convenient visual models, mathematically the transition matrices corresponding to them are more easily handled. The meaning of such matrices can be considered geometrically. Consider a system with two entities and a single property. This can be represented as a point on a graph for any state. If the system changes due to change of an exogenous variable, then the point representing the system is displaced. A series of changes would trace a line, and the transition matrix contains the information describing this line. Of course in most models the graph is not in two dimensions, but the properties of the transition matrix still hold (see Keeney *et al.* 1967 for an extended description of this "state space" model).

The state of the system is a static description and the dynamics of changes in state are incorporated into the model by the processes. While some systems may only show changes in response to changes in exogenous variables, in many systems and certainly in ecosystems the changes in state are partly determined by the previous states of the system, that is, by its history, by means of "feedback" or "memory". This is of course also included in the processes by making these employ previous values of the endogenous variables in the calculations. If these processes themselves employ parameters which change with time, the system is evolutionary, whereas if the parameters do not change with time, the process is stationary. The difficulties introduced by considering evolutionary processes are such that the majority of models employ station-

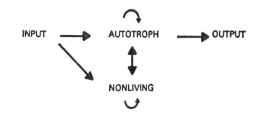

**a. Perfect Autotroph Crop**

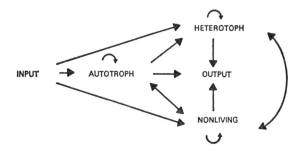

**Figure 15.4** Developments of the model for non-demographic systems.

ary processes, although it is fairly clear that real ecosystems are strictly evolutionary. There is little work on the mathematics of evolutionary processes, and most of this is recent and at a somewhat advanced mathematical level. It would certainly be possible to permit evolutionary processes in simulation models, but this would involve a large increase in time and effort in an already time-consuming method, since the initial state of the system must be specified very carefully for evolutionary processes. For many practical purposes over moderate time intervals the assumption of stationarity may be justified, although, as with multivariate models, the possibility of increasing fidelity by employing evolutionary models must be considered.

## *Analysis*

The final stage of the systems approach is the analysis proper. This involves the solution of the model, in some sense, and the validation of the model outputs by comparing them to the real system outputs. In a few simple cases the model may be solved analytically using standard mathematical techniques. Models employing linear differential equations, for example, may be soluble, and in this case the sensitivity of the model to small changes in parameter values can also be calculated (Wilkins 1966). In general, however, no analytic solution will be available, and recourse must be made to the somewhat time-consuming simulation approach.

The likelihood that high fidelity will be desired suggests that stochastic models, incorporating random processes, will be preferable to deterministic models. This is due to the more realistic incorporation of variability in stochastic models and to the availability of estimates of the expected variability of the outputs. As an example of the greater realism of stochastic models, consider the spread of an infection through a population. Deterministic models sug-

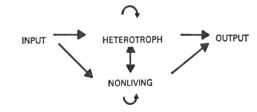

**b. Cavernicolous or Hypogean System**

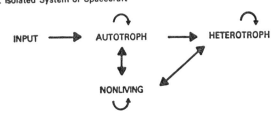

**c. Isolated System or Spacecraft**

**Figure 15.5** Examples of restricted systems.

gest the existence of a critical population size at which there is a change from "no epidemic" to "epidemic" and the epidemic is of a fixed size. Stochastic models not only permit the epidemic to be variable in size, but also provide that, whatever the population size, there is an estimable chance of an epidemic occurring, and conversely of its not occurring (Bartlett 1960).

Simulation methods have been widely used both with analogue and with digital computers (Clymer and Graber 1964, International Business Machines Corporation 1966). Most of the ecological applications have used constant time increments, calculating the state of the model periodically. Less commonly event-orientated models have been attempted (Holling 1966). These essentially calculate the time interval between changes in state, so that periods when no change in state occurs require a constant computational effort independent of the length of the interval. Event orientation emphasizes the importance of recurrence intervals, which are ecologically important in determining survival times, where the event of "successful reproduction" and the event of "death" mark the intervals. Recurrence intervals are also important in migration and have been found useful in sampling vegetation (Williams, *personal communication*). Even if there are strongly periodic phenomena such as diurnal or annual cycles, an attempt to define events may force the modeller to consider his system in greater detail.

After a model of the system has been established and some means of investigating its responses has been provided, the crucial problem of the validation of the model remains. Validation may involve the functional form of the processes and the parameters supplied as constants to these processes, but primarily the interest lies in how well the model outputs mimic those of the real system, that is, in the fidelity of the model over the range of interest. If high fidelity is required there will usually be a process of successive approximation, with the model being progressively altered until the desired fidelity is obtained. This requires, of course, some measure of fidelity to assess the disparity between model and reality. Since the processes usually involve subsystems of the model, validating the processes is essentially also a process of measuring the fidelity of a system, in that the outputs of the subsystems to the complete system should presumably also be of high fidelity.

The difficulty of validating outputs depends on the features which it is desired to mimic. If only mean values must be estimated, the disparity can be measured by a test akin to Students' $t$, and various techniques are available to increase the precision of the comparison, mostly developed in Monte-Carlo studies (Hammersley and Morton 1956). These include such methods as Russian roulette, antithetic variables, and regression. If, however, the variance of the outputs or features of the transient response of outputs to particular changes in exogenous variables is required, the problem is more complex. The outputs form a correlated series of observations, and the comparison and investigation of such series present considerable statistical problems (see Quenouille 1957, Robinson 1967, Jenkins and Watt 1968). Rarely do ecological models specify which features of the output are to be reproduced by the model. Watt (1961) has provided examples of functions which produce outputs of given forms, and the use of least-squares surface fitting can also aid in the selection of possible functions to provide specific output forms. Perhaps the most general techniques are those of Wiener (1949), though these require a large amount of data.

Validation of the parameters of the processes involves searching the response surface of the model to obtain "best" estimates. A variety of techniques might be of use here, including those due to Hooke and Jeeves (1961), Spang (1962), and Marquardt (1963). The general problem of estimation in simulation studies has received most attention in engineering and management studies (e.g., Burdick and Naylor 1966, Fishman 1967, Fishman and Kiviat 1967), but it must be remembered that even if the model is validated, extrapolation beyond the limits of such validation is the responsibility of the ecologist. It would be foolish to say that such extrapolation is never justified, but the justification is not mathematical or statistical.

## An autotroph system

A diagrammatic representation of a precipitation–evapotranspiration (PET) system is used as an example of the models employed in systems analysis (Figure 15.6). This is not the only model of this system since both Crawford and Linsley (1966) and Hufschmidt and Fiering (1966) incorporate simple expressions in their larger models to represent the whole of the PET system. Equally, more detailed models might be built up from the equations describing the transfer of heat and water vapor between leaf and atmosphere, and corresponding detailed study of the distribution of stem and leaves. The fidelity of the model will depend on the specifications of the processes by which the transfers of the property, here water, between entities is to be made. Such specifications have been provided and the resulting model converted to a computer program. The diagram shows only the connections between entities which were considered in the modelling.

Two subsystems are easily identified, one modelling the entry of water into the soil, the other modelling its return to the atmosphere. These interact at two points, since changes in the amount of leaves (and their distribution) will affect interception, and changes in the amount of roots will affect water extraction from the soil by the plant. Conversely, both leaf and root growth will be dependent on water availability.

Three other systems are explicitly included. The photosynthetic system requires inputs from the leaves and will feedback to both leaves and roots. This feedback is accomplished by the growth system which is responsible for the partition of photosynthate between the parts of the plant. The atmospheric system provides the source of water and the radiation which finally controls the loss of water. A fourth system could easily be added to introduce the effects of topography on input and output of water as runoff to or from other areas, and possibly erosion effects of such runoff. All the systems here operate in parallel in that they all operate simultaneously.

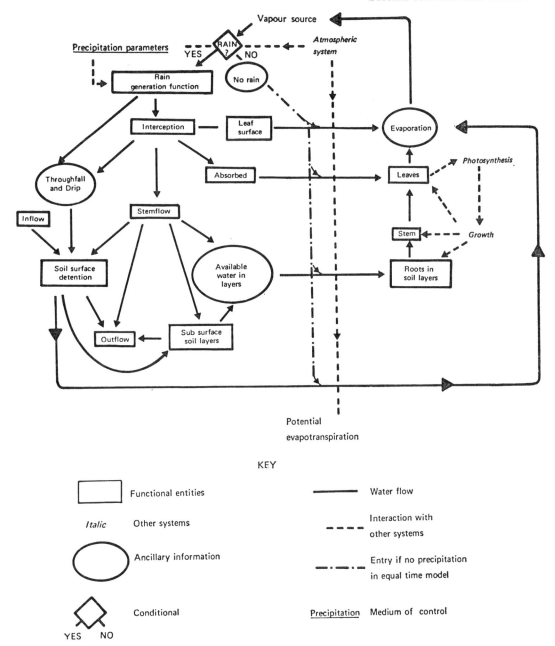

**Figure 15.6** The PET system.

An equal time model of this system would review the description of the entities, which in this case would be the water contents and size of plant parts, at periodic intervals recalculating when necessary. During these periods the state is assumed to be constant, but the interval can be arbitrarily small at the expense of more computation. Given the periodicity of instrumental recording this might be acceptable, but the existence of continuous recorders permits the event-orientated model to be investigated.

In the event-orientated model time is variable, but during the interval between events the processes are assumed to proceed in a determinate manner. The events here would mostly be effects on the rates of water movement and on the growth rates. The systems and subsystems need not operate synchronously, each having its own event timing. Thus the photosynthetic system would show no events during darkness, and the growth system might show seasonal and ontogenetic effects. Dahl and Nygaard (1966) present a simple event model of an epidemic which illustrates the computer-programming techniques required. The event technique operates as if it followed small packages of water through the system and in this way transforms the parallel operation of the systems to a sequential operation. The choice between the two models, event or periodic time, will finally depend on the information available and the user's preferences. The PET system has in fact been programmed in both periodic and event-time forms (Cooper, *personal communication*), with the latter proving computationally more efficient.

With either approach to modelling the models may be deterministic or stochastic. The stochastic model effectively replaces certain constants in the deterministic model with random variables drawn from appropriate statistical distributions. This drawing need not in fact be strictly random since by careful manipulation of the technique of drawing, the precisions of comparisons between the performance of the model under varying conditions may be increased. The technique is related to stratified sampling. While the appropriate distributions to use are relatively specific to individual problems and, indeed, form one of the most difficult parts of model building, for very rare events it may be possible to make use of the fact that extreme values have only three possible distributions (Gumbel 1958). This might appear a marginal advantage as there remains some choice to be made. However, this particular problem is usually solved by an automatic choice of the exponential distribution probably because of its ease of computation, and without regard for the alternatives. The systems analyst may indeed accept the simple exponential distribution, but he should be aware of the alternatives.

One of the interesting possibilities of controlling the "random" numbers depends on the nonexistence of such numbers. Random numbers are, in fact, pseudorandom in that they pass some of the tests of randomness which are possible, but not all. The infinite number of such tests makes it impossible to know if any set of numbers is random. Provided that the numbers are random for the tests employed, nonrandomness can be incorporated to reduce the effects of unimportant sources of variation. Tocher (1963) considers the possibilities in some detail.

## Experimentation control and optimization

The techniques and considerations of the previous sections will hopefully lead to a valid model of the ecosystem. We will now consider means of using such a model of a single system as a guide to the management of the real system. This will involve experimenting with the real and model systems, identifying the parameters of the system which will enable it to be controlled, choosing a value function by which the performance of the system is to be measured, selecting the route to some desired state, and maintaining the system at or near this desired point. The advantages of using the model system lie in the ease and rapidity with which experiments may be carried out, and the possibility of including experiments which might be totally destructive in the real system. The disadvantages lie in the restricted range of confirmed validity of the model and in its fidelity even within this range to the real system which it is desired to control.

Designing experiments for model systems will necessarily involve use of the techniques developed in statistics for efficient experimenting, though often in an unusual form. The output of the experiments forms a response surface, and special experimental designs have been developed for studying there (Box and Draper 1959, Cochran 1963, Draper and Lawrence 1965). Since the response is a correlated sequence of values, the "growth curve" techniques of Rao (1965) and Potthof and Roy (1964) may be of assistance (see also Whittle 1963, Phattaford 1965, Spent 1967). The response may of course be multivariate, and correspondingly so must the methods of analysis (see, e.g., Seal 1964), and may equally involve relaxation of assumptions of normality thus necessitating the use of non-parametric methods (Box and Watson 1962, Mood and Graybill 1963, Tiku 1964). Because the experiments are carried out on the model, efficiency and precision may be improved by restrictions imposed on the model which could not be imposed on the real system. One technique would be restrictions on the choice of "random" numbers as mentioned in the previous section, such as repeating the same sequence of "random" numbers both in the control and the experimental model solutions. A computer aid design may also be used in some cases (Kennard and Stone 1969).

The experiments lead towards control of the system, enabling a manager to manipulate the system towards some point and to maintain the system in the neighborhood of this point. Almost always there will be constraints on the actions available to the manager, such as avoiding certain states, restrictions on materials, and so on. General mathematical control principles are known (e.g., Pontryagin's continuous maximization principle, for which see Fan 1966), but these have proved difficult to apply in practice. Control implies the existence of a desired state and some means of assessing the importance and hence the size of any deviation from this state. Related to this is the need to measure the effects of any control operation. These subjects have been studied in detail in operations research (Bellman 1961, Muhzam 1963, Box and Tiao 1965). Maintenance of the system near the desired point means the control of variations in the outputs of the system. For example, management of a watershed to have flow proportional to demand would be ideal for hydroelectric power generation, where overproduction is worth little and underproduction is extremely costly. The quest for high fidelity models seems to result from the detailed control necessary, coupled with an assumption that the control of endogenous variables will be more selective, more efficient, and less expensive than control of exogenous variables. The truth of this assumption is debatable since the cost of obtaining the required detail in the model must also be considered. Both endogenous and exogenous variables can be manipulated in many systems.

Efficient control will usually imply the selection of important variables for which several techniques have been developed. Sensitivity analysis (Radanovic 1966, Wilkins 1966) is widely used to study the effects of small perturbations where the effects can be assumed to be nearly linear. Other approaches for isolating important variables exist, such as stepwise multiple regression, canonical correlation analysis (Kendall 1957), multiple predictive analysis, and two-parameter numerical taxonomy (Macnaughton-Smith 1965) or factor analysis (Lawley 1940, Harman 1966). Box and Jenkins (1962) have considered some statistical aspects of control.

The development of optimal control policies is one portion of the overall control process. The goal is provided by a "supersystem", and in this case the individual optimality of subsystems does not ensure the optimality of the system as a whole. An ecosystem might be evaluated in turn (in an appropriately organized society) by an administrative system, a political system, and a social system which employs a judicial system to enforce its control measures (Price 1965, Bulkley and McLaughlan 1966). The goals of all these evaluating systems must be defined and may often be conflicting. For the ecologist it is an evaluating function which is required rather than the goal itself, and this function may constrain the operation of the model and the operations of the managers. The existence of such an evaluating function is crucial, but two further problems are also apparent.

The first of these concerns the existence of "local" optima, which makes the search for the overall optimum more complex. Methods such as linear programming and

its extensions to integer, quadratic, stochastic, and dynamic programming (Bellman 1957, Churchman, Ackoff, and Arnoff 1961, Wolfe, 1962, Dantzig 1963, Watt 1963) have proved useful initial guides even if the system models do not always precisely fit the mathematical specifications (see Serck-Hanssen 1963, Watt 1963, Petrini 1964, Heady and Egbert 1964). Other workers have used statistical decision theory in efforts to determine optimal policies for action (e.g., Dillon and Heady 1960, Findler 1966).

The second problem is that of moving from the present state to the optimal one. Here the techniques of network analysis as planning aids are useful, including critical path analysis, resource allocation scheduling, program evaluation, and review techniques and transportation methods (Hein 1967, Hasse 1960, Davis 1965, Martino 1965, Davis 1968). Since the majority of these methods require computer assistance with the calculation and the systems model itself will often be in the form of a computer program, it is interesting to speculate on what additional information is required to enable the computer to design its own experiments, and after analysis to report both the optimal point and the method of reaching it. Certainly cost functions, value functions, and constraints are required, but whether this is sufficient information is not known. As yet the evaluation of ecosystems is at a fairly gross level, and the ecologist is educating himself and others in the extent and degree of complexity inherent in ecosystem management, while avoiding the grosser catastrophes.

## Comparison and organization of ecosystems

Some of the problems of comparing ecosystems will be considered briefly. Such comparisons are desirable partly because of the spatial and temporal variation between systems, and partly because as a "pure" science ecology will include the study of patterns in ecosystems.

While it would be possible to extend the description of a system to include those with which it interacts, this will often be impracticable. The pattern of ecosystems with respect to environmental factor, and the processes of successional change are both areas where the comparison of ecosystems is desirable. Such comparisons have for the most part been made by comparing the diversity of the systems as measured by a single property. In vegetation studies this has commonly meant comparison of species lists. The emphasis placed on functional entities by Lindeman (1942) and the increasing use of indicator species has not replaced the taxonomic comparisons, and the success of floristic methods such as those of Heikurainen (1964) suggests that there is strong relationship between functional and taxonomic classes. For some purposes it may be necessary to reconsider presently unfashionable entities, such as the synusiae of Lipmaa (1939).

The process of comparison and the organization of the resulting information to exhibit the patterns of ecosystem structuring is itself a systems process. Clowes (1967), in discussing similar problems in the computer processing of pictures, again distinguishes the four phases: the definition of parts, the provision of a grammar of parts (parsing phase), the representation of this part in relationship to structure in the machine (modelling), and the final analysis of the picture representation (analysis phase). A formal process of comparing ecosystems will itself involve these four phases, although the last analytic phase will be some numerical organization method such as classification, ordination, or spectral analysis (Robinson 1967, Jenkins and Watt 1968). The ecological difficulties all lie in the selection of the entities or parts and the selection of the relationships between the parts which are of interest in the particular study. Simple examples of relationships important in some areas of ecology are the concept of "epiphyte", which involves the relationship "growing on", and the concept of stratification of vegetation involving the spatial relationships "above" and "below". Selection of the appropriate relationships from the many available is a major ecological problem.

While the processing of the ecosystem description is possible, this is not the place to discuss the means available to represent ecosystems and the techniques necessary to compare the complex structures. The majority of the problems so far encountered in this area have been solved, in the sense that something can be done, although the ecological implications of the available solutions is not always clear.

## Conclusion

The questions to be asked of this brief account of systems analysis fall into three categories. First, what additional knowledge must the ecologist acquire before he can use systems methods? Second, what ecological questions must be answered before he can apply the methods? Third, what can he hope to gain by using such methods? These will be considered in order.

It is apparent that systems analysis includes a wide variety of mathematical and statistical techniques and borders many areas, including computation, picture processing, language processing, and problem solving. The ecologist need not be fluent in all these areas, but some means of communicating between them seems desirable. The methods used in systems analysis are rarely phrased in ecological language, and the ecologist will certainly have to phrase his questions in non-ecological terms if the developers of the methods are to assist him.

The ecological questions rest on the need for this translation, for the ecologist defines the problems in which he is interested and must interpret them to the assisting workers. For systems he must specify the parts and the relationships and be prepared to modify these definitions in the light of data-collection problems and the fidelity requirement. If he is attempting to control or modify an ecosystem in the light of his models, he must have the desired objective stated, some means of evaluating departures from this state, and some idea of the external constraints imposed on the system and its managers. As an example where the objective function has been variously interpreted, consider the problem of controlling fire in forests. Australian foresters are at present recommending frequent controlled burning as a means of reducing fire hazards. Such a solution has one disadvantage, i.e., the frequency of burning increases due to the selection of rapidly recovering and fire-tolerant species. It also ignores the problems raised by loss of nutrients due to burning and the effects of such losses on the productivity of the trees, since the environment is already nutrient poor. As a solution to the problem of reducing fire risks immediately, controlled burning is probably acceptable, but this is in fact only part of the system.

The gains to be expected from a systems approach come from the precise statement of the problems and the discipline imposed by an ordered approach to the complexities of the real system. It is unlikely that an optimal solution to any problem will be attained directly, a process of successive approximation being likely. That the discipline is helpful can be seen from experience with one technique of management, the program evaluation and review technique (PERT, see Davis 1968). This technique has been credited with saving large sums of money, yet on closer inspection the method consists of little more than an explicit statement of what goes on and in what order! It should also be clear, however, that systems analysis is not a panacea, and its use will involve the ecologist in extending his knowledge, biological and other, before gaining much reward. Hopefully the use of systems methods will prevent ecologists from joining those "who saw the effect but not the cause".*

## Acknowledgments

It is a great pleasure to acknowledge the advice and aid of Professor C. F. Cooper under whose auspices I worked at

* St Augustine Contra Pelagium IV 60.

the University of Michigan as a participant in a research project sponsored by Cooperative Research, U.S. Department of Agriculture. It is also a pleasure to record my thanks to Dr. J. Olson of Oak Ridge National Laboratory and other members of the discussion group on systems analysis. My thanks to Professor Cooper again for permission to use the PET model and to Dr. D. J. Anderson of the Australian National University for the response surface diagram.

## Bibliography

Archibald, E. E. A. (1948) "Plant populations I. A new application Neyman's contagious distribution", *Ann. Bot.* (London) N.S. **12**, 221–35.

Bartlett, M. S. (1960) *Stochastic population models in ecology and epidemiology*, Methuen, London.

Bellman, R. (1957) *Dynamic programming*, Princeton Univ. Press, Princeton, N.J.

— (1961) *Adaptive control processes: a guided tour*, Princeton Univ. Press, Princeton, N.J.

Bellman, R., Kagiwada, H. and Kalaba, R. (1966) "Inverse problems in biology", *J. Theor. Biol.* **11**, 164–67.

Box, G. E. P., and Draper, N. R. (1959) "A basis for the selection of a response surface design", *J. Amer. Statist. Ass.* **54**, 622–54.

Box, G. E. P. and Jenkins, G. M. (1962) "Some statistical aspects of adaptive optimisation and control", *J. Roy. Statist. Soc.*, *Ser. B*, **24**, 297–343.

Box, G. E. P., and Tiao, G. C. (1965) "A change in level of a nonstationary time series", *Biometrika* **52**, pp. 181–92.

Box, G. E. P., and Watson, G. S. (1968) "Robustness to non-normality of regression tests", *Biometrika* **49**, 93–106.

Bulkley, J. W., and McLaughlan, R. T. (1966) *Simulation of political interaction in multiple purpose river basin development*, Mass. Inst. Technol., Dep. Civil Eng. Hydrodyn. Lab. Rep. 100.

Burdick, D. S., and Naylor, T. H. (1966) "Design of computer simulation experiments for industrial systems", *Commun. Ass. Comput. Mach.* **9**, 329–39.

Bush, R. R., and Mosteller, F. (1955) *Stochastic models for learning*, John Wiley and Sons, Inc., New York.

Churchman, C. W., Ackoff, R. L. and Arnoff, E. L. (1961) *Introduction to operations research*, John Wiley and Sons, Inc., New York.

Clowes, M. B. (1967) "Perception, picture processing and computers". Collins, N. L. and Mitchie, D. (ed.) *Machine intelligence I*, Oliver and Boyd, Edinburgh & London.

Clymer, A. B. and Graber, G. F. (1964) "Trends in the development and applications of analog simulations in biomedical systems", *Simulation* **4**, 41–58.

Cochran, W. G. (1963) *Sampling techniques*, John Wiley and Sons, Inc., New York.

Cooper, C. F. (1969) "Ecosystem models in watershed management". Van Dyne, G. M. (ed.) *The ecosystem concept in natural resource management*. Academic Press, New York.

Crawford, N., and Linsley, R. (1966) *Digital simulation in hydrology. Stanford Watershed Model IV*. Stanford Univ., Dept. Civil Eng. Tech. Rep. 39.

Dahl, O. J., and Nygaard, K. (1966) "SIMULA: an ALGOL-based simulation language", *Commun. Ass. Comput. Mach.* **9**, 671–78.

Dansereau, P., Buell, P. F., and Dagon, R. (1966) "A universal system for recording vegetation", *Sarracenia* **10**, 1–64.

Dantzig, G. S. (1963) *Linear programming and extensions*, Princeton Univ. Press, Princeton, N.J.

Davis, E. W. (1965) "Resource allocation in project network models: a survey", *J. Ind. Eng.* **14**, 177–88.

David, J. B. (1968) "Why not PERT for your next resource management problem", *J. Forest* **66**, 405–8.

Dillon, J. L., and Heady, E. O. (1960) "Theories of choice in relation to farmer decision", *Iowa State Univ. Agr. Exp. Sta. Res. Bull.* **485**.

Draper, N. R., and Lawrence, W. E. (1965) "Designs which minimise model inaccuracies: cuboidal regions of interest", *Biometrika* **52**, 111–18.

Fan, Liang-Tseng (1966) *The continuous maximum principle*. John Wiley and Sons, Inc., New York.

Feigenbaum, E. A., and Feldman, J. (1963) *Computers and thought*, McGraw-Hill Book Co., Inc., New York.

Findler, N. V. (1966) "Human decision-making under uncertainty and risk: computer based experiments and a heuristic simulation program", *Proc. A.F.I.P.S. 1965 Fall Joint Computer Conf.*, **1**, 737–52.

Fishman, G. S. (1967) "Problems in the statistical analysis of simulation experiments: the comparison of means and the length of sample records", *Commun. Ass. Comput. Mach.* **10**, 94–9.

Fishman, G. S., and Kiviat, P. J. (1967) "The analysis of simulation generated time series", *Manag. Sci.* **13**, 525–57.

Ford, L. R., Jr., and Fulkerson, D. R. (1962) *Flows in networks*, Princeton Univ. Press, Princeton, N.J.

Garfinkel, D. A. (1967a) "A simulation study of the effects on simple ecological systems of making rate of increase of population density dependent'', *J. Theor. Biol.* **14**, 46–58.

—— (1967*b*) "Effect on stability of Lotka-Volterra ecological systems of imposing strict territorial limits on populations", *J. Theor. Biol.* **14**, 325–27.

Glanzer, M., and Glaser, R. (1959) "Techniques for the study of group structure and behaviour. 1. Analysis of structure", *Psychol. Bull.* **56**, 317–32.

Golley, F. B. (1960) "Energy dynamics of a food chain of an old field community", *Ecol. Monogr.* **30**, 187–206.

Greig-Smith, P. (1964) *Quantitative plant ecology*, Butterworth, London.

Gumbel, E. L. (1958) *Statistics of extremes*, Columbia Univ. Press, New York.

Halmos, P. R., and Vaughan, H. E. (1950) "The marriage problem", *Amer. J. Math.* **72**, 214–15.

Hammersely, J. M., and Morton, K. W. (1956) "A new Monte Carlo technique: antithetic variables", *Proc. Camb. Phil. Soc.* **52**, 449–75.

Harary, F., and Lipstein, P. (1962) "The dynamics of brand loyalty: a Markovian approach", *Oper. Res.* **10**, 19–40.

Harary, F., Norman, R. Z., and Cartwright, D. (1965) *Structural models: An introduction to the theory of directed graphs*, John Wiley and Sons, Inc., New York.

Harman, H. H. (1966) *Modern factor analysis*, 2nd ed. Univ. Chicago Press, Chicago.

Hasse, M. (1960) "Über die Behandlung Graphen theoretischer Probleme unter Verwendung der Matrizenrechnung", *Wiss. Z. Tech. Univ. Dresden* **10**, 1313–16.

Heady, E. O., and Egbert, A. C. (1964) "Regional programming of efficient agricultural patterns", *Econometrika* **32**, 374–86.

Heikurainen, L. (1964) *Suptyypien Ojituskelpoisus: metsänkasvatusta silmälläpitäen*, Kirjayhytyma, Helsinki.

Hein, L. W. (1967) *The quantitative approach to managerial decision*, Prentice-Hall, New York.

Holling, C. S. (1966) "The functional response of invertebrate predators to prey density", *Mem. Ent. Soc. Can.* **48**, 1–85.

Hooke, R., and Jeeves, T. A. (1961) "Direct search solutions of numerical statistical problems", *J. Ass. Comput. Mach.* **8**, 212–29.

Hufschmidt, M. M., and Fiering, M. B. (1966) *Simulation techniques for design of water resource systems*, Harvard Univ. Press, Cambridge, Mass.

International Business Machines Corporation (1966) *Bibliography on simulation*, Report 320-0926-0, White Plains, N.Y.

Jacoby, J. E., and Harrison, S. (1962) "Multivariable experimentation and simulation models", *Naval Res. Log. Quart.* **9**, 121–36.

Jenkins, G. M., and Watt, D. G. (1968) *Spectral analysis and its applications*, Holden Day, San Francisco, Calif.

Keeney, M. G., Koenig, H. E., and Zemach, R. (1967) *State space models of educational institutions*, Michigan State Univ. Div. of Engineering Research, East Lansing, Mich.

Kendall, M. G. (1957) *A course in multivariate analysis*, Griffin, London.

Kennard, R. W., and Stone, L. A. (1969) "Computer aided design of experiments", *Technometrics* **11**, 137–48.

Kerner, E. H. (1957) "A statistical mechanics of interacting biological species", *Bull. Math. Biophys.* **19**, 121–46.

—— (1959) "Further considerations on the statistical mechanics of biological association", *Bull. Math. Biophys.* **21**, 217–55.

Lawley, D. N. (1940) 'The estimation of factor loadings by the method of maximum likelihood", *Proc. Roy. Soc. Edinb.*, a, **60**, 64–82.

Lindeman, R. L. (1942) "The trophic dynamic aspect of ecology", *Ecology* **23**, 399–418.

Lippmaa, T. (1939) "The unistratal concept of plant communities', *Amer. Midland Natur.* **21**, 111–45.

Macnaughton-Smith, P. (1965) *Some statistical and other techniques for classifying individuals*. Home Office Res. Unit Rep. 6, H.M.S.O., London.

Margalef, D. R. (1947) "Information theory in ecology". *Mems. R. Acad. Barcelona* **23**, 373–440. (*Trans. in Gen. Systems* **3**, 36–71. 1958.)

Marquardt, D. W. (1963) "An algorithm for least squares estimation of nonlinear parameters", *J. Soc. Ind. Appl. Math.* **11**, 431–41.

Martino, R. L. (1965) "Advances in network techniques: an introduction to MAP", *Data Process.* **8**, 231–57.

Mood, A. M., and Graybill, F. A. (1963) *Introduction to the theory of statistics*, McGraw-Hill Book Co., Inc., New York.

Morton, J. A. (1964) "From research to industry", *Int. Sci. Technol.*, May 1964, 82–92, 105.

Muhzam, H. (1963) *On multivariate trends*, Paper presented to the 5th Int. Biometric Conf., Cambridge, England.

Olson, J. S. (1963) "Energy storage and the balance of producers and decomposers", *Ecology* **44**, 322–31.

Orcutt, G. H. (1960) "Simulation of economic systems", *Amer. Econ. Rev.* **50**, 893–907.

Patten, B. C. (1965) *Community organization and energy*

*relationships in plankton.* Oak Ridge Nat. Lab. Rep. ORNL-3634.

Petrini, P. (1964) "Competition between agriculture and forestry under Swedish conditions", *Lantbrukshägskolansannalar* **30**.

Phattaford, R. M. (1965) "Sequential analysis of dependent observations", *Biometrika* **52**, 157–65.

Potthof, R. F., and Roy, S. N. (1964) "A generalized multivariate analysis of variance model useful especially for growth curve problems", *Biometrika* **51**, 313–26.

Priban, I. P. (1968) "Forecasting failure of health", *Sci. Cult.* **34**, 232–5.

Price, D. K. (1965) *The scientific estate*, Harvard Univ. Press, Cambridge, Mass.

Quenouille, M. H. (1957) *Analysis of multiple time series*, Griffin, London.

Radanovic, L. (ed.) (1966) "Sensitivity methods in control theory", *Proc. Int. Symp. Dubrovnik, Yugoslavia*, Pergamon Press, New York.

Rao, C. R. (1965) "Theory of least squares when the parameters are stochastic and its application to the analysis of growth curves", *Biometrika* **52**, 447–58.

Robinson, E. A. (1967) *Multichannel time series analysis*, Holden Day, San Francisco, Calif.

Rosen, R. (1958) "The representation of biological systems from the standpoint of the theory of categories", *Bull. Math. Biophys.* **20**, 317–41.

Ross, D. T. (1967) "The AED approach to generalized computer-aided design", *Proc. Ass. Comput. Mach. National Meeting 1967*, 367–85.

Seal, H. L. (1964) *Multivariate statistical analysis for biologists*, Methuen, London.

Serck-Hanssen, J. (1963) "A programming model for a fishing region in northern Norway", *Regional Science Association Papers* **12**, 107–18, Lund Congress.

Siegel, S. (1956) *Nonparametric statistics for the behavioural scientist*, John Wiley and Sons, Inc., New York.

Simon, H. A., and Newall, A. (1962) "Simulation of human thinking", 95–131, in M. Greenberger (ed.), *Computers and the world of the future*, Mass. Inst. Technol. Press, Cambridge, Mass.

Spang, H. A. (1962) "Review of minimization techniques for non-linear functions", *Soc. Ind. Appl. Math. Rev.* **4**, 363–5.

Spent, P. (1967) "Estimation of mean growth curves", *J. Theor. Biol.* **17**, 159–73.

Tiku, M. L. (1964) "Approximating the general non-normal variance ratio sampling distribution", *Biometrika* **51**, 83–95.

Tocher, K. D. (1963) *The art of simulation*, English Universities Press, London.

Van Dyne, G. M., Wright, R. G., and Dollar, J. F. (1968) *Influence of site factors on vegetation productivity.* ORNL-TM 1974 Contract No. W-7405-eng-26. Oak Ridge National Laboratory.

Watanabe, S., and Abraham, C. T. (1960) "Loss and recovery of information by coarse observation of stochastic chain", *Information and Control* **3**, 248–78.

Watt, K. E. F. (1961) "Mathematical models for use in insect pest control", *Can. Entomol. Suppl.* **19**, 1–62.

—— (1963) "Dynamic programming, 'Look Ahead' programming and the strategy of insect pest control", *Can. Entomol.* **95**, 525–36.

—— (1968) *Ecology and resource management: a quantitative approach*, McGraw-Hill Book Co., Inc., New York.

Whittle, P. (1962) "Topographic correlation, power-law covariance functions and diffusion", *Biometrika* **49**, 305–12.

—— (1963) *Prediction and regulation*, English Universities Press, London.

Wiener, N. (1962) *The extrapolation, interpolation and smoothing of stationary time series*, Mass. Inst. Technol. Press, Cambridge, Mass.

Wilkins, R. D. (1966) "General time varying systems error sensitivity analysis", *Commun. Ass. Comput. Mach.* **9**, 855–9.

Williams, W. T. (1967) "Numbers, taxonomy and judgement", *Bot. Rev.* **33**, 379–86.

Witherspoon, J. P., Auerbach, S. I., and Olson, J. S. (1964) "Cycling of caesium-134 in white oak trees", *Ecol. Monogr.* **34**, 403–20.

Wolfe, P. (1962) "Recent developments in non-linear programming", 156–87, in Alt, F. L., and Ruhinoff, M. (eds.), *Advances in computers* **3**.

Reprinted from Dale, M. B., *Systems Analysis and Ecology.* Reprinted by permission of the Publisher. Copyright 1970, Duke University Press, Durham, North Carolina.

## Section V
## Introduction

This last section contains four papers which show something of the application of systems ideas to practical planning or to operating systems. Kast and Rosenzweig deal with organizations and give examples of different structures and of the sub-systems within them. This article essentially sets the scene for the others by showing how the traditional structural approach is limited as far as revealing behaviour goes.

The second article, by Van Court Hare Jr., is concerned with the problem of implementing system changes and of achieving the desired ends when changes are introduced. Again there are a number of examples illustrating implementation and system operation problems.

The last two papers are specific studies, the first by de Neufville on New York City's water supply system, and the second by Blumberg on the city as a system. Both, we think, illustrate the value of adopting a systems approach.

## Associated reading

Unfortunately there is a lack of good case-study or application material about systems. The North American Power failure mentioned in Chapter 6, page 114, has been extensively analysed (there is a file of material on it in the Open University's Technology Foundation Course: T100, Unit 5, *Systems File*). Other case studies have been reported; in the *Journal of Systems Engineering*, for example, there is a paper by K. E. Shaw on a systems study of a college of Education, (**1**, 2, Summer 1970) and one by Taylor and Youle on optimization of a petrochemical complex (**1**, 1, Autumn 1969). A list of failed systems can be found in "Systems that failed", *Congressional Record*, Vol. 115, No. 59, April 15, 1969.

# 16 Organization structure

*by F. E. Kast and J. E. Rosenzweig*

Structural relationships are fundamental considerations of organization theorists and practicing managers. The technical system has an important effect upon the type of structure appropriate for task performance. In turn, the structure sets the framework for the psycho-social system and is inexorably interwoven with the managerial system. The primary emphasis, in this article, is on formal rather than on informal relationships. We are concerned with developing the concept of structure, investigating the variables affecting it, considering newer developments, such as horizontal relationships and program management, and examining the dynamics of structure in relationship to the other organizational subsystems. The following topics are discussed:

## Definition of structure

Very simply, structure may be considered as *the established pattern of relationships among the components or parts of the organization.* However, the structure of a social system is not visible in the same way as a biological or mechanical system. It cannot be seen but is inferred from the actual operations and behavior of the organization.

The distinction between *structure* and *process* in systems helps in understanding this concept. "The *structure* of a system is the arrangement of its subsystems and components in three-dimensional space at a given moment of time. . . . Process is dynamic change in the matter-energy or information of that system over time."[1]

In the biological system the structure of the organism may be studied separately from its processes. For example, the study of anatomy is basically the study of the structure of the organism. In contrast, physiology is concerned with the study of the functions of living organisms. In the study of a social system such as an organization, it is difficult if not impossible to make this clear-cut distinction. In fact, there are those who suggest that it is impossible to study the structure of the organization as separate from its processes. "A social system is a structuring of events or happenings rather than of physical parts and it therefore has no structure apart from its functioning."[2]

We agree that the structure of the organization cannot be looked at as completely separate from its functions; however, these are two separate phenomena. Taken together, the concepts of structure and process can be viewed as the static and dynamic features of the organization. In some systems the static aspects (the structure) are the most important for investigation; in others the dynamic aspects (the processes) are more important. Actually, structure and processes are correlative and not opposing aspects of the system. We will view the organization's structure as being the established pattern of relationships among the components in the organization. "Organization structure consists simply of those aspects of the pattern of behavior in the organization that are relatively stable and that change only slowly."[3]

In the complex organization, structure is set forth initially by the design of the major components or subsystems and then by the establishment of patterns of relationship among these subsystems. It is this internal differentiation and patterning of relationships with some degree of permanency which is referred to as structure. The formal structure is frequently defined in terms of:

1. The pattern of formal relationships and duties – the organization chart plus job descriptions or position guides.
2. Formal rules, operating policies, work procedures, control procedures, compensation arrangements, and similar devices adopted by management to guide employee behavior (including that of executives) in certain ways, within the structure of formal relationships.[4]

## Formal and informal organization

*Formal organization* is the planned structure and represents the deliberate attempt to establish patterned relationships among components which will meet the objectives effectively. The formal structure is typically the result of explicit decision making and is prescriptive in nature – a "blueprint" of the way activities should be accomplished. Typically it is represented by a printed chart and is set forth in organization manuals, position descriptions, and other formalized documents. Although the formal structure does not comprise the total organizational system, it is of major importance. It sets a general framework and delineates certain prescribed functions and the relationships between these activities.

Anyone who has participated in an organization recognizes that many interactions occur which are not prescribed by the formal structure. The *informal organization* refers to those aspects of the system that are not formally planned but arise spontaneously out of the activities and interactions of participants.

Informal relationships are vital for the effective functioning of the organization. Frequently groups develop spontaneous and informal means for dealing with important activities which contribute to overall performance. Often the formal organization is slow in responding to external forces such as technological changes, and informal relationships develop to deal with these new problems. Thus, the informal organization may be adaptive and serve to perform innovative functions which are not being adequately met by the formal structure. On the other hand, there are occasions in which the informal organization may operate to the detriment of goals – when work groups slow down or sabotage production, for example.

Traditional management theorists concentrated on the formal organization structure. The human relationists, in contrast, were concerned primarily with informal relationships. This diversity of interest led to the view that there is an actual separation between the formal and informal structures. However, they really are intermeshed.

It is impossible to understand the nature of a formal organization without investigating the networks of informal relations and the unofficial norms as well as the formal hierarchy of authority and the official body of rules, since the formally instituted and the informally emerging patterns are inextricably intertwined. The distinction between the formal and the informal aspects of organizational life is only an analytical one and should not be reified; there is only one actual organization.[5]

In this article we will discuss the formal structure and will consider the informal patterns and relationship in Part Four. We should keep continually in mind, however, that this cleavage is artificial. In the actual organization the informal and formal structures are so intertwined as to defy separation.

## Authority and organization structure

There is a direct interrelationship between organization structure and the pattern of authority. In fact, many traditionalists made the underlying assumption that authority relationships were synonymous with the organization structure. Inasmuch as structure is concerned with the establishment of positions and the relationships between positions, it does provide the framework for authority relationships. However, the authority pattern is just one part of the total structure.

Authority refers to a relationship between the participants in the organization and is not an attribute of one individual. The authority structure provides the basis for assigning tasks to the various elements in the organization and for developing a control mechanism to ensure that these tasks are performed according to plan. It provides for the establishment of formalized influence transactions among the members of the organization.

The concept of authority is closely related to the idea of the legitimate exercise of the power of a position and depends on the willingness of subordinates to comply with certain directives of superiors. Obviously, the structure and the positioning of participants in a hierarchical arrangement facilitate the exercise of authority.

## Organization charts

A typical way of depicting the structure is through printed organization charts which specify the formal authority and communication networks of the organization. Figure 16.1 presents a simplified chart for a manufacturing company. The title of the position on the chart broadly identifies its activities, and its distance from the top indicates its relative status. The lines between positions are used to indicate the prescribed formal interactions. Most organization charts are hierarchical and emphasize relationships between superiors and direct subordinates. They are frequently supplemented by position descriptions and organizational manuals which attempt to define the tasks of the various positions and the interactions between them more specifically.

The organization chart is usually a simplified, abstract model of the structure. It is not an exact representation of

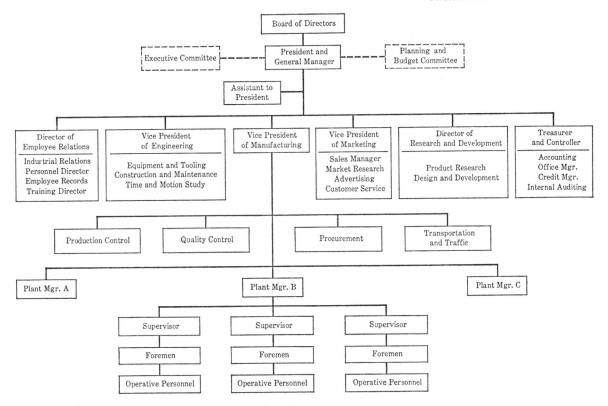

**Figure 16.1** Simplified organization chart for a manufacturing company.

the reality of the structure and has many limitations. It shows only a limited number of the relationships, even in the formal organization, and none of those in the informal organization. It does not, for example, indicate the degree of authority which a superior has over a subordinate. Does the superior have the right to hire and replace the occupant of a subordinate position? More importantly, it does not indicate the interactions between equals or the lateral relationships between people in different parts of the organization.

In spite of these limitations, the organization chart provides a useful starting point for the investigation of structure. It gives some indication of the hierarchical nature of positions and indicates the major activities performed. It prescribes certain patterns of formal interaction among positions. Thus, the chart communicates some important attributes of the structure. Its inaccuracy generally lies in its simplicity and in its lack of consideration of many other important aspects of the structure. "It usually errs by not reflecting the nuances of relationships within the organization; it usually deals poorly with informal control and informal authority, usually underestimates the significance of

personality variables in molding the actual system, and usually exaggerates the isomorphism between the authority system and the communication system." [6]

One problem of the organization chart is an inherent difficulty in trying to set forth in a simple, schematic two-dimensional plane the complex structural relationships existing in an organization. Conceptually, we would have a model closer to reality if we were able to utilize three-dimensional rather than two-dimensional charts. The requirement that the organization chart be confined to the printed page places limitations on developing schematic models.

## Traditional concepts of organization structure

Traditional management theorists were primarily concerned with the design of efficient organization. They emphasized such concepts as objectivity, impersonality, and structural form. The organization structure was designed for the most efficient allocation and coordination of activities. The positions in the structure, not the people, had the authority and responsibility for getting tasks accomplished. The

structure was emphasized as the most important and enduring characteristic of the organization. Many of the traditional concepts were based upon experiences with stable
organizations such as the military, church, and established
public bureaucracies. Industrial organizations were concerned with developing a structure geared to stable production. The emphasis was upon developing a rigid structure
with well-defined relationships and clearly established lines
of authority and communication. Let us consider some
"principles" of organization.

## Organizational specialization and division of labor

A basic concept of the traditional management theory is to
divide work into specialized tasks and to organize these
into distinct departments. Departmentalization with a
natural division of labor is emphasized. It is desirable to
determine the necessary activities for the accomplishment
of overall organizational objectives and then to divide these
activities on a logical basis into departments which perform
the specialized functions. The organization structure is the
primary means for achieving the technical and economic
advantages of specialization and division of labor.

## The scalar principle

The scalar principle states that authority and responsibility
should flow in a direct line vertically from the highest level
of the organization to the lowest level. It establishes the
hierarchical structure of the organization. It refers to the
vertical division of authority and responsibility and the
assignment of various duties along the scalar chain.
Primary emphasis is upon superior–subordinate relationships. Most organization charts indicate that this principle
is still used in designing the structure. The scalar principle
is complementary to the concept of unity of command, in
which each subordinate has only one superior.

## Authority, responsibility, and accountability

In the classical view, the legitimatization of authority at a
central source ensures that the superior "has the *right* to
command someone else and that the subordinate person
has the *duty* to obey the command. This is implied in the
notion of official legitimacy, legal in nature rather than
social and informal".[7] Authority is the right to invoke
compliance by subordinates on the basis of formal position
and control over rewards and sanctions. It is impersonal
and goes with the position rather than the individual.
Furthermore, authority and responsibility should be
directly linked, that is, if a subordinate is granted the

responsibility for carrying out an activity, he should also be
given the necessary authority. Accountability is associated
with the flow of authority and responsibility and is the
obligation of the subordinate to carry out his responsibility
and to exercise authority in terms of the established policies
and standards. This view of authority, responsibility, and
accountability provides the framework for much of
traditional management theory. It is the basis for legitimat-
izing organizational hierarchy and control systems and for
establishing many other concepts such as span of control
and line-staff relationships. Authority is the means for
integrating the activities of participants toward objectives
and provides the basis for centralized direction and control.

## Span of control

The span of control, or span of supervision, relates to the
number of subordinates which a superior can supervise
effectively. It is closely related to the hierarchical structure
and to departmentalization. Implicit in the span of control
concept is the necessity for the coordination of the activities
of the subordinates by the superior. It emphasizes superior-
subordinate relationships which allow for the systematic
integration of activities. Traditional theory advocates a
narrow span to enable the executive to provide adequate
integration of all the activities of subordinates. It does not
give recognition to the possibility of other means for
coordination.

## Line and staff

As organizations grew more complex, it was necessary to
integrate personnel with specialized knowledge and functions into the managerial system. This required modifications in the concepts of the scalar structure, unity of
command, and authority and responsibility. In many ways,
the line and staff concept can be viewed as a necessary
compromise in terms of the other classical principles. The
line organization is vested with the primary source of
authority and performs the major functions of the organization; the staff supports and advises the line. The staff is
an aid to the executive, an extension of his personality.
Through the use of specialized staffs, reporting directly to
the executive, it is possible to use their knowledge without
sacrificing the executive's coordinating function. This view
maintains the integrity of the line organization as central in
the scalar chain and as the source of authority.

Many modern management writers are critical of the
application of these traditional principles. However, they
do have a useful place if they are applied with discrimination. They are useful at a certain stage in the development

of an organization. They provide a basis for the initial formalizing of relationships as an organization grows from a small, informal operation. They also are appropriate where the organization is dealing with programmed and routine activities and has a stable technology and environment.

However, we would agree with the critics that absolute adherence to these principles is unrealistic. While they may serve as useful guidelines, organizations in a dynamic environment will generally need to have more fluid relationships. These principles were quite useful at the time of their formulation, during the early part of the twentieth century; however, with accelerating technology and new organizational requirements, they need to be modified.

These principles dealt with the two fundamentals of organizing – the differentiation of activities and their integration. Differentiation and integration are related to the broader scientific concepts of *analysis* – the separation of a whole into its constituent elements – and *synthesis* – the combination of parts or elements into a complex whole. Structure is concerned with both analysis and synthesis. However, these two forces are often working at cross purposes. One of the problems in establishing an appropriate organization structure is to provide the optimum balance between these forces.

## Differentiation of organizational activities

Complex organizations are characterized by a high degree of task specialization. Even the simplest enterprise, with just a few employees, has some division of labor among participants. In larger organizations this differentiation is carried much further. For example, a large university can have more specialization in course offerings and faculty personnel than the small liberal arts college which must concentrate on more general, less specialized subject matter. The total task of the organization is differentiated so that particular departments and units are responsible for the performance of specialized activities. "*Differentiation* is defined as the state of segmentation of the organizational system into subsystems, each of which tends to develop particular attributes in relation to the requirements posed by its relevant external environment." [8]

In the organization, this differentiation occurs in two directions: the vertical specialization of activities, represented by the organizational hierarchy, and the horizontal differentiation of activities, called departmentalization. Figure 16.1 illustrates these two bases of separation of activities. The vertical differentiation is represented by the hierarchy moving from the president to the vice-presidents,

plant managers, and supervisors, and finally to the operative level. The vertical differentiation establishes the managerial structure, whereas the horizontal differentiation establishes the basic departmentalization. Taken together, they set the formal structure of the organization.

## Vertical differentiation: hierarchy

The vertical division of labor establishes the hierarchy and the number of levels in the organization. Although organizations differ in the degree of their vertical divisions of labor and the extent to which it is made explicit and formalized, they all exhibit this characteristic. In the more formal organizations, such as the military, the vertical specialization is established by quite specific definitions of roles for the various positions, and there are significant status differences between levels. There is, for example, a basic separation between officers and enlisted personnel. Within the officer ranks, there is a distinct difference of role, status, and position in the hierarchy from second lieutenant to five-star general. Other organizations may not have such a clear-cut hierarchical differentiation of role and function. In the university there is a hierarchy from instructor to assistant professor to associate professor to full professor in the professorial ranks.* However, the beginning instructor may perform a teaching and research role quite similar to that of the full professor.

In the formal organization this hierarchy sets the basic communications and authority structure, the so-called "chain of command". In the business organization there are typically vertical differentiations of positions ranging from hourly employees to first-line supervisors, middle managers, and top executives. These levels are fairly well defined, with major differences in functions and status for the various positions.

There are substantial rewards for moving upward in the hierarchy. Position in the vertical dimension frequently determines the authority and influence, privilege, status, and rewards enjoyed by the incumbent. Theoretically, the further up the vertical hierarchy, the broader the considerations and the more strategic the decisions. Thus, the president should be concerned with broad institutional decisions, whereas his subordinates would be concerned with more narrowly confined decisions, and so forth down to the lower levels, where the concern is with technical operations. This vertical differentiation of activities also has the effect of creating the organizational pyramid. Inasmuch as each superior has more than one subordinate reporting to

* The British equivalent of American professorial appointments are lecturer, senior lecturer, and professor respectively.

him, the organization tends to broaden out (see Figure 16.1).

## Horizontal differentiation: departmentalization

Organizations typically have some basis for horizontal differentiation of activities. Even in a small retail store operation one partner often performs certain functions such as purchasing and inventory control, with the other in charge of advertising and sales promotion. In a small organization, this differentiation may be informal and may arise out of the natural interests and skills of the individuals involved. In a more complex organization, this horizontal specialization of activities is a necessity because of the need to perform particular functions effectively and efficiently.

The appropriate division of organizational activities into departments for purposes of administration was one of the fundamental concerns of traditional management theorists. Although there have been many criticisms of their emphasis on departmentalization and related prescriptions, the necessity for differentiation of activities is inherent in organizations.[9]

The three primary bases of departmentalization are (i) function, (ii) product, and (iii) location.[10] Departmentalization by *function* is shown in Figure 16.1, wherein the activities of the organization are divided into the primary functions to be performed – manufacturing, marketing, engineering, research and development, employee relations, and finance. This arrangement has the advantage of the specialization and concentration of similar activities within a departmental unit. It is the most prevalent form of departmentalization and is seen not only in business enterprises but in hospitals, governmental agencies, and many other kinds of organizations. The major problem associated with this form is the coordination of the specialized activities.

*Product* departmentalization has become increasingly important, especially for large, complex organizations. For example, companies such as General Electric, General Motors, and DuPont have major product divisions with substantial autonomy. This form has been used increasingly, particularly in the post-World War II period during which there has been a trend toward heterogeneous diversification.

A third primary basis for departmentalization is *location*. All the organizational activities performed in a particular geographic area are brought together and integrated into a single unit. This has been the pattern adopted by chain stores in establishing regional offices. The geographic basis of departmentation also has become an important form for

multi-national business corporations. Thus, many large-scale international companies such as IBM, Nestlé Corporation, and Unilever utilize this form.

In addition to these primary bases of departmentation, there are several others. Some organizations may departmentalize on a basis of *customers*, with separate units for retail and wholesale or for government and commercial sales. In many manufacturing organizations, departmentalization may relate to the *processes* or *equipment* utilized.

In the large organization, there is no one basis of departmentalization which is carried out uniformly throughout the entire enterprise. For example, at one level in the organization there may be the product divisions. At the next level, there may be functional specialization, and at the third level, departmentalization based upon geographic location or customer.

## The role of specialists

A traditional basis of differentiation of managerial activities has been in terms of line and staff functions. The line has direct command authority over the activities of the organization and is concerned with the primary functions. In contrast, the staff performs an advisory role and is concerned with supportive or adjutant activities. The development of the line-staff concept was necessary to provide some means of integrating the activities of numerous highly trained specialists who contribute important knowledge and skills.

The role of staff has changed substantially with greater specialization and complexities of many organizations. Staffs have come to play much more important roles. With the expansion of this role the clear delineation between line and staff activities is no longer possible. The view of line as having command authority and staff as only having an advisory role does not always hold true. The staff expert, because of knowledge and technical competence in a particular area of specialization, is frequently viewed as a source of authority and influence in the organization.[11] This is particularly true where the staff has functional authority. Functional authority resides within a specialized staff which exercises control over other operational units. Quite frequently, for example, the industrial relations department has functional authority over many personnel practices in all departments throughout the organization. Functional authority represents a substantial variation from the traditional emphasis upon the line structure and unity of command.

Etzioni suggests that in certain types of organizations,

such as research laboratories, hospitals, and universities, the roles of staff and line are reversed.

In full-fledged professional organizations the staff-professional line-administrator correlation, insofar as such distinctions apply at all, is reversed. Although administrative authority is suitable for the major goal activities in private business, in professional organizations administrators are in charge of secondary activities; they administer *means* to the major activity carried out by professionals. In other words, to the extent that there is a staff-line relationship at all, professionals should hold the major authority and administrators the secondary staff authority.[12]

Although many organizations, particularly business and the military, attempt to differentiate between the line and staff activities, it is our view that this distinction is becoming increasingly difficult to justify. Newer organizational forms, specifically developed to ensure the integration of activities, both on a vertical and horizontal basis, may be replacing the traditional line-staff form. While organizations with a uniform technology and operating in a stable environment may still find the differentiation of activities in terms of line and staff meaningful, organizations with dynamic technology and changing environment are finding this concept obsolete.

We have looked at some of the ways in which organizations differentiate activities. It appears that in all forms of complex organizations there has been a continual *trend toward the differentiation of activities into specialized subsystems.* Part of this has been a consequence of increased size, but even more significant has been the growing need for more specialization within organizations.

## NASA organizational structure

The National Aeronautics and Space Administration (NASA) provides an excellent example of the vertical and horizontal differentiation of organizational activities. NASA was established in 1958 as a civilian agency of the federal government to plan and conduct space exploration for peaceful purposes. In early 1961 the national space program was changed dramatically with the announcement of the objective of a manned moon landing and return by 1970, the Apollo program. NASA's yearly budget has been in excess of $5 billion, and the number of direct employees has been over 34,000. In addition, approximately 300,000 people employed by industry, universities, and research organizations have been working on NASA projects.

A NASA organization structure adapted to meeting the requirements of rapidly changing technology and of many diverse programs has evolved gradually. Figure 16.2 shows the overall NASA organization with the four major program areas – manned space flight, space science and applications, tracking and data acquisition, and advanced research and technology. These program areas are supported by a complex of functional activities reporting to the office of the administrator which are primarily at the *institutional* level and are concerned with relating NASA to its external environmental systems – such as the Department of Defense, Congress, universities, and industry.

Figure 16.3 shows a more detailed organization of the Office of Manned Space Flight. This is the program level within the NASA organization. The completed Mercury and Gemini programs were under this Office. Currently the major effort is in the Apollo program (manned lunar landing) and in advanced manned mission programs such as the orbital laboratory. Future programs under this office may include the manned space station and manned planetary exploration. In addition to these program activities there are a number of functional specialists reporting to the administrator of the Office of Manned Space Flight who develop broad policies and evaluate the effectiveness of the functional efforts on all programs. The technical task performance is carried out in the three space centers.

Figure 16.4 provides a detailed chart for one of these space centers, the George C. Marshall Space Flight Center in Huntsville, Alabama. This center is responsible for the management of all activities leading to the design, development, production, test, and delivery of large launch vehicles and related systems. The center comprises two major operating elements: research and development operations and industrial operations. The industrial operations are organized on a program basis with the Saturn I/IB Program, Saturn V Program, Engine Program, and Saturn/Apollo Applications Program. Many industrial contractors support these program efforts. For example, the Chrysler Corporation and the Boeing Company operate the Michoud Assembly Facility for the Saturn programs. The research and development operations are not organized by programs, but by disciplines or functional activities. These activities are also supported by industrial contractors. Therefore, in addition to the organization structure represented by these three charts, hundreds of industrial firms are integrated into the various NASA programs.

These charts indicate the three major vertical levels in the NASA organization – the office of the administrator, the four program areas, and the field centers. They also suggest

NATIONAL AERONAUTICS AND SPACE ADMINISTRATION

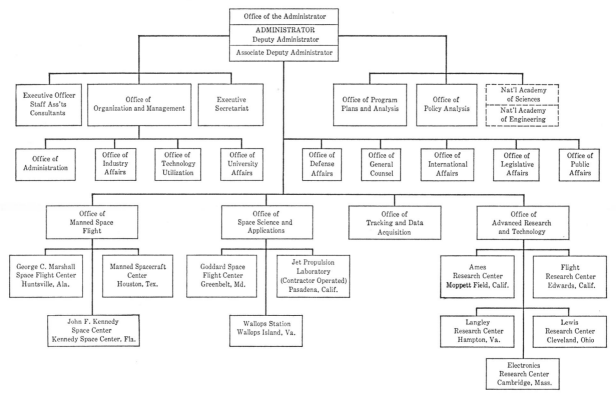

**Figure 16.2** Organization of the National Aeronautics and Space Administration (*NASA Authorization for Fiscal Year 1968,* Hearings before the Committee on Aeronautical and Space Sciences, U.S. Senate, 90th Cong., 1st Sess., 1967, p. 59).

the great specialization of activities required in the nation's space programs. NASA must coordinate the efforts of over 300,000 government, industrial, and university employees. Many of NASA's personnel are highly trained scientists and professionals – over 55 percent have college degrees or the equivalent in specialized experience. The complex technology and task requirements have necessitated the development of an exceedingly complex organization structure. In organizations such as NASA the increased differentiation of activities has magnified the problems of coordination.

## Integration of organizational activities

The second overall consideration in the design of organization structures is that of coordination of activities. "*Integration* is defined as the process of achieving unity of effort among the various subsystems in the accomplishment of the organization's task."[8] Through the processes of vertical and horizontal differentiation the activities required for organizational performance are separated. They then have to be integrated. The requirements of the environment and the technical system often determine the degree of coordina-

tion required. In some organizations, it is possible to separate activities in such a way as to minimize these requirements. This is typically true of chain store operations where each individual store unit has substantial autonomy. In other organizations, particularly those departmentalized functionally, integration is more important.

It is important to recognize the interaction between the need to specialize activities and the requirements for integration. The more differentiation of activities and specialization of labor, the more difficult the problems of coordination.

### Bases of Coordination

Organizations typically establish several different mechanisms for achieving coordination. Litterer suggests three primary means: through the hierarchy, the administrative system, and voluntary activities.[13] In *hierarchical* coordination, the various activities are linked together by placing them under a central authority. In Figure 16.1, the major functions are coordinated by the president. In the simple organization, this form of coordination might be sufficient.

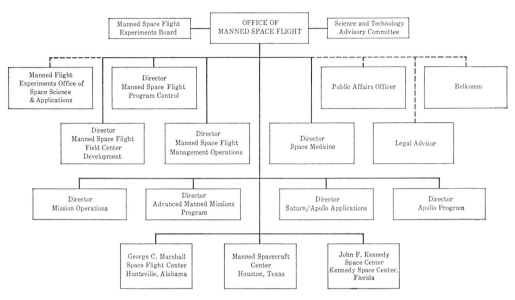

**Figure 16.3** Organization of the Office of Manned Space Flight (*1968 NASA Authorization*, Part 1, Hearings before the Committee on Science and Astronautics, U.S. House, 90th Cong., 1st Sess., 1967, p. 168).

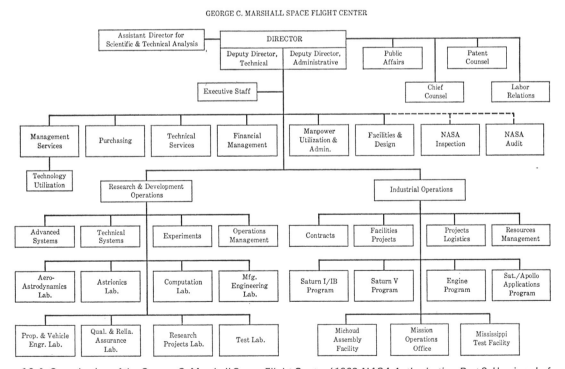

**Figure 16.4** Organization of the George C. Marshall Space Flight Center (*1968 NASA Authorization*, Part 2, Hearings before the Committee on Science and Astronautics, U.S. House, 90th Cong., 1st Sess., 1967, p. 933).

However, in the complex organizations such as NASA with many levels and numerous specialized departments, hierarchical coordination becomes more difficult. Although the typical pyramidal chart indicates that there is one central position which is a focal point for coordination of all the activities, this is impossible for the larger organization. It would be difficult for a top-level executive to cope with all the coordinating problems that might come up through the hierarchy. There are also major problems of communication up and down the hierarchy which make it difficult for the individual at the top to have the information required for the coordination of activities at lower levels. This is particularly true when there are many layers in the organization. Thus, coordination through the hierarchical structure must be supplemented by other means.

The *administrative* system provides a second mechanism for coordination of activities. "A great deal of coordinative effort in organization is concerned with a horizontal flow of work of a routine nature. *Administrative systems* are formal procedures designed to carry out much of this routine coordinative work automatically."[13] Many work procedures such as memos with routing slips help coordinate efforts of different operating units. To the extent that these procedures can be programmed or routinized, it is not necessary to establish specific means for coordination. For nonroutine and nonprogrammable events, specific units such as committees may be required to provide integration.

A third type of coordination is through *voluntary means.* "The individual or group of individuals sees a need, finds a program, and applies it when deemed necessary."[13] Much of the coordination may depend upon the willingness and ability of individuals or groups to voluntarily find means to integrate their activities with other organizational participants. Achieving voluntary coordination is one of the most important yet difficult problems of the manager. Voluntary coordination requires that the individual have sufficient knowledge of organizational goals and objectives, adequate information concerning the specific problem of coordination, and the motivation to do something on his own.

The problems of integration for the organization with a stable environment, a constant technology, and routine activities are substantially different from those for the organization facing rapidly changing environmental and technological forces. The stable organization can rely upon the hierarchical structure and established procedures to ensure coordination. The organization facing change must develop different mechanisms for integration.

## Development of means of integration

Problems of integrating diverse activities in complex organizations have stimulated the development of many coordinative mechanisms. One approach to integrating activities is the committee. Committees typically are made up of members from a number of different departments or functional areas and are concerned with problems requiring coordination. Many business organizations have established executive committees at the corporate level to provide integration.[14] The use of committees for purposes of coordination is a well-established approach in other institutions such as universities and hospitals. Committees can be viewed as a means for the organization to achieve coordination between diverse groups.

Additional means for integration have developed in many organizations. Lawrence and Lorsch studied six organizations operating in the chemical processing industry to determine how they achieved integration. These organizations used a technology which required highly differentiated and specialized activities but also a major degree of integration among them.[15] The study was concerned with how organizations achieve both substantial differentiation and tight integration when these forces seem paradoxical. They found that successful companies used task forces, teams, and project offices to achieve coordination. There was a tendency to formalize coordinative activities which had developed informally and voluntarily.

In the most successful organizations, the influence of the integrators stemmed from their professional competence rather than from their formal position. They were successful as integrators because of their specialized knowledge and because they represented a central source of information in the operation. These results suggest that it is possible for the complex organization to achieve both differentiation of activities and effective integration but that new organizational arrangements are required to do so.

Others have recommended new structural forms to help with the problems of integration. Likert says, "Increases in functionalization, in turn, make effective coordination both more necessary and even more difficult."[16] He suggests that one mechanism for achieving integration is by having people serve as "linking pins" between the various units in the organization. Horizontally, there are certain organizational participants who are members of two separate groups and serve as coordinating agents between them. On the vertical basis, individuals serve as linking pins between their own level and those above and below. Thus, through this system of linking pins, the "voluntary coordination" necessary to make the dynamic system operate effectively is achieved.

This constitutes a multiple, overlapping group structure in the organization. Likert says,

> To perform the intended coordination well a fundamental requirement must be met. The entire organization must consist of a multiple, overlapping group structure with *every* work group using group decision-making processes skillfully. This requirement applies to the functional, product, and service departments. An organization meeting this requirement will have an effective interaction-influence system through which the relevant communications flow readily, the required influence is exerted laterally, upward, and downward, and the motivational forces needed for coordination are created.[16]

## Elaboration of structure

One characteristic of large-scale organizations in every field of endeavor has been the increased elaboration and complexity of structure. This is true for business enterprises as well as hospitals, universities, and local, state, and federal governmental (including military) organizations. Although size may be a contributing factor to this elaboration, other forces are also significant.

### Impact of sociocultural environment

A number of writers have investigated the relationship between the sociocultural environment and organization structure. For example, Stinchcombe suggests that firms founded during the nineteenth century have a different structure than do automotive plants and other companies founded during the twentieth century. He says, "Extensive 'staff' departments made up of professionals trained in colleges and universities do not appear in industries founded before the twentieth century, while practically all industries whose organizational forms were developed within this century have extensive staff departments."[17] The specific structural form depends upon the social, cultural, environmental forces prevailing at the time the organization is established. Even though modifications are made over time, organizations seem to retain a strong flavor of their original form. He also suggests that organization structure cannot precede developments in the sociocultural environment which makes the particular forms possible.

> The organizational inventions that can be made at a particular time in history depend on the social technology available at the time. Organizations which have purposes that can be efficiently reached with the socially possible organizational forms tend to be founded during the period in which they become possible. Then, both because they can function effectively with those organizational forms, and because the forms tend to become institutionalized, the basic structure of the organization tends to remain relatively stable.[17]

There is substantial evidence to verify Stinchcombe's thesis. For example, the organization structure for NASA is significantly different from that of older governmental agencies. It has substantially more differentiation and specialization of activities and also has developed different means for achieving integration, such as the program orientation. NASA's organization is very dependent upon forces in the sociocultural environment. It would have been impossible to adopt the current structure without having highly trained technical specialists available in large numbers from our universities.

### Structural evolution in industrial organizations

For large-scale industrial organizations, certain patterns are evident in the structural changes that have occurred over periods of time. Chandler states that as firms developed new strategies in response to the changing social and economic environment, basic changes in structure have been required.[18] In an intensive study of four large corporations, E. I. du Pont de Nemours & Co., General Motors Corporation, Standard Oil Company of New Jersey, and Sears, Roebuck and Company, supported by a survey of seventy other large industrial firms, he found certain evolutionary patterns of structure. Changing population, income, technology, and other forces in the environment have led to the expansion of these firms into new fields. This strategy of diversification and expansion has required major modifications in structure. "A new strategy required a new or at least refashioned structure if the enlarged enterprise was to operate efficiently. . . . Unless new structures are developed to meet new administrative needs which result from an expansion of a firm's activities into new areas, functions, or product lines, the technological, financial, and personnel economies of growth and size cannot be realized."[18]

The pattern of development of large industrial enterprises led to the adoption of a multidivisional structure where the central corporate office plans and coordinates the activities of a number of operating divisions and makes allocations of personnel, facilities, funds, and other resources. The actual operations of the organization are decentralized to the operating divisions, which have a substantial degree of autonomy. This structural form has been the typical pattern adopted in the past several decades. This evolution is illustrated later in the chapter with a discussion of the Boeing Company.

## Growth of administrative structure

There is a general view that as organizations increase in size, the number of administrative personnel increases more than proportionately. However, research findings suggest that if anything, the ratio of administrative personnel to operative personnel decreases.[19] However, there is a relationship between the number of administrative personnel and the complexity of operations. In a survey of forty-one industries, Rushing found that the factor of size alone did not lead to an increase in the proportion of administrative personnel; however, the factor of complexity was directly related to the relative size of the administrative force.[19] These findings are consistent with the view that as an organization increases in specialization and complexity, the scope of the managerial coordination problems increases. Therefore, it seems logical that the number of people engaged in administrative tasks would also increase.

Within the administrative group there are three primary subgroups: management, clerical, and professional personnel. Management provides coordination through the managerial hierarchy. For professional personnel, the primary coordinative mechanism is expertise and knowledge. Clerical personnel are concerned with coordination of work flow and procedural communications. As complexity increases in the organization, the relative number of people in the professional and clerical subgroups increases more than that in the managerial group.

> With increases in the division of labor, managerial activities may be increasingly supplemented with the activities of clerical and professional personnel. Thus, relative to managerial authority and supervision, formal communication and professional authority may become increasingly important in coordination as industries become increasingly complex. Decisions may be made and coordination may be effected less and less on the basis of direct observation of the work process by the managerial hierarchy and more and more indirectly on the basis of information processed by professional and clerical personnel.[20]

These findings suggest that with the growing complexity and elaboration of organizations, different forms of integration may be utilized. Increasingly, coordination through professional authority and standard operating procedures maintained by clerical personnel may serve as substitutes for coordination through the managerial hierarchy.

## Horizontal and diagonal relationships

Most organization charts are drawn to emphasize the vertical hierarchy and superior–subordinate relationships. Very few indicate horizontal interactions, those integrative activities which flow between departments, units, or individuals at approximately the same level.

> Horizontal relationships are those whose functions are not primarily the passing down of orders or the passing up of information and whose nature and characteristics are not primarily determined by the fact that one actor is superior to the other in the organization's hierarchy. The function of horizontal relationships is to facilitate the solution of problems arising from division of labor, and their nature and characteristics are determined by the participants having different organizational subgoals but interdependent activities that need to intermesh.[21]

As organizations have become more complex, it has been impossible to provide the necessary coordination through the vertical hierarchy. For example, in the modern hospital, a great many horizontal interactions are required. Patient treatment may involve a number of departments and specialized units, many of which are highly technical. It would be impossible for any single superior to coordinate all the activities required. As Sayles and Strauss say, "The modern organization depends on lateral relationships precisely because there are so many specialized points of view and so many required contacts that no single manager could handle the communication flow alone."[22]

In the industrial organization, the need for establishing effective horizontal relationships is also important. For example, the required interaction between product research and manufacturing, between sales and inventory control, and between advertising and finance is evident. Increasingly, new organizational units such as operations research groups and data processing centers have been established. They can succeed only if they are able to establish effective horizontal relationships with numerous other units in the organization.

In a study of 142 purchasing agents in different firms, Strauss found that the relationships between purchasing and other departments could not be understood in terms of traditional superior–subordinate or line-staff concepts. The purchasing agents' internal relationships were almost entirely lateral. "They are with other functional departments of about the same rank in the organizational hierarchy – departments such as production scheduling, quality control, engineering, and the like. Most agents receive relatively little attention from their superiors; they must act on their own, with support being given by higher management only in exceptional cases."[23] While technically the purchasing department is classified as a staff department, it is much more involved than merely advising and for all practical purposes has authority over many of the workflow processes. Many conflicts developed between purchasing and other departments, and purchasing agents developed mechanisms for their resolution. Conflicts were rarely referred up the hierarchy to be resolved by a common superior. The purchasing agents used other means, primarily based upon their own expertise and personal influence, for coordinating activities with other departments.

Establishing effective means for dealing with the problems of horizontal integration in complex organizations is perhaps the single most important structural problem. Traditionally, lateral communications have been left to the informal structure. However, as the problems of integration have increased, formal means have been developed to supplement the informal relationships.

## Program management

The program management approach is geared to changing managerial requirements in the research, development, procurement, and utilization of large-scale military, space, and civilian projects. With the advent of newer, more complex programs, the military services as well as other government agencies and private companies have had to adapt their organizational structures away from traditional functional arrangements. The pressures of accelerating technology and short lead times have made it necessary to establish some formalized managerial agency to provide overall integration of the many diverse functional activities.

Various terms have been used to designate these integrated management functions such as *systems management, program management, weapon system management, product management,* and *project management.* Although there are some differences among these terms and their meanings, they have a thread of commonality – the integrated management of a specific program on a systems basis. Cleland says: "The project manager acts as a focal point for the concentration of attention on the major problems of the project. This concentration forces the channeling of major program considerations through an individual who has the proper perspective to integrate relative matters of costs, time, technology, and total product compatibility."[24]

This approach has been used in many major weapon systems and space programs.[25] For example, the Air Force sets up a system program office wherein the Air Force manager has the major responsibilities for integration of activities. The Navy established a program management type of organization in the form of the Special Projects Office for the Polaris system. The National Aeronautics and Space Administration has also used this approach in its more complicated projects, including the manned space flight program (see Figures 16.2, 16.3, and 16.4). This approach is being used throughout industry as well.[26]

### Functions of program manager

A program manager is responsible for organizing and controlling all activities involved in achieving the ultimate objective. He is usually superimposed upon the functional organization, creating new and complex relationships. This structural approach requires organizational modifications, emphasizes the integrative aspects, and requires the development of effective horizontal and diagonal information–decision networks.

There are various organizational approaches to program management. In the "staff" form the program manager is an adviser to the chief executive or general manager – he has little authority on his own. The functional managers retain the primary authority. At the other end of the spectrum, the program manager is granted complete authority over all the activities necessary to carry out the program. This is the approach used in many major military or space projects. Figure 16.3 shows that all the operational activities report directly to the Office of Manned Space Flight.

The matrix form is a compromise between these two extremes (see Figure 16.5). The functional managers such as manufacturing, engineering, and marketing are responsible to the general manager for their special activities. The project manager reports directly to the general manager on a line basis. He may have personnel assigned to his project from the various functional departments. Under the matrix form there are two primary flows of authority – the vertical flow of authority from the various functional managers and the horizontal flow of project authority.

### Authority relationships

The essence of program management is that it is interfunctional and is often in conflict with the normal organization structure. Thus, where the program management approach is used, there is a natural conflict system. Instead of an organization operating under the traditional view with a

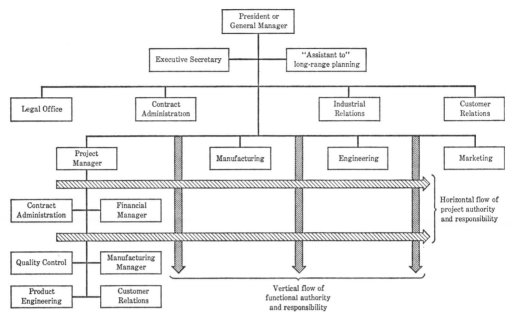

**Figure 16.5** Functional organization with project manager in a line capacity (Cleland, D. I. and King, W. R. (1968) *Systems Analysis and Project Management*, McGraw-Hill Book Company, New York, p. 177).

well-defined hierarchical structure, a unity of command, and clear-cut authority and responsibility relationships, the system is much more dynamic and less structured.

The program manager cannot operate effectively if he relies solely upon the formal authority of his position. Success is more likely to depend upon his ability to influence other organizational members. Because he is a focal point in the operation, he does have informational and communications inputs which provide him with a strong basis of influence. "One of the project manager's greatest sources of authority involves the manner in which he builds alliances in his environment – with his peers, associates, superiors, subordinates, and other interested parties. The building of alliances supplements his legal authority; it is the process through which the project manager can translate disagreement and conflict into authority (or influence power) to make his decisions stand."[27]

The program manager's authority and influence flow in different directions from hierarchical authority. They flow horizontally across vertical superior–subordinate relationships existing within the functional organization. Throughout the program, personnel at various levels and in many functions must contribute their efforts. For each new program, lateral information–decision networks must be established which differ significantly from the existing networks based upon the established structure. The organiza-

tion should be sufficiently flexible to allow for evolving relationships and networks as program requirements change.

## Other characteristics

The program manager's task is finite. He takes a project from the beginning and works it through to completion. Once completed, his task is over, and the program management group can be reassigned to new activities. Thus, by its very nature the function is temporary. The organizational structure is dynamic, and people must be prepared to accept change. The emphasis upon flexibility rather than permanency of relationships strongly affects the psycho-social and managerial systems.

The program manager and his staff usually serve as important boundary agents. Many activities, particularly in military and space programs, require interorganizational coordination. The program manager is the central point of the information–decision system regarding program activities, and he is the natural focal point for interorganizational coordination. "Rarely does the project manager find that the project activities are limited to his own organization; he usually must work with participants (or contributors) outside the company. He therefore has superior knowledge of the relative roles and functions of the individual parts of the project which makes him a logical person to take part in major interorganizational decisions affecting the project."[27]

Frequently the introduction of the program approach creates additional organizational units and more management positions as well. In several companies which adopted program management, Middleton found a significant increase in the number of departments, the number of vice-presidents and directors, and the number of second-level supervisors.[28]

Although program management has been primarily used in the defense and aerospace sectors, it will find increasing application in many other areas. Steiner and Ryan suggest forces that will influence this growth: "Our projection of greater use in the commercial world is predicated on several bases: increased sophistication of customer needs, increased complexity and size of business, increased pace of technological change, increased involvement of the Government as a customer in nondefense areas, and the changing needs of people in organizations."[26] Program management also will find increasing applications in the noncommercial sectors for dealing with problems such as transportation, urban renewal, and pollution control.[29] It is one of the most important innovations in the structure of organizations.

## An example of organization structure

Because of the great diversity among industrial organizations, it would be impossible to set forth a single structure as representative of American industry. For purposes of illustration we are showing the structure represented by organization charts for a large company in the aerospace industry, the Boeing Company.

This company is one of the largest industrial corporations in the United States, ranking among the upper twenty.[30] In 1967 the company had sales of nearly $3 billion, more than $2 billion in assets, and over 140,000 employees. It is one of the major firms in the aerospace industry and has been the contractor for many of the nation's major defense and space programs such as the B-47 and B-52 airplanes, the Minuteman missile system, and the Saturn booster program. It is the world's largest producer of commercial aircraft and is currently engaged in research and development on the SST (supersonic transport).

Over the past several decades the organization structure has become increasingly complex through continual differentiation and elaboration. This resulted from the expansion of the company into a number of new fields and program efforts and from the increasingly complex technology which requires greater specialization. One of the

basic trends has been the vertical elaboration of the structure through the establishment of separate divisions which specialize on particular program activities. Figure 16.6 shows the overall corporate structure and the major divisions.

The corporate headquarters, through the management council, establishes major policies and plans, coordinates the activities of the operating divisions, and makes allocations of personnel, facilities, funds, and other resources. The actual operations of the company are decentralized to the divisional level. The headquarters staff is composed of a number of functional vice-presidents who establish broad policies and coordinate the divisional efforts relating to their functions. They carry on many activities which have importance to the corporation as a whole.

The organization structure for the largest division, the Commercial Airplane Division, is shown in Figure 16.7. This division has over 80,000 employees and is engaged in the production of commercial and military aircraft and support systems including the SST program. It is divided into five branches and contains staff and functional personnel at the divisional headquarters who are counterparts to the vice-presidents in corporate headquarters. The major marketing and contract administration activities are located at the divisional level.

Figure 16.8 shows in more detail the structure of the largest branch in this division, the Renton branch. It is engaged in the production of 707, 720, and 727 commercial aircraft and in support programs for the KC-135 military transport. The divisions and the branches provide the integration of effort for specific programs.

These charts indicate the vertical levels in the organization. They do not, however, show all the program activities and the total structure. There are five other divisions in the corporation which are involved in more than twenty-five other major programs.

These charts present a general picture of the structure at one point in time. In reality, the structure is continually evolving and changing to meet new program requirements, changing technologies, and environmental influences. There have been scores of major changes in structure over the past twenty years and hundreds of changes throughout lower levels in the organization. An important new program effort such as the SST requires the reassignment of many personnel and a major restructuring of the organization. The organization must remain flexible in order to meet dynamic changes.

This multidivisional structure with program efforts in the divisions provides for both maintenance and adaptability

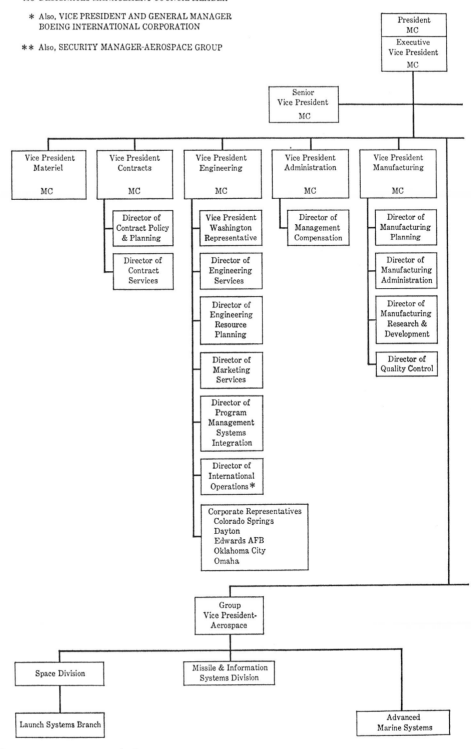

Figure 16.6 The Boeing Company corporate organization.

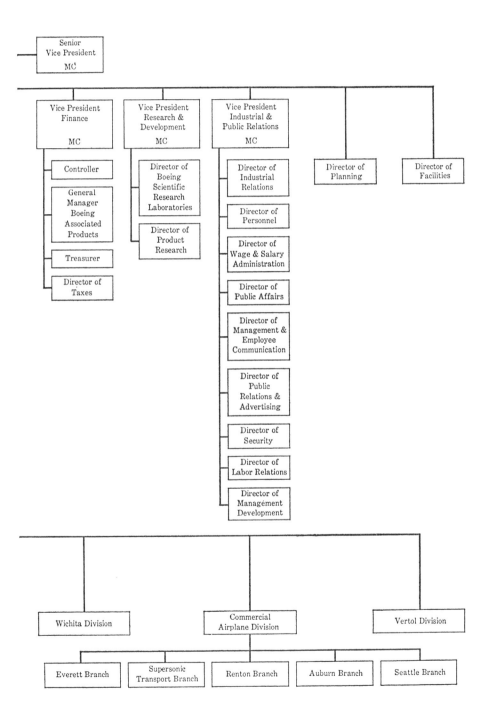

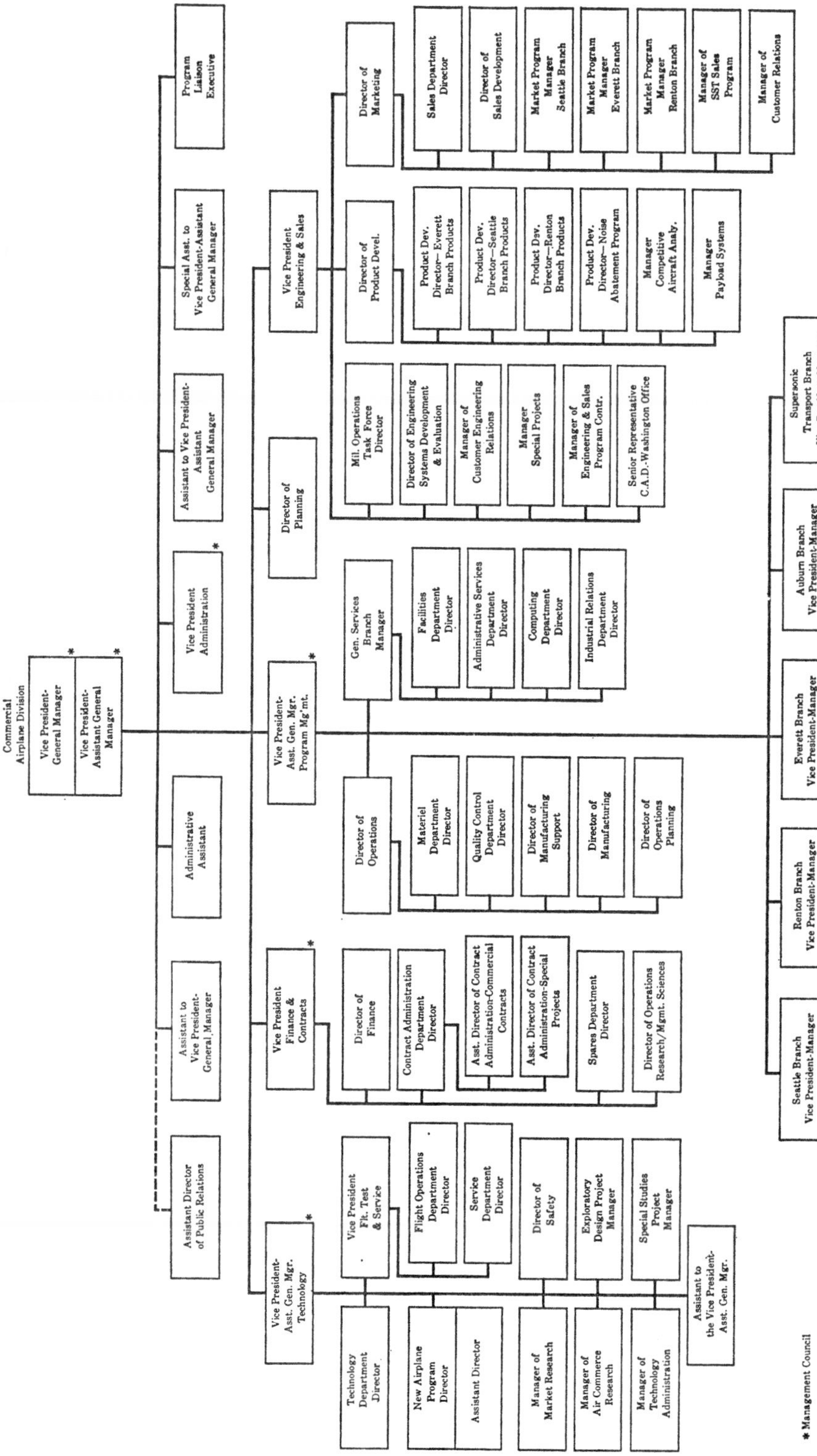

**Figure 16.7** The Boeing Company, Commercial Airplane Division.

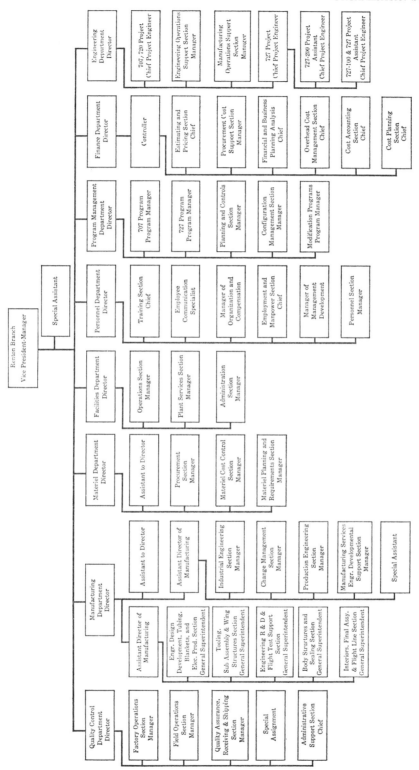

**Figure 16.8** The Boeing Company, Commercial Airplane Division, Renton Branch.

in the organization. The corporate headquarters operates at the institutional level and deals with environmental uncertainties. The divisions and branches operate at the technical level and are primarily concerned with specific programs. They have broad autonomy for the development of new program efforts. When the company undertakes a new program, it is possible to make the changes at the divisional and branch levels without upsetting the entire structure. This approach provides for the adaptability which is vital in the dynamic aerospace industry.

## Dynamics of organization structure

As a result of many forces most organizations undergo relatively frequent structural changes. A look at the organization of a modern metropolitan hospital will show that dramatic changes have occurred over the past two decades. Most universities are currently undergoing structural changes in order to meet the requirements of advancing knowledge.[31] In business organizations, the changes are equally dramatic. Daniel reported that in a recent three-year period at least two-thirds of the nation's top 100 industrial companies reported major organizational re-alignments.[32] He estimated that on the average, the larger industrial corporations have a t least one major restructuring every two years. Increasingly, industrial organizations are accepting the necessity for changing their structure as a fact of life and are establishing permanent departments

charged with the responsibility for organizational analysis and planning.[33]

The movement toward dynamic, flexible structures and away from the rigid bureaucratic form seems to be a trend in modern organizations. Table 16.1 summarizes the characteristics of adaptive-organic and bureaucratic-mechanistic systems. Instead of providing for permanent, structured positions as characteristic of the mechanistic system, the adaptive–organic system has less structuring, more frequent change of positions and roles, and more dynamic interplay among the various functions. The organic system requires more time and effort toward integration of diverse activities. The bureaucratic–mechanistic form provided for coordination through the hierarchical structure. In the adaptive–organic form, mechanisms for horizontal and diagonal integration are established. "The function of the 'executive' thus becomes *coordinator*, or 'linking pin' between various project groups. He must be a man who can speak the diverse languages of research and who can relay information and mediate among the groups. *People will be differentiated not vertically according to rank and role but flexibly according to skill and professional training.*"[34]

Obviously, the organic form, requiring a dynamic, changing structure, will not be feasible for all organizations. Many organizations can perform most effectively with a more mechanistic structure. These two organizational

**Table 16.1** Organizational characteristics of organic and mechanistic structures

| ORGANIZATIONAL CHARACTERISTICS INDEX | TYPES OF ORGANIZATION STRUCTURE | |
| | ORGANIC | MECHANISTIC |
| --- | --- | --- |
| Span of control | Wide | Narrow |
| Number of levels of authority | Few | Many |
| Ratio of administrative to production personnel | High | Low |
| Range of time span over which an employee can commit resources | Long | Short |
| Degree of centralization in decision making | Low | High |
| Proportion of persons in one unit having opportunity to interact with persons in other units | High | Low |
| Quantity of formal rules | Low | High |
| Specificity of job goals | Low | High |
| Specificity of required activities | Low | High |
| Content of communications | Advice and information | Instructions and decisions |
| Range of compensation | Narrow | Wide |
| Range of skill levels | Narrow | Wide |
| Knowledge-based authority | High | Low |
| Position-based authority | Low | High |

SOURCE: Hower, R. M. and Lorsch, J. W. (1968) "Organizational Inputs", in Seiler, J. A. *Systems Analysis in Organizational Behavior*, Richard D. Irwin, Inc., and The Dorsey Press, Homewood, Ill., p. 168.

forms represent polar points on a continuum. In many organizations it will be necessary to operate certain sections such as research and development by utilizing the organic system, and other sections (production operations) with a more mechanistic system.

A number of the organizational characteristics shown in Table 16.1 for organic and mechanistic systems are more closely related to the psycho-social and managerial systems than to structure. These are discussed in Article 1 of this collection of readings.

## Summary

Structure may be considered as the established pattern of relationships between the components or parts of the organization. Unlike mechanical or biological systems, the structure of the social organization is not visible; it is inferred from operations.

Organizations have both formal and informal structure. The formal structure is the result of explicit decision making concerning organizational patterns and is typically expressed in charts, manuals, and position descriptions. Organization charts are usually highly simplified, abstract models of the structure and deal with a limited number of relationships.

Traditional management theorists were vitally concerned with the design of efficient organization structures. Many principles were based on experiences with stable organizations such as the military, church, and established public bureaucracies. Some of the most important of these principles were: organization specialization and the division of labor; the scalar principle; concepts of authority, responsibility, and accountability; span of control, and line and staff relationships. Many modern writers are critical of these principles; however, they are still applicable in some organizations and in parts of others.

Complex organizations are characterized by a high degree of task specialization or division of labor. This differentiation occurs in two directions – the vertical, represented by the hierarchy; and the horizontal, represented by departmentalization. Increased differentiation has magnified the problems associated with integration. Organizations have developed many mechanisms for achieving coordination, such as the formal hierarchy, the administrative system, and voluntary means. Organizations facing a changing environment and accelerating technology have found it necessary to adopt new means for ensuring integration, such as committees, task forces, coordinating teams, and program managers.

Program management has been used effectively to provide the necessary integration of activities on a total systems basis. However, it creates many problems of organizational conflict, particularly between the program and functional managers.

Most modern organizations undergo frequent changes in structure. Instead of providing for permanent, highly structured relations as characteristic of the bureaucratic–mechanistic system, the adaptive–organic organization has less structuring, more frequent change of positions and roles, and a more dynamic interplay between the various functions. Obviously, however, the organic form is not feasible for all organizations. Many organizations, operating in a stable environment and with a uniform technology, can perform more effectively by utilizing a mechanistic structure.

## Review and research

1. What is the structure of an organization? How does this differ from the structure of a physical or biological system?

2. What are advantages and disadvantages of using charts to illustrate organization structure?

3. What is the distinction between the formal and the informal organization?

4. Evaluate the contributions of the traditional management theorists to the concept of structure.

5. Why have large organizations increasingly differentiated their activities?

6. Why is integration becoming more important in complex organizations? Discuss alternative means for achieving integration.

7. How is it possible for an organization to achieve both greater differentiation and more effective integration?

8. Investigate a specific organization to determine how it has developed both vertical and horizontal differentiation. Evaluate the means by which this organization achieves integration.

9. Why have large corporations followed a similar pattern in their structural evolutions? What is this pattern?

10. Why have horizontal and diagonal relationships become so important in the modern organization?

11. What is program management, and why has it evolved? How does the "authority" of the program manager differ from traditional line authority?

## References

1 Miller, G. (1965) "Living Systems: Basic Concepts", *Behavioral Science*, pp. 209–11.

2 Katz, D. and Kahn, R. L. (1966) *The Social Psychology of Organizations*, John Wiley & Sons, Inc., New York, p. 31.

3 March, J. G. and Simon, H. A. (1958) *Organizations*, John Wiley & Sons, Inc., New York, p. 170.

4 Hower, R. M. and Lorsch, J. W. (1967) "Organizational Inputs", in John A. Seiler, *Systems Analysis in Organizational Behavior*, Richard D. Irwin, Inc., and The Dorsey Press, Homewood, Ill., p. 157.

5 Blau, P. M. and Scott, W. R. (1962) *Formal Organizations*, Chandler Publishing Company, San Francisco, p. 6.

6 Cyert, R. M. and March, J. G. (1963) *A Behavioral Theory of the Firm*, Prentice-Hall, Inc., Englewood Cliffs, N.J., p. 289.

7 Pfiffner, J. M. and Sherwood, F. P. (1960) *Administrative Organization*, Prentice-Hall, Inc., Englewood Cliffs, N.J., p. 75.

8 Lawrence, P. R. and Lorsch, J. W. (1967) "Differentiation and Integration in Complex Organizations", *Administrative Science Quarterly*, June, pp. 3–4.

9 For a discussion and criticism of the traditional management theorists' emphasis upon departmentalization, see March and Simon, *op. cit.*, pp. 22–3. Their primary criticism was the lack of consideration of the problems of integration of activities between the various departments. They say: "One peculiar characteristic of the assignment problem, and of all the formalizations of the departmentalization problem in classical organization theory, is that, if taken literally, problems of coordination are eliminated. Since the whole set of activities to be performed is specified in advance, once these are allocated to organization units and individuals the organization problem posed by these formal theories is solved." March and Simon, *op. cit.*, pp. 25–6.

10 Material in this section relies on Dale, E. (1952) *Planning and Developing the Company Organization Structure*, American Management Association, New York, pp. 28–49; and Newman, W. H., Summer, C. E. and Warren, E. K. (1967) *The Process of Management*, 2nd ed., Prentice-Hall, Inc., Englewood Cliffs, N.J., pp. 43–59.

11 Pfiffner and Sherwood make an interesting distinction between line and staff. The line is *substantive* (direct) in its contribution to the organization's overall objectives, and the staff is *adjective* (indirect) in its contribution. Staff activities are frequently intellectual processes. "The staff person has his time freed to gather data, study, reflect, and come up with solutions arrived at through intellectual processes. He is the thinking and planning arm of the organization. He must inevitably wield power." Pfiffner and Sherwood, *op. cit.*, p. 173.

12 Etzioni, A. (1964) *Modern Organizations*, p. 81. Reprinted by permission of Prentice-Hall, Inc., Englewood Cliffs, N.J.

13 Litterer, J. A. (1965) *The Analysis of Organizations*, John Wiley & Sons, Inc., New York, pp. 223–32.

14 For a discussion of different types of committees in business organizations, see Dale, E. (1967) *Organization*, American Management Association, New York, chap. 10, "Coordination Through Committee", pp. 163–78.

15 Lawrence and Lorsch, *op. cit.*, pp. 1–47. For a detailed look at the relationship between differentiation and integration in a number of other organizations, see Lawrence, P. R. and Lorsch, J. W. (1967) *Organization and Environment*, Division of Research, Graduate School of Business Administration, Harvard University, Boston.

16 Likert, R. (1967) *The Human Organization*, McGraw-Hill Book Company, New York, p. 156.

17 Stinchcombe, A. L. (1965) "Social Structure and Organizations", in March, J. G. (ed.), *Handbook of Organizations*, Rand McNally & Company, Chicago, pp. 143–4.

18 Chandler, A. D., Jr. (1962) *Strategy and Structure*, The MIT Press, Cambridge, Mass.

19 For a discussion of the research on this relationship, see Rushing, W. A. (1967) "The Effects of Industry Size and Division of Labor on Administration", *Administrative Science Quarterly*, September, pp. 273–95.

20 *Ibid.*, p. 292. Also see Rushing, W. A. (1967) "Two Patterns of Industrial Administration", *Human Organization*, Spring–Summer, p. 37.

21 Landsberger, H. A. (1961) "The Horizontal Dimension in Bureaucracy", *Administrative Science Quarterly*, December, p. 300.

22 Sayles, L. R. and Strauss, G. (1966) *Human Behavior in Organizations*, Prentice-Hall, Inc., Englewood Cliffs, N.J., p. 424.

23 Strauss, G. (1962) "Tactics of Lateral Relationship: The Purchasing Agent", *Administrative Science Quarterly*, September, p. 162.

24 Cleland, D. I. (1964) "Why Project Management?", *Business Horizons*, Winter, p. 83.

25 For a discussion of the evolution of the program man-

agement concept, see Kast, F. E. and Rosenzweig, J. E. (1965) "Organization and Management of Space Programs", in Ordway, F. I., III (ed.), *Advances in Space Science and Technology*, Academic Press, Inc., New York, pp. 273–364; and Johnson, R. A., Kast, F. E. and Rosenzweig, J. E. (1967) *The Theory and Management of Systems*, 2nd ed., McGraw-Hill Book Company, chap. 7, "Program Management: Weapon and Space Systems", pp. 133–72.

26 For an extensive report on project management in the aerospace industry, see Steiner, G. A. and Ryan, W. G. (1968) *Industrial Project Management*, The Macmillan Company, New York.

27 Cleland, D. I. and King, W. R. (1968) *Systems Analysis and Project Management*, McGraw-Hill Book Company, New York, p. 239.

28 Middleton, C. J. (1967) "How to Set up a Project Organization", *Harvard Business Review*, March–April, pp. 81–2.

29 There have been numerous examples of the use of this form of management in areas other than the aerospace and defense industries. See, for example, Herrmann, C. C. (1966) "Systems Approach to City Planning", *Harvard Business Review*, September–October, pp. 71–80; and Horvath, W. J. (1966) "The Systems Approach to the National Health Problem", *Management Science*, June, pp. B-391–5.

30 "The 500 Largest U.S. Industrial Corporations", *The Fortune Directory*, June 15, 1968, pp. 2–3.

31 Rourke, F. E. and Brooks, G. E. (1966) *The Managerial Revolution in Higher Education*, The Johns Hopkins Press, Baltimore.

32 Daniel, D. R. (1966) "Reorganizing for Results", *Harvard Business Review*, November–December, p. 96.

33 For a discussion of the growth of these specialized departments, see Glueck, W. F. (1967) "Applied Organization Analysis", *Academy of Management Journal*, September, pp. 223–34.

34 Bennis, W. G. (1966) *Changing Organizations*, McGraw-Hill Book Company, New York, p. 12.

# 17 Analysis for implementation
## by Van Court Hare Jnr.

Most systems analysts find that they introduce change in the systems they study. They correct the faults of malfunctioning systems, or seek to improve an existing system. Or, they design new systems and seek to implement them, displacing older systems by new ones. Indeed, the systems analyst, probably has "the future in his bones", to use C. P. Snow's phrase. Otherwise, he would not have taken up his occupation.

Often such changes greatly broaden the scope of the systems analyst's problem and call upon his knowledge not only of technical possibilities but also of institution and culture.

When we consider this broader subject, discussions of the nature of man, a subject central to most of the great systems of human thought, eventually confront us. Based on assumptions or ideas, usually simplified to suit the times, the concepts of the rational man, the sinful man, the man of will and power, the economic man, and the Freudian man have all become the basis for arguments and theories of human behavior that are still with us in many forms.

The latest trend in building a picture of human nature is to consider "behavioral man", who is defined by the sum total of his observed actions, rather than by assumptions about his character. For our present discussion, this latter viewpoint provides a more varied picture of the human scene and a number of detailed observational results that can be used by the systems analyst. Because all operating systems at one or more stages of their definition, development, analysis, and use are affected by human individuals, knowledge of actual behavior patterns in different circumstances becomes an essential ingredient in understanding how systems come about and how they will be accepted and work in practice.

In what follows we present a sketch of a major cultural conflict and a corresponding discussion of behavioral science man that has meaning for the systems analyst who hopes to implement system change.[1]

## Social science and technological change
Social scientists have long been concerned with the problems of technological change and how they influence the society and the culture in which we live. The reverse problem, of course, is also important because the historical setting, and the tools and ideas presently known, affect the selection of projects considered worthwhile.

In viewing this grand process of technological advancement and social change we generally find a conflict between those who propose change and those who prefer the present state of affairs. In analyzing a given society, for example, it is useful to make a distinction between what Wheelis has called "the instrumental process" and "the institutional process". These are concepts representing two opposing clusters of activities, attitudes, and kinds of criteria for what "good" is. Both processes affect groups within society at a given time, and indeed to a greater or lesser extent they affect the individual at a given time. Thus, our understanding of these processes sheds much light on the ways in which system change may be acceptably introduced, so we shall consider each of them in turn.

## The instrumental process
The instrumental process, which is concerned with "the facts", stresses replication, verifiability, and usefulness in social life. "The authority of the instrumental process is rational, deriving from its demonstrable usefulness to the life process. The final appeal is to the evidence."[2]

The scientific method approximates the heart of the matter, but the instrumental process is a larger concept that concerns the development of tools and techniques (both physical and mental) used to solve problems. Electric saws *and* the differential calculus are both instruments for this purpose. It includes art, both fine and applied, because materials and methods are required in their completion. The instrumental process is bound to reality, facts are facts, it seems to say. Ignoring them is of no avail. Reality can be altered, particularly if it is clearly observed. Indeed, the better one understands it and the more tools one has to deal with it, the more radically it can be changed.[3]

We may not like the facts, but there they are – for better or for worse. Our job is to proceed with the project at hand. As we proceed with the instrumental process, we learn more and develop more tools, which, in turn, increase the output of the instrumental process and the number of possible combinations of what is already available.

The instrumental process is respected because it is useful, productive, growing, and bountiful in many, though not all, spheres of human life. Yet, from an individual or social viewpoint, for very personal reasons, the instrumental process "is often disparaged as mere problem-solving; for the security it creates, though real, is limited".[4] It may be respected, but not loved.

## The institutional process

The institutional process, on the other hand, builds certainty, not doubt, for the individual. It seeks stability, sure-footedness, a rock of ages. Change, particularly rapid change, is shunned.

Thus, both the individual and society build strong barriers, both conscious and unconscious, for protection against change. Most frequently, these barriers seek an authority, organization, or tradition – in short an institution – larger than self or even everyday reality. This institutional process is diametrically opposed to what we have previously called the instrumental process.

> Everything mundane is subject to change, and hence certainty is not to be found in the affairs of men. The searcher arrives at his goal [of certainty], therefore, in a realm of being superordinate to man. Solomon put it succinctly: "Trust in the Lord with all thine heart; and lean not unto thine own understanding." [5]

Although religion is one example of the institutional process, the concept is broader than that. The institutional process includes customs, taboos, rites, mores, ceremonial compulsions, magic, kinship, status, coercive power systems, and such modern institutions as private property and the sovereign state. As such, "The authority of the institutional process is arbitrary; the final appeal is to force."

> In particular, the institutional process is bound to human desire and fear. Wishing will make it so, it seems to say. It is unbearable that no one should care; so there must exist a heavenly Father who loves us. Activities of the institutional process do not, objectively, gratify any need or guard against any danger; incantation does not cause rain to fall or game to be plentiful. But such activities may engender a subjective sense of security, and this has always been a factor to be reckoned with – and, indeed, to be exploited. Honor and prestige accrue to the institutional process; for the security it creates, though illusory, is unlimited.[6]

## Some findings about behavioral science man

The matter is put in a slightly different way by Berelson and Steiner, who, after compiling an inventory of scientific findings in the social sciences, summarize that body of knowledge on "behavioral science man".[7]

> Perhaps the character of behavioral science man can be grasped through his orientation to reality. . . . First, he is extremely good at adaptive behavior – at doing or learning to do things that increase his chances for survival or for satisfaction. . . . But there is another way man comes to terms with reality when it is inconsistent with his needs or preferences. . . . In his quest for satisfaction, man is not just a seeker of truth, but of deceptions, of himself as well as others. . . . When man can come to grips with his needs by actually changing the environment he does so. But when he cannot achieve such "realistic" satisfactions, he tends to take the other path: to modify what he sees to be the case, what he thinks he wants, what he thinks others want.
>
> [In the latter case] he adjusts his social perception to fit not only the objective reality but also what suits his wishes and his needs . . . he tends to remember what fits his needs and expectations . . ., or what he thinks others will want to hear . . .; he not only works for what he wants but wants what he has to work for . . .; his need for psychological protection is so great that he has become expert in "defense mechanisms" . . . he will misinterpret rather than face up to an opposing set of facts or point of view . . .; he avoids the conflicts of issues and ideals whenever he can by changing the people around him rather than his mind . . ., and when he cannot, private fantasies can lighten the load and carry him through . . .; he thinks that his own organization ranks higher than it actually does . . .; and that his own group agrees with him more fully than it does . . .; and if it does not, he finds a way to escape to a less uncongenial world. . . .[8]

The introduction of change, particularly change that seems to the individual beyond his control and which therefore threatens, or reduces perceived security, elicits reactions that are not necessarily logical and that the systems analyst may expect in the course of his work. If the systems analyst proposes change, which is the essence of the instrumental process, he meets the proponents of status quo, for the essence of the institutional process is to stand pat.

Indeed, some institutional processes are so rigid, that the

innovator contests them at his peril. In his *Letters from Earth*, Samuel Clemens wrote,

> We do not know how or when it became custom for women to wear long hair, we only know in this country it *is* the custom, and that settles it. . . . Women may shave their heads elsewhere, but here they must refrain or take the uncomfortable consequences. . . . The penalty may be unfair, unrighteous, illogical, and a cruelty; no matter, it will be inflicted, just the same.[9]

And, some habits are so strongly ingrained that they are impervious to change. Many individuals work at night to avoid change. As one elderly worker, who had worked the night shift for forty years expressed it to the author:

> When I went to work there were no cars on the street, only horses. Wagons and horses. Now there are cars, and too many people. Too many. Why do I work at night? Things never change much at night. In the morning there are cars and people. But, things never change much at night. Who needs those cars and people?

It is interesting that the instrumental and institutional processes described above have been compared to the term *ego* and *superego* used in individual psychoanalysis.

In those terms, the ego represents the executive department of the human personality – the instrumental activities that recognize facts, marshall resources, devise plans of action, and get things done.

The superego is the judicial department, which performs a screening function, directs awareness, vetoes unacceptable proposals, and sets values and effectiveness measures used in goal formation. The superego is institutional in character, and derives its "conscience" from the culture, its customs, habits, and mores.

Most studies show that the conscience so formed is highly relative to the culture or society in which the individual lives.[10]

For many important issues, constraints upon the superego are set by a small group – those near home as it were. Thus, the constraints are greater where families live together for several generations than where they do not, greater in small towns than in large, greater at home than abroad, greater when there are strong religious beliefs or formal institutional ties than when there are none, greater when only one set of values is perceived than when there are many that seem relative to time or place. We are all familiar with acts and common phrases that illustrate these facts.

Things happen in motels that do not happen in homes, and towels are swiped in distant hotels by persons who would not steal a pin in their hometowns. Some persons, indeed, travel for just this purpose – to lose an unwanted reinforcement of conscience. For them wanderlust is not a lust for wandering but a wandering for lust.[11]

Similarly, methods exist for strengthening the superego or judicial function in the personality (and therefore the institutional function in the culture), and also for reducing its effect. Street lights reduce burglaries, and double-entry bookkeeping reduces embezzlement. Conversely, in surroundings where multiple values are evident and where institutional restrictions are consciously relaxed, the range of acceptable value and goal choices increases, leading to a greater variety of possible actions or considerations and to a greater potential for change. Thus, as institutional restrictions become less (and instrumental efforts are, relatively speaking, more respected), new proposals become more easily accepted by those who must approve and use them and vice versa.*

Note also that the capacity of the investigator or the individual to effect system change, or to alter his perception of the facts to suit his needs, is due to his capacity for the creation and manipulation of *symbols*. Language and abstraction form the concepts, ideas, and instructions that permit learning and the transfer of experience (and the very act of systems definition and analysis).

This capacity, which permits the analyst to generalize, also permits him to change the name of the game to suit his needs.

Although it would appear to be a fact that a rose by any other name would smell as sweet, for individuals who view a scene this invariance of description may not hold. A plain ham-and-cheese sandwich may taste better if it is described as a "wedge of cheddar wedded to a generous portion of prime Virginia ham surrounded by California tomatoes and Florida lettuce and a discrete portion of pure egg

---

* The converse effect has interesting psychological implications, although we cannot explore it in detail. For example, when the rate of instrumental change is high in a culture, that area of the individual personality controlled by the superego could be expected to diminish. The individual may thus be involved by a search for certainty in his changing world, yet finds few institutional guides acceptable to him. Wheelis, for example, cites the quest for group consensus and the appeal of mass movements for the individual as evidence of this change in the superego in complex societies. He derives many interesting results from this thesis, one of which is that psychiatry as practiced in many cases treats problems no longer relevant to the present scene. See Wheelis, *op. cit.*, pp. 87–9, and Chapter 7.

mayonnaise". Even though a simple yes or no might suffice, a problem solution may seem more impressive and convincing if crouched in mathematical symbols and presented with a slight but correct accent by a man with a Ph.D. from Cambridge.

But, because our symbols, our abstractions, and our ability to conjure up favorable or unfavorable impressions with a word or gesture are products of our culture, and because the participant-listener's symbols and abstractions are formed by his culture, a knowledge of how symbols are formed and held is the key to our understanding of culture.*

Finally, we should note that institutional problems are magnified as the instrumental process advances with time. Although institutions do change under the impact of technology and instrumental advances, they change slowly and reluctantly, ". . . and make peace, finally, with the conditions which altered them".[12]

But institutional change is *slower* than instrumental change. By the time the institutional process, or the culture, has made peace with instrumental change, ". . . technology has moved on, and the laggard is still trailing".[13] Indeed, the discrepancy between instrumental growth and institutional change becomes worse with time. The combinatorial possibilities of instrumental growth are geometric; more tools, more techniques, more facts, and more concepts lead to a cornucopia of new possibilities. The instrumental process is regenerative, but the institutional process does not partake of this bounty and holds steadfast, unless intimidated, coerced, and pummeled into movement.

The resulting effect is a cultural lag – an ever increasing gulf between what is possible and what is acceptable.[14]

## Introducing change

Changes that alter no dearly held belief, custom, or mode of habitual operation are often introduced with relative ease in highly technical areas. Tools may be redesigned, new production methods may be introduced, new weapons may be brought out; tactics, competitive goals, and impersonal means may all be changed with relative ease. However,

* A culture is most frequently defined by its community of understanding, and may be measured by the frequency of compatible interactions that occur between its members, as indicated by Deutsch, K. W. (1953) *Nationalism and Social Communication*, Technology Press and Wiley, New York. C. P. Snow expressed the same idea in literary terms: "Without thinking about it, they respond alike. That is what culture means." To speak of a cultural lag is perhaps not so descriptive as to speak of a cultural conflict or gap between the instrumental and institutional community of understanding.

primary group relations, territorial and religious stability, systems of prestige, customs, mores, and habits resist activation.

Change is easier to introduce in matters arranged on a scale with narrow intervals than in those arranged in a sharp dichotomy – i.e., when the only answer is black or white. Change is easier to introduce when the elements of change are congenial to the culture, and the society has roughly equivalent substitutes or existing alternatives. Change is easier to introduce through existing institutions rather than through new, through individuals of high prestige and status rather than low, through a third "disinterested" party rather than directly. Change is easier to introduce if it directly affects only a small segment of society, rather than the mass, if its side effects are imperceptible rather than pervasive, and if secrecy instead of full publicity is the rule. Change is easier to introduce in times of crises and stress than in more tranquil times.

In short, the introduction of change is eased if the symbols of change present no apparent alteration or modification of the culture's widely held symbols. Indeed, change is greatly facilitated if the culture's present symbols and instructions reinforce the proposed alterations in operation.

To exploit the cultural symbols of the time or to create others that are only slightly changed but useful, to present a carefully edited story, to obtain the approval of a high-status group for a project, to associate the new development with values already held dear – all of these activities help bridge the cultural gap and make a new proposal acceptable.

*Example:* Pharmaceutical firms have the problem of introducing and marketing new drugs as they are developed and tested. Because many new drugs of a specialized type are introduced each year, the physician is deluged with circulars, samples, and "detail men" explaining the virtues of their products, many of which compete for the same type of treatment. Several drug firms have organized this effort to exploit institutional values held by physicians. Extensive mailing lists are maintained with records on each physician (containing, for example, age, school attended, organizational affiliations, and the like). When a new drug is to be introduced, it is often possible to analyze this list and to compile a relatively shorter list of former professors or maestros who represent a higher status group. If the maestros react favorably to the new drug – and their smaller number makes them easier to convince with limited resources – then their approval can have a strong institutional influence in making the technological advance acceptable to the total list.

*Example:* The elimination of elevator operators (by the substitution of push buttons) to reduce operating costs may well be spoken of as an attempt to improve passenger service, to increase passenger comfort, and to reduce delays in the lobby. The acceptable symbols are stressed, and the less acceptable image of a mercenary landlord throwing old retainers out of work is played down.

Another benefit derives from these seemingly devious devices. Change is easier to introduce in form than in substance: When imposed "from the outside" the forced change may result in overt compliance, but covert resistance. If the proposed change can be made to come "from the inside" (or seem to), the form and the substance of change are more likely to coincide. The change is also more likely to be permanent and not to be a mere verbal acquiescence until the analyst has gone.

Anthropologists also tell us that in the evolution of a culture pattern action comes first and values second. We begin to like what we do. Thus, it is frequently easier to change the values of individuals concerned with a system by alteration of their activities rather than by a direct attack upon their beliefs.

*Example:* When a system's users are unfamiliar with it they may be afraid of it, and thus hold it in low esteem. However, *after* experiencing success with its use they become more optimistic about their ability to influence their own future, and the values employed by the users in assessment of the system change. Consequently, instead of describing the virtues of a new product or system, a demonstration model is put in the user's hands so that he may convince himself of its value.

Similarly, if behavior can be changed, a change in values usually follows more easily than if the reverse procedure is followed.

*Example:* These alternate approaches to change are evident in the policies of the Eisenhower and Johnson administrations with regard to racial discrimination. The Eisenhower policy was that social values would change with time, leading to later changes in behavior. The argument for this approach is that when the behavioral change does occur, it will be permanent because it is reinforced by the individual's value structure. The Johnson administration, on the other hand, in urging stronger legislation against discrimination, sought to change behavior from which a change in values would emerge. It is argued that the latter

course produces permanent social change more swiftly than the former, although covert resistance may be expected at the outset.

When introducing change in large-scale systems and organizations, policies are much easier to change than procedures. This observation, made by many professional administrators and systems analysts,[15] does not contradict what has just been said, but blends instrumental considerations with it.

First, the detail and variety of specific changes that must be made in procedures to obtain a given result frequently exceed the resources of the controller. And, because procedures usually adapt themselves to the demands of policy, much more can be accomplished in a given time with limited resources by the policy-change approach, leaving resources available for the adjustment of critical procedures when necessary.

But, perhaps more important, a change in policy rather than in detailed procedure, leaves some freedom, although it may be illusory, for the individual to adjust to the proposed change. His values and institutional roadblocks are not directly confronted, and he is more likely to accept "his own" adjustments as good ones.

For similar reasons, making a few large-scale policy changes is often easier and more effective than instituting many small changes. The few major changes can be controlled, and the individual does not develop the frustrations, confusions, and value disturbances that a series of harassing minor alterations will produce.

## Problems of implementation

Without going further, it would appear from what has been said that many repetitive difficulties arise when certain kinds of change are proposed and introduced, and that from this experience much has been learned about social and cultural changes. Moreover, numerous techniques and artifices may be used in easing the introduction of instrumental change and in mitigating institutional obstacles. Yet the field is an open one, and much remains to be done.

If this is so, it would appear reasonable to conduct analyses aimed at the implementation of specific systems, or at specific systems improvements – so-called action research – whenever system innovation and improvement are proposed.

For example, the efforts of political scientists and public relations firms to elect a given political candidate, to ease passage of a school bond issue to reduce racial discrimination, or to promote the fluoridation of drinking water represent research of this type in the social sciences. Market and advertising research also has the same "action" flavor. The same may be said for the use of psychological tests and research in personnel selection for given occupations. The research is not "disinterested" in its outcome; it is purposeful and goal directed.

Such activities, which we prefer to call analysis for implementation, are often shunned by the scientist (for reasons we shall mention hereafter), although, for a particular purpose and stated objective, analysis for implementation may greatly increase the success of a technical advance, discovery, or improvement.

For example, even relatively simple system changes may raise questions for which the uninitiated analyst is unprepared. The automobile owner hesitates to spend more funds on his car because his children are sick, so he believes the car will run another year – even though the mechanic knows objectively that the vehicle is potentially dangerous. What is the mechanic to do? The patient hesitates to have the clearly indicated operation and believes he will get better. Should the physician retire after stating the bald facts? Persons who have not experienced the disasters of a tornado, flood, or large explosion tend to deny or to disbelieve warnings that danger is near. They search for more information, and often ". . . interpret signs of danger as signs of familiar normal events until it is too late to take effective precautions." [16] Should the weather man report his scientific conclusions and make no interpretation or exhortation to his listeners to take care? A system that takes care of today's conditions is installed, but it does not provide for future contingencies or for "updating" the system as conditions change with time. Later the system efficiently performs functions no longer relevant to prevailing conditions, with possibly disastrous consequences. Should the analyst not concern himself with these problems of implementation and use?

## Should the analyst concern himself with the problems of cultural change?

There are many scientists, and thus many systems analysts, who would, on serious grounds, take issue with the proposal that the investigator concern himself with the use made of his work. Rational investigation and logical decision cannot take place, they argue, if one has a vested interest in obtaining a given outcome. This position is strongly held by science as an institution because of the historical struggle to free science, and the instrumental process, from the constraints, the dogma, and the myth-making of institutions.

There is yet another reason for the strength of this position. As older institutional constraints have been removed, others have come into play as the individual searches for the universal certainty which the rational process cannot supply.

For example, a vote of the majority or a mass movement may threaten the dispassionate scientific pursuit just as much as constraints imposed by a monarch or the clergy. The mathematician does not arrive at a problem solution by conducting a public opinion poll on the street and averaging the answers obtained, even if those polled are other mathematicians! The test is different. It depends upon the demands of a verifiable procedure, not the beliefs of any individuals, regardless of their reputation, their power, their eminence, or their number.* If in his choice of variables or the development of alternatives (both of which are subtle selection processes) the scientist consciously begins to favor or exclude one group of possibilities for institutional reasons, or if he must shade his thinking, model building, and verification to meet institutional constraints, he has abandoned the basic tenets of science. Surely, he says, many new discoveries that might otherwise be his will be lost, or worse he will be deluded and falsely evaluate what he observes.

The scientist may also argue that his energies are limited. To worry about implementation will not only debase his pursuit of knowledge but will also embroil him in a conflict of personal values that will consume his limited resources in a wasteful fashion. How can he simultaneously be a myth-maker and an iconoclast?

The dilemma presented by arguments for and against research for implementation is well known, and although exaggerated here for effect it is nevertheless real. The scientist–analyst may choose to avoid the problems of implementation altogether, but someone will implement the results of his work, or not, and the job may be done well, or poorly, depending upon how well the analyst and the implementer understand each other.†

---

* For example, one test for an instrumental versus an institutional process is whether a conclusion is validated by the success of a procedure or the agreement of an individual or group in society. Thus, if a surgeon sets a broken arm, that is first aid. If the nurse performs an appendectomy, that is nevertheless surgery. First aid and surgery are instrumental. If a priest administers the sacrament with wine and wafers, it is a holy ceremony; but if a lay person performs the same act, it is a sacrilege. A marriage performed by an unlicensed individual is invalid. The latter procedures are institutional.

† An interesting sidelight on this problem is the reluctance of professional people to engage in politics, an attitude encouraged by the Federal Tax Policy. ". . . Federal tax policy forbids

## Leadership and organization to bridge the cultural gap

One resolution of this difficulty – which almost always arises in applications of management science and operations research, to name one area of systems analysis – is to conduct a project with mixed teams of investigators, some of whom have instrumental skills, and others who have institutional skills. These skills when shared in the work group bridge the interface between the two worlds and permit a smoother transition between problem definition, analysis, and implementation.

Many organizations use similar devices to bridge the gap between instrumental and institutional requirements. For example, often an organization has two leaders instead of one, although one man may be apparently in charge. The role played by one leader is to institute instrumental change. The role played by the other leader is to represent the institutional requirements of the organization and the component individuals. When the instrumental leader causes friction, the institutional leader smooths it over or rephrases the requirements in more acceptable, warmer, more congenial, or more orthodox terms. It matters little who is the obvious leader, so long as the two cooperate (and can stand each other)! Together they will be able to produce more change in the organization than either could accomplish individually. The family unit, to come closer to home, offers a similar example of dual leader effectiveness in creating change in the habits of the young.

A final example from intelligence operations is interesting because it illustrates the power of the same approach, employed to different ends.

*Example:* Many of the intelligence services of the world employ a method of interrogation in which two interrogators, each employing a distinctly different role characterization, alternately confront the subject. The first man, for example, may affect a stern air, a military costume with riding boots and crop, a crew cut, an air of efficiency and dispatch, and a stern, cruel disposition. As the perfect martinet, he demands the subject talk at once or be shot at dawn, withdraws all physical comfort, inflicts various ap-

parent physical and mental tortures – just as the subject might anticipate. Finally, in exasperation, ordering the firing squad to be assembled, the first interrogator leaves the room. Very likely he has learned nothing, and expected to learn nothing, from the subject. After some time, the second interrogator enters. He is an entirely different type. Dressed in baggy tweeds, probably smoking a pipe, he seems distressed with the subject's plight, orders some food to be brought at once, produces cigarettes, offers apologies for the abruptness of his colleague, and settles down to commiserate with his unfortunate friend. He may offer some personal experiences of his own, some philosophies and observations on life and his friend's present plight. But then, he is unavoidably called from the room, and the subject is again alone. He did not expect this. As the night wears on, the alternate presences continue. First he is threatened, then he is consoled. In the end, although some time may be required, the subject begins to change: He sees the constraints of his former world as less important than before, his values begin to seem irrelevant to his present state, he may even be convinced of the error of his ways and seek to explain himself in his defense. Then he talks, as was intended, most likely to his tweedy friend who in fact was the instrument of the subject's change.*

Little more can be said here on this topic, but the administrator of systems analysis projects who seeks to blend instrumental and institutional skills for a given study can benefit from further study of the dual role approach to organization.

## Organization of data for implementation

To continue, let us suppose the investigator is concerned with the problems of implementation, and that his concern is to anticipate problems that may occur in a specific case, rather than to worry in general.

Many of the examples and points cited in our next few pages follow from underestimates of institutional power to affect routine and emergency operations of instrumental processes.

## Why are implementation data scarce?

In most specific cases, the selection of treatments and the anticipation of specific problems and reactions requires high technical competence and experience in a given field. Nevertheless, in a given field, the data of past experience can be organized in an orderly fashion and "what if"

---

charitable deductions of gifts to organizations engaged in promoting or opposing legislation. Thus, for example, the bulk of foundation money goes to organizations that conduct research, and financial aid for organizations that take public positions, however worthy, is hard to come by. As a result, lobbies representing private interests operate freely and effectively, while those groups that might represent the public interest stay out of politics." Abrams, C. (1965). "The City Planner and the Public Interest", *Columbia University Forum.*

* For an extensive discussion of interrogation and training methods in this form of intelligence operation, see Pinto O. (1952) *Spy-Catcher,* Harper, New York.

questions can be asked for specific analyses of implementation. For example, the collection of symptom–cause relationships described in Chapter 11 might be a typical example for this type of display. (Problem characteristics would then replace symptoms, and probable difficulties would replace causes.)

However, in collecting data for implementation, the purpose of the collection is expanded. The emphasis is not on the apparent difficulties and present symptoms, but on those that *might* appear in the future, or that have been known to occur in the past, given specified side conditions.

In medicine, for example, certain treatments or drugs are known to be "counterindicated" when the patient has a given past history, and these counterindications are reported and publicized in the profession.

In the same way, certain forms of system alteration or modification are known to raise given problems with great regularity. When information systems are installed, or when decision-making processes are analyzed and changed, we encounter the same problems over and over again.

Unfortunately, in the latter case, published warnings and admonitions are uncommon. The investigator who analyzes and installs business systems, for example, is seldom forewarned against probable pitfalls, and he seldom has organized, published data to aid his implementation work. We may have diagnostic aids for hardware maintenance, and for trouble-shooting in many fields. However, there has been little emphasis to date on the diagnosis of conceptual or decision-making failures on the part of the analyst when he implements systems change. Where such data are available, the files are kept secret or transmitted from one worker to another as an art – for institutional reasons which should be obvious from our previous discussion in this chapter.

For example, from the 35,000 or so electronic computer installations made in the United States in the past ten years much has been learned and published about electronic difficulties, hardware reliability, component failures, and design defects. Yet little, if anything, has been reported in an organized form about the many specific failures of the systems that have been installed – if those failures were due to faulty decision-making, inadequate system conception, or lack of individual experience and foresight. Little, if anything, has been published about the specific difficulties those systems have encountered as times have changed. Not only is the nature of such data collection and organization difficult, but institutional barriers also prevent publicity. The physician does not testify against his colleagues except within the instrumental framework and the

users and manufacturers of computing equipment are not likely to publicize their failures except when the onus can fall upon the hardware details, and frequently not then. The available data are locked in consultants' files, or in the notebooks of internal investigators. The auditor has his check list of devious practices to look for, but he is not likely to publish a statistical account of his, or his clients', difficulties and shortcomings.

The point of these illustrations is that such compilation of problems, even if maintained privately by the investigator, can be a powerful tool in anticipating and preventing a repetition of implementation difficulties. The construction of such a listing is thus one of the major steps in analysis for implementation. It is a valuable step if the result is only a list. It is an even more valuable tool for the analyst, in a given case, if the broad listing can be classified and cross referenced in a hierarchy of problem types, with specific classifications for the anticipated problems of specific system types. In such a tabulation it would be seen that many of the specified problem areas arise when instrumental and institutional processes meet at an interface, when man-and-machine or man-and-man meet.

## A problem anticipation file

To illustrate one such listing, we now present a selected group of implementation problems that are general enough to provide both a manageable list and a set of categories for further development. For each of these categories, we provide an example.

The reader may add his own examples to this outline. Our aim in the following presentation is to suggest a set of major problems to anticipate in a wide variety of systems implementations, and to leave further development to the reader. The categories chosen are taken from a composite of systems analysis problems in several fields, and are presented in the form of questions to stimulate further discussion and thought.

## 1 Are the objectives and constraints perceived by the investigator the same as those perceived by the organization?

Frequently, differences in cultural background and the conflict between professional and administrative interests cause the systems analyst to solve the wrong problem. This most subtle of systems mistakes happen too frequently – even when the problem of analysis is stated in writing and agreed to by the analyst and the user – that great care must be taken to reach a common understanding of what is needed.

The trouble is usually not so obvious as maximizing profit instead of minimizing cost, although that type of error is frequent enough. Usually, an objective is stated formally by the system user, but perhaps incorrectly or incompletely. So, the analyst may not at first perceive constraints that the user imposes upon acceptable solutions, or, conversely, he may anticipate constraints that are not in fact considered important. He may often be purposefully deluded.

*Example:* A major oil company sought a scientific procedure for locating filling stations as new stations were added to the distribution system. Initially, the objective was to locate stations that would return at least a minimum return on investment, as specified by the firm's management. A procedure that included many factors, among them estimated sales of petroleum products at the proposed stations, was developed. Check of the new procedure indicated that it would locate stations more consistently and reliably than less organized methods. However, the new procedure was rejected by the executives charged with station location. After some time these executives revealed the method was not suitable to them because it included forecasts of station sales, and this limited executive flexibility in acquiring new locations. As it turned out the true objective was to add 200–300 new stations to the system each year. Many proposed station locations could not make the required return on investment, and competition for good locations was severe. Knowing that the computed return on investment was based on internal transfer prices, which also included contributions to profit, the executives often inflated the estimate of station sales to get around what they felt was an unrealistic investment requirement and come up with the required number of new additions (which otherwise would not have been possible). Had the proposed method taken these facts into account, the systems analysis project might have been implemented, rather than rejected. It is not surprising in this instance that proposals for follow-up studies to compare predicted sales and investment return against actual values were also rejected.

The analyst may avoid this pitfall or sidestep it in many cases by investigating in advance alterations in constraints and objectives that may be of possible interest, and by determining how the problem solution is affected by alternate problem statements. He may find that the problem statement contains many noncritical factors, learn which factors are critical, and be prepared for the presentation of alternate proposals should they be required.

Because of his training and knowledge of methodology, the analyst may also tend to frame problem objectives and constraints to make his job easier, unwittingly leading also to the solution of the wrong problem. The work may be professionally competent and workmanlike in every respect, but it may also be irrelevant to the present need. The cliché that the right problem solved approximately is a better result than the wrong problem solved precisely is a fair warning. Most major problems of systems implementation are introduced at the beginning, when the wrong objectives and constraints are assumed in a system definition.*

There is another reason for looking carefully into the goals, objectives, and constraints to be used in a systems analysis project or design. The implications of the chosen goals, objectives, and constraints may not be clearly understood at the outset and a solution which seems desirable at first may in fact be fraught with difficulties that once commenced are difficult to overcome.

For example, when automatic or automated systems are given a goal, it is, as the late Norbert Wiener observed, like invoking a form of magic. The goal is interpreted literally, and the full implications of a given instruction or objective must be understood by the analyst if he is to stave off embarrassment and woe.

Folklore, for example, contains stories – ranging from the *Sorcerer's Apprentice* to the *Monkey's Paw* – in which magic, once begun, was difficult or impossible to turn off. The Apprentice learned the words to bring magic to the alleviation of his workday tasks, but forgot how to stop the magic broom and the magic pail of water from overdoing their appointed tasks. (Fortunately, he was saved by the Master's return.) In the *Monkey's Paw* and many similar tales, three wishes were granted. In each case, the first wish was fulfilled, but with unsuspected side effects. And usually in these stories the last two wishes were used to undo the horrors created by the fulfillment of the first.

Thus, at the outset, the analyst should beware lest he have King Midas' touch.

## 2 *Are the effectiveness measures used in the analyses appropriate?*

Since goals are formulated from sets of values or effectiveness measures, the measures used may be incorrectly chosen and throw off the analysis.

---

* "At first it is impossible for the novice to cast aside the minor symptoms, which the patient emphasizes as his major ones, and to perceive clearly that one or two facts that have been belittled in the narration of the story of the illness are in reality the stalk about which everything else in the case must be made to cluster." Herbert Amory Hare (1899) *Practical Diagnosis*, Lea Brothers, Philadelphia.

*Example:* A classic example, reported by Morse and Kimball [17] from their World War II experience, concerns the installation of antiaircraft guns on merchant vessels. On the one hand, guns installed on these ships were so "in-effective" as to be useless; on the other hand, they made the crews feel safer. Because the guns were expensive and were needed elsewhere, their removal was proposed. Indeed, data on equipped and nonequipped ships showed that only 4% of attacking planes were shot down, a dismal figure that served to indicate the guns were not worth installing or keeping aboard. On second thought, however, it was apparent that the percentage of planes shot down was not the correct effectiveness measure for the guns. Guns were installed on the ship *to protect the ship*, and the proper measure was whether the ship was damaged less with or without a gun. Analyses of the observed data in this light showed the guns definitely increased the ship's chance of survival. Even though the antiaircraft guns did not often shoot down the attacking planes, a gun's use lowered attack accuracy, reduced damage, and often saved the ship. The change of measure changed the decision, and the ships were equipped with guns.

A typical error in selecting effectiveness measures is to scale alternatives by their ability to reach a given objective without regard to the resources consumed, or to seek a resource measure only without regard to effectiveness. The property of "cost-effectiveness", which gives the contribution to effectiveness per unit resource, is often used to remove this problem. Even then, it is essential that the "effectiveness" measure be the one desired.[18]

### 3 *Are the attention and awareness functions of the system correctly oriented?*

Newly designed systems or organizations and those that have been in operation for some time can suffer from problems of incorrect awareness or goal rigidity, generally described as "fixation" problems. Goal-directed systems have some form of goal setting and holding function. And, because a system's awareness of alternate possible courses of action, forms of organization, and other goal and value possibilities limits the types of goals and values that will be formulated, goal setting and holding functions of a system can be affected by these factors.

*Example:* If the reader will tightly hold the thumb of his left hand in his closed left fist, and close his eyes, he will after a time "feel" that his thumb is larger than the other four fingers combined. This "perception" of the size or importance of the thumb, were it constant, could easily

alter the individual's work habits, selection of desirable jobs, and even his sensory view of the world about him. The pictures drawn by children, which seem distorted to adults but realistic to children, are another example of how awareness and perception affect the organization of behavior. The senses most acutely tuned to a given scene, and the "mix" of a system's sensory input types can greatly affect behavior and goal-setting functions. An analysis of the nerve structure of the pig would cause an analyst to believe that the pig considers his snout a very important information source. The pig thus "views the world through his nose". Several authors have discussed this problem of perception and awareness in different contexts.[19]

Difficulties arise if the data required to solve a given problem are not available, are not sought, or are not perceived "realistically", i.e., with respect to the system's survival and growth.

Similarly, the methods used for combining data, generating new goals and values, and updating presently used objectives may cause trouble. On the one hand, the goal setting process may be too rigid. Like the driver who locks his steering wheel and drives over the cliff, many systems can reach disaster if erroneous goal locking is present. On the other hand, lack of goal stability is also a problem. Then, the system acts like a small child who first picks up one toy, then another, in a succession of unrelated activities.

*Example:* During World War II, and even today, postmasters throughout the country are ordered to watch the mail of certain individuals. During the war individuals suspected of Nazi leanings were put on "watch lists". Ten years after the war, some of these lists were still in use because the original orders had not been withdrawn. Obsolete reports, procedures, and objectives may also be found in most large-scale systems.

The shortcomings illustrated in this section can be alleviated by improving the quality of system inputs, and by focusing attention on the procedures the system uses for formulating and updating goals to meet changed conditions.

### 4 *Have operating standards been developed for the system?*

If operating standards are not developed when a system is implemented and installed, particularly in lower level operations, errors or deviations cannot be corrected. As a result, even minor deviations create a crisis. Lack of specifications and documented standards for component operations can cause the system to get out of hand, and to deviate unexpectedly and unpredictably from its over-all purpose,

In short, planning, control, and design are virtually impossible without the use of standards.

Hardware systems analysts take great pains to provide detailed operating specifications and standards for their equipment. Of equal or greater importance are standards in procedure and information handling systems.

*Example:* The frequent underestimates of computer programing costs, research and development completion times, and the effort required to introduce new products are examples of cases where even approximate standards could have prevented implementation mistakes. Monitoring these processes against standards for segments of the total job can usually reduce the error between projected and actual cost, completion dates, and promised performance specifications. Should deviations be noted early in the procedure, the projected time, cost, or performance estimates can be revised, or corrective action can be taken early enough to prevent serious problems.[20]

## 5 *Are vital system processes protected against danger or failure?*

To lose a leg is not so serious as decapitation. In one instance you can carry on, in the other you cannot. The problem of guarding vital control and flow processes against loss or failure is equally serious for the human being, the organization, the hardware system, or the information system. Systems that do not protect these vital processes against damage and the vicissitudes of the environment do not survive, or have difficulty retaining stable continuity of operation.

*Example:* An extreme example is the protection provided for a military communications center. The new combat operations center of the North American Defense Command (NORAD) is buried deep inside Colorado's 9656 foot Chevenne mountain and protected against any predictable hazards from enemy sabotage to a direct hit by a nuclear bomb. Thirteen computers, each independent, are able to pick up the work of others in case of failure. The installation is shielded against radioactivity and the electromagnetic effects of nuclear explosions. Power, water, food, fuel, and other essential supplies are stored in gigantic reserves. Houses and rooms within the mountain are set on four-foot springs of three-inch steel to protect personnel and equipment from the shock of a blast or an earthquake. The tunnels and chambers that house the central communications and control center of the military defense effort for the nation are 1400 feet under the mountain top.[21]

Because critical, higher-order systems processes usually involve human operators, the continuity and stability of service of these individuals is often guarded or planned for in systems implementation.

*Example:* In one large order-processing system 90 sales officers were connected by teletype to a central office, where orders, received as punched paper tape, were re-routed and scheduled to plants through what is called a "torn-tape filter center". The operation of this center, which was current technology in the late 1950's, required operators to read, tear, and redispatch messages on short lengths of paper tape. These operators, at the heart of the information system, were clearly critical to the success of the operation. Employee turnover, divided loyalty, and similar problems that might affect the operation of this vital spot were virtually eliminated by recruiting as operators only divorced women with several children who had never worked for the company or with the equipment before. Trained in these special tasks and held together by their common economic need and background, the girls hired remained on the payroll for many years, and turnover, absences, and job dissatisfaction were astonishingly rare.

## 6 *Has adequate provision been made for updating the system?*

Installed systems often have many components or adjustable elements "set" at the time of installation. As time passes, these settings may no longer be appropriate to the system's condition of operation, so the system fails.

*Example:* The November 9, 1965, electrical blackout of the eastern seaboard was traced to a relay located at the Ontario Hydroelectric Commission's distribution plant at Queenston, Ontario, near Niagara Falls. According to the Federal Power Commission's report, the Ontario relay was set to operate a circuit breaker if the power load exceed 375 million watts. It was set at this point in 1963 and was not reviewed. Subsequently, the average power load on the line controlled by the relay increased to 356 million watts, and thus an ordinary upward fluctuation in power tripped the relay and started the whole blackout.[22]

Similar difficulties occur in systems and operating organizations when policies have not been reviewed and are no longer appropriate, when decision making is based on obsolete data, when component operation has deteriorated from design values, when system structure has changed with time but without the analyst's knowledge, or when the goals and values of the system are not kept current with present requirements.

## 7 Is the system protected against direct falsification or illicit interruption?

Although information errors can occur in many parts of a system, either from mechanical failure or human mistake, there are usually several ways in which to introduce false information into the system purposefully or to intercept confidential information for competitive purposes.

*Example:* Inventory control systems depend upon correct reports of sales so that orders may be related to demand. However, when reports of sales are made by distributors or agents who have inventory "on consignment" and who collect from customers before remitting to a central source, some direct or indirect alteration of the data may be expected.

For example, commission agents frequently delay reports of sales and use the collected funds as working capital as long as possible. In other situations commission agents were found to be reporting and paying for bulk sales when in fact package goods of the same item were often sold at a higher price. The difference was eventually detected, but the errors were blamed on the computing and inventory system. Similar shading of input data may be expected if there is a strong conflict of objectives and values at an information interface. For this reason, some manufacturers operate their own distribution facilities so that accurate data inputs to data control systems can be assured.

In a similar way, when the competitive objective of organization and system differ strongly, information protection problems arise.[23]

*Example:* Communications systems, such as telephone lines, computers, teleprinters, and similar devices, all radiate energy as they work. These signals can often be captured and decoded by an industrial spy, usually with little chance of detection. For example, a teletype machine generates sparks as it prints. Even when located in a shielded room, its signals can be detected from several miles away, and reproduced with suitable equipment if security precautions are not taken. The problem of information protection is increased when information processing facilities are shared, as is the case in real-time computing centers. Planning for the World Trade Center in New York, where computer systems on every ten floors will be shared, includes protection against monitoring systems. Every computer system for defense operations must be protected against monitoring, according to the specification of FED-STD-222 and DCAENS 422-5s, the contents of which are known only to those with clearance. Less exotic forms of data falsification and theft (as well as material spoilage and theft) often present difficulties that are overlooked. For example, material theft, damage, hoarding, and similar activities can cause major data errors in inventory control systems.

## 8 Are operators actually performing according to the system definition and plan?

Many systems have not performed as predicted because an essential operation was not performed by an operator or group of operators according to the plan assumed by the systems analyst.

*Example:* Electronic computers are often used to calculate minimum-flight-time and minimum-fuel flight plans for commercial aircraft. These plans take into account weather, wind, load, and similar factors, and are prepared for the pilot just before takeoff. When first introduced, the time and fuel reductions predicted by these schemes failed to materialize. The question arose as to whether the optimizing computations were in error or whether pilot adherence to the computer plan was unsatisfactory. An investigation of the latter problem led to increased pilot cooperation, and the predicted savings were at last obtained.

## 9 Will the system accept and act upon signs of impending disaster?

Although the desire for survival and perpetuation is often strong in organizations and individuals, and is often designed into procedural and hardware systems, this survival or continuity of operation is often threatened when the system fails to act or delays action in response to clear signs of danger.

There are cases in which the system is not "aware" of impending danger because such input data are not received or sought. But even when such data are in hand, many technical and institutional blocks can prevent correct evaluation and acceptance in time for adequate action. For example, the required pieces of intelligence information may be on the "desks" of several intelligence analysts who do not individually see the emerging pattern of danger and dismiss the isolated pieces of intelligence as unimportant. The organizational leader may have surrounded himself with weak yes-men who fail to tell him the truth. There may be technical delays in transmission, reception, and decoding and possible mistakes along the way. But even when these faults are overcome, the executive, the operator, or the control system often cannot, or will not, accept and act quickly upon the fact that disaster is at hand.

The following is reported in some detail as a modern and classic example of this often neglected implementation problem.

*Example:* In the major eastern power failure of November 9, 1965, previously mentioned, the first signs of failure were at 5.16.11 pm when service was interrupted to only portions of upstate New York and Ontario.

There was a period of some 7 minutes to 12 minutes between the initial disturbance at 5.16 pm when the service to the various portions of southern New York and New England finally collapsed. The operators at the various dispatching centers all knew after 5.16 on November 9 that the frequency on their system was going down and that the load had reversed and was placing a large drain on their generating reserves. . . .

The night of the blackout a 62-year-old Con Edison Engineer, Edwin J. Nellis, who has been with the [New York City] utility for 41 years, was on duty at Con Edison's automated Energy Control Center on Manhattan's West Side. At 5.16 pm, the lights dimmed, and Mr. Nellis called for an instrument check, which showed nothing wrong with Con Edison's generating equipment.

Checking his instruments again, Mr. Nellis noticed a surge of power in from the north, then a surge outward. Con Edison officials report that he immediately called the Niagara Mohawk Company in Syracuse to determine what the trouble was. At the same time he was ordering all 12 Con Edison generating plants to peak power output – to handle any extra demand should the trouble be serious.

Meanwhile, three other stations in the power network, or grid – a station in Flushing, Queens, one in Rockland County and one in Orange County – were reporting troubles of their own to Mr. Nellis.

It was then that the lights dimmed a second time, and instruments showed a tremendous surge of power into New York, then out again. Mr. Nellis was now on the phone to Syracuse, which told him "of trouble to the north".

On hearing this, he told Syracuse, "I'm going to cut clear of you," and began pushing the first of eight buttons to cut Con Edison away from the rest of the grid. He also began ordering Con Edison's network stations – 42 in all – to shed their loads. He was too late, and in just 2.5 seconds New York City was blacked out – at 5.28 pm.

. . . In retrospect," the [Federal Power Commission] report said, "it seems likely that a timely shedding of the load in some sections of New York might have avoided a citywide blackout and the breakdown of service elsewhere, as well as facilitating restoration of service. But whether because of lack of clarity in the control room instrumentation or for other reasons, the system operator did not make an immediate clear-cut decision in this emergency."

In reply, Charles E. Eble, president of Con Edison, insisted that the company's operators "followed established procedures and in our opinion made proper and timely decisions in the short space of time available to them".

However, the automatic controls on Con Edison's generators, as T. H. White aptly observed for *Life Magazine*, were quicker "to protect their own". They cut out by themselves when the survival of their generators was threatened by the massive heat of extreme overload.[24]

## 10 *Have potential difficulties at the boundaries of functions, departments, components or modules have adequately "bridged"?*

The analyst may in general expect difficulty in system implementation when his system crosses functions or boundaries. Although this statement is true of hardware systems – more interfaces or intercommunications between components generally mean more potential trouble – it is particularly true for procedural and information processing systems that cut across organizational boundaries. Additional care in implementation is always needed to bridge these sources of potential system disruption. Severe measures or implementation decisions may be required if the "boundary problem" is aggravated by a man-machine interface.

*Example:* To avoid such boundary problems at the outset, many systems analysts take the position that a new procedural or information system should be designed either to be completely manual and so simple that any operator can understand it or, at the other extreme, so automated that no human intervention is required in the intermediate steps from input to output. Many failures with combinations of manual and automated steps are the basis for this conclusion.

## 11 Has the analyst correctly evaluated his own resources in relation to the task of analysis and implementation?

Gross underevaluation of the time, cost, and personnel requirements for system development and installation is unfortunately the rule for projects specified by performance standards. Similarly, overoptimism is often the rule when a systems project is proposed with fixed resources. Usually too much is attempted with too little, with the frequent result that the project flounders, and this leads to general disappointment and losses.

*Example:* The installation of even a modest data processing facility will take about two years, on the average, although many firms, to their regret, frequently make estimates of a year or less. The many steps required in preparing for a changeover to the computer system invariably bring snags that prolong the effort and raise its cost beyond what was expected.

Similar problems occur when the analysts' range of actions is smaller than is required to handle the system he confronts, and an assessment of this relationship – discussed further in Chapter 6 of the original book – is in order, particularly when implementation, with its greater variety of difficulties, is confronted.

Finally, systems implementation is subject to many threshold effects that raise questions of resource availability. Often a little implementation does no good, and a basic minimum of resources must be committed to assure any degree of success. If this minimum is not available, attempts at implementation are usually wasted, an economic fact of life of which the analyst should be aware.

## 12 Is the system chosen for analysis and implementation big enough?

The scope of a system considered may not be large enough to result in any major improvement, or worse, it may lead to unwanted suboptimization. In addition, the costs in-involved in system analyses and implementation are often relatively fixed after a certain threshold of resources is reached, and may not vary thereafter directly with the size of the system considered. Thus, major improvements or large-scale improvements may be no more costly than lesser efforts, although the payoff can be much greater.

*Example:* The design of an inventory control system for a small company with 1000 items requires almost as much effort as one for a larger company with 10,000 or 100,000 items, although the absolute dollar improvements in the latter case will usually be much greater. The hardware and paper conversion will be somewhat more costly in the latter case, but development problems, personnel problems, and the political problems of installation are essentially the same. This fact usually places the larger firm in a better position to use systems analysis than the smaller firm.

In the same way, the analyst within an organization should look for systems improvements that will produce the largest payoff first, and should shun forms of implementation that offer a small return in relation to the cost of analysis and implementation.

For institutional reasons, the reverse strategy is often unwisely chosen. ("Do a series of small projects to prove the worth of research to the organization.") Although this may appear at first to make good political sense, the result is often not as expected. Both the analysts and the organization become discouraged with the lack of demonstrable and dramatic return from the costs incurred after a time. The bold choice carries the risk of dramatic failure as well as dramatic gain; but the piecemeal approach carries the risk that the results of the smaller efforts are not measurable above the noise inherent in a system's reporting and evaluation procedures.

Thus, there is a minimum size for systems analysis projects set, on the one hand, by the threshold cost of analysis and implementation and, on the other hand, by the need for measurable results, which often must be dramatic to be noticed.

## References

[1] This discussion is abstracted basically from two sources: Wheelis, A. (1958) *The Quest for Identity*, Norton, New York, and Victor Gollancz Ltd., London, especially Chapter III, and Berelson, B. and Steiner, G. A. (1964) *Human Behavior: An Inventory of Scientific Findings*, Harcourt, Brace & World, New York. The Wheelis book is a discussion of current psychiatric and cultural problems. Berelson and Steiner report 1045 experimental and observational findings from which general conclusions are drawn in Chapter 17. There, confirming cross references to the literature may be found in abundance.

[2] Wheelis, *op. cit.*, p. 74.

[3] Wheelis, *op. cit.*, p. 75.

[4] Wheelis, *op. cit.*, p. 75.

[5] Wheelis, *op. cit.*, p. 74.

[6] Wheelis, *op. cit.*, p. 75.

[7] Berelson and Steiner, *op. cit.*, Chapter 17.

[8] Berelson and Steiner, *op. cit.*, pp. 663–4.

[9] Clemens, S., *Letters from Earth* as quoted in Berelson and Steiner, *op. cit.*, p. 642.

[10] For example, see the cases summarized by Berelson and Steiner, *op. cit.*, Chapter 17.

[11] Wheelis, *op. cit.*, p. 101. In 10 months of 1965 the Americana

Hotel in New York City is reported to have lost 38,000 demitasse spoons, 20,000 towels, and 475 bibles to its guests. *New York Daily News*, January 24, 1966, p. 23.

[12] Wheelis, *op. cit.*, p. 82.

[13] Wheelis, *op. cit.*, p. 82.

[14] The culture lag was first discussed in length by Ogburn, W. F. (1927) *Social Change*, Dell, New York.

[15] Hitch, C. J. (1965) *Decision-Making for Defense*, University of California Press, Berkeley. (This is a series of four lectures by the former Comptroller of the Defense Establishment.) The reader may also find two other works of interest in the same vein, Kaufman, W. W. (1964) *The McNamara Strategy*, Harper, and Quade, E. S. (1965) *Analysis for Military Decisions*, Rand McNally.

[16] Fritz, C. E. (1961) "Disaster", in Merton, R. K. and Nisbit, R. A. (eds.), *Contemporary Social Problems*, 1st ed., Harcourt, Brace & World, p. 665.

[17] Morse, P. M. and Kimball, G. E. (1951) *Methods of Operations Research*, Technology Press, and Wiley, New York, pp. 52–3.

[18] See also Hitch, C. J. and McKean, R. N. (1960) *The Economics of Defense in a Nuclear Age*, Harvard University Press, Cambridge, Mass., and Hitch, C. J. (1965) *Decision-Making for Defense*, University of California Press, Berkeley. The Operations Research Society of America has a "Cost Effectiveness" Section, which concentrates on problems of measure selection and use.

[19] See Adrian, E. D. (1928) *The Basis of Sensation: The Action of the Sense Organs*, Norton, New York, and the same author's *The Physical Background of Perception*, (1947) Clarendon Press, Oxford. Also, Hebb, D. O. (1949) *The Organization of Behavior*, Wiley, New York, and Penfield, W. and Rasmussen, T. (1950) *The Cerebral Cortex of Man*, Macmillan, New York. In a completely different vein, the works of Marshall McLuhan are based upon changes in the ratio of sensory inputs from different media, such as the printed page versus television, and their effects upon the individual and society. See *The Gutenberg Galaxy* (1962) University of Toronto Press, Toronto, and *Understanding Media* (1964) McGraw-Hill, New York.

[20] As one example, see Brandon, D. (1963) *Management Standards for Data Processing*, Van Nostrand, Princeton, N.J. Critical Path Methods and PERT Networks are planning tools often used to introduce project control.

[21] *Time*, June 28, 1966, pp. 52–3.

[22] *New York Times*, December 7, 1965, p. 41.

[23] Sarafin, E. E. (1965) "Information Protection", *Control Engineering*, pp. 105–7.

[24] From the Federal Power Commission Report, reprinted in the *New York Times*, December 7, 1965, p. 40, and the report by *Times* reporter Thomas O'Toole describing the sequence of events in New York, p. 41. Copyright 1965 by The New York Times Company. Reprinted by permission. One may well ask what good is an automated information or control system if the operators who have the final word on system action fail to take action or veto the action clearly indicated by the system itself?

# 18 Systems analysis of large-scale public facilities: New York City's water supply network as a case study

*by Richard de Neufville*

## Summary

This report explores the strengths and limitations of systems analysis by means of a case study of work carried out under the author's direction. The particular problem was that of designing a large-scale civil engineering facility, the billion-dollar additions to New York City's water supply system, but it is suggested that the kind of problems encountered, and successes achieved, have widespread generality.

The systems analysis indicated that economies of up to 50% were possible over the anticipated cost of the original proposal generated by the traditional engineering design process. These opportunities became apparent through the use of mathematical models of the system which could be used, in a computer, to explore hundreds of possible configurations. The computer also made it possible to calculate several measures of effectiveness for each trial design and to evaluate the trade-offs between each of these criteria. The planners could then specifically choose what kind of design they wanted and thus achieve significant increases in design effectiveness.

Significant institutional constraints did, however, preclude the use of some forms of economically desirable systems. To many it always appears perverse that public agencies are so often immune to analytic rationality. It might more sensibly be argued, however, that analysts simply fail to appreciate the more complex rationality of interest groups and social organizations.[1] Until they do, it would seem wise to recognize that environmental restrictions, whether social, economic or physical, are pervasive and characteristic of systems problems. Their overall effect is to limit the amount of savings that can be realized. In this case the overall economies achieved were about 100 million dollars (about 40 million pounds) or two-thirds of what might have been technically possible.

## Problem formulation

*On being drawn into the fire*

The first lesson to be drawn from the New York City experience concerns the manner in which it was posed to the analysts. It came to us after extensive preliminary designs had been prepared by a traditional design agency; after their proposal had been rebuffed fairly unceremoniously by the authorities; in short after a fair amount of bad blood. Positions had polarized around particular concepts leaving little room for discussion about the merits of alternatives. These are clearly not the most advantageous working conditions for rational analysis. But it would seem that such situations will be typical so long as systems analysts are in short supply and their use a rarity.

A little introspection soon indicates why it is unlikely that systems analysis will generally not, in the foreseeable future, be an integral part of the design or planning process from the start. Most groups do not now employ systems analysts. They would not even if they wanted to, there are not enough around. Most organizations would consequently have to make a special effort to use* systems analysis as part of its regular planning or design. They will not do this unless they sense that there is some problem as a motivation to do so. As one's problems are generally perceived by comparing oneself to one's peers (the "I-don't-care-if-I'm-mediocre-so-long-as-I'm-above-average" syndrome), the need to bring powerful analysis to bear on a problem will generally not be felt until major difficulties are encountered in the conventional design process. By then the fat is in the fire. It is tempting to argue that this will continue to be the case so long as there are few qualified professional analysts.

This reasoning certainly applied to the use of systems analysis on New York City's water supply network. A conventional municipal design agency, the Board of Water Supply, was allowed to proceed with its design and to spend several hundreds of thousands of pounds preparing a

---

\* Using analysts is also different from simply having them on the staff. Tame in-house analysts or computer experts, docile enough not to ask threatening questions, are catchy institutional adornments which are fun to trot out before stockholders or ministers. Between times they can be conveniently tucked away in computer centers or long-range corporate planning units and have essentially no effect whatsoever on what actually happens.

specific plan. They developed a proposal for a five-stage addition to the existing water supply system which would cost about 400 million pounds. This price tag brought about an immediate reaction from the budgetary authorities. They claimed that the initial design, predicated upon a 25% population growth of New York City, was contrary to the evident stagnation of the central city.* The plan was therefore extravagant and no additions were needed. The Board of Water Supply claimed that it was reasonable and conservative to allow for growth over the next forty years. The battle was joined. The MIT systems analysts were then brought in.

The evidence indicates that the situation is quite similar in England. The planning for the Third London Airport had to reach a substantial deadlock over a particular design (the Stanstead site in this instance) before the authorities commissioned an extensive research effort into the problem. As with the MIT analysis for New York City, the Roskill commission on the Third London Airport brought together analysts for a one-time analysis in the middle of a controversy. The effort could be neither as dispassionate nor as organized as desirable.

The contention here is that systems analysts will often be confronted with messy, controversial situations. That they will practise in this arena as often, if not more often, as they will be able to work in carefully organized developmental programs. In short, a neatly ordered design process, of the kind we so often talk or write about, may be the exception rather than the rule.

## The problem as presented

The original perception of the design problem was created by the traditional, institutionalized processes, as might be expected. In this case they were represented by the Board of Water Supply, the municipal agency responsible for supplying potable water to New York City.

The Board postulated that the City required substantial additions to its capacity for distributing water throughout the City.[2] The need for the new facilities was based on two basic assumptions:

1. That the population of the city itself would increase steadily over the next forty years; and

* In the United States, which does not have a Green Belt policy or even much land use control, the growth of metropolises such as New York has occurred in suburbs 15 miles or more from the business centers. These suburbs are governed by separate, independent councils and may even be in different states. Coordination of public utilities is then extremely difficult and impractical.

2. That the existing facilities would or did require extensive rehabilitation.

The postulated need for additional capacity then led the Board of Water Supply to evolve a plan to provide the facilities required. The Board was and is responsible by law to do so. Anticipating the next section, it is worth noting that this legislative delegation of authority unwittingly implied a significant design decision. Indeed, the Board was responsible for supplying potable water, not for distributing it. In practice, this meant that the Board was in charge of the so-called primary water supply network (aqueducts ten feet in diameter or larger) and that another municipal agency built and maintained the secondary and tertiary water supply network (six feet in diameter water mains and all the smaller conduits). Responsibility for the water system was legally divided. Therefore if the Board of Water Supply was to design additional capacity, it was essentially constrained to design additions to the primary system, whether or not these represented the most desirable investment to make in the system!

The preliminary design developed by the Board of Water Supply consisted of about 50 miles of tunnels up to 28 feet in diameter. It was estimated in 1967 to cost about one billion dollars and was slated to be built in five stages. The first stage was intended to comprise the largest tunnels and was estimated to cost 323 million dollars. The whole affair was to be one of the biggest, if not the biggest, single civil works projects ever.

Apart from the size of the project, the development of the design proceeded much like most other designs. There were some fairly sweeping fundamental assumptions and institutional factors which shaped the overall concept of the solution. The parallel with the evaluation of the plans for the Third London Airport is reasonably close. In that case the British Airports Authority assumed that airline traffic would grow steadily and should be encouraged; from this it followed that additional capacity would have to be found and further that, since the Airports Authority was involved, this capacity would be provided by means of an additional airport rather than any of the other possible alternatives. The similarity between these two cases, and indeed the generality of the points to be made by examining the New York City example, is enhanced by comparison of the detailed assumptions made in the design.

The preliminary design prepared by the Board of Water Supply was, in effect, based on several specifications:

1. A single geometrical configuration was considered as a possible location;

2. A single criterion of evaluation was used; namely that water be delivered at a pressure of 40 pounds per square inch at the end of the tertiary network;

3. The design horizon was 40 years, that is, the facilities were supposed to meet the conditions anticipated for the year 2010; and

4. The water would be forced through the network by gravity alone.

These simple specifications, as those made about other plans, may sound innocuous enough. But they were quite arbitrary insofar as they were not based on any assessment of their implications for the operation or the cost of the system to be designed. Most of them needed to be changed. This paper would argue that similarly arbitrary design or planning decisions need to be examined carefully and, in general, also adjusted.

This was the essence of the problem presented to the author and his colleagues at MIT. They were asked to do a systems analysis of the additions to the water supply system prepared by the Board of Water Supply. They were expected to determine the most relevant criteria for evaluation; to develop appropriate models of the system so that alternatives could be explored; and to recommend an optimal design and implementation strategy.

## Institutional constraints

Design is, as politics, an art of the possible. Good design must therefore recognize what limitations are placed upon it. Some of the restrictions on the design of public facilities are always physical; these are generally searched out carefully by the designers who are accustomed to deal in material terms. Many of the constraints are also, however, economic or social.

The first limitation on the systems analysis described here was in the nature of its power: it was essentially only negative. The systems analysis process as usually constituted serves many advisory functions: it can ask probing questions, provide means to explore alternatives, and suggest optimal solutions to a problem. But in terms of actual power, the analysts can usually only hold up bad decisions, they rarely can actually make people accept a plan they prefer. This, certainly, was the situation in the United States Department of Defense, where systems analysis was carried out on a grand scale with extensive executive backing.[3]

In the New York City case, the systems analysts were brought in to work for the budgetary or review authorities. Through their clients, they could delay the approval of the project as advocated by the Board of Water Supply. But neither the analysts nor the budgetary process could substitute a different scheme without the consent of the Board of Water Supply. The Board had an effective monopoly of the detailed engineering data required in order to design and construct the project. The Board of Water Supply also had a veto power over what gets accomplished, as do most of the traditional design agencies.

Faced with this array of forces, the systems analyst can at most hope to achieve a compromise. At some later date, when systems analysis may be more widespread, one might hope for better. Meanwhile, it is perhaps best to use the analysis process to determine which aspects are most critical to achieving improvements in the design, and to use this knowledge to advantage in the negotiations that will lead to the ultimate compromise. This was what was done in this instance, as is described below.

The second pervasive limitation on the application of systematic analysis which it is relevant to mention here arises in connection with the manner in which projects are funded. In the United States and, one suspects, elsewhere it is common for there to be institutional mechanisms which bias investments in favor of capital-intensive projects. Certain agencies may, for example, be exempt from taxation and thereby cause capital-intensive designs to be substituted for more economical projects with relatively high operating costs. The individual Port Authorities responsible for most American airports constitute such a tax shelter: this accounts in part for the fact that American airports use extensive terminal buildings where European airports (London, Paris, Lisbon, etc . . .) often use vehicles to carry passengers to and from aircraft.

In New York, the uneconomical bias toward capital-intensive projects exist in a different, but equally insidious, form. The city can raise money from three different sources in a system which inherently promotes monumentalism. These sources are:

1. Current revenues (mostly taxes) which must pay for all operating and maintenance expenses of the city. Most of any government's current revenues are entailed to specified commitments (salaries, social security, public welfare, etc.).[4] Politicians are furthermore loath to raise taxes, so there is thus relatively little money to be had from this source and much competition for it. Designs which imply heavy operating expenses therefore have little chance of approval.

2. Funds raised by bonds issued within the debt limit. These may pay for capital expenses, but their total amount is commonly limited by law as a device to im-

pose financial responsibility. The competition for this money exists, but is much less severe than that for current revenues.

3. Funds raised by bonds for purposes which are exempt from the bond limit. For special kinds of capital investments and, importantly, for projects sponsored by the Board of Water Supply, the city can issue bonds freely. The money raised in this manner is quite costless, politically. The tendency is to use it whenever possible, to build monumental civil works even if they are not economical.

## The systems analysis approach
### A five-step iterative process
The approach outlined here is essentially that described by the author elsewhere.[5] For convenience it is described as consisting of five steps. The particular categorization of the activities is clearly arbitrary, however, and others are equally plausible.

The steps suggested are as follows:

1. Definition of the objectives or, equivalently, of the criteria of evaluation;
2. Specification of measures of effectiveness, the quantitative indices by which one can evaluate the degree to which objectives have been attained;
3. Generation of alternatives, both by overall types or class and exhaustively, especially if computer models are used, within each class;
4. Evaluation of the alternatives according to their achievement in terms of the measures of effectiveness; and
5. Selection, as the result of a careful weighting of the several achievements of each alternative, of the best solution.

Overall, the analysis process was, and is, visualized as a search for optimal designs. Since clumsy or even false starts are inevitable, the process was also visualized as a learning experience in which the analysis team gains greater understanding of the system being examined, of its points of leverage, and of how optimal plans for it can best be formulated. In short, the analysis effort is seen as an iterative process in which one may cycle through the several steps of the analysis several times.

In the New York City case for example, the preliminary analyses helped us identify critical issues, such as reliability, which required their own measures of effectiveness. They also helped identify new classes of alternatives which could be considered to advantage. The discussion that follows

could not hope, and does not try to document this iterative process. For simplicity, the steps are discussed in sequence, although each of them did not develop fully before the subsequent one begun.

### Definition of objectives
The Board of Water Supply, as most design agencies today, used a single primary standard to evaluate the performance of their design. In particular, they specified that they had to deliver water at a pressure of 40 pounds per square inch at the curb, which is equivalent to 100 feet of water. As can be imagined, such a standard is a sparse description of the quality of the water delivered.

Most realistic descriptions of the outputs of a system must be in terms of many attributes. Municipal water, for example, serves many purposes. A fraction of it, about a quarter, is used by individuals at home. Most of it is actually used industrially as in the cooling of steam in electric power plants or in breweries; and the remainder is sprayed on fires or used to wash the streets. The users of the water are concerned, in varying degrees, about many aspects of its quality. For drinking purposes it should be sanitary and have a reasonable taste and color; the industrial users may be concerned about the total amount available and its chemical or corrosive properties; the fire department will naturally be most anxious about the reliability of its supply; the municipal council will naturally be concerned with the proper distribution of the services provided; and so on. A complete analysis should naturally consider each of the important dimensions.

One of the first tasks of the systems analysis of the proposed Third City Tunnel was, therefore, to lay out explicitly what the several objectives of this large project could or should be. Objectively, some five to ten major objectives might reasonably be ascribed to the proposed facility. But the analysis was not able to consider as many for two reasons, which are probably typical of such an enterprise.

First, the terms of reference of our study were written quite restrictively, apparently as a result of political pressure generated by anxiety over what we might find. We were prohibited, for example, to question whether or not there would ever be enough water to supply the demands the new tunnels were supposed to fulfill. Although legal compacts with the other states cast doubt on whether the additional water could be obtained,[6] we were explicitly instructed not to concern ourselves with the availability of water. A parallel situation has recently been observed in England in the case of the Third London Airport. Although there was no national strategy for the location and development of airports, the inquiry and the study team set up to review the question of the Third London Airport (The Roskill Commission) was instructed to assume that a new airport was, in fact, needed. A systems analysis born out of controversy, as that one and ours were, will almost certainly be overly restricted in scope and precluded from examining some of the fundamental objectives.

Second, the number of objectives we considered explicitly was restricted by our own limited capabilities and resources. Appropriate, quantifiable models were neither available nor possible to develop for several aspects of the water supply system. The available time and manpower likewise prevented us from doing all that appeared desirable. Our position in this respect was clearly typical. The objectives that we finally considered were both qualitative and distributional. Specifically, the analysis focussed on:

1. Overall performance of system;
2. Distribution of the service over the municipal area;
3. Reliability of the service; and
4. Total cost of construction and operation.

## Measures of effectiveness

The degree to which objectives were attained by alternative designs was estimated using objective indices. In general such measures of effectiveness should be chosen carefully as their very nature may easily bias the outcome of the planning process. If the cheapness of a transportation system is measured by the cost per ride instead of the cost per mile for example, short compact systems will be preferred over ones with longer routes and greater economies of scale. The choice of the measures of effectiveness is therefore not trivial.

In the New York City case, the effective range of choice of the measures of effectiveness was limited by what we could extract conveniently from our mathematical models of the system. The measures actually used were therefore somewhat crude. They nevertheless made it possible to explore the most important aspects of the design problem.

As a first-order estimate, performance was evaluated in terms of the pressure at which water could be supplied. Since static pressure measures the energy contained in the water, it can be transformed into velocity and rate of supply and is, therefore, a reasonable proxy for the quality, in a mechanical way, of the water. Overall performance was taken as an average of the performance, $p_i$, at the several key points of the water supply network, weighted by the quantity, $q_i$, of water desired at each of these $i$ nodes. Specifically, the index was:

$$\text{Overall Performance} = \sum_i p_i q_i / \sum q_i \sum$$

and was given in units of pressure.

A distributional measure of effectiveness should always accompany any index of overall performance. A situation which is satisfactory on the average may be attained at the expense of a number of extremely poor conditions. (As illustrated by the proverbial man with one foot in boiling water and the other in ice who should, on the average, be comfortable.) The measure used in this analysis was simply that of the performance at the extreme end of the supply network where performance would inevitably be lowest.

The reliability was estimated in terms of the performance that could be expected if a major failure of the system, such as the closure of one of the three main tunnels, occurred. Rather than attempt to guess at the probability of failure, a usual measure of reliability but one which would be extremely subjective in this instance, it was felt best to focus directly on the quality of the failure mode. The measure of reliability used was, in fact, an index of whether the performance of the water supply network would degrade catastrophically or gracefully.

The total cost of the alternative designs investigated was expressed in terms of the present values, taken to a convenient base year, of the discounted expenditures. This is one of the two standard measures, the other being the annualized costs which can be obtained by a simple mathematical manipulation. But traditional design agencies or planning groups, which must justify present expenditures, are naturally reluctant to discount future benefits. Many of them, and the New York City Board of Water Supply in particular, thus do not discount future cash flows. This failure biases planning toward overinvestment and monumentalism. Analysts need to be sure that the time streams of costs and benefits are always properly discounted.

The validity of the principle of discounting future costs and benefits is certain. The technical argument revolves around what annual rate should be used. Theoreticians are agreed that the appropriate rate is the opportunity cost of the capital invested, but have so far not been able to provide accurate estimates of the quantity. The discount rate used thus varies significantly from place to place, from agency to agency. In general the discount rate used for public investment in the United Kingdom and Europe, about 10%, is about twice that used in the United States. The lower American figure appears to represent weaker central planning which is unable to make its logical arguments overcome the reluctance of the construction groups,[7] rather than a true difference in the opportunity cost of capital.

The discount rate used to determine total cost for the New York City analysis was 5% per year. While it seems that the true opportunity cost for New York City is closer to 10 or even 15% at the present time, the 5% rate was, in a perverse way, not too inaccurate given the particular way in which water supply projects could be funded. The use of the 5% discount rate in the systems analysis in any case represented an improvement over the previous design which had not discounted at all.

## Alternatives

Although systems analysis is, in many respects, not much more than the organized, possibly computer-based application of common sense, good systems analyses are hard to achieve. The difficulties lie not so much in the organization of the process, which is really quite simple, but in the choices that must be made. The analyst is constantly faced with choices between different forms of analysis. Some of these will be tedious and unproductive while others may be very efficient. To be effective, the analyst must make good use of the limited resources at his disposal. The way a problem is formulated can be critical.

The importance of problem formulation is perhaps nowhere more evident than in the analysis of alternatives. This is where most of the resources are consumed. Here is where insightful choices can have the greatest significance.

The search for an optimal design for a system needs to look broadly at many different classes of alternatives and, within each class, iteratively at the different possibilities. The questions are: which are the most important classes or kinds of alternatives? and how can one identify the most promising individual designs?

The choice of which classes of alternatives to investigate, while important, maybe even crucial, cannot be decided by mathematical rule. A good choice will be one that provides the principal opportunities to improve the design. It may be the product of purely accidental qualities: insight, experience or luck. The improvement of the choice requires that one searches aggressively for attractive classes of alternatives, allow time for them to be found, and not foreclose the opportunity to examine them.

Considerable thought was devoted to the determination of the appropriate classes of alternatives for the design of any additions to the water supply system. Ultimately we came to three which may have extensive generality. These involved:

1. The physical configuration of the facilities themselves; in this case the route of the tunnels, their length, width and type of construction;

2. The phasing over time of the provision of the capacity, being an exploration of which design horizon is the most economical; and

3. The substitution of operating capabilities for constructed facilities, which would here be the improvement of performance (defined in terms of pressure) by use of pumps rather than by more tunnels.

The last two categories covered alternatives which had not previously been considered explicitly. The recognition of this omission in the systems analysis process led to substantial improvements in design, as shown below.

Sensitivity analyses were used to search for ways to improve alternatives within any given class. With regard to the configuration of the tunnel for example, the expression for energy loss in terms of the tunnel characteristics was differentiated so that one could estimate the most efficient ways to reduce pressure drops and, consequently, to increase performance.

## Evaluation of the alternatives

The primary vehicle for the evaluation of the alternatives in terms of the several objectives was a computer model. Specifically we had the capability, available as part of the ICES (Integrated Civil Engineering System) developed at MIT, to represent networks and to calculate flows and pressures at desired points.[8] This model enabled us to investigate in a few minutes alternative designs which would take trained engineers several days to evaluate manually. Since the model was, furthermore, time-shared on an IBM 360/67, it was easy to follow-up on effective improvements quickly. The systems analysis was therefore able to investigate literally hundreds of configurations where the traditional planning process has been limited to a very few.

The evaluation was conducted in terms of a cost-effectiveness analysis.[9] The success of each alternative in terms of meeting the objectives was plotted to define a region of feasible design. The outermost limit of possibilities, which was the locus of the best performance that could be achieved for every level of cost, represented the cost-effectiveness function. (Technically, the cost-effectiveness function is a simplified version of the more general production function, the latter being the locus of the most effective possible designs given in terms of the physical resources used rather than the cost.) Once the cost-effectiveness func-

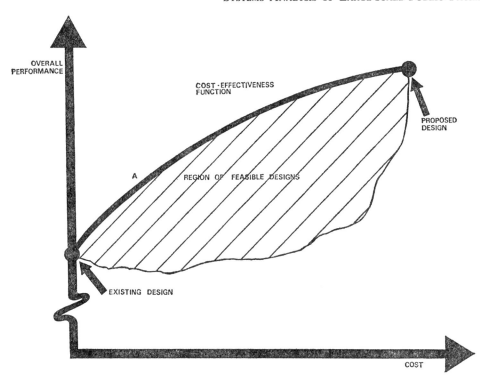

**Figure 18.1** Cost-effectiveness function in terms of overall performance.

tion was available it became possible to consider and choose the best design, the one that met all the objectives satisfactorily at a minimum cost.

The cost-effectiveness function in terms of overall performance is shown in Figure 18.1. As expected theoretically, it conforms to the empirical law of diminishing marginal returns: less and less improvement in design can be obtained for the same extra cost as the design becomes more costly. In such situations, which are pervasive, it is reasonable as a general rule to select a design or plan which is in the region where the money is well spent, such as the one indicated by point A. It certainly is not economically desirable to build a system where money is spent relatively unproductively, as occurred for the preliminary design of the Third City Water Tunnel. As a first result, then, the systematic use of computer models had revealed that it might be possible to save 30% of the total cost. This large saving could be attained by reducing the size of the planned facilities without thereby significantly altering performance.

To validate this initial conclusion, a cost-effectiveness analysis was carried out for the second measure of effectiveness: the performance at the extremities of the system (Figure 18.2). This analysis indicated that it was still possible to obtain an effective design at substantially re-

duced cost. It also showed that there were two different types of configuration, 1 and 2, and that it was important, regardless of the level of design, to choose the latter. Inspection of the alternatives showed that the group 2 designs were ones in which there were redundant tunnels. The existence of such facilities, like the proposed Third City Tunnel parallel to the previous two, evened out the loss of pressure and thus improved performance over the entire system.

The necessity for a Third City Tunnel of some size was finally confirmed by examining the reliability of the system (Figure 18.3). Unless some form of parallel tunnel were provided it appeared quite possible that the city would be in danger of losing a major part of its supply as the existing tunnels continued to deteriorate. The Board of Water Supply was thus quite correct in asserting the urgency of some form of tunnel. But, as indicated again by the region A, it was still quite possible to achieve substantial reductions in total cost.

With regard to the second class of alternatives, those referring to time-phasing of additions to capacity, it is possible to use a fairly standard approach. The essential trade-off is between possible economies of scale, and the discount rate. The presence of economies of scale impel a

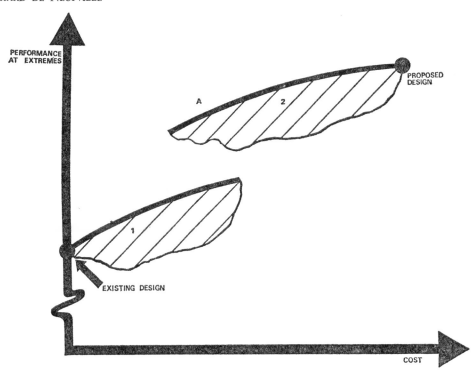

**Figure 18.2** Distributional objective : Cost-effectiveness function for the performance at the extremeties of the system.

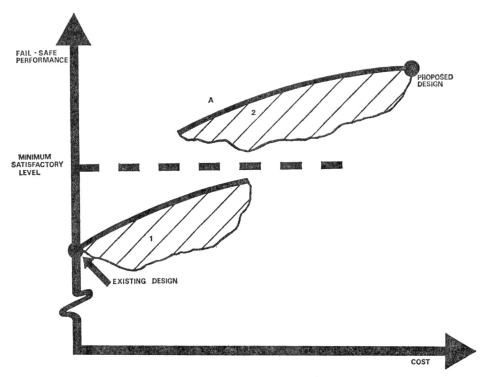

**Figure 18.3** Reliability objective : Cost-effectiveness function for fail-safe performance.

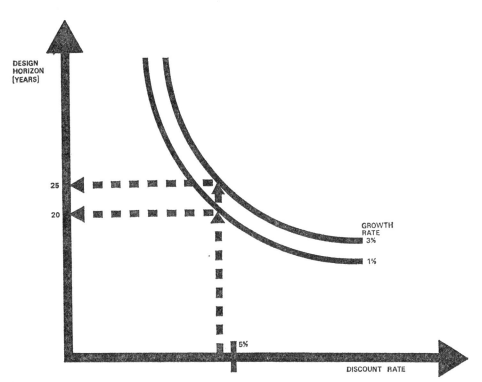

**Figure 18.4** Nomograph for the determination of the best design horizon (economy of scale factor, $\alpha = 0.6$).

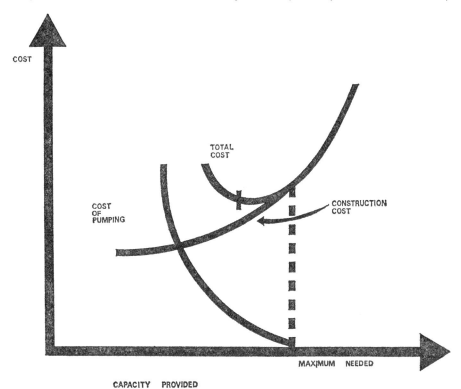

**Figure 18.5** The most economical design for a water supply system is, in general, one that includes pumping to take care of peak loads.

designer to plan larger facilities so as to increase the capacity obtained per dollar invested. The existence of a discount rate on the other hand encourages him to defer expenses as much and as far into the future as possible. If there were no discounting of future costs, it would be wise to build as large a facility as might ever be needed. If there were no economies of scale, it would be rational to defer construction until the moment it were needed.

The optimal design horizon for different situations has been determined by Manne.[10] His solutions are given in terms of the discount rate, the rate of growth of demand, and the economy of scale factor, $\alpha$. The latter has to be determined empirically by calibration of the formula:

$$\text{Cost} = (\text{Constant}) \times (\text{Capacity Size})^{\alpha}$$

For tunnels it appears that $\alpha \sim 0.6$. The most economical design horizon can then be determined from Figure 18.4.

The most economical period between additions to capacity turns out to be between 20 and 25 years. This is roughly half of what is assumed in the construction of many large-scale projects. By using this design period, it is possible to capture substantial savings not possible if the longer period is used, as was originally planned for the Third City Tunnel. These results were used to confirm the desirability of substantially reducing the designed size of proposed tunnels.

The statement that a twenty-year horizon is most desirable is not the same as saying that the larger, 40-year, capacity will not be needed. It is merely to say that it will be cheaper to build this capacity in two installments, each planned for twenty years worth of growths.

Construction in smaller stages is not only more economical, it is also more flexible. If the projected growth somehow fails to materialize, further substantial savings can be achieved by merely not building the capacity that is now known to be unnecessary. Even if the demand does occur, it may very well be of a different kind and in a different place than originally anticipated. The shorter design horizon then permits the planner to adjust his program.

Consideration of the final overarching class of alternatives, the use of operating improvements instead of additional capacity, indicated that further savings could be achieved. This is often the case. Experience indicates that engineers have a tendency to think of construction solutions to operational problems.

The basic operational problem of the water supply system is, as it is in many other systems, the existence of peak loads 20 to 30% above the average. The system must operate at particularly high levels for relatively short periods. In the New York City case, the system was designed to operate with degration of quality at the peak hour on the peak day, which occurs with a frequency of about ·0001. The capacity provided to meet this peak is thus wasted 99·98% or more of the time.

To meet peak demands by providing capacity that will be available all the time, rather than by using standby capabilities that will rarely be used, can be expensive. The operation of small scale, relatively inefficient facilities over extended periods can likewise be costly. The most appropriate design represents a balance between operating costs and fixed investments (Figure 18.5).[11]

For the New York City water supply system and the particular kind of peak loads it carried, a 30% reduction in total cost could be obtained by using pumping plants to provide the pressure (and performance) desired at peak hours. It should be noted that the role of pumping and similar operational measures is quite limited. Their costs rise quite rapidly when they begin to be used to meet continual, base-load demands.

## Implementation

The plan ultimately selected for implementation was a compromise, as was to be anticipated. For the record, it is appropriate to describe the plan settled upon. In a larger sense, however, it is more pertinent to indicate why the compromise design took the particular form it did and how it came about. These elements constitute the guidelines for the future.

The final design for the first stage of the Third City Tunnel, the one now being implemented, was as follows:

1. It was located along the same plan and elevation as the preliminary design;
2. It was designed without pumping, just as the original design; but
3. It was only 3/5ths the size, being 20 to 22 feet in diameter instead of the 26 to 28 feet originally planned. As a result of this single change the cost of the first stage was reduced from an estimated $323 million to $223 million for a net savings of $100 million or £40 million.[12]

It is revealing to examine the nature of the compromise. In many superficial aspects, route and scheme of operation, there was no change at all. This was important from the point of view of the Board of Water Supply; they had laid much of their prestige on the line in laying out their original concept and could hardly retreat from their position without severe loss of face. Being an engineering group, however, they could give much more easily on the cost aspects of the plan which, one might say (although I would not), were not really technical or engineering matters. For the Board of Water Supply to reduce the size of the project was the easiest thing it could do. As it happened, it was also the step that the budgetary review authorities, with whom the Board of Water Supply were in conflict, most demanded. The compromise was arrived at, as might be expected, on the basis of mutual expediency. Optimality of the resultant design was not the prime mover of the compromise.

The significant reduction in the net cost was reason enough to justify the systems analysis, which cost only $50,000. But it would be a gross oversimplification to believe that the analysis was, or could be, primarily responsible for this outcome. No significant savings could have been achieved if the budgetary authorities had not been prepared to wage an administrative battle. Conversely, greater savings could have been accomplished if the construction money had not been so easy to obtain (as explained previously) and thus if the Budget Bureau had been more determined.

The role of the analysis reported here, and perhaps the role of all like systems analysis, was to clarify issues and to indicate points of leverage in the preliminary plans. The analysis provided ammunition that might be used. The effectiveness of this ammunition depended, and depends in general, on many other factors besides the quality of the analytical work. Many of these factors would appear to be set in advance, before the analysis begun. It is then inappropriate to judge the analysis itself on the size of the net results that occurred after the analysis was completed.

The analysis can, however, have significant longer term effects, as did the New York City Study. In the first instance, it may be expected that the agencies that were participants in the debate which the systems analysis was called in to investigate will develop more modern analytic capabilities. This was certainly the case in the Department of Defence during the McNamara period. It was also, apparently, true for the Board of Water Supply. Since the debate occurred, they are reported to have begun to use the concept of opportunity cost and to implement a few computer models of their network. Secondly, the analysis may draw attention to important problems that management needs to face. In this case the MIT effort emphasized the need to pay attention to the secondary pipe networks in the city; the volume of construction on these systems has increased since then by five-fold.[13] Such secondary benefits may, ultimately, be equally as important as the immediate, more obvious primary results.

## References

1 Simon, H. A. (1959) *Administrative Behavior*, The Macmillan Co., New York.

2 "Report of the Board of Water Supply of the City of New York on the Third City Tunnel First Stage", July 1966.

3 Hiton, C. (1965) *Decision-Making for Defense*, University of California Press, Berkeley.

4 Crecine, J. P. (1967) "A Computer Simulation Model of Municipal Budgeting", *Management Science*, **13**, 11.

5 de Neufville, R. and Stafford, J. H. (1971) *Systems Analysis for Engineers and Managers*, McGraw-Hill, New York.

6 Hirshliefer, J., DeHaven, J. C., and Williman, J. W. (1960) *Water Supply: Economics, Technology, and Policy*, University of Chicago Press, Chicago.

7 Fox, J. K., and Herfindahl, O. C. (1964) "Attainment of Efficiency in Satisfying demands for Water Resources", *American Economic Review*, **54**, 3, 198.

8 Liu, K. T. (1968) *Pipe Network Analysis in Integrated Civil Engineering Systems* (*ICES*), IBM Cambridge Scientific Center, Cambridge, Mass.

9 de Neufville, R. (1970) "Cost-Effectiveness Analysis of Civil Engineering Systems: New York City's Primary Water Supply", *Operations Research*, **18**, 5, 785–804.

10 Manne, A. S. (1967) *Investments for Capacity Expansion*, The MIT Press, Cambridge, Mass.

11 Bayer, B. (1970) *Tradeoffs Between Tunnel Size and Pumping Capacity in Primary Water Distribution Systems*, M.S. Thesis, Department of Civil Engineering, MIT, Cambridge, Mass.

12 "Tunnel Goes for Record $222·6 Million", *Engineering News-Record*, pp. 13–14, Jan. 15, 1970.

13 "Pollution Fighter Marty Lang does Battle in 'Wicked Gotham'", *Engineering News-Record*, pp. 24–6, Mar. 4, 1971.

Reprinted from De Neufville, R. (1971) "New York City's Water Supply Network as a Case Study", *Journal of Systems Engineering*, **2, 1.**

# 19 The city as a system
## by Donald F. Blumberg

## Introduction

For people in decision-making or planning capacities who are dealing with real problems in real cities, the concept of a city system deserves some discussion. Is it really essential to deal with the city as a system? In order to fully understand the value of the concept, we must first define the types of functions or environmental elements which exist in an urban area.

The most familiar is the view of the city as a land-use subsystem, a series of *physical structures* making up the core and the outlying regions, the places where people live and work. We can also think of *functioning elements* of the city in terms of the social and economic environment, i.e., how the people live, where they receive their economic gain, their health characteristics, their patterns of housing use, the incidence of their juvenile delinquency, their educational and racial composition, and so forth. Emphasis is, in other words, primarily on the living population.

A third view must concentrate on the *transportation environment's elements* which move things and people from one place to another. The rail, road, and the air nets in the urban area and connecting this particular urban area with all others.

Lastly, one can view the city in terms of its *services*: the water system, the sewage system, the electric utilities, the hospitals, and the variety of other facilities which support the urban area.

These four separate "slices" or environmental elements represent, in general, the way that many people have, in the past, been looking at our urban areas – as slices rather than as an integrated whole. The thesis which we will propose, and the techniques that we will discuss, deal with bringing these four classes of subsystems or subenvironments together into one overall structure – the city viewed as a system.

However, we must also discuss the dynamically changing structure of the city. The basic problem in the city is not just the four individual subsystems as discussed above, but also the problem of dynamic change. The planning and the decision-making vary in time for each of these four classes of problem area – the physical, the social and economic, the transportation, and the service nets.

In summary, we view these four environmental groups, interacting with each other and in time, as the *city system*. In looking at a variety of large urban areas, we found that a basic problem was the inability of decision-makers and decision-making mechanisms to come to grips with these interacting factors and with their dynamics. In essence, they were unable to deal with the entire problem because their focus was on elements of the city system, rather than on the city system as a whole.

To give some feeling for the complexity and scope of this planning gap in the city system, it is of interest to examine the types of planners that are normally found in an urban area.

Typical examples are the city planner and the architect-engineer, both of whom emphasize land use and population growth. Their planning horizon extends over a period of 30 to 40 years and their reaction time in terms of construction starts covers a five-year-or-greater period of time. Next, we have the transportation engineer, whose emphasis is primarily on the existing transportation, the networks, and the demand for transportation. The transportation engineer has a somewhat different planning horizon and also a different feeling about the length of time that actions should take. The facilities planner, again, has a different focus.

In most urban areas in the United States, there are also the market planners – the people who are employed by large retail or wholesale organizations, or who are acting as consultants. Their emphasis is on population growth and market demand. Their planning horizon is narrower, and their action and reaction time concerning, for example, the initiation of a new supermarket or retail store, is on a different time frame from that of other types of planners. Market planners working in construction or investment fields also have a somewhat different focus, and the same changed focus holds for service planners in the area of education, health, welfare, social service, and police enforcement.

Each of these classes of planners in the city system is working for a decision-maker on a continuing basis. Each of these independent organizations is making decisions and taking actions which affect the urban area over time. If possible, it would be desirable to examine the actions taken by each of these planners, in turn, and define their mutual effects on the framework, structure, and type of the urban area or city system. We would like to have a methodology which would enable us to capture all these various outlooks and to perceive the dynamism which exists in the relations between subsystems.

City systems contain many interacting elements that are affected by randomness and unpredictability. These elements include activities which have extensive time lags; they involve very complex policies, rules, and procedures; they continually create a host of data; they involve many conflicting objectives; and they embody many component organizations. Lastly, the city system is impacted *by* and will have an impact *on* the local systems which are part of the urban area, the regional systems in which the urban area resides, and the larger national system.

## Techniques for modeling the city as a system

We have been using the term "systems" to deal with the urban area or city. We can draw upon the same systems approach to assist in planning for urban and social changes in the "city system". Up to this point, we have been talking in a theoretical framework about the city system. Let us get a little more specific. About two years ago we began to look at the process of planning as described by these various classes of planners in several separate cities. These cities were selected because they represented a geographical dispersion and because they represented areas in which, to some extent, sophisticated planning was being attempted. We went into each of these cities, talked to city planners, examined their problems, and tried to make an estimate of the degree to which improved or more advanced techniques for planning could have improved the situation, or could have helped achieve a better goal. With few exceptions, we found that improvements could have been significant.

With this challenge in mind, we began to explore the idea of developing more sophisticated techniques to improve the planning and decision-making process in city systems. There has been a significant amount of work done over the last 50 years in development of analytical techniques for planning and analysis. In urban areas, a considerable amount of work has been done in the area of statistical analysis, using multivariant factor analysis, components,

and cluster analysis. Within the last 20 or 30 years, a considerable amount of work has also been done in the fields of economic and demographic analysis, and in the use of interindustry and input/output trade area analysis and housing-demand models. Within the last few years, a good deal of work has been done in the area of simulation techniques as applied to city planning. Land-use models and Markov-type prediction models have been successfully developed. Three interesting simulation-type forecasting systems (outlined below) have been constructed within the last five years.

In the 1950s, the states of Pennsylvania and New Jersey banded together, forming a special compact to study the requirements for new transportation facilities and capabilities in the Delaware Valley area. In the effort, a supporting program, known as the Penn–Jersey Transportation Study, began to use some of these advanced techniques. The Penn–Jersey study team undertook development of a computer-based simulation model, called a regional growth model, which would allow them to forecast the future in terms of new highway facilities initiated in the Delaware Valley area. The model was designed to study the question, "Why do people make use of transportation, and what is the effect of initiating new transportation facilities?"

About the same time, in Pittsburgh, under urban renewal grants from the Federal government, another team began to develop an approach to planning the Golden Triangle. Supported by the University of Pittsburgh's professors and other consultants, they developed a computer-based simulation to study what happens when people live in an area, i.e., how much secondary industry is developed and what happens as the population of the area fluctuates. The first model was oriented more toward the physical facilities and the transportation system. The second model was oriented toward the people living in the area and toward social and economic subsystems.

San Francisco at approximately the same time (also supported by Federal funds) employed a management consulting firm to develop a computer simulation to model the physical characteristics of the housing in the area. This simulation attempted to deal with the question of what would happen if housing characteristics of the San Francisco area were affected by changes in housing codes and to estimate the impact of the type of decision. This third class of models was oriented toward the land-use elements of the city system.

We looked at these three classes of models and felt enough had been done to enable us to take a first step toward developing a new set of models aimed at describing the city system as a whole. The system developed (Figure 19.1) was designed to describe a community, an urban area, at some point in time. The models were designed to work on a time-increment basis, taking into consideration the changes that will occur in an urban area over time.

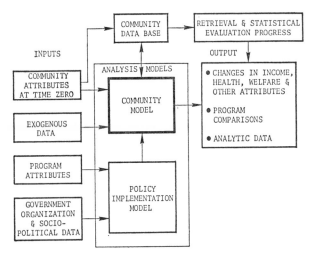

**Figure 19.1** Planning-simulation system.

## Structure of the community model

One initial class of inputs was provided by data covering a two-year period and describing the city system at a point in time. A second class of inputs consisted of exogenous data which described the style and character of the particular urban area. The model was developed to be of general use for any major urban area in the United States, and the exogenous data attempted to describe the differences between this particular city system and another. Both these data sources served as inputs to the "community model". The outputs from the community model consisted of predictions of dynamic changes in the city system over time. These were printed out directly by a computer, or stored in a data bank and later extracted.

The other portion of the system was designed to receive as inputs (i) the social and physical programs and attributes of programs to be initiated, (ii) the characterization of the government organizations, and (iii) characterization of other social and political agencies which existed within the community. These inputs were then used to analyze the effects that implementing a policy (or change in policy) would have on the city system. This could be done by including the policy model with the community model in the analysis model (Figure 19.1) to provide outputs showing the comparative results of different programs and to pro-

vide other analytical data concerning the impact of these programs.

The community model consists of a series of smaller models. The first of these, a small area submodel, was an attempt to describe a neighborhood in detail. It gave an account of the manner in which people live, including the secondary employment generated as a result of their living in that area, and their general social and economic patterns over a time period. The outputs from the small neighborhood-area model serve as the inputs to an area submodel, which describes in more physical terms what takes place in the community as a whole. Outputs from this model are the inputs to an individual submodel which relates what happens to an aggregate class of individuals within the urban area in terms of births, aging, deaths, education, etc. The outputs of that model, in turn, become inputs to a household model, which determines what the household incomes are, where these households reside, etc. Finally, the outputs of that model then become, in the next time frame, the inputs to the small area submodel. This begins the next cycle, and the system continues on in that manner.

The community models are basically made up of a series of equations, both logical and mathematical, based primarily on transition probabilities. For example, if there are 100 people at age 20 in a community in 1962, then, based on the given birth and death probabilities, in 1963 there should be, at age 21, some percentage of these 100 people who existed in the previous year.

A series of such equations in the community model were used to delineate these transition effects in the areas of housing, employment, education, health, and welfare. The outputs of these predictions form the inputs to an urban area-wide forecast, which is in turn used to calculate how many people are employed within the city and within the region supporting the city. These outputs are then applied to arrive at the number of people employed in each neighborhood. In turn, these estimates are utilized to obtain numbers on each population group by age, race, and employment in each small area.

These statistics, then, become the basis for an estimate of the occupations that are available or being filled, and also the basis for the means of obtaining numbers of households by race and sex. Finally, these figures are used to estimate family income, first by family and then by neighborhood. These inputs are used in the next time period as the setting points for these equations.

The "policy implementation model" (Figure 19.2) is a first-cut attempt at trying to model the process of government action within the community. Whereas the previous

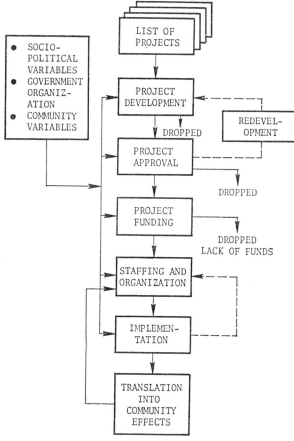

Figure 19.2 Policy implementation model.

model was a combination of equations, logical formulas, and statistical techniques, this policy model is an event-type simulation. It takes a list of projects to be initiated and goes through the whole development process of the project: the approval, if necessary, by the voters or government agencies, the funding and staffing, the organization and implementation, and the ultimate translation of these individual

steps into community effects. Each of these logical stages is affected by the social and political variabilities. However, the policy implementation model is still very naïve and considerable amount of work has yet to be done in the area of simulating the implementation of government policies and programs.

These models, and all the computer programs, are tied together through an executive computer program (see Figure 19.3), which controls the system and allows one to make changes in any of the submodels without major effects to the other submodels. This "executive" divides the models into a number of submodels: the data retrieval and printout system, the community and individual submodels, the small-area submodels, the government-action model, and the input subsystem. Each of these segments could be run either sequentially or in parallel on a large machine.

## Information obtained from the community model simulation

Up to this point we have been talking about the structure of this city system model in terms of its technical design. Let us now look at the type of information which could be generated by this type of mechanism. Given the appropriate inputs, a printout, as shown in Figure 19.4a could be generated. The output is being run for the City of Toronto, based on twenty-five neighborhoods or small areas. This particular set of runs assumes a particular mix of governmental programs and projects, targeted in specific ways.

The printouts depict the city at a certain point in time (similar printouts are produced for each year) as a function of this particular set of programs and assumptions. Shown are typical printouts for the year 1974. The system could, however, generate similar information for any year over which the models are run. Demographic and housing data are provided, as well as a considerable amount of information on ethnic groups; for example, as shown in Figure 19.4b the people living in Toronto are broken down into

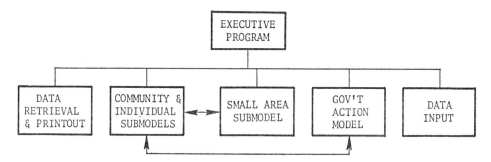

Figure 19.3 Simulation system organization.

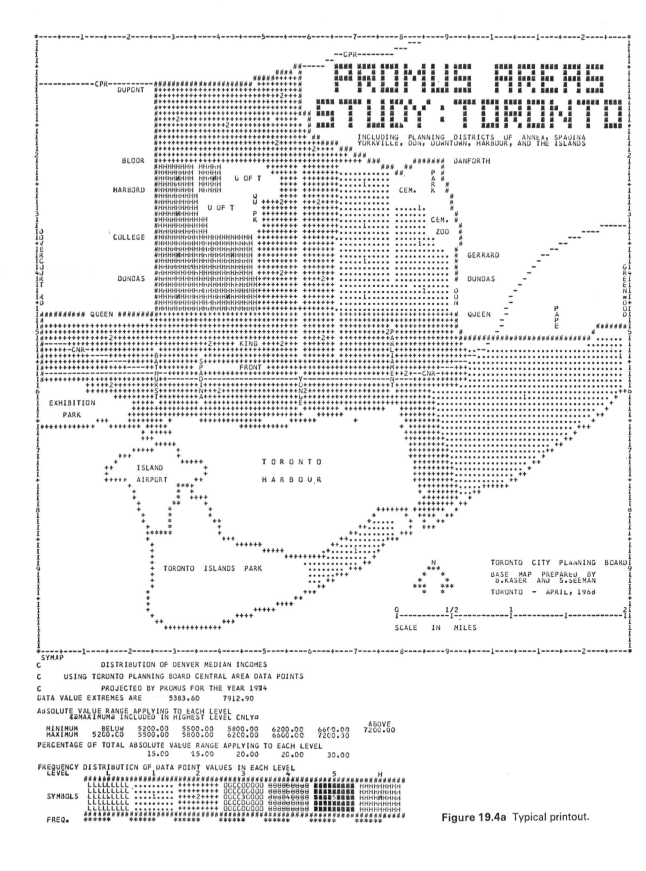

**Figure 19.4a** Typical printout.

three ethnic groups of males and females by age groups.

Breakdowns can also be provided on ethnic groups by occupation. Although in this particular study, only three groupings were considered, others could be added. And while only four occupation groupings were made, this could be increased to ten or fifteen occupations. As is shown in Figure 19.4c, we also have a considerable amount of detail on education, such as the number of people who are 5 to 35 years of age in kindergarten, elementary school, high school, etc., and information on the people 25 years of age and older in school.

Why are we using these particular breakdowns instead of others? In our survey of cities, we began to develop a pattern of the kind of data currently available. Our initial approach was to make use of the available data, recognizing that as experience in using the model grew, there would be a greater need for disaggregation. In general, the data base was developed on the basis of data normally found or reasonably obtainable in most urban communities. The classification of data is enough to indicate that a fairly large amount of information is required for statistical description of a city system.

## Dynamic effects of decisions

Let us get down to the more specific issue – the dynamic effects, in terms of this model structure, of decisions made in the city system. In studying the dynamically changing structure of the city system, we should recognize that people tend to reflect their own values and judgments as they evaluate data.

They impute special significance to certain data and often draw results out of context. In order to avoid this type of bias, we attempted to develop a data base or framework for our analysis that was reasonable, i.e., representative of the average city and yet not data drawn from a specific city. We took data from a group of cities, at random, and generated a realistic, but nevertheless hypothetical city named Capsburg (see Figure 19.5).

Capsburg has an elaborate data base to describe its seven neighborhoods. Just to give some idea of how one must get into the style and character of an area, we can take two neighborhoods, Area 3 and Area 7 in Capsburg. Let us contrast them. Both areas have the same population and roughly the same number of housing units, 1875 versus 1938. But Area 7 is a more dense area, with 6,000 square feet versus 31,500 square feet. Population density by itself, however, provides no good measure of character; spend a few days in selected areas of Manhattan and that will be obvious! Let us look a little further. In Area 3 the median

family income is $7,500 versus $3,200 in Area 7. There are 21 percent unemployed in Area 7 versus 2·9 per cent in Area 3.

With the type of data base available in a variety of different categories, it is possible to begin to form a qualitative description of each neighborhood. Our Area 3 is a typical old, very high income professional community. Given enough different data, enough variations, and enough measures, it is possible to begin to develop a one-for-one comparison between the quantitative estimates, as statistically described in the data base, and the qualitative feeling of the style and character of the city system. For analysis purposes, we will use this hypothetical, but quite realistic, data base to discuss dynamic change.

We have now defined our city system; but we have not yet explored the impact of the change on the system itself. To illustrate this type of change, let us take the results of the runs made on the model described above for the hypothetical city of Capsburg over the period of 1966 to 1982. Starting with a data base of 1960 to 1961, we would like to explore the impact of a series of possible programs that could be implemented (Figure 19.6). In order to do this, we placed ourselves in the role of a planner for the city system and we then generated a series of seven projects, focused or targeted in certain discrete areas. We also set up various mixes of these projects and budgeted them in various ways. We wanted to determine, for this purely illustrative mix of programs, what constituted the "best" mix and which budget level would achieve the optimum results in the city of Capsburg.

Although illustrative, these programs were primarily related to social change; and they could just as easily have involved urban renewal projects. One of the results (see Figure 19.7) illustrates what happens in Area 7 (the slum) for nonwhite incomes of less than $3,000 over the period 1966 to 1982. This is assuming we are given two budget mixes: one at $775,000 per year, and the other at $380,000 per year, as opposed to no program. When we first saw the results of this run, we felt that these projections could not be accurate. These sets of curves suggested that there was very little, if any, difference between the two mixes of funded programs as compared to no program whatsoever. We immediately began searching the model structure for errors, and we subsequently arrived at an interesting thesis – the "Lake Mead analogy".

A man decides to fill Lake Mead, using a bucket. Relative to his own size, there is a lot of water in the bucket. He takes the bucket of water to Lake Mead and throws the water into the lake; the water level does not rise.

HOUSING AND POPULATION ATTRIBUTES FOR TIME PERIOD ,1974
NUMBER IN POPULATION GROUPS BY AGE

### ETHNIC GROUP 1

| AREAL UNIT | MALES AGE GRP 1 | AGE GRP 2 | AGE GRP 3 | AGE GRP 4 | AGE GRP 5 | SUB TOTAL | FEMALES AGE GRP 1 | AGE GRP 2 | AGE GRP 3 | AGE GRP 4 | AGE GRP 5 | SUB TOTAL |
|---|---|---|---|---|---|---|---|---|---|---|---|---|
| 1 | 8145 | 7239 | 8128 | 4206 | 1911 | 29629 | 7755 | 6605 | 7586 | 4701 | 2865 | 29512 |
| 2 | 2577 | 789 | 1998 | 1126 | 540 | 7030 | 2416 | 791 | 2063 | 1131 | 526 | 6927 |
| 3 | 7772 | 2585 | 6383 | 3152 | 929 | 20821 | 7377 | 2775 | 6505 | 2968 | 964 | 20589 |
| 4 | 3258 | 2229 | 2787 | 1831 | 692 | 10837 | 2924 | 1410 | 2635 | 1733 | 763 | 9465 |
| 5 | 7052 | 2789 | 6059 | 4761 | 1540 | 22201 | 6958 | 3143 | 6688 | 4735 | 1939 | 23463 |
| 6 | 8742 | 3354 | 7086 | 4360 | 1330 | 24872 | 8323 | 3232 | 7398 | 4144 | 1394 | 24491 |
| 7 | 883 | 346 | 643 | 577 | 270 | 2719 | 831 | 347 | 669 | 528 | 284 | 2659 |
| 8 | 5957 | 1678 | 5064 | 2095 | 610 | 15444 | 5892 | 1832 | 5104 | 1939 | 741 | 15508 |
| 9 | 1783 | 521 | 1300 | 462 | 136 | 4202 | 1404 | 531 | 1246 | 427 | 149 | 3757 |
| 10 | 5635 | 2377 | 4638 | 3327 | 1904 | 17881 | 5441 | 2529 | 4879 | 3286 | 1686 | 17821 |
| 11 | 14479 | 4094 | 11048 | 4723 | 1188 | 35532 | 13432 | 4738 | 11634 | 4526 | 1321 | 35651 |
| 12 | 6406 | 3240 | 5713 | 4584 | 1812 | 21755 | 6265 | 3282 | 6176 | 5085 | 2470 | 23278 |
| 13 | 5000 | 2133 | 3868 | 3049 | 1375 | 15425 | 5070 | 2371 | 4227 | 3211 | 1631 | 16510 |
| 14 | 8569 | 4583 | 7207 | 7970 | 4438 | 32767 | 8391 | 4706 | 7998 | 9242 | 6112 | 36449 |
| 15 | 4551 | 2572 | 3859 | 5401 | 3828 | 20211 | 4474 | 2910 | 4176 | 5854 | 4172 | 21586 |
| 16 | 5590 | 4475 | 9679 | 11104 | 7798 | 38646 | 5512 | 5587 | 2212 | 11727 | 10965 | 36003 |
| 17 | 7348 | 2636 | 6177 | 4347 | 1759 | 22267 | 7142 | 2740 | 6616 | 4834 | 2596 | 23928 |
| 18 | 7303 | 7071 | 8106 | 6325 | 2775 | 31580 | 6950 | 4220 | 8274 | 7611 | 3811 | 30866 |
| 19 | 4741 | 1871 | 4089 | 3516 | 1494 | 15711 | 4601 | 2393 | 4577 | 3901 | 1979 | 17451 |
| 20 | 4572 | 1823 | 4222 | 1640 | 407 | 12664 | 4302 | 1968 | 4107 | 1627 | 532 | 12536 |
| 21 | 7646 | 2360 | 6086 | 2381 | 593 | 19066 | 7445 | 2777 | 6368 | 2243 | 715 | 19548 |
| 22 | 948 | 310 | 633 | 468 | 108 | 2467 | 882 | 259 | 758 | 423 | 131 | 2453 |
| 23 | 2488 | 975 | 1926 | 1175 | 573 | 7137 | 2362 | 1052 | 1928 | 1128 | 598 | 7068 |
| 24 | 13378 | 3658 | 10638 | 3167 | 721 | 31562 | 12755 | 4281 | 10379 | 2869 | 761 | 31045 |
| 25 | 6677 | 2237 | 4457 | 2163 | 597 | 16131 | 6384 | 2493 | 4425 | 1847 | 509 | 15658 |
| AREA TOTAL | 151580 | 67945 | 131794 | 87910 | 39328 | 478557 | 145288 | 68972 | 128628 | 91720 | 49614 | 484222 |

### ETHNIC GROUP 2

| AREAL UNIT | MALES AGE GRP 1 | AGE GRP 2 | AGE GRP 3 | AGE GRP 4 | AGE GRP 5 | SUB TOTAL | FEMALES AGE GRP 1 | AGE GRP 2 | AGE GRP 3 | AGE GRP 4 | AGE GRP 5 | SUB TOTAL |
|---|---|---|---|---|---|---|---|---|---|---|---|---|
| 1 | 30 | 24 | 30 | 7 | 3 | 94 | 30 | 25 | 32 | 8 | 3 | 98 |
| 2 | 3 | 0 | 1 | 0 | 0 | 4 | 3 | 1 | 2 | 0 | 0 | 6 |
| 3 | 10 | 5 | 7 | 3 | 1 | 26 | 10 | 5 | 8 | 3 | 1 | 27 |
| 4 | 6 | 8 | 6 | 2 | 0 | 22 | 7 | 8 | 6 | 2 | 0 | 23 |
| 5 | 8 | 2 | 6 | 2 | 0 | 18 | 8 | 2 | 7 | 2 | 0 | 19 |
| 6 | 14 | 19 | 12 | 2 | 0 | 47 | 15 | 20 | 13 | 3 | 0 | 51 |
| 7 | 0 | 0 | 0 | 0 | 0 | 0 | 0 | 0 | 0 | 0 | 0 | 0 |
| 8 | 4 | 1 | 5 | 1 | 0 | 11 | 4 | 1 | 6 | 1 | 0 | 12 |
| 9 | 3 | 0 | 1 | 0 | 0 | 4 | 3 | 0 | 1 | 0 | 0 | 4 |
| 10 | 20 | 7 | 14 | 7 | 3 | 51 | 20 | 7 | 15 | 7 | 4 | 53 |
| 11 | 65 | 21 | 43 | 10 | 2 | 141 | 66 | 21 | 45 | 11 | 2 | 145 |
| 12 | 14 | 13 | 16 | 4 | 0 | 47 | 14 | 13 | 17 | 4 | 1 | 49 |
| 13 | 225 | 75 | 118 | 43 | 15 | 476 | 228 | 75 | 125 | 43 | 15 | 486 |
| 14 | 279 | 102 | 136 | 54 | 23 | 594 | 282 | 103 | 144 | 55 | 24 | 608 |
| 15 | 1879 | 718 | 1465 | 893 | 343 | 5298 | 1904 | 789 | 1607 | 968 | 379 | 5647 |
| 16 | 235 | 101 | 213 | 136 | 59 | 744 | 229 | 117 | 194 | 77 | 29 | 646 |
| 17 | 19 | 3 | 16 | 8 | 0 | 46 | 27 | 15 | 30 | 13 | 5 | 90 |
| 18 | 86 | 147 | 158 | 40 | 13 | 444 | 91 | 53 | 103 | 45 | 16 | 308 |
| 19 | 326 | 120 | 299 | 183 | 52 | 980 | 332 | 143 | 240 | 143 | 73 | 931 |
| 20 | 24 | 17 | 31 | 7 | 0 | 79 | 24 | 12 | 31 | 6 | 1 | 74 |
| 21 | 14 | 6 | 11 | 5 | 2 | 38 | 14 | 3 | 20 | 6 | 3 | 46 |
| 22 | 10 | 1 | 4 | 5 | 0 | 20 | 12 | 4 | 10 | 7 | 0 | 33 |
| 23 | 33 | 16 | 31 | 14 | 9 | 103 | 48 | 14 | 30 | 14 | 8 | 114 |
| 24 | 69 | 21 | 49 | 15 | 6 | 160 | 71 | 21 | 52 | 15 | 6 | 165 |
| 25 | 59 | 18 | 37 | 23 | 6 | 143 | 54 | 19 | 42 | 16 | 3 | 134 |
| AREA TOTAL | 3435 | 1445 | 2709 | 1464 | 537 | 9590 | 3496 | 1471 | 2780 | 1449 | 573 | 9769 |

### ETHNIC GROUP 3

| AREAL UNIT | MALES AGE GRP 1 | AGE GRP 2 | AGE GRP 3 | AGE GRP 4 | AGE GRP 5 | SUB TOTAL | FEMALES AGE GRP 1 | AGE GRP 2 | AGE GRP 3 | AGE GRP 4 | AGE GRP 5 | SUB TOTAL |
|---|---|---|---|---|---|---|---|---|---|---|---|---|
| 1 | 70 | 46 | 60 | 20 | 2 | 198 | 71 | 49 | 58 | 19 | 2 | 199 |
| 2 | 107 | 44 | 55 | 30 | 14 | 250 | 107 | 45 | 54 | 29 | 11 | 246 |
| 3 | 62 | 28 | 44 | 18 | 2 | 154 | 63 | 30 | 43 | 18 | 1 | 155 |
| 4 | 47 | 21 | 32 | 13 | 1 | 114 | 47 | 21 | 32 | 13 | 1 | 114 |
| 5 | 79 | 35 | 56 | 23 | 3 | 196 | 79 | 38 | 54 | 23 | 2 | 196 |
| 6 | 89 | 41 | 63 | 26 | 4 | 223 | 90 | 42 | 62 | 25 | 3 | 222 |
| 7 | 0 | 0 | 0 | 0 | 0 | 0 | 0 | 0 | 0 | 0 | 0 | 0 |
| 8 | 51 | 19 | 28 | 12 | 2 | 112 | 51 | 20 | 27 | 12 | 2 | 112 |
| 9 | 37 | 14 | 19 | 9 | 2 | 81 | 37 | 15 | 19 | 9 | 1 | 81 |
| 10 | 74 | 31 | 50 | 21 | 4 | 180 | 74 | 32 | 50 | 21 | 4 | 181 |
| 11 | 596 | 206 | 337 | 131 | 35 | 1305 | 597 | 215 | 331 | 129 | 29 | 1301 |
| 12 | 74 | 25 | 42 | 16 | 4 | 161 | 75 | 26 | 41 | 16 | 3 | 161 |
| 13 | 1080 | 419 | 548 | 187 | 79 | 2313 | 1082 | 439 | 540 | 184 | 65 | 2310 |
| 14 | 1455 | 598 | 740 | 310 | 117 | 3220 | 1459 | 628 | 730 | 308 | 96 | 3221 |
| 15 | 1584 | 661 | 866 | 494 | 188 | 3793 | 1589 | 693 | 854 | 489 | 155 | 3780 |
| 16 | 1385 | 608 | 679 | 328 | 178 | 3178 | 1390 | 639 | 672 | 324 | 143 | 3168 |
| 17 | 62 | 21 | 36 | 13 | 3 | 135 | 63 | 22 | 34 | 13 | 2 | 134 |
| 18 | 250 | 109 | 122 | 59 | 31 | 571 | 249 | 115 | 121 | 58 | 25 | 568 |
| 19 | 120 | 49 | 65 | 37 | 13 | 284 | 120 | 52 | 64 | 36 | 11 | 283 |
| 20 | 35 | 9 | 27 | 7 | 3 | 81 | 39 | 16 | 22 | 7 | 2 | 86 |
| 21 | 54 | 27 | 48 | 11 | 1 | 141 | 54 | 29 | 47 | 10 | 0 | 140 |
| 22 | 6 | 2 | 3 | 1 | 0 | 12 | 6 | 2 | 3 | 1 | 0 | 12 |
| 23 | 348 | 153 | 143 | 77 | 29 | 750 | 293 | 149 | 126 | 65 | 30 | 663 |
| 24 | 507 | 147 | 314 | 75 | 15 | 1058 | 507 | 153 | 307 | 73 | 12 | 1052 |
| 25 | 399 | 148 | 189 | 77 | 10 | 823 | 377 | 154 | 206 | 62 | 5 | 804 |
| AREA TOTAL | 8571 | 3461 | 4566 | 1995 | 740 | 19333 | 8519 | 3624 | 4497 | 1944 | 605 | 19189 |

**Figure 19.4b** Typical printout.

HOUSING AND POPULATION ATTRIBUTES FOR TIME PERIOD ,1974
EDUCATION IN DECIMAL PERCENT EXCEPT MEDIAN
5 TO 35 YEARS OF AGE

| AREAL UNIT | KINDER | ELEM. | HIGH SCHOOL | JUNIOR COLLEGE | COLLEGE | VOC. EDUCATE. | H.S. DROP OUT | NOT CLASSIFIED | ADULT 15-65 EDUCATION |
|---|---|---|---|---|---|---|---|---|---|
| 1 | 0.0242 | 0.2428 | 0.1054 | 0.2387 | 0.2037 | 0.1417 | 0.0434 | 0.0 | 0.0 |
| 2 | 0.0501 | 0.4133 | 0.0989 | 0.2212 | 0.0328 | 0.1383 | 0.0453 | 0.0 | 0.0 |
| 3 | 0.0367 | 0.4120 | 0.1497 | 0.2624 | 0.0314 | 0.0407 | 0.0671 | 0.0 | 0.0 |
| 4 | 0.0291 | 0.3592 | 0.1263 | 0.2658 | 0.0908 | 0.0366 | 0.0922 | 0.0 | 0.0 |
| 5 | 0.0391 | 0.4231 | 0.1384 | 0.2605 | 0.0262 | 0.0353 | 0.0774 | 0.0 | 0.0 |
| 6 | 0.0392 | 0.4266 | 0.1455 | 0.2661 | 0.0340 | 0.0339 | 0.0547 | 0.0 | 0.0 |
| 7 | 0.0 | 0.5083 | 0.1516 | 0.2757 | 0.0120 | 0.0 | 0.0524 | 0.0 | 0.0 |
| 8 | 0.0465 | 0.4476 | 0.1299 | 0.2633 | 0.0299 | 0.0250 | 0.0578 | 0.0 | 0.0 |
| 9 | 0.0339 | 0.4527 | 0.1127 | 0.2646 | 0.0190 | 0.0301 | 0.0870 | 0.0 | 0.0 |
| 10 | 0.0110 | 0.4408 | 0.1241 | 0.2651 | 0.0199 | 0.0321 | 0.1069 | 0.0 | 0.0 |
| 11 | 0.0394 | 0.4272 | 0.1047 | 0.2585 | 0.0264 | 0.0788 | 0.0650 | 0.0 | 0.0 |
| 12 | 0.0190 | 0.3268 | 0.1350 | 0.2681 | 0.0924 | 0.0746 | 0.0841 | 0.0 | 0.0 |
| 13 | 0.0351 | 0.4161 | 0.1082 | 0.2359 | 0.0190 | 0.0848 | 0.1010 | 0.0 | 0.0 |
| 14 | 0.0182 | 0.3824 | 0.1186 | 0.2477 | 0.0252 | 0.0801 | 0.1278 | 0.0 | 0.0 |
| 15 | 0.0328 | 0.4473 | 0.1093 | 0.1597 | 0.0147 | 0.0841 | 0.1521 | 0.0 | 0.0 |
| 16 | 0.0109 | 0.3249 | 0.1201 | 0.2480 | 0.0474 | 0.0873 | 0.1614 | 0.0000 | 0.0 |
| 17 | 0.0346 | 0.3606 | 0.1375 | 0.2655 | 0.0477 | 0.0823 | 0.0719 | 0.0 | 0.0 |
| 18 | 0.0139 | 0.3555 | 0.1385 | 0.2621 | 0.0619 | 0.0888 | 0.0793 | 0.0 | 0.0 |
| 19 | 0.0226 | 0.3627 | 0.1249 | 0.2504 | 0.0542 | 0.0758 | 0.1095 | 0.0 | 0.0 |
| 20 | 0.0 | 0.4072 | 0.1216 | 0.2411 | 0.0344 | 0.1359 | 0.0599 | 0.0 | 0.0 |
| 21 | 0.0 | 0.4501 | 0.1399 | 0.2757 | 0.0338 | 0.0380 | 0.0625 | 0.0 | 0.0 |
| 22 | 0.0787 | 0.4185 | 0.1449 | 0.2671 | 0.0214 | 0.0258 | 0.0437 | 0.0 | 0.0 |
| 23 | 0.0267 | 0.4185 | 0.1125 | 0.2180 | 0.0141 | 0.1369 | 0.0734 | 0.0 | 0.0 |
| 24 | 0.0380 | 0.4172 | 0.1036 | 0.2229 | 0.0156 | 0.1252 | 0.0774 | 0.0 | 0.0 |
| 25 | 0.0 | 0.4693 | 0.1006 | 0.2260 | 0.0098 | 0.1334 | 0.0609 | 0.0 | 0.0 |
| AREA AVE. | 0.0261 | 0.3938 | 0.1222 | 0.2472 | 0.0457 | 0.0803 | 0.0846 | 0.0846 | 0.0 |

25 + YEARS OF AGE

| AREAL UNIT | NO SCHOOL | 1-7YRS COMPLETE | 8YRS COMPLETE | 9-11YRS COMPLETE | 12YRS COMPLETE | 1-3YRS COLLEGE | 4+YRS COLLEGE | MEDIAN SCH YRS |
|---|---|---|---|---|---|---|---|---|
| 1 | 0.0023 | 0.0366 | 0.1022 | 0.1250 | 0.2436 | 0.2194 | 0.2709 | 12.9540 |
| 2 | 0.0104 | 0.1120 | 0.1265 | 0.1272 | 0.2444 | 0.2701 | 0.1094 | 12.5086 |
| 3 | 0.0163 | 0.0495 | 0.0056 | 0.0396 | 0.4959 | 0.2126 | 0.1804 | 12.7952 |
| 4 | 0.0026 | 0.0434 | 0.1498 | 0.1738 | 0.3178 | 0.1621 | 0.1505 | 12.4092 |
| 5 | 0.0038 | 0.0328 | 0.1108 | 0.1616 | 0.3852 | 0.1594 | 0.1464 | 12.4986 |
| 6 | 0.0015 | 0.0375 | 0.0020 | 0.1800 | 0.4181 | 0.1903 | 0.1706 | 12.6683 |
| 7 | 0.0040 | 0.0690 | 0.2066 | 0.1788 | 0.3858 | 0.0867 | 0.0691 | 12.1128 |
| 8 | 0.0013 | 0.0172 | 0.0830 | 0.1349 | 0.3578 | 0.1829 | 0.2230 | 12.7372 |
| 9 | 0.0049 | 0.0761 | 0.1348 | 0.1845 | 0.3541 | 0.1175 | 0.1282 | 12.2830 |
| 10 | 0.0025 | 0.0655 | 0.1647 | 0.1858 | 0.3546 | 0.1287 | 0.0982 | 12.2307 |
| 11 | 0.0039 | 0.0707 | 0.1377 | 0.2141 | 0.3649 | 0.1196 | 0.0893 | 12.2032 |
| 12 | 0.0026 | 0.0413 | 0.1269 | 0.1516 | 0.3028 | 0.1951 | 0.1796 | 12.5870 |
| 13 | 0.0602 | 0.1461 | 0.1824 | 0.2271 | 0.2713 | 0.0590 | 0.0538 | 10.4962 |
| 14 | 0.0314 | 0.1393 | 0.2151 | 0.2187 | 0.2714 | 0.0736 | 0.0504 | 10.5793 |
| 15 | 0.0376 | 0.2332 | 0.1642 | 0.2144 | 0.2215 | 0.0789 | 0.0503 | 9.9265 |
| 16 | 0.0179 | 0.1234 | 0.1668 | 0.1910 | 0.2930 | 0.1136 | 0.0943 | 12.0141 |
| 17 | 0.0012 | 0.0068 | 0.0978 | 0.1509 | 0.3339 | 0.2089 | 0.2005 | 12.7291 |
| 18 | 0.0051 | 0.0202 | 0.1039 | 0.1490 | 0.3342 | 0.1824 | 0.2053 | 12.6654 |
| 19 | 0.0048 | 0.0205 | 0.3112 | 0.1188 | 0.2346 | 0.1626 | 0.1476 | 12.1917 |
| 20 | 0.0012 | 0.0235 | 0.1166 | 0.1813 | 0.4075 | 0.1621 | 0.1078 | 12.4361 |
| 21 | 0.0025 | 0.0231 | 0.1135 | 0.1753 | 0.4001 | 0.1687 | 0.1168 | 12.4653 |
| 22 | 0.0024 | 0.0075 | 0.0767 | 0.1038 | 0.2310 | 0.2275 | 0.3512 | 14.0239 |
| 23 | 0.0125 | 0.1710 | 0.2383 | 0.1678 | 0.2617 | 0.0787 | 0.0699 | 10.4182 |
| 24 | 0.0025 | 0.0454 | 0.1189 | 0.2037 | 0.4154 | 0.1255 | 0.0886 | 12.3129 |
| 25 | 0.0134 | 0.1293 | 0.2218 | 0.2613 | 0.3046 | 0.0473 | 0.0222 | 10.5407 |
| AREA AVE. | 0.0121 | 0.0763 | 0.1385 | 0.1750 | 0.3258 | 0.1439 | 0.1284 | 11.9976 |

Figure 19.4c Typical printout.

He runs back, fills the bucket, brings it back to Lake Mead, and again throws the water into the lake. The water level still does not rise. The water that he is throwing into the lake isn't going to fill the lake for a long time. The water level is going to stay pretty much the same. To conclude the analogy, we found that the amount of money we were targeting for improvement in the slum area was just a drop in the bucket – inadequate to solve a problem of that size. Thus, the slight difference between the two budget mixes could be explained quantitatively.

Let us look at another factor in the city, education (see Figure 19.8). Whereas the income change for two programs as opposed to no program seemed to produce minor results, in the area of education the results produced are

CAPSBURG COMMUNITY PROFILE*
(Original time period - 1960)

*General
Characteristics*

| Area | Neighborhood Communities | | | | | | | |
|---|---|---|---|---|---|---|---|---|
| | 1 | 2 | 3 | 4 | 5 | 6 | 7 | Total |
| Population | 4133 | 4751 | 5869 | 7733 | 7078 | 3753 | 5787 | 39,104 |
| Housing unit | 1432 | 1577 | 1875 | 2716 | 2000 | 1077 | 1938 | 12,615 |
| Area (1000 sq.ft.) | 8000 | 8000 | 31500 | 13000 | 16000 | 25000 | 6000 | 101,500 |

*Population
Characteristics*

| | | | | | | | | |
|---|---|---|---|---|---|---|---|---|
| Pop./H.Hold | 3.0 | 3.3 | 3.2 | 3.0 | 3.7 | 3.6 | 2.9 | |
| Pop./1000 sq.ft. | .5 | .6 | .2 | .6 | .4 | .1 | 1.0 | |
| Pop. 25 yr. + W H. School + (%) | 48 | 30 | 60 | 19 | 38 | 50 | 12 | |
| Non-white (%) | 4 | 94 | -0- | 3 | -0- | 1 | 98 | |
| Pop. owning H. units (%) | 40 | 45 | 58 | 42 | 69 | 84 | 21 | |
| Pop. renting H. units (%) | 56 | 53 | 39 | 54 | 28 | 12 | 77 | |

*Source: All data directly from 1960 census for actual metropolitan areas or derived from actual census data.

**Figure 19.5** Community projects – under steady employment assumption.

COMMUNITY PROJECTS - UNDER STEADY EMPLOYMENT ASSUMPTION

| Project No. | Project Description | Target Area | Funding (thousand $) | | | | | |
|---|---|---|---|---|---|---|---|---|
| | | | Max A Level | | | Max B Level | | |
| | | | 1 | 2 | 3 | 1 | 2 | 3 |
| 1 | Small business development | City wide | 7 | 15 | 30 | 7 | 15 | 30 |
| 2 | Job development project | Area 7 | 22 | 45 | 90 | 0 | 0 | 0 |
| 3 | Head start | City wide | 0 | 12 | 25 | 0 | 0 | 0 |
| 4 | Remedial education in elementary school | City wide | 11 | 22 | 45 | 11 | 22 | 45 |
| 5 | Year-round preschool | Area 7 | 6 | 22 | 25 | 6 | 12 | 25 |
| 6 | Drop-out counseling in high schools | City wide | 70 | 140 | 280 | 0 | 0 | 0 |
| 7 | Work study program | Area 7 | 70 | 140 | 280 | 70 | 140 | 280 |
| | Total Budget (thousands) | | 186 | 396 | 775 | 94 | 189 | 380 |

**Figure 19.6** Community projects under steady-employment assumption.

quite dramatic. Initiation of an education program, as compared to no education program at all, causes dramatic improvements. However, there was little *difference* between the two funded programs. Look at the number of students who are in Area 7 and at the way the two mixes have been targeted. You will find little difference in the amount of money spent for education; one amount is roughly about $100 more per student per year than the other. Why does it take such a long period of time before the influence of a good program is felt in a slum area? Shouldn't we obtain beneficial results immediately?

First, it takes a considerable amount of time before a program can be fully implemented. In Capsburg, not enough teachers were available to initiate the programs. In the runs made, approximately two years were required to recruit and hire the people and to get the programs approved by the electorate. Measuring improvement in people with more than eight years of schooling, at least eight years also passed before the students got through the program. Our intuitive guess about the city suggested that initiating programs in education would result in dramatic improvements in the educational process. It didn't! In this example, it took a much longer time than we anticipated.

There is an "almost infinite" variety of programs that could be analyzed. There is no particular reason why we selected these two programs. However, an examination of them raises an important question: Is it better to take action with respect to *immediate* outcome, or with respect to relative educational improvement? Because of the dynamic interaction of the city system, the question of real values becomes extremely important. This question can be answered by a cost-benefit analysis, that is, by taking a set of program mixes and by varying the budget levels, at a given period of time, to determine the effect of marginally increasing or decreasing the budget levels relative to particular objectives or values. An example is the case depicted, showing the percentages of people with less than eight years in school (Figure 19.9). This analysis suggests that an increase above the $400,000 level provides little increase in performance; the budget level must be significantly greater before any significant improvements in results are produced.

## Combinations of programs

After making this analysis, we began to realize that a logical and comprehensive analysis of the city system could give us much more information than our own individual and intuitional views of the city as a series of subsystems. We then began to develop a plan to pool projects and program mixes in order to develop a strategy for program formulation in the city system. We set about developing different mixes of projects (see Figure 19.10) with long-term results for improving either the educational or the income levels through manpower development and utilization. Then, we ran these programs in the city system model. One interesting finding concerned the percentage of people in two key employment groups: Group 3, the skilled blue-collar workers, and Group 4, the laborers. The outcome of the programs (Figure 19.11) for these two groups suggests that there is a difference in manpower orientation versus educational programs.

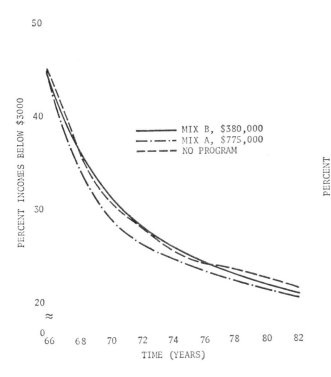

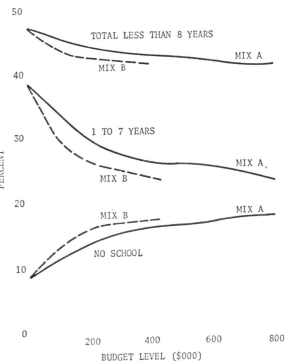

**Figure 19.7** Capsburg income attributes – Area 7 percent nonwhite income less than $3000 for two cap project mixes.

**Figure 19.8** Capsburg education attributes – 1982 Area 7 cap budget vs percent with less than 8 years of school.

Because of the particular way in which the programs were targeted (i.e., heavy focus on Area 7), the suggestion seemed to emerge that in Area 7 in 1968, it would be nearly impossible to get a shoeshine, for example, since no laborers or service workers were available. However, by 1972, the situation would appear to have returned to normal. In order to explain this apparently unrealistic situation, we examined the model structures, the targeting, and the budgeting involved and found that the programs were generating more jobs in Area 7 for Groups 1, 2, and 3 occupation levels than there were people available to fill. In effect, then, the shoeshine boy could get a job as a skilled blue-collar worker even though he was not qualified. In other words, although the shoeshine jobs were available, the manpower to shine the shoes was not. If such was the case, and if an improvement was made in the area, why did the situation return to its normal state?

The model structure took into account the mobility of the population. The skilled blue-collar worker in Area 7 was able to work at the next higher occupational level, now; and his income was increased. The increased income then enabled him to "escape" the slum, by moving out. The shoeshine boy also had more money and could now afford a slightly higher standard of living. Who, then, occupied the vacant housing left by the blue-collar worker? The model suggests that a new individual from outside the core community, an individual at a lower poverty level than the man who had previously lived there, then moved in. For this particular example, what has been done is to bring into the slums people whose income levels, health, and education levels are worse than such levels for the people who had previously lived there. By trying to improve social and economic conditions through targeting programs in the "slum area" we have simply "moved the poverty around".

As new people move into Area 7, people become available to shine shoes and the situation returns to normal. We assumed, as do many planners, that if the neighborhood were improved it would be better off. We neglected to take into consideration the fact that, in the dynamic city system, people move about and have the ability to migrate from one place to another. Through this particular set of programs, we could improve the lot of the people in the area; but there would still remain other unimproved areas. In general, the population in Area 7 remained constant over time; but the nonwhite population in Area 3 and in Area 6 grew dramatically.

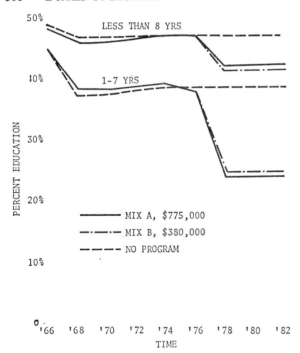

**Figure 19.9** Capsburg education attributes – area 7 percent with less than 8 years of school for two project mixes.

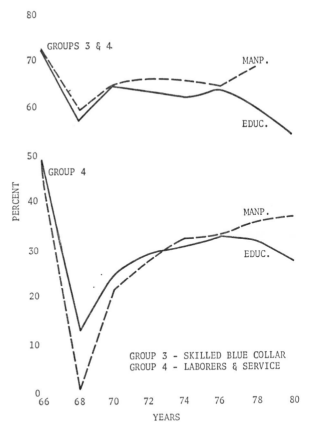

**Figure 19.11** Capsburg employment attributes – Area 7 percent nonwhite males in occupation groups 3 & 4 for two project mixes.

COMMUNITY PROJECTS - RISING EMPLOYMENT

| Project No. | Project Description | Target Area | Funding level (thousands) Education | Manpower |
|---|---|---|---|---|
| 1 | Day care for children of working mothers | City-wide | $200 | $200 |
| 2 | Basic education for the unemployed | City-wide | 490 | 490 |
| 3 | Small business development | Area 7 | 30 | 30 |
| 4 | Adult education and vocational training | Area 7 | 0 | 90 |
| 5 | Job development project | Area 7 | 0 | 640 |
| 6 | Head start | City-wide | 25 | 25 |
| 7 | Remedial education in elementary school | City-wide | 45 | 0 |
| 8 | Year-round preschool | Area 7 | 25 | 25 |
| 9 | Upward bound | Area 7 | 25 | 0 |
| 10 | Drop-out counseling, in high schools | City-wide | 280 | 280 |
| | Total budget (thousands) | | $1,120 | $1,780 |

**Figure 19.10**

## Conclusions

The examples discussed are only illustrations of a hypothetical community, but they demonstrate the value of looking at the whole system in planning for change. City system models, such as the one described here, can be extremely useful in planning for urban and social change. An overview of the application of such a simulation model is shown in Figure 19.12.

One of the extremely important consequences of this approach is that it allows one to obtain data on the effects of implementing particular policies and to begin to compare this data with the actual occurrences at a future time. In most cities today there is little opportunity to compare the assumptions which initiated the planning and decision process for social change with the final results.

The city system model also provides the guidelines for further research. It acts as a vehicle for further analytical refinements, checks, and reexamination of the decision and the constraints. This type of model technique is now being

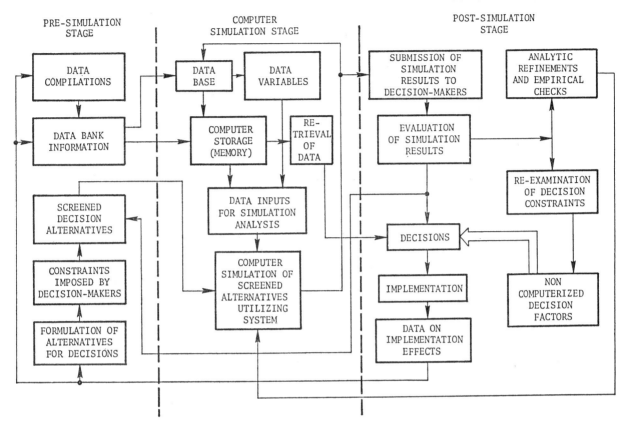

**Figure 19.12** Application of the computer-based system in urban planning and decision process.

applied in a few limited cases. It is still a long way from practical use, but it represents an approach to viewing the city as a system.

A number of problems exist in using this type of technique. First of all, the logic of the model has not yet been fully tested over time; further detailing is required, particularly in the areas of education, health, and welfare. In addition, there is a need for the creation of a regional or rural subsystem to adequately consider migration from the city core. At present, we can only view this city as an isolated system, and we can't consider the impact of the city on the surrounding area. For this reason, one needs to build an area model. As for the policy or government action model, it will require extensive analysis and definition before it can become a useful tool. Lastly, a technique is required to generate exogenous parameters, i.e., the specific descriptions which identify the differences in an urban area and which characterize it quantitatively, or, to put it differently, to identify those differences which separate one city from another (in contrast to those characteristics which cities share in general).

There are many advantages to the model city system approach. First of all, this approach focuses on action. Second, it provides a mechanism for considering alternative plans and priorities; many approaches to city planning consider only one plan, or a few variations on a single plan, ignoring alternative ways of achieving the same goals. Third, it forces a quantitative consideration of both the short-run and long-run effects. In many practical cases, the emphasis is on the short range and ignores the long range, or is on the long range and ignores the short range. The city system model forces one to consider both time frames at the same level of detail. This approach tends to reduce areas of potential conflict due to intuition (which, as noted above, is frequently wrong), and it allows more emphasis to be placed on the basic objectives and values. The city system model also provides a basis for organizing data and for utilizing the decisions to be made. It acts as a model structure and mechanism for deciding how aggregated or how disaggregated a data structure needs to be.

In summary, we have described an approach, a first attempt to quantitatively structure the city as a dynamic system, using computer and operations-research techniques. The methodology allows us to *begin* the exceedingly difficult task of predicting community characteristics over time, of exploring the types of government action, and of examining the future impact of individual projects, alternative project mixes, and budget levels. It provides us with a launching point for the examination of alternate organizations and types of communities.

As an approach it is only in the early stages of development. But new techniques like these are now becoming available and will in time provide the basis for operating the city as a system.

## Bibliography

1 Alonso, W. (1964) *Location and land use*, Harvard University Press, Cambridge, Massachusetts.

2 Barnes, C. F. Jr (1961) *Integrating land use and traffic forecasting*, presented at the 40th Annual Meeting of the Highway Research Board.

3 Berry, B. J. L. (1963) *Commercial structure and commercial blight*, University of Chicago, Department of Geography, Research Paper **86**.

4 Blumberg, D. F. (1966) *Systems for planning urban and social change – an operations research approach*, Philco-Ford Corporation.

5 Bogue, D. J. (1948) *The structure of the metropolitan community*, Ph.D. thesis at University of Michigan.

6 Bruck, H. W. (1963) "The simplified distribution model", *Penn–Jersey Transportation Study P–J Program Review Memo No 5*.

7 Chapin, F. S. Jr and Weiss, S. F. (1962) *Urban growth dynamics*, University of North Carolina.

8 "Chicago area transportation study" (1960) **11**, *Data Projections*.

9 "CPR experience in major cities" (1964) sponsored by the *Urban Renewal Administration* and by the *National Association of Housing and Renewal Officials*, Washington, D.C.

10 de Cani, J. S. (1961) "On the construction of stochastic models of population growth and migration", *Journal of the Regional Science Association*.

11 "Employment, income, and population submodels" (1964) *Community Renewal Program*, Pittsburgh, Pennsylvania.

12 Fisher, F. M. and Lefeber, L. (1964) *Review and evaluation of the work undertaken by Traffic Research Corporation for the Boston Regional Planning Project*, a Report to the Boston, Mass., Transportation Committee.

13 Garrison, W. L. (1960) "Toward simulation models of urban growth and development", *Northwestern University Proceedings of the IGU in Urban Geography, Lund*.

14 Hansen, W. B. (1961) "An approach to the analysis of metropolitan residential extension", *Journal of Regional Science* **3**.

15 Horwood, E. M. (1962) "A three dimensional calculus model of urban settlement", University of Washington HRB Bulletin **347**.

16 Kain, J. F. and Meyer, J. R. (1961) *A first approximation to a Rand model for study of urban transportation*, The RAND Corporation.

17 Lowrey, I. S. (1964) *A model of metropolis*, RAND Research Memorandum **RM-4035-RC**.

18 Mindlin, A. (1963) *Tract facts and housing discrimination – the use of census tract data in assessing the need for fair housing legislation*, Papers presented at the Census Tract Conference. Working paper **17** U.S. Department of Commerce, Bureau of Assessors.

19 Morse, P. M. (ed.) (1967) *Operations research for public systems*, MIT Press.

20 Muth, R. F. (1960) *The spatial structure of the housing market*, presented before the Econometric Society and the Regional Science Association.

21 Orcutt, G. H. (1964) *Simulation of economic systems: model description and solution*, presented at the IBM Conference on Simulation Models, New York.

22 Pendleton, W. C. (1962) *The value of highway accessibility*, presented to the 41st Annual Meeting of the Highway Research Board.

23 Pitts, F. R. (1964) *Scale and purpose in urban simulation models*, discussion paper prepared for the Conference on Strategy for Regional Growth, Iowa.

24 *Project SCANCAP* (1966) final reports on Contract No. OEO633 by Blumberg, D. F., Whorf, R., Goldmard, T. *et al.*, Philco-Ford Corporation Operations Research and Long Range Planning Activity Report to the Office of Economic Opportunity Research and Planning Directorate.

25 Seidman, D. R. (1964) *Report on the Activities Allocation Model*, Penn–Jersey Transportation Study.

26 Seidman, D. R. (1964) *An operational model of the residential land market*, paper presented at the Seminar on Models of Metropolitan Land Use Development, University of Pennsylvania.

27 Steger, W. A. (1964) *Data and information management in a large scale modeling effort: the Pittsburgh Urban Renewal Simulation Model*, CONSAD Research

Corporation Seminar on Models of Metropolitan Land Use Development, University of Pennsylvania.

28 Stevens, B. B. and Coughlin, R. E. (1959) "A note on inter-areal linear programming for a metropolitan region", *Journal of the Regional Science Association*.

29 Traffic Research Corporation (1963) *Review of existing land use forecasting techniques*, prepared for the Boston Regional Planning Project and others.

30 Van Huyck and Horning (1962) *The citizens guide to urban renewal*, Chandler Davis.

31 Voorhees, A. M. (1959) "The nature and uses of models in city planning", Alan M. Voorhees and Associates, Special Issue of *AIP Journal*.

32 Wingo, L. Jr (1961) *Transportation and urban land*, Resources for the Future Inc.

33 Wolfe, H. B. and Ernst, M. L. "A model of San Francisco housing market", Technical Paper **8** Arthur D. Little Inc., Boston, Mass.

34 Wood, R. C. and Almendinger, V. (1960) *1400 Governments*, Cambridge, Harvard University Press.

35 Zwick, C. J. (1962) *Models of urban change: their role in urban transportation research*, the RAND Corporation.

# Glossary

*Amplifier* An amplifier is a device or system which increases either the effort, flow, or the power level of a signal or physical quantity.

*Amplitude* The maximum departure from an equilibrium value. Used to define one of the major characteristics of a wave, its maximum value above or below an equilibrium value.

*Anabolism* The conversion of simple compounds into living, organized substance. Also called Constructive Metabolism (cf. catabolism).

*Artificial Intelligence* The use of computers or electro-mechanical or electro-chemical devices to perform operations analogous to the human abilities of learning and decision making.

*Autotrophe* An organism which is independent of outside sources of organic substances for the provision of its own organic constituents. It can manufacture its own organic substances from inorganic material, e.g. certain bacteria and some plants.

*Biosphere* The part of the Earth's atmosphere in which life can exist.

*Black Box* A component of a system that is only considered in terms of its inputs and outputs. Its internal mechanisms may be unknown or ignored.

*Catabolism* The conversion of living, organized substance into simpler compounds also termed Destructive Metabolism (cf. anabolism).

*Closed Loop* A system where part of the output is fed back to the input so that the system's output can affect its input or some of its operating characteristics.

*Closed System* A system which does not take in or give out anything to its environment.

*Cluster-analysis* A specific type of multi-variate analysis (see multi-variate).

*Constraint* A requirement that a system has to satisfy, or a limit or set of limits restricting its behaviour.

*Core Temperature* Internal body temperature.

*Cost–Benefit Analysis* A method for comparing the outcomes (benefits and disbenefits) of different courses of action in monetary terms.

*Cost Function* An equation which relates cost to the variables in a given situation.

*Cybernetics* The study of control and communication in living beings and machines.

*Damping* Suppression of the degree of movement or change of a variable.

*Demography* The field of human population analysis, also applied to the study of other animal populations.

*Deterministic* Having a specific outcome or where outcomes must follow from specific courses of action or inputs (compare stochastic).

*D.N.A.–Deoxyribonucleic acid* Long thread-like molecules, found in chromosomes and viruses, responsible for storing the genetic code.

*Ecology* The study of the relation of plants and animals to their environment.

*Econometric* The branch of economics which expresses theories in mathematical terms in order to verify them by statistical methods.

*Ecosystem* A natural unit of living and nonliving elements which interact to produce a stable system.

*Endogenous* Originating within the organism, e.g. endogenous metabolism is concerned with tissue waste and growth.

*Entropy* The entropy of a system is a measure of its degree of disorder.

*Environment* The totality of external conditions which affect the behaviour of a system.

*Epiphyte* Plant attached to another plant, not growing parasitically upon it but merely using it for support, e.g. lichens on trees.

*Epistemology* The theory of knowledge.

*Equilibrium* A state of balance.

*Exogenous* Originating outside the organism, e.g. exogenous metabolism concerned with effector activities and temperature.

*Feedback* The return of some of the output of a system as input or where the input to a system is affected by the present output (cf. closed loop).

*Frequency* The rate at which a repeated event or change occurs expressed as the number of occurrences in a standard time interval.

*Game Theory* A mathematical approach to idealized problems of competitive conflict or games.

*Heterotrophe* An organism requiring a supply of organic material (food) from its environment from which to make most of its own organic constituents. Depends ultimately on synthetic activities of autotrophic (q.v.) organisms, e.g. all animals and fungi, most bacteria, and a few plants.

*Hill-climbing* A method of finding the highest or lowest values of a function, by changing individual variables and noting the effect.

*Holistic* Pertaining to totality, or to the whole.

*Homeostasis* The maintenance of static or dynamic stability irrespective of external effects.

*Isomorphism* Similarity or identity in form.

*Iterative* Repeated application of a procedure or method.

*Markov Chains* Chains of successive events forming a stochastic process. The particular property of a Markov chain is that the probability of the next event to come depends only on the present state *not* of any previous event.

*Metaphysics* The branch of speculative philosophy which deals with the ultimate nature of things.

*Morphogenesis* The origination of morphological characters, i.e. characteristics of form.

*Multi-variate Factor Analysis* A mathematical method of analysing sets of data to discover which variables are statistically linked, by causative or other factors.

*Multi-variate Analysis* The branch of statistical analysis concerned with the relationship of sets of dependent variates.

*Noise* Any disturbance which does not represent any part of a message from a specified source. Usually used to refer to random disturbances.

*Nomothetic* Relating to the formulation of laws.

*Norm* A standard, or model, or pattern, or type to which individuals in a group tend to conform.

*Onteogeny or Ontogeny* The developmental history of the individual organism (compare *phylogeny*).

*Open Loop* A control system in which corrective action is not automatic, but depends on external intervention. Control actions are made without reference to the present output of the system.

*Open System* A system that is connected to, and interacts with, its environment.

*Optimization* Finding the "best" solution or situation in terms of some stated criteria.

*Paradigm* A pattern or example.

*P.E.R.T. (Program Evaluation and Review Technique)* A method of expressing sets of events and the time between them in a network, and of analysing the network to determine which sequence of events will determine the overall time taken to complete the set.

*pH* A measure of acidity, hydrion concentration.

*Photosynthesis* The process by which green plants manufacture their carbohydrates from atmospheric carbon dioxide and water in the presence of sunlight.

*Phylogeny* The evolutionary development of any organic type or species.

*Physiognomic* Relating the features of the face or form to a person's character.

*Phytosociological* Branch of botany comprising ecology (relationship between organism and its surroundings), chorology (biogeography), and genetics (hereditary and variation) of plant associations.

*Program(me)* A predetermined plan or set of instructions.

*Recursive* A procedure which includes itself within the procedure.

*Retina* The light-sensitive layer in the eye.

*Role* The part or character which a component has to play, undertake, or assume. Chiefly with reference to the part or parts played by a person in society or his life.

*Role Set* Refers to the set of social roles with which a person interacts by virtue of occupying a particular status. E.g. the status of a schoolteacher has a distinctive role set, relating the teacher to his pupils, to colleagues, to the school principal.

*Role-taking* Taking the role of the other. Role-taking attempts to explain how social interaction is possible as a sustained activity where each individual is able to take different roles successfully.

*R.N.A.–Ribonucleic Acid* Long thread-like molecules, found in living cells and viruses.

*Saccadic Movement* Sudden movement of the eyes from one fixation point to another.

*Sensitivity Analysis* A method of discovering by how much the estimates used in a model can vary without changing the result.

*Shannon's 10th Theorem* "If noise appears in a message, the amount of noise that can be removed by a correction channel is limited to the amount of information that can be carried by the channel."

*Signal* The physical embodiment of a message.

*Steady-state* A situation where inputs and outputs are constant.

*Stochastic* Having a probability attached to it. A stochastic process is one where the next event is probabilistically related to previous events.

*Syndrome* A complex set of various symptoms which are thought to be characteristic of a disease.

*Synergy* Special correlated action or co-operation resulting in unusual or unexpected results. Sometimes expressed as $2 + 2 = 5$, which is meant to illustrate that co-ordination of objects may give a larger result than their individual characteristics suggest.

*System* An entity which consists of interdependent parts.

*Taxon* A category in the taxonomic hierarchy (see *Taxonomy*).

*Taxonomy* The science of arranging organisms in logical and natural groups, in such a manner as to cast light on their evolution and affinities. Can be applied to the classification of other objects or items.

*Teleology* The doctrine of final causes or of adaptation to a definite purpose. Loosely, the idea that future states or goals can affect current behaviour.

*Thermodynamics: 2nd Law* The entropy of a closed system increases with time.

*Topology* A branch of geometry concerned with the interconnection of objects rather than with their size or shape.

*Vitalism* The theory that bodily functions are produced by a non-physical inner force called "vital force".

# Biographies of Authors

*F. E. Kast and J. E. Rosenzweig* are both Professors in the Department of Management and Organization at the University of Washington. They have together collaborated to write three books, *Science, Technology and Management*, *The Theory and Management of Systems*, and *Organization and Management*. They have both carried out consultancy work for many large American organizations including Boeing, Port of New York Authority, and the American Defense Department.

*L. von Bertalanffy* is Faculty Professor at the University of New York at Buffalo. He was a founder of the Society for General Systems Research, and has conducted experimental work in the fields of comparative physiology of growth and metabolism, cell physiology, biophysics, and cancer research.

*P. B. Checkland* joined I.C.I. in 1954 and spent fourteen years with the Company (but never worked on chemical problems). He was in the group developing the technology of melt spinning man-made fibres and worked on a number of new products in the fibres area. When he left I.C.I. he was manager of a Research Group. He joined the Systems Engineering Department of Lancaster University in 1969, becoming Head of Department in 1971.

*Gwilym M. Jenkins* is Professor of Systems Engineering in the Department of Systems Engineering at the University of Lancaster. He is the author of two books and numerous articles in applied statistics and systems engineering. Professor Jenkins has consulted for a large number of companies in the U.K. and the U.S.A. He is currently Chairman and Managing Director of I.S.C.O.L. Limited, a consultancy company set up by the University of Lancaster.

*R. L. Ackoff* is Professor of Operations Research at the University of Pennsylvania. He has held various academic positions at the University of Pennsylvania, Wayne State University, and Case Institute of Technology. He has published several books, the most recent of which is *A Concept of Corporate Planning*, and numerous articles in books and journals.

*Kenyon B. DeGreene* has taught at the University of Montana and at the University of California, and has travelled widely throughout the world, living and teaching in the Orient and Europe. He has held positions in systems analysis, design, and management at RAND Corporation, System Development Corporation, Northrop Corporation, and Aerospace Corporation, where he has had extensive experience in the development of large-scale systems, particularly computerized systems. He is Associate Professor of Human Factors, Institute of Aerospace Safety and Management, University of Southern California.

*G. A. Bekey* was Research Engineer with the Department of Engineering at UCLA for four years, and was Computer Applications Engineer and Manager of the Los Angeles Computation Centre of Beckman Instruments, Inc., for three years. He spent four years at the Space Technology Laboratories, Inc. (TRW, Inc.). He is currently Professor of Electrical Engineering and Computer Sciences at the University of Southern California, Los Angeles. His current research is in the fields of computers, human operator dynamics, and biomedical engineering. He is primarily interested in the application of automatic computer techniques to the identification and simulation of mathematical models of complex systems.

*Ida R. Hoos* is at present a member of the Social Sciences Group at the Space Sciences Laboratory. She is studying the sociological implications of technological change, especially the application of systems analysis to social problems. She has served as consultant to the U.S. Department of Health, Education and Welfare, the Ford Foundation, and the U.S. Civil Service Commission. Her articles have appeared in many learned journals, and her books include *Automation in the Office* (1961) and *Retraining the Workforce: Analysis of Current Experience* (1967).

*W. Buckley* received his Ph.D. from the University of Wisconsin and has taught at Brown University and Vassar College. He is Associate Professor of Sociology at the

University of California, Santa Barbara. He is the author of *Sociology and Modern Systems Theory*.

*D. Easton* is Professor of Political Science at the University of Chicago where he has taught since 1947. He is a Fellow of the American Academy of Arts and Science, a Member of the Division of Behavioral Sciences of the National Academy of Sciences-National Research Council, and a Member of the Council of American Political Science Association. He has been a Fellow of the Center for Advanced Study in the Behavioral Sciences at Stanford, a Consultant to the Brookings Institution, and a Ford Professor of Governmental Affairs. The author of numerous articles in a variety of learned journals, he has published the well-known book, *The Political System*, and recently *A Framework for Political Analysis*.

*Professor John H. Milsum* came from England to Canada in 1949, and worked on aircraft deicing problems at the National Research Council in Ottawa. He joined the McGill University faculty in 1961 as Abitibi Professor of Control Engineering in the Department of Electrical Engineering. His research and teaching interests include optimizing control, biological control, and general systems theory.

*Jay W. Forrester* is Professor of Management at M.I.T. where he directs research and teaching in the field of System Dynamics, was one of the nation's leading engineers in design and application of computers, and has made contributions to digital computer technology. He has written many papers in engineering and management. His books *Industrial Dynamics* (1961) and *Urban Dynamics* (1969) laid foundations for the application of System Dynamics to behaviour of complex social systems.

*W. B. Cannon* was George Higginson Professor of Physiology at Harvard Medical School from 1906 to 1942. During this period he served with the British and American expeditionary forces in 1917–18, as Exchange Professor to France in 1929 and Visiting Professor to Peiping in 1935. Researches dealt with the effects of emotion, excitement, internal secretions, and organic stabilization and first formulated in his book *Bodily Changes in Pain, Hunger, Fear and Rage* – a classic of Physiology.

*Dr. Ian P. Priban* is visiting Research Professor in Biomedical Engineering at the University of Virginia and Systems Research Consultant. From 1963 to 1969 he was head of a multi-disciplinary Systems Research Team – working at the National Physical Laboratory, which applied modern control engineering and advanced data processing methods in the identification and simulation of multivariable physiological systems. He is now developing this research further to provide modern prognostic techniques as part of the industrialization of health services facilities.

*Michael Dale* graduated in Botany from the University of Southampton in 1960. An undergraduate interest in computers led to a Ph.D. at Southampton, on multivariate analyses of heterogeneous data. This computational bias was quiescent for a few years spent at the University of Sheffield and lecturing at the University of Hull. In 1967 he was appointed Systems Ecologist with a Land Evaluation project in Australia, and after a few months at the University of Michigan, spent three years in Canberra. After a year at the Grassland Research Institute he returned to Australia as a Numerical Taxonomist.

*Van Court Hare Jnr.* is a Professor in the department of Management in the University of Massachusetts at Amherst. He has worked on the research staffs of several American Universities, and has published many articles and three books, *Systems Analysis: A Diagnostic Approach*, *Introduction to Programming: A Basic Approach*, and *Basic Programming*.

*Dr. Richard de Neufville* is Director of the Civil Engineering Systems Laboratory and Associate Professor at the Massachusetts Institute of Technology (M.I.T.) in Cambridge, Mass., U.S.A. He is the author of *Systems Analysis for Engineers and Managers*, and of numerous journal articles. He is particularly interested in how computer capabilities will lead planners to redefine the design and management process, and is currently applying systems analysis concepts to airport location and planning.

*Donald F. Blumberg*, President of Decision Sciences Corporation, has had extensive experience in the direction of major projects in urban and community planning and in the development of simulation models for regional and urban analysis. He has been a consultant to a number of government organizations such as the Office of Economic Opportunity, the Advanced Research Projects Agency, the City of Toronto, the Province of Ontario, Canada, and the Canadian Manpower Development Commission.

# Index

# Stem Cells

**The cover illustration** provided by P. M. Sharpe
and M. W. J. Ferguson is a transverse histological
section through the mid-plate region of a day 14
embryonic mouse. See chapter by Sharpe and
Ferguson for further details.
ISBN: 0 948601 16 7

# *Stem Cells*

Proceedings of the
British Society for Cell Biology – The Company of Biologists Limited Symposium
Bristol, April 1988

*Organized and edited by*

**Brian I. Lord**
**and**
**T. Michael Dexter**

*(Paterson Institute, Manchester)*

SUPPLEMENT 10   1988
JOURNAL OF CELL SCIENCE
Published by THE COMPANY OF BIOLOGISTS LIMITED, Cambridge

*Typeset, Printed and Published by*
THE COMPANY OF BIOLOGISTS LIMITED
Department of Zoology, University of Cambridge, Downing Street,
Cambridge CB2 3EJ

© The Company of Biologists Limited 1988

ISBN: 0 948601 16 7

# JOURNAL OF CELL SCIENCE SUPPLEMENTS

This volume is the latest in a continuing series on important topics in cell and molecular biology. All supplements are available free to subscribers to *Journal of Cell Science* or may be purchased separately from The Biochemical Society Book Depot, PO Box 32, Commerce Way, Colchester CO2 8HP, UK.

# PREFACE

When I was first approached by the British Society for Cell Biology to organize a meeting on stem cells, the original plan was for a one-day satellite symposium. This was later changed to a full $2\frac{1}{2}$ days 'theme' symposium for the joint meeting of the British Society for Cell Biology and the British Society for Developmental Biology in Bristol. I would like to believe that this change of mind occurred as a result of the many significant advances that have been made in stem cell research since the last symposium sponsored by the British Society for Cell Biology on this topic; a belief that is more than adequately justified by the papers presented at the meeting which are collected together in this book of the proceedings.

With the task of organizing the meeting before me, I naturally enlisted the help and advice of my colleague, Brian Lord, who I knew from past experience had the patience and organizational abilities to meet all the deadlines. The fact that so many first-rate workers, covering a diverse range of topics, were able to attend the meeting and to make their excellent contributions to this book, is due in large part to his efforts.

Was the symposium a success? I believe so; but no doubt the readers of this volume will make their own judgements based upon the contributions. But even for one as prejudiced as myself, it is clear that this area has evolved rapidly over the last few years. The structure of regenerating systems has been defined such that it is now possible, in many cases, to pinpoint precisely where a given cell should be placed in the continuum of development; many ill-defined 'factors' have been replaced by scientifically acceptable molecules of known amino acid structure; genes coding for important regulatory molecules have been cloned and expressed in prokaryote and eukaryote cells; at least some of the steps which are associated with malignant transformation and the generation of tumour stem cells have been characterized; and the intracellular events which are responsible for transducing an external stimulus into a cellular response are being slowly unravelled. But there is still a long way to go. The process of differentiation remains an enigma. Nonetheless, it is clear from these presentations that suitable model systems are now available with which the enthusiastic worker, with a little innovation, can begin to approach this fundamental problem. Meanwhile, as the reader will appreciate, whole new areas of developmental biology (with obvious theoretical and clinical implications) have been opened up by the participants in this symposium.

T. M. Dexter

*The Company of Biologists Limited* is a non-profit-making organization whose directors are active professional biologists. The Company, which was founded in 1925, is the owner and publisher of this and *The Journal of Experimental Biology* and *Development* (formerly *Journal of Embryology and Experimental Morphology*).

*Journal of Cell Science* is devoted to the study of cell organization. Papers will be published dealing with the structure and function of plant and animal cells and their extracellular products, and with such topics as cell growth and division, cell movements and interactions, and cell genetics. Accounts of advances in the relevant techniques will also be published. Contributions concerned with morphogenesis at the cellular and sub-cellular level will be acceptable, as will studies of micro-organisms and viruses, in so far as they are relevant to an understanding of cell organization. Theoretical articles and occasional review articles will be published.

### Subscriptions

*Journal of Cell Science* will be published 14 times in 1989 in the form of 3 volumes, each of 4 parts, and 2 Supplements. The subscription price of volumes 89, 90, 91 plus Supplements 9 and 10 is £355.00 (USA and Canada, US $780.00; Japan, £455.00) post free. Supplements may be purchased individually – prices on application to the Biochemical Society Book Depot. Orders for 1988 may be sent to any bookseller or subscription agent, or to The Biochemical Society Book Depot, PO Box 32, Commerce Way, Colchester CO2 8HP, UK. Copies of the journal for subscribers in the USA and Canada are sent by air to New Jersey for delivery with the minimum delay.

*Back numbers* of the *Journal of Cell Science* may be ordered through The Biochemical Society Book Depot. This journal is the successor to the *Quarterly Journal of Microscopical Science*, back numbers of which are obtainable from Messrs William Dawson & Sons, Cannon House, Park Farm Road, Folkestone, Kent CT19 5EE, UK.

### Copyright and reproduction

# STEM CELLS

# CONTENTS

*J. Cell Sci. Suppl. 10, 1–9 (1988)*
*Printed in Great Britain © The Company of Biologists Limited 1988ES*

# Stem cells: a problem in asymmetry

LEWIS WOLPERT

*Department of Anatomy and Developmental Biology, University College and Middlesex School of Medicine, Windeyer Building, London W1P 6DB, UK*

## Summary

The special property of stem cells is that their development is asymmetric. They give rise both to cells that are identical to themselves and to cells that are different. The mechanism that provides this asymmetry may be intrinsic or extrinsic. Such mechanisms are considered within the context of other systems where asymmetric development occurs. The specification of mating types in yeast provides a clear example of a stem cell system generated intrinsically. In fission yeast it appears that the asymmetry is due to chromosomal differences: this is the only known mechanism for intrinsic asymmetry. While there is good evidence for intrinsic asymmetry in both plants and invertebrates – particularly the nematode – the mechanism is not known. In insects and vertebrates there is no well established example of intrinsic asymmetry if one excludes asymmetric cytoplasmic localization during cleavage of the egg. Asymmetry is thus due to environmental influences. Stem cell systems are usually well structured and the cell's behaviour seems to be position-dependent. This is well established for the stem cells of hydra. By contrast it is claimed that the mammalian haemopoietic system is generated by an intrinsic, asymmetric, probabilistic mechanism – the validity of this view is questioned.

## Introduction

The egg can, in some ways, be thought of as a stem cell in that it multiplies and gives rise to many cell types and, most important, eventually, another egg. These two properties – generating one or more cell types different to the parent cell and self-renewal – are the key properties of a stem cell. It can be seen that, taken separately, each of these two properties are common to many different types of cell. In development it is commonplace for a cell to generate progeny different from the parent cell. That process may involve just maturation along a single lineage as in red blood cell differentiation after commitment to that lineage has been established, or it may involve generating daughter cells whose individual fate may be quite different as in nerve cell differentiation in the early neural tube. The other property, self-renewal, is the normal fate of cell division in a population of multiplying cells. The unique feature of stem cells is that they combine both properties to give asymmetric development and this presents special problems. One of the earliest uses of this concept of a stem cell was in relation to the development of germ cells (Wilson, 1906). The main evidence came from the studies of Boveri (see Wilson, 1906) on the development of *Ascaris* where there is chromatin loss during the early cleavages. Only the cell that gives rise to the germ cells kept its chromatin intact, and it behaves as a stem cell. These ideas are illustrated in Fig. 1.

How then is the asymmetry programmed into the stem cell so that it can generate

Key words: stem cells, asymmetric development, intrinsic asymmetry, microenvironment.

*L. Wolpert*

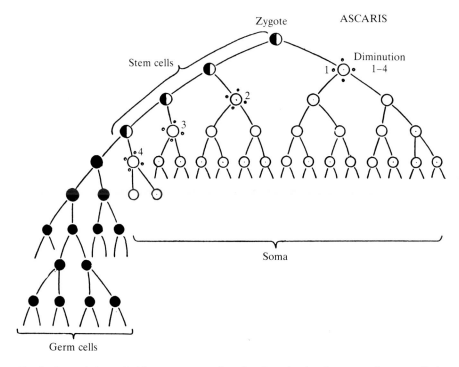

Fig. 1. One of the early ideas on stem cells related to the development of germ cells in Ascaris. This is from Wilson (1925).

offspring that are either like itself or different? The two ways, in principle, by which this can be achieved are (1) the cell may divide asymmetrically, one daughter being like itself, the other different; or (2), both daughters may be the same; but sometimes they will be like the parent cell, and sometimes different. In this case, the probability of being like the parent must be 0·5 or greater. Both these mechanisms will be considered within the context of known cellular mechanisms and evidence from other systems.

## Asymmetrical cell division

If a cell divides so that its daughters cells are different, the problem is how does this difference arise. The only two possibilities are that either there is an internal mechanism, autonomous to the cell, or the difference is imposed by external environmental conditions. The former is often discussed in terms of an autonomous lineage mechanism and the latter in terms of induction or positional signals.

There is very good evidence in early development, that is during cleavage of the egg, that the progeny of a cell division will be different, and that this difference may be ascribed to differences in the cytoplasm which the daughter cells acquire. Examples of this cytoplasmic localization are the polar granules that seem to specify germ cell development in both insects (Illmensee, 1976) and amphibia and the development of muscle in ascidian embryos (Jeffrey, 1983). Remarkably it has been shown that in cleavage-arrested one-cell ascidian embryos multiple-differentiation can occur within just one multinucleated cell (Crowther & Whittaker, 1986). Within the same cell there was ultrastructural evidence for epidermis, notochord, muscle and neural tissue. This presents something of a puzzle. How can these different characteristics develop within the same cell; it implies a not yet understood role for cytoplasmic components in bringing about such differentiation?

It is important to realize that in these cases we are dealing with cleavage of an egg and there is no growth but the subdivision of a cell into smaller units. In these cases the mechanism generating asymmetry is clearly an asymmetric localization of the cytoplasmic microenvironment within the egg. The question then is to what extent such an intrinsic lineage mechanism is involved in development at stages other than cell cleavage. To what extent is cell diversity generated by an intrinsic rather than extrinsic control? In general the evidence for an intrinsic mechanism for generating diversity is very weak in both vertebrates and insects, but rather strong in nematodes and yeasts.

## Intrinsic systems

Yeasts provide a fascinating example of developmental asymmetry in relation to mating types (Klar, 1987). Mating type switch in budding yeasts involves a transposition–substitution event in which the relevant DNA coding region is inserted at the *mat 1* locus. This involves a double stranded DNA break which is generated by a site–specific endonuclease coded for by the *HO* locus. The rules for changing from alpha to gamma mating type are: (i) only mother (older) cells can produce switched progeny. (ii) both progeny switch together. (iii) the switch occurs in most (80 %) cases.

It can be seen (Fig. 2) that the daughter cell behaves like a stem cell generating mother cells capable of switching. The pattern of switching is determined by the timing of HO transcription. It is transiently transcribed only in late $G_1$ in mother

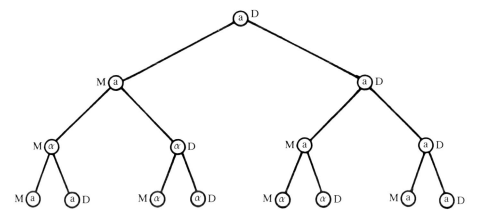

Fig. 2. The pattern of mating type inheritance in a budding yeast. M shows the mother cell, and D the daughter at each division. The mating types are **a** and $\alpha$. The inheritance of the **a** type in daughter cells in this figure follows a stem cell type lineage.

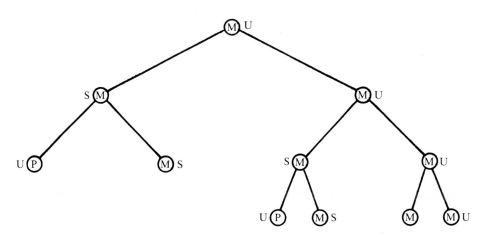

Fig. 3. The inheritance of mating types P and M in a fission yeast. S indicates that the mating type is switchable in one of the daughter cells at the next generation, and U that it is not.

cells and not in daughter cells. Both positive and negative regulatory genes have been described, and SWI5 is of central importance. The most recent evidence suggests that the SWI5 product itself, or something it affects, must be asymmetrically distributed at cell division.

In fission yeast (Fig. 3) the mating types are called P (plus) and M (minus). It too involves gene conversion analogous to the budding yeast switch. Cells may be characterized by whether they are able to switch (S) or unable to switch (U). In 72–94% of cell divisions one member of a pair of sister cells produces a *single* switched cell in the next generation. This gives the one in four rule in relation to mating type switching. The pattern of switchable (S), unswitchable (U) states gives the lineage the asymmetry characteristic of stem cells. It can be seen that the change from a switchable to an unswitchable state is just like a stem cell lineage, the mother cell remaining unswitchable and giving one switchable daughter at each division.

It has now been shown that the competence for switching in fission yeasts may be acquired through inheritance of a chromosome that was marked at the *mat 1* locus, one generation earlier (Klar, 1987). The basic idea is that just one strand of the DNA is imprinted by, for example, methylation and this provides the difference between daughter cells and permits switching to occur. This is the only known case where the mechanism for an internal asymmetry may have been established.

One of the clearest cases of asymmetric cell division of a stem cell is in the cambium of plants (Walbot & Holder, 1987). Whenever a cambial cell divides so that the larger daughter cell lies outwards that cell becomes phloem while the inner cell remains a cambial stem cell. Whenever the larger daughter cell lies on the inside such daughter cells become xylem. The mechanism is unknown. In volvox, similarly, there are large cells, the gonidia, which divide asymmetrically to generate new somatic cells, and further gonidia (Kirk, 1988). Experiments suggest that this is not just cytoplasmic localization but represents some cytoskeletal asymmetry.

The development of the nematode *Caenorhabditis elegans* is the paradigm for an animal whose development is determined by cell lineage. Considerable emphasis has been put on the invariance of its pattern of cleavage and the autonomy of the developing cells. It is thus an excellent example of cell division – albeit during cleavage – generating daughter cells with asymmetrical development. Thus some blastomeres, isolated early in development, continued to develop just as if they had remained in an intact embryo. There is, however, also considerable evidence for interactions between the cells even at early stages (Emmons, 1987). For example, Priess & Thomson (1987) studied muscle development using monoclonal antibodies to myosin, specific for body wall and pharyngeal muscle. In normal development both the anterior (AB) and the posterior (PI) cells of the two cell embryo produce both types of muscle cells. If the blastomeres are separated, PI continues to express both types but AB now expresses neither. The AB descendants need a signal from the anterior daughter to produce muscles. Moreover if the descendants of the two daughter cells of AB are interchanged their developmental fate is changed and normal development occurs even though their usual fate is quite different.

The development of the lateral hypodermis clearly has some of the characteristics of a stem cell (Sulston & Horvitz, 1977; Kimble, 1981). This lineage comprises a series of divisions in which one of the daughter cells, the anterior cell, forms a syncytial cell while the other divides again; the anterior cell again forms a syncytial cell and the posterior repeats the process, finally forming a seam cell. A very similar lineage is seen in the development of the grasshopper nervous system. Here a neuroblast divides asymmetrically and the smaller daughter cell gives rise to nerve cell whereas the larger mother cell divides several more times (Walbot & Holder, 1987).

There are a variety of mutants in the nematode which alter the pattern of cell division and can result in daughter cells being the same rather than different. Thus the lin-22 mutant causes the anterior cell of a division to resemble the posterior one. In spite of the very substantial amount of work on the asymmetrical divisions in the worm, however, the mechanism is not known. Unlike yeast, the DNA strands in the early nematode seem to segregate randomly (Ito & McGhee, 1987).

One way of thinking about the generation and maintenance of asymmetry may be in terms of membrane bound microfilaments. There is very good evidence for cytoplasmic localization in the ascidian embryo. Its development is regarded as being of the mosaic lineage type. In this egg, various cytoplasmic regions which become associated with particular cell types are recognizable. Following fertilization there is rearrangement of the cytoplasmic constituents such that the so-called myoplasm – that is, associated with the future muscle cells – becomes concentrated within one region of the egg. This seems to be associated with a localized increase in calcium which results in a localized contraction beneath the plasma membrane and this drags with it the filamentous structure attached to the membrane (Jeffrey, 1983). Microfilaments also are involved in the generation of an asymmetric distribution of cytoplasmic factors during the development of the nematode zygote (Strome & Hill, 1988).

## Extrinsic systems

In insects and vertebrates there is not a single well established case for intrinsic asymmetry of cell differentiation. (This excludes cytoplasmic localization during cleavage, which may specify the future germ cells.) In insects it is possible to mark a single cell using the technique of somatic recombination. All of the progeny of that cell can then be seen. Using this technique it has been shown that the wing of the insect develops from a group of about 20 cells. If one of these cells is marked at the time when these wing cells are specified then about one twentieth of the cells in one of the wings will be marked. However, it was possible to arrange the genetic constitution of the cells so that the marked cell grew much faster than the surrounding cells and the cell now formed not one twentieth but about half the wing. Yet, the pattern of the wing was completely normal even though the pattern of cell division in the wing was substantially altered (Garcia-Bellido *et al.* 1973). This clearly shows that the detailed pattern of cell division and the individual cell lineages are not important in the developing wing. It must mean that cell behaviour is determined by cell interactions or other environmental influences.

In vertebrates, a wide variety of experiments suggests that the specification of cell fate is determined by cell-to-cell interactions rather than by lineage (Rossant, 1984). This is particularly true in relation to organogenesis where there is extensive evidence for both induction (Gurdon, 1987) and positional signalling (Wolpert, 1981). For example, early development in amphibia clearly shows that induction of muscle occurs, and in chick limb development a mirror image limb can be caused to form by implanting an additional positional signal. A dramatic example is the ability of tooth mesenchyme to cause embryonic hind-limb epithelium to form enamel (Kratochwil, 1972). Temple & Raff (1985) have shown how the differentiation pathway of single glial cells is controlled by diffusible factors.

It is of interest to consider what might be thought of as embryonic stem cells, embryonic carcinoma cells. These cells have some of the properties of stem cells in that under appropriate conditions they can either proliferate or be made to give rise to a wide variety of cell types. In the latter case the cells do not do this in isolation as single cells but appear to need to go through a phase of cell aggregation which mimics the organization of the early mouse embryo. The clear implication is that interactions similar to those occurring in the early embryo are required in order for the cells to differentiate (Martin, 1975).

## Stem cell system

Interstitial cells in hydra are a multipotent stem cell system which gives rise during asexual growth to nerve cells and nematocysts (Heimfeld & Bode, 1981). On a daily basis, 10 % give rise to nerves, 30 % to nematocysts and 60 % to renewal. Nerve cell development is not related to density but to position along hydra (Venugopal & David, 1981). Thus, if a nerve free head is grafted onto a normal hydra, whose cells have been labelled with tritiated thymidine, the interstitial cells migrate in. If the head is then removed and the regenerated tip examined, the fraction of labelled nerve to other cell types is the same as in the control. It is possible that one of the factors involved is a neuropeptide (Holstein, Schaller & David, 1986). In more general terms the differentiation of interstitial cells is position-dependent. Stenotiles are produced in proximal regions whereas desmonemes are produced more distally (Bode & David, 1978). While such experiments show that the direction of stem cell differentiation can be environmentally directed, it leaves the question of asymmetry unanswered.

In a variety of vertebrate stem cell systems there is a well defined cellular arrangement in which the stem cells occupy a well defined position. This is particularly clear in skin, intestinal epithelia, lens growth and cartilage growth plates. In each case there is a region of proliferation adjacent to a region where there is no proliferation but cell differentiation, or maturation. It seems not unreasonable in all these cases to regard the stem cell properties as being environmentally determined though the mechanism is unknown.

The spatial organization characterizing stem cell population traditionally has been assumed to be absent in just one system – haematopoiesis. While there are models in which the microenvironment is regarded as determining stem cell behaviour, there is strong support for a stochastic model. The 'stochastic' model was first put forward by Till, McCulloch & Siminovitch (1964); a more detailed model is that of Korn *et al.* (1973). The model assumes that the decision of the pluripotent stem cell to self-renew or differentiate is a probabilistic event. Provided this probability is 0·5 then the stem cell population will be in steady state. A further assumption is that commitment of a cell to one or other of the lineages is also a probabilistic event. Ogawa *et al.* (1983) also regard haematopoiesis as involving a progressive and stochastic loss of potencies.

The main evidence for a stochastic model comes from experiments in which paired progenitor cells, derived from a single cell, were cultured individually and the haemopoietic colonies they generated analysed (Suda, Suda & Ogawa, 1983). Of the 387 paired cultures, 319 gave identical colonies whereas 68 gave dissimilar combinations of cells. They argue that this dissimilarity represents differences in intrinsic potential and represents a stochastic process. However, this evidence is not very persuasive and may reflect small differences in the microenvironment. Indeed there is now evidence that the haemopoietic cell populations do conform to a specific spatial organization also (Lord & Testa, 1988).

A stochastic model is quite different from all the mechanisms considered so far. It relies on an internal mechanism reliably to generate asymmetry with a well defined probability which can be altered by humoral factors. Stochastic models have been considered in relation to cell behaviour, particularly in relation to a transition probability model for entry into the cell-cycle (Brooks, 1985). However, it is not easy to see how one could reliably provide a given probability. One class of probabilistic models involves a small number of molecules occupying sites on a receptor. This could provide the probability but it leaves open the problem of how one could arrange reliably for a constant, yet small, number of molecules within the cell. We are remarkably ignorant as to how accurately cells can regulate molecules within the cell.

DNA is the exception – the number being fixed. This is part of a problem which we have considered elsewhere in relation to threshold models for cell commitment (Lewis *et al.* 1977). How can one arrange for an accurate threshold mechanism if the number of molecules varies significantly from cell to cell?

## Conclusions

The essential feature of stem cells is the asymmetry of their development. Such an asymmetry is clearly shown in nematodes and by yeasts in relation to mating type switching. In the fission yeasts the mechanism is thought to be due to imprinting of one of the DNA strands. This is the only case where the mechanism for an intrinsic asymmetry may be known. In vertebrates and insects – cytoplasmic localization apart – there are no clear examples for intrinsic asymmetry in development. All the evidence points to environmental influences. Stem cell systems in hydra and vertebrates strongly suggest the importance of spatial organization and thus extrinsic influences. The exception is the haemopoietic system where a probabilistic mechanism has been proposed, but the evidence is far from conclusive.

## References

BODE, H. R. & DAVID, C. N. (1978). Regulation of a multipotent stem cell, the interstitial cell in hydra. *Prog. Biophys. molec. Biol.* **33**, 198–206.

BROOKS, R. (1985). The transition probability model: successes, limitations and deficiencies. In *Temporal Order* (ed. L. Rensing & N. I. Jaeger), pp. 504–514. Berlin: Springer-Verlag.

CROWTHER, R. J. & WHITTAKER, J. R. (1986). Differentiation without cleavage: multiple cytospecific ultrastructural expressions in individual one-celled Ascidian embryos. *Devl Biol.* **117**, 114–126.

EMMONS, S. W. (1987). Mechanisms of *C. elegans* development. *Cell* **51**, 881–883.

GARCIA-BELLIDO, A., RIPOLL, P. & MORATA, G. (1973). Developmental compartmentalization in the wing disc of *Drosophila. Nature, New Biol.* **245**, 251–253.

GURDON, J. B. (1987). Embryonic induction – molecular prospects. *Development* **99**, 285–306.

HEIMFELD, S. & BODE, H. R. (1981). Regulation of interstitial cell differentiation in *Hydra attenuata*. VI. Positional pattern of nerve cell commitment is independent of local nerve cell density. *J. Cell Sci.* **52**, 85–98.

HOLSTEIN, T., SCHALLER, C. H. & DAVID, C. N. (1986). Nerve cell differentiation in hydra requires two signals. *Devl Biol.* **115**, 9–17.

ILLMENSEE, K. (1976). Nuclear and cytoplasmic transplantation in *Drosophila*. In *Insect Development*, (ed. P. A. Lawrence), pp. 76–96. Oxford: Blackwell's.

ITO, K. & McGHEE, J. D. (1987). Parental DNA strands segregate randomly during embryonic development of *Caenorhabditis elegans. Cell* **49**, 329–339.

JEFFREY, W. R. (1983). Messenger RNA localization and cytoskeletal domains in Ascidian embryos. In *Time, Space and Pattern in Embryonic Development* (ed. W. R. Jeffrey & R. A. Raff), pp. 241–259. New York: Alan R. Liss.

KIMBLE, J. (1981). Strategies for control of pattern formation in *Caenorhabditis elegans. Phil. Trans. Roy. Soc.* B **295**, 539–551.

KIRK, D. L. (1988). The ontogeny and phylogeny of cellular differentiation in Volvox. *Trends in Genetics* **4**, 32–36.

KLAR, A. J. S. (1987). Determination of the yeast cell lineage. *Cell* **49**, 433–435.

KORN, A. P., HENKELMAN, OTTENSMEYER, F. P. & TILL, J. E. (1973). Investigations of a stochastic model of haemopoiesis. *Expl Haemat.* **1**, 362–375.

KRATOCHWIL, K. (1972). Tissue interaction in embryonic development. General properties. In

*Inductive Tissue Interaction and Carcinogenesis* (ed. D. Tarin), pp. 1–47. London: Academic Press.

LEWIS, J. H., SLACK, J. M. W. & WOLPERT, L. (1977). Thresholds in development. *J. theor. Biol.* **65**, 579–590.

LORD, B. I. & TESTA, N. G. (1988). The hemopoietic system: Stucture and regulation. In *Hematopoietic: Long-term Effects of Chemotherapy and radiation* (ed. N. G. Testa & R. P. Gale), pp. 1–26. New York, Basel: Marcel Dekkar Inc.

MARTIN, C. R. (1975). Teratocarcinomas as a model system for the study of embryogenesis and neoplasia: review. *Cell* **5**, 229–243.

OGAWA, M., PORTER, P. N. & NAKAHATA, T. (1983). Renewal and commitment to differentiation of hemopoietic stem cells (an interpretive review). *Blood* **61**, 823–829.

PRIESS, J. R. & THOMSON, J. N. (1987). Cellular interactions in early *C. elegans* embryos. *Cell* **48**, 241–250.

ROSSANT, J. (1984). Somatic cell lineages in mammalian chimeras. In *Chimeras in Developmental Biology* (ed. N. Le Douarin & A. McLaren), pp. 89–109. London: Academic Press.

STROME, S. & HILL, D. P. (1988). Early embryogenesis in *Caenorhabditis elegans*: the cytoskeleton and the spatial organization of the zygote. *Bioessays* **8**, 145–149.

SUDA, T., SUDA, J. & OGAWA, M. (1983). Single-cell origin of mouse haemopoietic colonies expressing multiple lineages in variable combinations. *Proc. natn. Acad. Sci. U.S.A.* **80**, 6689–6693.

SULSTON, J. E. & HORVITZ, H. R. (1977). Post-embryonic cell lineages of the Nematode, *Caenorhabditis elegans*. *Devl Biol.* **56**, 110–156.

TEMPLE, S. & RAFF, M. C. (1985). Differentiation of a bipotential glial progenitor cell in a single cell microculture. *Nature, Lond.* **313**, 223–225.

TILL, J. E., MCCULLOUCH, E. A. & SIMINOVITCH, L. (1964). A stochastic model of stem cell proliferation based on the growth of spleen-colony forming cells. *Proc. natn. Acad. Sci. U.S.A.* **51**, 29–36.

VENUGOPAL, C. & DAVID, C. M. (1981). Nerve commitment in hydra. *Devl Biol.* **83**, 353–360.

WALBOT, V. & HOLDER, N. (1987). *Developmental Biology*. New York: Random House.

WILSON, E. B. (1906). *The Cell in Development and Inheritance* (2nd edn). New York: Macmillan.

WILSON, E. C. (1925). *The Cell in Development and Heredity* (3rd edn). New York: Macmillan.

WOLPERT, L. (1981). Positional information and pattern formation. *Phil. Trans. Roy. Soc., Ser.* B **295**, 441–450.

*J. Cell Sci. Suppl. 10, 11–27 (1988)*
Printed in Great Britain © The Company of Biologists Limited 1988

# Multi-lineage 'stem' cells in the mammalian embryo

R. L. GARDNER AND R. S. P. BEDDINGTON

*Imperial Cancer Research Fund, Developmental Biology Unit, Department of Zoology, University of Oxford, South Parks Road, Oxford OX1 3PS, UK*

## Summary

The term 'stem' cell has acquired a rather more restricted meaning in cell biology than in embryology as a result of studies on the growth kinetics of renewing tissues in mature organisms. It is normally used in an embryological context as a synonym for 'progenitor' cell.

Methods of establishing the existence of multi-lineage progenitor cells in mammals are examined briefly before the occurrence and properties of such cells in both embryonic and extra-embryonic tissues of the mouse conceptus are reviewed. Various attributes of 'stem' cells that can be obtained from outgrowths of blastocysts *in vitro* are also discussed.

## Introduction

Use of the term 'stem' cell has become rather more restricted in cell biology than in embryology in recent years. The term is generally used in an embryological context simply as a synonym for 'progenitor' cell (Balinsky, 1960; Hay, 1974). E. B. Wilson (1928), for example, referred to the blastomere which does not undergo chromatin diminution during cleavage in *Ascaris megalocephala* as the 'stem' cell of the germ-line. Restriction of the use of the term in cell biology has resulted from work on the growth kinetics of renewing tissues in adult organisms in which maintenance of a balance between loss of cells and their production is of central concern. In such tissues the task of making good all losses is believed to depend ultimately on the mitotic activity of a discrete subpopulation of relatively undifferentiated cells. A key attribute of these 'stem' cells is that they normally include among their progeny, cells which retain the same position as themselves in a particular lineage, together with those which progress further along it. The latter may, however, be capable of limited proliferation prior to differentiation (Wright & Alison, 1984). As discussed in one of the society's earlier symposia (Papaioannou *et al.* 1978), the 'stem' cell concept is not applicable to the early embryo when interpreted in this narrower sense. This is not due simply to the fact that the embryo is composed of expanding rather than renewing cell populations, but because one of the hallmarks of early development is a continuous, albeit often gradual, change in the status of cells. This is true even during cleavage where differences may be discernible between successive generations of blastomeres. In addition, early embryonic tissues typically display very high growth fractions and, particularly in those of the extra-embryonic membranes, there is no obvious partitioning of cells into dividing *versus* differentiating subpopulations.

The aim of this contribution is to consider the properties of the various types of

Key words: embryo, stem cells, mammal, clonal analysis, cell lineage.

multi-lineage 'progenitor' cells that have been identified in the early mammalian embryo, principally that of the mouse. Haemopoietic lineages are not discussed because they are dealt with specifically elsewhere (see Dieterlen-Lievre *et al*. 1989).

Unlike the situation in *Ascaris* and certain other metazoa, tissues of the mammalian conceptus and adult evidently originate from the progeny of more than one cell (Mintz, 1972; McLaren, 1976*a*; Gardner, 1978). This means that a clonal approach to fate mapping is needed to demonstrate the existence of multi-lineage progenitor cells in mammals. Strictly speaking, the normal lineage of cells can be established only by following their fate *in situ* in conditions in which cellular relationships within the embryo are not perturbed. This can often be achieved by intracellular injection of enzymes or fluorochrome-containing molecules in cases where it is not practicable to observe the division and deployment of cells directly in living embryos (Weisblat *et al*. 1978; Gimlich & Braun, 1985; Dale & Slack, 1987; Kimmel & Warga, 1987). Unfortunately, such cell labelling techniques are of rather limited value in mammalian embryos because of the rapidity with which the various molecules are diluted or degraded. It has therefore been necessary to rely mainly on the use of genes as cell markers in mammals. Until recently, the only way this could be done was by transplanting cells between embryos which differ in genotype at suitable 'marker' loci (Gardner & Lyon, 1971). The validity of this approach obviously rests on the assumption that the fate of donor cells is approximately normal, notwithstanding their isolation and transplantation. While this is probably the case when orthotopic grafts are made between synchronous embryos, it is less likely where there is marked disparity in age between the donor and host. Such disparity is inevitable using donor cells from post-implantation embryos since the blastocyst is the most advanced host stage which will develop normally *in vivo* following manipulation *in vitro*.

Recently, a novel stratagem has been devised whereby genes can be harnessed as *in situ* cell markers for clonal analysis of lineage in mammals. It depends on the use of recombinant retroviruses to mediate the transfer of foreign genes into cells. Viruses that are unable to replicate are used so that, whenever integrated, their genome should be transmitted only to the clonal descendants of the infected cell (Sanes *et al*. 1986; Price *et al*. 1987). This viral stratagem looks most promising at present as a solution to the hitherto intractable problem of the long-term study of cell lineage in the post-implantation conceptus. It has, indeed, already been used to investigate lineage in the mesoderm of the visceral yolk sac and epidermis in the mouse, as well as in the rat neural retina (Sanes *et al*. 1986; Price *et al*. 1987). Nevertheless, more work needs to be done before its potential can be fully assessed. For example, it remains to be established whether all cells are susceptible to such virally mediated alteration in genotype.

The problems of lineage analysis in mammals have been considered at some length because an awareness of them is essential for critical evaluation of the findings discussed below.

At least some descendants of most, if not all, cells of the early mammalian embryo participate in the development of extra-embryonic tissues. These are a structurally

Table 1. *Types of trophoblasts found in the mouse conceptus*

Primary trophoblastic giant cells
Secondary trophoblastic giant cells
Tertiary trophoblastic giant cells
Ectoplacental cone (core)
Extra-embryonic ectoderm
Chorionic ectoderm
Labyrinthine-layer I (cellular)
Labyrinthine-layer II (syncytial)
Labyrinthine-layer III (? syncytial)
Spongiotrophoblasts

and functionally diverse collection of tissues which, while playing vital roles in establishing and maintaining intra-uterine conditions necessary for development of the foetus, are discarded entirely at birth. They have attracted increasing attention lately both by virtue of marked expression of various so-called 'proto-oncogenes' (Adamson, 1987*a*,*b*) and because of growing evidence that some of them may differ from foetal tissues in the regulation of gene activity (Chapman, 1986; Surani, 1986; Monk *et al.* 1987). All components of the later conceptus originate from one of 3 tissues, the trophectoderm, primitive endoderm or primitive ectoderm, which have differentiated by the late blastocyst stage in the mouse. The aim of this contribution is to review the occurrence and properties of multi-lineage progenitor cells in each of these tissues in turn.

## Trophectoderm

The trophectoderm is the first extra-embryonic tissue to differentiate. It is a 'tight' attenuated epithelium forming the outer cell layer of the blastocyst. Its differentiation is presaged by the polarization of blastomeres at the 8-cell stage (Johnson & Ziomek, 1981), approximately 2-cell cycles before it matures as a transporting epithelium in the mouse (Borland *et al.* 1977). The trophectoderm is generally held to be the precursor tissue for all types of trophoblast cell encountered later in development both in the chorioallantoic placenta and elsewhere in the periphery of the conceptus. A list of the various trophoblasts found in the mouse is presented in Table 1. The classification of these cells is not ideal at present because it depends almost entirely on morphological and topographical criteria. It is, for example, not clear whether the successive generations of trophoblastic giant cells are functionally equivalent or not. Similar reservations apply to the two syncytial cell layers forming part of the exchange surface of the placental labyrinth (Table 1). However, with increasing use of specific molecular probes to study the placenta (Hall & Talamantes, 1984; MacPherson *et al.* 1985; Zuckerman & Head, 1986; Sasagawa *et al.* 1987), a more satisfactory system of classification will undoubtedly emerge.

Notwithstanding the present uncertainties, there clearly are several distinct types of trophoblast cells. If most or all of these do, indeed, originate from the trophectoderm, this tissue is a likely source of multi-lineage progenitor cells. In the mouse it is, in fact, only in the polar region of the trophectoderm to which the inner cell mass (ICM) is attached that cell division continues beyond the blastocyst stage. Beginning at implantation a terminal process of primary giant cell formation occurs throughout the remaining, mural trophectoderm. This process is accompanied by repeated endoreduplication of DNA whereby the cells become polytene rather than polyploid (Brower, 1987; Varmuza *et al.* 1988). Therefore, it is with the origin and fate of the polar trophectoderm that the following discussion is primarily concerned.

The distinct fates of mural and polar trophectoderm are not due to intrinsic differences between them but rather a consequence of their disposition with respect to the ICM. This is evident from two experimental findings. First, mural trophectoderm can substitute for polar providing ICM tissue is placed inside it before giant cell formation begins (Gardner *et al.* 1973; R.L. Gardner, unpublished observations). Second, polar trophectoderm behaves like mural when deprived of contact with the ICM (R. L. Gardner & J. Nichols, unpublished observations). These findings imply that close contact with ICM cells is essential for maintenance of trophectoderm proliferation in the mouse. As will be mentioned later, this is evidently not the case in all mammals.

It is very likely that the entire trophectoderm of the early blastocyst is derived from cells occupying an external location in the morula (Johnson & Maro, 1986; Pedersen, 1986). What is more contentious at present is whether the ICM contributes cells to the polar trophectoderm thereafter (Handyside, 1978; Cruz & Pedersen, 1985). ICM tissue can undoubtedly form trophectoderm *in vitro* following its isolation from early blastocysts (Hogan & Tilly, 1978; Handyside, 1978; Spindle, 1978; Rossant & Tamura-Lis, 1979; Nichols & Gardner, 1984). The conclusion that it also does so during normal development is based principally on the results of experiments in which central polar trophectoderm cells were marked by injection with horseradish peroxidase (HRP). Labelled cells were found consistently to have been displaced towards or into the mural trophectoderm when injected blastocysts were examined following culture for 48 h (Cruz & Pedersen, 1985). Dyce *et al.* (1987) were able to confirm these findings. However, using endocytosed fluorescent microspheres to pre-label the entire trophectoderm, these workers found no evidence that displacement of HRP-injected cells was accompanied by recruitment of ICM cells into the polar region. A notable feature of both studies was that the labelled cells seldom divided during the first 24 h after injection with enzyme, although they normally did so thereafter. It is conceivable, therefore, that temporary interruption of the cycling of injected cells led to their displacement as a result of the sustained proliferative activity of their uninjected neighbours (Copp, 1978; Dyce *et al.* 1987; Gardner, 1988). Dyce *et al.* (1987) did, in fact, find evidence of a two-way traffic of cells between the trophectoderm and ICM, albeit in only a small proportion of blastocysts. Interestingly, they were unable to enhance the movement of cells from ICM to polar trophectoderm by destroying one or two cells in the latter tissue.

Caution is warranted in interpreting such short-term *in vitro* experiments for two reasons. First, the blastocysts were cultured for up to two days on a surface to which they could not adhere. *In vivo*, blastocysts normally attach to the uterine epithelium within 24 h of cavitation: they enter a quiescent state if this is prevented by ovariectomy or concurrent lactation (McLaren, 1968; Bergstrom, 1978). Second, where cells did appear to have moved between the ICM and trophectoderm, proof is lacking that they actually survived to contribute to the growth of their adoptive tissue or, indeed, even underwent an appropriate change in phenotype.

The only experiments bearing on the question of what happens *in vivo* are those in which blastocysts, reconstituted from genetically dissimilar trophectoderm and ICM, have been transferred to the uterus. The chorionic ectoderm, ectoplacental cone and secondary giant cells of resulting 9th day or mid-gestation conceptuses typically consist entirely of cells of the trophectoderm donor in genotype (Gardner *et al.* 1973; Papaioannou, 1982; Barton *et al.* 1986). Hence, if the ICM does indeed contribute cells to the polar trophectoderm during normal development *in vivo* it probably does so only sporadically and at an early stage following blastulation (Rossant & Tamura-Lis, 1979; Rossant & Croy, 1985).

As the blastocyst implants, the polar trophectoderm transiently loses its epithelial organization and grows inwards, thereby displacing the ICM into the blastocoelic cavity. Once inside the conceptus it rapidly becomes re-established as a cylindrical columnar epithelium, the extra-embryonic ectoderm, which is closed at its outer extremity where a secondary outgrowth called the ectoplacental cone soon forms (Snell & Stevens, 1966). It is from the periphery of this cone that secondary giant cells emerge which will eventually surround the conceptus. Later the extra-embryonic ectoderm accquires a mesodermal lining and becomes reflected against the base of the ectoplacental cone as the chorionic ectoderm which is then gradually incorporated into the structure of the nascent chorioallantoic placenta (Snell & Stevens, 1966). Following union of the distal tip of the allantois with the chorion and formation of the extra-embryonic endodermal sinuses (Duval, 1892), the various tissues of the placenta are too intimately intermingled to be resolved by dissection.

Some progress in unravelling cell lineage relationships of the chorioallantoic placenta later in development has been made by Rossant & Croy (1985). These workers employed a probe specific for a *Mus musculus* satellite DNA sequence on placental sections of conceptuses developing from blastocysts composed of *M. caroli* ICM and *M. musculus* trophectoderm. Using this *in situ* marker in conjunction with a second intra-specific marker giving much poorer spatial resolution, they showed that a substantial majority of foetal cells in the placenta, including spongiotrophoblasts, were of trophectodermal origin. The ICM contribution was confined mainly to the endothelial and mesenchymal components in the labyrinth. However, as noted elsewhere (Gardner, 1985a), an *in situ* marker that can be visualized by electron microscopy seems essential if the provenance of all mature cell types in the placenta is to be determined.

So far, the origin and fate of the polar trophectoderm as a whole has been considered. Recently, however, early trophectoderm cells have been cloned by blastocyst injection (R. L. Gardner, unpublished data). The cloning efficiency of these cells is low compared with those of the ICM, partly because a significant proportion end up in the mural rather than polar trophectoderm. Nevertheless, individual clones have been found which span the extra-embryonic ectoderm, ectoplacental cone and secondary giant cells in early post-implantation host conceptuses. Hence, it is indeed likely that the polar trophectoderm represents a population of multi-lineage progenitor cells. Colonization of blastocysts has also been obtained with extra-embryonic ectoderm cells from early post-implantation conceptuses although, so far, only small clumps of tissue rather than single cells have been transplanted (Rossant *et al.* 1978).

It is evident from both cell transplantation experiments (Rossant *et al.* 1978) and biosynthetic studies (Johnson & Rossant, 1981) that the extra-embryonic ectoderm/ chorionic ectoderm constitutes the primary pool of trophectoderm-derived cells in the post-implantation conceptus. It is composed entirely of diploid cells, as is the core of the ectoplacental cone, and exhibits a high mitotic index (Rossant & Ofer, 1977). However, at all stages up to the 9th day of gestation when this diploid mitotically active trophoblast tissue can be isolated cleanly, it behaves in essentially the same way following removal from the conceptus. There is a rapid decline in the incidence of mitoses accompanied by the onset of endoreduplication of DNA and enlargement of a substantial proportion of cells (Gardner & Papaioannou, 1975; Rossant & Ofer, 1977; Ilgren, 1981; Rossant & Tamura-Lis, 1981; Varmuza *et al.* 1988). Throughout the period of development in question and beyond, the proliferative component of the trophoblast is associated with the ICM or certain of its derivatives. This has prompted speculation that maintenance of the cycling of trophoblast cells depends on ICM tissue from the blastocyst stage onwards (Gardner *et al.* 1973; Gardner, 1975). As noted by Rossant & Ofer (1977), the role of the ICM might be to hold adjacent trophoblast in a particular configuration rather than to secrete molecules necessary for its growth. So far, however, attempts to distinguish between these possibilities have yielded inconclusive results (Ilgren, 1981; Rossant & Tamura-Lis, 1981). Exploiting mutations that affect the growth of trophoblast may offer another approach to this problem. One of a series of deletions affecting the albino locus on chromosome 7 seems particularly promising in this connection. When homozygous, this deletion results in deficient growth and disorganization of the extra-embryonic ectoderm (Lewis *et al.* 1976). Consequent failure of normal elongation of the egg-cylinder may account for the concomitant apparent overgrowth of the parietal endoderm (Niswander *et al.* 1988). However, development of ICM derivatives may also be impaired (Niswander *et al.* 1988), possibly *via* another locus lying within the deletion.

An obvious question is whether ICM control of trophoblast growth is a general phenomenon in eutherian mammals. This is difficult to answer because of the dearth of relevant comparative studies and also because the term 'trophectoderm vesicle' is often used rather loosely to include structures that have already acquired a lining of endoderm derived from the ICM. Until recently, the only other species in which the fate of 'pure' trophectoderm had been investigated was the guinea-pig, which gave similar results to the mouse (Ilgren, 1980). However, comparable experiments have now been done using blastocysts of the common marmoset (Summers *et al.* 1988). In this species vesicles of mural trophectoderm showed a marked increase in cell number on culture *in vitro* providing they contained at least 30 cells initially. Those containing less than 20 cells at explantation formed monolayers in which only limited proliferation was observed. Whether the situation in the human resembles that in this lower primate rather than the rodent remains to be seen.

## Primitive endoderm

The primitive endoderm or hypoblast differentiates on the blastocoelic surface of the ICM shortly before the blastocyst begins to implant (Nadjicka & Hillman, 1974; Gardner *et al.* 1988). Like the trophectoderm, this tissue evidently gives rise only to extra-embryonic components of the post-implantation conceptus, namely the endoderm of both the parietal and visceral yolk sac (Snell & Stevens, 1966; Gardner, 1985*b*). Clones obtained by transplanting primitive endoderm cells between blasto-cysts can span both these extra-embryonic endoderm layers (Gardner, 1982, 1984). Hence, assuming regional heterogeneity within the two layers reflects phenotypic modulation rather than the existence of distinct types of cell (Dziadek, 1978), the primitive endoderm would appear to be composed of bi-potential progenitors.

According to the results of recent cloning experiments, the majority of cells comprising the visceral endoderm remain bi-potential for between 1 and 2 days after the primitive endoderm is first evident (Cockroft & Gardner, 1987). In certain experimental situations the visceral endoderm has been found to retain the option of forming parietal cells for at least the first 3 days of its existence (Solter & Damjanov, 1973; Diwan & Stevens, 1976; Hogan & Tilly, 1981; R. L. Gardner, unpublished observations). Impressed by the transitional cellular morphology of the junction between the two tissues, Hogan & Newman (1984) have argued that recruitment of cells to parietal from visceral endoderm may take place during normal development. This possibility has been explored by examining the junctional region in conceptuses in which the visceral endoderm was either chimaeric or selectively labelled *in vivo* by uptake of maternally injected HRP (Gardner & Davies, unpublished). The results suggest that such movement of cells may indeed occur, but only within 18 h or so of the beginning of parietal endoderm formation.

## Primitive ectoderm

The primitive ectoderm or epiblast accounts for all remaining cells in the mature blastocyst that belong neither to the trophectoderm nor the primitive endoderm. It is first discernible as a discrete population of cells within the ICM following differentiation of the primitive endoderm on the 5th day of gestation. Contrary to various earlier claims, the primitive ectoderm appears to be restricted in develop-mental potential from the outset (Gardner, 1985*b*). In common with the other two tissues of the blastocyst, it makes a contribution to certain extra-embryonic components of the conceptus by providing all their mesoderm as well as the ectoderm of the amnion. It is, in addition, the founder tissue of both the entire foetal soma and the germ-line (see Beddington, 1986, for a review). These conclusions regarding the normal fate of the primitive ectoderm are based mainly on data obtained by injecting 5th day tissue or cells into blastocysts (Gardner & Rossant, 1979; Gardner, 1985*b,c*).

Single cell injections were particularly instructive in demonstrating that individual primitive ectoderm clones can contribute to all derivatives of the parent tissue (Gardner, 1985c; Gardner *et al.* 1985). Hence, when it first differentiates the primitive ectoderm is probably composed of a homogeneous population of multilineage progenitor cells.

Unfortunately, attempts to investigate the fate of post-implantation primitive ectoderm by blastocyst injection have been unsuccessful. Even using *in situ* markers which would enable detection of very low levels of chimaerism (Lo, 1986; Varmuza *et al.* 1988), no evidence of survival of such cells following transplantation has been found (R. S. P. Beddington & J. Rossant, unpublished results). Since the retroviral stratagem outlined earlier has yet to be tested on primitive ectoderm, the developmental status of cells in this tissue beyond the 5th day is uncertain. As one might expect, different prospective foetal tissues show an orderly topographical origin which can be mapped on the primitive ectoderm during gastrulation (Beddington, 1981, 1982; Tam & Beddington, 1987). However, this map does not seem to be correlated with any prior restriction in developmental potential of cells within the tissue (Beddington, 1982, 1983). Indeed, in terms of its behaviour in various experimental situations, primitive ectoderm isolated during gastrulation on the 8th day of gestation is indistinguishable from its counterpart in the blastocyst (Beddington, 1986).

It would be mistaken, however, to assume that retention of multipotency depends on the maintenance of complete developmental stasis in the primitive ectoderm. Not only does the tissue begin to grow rapidly once implantation is under way, but it also exhibits other changes including conversion from a solid mass of cells to a pseudostratified epithelium (Jolly & Ferester-Tadie, 1936; Snell & Stevens, 1966; Batten & Haar, 1979). This structural reorganization which leads to the formation of a central proamniotic cavity, may involve extensive cell mingling within the tissue (Gardner, 1986). Certain antigenic determinants on the cell surface also change following implantation (Stinnakre *et al.* 1981; Pennington *et al.* 1985) and minor changes can be detected in the profile of newly synthesized polypeptides resolved by 2-dimensional gel electrophoresis (Evans *et al.* 1979). In addition, X-chromosome inactivation occurs in the primitive ectoderm of female conceptuses soon after implantation, but probably before gastrulation commences (Kozak & Quinn, 1975; Monk & Harper, 1979; Rastan, 1982; Gardner *et al.* 1985). Finally, as mentioned earlier, the ability of primitive ectoderm cells to colonize the blastocyst is lost, a change that is presaged by a decline in their cloning efficiency as implantation progresses during the 5th day (Gardner *et al.* 1985).

Growth of the primitive ectoderm accelerates once implantation begins (McLaren, 1976b; Snow, 1977), the cell cycle time averaging about 6 h during gastrulation (Solter *et al.* 1971; Snow, 1976, 1977; Poelmann, 1980). There may, however, be certain regional differences in its proliferative activity. For example, lateral ectoderm has a high mitotic index and in contrast to the frontal region, all its cells appear to be cycling (Poelmann, 1980). Furthermore, a population of cells with a cycle length of only 2–3 h has been identified just in front of the primitive streak (Snow, 1977).

While such regional variations in cell proliferation may play a role in morphogenesis during gastrulation (Poelmann, 1980), evidence that they are also implicated in the segregation of specific lineages remains circumstantial (Snow & Bennett, 1978). When exposed before gastrulation, or during its early stages, to teratogens which kill cells indiscriminately, embryos typically either die or make good the losses so effectively that no specific defects become apparent later (Austin, 1973). The extent to which the primitive ectoderm can regulate its development is dramatically illustrated by experiments in which a majority of gastrulating embryos was found to be able to withstand destruction of approximately 85 % of cells following maternal injection of mitomycin C (Snow & Tam, 1979). It is unlikely in view of such findings that sub-sets of cells are already assigned to particular lineages, or that there is any fixed relationship between number or pattern of cell divisions and allocation of cells to different lineages within the primitive ectoderm.

A primitive ectoderm derivative which might be expected to show precocious segregation is the germ-line. As is well known, primordial germ cells are set aside early in the development of nematodes, insects, and certain amphibians (see Eddy, 1975, for a review). In mammals, however, there is no distinctive germ plasm to assist in localizing the germ cell lineage. The earliest convincing sighting of primordial germ cells in the mouse is at the posterior end of the late primitive streak and base of the adjoining allantoic bud (Mintz & Russell, 1957; Ozdzenski, 1967). Obviously, failure to detect such cells earlier by current means does not exclude the possibility that the germ-line segregates before gastrulation is well advanced. Fifth day primitive ectoderm cells can form clones which colonize the germ-line as well as somatic tissues following injection into blastocysts. Furthermore, more than one cell from a donor blastocyst is capable of doing so (Gardner *et al.* 1985). Therefore, the germ-line evidently does not segregate until after the conceptus has implanted. What is less clear is whether it does so before the definitive germ layers of the foetus are formed. Indirect evidence from studies on genetic mosaics is somewhat conflicting.

Analysis of X-inactivation mosaics suggest that the foetal soma and germ-line are derived from a common, fairly large, pool of primitive ectoderm cells (McMahon *et al.* 1983). However, cases of germ-line mosaicism without accompanying somatic mosaicism have been found among genetic mosaics produced by irradiation (Searle, 1978), infection of preimplantation embryos with retroviruses (Soriano & Jaenisch, 1986), or injection of DNA into pro-nuclei (Wilkie *et al.* 1986). Mosaics produced by these methods might be expected to provide a more sensitive screen for lineage segregation than those resulting from X-inactivation because they exhibit a greater range in mosaicism. However, while these exceptional mosaics raise the possibility that the germ-line originates from a different group of cells than the foetal soma, it is important to note that not all primitive ectoderm derivatives were examined for mosaicism. The principal omission was the extra-embryonic mesoderm. This arises from the posterior end of the primitive streak where, it will be recalled, primordial germ cells are first seen (Snow, 1981; Beddington, 1982; Copp *et al.* 1986; Tam & Beddington, 1987). Furthermore, cases of chimaerism in either the extra-embryonic mesoderm or foetus, rather than both, have been encountered among conceptuses produced by aggregating morulae or injecting ICM cells into blastocysts (West *et al.* 1984; R. L. Gardner, unpublished observations). Therefore, restriction of mosaicism to the germ cells post-natally may be due to limited cell mingling between the region destined to form both primordial germ cells and extra-embryonic mesoderm and the remainder of the primtive ectoderm rather than segregation of the germ-line *per se.*

Up to gastrulation the primitive ectoderm probably continues to grow and, to a limited extent, differentiate as a homogeneous population of multipotential cells. Hence, in terms of growth kinetics, this tissue appears to behave more like a collection of transition cells than true 'stem' cells. However, if transplanted ectopically prior to the end of gastrulation, it can give rise to transplantable tumours called teratocarcinomas (Stevens, 1970; Damjanov *et al.* 1971; Diwan & Stevens, 1976; Beddington, 1983). These tumours contain nests of embryonal carcinoma (EC) cells as well as an assortment of differentiated tissues. When cloned either *in vivo* (Kleinsmith & Pierce, 1964) or *in vitro* (Jami & Ritz, 1974; Kahan & Ephrussi, 1970; Rosenthal *et al.* 1970; Martin & Evans, 1975), EC cells clearly reproduce themselves in addition to generating more differentiated progeny. More recently, similar cells known as embryonic stem (ES) cells have been obtained from preimplantation embryos maintained in culture (Evans & Kaufman, 1981; Martin, 1981). These too are multipotential tumorigenic cells which, like EC cells, resemble stem cells (in the restricted sense) in terms of their mode of growth.

The developmental status of EC and ES cells is uncertain. While it has been argued that their closest counterpart in the embryo is 6th day primitive ectoderm (Evans *et al.* 1979; Evans & Kaufman, 1981), they evidently do not share the restriction in developmental potential exhibited by cells of this tissue (Hogan *et al.* 1983; Gardner & Rossant, 1979; Gardner, 1985*a,b*). This is particularly true of ES cells which have been reported to produce trophoblast giant cells as well as extra-embryonic endoderm *in vitro* (Evans & Kaufman, 1983; Robertson & Bradley, 1986; Robertson, 1987; Doetschman *et al.* 1985). However, such claims are based mainly on the gross appearance of the cells rather than use of more specific markers of differentiation.

Recently, the developmental potential of ES cells derived from a delayed blastocyst has been assayed more critically by determining the distribution of their progeny in host conceptuses following blastocyst injection (Beddington & Robertson, 1989). A total of 12 clones were obtained in single cell transplantations in which the cloning efficiency was 17%. Eleven of the clones were found exclusively in primitive ectoderm derivatives, while the 12th had contributed to the extra-embryonic endoderm as well. In terms of both the frequency and extent of chimaerism, a marked bias towards primitive ectodermal colonization was also evident in multiple cell injections. Sixteen out of 43 conceptuses were chimaeric in these experiments. While one chimaera showed colonization of trophoblast only, each of the remaining 15 were chimaeric in derivatives of the primitive ectoderm. Three of the 15 also exhibited chimaerism in primitive endoderm derivatives, two in trophectoderm derivatives and, in one case, derivatives of all three tissues were colonized. These findings suggest that ES cells resemble early ICM cells more closely in pattern of colonization than those of the primitive ectoderm (Gardner, 1985*c*). Hence, in deriving ES lines one may either be selecting for the retention of any persisting early ICM cells, or encouraging reversion of the primitive ectoderm to a more primitive state. It is relevant to note that while primitive ectoderm clearly exhibits restriction in developmental potential following both blastocyst injection and maintenance in short-term culture (Gardner, 1985*a*,*b*), there is no evidence that this state can be propagated clonally *in vitro*: indeed, the fact that ES cells exist argues that it probably cannot.

The stage at which cells contributing to the somatic lineages of the foetus finally lose their multipotency is difficult to define. This is because, unlike organisms whose body plan is laid down fairly rapidly while they are still composed of relatively few cells, the mammalian embryo continues to extend its anteroposterior axis over several days (Rugh, 1968; Theiler, 1972). Thus, when the head already possesses its full complement of tissue primordia the tail has yet to form. Gastrulation, as defined by the continued presence of a primitive streak, lasts until closure of the posterior neuropore on the 10th day of gestation. Even then undifferentiated tissue persists in the tail bud which, in the chick embryo, has been clearly shown to generate a variety of axial structure such as neural tube, gut endoderm and somitic mesoderm (Schoenwolf, 1977, 1978, 1979; Bellairs & Sanders, 1986; Sanders *et al.* 1986; Tam, 1984; Shedden & Wiley, 1987). It is interesting to consider what determines the final cessation of axial elongation. However, even in the chick where this problem has been studied more extensively, it is not clear whether it is due to mechanical factors, tissue interaction or an intrinsic ageing process in the cells involved.

## Conclusion

During preimplantation mouse development there is clearly a sequential segregation of tissue lineages such that in the 5th day blastocyst there are three distinct tissue compartments: trophectoderm, primitive endoderm and primitive ectoderm. Within each compartment there is good evidence for the existence of multi-lineage progenitor, or stem cells. In the case of trophectoderm these appear to be maintained, at least initially, by continued interaction with the ICM and its derivatives. Likewise, the persistence of developmental lability in the primitive endoderm probably depends on local tissue interactions since only visceral endoderm, and not parietal endoderm, has been shown to be bipotent. In both these extra-embryonic tissues, progression of cells away from a particular location, and consequent alterations in their relations with neighbouring tissues, seems to result in a restriction in potency. This is reminiscent of the situation found in many adult stem cell systems. Primitive ectoderm cells may also retain their multipotency by virtue of their environment. However, little is known about this apart from the fact that continued production of new germ layer tissue is confined to the posterior end of the embryo. If the exacting tissue culture requirements for maintaining EC and ES cells are relevant, the key to sustained multipotency in primitive ectoderm cells may lie in their homotypic interactions and insulation from communication with other cell types in the conceptus.

We wish to thank Mrs Jo Williamson for help in preparing the manuscript, and the Royal Society, Imperial Cancer Research Fund and the Lister Institute of Preventive Medicine for support.

## References

ADAMSON, E. D. (1987*a*). Oncogenes in development. *Development* **99**, 449–471.

ADAMSON, E. D. (1987*b*). Expression of proto-oncogenes in the placenta. *Placenta* **8**, 449–466.

AUSTIN, C. R. (1973). Embryo transfer and sensitivity to teratogenesis. *Nature, Lond.* **244**, 333–334.

BALINSKY, B. I. (1960). *An Introduction to Embryology.* Philadelphia: W. B. Saunders.

BARTON, S. C., ADAMS, C. A., MORRIS, M. L. & SURANI, M. A. H. (1986). Development of gynogenetic and parthenogenetic inner cell mass and trophectoderm tissues in reconstituted blastocysts in the mouse. *J. Embryol. exp. Morph.* **90**, 267–285.

BATTEN, B. E. & HAAR, J. L. (1979). Fine structural differentiation of germ layers in the mouse at the time of mesoderm formation. *Anat. Rec.* **194**, 125–142.

BEDDINGTON, R. S. P. (1981). An autoradiographic analysis of the potency of embryonic ectoderm in the 8th day postimplantation mouse embryo. *J. Embryol. exp. Morph.* **64**, 87–104.

BEDDINGTON, R. S. P. (1982). An autoradiographic analysis of tissue potency in different regions of the embryonic ectoderm during gastrulation in the mouse. *J. Embryol. exp. Morph.* **69**, 265–285.

BEDDINGTON, R. S. P. (1983). Histogenic and neoplastic potential of different regions of the mouse embryonic egg cylinder. *J. Embryol. exp. Morph.* **75**, 189–204.

BEDDINGTON, R. S. P. (1986). Analysis of tissue fate and prospective potency in the egg cylinder. In *Experimental Approaches to Mammalian Embryonic Development* (ed. J. Rossant & R. A. Pedersen), pp. 121–147. New York: Cambridge University Press.

BEDDINGTON, R. S. P. & ROBERTSON, E. J. (1989). An assessment of the developmental potential of embryonic stem cells in the mid-gestation mouse embryo. *Development* (in press).

BEDDINGTON, R. S. P. & ROBERTSON, E. J. (1988). Manuscript in preparation.

BELLAIRS, R. & SANDERS, E. J. (1986). Somitomeres in the chick tail bud: an SEM study. *Anat. Embryol.* **175**, 235–240.

BERGSTROM, S. (1978). Experimental delayed implantation. In *Methods in Mammalian Reproduction* (ed. J. C. Daniel), pp. 419–435. New York: Academic Press.

BORLAND, R. M., BIGGERS, J. D. & LECHENE, C. P. (1977). Studies on the composition and formation of mouse blastocoele fluid using electron probe microanalysis. *Devl Biol.* **55**, 1–8.

BROWER, D. (1987). Chromosome organization in polyploid mouse trophoblast nuclei. *Chromosoma* **95**, 76–80.

CHAPMAN, V. M. (1986). X-Chromosome regulation in oogenesis and early mammalian development. In *Experimental Approaches to Mammalian Embryonic Development* (ed. J. Rossant & R. A. Pedersen), pp. 365–398. New York: Cambridge University Press.

COCKROFT, D. L. & GARDNER, R. L. (1987). Clonal analysis of the developmental potential of 6th and 7th day visceral endoderm cells in the mouse. *Development* **101**, 143–155.

COPP, A. J. (1978). Interaction between inner cell mass and trophectoderm of the mouse blastocyst. 1. A study of cellular proliferation. *J. Embryol. exp. Morph.* **48**, 109–125.

COPP, A. J., ROBERTS, H. M. & POLANI, P. E. (1986). Chimaerism of primordial germ cells in the early postimplantation mouse embryo following microsurgical grafting of posterior primitive streak cells *in vitro. J. Embryol. exp. Morph.* **95**, 95–115.

CRUZ, Y. P. & PEDERSEN, R. A. (1985). Cell fate in the polar trophectoderm of mouse blastocysts as studied by microinjection of cell lineage tracers. *Devl Biol.* **112**, 73–83.

DALE, L. & SLACK, J. M. W. (1987). Fate map for the 32-cell stage of *Xenopus laevis. Development* **99**, 527–551.

DAMJANOV, I., SOLTER, D. & SKREB, N. (1971). Teratocarcinogenesis as related to the age of embryos grafted under the kidney capsule. *Wilhelm Roux Arch. EntwMech. Org.* **173**, 228–234.

DIETERLEN-LIEVRE, F., PARDANAUD, L., YASSINE, F. & CORMIER, F. (1989). Early haemopoietic stem cells in the avian embryo. *J. Cell Sci. Suppl.* **10**, 29–44.

DIWAN, S. B. & STEVENS, L. C. (1976). Development of teratomas from the ectoderm of mouse egg cylinders. *J. natn. Cancer Inst.* **57**, 937–942.

DOETSCHMAN, T. C., EISTETTER, H., KATZ, M., SCHMIDT, W. & KEMLER, R. (1985). The *in vitro* development of blastocyst-derived embryonic stem cell lines: formation of visceral yolk sac, blood islands and myocardium. *J. Embryol. exp. Morph.* **87**, 27–45.

DUVAL, M. (1892). *Le Placenta des Rongeurs*. Extrait du journal de l'Anatomie et de la Physiologie Années 1889–1892 (ed. F. Alcan). Paris: *Anncienne Librarie Gemner Baillière*.

DYCE, J., GEORGE, M., GOODALL, H. & FLEMING, T. P. (1987). Do trophectoderm and inner mass cells in the mouse blastocyst maintain discrete lineages? *Development* **100**, 685–698.

DZIADEK, M. (1978). Modulation of alphafetoprotein synthesis in the early post-implantation mouse embryo. *J. Embryol. exp. Morph.* **46**, 135–146.

EDDY, E. M. (1975). Germ plasm and the differentiation of the germ cell line. *Int. Rev. Cytol.* **43**, 229–280.

EVANS, M. J. & KAUFMAN, M. H. (1981). Establishment in culture of pluripotential cells from mouse embryos. *Nature, Lond.* **292**, 154–156.

EVANS, M. J. & KAUFMAN, M. H. (1983). Pluripotential cells grown directly from normal mouse embryos. *Cancer Surveys* **2**, 186–207.

EVANS, M. J., LOVELL-BADGE, R. H., STERN, P. L. & STINNAKRE, M. G. (1979). Cell lineage of the mouse embryo and embryonal carcinoma cells: Forssman antigen distribution and patterns of protein synthesis. In *Cell Lineages, Stem Cells and Cell Determination (INSERM Symposium No. 10)* (ed. N. Le Douarin), pp. 115–129. Amsterdam: Elsevier/North-Holland Biomedical Press.

GARDNER, R. L. (1975). Origins and properties of trophoblast. In *Immunobiology of Trophoblast* (ed. R. G. Edwards, C. W. S. Howe & M. H. Johnson), pp. 43–61. Cambridge: University Press.

GARDNER, R. L. (1978). The relationship between cell lineage and differentiation in the early mouse embryo. In *Genetic Mosaics and Cell Differentiation* (ed. W. J. Gehring), pp. 205–241. Berlin: Springer-Verlag.

GARDNER, R. L. (1982). Investigation of cell lineage and differentiation in the extraembryonic endoderm of the mouse embryo. *J. Embryol. exp. Morph.* **68**, 175–198.

GARDNER, R. L. (1984). An *in situ* cell marker for clonal analysis of development of the extraembryonic endoderm in the mouse. *J. Embryol. exp. Morph.* **80**, 251–288.

GARDNER, R. L. (1985*a*). Origin and development of the trophectoderm and inner cell mass. In *Implantation of the Human Embryo: 2nd Bourne Hall Meeting* (ed. R. G. Edwards, J. M. Purdy & P. C. Steptoe), pp. 155–178. London: Academic Press.

GARDNER, R. L. (1985*b*). Regeneration of endoderm from primitive ectoderm in the mouse embryo: fact or artifact? *J. Embryol. exp. Morph.* **88**, 303–326.

GARDNER, R. L. (1985*c*). Clonal analysis of early mammalian development. *Phil. Trans. R. Soc.* B **312**, 163–178.

GARDNER, R. L. (1986). Cell mingling during mammalian embryogenesis. *J. Cell Sci. Suppl. 4*, 337–356.

GARDNER, R. L. (1988). Cell fate in the developing embryo. In *Fetal and Neonatal Development – Proceedings of the conference in Oxford. England 2nd–7th August 1987* (ed. C. T. Jones). New York: Perinatology Press, Ithaca (in press).

GARDNER, R. L. & LYON, M. F. (1971). X-chromosome inactivation studied by injection of a single cell into the mouse blastocyst. *Nature, Lond.* **231**, 385–386.

GARDNER, R. L., DAVIES, T. J. & CAREY, M. S. (1988). Effect of delayed implantation on differentiation of the extra-embryonic endoderm in the mouse blastocyst. *Placenta* **9**, 343–359.

GARDNER, R. L., LYON, M. F., EVANS, E. P. & BURTENSHAW, M. D. (1985). Clonal analysis of X-chromosome inactivation and the origin of the germ line in the mouse embryo. *J. Embryol. exp. Morph.* **88**, 349–363.

GARDNER, R. L. & PAPAIOANNOU, V. E. (1975). Differentiation in the trophectoderm and inner cell mass. In *The Early Development of Mammals: 2nd Symposium of the British Society for Developmental Biology* (ed. M. Balls & A. E. Wild), pp. 107–132. Cambridge: University Press.

GARDNER, R. L., PAPAIOANNOU, V. E. & BARTON, S. C. (1973). Origin of the ectoplacental cone and secondary giant cells in mouse blastocysts reconstituted from isolated trophoblast and inner cell mass. *J. Embryol. exp. Morph.* **30**, 561–572.

GARDNER, R. L. & ROSSANT, J. (1979). Investigation of the fate of 4·5 day *post-coitum* mouse inner cell mass cells by blastocyst injection. *J. Embryol. exp. Morph.* **52**, 141–152.

GIMLICH, R. L. & BRAUN, J. (1985). Improved fluorescent compounds for tracing cell lineage. *Devl Biol.* **109**, 509–514.

HALL, J. & TALAMANTES, F. (1984). Immunocytochemical localization of mouse placental lactogen in mouse placenta. *J. Histochem. Cytochem.* **32**, 379–382.

HANDYSIDE, A. H. (1978). Time of commitment of inside cells isolated from preimplantation mouse embryos. *J. Embryol. exp. Morph.* **45**, 37–53.

HAY, E. D. (1974). Cellular basis of regeneration. In *Concepts of Development* (ed. J. Lash & J. R. Whittaker), pp. 404–428. Stamford: Sinauer Associates, Inc.

HOGAN, B. L. M., BARLOW, D. P. & TILLY, R. (1983). F9 teratocarcinoma cells as a model for the differentiation of parietal and visceral endoderm in the mouse embryo. *Cancer Surveys* **2**, 115–140.

HOGAN, B. L. M. & NEWMAN, R. (1984). A scanning electron microscope study of the extraembryonic endoderm of the 8th-day mouse embryo. *Differentiation* **26**, 138–143.

HOGAN, B. L. M. & TILLY, R. (1978). *In vitro* development of inner cell masses isolated immunosurgically from mouse blastocysts. II. Inner cell masses from 3·5–4·0 day p.c. blastocysts. *J. Embryol. exp. Morph.* **45**, 107–121.

HOGAN, B. L. M. & TILLY, R. (1981). Cell interactions and endoderm differentiation in cultured mouse embryos. *J. Embryol. exp. Morph.* **62**, 379–394.

ILGREN, E. B. (1980). The control of trophoblastic growth in the guinea pig. *J. Embryol. exp. Morph.* **60**, 405–418.

ILGREN, E. B. (1981). On the control of the trophoblastic giant-cell transformation in the mouse: homotypic cellular interactions and polyploidy. *J. Embryol. exp. Morph.* **62**, 183–202.

JAMI, J. & RITZ, E. (1974). Multipotentiality of single cells of transplantable teratocarcinoma derived from mouse embryo graft. *J. natn. Cancer Inst.* **52**, 1547–1552.

JOHNSON, M. H. & MARO, B. (1986). Time and space in the mouse early embryo: a cell biological approach to cell diversification. In *Experimental Approaches to Mammalian Embryonic Development* (ed. J. Rossant & R. A. Pedersen), pp. 35–65. Cambridge: University Press.

JOHNSON, M. H. & ROSSANT, J. (1981). Molecular studies on cells of the trophectodermal lineage of the postimplantation mouse embryo. *J. Embryol. exp. Morph.* **61**, 103–116.

JOHNSON, M. H. & ZIOMEK, C. A. (1981). The foundation of two distinct cell lineages within the mouse morula. *Cell* **24**, 71–80.

JOLLY, J. & FERESTER-TADIE, M. (1936). Recherches sur l'oeuf du rat et de la souris. *Arch. Anat. Microsc. Morphol. Exp.* **32**, 323–390.

KAHAN, B. W. & EPHRUSSI, B. (1970). Developmental potentialities of cloned *in vitro* cultures of mouse testicular teratoma. *J. natn. Cancer Inst.* **44**, 1015–1036.

KIMMEL, C. B. & WARGA, R. M. (1987). Indeterminate cell lineage of the Zebrafish embryo. *Devl Biol.* **124**, 269–280.

KLEINSMITH, L. J. & PIERCE, G. B. (1964). Multipotentiality of single embryonal carcinoma cells. *Cancer Res.* **24**, 1544–1551.

KOZAK, L. P. & QUINN, P. J. (1975). Evidence for dosage compensation of an X-linked gene in the 6-day embryo of the mouse. *Devl Biol.* **45**, 65–73.

LEWIS, S. E., TURCHIN, H. A. & GLUECKSOHN-WAELSCH, S. (1976). The developmental analysis of an embryonic lethal ($C^{6H}$) in the mouse. *J. Embryol. exp. Morph.* **36**, 363–371.

LO, C. (1986). Localisation of low abundance DNA sequences in tissue sections by *in situ* hybridisation. *J. Cell Sci.* **81**, 143–162.

MACPHERSON, T. A., ZHENG, S-Y., GHANI, A. & GILL, T. J. (1985). The immunohistochemical localisation of pregnancy-specific $\beta_1$-glycoprotein in post-implantation rat trophoblast. *Placenta* **6**, 427–433.

MARTIN, G. R. (1981). Isolation of a pluripotent cell line from early mouse embryos cultured in medium conditioned by teratocarcinoma stem cells. *Proc. natn. Acad. Sci. U.S.A.* **78**, 7634–7638.

MARTIN, G. R. & EVANS, M. J. (1975). The differentiation of clonal lines of teratocarcinoma cells: formation of embryoid bodies *in vitro*. *Proc. natn. Acad. Sci. U.S.A.* **72**, 1441–1445.

MCLAREN, A. (1968). A study of blastocysts during delay and subsequent implantation in lactating mice. *J. Endocr.* **42**, 453–463.

McLaren, A. (1970). Early embryo-endometrial relationships. In *Ovo-implantation. Human Gonadotrophins and Prolactin* (ed. P. O. Hubinont, F. Leroy, C. Robyn & P. Leleux), pp. 18–33. Basel: S. Karger.

McLaren, A. (1976a). *Mammalian Chimaeras*. Cambridge: University Press.

McLaren, A. (1976b). Growth from fertilization to birth in the mouse. In *Embryogenesis in Mammals. Ciba Foundation Symposium 40 (new series),* (ed. K. Elliott & M. O'Connor), pp. 47–51. Amsterdam: Elsevier.

McMahon, A., Fosten, M. & Monk, M. (1983). X-chromosome inactivation mosaicism in the three germ layers and the germ line of the mouse embryo. *J. Embryol. exp. Morph.* **74**, 207–220.

Mintz, B. (1972). Clonal differentiation in early mammalian development. In *Molecular Genetics and Developmental Biology* (ed. M. Sussman), pp. 455–474. New Jersey: Prentice-Hall Inc.

Mintz, B. & Russell, E. S. (1957). Gene-induced embryological modifications of primordial germ cells in the mouse. *J. exp. Zool.* **134**, 207–238.

Monk, M. & Harper, M. (1979). Sequential X-chromosome inactivation coupled with cellular differentiation in early mouse embryos. *Nature, Lond.* **281**, 311–313.

Monk, M., Boubelik, M. & Lehnert, S. (1987). Temporal and regional changes in DNA methylation in the embryonic, extraembryonic and germ cell lineages during mouse embryo development. *Development* **99**, 371–382.

Nadjicka, M. & Hillman, N. (1974). Ultrastructural studies of the mouse blastocyst substages. *J. Embryol. exp. Morph.* **32**, 675–695.

Nichols, J. & Gardner, R. L. (1984). Heterogeneous differentiation of external cells in individual isolated early mouse inner cell masses in culture. *J. Embryol. exp. Morph.* **80**, 225–240.

Niswander, L., Yee, D., Rinchik, E. M., Russell, L. B. & Magnuson, T. (1988). The albino deletion complex and early postimplantation survival in the mouse. *Development* **102**, 45–53.

Ozdzenski, W. (1967). Observations on the origin of primordial germ cells in the mouse. *Zool. Pol.* **17**, 367–379.

Papaioannou, V. E. (1982). Lineage analysis of inner cell mass and trophectoderm using microsurgically reconstituted mouse blastocysts. *J. Embryol. exp. Morph.* **68**, 199–209.

Papaioannou, V. E., Rossant, J. & Gardner, R. L. (1978). Stem cells in early mammalian development. In *Stem Cells and Tissue Homeostasis: Symposium of the British Society for Cell Biology* (ed. B. I. Lord, C. S. Potten & R. J. Cole), pp. 49–69. Cambridge: University Press.

Pedersen, R. A. (1986). Potency, lineage, and allocation in preimplantation mouse embryos. In *Experimental Approaches to Mammalian Embryonic Development* (ed. J. Rossant & R. A. Pedersen), pp. 3–33. Cambridge: University Press.

Pennington, J. E., Rastan, S., Roelcke, D. & Feizi, T. (1985). Saccharide structures of the mouse embryo during the first eight days of development. Inferences from immunocytochemical studies using monoclonal antibodies in conjunction with glycosidases. *J. Embryol. exp. Morph.* **90**, 335–361.

Poelmann, R. E. (1980). Differential mitosis and degeneration patterns in relation to the alterations in the shape of the embryonic ectoderm of early postimplantation mouse embryos. *J. Embryol. exp. Morph.* **55**, 33–51.

Price, J., Turner, D. & Cepko, C. (1987). Lineage analysis in the vertebrate nervous system by retrovirus-mediated gene transfer. *Proc. natn. Acad. Sci. U.S.A.* **84**, 156–160.

Rastan, S. (1982). Timing of X-chromosome inactivation in post-implantation mouse embryos. *J. Embryol. exp. Morph.* **71**, 11–24.

Robertson, E. J. (1987). Embryo-derived stem cell lines. In *Teratocarcinomas and Embryonic Stem Cells: A Practical Approach* (ed. E. J. Robertson), pp. 71–112. Oxford: IRL Press.

Robertson, E. J. & Bradley, A. (1986). Production of permanent cell lines from early embryos and their use in studying developmental problems. In *Experimental Approaches to Mammalian Embryonic Development* (ed. J. Rossant & R. A. Pedersen), pp. 475–508. Cambridge: University Press.

Rosenthal, D., Wishnow, R. M. & Sato, G. H. (1970). *In vitro* growth and differentiation of clonal populations of multipotential mouse cells derived from a transplantable testicular teratocarcinoma. *J. natn. Cancer Inst.* **44**, 1001–1014.

Rossant, J. & Croy, B. A. (1985). Genetic identification of tissue of origin of cellular populations within the mouse placenta. *J. Embryol. exp. Morph.* **86**, 177–189.

ROSSANT, J., GARDNER, R. L. & ALEXANDRE, H. L. (1978). Investigation of the potency of cells from the postimplantation mouse embryo by blastocyst injection: a preliminary report. *J. Embryol. exp. Morph.* **48**, 239–247.

ROSSANT, J. & OFER, L. (1977). Properties of extra-embryonic ectoderm isolated from postimplantation mouse embryos. *J. Embryol. exp. Morph.* **39**, 183–194.

ROSSANT, J. & TAMURA-LIS, W. T. (1979). Potential of isolated mouse inner cell masses to form trophectoderm derivatives *in vivo*. *Devl Biol.* **70**, 255–261.

ROSSANT, J. & TAMURA-LIS, W. T. (1981). Effect of culture conditions on diploid to giant cell transformation in postimplantation mouse trophoblast. *J. Embryol. exp. Morph.* **62**, 217–227.

RUGH, R. (1968). *The Mouse.* Minneapolis: Burgess.

SANDERS, E. J., KHARE, M. K., OOI, V. C. & BELLAIRS, R. (1986). An experimental and morphological analysis of tail bud mesenchyme of the chick embryo. *Anat. Embryol.* **174**, 179–185.

SANES, J. R., RUBENSTEIN, J. L. R. & NICHOLAS, J-F. (1986). Use of a recombinant retrovirus to study post-implantation cell lineage in mouse embryos. *EMBO J.* **5**, 3133–3142.

SASAGAWA, M., YAMAZAKI, T., ENDO, M., KANAZAWA, K. & TAKEUCHI, S. (1987). Immunohistochemical localization of HLA antigens and placental proteins ($\alpha$hCG, $\beta$hCG, CTP, hPL and $SP_1$) in villous and extravillous trophoblast in normal human pregnancy: a distinctive pathway of differentiation of extravillous trophoblast. *Placenta* **8**, 515–528.

SCHOENWOLF, G. C. (1977). Tail (end) bud contributions to the posterior region of the chick embryo. *J. exp. Zool.* **201**, 227–246.

SCHOENWOLF, G. C. (1978). Effects of complete tail bud extirpation on early development of the posterior region of the chick embryo. *Anat. Rec.* **192**, 289–296.

SCHOENWOLF, G. C. (1979). Histological and ultrastructural observation of the tail bud formation in the chick embryo. *Anat. Rec.* **193**, 131–148.

SEARLE, A. G. (1978). Evidence from mutable genes concerning the origin of the germ line. In *Genetic Mosaics and Chimaeras in Mammals* (ed. L. B. Russell), pp. 209–224. New York: Plenum Press.

SHEDDEN, P. M. & WILEY, M. J. (1987). Early stages of development in caudal neural tube of the Golden Syrian hamster *(Mesocricetus auratus)*. *Anat. Rec.* **219**, 180–185.

SNELL, G. D. & STEVENS, L. C. (1966). Early embryology. In *Biology of the Laboratory Mouse*, 2nd edn (ed. E. L. Green), pp. 205–245. New York: McGraw-Hill.

SNOW, M. H. L. (1976). Embryo growth during the immediate postimplantation period. In *Embryogenesis in Mammals: CIBA Foundation Symposium 40 (new series)* (ed. K. Elliott & M. O'Connor), pp. 53–66. Amsterdam: Elsevier.

SNOW, M. H. L. (1977). Gastrulation in the mouse: growth and regionalization of the epiblast. *J. Embryol. exp. Morph.* **42**, 293–303.

SNOW, M. H. L. (1981). Autonomous development of parts isolated from primitive-streak-stage mouse embryos. Is development clonal? *J. Embryol. exp. Morph. Suppl.* **65**, 269–287.

SNOW, M. H. L. & BENNETT, D. (1978). Gastrulation in the mouse: the assessment of cell populations in the epiblast of $t^{w18}/t^{w18}$ embryos. *J. Embryol. exp. Morph.* **47**, 39–52.

SNOW, M. H. L. & TAM, P. P. L. (1979). Is compensatory growth a complicating factor in mouse teratology. *Nature, Lond.* **279**, 555–557.

SOLTER, D. & DAMJANOV, I. (1973). Explantation of extraembryonic parts of 7 day-old mouse egg cylinders. *Experientia* **29**, 701–702.

SOLTER, D., SKREB, N. & DAMJANOV, I. (1971). Cell cycle analysis in the mouse egg-cylinder. *Expl Cell Res.* **64**, 331–334.

SORIANO, P. & JAENISCH, R. (1986). Retroviruses as probes for mammalian development: allocation of cells to the somatic and germ cell lineages. *Cell* **46**, 19–29.

SPINDLE, A. I. (1978). Trophoblast regeneration by inner cell masses isolated from cultured mouse embryos. *J. exp. Zool.* **203**, 483–490.

STEVENS, L. C. (1970). Experimental production of testicular teratomas in mice of strains 129, A/He and their $F_1$ hybrids. *J. natn. Cancer Inst.* **44**, 923–929.

STINNAKRE, M. G., EVANS, M. J., WILLISON, K. R. & STERN, P. L. (1981). Expression of Forssman antigen in the post-implantation mouse embryo. *J. Embryol. exp. Morph.* **61**, 117–131.

SUMMERS, P. M., CAMPBELL, J. M. & MILLER, M. W. (1988). Normal *in vivo* development of marmoset monkey embryos after trophectoderm biopsy. *Human Reprod.* **3**, 389–393.

SURANI, M. A. H. (1986). Evidences and consequences of differences between maternal and paternal genomes during embryogenesis in the mouse. In *Experimental Approaches to Mammalian Embryonic Development* (ed. J. Rossant & R. A. Pedersen), pp. 401–435. Cambridge: University Press.

TAM, P. P. L. (1984). The histogenetic capacity of tissues in the caudal end of the embryonic axis of the mouse. *J. Embryol. exp. Morph.* **82**, 253–266.

TAM, P. P. L. & BEDDINGTON, R. S. P. (1987). The formation of mesodermal tissues in the mouse embryo during gastrulation and early organogenesis. *Development* **99**, 109–126.

THEILER, K. (1972). *The House Mouse.* Berlin: Springer-Verlag.

VARMUZA, S., PRIDEAUX, V., KOTHARY, R. & ROSSANT, J. (1988). Polytene chromosomes in mouse trophoblast giant cells. *Development* **102**, 127–134.

WEISBLAT, D. A., SAWYER, R. T. & STENT, G. S. (1978). Cell lineage analysis by intracellular injection of a tracer enzyme. *Science* **202**, 1295–1298.

WEST, J. D., BUCHER, T., LINKE,. I. M. & DUNNWALD, M. (1984). Investigation of variability among mouse aggregation chimaeras and X-chromosome inactivation mosaics. *J. Embryol. exp. Morph.* **84**, 309–329.

WILKIE, T. M., BRINSTER, R. L. & PALMITER, R. D. (1986). Germline and somatic mosaicism in transgenic mice. *Devl Biol.* **118**, 9–18.

WILSON, E. B. (1928). *The Cell in Development and Heredity,* 3rd edn. New York: MacMillan.

WRIGHT, N. & ALISON, M. (1984). *The Biology of Epithelial Cell Populations,* vol. 1. Oxford: Clarendon Press.

ZUCKERMAN, F. A. & HEAD, J. R. (1986). Isolation and characterization of trophoblast from murine placenta. *Placenta* **7**, 349–364.

*J. Cell Sci. Suppl. 10, 29–44 (1988)*
Printed in Great Britain © The Company of Biologists Limited 1988

# Early haemopoietic stem cells in the avian embryo

FRANÇOISE DIETERLEN-LIEVRE, LUC PARDANAUD, FOUZIA
YASSINE AND FRANÇOISE CORMIER

*Institut d'Embryologie Cellulaire et Moléculaire du CNRS et du Collège de France, 94736
Nogent s/Marne, France*

## Summary

Using 'yolk sac chimaeras', we have previously demonstrated that stem cells, destined to colonize haemopoietic organs other than the yolk sac, arise in the embryo proper. We have now investigated the emergence and potentialities of these cells *in vivo* and *in vitro*.

The *in vivo* approach consisted of interspecies grafting between quail and chick embryos. The cell progeny from the grafts was detected by means of QH1, a monoclonal antibody specific for the quail haemangioblastic lineage. When grafted into the dorsal mesentery of the chick embryo, which is a haemopoietic microenvironment, the region of the aorta from E3–E4 quail embryos generated large haemopoietic foci. When associated with a chick attractive thymic rudiment, cells left the quail aorta, entered this rudiment and underwent lymphopoiesis.

Cell suspensions prepared from 40–50 chick aortae, seeded in appropriate semi-solid media, yielded macrophage, granulocyte or erythrocyte clones. These colony forming cells were two to eight times more frequent than in cell preparations from hatchling bone marrow. By contrast, cells prepared from the whole embryonic body deprived of the aorta were not clonogenic.

By interspecies grafting of somatopleural (ectoderm + mesoderm, e.g. limb bud) or splanchnopleural rudiments (endoderm + mesoderm, e.g. lung, pancreas, intestine), the endothelial lining of blood vessels was shown to arise by two entirely different processes according to the rudiment considered: angiogenesis, i.e. invasion by extrinsic endothelial cells, in the limb bud, and vasculogenesis, i.e. *in situ* emergence of endothelial cells, in internal organs. The spleen, which first develops as a continuum to the pancreatic mesoderm, acquires its endothelial network by vasculogenesis, and is colonized by extrinsic haemopoietic stem cells. Granulopoietic cells in the pancreas and accessory cells in the lung are also extrinsic. Thus, in the case of endomesodermal rudiments, interspecies grafting reveals separate origins of endothelial and haemopoietic cells.

## Introduction

The emergence during embryonic life of the stem cells that colonize the rudiments of haemopoietic organs and found definitive blood cell lineages is still enigmatic in many respects. The process first occurs in the chick yolk sac during day 2 (E2) of incubation. At that time, solid groups of cells become committed to the 'haemangioblastic' lineage, which comprises haemopoietic and endothelial cells and their precursors. Within a few hours of their appearance, the central cells in these groups detach and evolve towards the erythroid pathway, while the peripheral cells take on the aspect of endothelium (Sabin, 1920; Kessel & Fabian, 1985; Pardanaud *et al.* 1987*a*; Péault *et al.* 1988). A new process initiated towards the end of day 2 (Dardick & Setterfield, 1978) culminates in the release of a different generation of red cells on day 5, at which time haemopoiesis becomes active in the embryo proper, beginning with the first colonization period of the thymic rudiment (reviewed by Le Douarin *et*

Key words: haemopoiesis, vasculogenesis, angiogenesis, quail-chick chimaeras.

al. 1984).

Using a chimaera model, consisting of a quail embryo grafted onto a chick yolk sac, we have demonstrated that this second phase of haemopoiesis depends on the emergence of a new set of stem cells, which are produced in the embryo proper rather than in the yolk sac (reviewed by Dieterlen-Lièvre, 1984).

We are now addressing the following questions. (1) What are the site of origin and potentialities of the intraembryonic stem cells that relay yolk sac stem cells? (2) Is there a common precursor for haemopoietic stem cells and endothelial cells?

The existence of this precursor, the haemangioblast according to the term coined by Murray (1932), has been postulated on descriptive grounds. First, a frequent observation in 1 to 3-day embryos, both in yolk sac blood islands and in intraembryonic blood vessels, is round cells that appear to have budded off from the endothelium (Sabin, 1920; Dieterlen-Lièvre & Martin, 1981; Péault et al. 1988). Second, endothelia and haemopoietic cells share common antigens, recognized in the quail by monoclonal antibodies (mAb). These antigens are strongly immunogenic, so that immunization with different preparations has induced the synthesis of several mAbs with a similar specificity for the quail hemangioblastic lineage. Two of these mAbs have been selected and extensively used in experiments with avian chimaeras. MBI (Péault et al. 1983; Péault, 1987) was obtained from immunization with the quail immunoglobulin $\mu$ chain. MB1 recognizes several glycoproteins of apparent molecular masses ranging from 80 to $200 \times 10^3$, among which is $\alpha2$ macroglobulin. The second antibody of this type, QH1 (Pardanaud et al. 1987a), has been obtained following immunization with 12-day embryonic quail bone marrow. Like MB1, it recognizes the haemangioblastic lineage of the quail and no cells of the chick. In Western blots carried out with bone marrow cell extracts, it recognizes several molecules ranging in $M_r$ between 150 and 220 ($\times 10^3$) (Pardanaud et al. 1987a). Both antibodies have similar specificities, though QH1 also recognizes quail primordial germ cells (Pardanaud et al. 1987b).

In the present report, we will consider two lines of experimental data; the first results from interspecific grafting of rudiments between quail and chick, followed by tracing cells of quail origin with antibody QH1. By this means: (1) stem cells that could be transplanted, and which displayed various haemopoietic potentialities, were shown to arise at E3–E4 in the para-aortic region; (2) evidence was obtained that some rudiments acquire independently their contingents of endothelial and haemo-poietic precursors.

The other class of results reviewed here relies on the analysis of haemopoietic potentialities present in various regions of the early embryo by the clonal culture system. This system has yielded definite proof of the primordial role of the para-aortic region in the production of intraembryonic stem cells (Cormier et al. 1986; Cormier & Dieterlen-Lièvre, 1988).


## Haemopoietic stem cells in the E3–E4 para-aortic region

Diffuse haemopoiesis occurs in the dorsal mesentery at E5–E7 in the quail embryo

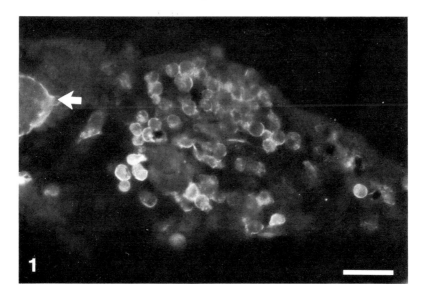

Fig. 1. QH1$^+$ progeny of an E4 quail aorta grafted for 3 days into the mesentery of a chick host. The structure of the grafted vessel has disappeared and dense aggregates of cells with a haemopoietic phenotype have developed. To the left of the field, a positive blood island-like structure is present (arrow). Bar, 25 $\mu$m.

and at E6–E8 in the chick embryo (Miller, 1913; Dieterlen-Lièvre & Martin, 1981). We thought that this site might be a favourable microenvironment for the multiplication and differentiation of cells with haemopoietic potentialities and we devised a technique for grafting rudiments to this site.

During normal development, the process of cell budding observed in various vessels is maximal in the dorsal aorta at E3. Dense mats of basophilic cells can be seen aggregated to the ventral aspect of the endothelium towards the lumen. This process also occurs on the tissue side of the aortic endothelium. Furthermore, similar basophilic cells (QH1$^+$ in the quail) are also scattered within the meshes of the dorsal mesenteric mesenchyme. In yolk sac chimaeras these cells are quail (Dieterlen-Lièvre & Martin, 1981). The aorta thus appears to be a likely candidate capable of producing the diffuse haemopoietic foci present in the paraaortic region.

The 'thoracic' segment of the dorsal aorta in the avian embryo is a large vessel, uncluttered by neighbouring organs between the levels of the aortic arches and the pro-/mesonephros. Until E5, the aortic endothelium in this free portion is surrounded by a muff of undifferentiated mesodermal cells. The whole segment with its mesodermal envelope can be dissected away with relative ease at this stage. When inserted ventral to the chick host aorta, the graft integrates into the mesentery. Three days later, it has given rise to a dense aggregate of cells that display the quail nucleolar marker and are positive with the quail haemangioblastic marker QH1 (Fig. 1). Exceptionally, a structure reminiscent of the engrafted vessel can be observed budding positive cells in the lumen (Fig. 2). Endothelial cells are sometimes present and these participate in the formation of chimaeric endothelial

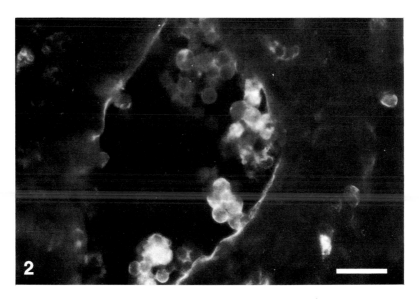

Fig. 2. In another graft similar to that of Fig. 1, the aorta has persisted as a hollow, endothelial-bound structure and round QH1$^+$ cells appear to be budding from the endothelium into the lumen. Bar, 25 $\mu$m.

structures. The aggregates of grafted haemopoietic cells are located in the vicinity of host blood-forming foci. The cells in these endogenous foci undergo erythropoiesis and less frequently granulopoiesis. Grafted quail cells usually differentiate as erythroblasts.

To determine whether progenitors with other potentialities were present in this region, the quail aorta, as defined above, was associated with a chick thymic rudiment. The thymus was taken at E6.5, when it becomes receptive to the first wave of colonizing stem cells. The two rudiments were co-cultured on an agar nutritive medium (Wolff & Haffen, 1952) for 12 h prior to grafting for 9 days in a chick host. Sequential sections of the transplants were treated with QH1 mAb and CT1 mAb, which is specific for thymocytes (Chen *et al.* 1984). Out of 10 associations, all but one harboured QH1$^+$ cells. Some of the thymic lobes that developed in each transplant were entirely populated by these quail cells (Fig. 3), while others were chimaeric. The CT1 antibody marked all thymocytes, irrespective of whether they were derived from the chick host or the quail aorta (Fig. 4). This experiment clearly demonstrates that precursors with T lymphocyte potentialities are present in the para-aortic region.

The question is still open as to whether haemopoietic cells deriving from the aortic rudiment are the progeny of either the endothelium or the mesoderm surrounding it. Only a partial answer can be given, because it is extremely difficult to dissect the endothelium cleanly. When the more or less bared endothelium is grafted, haemopoietic foci may develop, but their size is reduced.

Other rudiments were grafted to the same site: somites (from E2 embryos), liver, kidney, and another blood vessel, the common cardinal vein, (from E3 or E4). In

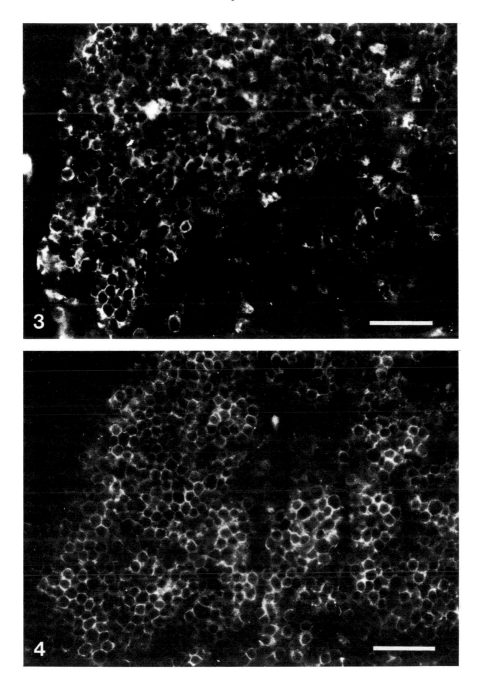

Fig. 3. Fifteen-day thymus developed from the association between a E6.5 chick thymus and an E4 quail aorta. Quail cells have entered the thymus and given rise to an abundant QH1$^+$ progeny which entirely fills the thymic cortex. The medulla is poorer in QH1$^+$ cells. Bar, 25 $\mu$m.

Fig. 4. A neighbouring section treated with CT1 mab. All the cells display the T lymphocyte antigen on their surface. Bar, 25 $\mu$m.

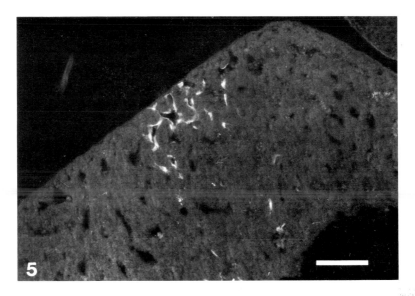

Fig. 5. Quail splanchnopleural mesoderm was grafted in an E3.5 chick embryo. Three days later, some cells from the graft, marked by the QH1 mAb, have reached the liver, where they assumed the endothelial phenotype. They coat the walls of sinusoids in typical fashion. Bar, 100 μm.

none of these cases, did haemopoietic cells ever develop. The cardinal vein gave rise to a thin sheet of quail cells inserted in the mesentery of the chick host. The vessel wall did not disintegrate as in the case of the aorta; however, no lumen persisted in these non-functional vessels.

## Haemopoietic stem cells in the E2 splanchnopleural mesoderm

In the E2 embryo, it is possible by mechanical means to dissect away the mesoderm either from the ectoderm or the endoderm with which it is associated. The splanchnopleural mesoderm from the area pellucida was divided into a number of segments along the cephalocaudal axis. When these segments were grafted to the chick dorsal mesentery, they gave rise to $QH1^+$ cells with extensive migratory behaviour. Cells from the grafted aorta gave rise to a solid aggregate of differentiating blood cells at the site of grafting in the mesentery; whereas, by contrast, the progeny of splanchnopleural mesoderm spread to different organs or tissues, mainly the mesentery, liver and kidney. These progeny were modest in number and the cells, identified by virtue of their QH1 affinity, adopted diverse phenotypes, apparently dictated by the environment in which they became arrested. For instance, cells that lodged in the liver or the kidney participated in the formation of chimaeric endothelia; in each location they became incorporated into the specific type of endothelium that characterizes that organ (Figs 5–6). Such specification imposed on invading foreign endothelial cells has been observed in grafts of mouse brain to the

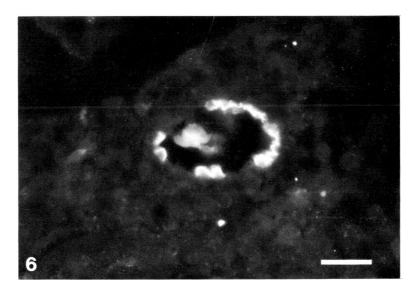

Fig. 6. In the same grafting conditions, these quail mesodermal cells became arrested in the dorsal mesentery of the chick host where they participated to a chimaeric endothelium. Note that these endothelial cells protrude in the lumen in typical fashion for an artery. The fluorescence visible in the lumen is probably due to haemopoietic cells of quail origin that are not in focus. Bar, 25 μm.

chick choriallantoic membrane (Risau *et al.* 1986). Cells that settled in the dorsal mesentery retained the round shape and the isolated status of haemopoietic cells (Dieterlen-Lièvre, 1984).

In some experimental series, mesodermal cells were not dissociated from the endoderm, so that the grafts contained cells from the two germ layers. Their fate was entirely different from that of isolated mesoderm. These grafts became implanted in the coelom and usually formed intestinal-like structures, associated with haemopoietic cell groups. These cell groups were dense aggregates of QH1$^+$ cells, reminiscent of aorta-derived haemopoietic cells. The splanchnopleural area corresponding to the level of somites 15–25 (Fig. 7) gave a particularly abundant QH1$^+$ progeny. This level is precisely the one that, in various types of interspecies chimaeras involving the *in ovo* transplantation of blastodisc territories, was found to be important for the formation of haemopoietic foci in the mesentery (Martin *et al.* 1980). In some of the splanchnopleural explants, the QH1$^+$ aggregates were spheres tightly bound by an endothelial envelope, i.e. blood islands.

Comparison of the derivatives yielded by the E3–E4 aortic region, E2 mesoderm or E2 mesoderm + endoderm indicates a positive influence of endoderm on the proliferation and, perhaps, the commitment of mesodermal cells to the haemopoietic pathway. Such an influence has been demonstrated earlier by Miura & Wilt (1970) in the case of extraembryonic endoderm, which promotes *in vitro* the growth of blood islands in the area vasculosa mesoderm.

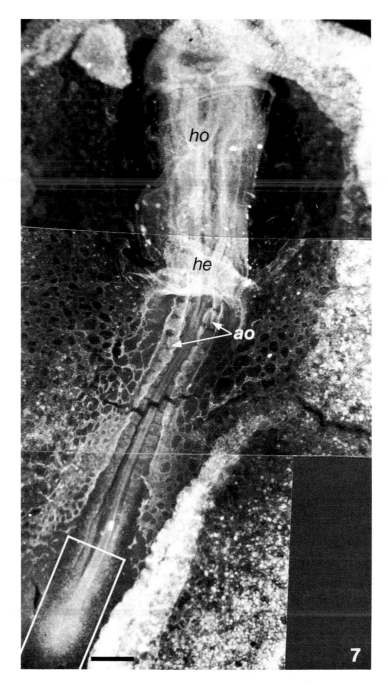

Fig. 7. A 15-somite quail embryo treated with QH1 antibody as a whole mount. Ventral view. The frame delineates the region whose splanchnopleura yields abundant haemopoietic cells, when engrafted in the chick mesentery. Embryonic structures and yolk granules exhibit a non-specific autofluorescence, that is easily distinguished from QH1 positivity. *ao*, aortae; *he*, heart; *ho*, ventral horns of the aorta. Bar, 100 μm.

## Assessment in clonal cultures of the concentration and types of progenitors in the para-aortic region

The art of cloning avian blood progenitors has lagged behind that achieved for mammalian cells. In particular, most growth factors remain unidentified. Mammalian growth factors do not cross-react functionally on avian haemopoietic cells. Usual media contain chicken serum, which favours powerfully the growth of macrophages and may even commit multipotential precursors to the monocytic pathway (Dodge & Sharma, 1985; Cormier & Dieterlen-Lièvre, 1988). The only avian growth factor available, c-MGF (Leutz *et al.* 1984), acts on monocytic precursors. Chicken anaemic serum is the usual source of avian erythropoietin. Our main goal was to detect whether progenitors with various potentialities were present in the wall of the aorta. To this end, Cormier devised a medium with only a minimal amount of serum that permits the growth and differentiation of granulocytic clusters. Another medium, supplemented with fibroblast-conditioned medium, supports the growth of monocytic and granulomonocytic colonies.

With the culture conditions available, we have been able to show that progenitors for monocytic, granulocytic and erythroid colonies are present in the wall of the aorta at E3 and E4 (Cormier *et al.* 1986; Cormier & Dieterlen-Lièvre, 1988). Strikingly, cell suspensions prepared from the embryo deprived of its aortic region yielded no progenitors. Furthermore, the progenitor concentration is two to eight times higher in the embryonic aorta wall than in the hatchling bone marrow (Fig. 8). We have not determined yet whether, depending on the culture conditions, the same precursors differentiate along various pathways or whether different, committed, precursors are recruited. In the latter case, the number of progenitors in the aortic wall would amount to the sum of individual precursors detected. We are devising culture conditions to search for pluripotential progenitors. This should enable us to enumerate more precisely the haemogenic capacities of this region. In any event, the clonal culture system yields critical evidence for the primordial role of this region in the emergence of haemopoietic stem cells at the period when yolk sac stem cells are first relayed by intraembryonic cells.

## Vasculogenesis, angiogenesis and haemopoiesis

Following Risau *et al.* (1988), it is convenient to distinguish vasculogenesis, the process by which endothelial cells arise *de novo*, from angiogenesis, the process by which normal or tumour tissues are invaded by pre-existing endothelial cells whose proliferation is stimulated by these tissues. We are currently mapping these processes in the developing embryo and attempting to relate them to the process of haemopoiesis.

The use of QH1 antibody on whole mounts (Fig. 7) (Pardanaud *et al.* 1987*a*) and of MB1 on sections (Péault *et al.* 1988) has revealed the very first steps of vasculogenesis, which were not distinguishable without a specific marker of endothelial cells. The two studies contribute different information on the emergence of the first endothelial cells. Vasculogenesis is initiated in the blastodisc at the head

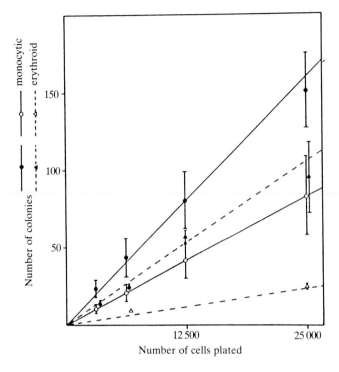

Fig. 8. Graph displaying the concentration of progenitors in the E4 chick aortic region (filled symbols) compared to the newborn bone marrow (open symbols). Both monocytic progenitors (grown in the presence of normal chicken serum and fibroblast conditioned medium) and erythroid progenitors (grown in the presence of anaemic serum) are more numerous in the aortic region.

process stage (Pardanaud et al. 1987a). The first positive cells appear in the area opaca at a median level, lateral to the first pairs of somites, and about 2 h later in the area pellicuda at the same level. Cells, first isolated, subsequently link up to form an extending network, which invests the blastodisc simultaneously in the cephalic and caudal directions. Caudalwards vascularization progresses parallel to segmentation. The caudal 'horseshoe' area vasculosa becomes established at the stage with five pairs of somites.

QH1[+] cells appear to emerge in situ all over the blastodisc; experimental evidence that there is no privileged site of formation of endothelial cells has also been obtained from the analysis of yolk sac chimaeras, in which quail and chick territories were associated surgically (Dieterlen-Lièvre, 1975; Martin et al. 1978). In these chimaeras the endothelia did not migrate from one area to another: in the chick yolk sac territory, endothelia were chick, while in the quail embryo territory endothelia were quail. Thus it is clear that no extensive migration of endothelial cells occurs in the horizontal plane of the blastodisc.

However, the vertical investment of the germ layers by endothelial cells proceeds differently. The pictures published by Péault et al. (1988) show that isolated MB1[+] cells first appear in ventral apposition to the mesoderm in contact with the endoderm.

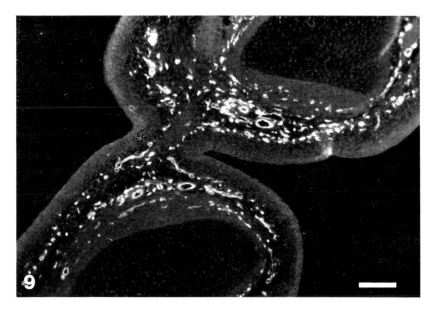

Fig. 9. Chick limb bud developed in a quail embryo host (stage HH 19–12 days). Endothelia in the limb tissues surrounding cartilaginous condensations are QH1$^+$, i.e of host origin. Bar, 100 μm.

By contrast, the somatopleural layer of the mesoderm is devoid of positive cells both in the area vasculosa and in the area pellucida. Péault *et al.* described the differentiation of intersegmental arteries by a proliferation of the aortae. These adventitious vessels penetrate between the somites, surround and eventually penetrate the neural tube. Whether endothelial cells also emerge *in situ* from the somatopleural mesenchyme cannot be surmised from these descriptive data.

In this regard it is interesting to note that the amnion, an ecto–mesodermal derivative, never acquires blood vessels. These considerations led us to study the respective origins of endothelial and haemopoietic cells in rudiments consisting of either endoderm or ectoderm associated with mesoderm. For the ecto-/mesodermal rudiment, the limb bud was selected. Jotereau & Le Douarin (1978) had previously demonstrated that haemopoietic cells, endothelial cells and osteosclasts were of host origin in chick limb buds explanted at stages 23–25 (Hamburger & Hamilton, 1951) and grafted to the somatopleura of quail hosts. To determine the host or graft origin of cells, these investigators used the quail nucleolar marker, which is difficult to identify in endothelial cells; furthermore, isolated cells from one or the other species cannot usually be detected. These problems are avoided by the use of monoclonal antibodies. Chick limb buds grafted to quail hosts displayed a rich QH1$^+$ endothelial network around cartilaginous condensations (Fig. 9). Bone marrow harboured endothelial and haemopoietic cells of the quail (Fig. 10). In the reverse association (quail limb buds grafted to chick hosts) any QH1$^+$ cell must have entered the rudiment prior to its retrieval from the donor embryo. Quail limb buds were taken

Fig. 11. Chick lung grafted in a quail (stage HH 15 – 11 days). QH1$^+$ isolated cells are probably macrophages. The arrow points to exceptional endothelial cells of host origin. Bar, 100 µm.

Fig. 12. Quail lung grafted in a chick (stage HH 21 – 12 days). The entire endothelial network is QH1$^+$, i.e. of host origin. QH1 has a slight affinity for quail endoderm. Bar, 100 µm.

Fig. 13. Chick pancreas grafted in a quail (stages HH 19 – 12 days). Dense aggregated of QH1$^+$ granulocytes infiltrate the wall of three blood vessels, that appear as dark circles. Bar, 100 µm.

Fig. 14. Quail pancreas grafted in a chick (stage HH 17 – 13 days). QH1$^+$ endothelia. Bar, 100 µm.

Fig. 15. Chick spleen grafted in a quail (stage HH 19 – 12 days). QH1$^+$ haemopoietic cells. Bar, 50 µm.

Fig. 16. Quail spleen grafted to the chick (stage HH 17 – 13 days). QH1$^+$ endothelial network. Arrow points to an artery in longitudinal profile. Erythrocytes display a non-specific yellow fluorescence. Bar, 50 µm.

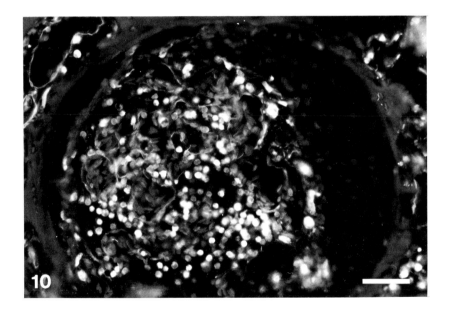

Fig. 10. Same graft as in Fig. 9 at bone marrow level. The bone marrow displays QH1$^+$ endothelia and haemopoietic cells. Bar, 100 µm.

from donors between the stages with 27 and 43 pairs of somites (HH16–21). They were grown until a total age of 13–16 days, when bone marrow differentiation is well under way. Two features were noted: (1) the bone marrow never contained positive cells; (2) scarce positive cells could be observed in the connective tissue surrounding the cartilage masses; they were usually isolated and occasionally inserted in a chimaeric vessels. The number of these cells was always very low (around 10) and was not significantly related to the stage at which the rudiment was obtained. These

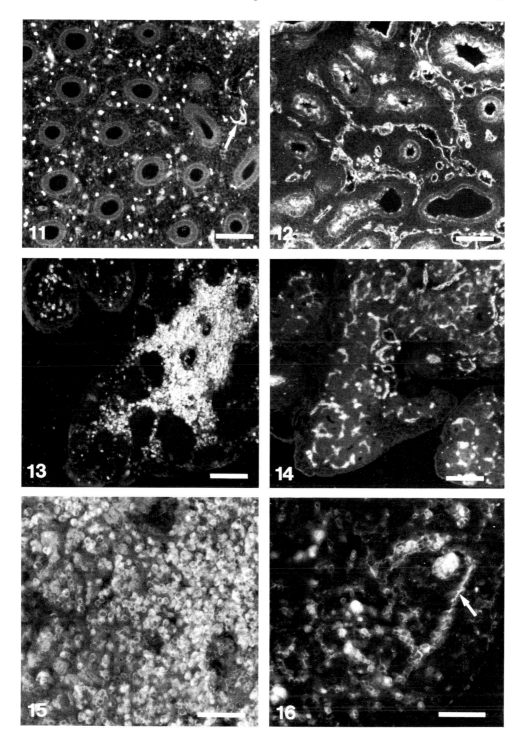

experiments enable us to conclude that endothelial cells and haemopoietic cells in the bone marrow both have an extrinsic origin, and that their ingress occurs after E4.

Various endo-/mesodermal rudiments were also grafted (Table 1). Some of these organs are not considered to have a haemopoietic function, but they harbour blood cells that exert specific functions, for instance macrophages in the lung. As for the chick pancreas, it is a very active site for granulopoiesis during embryonic life (Benazzi-Lentati, 1932; Dieterlen-Lièvre, 1965). Finally, the rudiment of the spleen carries out erythropoiesis and granulopoiesis during embryogenesis. Though purely mesodermal, it arises as an appendix to the pancreas and is thus subjected to interactions with endoderm.

All these organs developed according to the same rule. Endothelial cells and haemopoietic cells were distinct in origin; the first arose from precursors intrinsic to the rudiment, while the latter, provided by the host, invaded the rudiment. Concretely, when the rudiments were of the chick species, endothelial cells were QH1$^-$ and haemopoietic cells were positive (Figs 11, 13, 15). When rudiments came from the quail, endothelial cells were QH1$^+$ and haemopoietic cells were negative (Figs 12, 14, 16). The rudiments were obtained from donor embryos between 55 and 84 h of incubation, covering a range of stages between 25 and 43 pairs of somites (HH15 to -21). They were left to develop until they had reached a total age of 8–17 days. Regardless of the precise period of engraftment, the results were similar. It should be mentioned that chick rudiments grafted in quail hosts occasionally displayed a few endothelial profiles at the periphery of the explant (Fig. 11). This marginal ingression of host endothelia does not detract from the conclusion that the bulk of endothelial cell precursors arise within the mesoderm of these organs.

To summarize, interspecies grafting makes it possible to detect two independent processes during avian development: vasculogenesis in rudiments in which meso-derm is associated with endoderm, and angiogenesis in rudiments in which mesoderm is associated with ectoderm. Furthermore, haemopoiesis develops inde-pendently of vasculogenesis in the former rudiments.

Table 1. *Experimental demonstration of angiogenesis in ecto-/mesodermal organs and vasculogenesis in endo-/mesodermal organs*

| | QH1$^+$ haemopoietic (H) and endothelial (E) cells in interspecies grafts | | | | | | | | | | | |
| --- | --- | --- | --- | --- | --- | --- | --- | --- | --- | --- | --- | --- |
| | Limb buds | | | Lung | | | Intestine and pancreas | | | Spleen | | |
| | Total* | H† | E‡ | Total | H | E | Total | H | E | Total | H | E |
| Q→C | 23 | 0 | 0 | 11 | 0 | **11** | 6 | 0 | **6** | 61 | 0 | **61** |
| C→Q | 8 | **8** | **8** | 4 | **4** | 0 | 7 | **7** | 0 | 34 | **34** | 0 |

Values in bold face indicate the numbers of grants with QH1$^+$ cells of the type considered.
Donor embryos, 20–40 pairs of somites. Total age of grafts, 8–17 days.
* Number of grafts.
† Number of grafts with positive haemopoietic cells.
‡ Number of grafts with positive endothelial cells.

## Conclusion

We have dissected various events in the development of the avian haemopoietic system. First, a region of splanchnopleural mesoderm could be shown to produce haemopoietic cells. This region, though not precisely mapped yet, is located in the area pellucida, at the level of somites 10–25. Interactions between endoderm and mesoderm appear to exert a positive influence on the blood-forming properties of this region. It develops within 24 h in a tissue, surrounding the aorta, in which clonogenic cells of various blood lineages could be enumerated by culture in semi-solid media. Second, organ rudiments acquire their endothelial cell complement by two different processes, vasculogenesis or angiogenesis. Vasculogenesis, i.e. *in situ* emergence of endothelial cells, also appears to depend on the presence of endoderm interacting with the mesoderm. Where it occurs, haemopoietic stem cells have an independent origin from endothelial cells. Angiogenesis, i.e. colonization of a rudiment by extrinsic endothelial cell progenitors, occurs in the bone marrow, which is the definitive blood stem-cell reserve.

No experimental evidence is available concerning the link between endothelial and haemopoietic cell origins in the bone marrow. One of the questions about the development of the haemopoietic system deals with the existence of the haemangioblast, a putative common precursor to endothelial and haemopoietic lineages. If this precursor exists, its progeny diverge subsequently, as clearly indicated by the independent origins of the two lineages in endomesodermal organs.

We are indebted to Chen-lo Chen and Max Cooper for the kind gift of CT1 mab. This work was supported by the Centre National de la Recherche Scientifique and the Ministère de la Recherche et de la Technologie.

## References

BENAZZI-LENTATI, G. (1932). Sul focolaio eosinofilopoietico del pancreas di Uccelli. *Monitore Zool. Ital.* **43**, 115–118.

CHEN, C. H., CHANH, T. C. & COOPER, M. D. (1984). Chicken thymocyte-specific antigen identified by monoclonal antibodies: ontogeny, tissue distribution and biochemical characterization. *Eur. J. Immun.* **14**, 385–391.

CORMIER, F., DE PAZ, P. & DIETERLEN-LIEVRE, F. (1986). *In vitro* detection of cells with monocytic potentiality in the wall of the chick embryo aorta. *Devl Biol.* **118**, 167–175.

CORMIER, F. & DIETERLEN-LIEVRE, F. (1988). The wall of the chick embryo aorta harbors M-CFC, G-CFC, GM-CFC and BFU-E. *Development* **102**, 279–285.

DARDICK, I. & SETTERFIELD, G. (1978). Early origins of definitive erythroid cells in the chick embryo. *Tissue & Cell* **10**, 335–364.

DIETERLEN-LIEVRE, F. (1965). Etude morphologique et expérimentale de la différenciation du pancréas chez l'embryon de Poulet. *Bull. Biol. Fr. Belg.* **99**, 4–116.

DIETERLEN-LIEVRE, F. (1975). On the origin of haemopoietic stem cells in the avian embryo: an experimental approach. *J. Embryol. exp. Morph.* **33**, 607–619.

DIETERLEN-LIEVRE, F. (1984). Blood in Chimeras. In *Chimeras in Developmental Biology* (ed. N. Le Douarin & A. McLaren), pp. 133–163. London: Academic Press.

DIETERLEN-LIEVRE, F. & MARTIN, C. (1981). Diffuse intraembryonic hemopoiesis in normal and chimeric avian development. *Devl Biol.* **88**, 180–191.

DODGE, W. H. & SHARMA, S. (1985). Serum-free conditions for the growth of avian granulocyte and monocyte clones and primary leukemic cells induced by AMV, and the apparent conversion of granulocytic progenitors into monocytic cells by a factor in chicken serum. *J. cell. Physiol.* **123**, 264–268.

HAMBURGER, V. & HAMILTON, H. L. (1951). A series of normal stages in the development of the chick embryo. *J. Morph.* **88**, 49–92.

JOTEREAU, F. V. & LE DOUARIN, N. M. (1978). The developmental relationship between osteocytes and osteoclasts: A study using the quail–chick nuclear marker in endochondral ossification. *Devl Biol.* **63**, 253–265.

KESSEL, J. & FABIAN, B. C. (1985). Graded morphogenetic patterns during the development of the extraembryonic blood system and coelom of the chick blastoderm: a scanning electron microscope and light microscope study. *Am. J. Anat.* **173**, 99–112.

LE DOUARIN, N., DIETERLEN-LIEVRE, F. & OLIVER, P. (1984). Ontogeny of avian primary lymphoid organs and lymphoid stem cells. *Am. J. Anat.* **170**, 261–299.

LEUTZ, A., BEUG, H. & GRAF. T. (1984). Purification and characterization of cMGF, a novel chicken myelomonocytic growth factor. *EMBO J.* **3**, 3191–3197.

MARTIN, C., BEAUPAIN, D. & DIETERLEN-LIEVRE, F. (1978). Developmental relationships between vitelline and intra-embryonic haemopoiesis studied in avian "yolk sac chimaeras". *Cell Differ.* **7**, 115–130.

MARTIN, C., BEAUPAIN, D. & DIETERLEN-LIEVRE, F. (1980). A study of the development of the hemopoietic system using quail–chick chimeras obtained by blastoderm recombination. *Devl Biol.* **75**, 303–314.

MILLER, A. M. (1913). Histogenesis and morphogenesis of the thoracic duct in the chick; development of blood cells and their passage to the blood stream via the thoracic duct. *Am. J. Anat.* **15**, 131–198.

MIURA, Y. & WILT, F. H. (1970). The formations of blood islands in dissociated-reaggregated chick embryo yolk sac cells. *Expl Cell Res.* **59**, 217–226.

MURRAY, P. (1932). The development *in vitro* of the blood of the early chick embryo. *Proc. R. Soc. Lond.* **111**, 497–521.

PARDANAUD, L, ALTMANN,C., KITOS, P., DIETERLEN-LIEVRE, F. & BUCK, C. (1987*a*). Vasculogenesis in the early quail blastodisc as studied with a monoclonal antibody recognizing endothelial cells. *Development* **100**, 339–349.

PARDANAUD, L., BUCK, C. & DIETERLEN-LIEVRE, F. (1987*b*). Early germ cell segregation and distribution in the quail blastodisc. *Cell Differ.* **22**, 47–60.

PÉAULT, B. M. (1987). MB1, a quail leukocyte/vascular endothelium antigen: characterization of the lymphocyte-surface form and identification of its secreted counterpart as a α-2-macroglobulin. *Cell Differ.* **21**, 175–187.

PÉAULT, B., COLTEY, M. & LE DOUARIN, N. M. (1988). Ontogenic emergence of a quail leukocyte/endothelium cell surface antigen. *Cell Differ.* **23**, 165–174.

PÉAULT, B. M., THIERY, J. P. & LE DOUARIN, N. M. (1983). Surface marker for hemopoietic and endothelial cell lineages in quail that is defined by a monoclonal antibody. *Proc. natn. Acad. Sci. U.S.A.* **80**, 2976–2980.

RISAU, W., HALLMANN, R., ALBRECHT, U. & HENKE-FAHLE, S. (1986). Brain induces the expression of an early cell surface marker for blood–brain barrier-specific endothelium. *EMBO J.* **5**, 3179–3183.

RISAU, W., SARIOLA, H., ZERWES, H.-G., SASSE, J., EKBLOM, P., KEMLER, R. & DOETSCHMAN, T. (1988). Vasculogenesis and angiogenesis in embryonic-stem-cell-derived embryoid bodies. *Development* **102**, 471–478.

SABIN, F. (1920). Studies on the origin of the blood-vessels and of red-blood corpuscles as seen in the living blastoderm of chicks during the second day of incubation. *Contributions to Embryology*, vol. 9, pp. 214–262. Washington: Carnegie Instn.

WOLFF, E. & HAFFEN, K. (1952). Sur le développement et la différenciation sexuelle des gonades embryonnaires d'Oiseau en culture *in vitro*. *J. exp. Zool.* **119**, 381–404.

*J. Cell Sci. Suppl. 10, 45–62 (1988)*
*Printed in Great Britain © The Company of Biologists Limited 1988*

# Epithelial stem cells *in vivo*

C. S. POTTEN AND R. J. MORRIS

*Paterson Institute for Cancer Research, Christie Hospital, Manchester M20 9BX, UK and
The University of Texas System Cancer Center, Science Park, P.O. Box 389, Smithville, Texas
78957, USA*

## Summary

Cellular topography within the highly polarized surface epithelia can be used to identify the
location of the stem cells. In some instances, this can be quite precise and allows the characteristics
of stem cells to be studied. Our current knowledge of the stem cell population in murine epidermis
and small intestinal crypts is reviewed. In the epidermis, the stem cells would appear to make up
about 10 % of the basal layer and are distributed towards the centre of the basal layer component of
the epidermal proliferative unit. These cells have a long cell cycle and are probably the same cells
that retain both tritiated thymidine and radioactively labelled carcinogens for long periods of time.
This label retention permits the labelling of the putative stem cell compartment. Over recent years,
there has been an accumulation of information indicating various types of heterogeneity within the
basal layer, much of which can be interpreted in relation to cellular hierarchies. In the small
intestine, cell positions can be fairly precisely identified and the stem cell zone identified. Complex
modelling of a wide range of cell kinetic experiments suggests that each crypt contains between 4
and 16 steady state functional stem cells. Radiobiological experiments suggest that up to 32 cells
may be capable of clonal regeneration. The repopulation of the clonogenic cell compartment has
been determined and the doubling time measured to be 19·7 h. Such studies should throw further
light on the behaviour of stem cells and identify the timing of periods of increased and decreased
cell proliferation (activation and suppression of controls).

## Introduction

The constantly replacing epithelial tissues in the adult body are characterized by
having a high degree of structural order. The tissue is polarized as are the individual
cells also. Although epithelial tissues differ in structure and function they share a
unifying theme in that they all undergo continual lifelong cell turnover which is
characterized by specific patterns of proliferation within morphologically defined
units. The long life of these units, the patterns of proliferation and the radiobiological response (clonal regeneration) suggest the units contain stem cells. If the question
is asked 'where are the cells that are ultimately responsible for all the cell replacement
– the stem cells?' the superficial answer is generally quite clear. In simple flat
stratified epithelia such as the epidermis on the back skin of the mouse they must be
somewhere in the basal layer because cell proliferation occurs only in the basal layer.
In more complex undulating stratified epithelia where there are rete ridges or pegs,
and one example that has been particularly studied in the mouse is the dorsal surface
of the tongue and its filiform papilla (Hume & Potten, 1976), the answer is in the
basal layer but specifically in those regions of the basal layer that project deepest into

Key words: epithelial stem cells, epidermis, small intestine, clonogenic cells, division capacity,
label retention.

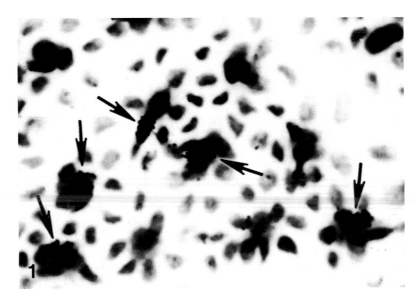

Fig. 1. Autoradiographs of a sheet of epidermis separated from the dermis by exposure to 0·5% acetic acid overnight. The epidermal sheet was prepared from a mouse that received twice daily injections of tritiated thymidine for 3 days starting on the third day after birth. The mouse was killed when it was 8 weeks old. The characteristic pattern of the clustered basal cells can be seen which relate to the EPU (see text). Cells which retain label can be easily seen (arrows). Many are centrally located in the cluster of EPU basal cells, i.e. at the putative stem cell location.

the connective tissue. Such an undulating stratified epithelium may be a model for all such epithelia including many regions of the epidermis in man and other regions of oral epithelia such as parts of the gingiva. In simple columnar epithelia such as the mucosa of the small intestine the answer is at the deepest part of the epithelium in the lamina propria which represents the origin of all the rapid cell displacement. In the small intestine this means near the base of the crypt immediately above, or scattered amongst, the Paneth cells. In the colon it may mean literally the cell or few cells right at the base of the crypt. Such precise topographical distribution for the stem cells means that they can be studied in a fairly direct manner. We should like to review our current understanding of some of the characteristics of these special cells.

It has not yet been determined whether the stem cells are merely proliferative cells which occur at special positions or whether they themselves differ intrinsically from other proliferative cells. If their function is merely determined by their position it is unclear what characterizes these positions, micro-environments or niches.

## The epidermis

The cells on the basal layer of the epidermis on mouse back skin are arranged in a particular pattern (Fig. 1) which is related to the columnar packing organization of the cells in the suprabasal strata (Fig. 2). These columns of cells are particularly evident from the surface appearance of the epidermis after silver staining of sheets of epidermis or in scanning electron micrographs or even in carefully prepared sections of murine skin. They represent the historical record of the proliferative activity of the group of about 10–11 basal cells immediately beneath the column and the whole unit, basal cells plus column, represents somewhat autonomous units of proliferation, called epidermal proliferative units (EPUs) (Fig. 2) (Potten, 1974, 1981, 1985). Studies on the effects of ionizing or ultraviolet irradiation of skin and various experiments involving tritiated thymidine labelling together with other morphological and functional cell studies suggest that the basal layer has considerable cellular heterogeneity (Table 1). Each basal cell has a characteristic position within the EPU. The position correlates with differences in proliferative activity and the response of the cells to tumour promoters. The radiobiological data suggest that each EPU probably possesses a single clonogenic cell, i.e. the stem or clonogenic cell compartment comprises about 10 % of the basal cells. Interpretation of cell kinetic experiments suggests that the cell replacement within the basal layer is best explained on the basis of a cell lineage comprising three generations of dividing transit cells. Taking the clonogenic cell estimates, the overall radiobiological observations and all the cell kinetic experiments the current most appropriate model for epidermis is illustrated in Fig. 2. There remains some doubt about the fine details of the structure of the hierarchy, and the position within the hierarchy of individual cells, but the stem cell population can be assumed to make up less than 20 % (probably 10 %) of the basal layer within which about 60 % of the cells are proliferative. The cell cycle of the stem cells is estimated to be about twice that of the transit cells with the overall average cell cycle time being about 125 h. The slow cell cycle of the stem cells may provide a means of identifying these cells (Fig. 1).

## Studies on label-retaining cells

Slowly cycling cells in mouse epidermis which are positioned towards the centre of the cluster of basal cells associated with each epidermal proliferative unit can be identified by continuous tritiated thymidine labelling studies (Potten, 1974) or by labelling basal cells and waiting for the label to dilute to background levels in the faster cycling cells (Fig. 1) (Bickenbach, 1981; Morris *et al.* 1985, 1986; Potten *et al.* 1982). This is most effective when the initial labelling protocol produces high labelling indices, such as after continuous labelling of young adult or neonatal mice. The cells that retain label for longer than the average (label-retaining cells, LRC) can be assumed to have divided less frequently, i.e. be more slowly cycling. Other cell kinetic analyses and modelling studies have suggested that the stem cells are more slowly cycling with a cell cycle time of 200 h (or about 8 days) and studies on the label-retaining cells show that most of these cells are located towards the centre of the EPU (Fig. 1), the site suggested for the stem cells.

The loss of label in the faster cycling cells could be attributed to the cell cycle

Mouse ∼10$^7$ cells/day/epidermis

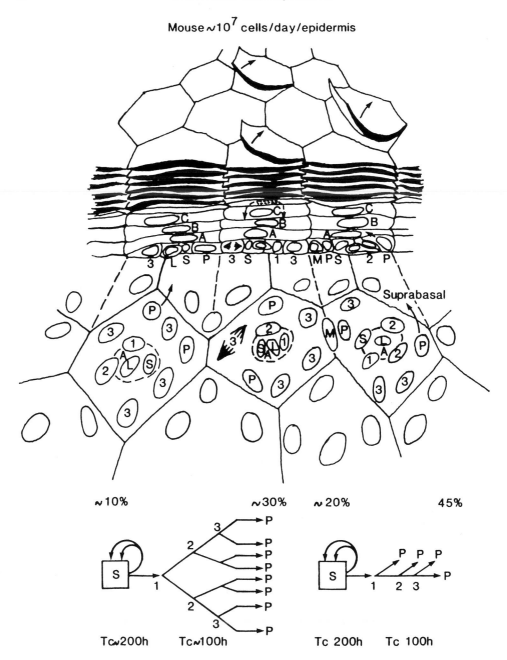

Fig. 2. Diagrammatic representation of the epidermal proliferative units (EPUs) in mouse epidermis as viewed from the surface (e.g. with SEM) – top of drawing; in section – middle portion; and in an epidermal sheet – lower portion (compare with Fig. 1). Two possible cell lineages that may explain the cell replacement process are shown below. A full lineage with three transit generations was deduced from an analysis of three cell kinetic experiments (Potten *et al.* 1982). An abbreviated lineage with differentiation from each transit generation was deduced from an analysis of the changing patterns with time of clusters of labelled cells (Loeffler *et al.* 1987).

Table 1. *Evidence for cellular heterogeneity in the epidermal basal layer (Clausen & Potten, 1988)*

| | | | |
|---|---|---|---|
| Morphological studies | Clear cells | Non-keratinocytes 10–12 % | Allen & Potten (1974) |
| | Dark cells | Decline with age – stem cells? | Klein-Szanto & Slaga (1981) |
| | Non-serrated cells | Slow cell cycle, base of rete ridge | Lavker & Sun (1982) |
| Functional studies | Clonogenic cells | 2–7 % – stem cells | Potten & Hendry (1973) |
| | Cells acutely sensitive to ionizing radiation | <10 % – stem cells? | Al-Barwari (1978) |
| | Phorbol ester-resistant mezerein-sensitive cells *in vitro* | ~10 % clonogenic cells | Parkinson *et al.* (1983, 1984) |
| | Small cells | Fast cell cycle, high self-replicative probability *in vitro* | Barrandon & Green (1985) |
| Cell kinetic studies | Continuous labelling and suprabasal labelling | Post-mitotic cells 20–40 % | Iversen *et al.* (1968) Potten *et al.* (1982) Loeffler *et al.* (1987) |
| | Slow cycling cells | 5–14 % *in vivo* cell kinetics – stem cells? retention of label – stem cells? | Potten *et al.* (1982) Bickenbach (1981) Morris *et al.* (1985, 1986) |
| | | Low RNA content – small cells | Eisinger *et al.* (1979) Staiano-Coico *et al.* (1986) Kimmel *et al.* (1986) |
| | Slow $G_2$ progression | 70 % of $G_2$ cells | Clausen *et al.* (1985) |
| | Slow S progression | 40 % of S cells, continuous | Clausen *et al.* (1985) |

duration alone or also to the fact that many of these cells may be dividing transit cells that emigrate from the basal layer and are exfoliated from the system. Based on our current cell kinetic model of epidermis, about half of the initially labelled cells would be expected to divide once and then leave the basal layer between 30 and 100 h. A second cohort would be expected to divide twice and leave the basal layer between about 145 and 200 h after the initial labelling. The final, third cohort of transit cells might also have a long cell cycle but nevertheless would be expected to emigrate between about 345 and 400 h after their third post-labelling cell division. However, during this period the stem cells originally labelled would have produced new transit cells with a labelling density half that observed initially. There are several points in time when it can be expected that the stem and early transit cells might have a higher grain density than the majority of cells. However, it is unlikely, based on currently assumed cell cycle differences, that this would ever be more than a two-fold difference in grain density, which is not consistent with the observations illustrated by Fig. 1. In order to obtain the grain differential commonly seen in LRC experiments it would be necessary to assume that the stem cells have a slower cell cycle than has been assumed previously or that other mechanisms operate to conserve radioactivity in the stem cells.

Transit cells, which characteristically have a limited life in the basal layer, are unlikely to be involved in carcinogenesis, which characteristically possesses a long latent period usually measured in months for mouse skin. It is interesting in this context that radioactively labelled carcinogens, tritiated or carbon-14-labelled benzo(a)pyrene (BP) (Morris *et al*. 1986) and tritiated dimethylbenze(a)anthracene (DMBA) (preliminary unpublished observations), are both retained in a few cells in the basal layer predominantly located towards the centre of the EPU. Other carcinogen label-retaining cells can be observed in the hair follicles as is also observed after the [³H]thymidine ([³H]dThd)-labelling protocols. Double labelling experiments with [³H]dThd and [¹⁴C]BP suggest both molecules are detecting the same slowly cycling population of cells.

Other preliminary unpublished data suggest that the cells retaining [³H]dThd label retaining cells behave in culture in a different manner to most pulse labelled cells. Cell suspensions that are prepared from skin which had been pulse labelled with tritiated thymidine produce clusters of cells (colonies) in culture which, if they contain labelled cells, have most of the labelled cells as isolated single labelled cells in a cluster of otherwise unlabelled cells, suggesting that they have been through no cell divisions. In contrast, suspensions prepared from skin which contain LRCs (as a consequence of a multiple labelling protocol one or more months earlier in life) produce colonies many of which have several lightly labelled cells, suggesting that the LRCs divided several times during the formation of the cluster of cells. The observations are consistent with the view that many of the [³H]dThd label-retaining cells possess an *in vitro* clonogenic capacity further supporting the view that the LRCs may be representative of a population of slow cycling stem cells. The LRCs are also the cells that can be seen to retain carcinogens for long periods of time and hence may be the cells that ultimately produce cancers.

## The significance of carcinogen label-retaining cells in two-stage murine cutaneous carcinogenesis

In two-stage carcinogenesis, benign and malignant cutaneous neoplasma are induced on the backs of mice following initiation with a subtumorigenic exposure to a carcinogen and subsequent repetitive exposure to a noncarcinogenic, hyperplasiogenic tumour promoter. Tumour initiation is thought to involve conversion of some epidermal cells into latent neoplastic cells; promotion elicits expression of the neoplastic change (Boutwell, 1974; Scribner & Suss, 1978; Slaga, 1984). Effective initiators of skin carcinogenesis such as polycyclic aromatic hydrocarbons have in common the capacity for covalent binding as activated electrophiles to cellular DNA and the ability to cause an irreversible alteration of the genome (Dipple *et al.* 1984; Miller & Miller, 1981; Osborn, 1984; Ashurst *et al.* 1982; Nakayama *et al.* 1984). The consequences of tumour initiation are essentially irreversible and not expressed in the absence of promotion. The tumour responses are evoked whether promotion is begun one week or one year after the exposure to the carcinogen (Boutwell, 1964; Roe *et al.* 1972; Stenbach *et al.* 1981; Van Duuren *et al.* 1975; Loehrke *et al.* 1983; Hennings & Boutwell, 1970; Argyris, 1985*a*) and are surprisingly similar for a tissue such as the epidermis which is characterized by continuous turnover and cyclic growth and regression of the hair follicles (Hennings & Yuspa, 1985; Argyris, 1963; Potten, 1983; Iversen *et al.* 1968; Leblond, 1964). Conceivably, any epidermal cell could become and remain initiated. Alternatively, a subpopulation having singular growth characteristics could be the target for the carcinogen. The identification of the target cells which maintain the lifelong potential to form tumours is consequently an objective with considerable significance.

Although previous studies had demonstrated the fairly uniform initial binding of radioactively labelled carcinogens throughout the epidermal basal layer (Borum, 1960; Bibby & Smith, 1977; Nakai & Shubik, 1964; Solun, 1970; Tarnowski, 1970) very little was known concerning possible relationships between keratinocyte maturity and the persistence of the radioactively labelled carcinogen. We therefore used [$^3$H]- and [$^{14}$C]benzo(a)pyrene to identify in the dorsal epidermis of mice carcinogen label-retaining cells. We compared them in number and distribution to two other distinct epidermal cell populations: (a) the slowly cycling, [$^3$H]thymidine label-retaining cells (Bickenbach, 1981; Mackenzie & Bickenbach, 1985; Morris *et al.* 1985; Potten, 1986), and (b) those with cellular kinetic features of maturing keratinocytes prior to displacement from the basal layer (Potten, 1986; Iversen *et al.* 1968; Mackenzie, 1970; Christophers, 1971).

The results (Morris *et al.* 1986) have demonstrated that a subset of epidermal basal cells retain radioactively labelled carcinogen much longer than most of the basal cells. These carcinogen label-retaining cells resembled the slowly cycling [$^3$H]thymidine LRCs rather than the 'maturing' basal cells (demonstrated four days after a single pulse of [$^3$H]thymidine at 8:00 am) in number, position in the tissue architecture, long turnover time, and in mitotic activation following an application of the tumour promoter 12-O-tetradecanoyl phorbol-13-acetate (TPA). Double emulsion autoradiographs prepared one month after continuous labelling with [$^3$H]thymidine for one week and treatment with $[^{14}C]B(a)P$ revealed doubly labelled nuclei and thus provided evidence that the carcinogen label was retained by the slowly cycling population.

These observations (Morris et al. 1986) are consistent with the hypothesis that radioactively labelled carcinogen persists in the slowly cycling cells because they are slow cycling. The observed reduction in the grain density and thus the number of labelled nuclei detected by autoradiography supports this hypothesis. However, the present data cannot exclude the possibilities that (1) all of the adduct might eventually be removed by repair, or (2) that low levels of the adduct might indeed by present but remain undetected by autoradiography. There are alternative possible explanations for the persistence of carcinogen label in a subpopulation of keratinocytes: (1) slowly cycling cells might have an inherently low or a carcinogen-induced reduction in their ability to repair adducts relative to other basal cells (Reddy et al. 1988), (2) the retained adducts might be hidden from the repair enzymes (Bustin et al. 1983; Lajtha, 1979) or, (3) some of the adducts might be irreparable. All of these possibilities deserve further investigation.

The persistence of radioactively labelled carcinogen in the slowly cycling cells is an observation of considerable significance for present and future investigations in skin carcinogenesis especially as it is related to tumour initiation (see below). The carcinogen LRCs may indeed be initiated cells, not necessarily because they retain carcinogen, but because they are stem cells affected before commitment to terminal differentiation (Lajtha, 1979; Buick & Pollak, 1984). Although the long-term presence of the adduct might possibly represent an enduring potential for the formation of initiated cells (Randerath et al. 1983) in the murine skin system, the similar tumour responses at one week and one year after initiation (Boutwell, 1964; Roe et al. 1972; Stenback et al. 1981; Van Duuren et al. 1975; Loehrke et al. 1983; Hennings & Boutwell, 1970; Argyris, 1985a) suggest that the initiated state is established quickly and then maintained.

The nature of the lesion that makes an epidermal cell a 'latent neoplastic cell' is not known although alterations affecting both terminal differentiation (Kulesz-Martin et al. 1980; Kawamura et al. 1985) or self-renewal of a stem cell population (Lajtha, 1979; Buick & Pollak, 1984) have been postulated. Elevated expression and point mutation of the Ha-ras proto-oncogene has been observed in murine papillomas after nine weeks of promotion; earlier detection was not possible with the present experimental techniques (Pelling et al. 1987). Other significant genetic lesions cannot be excluded at this time. Nor do we know the identity of the cell that receives and maintains the lesion, although an as yet unidentified epidermal stem cell has long been suggested as a likely candidate. Normal epidermal cells having some of the characteristics of stem cells such as the slowly cycling label-retaining cells and dark basal keratinocytes are consequently under intensive investigation. Admittedly, the possibility that a carcinogen might impose characteristics of slow cycling or delayed displacement upon cells that would not normally express these characteristics cannot be excluded at this time.

Why do initiated mice not develop tumours unless they are promoted? It is possible that the number of divisions required of a slowly cycling population to form a tumour might require a time longer than the lifespan of the initiated animal. Alternatively, there may be something about the process of tumour promotion, e.g. regenerative hyperplastic growth (Argyris, 1985*b*), inflammation, induction of dark cells (Slaga & Klein-Szanto, 1983), activation of stem cells (Lajtha, 1979; Buick & Pollak, 1984), that is needed to establish the condition of initiation or for an initiated cell to express its neoplastic potential. An eventual resolution of these problems will require a better understanding of how proliferation and maturation are regulated in continually renewing tissues such as epidermis.

## Small intestine

The crypt of the small intestine in the mouse is probably one of the most extensively studied mammalian epithelial systems from the point of view of its cell kinetics and possibly also from that of its radiation response. As a consequence the cell replacement process is now well understood and these crypts can be regarded as a model system for other sites in the gut. It is an extremely dynamic system with a cell dividing every 5 min in each crypt and the progeny moving rapidly from the crypts onto the villus and exfoliating within their short life span of about 3–4 days (Fig. 3). The cells ultimately responsible for the considerable cell loss are clearly to be found at the origin of all this cell migration, which can be traced to the base of the crypt. Unfortunately the details of the cell replacement at the crypt base are complicated by the presence of 20–30 mature functional Paneth cells. The lineage, or cell migration, ancestors – the stem cells – are to be found either immediately above the Paneth cells in an annulus that contains about 16–18 cells, not all of which are necessarily stem cells (Loeffler *et al.* 1986; Potten & Loeffler, 1987), or in this annulus and scattered amongst the Paneth cells (Cheng & Leblond, 1974; Bjerknes & Cheng, 1981). The entire structure and its cell proliferation can be summarized as shown in Fig. 3. The proliferative units here are the crypts, which are closed systems, derived from single cells during development, i.e. they are clones (Ponder *et al.* 1985), which in the adult contain several stem cells each with its own lineage of dividing transit cells. The number of stem cells remains unclear but is probably not less than about 4 per crypt and not more than 16 in steady state, but there may be as many as 32 clonogenic cells – the most recent value determined from several radiation experiments (Potten *et al.* 1987). It is believed that the stem cells in the crypt have a cell cycle time about twice that of the dividing transit cells (24 h *versus* 12 h).

## Heterogeneity in the stem cell population

There are studies that suggest that some of the crypt stem cells are very sensitive cells, easily killed by radiation (Potten, 1977), and that the cell cycle characteristics of the neighbouring unaffected cells may be very easily disturbed by minor cytotoxic insults including the internal weak beta irradiation resulting from the incorporation of trace levels of tritiated thymidine (Cheng & Leblond, 1974; Potten, 1977, 1986).

The cells killed by small doses of radiation number about 6 per crypt and

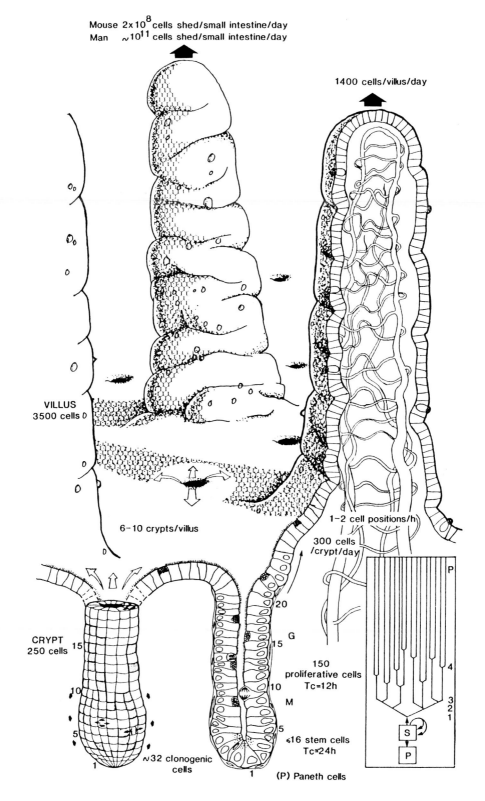

Mouse 2x10$^8$ cells shed/small intestine/day
Man   ~10$^{11}$ cells shed/small intestine/day

1400 cells/villus/day

VILLUS
3500 cells

6-10 crypts/villus

1-2 cell positions/h

300 cells
/crypt/day

CRYPT
250 cells

20

G

15

150
proliferative cells
Tc=12h

M

10

5

~32 clonogenic
cells

≤16 stem cells
Tc≈24h

(P) Paneth cells

P

4

3
2
1

S

P

Fig. 3. Diagrammatic representation of the spatial and proliferative organization of the mucosa in the small intestine of the mouse. The inter-relationship between the villi and longitudinal axis of the crypt is shown. Such sections can be used to analyse the changes that occur in proliferative activity with cell position. The base of the crypt can be identified by the presence of Paneth cells and the central crypt base cell is usually identified as at cell position one. There are usually about 20 cell positions along the side of the crypt (the crypt column). The crypt in total contains about 250 cells and its surface view is represented on the left. The cell lineage that most effectively explains the cell replacement is illustrated on the right. Cells of particular hierarchical status in this lineage can be related to cell positions within the crypt as indicated in the diagram. The cell replacement process in the crypt could be explained on the basis of up to 16 functional stem cells per crypt (Loeffler *et al.* 1986). It is likely that the crypt contains about 32 cells that possess a clonogenic capacity (Potten *et al.* 1987).

---

apparently die through apoptosis and can easily be recognized in H & E sections within 3–6 h. Yet other cells in the crypt base exhibit a high radiation sensitivity when $G_2$ progression (mitotic delay) is studied (Chwalinski & Potten, 1986). Others apparently can enter a reduced cell cycle time (e.g. 16 h instead of 24 h) very rapidly after minor perturbations (Potten, 1986). The cells that die after low doses of radiation exhibit differences in their circadian behaviour to that of the clonogenic population as a whole (Ijiri & Potten, 1988), suggesting they are a distinct subpopulation of cells which because of their position may be part of the stem cell compartment. These cells may have a sensitivity characterized by a $D_o$ value of 20–30 cGy while the clonogenic cells have a $D_o$ value of 135 cGy. Such observations lead to the conclusion that the stem/clonogenic pool is probably heterogeneous with either distinct subpopulations or a hierarchy (age structure) of cells.

## Regeneration of clonogenic cells in the intestine

Doses of radiation above about 8–9 Gy will completely sterilize some crypts and clonal regeneration assays have been developed (Withers & Elkind, 1969, 1970), which have been extensively used and from which the number of clonogenic cells can be estimated (Hendry & Potten, 1974; Potten & Hendry, 1975; Potten *et al.* 1987). The repopulation of the clonogenic cell population has recently been measured (Fig. 4) and this provides a doubling time of 19·7 h for the regenerating clonogenic cells (Potten *et al.* 1988). In principle the relationship between the clonogenic cell repopulation, the crypt repopulation and the crypt cell production rate would permit the true cell cycle time for the clonogenic cells and their self-maintenance probability $(P)$ to be estimated. At present the unknown element here is what changes occur, over these post-irradiation times, in the number of transit cell generations. In the normal steady state crypt (where $P = 0\cdot5$) the cell migration velocity per column $(V)$ is determined by the number of stem cells $(N_s)$, their cell cycle time $(T_c)$ and the number of transit cell divisions $(L)$ as follows:

$$V = \frac{N_s}{T_c} \cdot 2^L$$

as was demonstrated from a comprehensive mathematically based model of the crypt

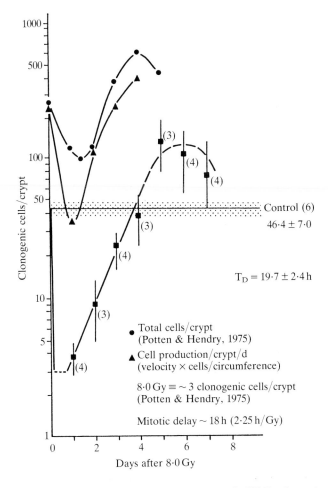

Fig. 4. The results of a recent experiment (Potten *et al.* 1988) where the number of clonogenic cells per crypt (arithmetic mean) has been calculated using the approach described by Hendry (1979) during the first 7 days after an initial dose of 8·0 Gy gamma radiation. In this experiment the control crypts contained $46 \pm 7$ clonogenic cells. The clonogenic cells repopulate the crypts with a doubling time of $19·7 \pm 2·4$ h. The data are consistent with an initial mitotic delay of about 18 h, i.e. about 2·25 h/Gy. On days 5–7 the number of clonogenic cells overshoots the control value by a factor of 2·2 (average for days 5–7). The regeneration of the clonogenic compartment can be compared with the total cellularity of the crypt and the cell output from the crypt. Such a comparison indicates that some clonogenic cells must differentiate into the transit population during the regeneration phase.

that we have developed (Loeffler *et al.* 1986; Potten & Loeffler, 1987). The model can be summarized as shown in Fig. 5.

## Carcinogenic target cells

One challenge for future research is to determine whether target cells for carcinogenesis are solely stem cells or whether cancer may also arise on occasions from

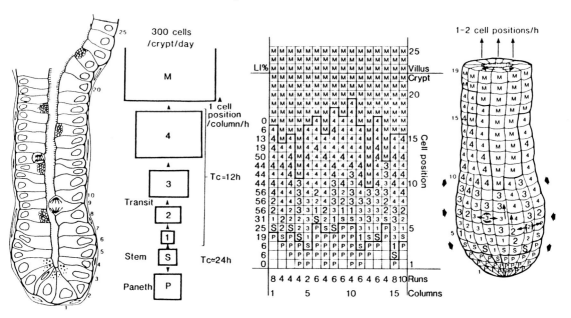

Fig. 5. The cell replacement process in the crypt can be mathematically modelled using a simple matrix to represent the crypts which can be regarded as slit-open and the sheet of cells laid flat (Loeffler *et al.* 1986; Potten & Loeffler, 1987). The best fit to all the available data is obtained with a cell lineage with up to 16 stem(s) cells and 4 transit generations (1–4). The matrix shows a representative distribution of labelled (S phase) cells (large numbers). The matrix can be reassembled to form a crypt (right-hand diagram). Consideration of the mitotic polarity in mathematical modelling suggests that the shape of the crypt and the cell production can be controlled by two interacting processes (forces): one which tends to reduce the circumference, squeezes the crypt and forces cells to move out of the top; and a counter balancing force, which can be attributed to the mitotic activity which tends to increase the circumference.

dividing transit cells. The arguments in favour of cancer being a disease solely of stem cells can be summarized as follows. The latent period between exposure to known carcinogens and the development of tumours is long, generally months in mice or decades in humans and involves several steps, the first of which is tumour initiation. Thus, initiated cells or their progeny must persist in epithelial tissues at least for these lengths of time. The initiation event is commonly thought of as a mutational event presumably one associated with the genes controlling cell proliferation generally or self-maintenance probability more specifically (expressed by some as a loss of commitment to terminal differentiation). Although such mutational events could in principle occur in any cell within the tissue, the high degree of structural polarity and rapid cell migration would mean that most such mutated cells would be irrevocably shed within a few days of being mutated. It is only the stem cells that are permanent residents and hence persist for long enough to account for the lag period (Potten, 1984). The argument against this would suggest that any cell could be a potential cancer producing cell. Any initiated mid crypt transit cell would have to resist further differentiation and emigration in order to produce a cancer.

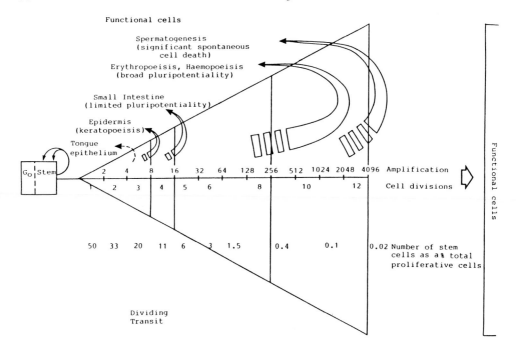

Fig. 6. The cellular hierarchies in epithelial tissues placed in the perspective of all replacing tissues. The precise number of amplifying transit cell divisions may be somewhat uncertain and variable. There may be up to 13 amplification transit cell divisions in the erythropoietic lineage in the bone marrow. In spermatogenesis there may be up to 12 mitotic cell divisions but there is also appreciable spontaneous cell death at certain points in the lineage, which reduces the effective amplification. The relationship between the number of transit cell divisions and the concentration of stem cells is illustrated.

This is hard to envisage for a tissue such as the intestine. It would imply that the initiation/mutational event affected not only some aspect of cell proliferation but simultaneously also affected the basement membrane and cell to cell relationships such that the cell no longer moved. Epithelial cells are tightly bound to each other by desomosomes and tight junctions and migrate as clusters or discrete columns of cells (Schmidt *et al*. 1985). It is hard to see how a cell in the gut could avoid the movement of its adjoining cells – how it could in fact step out of line of the moving column of cells in the epithelial sheet. It would be like trying to stop moving on an escalator packed solid with other moving people. Since, at least in some aspects, a transit cell could be considered to be differentiated, it would also imply that the single mutational event also resulted in the dedifferentiation of the cell.

## Stem cell division potential

In epithelial tissues the number of transit cell divisions lies between 2 and 4 as a consequence of which the stem cell population will comprise between 30 % and 10 % of the proliferative compartment of the tissue (see Fig. 6, which places epithelia within the general context of all replacing tissues). The cell cycle duration for the stem cells in the various replacing tissues of the mouse is generally poorly defined but approximate estimates are as follows (Potten, 1986); tongue – 24 h, epidermis – 200 h, small intestine – 24 h (16–30 h), colon 15–22 h, bone marrow – 100–120 h, testis > 60 h. Consequently, for a laboratory mouse that may live for up to 3 years (which may be up to 6 times its natural life expectancy in the wild) the stem cells will divide between about 100 times (epidermis) and about 1000 times (tongue and intestine); bone marrow – 200 to 300 times and testis up to 400 times. Bone marrow transplantation experiments (from old mice to lethally irradiated juveniles or juvenile $W/W^v$ mice, which have a bone marrow stem cell deficiency) suggest that the haemopoietic stem cells can be transplanted at least 5 times and that the stem cells then divide as many as 1000 times (Harrison, 1973; Schofield, 1978; Harrison & Astle, 1982), i.e. 5 times the number in the life span of a laboratory mouse. Thus these stem cells possess a division potential far in excess (up to 30 times) of what may be required for the life of an average wild mouse. The potential may be even higher since the act of transplanation may require extra divisions to overcome transplantation damage.

## References

AL-BARWARI, S. E. (1978). Cell and population kinetics in the irradiated skin. Ph.D. Thesis, University of Manchester.

ALLEN, T. D. & POTTEN, C. S. (1974). Fine structural identification and organisation of the epidermal proliferative units. *J. Cell Sci.* **15**, 291–319.

ARGYRIS, T. S. (1963). Hair growth cycles and skin neoplasia. *Nat. Cancer Inst. Monogr.* **10**, 23–43.

ARGYRIS, T. S. (1985*a*). Promotion of epidermal carcinogenesis by repeated damage to mouse skin. *Am. J. indust. Med.* **8**, 329–337.

ARGYRIS, T. S. (1985*b*). Regeneration and the mechanism of epidermal tumour promotion. *CRC Crit. Rev. Toxicol.* **14**, 211–258.

ASHURST, S. W., COHEN, G. M., NESNOW, S., DiGIOVANNI, J. & SLAGA, T. J. (1982). Formation of benzo(a)pyrene/DNA adducts and their relationship to tumour initiation in mouse epidermis. *Cancer Res.* **43**, 1024–1029.

BARRANDON, Y. & GREEN, H. (1985). Cell size as a determinant of the clone-forming ability of human keratinocytes. *Proc. natn. Acad. Sci. U.S.A.* **82**, 5390–5394.

BIBBY, M. C. & SMITH, G. M. (1977). High-resolution autoradiographic localization of 3-methylcholanthrene-³H in the skin of Balb/c mice after topical application. *Br. J. Derm.* **97**, 429–436.

BICKENBACH, J. R. (1981). Identification and behaviour of label-retaining cells in oral mucosa and skin. *J. Dent. Res.* **60**, 1611–1620.

BJERKNES, M. & CHENG, H. (1981). The stem cell zone of the small intestinal epithelium. I. Evidence from Paneth cells in the adult mouse. *Am. J. Anat.* **160**, 51–63.

BORUM, K. (1960). Localization of radioactivity in mouse skin following one application of ¹⁴C-labelled 9,10-dimethyl,1,2-benzanthracene. *Acta Un. int. Cancr.* **16**, 60–62.

BOUTWELL, R. K. (1964). Some biological aspects of skin carcinogenesis. *Prog. exp. Tumor Res.* **4**, 207–250.

BOUTWELL, R. K. (1974). The function and mechanism of promoters of carcinogenesis. *CRC Crit. Rev. Toxicol.* **2**, 419–443.

BUICK, R. N. & POLLAK, M. N. (1984). Perspectives on clonogenic tumour cells, stem cells, and oncogenes. *Cancer Res.* **44**, 4909–4918.

BUSTIN, M. B., KURTH, P. D., SLOR, H. & SEIDMAN, M. (1983). Immunological studies on the influence of chromatin structure on the binding of a chemical carcinogen to the genome. In

*Application of Biological Markers to Carcinogen Testing* (ed. H. A. Milman & S. Sell), pp. 349–371. New York: Plenum Publishing Corporation.

CHENG, H. & LEBLOND, C. P. (1974). Origin differentiation and renewal of four main epithelial cell types in the mouse intestine. V. Unitarian theory of the origin of the four epithelial cell types. *Am. J. Anat.* **141**, 537–563.

CHRISTOPHERS, E. (1971). Cellular architecture of the stratum corneum. *J. invest. Derm.* **56**, 165–170.

CHWALINSKI, S. & POTTEN, C. S. (1986). Radiation induced mitotic delay: duration, dose and cell position dependence in the crypts of the small intestine in the mouse. *Int. J. Rad. Biol.* **49**, 809–819.

CLAUSEN, O. P. F., KIRKHUS, B., ELGJO, K., PEDERSEN, S. & BOLUND, L. (1985). DNA synthesis rate changes during the S phase in mouse epidermis. *Cell Tiss. Kinet.* **18**, 445–455.

CLAUSEN, O. P. F. & POTTEN, C. S. (1988). Heterogeneity in epidermal cell proliferation. *J. Cutaneous Path.* (in press).

DIPPLE, A., MOSCH, R. C. & BIGGER, C. A. H. (1984). Polynuclear aromatic carcinogens. In *Chemical Carcinogens*, vol. 1, *ACS Monograph 182* (ed. C. E. Sealer), pp. 41–163. Washington, DC: American Chemical Society.

EISINGER, M., LEE, J. S., HEFTON, J. M., DARZYNKIEWICZ, Z., CHIAO, J. W. & DE HARVEN, E. (1979). Human epidermal cell cultures. Growth and differentiation in the absence of dermal components or medium supplements. *Proc. natn. Acad. Sci. U.S.A.* **76**, 5340–5344.

HARRISON, D. E. (1973). Normal production of erythrocytes by mouse bone marrow continues for 73 months. *Proc. natn. Acad. Sci. U.S.A.* **70**, 3184–3190.

HARRISON, D. E. & ASTLE, C. M. (1982). Loss of stem cell repopulating ability upon transplantation. *J. exp. Med.* **156**, 1767–1779.

HENDRY, J. H. (1979). A new derivation, from split-dose data, of the complete survival curve for clonogenic normal cells in vivo. *Rad. Res.* **78**, 404–414.

HENDRY, J. H. & POTTEN, C. S. (1974). Cryptogenic cells and proliferative cells in intestinal epithelium. *Int. J. Rad. Biol.* **25**, 583–588.

HENNINGS, H. & BOUTWELL, R. K. (1970). Studies on the mechanisms of Skin Tumor Promotion. *Cancer Res.* **30**, 312–320.

HENNINGS, H. & YUSPA, S. H. (1985). Two-stage promotion in mouse skin: an alternative interpretation. *J. natn. Cancer. Inst.* **74**, 735–740.

HUME, W. J. & POTTEN, C. S. (1976). The ordered columnar structure of mouse filiform papillae. *J. Cell Sci.* **22**, 149–160.

IJIRI, K. & POTTEN, C. S. (1988). Circadian rhythms in the incidence of apoptotic cells and number of clonogenic cells after radiation using normal and reversed light conditions. *Int. J. Rad. Biol.* **53**, 717–727.

IVERSEN, O. H., BJERKNES, R. & DEVIK, F. (1968). Kinetics of cell renewal, cell migration and cell loss in the mouse hairless dorsal epidermis. *Cell Tiss. Kinet.* **1**, 351–367.

KAWAMURA, H., STRICKLAND, J. E. & YUSPA, S. H. (1985). Association of resistance to terminal differentiation with initiation of carcinogenesis in adult mouse epidermal cells. *Cancer Res.* **45**, 2748–2757.

KIMMEL, M., DARZYNKIEWICZ, Z. & STAINO-COICO, L. (1986). Stathmo-kinetic analysis of human epidermal cells in vitro. *Cell Tiss. Kinet.* **19**, 289–304.

KLEIN-SZANTO, A. J. P. & SLAGA, T. J. (1981). Numerical variation of dark cells in normal and chemically induced hyperplastic epidermis with age of animal and efficiency of tumor promoter. *Cancer Res.* **41**, 4437–4440.

KULESZ-MARTIN, M. F., KOEHLER, B., HENNINGS, H. & YUSPA, S. H. (1980). Quantitative assay for carcinogen altered differentiation in mouse epidermal cells in culture. *Carcinogenesis* **1**, 995–1006.

LAJTHA, L. G. (1979). Stem cell concepts. *Differentiation* **14**, 23–24.

LAVKER, R. M. & SUN, T. T. (1982). Heterogeneity in epidermal basal keratinocytes: Morphological and functional correlations. *Science* **215**, 1239–1241.

LEBLOND, C. P. (1964). Classification of cell populations on the basis of their proliferative behaviour. *Nat. Cancer Inst. Monogr.* **14**, 119–150.

LOEFFLER, M., POTTEN, C. S. & WICHMANN, H. E. (1987). Epidermal cell proliferation. II. A comprehensive mathematical model of cell proliferation and migration in the basal layer predicts some unusual properties of epidermal stem cells. *Virchows Arch. B. Zellpath.* **53**, 286–300.

LOEFFLER, M., STEIN, R., WICHMANN, H. E., POTTEN, C. S., KAUR, P. & CHWALINSKI, S. (1986). Intestinal cell proliferation I. A comprehensive model of steady state proliferation in the crypt. *Cell Tiss. Kinet.* **19**, 627–646.

LOEHRKE, H., SCHWEIZER, J., DEDERER, E., HESSE, B., ROSENKRANZ, G. & GOERTTLER, K. (1983). On the persistence of tumor initiation in two-stage carcinogenesis on mouse skin. *Carcinogenesis* **4**, 771–775.

MACKENZIE, I. C. (1970). Relationship between mitosis and the structure of the stratum corneum in mouse epidermis. *Nature, Lond.* **226**, 653–655.

MACKENZIE, I. C. & BICKENBACH, J. (1985). Label-retaining keratinocytes and Langerhans cells in mouse epithelia. *Cell Tiss. Res.* **242**, 551–556.

MILLER, E. C. & MILLER, J. A. (1981). Searches for ultimate chemical carcinogens and their reactions with cellular macromolecules. *Cancer (Phila).* **47**, 2327–2345.

MORRIS, R. J., FISCHER, S. M. & SLAGA, T. J. (1985). Evidence that the centrally and peripherally located cells in the murine epidermal proliferative unit are two distinct cell populations. *J. invest. Derm.* **84**, 277–281.

MORRIS, R. J., FISCHER, S. M. & SLAGA, T. J. (1986). Evidence that a slowly cycling subpopulation of adult murine epidermal cells retains carcinogen. *Cancer Res.* **46**, 3061–3066.

NAKAI, J. & SHUBIK, P. (1964). Autoradiographic localization of tissue-bound tritiated 7,12-dimethylbenz[a]anthracene in mouse skin 24 and 48 hours after a single application. *J. natn. Cancer Inst.* **33**, 887–891.

NAKAYAMA, J., YUSPA, S. H. & POIRER, M. C. (1984). Benzo(a)pyrene-DNA adduct formation and removal in mouse epidermis *in vivo* and *in vitro*: relationship of DNA binding to initiation of skin carcinogenesis. *Cancer Res.* **44**, 4048–4095.

OSBORN, M. R. (1984). DNA interactions of reactive intermediates derived from carcinogens. In *Chemical Carcinogens*, vol. 1, *ACS Monograph 182* (ed. C. E. Searle), pp. 485–524. Washington DC: American Chemical Society.

PARKINSON, E. K., GRABHAM, F. & EMMERSON, A. (1983). A subpopulation of cultured human keratinocytes which is resistant to the induction of terminal differentiation-related changes by phorbol 12-myristate 13-acetate: Evidence for an increase in the resistant population following transformation. *Carcinogenesis* **4**, 857–861.

PARKINSON, E. K., PERA, M. F., EMMERSON, A. & GORMAN, P. A. (1984). Differential effects of complete and second-stage tumour promoters in normal but not transformed human and mouse keratinocytes. *Carcinogenesis* **5**, 1071–1077.

PELLING, J. C., FISCHER, S. M., NEADES, R., STRAWHECKER, J. & SCHWEICKERT, L. (1987). Elevated expression and point mutation of the Ha-ras proto-oncogene in mouse skin tumours promoted with benzoyl peroxide and other promoting agents. *Carcinogenesis* **8**, 1481–1484.

PONDER, B. A. J., SCHMIDT, G. H., WILKINSON, M. M., WOOD, M., MONK, M. & REID, A. (1985). Derivation of mouse intestinal crypts from single progenitor cells. *Nature, Lond.* **313**, 689–691.

POTTEN, C. S. (1974). The epidermal proliferative unit: the possible role of the central basal cell. *Cell Tiss. Kinet.* **7**, 77–88.

POTTEN, C. S. (1977). Extreme sensitivity of some intestinal crypt cells to X and $\gamma$ irradiation. *Nature, Lond.* **269**, 518–521.

POTTEN, C. S. (1981). Cell replacement in epidermis (keratopoiesis) via discrete units of proliferation. *Int. Rev. Cytol.* **69**, 271–318.

POTTEN, C. S. (1983). Stem cells in epidermis from the back of the mouse. In *Stem Cells: Their Identification and Characterization* (ed. C. S. Potten), pp. 200–232. New York: Churchill-Livingstone.

POTTEN, C. S. (1984). Clonogenic, stem and carcinogen-target cells in small intestine. *Scand. J. Gastroenterol.* **19**, suppl. 109, 3–14.

POTTEN, C. S. (1985). *Radiation and Skin*. London: Taylor-Francis.

POTTEN, C. S. (1986). Cell cycles in cell hierarchies. *Int. J. Rad. Biol.* **49**, 257–278.

POTTEN, C. S. & HENDRY, J. H. (1973). Clonogenic cells and stem cells in epidermis. *Int. J. Rad. Biol.* **24**, 537–540.

POTTEN, C. S. & HENDRY, J. H. (1975). Differential regeneration of intestinal proliferative cells and cryptogenic cells after irradiation. *Int. J. Rad. Biol.* **27**, 413–424.

POTTEN, C. S., HENDRY, J. H. & MOORE, J. V. (1987). New estimates of the number of clonogenic cells in crypts of murine small intestine. *Virchows. Arch. B. Zellpath.* **53**, 227–234.

POTTEN, C. S. & LOEFFLER, M. (1987). A comprehensive model of the crypts of the small intestine of the mouse provides insight into the mechanisms of cell migration and the proliferative hierarchy. *J. theor. Biol.* **127**, 381–391.

POTTEN, C. S., TAYLOR, Y. & HENDRY, J. H. (1988). The doubling time of regenerating clonogenic cells in the crypts of the small intestine. *Int. J. Rad. Biol.* (in press).

POTTEN, C. S., WICHMANN, H. E., LOEFFLER, M., DOBEK, K. & MAJOR, D. (1982). Evidence for discrete cell kinetic sub-populations in mouse epidermis based on mathematical analysis. *Cell Tiss. Kinet.* **15**, 305–329.

RANDERATH, E., AGRAWAL, H. P., REDDY, M. V. & RANDERATH, K. (1983). Highly persistent polycyclic aromatic hydrocarbon–DNA adducts in mouse skin: Detection by $^{32}$P-postlabeling analysis. *Cancer Lett.* **20**, 104–114.

REDDY, M. V., GUPTA, R. C., RANDERATH, E. & RANDERATH, K. (1983). $^{32}$P-postlabeling test for covalent DNA binding of chemicals *in vivo*: Application to a variety of aromatic carcinogens and methylating agents. *Carcinogenesis* **5**, 231–243.

ROE, F. J. C., CARTER, R. N., MITCHLEY, B. C. V., PETO, R. & HECKER, E. (1972). On the persistence of tumor initiation and the acceleration of tumor progression in mouse skin carcinogenesis. *Int. J. Cancer* **9**, 624–673.

SCHMIDT, G. H., WILKINSON, M. M. & PONDER, B. A. J. (1985). Cell migration pathway in the intestinal epithelieum: An in situ marker system using aggregation chimeras. *Cell* **40**, 425–429.

SCHOFIELD, R. (1978). The relationship between the spleen colony-forming cell and the haemopoietic stem cell. *Blood Cells* **4**, 7–25.

SCRIBNER, J. D. & SUSS, R. (1978). Tumor initiation and promotion. *Int. Rev. exp. Path.* **18**, 137–198.

SLAGA, T. J. (1984). Mechanisms involved in two-stage carcinogenesis in mouse skin. In *Mechanisms of Tumor Promotion*, vol. 2 (ed. T. J. Slaga), pp. 1–16. Boca Raton, FL: CRC Press Inc.

SLAGA, T. J. & KLEIN-SZANTO, A. J. P. (1983). Initiation-promotion versus complete carcinogenesis in mice: Importance of dark basal keratinocytes (stem cells). *Cancer Invest.* **1(5)**, 425–436.

SOLUN, S. (1970). High-resolution autoradiographic localization of 3,4-benzo(a)pyrene-$^3$H in mouse skin. *Cancer Res.* **30**, 1123–1128.

STAIANO-COICO, L., HIGGINS, P. J., DARZYNKIEWICZ, Z., KIMMEL, M., GOTTLIEB, A. B., PAGAN-CHERRY, I., MADDEN, M. R., FINKELSTEIN, J. L. & HEFTON, J. M. (1986). Human keratinocyte culture. Identification and staging of epidermal cell subpopulations. *J. clin. Invest.* **7**, 396–404.

STENBACK, F., PETO, R. & SHUBIK, P. (1981). Initiation and promotion at different stages and doses in 2200 mice. I. Methods and the apparent persistence of initiated cells. *Br. J. Cancer* **44**, 1–14.

TARNOWSKI, W. M. (1970). Autoradiographic localization of tritiated 7,12-dimethylbenz[a]anthracene in mast cells of hairless mouse skin. *Cancer Res.* **30**, 1163–1167.

VAN DURREN, B. L., SIVAK, A., KATZ, C., DEIDMAN, I. & MELCHIONNE, S. (1975). The effect of aging and interval delay between primary and secondary treatment in two-stage carcinogenesis on mouse skin. *Cancer Res.* **35**, 502–505.

WITHERS, H. R. & ELKIND, M. M. (1969). Radiosensitivity and fractionation response of crypt cells of mouse jejunum. *Rad. Res.* **38**, 598–613.

WITHERS, H. R. & ELKIND, M. M. (1970). Microcolony survival assay for cells of mouse intestinal mucosa exposed to radiation. *Int. J. Rad. Biol.* **17**, 261–268.

*J. Cell Sci. Suppl. 10, 63–76 (1988)*
*Printed in Great Britain © The Company of Biologists Limited 1988*

# Marrow stromal stem cells

MAUREEN OWEN*

*MRC Bone Research Laboratory, Nuffield Department of Orthopaedic Surgery, University of Oxford, Oxford OX3 7LD, UK*

## Summary

Evidence for the hypothesis that there are stromal stem cells present in the soft connective tissues associated with marrow and bone surfaces that are able to give rise to a number of different cell lines is reviewed. The lines are currently designated fibroblastic, reticular, adipocytic and osteogenic. Fibroblastic colonies, each derived from a single colony-forming unit fibroblastic (CFU-F), are formed when marrow cells are cultured *in vitro*. *In vivo* assays of tissue formed by CFU-F in open transplant or in diffusion chambers, have demonstrated that some CFU-F have a high ability for self renewal and multipotentiality whereas some have more limited potential. Preliminary investigations *in vitro* also support the hypothesis and have shown that CFU-F are a heterogeneous population of stem and progenitor cells and that their differentiation *in vitro* can be modified at the colony level. The stromal cells which survive and proliferate *in vitro* are highly dependent on culture conditions. The number and hierarchy of cell lines belonging to the stromal fibroblastic system are not yet fully elucidated and more specific markers and better assays for the different phenotypes are required before a greater understanding can be achieved. The possibility that the marrow stromal system is part of a wider stromal cell system of the body is proposed.

## Introduction

Marrow stromal tissue is a network of cells and extracellular matrix which physically supports the haemopoietic cells and influence their differentiation (Dexter, 1982). Macrophages and endothelial cells are often included in the stromal cell population (Allen & Dexter, 1982, 1984). However, in the present chapter, the term stromal will be restricted to cells of the stromal 'fibroblastic' system of marrow. By definition these include osteoblasts and preosteoblasts found near to bone surfaces, fibroblasts and reticular cells, terms commonly used for the soft connective tissue cells of marrow and blood vessel walls, and marrow adipocytes (Owen, 1985). Current evidence suggests that haemopoietic, stromal and endothelial cellular systems are histogenetically distinct in the post-natal animal under normal conditions (Le Douarin, 1979; Wilson, 1983; Simmons *et al.* 1987).

As a working hypothesis for differentiation in the marrow stromal system we have proposed a scheme analogous to that in the haemopoietic system, where stromal stem cells give rise to committed progenitors for different cell lines (Fig. 1) (Owen, 1978, 1985). The main evidence for stem cells comes from an *in vivo* assay of tissue formed following transplantation of stromal cells under the renal capsule or in diffusion chambers. The formation of fibroblastic colonies from a suspension of marrow cells

---

*\* Member of Medical Research Council External Scientific Staff.

Key words: marrow stroma, stem cells, osteogenesis.

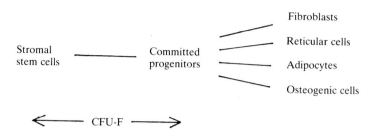

Fig. 1. Hypothetical diagram for lineage in the marrow stromal system. In analogy with the haemopoietic system it is proposed that (1) stromal stem cells generate progenitors committed to one or more cell lines, (2) the cells form a continuum where capability for self-renewal and multipotentiality decrease as lineage commitment increases, (3) CFU-F (FCFC) which form fibroblastic colonies *in vitro* are components of the stem and progenitor cell population.

plated *in vitro*, each colony being derived from a single fibroblastic colony forming cell (FCFC) or colony forming unit fibroblastic (CFU-F), was demonstrated more than a decade ago (Friedenstein *et al.* 1970; Friedenstein, 1976) but clonal *in vitro* assays, which have been so successful for investigating progenitor cells in the haemopoietic system, have been little explored for the stromal system. The number and hierarchy of the stromal fibroblastic lines in marrow are not yet completely identified. The proposed lines have been designated fibroblastic, reticular, adipocytic and osteogenic. Lines with these characteristics can be established *in vitro* from the soft connective tissues of marrow and bone surfaces. Osteogenic, fibroblastic and adipocytic lines have been derived both from new born mouse calvarial and marrow tissues (Kodama *et al.* 1982; Lanotte *et al.* 1982; Sudo *et al.* 1983; Zipori *et al.* 1985; Benayahu *et al.* 1987). In this paper, the evidence supporting the stromal system hypothesis will be reviewed.

## Differentiation of marrow stromal cells in diffusion chambers *in vivo*

The demonstration that suspensions of single cells derived from marrow form a fibrous osteogenic tissue when incubated within diffusion chambers implanted *in vivo* was an important advance. This showed that the differentiating capacity of marrow stromal cells was not dependent on the structural relationship of the cells *in situ* and that precursor cells determined in an osteogenic direction were present in marrow stroma (Friedenstein, 1973). Cells of the host do not penetrate the chambers and vascularization of the tissue does not occur. The resorbing cells of bone are derived from the haemopoietic system (Marks, 1983; Chambers, 1985) and there is no evidence of bone resorption within the chambers (Ashton *et al.* 1980). Consequently the diffusion chamber is suitable for studying differentiation of the stromal cells *per se*.

The stages of tissue formation when a suspension of about $10^7$ single marrow cells (rat or rabbit) is incubated within diffusion chambers implanted intraperitoneally is shown diagrammatically in Fig. 2 (Ashton *et al.* 1980; Bab *et al.* 1986; Mardon *et al.*

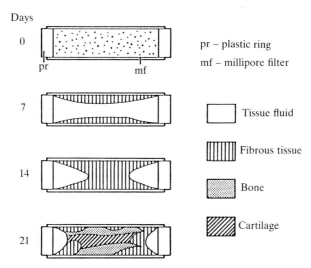

Fig. 2. Cross sections of diffusion chambers at different times after intraperitoneal implantation, $10^7$ marrow cells inoculated at day 0 through hole in plastic ring which is then sealed. Millipore filter has $0·45\,\mu$m pore size. Stromal fibroblastic cells attach and fibrous tissue grows from the chamber surfaces. By about 3 weeks bone and cartilage are well developed, see text and references.

1987). Within a few days stromal fibroblasts have attached to the millipore filter and fibrous tissue grows from this surface. Early signs of osteogenesis, from about 8 days onwards, are localized areas of fibroblastic cells which assume a more polygonal shape and express intense staining in the cytoplasmic membranes for alkaline phosphatase activity (Fig. 3). By about 3 weeks both bone and cartilage have developed in association with these areas and the tissue is morphologically identical to its skeletal counterparts according to both light and electron microscopic criteria (Ashton *et al.* 1980; Bab *et al.* 1984).

The fibrous tissue formed initially, stains strongly for type III collagen, laminin and fibronectin, weakly for type I and is negative for type II collagen. However, as osteogenesis develops within the fibrous anlage, collagen types I and II are found exclusively in bone and cartilage respectively. Fibrous tissue which does not become osteogenic continues to stain for type III; in fact loss of expression of collagen type III is considered a good marker for the appearance of the osteoblastic phenotype. Staining for laminin and fibronectin also decreases to negligible levels as osteogenic tissue develops. The sequential expression of these extracellular matrix components is similar to that seen in osteogenesis in the embryo and it was concluded that connective tissue generation in diffusion chambers from precursor cells present in adult marrow resembles a bone developmental process (Mardon *et al.* 1987).

Using histomorphometric techniques analysis of cell kinetics in chambers inoculated with $10^7$ marrow cells showed that there was an increase in the total stromal cell population by more than six orders of magnitude between 3 and 20 days (Bab *et al.* 1986). The number of haemopoietic cells decreased to $0·05\%$ of the initial inoculum

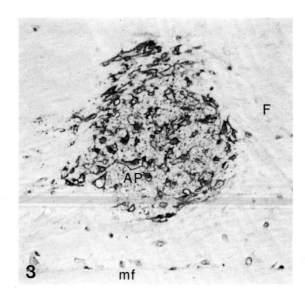

Fig. 3. Section of tissue in chamber inoculated with $10^7$ rabbit marrow cells and implanted for 14 days, stained for alkaline phosphatase activity, von Kossa reaction and with Mayer's Haematoxylin. Fibrous tissue (F), localized area of cells with cytoplasmic membranes well stained for the enzyme (AP), von Kossa reaction is negative, millipore filter (mf). ×320.

during the same period. At 3 days an average of only 15 stromal fibroblastic cells was identified within the chamber and it was concluded that the mixture of connective tissues formed is generated by a small number of cells with high capacity for proliferation and differentiation, i.e. cells with the characteristics of stem cells.

## Differentiation of marrow stromal cells in open transplant *in vivo*

When an intact piece of marrow is transplanted ectopically, for example either subcutaneously or under the renal capsule, stromal cells survive, proliferate and differentiate into bone and marrow stroma and provide the appropriate micro-environment for haemopoiesis by invading host haemopoietic stem cells, resulting in formation of a bone and marrow organ (Tavassoli & Crosby, 1968; Friedenstein, 1976). By the use of different antigenic and chromosomal markers in donor and host it was shown that the marrow stromal cells of the newly formed bone and marrow organ are derived from the donor and the haemopoietic tissue from the host (Friedenstein *et al.* 1978). Freshly isolated suspensions of marrow cells or fibroblastic cells cultured from marrow, grafted under the kidney capsule within porous sponges, also form a bone and marrow organ in heterotopic transplants (Friedenstein *et al.* 1982). With the morphological methods used it was not possible to be certain of the exact sequence of events in regeneration of bone and marrow tissue. A review of the relevant literature suggested that initially the stromal elements differentiate into osteoid and bone trabeculae and later reconstruct the connective tissue lining cells of the microvasculature (Owen, 1980).

## Evidence for stromal stem cells

The clonal origin of the fibroblastic colonies formed when suspensions of dispersed marrow cells are cultured *in vitro* (Friedenstein *et al.* 1970; Castro-Malaspina *et al.* 1980) has been confirmed using thymidine labelling, time-lapse photography and chromosome markers (Friedenstein, 1976; Friedenstein *et al.* 1987; Latsinik *et al.* 1987). A definitive answer to the question of whether stem cells are present in the stroma of bone and marrow must come from an analysis based on the self-replicating ability and multipotentiality of individual FCFC or CFU-F. This has been investigated by assay of single colonies in open transplant and diffusion chambers *in vivo* (Friedenstein, 1980; Friedenstein *et al.* 1987). By transplanting individual clones under the renal capsule it is possible to examine whether a single cell gives rise to the variety of cell lines of bone and marrow stroma necessary to support haemopoiesis.

Friedenstein and his colleagues have studied the potential for differentiation in open transplant of single fibroblastic clones grown *in vitro* from mouse marrow cells (Friedenstein, 1980). Clones were grown for 16 to 30 days on thin collagen gels. Individual clones were excised, placed between small pieces of millipore filter and grafted under the renal capsule of syngeneic recipients. The tissue formed was examined histologically. About 15 % of the fibroblastic clones transplanted produced a bone and marrow organ, containing osteogenic tissue, typical adipose cells, and a well-formed microvasculature together with associated host-derived haemopoiesis. About 15 % of the clones yielded only bone tissue. The remaining clones formed a soft connective tissue or did not form any tissue (Friedenstein, 1980).

It is proposed that the clonogenic precursors which yielded a bone marrow organ, i.e. gave rise to several different stromal lines, are putative stromal stem cells. Clones producing either bone or soft connective tissue only arise from precursor cells with limited potential. A proportion of clones has a low proliferative activity and does not survive. Although these results provide strong circumstantial evidence for the existence of a stromal cell system and stromal stem cells, more definitive proof of the clonality of colonies capable of forming the mixture of bone and marrow stromal lines is necessary and requires the use of uniquely marked stem cells in the donor material.

Using cultures of rabbit marrow cells a high ability of CFU-F to self-renew was demonstrated (Friedenstein *et al.* 1987). Fibroblasts were grown to confluence in culture from a number of CFU-F (FCFC) and after about eighteen passages *in vitro* these cells were assayed in diffusion chambers. The inoculum of harvested fibroblasts able to form fibrous-osteogenic tissue in the chamber was defined as one osteogenic unit. The number of osteogenic units which could be harvested from culture after passaging ranged up to more than a thousand times the number of initiating CFU-F, thus demonstrating that precursors of the fibrous-osteogenic tissues are highly proliferative and that they retain their capacity for differentiation after extensive culture and passaging *in vitro*. The ability of fibroblasts grown from a single colony *in vitro*, harvested after two or three passages, to form osteogenic tissue in diffusion chambers was demonstrated and evidence for a common precursor for bone and cartilage was also obtained in these experiments by assay of clonal progeny in conditions where either bone only or both bone and cartilage are formed.

## Differentiation of single colonies *in vitro*

*In vitro* colony assays have been used to study both multipotent and lineage-committed progenitor cells in the haemopoietic system (Metcalf, 1984). Recent studies to investigate differentiation of CFU-F at the colony level have been initiated with a view to developing *in vitro* clonal methods for studying lineage in the marrow stromal system (Owen *et al.* 1987). When a suspension of rabbit marrow cells was cultured *in vitro* with foetal calf serum the fibroblastic colonies formed varied widely in size and level of expression of alkaline phosphatase activity (Fig. 4). The enzyme was used as an osteogenic marker, since its appearance is an early indicator of developing osteogenic tissue when rabbit marrow cells are cultured in diffusion chambers *in vivo* (Bab *et al.* 1986). Alkaline phosphatase activity appeared to originate in the centre of the colony where the cells first reach confluence and where cell growth is arrested. Labelling with tritiated thymidine showed growing cells located mainly at the edge of the colony (Owen & Friedenstein, 1988). The level of enzyme expression varied: some colonies were entirely negative, whereas in others a large proportion of the cells was positive for the enzyme (Fig. 4).

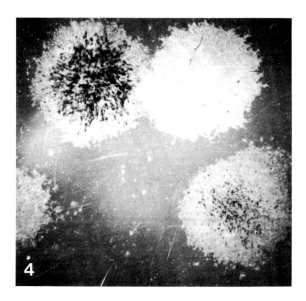

Fig. 4. Fibroblastic colonies formed when a suspension of single rabbit marrow cells ($10^7$ cells/25 cm$^2$ flask) is cultured in BGJ$_b$ medium with 10% foetal calf serum, fixed and stained for alkaline phosphatase activity (black) at 16 days. Details, see Owen *et al.* (1987). Colonies top left and bottom right are well and lightly stained for the enzyme respectively, other colony is negative. ×6.

The heterogeneity of the colonies formed is consistent with their derivation from a population of stem and progenitor cells at different stages of a tissue developmental system, (Fig. 1). It was assumed that colonies expressing a high level of alkaline phosphatase activity were initiated by CFU-F approaching committed progenitor status for the osteogenic line. Only 2·5 % of colonies fell into this category and although not proven it seemed likely that the majority of colonies in the cultures are probably from relatively early precursors with more than one lineage potential. In these cultures hydrocortisone (HC), which is known to increase alkaline phosphatase activity in a number of osteogenic systems (Rodan & Rodan, 1984), stimulated the number of colonies formed in all size ranges and the enzyme in colonies at all levels of expression (Fig. 5A). Addition of epidermal growth factor (EGF) increased average colony size and reduced expression of the enzyme in colonies at all levels to negligible amounts (Fig. 5B). These results indicate that both HC and EGF act on a spectrum of early precursors in the stromal system.

As is well known the survival of cell populations in culture is highly dependent on culture conditions. In the current literature culture conditions for marrow stromal cells fall mainly into two categories. (1) As in the experiment just described, marrow cells cultured in medium with foetal calf serum form fibroblastic colonies from precursors designated CFU-F. Under these conditions adipogenesis is rarely seen and the cells are commonly referred to as marrow fibroblasts (Castro-Malaspina *et al.* 1980). (2) Using the conditions which establish the microenvironment necessary for support of haemopoietic stem cells in long term marrow cultures (horse serum with HC), reticular-type cells with a high capacity for adipogenesis are predominant in the cell layer and few fibroblastic cells are present (Dexter *et al.* 1977; Singer *et al.* 1985). With a modification of these conditions, the growth of colonies with a reticular-fibroblastoid morphology, many with lipid inclusions, from precursors designated CFU-RF has been reported (Lim *et al.* 1986). In the latter study a comparison of macromolecules synthesized by progeny from CFU-F and CFU-RF was made using immunofluorescent antibody techniques. Both cell populations were positive for collagen types I, III and V; however, cells from CFU-RF were, in addition, positive for collagen type IV and laminin. The cells of both populations were negative for markers for endothelial and myeloid cells. It is not known how CFU-F are related to CFU-RF and the possibility cannot be ruled out that they are derived from common precursors and that the different patterns of macromolecules synthesized are a result of culture conditions.

## Relationship of cells *in vitro* and *in vivo*

An important question is, how are cells in culture related to their *in vivo* counterparts (Fig. 6)? Unfortunately there is no standard terminology for the different cell types. The best characterized cells of the marrow stromal system are osteogenic cells. Both *in vivo* and *in vitro* they are identified by high levels of alkaline phosphatase activity, synthesis of type I collagen (Sandberg & Vuorio, 1987), and of the bone-specific protein, osteocalcin (Bronckers *et al.* 1987), and the presence of

*M. Owen*

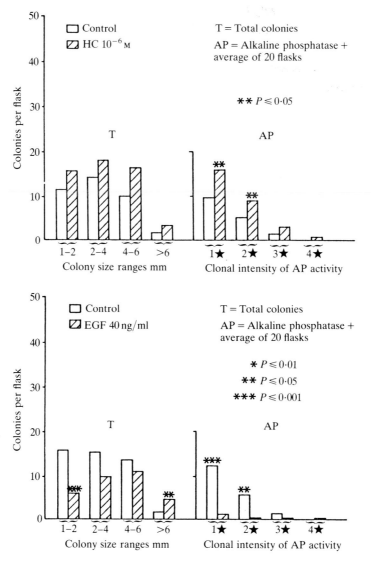

Fig. 5. Effect of HC (A) and EGF (B) on the total number of colonies formed (T) for different size ranges and on the number positive for alkaline phosphatase activity (AP) for four different levels of staining for the enzyme. HC and EGF were present from day 0, culture conditions same as in legend to Fig. 4; details, see Owen *et al.* (1987). *P* values are for comparison with control.

receptors for parathyroid hormone (Rodan *et al.* 1988). By comparison there has been little characterization of other stromal cell types. Collagen types I and III are found *in situ* throughout the reticular-fibroblastic network and connective tissues of blood vessel walls (Bentley *et al.* 1981, 1984). Type IV collagen and laminin are mainly associated with basement membrane and localized in the walls of small blood

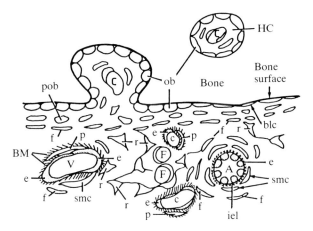

Fig. 6. Diagrammatic representation of stromal cells of bone and marrow and the microvasculature *in vivo*. Osteoblasts (ob), preosteoblasts (pob) and bone lining cells (blc) on bone surfaces and within haversian canal (HC), arteriole (A), venule (V), capillaries (c), endothelial cells (e), fibroblastic cells (f), reticular cells (r), smooth muscle cells (smc), pericytes (p) surrounded by basement membrane (BM), internal elastic lamina (iel), fat cell (F).

vessels. It might be speculated that stromal cells which synthesize collagen type IV and laminin *in vitro* may be derived from perivascular cells.

There is little understanding of the relationship of perivascular cells (pericytes, smooth muscle cells and fibroblasts of vessel walls) to other cells of the stromal system (Fig. 6). Cells which express muscle actin have been identified in long term marrow cultures (Charbord *et al.* 1985) and a cloned cell line derived from foetal rat calvaria was reported to have myogenic, osteogenic and adipocytic potential in culture (Grigoriadis *et al.* 1986). Pericytes are thought to be precursors of smooth muscle cells (Ham, 1974*a*). Whether a myogenic cell line is a component of the marrow stromal system however, must await the outcome of future experiments. Stromal stem cells are not identifiable morphologically and their location in bone marrow is not known. In young adult rabbits the CFU-F are more concentrated in the cell layers near bone surfaces than throughout the marrow cavity (Ashton *et al.* 1984). On the basis of morphological evidence, it has been suggested in the past that pluripotential mesenchymal cells are present in soft connective tissues throughout the body often in perivascular locations (Ham, 1974*b*).

## Concluding comments

The best available assay for marrow stromal stem cells is tissue analysis following transplantation in an open system under the renal capsule where all cell lines of a bone and marrow organ may be formed. The most direct evidence for stromal stem cells has been obtained from assay of single colonies using this system. Studies with diffusion chambers and preliminary investigations *in vitro* also support the stromal system hypothesis. However, for more rigorous proof of the stem cell hypothesis, marked stem cells and an ability to follow the marker in the stem cell progeny is necessary (Abramson *et al.* 1977). Gene transfer techniques which have recently been used for haemopoietic stem cells could be applied in the present case (Lemischka *et al.* 1986; Price, 1987).

Few experiments have been made to investigate the possibility of developing clonal *in vitro* assays for the stromal system but preliminary studies indicate their feasibility (Owen *et al.* 1987). In liquid cultures with foetal calf serum a proportion of colonies formed appears to be derived from early precursors and investigations *in vitro* of events occurring prior to production of committed progenitor cells should be possible. The existence of irreversibly committed progenitor cells for the different cell lines of the marrow stromal system is still hypothetical. Nor is there any solid information on the hierarchy of the different lines in this system, e.g. whether committed progenitors exist for each cell line or are common to two or more lines is not known. The availability of more markers for the different cell lines of the stromal system and of culture methods which allow their differentiation *in vitro* are needed before the stimulatory factors necessary for the development of specific phenotypes can be fully identified. In this respect the use of soft-gel media (Ernst & Froesch, 1987; Guenther *et al.* 1988) and the bone nodule method (Bellows *et al.* 1986, 1987) are giving promising results.

It is possible that the stromal fibroblastic system of bone and marrow is part of a wider stromal cell system of the body, each organ containing pluripotent and restricted stem cells which generate the cell lines of the particular organ concerned (Fig. 7). In discussing this an attempt will be made to clarify some of the current nomenclature. In one known situation, stromal cells can be induced to differentiate in a direction different from the tissue in which they are located. This is induction of osteogenesis in many tissues outside the skeleton, by factors derived from bone matrix and transitional epithelium (Friedenstein, 1973; Reddi, 1981; Urist *et al.*

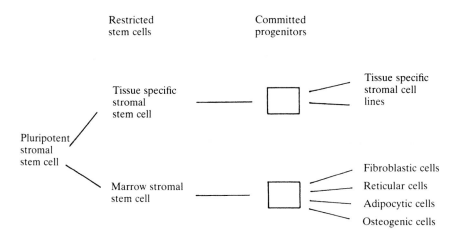

Fig. 7. Hypothetical diagram for the stromal system of the body. It is proposed that pluripotent stem cells are present throughout the loose connective tissues of many organs and that organs also contain stem cells restricted to the cell lines of the organ concerned.

1983). The cells involved were named inducible osteogenic precursor cells (IOPC); on the other hand the cells in marrow which form bone spontaneously in ectopic transplants and in diffusion chambers *in vivo* were called determined osteogenic precursor cells (DOPC) (Friedenstein, 1973) and more recently osteogenic stem cells (Friedenstein *et al.* 1987). In our present state of knowledge it is not possible to distinguish between DOPC, osteogenic stem cells and the marrow stromal stem cells of the present chapter. All are components of a population which contain specific stem cells and early progenitors of bone and marrow stromal lines whereas IOPC are likely to be components of a pluripotent stromal stem cell compartment (Fig. 7). There is little information on the stromal cell system in organs other than bone and marrow except that in haemopoietic organs stromal cells are specific for their organ of origin in terms of the type of haemopoiesis which they support (Friedenstein *et al.* 1974; Trentin, 1976).

Finally, little is known about the relative numbers of marrow stromal stem cells with age or in different diseases and their role in normal physiology. Marrow CFU-F are practically non-cycling *in vivo* (Keilis-Borok *et al.* 1971) and the importance of stromal stem cells therefore may lie mainly in the role they play in connective tissue regeneration, e.g. in re-establishment of the haemopoietic microenvironment and in bone repair, and possibly in certain connective tissue diseases.

## References

ABRAMSON, S., MILLER, R. G. & PHILLIPS, R. A. (1977). The identification in adult bone marrow of pluripotent and restricted stem cells of the myeloid and lymphoid systems. *J. exp. Med.* **145**, 1567–1579.

ALLEN, T. D. & DEXTER, T. M. (1982). Ultrastructural aspects of erythropoietic differentiation in long-term bone marrow culture. *Differentiation* **21**, 86–94.

ALLEN, T. D. & DEXTER, T. M. (1984). The essential cells of the haemopoietic microenvironment. *Expl Haem.* **12**, 517–521.

ASHTON, B. A., ALLEN, T. D., HOWLETT, C. R., EAGLESOM, C. C., HATTORI, A. & OWEN, M. (1980). Formation of bone and cartilage by marrow stromal cells in diffusion chambers *in vivo*. *Clin. Orthop. rel. Res.* **151**, 294–307.

ASHTON, B. A., EAGLESOM, C. C., BAB, I. & OWEN, M. E. (1984). Distribution of fibroblastic colony-forming cells in rabbit bone marrow and assay of their osteogenic potential by an *in vivo* diffusion chamber method. *Calc. Tiss. Int.* **36**, 83–86.

BAB, I., ASHTON, B. A., GAZIT, D., MARX, G., WILLIAMSON, M. C. & OWEN, M. E. (1986). Kinetics and differentiation of marrow stromal cells in diffusion chambers *in vivo*. *J. Cell Sci.* **84**, 139–151.

BAB, I., HOWLETT, C. R., ASHTON, B. A. & OWEN, M. E. (1984). Ultrastructure of bone and cartilage formed *in vivo* in diffusion chambers. *Clin. Orthop. rel Res.* **187**, 243–254.

BELLOWS, C. G., AUBIN, J. E. & HEERSCHE, J. N. M. (1987). Physiological concentrations of glucocorticoids stimulate formation of bone nodules from isolated rat calvaria cells *in vitro*. *Endocrinology* **121**, 1985–1992.

BELLOWS, C. G., AUBIN, J. E., HEERSCHE, J. N. M. & ANTOSZ, M. E. (1986). Mineralized bone nodules formed *in vitro* from enzymatically released rat calvaria cell populations. *Calc. Tiss. Int.* **38**, 143–154.

BENAYAHU, D., KLETTER, Y., ZIPORI, D. & WIENTROUB, S. (1987). Osteoblastic expression of marrow stromal derived cell line: *In vitro* and *in vivo*. *Calc. Tiss. Int.* **41**, Suppl. 2, 81.

BENTLEY, S. A., ALABASTER, O. A. & FOIDART, J. M. (1981). Collagen heterogeneity in normal human bone marrow. *Br. J. Haemat.* **48**, 287–291.

BENTLEY, S. A., FOIDART, J.-M. & KLEINMAN, H. K. (1984). Connective tissue elements in rat bone marrow: Immunofluorescent visualization of the hematopoietic microenvironment. *J. Histochem. Cytochem.* **32**, 114–116.

BRONCKERS, A. L. J. J., GAY, S., FINKELMAN, R. D. & BUTLER, W. T. (1987). Developmental appearance of Gla proteins (osteocalcin) and alkaline phosphatase in tooth germs and bones of the rat. *Bone Miner.* **2**, 361–373.

CASTRO-MALASPINA, H., GAY, R. E., RESNICK, G., KAPOOR, N., MEYERS, P., CHIARIERI, D., McKENZIE, S., BROXMEYER, H. E. & MOORE, M. A. S. (1980). Characterization of human bone marrow fibroblast colony-forming cells (CFU-F) and their progeny. *Blood* **56**, 289–301.

CHAMBERS, T. J. (1985). The pathobiology of the osteoclast. *J. clin. Path.* **38**, 241–252.

CHARBORD, P., GOWN, A. M., KEATING, A. & SINGER, J. W. (1985). CGA-7 and HHF, Two monoclonal antibodies that recognize muscle actin and react with adherent cells in human long-term bone marrow cultures. *Blood* **66**, 1138–1142.

DEXTER, T. M. (1982). Stromal cell associated haemopoiesis. In *J. cell. Physiol. Suppl. 1, Proc. Symp. cell. molec. Biol. of Hemopoietic Stem Cell Differentiation*, pp. 87–94.

DEXTER, T. M., ALLEN, T. D. & LAJTHA, L. G. (1977). Conditions controlling the proliferation of haemopoietic stem cells *in vitro*. *J. cell. Physiol.* **91**, 335–344.

ERNST, M. & FROESCH, E. R. (1987). Osteoblast like cells in a serum-free methylcellulose medium form colonies: Effects of insulin and insulin-like growth factor I. *Calc. Tiss. Int.* **40**, 27–34.

FRIEDENSTEIN, A. J. (1973). Determined and inducible osteogenic precursor cells. In *Hard Tissue Growth, Repair and Remineralization, Ciba Fdn Symp.*, vol. 11, pp. 169–185. North-Holland, Amsterdam: Elsevier-Excerpta Medica.

FRIEDENSTEIN, A. J. (1976). Precursor cells of mechanocytes. *Int. Rev. Cytol.* **47**, 327–355.

FRIEDENSTEIN, A. J. (1980). Stromal mechanisms of bone marrow: cloning *in vitro* and retransplantation *in vivo*. In *Immunobiology of Bone Marrow Transplantation* (ed. S. Thienfelder), pp. 19–29. Berlin: Springer-Verlag.

FRIEDENSTEIN, A. J., CHAILAKHYAN, R. K. & GERASIMOV, U. V. (1987). Bone marrow osteogenic stem cells: *In vitro* cultivation and transplantation in diffusion chambers. *Cell Tiss. Kinet.* **20**, 263–272.

FRIEDENSTEIN, A. J., CHAILAKHYAN, R. K. & LALYKINA, K. S. (1970). The development of fibroblast colonies in monolayer cultures of guinea pig bone marrow and spleen cells. *Cell Tiss. Kinet.* **3**, 393–402.

FRIEDENSTEIN, A. J., CHAILAKHYAN, R. K., LATZINIK, N. V., PANASYUK, A. F. & KEILISS-BOROK, I. V. (1974). Stromal cells responsible for transferring the microenvironment of the hemopoietic tissues. *Transplantation* **17**, 331–340.

FRIEDENSTEIN, A. J., IVANOV-SMOLENSKI, A. A., CHAJLAKJAN, R. K., GORSKAYA, U. F., KURALESOVA, A. I., LATZINIK, N. W. & GERASIMOW, U. W. (1978). Origin of bone marrow stromal mechanocytes in radiochimeras and heterotopic transplants. *Expl Hem.* **6**, 440–444.

FRIEDENSTEIN, A. J., LATZINIK, N. W., GROSHEVA, A. G. & GORSKAYA, U. F. (1982). Marrow microenvironment transfer by heterotopic transplantation of freshly isolated and cultured cells in porous sponges. *Expl Hem.* **10**, 217–227.

GRIGORIADIS, A. E., AUBIN, J. E. & HEERSCHE, J. N. M. (1987). Glucocorticoid induces the differentiation of progenitor cells present in a clonally-derived fetal rat calvaria cell population. In *Calcium Regulation and Bone Metabolism: Basic and Clinical Aspects*, vol. 9 (ed. D. V. Cohn *et al.*), p. 646. Amsterdam: Excerpta Medica.

GUENTHER, H. L., HOFSTETTER, W., MUHLBAUER, R., STUTZER, A. & FLEISCH, H. (1988). Clonal rat calvarial cell populations established from TGF-induced cell colonies (soft agarose) express different phenotypes. *Calc. Tiss. Int.* **42**, Suppl., abs. 17, p. A5.

HAM, A. W. (1974*a*). *Histology*, seventh edn, p. 577. Philadelphia and Toronto: J. B. Lippincott Co.

HAM, A. W. (1974*b*). *Histology*, seventh edn, p. 249. Philadelphia and Toronto: J. B. Lippincott Co.

KEILIS-BOROK, I. V., LATSINIK, N. V., EPIKHINA, S. Y. & FRIEDENSTEIN, A. J. (1971). Dynamics of the formation of fibroblast colonies in monolayer cultures of bone marrow, according to $^3$H-thymidine incorporation experiments. *Cytologia* **13**, 1402–1409.

KODAMA, H.-A., AMAGAI, Y., KOYAMA, H. & KASAI, S. (1982). Hormonal responsiveness of a preadipose cell line derived from newborn mouse calvaria. *J. cell. Physiol.* **112**, 83–88.

LANOTTE, M., SCOTT, D., DEXTER, T. M. & ALLEN, T. D. (1982). Clonal preadipocyte cell lines with different phenotypes derived from murine mouse stroma: Factors influencing growth and adipogenesis *in vitro*. *J. cell. Physiol.* **111**, 177–186.

LATSINIK, N. V., GROSHEVA, A. G., NAROVLYANSKII, A. N., PAVLENKO, R. G. & FRIEDENSTEIN, A. J. (1987). Clonal nature of fibroblast colonies formed by bone marrow stromal cells in culture. *Bull. exp. Biol. Med. (Engl. Trans. Byull. Eksp. Biol. Med.)* **103**, 356–358.

LE DOUARIN, N. M. (1979). Dependence of myeloid and lymphoid organ development on stem-cell seeding: Investigations on mechanisms in cell marker analysis. In *Mechanisms of Cell Change* (ed. J. Ebert & T. Okada), pp. 293–326. New York: Wiley.

LEMISCHKA, I. R., RAULET, D. H. & MULLIGAN, R. C. (1986). Developmental potential and dynamic behavior of hematopoietic stem cells. *Cell* **45**, 917–927.

LIM, B., ISAGUIRRE, C. A., AYE, M. T. *et al.* (1986). Characterisation of reticulofibroblastoid colonies (CFU-RF) derived from bone marrow and long-term marrow culture monolayers. *J. cell. Physiol.* **127**, 45–54.

MARDON, H. J., BEE, J., VON DER MARK, K. & OWEN, M. E. (1987). Development of osteogenic tissue in diffusion chambers from early precursor cells in bone marrow of adult rats. *Cell Tiss. Res.* **250**, 157–165.

MARKS, S. C. (1983). The origin of osteoclasts. *J. oral Path.* **12**, 226–256.

METCALF, D. (1984). *Hemopoietic Colony Stimulating Factors*. Amsterdam, New York, London: Elsevier.

OWEN, M. (1978). Histogenesis of bone cells. *Calc. Tiss. Int.* **25**, 205–207.

OWEN, M. (1980). The origin of bone cells in the postnatal organism. *Arthritis Rheum.* **23**, 1073–1080.

OWEN, M. E. (1985). Lineage of osteogenic cells and their relationship to the stromal system. In *Bone and Mineral Research*, vol. 3 (ed. W. A. Peck), pp. 1–25. Amsterdam, New York, Oxford: Elsevier.

OWEN, M. E., CAVE, J. & JOYNER, C. J. (1987). Clonal analysis *in vitro* of osteogenic differentiation of marrow CFU-F. *J. Cell Sci.* **87**, 731–738.

OWEN, M. & FRIEDENSTEIN, A. J. (1988). Stromal stem cells: marrow derived osteogenic precursors. *Ciba Fdn Symp.* **136,** 42–60.

PRICE, J. (1987). Retroviruses and the study of cell lineage. *Development* **101**, 409–419.

REDDI, A. H. (1981). Cell biology and biochemistry of endochondral bone development. *Coll. Res.* **1**, 209–226.

RODAN, G., HEATH, J. K., YOON, K., NODA, M. & RODAN, S. B. (1988). Diversity of osteoblast phenotypes. *Ciba Fdn Symp.* **136**, in press.

RODAN, G. A. & RODAN, S. B. (1984). Expression of the osteoblastic phenotype. In *Bone and Mineral Research*, vol. 2 (ed. W. A. Peck), pp. 244–285. Amsterdam, New York, Oxford: Elsevier.

SANDBERG, M. & VUORIO, E. (1987). Localization of types I, II, III collagen mRNAs in developing human skeletal tissues by *in situ* hybridization. *J. Cell Biol.* **104**, 1077–1084.

SIMMONS, P. J., PRZEPIORKA, D., THOMAS, E. D. & TOROK-STORB, B. (1987). Host origin of marrow stromal cells following allogeneic bone marrow transplantation. *Nature, Lond.* **328**, 429–432.

SINGER, J. W., KEATING, A. & WIGHT, T. N. (1985). Human haemopoietic microenvironment. In *Recent Advances in Haematology*, No. 4 (ed. A. V. Hoftbrand), pp. 1–25. Churchill Livingstone.

SUDO, H., KODAMA, H-A., AMAGAI, Y., YAMAMOTO, S. & KASAI, S. (1983). *In vitro* differentiation and calcification in a new clonal osteogenic cell line derived from newborn mouse calvaria. *J. Cell Biol.* **96**, 191–198.

TAVASSOLI, M. & CROSBY, W. H. (1968). Transplantation of marrow to extramedullary sites. *Science* **161**, 54–56.

TRENTIN, J. J. (1976). Hemopoietic inductive microenvironments. In *Stem Cells* (ed. A. B. Cairnie, P. K. Lala & D. G. Osmond), pp. 255–261. New York: Academic Press.

URIST, M. R., DELANGE, R. J. & FINERMAN, G. A. M. (1983). Bone cell differentiation and growth factors. *Science* **220**, 680–686.

WILSON, D. (1983). The origin of the endothelium in the developing marginal vein of the chick wing-bud. *Cell Differ.* **13**, 63–67.

ZIPORI, D., DUSKIN, D., TAMIR, M., ARGAMAN, A., TOLEDO, J. & MALIK, Z. (1985). Cultured mouse marrow stromal cell lines. II. Distinct subtypes differing in morphology, collagen types, myelopoietic factors, and leukemic cell growth modulating activities. *J. cell. Physiol.* **122**, 81–90.

*J. Cell Sci. Suppl. 10, 77–83 (1988)*
*Printed in Great Britain © The Company of Biologists Limited 1988*

# Differentiation of a bipotential glial progenitor cell: what controls the timing and the choice of developmental pathway?

MARTIN C. RAFF AND LAURA E. LILLIEN

*Medical Research Council Developmental Neurobiology Programme, Biology Department, Medawar Bulding, University College London, London WC1E 6BT, UK*

## Summary

In the rat central nervous system (CNS) oligodendrocytes and type-2 astrocytes are thought to develop from a common precursor – the O-2A progenitor cell. Oligodendrocytes develop first and make myelin; type-2 astrocytes develop later and extend processes to nodes of Ranvier. The timing of differentiation of O-2A progenitor cells seems to depend on chemical signals secreted by another type of glial cell – the type-1 astrocyte. Type-1 astrocytes secrete platelet-derived growth factor (PDGF), which stimulates O-2A progenitor cell proliferation and drives the clock that controls the onset of oligodendrocyte differentiation, which is the constitutive pathway of progenitor cell development. Later, type-1 astrocytes are thought to secrete a CNTF-like protein that initiates type-2 astrocyte differentiation.

## Introduction

The many types of nerve cells and supporting (glial) cells in the mammalian central nervous system (CNS) develop on a predictable schedule from the neuroepithelial cells of the neural tube. The mechanisms responsible for controlling the direction and timing of neuroepithelial cell differentiation, however, are largely unknown. We have been studying the control of glial cell differentiation in the rat CNS – in the optic nerve, one of the simplest parts of the CNS, and in the brain, the most complex organ in the body. Here we briefly review some of the main findings.

## The rat optic nerve contains three types of macroglial cells

The optic nerve is simple because it contains no nerve cells. It does, however, contain the axons of the retinal ganglion cells that project from the eye to the brain. Three types of macroglial cells structurally and functionally support the axons in the nerve: oligodendrocytes and two types of astrocytes, called type 1 and type 2 (Raff *et al.* 1983*a*). *Oligodendrocytes* myelinate the axons. *Type-1 astrocytes* extend processes that run at right angles to the axons: some of these processes terminate on the surface of the nerve, forming a 'glial limiting membrane' (Miller *et al.* 1989); others terminate on the surface of blood vessels (Miller *et al.* 1989) and apparently (Janzer & Raff, 1987) induce the underlying endothelial cells to form extensive tight junctions with one another, which are the basis of the blood–brain barrier (Reese & Karnovsky, 1967). *Type-2 astrocytes* extend processes that run parallel to the axons

Key words: glial cell differentiation, oligodendrocytes, astrocytes.

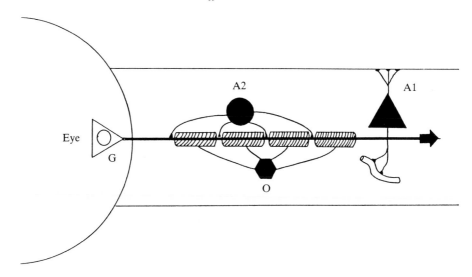

Fig. 1. Schematic drawing of rat optic nerve showing a retinal ganglion cell (G), an oligodendrocyte (O), a type-1 astrocyte (A1), and a type-2 astrocyte (A2). Type-1 astrocytes extend radial processes to the surface of the nerve and to blood vessels. Oligodendrocytes and type-2 astrocytes collaborate in ensheathing each retinal ganglion cell axon: oligodendrocytes wrap around the axon to form an insulating myelin sheath, while type-2 astrocytes extend fine longitudinal processes that contact the axon where the myelin sheath is interrupted at nodes of Ranvier.

and terminate at nodes of Ranvier (ffrench-Constant & Raff, 1986a; Miller *et al.* 1989), where the myelin sheath is interrupted and the electrical activity of the axon is confined. By enveloping the exposed axons at nodes of Ranvier, type-2 astrocytes collaborate with oligodendrocytes in ensheathing the axons and constructing the nodes (Fig. 1).

## The three types of macroglial cells in optic nerve cultures arise from two cell lineages

Experiments in culture suggest that the three types of macroglial cells in the nerve arise from two distinct lineages: oligodendrocytes and type-2 astrocytes develop from a common, bipotential *O-2A progenitor cell* (Raff *et al.* 1983b), whereas type-1 astrocytes develop from a different precursor cell (Raff *et al.* 1984a). Type-1 astrocytes first appear at embryonic day 16 (E16), oligodendrocytes on the day of birth (E21), and type-2 astrocytes between postnatal days 8 and 10 (P8–10) (Miller *et al.* 1985). Both kinds of precursor cells divide rapidly before they differentiate; while type-1 astrocytes continue to divide for at least a week or so after they develop, oligodendrocytes, and probably type-2 astrocytes, divide infrequently, if at all, after they are formed (Skoff *et al.* 1976a,b; Miller *et al.* 1985; Noble & Murray, 1984).

Recent experiments suggest that O-2A progenitor cells migrate into the developing optic nerve from the brain (Small *et al.* 1987). This implies that the neuroepithelial cells of the optic stalk (the part of the neural tube that will form the optic nerve) gives rise only to type-1 astrocytes.

We have focused our attention on the O-2A cell lineage and have tried to answer two related questions: what determines whether an individual O-2A progenitor cell develops into an oligodendrocyte or a type-2 astrocyte, and what controls when a progenitor cell differentiates?

## Oligodendrocyte differentiation is the constitutive pathway of O-2A progenitor cell development

Whereas most O-2A progenitor cells in the developing optic nerve proliferate for a week or more before differentiating, when they are grown in dissociated cell culture, they stop dividing and differentiate within 2–3 days: if they are cultured without foetal calf serum (FCS), they become oligodendrocytes, while in the presence of FCS they become type-2 astrocytes (Raff *et al.* 1983*b*, 1984*b*). Clearly, environmental conditions can profoundly influence both the timing and direction of O-2A progenitor cell differentiation.

If a single O-2A progenitor cell is cultured alone in a microwell in the absence of FCS, it immediately stops dividing and differentiates into an oligodendrocyte (Temple & Raff, 1985). This suggests that oligodendrocyte differentiation is the constitutive pathway of O-2A progenitor cell development, which is automatically triggered when the cell is deprived of signals from its neighbours.

The normal timing of oligodendrocyte development can be reconstituted *in vitro* if O-2A progenitor cells from embryonic optic nerve are cultured together with an excess of purified type-1 astrocytes in the absence of FCS. The astrocytes secrete a growth factor(s) that keeps the progenitor cells dividing in these mixed cultures (Noble & Murray, 1984), and the progenitors now give rise to oligodendrocytes beginning on the equivalent of the day of birth, just as *in vivo* (Raff *et al.* 1985). A crucial growth factor that type-1 astrocytes secrete in culture in order to keep progenitor cells dividing is platelet-derived growth factor (PDGF) (Richardson *et al.* 1988; Noble *et al.* 1988). Adding excessive amounts of PDGF to cultures of embryonic optic nerve, however, does not prevent the first oligodendrocytes from developing on schedule (Raff *et al.* 1988). Apparently, O-2A progenitor cells can divide only a limited number of times (or for a limited period of time) before they become unresponsive to PDGF and differentiate into non-dividing oligodendrocytes, and the first cells reach this point on the day of birth, or its equivalent in culture.

## Type-2 astrocyte differentiation is initiated by a specific inducing protein

Unlike oligodendrocyte differentiation, type-2 astrocyte differentiation does not occur when O-2A progenitor cells are cultured in serum-free medium (Raff *et al.* 1983*b*; Temple & Raff, 1985). Progenitor cells can be induced to differentiate into type-2 astrocytes, however, if they are cultured in FCS (Raff *et al.* 1983*b*; Temple & Raff, 1985). Moreover, and of more relevance to normal development, type-2 astrocyte differentiation can be initiated in culture by a 20 000–25 000 $M_r$ protein that greatly increases in concentration in the rat optic nerve after the first postnatal week, when type-2 astrocyte development begins (Hughes & Raff, 1987). Since the protein acts on O-2A progenitor cells isolated from E17-18 optic nerve, which is more than 10 days before these cells normally develop into type-2 astrocytes, it seems that it is the increase in the inducing protein rather than the onset of progenitor cell responsiveness that is responsible for timing type-2 astrocyte differentiation in the developing nerve.

Recent evidence (Hughes *et al.* 1988) indicates that the type-2 astrocyte-inducing protein is very similar or identical to ciliary neurotrophic factor (CNTF), a protein that promotes the survival of some types of peripheral neurones *in vitro*, including ciliary ganglion neurones (Helfand *et al.* 1976; Barbin *et al.* 1984; Manthorpe *et al.* 1986). Cultures of purified type-1 astrocytes can produce CNTF or a closely related molecule (Rudge *et al.* 1985; Lillien *et al.* 1988). Thus, by secreting PDGF and CNTF, type-1 astrocytes apparently regulate the timing of both oligodendrocyte and type-2 astrocyte development.

## Macroglial cells develop on schedule in dissociated cell cultures of embryonic rat brain

O-2A lineage cells are not confined to the optic nerve; they are presumably present wherever CNS axons are myelinated. It is not surprising, therefore, that O-2A progenitor-like cells have been found in perinatal brain (Williams *et al.* 1985; Goldman *et al.* 1986; Lillien *et al.* 1988), cerebellum (Levi *et al.* 1986), and spinal cord (L. E. Lillien, unpublished). When cells dissociated from embryonic rat brain from E10 onwards are cultured in FCS, type-1-like astrocytes, oligodendrocytes and type-2 astrocytes develop on precisely the same schedule as they do in the developing brain (Abney *et al.* 1981; Williams *et al.* 1985), which is virtually identical to the schedule in the optic nerve. This suggests that the mechanisms controlling glial cell diversification from E10 onwards operate independently of brain morphogenesis.

Since FCS itself can induce type-2 astrocyte differentiation, its presence complicates the analysis of type-2 astrocyte development in such cultures. We therefore developed a system in which oligodendrocytes and type-2 astrocytes develop on schedule in cultures of embryonic rat brain cells in the absence of FCS (Lillien *et al.* 1988). Just at the time type-2 astrocytes begin to develop in such cultures, a CNTF-like protein appears in the culture medium that is capable of prematurely inducing type-2 astrocyte differentiation if added to younger cultures (Lillien *et al.* 1988). Moreover, extracts of cultures in which type-2 astrocytes have started to develop contain at least 50-fold more of the inducing protein than extracts of younger cultures. Thus, as in the optic nerve, it is apparently the production of a CNTF-like inducing protein rather than the responsiveness of the O-2A progenitor cells that controls the timing of type-2 astrocyte differentiation in the brain. The ability to reconstitute the timing *in vitro* should facilitate the task of determining how the synthesis and/or release of the inducing protein is controlled.

## Where are the stem cells for the O-2A lineage?

Although oligodendrocytes and type-2 astrocytes are thought to divide infrequently, if at all, there are dividing O-2A progenitor cells in the adult rat optic nerve, where they presumably mediate a slow turnover of O-2A lineage cells (ffrench-Constant & Raff, 1986*b*; Wolswijk & Nobel, 1988). Where do the dividing progenitor cells come from in the adult nerve? One possibility is that they are continuously produced from dividing subventricular cells in the brain, the main population of stem cells in the adult rat CNS (Hommes & Leblond, 1967); this would imply that newly formed O-2A progenitor cells continuously migrate into the adult optic nerve from the brain. Another possibility is that the O-2A progenitor cells in the adult nerve are themselves stem cells, which continuously produce new progenitor cells as well as oligodendrocytes and type-2 astrocytes. There is evidence that perinatal O-2A progenitor cells, which produce oligodendrocytes *in vitro* mainly after a limited number of symmetrical proliferative divisions (Temple & Raff, 1986), can transform in culture into adult-type O-2A progenitor cells, which produce oligodendrocytes by asymmetrical, self-renewing divisions (S. Wren, G. Wolswijk & M. Noble, personal communication).

## Glial cell diversification in perspective

One of the central challenges in developmental biology is to understand how a fertilized egg gives rise to the diverse cell types in the adult organism. In the CNS, the comparable challenge is to understand how the neuroepithelium of the neural plate and tube, composed initially of morphologically homogeneous cells, gives rise to the great diversity of nerve and glial cells. An early step must involve the division of the continuous neuroepithelium into regions that will later give rise to the characteristic set of cells of the retina, forebrain, midbrain, hindbrain, spinal cord, and so on, a process that may be analogous to dividing the blastoderm of a *Drosophila* embryo into segments (Nüsslein-Volhard *et al.* 1985; Ingham, 1988) and may depend on gradients and positional information (Wolpert, 1971). Our studies of glial cell differentiation are concerned with much later steps in cell diversification, in which positional cues may be less important. Cell diversification at these later stages seems to depend on cell–cell interactions in which each cell type that differentiates influences the subsequent course of cell diversification in the region.

It would be surprising if some of the general principles underlying glial cell diversification do not also apply to the diversification of neurones and to many non-neural cells as well. It is especially encouraging that many of the same families of signalling molecules and receptors are being found to mediate cell–cell interactions in the development of a variety of tissues and organisms.

## References

ABNEY, E., BARTLETT, P. & RAFF, M. C. (1981). Astrocytes, ependymal cells, and oligodendrocytes develop on schedule in dissociated cell cultures of embryonic rat brain. *Devl Biol.* **83**, 301–310.

BARBIN, G., MANTHORPE, M. & VARON, S. (1984). Purification of the chick eye ciliary neuronotrophic factor (CNTF). *J. Neurochem.* **43**, 1468–1478.

FFRENCH-CONSTANT, C. & RAFF, M. C. (1986a). The oligodendrocyte – type-2 astrocyte cell lineage is specialized for myelination. *Nature, Lond.* **323**, 335–338.

FFRENCH-CONSTANT, C. & RAFF, M. C. (1986b). Proliferating bipotential glial progenitor cells in adult rat optic nerve. *Nature, Lond.* **319**, 499–502.

GOLDMAN, J. E., GEIRER, S. S. & HIRANO, M. (1986). Differentiation of astrocytes and oligodendrocytes from germinal matrix cells in primary culture. *J. Neurosci.* **6**, 52–60.

HELFAND, S. L., SMITH, G. A. & WESSELLS, N. K. (1976). Survival and development in culture of dissociated parasympathetic neurons from ciliary ganglion. *Devl Biol.* **50**, 541–547.

HOMMES, O. R. & LEBLOND, C. P. (1967). Mitotic division of neuroglia in the normal adult rat. *J. comp. Neurol.* **129**, 269–278.

HUGHES, S. M., LILLIEN, L. E., RAFF, M. C., ROHRER, H. & SENDTNER, M. (1988). Ciliary neurotrophic factor (CNTF) induces type-2 astrocyte differentiation in culture. *Nature, Lond.* **335**, 70–73.

HUGHES, S. M. & RAFF, M. C. (1987). An inducer protein may control the timing of fate switching in a bipotential glial progenitor cell in rat optic nerve. *Development* **101**, 157–167.

INGHAM, P. W. (1988). The molecular genetics of embryonic pattern formation in *Drosophila*. *Nature, Lond.* **335**, 25–34.

JANZER, R. C. & RAFF, M. C. (1987). Astrocytes induce blood–brain barrier properties in endothelial cells. *Nature, Lond.* **325**, 253–257.

LEVI, G., GALLO, V., WILKINS, G. P. & GHEN, J. (1986). Astrocyte subpopulations and glial precursors in rat cerebellar cell cultures. *Adv. Biosci.* **61**, 21–30.

LILLIEN, L. E., HUGHES, S. M., ROHRER, H., SENDTNER, M. & RAFF, M. C. (1988). Type-2 astrocyte differentiation is initiated in culture by a CNTF-like protein produced by type-1 astrocytes. *Neuron* **1**, 485–494.

MANTHORPE, M., SKAPER, S. D., WILLIAMS, L. R. & VARON, S. (1986). Purification of adult rat sciatic nerve ciliary neuronotrophic factor. *Brain Res.* **367**, 282–286.

MILLER, R. H., DAVID, S., PATEL, R., ABNEY, E. R. & RAFF, M. C. (1985). A quantitative immunohistochemical study of macroglial cell development in the rat optic nerve: in vivo evidence for two distinct astrocyte lineages. *Devl Biol.* **111**, 35–41.

MILLER, R. H., FULTON, B. P. & RAFF, M. C. (1989). A novel type of glial cell associated with nodes of Ranvier in rat optic nerve. *Eur. J. Neurosci.* (in press).

NOBLE, M. & MURRAY, K. (1984). Purified astrocytes promote the *in vitro* division of a bipotential glial progenitor cell. *EMBO J.* **3**, 2243–2247.

NOBLE, M., MURRAY, K., STROOBANT, P., WATERFIELD, M. & RIDDLE, P. (1988). Platelet-derived growth factor promotes division and motility, and inhibits premature differentiation of the oligodendrocyte – type-2 astrocyte progenitor cell. *Nature, Lond.* **333**, 560–562.

NÜSSLEIN-VOLHARD, C., KLUDING, H. & JÜRGENS, G. (1985). Genes affecting the segmental subdivisions of the *Drosophila* embryo. In *Molecular Biology of Development. Cold Spring Harbor Symp. quant. Biol.* vol. 50, pp. 145–154. NY: Cold Spring Harbor.

RAFF, M. C., ABNEY, E. R., COHEN, J., LINDSAY, R. & NOBLE, M. (1983a). Two types of astrocytes in cultures of developing rat white matter: differences in morphology, surface gangliosides and growth characteristics. *J. Neurosci.* **3**, 1289–1300.

RAFF, M. C., ABNEY, E. R. & FOK-SEANG, J. (1985). Reconstitution of a developmental clock *in vitro*: a critical role for astrocytes in the timing of oligodendrocyte differentiation. *Cell* **42**, 61–69.

RAFF, M. C., ABNEY, E. R. & MILLER, R. H. (1984a). Two glial cell lineages diverge prenatally in rat optic nerve. *Devl Biol.* **106**, 53–60.

RAFF, M. C., LILLIEN, L. E., RICHARDSON, W. D., BURNE, J. & NOBLE, M. D. (1988). Astrocyte-derived PDGF drives the clock that times oligodendrocyte development in culture. *Nature, Lond.* **333**, 562–565.

RAFF, M. C., MILLER, R. & NOBLE, M. (1983b). A glial progenitor cell that develops in vitro into an astrocyte or an oligodendrocyte depending on the culture medium. *Nature, Lond.* **303**, 390–396.

RAFF, M. C., WILLIAMS, B. P. & MILLER, R. H. (1984b). The in vitro differentiation of a bipotential glial progenitor cell. *EMBO J.* **8**, 1857–1864.

REESE, T. S. & KARNOVSKY, M. J. (1967). Fine structural localization of a blood brain barrier to exogenous peroxidase. *J. Cell Biol.* **34**, 207–217.

RICHARDSON, W. D., PRINGLE, N., MOSLEY, M., WESTERMARK, B. & DUBOIS-DALCQ, M. (1988). A role for platelet-derived growth factor in normal gliogenesis in the central nervous system. *Cell* **53**, 309–319.

RUDGE, J. S., MANTHORPE, M. & VARON, S. (1985). Output of neuronotrophic and neurite-promoting agents from rat brain astroglial cells: a microculture method for screening potential regulatory molecules. *Devl Brain Res.* **19**, 161–172.

SKOFF, R., PRICE, D. & STOCKS, A. (1976a). Electron microscopic autoradiographic studies of gliogenesis in rat optic nerve. I. Cell proliferation. *J. comp. Neurol.* **169**, 291–312.

SKOFF, R., PRICE, D. & STOCKS, A. (1976b). Electron microscopic autoradiographic studies of gliogenesis in rat optic nerve. II. Time of origin. *J. comp. Neurol.* **169**, 313–333.

SMALL, R. K., RIDDLE, P. & NOBLE, M. (1987). Evidence for migration of oligodendrocyte – type-2 astrocyte progenitor cells into the developing rat optic nerve. *Nature, Lond.* **329**, 155–157.

TEMPLE, S. & RAFF, M. C. (1985). Differentiation of a bipotential glial progenitor cell in single cell culture. *Nature, Lond.* **313**, 223–225.

TEMPLE, S. & RAFF, M. C. (1986). Clonal analysis of oligodendrocyte development in culture: evidence for a developmental clock that counts cell divisions. *Cell* **44**, 773–779.

WILLIAMS, B. P., ABNEY, E. R. & RAFF, M. C. (1985). Macroglial cell development in embryonic rat brain: studies using monoclonal antibodies, fluorescence activated cell sorting and cell culture. *Devl Biol.* **112**, 126–134.

WOLPERT, L. (1971). Positional information and pattern formation. *Curr. Top. devl Biol.* **6**, 183–224.

WOLSWIJK, G. & NOBLE, M. (1988). Identificaton of an adult-specific glial progenitor cell. *Development* (in press).

J. Cell Sci. Suppl. 10, 85–94 (1988)
Printed in Great Britain © The Company of Biologists Limited 1988

# Epidermal stem cells in culture

FIONA M. WATT

*Keratinocyte Laboratory, Imperial Cancer Research Fund, PO Box 123, Lincoln's Inn Fields, London WC2A 3PX, UK*

## Summary

Cultures of human epidermal keratinocytes retain many of the characteristics of the tissue from which they are derived, and are therefore useful as an experimental model for studying stem cell properties. The cultures provide evidence that the mechanisms regulating keratinocyte proliferation are complex. The dividing cell compartment is heterogeneous, containing some cells with stem cell characteristics and others that may correspond to transit amplifying cells. The overall growth rate of the cultures is influenced by a wide range of growth stimulatory and inhibitory molecules, but it is not clear whether responsiveness to these factors differs between the different subpopulations of dividing cells. Furthermore, keratinocytes are able to express molecules that regulate their own growth. The cultures are able to achieve at least a partial homeostatic balance between proliferation and terminal differentiation and can regenerate the suprabasal cell layers following injury. Finally, a range of new experimental approaches hold promise for future studies of how keratinocyte proliferation and terminal differentiation are controlled.

## Introduction

The epithelial cells of the epidermis are called keratinocytes. They are organized into multiple layers, the deepest of which (the basal layer) is attached to a basement membrane, while the outermost is exposed to the air. The majority of proliferating keratinocytes are located in the basal layer and cells undergo terminal differentiation as they move through the suprabasal layers towards the tissue surface.

Several different stages of epidermal terminal differentiation can be distinguished. During the early stages the postmitotic keratinocytes are metabolically active and increase in size and protein content. Late in terminal differentiation the cells undergo degenerative changes: the nucleus and cytoplasmic organelles are lost and an insoluble protein envelope, the cornified envelope, is assembled at the inner surface of the plasma membrane. These anucleate cornified cells (squames) protect the underlying living layers from desiccation and mechanical damage.

Squames are continually shed from the outer epidermal layers and are replaced through proliferation in the basal layer. A balance between proliferation and terminal differentiation ensures that the epidermis maintains a constant thickness. Furthermore, the epidermis is able to regenerate and re-establish homeostasis following injury (Pinkus, 1952; Potten, 1981).

Since the epidermis is renewed throughout adult life and proliferation is confined to a distinct subpopulation of cells, that subpopulation must contain stem cells. Stem cells are defined here as cells that have the capacity for unlimited self-renewal, whose

Key words: keratinocytes, stem cells, proliferation, terminal differentiation.

daughters may either be stem cells or else be committed to undergo terminal differentiation and (ultimately) become a squame. Epidermal homeostasis requires that the rate of production of new cells in the basal layer must be balanced by the rate of loss of terminally differentiated cells from the tissue surface; thus, on average, for every stem cell division, one daughter will remain a stem cell and the other will terminally differentiate.

An understanding of how proliferation of keratinocytes is regulated in normal epidermis is important if we are to understand what goes wrong in neoplasia and in benign hyperproliferative disorders such as psoriasis. Experiments *in vivo* have, for obvious reasons, concentrated on animal, rather than human, epidermis (see Potten & Morris, 1989). However, the development of methods for recreating human epidermis in culture (see Fusenig, 1986, for review) makes human keratinocytes accessible for investigation. In this article I shall review what is known about the proliferation of human epidermal keratinocytes in culture and discuss promising directions for future research.

## Human keratinocyte cultures

Human keratinocytes from epidermis, or other stratified squamous epithelia, can be grown in culture in the presence of a feeder layer of 3T3 cells and medium supplemented with a range of additives (see below) that prolong the lifespan and increase the growth rate of the cultures (Rheinwald & Green, 1975; Rheinwald, 1980). After isolation from the epidermis, cells originating from the basal layer attach to the culture dish, divide and give rise to individual colonies of cells. With time, individual colonies expand and adjacent colonies merge with one another, displacing the feeder cells. At confluence each dish is covered with a continuous stratified sheet of cells, approximately 6 to 8 layers thick. Human keratinocytes can be passaged several times before they undergo senescence and do not, with rare exceptions (Baden *et al.* 1987; Boukamp *et al.* 1988), undergo spontaneous transformation.

To what extent do these stratified sheets of keratinocytes resemble normal epidermis? They retain the fundamental characteristics of the tissue, in that they are stratified, with proliferation restricted to the basal layer and cells undergoing terminal differentiation as they move through the upper layers (Green, 1980; Watt, 1988). The overall morphology of the cultures is rather poor compared with normal epidermis; the basal cells tend to be flattened and layers of squames do not accumulate. Nevertheless, culture morphology can be improved substantially by conditions that more closely approximate the normal epidermal environment, such as feeding from below and exposure to air (Fusenig, 1986; Watt *et al.* 1987).

Another essential property of normal epidermis is its ability to maintain a balance between proliferation and terminal differentiation and to re-establish that balance following injury (Pinkus, 1952; Potten, 1981). The kinetics of proliferation and terminal differentiation in culture can be monitored using, as a differentiation marker, involucrin, the major precursor of the cornified envelope. By the criteria of constant cell number and proportion of involucrin-positive cells, homeostasis is

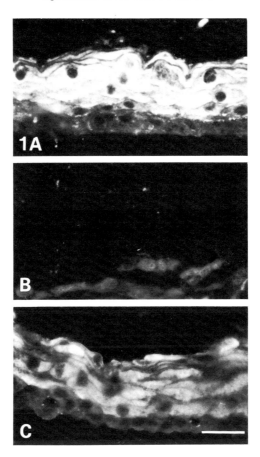

Fig. 1. Sections through human keratinocyte cultures stained with antiserum to involucrin. A. Confluent dish, 22 days after seeding. B. Culture stripped of all the suprabasal
layers. C. Stripped culture after 13 days of recovery. Suprabasal, involucrin-positive
layers have been regenerated. Bar, (A,C) 50 $\mu$m and (B) 34 $\mu$m. Reproduced from Read
and Watt (1988), with permission of Elsevier Science Publishing Co. Inc. Copyright 1988
by The Society for Investigative Dermatology, Inc.

achieved approximately four days after confluence, although it is not clear how long it
is maintained (Read & Watt, 1988). If the suprabasal, involucrin-positive cell layers
are stripped off (Fig. 1A,B) the remaining basal layer can regenerate a tissue of
approximately the same thickness as controls (Fig. 1C) (Read & Watt, 1988; Jensen
& Bolund, 1988). Thus, cultured epidermis has some capacity for homeostasis and
regeneration following injury.

In conclusion, the behaviour of human epidermal keratinocytes in culture
resembles normal epidermis sufficiently to provide a useful experimental model in
the quest for stem cells.

## Heterogeneity of dividing keratinocytes

Before discussing the behaviour of epidermal stem cells in culture, we must consider what is known of their properties *in vivo*. Kinetic studies suggest that the dividing population of keratinocytes in the epidermis is heterogeneous and that not all dividing cells are stem cells (Potten, 1981; Potten *et al.* 1982). A model has been put forward in which the daughters of stem cells that are committed to terminally differentiate nevertheless may go through a limited number of further divisions before becoming post-mitotic; these cells have been called transit amplifying cells (Potten, 1981; Potten *et al.* 1982). The existence of transit amplifying cells has profound implications for understanding how proliferation in the epidermis is controlled, since stem and transit amplifying cells might respond in different ways to carcinogens or epidermal wounding.

In order to test models of the kinetic organization of the epidermis, it would be useful to be able to distinguish between stem cells and transit amplifying cells by criteria other than their proliferative capacity. There is some evidence *in vivo* that the two populations may differ in cell cycle parameters, with stem cells having a longer cycle time and shorter S phase than transit amplifying cells (Potten *et al.* 1982). It is also possible that the cells occupy different positions, or 'niches' in the basal layer (Schofield, 1978; Potten, 1981; Lavker & Sun, 1983). So far no molecular markers of the two types of keratinocyte have been identified.

The fact that keratinocyte cultures eventually senesce after several passages might suggest that stem cells do not exist in culture. However, cultures grafted onto suitable recipients form normal epidermis that survives for years and thus stem cells must persist, at least in early passage cultures (Gallico *et al.* 1984). There is, furthermore, strong evidence for proliferative heterogeneity in culture. Subpopulations of keratinocytes that differ in cell cycle time and rate of DNA synthesis have been identified (Dover & Potten, 1983; Jensen *et al.* 1985*b*; Albers *et al.* 1986) and withdrawal from the cell cycle has been shown to occur in a specific subset of dividing cells (Albers *et al.* 1987). The proliferative potential of individual keratinocytes is inversely correlated with their size (Barrandon & Green, 1985) and may be influenced by their neighbours (Hall and Watt, in preparation).

Three distinct types of colony are formed by individual keratinocytes in culture (Barrandon & Green, 1987*a*). One, known as a holoclone, is distinguished by a high reproductive capacity in the absence of terminal differentiation (Fig. 2A). A second, the paraclone, consists of cells which stop dividing after a few rounds of mitosis and undergo terminal differentiation (Fig. 2C). Meroclones (Fig. 2B) are a mixture of cells of different growth potential and represent a transitional stage between a holoclone and a paraclone. The transitions from holo- to mero- to paraclone are unidirectional and result in a progressive restriction of growth potential (Barrandon & Green, 1987*a*). If the founder cells of holoclones are stem cells and those of paraclones transit amplifying cells this would fit well with the kinetic models of epidermis *in vivo* (e.g. Potten, 1981).

## Growth stimulators and inhibitors

Proliferation in the epidermis depends not only on the nature and size of the

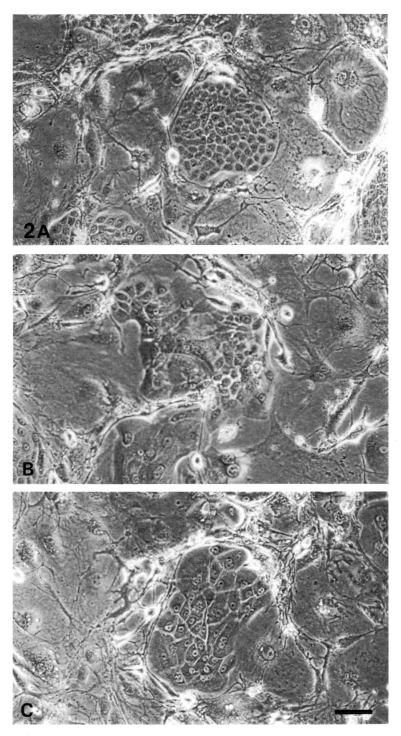

Fig. 2. Keratinocyte colonies of different morphologies, surrounded by a feeder layer of 3T3 cells (nomenclature of Barrandon and Green, 1987*a*): A. Holoclone. B. Meroclone. C. Paraclone. Bar, 100 μm. A. Reproduced from Watt (1988), with permission from Cambridge University Press.

proliferative cell compartment, but also on the growth regulatory molecules to which it responds. A number of careful studies of the growth requirements of human epidermal keratinocytes in culture have identified a range of factors that stimulate growth rate (Rheinwald & Green, 1975; Green, 1978; Boyce & Ham, 1983; Allen-Hoffmann & Rheinwald, 1984). Cholera toxin, for example, has a potent effect in increasing the overall rate of cell proliferation and increases the proportion of small cells in the colonies (Green, 1978). EGF and the related growth factor, TGFα, prolong the number of cell generations before senescence without affecting the growth rate; these molecules act indirectly by stimulating lateral migration of cells in the dividing peripheral zone of expanding colonies (Rheinwald & Green, 1977; Barrandon & Green, 1987b). In contrast to these stimulating effects, TGFβ inhibits keratinocyte proliferation and causes cells to accumulate in $G_1$ (Shipley et al. 1986).

Observations of the effect of factors on the overall growth rate of the cultures do not provide information as to how those factors act. Thus, since the dividing population is heterogeneous we need to know whether the different categories of dividing cells respond differently to each growth stimulator or inhibitor (Jensen et al. 1985a). It is also important to know whether such molecules act by reducing the cell cycle time of cells already in cycle or by recruiting more cells into the dividing population (Green, 1978).

Evidence for further complexity in the mechanisms regulating keratinocyte proliferation comes from the discovery that keratinocytes synthesize molecules that are known to regulate their own growth. Thus, normal keratinocytes in culture express TGF α and β and also have receptors for them (Shipley et al. 1986; Coffey et al. 1987; Nanney et al. 1984; Green & Couchman, 1985; Taylor et al. 1985). Exogenous TGFα stimulates endogenous TGFα synthesis (Coffey et al. 1987). These observations would be compatible with a model of autocrine growth control, as proposed by Sporn & Todaro (1980).

## Co-ordination of proliferation and terminal differentiation: epidermal homeostasis

When the epidermis is in a steady state, such that the rates of cell production and loss are equal, then the probability that the daughter of a stem cell division will enter the terminal differentiation pathway is 1 in 2 or 0·5. This value would be expected to change under some conditions; for example it would decrease during the wave of proliferation that follows injury (e.g. see Pinkus, 1952).

The differentiation rate and differentiation probability can be calculated for keratinocytes growing as a monolayer in medium containing a low concentration of calcium ions, by measuring the rate of appearance of [³H]thymidine-labelled involucrin-positive cells with time after a pulse of [³H]thymidine. Under those conditions approximately 4 cells per 5000 cells start to express involucrin every hour and the differentiation probability is 0·02, indicating a bias towards self-renewal at the expense of terminal differentiation (Dover & Watt, 1987). Treatment of cells with TPA, which is known to induce premature terminal differentiation (Parkinson

& Emmerson, 1982) causes a dramatic and dose-dependent increase in the differentiation rate (Watt and Dover, in preparation).

Although withdrawal from the cell cycle is the first stage in terminal differentiation, growth arrest may not be a sufficient signal for induction of differentiation, since, for example, growth arrest by TGF$\beta$ is reversible (Shipley *et al.* 1986) and arrest in [$^3$H]thymidine does not increase the proportion of cells expressing involucrin (Watt *et al.* 1988). A number of potential signals for terminal differentiation have been identified, including cell enlargement (Watt & Green, 1981) and restricted substratum contact (Watt *et al.* 1988); how these signals may be linked is currently the subject of speculation (Watt, 1988).

The ability of the epidermis to modulate its proliferation and terminal differentiation rates in response to signals such as wounding argues for some form of communication between the dividing and differentiating cell compartments. In one model put forward many years ago, it was proposed that the terminally differentiating cells secrete a factor that inhibits proliferation in the dividing cell compartment; loss of terminally differentiated cells through injury would relieve the inhibition until increased proliferation had restored the size of the differentiation compartment (Bullough, 1962). One candidate for such a factor is TGF$\beta$: in normal mouse epidermis the level of expression is low, but when the epidermis is treated with TPA, TGF$\beta$ is transiently induced at high levels in the terminally differentiated cells; this coincides with the transient inhibition of DNA synthesis in the basal layer that precedes TPA-induced hyperplasia (Akhurst *et al.* 1988). Also of interest is the observation that TGF$\alpha$ transcripts are expressed in all the layers of human epidermis (Coffey *et al.* 1987) but that EGF/TGF$\alpha$ receptors are lost from the cell surface during terminal differentiation (Nanney *et al.* 1984; Green & Couchman, 1985). A further potential regulator of homeostasis is a pentapeptide, purified from mouse epidermis, that inhibits proliferation of mouse and human keratinocytes in culture (Elgjo *et al.* 1986; Watt and Elgjo, in preparation). Finally, since junctional communication is lost during terminal differentiation, a role in regulating homeostasis has been proposed for gap junctions (Kam *et al.* 1987). Clearly, further experiments are required to test these ideas.

## Future prospects

It is clear that there has been some progress towards identifying epidermal stem cells in culture; towards analysing the factors that regulate their proliferation; and towards discovering how proliferation and terminal differentiation are co-ordinated. Several new experimental tools offer promise for future research. These include retroviral lineage markers (Price, 1987); keratinocytes in which terminal differentiation is partially or completely blocked (Rheinwald & Beckett, 1980; Taylor-Papadimitriou *et al.* 1982; Adams & Watt (1988); and immortal lines that nevertheless contain cells capable of undergoing terminal differentiation (Baden *et al.* 1987; Boukamp *et al.* 1988). For example, retroviral vectors carrying bacterial $\beta$-galactosidase as a marker gene can be introduced into keratinocytes and their progeny identified using a histochemical stain for $\beta$-galactosidase (Fig. 3; Price *et al.* 1987; Hall and Watt, in preparation); this allows analysis of the fate of the progeny of individual cells without having to work with isolated clones. Such approaches may shed light on the old question of the extent to which stem cell divisions are driven by an internal clock or subject to environmental regulation (see Wolpert & Lillien, 1989; Raff, 1989).

## References

ADAMS, J. C. & WATT, F. M. (1988). An unusual strain of human keratinocytes, which do not stratify or undergo terminal differentiation in culture. *J. Cell Biol.* **107**, 1927–1938.

AKHURST, R. J., FEE, F. & BALMAIN, A. (1988). Localized production of TGF-$\beta$ mRNA in tumour promoter-stimulated mouse epidermis. *Nature, Lond.* **331**, 363–365.

ALBERS, K. M., GREIF, F., SETZER, R. W. & TAICHMAN, L. B. (1987). Cell-cycle withdrawal in cultured keratinocytes. *Differentiation* **34**, 236–240.

ALBERS, K. M., SETZER, R. W. & TAICHMAN, L. B. (1986). Heterogeneity in the replicating population of cultured human keratinocytes. *Differentiation* **31**, 134–140.

ALLEN-HOFFMANN, B. L. & RHEINWALD, J. G. (1984). Polycyclic aromatic hydrocarbon mutagenesis of human epidermal keratinocytes in culture. *Proc. natn. Acad. Sci. U.S.A.* **81**, 7802–7806.

BADEN, H. P., KUBILUS, J., KVEDAR, J. C., STEINBERG, M. L. & WOLMAN, S. R. (1987). Isolation and characterization of a spontaneously arising long-lived line of human keratinocytes (NM1). *In Vitro* **23**, 205–213.

BARRANDON, Y. & GREEN, H. (1985). Cell size as a determinant of the clone-forming ability of human keratinocytes. *Proc. natn. Acad. Sci. U.S.A.* **82**, 5390–5394.

BARRANDON, Y. & GREEN, H. (1987a). Three clonal types of keratinocyte with different capacities for multiplication. *Proc. natn. Acad. Sci. U.S.A.* **84**, 2302–2306.

BARRANDON, Y. & GREEN, H. (1987b). Cell migration is essential for sustained growth of keratinocyte colonies: the roles of transforming growth factor-$\alpha$ and epidermal growth factor. *Cell* **50**, 1131–1137.

BOUKAMP, P., PETRUSSEVSKA, R. T., BREITKREUTZ, D., HORNUNG, J., MARKHAM, A. & FUSENIG, N. E. (1988). Normal keratinization in a spontaneously immortalized aneuploid human keratinocyte cell line. *J. Cell Biol.* **106**, 761–771.

BOYCE, S. T. & HAM, R. G. (1983). Calcium-regulated differentiation of normal human epidermal keratinocytes in chemically defined clonal culture and serum-free serial culture. *J. invest. Derm.* **81**, 33s–40s.

BULLOUGH, W. S. (1962). The control of mitotic activity in adult mammalian tissues. *Biol. Rev.* **37**, 307–342.

COFFEY, R. J. JR, DERYNCK, R., WILCOX, J. N., BRINGMAN, T. S., GOUSTIN, A. S., MOSES, H. L. & PITTELKOW, M. R. (1987). Production and auto-induction of transforming growth factor-$\alpha$ in human keratinocytes. *Nature, Lond.* **328**, 817–820.

DOVER, R. & POTTEN, C. S. (1983). Cell cycle kinetics of cultured human epidermal keratinocytes. *J. invest. Derm.* **80**, 423–429.

DOVER, R. & WATT, F. M. (1987). Measurement of the rate of epidermal terminal differentiation: expression of involucrin by S phase keratinocytes in culture and in psoriatic plaques. *J. invest. Derm.* **89**, 349–352.

ELGJO, K., REICHELT, K. L., HENNINGS, H., MICHAEL, D. & YUSPA, S. H. (1986). Purified epidermal pentapeptide inhibits proliferation and enhances terminal differentiation in cultured mouse epidermal cells. *J. invest. Derm.* **87**, 555–558.

FUSENIG, N. E. (1986). Mammalian epidermal cells in culture. In *Biology of the Integument*, vol. 2 (ed. J. Bereiter-Hahn, A. G. Matoltsy & K. S. Richards), pp. 409–442. Berlin: Springer-Verlag.

GALLICO, G. G. III, O'CONNOR, N. E., COMPTON, C. C., KEHINDE, O. & GREEN, H. (1984). Permanent coverage of large skin wounds with autologous cultured human epithelium. *New Engl. J. Med.* **311**, 448–451.

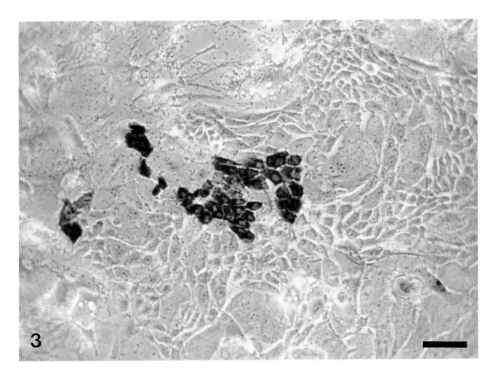

Fig. 3. Keratinocytes infected with a retroviral lineage marker encoding $\beta$-galactosidase. Infected cells are stained blue. Bar, 100 $\mu$m.

GREEN, H. (1978). Cyclic AMP in relation to proliferation of the epidermal cell: a new view. *Cell* **15**, 801–811.

GREEN, H. (1980). The keratinocyte as differentiated cell type. *Harvey Lectures* **74**, 101–139.

GREEN, M. R. & COUCHMAN, J. R. (1985). Differences in human skin between the epidermal growth factor receptor distribution detected by EGF binding and monoclonal antibody recognition. *J. invest. Derm.* **85**, 239–245.

JENSEN, P. K. A. & BOLUND, L. (1988). Low $Ca^{2+}$ stripping of differentiating cell layers in human epidermal cultures: an *in vitro* model of epidermal regeneration. *Expl Cell Res.* **175**, 63–73.

JENSEN, P. K. A., NØRGÅRD, J. O. R. & BOLUND, L. (1985*a*). Changes in basal cell subpopulations and tissue differentiation in human epidermal cultures treated with epidermal growth factor and cholera toxin. *Virchows Arch. Zellpath.* **49**, 325–340.

JENSEN, P. K. A., PEDERSEN, S. & BOLUND, L. (1985*b*). Basal-cell subpopulations and cell-cycle kinetics in human epidermal explant cultures. *Cell Tiss. Kinet.* **18**, 207–215.

KAM, E., WATT, F. M. & PITTS, J. D. (1987). Patterns of junctional communication in skin: studies on cultured keratinocytes. *Expl Cell Res.* **173**, 431–438.

LAVKER, R. M. & SUN, T.-T. (1983). Epidermal stem cells. *J. invest. Derm.* **81**, 121s–127s.

NANNEY, L. B., MAGID, M., STOSCHEK, C. M. & KING, L. E. JR (1984). Comparison of epidermal growth factor binding and receptor distribution in normal human epidermis and epidermal appendages. *J. invest. Derm.* **83**, 385–393.

PARKINSON, E. K. & EMMERSON, A. (1982). The effects of tumour promoters on the multiplication and morphology of cultured human epidermal keratinocytes. *Carcinogenesis* **3**, 525–531.

PINKUS, H. (1952). Examination of the epidermis by the strip method. II. Biometric data on regeneration of the human epidermis. *J. Invest. Dermatol.* **19**, 431–447.

POTTEN, C. S. (1981). Cell replacement in epidermis (keratopoiesis) via discrete units of proliferation. *Int. Rev. Cytol.* **69**, 271–318.

POTTEN, C. S. & MORRIS, R. J. (1989). Epithelial stem cells *in vivo. J. Cell Sci. Suppl. 10*, 45–62.

POTTEN, C. S., WICHMANN, H. E., LOEFFLER, M., DOBEK, K. & MAJOR, D. (1982). Evidence for discrete cell kinetic subpopulations in mouse epidermis based on mathematical analysis. *Cell Tiss. Kinet.* **15**, 305–320.

PRICE, J. (1987). Retroviruses and the study of cell lineage. *Development* **101**, 409–419.

PRICE, J., TURNER, D. & CEPKO, C. (1987). Lineage analysis in the vertebrate nervous system by retrovirus-mediated gene transfer. *Proc. natn. Acad. Sci. U.S.A.* **84**, 156–160.

RAFF, M. C. & LILLIEN, L. E. (1989). Differentiation of a bipotential glial progenitor cell: what controls the timing and choice of developmental pathway? *J. Cell Sci. Suppl. 10*, 77–83.

READ, J. & WATT, F. M. (1988). A model for in vitro studies of epidermal homeostasis: proliferation and involucrin synthesis by cultured human keratinocytes during recovery after stripping off the suprabasal layers. *J. invest. Derm.* **90**, 739–743.

RHEINWALD, J. G. (1980). Serial cultivation of normal human epidermal keratinocytes. *Meth. Cell Biol.* **21**, 229–254.

RHEINWALD, J. G. & BECKETT, M. A. (1980). Defective terminal differentiation as a consistent and selectable character of malignant human keratinocytes. *Cell* **22**, 629–632.

RHEINWALD, J. G. & GREEN, H. (1975). Serial cultivation of strains of human epidermal keratinocytes: the formation of keratinizing colonies from single cells. *Cell* **6**, 331–344.

RHEINWALD, J. G. & GREEN, H. (1977). Epidermal growth factor and the multiplication of cultured human epidermal keratinocytes. *Nature, Lond.* **265**, 421–424.

SCHOFIELD, R. (1978). The relationship between the spleen colony-forming cell and the haemopoietic stem cell. A hypothesis. *Blood Cells* **4**, 7–25.

SHIPLEY, G. D., PITTELKOW, M. R., WILLE, J. J. JR, SCOTT, R. E. & MOSES, H. L. (1986). Reversible inhibition of normal human prokeratinocyte proliferation by type $\beta$ transforming growth factor – growth inhibitor in serum-free medium. *Cancer Res.* **46**, 2068–2071.

SPORN, M. B. & TODARO, G. J. (1980). Autocrine secretion and malignant transformation of cells. *New Engl. J. Med.* **303**, 878–880.

TAYLOR, A., HOGAN, B. L. M. & WATT, F. M. (1985). Biosynthesis of EGF receptor, transferrin receptor and colligin by cultured human keratinocytes and the effects of retinoic acid. *Expl Cell Res.* **159**, 47–54.

TAYLOR-PAPADIMITRIOU, J., PURKIS, P., LANE, E. B., MCKAY, I. A. & CHANG, S. E. (1982).

Effects of SV40 transformation on cytoskeleton and behavioural properties of human keratinocytes. *Cell Differ.* **11**, 169–180.

WATT, F. M. (1988). The epidermal keratinocyte. *BioEssays* **8**, 163–167.

WATT, F. M., BOUKAMP, P., HORNUNG, J. & FUSENIG, N. E. (1987). Effect of growth environment on spatial expression of involucrin by human epidermal keratinocytes. *Arch. Derm. Res.* **279**, 335–340.

WATT, F. M. & GREEN, H. (1981). Involucrin synthesis is correlated with cell size in human epidermal cultures. *J. Cell Biol.* **90**, 738–742.

WATT, F. M., JORDAN, P. W. & O'NEILL, C. H. (1988). Cell shape controls the terminal differentiation of human epidermal keratinocytes. *Proc. natn. Acad. Sci. U.S.A.* **85**, 5576–5580.

WOLPERT, L. (1989). Stem cells: a problem in asymmetry. *J. Cell Sci. Suppl.* *10*, 1–9.

*J. Cell Sci. Suppl. 10, 95–114 (1988)*
*Printed in Great Britain © The Company of Biologists Limited 1988*

# Stem cells in mammary gland differentiation and cancer

PHILIP S. RUDLAND AND ROGER BARRACLOUGH

*Cancer and Polio Research Fund Laboratories, Department of Biochemistry, University of Liverpool, PO Box 147, Liverpool L69 3BX, UK*

## Summary

Evidence based on ultrastructure and immunocytochemical staining suggests that morphological gradations between epithelial and myoepithelial cells, and possibly between epithelial and alveolar-like cells, can occur in terminal ductal structures of rat and human mammary glands. In neoplastic disease the benign, carcinogen-induced rat and benign, human mammary tumours can contain epithelial, myoepithelial-like and alveolar-like cells, whereas their malignant counterparts mainly contain only epithelial-like cells. Clonal epithelial cell lines from normal rat mammary glands, from benign tumours and from SV40-transformed human mammary cultures can differentiate to either myoepithelial-like or alveolar-like cells. In those of the rat, the differentiation processes occur in steps, intermediate cells along the myoepithelial-like pathway resemble the morphological intermediates in the terminal ductal structures *in vivo*. Changes in specific polypeptides characterize each of the intermediate cells *in vitro*. One of the earliest increases observed in the myoepithelial-like pathway *in vitro* is that due to a novel protein p9Ka, whereas the major increases in Thy-1 antigen and the basement membrane proteins laminin and type IV collagen occur at later steps. The nucleotide sequence of the gene for p9Ka is related to that of the small, regulatory calcium-binding proteins, and antibodies raised to synthetic fragments of its predicted amino acid sequence react with only myoepithelial cells within the rat mammary parenchyma. Increases in the production of p9Ka and Thy-1 are largely due to increases in their messenger RNAs, possibly arising at the level of transcription of the DNA, whereas the increases in production of laminin and type IV collagen occur at a post-transcriptional level. The normal transcriptional promoter sequences of TATA or CAAT are not found adjacent to the genes for p9Ka or Thy-1. Cells and cell lines from malignant rat mammary tumours of increasing metastatic potential and from malignant areas of human ductal carcinomas largely fail to yield fully differentiated myoepithelial-like or alveolar-like cells in culture; however, weakly metastasizing rat cells yield variants which may retain a vestige of the myoepithelial phenotype. It is suggested that novel regulatory transcriptional element(s) may control the production of some of the proteins along the normal myoepithelial-like pathway, and that these elements may be relatively unique in their capacity to become inoperative in the malignant breast cancer cell.

## Identification of cell types and development of the normal mammary gland

The mammary glands of both adult rats and humans consist of a system of branching ducts terminating in alveoli and embedded in a fatty stroma (Raynaud, 1961). The mammary ducts are composed of one or more layers of cuboidal, epithelial cells, some of which border a lumen that is continuous throughout the ductal system. The epithelial cells are surrounded by a layer of elongated, myoepithelial cells (Hollman, 1974; Vorherr, 1974). These two fully differentiated cell types have been distinguished in the past by their characteristic ultrastructural morphologies. The ductal epithelial cells possess apical microvilli and specialized junctional complexes

Key words: mammary gland, stem cells *in vivo* and *in vitro*, differentiation and cancer.

with associated desmosomes, whereas the myoepithelial cells possess smooth muscle-like myofilaments with pinocytotic vesicles and basement membranes on their basal surfaces. A third functionally differentiated cell type, the secretory cell, is found in the mammary alveoli. This cell type is characterized by its ultrastructure and, during lactation, by the synthesis and secretion of milk products (Ozzello, 1971; Radnor, 1971).

More recently, immunocytochemical stains have been used to distinguish between the different cell types (Table 1). In the rat, the epithelial cells are stainable by antisera to milk fat globule membrane (MFGM) (Warburton *et al.* 1982*a*) and keratin monoclonal antibody (MAB) LE61 (Taylor-Papadimitriou *et al.* 1983). The myoepithelial cells can be stained by antisera to vimentin, actin, myosin (Dulbecco, 1982; Warburton *et al.* 1982*a*), keratin MAB LP34 (Taylor-Papadimitriou *et al.* 1983; Warburton *et al.* 1987), and by the lectins *Griffonia simplicifolia*-1 (GS-1) and pokeweed mitogen (Hughes, 1988). The basement membrane, which is probably synthesized at least in part by the myoepithelial cells, stains with antisera to laminin, type IV collagen and Thy-1 antigen (Dulbecco, 1982; Rudland *et al.* 1982; Warburton *et al.* 1982*a*; Monaghan *et al.* 1983). In the human gland, antisera (Heyderman *et al.* 1979) and MABs (Foster *et al.* 1982; Taylor-Papadimitriou *et al.* 1983) to MFGM are primarily against a single glycoprotein termed epithelial membrane antigen (EMA) (Ormerod *et al.* 1984; McIlhinney *et al.* 1985), whilst the two lectins (Hughes, 1988) and the antiserum to human keratin (Gusterson *et al.* 1982) fail to show any discriminatory staining. MAB LICR-LON-23.10 which recognizes basal cells of the skin and blood vessels (Gusterson *et al.* 1985) and MABs to the common acute lymphoblastic leukaemia antigen (CALLA) (Gusterson *et al.* 1986) preferentially recognize the human myoepithelial cells. The secretory alveolar cells from both species are characterized by being stainable by peanut lectin (Newman *et al.* 1979) and, during lactation, by antisera to their respective caseins (Rudland *et al.* 1983*a*; Earl & McIlhinney, 1985) (Table 1).

Table 1. *Summary of the immunocytochemical staining patterns of rat and human mammary cells* in vivo

| Reagent[a] | Epithelial cells | Myoepithelial cells | Alveolar cells |
|---|---|---|---|
| Anti-MFGM[b], EMA[c]; MABs to EMA | + | − | + |
| Peanut lectin alone | − | − | + |
| Anti-caseins[b,c] | − | − | + |
| Keratin MAB LE61 | + | − | + |
| | | | |
| Anti-actin/myosin | − | + | − |
| Keratin MAB LP34 | −[b](±)[c] | + | − |
| MAB LICR-LON-23.10 | − | +[c] | − |
| MABs to CALLA | − | + | − |
| GS-1/PWM lectins | − | +[b] | − |
| Anti-laminin/type IV collagen/Thy-1[b,c] | − | +[d] | − |

[a] Abbreviations as used in text; MAB, monoclonal antibody ±, weakly stained; [b] rat; [c] human; [d] basement membrane adjacent to myoepithelial cells.

The development of the mammary parenchyma takes place predominantly after birth, but prior to puberty (Myers, 1919; Dawson, 1934), by the lengthening and branching of primative ducts within the mammary fat pad. During this period of growth, the ducts terminate in globular structures called terminal end buds in rats (TEBs), which contain most of the dividing parenchymal cells (Dawson, 1934; Russo *et al.* 1982). The number of globular structures reaches a maximum in rats of about 20 days old (Russo *et al.* 1982), and in humans of about 13 years old (Dawson, 1934) (Fig. 1A). Thereafter the number rapidly declines as the globular structures differentiate to terminal ducts and alveolar buds in rats (Russo & Russo, 1978) or to terminal ductal alveolar units (TDLUs) in humans (Dawson, 1934) (Fig. 1B). The alveolar buds and TDLUs are the direct precursors of the secretory alveoli. In rats the TEBs and to a lesser extent the alveolar buds consist of a heterogeneous collection of cells which show a gradation in ultrastructural and immunocytochemical-staining characteristics towards the epithelial cells on the one hand, and to the myoepithelial cells of the subtending duct on the other hand (Williams & Daniel, 1983; Ormerod & Rudland, 1984). Some of the terminal structures in humans also show some evidence for similar morphological gradations (Stirling & Chandler, 1976; Smith *et al.* 1984; Rudland& Hughes, 1989). Thus some evidence exists *in vivo* relating epithelial cells

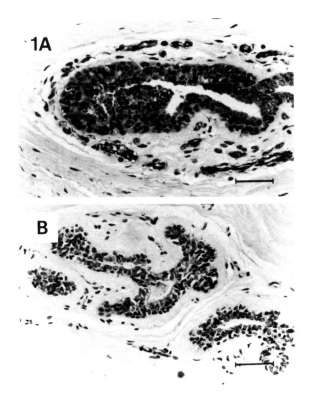

Fig. 1. Histological sections of human terminal ductal structures. Mammary gland from: A, 13 year old girl showing a terminal end-bud in longitudinal section; B, 14 year old girl showing a terminal ductal-lobuloalveolar unit. Bars, 50 μm.

to myoepithelial cells on the one hand and to alveolar cells on the other hand, although this evidence is stronger in the rat than in the human at present.

## Development and cellular structure of mammary tumours

The susceptibility of the rat mammary gland to chemical carcinogenesis correlates with the presence in the gland of TEBs and terminal ducts (Russo *et al.* 1977). The tumours induced by dimethyl-benzanthracene (DMBA) (Huggins *et al.* 1961) or nitrosomethyl urea (NMU) (Gullino *et al.* 1975) are predominantly cytologically benign in the authors' experience (Williams *et al.* 1981). These relatively benign tumours contain areas of epithelial and elongated, myoepithelial-like cells in duct-like arrangements (Murad & von Haam, 1972). However, many of the elongated, myoepithelial-like cells possess a more undifferentiated appearance than the myoepithelial cells of mature mammary ducts (Dunnington *et al.* 1984*a*). Hormonal stimulation of the host leads to production of a small proportion of alveolar-like cells which can synthesize casein (Supowit & Rosen, 1982). However, the amount of casein and casein mRNA produced by these cells is only 1–5 % of that produced by the alveolar cells of the lactating mammary glands in normal rats, when animals bearing the tumours are subsequently mated (Herbert *et al.* 1978; Supowit & Rosen, 1982; Rudland *et al.* 1983*a*). Chemical induction in partially immune-deficient rats that are then subjected to nonspecific immunostimulation can produce metastatic tumours (Table 2) which disseminate widely, some like the human disease (Kim, 1979). However, no cells with any myoepithelial characteristics are seen in such malignant carcinomas (Dunnington *et al.* 1984*a*).

The primary carcinogens which induce mammary tumours in humans are

Table 2. *Origins of the mammary cell lines discussed*

| Mammary tissue | Cell line | Identity |
|---|---|---|
| Normal rat | Rama 704 | epithelial |
| | Rama 704E | myoepithelial-like |
| | Rama 401 | myoepithelial-like |
| Benign DMBA rat tumour | Rama 25 | epithelial |
| | Rama 25-I | epithelial/myoepithelial intermediates |
| | Rama 29 | myoepithelial-like |
| Benign DMBA syngeneic rat tumour | Rama 37 | epithelial |
| | Rama 37E5 | myoepithelial-like |
| Weakly metastasizing rat tumour, TR2CL | Rama 600 | epithelial |
| Moderately metastasizing rat tumour, TMT-081 | Rama 800 | anaplastic epithelial |
| Strongly metastasizing rat tumour, SMT-2A | Rama 900 | anaplastic epithelial |
| Normal human transformed by SV40 | SVE3 | epithelial |
| | Huma 7 | epithelial |
| | Huma 25 | myoepithelial-like |
| | Huma 62 | myoepithelial-like |
| Human ductal carcinoma | Ca2-83 | epithelial |

completely unknown, apart from two exceptions where women had been exposed to high doses of radiation after atomic bomb explosions at Hiroshima and Nagasaki (McGregor *et al.* 1977). As in rats, the most susceptible developmental stage for these radiation-induced breast cancers is probably in prepubertal/adolescent females (McGregor *et al.* 1977). The specific phenotypic feature which best correlates with increased risk of neoplastic disease in humans is the presence of atypical epithelial cell proliferations in terminal ductal structures (Wellings *et al.* 1975). These atypical structures probably represent a spectrum from benign lesions to carcinoma-in-situ (Wellings & Yang, 1983), the direct precursor to mammary carcinoma, although there are contrary views (Azzopardi, 1979). Ultrastructural (Ahmed, 1978; Azzopardi, 1979; Macartney *et al.* 1979; Gould *et al.* 1980) and immunocytochemical techniques (Albrechstein *et al.* 1981; Barsky *et al.* 1982; Bussolati *et al.* 1980; Macartney *et al.* 1979; Gusterson *et al.* 1982; 1985; 1986) have shown that some myoepithelial cells are always present in the major categories of benign breast disease (epitheliosis, adenosis and fibroadenoma), but they are almost entirely lost in infiltrating ductal carcinomas. Similarly, in the few cases examined with well-characterized reagents, pregnant/lactating women bearing benign tumours can produce neoplastic cells that secrete casein, whereas none were seen in malignant carcinomas (Earl & McIlhinney, 1985; Earl, 1987). Thus the broad pattern of malignant cell types in human breast neoplasms is similar, to some extent, to that found in the corresponding rat mammary tumours; both the myoepithelial cell and the putative alveolar cells are lost in malignant compared with nonmalignant tumours.

## Differentiation of cultured stem cell lines isolated from normal and benign neoplastic mammary glands

To determine whether one cell type can give rise to another cell type directly, it is frequently necessary to obtain immortalized cell lines cloned from a single cell, and to observe the different cell types that such a system will generate.

In the rat, limited digestion of mammary glands or carcinogen-induced mammary tumours yields 'organoids' that can subsequently adhere to the surface of a tissue culture vessel and produce growing cultures of epithelial cells (Hallowes *et al.* 1977*b*; Rudland *et al.* 1977). After a few passages most of these cells die out, but the occasional spontaneously transformed, immortalized epithelial cell is generated which can eventually be cloned (Bennett *et al.* 1978). In this way single-cell-cloned epithelial cell lines have been obtained from the normal mammary glands of 7-day-old inbred, Furth-Wistar rats (Ormerod & Rudland, 1985), from DMBA-induced benign tumours of out-bred, Sprague-Dawley rats (Bennett *et al.* 1978), or inbred, Furth-Wistar rats (Dunnington *et al.* 1983) and from an NMU-induced rat mammary tumour (Dulbecco *et al.* 1981) (summarized in Table 2). Cultures of mammoplasty specimens from otherwise normal human breasts that have been obtained in virtually the same way as those from the rat mammary glands, however, fail to undergo spontaneous transformation events, and eventually die out after several passages in culture (Hallowes *et al.* 1977*a*; Stampfer *et al.* 1980; Easty *et al.* 1980; Rudland *et al.* 1989*a*). To obviate this problem, human epithelial cells have been immortalized by transforming them with simian virus 40 (SV40) (Fig. 2) (Chang *et al.* 1983; Rudland *et al.* 1989*b*). All the rat and human epithelial cell lines discussed above behave in a similar manner (Table 2), and thus the results of one, rat mammary 25 (Rama 25) from a benign rat mammary tumour, is described in detail below.

The epithelial cell lines, both rat and human, are conveniently cultured on a plastic substratum where they grow with a cuboidal morphology (Fig. 2A). When such cultures become densely packed, small, dark, polygonal cells are formed (Fig. 2B) which can contain vacuoles or 'droplets' at their peripheries (droplet cells) (Fig. 2F) (Bennett *et al.* 1978). These droplet cells form hemispherical blisters or domes (Fig. 2F) that arise from the unidirectional pumping action of the ouabain-sensitive sodium/potassium ATPase (Paterson *et al.* 1985*a*). The overall process can be accelerated with the erythroleukaemic differentiating agent, dimethyl sulphoxide (Friend *et al.* 1971; Bennett *et al.* 1978), or retinoic acid (Rudland *et al.* 1983*b*) in the presence of the mammotrophic hormones, prolactin, estrogen, hydrocortisone and insulin. Such cultures of Rama 25 produce authenticated rat $\beta$-casein, although the small amounts (50–100× less than in lactating rat mammary glands) may reflect the neoplastic origins of this particular cell line (Warburton *et al.* 1983). The discrete morphological stages observed in the formation of the casein-secreting, doming cultures *in vitro* (Paterson *et al.* 1985*b*) are paralleled by changes in a small number of specific polypeptides (Paterson & Rudland, 1985*a*). The final casein-secreting stage resembles alveolar-like cells, particularly those found in the benign rat mammary tumours (Rudland *et al.* 1983*a*). In addition, the human mammary epithelial cell lines can also keratinize in culture (Fig. 2E), whereas this is observed infrequently in the corresponding rodent cell lines (Rudland *et al.* 1989*b*).

Although the epithelial cell lines have been single-cell cloned at least once, confluent cultures at high passage-number yield ridges of elongated cells and subconfluent cultures yield from 0·1 % (human cell lines: Rudland *et al.* 1989*b*) up to 3 % (rat cell lines: Warburton *et al.* 1982*b*; Ormerod & Rudland, 1985) of clones of cells with an elongated morphology (Fig. 2C). Similar morphological forms occur in epithelial cell lines of mouse mammary tumours (Sanford *et al.* 1961; Dexter *et al.* 1978; Hager *et al.* 1981). From a comparison of the ultrastructure and immunocyto-chemical-staining characteristics of histological sections of rat (Ormerod & Rudland, 1982; Warburton *et al.* 1982*b*) and human mammary glands (Gusterson *et al.* 1982, 1985, 1986) and of their primary cultures (Warburton *et al.* 1985; Rudland *et al.* 1989*a,b*), the elongated cells derived from such cultures are thought to be related to myoepithelial cells rather than to fibroblasts (Fig. 2D). However, the final pheno-type of these elongated cells can vary. In general, cells of a more mature myoepithelial phenotype have been derived from the epithelial cells of normal mammary glands, e.g. the rat cell lines Rama 704E (Ormerod & Rudland, 1985) and Rama 401 (Warburton *et al.* 1981*b*), than from the epithelial cells of mammary tumours, e.g. the rat cell lines Rama 29 (Bennett *et al.* 1978) and Rama 37E5

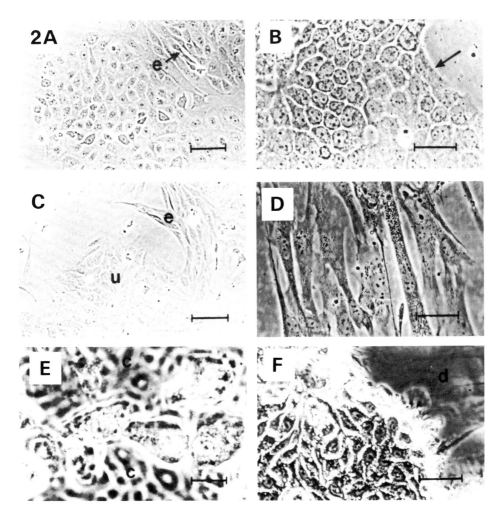

Fig. 2. Phase-contrast morphology of SV40-transformed normal human mammary cells in culture. The morphology of the corresponding rat cells is identical unless otherwise specified. A. Colony of cuboidal epithelial cells from the SV40-transformed cell line SVE3 showing the very occasional elongated cell (e). B. Cuboidal epithelial cells of a subclone of SVE3, human mammary (Huma) 7 showing more compact gray cells (<——) and dark cells. C. Elongated, myoepithelial-like cells derived from SVE3, Huma 25 which, when sparse are very elongated in appearance (e), but when more confluent appear pseudocuboidal (u) due to over-and-underlapping of cellular processes. D. Mammary fibroblastic cells. E. SVE3 cuboidal epithelial cells (c) undergoing desquamation by shedding thin, enucleated cellular residues into the medium; this rarely occurs in the corresponding rat cells. F. Small, dark, 'droplet cells' with associated hemispherical blister or dome (d) in the sheet of SVE3 cells (Rudland *et al.* 1989*b*). Bars: A,C, 100 μm; B,D,F, 50 μm; E, 20 μm.

(Dunnington *et al.* 1983) (Table 2). This result is consistent with the finding in the previous section that the better differentiated myoepithelial cells occur in normal rat mammary glands rather than in their tumours. Thus, based on the above results, the

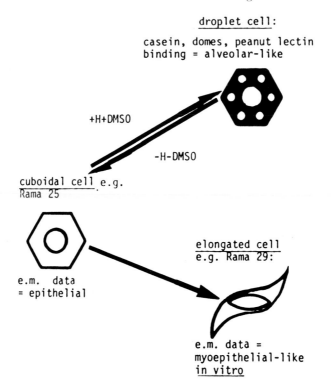

Fig. 3. Diagram of the intercellular conversions of Rama 25 epithelial cells. Rama 25 cuboidal, epithelial cells derived from a benign rat mammary tumour can differentiate to droplet cell/doming-alveolar-like cells with mammatrophic hormones prolactin, estrogen, hydrocortisone, insulin and dimethyl sulphoxide (DMSO) or to elongated, myoepithelial-like cells (e.g. the cell line Rama 29). e.m., electron microscopic.

majority of the more-elongated cells *in vitro* are classified as myoepithelial-like rather than as mature myoepithelial cells (Rudland *et al.* 1980, 1989*b*).

The epithelial cell lines can thus give rise to both alveolar-like cells and myoepithelial-like cells (Fig. 3). They are therefore possible candidates for stem cells for the mammary gland, since they can undergo *in vitro* the morphological transitions observed in terminal ductal structures *in vivo* (pp. 97–98) and in primary cultures *in vitro* (Rudland, 1987). Moreover, when grown on floating collagen gels which mimic the stromal matrix of the mammary gland, such epithelial cell lines form branched, duct-like structures reminiscent of the immature ducts found in neonatal mammary glands (Bennett, 1980; Ormerod & Rudland, 1982, 1985, 1988), further confirming their possible stem-cell properties.

## Identification and regulation of discrete differentiation stages to myoepithelial-like cells *in vitro*

Cloned cell lines that are intermediate (I) in morphology and known marker content between Rama 25 epithelial cells and elongated, myoepithelial-like cells have been

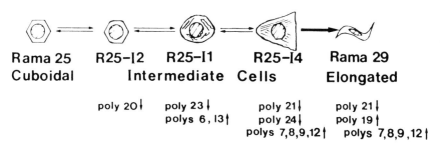

Fig. 4. Diagram of the differentiation of Rama 25 epithelial cells along a myoepithelial-like pathway. The cell lines intermediate in morphology between Rama 25 cuboidal epithelial and elongated, myoepithelial-like cells (e.g. Rama 29) are designated by R25-I etc. (Rudland *et al.* 1986). They are also thought to resemble similar cells in the direct conversion of Rama 25 cuboidal cells to elongated cells. Only the last stage is irreversible. The polypeptide changes associated with each stage are also shown; the numbers correspond to those reported previously (Paterson & Rudland, 1985*b*); polypeptide 13 is p9Ka (Barraclough *et al.* 1982).

isolated, and they form a series in the order: Rama 25 cuboidal cells, Rama 25-I2, Rama 25-I1, Rama 25-I4, and elongated cells, e.g. Rama 29 (Table 2; Fig. 4: Rudland *et al.* 1986). When grown on floating collagen gels, the intermediate cell line Rama 25-I2 forms more-mature, duct-like structures than the parental Rama 25, and ultrastructural and immunocytochemical analysis suggests that Rama 25-I1 and Rama 25-I4 resemble the intermediate cells of the terminal ductal structures *in vivo* (Rudland *et al.* 1986). The intermediate cell lines *in vitro* thus may represent the heterogeneous cells observed earlier (pp. 97–98) in budded structures *in vivo*. The above cellular order is maintained for increasing abundance of 7 polypeptides which are characteristic of elongated, myoepithelial-like cells and decreasing abundance of 4 polypeptides which are characteristic of cuboidal epithelial cells (Fig. 4) (Paterson & Rudland, 1985*b*; Rudland *et al.* 1986). The majority of these new proteins do not correspond to the known proteinaceous markers of the myoepithelial cells since the two dimensional-gel systems used to identify them cannot easily detect the lower levels of most of the known marker proteins of the myoepithelial cell.

One of the earliest detectable increases in a protein along the myoepithelial-like differentiation pathway is that due to polypeptide 13 (Fig. 4) (Rudland *et al.* 1986), a novel protein of 9000 mol.wt. termed p9Ka by Barraclough *et al.* (1982, 1984*a*). The nucleotide sequence of its gene (Fig. 5) suggests that it may be related to a class of small, regulatory, calcium-binding proteins (Fig. 6) (Barraclough *et al.* 1987*b*). The p9Ka protein may therefore serve to trigger the changes in the cytoskeleton (Paterson & Rudland, 1985*b*) which have been observed along this pathway to myoepithelial-

```
        10        20        30        40        50        60        70        80        90
GGATCCAGATGAGAGATTCTGGTACGGAGGTGTGTGTGTGTGTGTGTGTGTGTGTGTGTGTGTGTGTGTGTGTATTGCACAAGA

       100       110       120       130       140       150       160       170       180
ATGAAAACTGAAAAACAAGCAGTATATAAATGGCTCCCGGAGATTCTGAGATGCTGAGGCTTGCTTGTATGTTGCTATAGTGTATGTTGG

       190       200       210       220       230       240       250       260       270
TGCTTGGGAGCCACTGTCATGGATAGGTATGTTGCTGGGTCATCCAAGCCAGTGTGTGGACACTCAGGTACAGGAAGCAAAGTGAAGGCA

       280       290       300       310       320       330       340       350       360
TCAGCAGGCATTTTTGTTTTACGATGTTTAAATTACACTTATTTTATTTGTGTGTACGAGTGTATGGGTGGGGATGGGGCAAATGCCAAG

       370       380       390       400       410       420       430       440       450
GGGCACTTCTTGTGAGAGTCAATCTGTTCCTTCTAGCATGTGGGCTCTGGAGATCAAACTCAGGTCATTGAGCTTGGTGGCAAGCACCTC

       460       470       480       490       500       510       520       530       540
TACCTACTGAGCCACCTGTTCAACACCCACCTGTAGGCATTTGTGTTCATAGTAGTTCATAGCCCTATGAACATATAGCACCTAGGCCAA

       550       560       570       580       590       600       610       620       630
GAGAGCCTGGCTTCCCCACCCCCTCCCCTTGTACCCCAACCTCTGCCACTTCATCTCACTCCTACTAGGCAGCTGGGTTTTTTCCCTCAC

       640       650       660       670       680       690       700       710       720
TGTAGGCCCCTGGGCAGGCAGCCAGCAGCCGCGCCCAACGCTGGGAGGGAGAAGAATGGGTCAGAGGCTGGAGCTTGTGGTTGAGTTGGG

       730       740       750       760       770       780       790       800       810
GAGTGAGTAAGCTGAGTGAGGGATGGAAAACTGCTGTTGTTGAGGCCAGGCCTGGGGGGGGAGGCACAGAAGGCTGCTGGCATGAATTTCT

       820       830       840       850       860       870       880       890       900
AGAGTTTGAGTGGTAAGTTTTGCAAGTTTCAGAGCTTGAAGCACATATGAGCTTCTTGCCATCAGTGGGTACCACTCCTCTGATCTCCCT
                     ↑       ↑        ↑ ↑              ↑         ↑
       910       920       930       940       950       960       970       980       990
GGGAGTGAGGTCGGTCTCTGGAAGTGCTCTTAGAGAGTAGGTTGGAGTAGAGCACTAAAAACGGGGACAGACTGAGTGTGACTTGAGTGA

      1000      1010      1020      1030      1040      1050      1060      1070      1080
TGCCTAGCAACATATATCCAGCTCTCAACACACTGTTGGTGTGGGTTGGAGAAGGCTACTTTTGTGTCTCCTGCCCCTAGGTCTCAACGG

      1090           1100           1110           1120           1130           1140
TCACCATG GCG AGA CCC TTG GAG GAG GCC CTG GAT GTA ATA GTG TCC ACC TTC CAC AAA TAC TCA GGC
         Met Ala Arg Pro Leu Glu Glu Ala Leu Asp Val Ile Val Ser Thr Phe His Lys Tyr Ser Gly

            1160           1170           1180           1190           1200           1210
AAC GAG GGT GAC AAG TTC AAG CTG AAC AAG ACA GAG CTC AAG GAG CTA CTG ACC AGG GAG CTG CCT AGC
Asn Glu Gly Asp Lys Phe Lys Leu Asn Lys Thr Glu Leu Lys Glu Leu Leu Thr Arg Glu Leu Pro Ser

            1230      1240      1250      1260      1270      1280      1290      1300
TTC CTG GGG gtgagtggatcctgtctgtgtattgcatatgtgatgcatccccaggaggaggctggggctggagatatctatctatct
Phe Leu Gly

      1310      1320      1330      1340      1350      1360      1370      1380      1390
atctatctatctatctatctatctatctatctatctatctatctatctatctatctatatctatatcatctatctatatctatctatctatcta

      1400      1410      1420      1430      1440      1450      1460      1470      1480
catatatatatatatatatatatatatatatatatatatatatatatctctccctactcctggcgcttggtatggaaccacaatga

      1490      1500      1510      1520      1530      1540      1550      1560      1570
accatctacttcacaccagcccccgttgagacaaggcttagaatgaagttaactgaagtggcacaggaaaaccacattaggtagtcagt

      1580      1590      1600      1610      1620      1630      1640      1650      1660
gtctgaaagcacagccctagatcaggacagtctttccggtgatgtgcaacagaaatcgagtttctgcttgtgaagacatgattgtggaggc

      1670      1680      1690      1700      1710      1720      1730      1740      1750
acacaaatgcctgcagatcttcccctcaatgacaccttatcttagttaacacctccttgtcatgacagttacctatagacatagttaaaa

      1760      1770      1780      1790      1800      1810      1820      1830      1840
caagcgtggggaagatgtggtcacatcctttcccagctagcccatgtgctcatctcacagttgagccctgaggctagcacggtgtctgca

      1850      1860      1870      1880      1890      1900      1910           1920
agccttcctgagctcctggctggaggtggcgtctaactgtacctcttctacctccag AGA AGG ACA GAC GAA GCT GCA TTC
                                                           Arg Arg Thr Asp Glu Ala Ala Phe
```

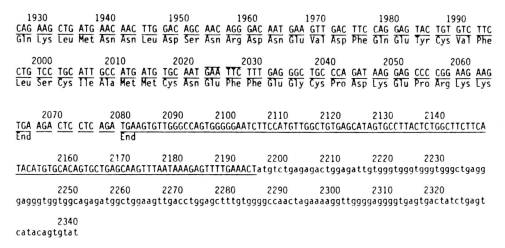

Fig. 5. The nucleotide sequence of the p9Ka gene. The sequence of the strand of DNA corresponding to the mRNA of p9Ka is shown. The arrows represent the multiple 5′ start sites of this mRNA, and the single intron and region beyond the 3′ terminus of the non-poly(A)-portion of the mRNA are shown in lower case letters. The potential p9Ka coding region is also shown with the corresponding amino acid residues beneath. The sequence corresponding to the particular complementary DNA to the mRNA for p9Ka that was used to isolate the genomic fragments is underlined. The numbers above the nucleotide sequence refer to the nucleotide immediately below the last digit (Barraclough *et al.* 1987*b*).

like cells (Warburton *et al.* 1981*a,b*). Antibodies to purified p9Ka and to a synthetic peptide corresponding to a short stretch of its deduced amino acid sequence (Barraclough *et al.* 1987*b*) bind only to myoepithelial cells in the rat mammary parenchyma, confirming the myoepithelial origins of p9Ka (Haynes, 1988). This protein and its messenger RNA coordinately increase initially in the intermediate Rama 25-I1 cells (Barraclough *et al.* 1984*a,b*; Rudland *et al.* 1986; B. R. Barraclough, unpublished results). Similarly Thy-1 protein and mRNA coordinately increase, but this increase occurs mainly in the Rama 25-I4 and elongated cells (Rudland *et al.* 1986; Barraclough *et al.* 1987*a*). These results suggest that asynchronous or stepwise regulation of the production of marker proteins for the myoepithelial-like cell is controlled mainly at the level of transcription of the DNA. This is not always the case. Thus the increase in laminin and type IV collagen which occurs mainly in the Rama 25-I1 and Rama 25-I4 cells (Rudland *et al.* 1986) is not due to major changes in their levels of mRNA (Warburton *et al.* 1986; Barraclough *et al.* 1987*a*) but, in the case of type IV collagen, to decreases in its rate of intracellular degradation (Warburton *et al.* 1986).

In the case of p9Ka, preliminary evidence suggests that at least part of the increase in its accumulation in the myoepithelial-like cells *in vitro* arises from an increased rate of transcription of its mRNA (B.R. Barraclough, unpublished observation). In many genes, regions of DNA which are important in controlling the synthesis of their mRNAs are often located immediately adjacent to those sequences that correspond to the 5′ end of their mRNAs. However, these regions, such as the TATA (Breathnach

```
p9Ka     Ala-Arg-Pro-Leu-Glu-Glu-Ala-Leu-Asp-Val-Ile-Val-Ser-Thr-Phe-His-Lys-Tyr-
                                  •                            •       •   •
BOV.     Lys-Ser-Pro-   Glu-Glu-   Leu-Lys-Gly-Ile-              Phe-Glu-Lys-Tyr-
CaBP.


         19
P9Ka     Ser-Gly-Asn-Glu-Gly-Asp-Lys-Phe-Lys-Leu-Asn-Lys-Thr-Glu-Leu-Lys-Glu-Leu-Leu-Thr-Arg-Glu-
                     ••     ••      •• G          • ••        •• •           •  •            •
BOV.     Ala-Ala-Lys-Glu-Gly-Asp-Pro-Asn-Gln-Leu-Ser-Lys-Glu-Glu-Leu-Lys-Leu-Leu-Leu-Gln-Thr-Glu-
CaBP.


         41
p9Ka     Leu-Pro-Ser-Phe-Leu-Gly-Arg-Arg-Thr-Asp-Glu-Ala-Ala-Phe-Gln-Lys-Leu-Met-Asn-Asn-Leu-
                                                                •        •  •            •
BOV.     Phe-Pro-Ser-Leu-Leu-   Lys-   Gly-   Pro-Ser-Thr-Leu-Asp-Glu-Leu-Phe-Glu-Glu-Leu-
CaBP.


         62
p9Ka     Asp-Ser-Asn-Arg-Asp-Asn-Glu-Val-Asp-Phe-Gln-Glu-Tyr-Cys-Val-Phe-Leu-Ser-Cys-Ile-Ala-Met-Met-
         ••      ••      ••  G      •  ••          •• •
BOV.     Asp-Lys-Asn-Gly-Asp-Gly-Glu-Val-Ser-Phe-Glu-Glu-Phe-Gln-Val-      Leu-         Val-
CaBP.


         85
p9Ka     Cys-Asn-Glu-Phe-Phe-Glu-Gly-Cys-Pro-Asp-Lys-Glu-Pro-Arg-Lys-Lys   COOH

BOV.         Lys-                                 Lys Ile Ser Gln
CaBP.
```

Fig. 6. The potential amino acid sequence of p9Ka and its relationship to the class of small, regulatory calcium-binding proteins. Amino acids are shown using the three letter code and are arranged to maximize the homology with the bovine intestinal calcium-binding protein (BOV CaBP), common residues are shown in bold type. The stars between the sequences show the preferred types of amino acid side chains in the general structure of the calcium-binding region of the small regulatory calcium-binding proteins: *, hydrophobic residue; **, oxygen-containing residue; and G, glycine. The helix, loop, helix arrangements of the calcium-binding sites are indicated by underscoring: helix, thin line; calcium-binding loop, thick line; and linker sequence, broken line (residues 41–53) (Barraclough & Rudland, 1988).

& Chambon, 1981) and CAAT (Benoist *et al.* 1980) consensus sequences are not found close to the p9Ka gene corresponding to p9Ka mRNA. In at least two other such cases, the murine Thy-1 gene (Giguere *et al.* 1985; Ingraham & Evans, 1986) and the 3-hydroxy-3-methylglutaryl coenzyme A reductase gene (Reynolds *et al.* 1984), multiple initiation sites for the transcription of the mRNAs have been reported, and this is also the case for the mRNA for p9Ka (Barraclough *et al.* 1987*b*). Thus it is possible that the genes for p9Ka and Thy-1 may contain a common or closely related novel promoter which regulates their expression between epithelial and myoepithelial-like cells.

## Carcinoma cells are characterized by their failure to differentiate to myoepithelial cells

In the rat, a variety of epithelial cell lines have been obtained from different transplantable tumours of the mammary gland, and these show similar metastatic potentials to those of their parental tumours (Table 2). These rat cell lines have been

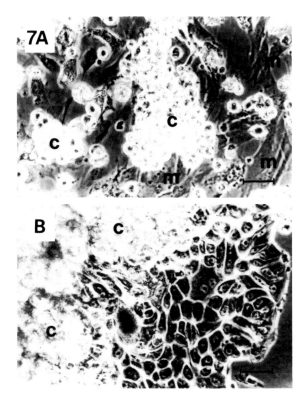

Fig. 7. Phase-contrast morphology of malignant mammary cell lines in culture. A. Clumps of cells of the cell line Rama 900 (c), isolated from the highly metastatic SMT-2A transplantable rat mammary tumour and growing with mesothelial-like feeder cells (m). B. Clumps of cells of the cell line Ca2-83 (c), isolated from a malignant human breast cancer, showing limited attachment and spreading of the epithelial cells on the substratum. Bars, 50 μm.

obtained with difficulty and grow as loosely-adherent colonies (Fig. 7A) much more slowly than cells from normal glands or benign tumours (Rudland, 1987). In contrast to cultured cells from normal and benign rat mammary glands, those from our metastasizing rat mammary carcinomas, as well as any cell lines developed from them, yield no myoepithelial cells nor any casein-producing, alveolar-like cells under the requisite hormonal conditions (Dunnington *et al.* 1984*b*; Williams *et al.* 1985; Rudland *et al.* unpublished). The weakly metastasizing Rama 600 cell line (Table 2) does contain a more elongated cellular component, but if this represents differentiation to a myoepithelial cell it is of a partial and incomplete nature, and probably reflects only a vestige of the complete pathway (Williams *et al.* 1985). Similarly, Rama 600 cells also appear to retain only a vestige of the differentiation pathway to alveolar cells (Rudland, 1988). Perhaps neoplastic transformation of the epithelial/intermediate cells results in a truncation of both differentiation pathways, and this truncation occurs earlier with increasing metastatic potential (Rudland, 1987).

Like most of the metastasizing rat mammary tumours, the culture of human mammary carcinomas has been extremely difficult (Hallowes *et al.* 1977*a*; Kirkland *et al.* 1979). Routine digestion of over 100 primary infiltrating ductal carcinomas with collagenase, by slight modifications of the methods used for the benign rat mammary tumours (pp. 99–102), yields loosely adherent, malignant-looking cell clusters (Fig. 7B) and fast-adherent, less malignant-looking epithelium on collagen gels (Hallowes *et al.* 1983; Rudland *et al.* 1985). Metastases in axillary lymph nodes and pleural effusions yield only the loosely adherent clusters, whilst normal mammary glands and benign fibroadenomas yield only fast-adherent colonies (Hallowes *et al.* 1983; Rudland *et al.* 1985). These results suggest that the fast-growing adherent sheets of epithelium from primary ductal carcinomas (Smith *et al.* 1981) do not usually represent the most-metastasizing cell populations but, as in the rat above, the latter are best represented by the slow-growing, loosely adherent aggregates (Rudland, 1987). Continued passage of one preparation of loosely adherent cell clusters has yielded a continuously growing cell strain, Ca2–83 (Table 2; Fig. 7B), which has not yet undergone a period of crisis (Rudland *et al.* 1985), unlike most other cell lines established from malignant breast cancer cells (Semen *et al.* 1976; Lasfargues *et al.* 1978; Engel *et al.* 1978). Since the fast-adherent sheets of epithelium from cultures of different human mammary tissues always contain elongated, myoepithelial-like cells, but the loosely adherent clusters do not, myoepithelial-like cells are usually found in cultures of fibroadenomas and uninvolved peritumoral tissue adjacent to carcinoma (Rudland *et al.* 1985). However, they are almost invariably missing from cultures of metastases, from the cultures of the malignant cell strain Ca2-83, and from cultures of the loosely adherent aggregates of malignant cells of ductal carcinomas (Rudland *et al.* 1985). Moreover, Ca2-83 cells fail to produce casein and alveolar-like cells under the requisite hormonal conditions (Rudland, 1987).

The retention of the differentiating ability of the benign neoplastic cells from human breasts and its loss in human carcinoma cells in culture are facts which are consistent with both the pathology of neoplastic breast disease in humans (pp. 98–99) and the above findings from culturing the equivalent rat mammary tumours. The presence of abnormal organoidal structures of epithelial and myoepithelial-like cells in some of the primary ductal carcinomas and their absence in metastatic tumours (Rudland *et al.* 1985) probably reflects progression of the primary tumour from a less-malignant to a more-malignant phase. As in the rat, these findings in humans are also more likely to be consistent with a mutational event occurring in an epithelial stem cell with gradual truncation of its differentiation pathways during the progressive phase of the disease (Rudland, 1987) than with mutational events occurring simultaneously in the epithelial stem cell and an adjacent nondifferentiat-ing epithelial cell that ultimately gives rise to the malignancy (Taylor-Papadimitriou *et al.* 1983). The loss of differentiating ability of epithelial stem cells to myoepithelial cells in the normal breast seems to be one of the few consistent changes wrought in the malignant breast cancer cell (Rudland, 1987). Thus the novel regulatory elements postulated in the previous section for transcriptional control of some of the events in the process of differentiation to myoepithelial cells may also be relatively unique in their capacity to become inactivated in the malignant breast cancer cell.

We thank our former colleagues of the now defunct Sutton Branch of the Ludwig Institute for Cancer Research for assistance and helpful discussions, Christine Hughes for expert histological and immunocytochemical assistance, and the North Western Cancer Research and the Cancer and Polio Research Funds for support in Liverpool.

# References

AHMED, A. (1978). *Atlas of the Ultrastructure of Human Breast Diseases.* Edinburgh: Churchill Livingstone.

ALBRECHSTEIN, R., NIELSON, M., WEWER, R., ENGVALL, E. & RUOSLAHTI, E. (1981). Basement membrane changes in breast cancer detected by immunohistochemical staining for laminin. *Cancer Res.* **41**, 5076–5081.

AZZOPARDI, J. G. (1979). *Problems in Breast Pathology.* Philadelphia: W. B. Saunders and Co.

BARRACLOUGH, R., DAWSON, K. J. & RUDLAND, P. S. (1982). Control of protein synthesis in cuboidal rat mammary epithelial cells in culture: changes in gene expression accompany the formation of elongated cells. *Eur. J. Biochem.* **129**, 335–341.

BARRACLOUGH, R., DAWSON, K. J. & RUDLAND, P. S. (1984a). Elongated cells derived from rat mammary cuboidal epithelial cell lines resemble cultured mesechymal cells in their pattern of protein synthesis. *Biochem. biophys. Res. Commun.* **120**, 351–358.

BARRACLOUGH, R., KIMBELL, R. & RUDLAND, P. S. (1984b). Enhanced expression of normal cell mRNA sequences accompanies the conversion of rat mammary cuboidal epithelial cells to an elongated morphology in culture. *Nucl. Acids Res.* **12**, 8097–8114.

BARRACLOUGH, R., KIMBELL, R. & RUDLAND, P. S. (1987a). Differential control of mRNA levels for Thy-1 antigen and laminin in rat mammary epithelial and myoepithelial-like cells. *J. cell. Physiol.* **131**, 393–401.

BARRACLOUGH, R. & RUDLAND, P. S. (1988). Differentiation of mammary stem cells in vivo and in vitro. In *Regulation of Differentiation in Eukaryotic Cells* (ed. A. M. Jetten). Washington: NIH Publications (in press).

BARRACLOUGH, R., SAVIN, J., DUBE, S. K. & RUDLAND, P. S. (1987b). Molecular cloning and sequence of the gene for p9Ka, a cultured myoepithelial cell protein with strong homology to S-100, a calcium-binding protein. *J. molec. Biol.* **198**, 13–20.

BARSKY, S. H., SEGAL, G. P., JANOTTA, F. & LIOTTA, L. A. (1982). Loss of basement membrane components by invasive tumours but not by their benign counterparts. *Lab. Invest. Abstract* p7A.

BENNETT, D. C. (1980). Morphogenesis of branching tubules in cultures of cloned mammary epithelial cells. *Nature, Lond.* **285**, 657–659.

BENNETT, D. C., PEACHEY, L. A., DURBIN, H. & RUDLAND, P. S. (1978). A possible mammary stem cell line. *Cell* **15**, 283–298.

BENOIST, C., O'HARE, K., BREATHNACH, R. & CHAMBON, P. (1980). The ovalbumin gene – sequence of putative control regions. *Nucl. Acids Res.* **8**, 127–142.

BREATHNACH, R. & CHAMBON, P. (1981). Organisation and expression of eucaryotic split genes coding for proteins. *A. Rev. Biochem.* **50**, 349–383.

BUSSOLATI, G., ALFANI, V., WEBER, K. & OSBORN, M. (1980). Immunocytochemical detection of actin on fixed and embedded tissues: its potential use in routine pathology. *J. Histochem. Cytochem.* **28**, 169–173.

CHANG, S. E., KEEN, J., LANE, E. B. & TAYLOR-PAPADIMITRIOU, J. (1983). Establishment and characterisation of SV40-transformed human breast epithelial cell lines. *Cancer Res.* **42**, 2040–2053.

DAWSON, E. K. (1934). A histological study of the normal mamma in relation to tumour growth. I. Early development to maturity. *Edinburgh Med. J.* **41**, 653–682.

DEXTER, D. L., KOWALSKI, H. M., BLAZER, B. A., FLIGIEL, S., VOGEL, R. & HEPPNER, G. H. (1978). Heterogeneity of tumor cells from a single mouse mammary tumor. *Cancer Res.* **38**, 3174–3181.

DULBECCO, R. (1982). Immunological markers in the study of development and oncogenesis in the rat mammary gland. *J. cell. Physiol.* (Suppl. 2), 19–22.

DULBECCO, R., HENAHAN, M., BOWMAN, M., OKADA, S., BATTIFORA, H. & UNGER, M. (1981). Generation of fibroblast-like cells from cloned mammary cells *in vitro*: a possible new cell type. *Proc. natn. Acad. Sci. U.S.A.* **78**, 2345–2349.

DUNNINGTON, D. J., KIM, U., HUGHES, C. M., MONAGHAN, P., ORMEROD, E. J. & RUDLAND, P. S. (1984a). Loss of myoepithelial cell characteristics in metastasizing rat mammary tumors relative to their nonmetastasizing counterparts. *J. natn. Cancer Inst.* **72**, 455–466.

DUNNINGTON, D. J., KIM, U., HUGHES, C. M., MONAGHAN, P. & RUDLAND, P. S. (1984b). Lack of production of myoepithelial variants by cloned epithelial cell lines derived from the TMT-081 metastasizing rat mammary tumor. *Cancer Res.* **44**, 5338–5346.

DUNNINGTON, D. J., MONAGHAN, P., HUGHES, C. M. & RUDLAND, P. S. (1983). Phenotypic instability of rat mammary tumor epithelial cells. *J. natn. Cancer Inst.* **71**, 1227–1240.

EARL, H. M. (1987). Markers of human breast differentiation and breast carcinomas, and characterisation of monoclonal antibodies to human casein. Ph.D. thesis, University of London.

EARL, H. M. & MCILHINNEY, R. A. J. (1985). Monoclonal antibodies to human casein. *Molec. Immun.* **22**, 981–991.

EASTY, G. C., EASTY, D. M., MONAGHAN, P., ORMEROD, M. G. & NEVILLE, A. M. (1980). Preparation and identification of human breast epithelial cells in culture. *Int. J. Cancer* **26**, 577–584.

ENGEL, L. W., YOUNG, M. A., TRALKA, T. S., LIPMANN, M. E., O'BRIEN, S. J. & JOYCE, M. J. (1978). Establishment and characterisation of three new continuous cell lines derived from human breast carcinomas. *Cancer Res.* **38**, 3352–3364.

FOSTER, C. S., EDWARDS, P. A. W., DINSDALE, E. A. & NEVILLE, A. M. (1982). Monoclonal antibodies to the human mammary gland. I. Distribution of determinants in non-neoplastic and extramammary tissues. *Virchows Arch. A. Cell path.* **394**, 279–293.

FRIEND, C., SCHER, W., HOLLAND, J. G. & SATO, T. (1971). Hemoglobin synthesis in murine virus-induced leukemic cells in vitro: stimulation of erythroid differentiation by dimethyl sulfoxide. *Proc. natn. Acad. Sci. U.S.A.* **68**, 378–382.

GIGUERE, V., ISOBE, K-I. & GROSVELD, F. (1985). Structure of the murine Thy-1 gene. *EMBO J.* **4**, 2017–2024.

GOULD, V. E., JAO, W. & BATTIFORA, H. (1980). Ultrastructural analysis in the differential diagnosis of breast tumours. *Pathol. Res. Pract.* **167**, 45–70.

GULLINO, P. M., PETTIGREW, H. M. & GRANTHAM, F. H. (1975). *N*-nitrosomethylurea as mammary gland carcinogen in rats. *J. natn. Cancer Inst.* **54**, 401–414.

GUSTERSON, B. A., MCILHINNEY, R. A. J., PATEL, S., KNIGHT, J., MONAGHAN, P. & ORMEROD, M. G. (1985). The biochemical and immunocytochemical characterisation of an antigen on the membrane of basal cells of the epidermis. *Differentiation* **30**, 102–110.

GUSTERSON, B. A., MONAGHAN, P., MAHENDRAN, R., ELLIS, J. & O'HARE, M. J. (1986). Identification of myoepithelial cells in human and rat breasts by anti-common acute lymphoblastic leukemia antigen antibody A12. *J. natn. Cancer Inst.* **77**, 343–349.

GUSTERSON, B. A., WARBURTON, M. J., MITCHELL, D., ELLISON, M., NEVILLE, A. M. & RUDLAND, P. S. (1982). Distribution of myoepithelial cells and basement membrane proteins in the normal breast and in benign and malignant breast diseases. *Cancer Res.* **42**, 4763–4770.

HAGER, J. C., FLIGIEL, S., STANLEY, W., RICHARDSON, A. M. & HEPPNER, G. H. (1981). Characterization of a variant producing tumor cell line from a heterogeneous strain Balb/cfC₃H mouse mammary tumor. *Cancer Res.* **41**, 1293–1300.

HALLOWES, R. C., MILLIS, R., PIGOTT, D., SHEARER, M., STOKER, M. G. P. & TAYLOR-PAPADIMITRIOU, J. (1977a). Results on a pilot study of cultures of human lacteal secretions and benign and malignant breast tumors. *J. clin. Oncol.* **3**, 81–90.

HALLOWES, R. C., PEACHEY, L. A. & COX, S. (1983). Epithelium from human breast cancers in culture: is it really cancer. *In Vitro* **19**, 286.

HALLOWES, R. C., RUDLAND, P. S., HAWKINS, R. A., LEWIS, D. J., BENNETT, D. C. & DURBIN, H. (1977b). Comparison of the effects of hormones on DNA synthesis in cell cultures of non-neoplastic and neoplastic mammary epithelium from rats. *Cancer Res.* **37**, 2492–2504.

HAYNES, G. A. (1988). Studies on a possible myoepithelial cell marker protein. Ph.D. thesis, University of London.

HERBERT, D. C., BURK, R. E. & MCGUIRE, W. L. (1978). Casein and α-lactalbumin detection in breast cancer cells by immunocytochemistry. *Cancer Res.* **38**, 221–223.

HEYDERMAN, E., STEELE, K. & ORMEROD, M. G. (1979). A new antigen on the epithelial membrane: its immunoperoxidase localisation in normal and neoplastic tissue. *J. clin. Path.* **32**, 35–39.

HOLLMAN, K. H. (1974). Cytology and fine structure of the mammary gland. In *Lactation: A Comprehensive Treatise* (ed. B. L. Larson & V. R. Smith), vol. 1, pp. 3–37. New York: Academic Press.

HUGGINS, C., GRAND, L. C. & BRILLANTES, F. P. (1961). Mammary cancer induced by a single feeding of polynuclear hydrocarbons and its suppression. *Nature, Lond.* **189**, 204–207.

HUGHES, C. M. (1988). Lectin staining of the rat mammary gland. M.Phil. thesis, University of London.

INGRAHAM, H. A. & EVANS, G. A. (1986). Characterization of two atypical promoters and alternate mRNA processing in the mouse Thy-1.2 glycoprotein gene. *Molec. cell. Biol.* **6**, 2923–2931.

KIM, U. (1979). Factors influencing metastasis of breast cancer. In *Breast Cancer* (ed. W. L. McGuire), vol. 3, pp. 1–49. New York: Plenum Publishing Corp.

KIRKLAND, W. L., YANG, N.-S., JORGENSEN, T., LONGLEY, C. & FURMANSKI, P. (1979). Growth of normal and malignant human mammary epithelial cells in culture. *J. natn. Cancer Inst.* **63**, 20–41.

LASFARGUES, E. Y., COUTINKO, W. G. & REDFIELD, E. S. (1978). Isolation of two human tumor epithelial cell lines from solid breast carcinomas. *J. natn. Cancer Inst.* **61**, 967–978.

MACARTNEY, J. C., ROXBURGH, J. & CURRAN, R. C. (1979). Intracellular filaments in human cancer cells: a histological study. *J. Path.* **129**, 13–20.

MCGREGOR, D. H., LAND, C. E., CHOI, K., TOKUOKA, S. & LIV, P. I. (1977). Breast cancer incidence among atomic bomb survivors, Hiroshima and Nagasaki, 1950–1969. *J. natn. Cancer Inst.* **59**, 799–811.

MCILHINNEY, R. A. J., PATEL, S. & GORE, M. E. (1985). Monoclonal antibodies recognise epitopes carried on both glycolipids and glycoproteins of the human milk fat globule membrane. *Biochem. J.* **227**, 155–162.

MONAGHAN, P., WARBURTON, M. J., PERUSINGHE, N. & RUDLAND, P. S. (1983). Topographical arrangement of basement membrane proteins in lactating rat mammary gland: comparison of type IV collagen, laminin, fibronectin and Thy-1 at the ultrastructural level. *Proc. natn. Acad. Sci. U.S.A.* **80**, 3344–3348.

MURAD, T. M. & VON HAAM, E. (1972). The ultrastructure of DMBA-induced breast tumors in Sprague Dawley rats. *Acta cytol.* **16**, 447–453.

MYERS, J. A. (1919). Studies on the mammary gland. IV. The histology of the mammary gland in male and female albino rats from birth to ten weeks of age. *Am. J. Anat.* **25**, 394–435.

NEWMAN, R. A., KLEIN, P. J. & RUDLAND, P. S. (1979). Binding of peanut lectin to breast epithelium, human carcinomas and a cultured rat mammary stem cell and its use as a marker of mammary differentiation. *J. natn. Cancer Inst.* **63**, 1339–1346.

ORMEROD, E. J. & RUDLAND, P. S. (1982). Mammary gland morphogenesis in vitro: formation of branched tubules in collagen gels by a cloned rat mammary cell line. *Devl Biol.* **91**, 360–375.

ORMEROD, E. J. & RUDLAND, P. S. (1984). Cellular composition and organisation of ductal buds in developing rat mammary glands: evidence for morphological intermediates between epithelial and myoepithelial cells. *Am. J. Anat.* **170**, 631–652.

ORMEROD, E. J. & RUDLAND, P. S. (1985). Isolation and characterisation of cloned epithelial cell lines from normal rat mammary glands. *In Vitro* **21**, 143–153.

ORMEROD, E. J. & RUDLAND, P. S. (1988). Mammary gland morphogenesis in vitro: extracellular requirements for the formation of tubules in collagen gels by a cloned rat mammary epithelial cell line. *In Vitro* **24**, 17–27.

ORMEROD, M. G., STEELE, K., EDWARDS, P. A. W. & TAYLOR-PAPADIMITRIOU, J. (1984). Monoclonal antibodies that react with epithelial membrane antigens. *J. exp. Path.* **1**, 263–271.

OZZELLO, L. (1971). Ultrastructure of the human mammary gland. *Pathol. Ann.* **6**, 1–58.

PATERSON, F. C., GRAHAM, J. M. & RUDLAND, P. S. (1985*a*). The effect of ionophores and related agents on the induction of doming in a rat mammary epithelial cell line. *J. cell. Physiol.* **123**, 89–100.

PATERSON, F. C. & RUDLAND, P. S. (1985*a*). Identification of novel, stage-specific polypeptides associated with the differentiation of mammary epithelial stem cells to alveolar-like cells in culture. *J. cell. Physiol.* **124**, 525–538.

PATERSON, F. C. & RUDLAND, P. S. (1985*b*). Microtubule-disrupting drugs increase the frequency of conversion of a rat mammary epithelial stem cell line to elongated, myoepithelial-like cells in culture. *J. cell. Physiol.* **125**, 135–150.

PATERSON, F. C., WARBURTON, M. J. & RUDLAND, P. S. (1985*b*). Differentiation of mammary epithelial stem cells to alveolar-like cells in culture: cellular pathways and kinetics of the conversion process. *Devl Biol.* **107**, 301–313.

RADNOR, C. J. P. (1971). A cytological study of the myoepithelial cells in the rat mammary gland. M.Sc. thesis, University of Manchester.

RAYNAUD, A. (1961). Morphogenesis of the mammary gland. In *Milk, the Mammary Gland and its Secretions* (ed. S. K. Kon & A. T. Cowie), vol. 1, pp. 3–46. New York: Academic Press.

REYNOLDS, G. A., BASU, S. K., OSBORNE, T. F., CHIN, D. J., GIL, G., BROWN, M. S., GOLDSTEIN, J. K. & LUSKEY, K. L. (1984). HMG CoA reductase: a negatively regulated gene with unusual promotor and 5′ untranslated regions. *Cell* **38**, 275–285.

RUDLAND, P. S. (1987). Stem cells and the development of mammary cancers in rats and in humans. *Cancer Metast. Rev.* **6**, 55–83.

RUDLAND, P. S. (1988). Stem cells in mammary development and cancer. In *Cellular and Molecular Biology of Experimental Mammary Cancer* (ed. D. Medina, W. Kidwell, G. Heppner & E. Anderson), pp. 9–28. NY: Plenum.

RUDLAND, P. S., BENNETT, D. C., RITTER, M. A., NEWMAN, R. A. & WARBURTON, M. J. (1980). Differentiation of a rat mammary stem cell line in culture. In *Control Mechanisms in Animal Cells* (ed. L. Jimenez de Asua, R. Levi-Montalcini, R. Shields & S. Iacobelli), pp. 341–365. New York: Raven Press.

RUDLAND, P. S., HALLOWES, R. C., COX, S. A., ORMEROD, E. J. & WARBURTON, M. J. (1985). Loss of production of myoepithelial cells and basement membrane proteins but retention of response to certain growth factors and hormones by a new malignant human breast cancer cell strain. *Cancer Res.* **45**, 3864–3877.

RUDLAND, P. S., HALLOWES, R. C., DURBIN, H. & LEWIS, D. (1977). Mitogenic activity of pituitary hormones on cell cultures of normal and carcinogen-induced tumor epithelium from rat mammary glands. *J. Cell Biol.* **73**, 561–577.

RUDLAND, P. S. & HUGHES, C. M. (1989). Immunocytochemical identification of cell types in the human mammary gland: variations in cellular markers are dependent on glandular topography and differentiation. *J. Histochem. Cytochem.* (in press).

RUDLAND, P. S., HUGHES, C. M., FERNS, S. A. & WARBURTON, N. J. (1989*a*). Characterisation of human mammary cell types in primary culture: immunofluorescent and immunocytochemical indicators of cellular heterogeneity. *In Vitro* (in press).

RUDLAND, P. S., HUGHES, C. M., TWISTON DAVIES, A. C. & WARBURTON, M. J. (1983*a*). Immunocytochemical demonstration of hormonally regulable casein in tumors produced by a rat mammary stem cell line. *Cancer Res.* **43**, 3305–3309.

RUDLAND, P. S., OLLERHEAD, G. & BARRACLOUGH, R. (1989*b*). Isolation of simian virus 40 transformed human mammary epithelial stem cell lines: differentiation to myoepithelial-like cells is associated with increased expression of large T antigen. *Devl Biol.* (in press).

RUDLAND, P. S., PATERSON, F. C., MONAGHAN, P., TWISTON DAVIES, A. C. & WARBURTON, M. J. (1986). Isolation and properties of rat cell lines morphologically intermediate between cultured mammary epithelial and myoepithial cells. *Devl Biol.* **113**, 388–405.

RUDLAND, P. S., PATERSON, F. C., TWISTON DAVIES, A. C. & WARBURTON, M. J. (1983*b*). Retinoid-specific induction of differentiation and reduction of the DNA synthesis and tumor-forming ability of a stem cell line from a rat mammary tumor. *J. natn. Cancer Inst.* **70**, 949–958.

RUDLAND, P. S., WARBURTON, M. J., MONAGHAN, P. & RITTER, M. A. (1982). Thy-1 antigen on normal and neoplastic rat mammary tissue: changes in location and amount of antigen during differentiation of cultured stem cells. *J. natn. Cancer Inst.* **68**, 799–811.

RUSSO, I. H. & RUSSO, J. (1978). Developmental stage of the rat mammary gland as determinant of its susceptibility to 7,12-dimethylbenz[a]anthracene. *J. natn. Cancer Inst.* **61**, 1439–1449.

RUSSO, J., SABY, J., ISENBURG, W. M. & RUSSO, I. H. (1977). Pathogenesis of mammary carcinomas induced in rats by 7,12-dimethylbenz[a]anthracene. *J. natn. Cancer Inst.* **59**, 435–445.

RUSSO, J., TAY, L. K. & RUSSO, I. H. (1982). Differentiation of the mammary gland and susceptibility to carcinogenesis. *Breast Cancer Res. & Treat.* **2**, 5–73.

SANFORD, K. K., DUNN, T. B., WESTFALL, B. B., COVALESKY, A. B., DUPREE, L. T. & EARLE, W. R. (1961). Sarcatomous change and maintenance of differentiation in long-term cultures of mouse mammary carcinoma. *J. natn. Cancer Inst.* **26**, 1139–1161.

SEMEN, G., HUNTER, S. J., MILLER, R. C. & DMOCHOWSKI, L. (1976). Characterisation of an established cell line (SH-3) derived from pleural effusion of a patient with breast cancer. *Cancer* **37**, 1814–1824.

SMITH, C. A., MONAGHAN, P. & NEVILLE, A. M. (1984). Basal clear cells of the normal human breast. *Virchows Arch. A. Cell. path.* **402**, 319–329.

SMITH, H. S., LAN, S., CERIANI, R., HACKETT, A. J. & STAMPFER, M. R. (1981). Clonal proliferation of nonmalignant and malignant breast epithelia. *Cancer Res.* **41**, 4637–4643.

STAMPFER, M., HALLOWES, R. C. & HACKETT, A. J. (1980). Growth of normal human mammary cells in culture. *In Vitro* **16**, 414–425.

STIRLING, J. W. & CHANDLER, J. A. (1976). The fine structure of the normal, resting terminal ductal-lobular unit of the female breast. *Virchows Arch. A. Cell. path.* **372**, 205–226.

SUPOWIT, S. C. & ROSEN, J. M. (1982). Hormonal induction of casein gene expression is limited to a small subpopulation of 7,12-dimethylbenz[a]anthracene-induced mammary cells. *Cancer Res.* **42**, 1355–1360.

TAYLOR-PAPADIMITRIOU, J., LANE, E. B. & CHANG, S. E. (1983). Cell lineages and interactions in neoplastic expression in the human breast. In *Understanding Breast Cancer, Clinical and Laboratory Concepts* (ed. M. A. Rich, J. C. Hager & P. Furmanski), pp. 215–246. New York: Marcell Dekker Inc.

VORHERR, H. (1974). *The Breast, Morphology, Physiology and Lactation*, pp. 1–18. New York: Academic Press.

WARBURTON, M. J., FERNS, S. A., HUGHES, C. M. & RUDLAND, P. S. (1985). Characterisation of rat mammary cell types in primary culture: lectin and antisera to basement membrane and intermediate filament proteins as indicators of cellular heterogeneity. *J. Cell Sci.* **79**, 287–304.

WARBURTON, M. J., FERNS, S. A., HUGHES, C. M., SEAR, C. H. J. & RUDLAND, P. S. (1987). Generation of cell types with myoepithelial and mesenchymal phenotypes during the conversion of rat mammary tumor epithelial stem cells into elongated cells. *J. natn. Cancer Inst.* **78**, 1191–1201.

WARBURTON, M. J., FERNS, S. A. & RUDLAND, P. S. (1982b). Enhanced synthesis of basement membrane proteins during the differentiation of rat mammary tumour epithelial cells into myoepithelial-like cells *in vitro*. *Expl Cell Res.* **137**, 373–380.

WARBURTON, M. J., HEAD, L. P., FERNS, S. A. & RUDLAND, P. S. (1983). Induction of differentiation in a rat mammary epithelial stem cell line by dimethyl sulphoxide and mammatrophic hormones. *Eur. J. Biochem.* **133**, 707–715.

WARBURTON, M. J., HEAD, L. & RUDLAND, P. S. (1981a). Redistribution of fibronectin and cytoskeletal proteins during the differentiation of rat mammary tumour cells. *Expl Cell Res.* **132**, 57–66.

WARBURTON, M. J., KIMBELL, R., RUDLAND, P. S., FERNS, S. A. & BARRACLOUGH, R. (1986). Control of type IV collagen production in rat mammary epithelial and myoepithelial-like cells. *J. cell. Physiol.* **128**, 76–84.

WARBURTON, M. J., MITCHELL, D., ORMEROD, E. J. & RUDLAND, P. S. (1982a). Distribution of myoepithelial cells and basement membrane proteins in the resting, pregnant, lactating, and involuting rat mammary gland. *J. Histochem. Cytochem.* **30**, 667–676.

WARBURTON, M. J., ORMEROD, E. J., MONAGHAN, P., FERNS, S. & RUDLAND, P. S. (1981b). Characterisation of a myoepithelial cell line derived from a neonatal rat mammary gland. *J. Cell Biol.* **91**, 827–835.

WELLINGS, S. R., JENSEN, H. M. & MARCUM, R. G. (1975). An atlas of subgross pathology of the human breast with special reference to possible precancerous lesions. *J. natn. Cancer Inst.* **25**, 231–275.

WELLINGS, S. R. & YANG, J. (1983). Human mammary pathology: a guide to breast cancer biology. In *Understanding Breast Cancer, Clinical and Laboratory Concepts* (ed. M. A. Rich, J. C. Hager & P. Furmanski), pp. 27–41. New York: Marcell Dekker Inc.

WILLIAMS, J. C., GUSTERSON, B., HUMPHREYS, J., MONAGHAN, P., COOMBES, R. C., RUDLAND, P. S. & NEVILLE, A. M. (1981). N-methyl-N-nitrosourea-induced rat mammary tumors: hormone responsiveness but lack of spontaneous metastasis. *J. natn. Cancer Inst.* **66**, 147–155.

WILLIAMS, J. C., GUSTERSON, B. A., MONAGHAN, P., COOMBES, R. C. & RUDLAND, P. S. (1985). Isolation and characterization of clonal cell lines from a transplantable metastasizing rat mammary tumor, TR2CL. *J. natn. Cancer Inst.* **74**, 415–428.

WILLIAMS, J. M. & DANIEL, C. W. (1983). Mammary ductal elongation: differentiation of myoepithelium and basal lamina during branching morphogenesis. *Devl Biol.* **97**, 274–290.

*J. Cell Sci. Suppl. 10*, 115–130 (1988)
Printed in Great Britain © The Company of Biologists Limited 1988

# Differentiation of fibroblast stem cells

KLAUS BAYREUTHER*, H. PETER RODEMANN, PAL. I. FRANCZ AND
KATHARINA MAIER

*Institut für Genetik, Universität Hohenheim, D 7000 Stuttgart 70, Federal Republic of Germany*

## Summary

Primary human skin fibroblasts derived from the abdomen of 45 female donors of the four age groups 1–20, 20–40, 40–60, and 60–80 years were studied in primary explant, in primary low-density mass cultures, and in primary clonal populations *in vitro*. As a function of the age of the donor, primary mitotic and postmitotic fibroblasts in the three primary cell systems analysed represent heterogeneous populations with reproducible changes in the proportions of the mitotic fibroblasts MF I, MF II, MF III, and postmitotic fibroblasts PMF IV, PMF V, PMF VI, and PMF VII. These findings make it very likely that equivalent cell types exist in the connective tissue of skin *in vivo*, and that these cells undergo reproducible changes in the proportions of the mitotic and postmitotic counterparts *in vivo* as a function of the age of the donor. Secondary mitotic human skin fibroblast populations of the cell line HH-8 *in vitro* underwent 53·6 ± 6·0 cumulative population doublings (CPD) in 302 ± 27 days. If appropriate methods are applied, mitotic fibroblasts differentiate spontaneously into postmitotic fibroblasts which are kept in stationary cultures for up to 305 ± 41 additional days. As a function of the CPD level and of the duration of stationary culture, secondary mitotic and postmitotic fibroblast populations are heterogeneous populations with reproducible changes in the proportions of mitotic fibroblasts MF I, MF II, and MF III, and postmitotic fibroblasts PMF IV, PMF V, PMF VI, and PMF VII. The seven secondary fibroblast cell types show differentiation-dependent and cell-type specific patterns of [$^{35}$S]methionine polypeptides in total soluble cytoplasmic and nuclear proteins, in secreted proteins, and in membrane bound proteins. These findings make it very likely that the morphologically recognizable primary and secondary fibroblasts differentiate spontaneously along a seven stage terminal cell lineage MF I – MF II – MF III – PMF IV – PMF V – PMF VI – PMF VII in three compartments of the fibroblast stem cell system.

## Introduction

The ontogenetic development of the normal fibroblast cell system in vertebrate and mammalian organisms *in vivo* and *in vitro* is not fully understood. *In vivo*, a metabolically inactive and a metabolically active fibroblast (Ross, 1968; Gabbiani & Rungger-Brändle, 1981), and in primary *in vitro* cell systems a differentiation sequence of three mitotic fibroblasts MF I – MF II – MF III with distinct cell-biological and biochemical properties in BN rat skin (Mollenhauer & Bayreuther, 1986) are described.

*In vitro*, normal secondary fibroblast populations have a finite mitotic lifespan which in a number of species, e.g. chicken and man is followed by cellular degeneration (Macieira-Coelho *et al.* 1976; Hayflick & Moorhead, 1961), and in

---

* To whom reprint requests and correspondence should be addressed.

Key words: primary human skin fibroblasts, secondary human skin fibroblasts, fibroblast morphotypes.

other species, e.g. mouse and rat, is succeeded by cellular transformation (Todaro & Green, 1963; Kontermann & Bayreuther, 1979). Distinct morphotypes and qualitative and/or quantitative disparities for a multitude of biochemical parameters are recorded for secondary human fibroblasts in early and late passages *in vitro* (Hayflick, 1981; Smith & Pereira-Smith, 1985; Schneider, 1985). Until now, no attempts have been undertaken to correlate the distinct fibroblast cell types with dissimilarities in biochemical parameters in secondary human fibroblast populations at non-identical cumulative population doublings levels (CPDL). As a consequence, in cell-biological and biochemical studies, secondary fibroblast populations have very often been dealt with like homogeneous, non-differentiating cell systems. Secondary BN rat fibroblast populations *in vitro* have been shown to be composed of three mitotic fibroblasts, the fibroblast cell types MF I, MF II, and MF III, which exhibit cell type-specific cell-biological and biochemical dissimilarities (Kontermann & Bayreuther, 1979). The frequencies of the different mitotic fibroblasts MF I, MF II, and MF III is a function of the CPDL of the secondary mass populations studied (Kontermann & Bayreuther, 1979).

For secondary fibroblast populations of various species (Raes & Remacle, 1983; Razin *et al.* 1977; Pereira-Smith & Smith, 1982), postmitotic fibroblasts have been shown to live for longer periods in stationary culture *in vitro*. Based on these findings it has been hypothesized that fibroblast cell systems are terminally differentiating stem cell systems (Martin *et al.* 1974; Bell *et al.* 1978).

We have provided morphological and biochemical evidence that secondary human skin fibroblasts of the cell line HH-8 *in vitro* differentiate along a terminal stem cell-like lineage with the mitotic fibroblasts MF I – MF II – MF III, the postmitotic fibroblasts PMF IV – PMF V – PMF VI, and the postmitotic and degenerating PMF VII in the three morphologically recognizable differentiating cell compartments of the fibroblast stem cell system (Bayreuther *et al.* 1988; Rodemann *et al.* 1988; Francz *et al.* 1988).

Cell-biological data obtained from studies of primary fibroblasts of the dermis of the abdomen of 45 female donors, ranging from 1 to 78 years of age, in primary explant cultures, primary low density mass culture populations, and primary clonal populations make it very likely that equivalents of the primary fibroblast cell types MF I, MF II, MF III, PMF IV, PMF V, PMF VI, and PMF VII are present in the connective tissue of the skin. Mitotic fibroblasts MF I and MF II are progressively depleted from the dermis as a function of the age of the donor. The data of comparative studies of the cell biology and biochemistry of the developing primary skin fibroblasts and of the evolving secondary skin fibroblasts in both *in vivo–in vitro* and *in vitro* cell systems make it very likely that the differentiation sequences described represent parts of a general fibroblast stem cell system.

## Materials and methods

*Primary human skin fibroblasts*

Skin biopsies from the lower abdomen of 45 female donors in the age groups of 1–20, 20–40,

40–60, and 60–80 years with 19, 7, 8, and 11 donors respectively were obtained. Parts of the biopsies were placed onto tissue culture dishes (Falcon) as explants, other parts were dissociated by enzyme treatment (collagenase/trypsin) and the cells were seeded into tissue culture dishes as primary low-density populations at low cell concentration or primary clonal populations (Rodemann & Bayreuther, 1984; Mollenhauer & Bayreuther, 1986). The three primary cell systems were cultured in DME medium, supplemented with 10 % foetal calf serum (fcs, Boehringer, lot nos. 139, 182, 881) and standard amounts of antibiotics (Rodemann & Bayreuther, 1984) in humidified $CO_2$-incubator at $37 °C$. Explant cultures were incubated for 10 days. Thereafter, they were fixed and stained as described elsewhere (Bayreuther *et al.* 1988). Low concentration cultures were seeded at a density of $1·5×10^4$ cells/cm$^2$ and maintained for 4 days: thereafter the cells were fixed and stained. For primary clonal populations, 500 cells/cm$^2$ (age group 1 and 2), 1000 cells/cm$^2$ (age group 3), and 1500 cell/cm$^2$ (age group 4) were seeded and cultured for 14 days, fixed and stained.

## Secondary human skin fibroblasts

As described elsewhere (Bayreuther *et al.* 1988), primary skin fibroblast populations of the cell line HH-8 were established and serially subcultured as secondary fibroblast populations. Preconditions and methods for the analysis of fibroblast morphology, fibroblast cell type frequencies, clone type morphology, clone type frequencies, and for the reproducible spontaneous transition of mitotic to postmitotic fibroblast populations have been reported in detail elsewhere (Bayreuther *et al.* 1988). The treatment protocols and time schedules for the experimentally induced differentiation of mitotic mass populations to postmitotic mass populations are also described elsewhere (Rodemann *et al.* 1988).

## Results

### Primary human skin fibroblasts in vitro

Primary human skin fibroblast populations were established from the abdominal skin of 45 female donors of four age groups: 1–20, 20–40, 40–60, and 60–80 years. Primary skin fibroblasts were studied in quantitative primary explant, in primary cultures of low cell density, and in primary clonal populations *in vitro*. Primary skin fibroblast populations were found to be composed of seven fibroblast cell types, the mitotic fibroblast cell types MF I, MF II, MF III, and the postmitotic fibroblasts PMF IV, PMF V, PMF VI, and the postmitotic and degenerating fibroblasts PMF VII. The mitotic fibroblast MF I is a small spindle shaped cell (Fig. 1A); fibroblast MF II is a small epithelioid cell (Fig. 1B); fibroblast MF III is a larger epithelioid cell (Fig. 1C); the postmitotic fibroblast PMF IV is a large spindle shaped cell (Fig. 1D); PMF V is a large epithelioid cell (Fig. 1E); PMF VI is the largest epithelioid cell (Fig. 1F). Fibroblast PMF VII is the degenerating cell of the fibroblast sequence (not shown). The composition of primary fibroblast populations that migrate within 7 days from the skin explants is a function of the age of the donor. Populations migrating from explants of a seven year old donor are heterogeneous populations, predominantly made up of MF II (Fig. 2A₁), that from a 30 year old donor are heterogeneous populations predominantly composed of MF II and MF III (Fig. 2B₁), and primary explant populations of a 78 year old donor are predominantly made up of MF III, PMF IV, PMF V, PMF VI (Fig. 2C₁). The age correlated changes in cell type frequencies of primary mitotic and postmitotic fibroblast cell types MF I, MF II, MF III, PMF IV, PMF V, and PMF VI in primary explant cultures is shown in Fig. 3.

Primary postmitotic fibroblast cell types can sometimes not be distinguished

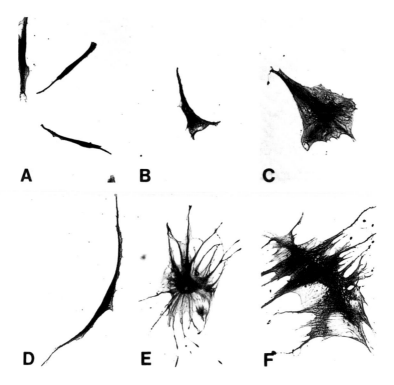

Fig. 1. Mitotic and postmitotic fibroblast morphotypes found in primary explant cultures or primary low density mass populations. A. Mitotic fibroblast MF I. B. Mitotic fibroblast MF II. C. Mitotic fibroblast MF III. D. Postmitotic fibroblast PMF IV. E. Postmitotic fibroblast PMF V. F. Postmitotic fibroblast PMF VI. Magnification: ×100.

definitely by morphological criteria. Monoclonal antibodies have therefore been raised against cytoplasmic and membrane bound antigens of primary and secondary human skin fibroblast cell types. Work is in progress to identify the fibroblast cell types *in vivo* and in primary and secondary fibroblast populations *in vitro* by the use of these antibodies.

The composition of primary low density cultures of skin fibroblast populations, extracted from skin specimens of donors of different age by collagenase/trypsin treatment can be analysed four days after seeding the cells, when the fibroblasts have expressed their morphological characteristics best and have not yet started to divide.

Primary low cell density cultures of fibroblast populations of the same donors as used for primary explant populations are shown in Fig. $2A_2$–$C_2$. Primary low cell density cultures of fibroblast populations of the seven year old donor contained heterogeneous populations predominantly made up of MF II (Fig. $2A_2$), that of the 30 year old donor contained heterogeneous populations mainly composed of MF II and MF III (Fig. $2B_2$), and primary low cell density populations of the 78 year old donor contained heterogeneous populations predominantly made up of MF III, PMF IV, PMF V, and PMF VI (Fig. $2C_2$). The age-dependent changes in the cell

Fig. 2. Primary explant populations of primary fibroblasts migrated within 7 days from skin explants of a 7 year old female donor ($A_1$), of a 30 year old female donor ($B_1$), and of a 78 year old female donor ($C_1$). Before fixation and staining the primary fibroblasts, skin explants were removed from the tissue culture dishes. Magnification: ×26. Low density populations of primary fibroblasts extracted by collagenase/trypsin treatment from skin biopsy of a 7 year old female donor ($A_2$), of a 30 year old female donor ($B_2$), and of a 78 year old female donor ($C_2$). Magnification: ×26.

type frequencies of mitotic and postmitotic fibroblast cell types in primary low density populations are demonstrated in Fig. 4. The changes documented are similar to those observed in primary human skin fibroblast explant cultures (Fig. $2A_1-C_1$, Fig. 3). In addition, they are similar to those found in secondary, human skin fibroblast, low cell density populations of the cell line HH-8 in the morphologically recognizable mitotic and differentiating progenitor compartments and in the morphologically recognizable postmitotic and maturing compartments *in vitro* (Fig. 8, Table 1).

Five different clone types arose in primary clonal cultures established from primary fibroblasts extracted from the dermis of a seven year old female donor. 14 days after seeding, the clones consisted either of a homogeneous population of MF I (Fig. 5A), MF II (Fig. 5C), or MF III (Fig. 5E), or of a heterogeneous population of either MF I and MF II (Fig. 5B) or MF II and MF III (Fig. 5D). For these clone types the following designations have been proposed (Rodemann *et al.* 1988): CTF I (Fig. 5A), CTF I/II (Fig. 5B), CTF II (Fig. 5C), CTF II/III (Fig. 5D), and

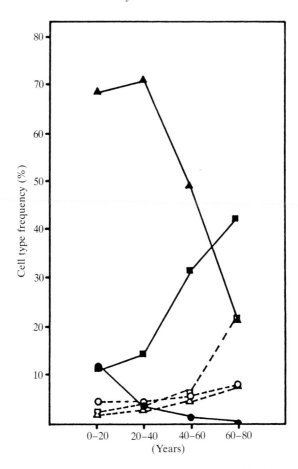

Fig. 3. Age correlated changes in the frequencies of primary fibroblast cell types MF I (●), MF II (▲), MF III (■), PMF IV (○), PMF V (△), and PMF VI (□) migrating out from skin explants of human donors of 4 different age groups. Numbers shown represent the mean values of at least 7 experiments in each group.

CTF III (Fig. 5E). Fig. 6 documents the age correlated changes in the clone type frequencies in clonal populations of the four age groups studied. Fibroblasts in a postmitotic differentiation state at the time of seeding into clonal cultures form plated cells of the cell types PMF V or PMF VI, as demonstrated in Fig. 5F. The changes in primary clone type frequencies were similar to those found for the cell type frequencies in primary low cell density populations (Fig. 4) or in primary explant populations (Fig. 3). Furthermore, these changes can also be correlated to the changes in cell type and clone type frequencies found in secondary low cell density cultures or secondary clonal populations as a function of the CPDL of the fibroblast cell line HH-8 (Tables 1 and 2) in the morphologically recognizable mitotic and differentiating progenitor compartment and in the morphologically recognizable postmitotic and maturing compartment (Bayreuther et al. 1988; Rodemann et al. 1988).

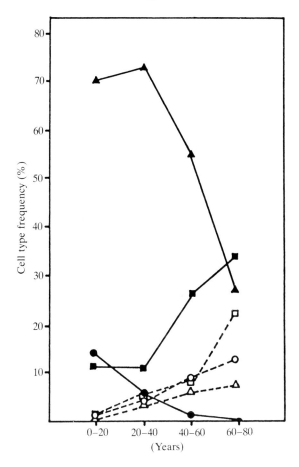

Fig. 4. Age correlated changes in the cell type frequencies of fibroblasts MF I (●), MF II (▲), MF III (■), PMF IV (○), PMF V (△), and PMF VI (□) in primary low density mass populations of skin fibroblasts isolated from skin biopsies of human donors of 4 different age groups. Numbers shown represent the mean value of at least 7 experiments in each group.

Studies are in progress to analyse the [$^{35}$S]methionine polypeptide pattern of homogeneous primary clonal populations of MF I, MF II, and MF III by two-dimensional gel electrophoresis. The biochemical characterization of primary postmitotic fibroblasts PMF IV, PMF V, and PMF VI in low cell density populations will be undertaken when cell type-specific monoclonal antibodies that make cell sorting possible are found.

### *Secondary human skin fibroblasts* in vitro

Secondary mitotic human skin fibroblast populations of the cell line HH-8 *in vitro* underwent $53.6 \pm 6.0$ cumulative population doublings (CPD) in $302 \pm 27$ days. When the growth capacity of the mitotic fibroblasts is exhausted and if appropriate methods are applied, mitotic fibroblasts differentiate spontaneously into postmitotic fibroblast populations. Postmitotic fibroblast populations can be kept in stationary culture for up to 305 ± 41 additional days. The maximum lifespan of the postmitotic HH-8 cells in stationary cultures has not been determined yet (Bayreuther *et al.* 1988; Rodemann *et al.* 1988).

Mitotic and postmitotic secondary fibroblast populations are heterogeneous populations with reproducible changes in the proportions of all stages of mitotic and postmitotic fibroblasts (Figs 7, 8, Table 1). As described for primary fibroblasts, the secondary fibroblast MF I (Fig. 7A) is a small spindle shaped cell, MF II (Fig. 7B)

Table 1. *Cell type frequencies of secondary mitotic and postmitotic fibroblasts as a function of the CPDL and the duration of the stationary culture*

| | | Fibroblast cell types (%) | | | | | | |
| | | MF I | MF II | MF III | PMF IV | PMF V | PMF VI | PMF VII |
|---|---|---|---|---|---|---|---|---|
| **MF population at** | | | | | | | | |
| CPD | Days | | | | | | | |
| 12·1 | 35 | 16·0 | 72·0 | 10·0 | 1·0 | 0·5 | 0·5 | — |
| 23·4 | 70 | 5·5 | 80·5 | 11·0 | 1·5 | 0·5 | 1·0 | — |
| 33·2 | 105 | 2·0 | 81·0 | 13·0 | 2·0 | 0·5 | 1·5 | — |
| 40·7 | 145 | 0·5 | 35·5 | 47·5 | 12·0 | 2·0 | 2·5 | — |
| 52·2 | 245 | — | 0·5 | 80·5 | 14·0 | 2·0 | 3·0 | — |
| **PMF populations at** | | | | | | | | |
| Week | Days | | | | | | | |
| 1 | 7 | — | — | 28·5 | 21·0 | 38·5 | 12·5 | — |
| 3 | 21 | — | — | 2·0 | 32·5 | 41·5 | 24·0 | — |
| 6 | 42 | — | — | — | 12·5 | 34·0 | 51·5 | 2·0 |
| 12 | 84 | — | — | — | 3·0 | 5·5 | 86·5 | 4·5 |
| 24 | 168 | — | — | — | — | 2·0 | 87·5 | 10·5 |
| 42 | 294 | — | — | — | — | — | 81·5 | 18·5 |

Cell type frequencies of mitotic (MF) and postmitotic (PMF) fibroblast populations were determined in low density mass cultures. The relative proportions of the different fibroblast cell types were analysed by identifying the cells by morphological criteria. At different time points (CPDL, cumulative population doublings level, or days in stationary culture) at least 4000 cells were analysed in random microscopic fields.

Table 2. *Frequencies of secondary fibroblast clone types as a function of the CPDL*

| | Clone types (%) | | | | | |
| CPD | CTF I | CTF I/II | CTF II | CTF II/III | CTF III | CEF |
|---|---|---|---|---|---|---|
| 12·1 | 6·5 | 7·5 | 39·0 | 38·5 | 8·5 | 19·0 |
| 23·4 | 4·2 | 5·3 | 39·5 | 32·3 | 18·7 | 15·5 |
| 33·2 | 1·1 | 2·4 | 27·8 | 35·9 | 32·8 | 10·5 |
| 40·7 | 0 | 0 | 10·3 | 16·4 | 73·3 | 8·0 |
| 52·2 | 0 | 0 | 0 | 1·5 | 88·5 | 3·0 |

At the CPDL (cumulative population doubling level) indicated, secondary skin fibroblast populations were seeded as clonal cultures as described in Materials and methods. Cells were cultured 14 days. Thereafter, clonal cultures were fixed and stained, and the frequencies of the different clone types were determined by morphological criteria. For quantification, 5000 clones were classified at each CPDL. CEF, cloning efficiency represents the proportion of originally seeded cells grown out to clonal populations.

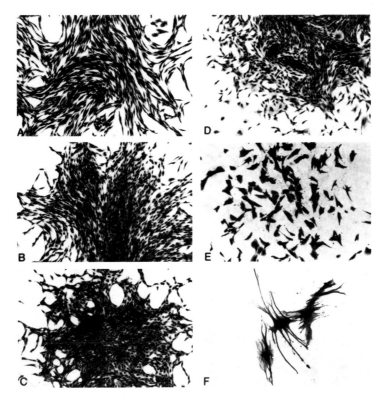

Fig. 5. Primary clone types established from primary fibroblasts extracted from skin biopsies of a 7 year old female donor. A. Clone type CTF I. B. Clone type CTF I/II. C. Clone type CTF II. D. Clone type CTF II/III. E. Clone type CTF III. F. Plated cells of postmitotic differentiation states PMF VI. Magnification: ×14 (A–E); ×26 (F).

is a small epitheloid cell, MF III is a larger pleiomorphic epitheloid cell (Fig. 7C). Secondary postmitotic fibroblast PMF IV (Fig. 7D) is a large spindle shaped cell, PMF V (Fig. 7E) is a larger pleiomorphic epitheloid cell, PMF VI is the largest pleiomorph epitheloid cell of the fibroblast series (Fig. 7F). The postmitotic fibroblast PMF VII (Fig. 7G) is the degenerating fibroblast. The reproducible changes in the proportions of mitotic and postmitotic fibroblast make it very evident that the fibroblasts differentiate along the seven stage terminal cell lineage MF I → III → PMF IV → VII. The shifts in the frequencies of mitotic and postmitotic fibroblasts in mass populations are accompanied by alterations in the [$^{35}$S]methionine polypeptide pattern of developing mass populations (Bayreuther *et al.* 1988). The [$^{35}$S]methionine polypeptide pattern of homogeneous subpopulations of MF I, MF II, MF III, PMF IV, PMF V, and PMF VI, isolated from heterogeneous mass populations by the glass ring technique, revealed that the six fibroblast morphotypes studied express their cell type-specific polypeptide pattern in the mixed populations (Bayreuther *et al.* 1988). Thus, the [$^{35}$S]methionine polypeptide patterns of the mixed populations of the cell line HH-8 are the sums of the polypeptide pattern of the distinct fibroblast cell types that make up the total populations at different stages

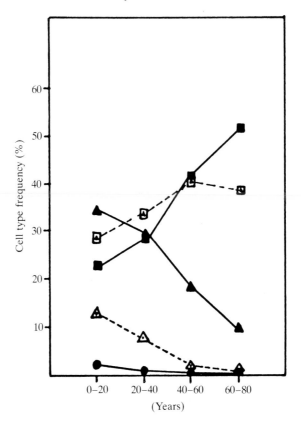

Fig. 6. Age correlated changes in the clone type frequencies of primary clone type CTF I (●), CTF I/II (△), CTF II (▲), and CTF II/III (▣), and CTF III (■) in primary clonal cultures isolated from human donors of four different age groups. Numbers shown represent the mean values of at least 7 experiments in each group.

of development (Bayreuther *et al.* 1988; Rodemann *et al.* 1988; Francz *et al.* 1988). Methods have been developed for the selective enrichment of the three mitotic and the four postmitotic fibroblasts from heterogeneous mitotic populations (Rodemann *et al.* 1988). MF II are enriched to 75–85 % at the CPDL 28–34, and MF III to 73–86 % at the CPDL 48–53. Another cell system suited for the analysis of cell-biological and biochemical changes accompanying the cytodifferentiation in the cell lineage MF I–III is the quantitative clonal culture system. As described for primary clonal populations, five different types of clones arise in secondary clonal cultures (Fig. 9). These colonies consist either of uniform populations of MF I in CTF I (Fig. 9A), MF II in CTF II (Fig. 9C), and MF III in CTF III (Fig. 9E), or of mixtures of MF I and MF II in CTF I/II (Fig. 9B), and MF II and MF III in CTF II/III (Fig. 9D).

When mixed populations at different CPDL were seeded into clonal cultures, changes in the frequencies of the different clone types can be observed as a function of the CPDL of the original population (Table 2). In order to achieve a selective

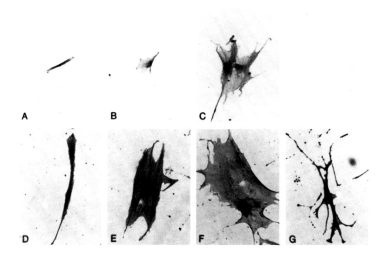

Fig. 7. Mitotic and postmitotic morphotypes of secondary fibroblasts of the cell line HH-8. A. Mitotic fibroblast MF I. B. Mitotic fibroblast MF II. C. Mitotic fibroblast MF III. D. Postmitotic fibroblast PMF IV. E. Postmitotic fibroblast PMF V. F. Postmitotic fibroblast PMF VI. G. Postmitotic fibroblast and degenerating fibroblast PMF VII. Magnification: ×52.

enrichment of the four postmitotic fibroblast cell types, methods have been worked out for the experimental induction of the differentiation from a lower state (MF II, MF III) to a higher state (PMF IV, PMF V, PMF VI, and PMF VII) in the fibroblast stem cell system by physical (UV) and chemical (mitomycin C) agents (Fig. 10) (Rodemann *et al.* 1988). The [$^{35}$S]methionine polypeptide pattern of nearly homogeneous sub- or total populations of mitotic fibroblasts MF I, MF II, MF III and their corresponding clone types CTF I, CTF II, and CTF III are identical (Rodemann *et al.* 1988). Likewise, postmitotic fibroblast cell types PMF IV, PMF V, PMF VI, and PMF VII that arose spontaneously and the experimentally induced corresponding postmitotic fibroblast cell types show identical [$^{35}$S]methionine polypeptide pattern (Rodemann *et al.* 1988; Francz *et al.* 1988). Differentiation associated changes in the total soluble cytoplasmic and nuclear proteins, secreted proteins, and membrane bound proteins have been demonstrated for 'spontaneous' and experimentally induced populations of mitotic and postmitotic fibroblast cell types by two-dimensional gel electrophoresis (Francz *et al.* 1988). These data provide conclusive evidence for the seven stage differentiation sequence MF I – MF II – MF III – PMF IV – PMF V – PMF VI – PMF VII of human skin fibroblast populations *in vitro* (Bayreuther *et al.* 1988; Rodemann *et al.* 1988; Francz *et al.* 1988).

## Discussion

Comparative cell-biological and biochemical studies of primary BN rat skin and lung fibroblasts of four age groups and of secondary BN rat skin fibroblasts as a function of

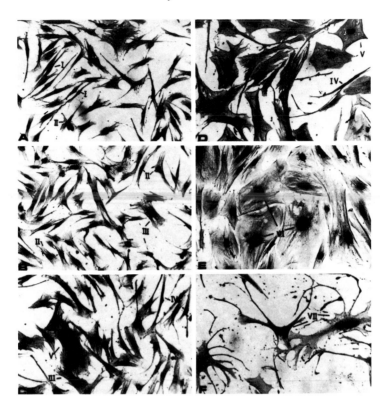

Fig. 8. Cell type composition of mitotic and postmitotic fibroblast populations. A. Mitotic population CPDL 15. B. Mitotic populations CPDL 32. C. Mitotic population CPDL 51. D. Postmitotic population, 3 weeks of stationary culture. E. Postmitotic population 20 weeks of stationary culture. F. Postmitotic population, 40 weeks of stationary culture. Magnification: ×52.

the CPDL *in vitro* have been undertaken (Mollenhauer & Bayreuther, 1986; Kontermann & Bayreuther, 1979). In primary explant, mass and clonal populations established from BN rat skin and lung of four age groups, three distinct mitotic fibroblast (MF) cell types, i.e. MF I, MF II, and MF III, could be identified on the basis of their morphological, proliferative, and biochemical properties *in vitro*. Since MF I, MF II, and MF III cells were demonstrable in each of the three primary cell culture systems employed, it is likely that corresponding cell types also exist *in vivo*. In primary explant, mass and clonal populations *in vitro*. the relative proportions of MF I, MF II, and MF III were found to change as a function of the age of the donor animal. These observations indicate that the primary mitotic BN rat fibroblasts differentiate *via* a three stage differentiation sequence: MF I – MF II – MF III *in vivo* and *in vitro* (Mollenhauer & Bayreuther, 1986). In secondary mass and clonal populations established from embryonic BN rat skin fibroblasts *in vitro*, distinct mitotic fibroblast cell types, i.e. MF I, MF II, and MF III, have been characterized by morphological, cell biological, and biochemical characteristics. The relative proportions of MF I, MF II, and MF III were found to change as a function of the

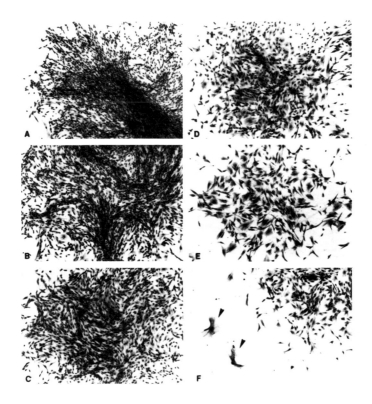

Fig. 9. Clonal populations of mitotic secondary fibroblast cell types MF I, MF II, and MF III. A. Clone type CTF I. B. Clone type CTF I/II. C. Clone type CTF II. D. Clone type CTF II/III. E. Clone type CTF III. F. Plated cells of postmitotic differentiation state PMF VI (indicated by arrowheads). Magnification: ×12.

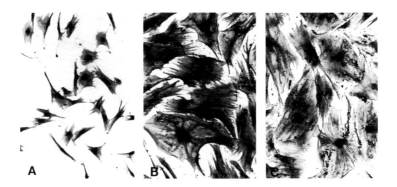

Fig. 10. Experimentally induced postmitotic fibroblast populations of the cell line HH-8, predominantly made up of postmitotic fibroblast PMF VI. A. Mitotic low density mass population, CPDL 30, predominantly made up of MF II. Fibroblast populations of this cell type composition were used for experimental induction of postmitotic fibroblast populations, predominantly made up of PMF VI, either by UV irradiation (B), or mitomycin C treatment (C) (Rodemann *et al.* 1988). Magnification: ×52.

CPDL of the secondary mass populations *in vitro*. indicating that secondary mitotic BN rat fibroblasts *in vitro* differentiate also along a three stage differentiation sequence: MF I – MF II – MF III (Kontermann & Bayreuther, 1979).

In the meantime cell-biological and biochemical studies with improved methods of the primary and secondary BN rat skin fibroblasts *in vitro* have revealed that primary as well as secondary fibroblasts of the BN rat differentiate spontaneously along a seven stage terminal cell lineage starting with the mitotic fibroblasts MF I–III, through the postmitotic fibroblasts PMF IV–VI to the postmitotic and degenerating fibroblast PMF VII. Identical data have been obtained from cell-biological and biochemical studies of primary and secondary skin fibroblasts of C3H mice and Valo chicken (Bayreuther *et al.* unpublished data).

Cell-biological data obtained from studies of primary fibroblasts of the abdominal dermis of 45 female human donors, ranging from 1 to 78 years of age, in primary explant populations, primary low cell density populations, and primary clonal populations make it very likely that equivalents of all the primary fibroblast cell types MF I to PMF VII are present in the connective tissue of the skin *in vivo*. As a function of the age of the donor, primary mitotic fibroblasts MF I and MF II are progressively depleted from the dermis. In previous presentations we have provided morphological and biochemical evidence that secondary human skin fibroblasts of the cell line HH-8 *in vitro* differentiate along a terminal stem cell system-like cell lineage through the same morphological stages (Bayreuther *et al.* 1988; Rodemann *et al.* 1988; Francz *et al.* 1988).

The morphological and biochemical cytodifferentiation of the primary and secondary human skin fibroblasts speaks for a seven stage cell lineage controlled by distinct genetic programs (Bayreuther *et al.* 1988; Rodemann *et al.* 1988; Francz *et al.* 1988). Analogous "seven stage" differentiation sequences have been found in primary and secondary prenatal and postnatal skin and lung fibroblast populations of Valo chicken, C3H mice, and BN rats (Bayreuther *et al.* unpublished data; Kontermann & Bayreuther, 1979; Mollenhauer & Bayreuther, 1986). Similarities in the design of the multi-stage differentiation sequence in the four species studied (chicken, mouse, rat, and man) make it very likely that the differentiation sequences described represent parts of a general fibroblast stem cell system, which seems to resemble that of the haemopoietic stem cell system (Bayreuther *et al.* 1988). Since the morphological and biochemical characteristics of the fibroblast stem cells *in vivo* and *in vitro* are not yet known, it remains open whether these cells can be propagated and induced to differentiate under the cell culture conditions employed. Under modified cell culture conditions described, connective tissues of chicken, mouse, rat and man give rise to the mitotic committed stem cells or progenitor cells MF I, MF II, and MF III, which proliferate and differentiate along the cell lineage MF I–MF II–MF III in the morphologically recognizable differentiating progenitor compartment. When the mitotic capacity of MF III is exhausted, fibroblast MF III becomes a member of the postmitotic and maturing compartment in which the cells differentiate along the sequence PMF IV–VI. Fibroblast PMF VI, the terminally differentiated end cell of the fibroblast differentiation sequence, is the cell with the greatest number of proteins synthesized (Bayreuther *et al.* 1988). After a long postmitotic lifespan, fibroblast PMF VI differentiates into fibroblast PMF VII, the degenerating fibroblast. The data presented demonstrate a morphological and biochemical seven stage differentiation sequence of cellular aging and death of primary and secondary human fibroblasts *in vitro* in the three morphologically recognizable differentiating cell compartments of the fibroblast stem cell system (Bayreuther *et al.* 1988; Rodemann *et al.* 1988; Francz *et al.* 1988; Bayreuther *et al.* unpublished data; Kontermann & Bayreuther, 1979; Mollenhauer & Bayreuther, 1986).

This work was supported by grants from the Deutsche Forschungsgemeinschaft (Ba 526/4), the Fritz-Thyssen-Stiftung, the Breuninger Stiftung, and the Cosmital S.A., CH-1723 Marly. H. Peter Rodemann is a recipient of a Heisenberg grant from the Deutsche Forschungsgemeinschaft (Ro 527/2-1).

## References

BAYREUTHER, K., RODEMANN, H. P., HOMMEL, R., DITTMANN, K., ALBIEZ, M. & FRANCZ, P. I. (1988). *Proc. natn. Acad. Sci. U.S.A.* **85**, 5112–5116.

BELL, E., MAREK, L. F., LEVINSTONE, D. S., MERRILL, C., SHER, S., YOUNG, I. T. & EDEN, M. (1978). Loss of division potential in vitro: Aging or differentiation? *Science* **202**, 1158–1163.

FRANCZ, P. I., BAYREUTHER, K. & RODEMANN, H. P. (1988). Cytoplasmic, nuclear, membrane-bound and secreted [$^{35}$S]methionine-labelled polypeptide pattern in differentiating fibroblast stem cells *in vitro*. *J. Cell Sci.* **92**, (in press).

GABBIANI, G. & RUNGGER-BRÄNDLE, E. (1981). The fibroblast. In *Handbook of Inflammation*, vol. III: *Tissue Repair and Regeneration* (ed. L. E. Glynn), pp. 1–50. Amsterdam: Elsevier, North Holland Biomedical Press.

HAYFLICK, L. (1981). Cell death in vitro. In *Cell Death in Biology and Pathology* (ed. D. Brown & R. A. Lockshin), pp. 243–285. London: Chapman & Hall.

HAYFLICK, L. & MOOREHEAD, P. S. (1961). The serial cultivation of human diploid cell strains. *Expl Cell Res.* **25**, 585–621.

KONTERMANN, K. & BAYREUTHER, K. (1979). The cellular aging of rat fibroblasts in vitro is a differentiation process. *Gerontology* **25**, 261–274.

MACIEIRA-COELHO, A., DIATLOFF, C. & MALAISSE, E. (1976). Doubling potential of fibroblasts from different species after ionising radiation. *Nature, Lond.* **261**, 586–588.

MARTIN, G. M., SPRAGUE, L. A., NORWOOD, T. H. & PENDERGRASS, W. R. (1974). Clonal selection, attenuation and differentiation in an in vitro model of hyperplasia. *Am. J. Path.* **74**, 137–154.

MOLLENHAUER, J. & BAYREUTHER, K. (1986). Donor-age-related changes in the morphology, growth potential, and collagen biosynthesis in rat fibroblast subpopulations in vitro. *Differentiation* **32**, 165–172.

PEREIRA-SMITH, O. M. & SMITH, J. R. (1982). Phenotype of low proliferative potential is dominant in hybrids of normal human fibroblasts. *Somat. Cell Genet.* **6**, 731–742.

RAES, M. & REMACLE, J. (1983). Ageing of hamster embryo fibroblasts as the result of both differentiation and stochastic mechanisms. *Expl Gerontol.* **18**, 223–240.

RAZIN, S., PFENDT, E. A., MATSUMURA, T. & HAYFLICK, L. (1977). Comparison by autoradiography of macromolecular biosynthesis in "young" and "old" human diploid fibroblast cultures. *Mech. Ageing Dev.* **6**, 379–382.

RODEMANN, H. P. & BAYREUTHER, K. (1984). Abnormal collagen metabolism in cultured skin fibroblasts from patients with Duchenne muscular dystrophy. *Proc. natn. Acad. Sci. U.S.A.* **81**, 5130–5134.

RODEMANN, H. P., BAYREUTHER, K., FRANCZ, P. I., DITTMANN, K. & ALBIEZ, M. (1988). Selective enrichment and biochemical characterisation of seven fibroblast cell types of human skin fibroblast populations in vitro. *Expl Cell Res.* (in press).

Ross, R. (1968). The connective tissue fiber forming cell. In *Treatise in Collagen* (ed. B. S. Gould), pp. 1–82. New York, London: Academic Press.

Schneider, E. L. (1985). Human skin derived fibroblast like cells in culture. In *Handbook of Cell Biology and Aging* (ed. V. J. Cristofalo), pp. 425–433. Boca Raton, FL: CRC Press.

Smith, J. R. & Pereira-Smith, O. M. (1985). Lung derived fibroblast like human cells in culture. In *Handbook of Cell Biology and Aging* (ed. V. J. Cristofalo), pp. 375–425. Boca Raton, FL: CRC Press.

Todaro, G. J. & Green, H. (1963). Quantitative studies of the growth of mouse embryo cells in culture and their development into established lines. *J. Cell Biol.* **17**, 299–313.

*J. Cell Sci. Suppl. 10, 131–144 (1988)*
*Printed in Great Britain © The Company of Biologists Limited 1988*

# Recombinant retrovirus-mediated gene transfer to normal haemopoietic cells

G. R. JOHNSON

*Cancer Research Unit, The Walter and Eliza Hall Institute of Medical Research, P.O. Royal Melbourne Hospital, 3050 Victoria, Australia*

## Summary

Several of parameters seeking to increase the infection frequency of normal haemopoietic cells by recombinant retroviruses containing a drug selectable marker and/or a haemopoietic growth factor gene have been compared. By using bone marrow cells pretreated with 5-fluorouracil, cocultivation of cells for at least 4 days with virus producing fibroblasts, and addition of pokeweed mitogen stimulated spleen cell conditioned medium, from 30 to 100% of haemopoietic spleen colony forming cells (CFU-S) could be infected.

Because drug (G-418) selection was found to select subsets of CFU-S, a retrovirus lacking the drug selectable marker Neo[r], but containing a GM-CSF gene, was used to study the effects of endogenous GM-CSF production on CFU-S differentiation. Infected CFU-S produced equivalent numbers of erythroid and neutrophil–macrophage committed progenitor cells to control uninfected CFU-S. However, the progeny of infected CFU-S produced GM-CSF, some cells grew autonomously and neutrophil numbers were greatly increased at the expense of erythroblasts. These results suggest that unregulated GM-CSF production, although not altering commitment, alters the amplication phase following commitment.

## Introduction

The haemopoietic colony stimulating factors (CSFs) are growth factors that, *in vitro*, stimulate the proliferation, differentiation and functional activation of neutrophils, macrophages, eosinophils, megakaryocytes and erythroid cells (reviewed by Metcalf, 1984). Proliferation and differentiation of these cell lineages is due directly to the ability of the CSF's to stimulate a subset of multipotential cells and their immediate progeny, the committed progenitor cells (*in vitro* colony-forming cells, CFC) (reviewed by Metcalf, 1984, 1986). Each of the four known CSFs has been molecularly cloned allowing production of large quantities of these glycoproteins, for studies, which have provided evidence for their *in vivo* function (Kindler *et al.* 1986; Metcalf *et al.* 1987*a,b*; Nienhuis *et al.* 1987; Groopman *et al.* 1987; Welte *et al.* 1987).

One of these haemopoietic growth factors, granulocyte–macrophage colony stimulating factor (GM-CSF) has been implicated in the development of leukaemia due to the detection of GM-CSF mRNA in cells from certain human myeloid leukaemias (Young & Griffin, 1986; Cheng *et al.* 1988). In addition the factor-dependent and non-tumourigenic murine cell line, FDC-P1, became tumorigenic when infected with a retrovirus expressing GM-CSF (Lang *et al.* 1985), although it

Key words: haemopoietic growth factors, retrovirus, gene transfer.

is not clear that unregulated GM-CSF expression alone, was responsible (Laker *et al*. 1987).

Infection of normal haemopoietic cells with recombinant retroviruses containing haemopoietic growth factor genes should allow experiments in which it can be determined whether autocrine production of growth factors by normal haemopoietic cells *in vivo* can lead to leukaemia induction.

To obtain long-term expression of the introduced gene, it is desirable to infect haemopoietic pluripotential cells which have the ability to reconstitute the entire haemopoietic system. Such repopulation is readily observed when bone marrow cells are transplanted into lethally irradiated recipients. Although these haemopoietic repopulating cells cannot be enumerated directly, a population of multipotential cells which are probably their immediate descendants can be assayed. These cells, termed spleen colony-forming units (CFU-S) form colonies of haemopoietic cells when transplanted into lethally irradiated recipients.

Haemopoietic spleen colony formation offers a number of advantages for studies aimed at introducing new genetic material into normal blood cells. Being clones, the frequency of infected cells is readily determined and if studied 12 – 14 days after transplantation sufficient cells can be obtained to allow both cellular and molecular studies. In the present manuscript a series of experiments utilizing spleen colony formation are described. The procedures developed allow the efficient infection and subsequent expression of a haemopoietic growth factor gene in the progeny of normal haemopoietic multipotential cells.

## Materials and methods

### Animals

Animals used were 2- to 3-month old C57BL/6/J WEHI or CBA/CaH/WEHI mice from stocks maintained at The Walter and Eliza Hall Institute of Medical Research. For transplantation studies, animals were subjected to whole body irradiation (9·0–9·5 Gy, $\gamma$ rays generated by cobalt[60] at 0·39 Gy min$^{-1}$ at 1·5 m) and transplanted intravenously with the required number of cells within 3 h of irradiation.

### Haemopoietic multipotential and committed progenitor cell assays

To obtain spleen colonies, lethally irradiated animals were injected intravenously with 0·25 to $1 \times 10^5$ syngeneic cells and 12 to 14 days later, animals were killed by cervical dislocation. Individual spleen colonies were dissected from non-confluent spleens and single cell suspensions prepared as described previously (Lala & Johnson, 1978).

The number of neutrophil, neutrophil–macrophage, macrophage or eosinophil committed progenitor cells (*in vitro* colony-forming cells, CFC) in haemopoietic tissues was determined by culturing cells in triplicate 1 ml agar-medium cultures as described previously (Johnson, 1980). Where required, cultures were maximally stimulated by the addition of 0·1 ml pokeweed mitogen stimulated spleen cell conditioned medium (PWM-SCM) (Metcalf & Johnson, 1978; Cutler *et al*. 1985*b*) as a source of haemopoietic growth factors.

Colonies derived from committed erythroid progenitor cells (burst-forming units erythroid, BFU-E) were scored after 7 days' incubation using 1·0 ml methylcellulose cultures as described previously (Johnson & Barker, 1985). Colony formation was stimulated by the addition of PWM-SCM and erythropoietin (1·6 units) prepared from human urine (Cutler *et al*. 1985*a*).

To select for haemopoietic cells expressing Neo$^R$, G418 (Geneticin, Gibco, USA) at a final concentration of 1 mg ml$^{-1}$ was added to cultures.

*Granulocyte–macrophage colony stimulating factor (GM-CSF) assay*

GM-CSF was assayed using FDC-P1 cells as described previously (Metcalf, 1985). The number of units of GM-CSF activity was calculated by assigning 50 units to the amount added to cultures resulting in 50 % of maximum stimulation.

*Preparation of conditioned media*

Cell suspensions obtained from spleen colonies were incubated at 37°C in 2 ml of Dulbecco's Modified Eagle's Medium (DME) containing 10 % foetal calf serum (FCS). After 7 days, the medium was harvested and assayed for GM-CSF. To obtain conditioned media from infected FDC-P1 cells, pools (5–10 clones) of autonomously growing cells were incubated ($1\times10^5$ cells ml$^{-1}$) in 5 mls of DME containing 10 % FCS for 3 days.

*Infection of normal haemopoietic cells*

Detailed conditions for the infection of normal haemopoietic cells have been described previously (Bowtell *et al.* 1987). Briefly, normal bone marrow ($1\times10^6$) or post 5-fluorouracil-treated ($150\,\mathrm{g\,kg}^{-1}$) bone marrow cells (minimum of $2\times10^6$ cells – 2 femur equivalents) were cocultivated for 2–8 days in 10 ml of DME and 20 % FCS with virus-producing $\psi$-2 cells plated 24 h previously at $5\times10^4$ per 10 cm dish. Prior to assay all haemopoietic cells were washed ($\times$3) in factor-free medium.

*Construction of retroviruses and analysis of viral DNA*

Detailed procedures for the construction of the retroviruses (DolNeo, MPDolNeo, ZipNeo, MPZipNeo, ZipNeo(GM-CSF), MPZen(GM-CSF) and NAc(GM-CSF)) have been provided previously (Bowtell *et al.* 1987; Bowtell *et al.* 1988; Cepko *et al.* 1984; Korman *et al.* 1987; Johnson *et al.* 1989). Fibroblast lines secreting virus free of helper virus were produced by calcium phosphate transfection of the $\psi$-2 packaging line (Mann *et al.* 1983) followed by selection in G418 ($400\,\mu\mathrm{g\,ml}^{-1}$). Individual colonies were then picked and expanded for assay. DNA was isolated from guanidine·HCl lysates and Southern blot analysis performed as described previously (Bowtell *et al.* 1987).

## Results

*Optimization of methods for the infection of normal haemopoietic cells*

To optimize infection of the cells forming spleen colonies, a series of preliminary experiments were performed. The possibility of using supernatants from virus-producing $\psi$-2 cell lines was compared to direct cocultivation of $\psi$-2 cells with haemopoietic cells. Only rarely were low numbers of haemopoietic cells infected when supernatants were used and the cocultivation method was applied for all further experiments. To maintain CFU-S and their progeny during the infection phase, pokeweed mitogen spleen cell conditioned medium (PWM-SCM) was added to the cultures. At the minimum, this source of conditioned medium contains IL-3, GM-CSF, and IL-1, all haemopoietic growth factors which are, either singly or in combination, able to stimulate either CFU-S or their progeny. The validity of adding PWM-SCM during the infection phase was confirmed by comparison with cultures containing only medium. In these latter cultures, CFU-S and progenitor cells were not detected if the cocultivation period exceeded 3 days.

Because CFU-S are normally not actively cycling and since retroviral infection is more efficient with dividing cells, the bone marrow cells used as a source of CFU-S

Table 1. *Comparison of cocultivation times for infection of CFU-S*

| Virus | Days of cocultivation | Fibroblast titre | Spleen colonies DNA + ve/Total assayed |
|---|---|---|---|
| MPDolNeo | 2 | $7 \cdot 2 \times 10^4$ | 1/40 |
| MPDolNeo | 5 | $7 \cdot 2 \times 10^5$ | 11/56 |
| DolNeo | 2 | $2 \cdot 4 \times 10^5$ | 1/20 |
| DolNeo | 5 | $2 \cdot 4 \times 10^5$ | 6/18 |

Day 5 post 5-FU treated bone marrow cells incubated for 2 or 5 days prior to transplantation.

were obtained from animals pretreated with the cytotoxic drug, 5-fluorouracil (5-FU). This agent selectively kills cycling cells, resulting in subsequent activation and cycling of multipotential cells to replenish the depleted marrow haemopoietic populations. Experiments were also performed in which bone marrow cells were removed from animals at varying intervals after treatment with 5-FU (2–8 days) and cocultured from 2–8 days. The infection frequency of CFU-S and haemopoietic progenitor cells (CFC) was directly related to the time after 5-FU treatment and the length of the cocultivation period (Bowtell *et al.* 1987). An example of this is shown in Table 1 where 5 day post-5-FU bone marrow cells were cocultured with two different viral-producing cell lines for 2 or 5 days. The number of spleen colonies subsequently found to contain viral DNA was significantly higher with the longer cocultivation period (Table 1).

Although the infection frequency was increased by these procedures, the ability of cells to repopulate lethally irradiated recipients declined if cells were taken from animals more than 4 days after treatment with 5-FU and cocultured for greater than 2 days (Bowtell *et al.* 1987). Therefore if both long-term repopulation and CFU-S studies were required, the infection protocol outlined in Fig. 1 was used. This procedure enabled sufficient numbers of infected CFU-S and CFC to be obtained for further studies, as well as providing sufficient cells for long term repopulation studies in lethally irradiated recipients (Bowtell *et al.* 1987; Johnson *et al.* 1989).

*Parameters affecting expression of a drug resistance gene in normal haemopoietic cells*

In most instances viruses used for infection of normal haemopoietic cells have been based on the Moloney murine leukaemia virus (see for example, Williams *et al.* 1984; Keller *et al.* 1985; Dick *et al.* 1985). To determine whether expression of the drug selectable gene (Neo$^R$) could be increased by exchanging viral enhancer sequences, viruses containing either Moloney (ZipNeo) or myeloproliferative sarcoma virus (MPZipNeo) LTR sequences (Bowtell *et al.* 1987) were compared. Bone marrow cells obtained from animals pretreated with 5-FU were cocultured with $\psi$-2 virus-producing lines, harvested and cultured in semisolid cultures and the numbers of G418-resistant haemopoietic colonies determined. In the absence of drug selection, no significant differences were detected in the numbers, or types, of haemopoietic progenitor cells recovered. However, in the presence of G418, significant differences

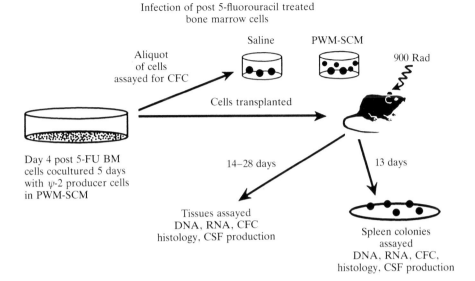

Fig. 1. Protocol for infecting normal bone marrow cells to produce spleen colonies and repopulated haemopoietic tissues.

Table 2. *Effect of modification of viral LTR on ability of virus to confer drug resistance to post-5-fluorouracil-treated bone marrow cells*

| Virus | Virus titre on fibroblasts | Number of $\psi$-2 fibroblasts used for cocultivation ($\times 10^{-3}$) | Per cent drug-resistant colonies | | |
| | | | Pure erythroid | Mixed-erythroid | Non-erythroid |
|---|---|---|---|---|---|
| ZipNeo | $1\times10^5$ | 5 | 0 | 0 | 1 |
| | | 10 | 0 | 0 | 3 |
| | | 50 | 0 | 0 | 3 |
| MPZipNeo | $6\times10^4$ | 5 | 0 | 5 | 9 |
| | | 10 | 0 | 7 | 40 |
| | | 50 | 0 | 25 | 51 |
| — | — | — | 0 | 0 | 0 |

Bone marrow cells (7 days post-5-FU treatment) cocultivated for 7 days with varying number of $\psi$-2 cells producing indicated viruses.

in the numbers of resistant colonies were observed (see Table 2). For each viral construct, the cocultivations were initiated with from 5 to $50\times10^3$ fibroblasts. At all starting numbers of $\psi$-2 cells, the percentage of drug-resistant colonies was greatest for cells infected with MPZipNeo, even though the titre of this virus was lower than ZipNeo, as measured in a fibroblast infection assay (Table 2). These data suggest that expression of the Neo$^R$ gene was enhanced by inclusion of MPSV sequences in the viral construct.

Historically, it has been convenient to use drug resistance to select cells infected with a recombinant retrovirus. By using drug resistance as a preselection step, it has been possible to enrich for infected cells, which may be desirable if the level of infection is low (Keller *et al.* 1985). However, if the infection frequency is high enough, and it appears that this can be achieved by manipulating the parameters during the infection phase (see above and Bowtell *et al.* 1987), preselection may not be required. To fulfil the requirements of preselection, most recombinant retroviruses have been designed to express two genes, the selectable marker and the second gene for which the biological activity is to be investigated. Two types of retroviral construct have therefore been produced for coexpression of the two genes. In one form, the two genes are expressed by alternate splicing, and in the second form one of the two genes is expressed *via* an internal promotor. In comparative studies, however, none of these vectors was able to express the second gene at levels equivalent to those in the parental vector containing only the selectable marker gene (Bowtell *et al.* 1987; Bowtell *et al.* 1988).

When preselection is used, it is expression of the selectable marker that determines survival of the cells. This may not, however, reflect the expression of the second gene, which is the gene of interest. Additionally, preselection, if efficient, should ideally result in all cell populations being equally selected. This may not be the case, as is shown by the data presented in Table 3. Bone marrow cells obtained 7 days after 5-FU injection, were cultured for 4 days with $\psi$-2 cells producing the MPZipNeo virus, followed by culturing for a further 3 days with or without G418. Thirteen days after transplantation of the cells into lethally irradiated recipients, 5 sequential spleen colonies were dissected from each group, and the cells from each spleen colony cultured in semisolid medium with or without G418 addition. Preselection of the cells prior to transplantation appeared to select a population of CFU-S with a reduced capacity to produce CFC (Table 3), although when CFC were present in a spleen colony, a higher percentage of them were drug resistant (Table 3).

*Development of protocols for screening recombinant retroviruses containing haemopoietic growth factor genes without a drug selectable marker*

To overcome some of the problems discussed above, a new retroviral vector pMPZen has been developed (Johnson *et al.* 1988) by removal of the selectable marker gene (Neo[R]), together with nearby SV40 and plasmid sequences from pZipNeoSV(X), and replacement of the enhancer in the LTR by that from the myeloproliferative sarcoma virus. A murine GM-CSF cDNA (pGM3′Δ1.11, Gough *et al.* 1987) was chosen for insertion into the vector (termed MPZen(GM-CSF) because it lacks sequences recently implicated in mRNA instability (Shaw & Kamen, 1986). Due to the absence of the selectable marker, new strategies had to be developed to select $\psi$-2 lines containing the construct, and to determine which $\psi$-2 clone produced the most virus. Fibroblast lines were therefore transfected with a mixture of retroviral construct and pSV2 Neo plasmid DNA at a ratio of 20:1 (w/w). Cotransfection of the $\psi$-2 cells with the pSV2 Neo plasmid enabled G418 selection of the fibroblasts incorporating this plasmid. Because of the large excess of retroviral DNA, this

Table 3. *Effect of drug selection prior to transplantation of bone marrow cells for CFU-S assay*

| Pre-selection | Spleen colony erythroid | Addition of G418 to CFC culture | Number of CFC per spleen colony | | |
|---|---|---|---|---|---|
| | | | Pure | Mixed erythroid | Non-erythroid |
| No | 1 | NO | 28 | 8 | 198 |
| | | YES | 8 | 0 | 90 |
| | 2 | NO | 88 | 18 | 1020 |
| | | YES | 58 | 8 | 528 |
| | 3 | NO | 88 | 18 | 782 |
| | | YES | 66 | 12 | 790 |
| | 4 | NO | 0 | 0 | 0 |
| | | YES | 0 | 0 | 0 |
| | 5 | NO | 0 | 0 | 10 |
| | | YES | 0 | 0 | 4 |
| Yes | 1 | NO | 12 | 6 | 82 |
| | | YES | 8 | 0 | 92 |
| | 2 | NO | 0 | 2 | 36 |
| | | YES | 0 | 0 | 32 |
| | 3 | NO | 22 | 0 | 36 |
| | | YES | 0 | 0 | 0 |
| | 4 | NO | 12 | 0 | 128 |
| | | YES | 12 | 0 | 110 |
| | 5 | NO | 6 | 0 | 48 |
| | | YES | 6 | 0 | 20 |

CFC assayed from individual spleen colonies obtained from day 7 post-5U-treated bone marrow cells cocultivated with MPZipNeo virus-producing $\psi$-2 cells for 4 days, and then cultured for a further 3 days with or without $1\,\mathrm{mg\,ml}^{-1}$ G418 prior to transplantation.

ensured that a high proportion of the drug-resistant $\psi$-2 clones also contained the retroviral DNA. Selected $\psi$-2 clones were then expanded and medium conditioned by them was assayed for GM-CSF, positive clones being due to integration of the MPZen(GM-CSF) construct. To determine the amount of MPZen(GM-CSF) virus produced, the GM-CSF-dependent haemopoietic cell line FDC-P1 was cocultured with each fibroblast clone. The FDC-P1 cells were harvested, washed, and cultured in semisolid agar cultures at a variety of cell densities, in the presence or absence of PWM-SCM. The number of FDC-P1 colonies was determined after 7 days' incubation. Those $\psi$-2 clones producing the highest proportion of autonomously growing FDC-P1 cells, at the lowest FDC-P1 plating density (to eliminate the possibility of infected FDC-P1 cells secreting sufficient GM-CSF to stimulate uninfected cells), were considered to have the highest viral titre (see Fig. 2).

With the MPZen(GM-CSF) virus, the fact that FDC-P1 cells grew autonomously when infected, aided selection of $\psi$-2 clones with the highest viral titre. Infection of FDC-P1 cells with MPZen constructs containing G-CSF (which does not stimulate

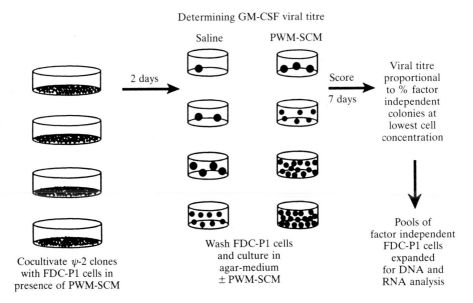

Fig. 2. Method for determining viral titre of different fibroblast clones producing virus containing a GM-CSF gene, but no drug selectable marker gene.

FDC-P1 cells), has also been used to successfully select virus-producing ψ-2 clones (Johnson, G. R. and Chang, J., unpublished results). In this instance sequential FDC-P1 clones were expanded and the proportion capable of producing G-CSF in conditioned media was indicative of the viral titre.

The MPZen(GM-CSF) was compared to the splicing vector Zip Neo(GM-CSF) and the β-actin internal promotor vector NAc(GM-CSF). FDC-P1 cells were cocultivated with the virus-producing cell lines, washed, and cultured at low cell numbers. Autonomously growing colonies were picked and pools of 10 colonies expanded. Equal numbers of cells from each pool were then used to condition medium, which was subsequently assayed for GM-CSF, IL-3, M-CSF and G-CSF (see Fig. 3). Only GM-CSF was detected and MPZen(GM-CSF)-infected FDC-P1 cells produced considerably more GM-CSF (at least 10-fold) than either Zip Neo(GM-CSF) or NAc(GM-CSF)-infected FDC-P1 cells (Table 4).

*Infection of normal haemopoietic cells with a retrovirus containing a haemopoietic growth factor gene*

Bone marrow cells were taken from animals 4 days after injection with 5-FU and cocultivated with either MPZen(GM-CSF) virus-producing ψ-2 or control ψ-2 cells, for 5 days. The cells were then transplanted into lethally irradiated recipients at 25 to $75 \times 10^3$ cells and 13 days later individual sequential spleen colonies dissected. A portion of each spleen colony was taken for counting and morphological analysis of cells, portion for conditioning of media, portion for enumeration of CFC and the remaining cells (80%) for DNA analysis. Of the 11 colonies examined from the virus-infected group, 9 were positive for MPZen(GM-CSF) DNA by Southern blot

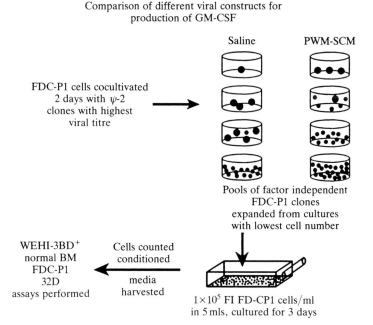

Fig. 3. Procedure for determining the amount of GM-CSF produced following infection of FDC-P1 cells with different viral constructs.

Table 4. *Comparison of GM-CSF activity in media conditioned by haemopoietic cell lines infected with different viral constructs*

| Virus | GM-CSF activity (units per $10^6$ infected cells)* |
|---|---|
| ZipNeo(GM-CSF) | 2 000 |
| ZipNeo(GM-CSF) | 2 200 |
| MPZen(GM-CSF) | 27 800 |
| MPZen(GM-CSF) | 29 700 |
| NAc(GM-CSF) | 100 |
| NAc(GM-CSF) | 130 |

* Number of units calculated by assigning 50 units to the dilution giving 50 % of maximum stimulation in the bioassay.

analysis. The mean total number of cells in viral DNA-positive colonies did not differ significantly from control colonies. Similarly, no significant differences were seen in the proportion of spleen colonies containing committed erythroid (BFU-E) or neutrophil–macrophage (GM-CFC) progenitor cells (Table 5), nor in the total numbers of these cells in infected or uninfected spleen colonies (Table 5). When spleen colony cells were assayed for their ability to produce GM-CSF, only medium conditioned by cells from viral DNA-positive colonies contained readily detectable

Table 5. *Committed progenitor cell numbers in spleen colonies infected with MPZen(GM-CSF) virus*

| Number of colonies | Number of colonies positive for viral DNA | Per cent colonies containing | | Mean number of progenitor cells per spleen colony | |
|---|---|---|---|---|---|
| | | BFU-E | GM-CFC | BFU-E | GM-CFC |
| 14 | 0 | 57 | 93 | $75 \pm 85$ | $1400 \pm 1500$ |
| 9 | 9 | 44 | 100 | $100 \pm 180$ | $2000 \pm 1800$ |

Spleen colonies assayed 13 days after transplantation.

Table 6. *Presence of autonomously growing GM-CFC and GM-CSF production in MPZen(GM-CSF) virus-infected spleen colonies*

| Number of colonies | Number of colonies positive for viral DNA | Number of colonies with autonomous CFC | Number of colonies producing GM-CSF |
|---|---|---|---|
| 14 | 0 | 0 | 0 |
| 9 | 9 | 8 | 9 |

Spleen colonies assayed 13 days after transplantation.

GM-CSF (Table 6). These same spleen colonies also contained variable numbers of autonomously growing neutrophil and macrophage colonies (0–100 % of the number in parallel cultures containing PWM-SCM (Table 6)). That some of these colonies contained GM-CFC that were producing sufficient GM-CSF for autostimulation, was proven by removing individual colonies after 7 days of incubation, washing the cells and culturing in medium. Approximately 10 % of the clones treated in this way, contained cells which continued to proliferate for a further 7 days, after which macrophages persisted for up to 12 weeks. At all times, GM-CSF was readily detectable in the medium from these cultures.

All of the spleen colonies (both virus-infected and control) contained varying proportions of erythroblasts, neutrophils, monocytes, eosinophils and blast cells, confirming the multipotentiality of the CFU-S initiating the spleen colonies. However, significant differences were observed in the distribution of cell types, when virally infected clones were compared to control clones (Fig. 4). In colonies expressing the virally derived GM-CSF, the mean percentage of erythroblasts was 51 % (controls 83 %), neutrophils 38 % (controls 6 %), monocytes 5 % (controls 4 %), eosinophils 1 % (controls 0 %) and blast cells 4 % (controls 8 %). Since the mean number of cells in virally infected and control colonies was not significantly different these data suggest that there was an increase in the absolute numbers of neutrophils, eosinophils and monocytes at the expense of erythroblasts and blast cells.

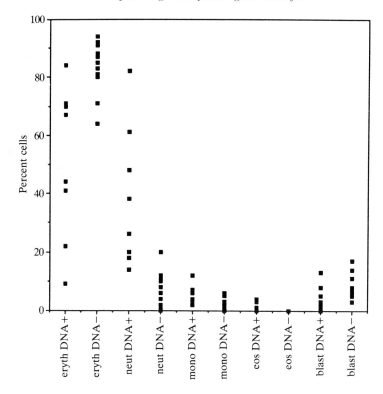

Fig. 4. Percent erythroblasts (eryth), neutrophils (neut), monocytes–macrophages (mono), eosinophils (eos), and blast cells in individual day 13 spleen colonies, either infected (DNA+) or uninfected (DNA−) with the MPZen(GM-CSF) retrovirus.

## Discussion

As shown previously (Williams *et al.* 1984; Keller *et al.* 1985; Dick *et al.* 1985; Bowtell *et al.* 1987), retroviral vectors provide an efficient method for infecting haemopoietic cells even if the cell types are present in low frequency, e.g. multipotential cells. These studies have utilized a drug selectable marker, Neo[R] but when a second gene is incorporated into these same vectors, its expression is very low (Bowtell *et al.* 1987; Bowtell *et al.* 1988).

Although the presence of a selectable marker can facilitate selection of low frequency infected cells, this does not necessarily select cells expressing the second gene. In addition, as shown in Table 3, prior drug treatment may lead to selection of subsets of cells, which may not be desirable. The infection frequency of haemopoietic multipotential cells can be increased by prolonging the cocultivation period (infection phase), by depleting the bone marrow population with cytotoxic drugs and allowing partial regeneration to occur prior to harvest of cells, and by having a source of haemopoietic growth factors present during the cocultivation phase. When combined, these procedures allow infection of up to 100 % of CFU-S (Bowtell *et al.* 1987).

Previous experiments have shown that expression of the virally introduced gene can be increased by incorporation of MPSV-derived enhancer sequences (Bowtell *et al.* 1987) and this manipulation was performed to produce the MPZen(GM-CSF) virus used in the present experiments. In addition, the 3′ untranslated region of the GM-CSF cDNA was removed to minimize possible mRNA instability (Shaw & Kamen, 1986). The resultant construct produced considerably more GM-CSF than either ZipNeo(GM-CSF) or NAc(GM-CSF) infected FDC-P1 cells. Although the latter two vectors contained a GM-CSF cDNA that contained the mRNA instability sequences, subsequent experiments in which MPZen(GM-CSF) and ZipNeo(GM-CSF) have both been constructed with the shortened GM-CSF cDNA clone, have confirmed that GM-CSF expression is higher from the MPZen construct (Gonda, T. J. and Johnson, G. R., unpublished observations). It remains unclear at this stage why expression from MPZen constructs is higher, but preliminary experiments suggest that it is related to the efficiency of translation.

Lacking a drug selectable marker, procedures have been developed for determining the viral titre of $\psi$-2 cells producing MPZen(GM-CSF). This has allowed the successful infection of CFU-S which produce spleen colonies producing readily detectable GM-CSF. Control uninfected colonies do not produce this growth factor. Intriguingly, one result of GM-CSF expression within a developing spleen colony appears to be an increase in the numbers of neutrophils produced and a decrease in the numbers of erythroblasts (see Fig. 4). This change in differentiation patterns does not appear to involve changes in commitment, since the numbers of erythroid and neutrophil committed progenitor cells per spleen colony appear to be unchanged. One possibility is that internally produced GM-CSF is able to amplify neutrophil production from committed progenitor cells, above that seen with exogenously acting GM-CSF and is by some, as yet unknown mechanism, inhibitory for BFU-E differentiation. To test this hypothesis, attempts are being made to infect primary skin cells with MPZen(GM-CSF), followed by grafting in the hope of producing animals with high circulating levels of GM-CSF. Such animals can then be used for spleen colony studies with normal uninfected cells, to determine whether differentiation patterns can be altered by high exogenous levels of the growth factor.

In addition MPZen viruses have been constructed containing other haemopoietic growth factor genes (G-CSF, IL-3, Epo and IL-5) and future experiments will compare the effect of unregulated expression of each of these on spleen colony development and in long-term repopulated mice.

The author is indebted to Dr N. Gough for suggesting and constructing the GM-CSF cDNA and Drs D. Bowtell, T. J. Gonda and I. K. Hariharan for making available the viral constructs used in these studies, and Dr S. Cory for performing the Southern blot analysis of spleen colony cells. This work was supported by the National Health and Medical Research Council, Canberra, The Anti-Cancer Council of Victoria and the National Institutes of Health, Washington, Grant No. CA-25972.

# References

Bowtell, D. D. L., Cory, S., Johnson, G. R. & Gonda, T. J. (1988). A comparison of expression in hemopoietic cells by retroviral vectors carrying two genes. *J. Virol.* **62**, 2464–2473.
Bowtell, D. D. L., Johnson, G. R., Kelso, A. & Cory, S. (1987). Expression of genes

transferred to haemopoietic stem cells by recombinant retroviruses. *Molec. Biol. Med.* **4**, 229–250.

CEPKO, C. L., ROBERTS, B. E. & MULLIGAN, R. C. (1984). Construction and applications of a highly transmissible retrovirus shuttle vector. *Cell* **37**, 1053–1062.

CHENG, G. Y. M., KELLEHER, C. A., MIYAUCHI, J., WANG, C., WONG, G., CLARK, S. C., McCULLOCH, E. A. & MINDEN, M. D. (1988). Structure and expression of genes for GM-CSF and G-CSF in blast cells from patients with acute myeloblastic leukemia. *Blood* **71**, 204–208.

CUTLER, R. L., JOHNSON, G. R. & NICOLA, N. A. (1985a). The preparation of human erythropoietin for tissue culture. *Expl Hemat.* **13**, 796–801.

CUTLER, R. L., METCALF, D., NICOLA, N. A. & JOHNSON, G. R. (1985b). Purification of a multipotential colony stimulating factor from pokeweed mitogen-stimulated mouse spleen cell conditioned medium. *J. biol. Chem.* **260**, 6579–7587.

DICK, J. E., MAGLI, M. C., HUSZAR, D., PHILLIPS, R. A. & BERNSTEIN, A. (1985). Introduction of a selectable gene into primitive stem cells capable of long-term reconstitution of the hemopoietic system of W/W$^v$ mice. *Cell* **42**, 71–79.

GOUGH, N. M., GRAIL, D., GEARING, D. P. & METCALF, D. (1987). Mutagenesis of murine granulocyte–macrophage colony stimulating factor reveals critical residues near the N-terminus. *Eur. J. Biochem.* **169**, 353–358.

GROOPMAN, J. E., MITSUYASU, R. T., DeLEO, M. J., OETTE, D. H. & GOLDE, D. W. (1987). Effect of recombinant human granulocyte–macrophage colony-stimulating factor on myelopoiesis in the acquired immunodeficiency syndrome. *New Eng. J. Med.* **317**, 593–598.

JOHNSON, G. R. (1980). Colony formation in agar by adult bone marrow multipotential hemopoietic cells. *J. cell. Physiol.* **103**, 371–383.

JOHNSON, G. R. & BARKER, D. C. (1985). Erythroid progenitor cells and stimulating factors during murine embryonic and fetal development. *Expl Hemat.* **13**, 200–208.

JOHNSON, G. R., GONDA, T. J., METCALF, D., HARIHARAN, I. K. & CORY, S. (1989). A lethal myeloproliferative syndrome in mice transplanted with bone marrow cells infected with a retrovirus expressing granulocyte-macrophage colony stimulating factor. *EMBO J.* (in press).

KELLER, G., PAIGE, C., GILBOA, E. & WAGNER, E. F. (1985). Expression of a foreign gene in myeloid and lymphoid cells derived from multipotential precursors. *Nature, Lond.* **318**, 149–154.

KINDLER, V., THORENS, B., DE KOSSODO, S., ALLET, B., ELIASON, J. F., THATCHER, D., FARBER, N. & VASSALLI, P. (1986). Stimulation of hematopoiesis in vivo by recombinant bacterial murine interleukin 3. *Proc. natn. Acad. Sci. U.S.A.* **83**, 1001–1005.

KORMAN, A. J., FRANTZ, J. D., STROMINGER, J. L. & MULLIGAN, R. C. (1987). Expression of human class 11 major histocompatibility complex antigens using retrovirus vectors. *Proc. natn. Acad. Sci. U.S.A.* **84**, 2150–2154.

LAKER, C., STOCKING, C., BERGHOLZ, U., HESS, N., DELAMARTER, J. F. & OSTERTAG, W. (1987). Autocrine stimulation after transfer of the granulocyte/macrophage colony-stimulating factor gene and autonomous growth are distinct but interdependent steps in the oncogenic pathway.

LALA, P. K. & JOHNSON, G. R. (1978). Monoclonal origin of B-lymphocyte colony forming cells in spleen colonies formed by multipotential hemopoietic stem cells. *J. exp. Med.* **148**, 1468–1477.

LANG, R. A., METCALF, D., GOUGH, N. M., DUNN, A. R. & GONDA, T. J. (1985). Expression of a hemopoietic growth factor cDNA in a factor-dependent cell line results in autonomous growth and tumorigenicity. *Cell* **43**, 531–542.

MANN, R., MULLIGAN, R. C. & BALTIMORE, D. (1983). Construction of a retrivirus packaging mutant and its use to produce helper free defective retrovirus. *Cell* **33**, 153–159.

METCALF, D. (1984). *The Hemopoietic Colony Stimulating Factors.* Amsterdam: Elsevier.

METCALF, D. (1985). Molecular control of granulocyte and macrophage production. In *Experimental Approaches for the Study of Hemoglobin Switching* (ed. G. Stamatoyannopoulos & A. W. Nienhuis), *Prog. Clin. Biol. Res.* **191**, 323.

METCALF, D. (1986). The molecular biology and functions of the granulocyte-macrophage colony stimulating factors. *Blood* **67**, 257–267.

METCALF, D., BEGLEY, C. G., JOHNSON, G. R. & NICOLA, N. A. (1987a). Quantitative responsiveness of hemopoietic populations in mice to injected recombinant Multi-CSF (IL-3). *Expl Hemat.* **15**, 288–295.

METCALF, D., BEGLEY, C. G., WILLIAMSON, D. J., NICE, E. C., DELAMARTER, J., MERMOD, J-J.,

THATCHER, D. & SCHMIDT, A. (1987*b*). Hemopoietic responses in mice injected with purified recombinant murine GM-CSF. *Expl Hemat.* **15**, 1–19.

METCALF, D. & JOHNSON, G. R. (1978). Production by spleen and lymph node cells of conditioned medium with erythroid and other hemopoietic colony stimulating activity. *J. cell. Physiol.* **96**, 31–42.

NIENHUIS, A. W., DONAHUE, R. E., KARLSSON, S., CLARK, S. C., AGRICOLA, B., ANTINOFF, N., PIERCE, J. E., TURNER, P., ANDERSON, W. F. & NATHAN, D. G. (1987). Recombinant human granulocyte–macrophage colony-stimulating factor (GM-CSF) shortens the period of neutropenia after autologous bone marrow transplantation in a primate model. *J. clin. Invest.* **80**, 573–577.

SHAW, G. & KAMEN, R. (1986). A conserved AU sequence from the 3′ untranslated region of GM-CSF mRNA mediates selective mRNA degradation. *Cell* **46**, 659–667.

WELTE, K., BONILLA, M. A., GILLIO, A. P., BOONE, T. C., POTTER, G. K., GABRILOVE, J. L., MOORE, M. A. S., O'REILLY, R. J. & SOUZA, L. M. (1987). Recombinant human granulocyte colony-stimulating factor. Effects on hematopoiesis in normal and cyclophosphamide-treated primates. *J. exp. Med.* **165**, 941–948.

WILLIAMS, D. A., LEMISCHKA, I. R., NATHAN, D. G. & MULLIGAN, R. C. (1984). Introduction of new genetic information into pluripotent haematopoietic stem cells of the mouse. *Nature, Lond.* **310**, 476–480.

YOUNG, D. C. & GRIFFIN, J. D. (1986). Autocrine secretion of GM-CSF in acute myeloblastic leukemia. *Blood* **68**, 1178–1181.

*J. Cell Sci. Suppl. 10*, 145–155 (1988)
Printed in Great Britain © The Company of Biologists Limited 1988

# *Cis* and *trans* control of erythroid cell-specific gene expression during erythropoiesis

P. R. HARRISON\*, M. PLUMB, J. FRAMPTON, I. CHAMBERS,
D. LLEWELLYN, J. CHESTER, K. MACLEOD, J. FLEMING, J. O'PREY,
M. WALKER AND H. WAINWRIGHT

*The Beatson Institute for Cancer Research, Garscube Estate, Switchback Road, Bearsden, Glasgow G61 1BD, UK*

## Summary

The overall aim of our group's work is to investigate the molecular mechanisms regulating erythroid cell-specific gene expression during erythroid cell differentiation. We have been successful in cloning two non-globin genes of interest: the first encodes the rabbit red cell-specific lipoxygenase (LOX), which has a role in degrading mitochondrial lipids during maturation of the reticulocyte to the erythrocyte; and the second, mouse glutathione peroxidase (GSHPX), an important seleno-enzyme responsible for protection against peroxide-damage. Characterization of the GSHPX gene revealed that the seleno-cysteine residue in the active site of the enzyme is encoded by UGA, which usually functions as a translation-termination codon. This novel finding has important implications regarding the role of mRNA sequence context effects in codon recognition.

In contrast with the $\beta$-globin locus, very little is known about the mechanisms responsible for the erythroid-specific expression of the $\alpha$-globin genes. By a combination of functional transfection assays and studies of the interactions of nuclear sequence-specific DNA-binding proteins with promoter sequences *in vitro*, we have recently defined two regions upstream of the mouse $\alpha$-globin gene involved in its erythroid-specific expression: one contains a sequence motif (GATAAG) that binds to a species-conserved and erythroid-specific factor both *in vitro* and *in vivo*. Interestingly, GATAAG motifs binding the same factor are found also in the mouse and chicken adult $\beta$-globin gene promoters, the erythroid-specific promoter of the haem pathway enzyme, porphobilinogen (PBG) deaminase and the chicken $\beta$-globin 3' enhancer. We are now commencing purification of this erythroid-specific GATAAG-binding factor, investigating in more detail how it functions in relation to other globin gene control regions and determining whether GATAAG-like regions have a functional role in the erythroid-specific expression of other genes.

We have begun to investigate the regulation of the GSHPX and red cell LOX genes. The presence of tissue-specific 3' DNase I-hypersensitive sites (DHSS) suggests that different 3' flanking regions of the GSHPX gene may be important in its regulation in the various cell types in which it is highly expressed, i.e. erythroid cells, liver and kidney. As far as the RBC LOX gene is concerned, its transcription unit has been defined and 5' and 3' flanking regions are being investigated for erythroid-specific regulatory elements: the available 2·7 kb of 5' LOX gene flanking sequence gives increased expression of a linked chloramphenicol acetyltransferase (CAT) gene when transfected into a mouse erythroid cell line compared to non-erythroid cell lines; but we have not yet located the regions responsible, except that they are upstream of −154 nucleotides. The limits of the LOX gene chromosomal domain, and regions involved in its activation in erythroid cells, are also being investigated by DNase I digestion studies.

\*Author for correspondence.

Key words: gene regulation, erythropoiesis, cell differentiation, *trans*-factors, *cis*-control.

## Introduction

Understanding how development is regulated revolves round three major questions (see Harrison (1988) for a recent general review of the subject): how cell proliferation is controlled to maintain homeostasis; how cell differentiation is regulated; and finally how spatial organization is established. Haematopoiesis (and erythropoiesis in particular) provides a useful experimental system in which to explore such questions at the molecular level and in particular the inter-relationship between cell growth and differentiation.

Erythroid cells are derived from multipotential haemopoietic stem cells *via* a series of intermediate progenitor cells with increasingly restricted developmental potential (reviewed by Harrison (1982*a,b*); Dexter & Spooncer (1987) – see Fig. 1). Early progenitor cells require growth factors that are probably presented by stromal cells in the tissue micro-environment; but later progenitors become responsive to the erythroid-lineage-specific growth factor, erythropoietin, presumably due to acquisition of receptors for the hormone. During this late stage of erythroid differentiation, various characteristic erythroid proteins are synthesized: the cytoskeletal

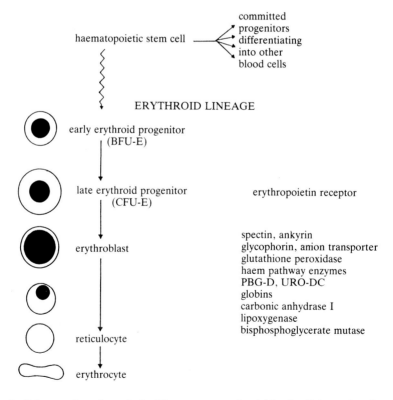

Fig. 1. Scheme of erythropoiesis. The ontogeny of red blood cell formation from the haemopoietic stem cell via the intermediate progenitor cells (BFU-Es and CFU-Es) is summarized, with an illustration of the characteristic morphological changes and red blood cell proteins expressed at various stages of differentiation. PBG-D: porphobilinogen deaminase; URO-DC: uroporphyrinogen decarboxylase.

proteins (the $\alpha$- and $\beta$-spectrins, ankyrin and band 4.1); the transmembrane sialoglycoproteins (glycophorins) and major anion exchange protein (band 3); the globins; the haem pathway enzymes (particularly porphobilinogen (PBG)-deaminase and uroporphyrinogen decarboxylase, both of which are elevated in red blood cells (RBCs)); and other families of enzymes of which particular isozymes are exclusive to red cells (the RBC lipoxygenase, carbonic anhydrase I and bisphosphoglycerate mutase) or are greatly elevated in RBCs (glutathione peroxidase (GSHPX)) (reviewed by Harrison, 1984). The aim of our work over the past few years has been to try to elucidate some of the control mechanisms responsible for activating the expression of this set of genes during erythroid cell differentiation, focusing mainly on the $\alpha$-globin, RBC lipoxygenase and GSHPX genes. Our basic working hypothesis has been that such genes must possess some common features that respond to the erythroid cell environment: our recent results seem to have identified one component that may be involved in this process.

## Cloning and characterization of genes

### The GSHPX gene

Some time ago, we cloned a mRNA expressed at a 50-fold higher level in mouse erythroblasts, liver and kidney compared to other cell types tested that encodes a $20 \times 10^3 M_r$ polypeptide and then subsequently we isolated the corresponding gene (Affara *et al.* 1983; Goldfarb *et al.* 1983). This has since been identified as encoding GSHPX (Chambers *et al.* 1986). One entirely novel point of interest to emerge was that the selenocysteine residue (Se-Cys) in the active site of the mouse enzyme is encoded by the 'termination codon', TGA (Chambers *et al.* 1986). More recently, this codon assignment for Se-Cys has been shown to be conserved in the human GSHPX gene and also in a bacterial seleno-enzyme, formate dehydrogenase (fdhF). This makes sense of earlier work suggesting that Se-Cys is incorporated into GSHPX co-translationally, possibly involving a specific tRNA. However, it raises intriguing questions as to how the UGA triplet is recognized as encoding Se-Cys in one mRNA but translation termination in another. One clue as to the basis for the 'mRNA context effect' for Se-Cys incorporation may be that Se-Cys is derived from serine, probably *via* substitution of the phosphate group in phosphoserine by selenite: thus Se-Cys-tRNA could be derived from a UGA-suppressor seryl-tRNA, which is known to exist (discussed by Chambers & Harrison, 1987). Presumably this suppressor tRNA must recognize other sequences in certain mRNAs other than the UGA codon itself. Very recently this idea has received strong confirmation by the isolation of an *Escherichia coli* gene required for seleno cysteine synthesis that encodes a minor serine-tRNA species (Leinfelder *et al.* 1988).

### The RBC LOX gene

Using oligonucleotides derived from the *N*-terminal amino acid sequence of the rabbit reticulocyte LOX enzyme (obtained in collaboration with Dr B. Thiele from Professor S. Rapaport's group in Berlin) to screen rabbit reticulocyte cDNA libraries, we obtained first a short cDNA recombinant whose sequence encodes the $N$-terminal 30 amino acid sequence (Thiele *et al.* 1987*a*) and later cDNAs derived from the 3' end of the LOX mRNA. By Northern blot analysis with LOX cDNAs, the RBC LOX mRNA is expressed late in erythroid differentiation and in a tissue-specific manner, not being detectable in bone marrow, heart, spleen, lung and brain cells (Thiele *et al.* 1987*b*). This represents the first report of the cloning of any mammalian LOX mRNA, though the cloning of the human leucocyte 5-LOX mRNA has since been reported (Matsumoto *et al.* 1988; Dixon *et al.* 1988).

Using the LOX cDNAs to screen a rabbit genomic DNA library, a 17 kb genomic DNA recombinant has been isolated that contains the RBC LOX gene (Thiele *et al.* 1987*b*). Using hybridization conditions of moderate stringency, the RBC LOX gene seems to be unique in the genome since the pattern of hybridization of 5' and 3' RBC LOX cDNAs to total genomic DNA digested with various restriction enzymes is fully explained by the restriction map of the 17 kb genomic DNA recombinant containing the LOX gene. This most probably means that the genes encoding the LOX isozymes of other tissues are not very closely related to the RBC LOX gene, though the various LOX proteins seem to be recognizably similar in terms of amino acid sequence. Alternatively, the various LOXs may be encoded by mRNAs generated by the splicing of alternative tissue-specific exons onto a set of common exons, as is the situation for the erythroid-specific and non-erythroid forms of PBG-deaminase (Chretien *et al.* 1988).

The transcriptional unit of the RBC LOX gene has now been defined. The site of transcription initiation has been mapped by a combination of S1 nuclease mapping experiments with genomic fragments and primer extension/sequencing using the LOX mRNA and correlating the primer extension sequence with the genomic DNA sequence in the region of transcription initiation predicted by the S1 mapping experiments. Furthermore, a fragment containing the first 154 nucleotide (nt) upstream of the site of transcription initiation, functions equally well as a promoter when linked to the chloramphenicol acetyltransferase (CAT) gene and tested in transient expression assays after transfection into mouse erythroleukaemia or non-erythroid cell lines. The 3' end of the gene has also been defined in the genomic recombinants by hybridization with 3'LOX cDNAs followed by sequencing of the appropriate genomic DNA region. The RBC LOX gene contains at least two introns, and the available genomic DNA recombinants contain about 2·5 kb and 6·5 kb of 5' and 3' flanking DNA, respectively.

## Developmental changes in upstream transcripts from globin and non-globin genes

Much evidence in the literature shows that the chromatin structure around gene control regions is often in a highly accessible conformation in cell types in which the gene is active as defined by the appearance of DNase I-hypersensitive sites (DHSS). When located 5' to the gene, such active control regions are also often the sites of minor transcripts: but whether such transcripts have a function in regulation *per se* or are simply diagnostic of the altered chromosome structure associated with the active gene is still far from clear.

To begin to explore such questions, we monitored the appearance of minor upstream transcripts from the mouse α- and β-globin genes and the GSHPX gene during erythroid cell differentiation. To do this, we analysed haemopoietic stem cell lines (from Prof. T. M. Dexter, Paterson Laboratory, Manchester), committed erythroid precursor cells (CFU-Es) purified from the spleens of anaemic mice, erythroleukaemia cells at various stages of differentiation, reticulocytes and various other haemopoietic and non-haemopoietic cells. For each gene, we found that upstream transcripts occurr at distinct clusters of sites at different stages of erythropoiesis: some occur only during early erythropoiesis; some occur early and persist to the terminal stages; while others accumulate roughly in parallel with the main transcript (Frampton *et al.* 1987*a*). This suggests that the minor transcripts that appear early in erythropoiesis may be associated with activation of the globin genes prior to onset of active transcription from the cap site.

The initiation sites for certain of these minor transcripts lie within developmentally regulated DNase I-hypersensitive sites whose occurrence correlates with transcription of the genes modulated by *trans*-acting factors present in expressing *versus* non-expressing cell hybrids (Affara *et al.* 1985); they are also close to sequences known to be involved in globin gene regulation (for example, the TATA, CAAT and CACCCT motifs). In particular, one group of β-globin minor transcripts arise at a previously unnoticed 13 nt sequence conserved amongst adult mammalian globin genes (Frampton *et al.* 1987*a,b*) (the B box, see Fig. 2), which has recently been shown to be an erythroid-specific control element, by Antoniou *et al.* (1988). Other groups of upstream transcripts originate from other control regions we have since identified (see below).

## Regulation of the mouse α-globin gene

There has been little evidence published about the mechanisms responsible for the erythroid-specific expression of the α-globin genes. What is known suggests that in many respects they are regulated differently from the β-globin genes: for example, transcription of transfected human α-globin genes in mouse erythroleukaemia cells is not greatly increased as the cells are induced to differentiate, whereas that of transfected human β-globin genes is. We considered it worthwhile, therefore, to try to elucidate the transcriptional mechanisms responsible for the erythroid-specific expression of the mouse α-globin gene with a view to comparing its mode of regulation with that of the much more extensively studied β-globin genes. In particular, we decided to investigate *cis*-control regions responsible for its erythroid-specific regulation by a combination of functional transfection assays and studies of the interactions of nuclear proteins with the α-globin gene promoter, by comparing erythroid and non-erythroid cells (Frampton *et al.* 1988).

*Functional analysis of the α-globin gene promoter*

Progressive deletions of 4 kb of the mouse α-globin gene 5′ flanking sequence have been inserted upstream of the CAT gene under the control of a minimal 52 bp α-globin promoter (containing only sequences from the TATA motif to the cap site) and then transfected into mouse erythroleukaemia or fibroblast (STO) cells. The extent of expression of the CAT gene has been monitored mainly by transient assays, but in some cases also in stable cell lines derived by co-transfection with the selectable neomycin-resistance gene. CAT gene expression is assayed usually by enzyme activity but RNA transcripts are measured by the S1 protection technique to check important conclusions. The 52 bp α-globin minimal promoter does not act in a tissue-specific way when compared to a minimal SV40 promoter (containing the 21 bp repeats but not the enhancer).

The 4 kb of α-globin 5′ flanking DNA confers a 20-fold erythroid-specific increase in CAT gene expression in transient assays and this is due to at least two separate regions: a proximal region between −197 to −52 nt; and a distal region at about −2 kb (Frampton *et al.* unpublished). So far a tissue-specific enhancer has not been identified in the 3′ flanking region of the α-globin gene.

*DNA–protein interactions within the α-globin promoter*

*The proximal region: the CCAAT and CACCC motifs.* The most proximal regulatory region (−52 to −197 nt), which confers a 4- to 5-fold increased transcription in erythroblasts compared to fibroblasts as described above, contains the previously identified CCAAT and CCACCC regulatory elements (Fig. 2). Three proteins binding to this region *in vitro* have been identified: (1) a CCAAT-binding protein; (2) a CACCC-binding protein; and (3) a protein which displaces the CCAAT-binding protein when it binds to an overlapping sequence. Although the CCAAT-binding protein is present in all tissues examined, footprint analysis with nuclear proteins from different tissues reveals two patterns: either the CCAAT-

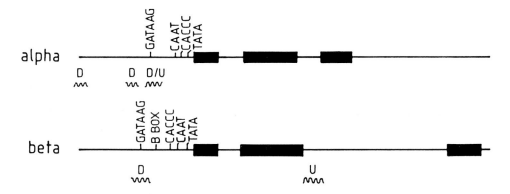

Fig. 2. Map of control sequences surrounding the mouse α- and β-globin genes. Various sequence motifs discussed in the text are shown together with the locations of DNase I-hypersensitive sites present in erythroblasts (mouse erythroleukaemia cells) (U) or in erythroblasts that have been induced to undergo erythroid maturation (D).

binding protein alone (in liver, spleen and erythroleukaemia cells induced to undergo erythroid maturation); or the displacement protein plus the CACCC-binding protein (in kidney, brain and undifferentiated erythroleukaemia cells).

There is increasing evidence that general transcription factors can contribute to specific gene control either as a consequence of post-translational modifications and/or due to a change in the relative concentrations of proteins which compete for binding to the same sequence. Experiments are in progress to try to elucidate how the combination of the three proteins (and any others not yet detected) contribute to the erythroid-specificity of this region of the α-globin promoter.

*The α-globin GATAAG motif.* Footprint and gel-shift analysis of the erythroid-specific regulatory element between −129 and −197 nt with mouse and human nuclear extracts revealed an erythroid-specific protein which binds to a GATAAG motif. The factor is found only in erythroid cells and is conserved between species: it is found in mouse erythroleukaemia cells, chicken erythrocytes and human erythroid cell lines K562 and KMOE; but not in mouse brain, kidney and spleen or HeLa cells – mouse liver contains a protein binding to the GATAAG region but it seems to be different from the factor present in erythroid cells (Plumb *et al.* 1989). In all cases specificity of DNA−protein interactions was confirmed by competition experiments with specific oligonucleotides.

## The role of the GATAAG motif in erythroid cell-specific gene expression

### Globin genes

A GATAAG motif is also present about 200 nt upstream of the mouse β-major globin gene (Fig. 2) and it also is footprinted by the same factor (Plumb *et al.* 1989). Since both the α- and β-globin GATAAG regions lie within erythroid-specific DNase I-hypersensitive sites *in vivo*, both globin GATAAG sequences probably bind to the GATAAG-binding factor *in vivo* in an erythroid-specific manner. GATAAG motifs are also present upstream of certain other globin genes: some of these have been shown to bind an erythroid-specific factor, for example the chicken α-pi, α-D, and β-rho globin genes, as reported by Kemper *et al.* (1987); and we have shown that this chicken factor also binds to the mouse α- and β-GATAAG elements (Plumb *et al.* 1989).

The roles the GATAAG regions of the α- and β-globin genes play in regulating their erythroid-specific transcription have also been investigated. It may be of significance that the α- and β-globin GATAAG regions are sites of erythroid-specific upstream transcripts (Frampton *et al.* 1987*a*) (Fig. 2). Deletion of a 60 nt region of the α-globin promoter containing the GATAAG element from a long promoter fragment (from the cap site to −700 nt) linked to the CAT gene reduces the promoter activity 2-fold in transient transfection assays with erythroblasts but not with fibroblasts. Consistent with this, linking one or two copies of the deleted GATAAG fragment to the minimal 52 nt α-globin promoter increases its promoter activity in erythroblasts 2- to 3-fold but not in fibroblasts: intriguingly, a single copy of the same GATAAG region inserted in the reverse orientation gives a 10-fold erythroid-specific increase. Similar experiments with the $\beta$-globin promoter show that a single copy of a 60 nt fragment containing the $\beta$-globin GATAAG region also gives an erythroid-specific increase in promoter activity, but in this case the effect is large (12-fold) irrespective of orientation (unpublished data). The reasons for the different functional activities of these short $\alpha$- or $\beta$-globin GATAAG-containing fragments are presently unclear: it is still possible that nearby sequences modulate their effects; alternatively, the $\alpha$- and $\beta$-GATAAG motifs may have different affinities for the available factor or they could function at different stages of differentiation. Since it is not feasible for technical reasons to perform transient assays in erythroleukaemia cells induced to undergo differentiation, the function of the $\alpha$- and $\beta$-globin GATAAG regions are being tested in erythroleukaemia cells stably transfected with the appropriate constructs.

GATAAG-like motifs are also present upstream of several other globin genes, in the 3′ enhancer of the chicken adult $\beta$-globin gene and in a putative enhancer in the erythroid-specific DNase I-hypersensitive site in the second intron of the mouse $\beta^{major}$-globin gene. Recent results using gel retardation assays have shown that the GATAAG motif in the chicken $\beta$-globin 3′ enhancer interacts strongly with the 5′ globin GATAAG-binding protein (Plumb *et al.* 1989): this suggests that the GATAAG-binding factor may interact cooperatively with both 5′ and 3′ globin control regions.

*Other genes*

Both the GSHPX gene promoter and the erythroid-specific promoter of the gene encoding the haem pathway enzyme, PBG-deaminase, contain exact GATAAG motifs, and the latter binds *in vitro* to the mouse and human globin gene GATAAG-binding factors (Plumb *et al.* 1989). Footprinting of the GATAAG motif in the GSHPX promoter has not yet been attempted, but it seems to be of some significance since it is the only sequence upstream of the coding region, apart from the TATA-like motif and one other sequence, that is conserved between the mouse and human genes. Although it does not contain an exact GATAAG sequence, the LOX gene promoter could still bind the GATAAG-binding factor since the consensus sequence for the GATAAG-binding factor is not yet known.

The major thrust of our future work in this area is to purify the GATAAG-binding protein by affinity chromatography and other means in order ultimately to clone the gene that encodes it so as to be able to elucidate further its putative role in erythroid cell-specific gene expression and how it functions in relation to other control regions. In the longer term, it will be worthwhile to investigate the function of the GATAAG-binding protein in relation to other transcription factors in *in vitro* transcription systems or in permeabilized cells.

## Regulation of non-globin genes

*The GSHPX gene*

The GSHPX mRNA is expressed at high levels in erythroid cells, kidney and liver compared to the low basal level in other cell types tested (Affara *et al.* 1983, 1985). This control seems to be primarily at the transcription level since the tissue-specific changes in mRNA levels are reflected in similar changes in the level of the GSHPX primary transcript, as determined using total cellular RNA in S1 protection experiments with an intron-specific probe (I. Chambers & P. R. Harrison, unpublished results).

In terms of established transcriptional control signals, the 5' flanking region of the mouse GSHPX gene has a TATA-like box but no CAAT-box and is G+C-rich, containing several potential binding sites for the transcription factor, Sp1 (Chambers *et al.* 1986). There are also tissue-specific anti-sense transcripts from the GSHPX promoter region (J. Frampton, unpublished data) and the promoter region is a site of DNase I hypersensitivity in the chromatin of both high- and low-expressing tissues (Affara *et al.* 1985). In these respects, it has characteristics of other 'housekeeping' genes that are expressed in all cells, though often more highly in some than others. The 5' flanking region also contains the species-conserved GATAAG motif noted above. The 3' flanking region contains a perfect SV40 core enhancer sequence flanked by potential Sp1-binding consensus sites. To test whether the GSHPX promoter itself is responsible for the elevated expression of the gene in erythroid cells, 680 bp of 5' flanking DNA sequence was linked to the CAT gene and tested for promoter function in transient assays when transfected into erythroleukaemia cells or fibroblasts. However, the GSHPX promoter functioned equally well in both cell types when compared to the minimal SV40 promoter.

Our earlier experiments showed that the GSHPX gene possesses tissue-specific DHSSs in the 3' flanking region in erythroblasts (Affara *et al.* 1985). Subsequent work has mapped these DHSS more accurately and showed that other high-expressing tissues like liver and kidney also have a broad 3' DHSS (2·2–2·6 kb from the polyadenylation site) like erythroid cells; but erythroid cells possess other 3' DHSS in addition, about 200–300 nt and 700–800 nt 3' to the polyadenylation site (I. Chambers and P.R.H., unpublished data). Unfortunately, these 3' DHSS lie outside the fragments of the GSHPX gene present in the genomic recombinants available, but once 3' overlapping genomic fragments have been isolated the 3' flanking DNA in the regions of the tissue-specific DHSS will be tested for enhancer activity in functional transfection assays and any tissue-specific proteins that interact with functionally important regions identified.

## The RBC LOX gene

Sequencing of the immediate upstream region has revealed a TATA-like motif at $-30$ nt but no CAAT nor GATAAG motifs. To locate possible control regions, two approaches are being adopted. First, the limits of the LOX gene chromosomal domain and the location of DNase I-hypersensitive sites (DHSS) within it in the chromatin of erythroid and non-erythroid cells are being investigated. Second, various fragments of the 2·7 kb 5' flanking region of the LOX gene have been cloned upstream of the CAT gene driven by the 154 nt LOX gene promoter and the constructs tested for functional activity when introduced into erythroid or non-erythroid cells by transient or stable transfection methods. The results show that the entire 2·7 kb of 5′ flanking LOX DNA gives an 8-fold increase in expression of a linked CAT gene in transient transfection assays with mouse erythroleukaemia cells compared to mouse fibroblasts; whereas the first 154 nt of 5′ flanking sequence has no such erythroid-specific promoter activity (Chester *et al.* manuscript in preparation). The 6·5 kb 3′ flanking region of the LOX gene has also been cloned 3′ to the LOX promoter/CAT gene construct and introduced into erythroid and fibroblast cell lines but no 3′ enhancer has yet been detected. It is anticipated that these ongoing experiments will reveal interesting information about the tissue-specific regulation of the RBC LOX gene vis-à-vis the globin, GSHPX and PBG-deaminase genes.

## References

AFFARA, N., FLEMING, J., BLACK, E., GOLDFARB, P. S., THIELE, B. & HARRISON, P. R. (1985). Chromatin changes associated with the expression of globin and non-globin genes in cell hybrids between erythroid and other cells. *Nucl. Acids Res* **13**, 5629–44.

AFFARA, N., GOLDFARB, P. S., YANG, Q.-S. & HARRISON, P. R. (1983). Patterns of expression of erythroblast non-globin mRNAs. *Nucl. Acids Res.* **11**, 931–945.

ANTONIOU, M., DEBOER, E., HABITS, G. & GROSVELD, F. (1988). The human beta-globin gene contains multiple regulatory regions: identification of one promoter and two downstream enhancers. *EMBO J.* **7**, 377–384.

CHAMBERS, I., FRAMPTON, J., GOLDFARB, P., AFFARA, N., McBAIN, W. & HARRISON, P. R. (1986). The structure of the mouse glutathione peroxidase gene: the selenocysteine in the active site is encoded by the 'termination codon', TGA. *EMBO J.* **5**, 1221–1227.

CHAMBERS, I. & HARRISON, P. R. (1987). A new puzzle in selenoprotein biosynthesis: selenocysteine seems to be encoded by the stop codon, UGA. *Trends Biochem Sci.* **12**, 255–256.

CHRETIEN, S., DUBART, A., BEAUPAIN, D., RAICH, N., GRANDCHAMP, B., ROSA, J., GOOSSENS, M. & ROMEO, P.-H. (1988). Alternative transcription and splicing of the human porphobilinogen deaminase gene result either in tissue-specific or in house-keeping expression. *Proc. natn. Acad. Sci. U.S.A.* **85**, 6–10.

DEXTER, T. & SPOONCER, E. (1987). Growth and differentiation in the hemopoietic system. *A. Rev. Cell Biol.* **3**, 423–441.

DIXON, R. A. F., JONES, R. E., DIEHL, R. E., BENNETT, C. D., KARGMAN, S. & ROUZER, C. A. (1988). Cloning of the cDNA for human 5-lipoxygenase. *Proc. natn. Acad. Sci. U.S.A.* **85**, 416–420.

FRAMPTON, J., CHAMBERS, I., CONKIE, D. & HARRISON, P. R. (1987b). The regulation of erythroid cell-specific gene expression. In *Molecular Approaches to Developmental Biology, UCLA Symp. Molecular Cellular Biol., New Series* (ed. R.A. Firtel & E.H. Davidson), vol. 151, pp. 533–545. New York: A. R. Liss.

FRAMPTON, J., CONKIE, D., CHAMBERS, I., McBAIN, W., DEXTER, M. & HARRISON, P. R. (1987a). Changes in minor transcripts from the α1- and β^{maj}-globin and glutathione peroxidase genes during erythropoeisis. *Nucleic Acids Res* **15**, 3671–3688.

GOLDFARB, P. S., O'PREY, J., AFFARA, N., YANG, Q-S. & HARRISON, P. R. (1983). Isolation of non-globin genes expressed preferentially in mouse erythroid cells. *Nucl. Acids Res.* **11**, 3517–3530.

HARRISON, P. R. (1982a). Stem cell regulation in erythropoiesis. *Nature, Lond.* **295**, 454–455.

HARRISON, P. R. (1982b). Regulation of differentiation in retrovirus-induced erythroleukaemias. *Cancer Surveys* **1**, 232–277.

HARRISON, P. R. (1984). Molecular analysis of erythropoieisis. *Expl Cell Res.* **155**, 321–344.

HARRISON, P. R. (1988). Molecular mechanisms involved in the regulation of gene expression during cell differentiation: a review. In *Colony Stimulating Factors: Molecular and Cellular Biology* (ed. T.M. Dexter, J. Garland & N. Testa). New York: Marcel Dekker (in press).

KEMPER, B., JACKSON, P. O. & GROSVELD, G. (1987). Protein-binding sites within the 5′ DNase I-hypersensitive region of the chicken-alpha-D globin gene. *Molec. Cell. Biol.* **7**, 2059–2069.

LEINFELDER, W., ZEHELIN, E., MANDRAND-BERTHELOT, M.-A. & BOCK, A. (1988). Gene for a novel tRNA species that accepts L-serine and cotranslationally inserts selenocysteine. *Nature, Lond.* **331**, 723–725.

MATSUMOTO, T., FUNK, C. D., RADMARK, O., HOOG, J.-O., JORNVALL, H. & SAMUELSSON, B. (1988). Molecular cloning and amino acid sequence of human 5-lipoxygenase. *Proc. natn. Acad. Sci. U.S.A.* **85**, 26–30.

PLUMB, M., FRAMPTON, J., WAINWRIGHT, H., WALKER, M., MACLEOD, K., GOODWIN, G. & HARRISON, P. R. (1989). GATAAG; a *cis*-control region binding an erythroid-specific nuclear factor with a role in globin and non-globin gene expression. *Nucl. Acids Res.* (in press).

THIELE, B. J., FLEMING, J., KASTURI, K., BLACK, E., CHESTER, J., O'PREY, J., RAPOPORT, S. M. & HARRISON, P. R. (1987b). Cloning of a rabbit erythroid cell-specific lipoxygenase mRNA. *Gene* **57**, 111–119.

THIELE, B. J., HOHNE, M., NACK, B., HARRISON, P. R. & RAPOPORT, S. M. (1987a). Lipoxygenase mRNA during development of red blood cells studied with a cloned probe. *Biomed. biochim. Acta* **46**, 124–125.

J. Cell Sci. Suppl. 10, 157–169 (1988)
Printed in Great Britain © The Company of Biologists Limited 1988

# The *ras* oncogenes

C. J. MARSHALL

*Institute of Cancer Research: Royal Cancer Hospital, Chester Beatty Laboratories, Fulham Road, London SW3 6JB, UK*

## Summary

Oncogenic forms of the p21*ras* genes have been found in a large variety of human malignancies and tumours induced in animals by chemical carcinogens or irradiation. The active form of the p21 *ras* proteins is the GTP bound state and oncogenic mutations result in the protein being constitutively in the GTP bound active state. There is evidence to suggest that activating mutations can occur either as initiating steps in carcinogenesis or as later events in the evolution to frank neoplasia. To transduce a signal for proliferation and transformation the active GTP form of p21*ras* must interact with one or more cellular targets. Genetic experiments suggest that one potential effector molecule is the GTPase activating protein GAP. However, the mechanism by which interaction with GAP results in proliferation and transformation remains to be elucidated.

## Introduction

The H, N and K *ras* genes encode closely related $21 M_r \times 10^3$ proteins that are localized on the inner surface of the plasma membrane, bind and hydrolyse guanosine triphosphate (GTP). These genes and proteins have received much attention because in a large fraction of some human malignancies a *ras* proto-oncogene is activated to a transforming gene (oncogene) by a single point mutation. Although it has been possible to analyse the pattern of *ras* gene mutations in great detail, understanding the function of both the normal and transforming proteins has proved more elusive.

## Pattern of *ras* gene mutations in human malignancy

Early studies of *ras* oncogenes in malignancies made use of calcium phosphate coprecipitation to introduce DNA into NIH-3T3 cells to search for transforming genes able to cause focus formation on a confluent layer (Shih *et al.* 1979). Subsequently, efforts were made to extend the sensitivity of the transfection assay by cotransfection with a dominant selectable marker followed by injection of the transfected cells into nude mice to assay for tumorigenic cells (Fasano *et al.* 1984). This cotransfection assay appears to allow detection of mutant *ras* genes, when they are present in only a minor fraction of cells, and transforming alleles that are poor at focus production (Bos *et al.* 1985; Toksoz *et al.* 1987). However, while the transfection assays are very sensitive they are very time consuming and have been superseded for most studies by direct DNA analysis. Allele-specific oligonucleotide probes have proved extremely useful in analysing the natural history of *ras* gene

Key words: p21 *ras*, oncogenic mutation, transformation.

mutations, first by direct probing of genomic DNA (Bos *et al.* 1984) and then with much more ease and sensitivity on *ras* target sequences amplified by the Polymerase Chain Reaction (PCR) (Saiki *et al.* 1985). Using the PCR and oligonucleotide probing it is possible to analyse large numbers of samples easily.

Analysis of *ras* gene mutations has lead to the conclusion that some tumours such as breast carcinomas show very little evidence of *ras* gene mutation (Bos, 1988) while in others such as colorectal cancer (Bos *et al.* 1987; Forrester *et al.* 1987), acute myeloid leukaemia (Farr *et al.* 1988*a*) and pancreatic carcinoma (Almoguerra *et al.* 1988) the incidence of mutation is 25–50 % or higher. In these situations where there is a high incidence of mutation there is very pronounced bias to one or other particular *ras* gene being mutated. Thus in AML the mutations are invariably in N-*ras* while in colorectal and pancreatic cancer the majority of mutations are in K-*ras*. The reason for this bias is unknown. At present we have no evidence for functional differences between the *ras* proteins, so it is unclear whether the pattern of activation reflects physiological differences between the proteins. Neither is it clear whether the pattern of activation is a consequence of differential expression of the three genes. The restriction to only one of the three genes being mutated in a particular form of malignancy is paralled by the pattern of activation of *ras* genes by chemical carcinogens in animal experiments. In these experiments the vast majority of tumours show the same *ras* gene being activated by the same mutation (Sukumar *et al.* 1983; Quintanilla *et al.* 1986). These results suggest that the specificity of mutations could reflect the nature of the interaction between DNA sequence and a particular carcinogen.

An important question in *ras* gene activation is the timing of the mutational event in relation to tumour initiation and progression. Studies using short lived carcinogens to induce tumours in rodents argue that *ras* gene mutation is an early, possibly initiating event in carcinogenesis (Sukumar *et al.* 1983). Similar conclusions about the timing of *ras* gene mutations have been made from studies of premalignant papillomas in rodent skin carcinogenesis (Balmain *et al.* 1984) and premalignant polyps in human colorectal cancer (Bos *et al.* 1987). Although these observations point to an early involvement of *ras* mutations in neoplastic transformation they do not necessarily imply that it is the initiating event. Strong support for *ras* gene mutations not being the initiating event comes from studies on acute myeloid leukaemia from the same patient in presentation and relapse. Farr *et al.* (1988) and Farr *et al.* (1988*b*) have found in five cases that the presentation AML may carry a *ras* gene mutation but relapses either do not contain any detectable mutations or bear a different mutation. Since relapses appear to be derived from the same leukaemic clone as the presentation (Fearon *et al.* 1986), these results argue that *ras* gene mutation is occurring after some other initiating leukaemic event. Therefore in these leukaemias *ras* gene mutation is more likely to play a role after the initial event(s) in neoplastic transformation.

Similar conclusions can also be drawn from studies on mutation in colorectal polyps where the smallest, most benign polyps do not contain *ras* gene mutations (Farr *et al.* 1988*b*). It is possible however, that while *ras* gene mutation is not the initiating genetic event it does occur early rather than very late in neoplastic progression because *ras* gene mutation is frequent in the preleukaemic myelodysplastic syndromes (Hirai *et al.* 1987; Padua *et al.* 1988).

## Biochemical properties of p21*ras* molecules

*Membrane localization*

The p21*ras* molecules are synthesized in the cytosol and are then found associated with the plasma membrane. The membrane bound form migrates on SDS–PAGE genes with an apparent molecular weight approximately $1-2\times10^3$ less than the cytosolic form of the protein. The mechanism and significance of this mobility shift remains obscure. It does not appear to be caused by the addition of the fatty acid palmitoyl residue to Cys186 since removal of the palmitoyl group by hydrazine does not shift the mobility of the membrane bound form to that of the cytosolic (McGhee *et al.* 1987).

Addition of a palmitoyl group to Cys186 appears to be a central step in the localization of p21*ras* molecules to the membrane. Mutation of the Cys186 to Ser186 which cannot form the thioester bond to palmititic acid results in a protein which cannot go to the plasma membrane and is incapable of transforming cells (Willumsen *et al.* 1984). Such data strongly argue that the site of action of the active p21*ras* molecule is at the membrane and implies that whatever is the target of p21*ras* must be localized in the membrane. Interestingly the palmitoyl group on Cys186 turns over rapidly with a half life of 10–20 min (McGhee *et al.* 1987) compared to the 20 h half life of the protein (Ulsh & Shih, 1984). The functional significance of this turnover is unclear and it remains to be resolved whether the cycles of removal and addition of palmititic acid are reflected in shuttling of the proteins between membrane and cytosol.

*Guanine nucleotide binding*

The purification of p21*ras* proteins from recombinant expression systems has permitted a detailed analysis of guanine nucleotide binding. Most workers report affinities for binding GTP or GDP in the $10^{-8}$ to $10^{-9}$ M range (McGrath *et al.* 1984; Trahey *et al.* 1987). However, higher affinities of around $10^{-11}$ M have been reported for proteins that have been prepared nucleotide free (Feuerstein *et al.* 1987). Comparison of the sequences of other guanine nucleotide binding proteins together with X-ray crystallographic analysis has delineated the structural features necessary for guanine nucleotide binding. At present only the crystal structure of the GDP form of p21*ras* has been solved (DeVos *et al.* 1988). GDP is bound in a pocket by four of the nine loops which interconnect $\alpha$ strands, or $\beta$ strands to helix. The residues of loop 1 which include amino acids 12 and 13 are near the $\beta$ phosphate of GDP, amino acid 30 of loop 2 is adjacent to the ribose of GDP, while amino acids 116, 117, 119 and 120 of loop 7 together with amino acids 145 and 147 of loop 9 form part of the pocket for the guanine of GDP. As will be discussed later mutations in loop 1 affect guanine nucleotide hydrolysis and loop 7 binding.

Since the active form of p21*ras* appears to be the GTP bound state (Trahey & McCormick, 1987), solution of the structure of the GTP form will be necessary to determine how binding of GTP to p21*ras* and conversion to the active state modifies the structure of the molecule. One level for regulating the activity of p21*ras* proteins is at the level of bound nucleotide. This could be achieved either by regulating the rate at which bound nucleotide is exchanged or by the rate of hydrolysis of bound GTP. Measurements of exchange rates on purified proteins show that in the presence of $Mg^{2+}$ the exchange rate is slow with a half life of around 40 min. The rate of exchange can be considerably increased *in vitro* by decreasing the $Mg^{2+}$ concentration (Hall & Self, 1986). Although it is an attractive idea that the exchange rate of guanine nucleotide is regulated *in vivo* in an analogous way to receptor-bound G proteins, no evidence has been adduced at present to show a stimulated exchange on p21*ras* proteins *in vivo*.

## GTP hydrolysis

GTP bound to purified normal p21*ras* proteins is hydrolysed slowly with a half life of around 50 min (Hall & Self, 1986). Oncogenic transforming mutations at codon 12 or 61 reduce this rate about 10-fold (McGrath *et al.* 1984). Structural determination of the GDP form of *ras* shows that the amino acids of loop 1 (10–15) are located just below the phosphate of GDP and presumably in the GTP form straddle the phosphate linkage (DeVos *et al.* 1988). The mechanics of catalysis of hydrolysis of the $\beta$–$\gamma$ bond are still unresolved. However, the fact that loop 1 has a highly constrained conformation explains why virtually any mutation at aa 12 or 13 leads to an inhibition of intrinsic GTPase. Although amino acid 61 of loop 4 is not in contact with the phosphates of GDP it is in contact with loop 1, presumably mutations at this site produce conformational changes in loop 1 and thereby result in reduced intrinsic GTPase activity.

It has been recently found that the rate of GTP hydrolysis by the purified normal proteins does not reflect the true rate in the cell. The rate of GTP hydrolysis by normal p21*ras* is at least 100-fold higher *in vivo* because the normal *ras* proteins interact with a protein called GTPase activity protein (GAP) to elevate the rate of hydrolysis (Trahey & McCormick, 1987). The rate of hydrolysis by the codon 12 and 61 mutants is unaffected by GAP, thus GAP only appears able to enhance the GTPase activity of proteins which already have a sufficient level of intrinsic activity. The mechanism by which GAP enhances GTPase activity remains to be elucidated. Furthermore, the precise role of GAP in the physiology of the *ras* proteins is not yet fully understood. One possibility is that GAP may act as a regulator of the amount of GTP bound to normal p21*ras* proteins and thereby regulate the activity of p21*ras*. Inhibiting the activity of GAP, perhaps as a result of growth factor stimulation, would then lead to an increase in the amount of bound GTP. However, genetic experiments to be described later argue that GAP may be involved in the effector functions of p21*ras*. The role of GTPase activation would therefore be to terminate the effector function.

## Transforming mutations in p21*ras* proteins

Since the active form of p21*ras* is the GTP bound state (Trahey & McCormick, 1987; Field *et al.* 1987) any mutation that increases the level of GTP bound to p21*ras* might be expected to lead to a transforming allele. In addition to mutations that lead to transforming activity, overexpression of normal *ras* proteins at 10–50 times the normal level can lead to transformation in some (e.g. see McKay *et al.* 1986) but not all cell types (Ricketts & Levinson, 1988). However, by far the major route to oncogenesis involving *ras* genes in human malignancy results from point mutations, reducing GTPase activity. Amplification and overexpression of normal *ras* genes appear to be rather infrequent.

## Mutations resulting in a reduction of intrinsic GTPase activity

The first transforming mutation that was identified in a *ras* oncogene detected by transfection with DNA from a human tumour was the Val$^{12}$ mutation in the H-*ras* gene of the T24 bladder carcinoma (Tabin *et al.* 1982; Reddy *et al.* 1982). Subsequently, all possible single base changes leading to a transforming mutation at codon 12 have been detected in human malignancies (Bos, 1988). However, the single most common mutation appears to be Asp$^{12}$ resulting from a G → A transition at the 2nd base of codon 12 (Farr *et al.* 1988; Bos, 1988). Site-directed mutagenesis experiments have shown that replacement of Gly$^{12}$ with any amino acid other than proline leads to a transforming protein (Seeburg *et al.* 1984). Interestingly, this study also showed that different replacements lead to transforming alleles with different potencies. For all cases so far studied, codon 12 replacement leads to a reduction in intrinsic GTPase activity (Colby *et al.* 1986), therefore the explanation of the different transforming strengths of different alleles remains to be seen.

Mutations at codon 12 appear to be the largest single class of *ras* gene mutations in human malignancy. However, mutations have also been detected at codon 13 and 61. The codon 13 mutations that have been found in human malignancy seem to fall into the class of weak transforming alleles, since they are more readily detected in transfection assays using the cotransfection/tumorigenicity assay (Bos *et al.* 1985; Hirai *et al.* 1987). Eighteen of the nineteen possible substitutions at codon 61 lead to reductions in intrinsic GTPase activity, although some of these proteins seem no more transforming than the normal allele (Der *et al.* 1986). For the few codon 13 mutations that have been examined intrinsic GTPase activity also seems to be reduced (C. Calés, personal communication).

The mechanism by which mutations at codons 12, 13 or 61 reduce the instrinsic GTPase is not fully understood. The observation that virtually any substitution at these sites and even deletions around codon 12 (Chipperfield *et al.* 1985) cause a reduction in GTPase is consistent with the idea that the mutations destroy a function. However, the precise mechanisms of the hydrolysis of the $\beta$–$\gamma$ phosphate link is not clear. This terminal phosphate is probably buried deep in the loop forming the phosphoryl binding region (DeVos *et al.* 1988). Which residues in this loop are involved in the catalysis of the hydrolysis is not known but it has been argued that it is likely to be the positioning of the peptide backbone rather than the side chains which is critical (DeVos *et al.* 1988). Mutation at codons 12, 13 or 61 is likely to move the peptide backbone away from the $\beta$–$\gamma$ phosphate bond.

None of the proteins with transforming mutations at codons 12 or 61 appears to interact with GAP to enhance their GTPase activity (Trahey & McCormick, 1987; C. Calés, personal communication). This result resolves the apparent paradox that some proteins such as Asp[12] have an intrinsic GTPase activity which is almost 50 % of normal yet are as fully transforming as proteins with only 10 % of wild type activity (Trahey *et al.* 1987). In the presence of GAP, Asp[12] has less than 1 % of the GTPase activity of normal p21*ras*.

## Guanine nucleotide exchange mutants

Since the rate of nucleotide exchange on p21*ras* is slow in physiological divalent cation concentrations ($t_{\frac{1}{2}} = 50$ min) (Hall & Self, 1986) and because the rate of GTP hydrolysis in the presence of GAP is high, the guanine necleotide bound to normal p21*ras* is probably GDP. Increasing the rate of guanine nucleotide exchange will drive more of the protein into the active GTP state because the concentration of intracellular GTP greatly exceeds that of GDP. There may be physiological mechanisms that speed up this exchange but it is also clear that some mutations enhance the rate of exchange and lead to transforming alleles. Mutations at codons 116 a.s.p. or 119 asparagine which are involved in binding of the guanine ring (DeVos *et al.* 1988) vastly increase the rate of nucleotide exchange and lead to transforming alleles (Walter *et al.* 1986). Similarly the Ala59 to Thr59 substitution which is found together with codon 12 substitution in the *ras* oncogenes of the Harvey and Kirsten murine sarcoma viruses leads to a 5- to 10-fold increase in guanine nucleotide exchange (Lacal & Aaronson, 1986). Curiously, none of these exchange mutants has yet been found in human malignancy (Farr *et al.* 1988; C. Farr, personal communication), although they have been seen in rodent tumours (Wiseman *et al.* 1986). One explanation may be that the exchange mutants are insufficiently potent in transforming activity *in vivo*. In our hands the exchange mutations are even weaker in NIH-3T3 focus assays than Val[13] mutations, which is the weakest transforming mutations we have found in human malignancies (Bos *et al.* 1985; G. Mbamulu and C.J. Marshall unpublished results).

## Effector functions of p21*ras*

The disturbances of growth regulation expressed in transformed cells suggests that proto-oncogenes and oncogenes are involved in growth control. Although some oncogenes which are derived from growth factors or growth factor receptors (Waterfield *et al.* 1983; Downward *et al.* 1984) clearly have an obvious role in growth control, the precise mechanism of *ras* transformation remains unclear. Like most transformed fibroblasts, *ras* transformed fibroblasts have reduced requirements for serum growth factors. In part, this reduced requirement may result from the production of autocrine transforming growth factors (Marshall *et al.* 1985), but may also reflect altered proliferative signals coming directly from transforming mutations. It is therefore of fundamental significance to understand the role of normal p21*ras* in proliferative signals and how this role is perverted by transforming *ras* mutations.

## Role of normal p21*ras*

The only experimental approach that has been successful in attempting to analyse the functions of normal p21*ras* proteins has been the injection of the antibody Y13–259 into a variety of cells. This antibody recognizes an epitope contained in amino acids 63–73 of loop 4 of all three p21*ras* proteins (Sigal *et al.* 1986). Binding of Y13–259 blocks nucleotide exchange on p21*ras* and interferes with the stimulation of GTPase activity by GAP (Adari *et al.* 1988). Microinjection of Y13–259 into *ras*-transformed cells reverts the transformed phenotype (Mulcahy *et al.* 1985). Thus this antibody appears to be able to neutralize the effects of p21 *ras*.

When Y13–259 is injected into quiescent non-transformed 3T3 fibroblasts subsequent serum stimulation of DNA synthesis is blocked (Mulcahy *et al.* 1985). Whatever process mediated by *ras* the antibody is blocking appears to be activated shortly after growth factor stimulation and to continue right up until S phase. Microinjection of Y13–259 blocks the early stimulation of c-*fos* expression which occurs 30 min–1 h after adding growth factors (Stacey *et al.* 1987) and inhibition of DNA synthesis is observed even if the antibody is added as late as 1–2 h before the commencement of S phase (Mulcahy *et al.* 1985). One likely interpretation of these results is that normal p21*ras* is involved in transmitting signals from growth factor receptors activated by ligand binding. It is known that not only does growth factor binding initiate rapid events but also that growth factors need to be present for 6–8 h to cause DNA synthesis. At present there appears to be no evidence for specificity of different polypeptide growth factors in this process. DNA synthesis stimulated by the mixture of growth factors in serum, pure PDGF or EGF is blocked by microinjection of Y13–259. Furthermore, in *Xenopus* oocytes maturation stimulated by insulin is inhibited by microinjection of the neutralizing antibody (Deshpande & Kung, 1987).

Strikingly, DNA synthesis stimulated by activation of protein kinase C by phorbol ester treatment is also inhibited by Y13–259 (Yu *et al.* 1988). Since a variety of different stimuli of DNA synthesis which appear to work through different routes (Rozengurt, 1986) are all blocked by inhibiting p21*ras* the site of action of normal p21*ras* may be a point of convergence for all routes to stimulate DNA synthesis. Alternatively p21*ras* may be involved in the generation of a signal which growth factor-activated pathways do not produce but with which they must interact to stimulate DNA synthesis.

## Second messenger systems and p21*ras*

Observations that p21*ras* appears to be involved in growth factor signalling pathways coupled with the analogy with classical G proteins (Gilman, 1984) of a regulatory GTPase activity has prompted the search for the involvement of p21*ras* with known second-messenger generating systems. Because of the ease of molecular genetics with yeast much of the work on the functions of the *ras* proteins has been carried out in yeast rather than mammalian cells. The difficulties in doing biochemistry on microinjected cells has meant that most work on vertebrate cells has had to rely mainly on using cells containing transforming mutant *ras* proteins or overexpressing normal p21*ras* proteins.

Elegant genetic and biochemical experiments show that in the yeast *Saccaromyces cerevisiae ras* is involved in regulating adenylate cyclase activity by a direct interaction between *ras* and adenylate cyclase (Toda *et al.* 1988). However, no evidence has been found for such a role in higher organisms, since p21*ras* does not appear to activate adenylate cyclase in vertebrate cells (Beckner *et al.* 1985; Birchmieir *et al.* 1985).

Attention has therefore been focused on the other well-characterized second-messenger system resulting from activation of receptors, the breakdown of phosphatidylinositol 4,5-bisphosphate (PIP2). Phospholipase C action on PIP2 results in the formation of inositol trisphosphate (IP3), which releases $Ca^{2+}$ from intracellular stores, and diacylglycerol, which activates protein kinase C. Studies on a cell line (TI5) overexpressing a normal N-*ras* gene from an inducible promoter has shown that these cells are sensitized to bombesin as an agonist for PIP2 breakdown (Wakelam *et al.* 1986). These results were first interpreted as indicating that a normal *ras* protein can function as a coupling protein between an activated receptor and a second-messenger generating system in a way analogous to classical G proteins. However, subsequent studies have shown that the situation in this cell line is unusual and other cell lines overexpressing normal N-*ras* do not show such responses (Lloyd *et al.* 1988). In general, responses to PIP2 breakdown agonists appear to be downregulated in *ras*-transformed cells (Parries *et al.* 1987; A. Lloyd, M. Whittaker and C. J. Marshall, unpublished results). Reports from several, but not all (Seuwen *et al.* 1988), studies have shown small but reproducible increases in the turnover of inositol phospholipids in *ras*-transformed cells (Fleischmann *et al.* 1986; Hancock *et al.* 1988). These effects appear dependent on p21*ras* being in the active GTP state since when cells transformed by overexpressing normal *ras* proteins are studied under conditions in which the bound GTP will have been hydrolysed to GDP, no activation of PI turnover is found (Hancock *et al.* 1988). However, it is not clear from these experiments whether p21*ras* activates phospholipase C directly or whether the activation is more indirect involving 'cross talk' between signalling pathways.

Studies relying on the behaviour of comparisons of *ras*-transformed cells with their normal counterparts are fraught with difficulties because of unselected and unknown divergence between cell lines during prolonged tissue culture. Transformation may also indirectly alter many aspects of cell physiology. We have therefore turned to an alternative approach to assay more immediate effects following the introduction of *ras* proteins into cells. By the use of the scrape loading technique (McNeil *et al.* 1984) purified recombinant p21*ras* proteins can be introduced into large numbers of cells at high efficiency (Morris *et al.* 1988). Within five minutes of introducing a transforming Val$^{12}$ *ras* protein, activation of protein kinase C can be observed (Morris *et al.* 1988). However, there is no measurable increase in inositol phospholipid breakdown indicating that *ras* may be involved in generating messengers which activate protein kinase C from other sources of diacylglycerol (Lacal *et al.* 1987*b*).

The activation of protein kinase C following the introduction of transforming *ras* proteins suggests that p21*ras* is 'upstream' of protein kinase C. However, this is at variance with the observation that blocking normal p21*ras* by microinjection of neutralizing antibody Y13–259 inhibits phorbol ester-stimulated DNA synthesis, which is presumably mediated *via* protein kinase C (Yu *et al.* 1988). The microinjection experiments indicate therefore that normal p21*ras* functions after protein kinase C activation. One resolution of this paradox is that there may be differences between the pathways activated by normal and transforming p21*ras* proteins. Such differences, which may be quantitative rather than qualitative, are possible because the activity of normal p21*ras* is regulated by hydrolysis of GTP whereas transforming mutants are not subject to such regulation. The argument that at least part of the transforming activity of p21*ras* is channelled *via* protein kinase C is supported by the observation that down regulation of protein kinase C blocks *ras*-stimulated DNA synthesis in either microinjected (Lacal *et al.* 1987*a*) or scrape-loaded cells (Morris *et al.* 1988). Furthermore, both p21*ras* and protein kinase C activation by phorbol esters stimulates inactive enhancers presumably *via* the AP1c-jun site (Wasylyk *et al.* 1987).

## Is GAP the p21*ras* effector?

Single amino acid substitutions or deletions in the region of amino acids 30–40 (loop 2) of p21*ras* leads to a protein which is transformation defective but still localizes to the membrane, binds guanine nucleotides and has unaltered intrinsic GTPase (Sigal *et al.* 1986; Willumsen *et al.* 1986; Cales *et al.* 1988). Two groups have asked the question whether this class of mutation, which presumably affects the interaction of p21*ras* with its target molecule, alters the interaction with GAP. Effector site mutations that destroy transforming activity also destroy the ability of GAP to enhance GTPase activity but substitutions in this region which do not affect transformation do not affect GAP activity (Calés *et al.* 1988; Adari *et al.* 1988). Mutations at other sites of the molecule do not affect the GAP interaction. Thus the regions defined genetically as being the site at which p21*ras* interacts with its target also seems to be the site at which p21*ras* interacts with GAP. This result therefore provides strong evidence that GAP is the next step in the pathway mediating signal transduction through p21*ras*. The role of GAP in enhancing the GTPase of p21*ras* would then be to turn off its own activation. This model for p21*ras*–GAP interaction predicts that the oncogenic transforming proteins also will interact with GAP to activate it (Vogel *et al.* 1988).

The nature of GAP has yet to be defined. Its likely role as the target of p21*ras* suggests that it will be a regulatory enzyme, perhaps a phospholipase or a kinase.

Furthermore, it also remains to be demonstrated how GAP is involved in the activation of protein kinase C, which is an essential component of the *ras*-mediated proliferative signal.

## References

ADARI H., LOWY, D. R., WILLUMSEN, B. M., DER, C. J. & McCORMICK, F. (1988). Guanosine triphosphatase activating protein GAP interacts with the p21 *ras* effector binding domain. *Science* **240**, 518–521.

ALMOGUERRA, C., SHIBATA, D., FORRESTER, K., MARTIN, J., ARNHEIM, N. & PERUCHO, M. (1988). Most human carcinomas of the Exocrine Pancreas contain mutant c-k *ras* genes. *Cell* **53**, 549–554.

BALMAIN, A., RAMSDEN, M., BOWDEN, G. T. & SMITH, J. (1984). Activation of the mouse cellular Harvey-*ras* gene in chemically induced benign skin papillomas. *Nature, Lond.* **307**, 658–660.

BARBACID, M. (1987). *ras* genes. *A. Rev. Biochem.* **56**, 779–827.

BECKNER, S. K., HATTORI, S. & SHIH, T. Y. (1985). The *ras* oncogene product is not a regulatory component of adenylate cyclase. *Nature, Lond.* **317**, 71–72.

BIRCHMEIER, C., BROEK, D. & WIGLER, M. (1985). *Ras* proteins can induce meiosis in *Xenopus* oocytes. *Cell* **43**, 615–621.

BOS, J. L. (1988). The *ras*-gene family and human carcinogenesis. *Mutat. Res.* **195** (3) 255–271.

BOS, J. L., FEARON, E. R., HAMILTON, S. R., VERLAAN DE VRIES, M., VAN BOOM, J. H., VAN DER EB, A. J. & VOGELSTEIN, B. (1987). Prevalance of *ras* gene mutations in human colorectal cancer cells. *Nature, Lond.* **327**, 293–297.

BOS, J. L., TOKSOZ, D., MARSHALL, C. J., VERLAAN DE VRIES, M., VEENEMAN, G. H., VAN DER EB, A., VAN BOOM, J. H., JANSSEN, J. W. G. & STEENVOORDEN, A. C. M. (1985). Amino-acid substitution at codon 13 of the N-*ras* oncogene in human acute myeloid leukaemia. *Nature, Lond.* **315**, 726–730.

BOS, J. L., VERLAAN-deVRIES, M., JANSEN, A. M., VEENEMAN, G. H., VAN BOOM, J. H. & VAN DER EB, A. J. (1984). Three different mutations in codon 61 of the human N-*ras* gene detected by synthetic oligonucleotide hybridization. *Nucl. Acids Res.* **12**. 9155–9163.

CALÉS, C., HANCOCK, J. F., MARSHALL, C. J. & HALL, A. (1988). The cytoplasmic protein GAP is implicated as the target for regulation by the *ras* gene product. *Nature, Lond.* **332**, 548–551.

CHIPPERFIELD, R. G., JONES, S. S., LO, K. M. & WEINBERG, R. A. (1985). Activation of Ha-*ras* p21 by substitution, deletion and insertion mutations. *Molec. Cell Biol.* **5**, 1809–1813.

COLBY, W. W., HAYFLICK, J. S., CLARK, S. G. & LEVINSON, A. D. (1986). Biochemical characterisation of polypeptides encoded by mutated human Ha-*ras*-1 genes. *Molec. cell Biol.* **6**, 730–734.

DER, C., FINKEL, T. & COOPER, G. M. (1986). Biological and biochemical properties of human *ras*- genes mutated at codon 61. *Cell* **44**, 167–176.

DESHPANDE, A. K. & KUNG, H. F. (1987). Insulin induction of *Xenopus laevis* oocyte maturation is inhibited by monoclonal antibody against p21 *ras* proteins. *Molec. Cell Biol.* **7**, 1285–1288.

DeVOS, A. M., TONG, L., MILBURN, M. V., MATIAS, P. M., JANCARIK, J., NOGUCHI, S., NISHIMURA, S., MIURA, K., OHTSUKA, E. & KIM, S. H. (1988). Three dimensional structure of an oncogene protein: catalytic domain of human c-H-*ras* p21. *Science* **239**, 888–893.

DOWNWARD, J., YARDEN, Y., MAYES, E., SCRACE, G., TOTTY, N., STOCKWELL, P., ULLRICH, A., SCHLESSINGER, J. & WATERFIELD, M. D. (1984). Close similarity of epidermal growth factor receptor and v-*erb*-B oncogene protein sequence. *Nature, Lond.* **307**, 521–527.

FARR, C. J., MARSHALL, C. J., EASTY, D. J., WRIGHT, N. A., POWELL, S. C. & PARASKERA, C. (1988b). A study of *ras* gene mutations in colonic adenomas from familial polyposis coli patients. *Oncogene* **3**, 673–678.

FARR, C., SAIKI, R., ERLICH, H., McCORMICK, F. & MARSHALL, C. J. (1988a). Analysis of *ras* gene mutations in acute myeloid leukaemia using the polymerase chain reaction and oligonucleotide probes. *Proc. natn. Acad. Sci. U.S.A.* **85**, 1629–1633.

FASANO, O., BIRNBAUM, D., EDLUND, L., FOGH, J., & WIGLER, M (1984). New Human Transforming Genes detected by a tumorigenicity assay. *Molec. Cell Biol* **4**, 1695–1705.

FEARON, E. R., BURKE, P. J., SCHIFFER, C. A., ZEHNBAUER, B. A. & VOGELSTEIN, B. (1986).

Differentiation of leukaemia cells to polymorphonuclear leukocytes in patients with acute nonlymphocytic leukaemia. *N. Engl. J. Med.* **315**, 15–24.

FEUERSTEIN, J., GOODY, R. S. & WITTINGHOFER, A. (1987). Preparation and characterisation of nucleotide free and metal iron free p21 'apoprotein'. *J. biol. Chem.* **262**, 8455–8460.

FIELD, J., BROEK, D., KATAOKA, T. & WIGLER, M. (1987). Guanine nucleotide activation of and competition between *ras* proteins from Saccharomyces cerevisiae. *Molec. cell Biol.* **7**, 2128–2133.

FLEISCHMANN, L. F., CHAWALA, S. B. & CANTLEY, L. (1986). Ras transformed cells: altered levels of phosphatidylinositol – 4,5-bisphosphate and catabolites. *Science* **231**, 407–410.

FORRESTER, K., ALMOGUERA, C., HAN, K. & PERUCHO, M. (1987). Detection of high incidence of K-*ras* oncogenes during human colon tumorigenesis. *Nature, Lond.* **327**, 298–303.

GILMAN, A. G. (1984). G Proteins and dual control of adenylate cyclase. *Cell* **36**, 577–579.

HALL, A. & SELF, A. (1986). The effect of $Mg^{2+}$ on the guanine nucleotide exchange rate of p21 N-*ras*. *J. biol. Chem.* **261**, 10963–10965.

HANCOCK, J. F., MARSHALL, C. J., MCKAY, I. A., GARDINER, S., HOUSLAY, M. D., HALL, A. & WAKELAM, M. J. O. (1988). Mutant but not normal p21 *ras* elevates inositol phospholipid breakdown in two different cell systems. *Oncogene* **3**, 187–193.

HIRAI, H., KOBAYASHI, Y., MANO, H., HAGIWARAK, MARA, Y., OMINE, M., MIZOGUCHI, H., NISHIDA, J. & TAKAKU, F. (1987). A point mutation at codon 13 of the N-*ras* oncogene in myelodysplastic syndrome. *Nature, Lond.* **327**, 430–432.

LACAL, J. C. & AARONSON, S. A. (1986). Activation of *ras* p21 transforming properties associated with an increase in the release rate of bound guanine nucleotide. *Molec. cell. Biol.* **6**, 4214–4220.

LACAL, J. C., FLEMING, T. P., WARREN, B. S., BLUMBERG, P. M. & AARONSON, S. A. (1987*a*). Involvement of functional protein kinase C in the mitogenic response to the H-*ras* oncogene product. *Molec. cell. Biol.* **7**, 4146–4149.

LACAL, J. C., MOSCAT, J. & AARONSON, S. A. (1987*b*). Novel source of 1,2 diacylglycerol elevated in cells transformed by Ha-*ras* oncogenes. *Nature, Lond.* **330**, 269–272.

LLOYD, A., DAVIES, S., CROSSLEY, I., WHITTAKER, M. J., WAKELAM, M., HALL, A. & MARSHALL, C. J. (1988). Bombesin stimulation of TI5 cells overexpressing N-*ras* causes an increase in the production of IP₃ and a corresponding increase in the release of intracellular calcium. *Biochem. J.* (in press).

MAGEE, A. I., GUTIERREZ, L., MCKAY, I. A., MARSHALL, C. J. & HALL, A. (1987). Dynamic fatty acylation of p21 N-*ras*. *EMBO J.* **6**, 3353–3357.

MARSHALL, C. J., VOUSDEN, K. & OZANNE, B. (1986). The involvement of activated *ras* genes in determining the transformed phenotype. *Proc. R. Soc. Lond.* B **226**, 99–106.

MCGRATH, J. P., CAPON, D. J., GOEDDEL, D. V. & LEVINSON, A. D. (1984). Comparative biochemical properties of normal and activated human *ras* p21 protein. *Nature, Lond.* **310**, 644–649.

MCKAY, I. A., MARSHALL, C. J., CALÉS, C. & HALL, A. (1986). Transformation and stimulation of DNA synthesis in NIH-3T3 cells are a titratable function of normal p21 N-*ras* expression. *EMBO J.* **5**, 2617–2621.

MCNEIL, P. L., MURPHY, R. F., LANNI, F. & TAYLOR, D. L. (1984). A method for incorporating macromolecules into adherent cells. *J. Cell Biol* **98**, 1556–1564.

MORRIS, J. D. H., PRICE, B., LLOYD, A. C., SELF, A. J., MARSHALL, C. J. & HALL, A. (1989). Scrape loading of Swiss 3T3 cells with *ras* protein induces rapid activation of protein kinase C followed by DNA synthesis. *Oncogene* (in press).

MULCAHY, L. S., SMITH, M. R. & STACEY, D. W. (1985). Requirement for *ras* proto-oncogene function during serum-stimulated growth of NIH-3T3 cells. *Nature, Lond.* **313**, 241–243.

PADUA, R. A., CARTER, G., HUGHES, D., GOW, J., FARR, C., OSCIER, D., MCCORMICK, F. & JACOBS, A. (1988). *Ras* mutations in myelodysplasia detected by amplification and oligonucleotide hybridisation. *Leukaemia Res.* (in press).

PARRIES, G., HOEBEL, R. & RACKER, E. (1987). Opposing effects of a *ras* oncogene on growth factor stimulated phosphoinositide hydrolysis – Desensitisation to platelet–derived growth factor and enhanced sensitivity to bradykinin. *Proc. natn. Acad. Sci. U.S.A.* **84**, 2648–2652.

QUINTANILLA, M., BROWN, K., RAMSDEN, M. & BALMAIN, A. (1986). Carcinogen specific mutation and amplification of Ha-*ras* during mouse skin carcinogenesis. *Nature, Lond.* **322**, 78–80.

REDDY, E. P., REYNOLDS, R. K., SANTOS, E. & BARBACID, M. (1982). A point mutation is responsible for the acquisition of transforming properties of the T24 human bladder carcinoma oncogene. *Nature, Lond.* **300**, 149–152.

RICKKETS, M. H. & LEVINSON, A. D. (1988). High level expression of c-H-*ras* fails to fully transform Rat-1 cells. *Molec. cell. Biol* **8**, 1460–1468.

ROZENGURT, E. (1986). Early signals in the mitogenic response. *Science* **234**, 161–166.

SAIKI, R., SCHARF, S., FALOONA, F., MULLIS, K. B., HORN, G. T., ERLICH, H. A. & ARNSTEIN, N. (1985). Enzymatic amplification of $\beta$ globin genomic sequences and restriction site analysis for diagnosis of sickle cell anemia. *Science* **230**, 1350–1354.

SEEBURG, P. H., COLBY, W. W., CAPON, D. J., GOEDDEL, D. V. & LEVINSON, A. D. (1984). Biological properties of human c-Ha-*ras*-1 genes mutated at codon 12. *Nature, Lond.* **312**, 71–75.

SEUWEN, K., LAGARDE, A. & POUYSSEGUR, J. (1988). Deregulation of hamster fibroblast proliferation by mutated *ras* is not mediated by constitutive activation of phospholipase C. *EMBO J.* **7**, 161–168.

SHIH, C., SHILO, B., GOLDFARB, M. P., DANNENBERG, A. & WEINBERG, R. A. (1979). Passage of phenotypes of chemically transformed cells via transfection of DNA and chromatin. *Proc. natn. Acad Sci. U.S.A.* **76**, 5714–5718.

SIGAL, I. S., GIBBS, J. B., D'ALONZO, J. S. & SCOLNICK, E. M. (1986). Identification of effector residues and a neutralizing epitope of Ha-*ras* encoded p21. *Proc. natn. Acad. Sci. U.S.A.* **83**, 4725–4729.

STACEY, D. W., WATSON, T., KUNG, H-F. & CURRAN, T. (1987). Microinjection of transforming *ras* protein induces c-*fos* expression. *Molec. cell. Biol.* **7**, 523–527.

SUKUMAR, S., NOTARIO, D., MARTIN-ZANCA, D. & BARBACID, M. (1983). Induction of mammary carcinomas in rats by nitroso-methylurea involves malignant activation of H-*ras*-1 by single point mutations. *Nature, Lond.* **306**, 658–661.

TABIN, C. J., BRADLEY, S. M., BARGMANN, C. I., WEINBERG, R. A., PAPAGEORGE, A. G., SCOLNICK, E. M., DHAR, R., LOWY, D. R. & CHANG, E. H. (1982). Mechanism of activation of a human oncogene. *Nature, Lond.* **300**, 143–149.

TODA, T., UNO, I., ISHIKAWA, T., POWERS, S., KATAOKA, T., BROEK, D., BROACH, J., MATSUMOTO, K. & WIGLER, M. (1988). In Yeast, RAS proteins are controlling elements of the cyclic AMP pathway. *Cell* **40**, 27–36.

TOKSOZ, D., FARR, C. J. & MARSHALL, C. J. (1987). *ras* gene activation in a minor population of the blast population in acute myeloid leukaemia. *Oncogene* **1**, 409–413.

TRAHEY, M. & MCCORMICK, F. (1987). Cytoplasmic protein stimulates normal N-*ras* p21 GTPase but does not affect oncogenic mutants. *Science* **238**, 542–545.

TRAHEY, M., MILLEY, R. J., COLE, G., INNIS, M., PATERSON, H., MARSHALL, C. J., HALL, A. & MCCORMICK, F. (1987). Biochemical and biological properties of the human N-*ras* protein. *Molec. cell. Biol.* **7**, 541–544.

ULSH, L. S. & SHIH, T. Y. (1984). Metabolic turnover of human c-ras$^{\text{H}}$ p21 protein of EJ bladder carcinoma and its normal cellular and viral homologs. *Molec. cell. Biol.* **4**, 1647–1655.

VOGEL, U. S., DIXON, R. A. F., SCHABER, M. D., DIEHL, R. E., MARSHALL, M. S., SCOLNICK, E. M., SIGAL, T. S. & GIBBS, J. B. (1988). Cloning of bovine GAP and its interaction with oncogenic *ras* p21. *Nature, Lond.* **335**, 90–93.

WAKELAM, M. J. O., DAVIES, S. A., HOUSLAY, M. D., MCKAY, I., MARSHALL, C. J. & HALL, A. (1986). Normal p21 N-*ras* couples the combesin and other growth factor receptors to inositol phosphate production. *Nature, Lond.* **323**, 173–176.

WALTER, M., CLARK, S. G. & LEVINSON, A. D. (1986). The oncogenic activation of human p21 *ras* by a novel mechanism. *Science* **233**, 649–652.

WASYLYK, C., IMLER, J. C., PEREZ-MUTUL, J. & WASYLYK, B. (1987). The c-Ha-*ras* oncogene and a tumour promoter activate the polyoma virus enhancer. *Cell* **48**, 525–534.

WATERFIELD, M. D., SCRACE, G. T., WHITTLE, N., STROOBANT, P., JOHNSON, A., WASTESON, A., WESTERMARK, B., HELDIN, C. H., HUANG, J. S. & DUEL, T. F. (1983). Platelet-derived growth factor is structurally related to the putative transforming protein p28$^{\text{sis}}$ of simian sarcoma virus. *Nature, Lond.* **304**, 35–39.

WILLUMSEN, B. M., CHRISTENSEN, A., HUBBERT, N. L., PAPAGEORGE, A. G. & LOWY, D. R. (1984). The p21ras C-terminus is required for transformation and membrane association. *Nature, Lond.* **310**, 583–586.

WILLUMSEN, B. M., PAPAGEORGE, A. G., KUNG, H. F., BEKESI, E., ROBINS, T., JOHNSEN, M., VASS, W. C. & LOWY, D. R. (1986). Mutational analysis of a *ras* catalytic domain. *Molec. cell. Biol.* **6**, 2646–2654.

WISEMAN, R. W., STOWERS, S. J., MILLER, E. C., ANDERSON, M. W. & MILLER, J. A. (1986). Activating mutations of the c-Ha-*ras* proto-oncogene in chemically induced hepatomas of the male B6C3F1 mouse. *Proc. natn. Acad. Sci. U.S.A.* **83**, 5825–5834.

YU, C. L., TSAI, M. H. & STACEY, D. W. (1988). Cellular *ras* activity and phospholipid metabolism. *Cell* **52**, 63–71.

*J. Cell Sci. Suppl. 10, 171–180 (1988)*
*Printed in Great Britain* © *The Company of Biologists Limited 1988*

# Tumour suppressor genes

GEORGE KLEIN

*Department of Tumor Biology, Karolinska Institute, Box 60 400, S-104 01 Stockholm, Sweden*

## Summary

Genes that can inhibit the expression of the tumorigenic phenotype have been detected by the fusion of normal and malignant cells, the phenotypic reversion of *in vitro* transformants, the induction of terminal differentiation of malignant cell lineages, the loss of 'recessive cancer genes', the discovery of regulatory sequences in the immediate vicinity of certain oncogenes, and the inhibition of tumour growth by normal cell products. Such tumour suppressor genes will probably turn out to be as, if not more, diversified as the oncogenes. Consideration of both kinds of genes may reveal common or interrelated functional properties.

## Introduction

The category of genes that can suppress transformation or tumorigenicity may be as diversified as, or even more, diversified than the oncogenes. The constitutive activation of a 'growth-factor oncogene' for example, may be cancelled by the loss or dysfunction of the corresponding receptor, by a roadblock elsewhere within the complex pathway of signal transmission, and by changes in the responding target. Oncogene-induced blocks to cell maturation may be overcome by strong inducers or circumvented by the use of alternative pathways. In this article I will review the fragmentary but firm evidence that shows the existence of such mechanisms.

Tumour-suppressing genes have been detected in the following systems: (i) Fusion of normal and malignant cells leads to the suppression of the tumorigenic phenotype in the majority of the combinations where the hybrid maintains a relatively complete chromosome complement. Reappearance of tumorigenicity is accompanied by chromosome losses. The loss of certain normal parent-derived chromosomes appears to be particularly important (Harris *et al.* 1969; Harris, 1971; Klein *et al.* 1971; Wiener *et al.* 1974; Stanbridge, 1987; Klinger, 1982; Klinger & Shows, 1983; Sager, 1985). (ii) Morphological and nontumorigenic revertants have been isolated from both virally and chemically induced transformants (Bassin & Noda, 1987; Sachs, 1987). They are not necessarily generated by the loss or down-regulation of the original transforming gene. (iii) Differentiation blocks can be bypassed by the temporary down-regulation of temperature-sensitive oncogenes or by exposure to strong differentiation-inducing signals. (iv) Loss or mutational inactivation of 'recessive cancer genes' plays an essential role in the genesis of retinoblastoma, Wilms' tumour, and osteosarcoma, indicating that the normal alleles of these genes can counteract neoplastic transformation in the corresponding tissues (Knudson, 1987; Benedict, 1987). (v) Regulatory sequences capable of preventing

Key words: stem cells, gene regulation, tumour suppression.

illegitimate activation (Vande Woude *et al*. 1987; Verma, 1986) have been identified in the immediate vicinity of certain oncogenes (for example, c-*mos* and c-*fos*). (vi) Tumour growth can be inhibited by diffusible products released by surrounding normal cells.

## Suppression of tumorigenicity by somatic hybridization

A large variety of spontaneous, virally, and chemically induced tumours become low- or nontumorigenic after fusion with fibroblasts, lymphocytes, or macrophages (Harris *et al*. 1969; Harris, 1971; Klein *et al*. 1971; Wiener *et al*. 1974; Stanbridge, 1987; Klinger, 1982; Sager, 1985; Bassin & Noda, 1987). Reappearance of tumorigenicity after chromosome loss was found to occur at variable rates, depending on the stability of each hybrid combination.

The suppression of tumorigenicity by cell hybridization can be discussed in genetic or epigenetic terms that are not mutually exclusive. If genetic losses play an essential role in the evolution of the malignant phenotype, the normal cell genome may act by genetic complementation. In cases where the neoplastic transformation is due to a blockage of maturation, for example, by a dominantly acting oncogene, the normal partner cell may impose its own differentiation program on the hybrid. Stanbridge has concluded that 'the hybrid cell takes on the phenotypic signature of the normal parental cell, regardless of the origin of the malignant parental cell' (Stanbridge, 1987).

The identification of chromosome pairs of the normal parent that are regularly lost from the high malignant segregants was helpful to map the location of the relevant suppressor genes. Human intraspecies hybrids were studied most extensively. Stanbridge *et al*. (1981) found that the reexpression of tumorigenicity in hybrids of HeLa cells and normal fibroblasts was associated with the loss of one copy of chr 11 and one copy of chr 14. Klinger's group (Kaelbling & Klinger, 1986; Klinger & Kaelbling, 1986; Kaelbling *et al*. 1986) provided similar evidence for human chr 11, whereas Benedict *et al*. (1984) implicated human chr 1 and possibly chr 4 in the suppression of the HT 1080 fibrosarcoma by normal fibroblasts. This is not necessarily a contradiction. The tumorigenic phenotype may be suppressed by functionally different mechanisms, depending on the transforming gene and the phenotype of the normal partner cell. The two malignant partners of these crosses, HeLa and HT 1080, produced nontumorigenic hybrids when fused with each other (Weissman & Stanbridge, 1983), suggesting genetic complementation between cells that carry different genetic lesions. HT 1080 carries a mutationally activated N-*ras* allele (Benedict *et al*. 1984). Corresponding losses were found in tumours that carry mutated *ras*, including chemically induced mouse skin carcinomas (Quintanilla *et al*. 1986), thymic lymphomas (Guerrero *et al*. 1985) and a variety of human tumours and derived cell lines (Taparowsky *et al*. 1982; Santos *et al*. 1984; Kraus *et al*. 1984; Fearon *et al*. 1985). It is therefore conceivable that the normal *ras* may antagonize the tumorigenic effect of the mutated allele. It was particularly suggestive that the progression of chemically induced mouse skin papillomas to carcinoma was accompanied by the amplification of the mutated *ras* or the loss of the normal allele or both (Quintanilla *et al.* 1986).

The suppression of tumorigenicity in hybrids between normal cells and tumour cells transformed by activated oncogenes may occur at different levels. Down-regulation of transcription has been demonstrated for v-*src* (Dyson *et al.* 1982; Wyke & Green, 1986), but it is more the exception than the rule. It is more frequent that suppression acts beyond the level of oncoprotein expression. This was found in the SV40 system (Sager, 1986; Howell, 1982) and particularly often in relation to *ras*-transformed cells.

Geiser *et al.* (1986) fused the human EJ bladder carcinoma line, which carries a transforming, mutation-activated *ras* gene, with normal fibroblasts. The hybrids retained the transformed phenotype *in vitro*, but did not grow in nude mice. Tumorigenic segregants appeared on serial cultivation. The mutated *ras* p21 protein was present at the same level in tumorigenic and nontumorigenic hybrids. Transfection with c-H-*ras*-expressing constructs increased the amount of p21, but did not induce tumorigenicity. Suppression of transformation in the absence of any change in p21 expression was also demonstrated in a Chinese hamster (Craig & Sager, 1985) and a mouse system (Rabinowitz & Sachs, 1970; Greenberger *et al.* 1976). In the latter study, flat revertants isolated from Kirsten sarcoma virus-transformed murine fibroblasts still contained a functionally intact viral oncogene, as shown by rescue experiments. Their p21 level was as high as in the original transformants, but they were resistant to retransformation by activated *ras* of either cellular or viral origin. Somatic hybridization of the revertants with both nontrans-formed and transformed cells of the same lineage generated nontransformed hybrids. The revertants could also suppress *src*, *fes*, K-, H-, and N-*ras* and mutated human H-*ras* transformants, but not *mos*, *sis*, *fms*, *ras*, polyoma, SV40, and chemically transformed cells of the same origin.

Src and *fes* encode oncoproteins unrelated to *ras*. The common suppression pattern suggests that the dominant reversion imposes a block on a transformation pathway that converges in these three transformants. *raf* and *mos* are believed to act at a level beyond the *ras*-dependent signalling pathway (Rapp *et al.* 1987). The analysis of the suppression patterns provides a new approach towards the definition of these pathways in cells transformed by different oncogenes. The mapping of suppressor genes by the relatively cumbersome method of somatic hybridization will probably be replaced by the more direct microcell-mediated transfer of single chromosomes, as exemplified by the recent report of Weissman *et al.* (1987) on the suppression of Wilms' tumour cells by fusion with a minicell containing chromosome 11.

## Reversion

The isolation of nontransformed and/or nontumorigenic variants from cultures of transformed cells has provided another source of information on tumour suppressor genes. It is easy to see that many different types of revertants must exist. Each regulatory or structural change that pushes the cell forward along the pathway of progression must have a counterpart that may cause reversion. Reversion can only be detected at the population level if the growth of the original malignant cell is inhibited, however. This requires special techniques. Bassin & Noda (1987) have subdivided revertants into an oncoprotein-related and a target-related category. The former arise by the loss or inactivation of a transforming gene, whereas the latter continue to express the transforming protein, but are phenotypically normal or quasi-normal.

Revertants with a defective oncoprotein are relatively trivial. They usually arise in cultures of virally transformed cells and are susceptible to retransformation by the same agent. Target-related revertants are resistant to retransformation. Noda *et al.* (1983) increased the probability of isolating such revertants by starting with doubly infected cells that carried two copies of the viral v-Ki *ras* gene. $N'$-methyl-$N$-nitrosoguanidine (MNNG)-mutagenized cultures contained approximately $10^{-7}$ revertants that were more flattened, cloned less well in agarose, lacked tumorigenicity, and had an increased chromosome number. They contained the same two v-Ki *ras* copies as the transformant, grew equally well in low serum and produced the same high amounts of the p21 *ras* protein and transforming growth factor-alpha (TGF-alpha). It was suggested that they had arisen by a change in the transformation pathway, occurring at some point beyond the interaction of TGF with its receptor. A possible clue about the nature of this change was provided by the finding that the characteristically reduced tropomyosin content of the *ras*-transformed cells was restored to the control level in the revertants (Cooper *et al.* 1985).

Another study by the same group (Noda *et al.* 1985) has shown that the same gene can act in a transforming or a suppressing capacity, depending on the target cell. Activated *ras* and v-*src* genes can transform fibroblasts, but suppress growth of PC 12 cells, which were derived from rat pheochromocytoma. PC 12 cells can multiply indefinitely in growth medium, but differentiate into sympathetic neurones after exposure to nerve growth factor. The two viral oncogenes mimic the activities of NGF. It was suggested that they may induce the same intracellular signals in both kinds of cells, but elicit different responses, depending on the properties of the target cell.

## Recessive cancer genes – a special category of tumour suppressor genes?

Molecular analysis has fully confirmed the ingenious theory of Knudson that retinoblastoma arises by the loss of both alleles at the same locus (RB-1). The gene is localized at 13q14 on the human chromosome map (for review see Knudson, 1987). In familial retinoblastoma, a defective RB-1 allele is transmitted through the germline. It may be associated with a deletion at 13q14.2, but is more frequently invisible at the cytogenetic level. The second change occurs during somatic development. It may arise by the loss of one chr 13 with or without the duplication of the other, or, less frequently, by somatic crossing over or by interstitial deletion (Cavenee *et al.* 1983).

Recently, a cDNA fragment that corresponds to a gene that spans over at least 70 kb of human chr 13q14 has been cloned. The gene was sequenced and identified as the retinoblastoma susceptibility gene (Friend *et al.* 1986; Lee *et al.* 1987; Fung *et al.* 1987). It is expressed in many tumour cells and also in foetal retina, but not at all, or only in a truncated form, in retinoblastomas and osteosarcomas. It remains to be shown whether this gene is capable of reverting some of the malignant properties of retinoblastoma and osteosarcoma, when introduced in an appropriately active form.

A gene localized at 11p13 appears to play a similar role in Wilms' tumour (Francke *et al.* 1979; Ladda *et al.* 1974; Riccardi *et al.* 1980) and perhaps in hepatoblastoma and embryonal rhabdomyosarcoma as well (Koufos *et al.* 1985). Similar genetic losses may be involved in some solid tumours in adults. The 3p14 region is frequently deleted in renal carcinoma and in small cell carcinoma of the lung (Wang & Perkins, 1984; Pathak *et al.* 1982; Kovacs *et al.* 1987; Kovacs *et al.* 1988; Heim & Mitelman, 1987; Yoshida *et al.* 1986; Whang-Peng *et al.* 1982). A recessive locus on chr 13 may be involved in the genesis of ductal breast carcinomas and the loss of an allele on chr 5 may occur in colonic carcinomas (Lundberg *et al.* 1987; Solomon *et al.* 1987).

How can gene losses lead to tumour development? Comings (1973) has suggested that every cell contains structural 'transforming' genes, active during embryogenesis but suppressed during differentiation by dominant 'suppressor' or 'regulatory' genes. Loss of both copies of the latter may lift the suppression, with continuous expression of the transforming gene and tumour development as the result. Comings' theory is essentially consistent with the modern development, at least for retinoblastoma. Normally, the retinoblast differentiates into a retinocyte that has irreversibly lost the ability to divide. Children who inherit the deletion of one RB-1 allele from one of their parents run the risk of developing retinoblastoma only during their first years of life. If the second allele is not lost by a somatic change by the age of five, all retinocytes will have differentiated terminally. It is therefore likely that the wild-type RB-1 allele is essential for the terminal step, in a structural or a regulatory capacity.

## Suppression by diffusible products of normal cells

Paul (1988) has recently summarized evidence indicating that small molecules, produced by normal cells, can diffuse in solid tissues through gap junctions and exert a damping effect on tumour cell precursors that contain activated oncogenes. If so, a second event may involve a reduction of the damping effect by modulating the gap junctions, or by creating a critical mass of transformed cells. Land *et al.* (1986) have shown that both *myc*- and *ras*-transformed rat fibroblasts can be suppressed by surrounding normal cells. Similar observations were made earlier by Stoker (1964) in relation to polyoma-transformed cells. Growth regulatory polypeptides that can inhibit the replication of certain cells, but may stimulate the growth of others have been demonstrated experimentally in several systems (Zarling *et al.* 1986; Newmark,

1987; Keski-Oja & Moses, 1987). They include an increasing number of known cellular products such as TGF-beta and members of the interferon family (Todaro, 1988).

## Concluding remarks

It is widely accepted that tumour development and progression are due to sequential changes at the DNA level (for review see Klein & Klein, 1985). This is reflected by the 'reassortment of unit characteristics' at the phenotypic level (Foulds, 1954). Several of the currently known oncogenes can block specific steps in the maturation progress. Constitutively activated growth factors may inhibit maturation by urging their target cell to proliferate. Truncated growth factor receptors or faulty signal transducers may achieve a similar effect by emitting a continuous 'go' signal in the absence of external simulation. DNA-binding proteins like *myc* or *myb* may block maturation by interfering with the condensation of chromatin that is the hallmark of terminal differentiation in many cell lineages.

The category of genes described as anti-oncogenes, tumour suppressor genes, or emergenes can antagonize tumorigenic behaviour at various levels. Somatic hybridization of normal cells with malignant ones has provided evidence that the normal genome may provide the tumour cell with the ability to respond to appropriate differentiation-inducing stimuli *in vivo*.

The differentiation block imposed by temperature sensitive v-*src*, a membrane associated tyrosine kinase, or v-*erb B*, a truncated growth factor receptor, may be permanently lifted by the temporary down regulation of the oncoprotein. Reexpression of the oncoprotein cannot halt or reverse the process; the potential 'go'-signal is apparently inactive when the cell has moved out from the sensitive 'maturation window'. Signals induced by physiological or chemical differentiation (or both) may down-regulate other highly expressed oncoproteins and thereby lift the maturation block. Such signals may even override the high expression of amplified *myc* genes.

Revertants fall into several categories. Deletion or mutational inactivation of viral oncogenes is relatively trivial. Cellular genes that can act beyond the level of oncoprotein expression are more interesting. They have been best documented in revertants isolated from *ras*-transformed fibroblasts. In the most extensively studied case (Bassin & Noda, 1987), the transformed and tumorigenic phenotype of v-Ki-*ras* infected fibroblasts was reverted by dominantly acting cellular gene or genes in spite of the continued presence of wild-type transforming virus and full expression of the p21 *ras* protein. The same gene(s) could also cancel the transforming action of *src*, *fes*, and all members of the *ras* family, but not *sis*, *fms*, *raf*, polyoma and SV40. This approach may provide new leads for a functional oncogene classification, based on suppressor sensitivity.

The oncogene terminology has evolved through a series of historical accidents and is actually a misnomer, but it is here to stay. It embraces a wide variety of genes that can influence the cell cycle at different levels. The consensus to collect a variety of normal genes under a common, cancer related name is based on the fact that they may contribute to tumour development when they get out of hand. As long as this is so, we might just as well refer to the normal genes that can antagonize them in one system or another by the common name of 'emerogenes', as suggested by one of the originators of the oncogene terminology, George Todaro (1988) (*emero*: to tame, to domesticate). Some of them may control cell maturation. They, and/or other genes that act at different levels, may overrule the transforming action of highly expressed oncoproteins. They, or other genes that act at different levels, may overrule the transforming action of highly expressed oncoproteins. They or the normal alleles of the recessive cancer genes may also prevent tumours by obstructing the development of progression of preneoplastic cells. The study of the emerogenes is experimentally more difficult than the pursuit of the oncogenes, but it may turn out to be even more rewarding.

# References

BASSIN, R. H. & NODA, M. (1987). Oncogene inhibition by cellular genes. *Adv. Viral Oncol.* **6**, 103–127.

BENEDICT, W. F. (1987). Recessive human cancer susceptibility genes (retinoblastoma and Wilms' loci). *Adv. Viral Oncol.* **7**, 19–34.

BENEDICT, W. J., WEISSMAN, B. E., MARK, C. & STANBRIDGE, E. J. (1984). Tumorigenicity of human HT1080 fibrosarcoma × normal fibroblast hybrids; Chromosome dosage dependency. *Cancer Res.* **44**, 3471–3479.

CAVENEEE, W. K., DRYJA, T. P., PHILIPS, R. A., BENEDICT, W. F., GODBOUT, R., GALLIE, B. L., MURPHREE, A. L., STRONG, L. C. & WHITE, R. L. (1983). Expression of recessive alleles by chromosomal mechanisms in retinoblastoma. *Nature, Lond.* **305**, 779–784.

COMINGS, D. E. (1973). A general theory of carcinogenesis. *Proc. natn. Acad. Sci. U.S.A.* **70**, 3324–3328.

COOPER, H. L., FEUERSTEIN, N., NODA, M. & BASSIN, R. H. (1985). Suppression of tropomyosin synthesis, a common biochemical feature of oncogenesis by structurally diverse retroviral oncogenes. *Molec. cell. Biol.* **5**, 952–983.

CRAIG, R. W. & SAGER, R. (1985). Suppression of tumorigenicity in hybrids of normal and oncogene-transformed CHEF cells. *Proc. natn Acad. Sci. U.S.A.* **82**, 2062–2066.

DYSON, P. J., QUADE, K. & WYKE, J. A. (1982). Expression of the ASV src gene in hybrids between normal and virally transformed cells: Specific suppression occurs in some hybrids but not others. *Cell* **30**, 491–498.

FOULDS, L. (1954). The experimental study of tumor progression: a review. *Cancer Res.* **14**, 327–339.

FRANCKE, U., HOLMES, L. B., ATKINS, L. & RICCARDI, V. K. (1979). Aniridia-Wilms' tumor association: evidence for specific deletion llp13. *Cytogenet. Cell Genet.* **24**, 185–192.

FRIEND, S., BERNARDS, R., ROGELJ, S., WEINBERG, R. A., RAPAPORT, J. M., ALBERT, D. M. & DRUJA, T. P. (1986). A human DNA segment with properties of the gene that predisposes to retinoblastoma and osteosarcoma. *Nature, Lond.* **323**, 643–646.

FUNG, Y.-K. T., MURPHREE, A. L., JIN-QUIAN, A. T., HINRICHS, S. T. & BENEDICT, W. F. (1987). Structural evidence for the authenticity of the human retinoblastoma gene. *Science* **236**, 1657–1661.

GEISER, A. G., DER, C. J., MARSHALL, C. J. & STANBRIDGE, E. J. (1986). Suppression of tumorigenicity with continued expression of the c-Ha-ras oncogene in EJ bladder carcinoma-human fibroblast hybrid cells. *Proc. natn. Acad. Sci. U.S.A.* **83**, 5209–5213.

GREENBERGER, J. S., BENSINGER, W. I. & AARONSON, S. A. (1976). Selective techniques for the isolation of morphological revertants of sarcoma virus-transformed cells. In *Methods in Cell Biology* (ed. D. M. Prescott), pp. 237–249. New York: Academic Press.

GUERRERO, I., VILLASANTE, A., CORCES, S. V. & PELLICER, A. (1985). Loss of the normal N-ras allele in a mouse thymic lymphoma induced by a chemical carcinogen. *Proc. natn. Acad. Sci. U.S.A.* **82**, 7810–7814.

HARRIS, H. (1971). Cell fusion and analysis of malignancy: The Croonian lecture. *Proc. R. Soc. Lond.* B **179**, 1–20.

HARRIS, H., MILLER, O. J., KLEIN, G., WORST, P. & TACHIBANA, T. (1969). Suppression of malignancy by cell fusion. *Nature, Lond.* **223**, 363–368.

HEIM, S. & MITELMAN, F. (1987). *Cancer Cytogenetics*, pp. 1–309. New York: Alan R. Liss.

HOWELL, N. (1982). Suppression of transformation and tumorigenicity in interspecies hybrids of human SV40-transformed and mouse 3T3 cell lines. *Cytogenet. Cell Genet.* **34**, 215–229.

KAELBLING, M. & KLINGER, H. P. (1986). Suppression of tumorigenicity in somatic cell hybrids. III. Cosegregation of human chromosome 11 of a normal cell and suppression of tumorigenicity in intraspecies hybrids of normal diploid × malignant cells. *Cytogenet. Cell Genet.* **42**, 65–70.

KAELBLING, M., ROGINSKI, R. S. & KLINGER, H. P. (1986). Polymorphisms indicate loss of heterozygosity for chromosome 11 of D98AH2 cells. *Cytogenet. Cell Genet.* **41**, 240–244.

KESKI-OJA, J. & MOSES, H. L. (1987). Growth inhibitory polypeptides in the regulation of cell proliferation. *Med. Biol.* **65**, 13–20.

KLEIN, G., BREGULA, U., WIENER, F. & HARRIS, H. (1971). The analysis of malignancy by cell fusion. I. Hybrids between tumor cells and L cell derivatives. *J. Cell Sci.* **8**, 659–672.

KLEIN, G. & KLEIN, E. (1985). Evolution of tumors and the impact of molecular oncology. *Nature, Lond.* **315**, 190–195.

KLINGER, H. P. (1982). Suppression of tumorigenicity. *Cytogenet. Cell Genet.* **32**, 68–84.

KLINGER, H. P. & KAELBLING, M. (1986). Suppression of tumorigenicity in somatic cell hybrids. IV. Chromosomes of normal human cells with suppression of tumorigenicity in hybrids with D98AH2 carcinoma cells. *Cytogenet. Cell Genet.* **42**, 225–235.

KLINGER, H. P. & SHOWS, T. B. (1983). Suppression of tumorigenicity in somatic cell hybrids. II. Human chromosomes implicated as suppressors of tumorigenicity in hybrids with Chinese hamster ovary cells. *J. natn. Cancer Inst.* **71**, 559–569.

KNUDSON, A. G. (1987). A two-mutation model for human cancer. *Adv. viral Oncol.* **7**, 1–17.

KOUFOS, A., HANSEN, M. F., COPELAND, N. G., JENKINS, N. A., LAMPKIN, B. C. C. & CAVENEE, W. K. (1985). Loss of heterozygosity in three embryonal tumours suggests a common pathogenetic mechanism. *Nature, Lond.* **316**, 330–334.

KOVACS, G., ERLANDSSON, R., BOLDOG, F., INGVARSSON, S., MULLER-BRECHLIN, R., KLEIN, G. & SUMEGI, J. (1988). Consistent chromosome 3p deletion and loss of heterozygosity in renal cell carcinoma. *Proc. natn. Acad. Sci.* **85**, 1571–1575.

KOVACS, G., SZUCS, S., DE RIESE, W. & BAUMGÄRTEL, H. (1987). Specific chromosome aberration in human renal cell carcinoma. *Int. J. Cancer* **40**, 171–178.

KRAUS, M. H., YUASA, Y. & AARONSON, S. A. (1984). A position 12-activated H-ras oncogene in all HS578T mammary carcinosarcoma cells but not normal mammary cells of the same patient. *Proc. natn. Acad. Sci. U.S.A.* **81**, 5384–5388.

LADDA, R., ATKINS, L., LITTLEFIELD, J., NEURATH, P. & MARIMUTHU, K. M. (1974). Computer-assisted analysis of chromosomal abnormalities: detection of a deletion in aniridia/Wilms' tumor syndrome. *Science* **185**, 784–787.

LAND, H., CHEN, A. C., MORGENSTERN, J. P., PARADA, L. F. & WEINBERG, R. A. (1986). Behaviour of myc and ras oncogenes in transformation of rat embryo fibroblasts. *Molec. Cell. Biol.* **6**, 1917–1925.

LEE, W.-H., BOOKSTEIN, R., HONG, F., YOUNG, L.-J. & LEE, E. Y.-H. P. (1987). Human retinoblastoma susceptibility gene: Cloning, identification, and sequence. *Science* **235**, 1394–1399.

LUNDBERG, C., SKOOG, L., CAVENEE, W. K. & NORDENSKJÖLD, M. (1987). Loss of heterozygosity in human ductal breast tumors indicates a recessive mutation on chromosome 13. *Proc. natn. Acad. Sci.* **84**, 2372–2376.

NEWMARK, P. (1987). Oncogenes and cell growth. *Nature, Lond.* **327**, 101–102.

NODA, M., KO, M., OGURA, A., DING-GAN LIU, T., AMANAO, T., TAKANO, T. & IKAWA, Y. (1985). Sarcoma viruses carrying ras oncogenes induce differentiation-associated properties in a neuronal cell line. *Nature, Lond.* **318**, 73–75.

NODA, M., SELINGER, Z., SCOLNICK, E. M. & BASSIN, R. H. (1983). Flat revertants isolated from

Kirsten sarcoma virus-transformed cells are resistant to the action of specific oncogenes. *Proc. natn. Acad. Sci. U.S.A.* **80**, 5602–5606.

PATHAK, S., STRONG, L. C., FERRELL, R. E. & TRINDADE, A. (1982). Familial renal cell carcinoma with a 3;11 chromosome translocation limited to tumor cells. *Science* **217**, 939–941.

PAUL, J. (1988). *Theories of Carcinogenesis* (ed. O. H. Iversen), pp. 45–60. Washington, DC: Hemisphere.

QUINTANILLA, M., BROWN, K., RAMSDEN, M. & BALMAIN, A. (1986). Carcinogen-specific mutation and amplification of HA-ras during mouse skin carcinogenesis. *Nature, Lond.* **322**, 78–80.

RABINOWITZ, Z. & SACHS, L. (1970). Control of the reversion of properties in transformed cells. *Nature, Lond.* **225**, 136–139.

RAPP, U. R., CLEVELAND, J., STORM, S. M., BECK, T. W. & HULEIHL, M. (1987). Transformation by raf and myc oncogenes. In *Oncogenes and Cancer* (ed. S. A. Aaronson *et al.*), pp. 55–57. Utrecht: Japan Scientific Soc. Press, Tokyo/VNU Science.

RICCARDI, V. M., HITTNER, H. M., FRANCKE, U., YUNIS, J. J., LEDBETTER, D. & BORGES, W. (1980). The Aniridia-Wilms' tumor association: the clinical role of chromosome band llp13. *Cancer Genet. Cytogenet.* **2**, 131–137.

SACHS, L. (1987). Development and suppression of malignancy. *Adv. viral Oncol.* **6**, 129–142.

SAGER, R. (1985). Genetic suppression of tumor formation. *Adv. Cancer Res.* **44**, 43–68.

SAGER, R. (1986). Genetic suppression of tumor formation: a new frontier in cancer research. *Adv. Cancer Res.* **46**, 1573–1580.

SANTOS, E., MARTIN-ZANCA, D., PREMKUMAR, REDDY, E., PIEROTTI, M. A., DELLA-PORTA, G. & BARBACID, M. (1984). Malignant activation of a K-ras oncogene in lung carcinoma but not in normal tissue of the same patient. *Science* **223**, 661–664.

SOLOMON, E., VOSS, R., HALL, V., BODMER, W. F., JASS, J. R., JEFFREYS, A. J., LUCIBELLO, F. C., PATEL, I. & RIDER, S. H. (1987). Chromosome 5 allele loss in human colorectal carcinoma. *Nature, Lond.* **328**, 616–619.

STANBRIDGE, E. J. (1987). Genetic regulation of tumorigenic expression in somatic cell hybrids. *Adv. viral Oncol.* **6**, 83–101.

STANBRIDGE, E. J., FLANDERMEYER, R. R., DANIELS, D. W. & NELSON-REES, W. A. (1981). Specific chromosome loss associated with the expression of tumorigenicity in human cell hybrids. *Somat. Cell Genet.* **7**, 699–712.

STOKER, M. (1964). Regulation of growth and orientation in hamster cells transformed by polyoma virus. *Virology* **24**, 165–174.

TAPAROWSKY, E., SVARD, Y., FASANO, O., SHIMIZY, K., GOLDFARB, M. & WIGLER, M. (1982). Activation of the T 24 bladder carcinoma transforming gene is linked to a single amino acid change. *Nature, Lond.* **300**, 762–765.

TODARO, G. (1988). *Theories of Carcinogenesis.* (ed. O. H. Iversen), pp. 61–80. Washington, DC: Hemisphere.

VANDE WOUDE, G. F., OSKARSSON, M., McGEADY, M. L., SETH, A., PROPST, F., SCHMIDT, M., PAULES, R. & BLAIR, D. G. (1987). Sequences that influence the transforming activity and expression of the mos oncogene. *Adv. viral Oncol.* **6**, 71–127.

VERMA, I. M. (1986). Proto-oncogene fos: a multifaceted gene. *Trends Genet.* **9**, 93–96.

WANG, N. & PERKINS, K. L. (1984). Involvement of band 3p14 in t(3;8) hereditary renal carcinoma. *Cancer Genet. Cytogenet.* **11**, 479–481.

WEISSMAN, B. E., SAXON, P. J., PASQUALE, S. R., JONES, G. R., GEISER, A. G. & STANBRIDGE, E. J. (1987). Introduction of a normal human chromosome 11 expression. *Science* **236**, 175–180.

WEISSMAN, B. E. & STANBRIDGE, E. J. (1983). Complementation of the tumorigenic phenotype in human cell hybrids. *J. natn. Cancer Inst.* **70**, 667–672.

WHANG-PENG, J., BUNN, P. A. JR, KAO-SHAN, C. S., LEE, E. C., CARNEY, D. N. & MINNA, J. D. (1982). A non random chromosomal abnormality, del 3p (14–23), in human small cell lung cancer (SCLC). *Cancer Genet. Cytogenet.* **6**, 119–134.

WIENER, F., KLEIN, G. & HARRIS, H. (1974). The analysis of malignancy by cell fusion. V. Further evidence of the ability of normal diploid cells to suppress malignancy. *J. Cell Sci.* **15**, 177–183.

WYKE, J. A. & GREEN, A. R. (1986). *Oncogenes and Growth Control* (ed. P. Kahn & T. Graf), pp. 340–343. New York: Springer-Verlag.

YOSHIDA, M. A., OHYASHIKI, K., OCHI, H., GIBAS, Z., EDSON PONTES, J., PROUT JR, G. R., HUBEN, R. & SANDBERG, A. A. (1986). Cytogenetic studies of tumor tissue from patients with nonfamilial renal cell carcinoma. *Cancer Res.* **46**, 2139–2147.

ZARLING, I. M., SHOYAB, M., MARQVARDT, H., HANSON, M. B., LIOUBIN, M. N. & TODARO, G. J. (1986). Oncostatin M: a growth regulator produced by differentiated histiocytic lymphoma cells. *Proc. natn. Acad. Sci. U.S.A.* **83**, 9739–9743.

J. Cell Sci. Suppl. 10, 181–194 (1988)
Printed in Great Britain © The Company of Biologists Limited 1988

# Regulation of the proliferation of spermatogonial stem cells

D. G. DE ROOIJ

*Department of Cell Biology, State University of Utrecht, Medical School, Utrecht, The Netherlands*

## Summary

The proliferating cells in the seminiferous epithelium can be subdivided into the (morphologically) undifferentiated and the differentiating spermatogonia. In turn the undifferentiated spermatogonia can be subdivided according to their topographical arrangement into clones consisting of one cell, the A-single ($A_s$) spermatogonia, two cells, the A-paired ($A_{pr}$) spermatogonia or groups of 4, 8 or 16 cells, the A-aligned ($A_{al}$) spermatogonia. Most likely the $A_s$ spermatogonia are the stem cells of spermatogenesis. When these cells divide their daughter cells can either migrate away from each other and become two new stem cells or stay together as $A_{pr}$ spermatogonia. The $A_{pr}$ spermatogonia can divide further to form $A_{al}$ spermatogonia.

Although suggestions have been made for the existence of a class of long-cycling stem cells with a higher probability for self-renewal, all cell kinetic data are still compatible with a homogeneous population of stem cells, the proliferative activity of which varies during the cycle of the seminiferous epithelium. Radiobiological studies have revealed that the radiosensitivity of the stem cells varies with their proliferative activity and that there is no particular class of radioresistant stem cells.

In both rat and Chinese hamster the cell cycle time of the undifferentiated spermatogonia appeared to be much longer than that of the differentiating spermatogonia. All types of undifferentiated spermatogonia have the same minimum cell cycle time. However, the $A_s$ spermatogonia, the stem cells, generally divide after longer intervals.

The proliferative activity of the undifferentiated spermatogonia varies during the cycle of the seminiferous epithelium. At a certain moment during the epithelial cycle the undifferentiated spermatogonia, including the stem cells, are stimulated to proliferate. After a period of active proliferation the $A_{pr}$ and $A_{al}$ spermatogonia are arrested in $G_1$ phase possibly by the production of a chalone by the differentiating spermatogonia. In both rat and Chinese hamster the $A_s$ spermatogonia are less sensitive towards this inhibition and continue to proliferate for some time longer.

In the normal epithelium the probability of self-renewal of the stem cells varies with their proliferative activity in such a way that is low during active proliferation. In the normal epithelium there appeared to be no regulatory mechanism to ensure an even density of the stem cells. A large variation in stem cell density was found between areas. However, after heavy cell loss, for example after irradiation, the probability of self-renewal was found to be close to 100%.

In primates the undifferentiated spermatogonia are composed of the so-called $A_p$ and $A_d$ spermatogonia. Studies after irradiation have revealed that these cells too, are composed of clones of 1, 2, 4, 8 or 16 cells. The $A_d$ spermatogonia are quiescent in the normal epithelium but they were found to transform into active $A_p$ spermatogonia after irradiation. Possibly the stimulation of the proliferative activity of the undifferentiated spermatogonia is very weak in primates, causing half of these cells to become arrested in $G_0$ phase for long periods of time and to acquire the dark appearance after staining with haematoxylin.

## Spermatogenesis in non-primates

In the wall of the seminiferous tubules, germ cells and Sertoli cells can be found (Fig. 1). The Sertoli cells are somatic cells that have an important supporting and

Key words: spermatogenesis, stem cell, proliferation, regulation.

possibly regulating function in the spermatogenic process (Parvinen, 1982). The germ cells can be subdivided into three categories: (1) the proliferating cells, called spermatogonia; (2) the spermatocytes that carry out the meiotic divisions; (3) the spermatids that transform into spermatozoa. All spermatogonia can be found on the basement membrane of the tubules. They can be subdivided into the (morphologically) undifferentiated and the differentiating spermatogonia. In turn the undifferentiated spermatogonia can be subdivided according to their topographical arrangement into clones consisting of one cell, the A-single ($A_s$) spermatogonia, two cells, the A-paired ($A_{pr}$) spermatogonia or groups of 4, 8 or 16 cells, the A-aligned ($A_{al}$) spermatogonia. As discussed previously (review by De Rooij, 1983), most likely the $A_s$ spermatogonia are the stem cells of spermatogenesis. When these cells divide their daughter cells can either migrate away from each other and become two new stem cells or stay together, interconnected by an intercellular bridge, as $A_{pr}$ spermatogonia (Fig. 2). The $A_{pr}$ spermatogonia can divide further to form chains of 4, 8 or 16 $A_{al}$ spermatogonia (Fig. 3).

Spermatogenesis takes place in a cyclic manner. At a particular moment during that cycle the undifferentiated spermatogonia are mostly quiescent and their number is low, only $A_s$, $A_{pr}$ and a few $A_{al}$ spermatogonia being present. Then the cells are stimulated and for a certain period of time, active proliferation occurs during which more and more $A_{al}$ spermatogonia are formed (Fig. 4). The total number of $A_s$ and $A_{pr}$ spermatogonia does not change much during the epithelial cycle. The period of

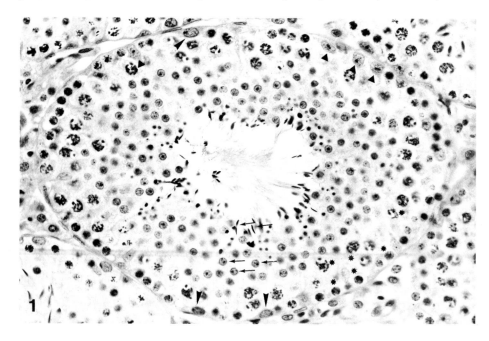

Fig. 1. Cross section of a mouse seminiferous tubule in which some of the cells have been indicated with symbols. Sertoli cells (triangles), A spermatogonia (arrowheads), two generations of spermatocytes (asterisks), and two generations of spermatids (arrows) one of which is about to leave the epithelium as spermatozoa. ×360.

active proliferation stops when most of the cells become arrested in $G_1$ phase. After a subsequent period of relative quiescence almost all of the $A_{al}$ spermatogonia formed during the period of proliferation, differentiate into the first generation of the differentiating type spermatogonia, in most animals called $A_1$ spermatogonia. These $A_1$ spermatogonia then start a series of six divisions and ultimately become spermatocytes.

The duration of the cycle of the seminiferous epithelium varies between 8 and 17 days but is always exactly similar in animals of a particular species. Also the duration of the various steps in the development of the spermatogenic cells is always the same within a particular species. As a consequence the same associations of generations of cells in particular developmental stages are always found together in the tubular wall. Thus, for example spermatids at a particular step in their transformation into spermatozoa are always found with spermatogonia and spermatocytes of a particular stage in their respective development. This makes it possible to divide the epithelial cycle into, mostly 12, stages according to steps in the development of one of the generations of spermatogenic cells, usually the spermatids (review by Courot *et al.* 1970).

## Identity of the spermatogonial stem cell

Huckins (1971*a*), Oakberg (1971), de Rooij (1973), Oud & De Rooij (1977) and Lok *et al.* (1982) have postulated that the $A_s$ spermatogonia are the stem cells of spermatogenesis in the rat, mouse, Chinese hamster and ram. However, Clermont &

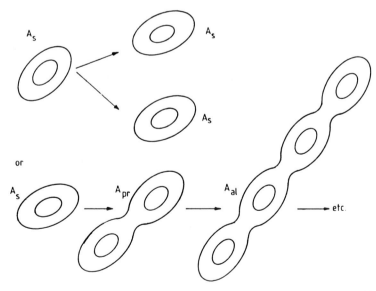

Fig. 2. In the upper part a self-renewing division of a spermatogonial stem cell, the $A_s$ spermatogonium. The daughter cells move away from each other and become two new stem cells. In the lower part a stem cell division that gives rise to a pair of cells that stay together as $A_{pr}$ spermatogonia and will divide further to form larger clones of $A_{al}$ spermatogonia that eventually will become spermatozoa.

Bustos-Obregon (1968), Clermont & Hermo (1975) and Bartmanska & Clermont (1983) consider the $A_s$ and the $A_{pr}$ spermatogonia to be resting reserve cells and the $A_1$ spermatogonia to be derived from the fourth generation of differentiating spermatogonia. As discussed previously, there are a number of data that do not fit in with this model (De Rooij, 1983). Furthermore Erickson (1981) and Erickson & Hall (1983) consider all types of undifferentiated spermatogonia to have stem cell properties. In this model, stem cell renewal takes place by breaking up of $A_{pr}$ and $A_{al}$ clones and in that process accidentally also $A_s$ spermatogonia are formed. Indeed the morphological appearances of the $A_s$, $A_{pr}$ and the $A_{al}$ spermatogonia are almost similar. However, breaking up of clones of $A_{al}$ spermatogonia in the normal epithelium does not seem to take place on a regular basis as Huckins (1971a) and Lok *et al.* (1982) found the clones of $A_{al}$ spermatogonia always to be composed of $2^n$ cells. Taken together the $A_s$ model still seems to fit best to the experimental data and will be used in this paper.

Assuming the $A_s$ spermatogonia to be the spermatogonial stem cells the important question arises whether or not these cells form a homogeneous population of cells. Huckins (1971c, 1978) has postulated the existence of so-called 'long cycling' stem cells. Thirteen days (i.e. one epithelial cycle in the rat) after injection of

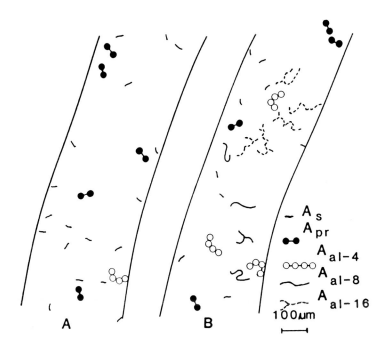

Fig. 3. Topographical arrangement of clones of undifferentiated spermatogonia on the basement membrane of two seminiferous tubules. The undifferentiated spermatogonia lie intermingled with differentiating spermatogonia and Sertoli cells, and in some epithelial stages with early spermatocytes. A. Seminiferous tubule in epithelial stage IX. Only $A_s$ and $A_{pr}$ spermatogonia and one clone of $A_{al}$ spermatogonia are present. B. Seminiferous tubule in epithelial stage IV which is just after the period of active proliferation of the undifferentiated spermatogonia. Many clones of $A_{al}$ spermatogonia have been formed.

[³H]thymidine, a small number of heavily labelled $A_s$ spermatogonia was found, while all other originally labelled stem cells had supposedly diluted their label beyond recognition by a number of divisions. Furthermore, the distribution of the labelled $A_s$ spermatogonia over the stages of the cycle of the seminiferous epithelium after 13 days was slightly different from that after 1 h. It was concluded that part of the $A_s$ spermatogonia divide less frequently than the rest and that the long-cycling stem cells proliferate during slightly different epithelial stages. The long-cycling stem cells were supposed to have a higher self-renewal probability than the fast cycling ones.

Furthermore, in rats and mice experiments were done in which labelling with [³H]thymidine was combined with irradiation (Oakberg & Huckins, 1976; Huckins, 1978; Huckins & Oakberg, 1978; Oakberg *et al.* 1986). The results were interpreted to mean that the long-cycling stem cells are more resistant to irradiation.

The existence of 'long-cycling' and radioresistant stem cells still is a matter of debate. Lok *et al.* (1984) performed a quantitative autoradiographic study in the Chinese hamster in which the labelling pattern of the undifferentiated spermatogonia was studied one epithelial cycle after injection of [³H]thymidine. After one epithelial cycle the number of [³H]thymidine-labelled stem cells was half that found at 1 h after injection. However, during steady state kinetics this should remain the same. Indeed this decrease in the number of labelled stem cells can be explained by a situation in

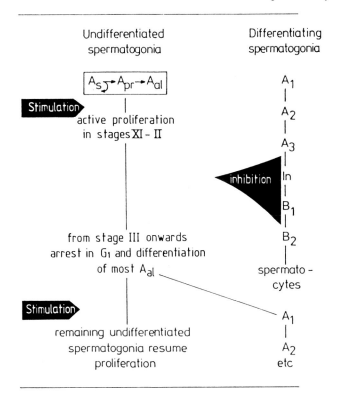

Fig. 4. Scheme of spermatogonial proliferation in the Chinese hamster.

which some of the stem cells proliferate rapidly and quickly differentiate into $A_{pr}$ spermatogonia, and others cycle only slowly having a higher probability of self-renewal. However, as discussed previously, this is certainly not the only explanation (Lok et al. 1984). Other factors may also be important or even explain the whole decrease in labelled $A_s$ spermatogonia after one epithelial cycle. First, those stem cells that were at the beginning or the end of S phase during the period of time in which [³H]thymidine was available, may have been scored unlabelled because of the dilution of their label after division. Second, influx of unlabelled components of so-called 'false' pairs (i.e. stem cells that at the time of [³H]thymidine injection were newly born and still had to migrate away from each other, mostly during $G_1$, and were scored as $A_{pr}$ spermatogonia at the 1 h interval). Third, selective segregation of DNA at stem cell mitosis as has been suggested for epidermal stem cells by Cairns (1975) and Potten et al. (1978). When this occurs many stem cells will loose their label after the second division. Fourth, irradiation death of radiosensitive labelled stem cells. Taken together, the concept of long-cycling stem cells is just one of a number of possibilities to explain the [³H]thymidine-labelling pattern observed.

Another important item is whether or not there exists a special kind of radioresistant stem cells as suggested by Oakberg & Huckins (1976), Huckins (1978), Huckins & Oakberg (1978) and Oakberg et al. (1986). Van Beek et al. (1986b) have determined the dose–response relationships of the stem cells for fast neutron irradiation in various stages of the epithelial cycle. It was found that in stages IX to XII of the epithelial cycle some of the stem cells are very radioresistant, in stages I–III almost all stem cells have an intermediate radiosensitivity and in stage VII virtually all stem cells are very radiosensitive. These results exclude the existence of a substantial separate population of radioresistant stem cells. More likely, the radiosensitivity of the stem cells varies with their proliferative behaviour.

In summary, in the non-primate testis all cell kinetic and radiobiological data are consistent with a homogeneous population of stem cells, the proliferative activity and the radiosensitivity of which varies during the epithelial cycle. To date no conclusive evidence is available for a more complicated composition of the stem cell population.

## The cell cycle properties of the undifferentiated spermatogonia

The cell cycle properties of the undifferentiated spermatogonia have been studied in the rat (Huckins, 1971b) and the Chinese hamster (Lok et al. 1983). In both species the duration of the cell cycle of the undifferentiated spermatogonia appeared to be considerably longer than that of the differentiating spermatogonia (Huckins, 1971d; Lok & De Rooij, 1983a). For example, in the Chinese hamster the duration of the cell cycle of the undifferentiated was found to be at least 90 h while that of the differentiating spermatogonia was found to be about 60 h. Furthermore, in both rat and Chinese hamster the second peak of the curve of the labelled mitoses of the $A_s$ spermatogonia was much lower than that of the $A_{pr}$ and $A_{al}$ spermatogonia. This shows that the $A_s$ spermatogonia divide slower than the $A_{pr}$ and $A_{al}$ spermatogonia although the minimum duration of the cell cycle of the undifferentiated spermato-

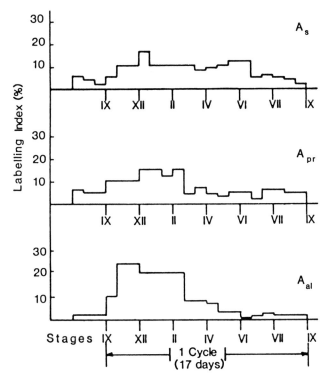

Fig. 5. [³H]thymidine-labelling index of the $A_s$, $A_{pr}$ and $A_{al}$ spermatogonia in various stages of the epithelial cycle in the Chinese hamster (Lok & De Rooij, 1983*b*).

gonia is the same. Hence, like in other tissues in the seminiferous epithelium, the stem cells also have a lower rate of proliferation than their more differentiated descendants (Lajtha, 1979).

## Stimulation of stem cell proliferation

The [³H]thymidine-labelling index (LI) of the undifferentiated spermatogonia throughout the epithelial cycle has been determined in the Chinese hamster (Lok & De Rooij, 1983*b*) and for part of the epithelial cycle in the rat (Huckins, 1971*b*). It was found that the $A_s$ spermatogonia have a varying LI (Fig. 5). In the Chinese hamster in stages VII–IX the LI was found to be low and to double during stage X. In the rat also the LI of the $A_s$ spermatogonia was found to vary with a period of a very low and one with a relatively high LI. So in both the Chinese hamster and the rat there is a period of active proliferation of the $A_s$ spermatogonia and a period of relative quiescence.

In the Chinese hamster the growth fraction during the active period was calculated to be about 60 %, and 30 % during the more quiescent period. As the LI of the $A_s$ spermatogonia increases in stage X it can be assumed that the stimulation of the proliferative activity of these cells takes place from stages VIII and/or IX onwards.

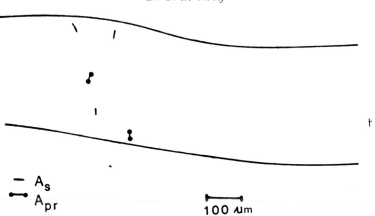

$-\mathrm{A_s}$
$\bullet\!-\!\bullet\ \mathrm{A_{pr}}$

$\longmapsto\!\!\!\bullet$
**100 Ам**

Fig. 6. Topography of the labelled undifferentiated spermatogonia in an autoradiograph of a whole mount of a seminiferous tubule of a Chinese hamster, 1 h after injection of [³H]thymidine. In this area, which was in epithelial stage XI, a cluster of 3 labelled $A_s$ spermatogonia and 2 pairs of $A_{pr}$ spermatogonia can be seen.

The source of the stimulating factors may well be the Sertoli cells that are known to produce a number of mitogenic factors (Bellvé & Feig, 1984; Holmes *et al*. 1986).

Autoradiographic studies after injection of [³H]thymidine on whole mounts of seminiferous tubules have revealed that the undifferentiated spermatogonia are triggered into cell cycle in a whole area of a seminiferous tubule at the same time (De Rooij & Janssen, 1988). The $A_s$ spermatogonia present in such an area react in the same way as the other types of undifferentiated spermatogonia as these cells too, are often found in the clusters of labelled clones of undifferentiated spermatogonia (Fig. 6). As yet no data are available about how this pattern of stimulation arises.

### Inhibition of spermatogonial proliferation

It has been shown by various groups that the proliferation of the undifferentiated spermatogonia can be partly inhibited by testicular extracts (Clermont & Mauger, 1974; Thumann & Bustos-Obregon, 1978; Irons & Clermont, 1979; De Rooij, 1980). The inhibiting factor, which was found to be tissue- but not species specific, was thought to be a chalone and has not been purified as yet.

In the normal seminiferous epithelium the proliferative activity of the undifferentiated spermatogonia is inhibited around stages III–IV in the mouse, rat and Chinese hamster. In the Chinese hamster it was found that when the differentiating spermatogonia were specifically removed from the epithelium this inhibition did not take place (Fig. 7; De Rooij *et al*. 1985). It was concluded that from stage III onwards the proliferation of the undifferentiated spermatogonia is inhibited by the In and B spermatogonia present in these stages by way of a negative feedback system (Fig. 4). This feedback regulation might work *via* the production of a chalone by the In and B spermatogonia. In this respect it is interesting that the inhibiting activity of the extracts was absent when they were made of testes from which all spermatogonia were removed (De Rooij *et al*. 1985).

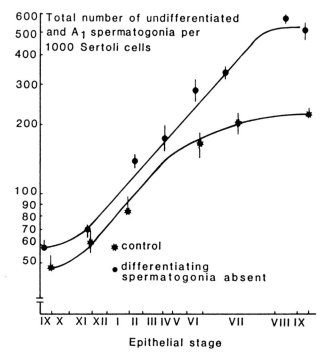

Fig. 7. Total number of undifferentiated and $A_1$ spermatogonia per 1000 Sertoli cells during the epithelial cycle in the normal Chinese hamster and in hamsters in which locally the differentiating spermatogonia were specifically removed with ara-C. In the latter situation the numbers of undifferentiating spermatogonia keep increasing, no inhibition taking place (De Rooij *et al.* 1985).

An important question is whether or not the stem cells are also inhibited in their proliferative activity by this feedback system. In the Chinese hamster the LI of the $A_{pr}$ and $A_{al}$ spermatogonia drops sharply in stage III while the LI of the $A_s$ spermatogonia drops in early stage VII (Lok & De Rooij, 1983*b*). In the rat the LI of the undifferentiated spermatogonia drops in stage II and that of the $A_s$ spermatogonia in stage V (Huckins, 1971*b*). Hence it can be concluded that the $A_s$ spermatogonia are much less sensitive or perhaps completely insensitive for the feedback regulation. In case these cells are insensitive we have to assume that the decrease in their proliferative activity later during the epithelial cycle is caused by a lack of stimulation. This would be consistent with the notion that the secretory activity of the Sertoli cells varies during the epithelial cycle (Parvinen, 1982).

## Probability of self-renewal and differentiation of stem cells

As yet not many data are available about the regulation of the ratio between self-renewal and differentiation of the stem cells. Cell counts in the normal mouse and the Chinese hamster revealed that during the period of active proliferation of the stem cells the number of these cells slowly decreases (Van Beek *et al.* 1984; De Rooij *et al.* 1985). This indicates that in such a situation more than 50% of the daughter cells

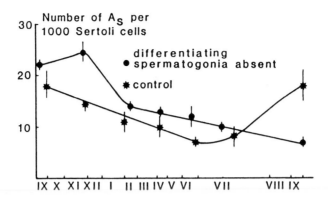

Fig. 8. Number of $A_s$ spermatogonia per 1000 Sertoli cells during the epithelial cycle in normal Chinese hamsters and in hamsters in which the inhibition of the proliferation of the undifferentiated spermatogonia did not take place because of the removal of the differentiating spermatogonia (De Rooij *et al.* 1985).

become $A_{pr}$ spermatogonia as a first step towards differentiation. Furthermore, when the period of active proliferation of the undifferentiated spermatogonia is prolonged the decrease in the number of $A_s$ spermatogonia also continues (Fig. 8). Hence there is a relationship between the proliferative activity in the epithelium and the probability of self-renewal of the stem cells.

Attempts have been made to detect a regulatory mechanism that would ensure an even density of stem cells and/or all the undifferentiated spermatogonia by way of changing the ratio between self-renewal and differentiation when necessary (De Rooij & Janssen, 1987). No trace of such a regulatory mechanism was found. Different areas could possess widely different numbers of $A_s$ spermatogonia and/or $A_{pr}$ and $A_{al}$ spermatogonia and consequently produce very many or few differentiating spermatogonia. It was found that an even distribution of spermatocytes in the epithelium was ensured by a density-dependent degeneration of differentiating spermatogonia in such a way that many of these cells degenerated in high-density areas and only few or none at all in low-density areas (De Rooij & Lok, 1987). Apparently in the normal epithelium there is no need for a precise regulatory mechanism to keep the density of the stem cells within close limits.

Nevertheless, in situations in which the number of stem cells gets very low, like after irradiation, the probability of self-renewal gets close to 100 %. This could be deduced from the observation that both after irradiation and after administration of busulfan isolated clones of $A_{al}$ spermatogonia were extremely rare (Van Keulen & De Rooij, 1975; Van Beek *et al.* 1986*a*). Isolated clones $A_{al}$ spermatogonia would arise when a surviving stem cell would directly differentiate into $A_{pr}$ spermatogonia instead of renewing himself.

## Spermatogonial stem cells in primates

Spermatogonial multiplication and stem cell renewal has been studied in the human

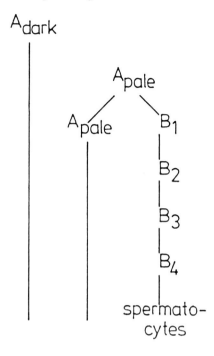

Fig. 9. Scheme of spermatogonial multiplication in the rhesus monkey (Clermont &
Leblond, 1959; Clermont & Antar, 1973).

(Clermont, 1966) and in four different species of monkeys (Clermont & Leblond,
1959; Clermont, 1969; Clermont & Antar, 1973; Chowdhury & Steinberger, 1976).
Although spermatogenesis in primates and non-primates has much in common, some
important differences exist in the way spermatogonial multiplication takes place.
Among the things they have in common is the presence of the type differentiating
spermatogonia. However, at the place in the spermatogenic lineage where in the non-
primates there is a class of undifferentiated spermatogonia, in primates so-called
A-pale ($A_p$) spermatogonia and A-dark ($A_d$) spermatogonia are described (review De
Rooij, 1983). The $A_p$ spermatogonia divide once every epithelial cycle giving rise to
differentiating spermatogonia and renewing themselves (Fig. 9). The $A_d$ spermatogonia were found to be quiescent in the normal epithelium and are supposed to be
reserve cells (Clermont, 1969; Clermont & Antar, 1973; Chowdhury & Steinberger,
1976).

Some recent data have provided more details about the nature of the $A_p$ and $A_d$
spermatogonia and their behaviour in unusual circumstances. Van Alphen *et al.*
(1988*a,b*) have studied the depletion and the repopulation of the seminiferous
epithelium of the rhesus monkey after X-irradiation. Normally the density of the $A_p$
and the $A_d$ spermatogonia is so high that it is not possible to see whether the
populations of these cells consist of clones of 1, 2, 4, 8 or 16 cells, like the
undifferentiated spermatogonia in the non-primates. However, after irradiation in
the early repopulating colonies, arising from surviving stem cells, the density of the

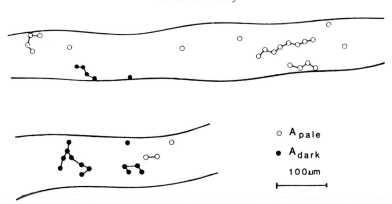

Fig. 10. Examples of repopulating colonies in the seminiferous epithelium of the rhesus monkey at 98 days after a dose of 2 Gy of X-irradiation. In this situation of low spermatogonial density it can be seen that both the $A_p$ and $A_d$ spermatogonia are composed of clones of one, two, four or eight cells like the undifferentiated spermatogonia in the non primates.

spermatogonia is still low. In this situation it was found that both the $A_p$ and $A_d$ spermatogonia consist of clones of 1, 2, 4, 8 or 16 cells (Fig. 10). Hence the $A_p$ and $A_d$ spermatogonia are not only similar to the non-primate undifferentiated spermatogonia with respect to their place in the spermatogenic lineage but also to their clonal composition. Further studies will be necessary to find out whether or not the single $A_p$ and $A_d$ spermatogonia are the stem cells in primates.

With respect to the behavioural properties of the $A_d$ spermatogonia it was found that these cells do not change in number during the first epithelial cycle after irradiation which takes 10·5 days in the rhesus monkey (De Rooij *et al.* 1986). Thereafter they gradually are activated to transform into $A_p$ spermatogonia, which then start to proliferate. This confirms the suggestion that the $A_d$ spermatogonia are reserve cells that become active after cell loss (Clermont & Hermo, 1976). They do not seem to be a special class of spermatogonia having their own way of renewing themselves but they may just be inactived $A_p$ spermatogonia acquiring their typical appearance by being in the $G_0$ phase for a long time.

Taken together these new data confirm the earlier speculations that together the $A_p$ and $A_d$ spermatogonia are similar to the undifferentiated spermatogonia in the non-primates (De Rooij, 1983). However, while the non-primate undifferentiated spermatogonia, including the stem cells, divide several times per epithelial cycle, in primates only the $A_p$ part of these cells divides and only once during each epithelial cycle. Apparently the stimulation of the proliferative activity of the A spermatogonia in primates is very weak. Another possible cause could be a stronger inhibition of the proliferative activity. However, after irradiation when the density of the spermatogonia was still very low, $A_d$ spermatogonia were already formed, suggesting that the stimulation of the proliferation in primates is very weak.

The author is grateful to Mr A. N. van Rijn for drawing the figures.

# References

BARTMANSKA, J. & CLERMONT, Y. (1983). Renewal of type A spermatogonia in adult rats. *Cell Tiss. Kinet.* **16**, 135–143.

BELLVÉ, A. R. & FEIG, L. A. (1984). Cell proliferation in the mammalian testis: biology of the seminiferous growth factor (SGF). *Rec. Progr. Horm. Res.* **40**, 531–567.

CAIRNS, J. (1975). Mutation selection and the natural history of cancer. *Nature, Lond.* **255**, 197–200.

CHOWDHURY, A. K. & STEINBERGER, E. (1976). A study of germ cell morphology and duration of spermatogenic cycle in the baboon, Papio anubis. *Anat. Rec.* **185**, 155–169.

CLERMONT, Y. (1966). Renewal of spermatogonia in man. *Am. J. Anat.* **118**, 509–524.

CLERMONT, Y. (1969). Two classes of spermatogonial stem cells in the monkey (Cercopithecus aethiops). *Am. J. Anat.* **126**, 57–72.

CLERMONT, Y. & ANTAR, (1973). Duration of the cycle of the seminiferous epithelium and the spermatogonial renewal in the monkey Macaca arctoides. *Am. J. Anat.* **136**, 153–166.

CLERMONT, Y. & BUSTOS-OBREGON, E. (1968). Re-examination of spermatogonial renewal in the rat by means of seminiferous tubules mounted "in toto". *Am. J. Anat.* **122**, 237–248.

CLERMONT, Y. & HERMO, L. (1975). Spermatogonial stem cells in the albino rat. *Am. J. Anat.* **142**, 159–176.

CLERMONT, Y. & HERMO, L. (1976). Spermatogonial stem cells and their behaviour in the seminiferous epithelium of rats and monkeys. In *Stem Cells of Renewing Cell Populations* (ed. A. B. Cairnie, P. K. Lala, & D. G. Osmond), pp. 273–286. New York: Academic Press.

CLERMONT, Y. & LEBLOND, (1959). Differentiation and renewal of spermatogonia in the monkey, Macacus rhesus. *Am. J. Anat.* **104**, 237–274.

CLERMONT, Y. & MAUGER, A. (1974). Existence of a spermatogonial chalone in the rat testis. *Cell Tiss. Kinet.* **7**, 165–172.

COUROT, M., HOCHEREAU-DE REVIERS, M. T. & ORTAVANT, R. (1970). Spermatogenesis. In *The testis* (ed. Johnson, A. D., Gomes, W. R. & Vandemark, N. L.), pp. 339–432. New York: Academic Press.

DE ROOIJ, D. G. (1973). Spermatogonial stem cell renewal in the mouse. I. Normal situation. *Cell Tiss. Kinet.* **6**, 201–207.

DE ROOIJ, D. G. (1980). Effect of testicular extracts on proliferation of spermatogonia in the mouse. *Virchows Arch. B. Zellpath.* **33**, 67–75.

DE ROOIJ, D. G. (1983). Proliferation and differentiation of undifferentiated spermatogonia in the mammalian testis. In *Stem Cells. Their Identification and Characterization* (ed. C. S. Potten), pp. 89–117. Edinburgh: Churchill Livingstone.

DE ROOIJ, D. G. & JANSSEN, J. M. (1987). The regulation of the density of spermatogonia in the seminiferous epithelium of the Chinese hamster. I. Undifferentiated spermatogonia. *Anat. Rec.* **217**, 124–130.

DE ROOIJ, D. G. & JANSSEN, J. M. (1988). Regulation of the proliferation of the undifferentiated spermatogonia in the Chinese hamster. *Ann. N. Y. Acad. Sci.* **513**, 296–298.

DE ROOIJ, D. G. & LOK, D. (1987). The regulation of the density of spermatogonia in the seminiferous epithelium of the Chinese hamster. II. Differentiating spermatogonia. *Anat. Rec.* **217**, 131–136.

DE ROOIJ, D. G., LOK, D. & WEENK, D. (1985). Feedback regulation of the proliferation of the undifferentiated spermatogonia in the Chinese hamster by the differentiating spermatogonia. *Cell Tiss. Kinet.* **18**, 71–81.

DE ROOIJ, D. G., VAN ALPHEN, M. M. A. & VAN DE KANT, H. J. G. (1986). Duration of the cycle of the seminiferous epithelium and its stages in the rhesus monkey (Macaca mulatta). *Biol. Reprod.* **35**, 587–591.

ERICKSON, B. H. (1981). Survival and renewal of murine stem spermatogonia following $^{60}$Co gamma radiation. *Radiat. Res.* **86**, 34–51.

ERICKSON, B. H. & HALL, G. G. (1983). Comparison of stem-spermatogonial renewal and mitotic activity in the gamma-irradiated mouse and rat. *Mutat. Res.* **108**, 317–335.

HOLMES, S. D., SPOTTS, G. & SMITH, R. G. (1986). Rat Sertoli cells secrete a growth factor that blocks epidermal growth factor (EGF) binding to its receptor. *J. biol. Chem.* **261**, 4076–4080.

HUCKINS, C. (1971a). The spermatogonial stem cell population in adult rats. I. Their morphology, proliferation and maturation. *Anat. Rec.* **169**, 533–558.

HUCKINS, C. (1971*b*). The spermatogonial stem cell population in adult rats. II. A radioautographic analysis of their cell cycle properties. *Cell Tiss. Kinet.* **4**, 313–334.

HUCKINS, C. (1971*c*). The spermatogonial stem cell population in adult rats. III. Evidence for a long-cycling population. *Cell Tiss. Kinet.* **4**, 335–349.

HUCKINS, C. (1971*d*). Cell cycle properties of differentiating spermatogonia in adult Sprague-Dawley rats. *Cell Tiss. Kinet.* **4**, 139–154.

HUCKINS, C. (1978). Behavior of stem cell spermatogonia in the adult rat irradiated testis. *Biol. Reprod.* **19**, 747–760.

HUCKINS, C. & OAKBERG, E. F. (1978). Morphological and quantitative analysis of spermatogonia in mouse testes using whole mounted seminiferous tubules. II. The irradiated testes. *Anat. Rec.* **192**, 529–542.

IRONS, M. I. & CLERMONT, Y. (1979). Spermatogonial chalone(s): Effect on the phases of the cell cycles of type A spermatogonia in the rat. *Cell Tiss. Kinet.* **12**, 425–433.

LAJTHA, L. G. (1979). Stem cell concepts. *Differentiation* **14**, 23–34.

LOK, D. & DE ROOIJ, D. G. (1983*a*). Spermatogonial multiplication in the Chinese hamster. I. Cell cycle properties and synchronization of differentiating spermatogonia. *Cell Tiss. Kinet.* **16**, 7–18.

LOK, D. & DE ROOIJ, D. G. (1983*b*). Spermatogonial multiplication in the Chinese hamster. III. Labelling indices of undifferentiated spermatogonia throughout the cycle of the seminiferous epithelium. *Cell Tiss. Kinet.* **16**, 31–40.

LOK, D., JANSEN, M. T. & DE ROOIJ, D. G. (1983). Spermatogonial multiplication in the Chinese hamster. II. Cell cycle properties of undifferentiated spermatogonia. *Cell Tiss. Kinet.* **16**, 19–29.

LOK, D., JANSEN, M. T. & DE ROOIJ, D. G. (1984). Spermatogonial multiplication in the Chinese hamster. IV. Search for long cycling stem cells. *Cell Tiss. Kinet.* **17**, 135–143.

LOK, D., WEENK, D. & DE ROOIJ, D. G. (1982). Morphology, proliferation and differentiation of undifferentiated spermatogonia in the Chinese hamster and the ram. *Anat. Rec.* **203**, 83–99.

OAKBERG, E. F. (1971). Spermatogonial stem-cell renewal in the mouse. *Anat. Rec.* **169**, 515–532.

OAKBERG, E. F., GOSSLEE, D. G., HUCKINS, C. & CUMMINGS, C. C. (1986). Do spermatogonial stem cells have a circadian rhythm? *Cell Tiss. Kinet.* **19**, 367–375.

OAKBERG, E. F. & HUCKINS, C. (1976). Spermatogonial stem cell renewal in the mouse as revealed by $^3$H-thymidine labeling and irradiation. In *Stem Cells of Renewing Cell Populations.* (ed. A. B. Cairnie, P. K. Lala & D. G. Osmond), pp. 287–302. New York: Academic Press.

OUD, J. L. & DE ROOIJ, D. G. (1977). Spermatogenesis in the Chinese hamster. *Anat. Rec.* **187**, 113–124.

PARVINEN, M. (1982). Regulation of the seminiferous epithelium. *Endocr. Rev.* **3**, 404–417.

POTTEN, C. S., HUME, W. J., REID, P. & CAIRNS, J. (1978). The segregation of DNA in epithelial stem cells. *Cell* **15**, 899–906.

THUMANN, A. & BUSTOS-OBREGON, E. (1978). An "in vitro" system for the study of rat spermatogonial proliferative control. *Andrologia* **10**, 22–25.

VAN ALPHEN, M. M. A., VAN DE KANT, H. J. G. & DE ROOIJ, D. G. (1988*a*). Depletion of the spermatogonia from the seminiferous epithelium of the rhesus monkey after X-irradiation. *Radiat. Res.* **113**, 473–486.

VAN ALPHEN, M. M. A., VAN DE KANT, H. J. G. & DE ROOIJ, D. G. (1988*b*). Repopulation of the seminiferous epithelium of the rhesus monkey after X-irradiation. *Radiat. Res.* **113**, 487–500.

VAN BEEK, M. E. A. B., DAVIDS, J. A. G. & DE ROOIJ, D. G. (1986*a*). Non-random distribution of mouse spermatogonial stem cells surviving fission neutron irradiation. *Radiat. Res.* **107**, 11–23.

VAN BEEK, M. E. A. B., DAVIDS, J. A. G. & DE ROOIJ, D. G. (1986*b*). Variation in the sensitivity of the mouse spermatogonial stem cell population to fission neutron irradiation during the cycle of the seminiferous epithelium. *Radiat. Res.* **108**, 282–295.

VAN BEEK, M. E. A. B., DAVIDS, J. A. G., VAN DE KANT, H. J. G. & DE ROOIJ, D. G. (1984). Response to fission neutron irradiation of spermatogonial stem cells in different stages of the cycle of the seminiferous epithelium. *Radiat. Res.* **97**, 556–569.

VAN KEULEN, C. J. G. & DE ROOIJ, D. G. (1975). Spermatogenetic clones developing from repopulating stem cells surviving a high dose of an alkylating agent. I. First 15 days after injury. *Cell Tiss. Kinet.* **8**, 543–551.

*J. Cell Sci. Suppl. 10, 195–230 (1988)*
Printed in Great Britain © The Company of Biologists Limited 1988

# Mesenchymal influences on epithelial differentiation in developing systems

P. M. SHARPE AND M. W. J. FERGUSON*

*Animal & Human Reproduction Development & Growth Research Group, Department of Cell & Structural Biology, University of Manchester, Coupland 3 Building, Manchester M13 9PL, England*

## Summary

Mesenchyme tissue: cells, matrix and soluble factors, influence the morphogenesis, proliferation and differentiation of a variety of embryonic epithelia, e.g. in the tooth, skin, mammary and salivary glands. Mesenchyme derivatives also 'maintain' adult epithelia, e.g. the local proliferation rate and cytokeratin composition of oral mucosa. Abnormalities in such epithelial–mesenchymal interactions lead to a variety of pathologies such as premalignant lesions, e.g. leukoplakia, tumours and psoriasis, whilst therapeutic manipulation of such interactions can prevent the exfoliation of dental implants. In all of these systems it is critical to understand, at the cellular and molecular levels, how the mesenchyme signals to the epithelium and how the latter processes and responds to such signals. We have investigated such questions using the developing embryonic palate both as a model system and as an important organ: failure of mesenchymal signalling leads to the common and distressing birth defect of cleft palate.

Bilateral palatal shelves arise from the maxillary processes of embryonic day 11 (E11) mice, grow initially vertically down the sides of the tongue, elevate on E13·8 to a horizontal position above the dorsum of the tongue and fuse with each other in the midline on E14. The medial edge epithelia of each shelf fuse with each other to form a midline epithelial seam, suprabasal cells die, and the basal (stem) cells synthesize extracellular matrix molecules and turn into mesenchymal cells. Simultaneously the oral epithelia differentiate into stratified squamous cells and the nasal epithelia into pseudostratified ciliated columnar cells. Oral, medial and nasal epithelial differentiation is specified by the underlying mesenchyme *in vivo* and *in vitro*. Signalling involves a bifurcating action of a combination of soluble growth factors e.g. TGF-$\alpha$, TGF-$\beta$, PDGF and FGF on palatal epithelia and mesenchyme. These factors stimulate the synthesis of specific extracellular matrix molecules by palate mesenchyme cells, and the appearance of receptors for such molecules on epithelial cells. In this way, a combination of mesenchymal soluble factors and extracellular matrix molecules direct palatal epithelial differentiation. These signals act on epithelial basal (stem) cells, causing them to synthesize unique proteins, which may direct subsequent differentiation of daughter cells. In the most extreme example, namely the medial edge epithelia, these signals result in the basal epithelial cells transforming into mesenchymal cells, thus demonstrating that they are indeed multipotential stem cells.

## Introduction

Epithelial–mesenchymal interactions are defined as tissue interactions that result in changes to one or both tissues which would not occur in the absence of these interactions.

In this paper we briefly discuss the common types of interaction which occur

* To whom all correspondence and reprint requests should be addressed.

Key words: mesenchyme signalling, embryonic palate, epithelial differentiation, growth factors.

during the differentiation and morphogenesis of most tissues and organs and consider possible mechanisms by which they occur. We then discuss our specific area of interest: the formation of the mammalian secondary palate, an organ which undergoes regional and temporal regulation of epithelial differentiation by the underlying mesenchyme. We do not intend to give a detailed review of palate development: several recent reviews are available (Ferguson, 1978, 1987, 1988; Greene & Pratt, 1976; Melnick *et al.* 1980; Pisano & Greene, 1986; Pratt, 1984; Pratt & Christiansen, 1980; Shah, 1979; Zimmerman, 1984). Instead we will concentrate on our current ideas, resulting from work in our own laboratory, on the mechanisms of signalling from mouse embryonic palatal mesenchyme (MEPM) cells to palate epithelial cells during the breakdown of the epithelial seam in secondary palate development.

## Mesenchymal–epithelial interactions: a role for the extracellular matrix (ECM)

Mesenchymal–epithelial interactions have been described during the development of a large number of organs, e.g. kidney (Ekblom *et al.* 1986), lens (Kratochwil, 1983), tooth (Kollar, 1983; Thesleff & Hurmerinta, 1981), otic capsule (McPhee & Van der Water, 1986), male and female accessory sexual glands (Cunha *et al.* 1981), skin (Dhouailly, 1975; McAleese & Sawyer, 1981; Sawyer, 1983; Saxen & Karkinen-Jaaskelainen, 1981), bone (Hall, 1984), mammary gland (Sakakura, 1983) and salivary glands (Bernfield *et al.* 1984). It is apparent from these studies that several types of interaction can occur from a strict 'instructive' mechanism resulting in the cells of a tissue developing a unique morphology and gene expression which would not normally be present, to 'permissive' effects whereby a tissue whose fate has already been determined is maintained and stabilized by another. Most developmental systems involve multistep inductive processes. In skin, for example, it is well established that the dermis gives an inductive signal specifying the size and distribution of appendage primordia, a signal which can be interpreted by epidermal tissue of another species (Dhouailly, 1975; Saxen & Karkinen-Jaaskelainen, 1981). The appendages, however, remain rudimentary and resemble those of epidermal origin, e.g. feather for bird, hair for mammal. Full development of the appendage cannot occur across species but requires another inductive signal which is species specific.

   A role for ECM molecules in tissue interactions has been reviewed several times (Bohnert *et al.* 1986; Bissell *et al.* 1982; Ekblom *et al.* 1986; Hay, 1977; Kollar, 1983). Such a role seems likely; after all the mesenchyme and epithelia are separated *in vivo* by the basement membrane, a specialized ECM structure. Since the basement membrane has been shown to have a stabilizing effect on epithelia, regulating cell shape (Sugrue & Hay, 1981) and inhibiting epithelial cell migration (Greenburg & Hay, 1988), it follows that one action of the mesenchyme might be to alter the composition of the basement membrane upon which epithelial cells are anchored and so exert an effect upon gene expression *via* transmembrane receptors, the cytoskeleton and the nuclear matrix (Bissell *et al.* 1982). Evidence for a role of the basement membrane in mesenchymal–epithelial interactions comes mainly from two types of study: firstly, subtraction of basement membrane or its constituents from interacting tissues; secondly, circumstantial evidence showing specific changes in basement membrane or the underlying ECM at precise developmental times.

Of the former studies, the simplest in identifying that the basement membrane was necessary for mesenchyme–epithelia signalling were transmembrane recombinations (reviewed by Hay, 1977). Essentially, induction in membrane-separated tissues occurred only if those tissues were in close proximity. This seemed to preclude a role for a freely diffusable factor, suggesting that the mesenchyme conditioned the separating membrane with ECM components, leading to induction. Interestingly, a reciprocal signalling effect can also be observed: Millipore filters conditioned by mandibular epithelia can induce mesenchyme cells to form bone (Hall & Van Exan, 1982). Mouse primary epidermal cell cultures grown on plastic or a collagen gel matrix do not differentiate or produce basement membrane components. Re-implantation or recombination *in vitro* with dermal mesenchyme resulted in near normal differentiation and basement membrane formation (Bohnert *et al.* 1986). Such studies strongly suggest that mesenchyme exerts effects on basement membrane structure and turnover but beg the question: which particular components are important?

One of the best described models for mesenchyme-induced changes in basement membrane composition is during salivary gland formation (Bernfield *et al.* 1984). The mesenchyme appears to induce morphogenesis by stimulating epithelial cell proliferation and glycosaminoglycan (GAG) degradation in distal tubules whilst GAGs and type I collagen are deposited within intralobular clefts. Deposition of collagen may stabilize cleft morphology, since a collagenase inhibitor stimulates cleft formation (Nakanishi *et al.* 1986). Work on other ECM components has tended to be of a rather descriptive nature, e.g. the transient expression of type II collagen during otocyst–periotic mesenchyme interaction leads one to suppose a role for this molecule in otic capsule determination (Thorogood *et al.* 1986; Van der Water & Galinovic-Schwartz, 1987). Similar studies have suggested an important role for fibronectin during tooth development (Lesot *et al.* 1981; Thesleff *et al.* 1981). In fact fibronectin is a good candidate as an intermediate molecule between the matrix and the cell, since it possesses both ECM and cell binding domains (Buck & Horwitz, 1987*a*,*b*; Hynes, 1987).

A second candidate molecule receiving a lot of attention is tenascin. This glycoprotein seems to have an interesting role by virtue of its distribution being limited to the mesenchyme surrounding epithelia undergoing morphological changes (Aufderhide *et al.* 1987; Chiquet-Ehrismann *et al.* 1986; Thesleff *et al.* 1987; Fyfe *et al.* 1988).

## Mesenchymal–epithelial interactions: a role for growth factors

Evidence that growth factors can have profound effects on developmental processes is rapidly accumulating, particularly from studies on the early amphibian embryo. Smith (1987) showed the ability of a substance produced by the vegetal pole of *Xenopus* blastulae to induce mesoderm formation in the normally ectodermal animal pole. Subsequently basic fibroblast growth factor (bFGF) has been shown to mimic this effect (Grunz *et al.* 1988; Slack *et al.* 1987) whilst transforming growth factor-$\beta$ (TGF-$\beta$) acts synergistically with bFGF on the inductive process (Kimelman & Kirschner, 1987). In fact it has been found that a second form of TGF-$\beta$, TGF-$\beta_2$, is a much stronger mesoderm inducing factor than either TGF-$\beta_1$ or FGF (Rosa *et al.* 1988). It thus seems highly likely that factors native to *Xenopus* will eventually be discovered with close homologies to mammalian growth factors; indeed a product of the *Xenopus* Vg 1 gene whose transcript has been isolated and shown to resemble TGF-$\beta$ is localized in the vegetal region (Weeks & Melton, 1987). Similarly a number of proto-oncogenes appear to be spatially and temporally regulated during mammalian embryogenesis (Adamson, 1987) and although no clear link to developmental processes has arisen it is encouraging to note that the proto-oncogene *int-2* (which codes for an FGF-like molecule) is differentially expressed during early tissue induction in the mouse embryo (Wilkinson *et al.* 1988). The *neu* oncogene which encodes for a receptor to a growth factor similar to EGF is also differentially expressed during rat development (Kokai *et al.* 1987). Growth factors and their receptors are present during mammalian embryogenesis (Adamson, 1983, 1987; Mercola & Stiles, 1988), suggesting some, as yet undefined, physiological role. Certainly their known effects on cell proliferation, cell migration, ECM synthesis and degradation and angiogenesis would proffer on them a suitable repertoire of effects to act as inductive signals during mesenchyme–epithelial interactions. Their possible role in such interactions will be more fully discussed in terms of palate development.

Growth factors and extracellular matrix molecules may interact in the signalling of mesenchymal–epithelial interactions. First, many growth factors bind to and remain physiologically active on extracellular matrix molecules (Fava & McClure, 1987; Roberts *et al.* 1988; Smith *et al.* 1982). This gives a possible mechanism for dissociating synthesis from effect with respect to developmental time. A population of cells could secrete a growth factor bound to a specific extracellular matrix molecule, e.g. TGF-$\beta$ and fibronectin. This complex could remain *in situ*, but have a profound effect when a second population of cells migrated onto this matrix (and altered it). Such effects may occur, for example, during neural crest cell migration and differentiation in the head (Newgreen & Erickson, 1986). The fact that TGF-$\beta$ may be bound in variable amounts to differing fibronectin preparations (Fava & McClure, 1987) means that many of the classical papers describing effects of fibronectin on neural crest cell migration and differentiation should be repeated to determine how many of these effects are due to bound growth factors. Similar considerations apply to heparan sulphate proteoglycan and FGF (Gospodarowicz *et al.* 1987) (and other heparin binding growth factors), collagens and EGF (Erickson & Turley, 1987). Indeed one of the functions of differentially localizing different extracellular matrix molecules spatially and temporally in the embryo and adult may be to achieve different localizations and concentration gradients of growth factors.

Second, some growth factors, e.g. FGF, have no signal peptide and so may be co-secreted from the cell bound to extracellular matrix molecules (Gospodarowicz *et al.* 1987).

Third, in the context of epithelial–mesenchymal interactions, growth factors can have completely divergent effects on the epithelium and the mesenchyme. Thus TGF-$\beta$ can stimulate the synthesis of specific extracellular matrix molecules, e.g. fibronectin, collagen IV, hyaluronic acid, by palate mesenchyme cells. The same growth factor can also stimulate the synthesis of cell adhesion receptors for such molecules (the integrins – Hynes, 1987; Buck & Horwitz, 1985*a*,*b*; Ruoslahti & Pierschabacher, 1987) on epithelial cells (Ignotz & Massague, 1987). Thus the same soluble factor can establish an interacting system between mesenchyme and epithelium *via* extracellular matrix molecules and their receptors. Layer onto this complexity the spatial and temporal heterogeneity of cells producing and responding to such soluble factors and extracellular matrix molecules and one has a very diverse system for regulating and specifying cellular interactions in time and space.

Fourth, it has recently been shown that certain pattern forming genes in lower organisms specify the synthesis of cell surface molecules, whose extracellular domains bear a remarkable homology to known growth factors (Kidd *et al.* 1986; Schejter *et al.* 1986). As pattern-forming genes presumably exert their effects *via* cell–cell interactions which involve cell surface molecules (e.g. cell adhesion molecules) it is easy to envisage how 'growth factors' could have evolved. Perhaps the extracellular domain of these molecules is cleared from the cell surface, after it has performed its function and 'dumped' on the extracellular tissues for degradation. This extracellularly dumped molecule may retain (or evolve) biological activity and so evolve into a class of soluble factors exerting their effects at short range. Additionally, extracellular matrix molecules, e.g. fibronectin, collagen type IV, are present in such lower organisms as *Drosophila* embryos and localize in time and space with important morphogenetic events (Mirre *et al.* 1988; Naidet *et al.* 1987). Soluble factors and extracellular matrix molecules, therefore, have played a role in specifying the pattern and type of differentiation by regulating cell–cell and cell–matrix interactions over a long phylogenetic time.

## Mesenchymal–epithelial interactions: a role for stem cells

Epithelial–mesenchymal interactions during development are usually reciprocal with respect to time, i.e. the epithelium signals to the mesenchyme which then signals to the epithelium etc. This reciprocal scenario is exemplified by tooth development (Thesleff & Hurmerinta, 1981) and serves to effect specific local control and co-ordination between cell proliferation, differentiation and morphogenesis of the two tissues. Such local control extends into adulthood and it is clear that epithelial–mesenchymal interactions play an important role in the maintenance of adult organs (Cunha *et al.* 1985). Thus the synthesis of site- and appendage-specific cytokeratins by epithelial cells is specified by the underlying adult dermis (Briggaman, 1982; Sawyer *et al*. 1984; Schweizer *et al*. 1984): deep connective tissues neither modulate histodifferentiation of epithelium nor facilitate its migration or growth (Heaney & Vowles, 1988). This latter property can be exploited to prevent the epithelialization and exfoliation of dental implants. Cyclical changes in the adult epithelia of the urogenital tract and mammary gland may be mediated by the underlying stroma (Cunha *et al*. 1985). Moreover the primary cellular pathology of a number of adult 'epithelial' disorders may relate to important initial changes in the underlying fibroblasts and their extracellular matrices, e.g. breast cancer (Schor *et al*. 1987; Sakakura, 1983), psoriasis (Saiag *et al*. 1985). Experimentally induced irritation of the dermis alone results in a hyperplastic epidermis (Stern, 1979) whilst basal cell carcinomas can be induced to re-express a normal pattern of differentiation and keratinization when isolated from their stroma and recombined with stroma from unaffected regions (Cooper & Pinkus, 1977). Unaffected stroma can also reverse hyperplastic and dysplastic epithelial changes in experimental oral carcinogenesis (Mahmoud *et al*. 1988). The clonal modulation of fibroblast subsets by extracellular matrix and soluble factors may be important in the spatial and temporal control of epithelial–mesenchymal interactions in the embryo and adult (Schor & Schor, 1987).

Ultimately these signals must act on stem cells to alter gene expression and thus morphology, proliferation rates and differentiation. It is unclear: (a) whether mesenchymal stem cells exist – these could be the originators of specific clones of fibroblasts, and (b) when, where and how stem cells become specified in the embryo – at early stages all embryonic cells are stem cells. Therefore, mesenchymal signals, e.g. soluble factors and extracellular matrix molecules, could be expected to act on epithelial stem cells.Remarkably few studies have addressed this question, which is peculiar in view of the known effects of soluble factors in controlling epithelial cell proliferation within a population of epithelium. Investigations of stem cells, epithelial kinetics and differentiation in heterotypically recombined epithelia and mesenchyme are urgently required. Moreover, if mesenchyme signals alter gene expression in epithelial stem cells, then they presumably do so *via trans*-acting factors. Stem cells are the place to look for such factors and the genes they regulate.

In certain regions of the embryo and at specific developmental times it is clear that the basal epithelial cells are indeed multipotential stem cells. Thus during neural crest cell migration (Newgreen & Erickson, 1986), midline palatal epithelial seam degeneration (Ferguson, 1988) and Mullerian duct regression (Trelstad *et al*. 1982) epithelial cells transform into mesenchyme cells, often in response to mesenchymally derived signals. Similar transformations in phenotype from epithelia to mesenchyme can be induced in embryonic corneal epithelia by *in vitro* culture with extracellular matrix molecules (Greenburg & Hay, 1986; Sugrue & Hay, 1986). These epithelial to mesenchymal transformations include the appearance of vimentin and the disappearance of cytokeratin intermediate filaments from within the cytoplasm of the cell. These transformations must surely indicate that mesenchyme signals, particularly extracellular matrix molecules, can profoundly alter gene expression in embryonic basal epithelial cells (stem cells).

## Palate development

Several detailed reviews of palate development are available (see Introduction): accordingly we intend only to give a brief outline of palate development emphasizing those points relevant to a discussion of epithelial–mesenchymal interactions. Mesenchyme cells of the neural crest migrate to the primitive oral cavity where, in association with cranio-pharyngeal ectoderm they form the bilateral maxillary processes. From these, at embryonic day 12 in mice, day 6 in chickens, day 17 in alligators and day 45 in man, arise bilateral palatal shelves. In mammals these shelves at first grow vertically down the sides of the tongue (Fig. 1) but at a precise developmental stage elevate to a horizontal position above the dorsum of the tongue (Fig. 2). Mechanisms of shelf elevation have recently been discussed by Ferguson (1988). The medial edge epithelia (MEE) of approximating shelves then fuse to form a midline epithelial seam (Fig. 2), which rapidly degenerates, resulting in mesenchymal continuity across the palate. At the same time epithelial cells on the nasal and oral aspects of the palate differentiate into pseudostratified ciliated columnar and stratified squamous, non-keratinizing cells, respectively.

In birds the process is different in that the palatal shelves develop horizontally and importantly the MEE do not adhere, fuse and die, but instead keratinize, resulting in a naturally cleft palate (Ferguson *et al.* 1984; Ferguson & Honig, 1984, 1985).

The crocodilians, unlike most reptiles, have an intact, mammal-like secondary palate but MEE fusion and cell death is not a feature of this development, rather mesenchymal continuity is attained mainly by a merging process with mesenchymal

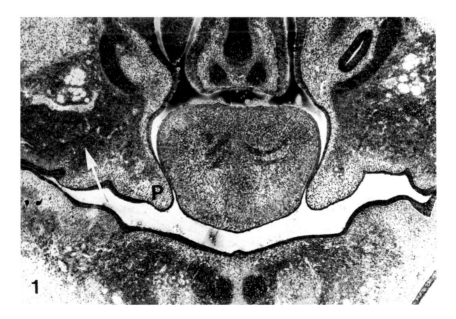

Fig. 1. Histological section silver/methionine-stained for GAGs (arrow) through the anterior-palatal region of a day 13 mouse embryonic head. Note the palatal shelves (P) lying vertically down the sides of the tongue. (×70).

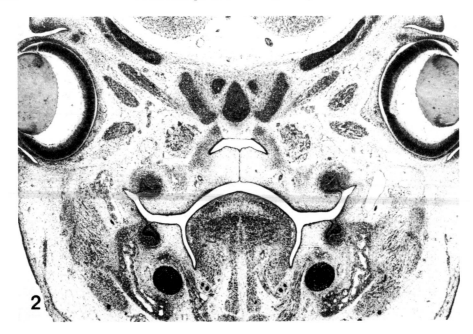

Fig. 2. Transverse histological section through the mid-palate region of a day 14 embryonic mouse. The section was stained with H & E and Alcian Blue. The palatal shelves have elevated to a horizontal position above the tongue and the midline epithelial seam has formed. (×70).

infilling and migration of MEE onto the nasal aspect of the palate (Ferguson, 1984, 1985). Organ culture experiments using single or homologous pairs of alligator, chick or mouse palatal shelves indicated that regionally specific epithelial differentiation occurred *in vitro* exactly as *in vivo* (Ferguson *et al.* 1984). Furthermore, MEE differentiation (migration in alligator, keratinization in chick and death in mouse) did not depend on shelf contact. Thus an experimental cross vertebrate system was available whereby nasal and oral epithelial differentiation were similar but MEE differentiation was species specific. This led to a series of experiments involving homologous, heterologous, heterochronic and isochronic combinations of mandibular, limb and palatal tissues both within and between mouse, chick and alligator embryos to determine the roles of mesenchyme and epithelia in palatal epithelial differentiation (Ferguson & Honig, 1984). In alligator and chick the situation is similar, the underlying mesenchyme signals oral, medial edge and nasal differentiation in a species specific manner even to heterologous epithelia. In the mouse the situation is slightly more complicated in that mouse epithelia seem to be 'biased' towards a palate-specific developmental fate. Thus a sheet of early embryonic mouse palatal epithelium will differentiate into nasal, medial and oral phenotypes when placed on a 'neutral' mesenchyme, e.g. mandibular. If, however, the mouse epithelial sheet is placed in a crossed recombination with alligator mesenchyme then the underlying mesenchyme completely respecifies nasal and oral aspects and induces a new medial edge migratory phenotype (typical of the alligator), but a line of cell death corresponding to the original medial edge will persist. Recombination experiments involving mouse epithelial sheets with their medial edges aligned to the medial edges of alligator or chick palatal mesenchyme results in complete respecification of nasal, medial and oral epithelial differentiation; this also occurs in crossed mouse/mouse recombinations. Mouse palate mesenchyme is always able to signal regionally specific epithelial differentiation to heterologous epithelia or to epithelia of other species. In summary, these recombination experiments demonstrate that regional differentiation of palatal epithelia is specified by the mesenchyme in a species-specific manner.

The question now arises: what is the nature of the mesenchymal signal? There are four main possibilities: (a) extracellular matrix molecules, (b) soluble factors, (c) cell–cell contact, (d) combinations of (a)–(c). Possibility (c) can be excluded as hundreds of TEM surveys of the epithelial–mesenchymal interface during each stage of mouse palate development have revealed that direct cell–cell contacts are extremely rare (Hall & Ferguson, unpublished). We thus propose that the mesenchymal signal is probably a combination of ECM molecules and soluble factors.

## Distribution of ECM during palate formation

We have conducted extensive immunocytochemical mapping at all stages of mouse and chick palate formation using polyclonal or monoclonal antibodies against: collagen types I–X, laminin, fibronectin, tenascin, heparan sulphate proteoglycan, chondroitin 0, 4, 6-sulphates (Fyfe & Ferguson, 1988; Fyfe *et al.* 1988). Essentially, most molecules are uninteresting either because they are absent (collagen types II, VIII and X), or are distributed ubiquitously at all developmental stages (collagen types I, III, chondroitin sulphates and fibronectin). Collagen type IV and laminin are present in basement membranes of palatal epithelia and blood vessels, their distribution during epithelial seam degeneration will be discussed later. Collagens V and VII are found in basement membranes and particularly around epithelia comprising the midline epithelial seam. The most interesting molecules appear to be tenascin and type IX collagen and the distribution of these molecules is particularly interesting around the time of mesenchyme to epithelium signalling.

Approximately 24–36 h prior to shelf fusion, mouse MEE cease DNA synthesis (Hudson & Shapiro, 1973). This process has been termed programmed epithelial cell death. It has been assumed that after shelf fusion and the accumulation of lysosomal enzymes (Mato *et al.* 1966) in seam cells, they rapidly die. We now believe, however, that although some cells (probably all the suprabasal cells) die, a significant proportion (probably the basal cells) transforms into mesenchyme cells and migrates into the mesenchyme.

The basement membrane on each side of the epithelial seam is remarkably conserved, remaining intact even when the seam is only 2–3 cells thick (Fig. 3A). Where the seam has disrupted and mesenchymal continuity is achieved the basal lamina is quickly reconstituted around the isolated epithelial fragments (Fig. 3B).

During seam disruption the basement membrane shows a progressive loss of laminin, whilst fibrils of tenascin and type III collagen become aligned in the sub-basement membrane zone perpendicular to the basement membrane (Fig. 4). Epithelial seam cells then migrate into the palatal mesenchyme, initially carrying along with them remnants of the basement membrane (Figs 5, 6). An obvious inference is that these cells are migrating along a suitable ECM pathway provided by tenascin/collagen type III bundles.

Indeed, we now have evidence that during seam disruption some midline epithelial cells secrete extracellular matrix molecules. They may be stimulated to do so by shelf fusion and contact with ECM molecules on both their surfaces: a process similar to that occurring experimentally in corneal epithelial sheets suspended within collagen gels (Greenburg & Hay, 1986; Sugrue & Hay, 1986). Soluble growth factors may also stimulate MEE cells to synthesize ECM molecules. Synthesis of a common matrix between epithelial and mesenchymal cells (and contributed by both) may

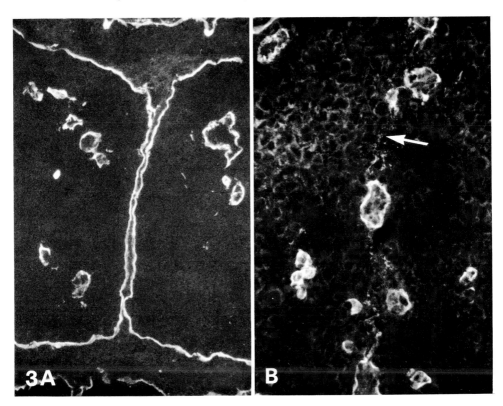

Fig. 3. A. Cryosection through the mid-line epithelial seam of an early day 14 mouse embryo. The section has been stained immunocytochemically for type IV collagen which localizes in the basement membrane. Note the intact basement membrane even where the seam is only 2–3 cells thick. (×280). B. Similar section, under higher power, of a late day 14 epithelial seam. Note that during degeneration of the seam (arrowed) small groups of epithelial cells migrate into the surrounding mesenchyme carrying with them clumps of basement membrane material. Residual epithelial cells remaining in the seam synthesize a new basement membrane around them. (×448).

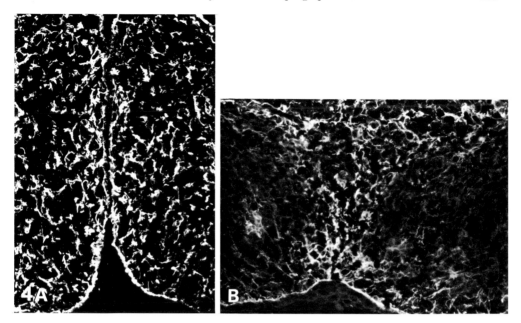

Fig. 4. A. Cryosection through a horizontal day 14 embryo palatal shelf immunostained with an antibody against type III collagen. Staining localizes to bundles of collagen throughout the mesenchyme, those adjacent to the medial edge basement membranes are orientated perpendicular to the latter in the sub-basement membrane zone. (×280). B. Cryosection of a degenerating epithelial seam in a late day 14 embryonic mouse stained immunocytochemically with an antibody to tenascin. Note strong localization particularly beneath the basement membrane around the area of seam disruption. Tenascin is located on fibrils of other extracellular matrix molecules including type III collagen. (×179).

facilitate epithelio–mesenchyme transformation. Once a break occurs in the midline epithelial seam, epithelial cells migrate into the mesenchyme and transform into mesenchyme cells (Fig. 5). These cells migrate preferentially on the mesenchyme side of the midline basement membrane up and down the length of the palate, so thinning the epithelial seam. These cells may be involved in specifically altering this basement membrane region, e.g. by synthesis or degradation of specific extracellular matrix molecules, so facilitating seam disruption at more posterior (or anterior) levels as development progresses. These changes mirror the developmental gradients in the palate with time.

It is interesting to note that chick palatal shelves do not develop these fibrils of tenascin and type III collagen and the medial edge epithelia do not migrate into the mesenchyme (Fyfe & Ferguson, 1988; Fyfe *et al.* 1988). The migratory mouse medial edge epithelial cells lose staining for cytokeratin intermediate filaments and gain vimentin staining, thus they quickly become indistinguishable from the rest of the palatal mesenchyme so that their ultimate developmental fate is unknown.

Type IX collagen is absent from basement membranes, mesenchymal and epithelial cell surfaces of vertical day 13 palates. However, just prior to shelf elevation, at the time of mesenchymal signalling of MEE differentiation, it is present on the cell surfaces of MEE cells (Fig. 7). Type IX collagen is present at intersections of collagens I and III fibrils with either themselves or the basal lamina (Fig. 8). It is absent from chick palates. Type IX collagen is a putative linker molecule which allows ECM molecules to interact with each other and with cell surfaces (Ferguson, 1988).

It is well known that, while epithelial cells will not invade type I collagen gels (Greenburg & Hay, 1986), suspension within such a gel precipitates cell migration and transformation to a migratory phenotype (Greenburg & Hay, 1982, 1986, 1988) even in adult cells (Greenburg & Hay, 1988). Such transformations do not occur in basal epithelial cells anchored to the basal lamina and indeed basement membrane molecules prevent epithelial transformation presumably by stabilizing epithelial cell ECM receptor expression (Greenburg & Hay, 1988). We propose that the above observations mirror those occurring during MEE migration and differentiation and provide insights into inductive mechanisms. These chiefly are: (a) modification of the basement membrane (e.g. loss of laminin). (b) Provision of a new microenvironment surrounding the epithelial cell (expression of type IX collagen, tenascin, type

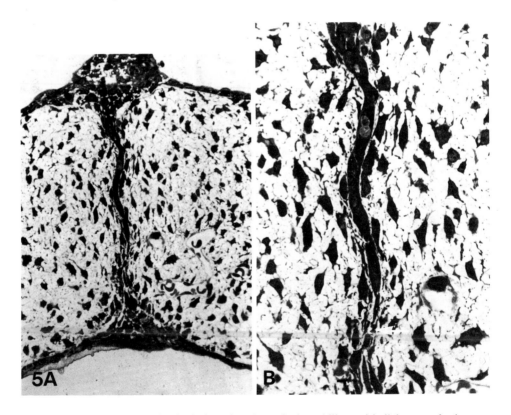

Fig. 5. A. Transverse histological section through the midline epithelial seam of a late day 14 embryonic mouse. Note the alignment of mesenchyme cells adjacent to the epithelial seam. (×280). B. Higher power representation of a similar section. Note that around the sites of seam degeneration (arrowed) epithelial cells appear to be migrating out of this zone and along the basement membrane. (×448).

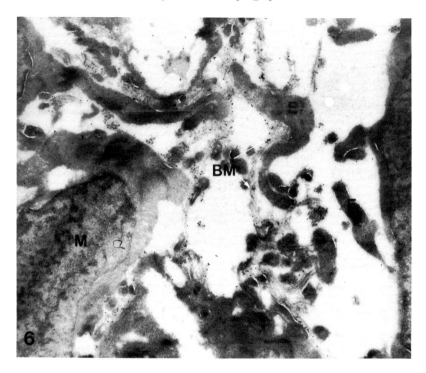

Fig. 6. Cryoelectron micrograph of a degenerating epithelial seam in a day 14 mouse embryo. The section has been prepared using 15 nm gold probes conjugated to a secondary antibody which detects the primary antibody to laminin. The basement membrane is localized. Note the disruption of laminin staining in the basement membrane (BM, arrowed) and migration of seam epithelial cells (E) into the mesenchyme M, carrying basement membrane molecules with them. (×20 000).

III collagen etc.). (c) Stimulation of extracellular matrix synthesis by the epithelial cells. (d) Induction of ECM receptors on the epithelial cell surface. The sum of these effects is that an epithelial cell which had been anchored to a stabilizing basement membrane now finds itself surrounded by a new microenvironment for which it feels a greater affinity than for the old environment of its fellow epithelial cells.

We thus propose that the 'programmed cell death' of MEE cells occurs chiefly in suprabasal and peridermal cells which are trapped within the mid-line seam during its formation. The migratory stimulus acts on a sub-population of MEE cells which are in contact with the basement membrane, namely the basal (stem) cells.

If such a hypothesis is true and MEE transformation results from the temporally and spatially regulated production of particular ECM molecules the question arises: what regulates ECM production?

## Growth factors and palate development

There are very few published data on the influence of soluble growth factors on palate development. It is known that palate mesenchyme cells have large numbers of receptors for epidermal growth factor (Yoneda & Pratt, 1985*a*,*b*) and that EGF, albeit at pharmacological doses, inhibits MEE cell death *via* an interaction with the underlying mesenchyme (Tyler & Pratt, 1980). Other soluble molecules included in our experiments have been: transforming growth factor $\alpha$ (TGF-$\alpha$), the presumptive embryonic homologue of EGF (Derynck, 1986); transforming growth factor B (TGF-$\beta$) a potent inhibitor of epithelial cell proliferation, which also has profound effects on ECM metabolism (Sporn *et al.* 1987); acidic and basic fibroblast growth factors (aFGF, bFGF), which can also cause changes in ECM biosynthesis (Gospodarowicz *et al.* 1987), and platelet derived growth factor (PDGF), which plays an important role in wound healing (Lynch *et al.* 1987) and is of potential interest in terms of epithelial seam formation and degeneration.

A range of experiments has been performed to assess the individual effects of these growth factors on mouse palate development in organ culture, mouse embryonic palate mesenchyme (MEPM), cell culture and mouse palatal epithelial cell culture. Most experiments to date have been conducted on MEPM cell culture and these will be discussed first. The stratagem for these experiments has first been to establish the optimal dose for each growth factor in terms of mitogenic response of MEPM cells cultured on plastic. Secondly, to assess the effects of this dose of the factor on cell proliferation and ECM biosynthesis when cells are cultured on plastic, on the surface of a collagen gel or within a three-dimensional collagen gel, the latter representing a more physiologically relevant substratum.

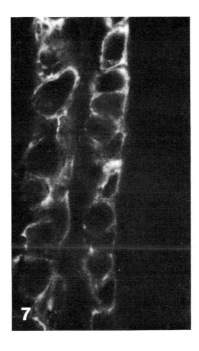

Fig. 7. Cryosection through the horizontal palatal shelves in the area of epithelial fusion in a day 14 embryonic mouse. Section was immunostained for type IX collagen. Note that staining occurs around the surfaces of medial edge epithelial cells. ($\times$448).

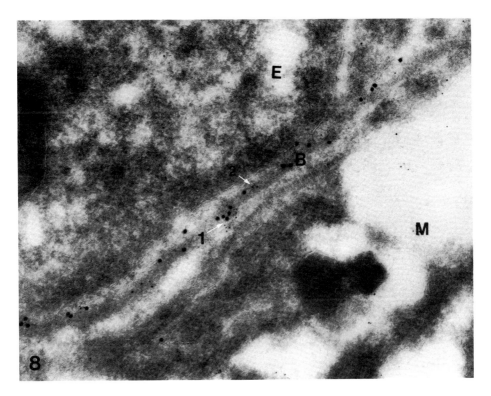

Fig. 8. Cryoelectron micrograph of the epithelial seam of a fused palate from a day 14 mouse embryo. Note the presence of a medial edge epithelial cell (E), basement membrane (B) and underlying mesenchyme (M). The section has been prepared with a 15 nm gold probe conjugated to a secondary antibody recognizing a primary antibody against laminin. Double labelling with a 5 nm gold probe conjugated secondary antibody recognizing a different primary antibody against type IX collagen was performed. Note that type IX collagen appears to be anchoring a fibril of type I collagen (arrow 1) and the cell itself (arrow 2) to the basement membrane. (×90 000).

In general EGF, TGF-α, aFGF, bFGF, PDGF all markedly stimulate MEPM cell proliferation when cultured on plastic and to a lesser extent on collagen (Fig. 9). However, none of these growth factors stimulated cell growth when cultured within a collagen gel (Fig. 9). TGF-β consistently inhibited cell proliferation independent of the substratum. These data suggest that in a physiological situation the mitogenic effects of these 'growth factors' are probably secondary to other effects on differentiation, e.g. ECM biosynthesis.

ECM biosynthesis has been assessed by immunocytochemistry, direct incorporation of labelled precursors into collagenous and non-collagenous proteins, SDS–gel electrophoresis under differing conditions, immunoprecipitation and indentification of individual GAGs using differential solubility assays. MEPM cells *in vitro* produce the full range of ECM molecules found *in vivo* when cultured on the three substrata (Fig. 10). Culture of cells on the surface or within collagen gels (Fig. 11) has indicated interesting responses in terms of ECM reorganization. In gel culture in the presence of high concentrations of donor calf serum (DCS) induces cell proliferation and ECM reorganization. Similar culture conditions in lower DCS concentrations in the presence or absence of growth factors results in less matrix reorganization. 'On gel' culture produces extensive invasion of the gel and reorganization of the gel just below the surface in a region where new extracellular matrix molecules are being synthesized (Fig. 10). As assessed immunocytochemically TGF-$\beta$ stimulates the synthesis of fibronectin (Fig. 12), laminin and collagen types III, IV, V and IX. This increase is the result of increasing synthesis in cells already producing the molecule (Sharpe *et al.* 1989) but also, in the case of type IV collagen, by switching on cells to make the molecule. TGF-$\beta$ is capable of stimulating collagen and total protein synthesis in MEPM cells cultured on all three substrata (Sharpe *et al.* 1989).

These experiments were, however, carried out in the presence of serum (Fig. 13), we have found that in the absence of serum, TGF-$\beta$ inhibits collagen type I synthesis

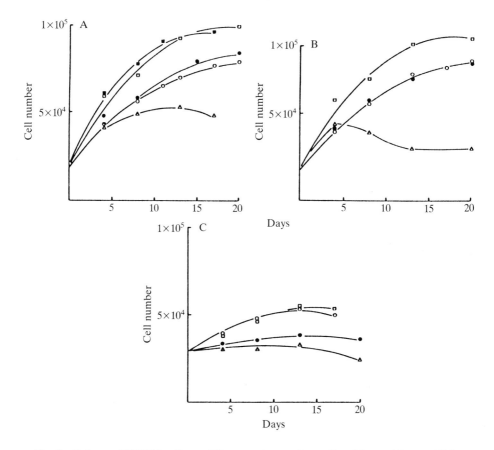

Fig. 9. Culture of MEPM cells on different substrata in media with or without addition of growth factors. MEPM cells were cultured either on plastic (A), on collagen (B) or within a collagen gel (C), in media containing 2·5% donor calf serum (DCS, ○) ± EGF (10 ng ml$^{-1}$, ●), TGF-$\alpha$ (10 ng ml$^{-1}$), PDGF (10 ng ml$^{-1}$, ■), aFGF (5 ng ml$^{-1}$), bFGF (10 ng ml$^{-1}$, □) or TGF-$\beta$ (1 ng ml$^{-1}$, △). Essentially, data for TGF-$\alpha$ and aFGF resembled those for EGF and bFGF, respectively.

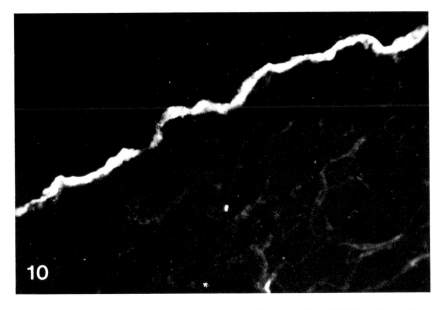

Fig. 10. Cryosection through a type I collagen gel upon which MEPM cells had been cultured in media containing 2·5% DCS + PDGF (1 ng ml$^{-1}$). The section was stained immunocytochemically for laminin. Note the intense localization just below the surface of the gel in a basement membrane-like structure. ($\times$448).

(Fig. 14) (Sharpe *et al.* 1989) although it still stimulates synthesis of minor collagens and non-collagenous proteins. This dimorphism of action must be due to interactions between TGF-$\beta$ and components of serum (probably other growth factors) which remain to be identified.

Analysis of GAG synthesis has shown that TGF-$\beta$ markedly stimulates hyaluronic acid (HA) and chondroitin sulphate production in sparse but not confluent MEPM cell cultures (Fig. 15; Foreman, Sharpe & Ferguson, unpublished). Interestingly TGF-$\beta$ also changes the proportions of size-classes of HA synthesized, stimulating the production of low molecular weight HA preferentially in serum-free conditions (Fig. 16; Foreman, Sharpe & Ferguson, unpublished). Such an effect may have important implications both in palatal shelf elevation (Ferguson, 1988) and in MEE migration from the epithelial seam, considering the large accumulation of HA around the seam basement membrane and the known effects of different size classes of HA on cell proliferation and morphogenesis (Caplan, 1987).

EGF (or TGF-$\alpha$) stimulates the synthesis of collagen types III, V and IX, as assessed immunocytochemically but inhibits type I collagen production (Dixon *et al.* unpublished). Preliminary experiments have established that EGF (or TGF$\alpha$) markedly stimulates GAG production as do a or bFGF (Foreman, Sharpe & Ferguson, unpublished). In addition a or bFGF has remarkable effects on MEPM cell morphology (Fig. 17; Foreman, Sharpe & Ferguson, unpublished). Such changes must involve profound alterations in cytoskeletal profile and it remains to be seen whether FGF exerts similar effects on palate epithelial cells, perhaps stimu-

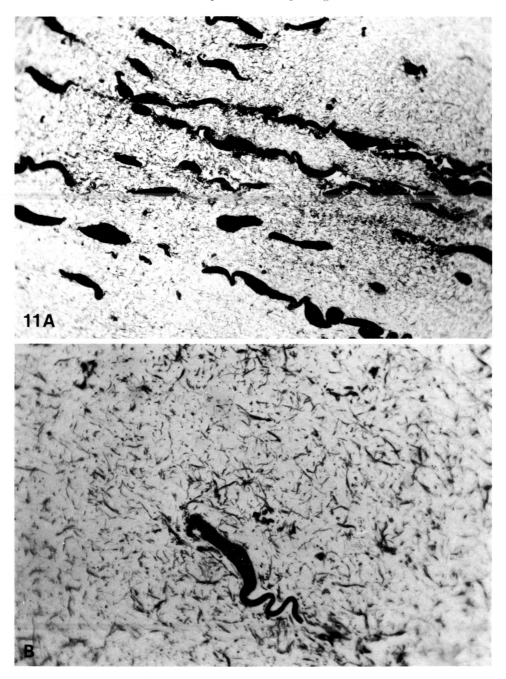

Fig. 11. Collagen gels containing MEPM cells cultured either on the surface (D) or within the matrix (A,B,C) were paraformaldehyde fixed, resin embedded and sections silver stained. A. Within gel culture in media containing 10% DCS. Note the large number of cells and their elongated appearance. Around the cell surfaces there is a marked reorganization of the gel matrix and the synthesis of new extracellular matrix molecules. (×280). B. In gel culture in media containing 2·5% DCS + 1 ng ml$^{-1}$ PDGF. (×280).

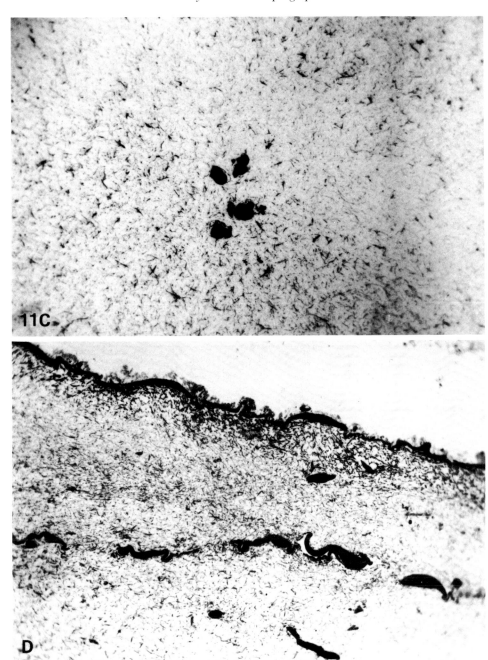

Fig. 11. C. In gel culture in media containing 2·5% DCS + 1 ng ml$^{-1}$ TGF-$\beta$. (×280). In both B and C very few cells are present and little reorganization occurs (compare with A). In the presence of TGF-$\beta$ the cells round up. D. On gel culture in media containing 10% DCS. (×280). Note the migration of cells into the gel and the reorganization and synthesis of extracellular matrix molecules just below the gel surface. This region corresponds exactly to those areas beneath the gel surface staining by immunocytochemical methods (Fig. 10).

lating their migration? PDGF has so far proved to be relatively uninteresting since it has not been found to alter any component of the ECM (Foreman, Sharpe & Ferguson, unpublished).

Organ culture experiments are at a preliminary stage but so far have revealed that submerged organ culture in EGF-supplemented medium results in excessive medial edge development, no inhibition of MEE cell death (in serum-free medium:

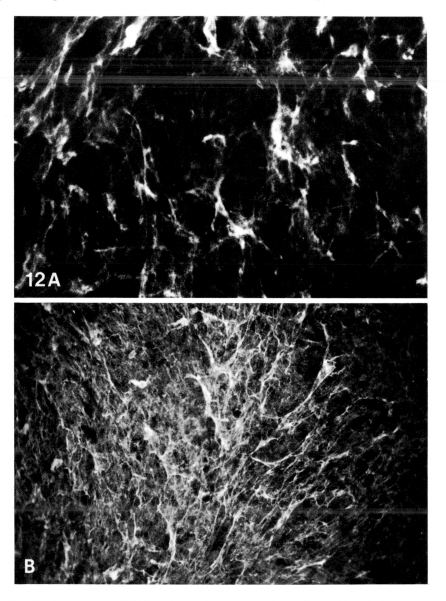

Fig. 12. Cultures of MEPM cells on the surface of a collagen film. Cultures were immunocytochemically stained for fibronectin. A. Cells cultured in media containing 2·5% DCS. (×280). B. Cells cultured in media containing 2·5% DCS + 1 ng ml$^{-1}$ TGF-$\beta$. Note the marked increase in fibronectin deposition induced by TGF-$\beta$. (×280).

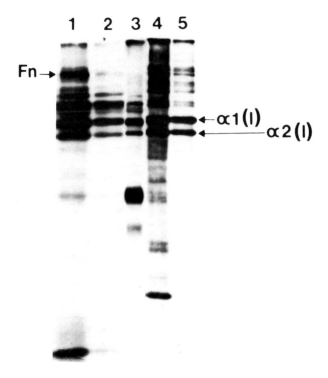

Fig. 13. Effect of TGF-$\beta$ on newly synthesized proteins of MEPM cells cultured on plastic in the presence of serum. Cells were labelled in the presence of 2·5% DCS ± 1 ng ml$^{-1}$ TGF-$\beta$. Labelled proteins in both the media and cell layer extracts were run reduced on 8% gels. Samples are: lane 1, TGF-$\beta$ medium; lane 2, control medium; lane 3, collagen type I and X standards; lane 4, TGF-$\beta$ guanidium hydrochloride (GuHCl) extract of cell layer; lane 5, control GuHCl extract. Reproduced from a paper submitted to *Development*.

inhibition only occurs in media containing serum) and increased quantities of ECM. With TGF-$\beta$ the epithelium was thin, MEE cell death enhanced and fibronectin content increased. These data are encouraging, since they indicate that the factors act in a similar way in organ culture as in cell culture and that physiological levels of these factors may well play a role in mouse palate development.

Epithelial cell culture has so far been restricted to plating isolated sheets of palatal epithelium onto the surface of collagen gels which have been conditioned by palatal mesenchyme (Ferguson, 1988). So far we have established that differentiation of these sheets is maintained in mesenchyme-free culture. The rationale behind such experiments is to induce various patterns of differentiation by gels conditioned with mesenchymal cells treated with various factors (TGF-$\beta$, EGF etc.).

## Regional heterogeneity of the palate

It is apparent that the palate mesenchyme is composed of a heterogeneous population, since different regions specify particular types of differentiation in the epithelium. The problem is in identifying how this heterogeneity is manifest and how it arises. It is certainly apparent that not all MEPM cells produce the same ECM components, and that not all cells are responsive to growth factors (Sharpe *et al.* 1989; Dixon *et al.* unpublished), perhaps because only certain cells contain receptors for these factors. It is also interesting to note that in confluent monolayers of MEPM 80–90 % will produce type III collagen (Sharpe *et al.* 1989) whilst in cells explanted directly from the palate less than 30 % do so (Fig. 18). Such an observation implies heterogeneity and also that some mechanism exists whereby either cell–cell or cell–matrix interactions induce production of ECM molecules. Moreover, when MEPM cells are cultured within collagen gels, extracellular matrix biosynthesis is stimulated more than when cells are placed at the surface of a collagen gel or on plastic under identical conditions (Sharpe *et al.* 1989; Dixon *et al.* unpublished). This implies that extracellular matrix molecules may stimulate the synthesis of more extracellular matrix molecules in either an autocrine or paracrine fashion. *In vitro* a

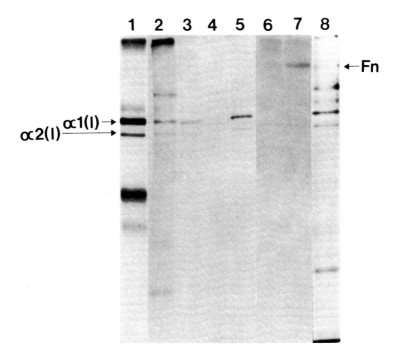

Fig. 14. Immunoprecipitation of collagen type I and fibronectin in the cell layer of MEPM cells cultured on plastic in the absence of serum. Immunoprecipitation was performed on the guanidium chloride extracts containing dpm's produced by $1 \times 10^5$ cells. Proteins were analysed on 8% SDS–polyacrylamide gels under reducing and non-reducing conditions. Samples are: lane 1, type 1 and ×collagen standards; lane 2, GuHCl extract; lane 3, control + rabbit anti-bovine type I collagen; lane 4, 1 ng ml$^{-1}$ TGF-$\beta$ + rabbit anti-bovine type I collagen; lane 5, 1 ng ml$^{-1}$ TGF-$\beta$ + 50 μg ml$^{-1}$ neutralizing antibody + rabbit anti-bovine type I collagen; lane 6, control + goat anti-mouse fibronectin; lane 7, 1 ng ml$^{-1}$ TGF-$\beta$ + goat anti-mouse fibronectin; lane 8, GuHCl extract. Lanes 2, 3, 4 and 5 are unreduced, lanes 6, 7 and 8 are reduced. Reproduced from a paper submitted to *Development*.

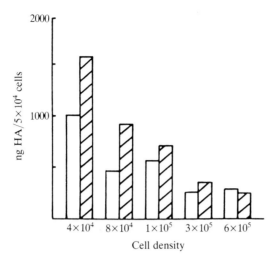

Fig. 15. Synthesis of hyaluronic acid (HA) by MEPM cells cultured on plastic in media containing 2·5% DCS (open boxes) or 2·5% DCS + TGF-$\beta$ (1 ng ml$^{-1}$, lined boxes). HA was detected using zip plate analysis, and production was quantified by laser densitometry. Note TGF-$\beta$ increases HA synthesis in sparse but not confluent cultures.

much higher percentage of these ECM molecules are in solution than *in vivo*: consequently an increase in the percentage of MEPM cells synthesizing a particular ECM molecule with time *in vitro* could be explained. *In vivo* this effect may be important in causing/amplifying the regional and temporal-specific clonal expansion of mesenchyme cells. Soluble growth factor might act on a certain population of mesenchyme cells causing them to synthesize more specific extracellular matrix molecules. These molecules in turn may induce adjacent cells to synthesize the same extracellular matrix molecules. Thus both soluble factors and ECM molecules may cause the clonal modulation and expansion of subsets of mesenchyme cells. At some point the system must self regulate, perhaps by the influence of large quantities of extracellular matrix molecules on the shape and adhesive properties of the mesenchyme cells, their expression of cell surface receptors for ECM and soluble molecules, and their response to soluble factors (which may now be matrix bound). Clearly this would imply that different cell surface receptors for different extracellular matrix molecules (Hynes, 1987; Buck *et al.* 1985a,b) may subserve different functions. Some may be involved solely with adhesion, thereby altering cell shape and facilitating or inhibiting cell migration. Other classes of receptor (or indeed the same receptors) may elicit important second messenger responses within the cells causing differential gene expression, e.g. stimulate the synthesis of extracellular matrix molecules. Similar events may occur in the wound-healing cascade. It follows that disorders in this clonal modulation/amplification system may be important in defective wound healing responses, excessive scarring, fibrotic disorders and maintenance of adult organs as well as in embryonic development and birth defects.

Heterogeneity within the palate may arise due to gradients of production of growth factors or growth factor receptors and extracellular matrix molecules and their

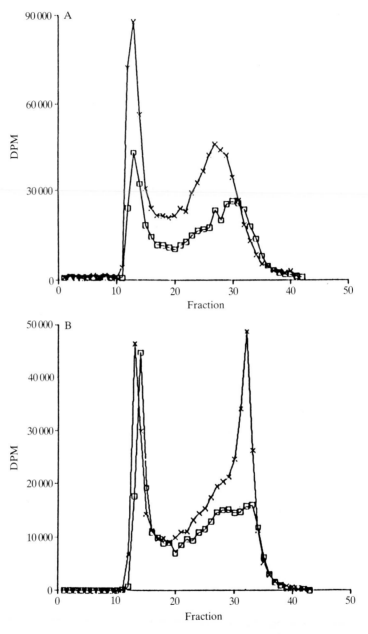

Fig. 16. GAG synthesis was assessed by the incorporation of $^3$H-labelled glucosamine. The size class of GAG produced was determined by separation, under reducing conditions, through a Sephadex 2B column. GAG production was measured in MEPM cells cultured on plastic in media containing: A. 2·5% DCS (□), 2·5% DCS + 1 ng ml$^{-1}$ TGF-$\beta$ (×); B, serum-free media (□), serum-free+1 ng ml$^{-1}$ (TGF-$\beta$ (×)). The peaks appearing in fractions 11–15 and 20–30 are due to hyaluronic acid (HA) synthesis, since their appearance is abolished by treatment with highly purified *Streptomyces* hyaluroni-dase. Note that in the presence of 2·5% DCS, TGF-$\beta$ stimulates the appearance of both high and low molecular weight HA. In serum-free conditions, however, TGF-$\beta$ increases the appearance of only low molecular weight HA. DPM, disints min$^{-1}$.

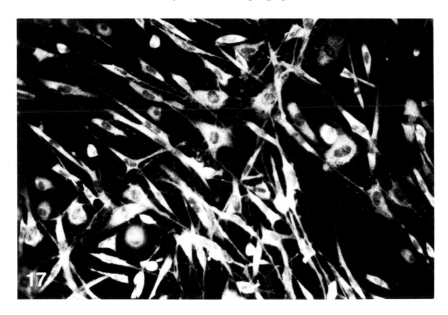

Fig. 17. MEPM cells cultured on a glass substratum in a medium containing 2·5% DCS + 5 ng ml$^{-1}$ aFGF. The culture was stained immunocytochemically with an antibody against laminin. Note the abnormal spindle-like appearance of the cells. (×448).

receptors. The distribution of such molecules and their receptors together with the clonal modulation of adjacent mesenchyme cells may account for regionally specific induction during mesenchymal signalling to the epithelium. Moreover there may be a corresponding heterogeneity in the responding epithelial cells in terms of production of receptors for, and response to, extracellular matrix and soluble molecules. Thus in cultures of isolated palatal epithelial sheets EGF stimulates proliferation of the oral and medial edge epithelium much more than the nasal epithelium (Grove & Pratt, 1984). We have demonstrated a difference in the cytokeratin profile and the distribution of cell-surface carbohydrate molecules (as evidenced by staining patterns with different lectins) in the oral, medial and nasal palatal epithelia (Ferguson, 1988). Moreover we have also produced monoclonal antibodies which recognize epitopes on oral, medial and nasal palatal epithelia, which are regionally and temporally expressed during critical phases of palate development (Dixon *et al.* 1989). These differences in part reflect an inherent heterogeneity of the palatal epithelium but for the most part they represent molecular markers of progressive regional epithelial differentiation. They may therefore represent a set of genes whose expression is regulated by mesenchymally derived factors.

Identification of these subsets of mesenchyme and epithelial cells and the ability to sort such cells (e.g. using FACS) by way of their unique cell surface markers allows one to establish defined clones of mesenchyme and epithelial cells. These clones can then be used in recombination or conditioning experiments to analyse better the mechanisms of epithelial–mesenchymal interactions in the developing palate.

To investigate aspects of palatal mesenchyme heterogeneity directly we have undertaken a series of experiments, namely: (a) *in situ* hybridization studies to localize sites of production of growth factors and ECM molecules during palate development. (b) Immunolocalization studies to determine sites of production,

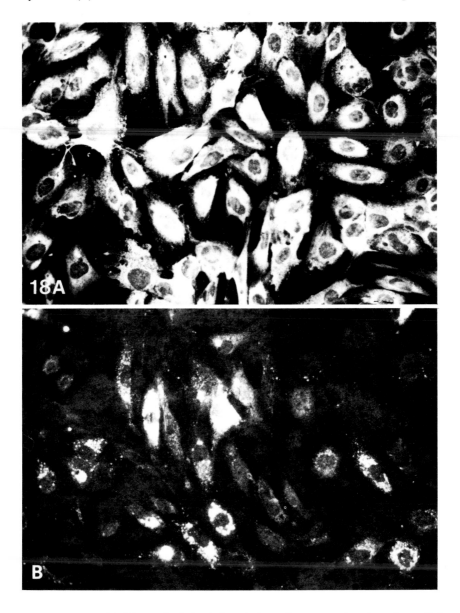

Fig. 18. Culture of MEPM cells derived directly from dissagregated entire palates. Cells were cultured for 72 h on a glass substratum in 2·5% DCS and were stained immunocytochemically for: A. Laminin. (×448). B. Type III collagen. (×448). Note the heterogeneity of the mesenchyme population, most cells synthesizing laminin but very few type III collagen. The percentage of cells staining for particular extracellular molecules varies, both for different molecules and for the same molecule with time *in vitro*.

sequestration and binding of various growth factors and growth factor receptors using both fluorescence and silver-enhanced immunogold labelling techniques. (c) Culture of regionally derived palate mesenchyme cells from the oral, medial edge and nasal aspects of embryonic mouse palatal shelves. (d) Production of monoclonal antibodies to regionally and developmentally specific areas of epithelia and mesenchyme. It is not known whether palatal cells can produce the common growth factors although TGF-$\beta$ has been localized in this region (Heine *et al.* 1987). What is certain is that the embryo does produce a range of growth factors, whilst similar and other growth factors of maternal origin can exert effects on embryogenesis (Mercola & Stiles, 1988). Maternally derived growth factors, e.g. EGF, may be important in palate development as the embryo and oral cavity are bathed in amniotic fluid (containing the maternally derived factors), which the embryo swallows. Gradients of penetration of these factors into the palatal shelves may exist. It will be interesting

Fig. 19. Histological section through the mid-line epithelial seam of a pair of fused palatal shelves in a day 14 mouse embryo. The section has been stained with an antibody against the EGF-receptor. These primary location sites are recognized by a secondary antibody bound to colloidal gold particles and visualized by epipolarized illumination, which reveals the EGF-receptor as a white spot. Note the accumulation of the receptor on mesenchyme cells close to the epithelial seam. (×280).

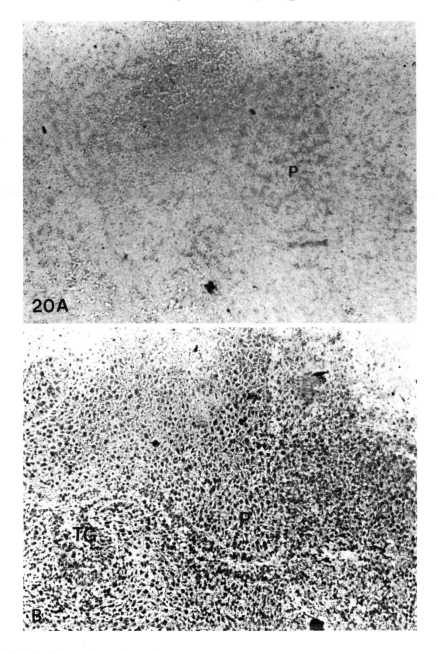

Fig. 20. Cryosections of day 13 (A,B, ×180) and day 14 (C,D, ×180) mouse embryos. Sections were stained with an immunogold-linked secondary antibody to a primary antibody which recognized TGF-$\beta$ (B,D). Control sections (A,C) were stained with secondary antibody alone. The gold particles were visualized by silver enhancement techniques. At day 13 there is localization within epithelia and mesenchyme of the palate (P) and tooth germ (TG). In the horizontal palate localization occurs primarily at the epithelial–mesenchymal interface. At day 14 TGF-$\beta$ is particularly localized in myotubes of the tongue (T), bone blastamata (B), cartilage (C) and the epithelia of Jacobsen's organ (J).

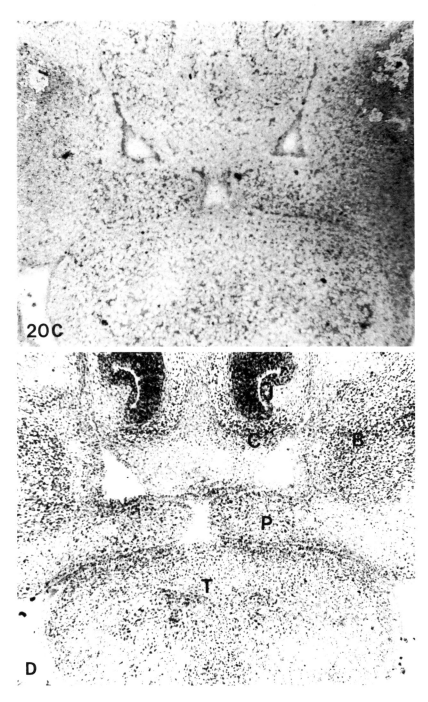

to examine whether the sites of production of the various growth factors correlate
with the sites of localization. Certainly in human foetal tissues insulin-like growth
factor (IGF) studies (D'Ercole, 1987) have suggested that the two sites are not
necessarily the same. Such observations suggest transport of a growth factor from a

site of production to a target site and imply a regulatory role for carrier proteins during development. This hypothesis is attractive for several growth factors. TGF-$\beta$, for example, binds to fibronectin (Fava & McClure, 1987), whilst FGFs, which have no signal peptide sequence, are thought to be co-secreted with an ECM molecule (Gospodarowicz *et al.* 1987). Specific binding proteins, as for the insulin-like growth factors, may also exist.

Immunolocalization studies are at an early stage but have already revealed temporal and spatial differences. Immunolocalization of the EGF receptor, for example, has shown that in the vertical palatal shelf EGF receptors are rare on the medial edge mesenchyme but are abundant in the same area at the time of shelf fusion and epithelial seam degeneration (Fig. 19). Likewise, immunolocalization of TGF$\alpha$ itself reveals that at embryonic day 12 it is sparsely and ubiquitously distributed in the palatal mesenchyme. At day 13, TGF$\alpha$ is concentrated around the future oral and medial edges of the palatal shelves, but sparse in the future nasal region, except in the region of future fusion of the palatal nasal epithelium with the nasal septum. This distribution is interesting in view of the differential effects of EGF on oral and medial edge epithelia as compared to nasal epithelia (Grove & Pratt, 1984). These localizations are most marked in the anterior one third of the palate, which is developmentally the most advanced and the first region to fuse *in vivo*. At day 14 TGF$\alpha$ remains concentrated in the medial edge mesenchyme particularly in the anterior one third of the palate. It remains localized in this region even after palatal fusion and degeneration of the midline epithelial seam. At this stage much TGF$\alpha$ is localized in the palatal seam. This differential distribution in the medial edge of the palatal shelf mesenchyme correlates (1) with the area of maximum cell division (Cleaton-Jones, 1976; Jelnick & Dostal, 1974; Nanda & Romeo, 1975), (2) with an area of altered ECM biosynthesis both before and after shelf fusion, (3) with the observation that EGF exerts its effect on palatal medial edge epithelial differentiation *via* an indirect effect on the underlying mesenchyme (Tyler & Pratt, 1980). The localization of TGF-$\beta$ is also developmentally regulated (Fig. 20). In the vertical palate of day 13 embryos TGF-$\beta$ is ubiquitously distributed throughout the palatal epithelia and mesenchyme. In early day 14 embryos, however, localization occurs primarily on the nasal aspect of the palate and, significantly, at the epithelial–mesenchymal interface, i.e. in basal epithelial cells and in mesenchyme underlying the basement membrane. This distribution pattern is the reverse of EGF, which is interesting in view of the inhibiting effects of TGF-$\beta$ on epithelial proliferation and the exact correlation of specific growth factor localizations with known epithelial proliferation rates.

Culture of cells from the oral, medial edge and nasal (OMEN) regions of the palate, although also in preliminary stages, has yielded encouraging results. Medial edge cells proliferate in culture far more quickly than those of oral and nasal origin, an observation which correlates with mitotic indices derived *in vivo* (Cleaton-Jones, 1976; Jelnick & Dostal, 1974; Nanda & Romeo, 1975). Such differences are maintained through several passages *in vitro*. We intend to investigate the nature of ECM production by the OMEN cells and any differential response to growth factors in terms of mitogenesis and ECM production. Ultimately we hope to repeat epithelial sheet/conditioned gel experiments (described previously) using regionally derived or cloned mesenchyme and epithelial cells.

## Conclusions

Epithelial differentiation during development of the palate is specified by the underlying mesenchyme. Epithelial differentiation is regionally specific and the mesenchyme consists of a heterogeneous population of cells and matrix molecules. Clonal modulation of this heterogeneity probably results in regionally and temporally specific mesenchymal signalling in terms of subtle changes in local ECM and basement membrane molecules regulated by soluble growth factors. The production of such growth factors may occur in palatal or extra-palatal tissues, these factors and the extracellular matrix molecules they stimulate acting in autocrine or paracrine fashion. The production of both growth factors and extracellular matrix molecules are regulated perhaps by interactive feedback loops. Moreover growth factors bind to such extracellular matrix molecules, so tending to further the localization of the former, and to enable the separation, in developmental time, of production of the signal and response to it by an appropriate target cell population. The specific inductive signal from palatal mesenchyme is unknown but we believe that it involves complex interactions between growth factors, ECM molecules and their receptors. The same growth factor can stimulate synthesis of specific ECM molecules by the mesenchyme and receptors for such molecules on the epithelium: an interacting system is thereby established. Epithelial response to such signals may also be influenced by clonal heterogeneity and result in differential gene expression. Such a system allows for complex interactive regulatory steps, e.g. growth factors may stimulate the production of a particular ECM molecule by cells, which alters the response of those cells to that growth factor.

Specifically, we suggest that during MEE cell migration tenascin, type III collagen and in particular type IX collagen may play important regulatory roles. The observations that TGF-$\beta$ and EGF can stimulate the synthesis of such molecules may be significant. TGF-$\beta$ is a good candidate for one physiologically relevant soluble molecule, as it has been localized in the embryonic palate (Heine *et al.* 1988), is a potent stimulator of ECM biosynthesis in palate mesenchyme (Sharpe *et al.* 1989) and can induce the expression of ECM receptors in epithelial cells (Ignotz & Massague, 1987). EGF or TGF-$\alpha$ may perform a similar role. Doubtless, the interactions of various growth factors are important *in vivo*, and add another layer of complexity to an already highly heterogeneous and interactive system.

Supported by grants from the MRC, Wellcome Trust, Birthright and Action Research for the Crippled Child. We acknowledge the help of Bill Moser, Martin Carrette, David Foreman, Mike Dixon, David Lyfe and Jill Garner.

## References

ADAMSON, E. D. (1983). Growth factors in development. In *The Biological Basis of Reproductive and Developmental Medicine* (ed. J. B. Warshaw), pp. 307–336. New York: Elsevier Press.

ADAMSON, E. D. (1987). Oncogenes in development. *Development* **99**, 449–471.

AUFDERHEIDE, E., CHIQUET-EHRISMANN, R. & EKBLOM, P. (1987). Epithelial–mesenchymal interactions in the developing kidney lead to expression of tenascin in the mesenchyme. *J. Cell Biol.* **105**, 599–608.

BERNFIELD, M., BANERJEE, S. D., KODA, J. E. & RAPRAEGER, A. C. (1984). Remodelling of the basement membrane as a mechanism of morphogenetic tissue interaction. In *The Role of Extracellular Matrix in Development* (ed. R. Trelstad), pp. 545–572. New York: A. R. Liss Inc.

BISSELL, M. J., HALL, G. & PARRY, G. (1982). How does the extracellular matrix direct gene expression? *J. theor. Biol.* **99**, 31–68.

BOHNERT, A., HORNUNG, J., MACKENZIE, I. C. & FUSENIG, N. E. (1986). Epithelial–mesenchymal interactions control basement membrane production and differentiation in cultured and transplanted mouse keratinocytes. *Cell Tiss. Res.* **244**, 413–429.

BRIGGAMAN, R. A. (1982). Epidermal–dermal interactions in adult skin. *J. invest. Derm.* **79**, 21–24.

BUCK, C. A. & HORWITZ, A. F. (1987*a*). Cell surface receptors for extracellular matrix molecules. *A. Rev. Cell Biol.* **3**, 179–205.

BUCK, C. A. & HORWITZ, A. F. (1987*b*). Integrin, a trans-membrane glycoprotein complex mediating cell–substratum adhesion. *J. Cell Sci. Suppl.* **8**, 231–250.

CAPLAN, A. I. (1987). The extracellular matrix is instructive. *Bioessays* **5**, 129–132.

CHIQUET-EHRISMANN, R., MACKIE, E. J., PEARSON, C. A. & SAKAKURA, T. (1986). Tenascin: an extracellular matrix protein involved in tissue interactions during fetal development and oncogenesis. *Cell* **47**, 131–139.

CLEATON-JONES, P. (1976). Radioautographic study of mesenchymal cell activity in the secondary palate of the rat. *J. dent. Res.* **55**, 437–440.

COOPER, M. & PINKUS, H. (1977). Intrauterine transplantation of rat basal cell carcinoma: a model for reconversion of malignant to benign growth. *Cancer Res.* **37**, 2544–2552.

CUNHA, G. R., BIGSBY, R. M., COOKE, P. S. & SUGIMURA, Y. (1985). Stromal–epithelial interactions in adult organs. *Cell Differ.* **17**, 137–148.

CUNHA, G. R., SHANNON, J. M., NEUBAUER, B. L., SAWYER, L. M., FUJII, H., TAGUCHI, O. & CHUNG, L. W. K. (1981). Mesenchymal–epithelial interactions in sex differentiation. *Hum. Genet.* **58**, 68–77.

D'ERCOLE, A. J. (1987). Somatomedins/insulin like growth factors and fetal growth. *J. dev. Physiol.* **9**, 481–495.

DERYNCK, R. (1986). Transforming growth factor: structure and biological activities. *J. Cell Biochem.* **32**, 293–304.

DHOUAILLY, D. (1975). Formation of cutaneous appendages in dermo-epidermal recombinations between reptiles, birds and mammals. *Willhelm Roux Arch. EntwMech. Org.* **177**, 323–340.

DIXON, M. W. J., WHITE, A. & FERGUSON, M. W. J. (1989). Monoclonal antibodies recognising stage and region specific epitopes on mouse palatal epithelium. *Differentiation* (in press).

EKBLOM, P., THESLEFF, I. & SARIOLA, H. (1986). The extra-cellular matrix in tissue morphogenesis and angiogenesis. In *The Cell in Contact* (ed. G. M. Edelman & J. P. Thiery), pp. 365–392. New York: J. Wiley & Sons.

ERICKSON, C. A. & TURLEY, E. A. (1987). The effects of epidermal growth factor on neural crest cells in tissue culture. *Expl Cell Res.* **169**, 267–279.

FAVA, R. A. & McCLURE, D. B. (1987). Fibronectin-associated transforming growth factors. *J. cell. Physiol.* **131**, 184–189.

FERGUSON, M. W. J. (1978). Palatal shelf elevation in the Wistar rat fetus. *J. Anat.* **125**, 555–577.

FERGUSON, M. W. J. (1984). Craniofacial development in *Alligator mississippiensis*. In *The Structure, Development and Evolution of Reptiles* (ed. M. W. J. Ferguson), pp. 223–273. London: Academic Press.

FERGUSON, M. W. J. (1985). The reproductive biology and embryology of crocodilians. In *Biology of the Reptilia*, vol. 14, *Development* (ed. C. Gans, F. S. Billett, & P. Maderson), pp. 454–720. New York: J. Wiley & Sons.

FERGUSON, M. W. J. (1987). Palate development: mechanisms and malformations (Conway Review Lecture). *Irish J. med. Sci.* **156**, 309–315.

FERGUSON, M. W. J. (1988). Palate development. *Development* **103 Suppl.**, 41–60.

FERGUSON, M. W. J. & HONIG, L. S. (1984). Epithelial–mesenchymal interactions during vertebrate palatogenesis. In *Current Topics in Developmental Biology*, vol. 19, *Palate Development: Normal and Abnormal, Cellular and Molecular Aspects* (ed. E. F. Zimmerman), pp. 137–164. New York: Academic Press.

FERGUSON, M. W. J. & HONIG, L. S. (1985). Experimental fusion of the naturally cleft embryonic chick palate. *J. craniofac. genet. devl Biol.* **S1**, 323–337.

FERGUSON, M. W. J., HONIG, L. S. & SLAVKIN, H. C. (1984). Differentiation of cultured palatal shelves from alligator, chick and mouse embryos. *Anat. Rec.* **209**, 231–249.

FYFE, D. & FERGUSON, M. W. J. (1988). Immunocytochemical localisation of collagen types I–XII, proteoglycans, laminin and fibronectin during mouse secondary palate development. *Devl Biol.* (in press).

FYFE, D., FERGUSON, M. W. J. & CHIQUET-EHRISMANN, R. (1988). Tenascin immunolocalisation during palate development in mouse and chicken embryos. *Anat. & Embryol.* (in press).

GOSPODAROWICZ, D., NEUFELD, G. & SCHWEIGERER, L. (1987). Fibroblast growth factor: structural and biological properties. *J. cell. Physiol., Suppl.* **5**, 15–26.

GREENBURG, G. & HAY, E. D. (1982). Epithelia suspended in collagen gels can lose polarity and express characteristics of migrating mesenchyme cells. *J. Cell Biol.* **95**, 333–339.

GREENBURG, G. & HAY, E. D. (1986). Cytodifferentiation and tissue phenotype change during transformation of embryonic lens epithelium to mesenchyme like cells in vitro. *Devl Biol.* **115**, 363–379.

GREENBURG, G. & HAY, E. D. (1988). Cytoskeleton and thyroglobulin expression change during transformation of thyroid epithelium to mesenchyme-like cells. *Development* **102**, 605–622.

GREENE, R. M. & PRATT, R. M. (1976). Developmental aspects of secondary palate formation. *J. Embryol. exp. Morph.* **36**, 225–245.

GROVE, R. I. & PRATT, R. M. (1984). Influence of epidermal growth factor and cyclic AMP on growth and differentiation of palatal epithelial cells in culture. *Devl Biol.* **106**, 427–437.

GRUNZ, H., MCKEEHAN, W. L., KNOCHEL, W., BORN, J., TIEDEMANN, H. & TIEDEMANN, H. (1988). Induction of mesodermal tissues by acidic and basic heparin binding growth factors. *Cell Differ.* **22**, 183–190.

HALL, B. K. (1984). Matrices control the differentiation of cartilage and bone. In *Matrices and Cell Differentiation* (ed. E. D. Hay), pp. 147–169. New York: Alan R. Liss Inc.

HALL, B. K. & VAN EXAN, R. J. (1982). Induction of bone by epithelial cell products. *J. Embryol. exp. Morph.* **69**, 37–46.

HAY, E. D. (1977). Cell–matrix interaction in embryonic induction. In *International Cell Biology.* (ed. B. R. Brinkley & K. R. Porter), pp. 50–57. Chicago: Rockefeller University Press.

HEANEY, T. G. & VOWLES, R. W. (1988). Morphometric analysis of epithelium on a deep connective tissue substratum. *J. dent. Res.* **67**S, 175.

HEINE, V. I., MUNOZ, E. F., FLANDERS, K. C., ELLINGSWORTH, L. P., LAM, P., THOMPSON, N. C., ROBERTS, A. B. & SPORN, M. B. (1987). The role of transforming growth factor beta in the development of the mouse embryo. *J. Cell Biol.* **105**, 2861–2867.

HUDSON, C. D. & SHAPIRO, B. L. (1973). An autoradiographic study of deoxyribonucleic acid synthesis in embryonic rat palatal shelf epithelium with reference to the concept of programmed cell death. *Arch. Oral Biol.* **18**, 77–84.

HYNES, R. O. (1987). Integrins: A family of cell surface receptors. *Cell* **48**, 549–554.

IGNOTZ, R. R. & MASSAGUE, J. (1987). Cell adhesion protein receptors as targets for transforming growth factor-B action. *Cell* **51**, 189–197.

JELNICK, R. A. & DOSTAL, M. (1974). Morphogenesis of cleft palate induced by exogenous factors. VII. Mitotic activity during formation of the mouse secondary palate. *Folia morph. (Praha)* **22**, 94–101.

KIDD, S., KELLEY, M. R. & YOUNG, M. W. (1986). Sequence of the notch locus of *Drosophilia melanogaster*: relationship of the encoded protein to mammalian clotting and growth factors. *Molec. cell. Biol.* **6**, 3094–3108.

KIMELMAN, D. & KIRSCHNER, M. (1987). Synergistic induction of mesoderm by FGF and TGF-B and the identification of an mRNA coding for FGF in the early *Xenopus* embryo. *Cell* **51**, 869–877.

KOKAI, Y., COHEN, J. A., DREBIN, J. A. & GREENE, M. I. (1987). Stage- and tissue-specific expression of the *neu* oncogene in rat development. *Proc. natn. Acad. Sci. U.S.A.* **84**, 8498–8501.

KOLLAR, E. J. (1983). Epithelial–mesenchymal interactions in the mammalian integument: tooth development as a model for instructive induction. In *Epithelial–Mesenchymal Interactions in Development* (ed. R. H. Sawyer & J. F. Fallow), pp. 27–49. New York: Praeger.

KRATOCHWIL, K. (1983). 'Embryonic induction'. In *Cell Interactions and Development Molecular Mechanisms* (ed. K. M. Yamada), pp. 99–122. New York: J. Wiley & Sons.

LESOT, H., OSMAN, M. & RUCH, J. V. (1981). Immunofluorescent localization of collagens, fibronectin and laminin during terminal differentiation of odontoblasts. *Devl Biol.* **82**, 371–381.

LYNCH, S. E., NIXON, J. C., COLVIN, R. B. & ANTONIADES, H. N. (1987). Role of platelet-derived growth factor in wound healing: Synergistic effects with other growth factors. *Proc. natn. Acad. Sci. U.S.A.* **84**, 7696–7700.

MAHMOUD, M., YAEGER, J. & KOLLAR, E. (1988). Stromal–epithelial interaction in experimental oral carcinogenesis. *J. dent. Res.* **67S**, 175.

MATO, M., AIKAWA, E. & KATAHIRA, M. (1966). Appearance of various types of lysosomes in the epithelium covering lateral palatine shelves during secondary palate formation. *Gunma J. med. Sci.* **15**, 46–56.

MCALEESE, S. R. & SAWYER, R. H. (1981). Correcting the phenotype of the epidermis from chick embryos homozygous for the gene scaleless (*sc/sc*). *Science* **214**, 1033–1034.

MCPHEE, J. R. & VAN DER WATER, T. R. (1986). Epithelial–mesenchymal tissue interactions guiding otic capsule formation: the role of the otocyst. *J. Embryol. exp. Morph.* **97**, 1–24.

MELNICK, M., BIXLER, D. & SHIELDS, E. D. (1980). *The Aetiology of Cleft Lip and Cleft Palate.* New York: Alan Liss.

MERCOLA, M. & STILES, C. D. (1988). Growth factor super families and mammalian embryogenesis. *Development* **102**, 451–460.

MIRRE, C., CECCHINI, J. P., LE PARCO, Y. & KNIBIEHLER, B. (1988). De novo expression of a type IV collagen gene in *Drosophilia* embryos is restricted to mesodermal derivatives and occurs at germ band shortening. *Development* **102**, 369–376.

NAIDET, C., SEMERWA, M., YAMADA, K. & THIERY, J. P. (1987). Peptides containing the cell attachment recognition signal Arg-Gly-Asp prevent gastrulation in *Drosophila* embryos. *Nature, Lond.* **325**, 348–350.

NAKANISHI, Y., SUGIURA, F., KISHI, J-I. & HAYAKAWA, T. (1986). Collagenase inhibitor stimulates cleft formatiton during early morphogenesis of mouse salivary gland. *Devl Biol.* **113**, 201–206.

NANDA, R. & ROMEO, D. (1975). Differential cell proliferation of embryonic rat palatal processes as determined by incorporation of tritiated thymidine. *Cleft Palate J.* **12**, 436–443.

NEWGREEN, D. & ERICKSON, C. R. (1986). The migration of neural crest cells. *Int. Rev. Cytol.* **103**, 89–145.

PISANO, M. M. & GREENE, R. M. (1986). Hormone and growth factor involvement in craniofacial development. *IRCS Med. Sci.* **14**, 635–640.

PRATT, R. M. (1984). Hormones, growth factors and their receptors in normal and abnormal prenatal development. In *Issues and Reviews in Teratology 2* (ed. H. Kalter), pp. 189–217. New York: Plenum Press.

PRATT, R. M. & CHRISTIANSEN, R. C. (1980). *Current Research Trends in Prenatal Craniofacial Development.* Amsterdam: Elsevier/North-Holland.

ROBERTS, R., GALLAGHER, J., SPOONCER, E., ALLEN, T. D., BLOOMFIELD, F. & DEXTER, T. M. (1988). Heparan sulphate bound growth factors: a mechanisms for stromal cell mediated haemopoiesis. *Nature, Lond.* **332**, 376–378.

ROSA, F., ROBERTS, A. B., DANIELPOUR, D., DART, L. L., SPORN, M. B. & DAWID, I. B. (1988). Mesoderm induction in amphibians: The role of TGF-Bbd2-like factors. *Science* **239**, 783–785.

RUOSLAHTI, E. & PIERSCHABACHER, M. D. (1987). New perspectives in cell adhesion: RGD and integrins. *Science* **238**, 491–497.

SAIAG, P., COULOMB, B., LEBRITAN, C., BELL, E. & DUBERTVET, L. (1985). Psoriatic fibroblasts induce hyperproliferation of normal keratinocytes in a skin equivalent model *in vitro*. *Science* **230**, 669–672.

SAKAKURA, T. (1983). Epithelial–mesenchymal interactions in mammary gland development and its perturbation in relation to tumorigenesis. In *Understanding Breast Cancer* (ed. M. A. Rich, J. C. Hager & P. Furmanski), pp. 261–284. New York: Marcel-Dekker Inc.

SAWYER, R. H. (1983). The role of epithelial–mesenchymal interactions in regulating gene expression during avian scale morphogenesis. In *Epithelial–Mesenchymal Interactions in Development* (ed. R. H. Sawyer & J. F. Fallon), pp. 115–146. New York: Praeger.

SAWYER, R. H., O'GUIN, W. M. & KNAPP, L. W. (1984). Avian scale development. X. Dermal induction of tissue specific keratins in extraembryonic ectoderm. *Devl Biol.* **101**, 8–18.

SAXEN, L. & KARKINEN-JAASKELAINEN, M. (1981). Biology and pathology of embryonic induction. In *Morphogenesis and Pattern Formation* (ed. L. L. Brinkley, B. Carlson & T. Connelly), pp. 21–48. New York: Raven Press.

SCHEJTER, E. D., SEGAL, D., GLAZER, L. & SHILO, B. Z. (1986). Alternative 5'Exons and tissue specific expression of the *Drosophilia* EGF receptor homolog transcripts. *Cell* **46**, 1091–1101.

SCHOR, S. L. & SCHOR, A. M. (1987). Clonal heterogeneity in fibroblast phenotype: implications for the control of epithelial-mesenchymal interactions. *Bioessays* **7**, 200–204.

SCHOR, S. L., SCHOR, A. M., HOWELL, A. & CROWTHER, D. (1987). Hypothesis: persistent expression of fetal phenotypic characteristics by fibroblasts is associated with an increased susceptibility to neoplastic disease. *Expl Cell Biol.* **55**, 11–17.

SCHWEIZER, J., WINTER, H., HILL, M. & MACKENZIE, I. (1984). The keratin polypeptide patterns in heterotypically recombined epithelia of skin and mucosa of adult mouse. *Differentiation* **26**, 144–153.

SHAH, R. M. (1979). Current concepts on the mechanism of normal and abnormal secondary palate formation. In *Advances in the Study of Birth Defects*, vol. 1, *Teratogenic Mechanisms* (ed. T. V. N. Persaud). Lancaster: M.T.P. Press Ltd.

SHARPE, P. M., FOREMAN, D., CARETTE, M. J. M., SCHOR, S. L. & FERGUSON, M. W. J. (1989). Transforming growth factor beta affects proliferation and extracellular matrix production by mouse embryonic palatal mesenchyme cells *in vitro*. *Development* (in press).

SLACK, J. M. W., DARLINGTON, B. G., HEATH, J. K. & GODSAVE, S. F. (1987). Mesoderm induction in early *Xenopus* embryos by heparin binding growth factors. *Nature, Lond.* **326**, 197–200.

SMITH, J. C. (1987). A mesoderm-inducing factor is produced by a *Xenopus* cell line. *Development* **99**, 3–14.

SMITH, J. C., SINGH, J. P., LILLQUIST, J. S., GOON, D. S. & STILES, C. D. (1982). Growth factors adherent to cell substrate are mitogenically active *in situ*. *Nature, Lond.* **296**, 154–156.

SPORN, M. B., ROBERTS, A. B., WAKEFIELD, L. M. & DE CROMBRUGGHE, B. (1987). Some recent advances in the chemistry and biology of transforming growth factor beta. *J. Cell Biol.* **105**, 1039–1045.

STERN, K. S. (1979). Epidermal hyperplasia induced in guinea pig flank skin by interdermal injection of sudan red. *Dermatologica* **159**, 307–315.

SUGRUE, S. P. & HAY, E. D. (1981). Response of basal epithelial cell surface and cytoskeleton to solubilized extracellular matrix molecules. *J. Cell Biol.* **91**, 45–54.

SUGRUE, S. P. & HAY, E. D. (1986). The identification of extracellular matrix (ECM) binding sites on the basal surface of embryonic corneal epithelium and the effect of ECM binding on epithelial collagen production. *J. Cell Biol.* **102**, 1907–1915.

THESLEFF, I., BARRACH, H. J., FOIDART, J. M., VAHERI, A., PRATT, R. M. & MARTIN, G. R. (1981). Changes in the distribution of type IV collagen, laminin, proteoglycan and fibronectin during mouse tooth development. *Devl Biol.* **81**, 182–192.

THESLEFF, I., MACKIE, E., VAINIO, S. & CHIQUET-EHRISMANN, R. (1987). Changes in the distribution of tenascin during tooth development. *Development* **101**, 289–296.

THESLEFF, J. & HURMERINTA, K. (1981). Tissue interactions in tooth development. *Differentiation* **18**, 75–88.

THOROGOOD, P., BEE, J. & VAN DER MARK, K. (1986). Transient expression of collagen type II at epithelio-mesenchymal interfaces during morphogenesis of the cartilagenous neurocranium. *Devl Biol.* **116**, 497–509.

TRELSTAD, R. L., HAYSHI, A., HAYASHI, K. & DONAHOE, P. K. (1982). The epithelial mesenchymal interface of the male rat Mullerian duct: loss of basement membrane integrity and ductal regression. *Devl Biol.* **92**, 27–40.

TYLER, M. S. & PRATT, R. M. (1980). Effect of epidermal growth factor on secondary palatal epithelium *in vitro*: tissue isolation and recombination studies. *J. Embryol. exp. Morph.* **58**, 93–106.

VAN DER WATER, T. R. & GALINOVIC-SCHWARTZ, V. (1987). Collagen type II in the otic extracellular matrix. *Hearing Res.* **30**, 39–48.

WEEKS, D. L. & MELTON, D. A. (1987). A maternal mRNA localized to the vegetal hemisphere in *Xenopus* eggs codes for a growth factor related to TGF-B. *Cell* **51**, 861–867.

WILKINSON, D. G., PETERS, G., DICKSON, C., MCMAHON, A. P. (1988). Expression of the FGF-related proto-oncogene int-2 during gastrulation and neurulation in the mouse. *EMBO J.* **7**, 691–695.

YONEDA, T. & PRATT, R. M. (1981a). Mesenchyme cells from the human embryonic palate are highly responsive to epidermal growth factor. *Science* **213**, 563–565.

YONEDA, T. & PRATT, R. M. (1981b). Interaction between glucocorticoids and EGF *in vitro* in the growth of palatal mesenchyme cells from the human embryo. *Differentiation* **19**, 194–198.

ZIMMERMAN, E. F. (1984). (ed.) *Palate Development: Normal and Abnormal Cellular and Molecular Aspects. Current Topics in Developmental Biology*, vol. 19. New York: Academic Press.

*J. Cell Sci. Suppl. 10, 231–242 (1988)*
*Printed in Great Britain © The Company of Biologists Limited 1988*

# Feedback regulators in normal and tumour tissues

B. I. LORD

*Paterson Institute for Cancer Research, Christie Hospital, Manchester M20 9BX, UK*

## Summary

Regulation of cell behaviour and population size is presumed to be not unlike classical regulation in non-biological systems, i.e. it is controlled by the cybernetic principle of negative feedback whereby the performance of progenitor cells depends inversely on a signal from their product, the size of which is proportional to the mass of the product. This signal may be inhibitory, acting directly on the progenitor cells. Alternatively, it may operate *via* an indirect and integrated inhibitor/stimulator feedback loop in which the one influences the production of the other. Illustrations taken from the various phases of haemopoietic development show the operation of these loops. Haemopoietic stem cells are under the direct influence of both inhibitor and stimulator but it is a feedback signal from the stem cell population that dictates the production of the one rather than the other. A second inhibitor acting at the stem cell level is a low molecular weight tetrapeptide which blocks the entry of cells into DNA synthesis, thus protecting them during a regimen of treatment with an S-phase cytotoxic drug. Proliferation of the maturing cells is also inhibited by feedback products of their fully mature descendants. Here, the effect is one of cell cycle modulation, whereas in the stem cell population the inhibitor and stimulator effect an on/off switch.

Attempts to characterize the molecules involved have been limited. A series of tri- to penta-peptides has been described for haemopoietic or epithelial cell inhibitors. A common feature of several is a pGlu-Glu end though whether this has any significance is not known.

In tumours it has been shown that some ascites are self-limiting and treatment of small tumours with cell-free fluid from a mature growth blocks their further growth. It appears that many tumour cells produce the feedback signals characteristic of their normal counterparts but are themselves less sensitive to it. The same is true of transforming growth factor-$\beta$ which is produced and detected by virtually all cell types. In this case, the factor, inhibiting in most cases, is produced in inactive form and achieves its target specificity by a localized capacity to activate it. Some tumours, while responding to exogenous active TGF-$\beta$ are incapable of activating the latent molecule.

It is concluded that the differential sensitivity of normal and neoplastic tissues to physiological feedback regulators is a potentially exploitable property in cancer therapy.

## Principles of feedback regulation

The cybernetic principle of negative feedback regulation to maintain a system in a steady state is one which has always been exploited by man, intuitively or systematically, to control life's inventions. Science, rather belatedly, is coming to recognize that the same principle can operate physiologically to maintain cell populations. Thus, while the speed of Watt's steam engine needed to be regulated by a govenor which reduced the input of steam in proportion to its speed, so the production of cells in a biological system needs to be limited by a feedback message(s) which depends on the size of the resultant population. Weiss & Kavenau (1957) introduced a theoretical concept of templates acting as catalysts for the

Key words: feedback regulators, normal tissue, tumour tissue, haemopoiesis, stem cells.

promotion of a process and antitemplates, produced by the product, to limit their function. When Bullough (1962) attempted to demonstrate the concept of feedback inhibition (the chalone hypothesis) in a biological system, however, it was not well received, mainly because of the difficulty of providing convincing 'negative' experimentation. Nevertheless, several groups did take the principle seriously and within a few years, inhibitors were described for epidermal and about a dozen more types of cell proliferation (see Forcher & Houck, 1973). In subsequent years, interest waned, probably due to the problems of obtaining pure factors. In 1979, Allen and Smith, reporting on attempts to purify the lymphocyte chalone demonstrated that its estimated molecular weight tended to be less with each successive publication and a graph of molecular weight plotted against the year of estimation would effectively have predicted its total disappearance by about 1982. They were not far wrong. Nevertheless, notably in haemopoietic and epithelial tissues, considerable efforts have been made to elucidate the significance of negative feedback processes in the regulation of cell proliferation, and cell population mass.

Fig. 1a illustrates the simplest form of negative feedback regulation. The product, P, elaborates an inhibitory factor, I, to act directly on the generator, G, and thus limit its output.

It may be noted that the principle of positive feedback, whereby more leads to even more which leads to ... *ad infinitum* is not a tenable concept in a control process. However, stimulatory processes may be involved as seen in Fig. 1b and 1c. In Fig. 1b, the inhibitory factor operates *via* a 'black box' to limit the output of a stimulatory factor. Alternatively it is also possible that the product factor may act as a stimulator of inhibitor production (Fig. 1c).

## Negative feedback regulatory loops in haemopoiesis

### Stem cells

Haemopoietic stem cells are conventionally assayed using the spleen colony technique described by Till & McCulloch (1961) and should strictly be identified by

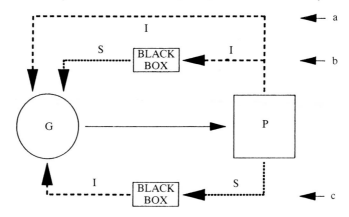

Fig. 1. The principle of negative feedback regulation. P is the product of a generator, G. I and S represent inhibitory and stimulatory processes.

their functional properties as CFU-S (colony forming units in the spleen) or spleen colony forming cells, CFC-S. As a population, *in vivo*, at least some of these cells are self-maintaining and multipotent in their capacity for differentiation. However, there is considerable heterogeneity in the population and it now seems clear that some, having a higher individual self-renewal capacity, are developmentally younger than others (Schofield, 1978; Schofield *et al.* 1980; Magli *et al.* 1982). There is now some question as to whether the most primitive stem cell can itself develop as a spleen colony or whether it exists as a pre-CFU-S (Hodgson & Bradley, 1979). Nevertheless, work on stem cell regulation has been conducted on this CFC-S population and two proliferation inhibitors, specific for it, have been described (Lord *et al.* 1976; Frindel & Guigon, 1977).

The first of these inhibitors is prepared by washing fresh, normal bone marrow (in which the majority of the CFC-S population is proliferatively quiescent) and obtaining a conditioned medium which contains the inhibitory activity. The background to this approach was laid by observations on mice that had been heavily irradiated but with one hind limb shielded (Gidali & Lajtha, 1972). In these experiments, it was found that the proliferative behaviour of CFC-S in the shielded and unshielded limbs is independent, leading to the conclusion that control is exercised locally. Rencricca *et al.* (1970) obtained a similar imbalance when following recovery from phenylhydrazine-induced anaemia. In their experiments, CFC-S migrated to the spleen and remained predominantly non-proliferating while increasing in number approximately fivefold. By contrast, a reduced number of CFC-S in the marrow was induced to proliferate rapidly. Again, localized CFC-S proliferation control was indicated.

The conditioned medium obtained from normal marrow, used either directly or as an Amicon Diaflo, semipurified and freeze-dried fraction (Lord *et al.* 1976; Wright & Lord, 1977), is found to block the entry of CFC-S into the DNA-synthesis phase of their proliferative cycle. Furthermore, this inhibition is confined specifically to the CFC-S population. It has no effect on the mixed *in vitro* colony-forming cells (multipotential cells considered to occupy the mature end of the CFC-S age spectrum) or on the committed progenitors of granulocytes, macrophages or erythroid cells (Lord *et al.* 1976; Tejero *et al.* 1984).

This inhibitor is not detected in marrow containing rapidly proliferating CFC-S but, by contrast, a stimulator is present (Lord *et al.* 1977a). Prepared and assayed in a similar way to the inhibitor, this stimulatory activity is capable of triggering cells from the $G_0$-phase directly into DNA synthesis and it, too, is specific for CFC-S (Tejero *et al.* 1984). A search for the cells which produce these inhibitory and stimulatory activities, using sorting techniques which included density separation, plastic adherence and fluorescence activated cell sorting, showed that two distinct subpopulations of macrophages are responsible, the one for inhibitor and the other for stimulator (Wright *et al.* 1980, 1982; Simmons & Lord, 1985). Furthermore, although only either one of these activities can be detected in any source of haemopoietic tissue and irrespective of the proliferative status of CFC-S in that tissue, both types of producer cell are always present (Wright & Lord, 1979).

Although only inhibitor or stimulator is produced at any one time, it was shown that each type of macrophage, on separation from the other, is capable of producing its specific factor (Wright & Lord, 1979). In addition, although the two factors are not mutually destructive, the presence of one blocks the synthesis of the other (Lord & Wright, 1982). A final feature of this interaction between inhibitor and stimulator is that while their effects are reversible, the proliferation reversion is not automatic on removal of the activity. The presence of the opposing factor is required to effect this proliferation switch (Lord et al. 1977a). In other words, the movement of CFC-S between a non-proliferative $G_0$-state and cell cycle requires an On/Off switching mechanism, two separate operations which appear to be provided by the inhibitor and stimulator. Fig. 2 thus summarizes these observations. The CFC-S population generates a range of haemopoietic cell lineages, including the macrophage subpopulations which produce inhibitor and stimulator. The inhibitor arm is identical to the mechanism illustrated in Fig. 1a. By contrast, since the stimulator on its own cannot act as a control mechanism, this arm must be considered a variation on that shown in Fig. 1b and require a feedback regulator to limit its production. Furthermore, since the production of stimulator is limited to a subpopulation of macrophages which is only one of many lines of CFC-S progeny, it is unlikely that this feedback can come from anywhere other than the mass of the CFC-S population itself. Thus, the macrophages become the black box in Fig. 1b and the inhibitor, in this process, becomes a feedback factor from the CFC-S population (Fig. 3).

By separating out a pure population of CFC-S (Lord & Spooncer, 1986) and treating a stimulator-producing bone marrow with the CFC-S or an extract from them, it was possible to demonstrate the existence of this feedback signal (Lord,

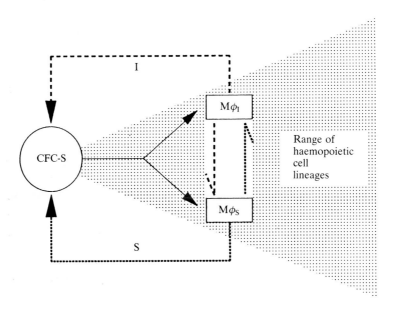

Fig. 2. Inhibitory (I) and Stimulatory (S) factors, generated by two macrophage (M$\phi$) subpopulations, influencing the proliferation of spleen colony forming cells (CFC-S).

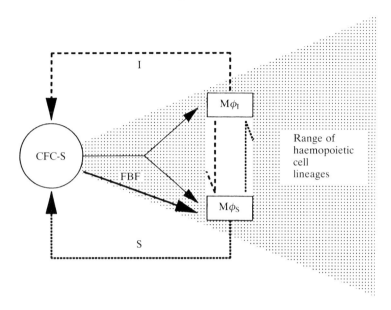

Fig. 3. The spleen colony forming cell (CFC-S) feedback factor (FBF) which determines the relative production of inhibitory (I) and stimulatory (S) factors (see Fig. 2).

1986). Furthermore, by separating the inhibitor-producing macrophages from the bulk population, it was shown that the effect of this feedback signal was directly to block stimulator production, rather than to induce inhibitor production.

The second inhibitor of CFC-S proliferation (Frindel & Guigon, 1977) was obtained as a dialysate from frozen bovine calf marrow and subsequently from frozen bovine foetal liver. This activity has been tested largely *in vivo* and was shown to block the recruitment of CFC-S from $G_0$ into cell cycle, a change which is normally induced by injection(s) of cytosine arabinoside (Guigon & Frindel, 1978; Guigon *et al*. 1980). It was originally considered to be specific for the CFC-S in the same way as the other inhibitor but recently, in its more purified form, some of this specificity appears to have been lost (Guigon, 1987), neonatal hepatocyte proliferation being inhibited, for example (Lombard *et al*. 1987). This group also reported stimulatory activity in damaged marrow (Frindel *et al*. 1976) but has not directly investigated any mechanism of action and interaction between the two activities. Nevertheless, they have, most importantly, demonstrated that the protection afforded by preventing CFC-S recruitment into cell cycle increases the survival from normally lethal single and multiple doses of S-phase cytotoxic agents (Guigon *et al*. 1982; Wdzieczak-Bakala *et al*. 1983).

*Committed and maturing cells*

While strictly outside the boundaries of stem cell regulation, feedback processes undoubtedly exist also in the more mature, single lineage compartments of haemopoietic tissue and, as will be shown below, may have some bearing on the processes involved at the stem cell level. In 1968, Rytömaa & Kiviniemi (1968a) reported an inhibitor of myelocyte proliferation present in medium conditioned by mature granulocytes. By a totally independent method, that of cell cycle-associated changes in fluorescence polarization (Cercek *et al.* 1973), it was shown that such conditioned media were able to induce changes specifically in the proliferating myelocytic cells (Lord *et al.* 1974*a*). Subsequently it was shown to reduce both the tritiated thymidine ([$^3$H]dThd) autoradiographic labelling index of myelocytes when injected into mice (Lord, 1975) but had little or no effect on their committed progenitors (Lord *et al.* 1977). Unlike the On/Off mechanism operating for CFC-S, a mechanism perhaps reserved for cells which under normal steady-state conditions reside in an out-of-cycle $G_0$-state, this inhibitor was reversible simply by washing it out (Lord *et al.* 1974*b*). From repeated [$^3$H]dThd-labelling experiments it was shown that the inhibitor merely reduced (not blocked) the rate of flow of cells into DNA-synthesis, thus limiting output by lengthening the $G_1$-phase of the cell cycle (Lord, 1975).

Maurer *et al.* (1978) found that similar preparations did in fact prevent colony formation *in vitro* by the granulocyte/macrophage committed progenitors (GM-CFC) and following its purification (Paukovits & Laerum, 1982) there is now some evidence that it may have an inhibitory effect on CFC-S similar to that described by Guigon (1987). It appears therefore, that this activity may affect a wider spectrum of cell stages, perhaps in a dose-dependent manner similar to that of some of the growth factors.

As will be discussed below, this material is a pentapeptide but it is only in its monomeric form that it is inhibitory to GM-CFC. The oxidation product of it, however, is a dimer and has been found to be stimulatory. Laerum & Paukovits (1987) speculated that the producer cells, the granulocytes, through their strong oxidizing and reducing capacity (Weiss *et al.* 1983; Watanabe & Bannai, 1987) can maintain an unstable equilibrium between the monomer and dimer, which may bring about a rapid and efficient modulation of granulopoiesis.

In parallel with this inhibitor(s) of granulopoiesis, two erythroid factors have been described. Kivilaakso & Rytömaa (1971) reported one obtained from mature erythrocytes and its activity was confirmed by the fluorescence polarization technique (Lord *et al.* 1974*a*) and autoradiography (Lord *et al.* 1977*b*). Its reversibility and mechanism of action appeared to be very comparable with that for the granulocyte extract. A second inhibitor, described by Axelrad and his colleagues (1987) was obtained from normal bone marrow. It appears to act very rapidly to block the erythroid committed burst-forming unit, BFU-E, in the S-phase of cycle. The blockage, however, is reversible, equally rapidly, on removing the factor.

The best recognized regulator of erythropoiesis, however, is erythropoietin, EPO. Although EPO promotes rapid proliferation of maturing normoblasts, its primary function appears to be the induction of haemoglobin synthesis so that cells can proceed to maturity. Nevertheless, as a stimulating regulatory molecule, its concentration, varying with the demand for erythropoiesis, is dependent on negative feed back. Although indirect in its action, EPO is produced by the kidney in inverse proportion to the oxygen tension developed there by the red cell mass.

Lactoferrin and acidic isoferritins have been implicated as further feedback regulators of GM-CFC growth and development (Broxmeyer *et al.* 1978, 1982). Elaborated by the mature granulocyte macrophage populations, they are reported to block the production of the appropriate colony-stimulating factors for GM-CFC development. Although they appear to be active at very low concentrations ($10^{-15}$ M or less) their role is somewhat controversial because of the relatively high concentrations normally found *in vivo* (Rich & Sawatzki, 1987).

## Characterization of feedback regulators

The chemical characterization of inhibitory molecules is very patchy and is limited to those shown in Table 1. Paukovits and his colleagues (1987) have isolated and characterized a pentapeptide as the so-called granulocyte chalone. Its structure differs in only one group from another pentapeptide inhibitor, that of epidermal keratinocyte proliferation (Elgjo *et al.* 1986), and also bears a striking similarity to a tripeptide with cell cycle inhibitory effects in the colon (Skraastad *et al.* 1987). Whether the PyroGglu component occurring at the end of each of these peptides has any common mechanistic significance is unknown.

The inhibitor of CFC-S described by Guigon & Frindel has recently been defined as a tetrapeptide (Lenfant *et al.* 1987) but has no structural similarity with the pentapeptide structure. This is perhaps surprising since Guigon, working also with the pentapeptide material, has suggested that it has similar properties to their own tetrapeptide (Guigon, 1987).

To date, there is no information on the proteinaceous inhibitors of CFC-S and BFU-E. Both have reported molecular weights in the range of 50K to 100K daltons (79000 for the BFU-E inhibitor) (Axelrad *et al.* 1987) and both are inactivated by trypsin. Currently they are both considered as glycoproteins but clearly they are still components of a fairly generalized 'soup'.

## Feedback inhibitors in tumours

The fact that tumour cell populations grow without apparent regard for the normal feedback processes raises the question whether tumour development is the result of

Table 1. *Peptide inhibitors of cell proliferation*

| Peptide structure | Target cells | Author |
|---|---|---|
| PyroGlu-Glu-Asp-Cys-Lys | Myelocytic?<br>GM-CFC<br>CFC-S | Paukovits *et al.* (1987) |
| PyroGlu-Glu-Asp-Ser-Gly | Keratinocytes | Elgjo *et al.* (1986) |
| PyroGlu-His-Gly | Colonic epithelial cells | Skraastad *et al.* (1987) |
| Lys-Pro-Asp-Ser | CFC-S<br>Neonatal hepatic cells | Lenfant *et al.* (1987)<br>Lombard *et al.* (1987) |

their failure to recognize the feedback signals and, if so, can this failure be exploited to improve therapy for the condition? There is evidence that some ascites tumours, at least, can be self-limiting in their growth. For example, Bichel (1972) showed that the hypotetraploid ascites tumours (JB-1 and Erlich) each grow to a maximum size of $10^9$ cells. The growth of each was quite independent because, grown together in one mouse, they reached a total of $2 \times 10^9$ cells. However, each could be limited independently by its own cell-free ascitic fluid (see Fig. 4). Treatment of a mouse bearing one of the tumours with cell-free fluid from the other tumour did not affect the flow of cells through mitosis. By contrast, cell-free fluid from a tumour of the same type did block entry to mitosis (see Bichel, 1972). Thus, a highly specific tumour product appears to be acting as a feedback regulator for that tumour.

It seems probable, however, that the sensitivity of a tumour cell to the inhibitory factor is lower than that of its normal counterpart. Rytömaa & Kiviniemi (1968*b*) found that Shay myelocytic chloroleukaemia cells generate large quantities of the granulocyte feedback inhibitor, release it very rapidly but are themselves considerably less sensitive to its effects. Nevertheless, regression of this tumour was obtained by large-dose treatments with granulocyte chalone (Rytömaa & Kiviniemi, 1969).

In a similar way, interleukin-3 (IL-3)-dependent, haemopoietic stem cell lines are inhibited, in a dose-related manner, by the bone-marrow extract described by Lord *et al.* (1976). A spontaneous leukaemic, IL-3-independent derivative of one of these lines, however, was highly resistant and continued to undergo rapid proliferation (Lord *et al.* 1987). In addition, Friend virus-induced polycythaemia was unresponsive to the negative regulatory protein for BFU-E (Axelrad *et al.* 1987).

Normal and neoplastic epithelial cells, too, appear to have a differential response to the epidermal inhibitory pentapeptide. Used in a dose range of $10^{-10}$ to $10^{-4}$ M, the autoradiographic labelling index of mouse tongue keratinocytes was reduced by an average of 28 %. That for a squamous carcinoma cell line (SCC-9) was reduced by only 3 % (Professor W. J. Hume, personal communication).

Guigon & Frindel (1981) studied the effects of the haemopoietic tetrapeptide

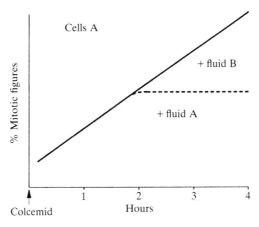

Fig. 4. Mitotic activity of ascites cells (type A) treated with cell-free ascitic fluid from type A or type B tumours. Adapted from Bichel (1972).

inhibitor in mice bearing EMT6 mammary-derived tumours. The inhibitor had no effect on the tumour response to treatment with cytosine arabinoside and the number of survivors was somewhat increased (Guigon & Frindel, 1981; Guigon *et al.* 1986; Guigon, 1987).

## Transforming growth factor-β (TGF-β)

Owing to its ubiquitous appearance in many tissues, TGF-β has become a much investigated molecule (see review by Sporn *et al.* 1987). It is a polypeptide of 25 000 molecular weight and virtually all cell types both produce and bear receptors for it. In addition, its effects may be either stimulating or inhibitory, depending upon the cell type it encounters. Although its mechanisms of action are still somewhat speculative, TGF-β is being given serious consideration as a widely operative and physiologically regulatory molecule.

Virtually all cells produce TGF-β in an *inactive* or latent form and it has been suggested that target specificity – one of the most important considerations for cell population control – may be critically determined by the ability of a cell to activate the latent complex. For example, unregulated epithelial growth may be the result of failure to activate the latent form of its autocrine feedback TGF-β. Thus a human A549 lung carcinoma cell, which has abundant TGF-β receptors and secretes large amounts of *inactive* TGF-β, continues to proliferate unless exogenous *active* TGF-β is made available. In contrast with the normal parent cell type, which is inhibited by the TGF-β that it generates, it appears that the tumour cell has lost its ability to activate the latent molecule.

Osteoblasts, on the other hand, are stimulated by TGF-β and it has been found that osteosarcoma cells respond similarly to exogenous material (Pfeilschifter *et al.* 1987). It appears that bone remodelling is under autocrine feedback control, its highly acidic microenvironment providing a mechanism for activation of the latent TGF-β produced and secreted by the osteoblasts (Sporn *et al.* 1987).

## Conclusion

The differential sensitivity of normal and neoplastic tissues to normal physiological feedback regulators is potentially an exploitable property in cancer therapy. Not only should it be possible to protect the bone marrow while treating distant tumours as in the experiments with EMT6 tumours but also, particularly with bone marrow, the relative insensitivity of tumour tissue compared to its normal counterpart, suggests that this same protection could be utilized when treating malignancies of the same origin. A greater understanding of the mechanisms of TGF-β action and activation would appear to be necessary before its widespread effects can be harnessed to modify the performance of specific cell types.

This work was supported by a grant from the Cancer Research Campaign.

## References

ALLEN, J. C. & SMITH, C. J. (1979). Chalones: A reappraisal. *Biochem. Soc. Trans.* **7**, 584–592.

AXELRAD, A. A., CROIZAT, H., DEL RIZZO, D., ESKINAZI, D., PEZZUTI, G., STEWART, S. & VAN DER GAAG, H. (1987). Properties of a protein NRP that negatively regulates DNA synthesis of the early erythropoietic progenitor cells BFU-E. In *The Inhibitors of Hematopoiesis*, vol. 162 (ed. A. Najman, M. Guigon *et al.*), pp. 79–92, London, Paris: Colloque INSERM/John Libby Eurotext Ltd.

BICHEL, P. (1972). Specific growth regulation in three ascitic tumours. *Eur. J. Cancer* **8**, 167–173.

BROXMEYER, H. E., BOGNACKI, J., RALPH, P., DORNER, M. H., LU, L. & CASTRO-MALASPINA, H. (1982). Monocyte–macrophage derived acidic isoferritins: normal feedback regulators of granulocyte–macrophage progenitor cells. *Blood* **60**, 595–607.

BROXMEYER, H. E., SMITHYMAN, A., EGER, R. R., MEYERS, P. A. & DE SONSA, M. (1978). Identification of lactoferrin as the granulocyte-derived inhibitor of colony-stimulating activity (CSA) production. *J. exp. Med.* **148**, 1052–1067.

BULLOUGH, W. S. (1962). The control of mitotic activity in adult mammalian tissues. *Biol. Rev.* **37**, 307–342.

CERCEK, L., CERCEK, B. & OCKEY, C. H. (1973). Structuredness of the cytoplasmic matrix and Michaelis–Menten constants for the hydrolysis of FDA during the cell cycle in Chinese hamster ovary cells. *Biophysik* **10**, 187–194.

ELGJO, K., REICHELT, K. L., HENNINGS, H., MICHAEL, D. & YUPSA, S. H. (1986). Purified epidermal pentapeptide inhibits proliferation and enhances terminal differentiation in cultured mouse epidermal cells. *J. invest. Derm.* **87**, 555–558.

FORCHER, B. K. & HOUCK, J. C. (eds) (1973). Chalones; concepts and current researches. *Natn. Canc. Inst. Monogr.* **38**, pp. 233.

FRINDEL, E., CROIZAT, H. & VASSORT, F. (1976). Stimulating factors liberated by treated bone marrow: *in vitro* effect on CFU kinetics. *Expl Hemat.* **4**, 56–61.

FRINDEL, E. & GUIGON, M. (1977). Inhibition of CFU entry into cycle by a bone marrow extract. *Expl Hemat.* **5**, 74–76.

GIDALI, J. G. & LAJTHA, L. G. (1972). Regulation of haemopoietic stem cell turnover in partially irradiated mice. *Cell Tiss Kinet.* **5**, 147–157.

GUIGON, M. (1987). Biological properties of low molecular weight pluripotent stem cell (CFU-S) inhibitors. In *The Inhibitors of Hematopoiesis*, vol. 162 (ed. A. Najman, M. Guigon *et al.*), pp. 241–251. London, Paris: Colloque INSERM/John Libby Eurotext Ltd.

GUIGON, M., ENOUF, J. & FRINDEL, E. (1980). Effects of CFU-S inhibitors on murine bone marrow during ARA-C treatment. *Leuk. Res.* **4**, 385–391.

GUIGON, M. & FRINDEL, E. (1978). Inhibition of CFU-S entry into cycle after irradiation and drug treatment. *Biomedicine* **29**, 176–178.

GUIGON, M. & FRINDEL, E. (1981). Inhibitors de la prolifération des cellules souches hématopoïétiques. Perspectives d'utilisation ou chimiotherapie. *Bull. Cancer* **68**, 150–153.

GUIGON, M., MARY, J. Y., ENOUF, J. & FRINDEL, E. (1982). Protection of mice against lethal doses of 1-β-D-arabinofuranosyl-cytosine by pluripotent stem cell inhibition. *Cancer Res.* **42**, 638–642.

GUIGON, M., WDZIECZAK-BAKALA, J., IZUMI, H., LENFANT, M. & FRINDEL, E. (1986). Protection de la souris normale ou portense de tumeur par un inhibiteur des CFU-S au cours d'un protocole letal de chimiotherapie (ARA-C). *Bull. Cancer* **7**, 408–415.

HODGSON, G. S. & BRADLEY, T. R. (1979). Properties of haematopoietic stem cells surviving 5-fluorouracil treatment: Evidence for a pre-CFU-S cell. *Nature, Lond.* **281**, 381–2.

KIVILAAKSO, E. & RYTÖMAA, T. (1971). Erythrocyte chalone, a tissue specific inhibitor of cell proliferation in the erythron. *Cell Tiss. Kinet.* **4**, 1–9.

LAERUM, O. D. & PAUKOVITS, W. R. (1987). Biological effects of myelopoiesis inhibitors. In *The Inhibitors of Hematopoiesis*, vol. 162 (ed. A. Najman, M. Guigon *et al.*), pp. 21–30. London, Paris: Colloque INSERM/John Libby Eurotext Ltd.

LENFANT, M., WDZIECZAK-BAKALA, J., GINGON, M., SOTTY, D., GUITTET, E., PROME, J. C. & FRINDEL, E. (1987). Purification and structure determination of a hematopoietic pluripotent stem cell proliferation inhibitor. *Expl Hemat.* **15**, p.508.

LOMBARD, M-N., WDZIECZAK-BAKALA, J., SOTTY, D., LENFANT, M., NADAL, C. & GUIGON, M. (1987). Effect on hepatocyte $G_1$-S transition of an inhibitor of CFU-S entry into DNA synthesis.

In *The Inhibitors of Hematopoiesis*, vol. 162 (ed. A. Najman, M. Guigon *et al.*), pp. 271–275. London, Paris: Colloque INSERM/John Libby Eurotext Ltd.

LORD, B. I. (1975). Modification of granulocytopoietic cell proliferation by granulocyte extracts. *Bull. d'Ist. Sieroter. Milanese Arch. Microbiol. Immunol.* **54**, 187–194.

LORD, B. I. (1986). Interactions of regulatory factors in the control of haemopoietic stem cell proliferation. In *Biological Regulation of Cell Proliferation*, Serono Symposium Publications, vol. 34 (ed. R. Baserya, P. Foa, D. Metcalf & E. E. Polli), pp. 167–171. New York: Raven Press.

LORD, B. I., CERCEK, L., CERCEK, B., SHAH, G. P., DEXTER, T. M. & LAJTHA, L. G. (1974a). Inhibitors of haemopoietic cell proliferation?: Specificity of action within the haemopoietic system. *Br. J. Cancer* **29**, 168–175.

LORD, B. I., CERCEK, L., CERCEK, B., SHAH, G. P. & LAJTHA, L. G. (1974b). Inhibitors of haemopoietic cell proliferation: reversibility of action. *Br. J. Cancer* **29**, 407–409.

LORD, B. I., LIU, FU-LU, POJDA, Z. & SPOONCER, E. (1987). Inhibitor of haemopoietic CFU-S proliferation: assays, production sources and regulatory mechanisms. In *The Inhibitors of Hematopoiesis*, vol. 162 (ed. A. Najman, M. Guigon *et al.*), pp. 227–239. London, Paris: Colloque INSERM/ John Libby Eurotext Ltd.

LORD, B. I., MORI, K. J. & WRIGHT, E. G. (1977a). A stimulator of stem cell proliferation in regenerating bone marrow. *Biomed. Exp.* **27**, 223–226.

LORD, B. I., MORI, K. J., WRIGHT, E. G. & LAJTHA, L. G. (1976). An inhibitor of stem cell proliferation in normal bone marrow. *Brit. J. Haemat.* **34**, 441–445.

LORD, B. I., SHAH, G. P. & LAJTHA, L. G. (1977b). The effects of red blood cell extracts on the proliferation of erythrocyte precursor cells *in vivo*. *Cell Tiss. Kinet.* **10**, 215–222.

LORD, B. I. & SPOONCER, E. (1986). Isolation of haemopoietic spleen colony forming cells. *Lymphokine Res.* **5**, 59–72.

LORD, B. I., TESTA, N. G., WRIGHT, E. G. & BANERJEE, R. K. (1977). Lack of effect of a granulocyte proliferation inhibitor on their committed precursor cells. *Biomedicine* **26**, 163–168.

LORD, B. I. & WRIGHT, E. G. (1982). Interaction of inhibitor and stimulator in the regulation of CFU-S proliferation. *Leuk. Res.* **6**, 541–551.

MAGLI, M. C., ISCOVE, N. N. & ODARTCHENKO, N. (1982). Transient nature of early haematopoietic spleen colonies. *Nature, Lond.* **295**, 527–529.

MAURER, H. R., HENRY, R. & MASCHLER, R. (1978). Chalone inhibition of granulocyte colony growth in agar: Kinetic quantitation by capillary tube scanning. *Cell Tiss. Kinet.* **11**, 129–138.

PAUKOVITS, W. R. & LAERUM, O. D. (1982). Isolation and synthesis of a hemoregulatory peptide. *Z. Naturf.* **37c**, 1297–1300.

PAUKOVITS, W. R., LAERUM, O. D., PAUKOVITS, J. B., GUIGON, M. & SCHANCHE, J.-S. (1987). Regulatory peptides inhibiting granulopoiesis. In *The Inhibitors of Hematopoiesis*, vol. 162 (ed. A. Najman, M. Guigon *et al.*), pp. 31–42. London, Paris: Colloque INSERM/John Libby Eurotext Ltd.

PFEILSCHIFTER, J., D'SOUZA, S. M. & MUNDY, G. R. (1987). Effects of transforming growth factor-$\beta$ on osteoblastic ostersarcoma cells. *Endocrinology* **121**, 212–218.

RENCRICCA, N. J., RIZZOLI, V., HOWARD, D., DUFFY, P. & STOHLMAN, F. JR. (1970). Stem cell migration and proliferation during severe anemia. *Blood* **36**, 764–771.

RICH, I. N. & SAWATZKI, G. (1987). The role of lactoferrin in regulating colony stimulating factor production. In *The Inhibitors of Hematopoiesis*, vol. 162 (ed. A. Najman, M. Guigon *et al.*), pp. 63–66. London, Paris: Colloque INSERM/John Libby Eurotext Ltd.

RYTÖMAA, T. & KIVINIEMI, K. (1968a). Control of granulocyte production. I. Chalone and antichalone, two specific humoral regulators. *Cell Tiss. Kinet.* **1**, 329–340.

RYTÖMAA, T. & KIVINIEMI, K. (1968b). Control of cell production in rat chloroleukaemia by means of the granulocyte chalone. *Nature, Lond.* **200**, 136–137.

RYTÖMAA, T. & KIVINIEMI, K. (1969). Chloroma regression induced by the granulocyte chalone. *Nature, Lond.* **222**, 995–996.

SCHOFIELD, R. (1978). The relationship between the spleen colony forming cells and the haemopoietic stem cell. A hypothesis. *Blood Cells.* **4**, 7–25.

SCHOFIELD, R., LORD, B. I., KYFFIN, S. & GILBERT, C. W. (1980). Self-maintenance capacity of CFU-S. *J. cell. Physiol.* **103**, 355–362.

SIMMONS, P. J. & LORD, B. I. (1985). Enrichment of CFU-S proliferation inhibitor-producing cells based on their identification by the monoclonal antibody F4/80. *J. Cell Sci.* **78**, 117–131.

SKRAASTAD, O., FORSLI, T., REICHELT, K. L. & CROMARTY, A. (1987). Purification of an endogenous inhibitor of cell proliferation in colon. In *XVth Meeting of European Study Group for Cell Proliferation.* Sundvolden, Norway. Abstracts p. 17.

SPORN, M. B., ROBERTS, A. B., WAKEFIELD, L. M. & DE CROMBRUGGHE, B. (1987). Some recent advances in the chemistry and biology of transforming growth factor-beta. *J. Cell Biol.* **105**, 1039–1045.

TEJERO, C., TESTA, N. G. & LORD, B. I. (1984). The cellular specificity of haemopoietic stem cell proliferation regulators. *Br. J. Cancer.* **50**, 335–341.

TILL, J. E. & McCULLOCH, E. A. (1961). A direct measurement of the radiation sensitivity of normal mouse bone marrow cells. *Radiat. Res.* **14**, 213–222.

WATANABE, H. & BANNAI, S. (1987). Induction of the cysteine transport activity in mouse peritoneal macrophages. *J. exp. Med.* **165**, 628–640.

WDZIECZAK-BAKALA, J., GUIGON, M., LENFANT, M. & FRINDEL, E. (1983). Further purification of a CFU-S inhibitor: in vivo effects after cytosine arabinoside treatment. *Biomed. Pharmacother.* **37**, 467–471.

WEISS, P. & KAVANAU, J. L. (1957). A model of growth and control in mathematical terms. *J. gen. Physiol.* **41**, 1–47.

WEISS, S. J., LAMPERT, M. B. & TEST, S. T. (1983). Long-lived oxidants generated by human neutrophils: characterization and bioactivity. *Science* **222**, 625–628.

WRIGHT, E. G., ALI, A. M., RICHES, A. C. & LORD, B. I. (1982). Stimulation of haemopoietic stem cell proliferation: characteristics of the stimulator producing cells. *Leuk. Res.* **6**, 531–539.

WRIGHT, E. G., GARLAND, J. M. & LORD, B. I. (1980). Specific inhibition of haemopoietic stem cell proliferation: characteristics of the inhibitor producing cells. *Leuk. Res.* **4**, 537–545.

WRIGHT, E. G. & LORD, B. I. (1977). Regulation of CFU-S proliferation by locally produced endogenous factors. *Biomed. Exp.* **27**, 215–218.

WRIGHT, E. G. & LORD, B. I. (1979). Production of stem cell proliferation regulators by fractionated haemopoietic cell suspensions. *Leuk. Res.* **3**, 15–22.

*J. Cell Sci. Suppl. 10, 243–255 (1988)*
*Printed in Great Britain © The Company of Biologists Limited 1988*

# Molecular events associated with the action of haemopoietic growth factors

WILLIAM L. FARRAR[1], STUART W. EVANS[1], ANNICK HAREL-BELLAN[1]
AND DOUGLAS K. FERRIS[2]

[1]*Laboratory of Molecular Immunoregulation, Biological Response Modifiers Program, National Cancer Institute, Building 560, Room 21-89A, Frederick, MD 21701-1013, USA*
[2]*Biological Carcinogenesis Development Program, Program Resources, Inc., NCI-Frederick Cancer Research Facility, Frederick, MD 21701-1013, USA*

## Summary

Haemopoietic growth factors stimulate a number of consensus biochemical and molecular events regardless of the specificity detailed by unique ligand and receptor structures. Analysis of three distinct colony stimulating factors, CSFs (IL-3, G-CSF, GM-CSF) and the lymphocytotropic growth factor IL-2 reveal remarkable similar distal subcellular biochemical signals although initial membrane 'signal transduction' may differ significantly. Both early progenitor cell growth factors, such as IL-3, and late acting factors such as CSF-1, stimulate tyrosine and serine-threonine substrate phosphorylations. One substrate (p68) is phosphorylated by many CSF stimulants, including IL-2, suggesting a highly conserved role in many unique receptor(s) signal transduction processes. The proliferative CSFs and IL-2 also stimulate the expression of many of the same genes including proto-oncogenes, ornithine decarboxylase and members of the ancient family of stress response genes. Although initial membrane events may differ among the respective proliferative stimulants, biochemical and molecular convergence on highly conserved cellular substrates and the programme of gene expression is seen.

## Introduction

Proliferation of bone marrow haemopoietic precursors *in vitro* is dependent upon the presence of specific growth factors (reviewed by Dexter, 1984; Nicola & Vadas, 1984). Several myeloid colony stimulating factors (CSF) have now been demonstrated to possess unique primary amino acid sequences and distinct biological activities. In primary bone marrow cultures, G-CSF induces granulocyte colonies (Nicola *et al.* 1983); GM-CSF (Sparrow *et al.* 1985) induces mixed colonies of granulocytes and monocytes, whereas IL-3 (or multi CSF) (Ihle *et al.* 1982) stimulates the proliferation of a pluripotent stem cell population. Growth factor-dependent mouse myeloid cell lines, recently developed, provide valuable resources for studying the intracellular effects of the interaction between myeloid cells and CSFs.

Signal transduction is the biochemical process by which ligand–receptor interactions simplify and amplify a series of chemical signals, which activate a myriad of enzymatic activities that regulate cell metabolism and macromolecular synthesis. A limited repertoire of signals generated at the membrane has been observed with a wide variety of hormones, neurotransmitters, or 'informational substances.' The

Key words: haemopoiesis, growth factors, colony stimulating factors.

number of second messengers is surprisingly small and remarkably universal. Two major signal pathways are now known. One employs cyclic adenosine monophosphate (cyclic AMP) and the other calcium ions and the phosphoinositide species, inositol triphosphate (IP3) and diacylglycerol. The paths have many common features. Both utilize specific protein recognition sites (receptors), which bind, with high affinity ($K_d = 10^{-9}-10^{-12}$ M), informational substances which may have peptic or organic structures. In order for the signal to be initiated the informational substance (ligand) must bind the receptor outside the plasma membrane with sufficient affinity to engage the interaction of a GTP-binding protein with the receptor within the transmembrane structure.

The GTP-binding protein (G protein) is activated by binding guanosine triphosphate (GTP) and then 'tranduces' the external information to an amplifying system, adenylate cyclase (AC), for cyclic AMP coupled transduction and phospholipase C (PL-C) for phosphoinositol coupled systems. The amplifier enzymes convert precursor molecules, usually with energy-rich phosphate groups, into second messengers. In the case of adenylate cyclase, ATP is converted into cyclic AMP, whereas PL-C hydrolyses phosphatidylinositol 4, 5-bisphosphate ($PIP_2$) into IP3 and diacylglycerol (DG). IP3 stimulates the release of intracellular stores of $Ca^{2+}$, effecting the activation of $Ca^{2+}$-dependent kinases such as $Ca^{2+}$-calmodulin-dependent protein kinase. Diacylglycerol stimulates the activation of a phospholipid-dependent protein kinase, protein kinase C (PK-C). The result of the activation of these kinase systems is to regulate the function of specific substrate proteins. Both pathways can be mimicked by pharmacological analogues. Stable derivatives of cyclic AMP, can readily penetrate the cell and activate PK-A. Release of intracellular $Ca^{2+}$ and $Ca^{2+}$ influx can be irreversibly achieved by the addition of $Ca^{2+}$ ionophores (ionomycin, A23187) to cell cultures. Likewise, a potent class of tumour promoters, phorbol esters, can penetrate the cell membrane and activate PK-C. These pharmacological stimulants have proven useful in cause–effect experimentation to elucidate the roles of the discrete second messengers in cellular functions and gene expression.

The mechanism(s) by which the external signal reaches the nucleus and results in specific gene transcription is unknown, but largely believed to involve protein phosphorylation. Although nuclear phosphoproteins for CSF or cytokine growth signals have not been investigated, we will discuss the available information regarding haemopoietic growth factor regulation of protein phosphorylation.

Mitogen stimulation of fibroblasts, lymphocytes and CSF-directed proliferation all result in the synthesis of consensus genes common to all cycling cells. Notable are the proto-oncogenes, ornithine decarboxylase (ODC) and heat shock proteins (Harel-Bellan & Farrar, 1987; Farrar *et al.* 1988*a*; Ferris *et al.* unpublished; Cleveland *et al.* 1987; Ferris *et al.* 1988). Many of these gene products can also be stimulated or repressed by pharmacological activitors of PK-C or PK-A. Conversely, anti-proliferative signals such as cyclic AMP or interferons can be shown to repress growth response genes such as c-*myc* or ODC (Farrar *et al.* 1988*b*; Harel-Bellan & Farrar, 1988; Farrar *et al.* 1987).

Here, we will present data summarizing some of the conserved biochemical events which are apparently involved in CSF mediated cellular proliferation and how these molecular targets may also be affected by anti-proliferative signals.

## Results and discussion

### *CSF regulation of protein phosphorylation*

While the importance of protein phosphorylation in regulating cellular metabolism has been well established, its precise role in growth factor-induced signal transduction is unclear.

Using two-dimensional gel electrophoresis, we have examined the proteins phosphorylated in several CSF-dependent murine lymphoid and myeloid cell lines following stimulation with the appropriate growth factor or a direct activator of PK-C, a synthetic analogue of diacyglycerol (OAG). We found that stimulation with OAG induced rapid phosphorylation of a $68 \times 10^3 \, M_r$ protein (p68) in each of the four cell lines tested and the same protein was also phosphorylated in response to growth factors (Evans *et al.* 1987). There was, however, an intriguing exception to the general finding that p68 phosphorylation was induced in all cells responding to an appropriate growth factor. One of the cell lines (NSF 60.8) can proliferate in response to either GM-CSF or G-CSF but p68 phosphorylation was induced only by G-CSF. This finding suggests the existence of an alternative pathway, involving protein phosphorylation, that leads to cell growth. Phosphorylation of p68 in two CSF-dependent clones is shown in Fig. 1. The NSF-60 cell line grows in response to G-CSF and IL-3 (multi-CSF). p68 was phosphorylated by both growth factors but not by GM-CSF or IL-2, which do not stimulate growth. The NSF 60.8 cell line responds to all three CSFs for proliferation and phosphorylation of p68. While p68 is the predominant protein phosphorylated in these cells in response to phorbol esters its biochemical function is still unknown. In addition to p68 a protein of $M_r \, 30 \times 10^3$ was also phosphorylated in response to IL-2 or OAG in IL-2-dependent T cells, while phosphorylation of p60 and p80 was stimulated only by IL-2 (Evans & Farrar, 1987).

More recently Ishii and coworkers (1988) have described the IL-2-dependent phosphorylation of proteins of 67 and $63 \times 10^3 \, M_r$ in human T-lymphocytes, that may be the human homologues of the murine proteins, p68 and p60, described above. Due to the different techniques used for the first-dimension separation (pH 3·5–10 non-equilibrating pH grandient gel electrophoresis used by us, *versus* pH 5–8 isoelectric focusing), it is uncertain how similar in charge these proteins are.

Whetton and coworkers (1986) showed activation of the hexose transport protein in the IL-3-dependent cell line, FDC-P1, both *in vitro* and *in situ* in response to TPA or IL-3. More recently they reported that TPA and a calcium ionophore can replace the maintenance requirement for IL-3 in these cells. They suggest that the increased glucose transport, perhaps resulting from phosphorylation of the transport protein in response to TPA/ionophore or IL-3, is important to both the survival and proliferation of FDC-P1 cells. Additionally, IL-3 has been shown to stimulate the

## Phosphorylation of p68 in NSF 60 and NSF 60.8 Myeloid Cell Lines

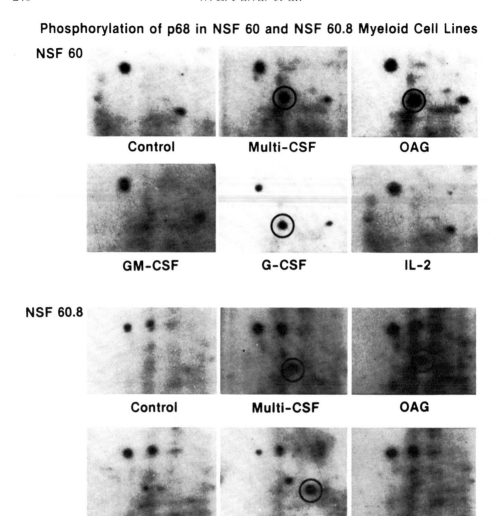

Fig. 1. CSF stimulation of p68 phosphorylation in NFS 60 and NSF-60.8 cell lines. Cells were washed free of conditioned medium and resuspended in phosphate/serum-free RPM I-1640. 300 $\mu$Ci 0-$^{32}$PO$_2$ was added and cells were stimulated with 1000 units/10$^7$ cells of each CSF for 10 min (Evans *et al.* 1987). Multi-CSF $\equiv$ IL-3. Shown in NEPHE$\times$SDS–PAGE of phosphoproteins in the location proximal to p68.

phosphorylation of a $33\times10^3\,M_r$ protein in several murine myeloid cell lines and the p33 was found to be constitutively phosphorylated in autonomous malignant clones (Garland, 1988). The p33 protein is localized in the endoplasmic reticulum and is phosphorylated on serine residues (J. Garland, personal communication).

Since the discovery in 1980 that the transforming gene product of the Rous sarcoma virus was a tyrosine kinase (Collett *et al.* 1980) a variety of viral oncogenes and their cellular counterparts, the proto-oncogenes, have been demonstrated to possess tyrosine kinase activity (Kolata, 1983; Hunter, 1984; Hunter & Cooper,

Table 1. *Intrinsic kinase*

| Receptor | | Size ($M_r \times 10^{-3}$) | Activity |
|---|---|---|---|
| EGF | | 170 | Yes |
| PDGF | | 180 | Yes |
| | $\alpha$ chain | 135 | |
| Insulin | | | Yes |
| | $\beta$ chain | 90 | |
| NGF | | 103 | ? |
| | $\alpha 2$ | | |
| IGF-1 | | | Yes |
| | $\beta 2$ | | |
| Bombesin | | 115 | Probably |
| IL-2 | | 55–58 | No |
| IL-3 | | 55 & 75 | ? |
| G-CSF | | 30 | ? |
| GM-CSF | | 51 | ? |
| M-CSF, CSF-1 | | 165 | Yes |

1985). The members of this family of proto-oncogenes are transmembrane proteins consisting of, at a minimum, an external receptor portion, a transmembrane section, and a cytoplasmic catalytic site. Included within this group are the epidermal growth factor (EGF) receptor, platelet-derived growth factor (PDGF) receptor, the insulin receptor, and the insulin-like growth factor (IGF-1) receptor (Hunter & Cooper, 1985). Other growth factor receptors may also possess tyrosine kinase activity, but it is clear from inspection of Table 1 that all of the currently identified receptors with kinase activity are fairly large proteins. With the exception of CSF-1, the receptor of which contains intrinsic kinase activity homologous to v-*fms* (Sherr *et al.* 1985), no other CSF receptor with tyrosine kinase activity has been formally demonstrated.

Using anti-phosphotyrosine rabbit anti-serum coupled to Sepharose beads we have used affinity-capture to address whether IL-3 can stimulate tyrosine phosphorylation of cellular proteins. We found that IL-3 rapidly stimulates tyrosine kinase activity in the FDC-P1 cell line, causing elevated phosphorylation of several substrates including p213, p141, p118, p81, p39, p37 and p35. Fig. 2 shows the amino acid hydrolysis patterns of phosphoproteins extracted from single-dimension PAGE of immunoaffinity purified cellular extracts.

Seven of the analysed proteins, p213, p141, p118, p81, p38, p37 and p35, contained some phosphotyrosine, but with the exception of p213 all of them also contained significant amounts of phosphoserine. Surprisingly, in no case did the ratio of phosphotyrosine to phosphoserine in a protein change after IL-3 stimulation. The relative contents of phosphotyrosine and phosphoserine for the 11 proteins analysed, are presented in Table 2. Since the ratio of phosphoserine to phosphotyrosine in a given protein did not change following increased phosphorylation, we conclude that IL-3 must induce rapid coactivation of both serine and tyrosine kinases. It is also clear that a variety of protein substrates are utilized in common by both types of phosphotransferase systems.

The presence of phosphoproteins containing only phosphoserine in the affinity

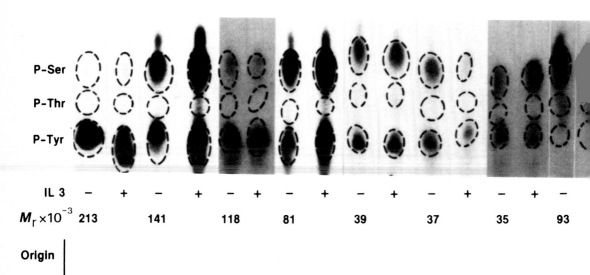

Fig. 2. Phosphoamino acid analyses of selected IL-3-modulated phosphoproteins. The selected proteins were sliced from either unstimulated (−) or 3 min IL-3 stimulated lanes (+). Following diffusion from gel slices the proteins were washed, acid hydrolysed and the phosphoamino acids separated by single-dimension, thin-layer, high voltage electrophoresis and visualized by autoradiography. The positions of unlabelled phosphoamino acid standards, visualized by staining with ninhydrin, are encircled by broken lines. Analyses of the 7 phosphotyrosine containing proteins are shown along with an analysis of pp93 (far right), which contained only phosphoserine, for comparison purposes.

Table 2. *Percentages\* of phosphoserine and phosphotyrosine in eleven IL-3-modulated phosphoproteins*

| Protein | % P-Tyr | % P-Ser |
|---------|---------|---------|
| pp213   | 99      | 1       |
| pp141   | 40      | 60      |
| pp118   | 90      | 10      |
| pp93    | 0       | 100     |
| pp81    | 30      | 70      |
| pp64    | 0       | 100     |
| pp58    | 0       | 100     |
| pp39    | 70      | 30      |
| pp37    | 40      | 60      |
| pp35    | 40      | 60      |
| pp29    | 0       | 100     |

\*Percentages were determined using a 2-dimensional scanning laser densitometer (LKB Ultrascan XL) and 2-dimensional analysis software (LKB 2400 GelScan IX) on a lab computer (AT&T PC6300).

purified extracts (p93, p64, p58 and p29) probably indicates that these proteins are associated with other proteins which do contain phosphotyrosine. Therefore, the apparent increases in phosphorylation of the phosphoserine proteins could also represent an increased association that is regulated by the phosphorylation state of a phosphotyrosine-containing protein.

Recently Koyasu and his coworkers (1987) reported on the IL-3 stimulated tyrosine and serine phosphorylation of a membrane glycoprotein of 150 000 $M_r$ (p150). The ratio of phosphoserine to phosphotyrosine (6:4) reported for p150 is identical to the ratio we found for a protein of similar molecular weight, p141. Interestingly, p150 was only phosphorylated in response to IL-3 although the cells could proliferate in response to IL-3, IL-4 or GM-CSF. Since the size of p150 is incompatible with the suspected size of the IL-3 receptor as determined by cross-linking ($60–75 \times 10^3 M_r$) they propose that p150 may be a tyrosine kinase distinct from, but associated with the IL-3 receptor, or that the IL-3 receptor itself may be a tyrosine kinase that phosphorylates p150 upon IL-3 binding. A third alternative mentioned is that p150 is phosphorylated by a tyrosine kinase that is regulated by the IL-3 receptor. Koyasu *et al.* (1987) conclude that the tyrosine phosphorylation of p150, which peaks at 3 min, is one of the earliest events specifically associated with IL-3 binding. While this conclusion may be correct, it also ignores the fact that there was apparently equally rapid serine phosphorylation of p150, thus leaving open the question of which phosphotransferase system is initially activated. This is not a trivial point because it is possible that these separate kinase systems are themselves regulated by phosphorylation.

Previously we speculated that the stimulated serine/threonine phosphorylation of a $68 \times 10^3 M_r$ protein by IL-3, IL-2, G-CSF or direct pharmacological activators of protein kinase C indicated that p68 represented a point of convergence for various growth factor signalling pathways and that activation of serine/threonine phosphorylation was an essential element in IL-2, IL-3 and G-CSF-mediated signal transduction. It is now clear that in addition to inducing serine/threonine phosphorylation, IL-3 also stimulates rapid phosphorylation of tyrosine in multiple proteins most of which are also phosphorylated on serine. Thus, it appears that coactivation of serine/threonine and tyrosine kinase activities plays a significant role in the biological regulation of myeloid cells by IL-3.

*CSF regulation of gene expression*

The intracellular effects of growth factors on their target cells have been extensively studied in different tissues such as fibroblastic cell lines induced to proliferate by serum or purified serum growth factors (epidermal growth factor (EGF); fibroblast growth factor (FGF); insulin, etc.) or else T cell lines induced to proliferate by IL-2 (Cleveland *et al.* 1987). At the nuclear level, growth factors rapidly induce major changes in the transcriptional programme of the cell. In particular, they induce the expression of the nuclear proto-oncogenes c-*fos* (Kruijer *et al.* 1984) and c-*myc* (Greenberg & Ziff, 1983; Muller *et al.* 1984) the cellular genomic counterparts of retroviral transforming genes (Cleveland *et al.* 1987; Bishop, 1985). These proto-oncogene protein products, being located in the nucleus, are believed to be, at least, part of the genetic elements involved in cell proliferation.

We have investigated the effect of growth factors on induction of nuclear proto-oncogenes in two growth factor-dependent mouse myeloid cell lines, one of which is induced to proliferate by each of the three biochemically unique CSFs: G-CSF, GM-CSF and IL-3.

In order to investigate the effects of CSFs on proto-oncogene mRNA induction, NSF-60.8 or FDC-P1 cells were arrested in $G_1$ phase of the cell cycle by deprivation of growth factors and reduced serum concentration for the appropriate periods of time, distinct for each cell line and then allowed to proceed into the cycle by addition of $100 \, \text{ng ml}^{-1}$ of r-mu-GM-CSF (NSF-60.8 cells ) or $(10 \, \text{ng ml}^{-1})$ r-mu-IL-3 ($\equiv$Multi-CSF) (FDC-P1 cells). At indicated time points, total RNA (or poly(A)$^+$ RNA, as indicated) was extracted from the cells and submitted to Northern analysis. For both cell lines, growth factors induced c-*fos* mRNA expression, visualized as a $2 \cdot 3 \, \text{kb}$ hybridizing species. This induction occurred rapidly, after 30 min of treatment with growth factor, and was transient, the steady state level of c-*fos* returning to background after 1 h (Fig. 3A). c-*myc* mRNA was also induced by growth factors in both cell lines, although with different kinetics. The maximum level of induction was reached only after 2–4 h of contact with growth factor (Fig. 3A,B), and the level of c-*myc* mRNA did not return to background level even by 20 h post CSF treatment (data not shown). c-*myb* mRNA level was high even in quiescent cells, when the level of c-*myc* or c-*fos* mRNA was minimal. It has to be noted that in NSF-60.8 cells, a genomic insertion has brought c-*myb* under the control of a retroviral promoter, which results in the transcription of a truncated c-*myb* message (kb instead of $3 \cdot 6 \, \text{kb}$). In those cells, the level of c-*myb* mRNA does not seem to be regulated throughout the cell cycle (Fig. 3B). However, in FDC-P1 cells, in which no genomic alteration of c-*myb* has been described, c-*myb* mRNA level was also high in quiescent cells, decreased rapidly, and increased again after 1 h of treatment with growth factor. The results seen with GM-CSF on NSF-60.8 cells were also observed when G-CSF was used as the stimulant (Harel-Bellan & Farrar, 1987).

Our results indicate that the three growth factors increased steady state levels of c-*fos* and c-*myc* on resting cells with the same kinetics. The induction of c-*myc* and c-*fos* seem therefore to occur in common with activation by a variety of growth factors in the different cell types studied so far, such as fibroblasts or lymphoid cells. This observation can now be extended to CSF-dependent myeloid cell lines, as shown for three different CSFs, IL-3, G-CSF or GM-CSF (Harel-Bellan & Farrar, 1987). It has to be noted that the level of induction of c-*fos* by CSF in myeloid cell lines is quantitatively less than what is observed in fibroblasts for example, the induction of c-*fos* being relatively low in meyloid cells so that its relevance to the proliferative process may be questionable.

In addition to CSF regulation of proto-oncogenes we have recently examined the effects of IL-3, G-CSF, GM-CSF on myeloid cell expression of ODC steady state mRNA synthesis and stimulation of heat shock protein synthesis (Farrar *et al.* 1988*a*; Ferris *et al.* unpublished). All the CSFs tested were capable of regulating

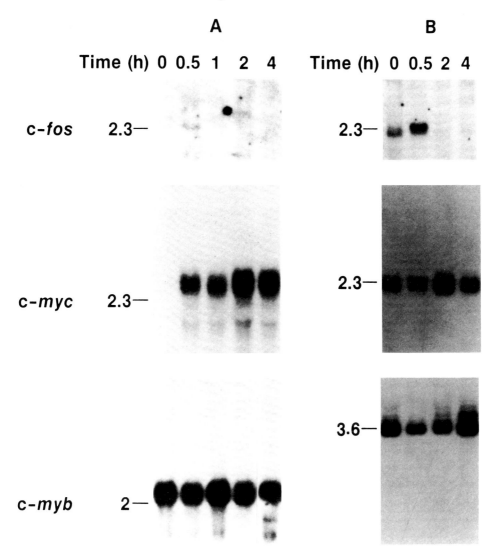

Fig. 3. Time course of nuclear proto-oncogene induction by CSF in CSF-dependent myeloid cell lines. Growth-arrested NSF-60.8 (A) or FDC-P1 (B) cells were allowed to proceed in the cell cycle by addition of 100 ng ml$^{-1}$ of r-mu-GM-CSF (A) or 1/20 dilution of r-mu-IL-3 ($\equiv$Multi-CSF) (B). At indicated time points, total RNA (A) or poly(A)$^+$ RNA (B) was extracted from the cells and subjected to Northern analysis. The same Northern blot was used with all the probes. mu = murine.

ODC mRNA expression and increased enzyme activity. ODC mRNA synthesis was increased as early as 1 h post CSF treatment in FDC-P1 or NSF-60.8 cells and enzyme levels steadily increased reaching a plateau approximately 6–8 h post stimulation.

The heat shock proteins are a family of genes more ancient than proto-oncogenes, found in all phyla in the plant and animal kingdoms (Subjeck & Shyy, 1986). We recently have shown that one member of the family, HSP 70, is modulated by IL-2 during lymphocyte growth (Ferris *et al.* 1988). We extended these observations to the study of myeloid growth factors and found that IL-3, GM-CSF and G-CSF could increase levels of two distinct gene products, HSP 90 and HSP 70, by transcriptional and post-transcriptional mechanisms (Farrar *et al.* 1988a). Although the function of heat shock proteins is unknown, they have been found in association with steroid receptors and $pp60^{src}$ and p53 oncogenes (Subjeck & Shyy, 1986). The finding that lymphoid and haemopoietic growth factors modulate their expression lends importance to their role in cell proliferation and further suggests that mechanism(s) involved in cellular proliferation have evolved from primitive stress-adaptation responses observed in eubacteria.

## Molecular effects of anti-growth signals

We have used the information deduced from CSF-directed gene modulation to study the molecular effects of potent anti-growth signals to myeloid and lymphoid cells dependent upon growth factors. The two anti-growth signals chosen were cyclic AMP and gamma interferon (IFN-gamma) (Farrar *et al.* 1988a; Harel-Bellan & Farrar, 1988; Farrar *et al.* 1987; Harel-Bellan *et al.* 1988). Both cyclic AMP and IFN-gamma inhibit NSF-60.8 cell line proliferation.

We investigated the effect of 8-Br-cyclic adenosine 3′:5′monophosphate (cyclic AMP), a pharmacological activator of cyclic AMP-dependent protein kinase, on the proliferation and the nuclear proto-oncogene induction in a murine granulocyte/macrophage colony stimulating factor-dependent myeloid cell line. Cells were growth-arrested by granulocyte macrophage colony stimulating factor and serum deprivation and allowed to proceed in the cell cycle by addition of the lymphokine in the presence or absence of 8-Br-cyclic AMP. [$^3$H]thymidine incorporation assays showed that addition of 8-Br-cyclic AMP inhibited the entry of cells into S phase and the subsequent proliferation. Northern analysis showed that 8-Br-cyclic AMP had opposite effects on c-*fos* and c-*myc* mRNA induction. 8-Br-cyclic AMP induced c-*fos* in the absence of any CSF. In the presence of CSF, c-*fos* mRNA was superinduced (30-fold induction compared to 4- to 5-fold by each signal alone). On the contrary, 8-Br-cyclic AMP was not able to induce c-*myc* in the absence of growth factor and hardly interfered with the induction of c-*myc* by CSF. As phorbol myristate acetate (PMA), a pharmacological activator of the lipid and $Ca^{2+}$-dependent protein kinase C, is known to induce nuclear proto-oncogene mRNA in CSF-dependent cell lines, we investigated the effect of 8-Br-cyclic AMP on PMA-induced c-*fos* and c-*myc* mRNA levels. When both cyclic AMP-dependent and lipid-dependent kinase systems were co-stimulated, in the absence of CSF, c-*fos* message was again, superinduced (60-fold induction). On the contrary, c-*myc* message induction by PMA was inhibited by 80 % by coactivation of cyclic AMP-dependent protein kinase with 8-Br-cyclic AMP (Harel-Ballan & Farrar, 1988).

When we tested the effects of 8-Br-cyclic AMP on ODC mRNA synthesis we found the cyclic AMP analogue inhibited ODC mRNA steady state accumulation

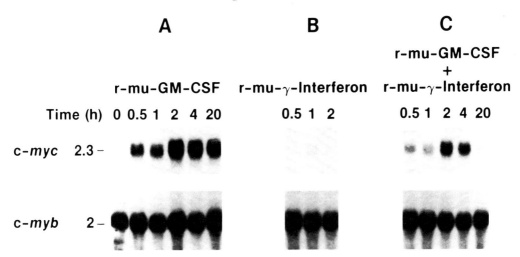

Fig. 4. Interferon gamma inhibits the CSF induced steady state level of c-*myc* message. NSF-60.8 cells were growth arrested and stimulated with 100 ng ml$^{-1}$ of r-mu-GM-CSF, 100 units ml$^{-1}$ of r-mu-g IFN or both as indicat- ed. At various time points, total RNAs were extracted and submitted to Northern analysis using a probe specific for c-*myc* mRNA or for c-*myb* mRNA as indicated. The size of the message, in kb, is indicated.

stimulated by either IL-2 with lymphocytes (Farrar *et al.* 1987) or CSF- stimulated NSF-60.8 cells (Farrar *et al.* 1988a).

IFN-gamma was examined for its effects on proto-oncogene expression and ODC steady state mRNA or enzyme levels. Stimultaneous addition of IFN-gamma with GM-CSF to NSF-60.8 cells markedly inhibits cellular proliferation within the first cell cycle (Farrar *et al.* 1988a; Harel-Bellan *et al.* 1988). GM-CSF stimulated ODC mRNA and enzyme levels were markedly reduced as early as 2 h after-treatment (Farrar *et al.* 1988a). The IFN-gamma did not affect accelerated ODC mRNA degradation suggesting a transcriptional inhibition of ODC mRNA.

The proliferation of NSF-60.8 cells is strongly inhibited by murine IFN-gamma. Northern analysis of growth arrested NSF-60.8 cells, activated by addition of GM-CSF in the presence of absence of gamma interferon, indicated that gammainter-feron inhibited the induction of c-*myc* mRNA steady state level by GM-CSF (Fig. 4). The effect was observed as early as 30 min after induction and the inhibition was complete after 20 h. Gamma interferon did not impair the transcriptional activation of c-*myc* gene, and had only a slight destabilizing effect on the mature c-*myc* message. Study of the processing steps of c-*myc* mRNA precursor indicated that in the presence of gamma interferon, a putative 3·6 kb splice intermediately accumulated instead of the mature message, suggesting that gamma interferon inhibits the splicing of c-*myc* precursor (Harel-Bellan *et al.* 1988).

The characterization of molecular events regulated by proliferative CSFs not only aid in our understanding of the mechanism(s) controlling the growth and differen-tiation of haemopoietic progenitors, but also serve operationally to examine the effects of potent anti-signals to the biological systems stimulated by growth factors.

For example, cyclic AMP and IFN-gamma, potent inhibitors of CSF-directed proliferation and potential differentiation agents, were shown to inhibit CSF stimulation of c-*myc* and ODC mRNA accumulation. The ability to examine at the biochemical and molecular level the fundamental elements which govern growth and anti-growth may provide new clues for examining the integrity or escape of these signals in blood cell malignancy. The recent advances in biotechnology and cell culture have nevertheless provided new tools in which to examine these fundamental questions common to all living organisms.

This project has been funded at least in part with Federal funds from the Department of Health and Human Services under contract number NO1-CO-74102 with Program Resources, Inc. The content of this publication does not necessarily reflect the views or policies of the Department of Health and Human Services, nor does mention of trade names, commercial products, or organizations imply endorsement by the U.S. Government.

## References

Bishop, J. M. (1985). Viral oncogenes. *Cell* **42**, 23–38.

Cleveland, J. L., Rapp, U. R. & Farrar, W. L. (1987). Role of c-myc and other genes in IL 2 regulated CT6 T lymphocytes and their malignant variants. *J. Immunol.* **138**, 3495–3504.

Collett, M. S., Purchio, A. F. & Erickson, R. L. (1980). Avian sarcoma virus-transforming protein, pp60$^{src}$, shows protein kinase activity specific for tyrosine. *Nature, Lond.* **285**, 167–171.

Dexter, T. M. (1984). Blood cell development. The message in the medium. *Nature, Lond.* **309**, 745–748.

Evans, S. W. & Farrar, W. L. (1987). Identity of common phosphoprotein substrates stimulated by interleukin 2 and diacylglycerol suggest a role of protein kinase C for IL 2 signal transduction. *J. Cell Biochem.* **37**, 47–59.

Evans, S. W., Rennick, D. & Farrar, W. L. (1987). Identification of a signal transduction pathway shared by hematopoietic growth factors with diverse biological specificity. *Biochem. J.* **244**, 683–691.

Evans, S. W., Rennick, D. & Farrar, W. L. (1986). Multi-lineage hematopoietic growth factor interleukin 3 and activators of protein kinase C stimulate phosphorylation of a common substrate. *Blood* **68**, 906–913.

Farrar, W. L., Bellan-Harel, A., Cleveland, J. L. & Vinocour, M. (1988*b*). Regulation of ornithine decarboxylase activity by IL 2 and cyclic AMP. *J. Immun.* (in press).

Farrar, W. L., Evans, S. W., Rapp, U. R. & Cleveland, J. L. (1987). Effects of antiproliferative cyclic adenosine 3'5' monophosphate on interleukin 2 stimulated gene expression. *J. Immunol.* **139**, 2075–2080.

Farrar, W. L., Vinocour, M. & Harel-Bellan, A. (1988*a*). Regulation of ornithine decarboxylase activity by colony stimulating factors and gamma interferon. *Blood*, (in press).

Ferris, D. K., Harel-Bellan, A., Morimoto, R. I., Welch, W. J. & Farrar, W. L. (1988). Mitogen and lymphokine stimulation of heat shock proteins in T lymphocytes. *Proc. natn. Acad. Sci. U.S.A.* **85**, 3820–3854.

Garland, J. M. (1988). Rapid phosphorylation of a specific 33-kDa protein (p33) associated with growth stimulated by murine and rat IL 3 in different IL 3-dependent cell lines, and its constitutive expression in a malignant independent clone. *Leukemia* **2**, 94–102.

Greenberg, M. E. & Ziff, E. B. (1983). Stimulation of 3T3 cells induces transcription of c-*fos* proto-oncogenes. *Nature, Lond.* **311**, 433–437.

Harel-Bellan, A., Brini, A. & Farrar, W. L. (1988). Gamma interferon inhibits c-*myc* gene expression by impairing the splicing process in a colony stimulating factor dependent murine cell line. *J. Immunol.* **141**, 1012–1017.

Harel-Bellan, A. & Farrar, W. L. (1987). Modulation of proto-oncogene expression by colony stimulating factors. *Biochem. biophys. Res. Commun.* **148**, 1001–1008.

Harel-Bellan, A. & Farrar, W. L. (1988). Regulation of proliferation in a murine CSF-dependent cell line: Super induction of c-fos by the growth inhibitor 8-Bromo-cAMP. *J. Cell Biochem.* (in press).

HUNTER, T. (1984). The proteins of oncogenes. *Sci. Am.* **251**, 70.

HUNTER, T. & COOPER, J. A. (1985). Protein-tyrosine kinases. *Annu. Rev. Biochem.* **54**, 897–902.

IHLE, J. N., KELLER, J., HENDERSON, L., KLEIN, F. & PALASZYNSKI, E. (1982). Procedures for the purification of interleukin 3 to homogeneity. *J. Immun.* **129**, 2431–2436.

ISHII, T., TAKESHITA, T., NUMATA, N. & SUGAMURA, K. (1988). Protein phosphorylation mediated by IL-2/IL-2 receptor β chain interaction. *J. Immun.* **141**, 174–179.

KOLATA, G. (1983). Is tyrosine the key to growth control. *Science* **219**, 378–381.

KOYASU, S., TOJO, A., MIYAJIMA, A., AKIYAMA, T., KASUGA, M., URABE, A., SCHREWS, J., ARAI, K., TAKAKU, F. & YAHARA, I. (1987). IL 3-specific tyrosine phosphorylation of a membrane glycoprotein of Mr 150,000 in multi-factor dependent myeloid cell lines. *EMBO J.* **6**, 3979–3984.

KRUIJER, W., COOPER, J. A., HUNTER, T. & VERMA, I. M. (1984). Platelet-derived growth factor induces rapid but transient expression of the c-fos gene and protein. *Nature, Lond.* **312**, 711–714.

MULLER, R., BRAVO, R., BURCKHARDT, J. & CURRAN, T. (1984). Induction of c-fos gene and protein by growth factors precedes activation of c-myc. *Nature, Lond.* **312**, 716–720.

NICOLA, N. A., METCALF, D., MATSUMOTO, M. & JOHNSON, G. R. (1983). Purification of a factor inducing differentiation in murine myelo-monocytic leukemia cells. *J. biol. Chem.* **258**, 9017–9023.

NICOLA, N. A. & VADAS, M. (1984). Haemapoietic colony stimulating factors. *Immunol. Today* **5**, 76–80.

SHERR, C. J., RETTENMIER, C. W., SACCA, R., ROUSSEL, M. F., LOOK, A. T. & STANLEY, E. R. (1985). The c-fms proto-oncogene is related to the receptor for the mononuclear phagocyte growth factor, CSF 1. *Cell* **41**, 665–670.

SPARROW, L. G., METCALF, D., HUNKAPILLER, M. W., HOOD, L. E. & BURGESS, A. W. (1985). Purification and partial amino acid sequence of asialo murine granulocyte–macrophage colony stimulating factor. *Proc. natn. Acad. Sci. U.S.A.* **82**, 292–296.

SUBJECK, J. R. & SHYY, T.-T. (1986). Stress protein systems of mammalian cells. *Am. J. Physiol.* **250** (*Cell Physiol.*), C1–C17.

WHETTON, A. D., HEYWORTH, C. M. & DEXTER, T. M. (1986). Phorbol esters activate protein kinase C and glucose transport and can replace the requirement for growth factor in interleukin-3-dependent multipotent stem cells. *J. Cell Sci.* **84**, 93–99.

*J. Cell Sci. Suppl. 10, 257–266 (1988)*
*Printed in Great Britain © The Company of Biologists Limited 1988*

# Regulatory factors of embryonic stem cells

JOHN K. HEATH AND AUSTIN G. SMITH

*Department of Biochemistry, University of Oxford, South Parks Rd, Oxford OX1 3QU*

## Summary

The analysis of factors which regulate cell proliferation and differentiation in early mammalian development has been facilitated by the existence of cell lines derived from pluripotential stem cells of the early embryo; embryonal carcinoma (EC) cells and embryonic stem (ES) cells. EC cells have proved to be a useful source of embryonic growth factors. A potent mitogen, ECDGF has been isolated from EC cell conditioned medium. ECDGF appears to be a novel member of the heparin binding growth factor family. A remarkable feature of heparin binding growth factors is their ability to induce mesodermal differentiation in *Xenopus laevis* animal pole explants. ES cell differentiation *in vitro* is controlled by exogenous factors, in particular a novel differentiation inhibitory factor DIA. Controlled bipotential differentiation of ES cells can be achieved by exposing ES cells to different combinations of regulatory signals.

## Introduction

It is becoming apparent from the study of a number of stem cell systems that soluble regulatory hormones and their associated cellular response mechanisms play a key role in coordinating and controlling both cell proliferation and developmental switching. The early phases of mammalian development are no exception. In this paper we discuss the expression of, and the response to, growth and differentiation factors by stem cells derived from the early mammalian embryo.

The direct analysis of growth and differentiation factor action in early mammalian development is complicated by two problems; at the time critical morphogenetic events occur *in vivo* the embryo is composed of a few thousand cells only and is sequestered in the relatively inaccessible environment of the maternal uterus. This means that direct biochemical analysis, by conventional techniques, of regulatory factor action and expression is very difficult. Furthermore, the embryo is composed of multiple cell types in close anatomical association. This renders direct experimental dissection of embryonic intercellular signalling processes complex. In order to begin to understand the identity of the signalling pathways that operate in the early phases of mammalian development *in vivo*, attention has focussed upon approaches which permit controlled biochemical analysis of embryonic polypeptide regulatory factors under experimentally favourable conditions. In this paper we shall consider two avenues that have been developed with this objective in mind: the use of multipotential cell lines derived directly, or indirectly, from pluripotential stem cells of the early embryo and the exploitation of species with experimentally accessible embryonic stages, in particular, amphibians. The expectation is that the information

Key words: embryonal carcinoma, embryonic stem cells, differentiation, growth factors, embryonic induction.

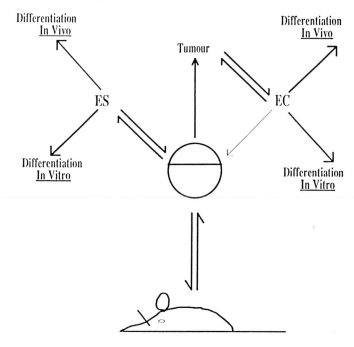

Fig. 1. The relationship between the normal mouse embryo, embryonal carcinoma (EC) cells and embryonic stem (ES) cells.

obtained from these surrogate systems can be used as a basis for the design of appropriate experiments to investigate the 'real' problem; the mammalian embryo itself.

## Embryonal carcinoma and embryonic stem cells

Multipotential cell lines can be derived from early mammalian embryos by two methods (Fig. 1). The first (reviewed by Stevens, 1983) depends upon either the natural occurrence of germ cell tumours in specific mouse strains or the induction of teratocarcinoma tumours from the primitive ectoderm of embryos transplanted to ectopic sites. The continued growth of these tumours is due to the existence of a tumorigenic, pluripotential stem cell population, the embryonal carcinoma (EC) cells. EC cells can be taken into culture and grown as permanent cell lines where they may, under appropriate circumstances, differentiate into cell types which phenotypically and behaviourally resemble the derivatives of normal embryonic primitive ectoderm. Reintroduction of cultured EC cells into host mice yields teratocarcinoma tumours containing differentiated derivatives of EC cell origin. The second approach involves the derivation of pluripotential stem cell lines directly from embryos cultured *in vitro* (reviewed by Evans & Kaufman, 1983). These embryonic stem (ES) cells in many, but not all, respects resemble EC cells derived by means of tumour induction.

It is important to appreciate that extrapolation of results obtained from the analysis of EC and ES cell lines to the normal embryo depends on the extent to which these cells can be shown to respond to normal developmental cues and signals. This can be tested by examining the developmental potential of the cells when re-incorporated into the normal embryo by blastocyst injection. From a large number of experiments of this type it is clear that EC cells are, in general, defective in their ability to differentiate correctly *in vivo* (Papaioannou & Rossant, 1983). Indeed, this inability of EC cells to differentiate efficiently *in vivo* may well be related to their tumour origin. ES cell lines, by contrast, can contribute to all tissues of the adult animal including the germ cell lineage (Bradley *et al.* 1984). ES cells are therefore without doubt genuine stem cells with pluripotential properties.

Thus EC cells, because of their embryonic origins, may be a valuable *source* of potential embryonic regulatory factors but are a less reliable guide to the possible *responses* of their normal embryonic counterparts. ES cells, on the other hand, appear to present a useful system for the identification of novel embryonic bioregulatory factors, since they are demonstrably capable of responding correctly to signals that exist in normal embryos.

## EC cell-derived growth factors

Certain EC cell lines, in particular PC13 EC, have been used extensively for the analysis of growth factor action and expression *in vitro* (reviewed by Heath & Rees, 1985). They provide, subject to the important considerations outlined above, a favourable experimental system since they are blocked in their capacity to undergo spontaneous differentiation *in vivo* and *in vitro*. They may thus be propagated as homogeneous EC cell populations *in vitro*, and are consequently well suited to experimental study. Differentiation of these cells *in vitro* can be induced by exposure of the cells to retinoic acid (RA) yielding an apparently uniform cell type PC13 END, which resembles extra-embryonic mesoderm of the normal embryo. PC13 is therefore a simple cell system which can be switched from the stem cell into a single differentiation pathway by an externally applied signal.

This RA-induced differentiation is accompanied by significant changes in the control of cell proliferation, including loss of tumorigenic potential, acquisition of dependency upon exogenous growth factors for multiplication and a finite proliferative lifespan. However, the principal relevance of this system to the identification of embryonic polypeptide regulatory factors lies in the fact that the expression of endogenous growth regulatory factors is also developmentally regulated. Thus EC differentiation into END cells is accompanied by the expression of insulin-like growth factors (IGFs) which have the capacity to exhibit both paracrine and autocrine growth effects on END cells and their EC progenitors (Heath & Rees, 1985; Heath & Shi, 1986). This identification of IGF expression by an early embryo-derived cell type has led to an examination of IGF expression in early mammalian embryos where it was observed that IGF-like molecules were expressed by extra-embryonic mesoderm and amnion in early postimplantation development. Subsequent *in situ* hybridization studies using oligonucleotide probes have both confirmed and extended these observations, revealing a specific tissue-limited expression of IGFs in the early postimplantation rodent embryo (Beck *et al.* 1987). This example clearly demonstrates the value of EC cells and their differentiated progeny as sources of embryonic polypeptide regulatory factors.

The ability to propagate PC13 EC cells as a homogeneous population *in vitro*, and the development of growth factor-free defined culture conditions (reviewed by Heath, 1987) permitted the analysis of bioregulatory factors secreted by EC stem cells. A potent, secreted, mitogenic activity was detected in serum-free PC13 EC cell conditioned medium whose expression ceased upon induction of differentiation (Isacke & Deller, 1983). The principal agent responsible for the mitogenic activity in PC13 EC cell conditioned medium was subsequently isolated and shown to be a single chain $M_r$ 17 500 molecule termed ECDGF (embryonal carcinoma-derived growth factor, Heath & Isacke, 1984).

A key biochemical characteristic of ECDGF is its strong affinity for heparin (Heath, 1987; Van Veggel *et al.* 1987), a property which is shared with at least two other important biological regulatory factors, acidic (aFGF) (Giminez-Gallego *et al.* 1985) and basic fibroblast growth factor (bFGF) (Esch *et al.* 1985) first identified in adult neuronal tissues. This similarity between FGFs and ECDGF in heparin affinity and apparent molecular weight has led to a more detailed appraisal of the structural and functional relationship between ECDGF, aFGF and bFGF.

It is significant that ECDGF is a secreted factor, indeed its presence in conditioned medium provided the means for its identification. Both acid and basic fibroblast growth factor seem to be closely cell-associated in cultured cell lines and are not readily detected in conditioned medium (e.g. see Jaye *et al.* 1988). This may be due to the apparent absence of a secretory signal sequence in the primary acid or basic FGF translation product (Abraham *et al.* 1986).

Detailed analysis of the biochemical characteristics of ECDGF and bovine brain-derived acidic and basic FGF also reveals significant overall differences between the three factors; thus ECDGF elutes at comparable salt concentrations (1·3 M-NaCl) on heparin-derived HPLC affinity columns to aFGF, but both factors elute earlier than bFGF under the same conditions. In contrast ECDGF elutes at higher salt concentrations (0·6 M-NaCl, 10 mM-phosphate, pH 6·8) than either acid or basic FGF on mono-S cation-exchange matrices. ECDGF is also significantly more retarded when analysed by reverse phase chromatography than either acid or basic FGF. In summary, ECDGF can be physically separated from either acidic or basic FGF by a variety of different biochemical techniques.

That these three heparin-binding growth factors are distinct molecular species is further supported by three additional lines of evidence. First, the amino acid composition of ECDGF (data not shown) is significantly different from either acidic or basic FGF. Second an extensive series of antibodies generated against peptides derived from either the acidic or basic FGF amino acid sequence (Baird *et al.* 1986; unpublished observations of J. Slack and J. K. Heath) have been tested for cross-reaction with ECDGF by Western blotting techniques. With the exception of antibodies directed against residues 16–24 of basic FGF (but curiously not residues 15–30 which span the same region), no cross reaction has been observed. Finally, distinct polypeptide maps are obtained from aFGF, bFGF and ECDGF when tryptic digests are analysed by microbore reverse phase HPLC.

All these findings therefore indicate that ECDGF is related to, but distinct from, the two 'prototype' heparin binding growth factors.

It has recently become apparent, however, that the 'FGF family' of growth factors is larger than had been hitherto suspected. A transforming oncogene *hst* has been isolated by standard NIH/3T3 transfection procedures from a human stomach tumour (Taira *et al.* 1987). An apparently identical gene *ks* has also recently been isolated from NIH/3T3 cells transfected with DNA taken from a Kaposi's sarcoma (Delli Bovi *et al.* 1987). The *ks/hst* gene encodes a functional mitogen with considerable sequence homology to the basic FGF prototype gene. A significant feature of *ks/hst* is the presence of a secretory signal sequence in the predicted primary translation product. Furthermore, this signal sequence appears to be functional since the product of the *ks/hst* gene can be shown to be secreted into the medium of cells when the gene is expressed under the control of a heterologous promotor (Delli-Bovi *et al.* 1987). Although expression of the *ks* gene in COS cells under the control of a heterologous promoter yields a secreted, functional *ks* protein of apparent $M_r 24000$, the predicted primary sequence of the protein contains a number of paired basic amino acid residues which, if acting as substrates for proteolytic processing, could in principle produce a molecule of the same approximate apparent molecular mass as ECDGF isolated from EC cell-conditioned medium.

A second oncogene, initially identified by virtue of its activation in mammary tumours by retrovirus insertion, is *int-2*. DNA sequence analysis of the *int-2* gene also reveals significant sequence homology with the basic FGF prototype gene (Dickson & Peters, 1987). *int-2* transcripts are also expressed at low levels in F9 EC cells, although the level of transcription increases upon differentiation (Smith *et al.* 1988). In addition *int-2* transcripts display a strikingly localized pattern of expression in early mouse development when studied by *in situ* hybridization techniques (Wilkinson *et al.* 1988). It must be noted, however, that the *int-2* gene has yet to be shown to encode a functional mitogen and its exact relationship to other heparin-binding growth factors remains to be determined.

These findings prompt the speculation that these additional members of the FGF gene family, ECDGF, *ks/hst* and *int-2*, may be 'embryonic' forms of the FGF family and that heparin binding growth factors as a class have an important functional role in early development. This view finds support from the somewhat unexpected discovery that FGF-like factors have powerful biological actions upon developmental switches in early amphibian development.

## Mesoderm induction

The differentiation of certain mesodermal tissues (such as muscle) in *Xenopus* appears to depend upon an inductive interaction between animal pole cells and the underlying vegetal endoderm, since isolated animal pole explants fail to generate muscle and other mesodermal structures unless recombined with vegetal tissues. This inductive interaction appears to be one of the earliest intercellular signalling events in amphibian development, and plays a key role in subsequent morphogenesis of the embryo. It is very significant therefore that the inducing property of vegetal tissues can be, at least partially, reproduced with exogenously added natural (basic or acidic) FGF, ECDGF, or *ks/hst* protein synthesized *in vitro* (Slack *et al.* 1987; unpublished observations of G. Paterno, L. Gillespie, J. Slack and J. K. Heath). The case for FGF-like factors being the primary mesoderm-inducing agents *in vivo* is further strengthened by the finding that a *Xenopus* homologue of the mammalian basic FGF gene exists, and RNA transcripts hybridizing with this gene have been found to be expressed in embryos at stages where mesoderm induction is taking place (Kimelman & Kirschner, 1987). However, it is not at present clear whether *Xenopus* FGF itself or the equivalent of another member of the heparin binding growth factor family such as ECDGF or *ks/hst* is the primary agent of *Xenopus* mesoderm induction *in vivo*.

It is not at all apparent that mammalian development involves a developmental event similar to the induction of mesoderm in *Xenopus*. Nevertheless, this unexpected biological property of ECDGF, along with its derivation from embryo-derived EC cells, indicates that it may play a role in regulating early developmental decisions in the early mouse embryo.

This involvement of FGF-like factors in amphibian mesoderm induction has several important consequences for further studies of growth factor action in mammalian development. First, in general terms it reveals that agents initially identified by virtue of their mitogenic properties may also have profound effects on cell differentiation and morphogenesis in particular circumstances. Second, it shows that growth factors from mammalian sources exhibit considerable evolutionary conservation. This not only opens up the novel approach of analysing the possible biological function of growth factors in mammalian embryos by experiments in other species, but also conversely suggests that the homologues of other extracellular bioregulatory factors found in *Xenopus*, such as the XTC cell-derived mesoderm-inducing factor (Smith, 1987) may have a biological role in mammalian development. Finally, the experimental accessibility of *Xenopus* embryos at early developmental stages compared to their mammalian counterparts suggests that they could have potential for the future identification of novel types of extracellular growth and differentiation regulatory factors from mammalian sources.

## Embryonic stem cell differentiation

As discussed above, murine embryo-derived ES cells offer certain advantages over EC cells as an *in vitro* test system for the analysis of the response of early embryonic cells to growth and differentiation factors. However, an important drawback exists which has hitherto limited their use in the investigation of bioregulatory factor action. ES cells readily undergo spontaneous differentiation *in vitro* unless cultured in the presence of a live heterologous feeder cell layer. Although this is very inconvenient from the experimental point of view, it may indicate something about the nature of the underlying mechanisms that control cell differentiation in this system. It appears that ES cells will enter a differentiation programme unless inhibited by a signal which can be provided by the feeder cells. This is in contrast to many teratocarcinoma-derived cell lines such as PC13, where entry into the differentiation programme is blocked unless an inducer, such as RA, is present.

It would obviously be of interest to understand the biochemical basis of the feeder cell effect on ES cell differentiation, since it would appear to affect mechanisms regulating a cellular decision to enter a differentiation programme which directly relates to a fundamental event in mammalian development, the differentiation of pluripotential primitive ectoderm. These mechanisms would, at least in part, appear to be the target for the changes underlying the loss of differentiation potential and acquisition of the malignant phenotype associated with EC cells. Indeed, rather as transformed fibroblasts lose the requirement for exogenous growth factor signals to maintain multiplication, it could be argued that EC cells have lost the requirement for exogenous differentiation inhibitory factors.

Isacke & Deller (1983) have demonstrated that the feeder cell effect, at least in the case of EC cells, is probably multifactorial, involving both cell contact-dependent and independent mechanisms. However, it is of some significance that the principal biological effect of feeder cells on ES cell differentiation can be reproduced by conditioned medium from various cell lines (Smith & Hooper, 1983; Koopman & Cotton, 1984). The medium from one cell line, Buffalo Rat Liver (BRL) has a particularly potent differentiation-inhibiting effect on multipotential EC and pluri-potential ES cells *in vitro* (Smith & Hooper, 1987). The effect of BRL conditioned medium is fully reversible, in that the cells can be maintained indefinitely in an undifferentiated state (in the absence of feeder cells) in its presence, but will rapidly differentiate at any time they are returned to normal unconditioned medium. Prolonged culture in BRL conditioned medium in the absence of feeder cells does not compromise the ability of ES cells to colonize the embryo in a chimaera or give rise to functional gametes. Hooper *et al.* (1987) have, for example, successfully used culture in BRL conditioned media to facilitate the isolation of hypoxanthine phosphoribosyl transferase-deficient ES cells which were used to generate ES cell derived germ line chimaeras transmitting HPRT-deficiency to progeny. The effect of BRL conditioned medium on ES cell differentiation is not reproduced by a variety of growth factors or growth modulators (such as IGF-II or TGF$\beta$) known to be secreted by BRL cells (Smith & Hooper, 1987).

The biological action of BRL cell conditioned medium on ES cell differentiation depends upon a specific secreted polypeptide differentiation regulatory factor (termed differentiation inhibitory activity, DIA) which acts specifically to supress ES cell differentiation *in vitro*. Further analysis of the structure of DIA and its mechanism of action will undoubtedly have important consequences for our knowledge of the mechanisms controlling ES cell differentiation. Furthermore, BRL conditioned medium has already found use as a practical tool for the experimental manipulation of ES cell proliferation and differentiation *in vitro*.

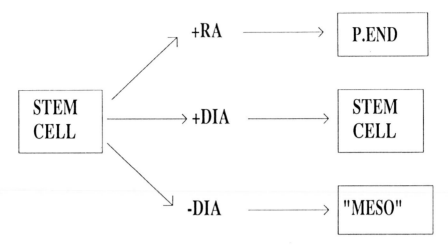

Fig. 2. The regulation of embryonic stem cell differentiation *in vitro* by differentiation inducers (RA) and differentiation inhibitors (DIA).

## Mixing signals

It has emerged that the regulation of ES cell and EC cell differentiation depends upon exogenous signals; DIA suppresses differentiation whereas agents like RA induce differentiation. It is conceivable therefore, that the actual pattern of differentiation may depend upon the balance between differentiation-inducing and differentiation-suppressing extracellular signals. This can be investigated by exposing ES cells, cultured at clonal densities, to combinations of signals and observing the effects of these treatments on differentiation.

The results of this type of experiment are unexpected (summarized Fig. 2). In the presence of BRL medium as a source of DIA activity, CP1/86 ES cell differentiation is suppressed, and the cells are maintained in the ES cell state. Removal of DIA from cells grown in monolayer results in differentiation into a new cell type with mesodermal characteristics ('Meso'). Addition of RA to cells grown in the presence of DIA also results in the induction of differentiation, but the cell type formed is distinct from that formed by removal of DIA exhibiting morphological and molecular characteristics of parietal endoderm (Heath *et al.* 1988).

The conclusion from these experiments is that RA not only overrides the differentiation inhibitory action of DIA but also influences the differentiation programme that is chosen. It is likely, however, that at least some of this response to extracellular differentiation regulatory signals is more complex and depends upon both the target cell itself and spatial relationships between cells or other forms of local cellular interactions. First, ES cell lines such as CCE exhibit different patterns of differentiation in response to RA induction (not shown) from CP1/86 and, secondly, differentiation of ES cells in aggregates or high cell densities yields a broader spectrum of differentiated cell types than occurs in low density monolayer culture.

It is interesting to view these results in the light of concepts derived from the observation of stem cell behaviour in other systems (for a more extensive treatment see Wolpert, 1989). It has often been argued that stem cells can be characterized by bifurcating cell divisions whereby a single stem cell divides to give rise to one differentiated daughter cell, and one daughter which retains the stem cell phenotype. In the case of ES cells, retention of the stem cell phenotype in these specific experimental conditions appears to be an 'all or none' property which is regulated by exogenous signals; both progeny of a single ES cell either enter a differentiation programme or do not. Clones comprising a mixture of ES cells and differentiated progeny are rarely, if ever, seen.

## Conclusion

Although the identification and characterization of regulatory factor expression and action in early mammalian development seems like a technically intractable problem it will be apparent that some progress is beginning to be made. In particular, the exploitation of EC and ES cells as surrogate embryonic stem cells has facilitated biochemical characterization of at least some candidate regulatory factors. The finding that embryo-derived regulatory factors control developmental processes in amphibians has opened up a system with accessible embryonic stages for experimental analysis. Finally, the identification of secreted polypeptide factors which regulate ES cell differentiation *in vitro* suggests that cell differentiation, as well as cell proliferation, may be controlled by soluble polypeptide factors. The characterization of their mechanisms of action may prove illuminating.

Research in the authors' laboratory is supported by the Cancer Research Campaign.

## References

ABRAHAM, J., WHANG, J., TUMULO, A., MERGIA, A., FRIEDMAN, J., GOSPODAROWICZ, D. & FIDDES, J. (1986). Human basic fibroblast growth factor: nucleotide sequence and genomic organisation. *EMBO J.* **5**, 2523–2528.

BAIRD, A., ESCH, F., MORMEDE, P., UENO, N., LING, N., BOHLEN, P., YING, S. & WEHRENBERG, W. (1986). Fibroblast growth factors. *Recent Prog. Hormone Res.* **42**, 146–203.

BECK, F., SAMANI, N. J., PENSCHOW, J., THORLEY, B., TREGEAR, G. & COGHLAN, J. (1987). Histochemical localisation of IGF-I and IGF-II mRNA in the developing rat embryo. *Development.* **101**, 175–184.

BRADLEY, A., KAUFMAN, M., EVANS, M. & ROBERTSON, E. (1984). Formation of germline chimeras from embryo-derived teratocarcinoma cell lines. *Nature, Lond.* **309**, 255–257.

DELLI-BOVI, P., CURATOLA, A. M., KERN, F., GRECO, A., ITTMANN, M. & BASILICO, C. (1987). An oncogene isolated by transfection of Karposi's sarcoma DNA encodes a growth factor that is a member of the FGF family. *Cell* **50**, 729–737.

DICKSON, C. & PETERS, G. (1987). Potential oncogene product related to growth factors. *Nature, Lond.* **326**, 833.

ESCH, F., BAIRD, A., LING, N., UENO, N., HILL, F., DENROY, L., KLEPPER, R., GOSPODAROEICZ, D., BOHLEN, P. & GUILLMAN, R. (1985). Primary structure of bovine pituitary basic fibroblast growth factor (FGF) and comparison with the amino-terminal sequence of bovine brain acidiac FGF. *Proc. natn. Acad. Sci. U.S.A.* **82**, 6507–6511.

EVANS, M. & KAUFMAN, M. (1983). Pluripotential cells grown directly from the mouse embryo. *Cancer Surveys.* **2**, 185–207.

GIMINEZ-GALLEGO, G., RODKEY, J., BENNETT, C., RIOS-CANDELORE, M., DISALVO, J. & THOMAS, K. (1985). Brain-derived acidic fibroblast growth factor: complete amino acid sequence and homologies. *Science* **230**, 1385–1388.

HEATH, J. K. (1987). Purification of embryonal carcinoma derived growth factor and analysis of teratocarcinoma cell multiplication. In *Teratocarcinomas and Embryonic Stem Cells: a Practical Approach* (ed. E. Robertson), pp. 183–206. Oxford: IRL Press.

HEATH, J. K. & ISACKE, C. (1984). Embryonal carcinoma derived growth factor. *EMBO J.* **3**, 2597–2962.

HEATH, J. K. & REES, A. R. (1985). Growth factors in mammalian embryogenesis. In *Growth Factors in Biology and Medicine* (ed. D. Evered & M. Stoker) Ciba Symp., vol. 116, 1–22.

HEATH, J. K. & SHI, W.-K. (1986). Developmentally regulated expression of insulin-like growth factors by differentiated murine teratocarcinomas and extra-embryonic mesoderm. *J.E.E.M.* **95**, 193–212.

HEATH, J. K., WILLS, A., EDWARDS, D. & SMITH, A. (1988). Growth factors in early development. In *Cell to Cell Signalling in Mammalian Development* (ed. S. deLaat, C. Mummery & J. Bluemink). Berlin: Springer (in press).

HOOPER, M., HARDY, K., HANDYSIDE, A., HUNTER, S. & MONK, M. (1987). HPRT-deficent (Lesch-Nyhan) mouse embryos derived from germline colonisation by cultured cells. *Nature, Lond.* **326**, 292–295.

ISACKE, C. M. & DELLER, M. J. (1983). Teratocarcinoma cells exhibit growth cooperativity in vitro. *J. cell. Physiol.* **117**, 407–414.

JAYE, M., LYALL, R., MUDD, R. & SCHLESSINGER, J. (1988). Expression of acidic fibroblast growth factor cDNA confers growth advantage and tumourgenesis to swiss 3T3 cells. *EMBO J.* **7**, 963–970.

KIMELMAN, D. & KIRSCHNER, M. (1987). Synergistic induction of mesoderm by FGF and TGFβ and the identification of an mRNA coding for FGF in the early Xenopus embryo. *Cell* **51**, 869–877.

KOOPMAN, P. & COTTON, R. (1984). A factor produced by feeder cells which inhibits embryonal carcinoma differentiation. *Expl Cell Res.* **154**, 233–242.

PAPAIOANNOU, V. E. & ROSSANT, J. (1983). Effects of the embryonic environment on proliferation and differentiation of embryonic carcinoma cells. *Cancer Surveys.* **2**, 165–184.

SLACK, J., DARLINGTON, B., HEATH, J. K. & GODSAVE, S. (1987). Mesoderm induction in *Xenopus* by heparin building growth factors. *Nature, Lond.* **326**, 197–200.

SMITH, A. G. & HOOPER, M. L. (1987). Buffalo rat liver cells produce a diffusible activity which inhibits the differentiation of murine embryonal carcinoma and embryonic stem cells. *Devl Biol.* **121**, 1–9.

SMITH, J. (1987). A mesoderm-inducing factor is produced by a *Xenopus* cell line. *Development* **99**, 3–14.

SMITH, R., PETERS, G. & DICKSON, C. (1988). Multiple RNAs expressed from the *int-2* gene in mouse embryonal carcinoma cells encode a protein with homology to fibroblast growth factors. *EMBO J.* **7**, 1013–1022.

SMITH, T. A. & HOOPER, M. L. (1983). Medium conditioned by feeder cells inhibits the differentiation of embryonal carcinoma cell cultures. *Expl Cell Res.* **145**, 458–462.

STEVENS, L. (1983). Testicular, ovarian and embryo-derived teratomas. *Cancer Surveys* **2**, 75–91.

TAIRA, T., YOSHIDA, Y., MIYAGAWA, K., SAKAMOTO, H., TEREDA, M. & SUGIMIRA, T. (1987). cDNA sequence of human transforming gene hst and identification of coding sequences required for transforming activity. *Proc. natn. Acad. Sci. U.S.A.* **84**, 2980–2984.

VAN VEGGEL, J., OOSTWARD, T., DELAAT, S. & VAN ZOELEN, E. (1987). PC13 embryonal carcinoma cells produce a heparin-binding growth factor. *Expl Cell Res.* **169**, 280–286.

WILKINSON, D., PETERS, G., DICKSON, C. & MACMAHON, A. (1988). Expression of the FGF-related proto-oncogene *int-2* during gastrulation and neurulation in the mouse. *EMBO J.* **7**, 691–695.

WOLPERT, L. (1989). Stem cells: a problem in symmetry. *J. Cell Sci. Suppl.* **10**, 1–9.

*J. Cell Sci. Suppl. 10*, 267–281 (1988)
Printed in Great Britain © The Company of Biologists Limited 1988

# Stem cell renewal and differentiation in acute myeloblastic leukaemia

E. A. McCULLOCH, M. D. MINDEN, J. MIYAUCHI*, C. A. KELLEHER
AND C. WANG

*The Division of Biological Research, The Ontario Cancer Institute, Toronto, Canada*

## Summary

The defining properties of stem cells are capacities for self-renewal and, after determination, a limited number of terminal divisions. The blast cells of acute myeloblastic leukaemia (AML) are maintained by stem cells with these two properties. Since renewal and differentiation can be assessed separately in cultures of AML blasts, these cancer cells provide a useful model for examining stem regulation; such studies have practical importance for future developments in the treatment of AML. This paper considers three aspects of blast cell biology. First, evidence is presented that self-renewal and differentiation are regulated by specific genes; further, the DNA encoding these genes has structural features that affect the chemosensitivity of self-renewal. This sensitivity varies from patient-to-patient and is an important attribute contributing to variation in treatment efficacy. Second, the effects of myelopoietic growth factors on blast stem cells are presented and discussed, as these bear on the regulation of the balance between renewal and differentiation. Finally, models of leukaemic haemopoiesis are considered in light of the experimental findings. The suggestion is advanced that leukaemia can be explained better by abnormalities of gene expression than by blocked differentiation.

## Introduction

Cell renewal systems achieve a steady state or controlled expansion by balancing growth-promoting stem cell renewal with growth-limiting differentiation. The regulation of the balance between self-renewal and determination, the first step in differentiation, is a significant biological problem, one that has attracted much attention. Several theories have been advanced in the context of haemopoiesis. In one, distribution of new stem cells among subclones was interpreted to mean that self-renewal and differentiation occur at random, governed only by definite 'birth' and 'death' probabilities (Nakahata *et al.* 1982; Till *et al.* 1964). In a different model, the effects of erythropoietin on haemopoiesis led to the suggestion that hormones 'instruct' stem cells to follow one or other course (Goldwasser, 1976). An inductive role for stromal cells in the bone marrow has been suggested, based on *in vivo* studies of genetically anaemic mice of genotype Sl/Sl^d (McCulloch *et al.* 1965) and the growth of marrow stem cells in long term cultures (Dexter *et al.* 1977).

New knowledge of genetic regulation provides a framework which may make it

*Present address: Department of Pathology, School of Medicine, Keio University, 35 Shinanomachi Shinjuku-Ku, Tokyo 160, Japan.

Key words: haemopoietic stem cells, self renewal, differentiation, acute myeloid leukaemia, blast cell clones possible to reconcile these views. Evidence is now available that the products of several genes play a role in the control of cell proliferation. Some, such as the proto-oncogenes *myc* and *fos* act in the nucleus, increasing in transcription as cells enter division (Marshall, 1987). Specific gene products may be required for either self-renewal or differentiation; for example an association has been reported between expression of p[53] and high self-renewal in leukaemic blasts (Smith *et al.* 1986). Other genes encode cell surface receptors for growth factors or hormones; c-*fms* product is the receptor for CSF-1 (Sherr *et al.* 1985), v-*erb*-B protein sequences have close homology to the epidermal growth factor receptor (Downward *et al.* 1984) and the thyroid hormone receptor is homologous to c-*erb*-A (Weinberger *et al.* 1986).

Molecular clones are available for the ligands of many of the receptors; the haemopoietic growth factors have been shown to be encoded by single copy genes (Clark & Kamen, 1987). When growth factors bind to their receptors, the complex is internalized. Inside the cell signal transduction mechanisms (Gilman, 1987; Majerus *et al.* 1987) lead to the initiation of nuclear events including cell division. Thus genetically determined signals connect the nucleus to the cellular environment. The apparent stochastic nature of self-renewal might be explained by a balance between gene products that determine 'birth' and 'death' probabilities. Nor is it necessary to postulate 'instruction' by environmentally derived growth factors; rather these select for cells that have expressed the genes for their receptors.

Malignant tumours whether of haemopoietic origin or from paremchymous organs, are usually cell renewal systems (Buick & McCulloch, 1985). Indeed, the long doubling time characteristic of cancer can be explained if a 'death' probability is introduced; if tumours grew at a rate determined only by the short generation time of mammalian cells they would be fatal in days rather than in months or years. Cancer cells, therefore, are useful for the study of stem cell function. They are particularly relevant to pathophysiology if the cells reflect the growth properties of populations *in vivo*. Many cell lines have limited value since their establishment was associated with very high rates of self renewal. The blast cells of acute myeloblastic leukaemia (AML) may be a good model, since renewal and differentiation can be assessed from cells freshly obtained from patients and these parameters may be retained by cells in culture for long time periods. These cancer cells provide the theme for this paper. Experiments will be described with the view of displaying both biological principles and potential for practical application.

## Abnormal clones in AML

AML may be considered as a clonal haemopathy (McCulloch *et al.* 1979); in each patient, blood cells are members of a single dominant clone (Fialkow, 1982; McCulloch *et al.* 1979), derived from a transformed primitive haemopoietic precursor; the cellular compositions of the clones are complex, consisting of one or more apparently normal myelopoietic lineages together with the characteristic blast population (Fialkow *et al.* 1987). These are arranged as a cellular hierarchy; cells at the apex of the hierarchy are pre-deterministic, and retain stem cell characteristics.

As in other renewal systems, blast stem cells are the points of origin of differentiation programmes, which conclude with non-dividing end cells analogous to the differentiated elements of normal haemopoiesis. Each cell division is a branch point from which a new programme begins. Prior to determination these divisions may lead to new stem cells and hence the origins of complete programmes. After determination, the programmes are limited to terminal divisions ending in proliferatively inert cells that retain blast morphology (Buick & McCulloch, 1985).

The balance between self-renewal and differentiation in AML blast clones may be estimated using two complementary cell culture methods. One, a clonogenic assay (Buick *et al.* 1977), measures principally terminal divisions, although minimal self-renewal can be detected by replating cells recovered from colonies (Buick *et al.* 1979). In the other, a suspension assay, clonogenic cells increase with time, a change that reflects self-renewal (Nara & McCulloch, 1985). Differentiation also occurs in suspension cultures, as is seen in the generation of adherent cells with many of the immunophenotypic characteristics of macrophages (Langley *et al.* 1986). These two complementary culture methods yield a number of parameters; the direct plating efficiency in methylcellulose ($PE_{mc}$) and the number of adherent cells generated during 7 days in suspension culture reflect the 'death' probability; the plating efficiency after suspension culture ($PE_s$) and the number of clonogenic cells recovered from suspension cultures are considered indicators of the 'birth' probability. These can be assessed singly or in combination as required by experimental design.

## The chemosensitivity of self-renewal

Using replating from methylcellulose as a way to assess self-renewal, data were obtained indicating that cytosine arabinoside (ara-C) was less toxic to primary colony-formation in methylcellulose than to the generation of secondary clonogenic cells within colonies (Buick *et al.* 1981; McCulloch *et al.* 1984). In contrast, colonies surviving in the presence of 5-azacytidine (5-aza) at concentrations capable of reducing primary colony formation to 10% of control, were found to replate at greater efficiencies than controls (Motoji *et al.* 1985). If, as proposed, the suspension assay depends on blast stem cell renewal, then measurements of drug sensitivity using this technique should reflect any selective drug action on renewal-specific DNA. In contrast, drug sensitivity measured with the clonogenic assay should reveal specificity for terminal divisions. These predictions led to comparisons of the drug survival curves measured in suspension and in methylcellulose. As expected, ara-C sensitivity was greater when measured in suspension than by colony-formation (Nara *et al.* 1986); for 5-aza, in contrast, sensitivity was greater using the clonogenic assay than the suspension assay (Wang & McCulloch, 1987). Adriamycin was tested as a control; this agent does not show specificity for self-renewal when tested using the replating assay. Adriamycin survival curves measured in suspension or by colony-formation were indistinguishable. Similar findings have been reported recently in experiments using a transplantable mouse leukaemia cell line (Nara *et al.* 1987). The

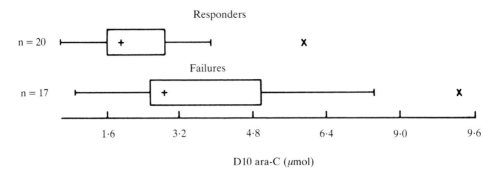

Fig. 1. Boxplots showing the distributions of ara-C blast sensitivities measured in suspension among responders (top) and failures (bottom) to chemotherapy with ara-C. The distributions are significantly different ($P = 0.03$). For description, see text.

findings were interpreted to support the hypothesis that the balance between self-renewal and determination is genetically-determined and that the specificity of certain drugs for one or other of the processes is based on selective activity for DNA segments carrying the relevant genes.

These observations might reflect only blast cell behaviour in culture. Evidence for *in vivo* relevance was sought by comparing drug sensitivities measured in suspension or in methylcellulose as attributes contributing to outcome variation. Clonogenic assays have been used by a number of investigators to compare sensitivity in culture to outcome; some (Park *et al.* 1980; Preisler, 1980) have observed associations, although usually small numbers of patients were included in the analyses. In our hands neither adriamycin nor ara-C sensitivity has been correlated with response to treatment when the measurements were made using the methylcellulose technique (Curtis *et al.* 1984; McCulloch *et al.* 1982*a*). In contrast, in a preliminary comparison of ara-C sensitivity, measured by the suspension and clonogenic assays, a significant association was found using the former but not the latter (Nara *et al.* 1986). A prospective study was then done, where blood was tested from 50 consecutive AML patients presenting at the Princess Margaret Hospital. Enough blast cells were obtained to permit the construction of survival curves from 39 of them, using the suspension culture method. The patients were all treated with a high-dose ara-C protocol (Curtis *et al.* 1987). The results are shown in Fig. 1 as boxplots. This graphic technique, from exploratory data analysis (Tukey, 1977), displays distributions; the box contains the interquartile range; the median is shown as (+) within the box. The lines extending to the right (high) or left (low) ends of the boxes extend to the largest observation within the 1·5 interquartile range of that end of the box, providing estimates of the skewness of the distributions. Outliers are shown as crosses. It is evident that responders were more sensitive to ara-C than failures; the difference is significant ($P = 0.03$), confirming the earlier finding in this larger series.

These clinical associations provide evidence that the suspension assay, but not the clonogenic assay, is measuring a cell parameter important for treatment outcome.

The question arises whether or not the parameter is drug specific. 5-azacytidine was used to examine this issue since 5-aza acts on DNA and is more toxic in culture for terminal than self-renewing divisions. A comparison was made of 5-aza survival curves measured by the clonogenic assay or in suspension for blasts from 21 freshly diagnosed AML patients (Wang *et al.* 1987). In agreement with previous findings, the blasts were more sensitive when tested using colony-formation rather than suspension culture. There was no association between 5-aza sensitivity of colony-formation and clinical outcome. For survival curves measured in suspension, the association was highly significant ($P = 0.008$). Since 5-aza was not used in the treatment of the patients, this finding cannot reflect a direct parallel between drug effects in culture and *in vivo*; rather, the data support the view that the sensitivity of self-renewal is a biological attribute, but one that does not have drug specificity. The postulate, then, is that DNA encoding genes regulating the balance between renewal and differentiation have structural characteristics that influence their sensitivity to chemotherapeutic agents generally.

## Myelopoietic growth factors

Most blast populations require growth factors to proliferate in culture; these may act on stem cells affecting the balance between renewal and differentiation. Media conditioned by the continuous cell line 5637 (5637-CM) is an effective source of factors, and usually gives maximal growth in culture (Hoang & McCulloch, 1985). 5637-CM is known to contain GM-CSF, G-CSF, IL-1 and IL-6 but not CSF-1 or IL-3. These factors have been described and named on the basis of their actions on normal haemopoiesis (Metcalf, 1986). As recombinant proteins became available, the cellular targets of growth factors have been re-assessed. Some factors, for example IL-1 (Jubinsky & Stanley, 1985; Mochizuki *et al.* 1987), IL-4 (Lee *et al.* 1986; Rennick *et al.* 1987), IL-5 (Campbell *et al.* 1987; Sanderson *et al.* 1986) and IL-6 (Garman *et al.* 1987; Ikebuchi *et al.* 1987), not only stimulated lymphocytes but also acted synergistically with myelopoiesis-specific factors on their target populations. Only erythropoietin and CSF-1 appear to be lineage and stage specific, acting on late erythropoietic and macrophage progenitors respectively. G-CSF (Nagata *et al.* 1986) is considered to be limited to granulopoiesis, but may act not only on committed progenitors but also at later stages. IL-3 (Yang *et al.* 1986) and GM-CSF (Gasson *et al.* 1985) normally stimulate early, predeterministic cells; their activities are then seen in all the progeny of such cells including red cell precursors. The activity of these early factors is not restricted to stem cells but continues throughout granulopoietic differentiation programmes. It seems that the role of growth factors in regulating haemopoiesis involves multiple activities, acting alone or, more usually, in combination, at sites that are not clearly related to cellular lineage diagrams.

## The response of AML blast cells to growth factors

Blast cells in culture usually respond to one or more of the myelopoietic growth factors described above. The clonogenic and suspension assays were used together to assess the effects of factors on blast renewal and determination using the following experimental design (Miyauchi et al. 1988a,b, 1987). Freshly obtained or cryopreserved blasts were cultured for two days in suspension in the presence of 5637-CM, which almost always gives a maximum response in both culture systems. A sample of the blasts was then plated with the growth factor(s) under test to obtain the primary plating efficiency in methylcellulose ($PE_{mc}$), a value reflecting terminal divisions. At the same time, suspension cultures were established with the growth factor(s) under examination. After 7 days the suspensions were harvested; adherent and non-adherent cells were counted separately. The adherent cells were taken with $PE_{mc}$ as indicators of the 'death' probability. The non-adherent populations were plated in 5637-CM to determine the maximum plating efficiency after suspension ($PE_s$). The product of $PE_s$ and the non-adherent cell count yielded the number of clonogenic blast cells present after suspension. Both $PE_s$ and clonogenic cell recovery were used to assess the "birth" probability.

The protocol yields a complex data set comprising four values, each with a different scale. Star diagrams, a graphic method from exploratory data analysis (Chambers et al. 1983), were used to depict and integrate the data. The diagrams consist of axes, radiating from a central point. Each axis was scaled for one of the four parameters measured experimentally. Values were plotted on each axis at the scaled distance from the central point; the points on each axis were joined to form a four-sided figure. The 'death'-related values, adherent cell number and $PE_{mc}$ were plotted on axes to the right and up; the 'birth'-related values, $PE_s$ and clonogenic cell recovery assigned axes to the left and down. Thus a star predominantly to the right and up showed a population growing under conditions that favoured differentiation while a star to the left and down reflected predominantly self-renewal events. Published tabular data (Miyauchi et al. 1988b) from experiments designed to test the effects of IL-3, GM-CSF, G-CSF and CSF-1, alone or in combination, are plotted in Fig. 2 as star diagrams.

In the figure, the stars are arranged as a matrix, with factor designations shown at the top on the left. Star diagrams alone the diagonal (cells 1, 3, 6 and 10) are drawn from data for each factor tested alone. The remaining diagrams are data for factors in combination, as indicated by the matrix labels. The cell insert at the top-right of the figure shows the scaled axes used to construct the star diagram together with the data obtained when no factor was added to the cultures. In Fig. 2 the insert shows that this blast clone had little or no spontaneous growth; the star diagrams in the cells of the matrix show that the blast cells responded to all of the culture conditions.

In general, there is marked clone-to-clone variation in responses of blasts to individual growth factors. In the example shown in Fig. 2, G-CSF had only modest activity and this was principally stimulation of self-renewal, as seen by a small star to the left and down in respect to the central point; we and others have observed examples where G-CSF also selected for differentiation (Miyauchi et al. 1987; Souza et al. 1986). The star diagram from GM-CSF alone (Fig. 2, cell 3) shows that both self-renewal and differentiation increased similarly in response to this factor, a finding in agreement with previous results (Griffin et al. 1986; Hoang et al. 1986).

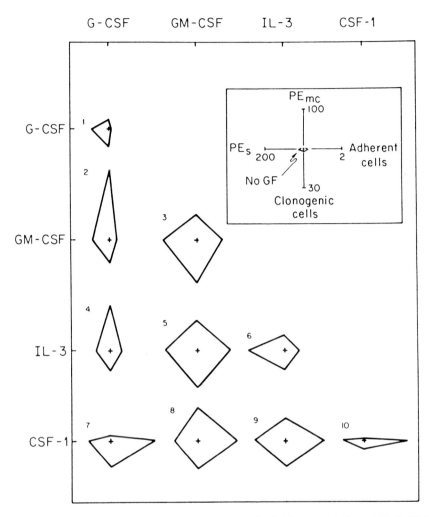

Fig. 2. Star diagrams depicting the responses of a single blast population of IL-3, GM-CSF, G-CSF and CSF-1, alone or in combination. The diagrams are arranged as a matrix, with a star diagram in each cell. The cells are numbered for easy reference to the text. The insert at the top right corner of the figure shows the scales and axes of the star, together with the response of the population when no factors were added to the cultures. The data are presented in tabular form in reference (Miyauchi *et al.* 1988*b*). For explanation, see text.

Next in the diagonal of the Fig. 2 matrix, the star diagram of IL-3 shows that this factor favoured renewal divisions, although some adherent cells were also formed; the effects are similar to those in other reports (Delwel *et al.* 1987; Miyauchi *et al.* 1987). The star diagram for CSF-1 is the last in the diagonal; it has the form of a triangle, with apex down, indicating that colonies did not form in methylcellulose (PE$_{mc}$) in response to this factor. However, in suspension, the 'death' probability emerged strongly, as seen by adherent cell formation, although some 'birth'-related events were also detected. This result is consistent with a previous report, showing that some, but not all, blast populations respond to CSF-1, but, when seen, the response was predominantly an increase in adherent cell formation (Miyauchi *et al.* 1988*a*).

The effects of combining each factor with one another are shown in the remaining star diagrams of Fig. 2. Interactions between factors are most evident at the left and bottom of the matrix. Cells 2, 4 and 7, on the left side, contain stars for G-CSF combined with GM-CSF, IL-3 and CSF-1. The changes in the star diagrams for each combination is evident by comparison with the diagram in cell 1 for G-CSF alone. GM-CSF and IL-3 had qualitatively similar synergistic effects when combined with G-CSF, both increasing the 'death' probability as seen as a shift of the star upwards, as $PE_{mc}$ became greater. The addition of CSF-1 to G-CSF increased the 'death' probability by promoting the generation of adherent cells. Similar, although less marked, CSF-1 effects are seen in the star diagrams on cells 8 and 9 at the bottom of the matrix, representing the combination of CSF-1 with GM-CSF and IL-3 respectively. Little interaction was seen when GM-CSF and IL-3 were combined. The star diagram for this combination seen in cell 5 is not different from that in the cell above it (cell 3), for GM-CSF alone. Similar results were obtained for 4 other blast clones (Miyauchi *et al.* 1988), where the combination of GM-CSF and IL-3 yielded an outcome not different from that of the most effective partner in the mixture; in the example shown in Fig. 2, this was GM-CSF.

The example presented in Fig. 2 is taken from clones of blasts with varied responses to growth factors. However, the clone of Fig. 1 is not atypical. IL-3, GM-CSF and G-CSF are active on most blasts; usually both self-renewal and differentiation are stimulated, although to varying degrees (Miyauchi *et al.* 1987). CSF-1 often does not increase colony-formation, but activity can be detected using suspension assays (Miyauchi *et al.* 1988*a*). The effects of CSF-1 are more consistent than those of the other factors, since differentiation is usually favoured. When the four factors are combined in pairs the pattern of Fig. 1 is seen regularly. The increase in the 'death' probability associated with CSF-1 persists and may be amplified when CSF-1 is combined with any of the other four hormones. The normally early-acting factors, IL-3 and GM-CSF are synergistic in combination with the late-acting G-CSF and CSF-1 (Kelleher *et al.* 1987), but, when used together, only the response to the most active factor is observed.

## CSF-1 expression

The responses of blast cells raises the question of the role of these hormones in regulation; specifically are autocrine mechanisms operative? Molecular cDNA clones for factors have been used to test for expression by Northern analysis. Some, but not all, populations were found to be positive and, of those, many did not secrete protein that could be detected by bioassays (Cheng *et al.* 1987; Young *et al.* 1987). For these a firm link was not established between expression and growth. The finding for CSF-1 was more revealing. About half of AML blasts were positive for CSF-1 expression by Northern analysis; of these only one secreted bioactive factor.

However, these expression positive clones were found to renew themselves significantly less well than expression negative populations (Wang *et al*. 1988). Thus expression of CSF-1, like exposure to the hormone exogenously, had an inhibitory effect on blast growth. Although CSF-1 protein has yet to be found in most CSF-1 expression positive populations, studies of *fms* expression support the view that the mechanism of inhibition by CSF-1 is similar for endogenous expression and exogenous exposure; only *fms* expression positive clones responded to CSF-1, as expected since the *fms* gene encodes the CSF-1 receptor (Sherr *et al*. 1985). Most CSF-1 expression positive clones were also *fms* expression positive. Regrettably, too few CSF-1 positive, *fms* negative examples were identified to test whether cells with this phenotype had different growth characteristics than the commoner *fms* positive type, although a trend towards better growth was seen in CSF-1 expression positive clones when *fms* was not expressed. Taken together, these data support the view that CSF-1 acts directly to inhibit blast growth by binding with its receptor, and that such interaction may take place intracellularly.

## Lineage infidelity

Throughout this paper, AML blasts have been considered as independent clones, maintained by stem cells. This view contrasts with the 'blocked differentiation' hypothesis of leukaemia and led to the prediction that phenotypes would be encountered on blasts that were not found in normal haemopoiesis; specifically, it was suggested that blast differentiation programmes might be assembled abnormally from normal components (McCulloch *et al*. 1978). Support for this abnormal gene expression model derived from studies of continuous cell lines. Friend cells, considered to be erythroleukaemic, were shown to express markers of granulopoiesis (Fioritoni *et al*. 1980); the human K562 line, also often described as an erythroleukaemia, was shown to express spontaneously erythropoietic and granulopoietic markers on single cells (Marie *et al*. 1981). Using histochemical or immunologically detected markers, several groups found markers usually associated with different lineages together on single leukaemic blasts (Lanham *et al*. 1984; McCulloch *et al*. 1982*b*; Mirro *et al*. 1985; Neame *et al*. 1985; Smith *et al*. 1983); it was suggested that 'lineage infidelity' was the basis for such phenotypes (Smith *et al*. 1983). An alternative possibility, 'Lineage Promiscuity', was suggested by Greaves and his colleagues. Their hypothesis was that early predeterministic stem cells might have latitude in expression of lineage-associated genes; such cells might express, transiently, genes for one lineage before becoming committed at determination irreversibly to a different differentiation pathway. Leukaemic transformation occurring in such cells might then 'immortalize' the 'promiscuous' predeterministic phenotype (Greaves *et al*. 1986). These authors wisely suggested that molecular techniques might resolve the issue when these new methods were applied to early events in haemopoiesis and to leukaemia. Soon data were published on rearrangements of immunoglobulin and T cell receptor genes in blasts that were considered on morphological and immunophenotypic grounds to be AML (Ackland *et al*. 1987;

Cheng et al. 1986; Norton et al. 1987). These data, while supporting the infidelity concept, did not rule out promiscuity as an explanation for early lymphoid molecular changes in myeloblastic cells; indeed, the findings were used to support the stem cell origin of leukaemia, regardless of phenotype (Norton et al. 1987).

The findings of blast cell responses to growth factors are relevant to the controversy over the nature of leukaemic blasts, provided certain conditions are met. The responses must be direct if they are to be construed as evidence for specific receptors on blast cells; receptors have been identified on bulk blast populations (Avalos et al. 1987; Kelleher et al. 1988; Mufson et al. 1987), and the observations of fms expression have been described earlier. It is also necessary to show that the receptors are on blast stem cells; the stimulation of self-renewal, a specific stem cell function, is strong, although indirect evidence. Finally, it must be demonstrated that different receptors are on the same cell. The synergistic effects of growth factors can be most readily understood if indeed each is acting on its own receptor on a common target stem cell.

If it can be accepted that the conditions outlined above are in place, the conclusion is that blast stem cells, which simultaneously express receptors for growth factors acting both throughout differentiation (IL-3 and GM-CSF) and the late stages (G-CSF and CSF-1), exist. It remains possible that normal cells may have this phenotype; the importance of CSF-1 should be considered in the context of recent data showing that only this factor can be detected in murine embryogenesis (Azoulay et al. 1987) and development of the placenta (Pollard et al. 1987), data that might indicate that abnormal gene expression is blast cells might include a reversion to more embryonic patterns. Nonetheless, observations of blast cells, expressing simultaneously surface and cytoplasmic markers of different lineage, undergoing lymphoid-associated gene rearrangements in association with AML characteristics and now with receptors for growth factors that act at different places in normal differentiation make it increasingly difficult to associate leukaemic phenotypes with any found in normal post-natal haemopoiesis. The data are more readily reconciled with a model that postulates abnormal gene expression.

## Conclusion

This paper contains a point of view about stem cell properties in general and particularly how these are reflected in acute myeloblastic leukaemia. The central tenet is that blasts comprise subclones within the leukaemic clones derived from transformed pluripotent stem cells. It follows that blast populations are maintained by a minority population of stem cells, able to renew themselves or pass through determination to terminal divisions. A practical conclusion is that stem cell self-renewal is the most sensitive target for curative chemotherapy. Indeed, one of the most active antileukaemic drugs, cytosine arabinoside may be effective because of its selective toxicity for cells that are self-renewing. Further, the chemosensitivity of self-renewal is a biological property that varies among leukaemic populations and contributes significantly to the probability that each will respond *in vivo* to chemotherapy.

A consideration of the regulation of self-renewal and differentiation leads to the conclusion that multiple, genetically controlled mechanisms affect the balance between these two stem cell functions. Among these mechanisms are receptors for growth factors and their ligands. A consideration of the postulated distribution of such receptors supports the view that leukaemic cells are not blocked in differentiation but rather follow abnormal differentiation pathways based on faulty expression of normal differentiation genes (lineage infidelity).

These practical and theoretic concepts have implications for the future. At the clinical level, growth factors may prove potent new weapons to use against leukaemia. Their deployment, however, will require new skills and new resources. Laboratories will be required to assess malignant clones in individual patients in order that the best combination of drugs and hormones may be used. Accurate measurements of blood levels will be needed. At the bedside, the administration of therapeutic regimens will be based on sound physiological principles and tailored to the needs of individual patients.

At the fundamental level, old questions take on new urgency. Precise knowledge of the mechanisms regulating stem cell function continues to be a priority requirement. At this time, it seems likely that advances will come from studies of the regulation of gene expression, regardless of the model. As the ideas develop, however, the cellular systems for testing them in human leukaemia will remain essential.

All of these considerations lead to the same strategic conclusion. Research on normal and leukaemic blood formation is a multi-disciplinary endeavour, where practical and fundamental work can be successfully melded. Clinical and biological observations are both needed; nor can one predict which source will provide the next major clue.

This work was supported by grants from the Medical Research Council of Canada and the National Cancer Institute of Canada.

# References

ACKLAND, S. P., WESTBROOK, C. A., DIAZ, M. O., LE BEAU, M. M. & ROWLEY, J. D. (1987). Evidence favoring lineage fidelity in Acute Nonlymphocytic Leukemia: absence of immunoglobulin gene rearrangements in FAB types M4 and M5. *Blood* **69**, 87–89.

AVALOS, B. R., HEDZAT, C., BALDWIN, G. C., GOLDE, D. W., GASSON, J. C. & DIPERSIO, J. F. (1987). Biological activities of human G-CSF and characterization of the human G-CSF receptor. *Blood* **70**, suppl. 1, 165a.

AZOULAY, M., WEBB, C. G. & SACHS, L. (1987). Control of hematopoietic cell growth regulators during mouse fetal development. *Molec. Cell Biol.* **7**, 3361–3364.

BUICK, R. N., CHANG, L. J.-W., MESSNER, H. A., CURTIS, J. E. & MCCULLOCH, E. A. (1981). Self renewal capacity of leukemic blast progenitor cells. *Cancer Res.* **41**, 4849–4852.

BUICK, R. N. & MCCULLOCH, E. A. (1985). The role of stem cells in normal and malignant tissue. In *Control of Animal Cell Proliferation, I* (ed. A. L. Boynton & H. L. Leffert), pp. 25–57. Orlando, FL.: Academic Press.

BUICK, R. N., MINDEN, M. D. & MCCULLOCH, E. A. (1979). Self-renewal in culture of proliferative blast progenitor cells in acute myeloblastic leukemia. *Blood* **54**, 95–104.

BUICK, R. N., TILL, J. E. & McCULLOCH, E. A. (1977). Colony assay for proliferative blast cells circulating in myeloblastic leukaemia. *Lancet* **1**, 862–863.

CAMPBELL, H. D., TUCKER, W. Q. J., HORT, Y., MARTINSON, M. E., MAYO, G., CLUTTERBUCK, E. J., SANDERSON, C. J. & YOUNG, I. G. (1987). Molecular cloning, nucleotide sequence, and expression of the gene encoding human eosinophil differentiation factor (interleukin 5). *Proc. natn. Acad. Sci. U.S.A.* **84**, 6629–6633.

CHAMBERS, J. M., CLEVELAND, W. S., KLEINER, B. & TUKEY, P. A. (1983). *Graphic Methods for Data Analysis*, pp. 157–161. Boston: Duxbury Press.

CHENG, G. Y. M., KELLEHER, C. A., MIYAUCHI, J., WANG, C., WONG, G., CLARK, S., McCULLOCH, E. A. & MINDEN, M. D. (1987). Structure and expression of genes of GM-CSF and G-CSF in blast cells from patients with Acute Myeloblastic Leukemia. *Blood* **71**, 204–208.

CHENG, G. Y. M., MINDEN, M. D., TOYONAGA, B., MAK, T. W. & McCULLOCH, E. A. (1986). T-cell receptor and immunoglobulin gene rearrangements in acute myeloblastic leukemia. *J. exp. Med.* **65**, 894–901.

CLARK, S. C. & KAMEN, R. (1987). The human hematopoietic colony-stimulating factors. *Science* **236**, 1229–1237.

CURTIS, J. E., MESSNER, H. A., HASSELBACK, R., ELHAKIM, T. M. & McCULLOCH, E. A. (1984). Contributions of host- and disease-related attributes to the outcome of patients with acute myelogeneous leukemia (AML). *J. clin. Oncol.* **2**, 253–259.

CURTIS, J. E., MESSNER, H. A., MINDEN, M. D., MINKIN, S. & McCULLOCH, E. A. (1987). High dose cytosine arabinoside in the treatment of acute myeloblastic leukemia: Contributions to outcome of clinical and laboratory attributes. *J. clin. Oncol.* **5**, 532–543.

DELWEL, R., DORSSERS, L., TOUW, I., WAGEMAKER, E. R. & LOWENBERG, B. (1987). Human recombinant multilineage colony stimulating factor (Interleukin-3): stimulator of acute myelocytic leukemia progenitor cells in vitro. *Blood* **70**, 333–336.

DEXTER, T. M., ALLEN, T. D. & LAJTHA, L. G. (1977). Conditions controlling the proliferation of hematopoietic cells in vitro. *J. cell. Physiol* **91**, 335–344.

DOWNWARD, J., YARDEN, Y., MAYES, E., SCRACE, G., TOTTY, N., STOCKWELL, P., ULRICH, A., SCHLESSINGER, J. & WATERFIELD, M. D. (1984). Close similarity of epidermal growth factor receptor and v-erb-B oncogene protein sequences. *Nature, Lond.* **307**, 521–527.

FIALKOW, P. J. (1982). Cell lineages in hematopoietic neoplasia studied with glucose-6-phosphate dehydrogenase cell markers in: *J. cell. Physiol.* (supplement 1) **111**, pp. 37–43. New York: Alan Liss.

FIALKOW, P. J., SINGER, J. W., RASKIND, W. H., ADAMSON, J. W., JACOBSON, R. J., BERSTEIN, D. I., DOW, L. D., NAJFELD, V. & VEITH, R. (1987). Clonal development, stem-cell differentiation and clinical remissions in acute nonlymphocytic leukemia. *N. Engl. J. Med.* **317**, 468–473.

FIORITONI, G., BERTOLINI, L. & REVOLTELLA, R. (1980). Cytochemical characteristics of leukopoietic differentiation in murine erythroleukemic (Friend) cells. *Cancer Res.* **40**, 866–872.

GARMAN, R. D., JACOBS, K. A., CLARK, S. C. & RAULET, D. H. (1987). B-cell-stimulatory factor 2 (beta 2 interferon) functions as a second signal for interleukin 2 production by mature murine T cells. *Proc. natn. Acad. Sci. U.S.A.* **84**, 7629–7633.

GASSON, J. C., GOLDE, D. W., KAUFMAN, S. E., WESTBROOK, C. A., HEWICK, R. M., KAUFMAN, R. J. & WONG, G. (1985). Molecular characterization and expression of the gene encoding erythroid-potentiating activity. *Nature, Lond.* **315**, 768–771.

GILMAN, A. G. (1987). G proteins: transducers of receptor-generated signals. *A. Rev. Biochem.* **56**, 615–649.

GOLDWASSER, E. (1976). Erythropoietin and the differentiation of red blood cells. *Fedn Proc. Fedn Am. Socs exp. Biol.* **34**, 2285–2292.

GREAVES, M. F., CHAN, L. C., FURLEY, A. J. W., WATT, S. M. & MOLGAARD, H. V. (1986). Lineage promiscuity in hemopoietic differentiation and leukemia. *Blood* **67**, 1–11.

GRIFFIN, J. D., YOUNG, D., HERRMAN, F., WIPER, D., WAGNER, K. & SABBATH, D. K. (1986). Effects of recombinant GM-CSF on the proliferation of clonogenic cells in acute myeloblastic leukemia. *Blood* **67**, 1448–1453.

HOANG, T. & McCULLOCH, E. A. (1985). Production of leukemic blast growth factor by a human bladder carcinoma cell line. *Blood* **66**, 748–751.

HOANG, T., NARA, N., WONG, G., CLARK, S., MINDEN, M. D. & McCULLOCH, E. A. (1986). The effects of recombinant GM-CSF on the blast cells of acute myeloblastic leukemia. *Blood* **67**, 313–316.

IKEBUCHI, K., WONG, G. G., CLARK, S. C., IHLE, J. N., HIRAI, Y. & OGAWA, M. (1987). Interleukin 6 enhancement of interleukin 3-dependent proliferation of multipotential haemopoietic progenitors. *Proc. natn. Acad. Sci. U.S.A.* **84**, 9035–9039.

JUBINSKY, P. T. & STANLEY, E. R. (1985). Purification of hemopoietin 1: A multilineage haemopoietic growth factor. *Proc. natn. Acad. Sci. U.S.A.* **82**, 2764–2768.

KELLEHER, C., MIYAUCHI, J., WONG, G., CLARK, S., MINDEN, M. D. & McCULLOCH, E. A. (1987). Synergism between recombinant growth factors, GM-CSF and G-CSF, acting on the blast cells of acute myeloblastic leukemia. *Blood* **69**, 1498–1503.

KELLEHER, C. A., WONG, G. G., CLARK, S. C., SCHENDEL, P. F., MINDEN, M. D. & McCULLOCH, E. A. (1988). Binding of iodinated recombinant human GM-CSF to the blast cells of acute myeloblastic leukemia. *Leukemia* **2**, 211–215.

LANGLEY, G. R., SMITH, L. J. & McCULLOCH, E. A. (1986). Adherent cells in cultures of blast progenitors in acute myeloblastic leukemia. *Leukemia Res.* **10**, 953–959.

LANHAM, G., BOLLUM, F. J., WILLIAMS, D. L. & STASS, S. A. (1984). Simultaneous occurance of terminal deoxynucleotidyl transferase and myeloperoxidase in individual leukemic blasts. *Blood* **64**, 318–320.

LEE, F., YOKOTA, T., OTSUKA, T., MEYERSON, P., VILLARET, D., COFFMAN, R., MOSMAN, T., RENNICK, D., ROEHM, N., SMITH, C., ZLOTNICK, A. & ARAI, K-I. (1986). Isolation and characterization of a mouse interleukin cDNA clone that expresses BSF-1 activities and T cell and mast cell stimulating activities. *Proc. natn. Acad. Sci. U.S.A.* **83**, 2061–2065.

MAJERUS, P. W., CONNOLLY, T. M., DECKMYN, H., ROSS, T. S., BROSS, T. E., ISHII, H., BANSAL, V. S. & WILSON, D. B. (1987). The metabolism of phosphoinositide-derived messenger molecules. *Science* **234**, 1519–1526.

MARIE, J. P., IZAGUIRRE, C. A., CIVIN, C. I., MIRRO, J. & McCULLOCH, E. A. (1981). The presence within single K-562 cells of erythropoietic and granulopoietic differentiation markers. *Blood* **58**, 708–711.

MARSHALL, C. J. (1987). Oncogenes and growth control 1987. *Cell* **49**, 723–725.

McCULLOCH, E. A., BUICK, R. N., MINDEN, M. D. & IZAGUIRRE, C. A. (1978). Differentiation programmes underlying cellular heterogeneity in the myeloblastic leukemias of man. In *Haemopoietic Cell Differentiation. ICN-UCLA Symposium on Molecular and Cellular Biology, X* (ed. D. W. Golde, M. J. Cline, D. Metcalf & C. F. Fox), pp. 317–333. New York: Academic Press.

McCULLOCH, E. A., CURTIS, J. E., MESSNER, H. A., SENN, J. S. & GERMANSON, T. P. (1982*a*). The contribution of blast cell properties to outcome variation in acute myeloblastic leukemia (AML). *Blood* **59**, 601–608.

McCULLOCH, E. A., HOWATSON, A. F., BUICK, R. N., MINDEN, M. D. & IZAGUIRRE, C. A. (1979). Acute myeloblastic leukemia considered as a clonal hemopathy. *Blood Cells* **5**, 261–282.

McCULLOCH, E. A., MOTOJI, T., SMITH, L. J. & CURTIS, J. E. (1984). Hemopoietic stem cells: Their roles in human leukemia and certain continuous cell lines. *J. cell. Physiol. Suppl.* **3**, 13–20.

McCULLOCH, E. A., RUSSELL, E. S., SIMINOVITCH, L., TILL, J. E. & BERNSTEIN, S. E. (1965). The cellular basis of the genetically determined hemopoietic defect in anemic mice of genotype $S1/S1^d$. *Blood* **26**, 399–410.

McCULLOCH, E. A., SMITH, L. J. & MINDEN, M. D. (1982*b*). Normal and malignant haemopoietic clones in man. *Cancer Surv.* **1**, 279–298.

METCALF, D. (1986). The molecular biology and functions of the granulocyte-macrophage colony-stimulating factors. *Blood* **67**, 257–267.

MIRRO, J., ANTOUN, G. R., ZIPF, T. F., MELVIN, S. & STASS, S. (1985). The E rosette-associated antigen of T cells can be identified on blasts from patients with acute myeloblastic leukemia. *Blood* **65**, 363–367.

MIYAUCHI, J., KELLEHER, C., WONG, G. G., CLARK, S. C., MINDEN, M. D. & McCULLOCH, E. A. (1988*a*). The effects of recombinant CSF-1 on the blast cells of acute myeloblastic leukemia. *J. cell. Physiol.* **135**, 55–62..

MIYAUCHI, J., KELLEHER, C. A., WONG, G. G., YANG, Y.-C., CLARK, S. C., MINKIN, S., MINDEN, M. D. & McCULLOCH, E. A. (1988*b*). The effects of combinations of the recombinant growth factors GM-CSF, G-CSF, IL-3 and CSF-1 on leukemic blast cells in suspension culture. *Leukemia* **2**, 382–387.

MIYAUCHI, J., KELLEHER, C., YANG, Y.-C., WONG, G. G., CLARK, S. C., MINDEN, M. D., MINKIN, S. & MCCULLOCH, E. A. (1987). The effects of three recombinant growth factors, IL-3, GM-CSF and G-CSF, on the blast cells of acute myeloblastic leukemia maintained in short term suspension culture. *Blood* **70**, 657–663.

MOCHIZUKI, D. Y., EISENMAN, J. R., CONLON, P. J., LARSEN, A. D. & TUSHINSKI, R. J. (1987). Interleukin-1 regulates hematopoietic activity, a role previously ascribed to hemopoietin-1. *Proc. natn. Acad. Sci. U.S.A.* **84**, 5267–5271.

MOTOJI, T., HOANG, T., TRITCHLER, D. & MCCULLOCH, E. A. (1985). The effect of 5-azacytidine and its analogues on blast cell renewal in acute myeloblastic leukemia. *Blood* **65**, 894–901.

MUFSON, R. A., GESNER, T. G., TURNER, K., NORTON, C., YANG, Y-C. & CLARK, S. (1987). Characterization of IL-3 receptors on human acute myelogenous leukemia cell line KG-1. *Blood* **70**, suppl 1, 118a.

NAGATA, S., TSUCHIYA, M., ASANO, S., KAZIRO, Y., YAMAZAKI, T., YAMAMOTO, O., HIRATA, Y., KUBOTA, N., OHEDA, M., NOMURA, H. & ONO, M. (1986). Molecular cloning and expression of cDNA for human granulocyte colony-stimulating factor. *Nature, Lond.* **319**, 415–417.

NAKAHATA, T., GROSS, A. J. & OGAWA, M. (1982). A stochastic model of self-renewal and committment to differentiation of the primitive hemopoietic stem cells in culture. *J. cell. Physiol.* **113**, 455–458.

NARA, N., CURTIS, J. E., SENN, J. S., TRITCHLER, D. L. & MCCULLOCH, E. A. (1986). The sensitivity to cytosine arabinoside of the blast progenitors of acute myeloblastic leukemia. *Blood* **67**, 762–769.

NARA, N. & MCCULLOCH, E. A. (1985). The proliferation in suspension of the progenitors of the blast cells in acute myeloblastic leukemia. *Blood* **65**, 1484–1493.

NARA, N., YAMASHITA, Y., MUROHASHI, I., TANIKAWA, S., IMAI, Y. & AOKI, N. (1987). The effects on leukemic clonogenic cells in murine myeloid leukemia of 1-beta-D-arabinofuranosylcytosine and the anthracyclines adriamycin, daunomycin, aclacinomycin and 4′-epidoxorubicin. *Cancer Res.* **47**, 2376–2379.

NEAME, P. B., SOAMBOONSRUP, P., BROWMAN, G., BARR, R. D., SAEED, N., CHAN, B. B., BERGER, A., WILSON, W. E. C., WALKER, I. R. & MCBRIDE, J. A. (1985). Simultaneous sequential expression of lymphoid and myeloid phenotypes in acute leukemia. *Blood* **65**, 142–148.

NORTON, J. D., CAMPANA, D., HOFFBRAND, A. V., JANOSSY, G., COUSTAN-SMITH, E., JAN, H., YAXLEY, J. C. & PRENTICE, H. G. (1987). Rearrangement of immunoglobulin and T cell antigen receptor genes in acute myeloblastic leukemia with lymphoid-associated markers. *Leukemia* **1**, 757–761.

PARK, C. H., AMARE, M., SAVIN, M. A., GOODWIN, J. W., NEWCOMB, M. M. & HOOGSTRATEN, B. (1980). Prediction of chemotherapy response in human leukemia using an in vitro chemotherapy sensitivity test on the leukemic colony-forming cells. *Blood* **55**, 595–601.

POLLARD, J. W., BARTOCCI, A., ARCECI, R., ORLOFSKY, A., LADNER, M. B. & STANLEY, E. R. (1987). Apparent role of the macrophage growth factor, CSF-1, in placental development. *Nature, Lond.* **330**, 484–486.

PREISLER, H. D. (1980). Prediction of response to chemotherapy in acute myelocytic leukemia. *Blood* **56**, 361–367.

RENNICK, D., YANG, G., MULLER-SIEBURG, C., SMITH, C., ARAI, N., TAKABE, Y. & GEMMELL, L. (1987). Interleukin 4 (B-cell stimulatory factor 1) can enhance or antagonize the factor-dependent growth of hemopoietic progenitor cells. *Proc. natn. Acad. Sci. U.S.A.* **84**, 6889–6893.

SANDERSON, C. J., O'GARRA, A., WARREN, D. J. & KLAUS, G. B. B. (1986). Eosinophil differentiation factor also has B-cell growth factor activity: proposed name interleukin 4. *Proc. natn. Acad. Sci. U.S.A.* **83**, 437–440.

SHERR, C. J., RETTENMIER, C. W., SACCA, R., ROUSSEL, M. F., LOOK, A. T. & STANLEY, E. R. (1985). The c-fms proto-oncogene product is related to the receptor for the mononuclear phagocyte growth factor, CSF-1. *Cell* **41**, 665–676.

SMITH, L. J., CURTIS, J. E., MESSNER, H. A., SENN, J. S., FURTHMAYR, H. & MCCULLOCH, E. A. (1983). Lineage infidelity in acute leukemia. *Blood* **61**, 1138–1145.

SMITH, L. J., McCULLOCH, E. A. & BENCHIMOL, S. (1986). The expression of the p53 oncogene in acute myeloblastic leukemia. *J. exp. Med.* **164**, 751–761.

SOUZA, L. M., BOONE, T. C., GABRILOVE, J., LAI, P. H., ZSEBO, K. M., MURDOCK, D. C., CHAZIN, V. R., BRUSZEWSKI, J., LU, H., CHEN, K. K., BARENDT, J., PLATZER, E., MOORE, M. A. S., MERTELSMANN, R. & WELTE, K. (1986). Recombinant human granulocyte colony-stimulating factor: effects on normal and leukemic myeloid cells. *Science* **232**, 61–65.

TILL, J. E., McCULLOCH, E. A. & SIMINOVITCH, L. (1964). A stochastic model of stem cell proliferation, based on the growth of spleen colony forming cells. *Proc. natn. Acad. Sci. U.S.A.* **51**, 29–36.

TUKEY, J. W. (1977). *Exploratory Data Analysis*, p. 39. Reading, MA.: Addison-Wesley.

WANG, C., CURTIS, J. E., SENN, J. S., TRITCHLER, D. L. & McCULLOCH, E. A. (1987). Response to 5-azacytidine of leukemic blast cells in suspension: a biological parameter associated with response to chemotherapy. *Leukemia* **1**, 753–756.

WANG, C., KELLEHER, C. A., CHENG, G. Y. M., MIYAUCHI, J., WONG, G. G., CLARK, S. C., MINDEN, M. D. & McCULLOCH, E. A. (1988). Expression of the CSF-1 gene in the blast cells of acute myeloblastic leukemia: association with reduced growth capacity. *J. cell. Physiol.* **135**, 133–138.

WANG, C. & McCULLOCH, E. A. (1987). The sensitivity to 5-azacytidine of blast progenitors in acute myeloblastic leukemia. *Blood* **69**, 553–559.

WEINBERGER, C., THOMPSON, C., ONG, E. S., LEBO, R., GRUOL, D. J. & EVANS, R. M. (1986). The c-erb-A gene encodes a thyroid hormone receptor. *Nature, Lond.* **324**, 641–646.

YANG, Y.-C., CIARLETTA, A. B., TEMPLE, P. A., CHUNG, M. P., KOVACIC, S., WITEK-GIANOTTI, J. S., LEARY, A. C., KRITZ, R., DONAHUE, R. E., WONG, G.-G. & CLARK, S. C. (1986). Human IL-3(Multi-CSF): Identification by expression cloning of a novel hemopoietic growth factor related to murine IL-3. *Cell* **47**, 3–10.

YOUNG, D. C., WAGNER, K. & GRIFFIN, J. D. (1987). Constitutive expression of the granuocyte-macrophage colony-stimulating factor gene in acute myeloblastic leukemia. *J. clin. Invest.* **79**, 100–106.

# INDEX